Colonial North America and the Atlantic World

A History in Documents

Brett Rushforth

Paul W. Mapp

Routledge
Taylor & Francis Group

LONDON AND NEW YORK

First published 2009 by Pearson Education, Inc.

Published 2016 by Routledge
2 Park Square, Milton Park, Abingdon, Oxon OX14 4RN
711 Third Avenue, New York, NY 10017, USA

Routledge is an imprint of the Taylor & Francis Group, an informa business

Copyright ©2009 Taylor & Francis.

Cover Design: Bruce Kenselaar

ISBN-13: 978-0-13-234237-7 (pbk)

Library of Congress Cataloging-in-Publication Data

Colonial North America : a history in documents / [edited by] Brett Rushforth, Paul W. Mapp.
    p. cm.
  Includes bibliographical references.

  ISBN-13: 978-0-13-234237-7

  1. North America—Colonization—Sources. 2. America—Early accounts to 1600. 3. North America—History—Colonial
period, ca. 1600-1775—Sources. 4. North America—Discovery and exploration—Spanish—Sources. 5. North America—
Discovery and exploration—French—Sources. 6. United States—History—Colonial period, ca. 1600-1775—Sources. 7. United
States—Social conditions—To 1865—Sources. 8. Indians of North America—First contact with Europeans—Sources.
I. Rushforth, Brett. II. Mapp, Paul W.
  E46.C65 2009
  970.01—dc22

                                                                                        2008012651

FOREWORD

During the summer of 1793, Alexander Mackenzie led a small expedition of Indians and French Canadians westward up a rocky and rapid river into the Canadian Rockies. Mackenzie sought an overland route to the Pacific to benefit his Montreal-based fur trading company. But his expedition stalled as the mountains proved higher, wider, and more complex than he had guessed. Mackenzie became lost in a world familiar to the local Sekani people. Then he noticed that the Sekani had some metal tools of British origin. Reasoning that the natives had obtained the tools from maritime traders along the Pacific coast, Mackenzie pursued, in his words, "that chain of connexion by which these people obtain their ironwork." The Pacific world of trade that was his goal also generated the tangible clues that drew his party to their destination. The eastward and overland passage of those goods revealed a long-standing web of intertribal connections otherwise invisible to the explorer. That web drew Mackenzie to the ocean along the shores of present-day British Columbia. A decade before the more famous Lewis and Clark expedition, Mackenzie was the first European to cross the continent—but he could not have done so without the combination of Indian guides and European trade.

In 1793, three centuries after Columbus, most of North America remained Indian country. European colonization had consolidated only in Mexico, along the Atlantic coast, and in pockets along the St. Lawrence and Mississippi Rivers and the Rio Grande. Nonetheless, as Mackenzie noted, the European invasion of the continent had already affected almost every corner of that vast Indian America. In addition to trade goods, disease pathogens had passed far beyond European hands through Indian intermediaries. During that same summer along the Northwest coast, British sailors found the signs of a massive smallpox epidemic: shrunken villages, bleaching skeletons scattered on the beaches, and native survivors with pocked faces. Empires possessed an intrusive power that reshaped the continent—but in unpredictable ways affected by the ability of Indians to adapt. While enduring invasion and disease, they seized new opportunities as trading partners, military allies, and missionary converts.

Mackenzie's story belongs to a new, more inclusive history of colonial America that embraces the entire continent. More than an English story confined to the fabled thirteen colonies of the Atlantic seaboard, the broader history of colonial America includes the Spanish heading north from Mexico and Cuba, the French probing the Great Lakes and the Mississippi River, the Dutch trading along the Hudson, and even the Russians coming eastward from Siberia into Alaska. These empires brought thousands of Africans, whose labor and cultures helped to reshape the continent. And as Mackenzie knew well, the colonizers of every stripe dealt with persistent and highly adaptable native people. Through the eighteenth century, natives remained critical to the construction of empires—and to the limits put to them. Indians belong at the center of the colonial story, just as they were at the pivot of Mackenzie's journey.

Teaching that story requires documents that introduce students to the broad array of peoples in colonial North America. As editors of this collection, Paul Mapp and Brett Rushforth have chosen and interpreted a lively array of revealing documents drawn from virtually every corner of the continent and across three centuries of time. Their selection and their interpretations provide a perfect complement to my own attempt to synthesize the continent's history in *American Colonies*. As with those tools among the Sekani, these documents can lead students to a rich discovery. In this case, they will recover a story of enduring and global importance: the transformation of the North American continent by Africans and European peoples, plants, and animals—in a dynamic interplay with the enduring natives.

Alan Taylor
University of California at Davis

CONTENTS

INTRODUCTION

Once understood as a brief prelude to the history of the United States, "colonial America" has undergone a rapid and remarkable transformation in recent years, emerging as a vibrant and complex era in its own right. Two trends have redefined the field of early American history over the past thirty years. Facing eastward, scholars taking an Atlantic approach have emphasized the swirling connections among the Americas, Europe, and Africa. Reciprocal cultural, economic, and demographic influences integrated these distant places into a common (if never fully coherent) "Atlantic world." Increasingly intertwined, the lands touching the Atlantic were drawn into networks of material and cultural exchange on a scale never before seen in any of the affected regions.

Facing westward, other scholars have grounded their work on the North American continent, arguing for the centrality of Native peoples to the story of early America. Rather than being passively absorbed into the colonial or Atlantic world, these scholars contend, Indians controlled much of the continent well into the eighteenth century. Indians thus powerfully shaped the continent's history throughout the period we label "colonial," raising questions about the appropriateness of that term for a time and place with so few colonies and so many independent peoples. Early North America differed profoundly both from what the continent would come to be in the nineteenth and twentieth centuries and from the impression created by exclusive focus on a narrow band of British coastal colonies.

Both of these trends reflect the interests and concerns of students in the twenty-first century. We live in an age of unprecedented globalization, and as student awareness of this reality has grown, so has student interest in the global dimensions of early American history. We have also become more aware of the need to appreciate and learn from the linguistic and cultural diversity characterizing contemporary North America. Early America offers no shortage of examples of this diversity and the challenges and opportunities it presents. Several hundred languages were spoken on the North American continent when Spanish ships first made landfall, and to those were added at least eight European languages and probably two-dozen African tongues. A great many colonial communities hosted peoples from Europe, Africa, and America, and the ways they worked out their relationships—or failed to do so—resonate in powerful ways in today's world.

But if these documents speak to contemporary concerns, they also underscore just how different the early American experience could be. Indian and European nations claimed territories crossing modern national boundaries, with much of what is now the United States considered part of Iroquoia, New Spain, or New France; and despite European claims to this territory, it was in reality controlled mostly by non-European peoples. The agricultural settlement patterns that dominated Native and European societies contrast sharply with today's predominantly urban and suburban lifestyles. Limited technology, communications, and geographic knowledge also set the colonial period apart from our own time in which global positioning satellites minutely map every mile of the continent. These and many other suggestive differences highlight the need to understand early America on its own terms rather than through our own hindsight or wishful thinking.

Incorporating documents from all regions of North America and including the perspectives of as many peoples as possible, this reader will give professors and students the tools they need to better understand the complexities of early American history, both those that relate to our own experience and those that belong entirely to another time.

A Note on the Documents

Four related principles have guided our selection of documents for this collection. First, we believe that reading, reflecting on, discussing, and writing about primary historical documents should form the core of most undergraduate history courses. The most lasting and profound insights into historical subjects come from working with the sources that historians themselves use as the building blocks of their interpretations. Consequently, our collection devotes no space to secondary writings, concentrating instead on giving students the raw materials to come to their own conclusions.

Second, we have found that students find large numbers of short documentary selections confusing, forgettable, and inadequate as a basis for historical argument. To develop a feel for a period different from their own, to come to know the authors of primary documents and to have enough exposure to them to discern their subtleties and idiosyncrasies, students need to spend time with individual primary sources. With these points in mind, we have chosen in most cases to offer one or two long or medium-length documents and one or two short documents per chapter. This provides both varied types of evidence for students to consider and sufficient content for students to think deeply about the sources and topics at hand. The variety of documents will allow professors a wide range of choices, perhaps assigning fewer documents per chapter in shorter terms or lower-level courses or requiring all the readings in longer semesters, upper-division courses, or classes with few secondary readings.

Third, the documents in each chapter correspond directly to the content of Alan Taylor's *American Colonies*. Not only do the documents illustrate the topics of Taylor's individual chapters, but wherever possible, we have selected readings specifically mentioned in his text. The documents will thus reinforce the ideas presented in the textbook, and perhaps more importantly, reveal to students the basis for many of Taylor's interpretations. Familiarity with the process through which scholars arrive at their ideas will inevitably encourage students to think critically as they form and reflect upon the interpretations they themselves have come to after reading the available evidence. For professors who adopt our text without adopting Taylor's, this selection criterion will still provide documents addressing core issues in current scholarship.

Finally, we have chosen documents we believe students will find interesting, exciting, and, though sometimes unpleasant, always rich in interpretive potential. We have tried to search for the gripping stories, the telling reflections, and the troubling dilemmas that make early America such a rewarding period to study. Through the force of their ideas, the resonance of their subjects, and the artfulness of their literary techniques, these documents will challenge students intellectually, and make historical inquiry both enjoyable and memorable.

Acknowledgments

We wish to thank the following instructors whose insightful comments were important to the development of this text:

David J. Silverman, George Washington University
Elsa A. Nystrom, Kennesaw State University
William H. Mulligan, Jr., Murray State University

1 Native North America

Combining written sources, archaeological findings, linguistic studies, and oral histories, historians and anthropologists have pieced together a surprisingly rich portrait of Native life in precolonial North America. The following documents—one a Native oral tradition and the others written by early Spanish conquistadors—provide glimpses of early Indian society in three distinct regions: the Northeast, the Southwest, and the Southeast.

1.1   Huron Creation Story*

This document, an oral tradition of the Huron Indians, offers an alternative explanation of the origins of North America's Native peoples. Such stories were frequently repeated at wintertime gatherings where they passed from one generation to the next. This account was related by a Huron woman named Catherine Johnson in 1912. In many versions of this tale, the woman, named Aataentsic, gives birth to the twin boys and dies during the delivery.

THE YOUNG WOMAN FALLEN FROM ABOVE

Several brothers and sisters were living together. The only meal they had every day consisted of a single basketful of corn, the daily yield of their corn-patch.

Tired of gathering the corn for every meal, the young woman one day thought to herself, "Now,

perhaps the easiest way is to cut the stalks [and gather the ears once for all]." So she cut down the corn-stalks and gathered them all. Her brothers, in their grief, spoke to her and said, "You have spoilt everything and ruined our subsistence! You have wasted it all!" They dropped her through a hole into the ocean.

Wild geese were roaming about on the waters. Their leader exclaimed, "A body is falling from above. Let us all gather close together!" And the woman from above fell gently upon the backs of the assembled geese, as they were together. After a while one of them said, "We are getting tired. Let someone else now take our place." The turtle, emerging from under the waters, said, "It is I, the next!" And the body of the woman fallen from above now rested upon the turtle's back.

Then the toad went [down] and came back with a mouthful of dirt. She gave the dirt to the woman fallen from above, saying, "Do this! Sprinkle it about at arm's length where you lie." The toad meant her to sprinkle the [grains of] earth all around her. So the woman did; and the

*Huron-Wyandot *Traditional Narratives: In Translations and Native Texts* (excerpt p.4), ed. Marius Barbeau, 1960. Canadian Museum of History, National Museums of Canada Bulletin, no.165.

land grew around her. She rose and began to walk about the new land.

The toad now gave the woman grains of corn, beans, pumpkin seeds, and seeds of all the plants that are reaped. That is what the toad did.

After a while the woman felt very lonely. She thought, "I wish to find a child." It so happened that she found twin boys. Very soon she noticed, as they were growing in size, that the younger of the twins was not good, and that he only cared for the rain of whatever his elder brother had undertaken. The elder brother made all that is found in the lap of our land. He created all the living beings and also the people. The Indian people were created by him, the Good One. His younger brother then came forward and said, "I too will make some people." And the monkeys he brought forth, as though they had been real human beings.

Of the twins, the elder is "Hamemdiju," and the younger one the "Underground-dweller."

Questions

1. How does this account differ from European explanations of the world's creation? How is it similar? What do these differences and similarities tell us about the values of each society?
2. How does this account fit into modern historical accounts of the peopling of North America? Is it possible to reconcile these two approaches to the continent's history?
3. What assumptions about gender and authority are implied in this account?
4. What can we learn from this tale about the relationship of the Hurons with their natural surroundings. If maize only reached the Northeast after about 700 A.D., why does it figure so prominently in a story of the world's creation?
5. Describe the relationship between good and evil in this story. What about the concepts of balance and reciprocity?

1.2   Coronado Visits a Pueblo Town*

Pedro de Castañeda de Nájera accompanied Coronado's 1540–1542 expedition into the American Southwest to Mexico and wrote one of the earliest European descriptions of the Pueblo Indians some years after his return.

Cíbola is seven villages. The largest is called Macaque. The houses are ordinarily three or four stories high, but in Macaque there are houses with four and seven stories. These people are very intelligent. They cover their privy parts and all the immodest parts with cloths made like a sort of table napkin, with fringed edges and a tassel at each corner, which they tie over the hips. They wear long robes of feathers and of the skins of hares, and cotton blankets. The women wear blankets, which they tie or knot over the left shoulder, leaving the right arm out. These serve to cover the body. They wear a neat well-shaped outer garment of skin.

They gather their hair over the two ears, making a frame which looks like an old-fashioned headdress.

The country is a valley between ridges resembling rocky mountains. They plant in holes. Maize does not grow high; ears from a stalk three or four to each cane, thick and large, of eight hundred grains, a thing not seen in these parts. There are large numbers of bears in this province, and lions, wildcats, deer, and otter. There are very fine turquoises, although not so many as was reported. They collect the pine nuts each year, and store them up in advance. A man does not have more than one wife. There are estufas or 'hot rooms' in the villages, which are the courtyards or places where they gather for consultation. They do not have chiefs as in New Spain, but are ruled by a council of the oldest men. They have priests who preach to them, whom they call papas. These are the elders. They go up on the highest roof of the village and preach to the village from there, like public criers, in the morning while the sun is rising, the whole village being silent and sitting in the galleries to listen. They tell them how they

*Frederick W. Hodge, ed., *Spanish Explorers in the Southern United States, 1528–1543* (New York: Charles Scribner's Sons, 1907), 350–366.

are to live, and I believe that they give certain commandments for them to keep, for there is no drunkenness among them nor sodomy nor sacrifices, neither do they eat human flesh nor steal, but they are usually at work. The estufas belong to the whole village. It is a sacrilege for the women to go into the estufas to sleep. They made the cross as a sign of peace. They burn their dead, and throw the implements used in their work into the fire with the bodies.

It is twenty leagues to Tusayan, going northwest. This is a province with seven villages, of the same sort, dress, habits, and ceremonies as at Cibola. There may be as many as 3,000 or 4,000 men in the fourteen villages of these two provinces. It is forty leagues or more to Tiguex, the road trending toward the north. The rock of Acuco, which we described in the first part, is between these.

CHAPTER 4

Of how they live at Tiguex, and of the province of Tiguex and its neighborhood.

Tiguex is a province with twelve villages on the banks of a large, mighty river; some villages on one side and some on the other. It is a spacious valley two leagues wide, and a very high, rough, snow-covered mountain chain lies east of it. There are seven villages in the ridges at the foot of this—four on the plain and three situated on the skirts of the mountain.

There are seven villages seven leagues to the north, at Quirix, and the seven villages of the province of Hemes are forty leagues northeast [northwest]. It is forty leagues north or east to Acha, and four leagues southeast to Tutahaco, a province with eight villages. In general, these villages all have the same habits and customs, although some have some things in particular which the others have not. They are governed by the opinions of the elders. They all work together to build the villages, the women being engaged in making the mixture and the walls, while the men bring the wood and put it in place. They have no lime, but they make a mixture of ashes, coals, and dirt which is almost as good as mortar, for when the house is to have four stories, they do not make the walls more than half a yard thick. They gather a great pile of twigs of thyme [sagebrush] and sedge grass and set it afire, and when it is half coals and ashes they throw a quantity of dirt and water on it and mix it all together. They make round balls of this, which they use instead of stones after they are dry, fixing them with the same mixture, which comes to be like a stiff clay. Before they are married the young men serve the whole village in general, and fetch the wood that is needed for use, putting it in a pile in the courtyard of the villages, from which the women take it to carry to their houses.

The young men live in the estufas, which are in the yards of the village. They are underground, square or round, with pine pillars. Some were seen with twelve pillars and with four in the centre as large as two men could stretch around. They usually had three or four pillars. The floor was made of large, smooth stones, like the baths which they have in Europe. They have a hearth made like the binnacle or compass box of a ship, in which they burn a handful of thyme at a time to keep up the heat, and they can stay in there just as in a bath. The top was on a level with the ground. Some that were seen were large enough for a game of ball. When any man wishes to marry, it has to be arranged by those who govern. The man has to spin and weave a blanket and place it before the woman, who covers herself with it and becomes his wife. The houses belong to the women, the estufas to the men. If a man repudiates his woman, he has to go to the estufa. It is forbidden for women to sleep in the estufas, or to enter these for any purpose except to give their husbands or sons something to eat. The men spin and weave. The women bring up the children and prepare the food. The country is so fertile that they do not have to break up the ground the year round, but only have to sow the seed, which is presently covered by the fall of snow, and the ears come up under the snow. In one year they gather enough for seven. A very large number of cranes and wild geese and crows and starlings live on what is sown, and for all this, when they come to sow for another year, the fields are covered with corn which they have not been able to finish gathering.

There are a great many native fowl in these provinces, and cocks with great hanging chins. When dead, these keep for sixty days, and longer in winter, without losing their feathers or opening, and without any bad smell, and the same is true of dead men.

The villages are free from nuisances, because they go outside to excrete, and they pass their water into clay vessels, which they empty at a distance from the village. They keep the separate houses where they prepare the food for eating and where they grind the meal, very clean. This is a separate room or closet, where they have a trough with three stones fixed in stiff clay. Three women go in here, each one having a stone, with which one of them breaks the corn, the next grinds it, and the third grinds it again. They take off their shoes, do up their hair, shake their clothes, and cover their heads before they enter the door. A man sits at the door playing on a fife while they grind, moving the stones to the music and singing together. They grind a large quantity at one time, because they make all their bread of meal soaked in warm water, like wafers. They gather a great quantity of brushwood and dry it to use for cooking all through the year. There are no fruits good to eat in the country, except the pine nuts. They have their preachers. Sodomy is not found among them. They do not eat human flesh nor make sacrifices of it. The people are not cruel, for they had Francisco de Ovando in Tiguex about forty days, after he was dead, and when the village was captured, he was found among their dead, whole and without any other wound except the one which killed him, white as snow, without any bad smell. I found out several things about them from one of our Indians, who had been a captive among them for a whole year. I asked him especially for the reason why the young women in that province went entirely naked, however cold it might be, and he told me that the virgins had to go around this way until they took a husband, and that they covered themselves after they had known man. The men here wore little shirts of tanned deerskin and their long robes over this. In all these provinces they have earthenware glazed with antimony and jars of extraordinary labor and workmanship, which were worth seeing.

CHAPTER 5

Of Cicuye and the villages in its neighborhood, and of how some people came to conquer this country.

We have already said that the people of Tiguex and of all the provinces on the banks of that river were all alike, having the same ways of living and the same customs. It will not be necessary to say anything particular about them. I wish merely to give an account of Cicuye and some depopulated villages which the army saw on the direct road which it followed thither, and of others that were across the snowy mountains near Tiguex, which also lay in that region above the river.

Cicuye is a village of nearly five hundred warriors, who are feared throughout that country. It is square, situated on a rock, with a large court or yard in the middle, containing the estufas. The houses are all alike, four stories high. One can go over the top of the whole village without there being a street to hinder. There are corridors going all around it at the first two stories, by which one can go around the whole village. These are like outside balconies, and they are able to protect themselves under these. The houses do not have doors below, but they use ladders, which can be lifted up like a drawbridge, and so go up to the corridors which are on the inside of the village. As the doors of the houses open on the corridor of that story, the corridor serves as a street. The houses that open on the plain are right back of those that open on the court, and in time of war they go through those behind them. The village is enclosed by a low wall of stone. There is a spring of water inside, which they are able to divert. The people of this village boast that no one has been able to conquer them and that they conquer whatever villages they wish. The people and their customs are like those of the other villages. Their virgins also go nude until they take husbands, because they say that if they do anything wrong then it will be seen, and so they do not do it. They do not need to be ashamed because they go around as they were born.

There is a village, small and strong, between Cicuye and the province of Quirix, which the Spaniards named Ximena, and another village almost deserted, only one part of which is inhabited. This was a large village, and judging from its condition and newness it appeared to have been destroyed. They called this the village of the granaries (*silos*), because large underground cellars were found here stored with corn. There was another large village farther on, entirely destroyed and pulled down, in the yards of which there were many stone balls, as big as twelve-quart bowls, which seemed to have been thrown by engines or catapults, which had destroyed the village. All that I was able to find out about them was that, sixteen years before, some people called Teyas had come to this country in great numbers and had destroyed these villages. They had besieged Cicuye but had not been able to capture it, because it was strong, and when they left the region, they had made peace with the whole country. It seems as if they must have been a powerful people, and that they must have had engines to knock down the villages. The only thing they could tell about the direction these people came from was by pointing toward the north. They usually call these people Teyas or brave men, just as the Mexicans say chichimecas or braves, for the Teyas whom the army saw were brave. These knew the people in the settlements, and were friendly with them, and they (the Teyas of the plains) went there to spend the winter under the wings of the settlements. The inhabitants do not dare to let them come inside, because they can not trust them. Although they are received as friends, and trade with them, they do not stay in the villages over night, but outside under the wings. The villages are guarded by sentinels with trumpets, who call to one another just as in the fortresses of Spain.

There are seven other villages along this route, toward the snowy mountains, one of which has been half destroyed by the people already referred to. These were under the rule of Cicuye. Cicuye is in a little valley between mountain chains and mountains covered with large pine forests. There is a little stream which contains very good trout and otters, and there are very large bears and good falcons hereabouts.

CHAPTER 6

Which gives the number of villages which were seen in the country of the terraced houses, and their population.

Before I proceed to speak of the plains, with the cows and settlements and tribes there, it seems to me that it will be well for the reader to know how large the settlements were, where the houses with stories, gathered into villages, were seen, and how great an extent of country they occupied. As I say, Cibola is the first:

Cibola, seven villages.
Tusayan, seven villages.
The rock of Acuco, one.
Tiguex, twelve villages.
Tutahaco, eight villages.
These villages were below the river.
Quirix, seven villages.
In the snowy mountains, seven villages.
Ximena, three villages.
Cicuye, one village.
Hemes, seven villages.
Aguas Calientes, or Boiling Springs, three villages.
Yuqueyunque, in the mountains, six villages.
Valladolid, called Braba, one village.
Chia, one village.

In all, there are sixty-six villages. Tiguex appears to be in the centre of the villages. Valladolid is the farthest up the river toward the northeast. The four villages down the river are toward the southeast, because the river turns toward the east. It is 130 leagues—ten more or less—from the farthest point that was seen down the river to the farthest point up the river, and all the settlements are within this region. Including those at a distance, there are sixty-six villages in all, as I have said, and in all of them there may be some 20,000 men, which may be taken to be a fair estimate of the population of the villages. There are no houses or other buildings between one village and another, but where we went it is entirely uninhabited. These people, since they are few, and their manners, government, and habits are so different from all the nations that have been seen and discovered in these western regions, must come from that part of Greater India, the coast of which lies to the west of this country, for they could have come down from that country, crossing the mountain chains and following down the river, settling in what seemed to them the best place. As they multiplied, they have kept on making settlements until they lost the river when it buried itself underground, its course being in the direction of Florida. It [the Rio Grande] comes down from the northeast, where they [Coronado's army] could certainly have found signs of villages. He [Coronado] preferred, however, to follow the reports of the Turk, but it would have been better to cross the mountains where this river rises. I believe they would have found traces of riches and would have reached the lands from which these people started, which from its location is on the edge of Greater India, although the region is neither known nor understood, because from the trend of the coast it appears that the land between Norway and China is very far up. The country from sea to sea is very wide, judging from the location of both coasts, as well as from what Captain Villalobos discovered when he went in search of China by the sea to the west, and from what has been discovered on the North Sea concerning the trend of the coast of Florida toward the Bacallaos, up toward Norway.

To return then to the proposition with which I began, I say that the settlements and people already named were all that were seen in a region seventy leagues wide and 130 long, in the settled country along the river Tiguex. In New Spain there are not one but many establishments containing a larger number of people. Silver metals were found in many of their villages, which they use for glazing and painting their earthenware.

CHAPTER 7

Which treats of the plains that were crossed, of the cows, and of the people who inhabit them.

We have spoken of the settlements of high houses which are situated in what seems to be the most level and open part of the mountains, since it is 150 leagues across before entering the level country between the two mountain chains which I said

were near the North Sea and the South Sea, which might better be called the Western Sea along this coast. This mountain series is the one which is near the South Sea. In order to show that the settlements are in the middle of the mountains, I will state that it is eighty leagues from Chichilticalli, where we began to cross this country, to Cibola; from Cibola, which is the first village, to Cicuye, which is the last on the way across, is seventy leagues; it is thirty leagues from Cicuye to where the plains begin. It may be we went across in an indirect or roundabout way, which would make it seem as if there was more country than if it had been crossed in a direct line, and it may be more difficult and rougher. This can not be known certainly, because the mountains change their direction above the bay at the mouth of the Firebrand (Tizon) River.

Now we will speak of the plains. The country is spacious and level, and is more than 400 leagues wide in the part between the two mountain ranges—one, that which Francisco Vazquez Coronado crossed, and the other that which the force under Don Fernando de Soto crossed, near the North Sea, entering the country from Florida. No settlements were seen anywhere on these plains.

In traversing 250 leagues, the other mountain range was not seen, nor a hill nor a hillock which was three times as high as a man. Several lakes were found at intervals; they were round as plates, a stone's throw or more across, some fresh and some salt. The grass grows tall near these lakes; away from them it is very short, a span or less. The country is like a bowl, so that when a man sits down, the horizon surrounds him all around at the distance of a musket shot. There are no groves of trees except at the rivers, which flow at the bottom of some ravines where the trees grow so thick that they were not noticed until one was right on the edge of them. They are of dead earth. There are paths down into these, made by the cows when they go to the water, which is essential throughout these plains. As I have related in the first part, people follow the cows, hunting them and tanning the skins to take to the settlements in the winter to sell, since they go there to pass the winter, each company going to those which are nearest, some to the settlements at Cicuye, others toward Quivira, and others to the settlements which are situated in the direction of Florida. These people are called Querechos and Teyas. They described some large settlements, and judging from what was seen of these people and from the accounts they gave of other places, there are a good many more of these people than there are of those at the settlements. They have better figures, are better warriors, and are more feared. They travel like the Arabs, with their tents and troops of dogs loaded with poles and having Moorish pack-saddles with girths. When the load gets disarranged, the dogs howl, calling someone to fix them right. These people eat raw flesh and drink blood. They do not eat human flesh. They are a kind people and not cruel. They are faithful friends. They are able to make themselves very well understood by means of signs. They dry the flesh in the sun, cutting it thin like a leaf, and when dry they grind it like meal to keep it and made a sort of sea soup of it to eat. A handful thrown into a pot swells up so as to increase very much. They season it with fat, which they always try to secure when they kill a cow. They empty a large gut and fill it with blood, and carry this around the neck to drink when they are thirsty. When they open the belly of a cow, they squeeze out the chewed grass and drink the juice that remains behind, because they say that this contains the essence of the stomach. They cut the hide open at the back and pull it off at the joints, using a flint as large as a finger, tied in a little stick, with as much ease as if working with a good iron tool. They give it an edge with their own teeth. The quickness with which they do this is something worth seeing and noting.

There are very great numbers of wolves on these plains, which go around with the cows. They have white skins. The deer are pied with white. Their skin is loose, so that when they are killed it can be pulled off with the hand while warm, coming off like pigskin. The rabbits, which are very numerous, are so foolish that those on horseback killed them with their lances. This is when they are mounted among the cows. They fly from a person on foot.

CHAPTER 8

Of Quivira, of where it is and some information about it.

Quivira is to the west of those ravines, in the midst of the country, somewhat nearer the mountains toward the sea, for the country is level as far as Quivira, and there they began to see some mountain chains. The country is well settled. Judging from what was seen on the borders of it, this country is very similar to that of Spain in the varieties of vegetation and fruits. There are plums like those of Castile, grapes, nuts, mulberries, oats, pennyroyal, wild marjoram, and large quantities of flax, but this does not do them any good, because they do not know how to use it. The people are of almost the same sort and appearance as the Teyas. They have villages like those in New Spain. The houses are round, without a wall, and they have one story like a loft, under the roof, where they sleep and keep their belongings. The roofs are of straw. There are other thickly settled provinces around it containing large numbers of men. A friar named Juan de Padilla remained in this province, together with a Spanish-Portuguese and a negro and a half-blood and some Indians from the province of Capothan, in New Spain. They killed the friar because he wanted to go to the province of the Guas, who were their enemies. The Spaniard escaped by taking flight on a mare, and afterward reached New Spain, coming out by way of Panuco. The Indians from New Spain who accompanied the friar were allowed by the murderers to bury him, and then they followed the Spaniard and overtook him. This Spaniard was a Portuguese, named Campo.

The great river of the Holy Spirit (Espiritu Santo), which Don Fernando de Soto discovered in the country of Florida, flows through this country. It passes through a province called Arache, according to the reliable accounts which were obtained here. The sources were not visited, because, according to what they said, it comes from a very distant country in the mountains of the South Sea, from the part that sheds its waters onto the plains. It flows across all the level country and breaks through the mountains of the North Sea, and comes out where the people with Don Fernando de

Soto navigated it. This is more than 300 leagues from where it enters the sea. On account of this, and also because it has large tributaries, it is so mighty when it enters the sea that they lost sight of the land before the water ceased to be fresh.

This country of Quivira was the last that was seen, of which I am able to give any description or information. Now it is proper for me to return and speak of the army, which I left in Tiguex, resting for the winter, so that it would be able to proceed or return in search of these settlements of Quivira, which was not accomplished after all, because it was God's pleasure that these discoveries should remain for other peoples and that we who had been there should content ourselves with saying that we were the first who discovered it and obtained any information concerning it, just as Hercules knew the site where Julius Caesar was to found Seville or Hispales. May the all-powerful Lord grant that His will be done in everything. It is certain that if this had not been His will Francisco Vazquez [Coronado] would not have returned to New Spain without cause or reason, as he did, and that it would not have been left for those with Don Fernando de Soto to settle such a good country, as they have done, and besides settling it to increase its extent, after obtaining, as they did, information from our army.

Terms

Cíbola—Zuñi
Tiguex—in the vicinity of Albuquerque
Cicuye—Pecos
Quivira—probably in northeastern part of the modern state of Kansas, in the region between the Arkansas and Kansas Rivers
North Sea—Atlantic Ocean
South Sea—Pacific Ocean
Great River—Missouri-Mississippi

Questions

1. Describe the Pueblo communities encountered by Coronado's expedition. How were they organized? What did they eat? How large was the population?
2. How might these communities have compared with contemporary Spanish towns?
3. What aspects of Pueblo culture might the Spanish have overlooked? Why?
4. How did the Plains Indians described by Castañeda differ from the Pueblos? What domestic animals did the Plains Indians employ?
5. Describe the character of relations among the different Indian communities.
6. What are the cattle Castañeda mentions?

1.3   The de Soto Expedition in the Southeast

The following description of the Mississippian peoples of the American Southeast derives from an account of the 1539–1543 Hernando de Soto expedition in Gonzalo Fernández de Oviedo y Valdés's Historia General y Natural de las Indias. *Oviedo drew his information from Rodrigo Ranjel, de Soto's private secretary on the expedition. The passage begins with the Spanish in what is now northwest Alabama and ends on the Mississippi River.*

AUTHOR'S PREFACE

Let not the reader marvel that the historian goes over in exact detail the days' marches and rivers

---

*Edward Gaylord Bourne, ed. and trans., Narratives of the Career of Hernando De Soto (London: David Nutt, 1905), vol. 2: 47–48, 120–145.

and crossings that this Commander and Governor Hernando de Soto encountered in these provinces and regions of the north, because among those gentlemen who were with the army all the time there was one named Rodrigo Ranjel, of whom mention has been made and will be made in the future, who served in this army and who, desiring to keep in mind what he saw and the course of his life, wrote down day by day at the end of his labours, every thing which happened, like a wise man, and also as a diversion, and also because every Christian ought to do so, to be able to confess, and to recall to memory his faults, especially those who are engaged in war; and also because those who have toiled and endured such heavy labours find comfort afterwards, as eyewitnesses, in sharing their experiences with their friends, and in giving an account of themselves as they ought to. And so this Rodrigo Ranjel, after all these things had happened, which have been and shall be narrated, came to this city of Santo Domingo, in the Island of Española, and gave an account to the royal audiencia of all these things, and it asked him and charged him that he should tell me in writing and give an account of everything in order that, as chronicler of their Majesties of these histories of the Indies, there might be gathered together and included in them this conquest and discovery in the North, that it might be known; since so many novelties and strange matters would be a delight for the judicious reader and a warning to many who are likely to lose their lives in these Indies following a governor who thus has control over the lives of others, as is apparent by these studies and writings of mine.

CHAPTER VII

In which is related what happened to the commander Hernando de Soto, in his intercourse with the chief of Tascaluca named Actahachi, who was such a tall man that he seemed a Giant; and also of the Skirmishes and tough Battles, and the assault made upon the Christians in the village called Mabila and further on in Chicaca. And other incidents noteworthy and appropriate to the history narrated in this chapter.

Sunday, October 10, the Governor entered the village of Tascaluca, which is called Athahachi, a recent village. And the chief was on a kind of balcony on a mound at one side of the square, his head covered by a kind of coif like the almaizal, so that his headdress was like a Moor's which gave him an aspect of authority; he also wore a *pelote* or mantle of feathers down to his feet, very imposing; he was seated on some high cushions, and many of the principal men among his Indians were with him. He was as tall as that Tony of the Emperor, our lord's guard, and well proportioned, a fine and comely figure of a man. He had a son, a young man as tall as himself but more slender. Before this chief there stood always an Indian of graceful mien holding a parasol on a handle something like a round and very large fly fan, with a cross similar to that of the Knights of the Order of St. John of Rhodes, in the middle of a black field, and the cross was white. And although the Governor entered the plaza and alighted from his horse and went up to him, he did not rise, but remained passive in perfect composure and as if he had been a king.

The Governor remained seated with him a short time, and after a little he arose and said that they should come to eat, and he took him with him and the Indians came to dance; and they danced very well in the fashion of rustics in Spain, so that it was pleasant to see them. At night he desired to go, and the commander told him that he must sleep there. He understood it and showed that he scoffed at such an intention for him, being the lord, to receive so suddenly restraints upon his liberty, and dissembling, he immediately despatched his principal men each by himself, and he slept there notwithstanding his reluctance. The next day the Governor asked him for carriers and a hundred Indian women; and the chief gave him four hundred carriers and the rest of them and the women he said he would give at Mabila, the province of one his principal vassals. And the Governor acquiesced in having the rest of that unjust request of his fulfilled in Mabila; and he ordered him to be given a horse and some buskins and a scarlet cloak for him to ride off happy. And now that the chief had given him four hundred carriers or rather slaves, and was to give him in Mabila a hundred women, and what they were most in need of, see how happy he could be made with those buskins and the cloak and with riding on a horse when he felt as if he were mounted on a tiger or a most savage lion, since this people held horses in the greatest terror!

At last, Tuesday, October 12, they departed from that village of Atahachi, taking along the chief as has been said and with him many principal men and always the Indian with the sunshade attending his lord, and another with a cushion. And that night they slept in the open country. The next day, Wednesday, they came to Piachi, which is a village high above the gorge of a mountain stream; and the chief of this place was evil intentioned, and attempted to resist their passage; and as a result, they crossed the stream with effort, and two Christians were slain, and also the principal Indians who accompanied the chief. In this village, Piachi, it was learned that they had killed Don Teodoro and a black, who came from the ships of Pamphilo do Narvaez.

Saturday, October 16, they departed thence into a mountain where they met one of the two Christians whom the Governor had sent to Mabila, and he said that in Mabila there had gathered together much people in arms. The next day they came to a fenced village, and there came messengers from Mabila bringing to the chief much bread made from chestnuts, which are abundant and excellent in that region.

Monday, October 18, St. Luke's day, the Governor came to Mabila, having passed that day by several villages, which was the reason that the soldiers stayed behind to forage and to scatter themselves, for the region appeared populous. And there went on with the Governor only forty horsemen as an advance guard, and after they had tarried a little, that the Governor might not show weakness, he entered into the village with the chief, and all his guard went in with him. Here the Indians immediately began an areyto, which is their fashion for a ball with dancing and song. While this was going on some soldiers saw them putting bundles of bows and arrows slyly among some palm leaves, and other Christians saw that above and below the cabins were full of people concealed. The Governor was informed of it and he put his helmet on his head and ordered all to go and mount their horses and warn all the soldiers that had come up. Hardly had they gone out when the Indians took the entrances of stockade, and there were left with the Governor, Luis de Moscoso and Baltasar de Gallegos, and Espindola, the Captain of the Guard, and seven or eight soldiers. And the chief went into a cabin and refused to come out of it. Then they began to shoot arrows at the Governor. Baltasar de Gallegos went in for the chief, he not being willing to come out. He disabled the

arm of a principal Indian with the slash of a knife. Luis de Moscoso waited at the door, so as not to leave him alone, and he was fighting like a knight and did all that was possible until, not being able to endure any more, he cried: "Señor Baltasar de Gallegos, come out, or I will leave you, for I cannot wait any longer for you." During this, Solis, a resident of Triana of Seville, had ridden up, and Rodrigo Ranjel, who were the first, and for his sins Solis was immediately stricken down dead; but Rodrigo Ranjel got to the gate of the town at the time when the Governor went out, and two soldiers of his guard with him, and after him came more than seventy Indians who were held back for fear of Rodrigo Ranjel's horse, and the Governor, desiring to charge them, a negro brought up his horse; and he told Rodrigo Ranjel to give aid to the Captain of the Guard, who was left behind, for he had come out quite used up, and a soldier of the Guard with him; and he with a horse faced the enemy until he got out of danger, and Rodrigo Ranjel returned to the Governor and had him draw out more than twenty arrows which he bore fastened in his armour, which was a loose coat quilted with coarse cotton. And he ordered Ranjel to watch for Solis, to rescue him from the enemy that they should not carry him inside. And the Governor went to collect the soldiers. There was great valour and shame that day among all those that found themselves in this first attack and beginning of this unhappy day; for they fought to admiration and each Christian did his duty as a most valiant soldier. Luis de Moscoso and Baltasar de Gallegos came out with the rest of the soldiers by another gate.

As a result, the Indians were left with the village and all the property of the Christians, and with the horses that were left tied inside, which they killed immediately. The Governor collected all of the forty horses that were there and advanced to a large open place before the principal gate of Mabila. There the Indians rushed out without venturing very far from the stockade, and to draw them on the horsemen made a feint of taking flight at a gallop, withdrawing far from the walls. And the Indians believing it to be real, came away from the village and the stockade in pursuit, greedy to make use of their arrows. And when it was time the horsemen wheeled about on the enemy, and before they could recover themselves, killed many with their lances. Don Carlos wanted to go with his horse as far as the gate, and they gave the horse an arrow shot in the breast. And not being able to turn, he dismounted to draw out the arrow, and then another came which hit him in the neck above the shoulder, at which, seeking confession, he fell dead. The Indians no longer dared to withdraw from the stockade. Then the Commander invested them on every side until the whole force had come up; and they went up on three sides to set fire to it, first cutting the stockade with axes. And the fire in its course burned the two hundred odd pounds of pearls that they had, and all their clothes and ornaments, and the sacramental cups, and the moulds for making the wafers, and the wine for saying the mass; and they were left like Arabs, completely stripped, after all their hard toil. They had left in a cabin the Christian women, which were some slaves belonging to the Governor; and some pages, a friar, a priest, a cook, and some soldiers defended themselves very well against the Indians, who were not able to force an entrance before the Christians came with the fire and rescued them. And all the Spaniards fought like men of great courage, and twenty-two died, and one hundred and forty-eight others received six hundred and eighty-eight arrow wounds, and seven horses were killed and twenty-nine others wounded. Women and even boys of four years of age fought with the Christians; and Indian boys hanged themselves not to fall into their hands, and others jumped into the fire of their own accord. See with what good will those carriers acted. The arrow shots were tremendous, and sent with such a will and force that the lance of one gentleman named Nuno de Tovar, made of two pieces of ash and very good, was pierced by an arrow in the middle, as by an auger, without being split and the arrow made a cross with the lance.

On that day there died Don Carlos, and Francis de Soto, the nephew of the Governor, and Johan de Gamez de Jaen, and Men Rodriguez, a fine Portugues gentleman, and Espinosa, a fine gentleman, and another named Velez, and one Blasco de Bar-

carrota, and many other honoured soliders; and the wounded comprised all the men of most worth and honour in the army. They killed three thousand of the vagabonds without counting many others who were wounded and whom they afterwards found dead in the cabins and along the roads. Whether the chief was dead or alive was never known. The son they found thrust through with a lance.

After the end of the battle as described, they rested there until the 14th of November, caring for their wounds and their horses, and they burned over much of the country. And up to the time when they left there, the total deaths from the time the Governor and his forces entered the land of Florida, were one hundred and two Christians, and not all, to my thinking, in true repentance.

Sunday, November 14, of the year already mentioned, the Governor left Mabila, and the Wednesday following came to a fine river. Thursday, the 28th, their way lay over bad places and through swamps, and they found a village with corn which was named Talicpacana. The Christians had discovered on the other side of the river a village which appeared to them from a distance to be finely situated.

On Sunday, the 21th of November, Vasco Gonçalez found a village half a league distant from this named Moculixa, from which they had transported all the corn to the other side of the river and had piled it in heaps covered with mats; and the Indians were across the river, and were making threats. A barge was constructed which was finished the 29th of the month, and they made a large truck to carry it to Moculixa; and when it was launched in the water sixty soldiers embarked in it. The Indians shot countless darts, or rather arrows. But when this great canoe reached the shore they took flight, and not more than three or four Christians were wounded. The country was easily secured, and they found an abundance of corn.

The next day, Wednesday, the whole force came to a village which was called Zabusta, and there they crossed the river in the boat and with some canoes that they had found in that place; and they tarried for the night in another village on the other side, because up above they found a fine one, and took the chief, whose name was Apafalaya, and carried him along as guide and interpreter; and this stream was called the river Apafalaya. From this river and town the Governor and his army set out in search of Chicaça on Thursday, December 9. The following Tuesday they arrived at the river of Chicaça, having traversed many bad passages and swamps and cold rivers.

And that you may know, reader, what sort, of a life these Spaniards led, Rodrigo Ranjel, an eye-witness, says that among many other great hard-ships that men endured in this undertaking he saw a knight named Don Antonio Osorio, brother of the Lord Marquis of Astorga, wearing a short gar-ment of the blankets of that country, torn on the sides, his flesh showing, no hat, bare-headed, bare-footed, without hose or shoes, a buckler on his back, a sword without a shield, amidst heavy frosts and cold. And the stuff of which he was made and his illustrious lineage made him endure his toil without laments such as many others made, for there was no one who could help him, although he was the man he was, and had in Spain two thou-sand ducats of income through the Church. And the day that this gentleman saw him he did not be-lieve that he had eaten a mouthful, and he had to dig for it with his nails to get something to eat.

I could hardly help laughing when I heard that this knight had left the Church and the in-come above mentioned to go in search of such a life as this, at the sound of the words of de Soto; because I knew Soto very well, and, although he was a man of worth, I did not suppose that he was so winning a talker or so clever, as to be able to de-lude such persons. What was it that a man like him wanted of a land unexplored and unknown? Nor did the Captain that took him know anything more than that in this land had perished John Ponce de Leon and the lawyer Lucas Vazquez de Allyón and Pamphilo de Narvaez and others abler than Hernando de Soto. And those that follow such guides have to go in that manner, since they found regions where they were able to make a set-tlement and rest and gradually push in and make their inferences and learn the country. But let us proceed, for the toil of this knight is little com-pared with those that are dying and escape.

The river of Chicaça they found overflowing its bed, and the Indians on the other side in arms with many white flags. Orders were given to make a barge, and the Governor sent Baltasar de Galle-gos with thirty horsemen, swimmers, to search the river up above for a good crossing place, and to fall suddenly upon the Indians; and it was per-ceived, and they forsook the passage and they crossed over very comfortably in the barge on Thursday, the 16th of the month. And the Gover-nor went on ahead with some horsemen, and they arrived late at night at a village of the lord which had been deserted by all the people. The next day Baltasar de Gallegos appeared with the thirty that went with him, and they spent that Christmas in Chicaça, and there was a snowstorm with a heavy fall of snow, just as if they had been in Burgos, and the cold was as severe, or more so. On Monday, January 3, 1541, the chief of Chicaça came prof-fering peace, and promptly gave the Christians guides and interpreters to go to Caluça, a place of much repute among the Indians. Caluça is a province of more than ninety villages not subject to any one, with a savage population, very warlike and much dreaded, and the soil is fertile in that section. In Chicaça the Governor ordered that half of his army make war on Sacchuma; and on their return the Chief Miculasa made peace, and mes-sengers came from Talapatica. In the meantime, while this war was going on, the time came to march, and they asked the chief for carriers; and the Indians raised such a tumult among themselves that the Christians understood it; and the settlement was that they would give them on the 4th of March, when they had to start, and that on that day they would come with them. On the evening of that day the Governor mounted his horse and found the Indians evilly disposed, and realizing their dangerous intentions he returned to the camp and said in public: "To-night is an Indian night. I shall sleep armed and my horse saddled." And they all said that they would do the same, and he called the Master of the Camp, who was Luis de Moscoso, and told him that they should take extra precautions that night in regard to the sen-tinels, since it was the last. The Governor as he went away from where he left those soldiers to whom he had given these warnings, lay down undressed on his couch, and neither was his horse saddled nor any other, and all those in the camp lay down to sleep without precautions and unarmed. The Master of the Camp put on the morning watch three horsemen, the most useless and with the poorest horses in the army. And on the day before mentioned, the 4th of March, when the Indian carriers had been promised them, at dawn, the Indians, fulfilling their word, entered the camp in many detachments, beating drums as if it had been in Italy, and setting fire to the camp, they burned and captured fifty-nine horses, and three of them they shot through both shoulders with arrows.

And the Christians were like heedless people on this occasion; and few arms, coasts-of-mail, lances and saddles remained after the fire; and all the horses had run off, escaping the fire and the noise. Only the commander was able to mount his horse, and they did not fasten the horse's girth, nor did he buckle his coat of arms, and Tapia de Valladolid was with him; and he fell over the first Indian that he thrust at who had thrust at him, saddle and all, and if the Indians had known how to follow up their victory, this would have been the last day of the lives of all the Christians of that army, and made an end of the demand for carriers.

Next the Spaniards went to a plain, a league from that village where they were; and they had cabins and supplies, and they set up the camp on a sloping hillside. And they made haste to set up a forge, and they made bellows of bear skins, and they retempered their arms, and made new frames for their saddles, and they provided themselves with lances for there were in that place very good ash-trees. And within a week they had everything repaired. There were slain in Chicaça and burned alive twelve Christians.

Tuesday, March 15, the morning watch, the Indians returned upon the Christians, determined to finish them up, and attacked them on three sides; and as necessity had made them cautious, and as they were informed and on the watch, they fought with them bravely and put the Indians to flight. And it pleased God that the Christians should not suffer much loss, and few

Indians perished. Some Spaniards displayed great valour that day, and no one failed to do his duty. And unfortunate was he on that occasion who did not well defend his life and who failed to prove to the enemy the quality and arms of the Christians.

CHAPTER VIII

In which the History narrates another encounter at a Barricade, in which the Commander fought with the Indians; and how he came to a very large river which the Christians crossed; and of the narration and discourse which the Chief of Casoui delivered in favour of the cross and the faith in the presence of the Commander and the Christians; and of the contention of this Chief with another, his enemy, named Pacaha, as to which ought to have precedence. Their departure from Utiangüe, and many other notable incidents.

Tuesday, April 26, in the year aforesaid, 1541, the Governor Hernando de Soto set out from the plain of Chicaça, and arrived at Limamu for the night; and there they searched for corn, because the Indians had hidden it, and they had to pass over a desert. And Thursday they came to another plain where the Indians had taken the position, having made a very strong barricade, and within it there were many Indian braves, painted red and decorated with other colours which appeared very fine (or rather, very bad, at least it meant harm to the Christians). And they entered the barricade by force, and with some loss by death and wounds on the part of the Commander and his army, and with a loss greater beyond comparison on the part of the conquered; and it would have been still more if the Indians had not taken flight.

Saturday, the last of April, the army set out from the place of the barricade and marched nine days through a deserted country and by a rough way, mountainous and swampy, until May 8, when they came to the first village of Quizqui, which they took by assault and captured much people and clothes; but the Governor promptly restored them to liberty and had everything restored to them for fear of war, although that was not enough to make friends of these Indians. A league beyond this village they came upon another with abundance of corn, and soon again after another league, upon another likewise amply provisioned. There they saw the great river. Saturday, May 21, the force went along to a plain between the river and a small village, and set up quarters and began to build four barges to cross over to the other side. Many of these conquerors said this river was larger than the Danube.

On the other side of the river, about seven thousand Indians had got together, with about two hundred canoes, to defend the passage. All of them had shields made of canes joined, so strong and so closely interwoven with such thread that a cross-bow could hardly pierce them. The arrows came raining down so that the air was full of them, and their yells were something fearful. But when they saw that the work on the barges did not relax on their account, they said that Pacaha, whose men they were, ordered them to withdraw, and so they left the passage free. And on Saturday, June 8, the whole force crossed this great river in the four barges and gave thanks to God because in His good pleasure nothing more difficult could confront them. Soon, on Sunday, they came to a village of Aquixo.

Tuesday, June 21, they went from there and passed by the settlement of Aquixo, which is very beautiful, or beautifully situated. The next day, Wednesday, they passed through the worst tract for swamps and water that they had found in all Florida, and on that day the toil of the soldiers was very heavy.

The next day following, Thursday, they entered the land of Quarqui, and passed through small villages; and the next day, Friday, St. John's day, they came to the village of the Lord of Casqui, who gave food and clothing to the army. It was Saturday when they entered his village, and it had very good cabins, and, in the principal one, over the door, were many heads of very fierce bulls, just as in Spain, noblemen who are sportsmen mount the heads of wild boars or bears. There the Christians planted the cross on a mound, and they received it and adored it with much devotion, and the blind and lame came to seek to be healed. Their faith, says Rodrigo Ranjel, would have

surpassed that of the conquerors if they had been taught, and would have brought forth more fruit than those conquerors did.

Sunday, June 26, they departed thence to go to Pacaha, an enemy of Casqui; and after passing several villages, they spent the night in one. And the following day they crossed a swamp over which the Indians had thrown a well-constructed bridge, broad and very cleverly built. On Wednesday they came to the village of Pacaha, a village and lord of wide repute and highly thought of in that country.

This town was a very good one, thoroughly well stockaded; and the walls were furnished with towers and a ditch round about, for the most part full of water which flows in by a canal from the river; and this ditch was full of excellent fish of divers kinds. The chief of Casqui came to the Christians when they were entering the village and they entertained him bravely. In Aquixo, and Casqui, and Pacaha, they saw the best villages seen up to that time, better stockaded and fortified, and the people were of finer quality, excepting those of Cofitachequi. The Commander and his soldiers remaining some days in Pacaha, they made some incursions further up country.

And the chief of Casqui, on one occasion, when he saw a chance for it, went off without seeking permission, on account of which the Governor tried to secure peace with Pacaha; and he came to the camp to recover a brother of his whom the Christians had taken when they entered the village; and an agreement was made with Pacaha that they should war against Casqui, which was very gratifying to Pacaha. But Casqui got wind of this resolve and came with fifty Indians of his in fine array, and he brought a clown for display, who said and did much that was amusing, making those who saw him laugh a good deal. The Governor assumed an air of irritation and sternness to please Pacaha, and sent word that Casqui should not come into the village. Casqui replied that he would not refrain from coming even if they cut off his head. Pacaha asked the Governor to allow him to give Casqui a slash in the face with a knife that he had in his hand, which the Christians had given him. But the Governor told Pacaha that he should do no such thing, nor do him any harm, for he would be angry at him; and he ordered Casqui to come so as to see what he wanted, and because he wished to ask him the reason why he had gone without his permission. Casqui came and spoke to the Governor as follows:—as it was reported by the interpreter Johan Ortiz and the other Indian interpreter that the Governor and the Christians had—"How is it, My Lord, possible, that after having given me the pledge of friendship, and without my having done any harm to you, or given any occasion, you desire to destroy me, your friend and brother? You gave me the cross for a defence against my enemies, and with it you seek to destroy me." (This he said because the Indians of Pacaha, his enemy, that went with the Christians, against him, wore crosses on their heads, high up, that they might be seen.) "Now, my Lord," said Casqui, "when God has heard us by means of the cross; when the women and boys and all those of my country threw themselves on their knees before it to pray for water to the God who you said suffered on it; and He heard us and gave us water in great abundance and refreshed our corn-fields and plantations; now, when we had the most faith in it and in your friendship, you desired to destroy these boys and women that are so devoted to you and your God. Why did you desire to use us with such cruelty without our deserving it from you? Why did you desire to destroy the faith and confidence which we had in you? Why did you desire to offend your God and us, when for Him, and in His name, you gave us assurances and received us for friends, and we gave you entire confidence and trust in the same God and His cross, and have it for our safeguard and protection, and hold it in the reverence and veneration which is proper? With what object or purpose were you actuated to do, or even to think of a thing so grievous against a people without blame, and friends of the cross and of yours?"

This said, he held his peace. The Governor, his eyes melting and not without trace of tears, considering the faith and words of this chief, replied to him, through the interpreters, in the presence of many of the Christian soldiers, who, attentively, and not without tears, overcome by such goodness and faith, had heard what was said, and spoke as follows: "Look you, Casqui, we are not come to destroy you, but to do for you what you know and understand is the work of the cross and our God, as you tell me. And these favours, which it has bestowed upon you, are a small thing in comparison with many others and very great ones, which it will secure you if you love it and believe in it. Be assured of this, and you will find it so and realize it better every day. And when you ran off without my permission I thought that you held the teaching we had given you of little account, and for that contempt that you had for it I wanted to destroy you; supposing that in pride you had gone off, for that is the thing which our God most abhors, and for which He punishes us the most. Now that you have come in humility, be assured that I wish you more good than you think; and if you have need of anything from me, tell me of it and you will see, since we do what our God commands us, which is not to lie; and, therefore, believe that I tell you the truth, since to speak a lie is a very great sin amongst us. For this good-will be not grateful to me or mine, since if you hold what you say, God, our Lord, commands that we love you as a brother, and that we treat you as such because you and yours are our brethren, and such is the injunction of our God."

The Indians, as much as the Christians, had heard with wonder what Casqui had said. It was now the hour for dinner and the commander sat down and ordered both chiefs to be seated. And between them there was much contention, as to which of them should sit on the right hand of the Governor. Pacaha said to Casqui: "You know well that I am a greater lord than you, and of more honourable parents and grandparents, and that to me belongs a higher place." Casqui replied as follows: "True it is that you are a greater lord than I, and that your forbears were greater than mine. And since this great lord here tells us that we must not lie, I will not deny the truth. But you know well that I am older and mightier than you, and that I confine you in your walls whenever I wish, and you never have seen my country." Finally this was left to the Governor to settle and he ordered that Pacaha should be seated on his right hand because he was a greater lord and more ancient in rank, and he showed in his good customs more of the manners of the courtier after their fashion.

Casqui had brought a daughter, a fine young girl, to the Governor. Pacaha gave him one of his wives, blooming, and very worthy; and he gave him a sister and another Indian woman of rank. The Governor made them friends and embraced them and ordered that there should be merchandising and business between one country and the other, and they agreed to it. And after this the Governor departed thence the 29th of July.

But I could wish that along with the excellencies of the cross and of the faith that this Governor explained to these chiefs, he had told them that he was married, and that the Christians ought not to have more than one wife, or to have intercourse with another, or to commit adultery; that he had not taken the daughter whom Casqui gave him, nor the wife and sister and the other woman of rank whom Pacaha gave him; and that they had not got the idea that the Christians, like the Indians, could have as many wives and concubines as they desired, and thus, like the Indians, live as adulterers.

Questions

1. Characterize the Indian societies encountered by de Soto's expedition. How large and dense were their populations? How were they organized? What kind of authority did their leaders possess? How would you describe relations among the Indian towns?

2. How were the Spanish able to survive the rigors of the march and the assaults of the many Indians they antagonized?

3. Describe Spanish-Indian relations in this account. How credible do you consider Ranjel's interpretation of their encounters? Why?

4. Discuss Native responses to the Spanish *entrada*.

5. What effects might de Soto's expedition have had on the Indians of the Southeast?

2 Europeans and the New World

Drawn by tales of fabulous wealth in far-off lands, growing numbers of European explorers, traders, and conquerors ventured into increasingly distant Atlantic waters in the fourteenth, fifteenth, and sixteenth centuries. They contributed to one of the signal developments of the early modern period: the intensifying contact among parts of the world that had been largely separate. The following documents display three steps in this process: fantastic European representations of the Indies, the first encounter between Columbus and the peoples of the Americas, and the catastrophic effects of Old World diseases on New World communities.

2.1 Marco Polo Describes the Riches of Asia*

Venetian merchant Marco Polo journeyed through Asia from 1271 to 1295. Captured after his return in a war between his home city and Genoa, Marco dictated his Travels *to another prisoner, the romance writer Rustichello of Pisa. Many have questioned the accuracy of the resulting account, but we are concerned here less with the journey's reality than with the book's reception. The* Travels *of Marco Polo became enormously popular in late medieval Europe, shaping European ideas about East and South Asia and fueling Europe's desire to tap the region's vast wealth. The city of Kinsai described in our selection is modern Hangzhou in eastern China.*

DESCRIPTION OF THE GREAT CITY OF KINSAY, WHICH IS THE CAPITAL OF THE WHOLE COUNTRY OF MANZI

When you have left the city of Changan and have traveled for three days through a splendid country,

passing a number of towns and villages, you arrive at the most noble city of KINSAY, a name which is as much as to say in our tongue "The City of Heaven," as I told you before.

And since we have got thither I will enter into particulars about its magnificence; and these are well worth the telling, for the city is beyond dispute the finest and the noblest in the world. In this we shall speak according to the written statement which the Queen of this Realm sent to Bayan the conqueror of the country for transmission to the Great Kaan, in order that he might be aware of the surpassing grandeur of the city and might be moved to save it from destruction or injury. I will tell you all the truth as it was set down in that document. For truth it was, as the said Messer Marco Polo at a later date was able to witness with his own eyes. And now we shall rehearse those particulars.

First and foremost, then, the document stated the city of Kinsay to be so great that it hath an hundred miles of compass. And there are in it

*Henry Yule, ed. and trans., *The Book of Ser Marco Polo* (London, 1903), vol. 1: 185–193, 200–208.

twelve thousand bridges of stone, for the most part so lofty that a great fleet could pass beneath them. And let no man marvel that there are so many bridges, for you see the whole city stands as it were in the water and surrounded by water, so that a great many bridges are required to give free passage about it. [And though the bridges be so high the approaches are so well contrived that carts and horses do cross them.]

The document aforesaid also went on to state that there were in this city twelve guilds of the different crafts, and that each guild had 12,000 houses in the occupation of its workmen. Each of these houses contains at least 12 men, whilst some contain 20 and some 40,—not that these are all masters, but inclusive of the journeymen who work under the masters. And yet all these craftsmen had full occupation, for many other cities of the kingdom are supplied from this city with what they require.

The document aforesaid also stated that the number and wealth of the merchants, and the amount of goods that passed through their hands, was so enormous that no man could form a just estimate thereof. And I should have told you with regard to those masters of the different crafts who are at the head of such houses as I have mentioned, that neither they nor their wives ever touch a piece of work with their own hands, but live as nicely and delicately as if they were kings and queens. The wives indeed are most dainty and angelical creatures! Moreover it was an ordinance laid down by the King that every man should follow his father's business and no other, no matter if he possessed 100,000 bezants.

Inside the city there is a Lake which has a compass of some 30 miles: and all round it are erected beautiful palaces and mansions, of the richest and most exquisite structure that you can imagine, belonging to the nobles of the city. There are also on its shores many abbeys and churches of the Idolaters. In the middle of the Lake are two Islands, on each of which stands a rich, beautiful and spacious edifice, furnished in such style as to seem fit for the palace of an Emperor. And when any one of the citizens desired to hold a marriage feast, or to give any other

entertainment, it used to be done at one of these palaces. And everything would be found there ready to order, such as silver plate, trenchers, and dishes [napkins and table-cloths], and whatever else was needful. The King made this provision for the gratification of his people, and the place was open to every one who desired to give an entertainment. [Sometimes there would be at these palaces an hundred different parties; some holding a banquet, others celebrating a wedding; and yet all would find good accommodation in the different apartments and pavilions, and that in so well ordered a manner that one party was never in the way of another.]

The houses of the city are provided with lofty towers of stone in which articles of value are stored for fear of fire; for most of the houses themselves are of timber, and fires are very frequent in the city.

The people are Idolaters; and since they were conquered by the Great Kaan they use paper-money. [Both men and women are fair and comely, and for the most part clothe themselves in silk, so vast is the supply of that material, both from the whole district of Kinsay, and from the imports by traders from other provinces.] And you must know they eat every kind of flesh, even that of dogs and other unclean beasts, which nothing would induce a Christian to eat.

Since the Great Kaan occupied the city he has ordained that each of the 12,000 bridges should be provided with a guard of ten men, in case of any disturbance, or of any being so rash as to plot treason or insurrection against him. [Each guard is provided with a hollow instrument of wood and with a metal basin, and with a time-keeper to enable them to know the hour of the day or night. And so when one hour of the night is past the sentry stikes one on the wooden instrument and on the basin, so that the whole quarter of the city is made aware that one hour of the night is gone. At the second hour he gives two strokes, and so on, keeping always wide awake and on the look out. In the morning again, from the sunrise, they begin to count anew, and strike one hour as they did in the night, and so on hour after hour.

Part of the watch patrols the quarter, to see if any light or fire is burning after the lawful hours; if they find any they mark the door, and in the morning the owner is summoned before the magistrates, and unless he can plead a good excuse he is punished. Also if they find any one going about the streets at unlawful hours they arrest him, and in the morning they bring him before the magistrates. Likewise if in the daytime they find any poor cripple unable to work for his livelihood, they take him to one of the hospitals, of which there are many, founded by the ancient kings, and endowed with great revenues. Or if he be capable of work they oblige him to take up some trade. If they see that any house has caught fire they immediately beat upon that wooden instrument to give the alarm, and this brings together the watchmen from the other bridges to help to extinguish it, and to save the goods of the merchants or others, either by removing them to the towers above mentioned, or by putting them in boats and transporting them to the islands in the lake. For no citizen dares leave his house at night, or to come near the fire; only those who own the property, and those watchmen who flock to help, of whom there shall come one or two thousand at the least.]

Moreover, within the city there is an eminence on which stands a Tower, and at the top of the tower is hung a slab of wood. Whenever fire or any other alarm breaks out in the city a man who stands there with a mallet in his hand beats upon the slab, making a noise that is heard to a great distance. So when the blows upon this slab are heard, everybody is aware that fire has broken out, or that there is some other cause of alarm.

The Kaan watches this city with especial diligence because it forms the head of all Manzi; and because he has an immense revenue from the duties levied on the transactions of trade therein, the amount of which is such that no one would credit it on mere hearsay.

All the streets of the city are paved with stone or brick, as indeed are all the highways throughout Manzi, so that you ride and travel in every direction without inconvenience. Were it not for this pavement you could not do so, for the country is very low and flat, and after rain 'tis deep in mire and water. [But as the Great Kaan's couriers could not gallop their horses over the pavement, the side of the road is left unpaved for their convenience. The pavement of the main street of the city also is laid out in two parallel ways of ten paces in width on either side, leaving a space in the middle laid with fine gravel, under which are vaulted drains which convey the rain water into the canals; and thus the road is kept ever dry.]

You must know also that the city of Kinsay has some 3000 baths, the water of which is supplied by springs. They are hot baths, and the people take great delight in them, frequenting them several times a month, for they are very cleanly in their persons. They are the finest and largest baths in the world; large enough for 100 persons to bathe together.

And the Ocean Sea comes within 25 miles of the city at a place called GANFU, where there is a town and an excellent haven, with a vast amount of shipping which is engaged in the traffic to and from India and other foreign parts, exporting and importing many kinds of wares, by which the city benefits. And a great river flows from the city of Kinsay to that sea-haven, by which vessels can come up to the city itself. This river extends also to other places further inland.

Know also that the Great Kaan hath distributed the territory of Manzi into nine parts, which he hath constituted into nine kingdoms. To each of these kingdoms a king is appointed who is subordinate to the Great Kaan, and every year renders the accounts of his kingdom to the fiscal office at the capital. This city of Kinsay is the seat of one of these kings, who rules over 140 great and wealthy cities. For in the whole of this vast country of Manzi there are more than 1200 great and wealthy cities, without counting the towns and villages, which are in great numbers. And you may receive it for certain that in each of those 1200 cities the Great Kaan has a garrison, and that the smallest of such garrisons musters 1000 men; whilst there are some of 10,000, 20,000 and 30,000; so that the total number of troops is something scarcely calculable. The troops forming these garrisons are not all Tartars. Many are from the province of Cathay, and good soldiers too. But you must not suppose they are by any means all of them cavalry; a very large proportion of them are foot-soldiers, according to the special requirements of each city. And all of them belong to the army of the Great Kaan.

I repeat that everything appertaining to this city is on so vast a scale, and the Great Kaan's yearly revenues therefrom are so immense, that it is not easy even to put it in writing, and it seems past belief to one who merely hears it told. But I *will* write it down for you.

First, however, I must mention another thing. The people of this country have a custom, that as soon as a child is born they write down the day and hour and the planet and sign under which its birth has taken place; so that every one among them knows the day of his birth. And when any one intends a journey he goes to the astrologers, and gives the particulars of his nativity in order to learn whether he shall have good luck or no. Sometimes they will say *no*, and in that case the journey is put off till such day as the astrologer may recommend. These astrologers are very skilful at their business, and often their words come to pass, so the people have great faith in them.

They burn the bodies of the dead. And when any one dies the friends and relations make a great mourning for the deceased, and clothe themselves in hempen garments, and follow the corpse playing on a variety of instruments and singing hymns to their idols. And when they come to the burning place, they take representation of things cut out of parchment, such as caparisoned horses, male and female slaves, camels, armour suits of cloth of gold (and money), in great quantities, and these things they put on the fire along with the corpse, so that they are all burnt with it. And they tell you that the dead man shall have all these slaves and animals of which the effigies are burnt, alive in flesh and blood, and the money in gold, at his disposal in the next world; and that the instruments which they have caused to be played at his funeral, and the idol hymns that have been chanted, shall also be produced again to welcome him in the next world; and that the idols themselves will come to do him honour.

Furthermore there exists in this city the palace of the king who fled, him who was Emperor of Manzi, and that is the greatest palace in the world, as I shall tell you more particularly. For you must know its demesne hath a compass of ten miles, all enclosed with lofty battlemented walls; and inside the walls are the finest and most delectable gardens upon earth, and filled too with the finest fruits. There are numerous fountains in it also, and lakes full of fish. In the middle is the palace itself, a great and splendid building. It contains 20 great and handsome halls, one of which is more spacious than the rest, and affords room for a vast multitude to dine. It is all painted in gold, with many histories and representations of beasts and birds, of knights and dames, and many marvelous things. It forms a really magnificent spectacle, for over all the walls and all the ceiling you see nothing but paintings in gold. And besides these halls the palace contains 1000 large and handsome chambers, all painted in gold and divers colours.

Moreover, I must tell you that in this city there are 160 *tomans* of fires, or in other words 160 *tomans* of houses. Now I should tell you that the *toman* is 10,000, so that you can reckon the total as altogether 1,600,000 houses, among which are a great number of rich palaces. There is one church only, belonging to the Nestorian Christians.

There is another thing I must tell you. It is the custom for every burgess of this city, and in fact for every description of person in it, to write over his door his own name, the name of his wife, and those of his children, his slaves, and all the inmates of his house, and also the number of animals that he keeps. And if any one dies in the house then the name of that person is erased, and if any child is born its name is added. So in this way the sovereign is able to know exactly the population of the city. And this is the practice also throughout all Manzi and Cathay.

And I must tell you that every hosteler who keeps an hostel for travellers is bound to register their names and surnames, as well as the day and month of their arrival and departure. And thus the sovereign hath the means of knowing, whenever it pleases him, who come and go throughout his dominions. And certes this is a wise order and a provident.

The position of the city is such that it has on one side a lake of fresh and exquisitely clear water (already spoken of), and on the other a very large river. The waters of the latter fill a number of canals of all sizes which run through the different quarters of the city, carry away all impurities, and then enter the Lake; whence they issue again and flow to the Ocean, thus producing a most excellent atmosphere. By means of these channels, as well as by the streets, you can go all about the city. Both streets and canals are so wide and spacious that carts on the one and boats on the other can readily pass to and fro, conveying necessary supplies to the inhabitants.

At the opposite side the city is shut in by a channel, perhaps 40 miles in length, very wide, and full of water derived from the river aforesaid, which was made by the ancient kings of the country in order to relieve the river when flooding its banks. This serves also as a defence to the city, and the earth dug from it has been thrown inwards, forming a kind of mound enclosing the city.

In this part are the ten principal markets, though besides these there are a vast number of others in the different parts of the town. The former are all squares of half a mile to the side, and along their front passes the main street, which is 40 paces in width, and runs straight from end to end of the city, crossing many bridges of easy and commodious approach. At every four miles of its length comes one of those great squares of 2 miles (as we have mentioned) in compass. So also parallel to this great street, but at the back of the market places, there runs a very large canal, on the bank of which towards the squares are built great houses of stone, in which the merchants from India and other foreign parts store their wares, to be handy for the markets. In each of the squares is held a market three days in the week, frequented by 40,000 or 50,000 persons, who bring thither for sale every possible necessary of life, so that there is always an ample supply of every kind of meat and game, as of roebuck, red-deer, fallow-deer, hares, rabbits, partridges, pheasants, francolins, quails, fowls, capons, and of ducks and geese an infinite quantity; for so many are bred on the Lake that for a Venice groat of silver you can have a couple of geese and two couple of ducks. Then there are the shambles where the larger animals are slaughtered, such as calves, beeves, kids, and lambs, the flesh of which is eaten by the rich and the great dignitaries.

Those markets make a daily display of every kind of vegetables and fruits; and among the latter there are in particular certain pears of enormous size, weighing as much as ten pounds apiece, and the pulp of which is white and fragrant like a confection; besides peaches in their season both yellow and white, of every delicate flavour.

Neither grapes nor wine are produced there, but very good raisins are brought from abroad, and wine likewise. The natives, however, do not much care about wine, being used to that kind of their own made from rice and spices. From the Ocean Sea also come daily supplies of fish in great quantity, brought 25 miles up the river, and there is also great store of fish from the lake, which is the constant resort of fishermen, who have no other business. Their fish is of sundry kinds, changing with the season; and, owing to the impurities of the city which pass into the lake, it is remarkably fat and savoury. Any one who should see the supply of fish in the market would suppose it impossible that such a quantity could ever be sold; and yet in a few hours the whole shall be cleared away; so great is the number of inhabitants who are accustomed to delicate living. Indeed they eat fish and flesh at the same meal.

All the ten market places are encompassed by lofty houses, and below these are shops where all sorts of crafts are carried on, and all sorts of wares are on sale, including spices and jewels and pearls. Some of these shops are entirely devoted to the sale of wine made from rice and spices, which is constantly made fresh and fresh, and is sold very cheap.

Certain of the streets are occupied by the women of the town, who are in such a number that I dare not say what it is. They are found not only in the vicinity of the market places, where usually a quarter is assigned to them, but all over the city. They exhibit themselves splendidly attired and abundantly perfumed, in finely gar-nished houses, with trains of waiting-women. These women are extremely accomplished in all the arts of allurement, and readily adapt their conversation to all sorts of persons, insomuch that strangers who have once tasted their attractions seem to get bewitched, and are so taken with their blandishments and their fascinating ways that they never can get these out of their heads. Hence it comes to pass that when they return home they say they have been to Kinsay or the City of Heaven, and their only desire is to get back thither as soon as possible.

Other streets are occupied by the Physicians, and by the Astrologers, who are also teachers of reading and writing; and an infinity of other pro-fessions have their places round about those squares. In each of the squares there are two great palaces facing one another, in which are estab-lished the officers appointed by the King to decide differences arising between merchants, or other inhabitants of the quarter. It is the daily duty of these officers to see that the guards are at their posts on the neighbouring bridges, and to punish them at their discretion if they are absent.

All along the main street that we have spoken of, as running from end to end of the city, both sides are lines with houses and great palaces and the gardens pertaining to them, whilst in the in-tervals are the houses of tradesmen engaged in their different crafts. The crowd of people that you meet here at all hours, passing this way and that on their different errands, is so vast that no one would believe it possible that victuals enough could be provided for their consumption, unless they should see how, on every market-day, all those squares are thronged and crammed with purchasers, and with the traders who have brought in stores of provisions by land or water; and everything they bring in is disposed of.

To give you an example of the vast consump-tion in this city let us take the article of *pepper*; and that will enable you in some measure to estimate what must be the quantity of victual, such as meat, wine, groceries, which have to be provided for the general consumption. Now Messer Marco heard it stated by one of the Great Kaan's officers of customs

that the quantity of pepper introduced daily for consumption into the city of Kinsay amounted to 43 loads, each load being equal to 223 lbs.

The houses of the citizens are well built and elaborately finished; and the delight they take in decoration, in painting and in architecture, leads them to spend in this way sums of money that would astonish you.

The natives of the city are men of peaceful character, both from education and from the example of their kings, whose disposition was the same. They know nothing of handing arms, and keep none in their houses. You hear of no feuds or noisy quarrels or dissensions of any kind among them. Both in their commercial dealings and in their manufactures they are thoroughly honest and truthful, and there is such a degree of good will and neighbourly attachment among both men and women that you would take the people who live in the same street to be all one family.

And this familiar intimacy is free from all jeal-ousy or suspicion of the conduct of their women. These they treat with the greatest respect, and a man who should presume to make loose proposals to a married woman would be regarded as an infa-mous rascal. They also treat the foreigners who visit them for the sake of trade with great cordiality, and entertain them in the most winning manner, affording them every help and advice on their business. But on the other hand they hate to see soldiers, and not least those of the Great Kaan's garrisons, regarding them as the cause of their having lost their native kings and lords.

On the Lake of which we have spoken there are numbers of boats and barges of all sizes for parties of pleasure. These will hold 10, 15, 20, or more persons, and are from 15 to 20 paces in length, with flat bottoms and ample breadth of beam, so that they always keep their trim. Any one who desires to go a-pleasuring with the women, or with a party of his own sex, hires one of these barges, which are always to be found completely furnished with tables and chairs and all the other apparatus for a feast. The roof forms a level deck, on which the crew stand, and pole the boat along whithersoever may be desired, for the Lake is not more than 2 paces in depth. The inside of this roof and the rest of the interior is covered with ornamental painting in gay colours, with windows all round that can be shut or opened, so that the party at table can enjoy all the beauty and variety of the prospects on both sides as they pass along. And truly a trip on this Lake is a much more charming recreation than can be enjoyed on land. For on the one side lies the city in its entire length, so that the spectators in the barges, from the distance at which they stand, take in the whole prospect in its full beauty and grandeur, with its numberless palaces, temples, monasteries, and gardens, full of lofty trees, sloping to the shore. And the Lake is never without a number of other such boats, laden with pleasure parties; for it is the great delight of the citizens here, after they have disposed of the day's business, to pass the afternoon in enjoyment with the ladies of their families, or perhaps with others less reputable, either in these barges or in driving about the city in carriages.

Of these latter we must also say something, for they afford one mode of recreation to the citizens in going about the town, as the boats afford another in going about the Lake. In the main street of the city you meet an infinite succession of these carriages passing to and fro. They are long covered vehicles, fitted with curtains and cushions, and affording room for six persons; and they are in constant request for ladies and gentlemen going on parties of pleasure. In these they drive to certain gardens, where they are entertained by the owners in pavilions erected on purpose, and there they divert themselves the livelong day, with their ladies, returning home in the evening in those same carriages.

Questions

1. What can you learn about thirteenth-century Europe from the way Marco Polo talks about China? What in Marco Polo's description of Kinsai might capture Europeans' attention?
2. How did the Europe of Columbus's day compare with the Asia of Marco Polo's account?
3. How might a European whose ideas about Asia came from Marco Polo be expected to act upon reaching lands he thought were part of that continent?

2.2   Columbus Reaches the New World*

This narrative of Columbus's famous 1492 voyage to the Americas comes from a digest of Columbus's logbook produced by historian Bartolomé de las Casas (1474–1566). It covers Columbus's journey from its departure to his encounter with the Lucayan Indians of the Bahamas.

IN THE NAME OF OUR LORD JESUS CHRIST

Whereas, Most Christian, High, Excellent and Powerful Princes, King and Queen of Spain and of the Islands of the Sea, our Sovereigns, this present year 1492, after your Highnesses had terminated the war with the Moors reigning in Europe, the same having been brought to an end in the great city of Granada, where on the second day of January, this present year, I saw the royal banners of your Highnesses planted by force of arms upon the towers of the Alhambra, which is the fortress of that city, and saw the Moorish king come out at the gate of the city and kiss the hands of your Highnesses, and of the Prince my Sovereign; and in the present month, in consequence of the information which I had given your Highnesses respecting the countries of India and of a Prince, called Great Can, which in our language signifies King of Kings, how, at many times he, and his predecessors had sent to Rome soliciting instructors who might teach him our holy faith, and the holy Father had never granted his request, whereby great numbers of people were lost, believing in idolatry and

*Christopher Columbus, *Journal of First Voyage to America*, ed. Van Wyck Brooks (New York: Albert & Charles Boni, 1924), 1–8, 17–32.

doctrines of perdition. Your Highnesses, as Catholic Christians, and princes who love and promote the holy Christian faith, and are enemies of the doctrine of Mahomet, and of all idolatry and heresy, determined to send me, Christopher Columbus, to the above-mentioned countries of India, to see the said princes, people, and territories, and to learn their disposition and the proper method of converting them to our holy faith, and furthermore directed that I should not proceed by land to the East, as is customary, but by a Westerly route, in which direction we have hitherto no certain evidence that any one has gone. So after having expelled the Jews from your dominions, your Highnesses, in the same month of January, ordered me to proceed with a sufficient armament to the said regions of India, and for that purpose granted me great favours, and ennobled me that thenceforth I might call myself Don, and be High Admiral of the Sea, and perpetual Viceroy and Governor in all the islands and continents which I might discover and acquire, or which may hereafter be discovered and acquired in the ocean; and that this dignity should be inherited by my eldest son, and thus descend from degree to degree forever. Hereupon I left the city of Granada, on Saturday, the twelfth day of May, 1492, and proceeded to Palos, a seaport, where I armed three vessels, very fit for such an enterprise, and having provided myself with abundance of stores and seamen, I set sail from the port, on Friday, the third of August, half an hour before sunrise, and steered for the Canary Islands of your Highnesses which are in the said ocean, thence to take my departure and proceed till I arrived at the Indies, and perform the embassy of your Hignesses to the Princes there, and discharge the orders given me. For this purpose I determined to keep an account of the voyage, and to write down punctually every thing we performed or saw from day to day, as will hereafter appear. Moreover, Sovereign Princes, besides describing every night the occurrences of the day, and every day those of the preceding night, I intend to draw up a nautical chart, which shall contain the several parts of the ocean and land in their proper situations; and also to compose a book to represent the whole by picture with latitudes and longitudes, on all which

accounts it behooves me to abstain from my sleep, and make many trials in navigation, which things will demand much labour.

Friday, Aug. 3d. 1492. Set sail from the bar of Saltes at 8 o'clock, and proceeded with a strong breeze till sunset, sixty miles or fifteen leagues S. afterwards S.W. and S. by W. which is the direction of the Canaries.

Saturday, Aug. 4th. Steered S.W. by S.

Sunday, Aug. 5th. Sailed day and night more than forty leagues.

Monday, Aug. 6th. The rudder of the caravel Pinta became loose, being broken or unshipped. It was believed that this happened by the contrivance of Gomez Rascon and Christopher Quintero, who were on board the caravel, because they disliked the voyage. The Admiral says he had found them in an unfavourable disposition before setting out. He was in much anxiety at not being able to afford any assistance in this case, but says that it somewhat quieted his apprehensions to know that Martin Alonzo Pinzon, Captain of the Pinta, was a man of courage and capacity. Made a progress, day and night, of twenty-nine leagues.

Tuesday, Aug. 7th. The Pinta's rudder again broke loose; secured it, and made for the island of Lanzarote, one of the Canaries. Sailed, day and night, twenty-five leagues.

Wednesday, Aug. 8th. There were divers opinions among the pilots of the three vessels, as to their true situation, and it was found that the Admiral was the most correct. His object was to reach the island of Grand Canary, and leave there the Pinta, she being leaky, besides having her rudder out of order, and take another vessel there, if any one could be had. They were unable to reach the island that day.

Thursday, Aug. 9th. The Admiral did not succeed in reaching the island of Gomera till Sunday night. Martin Alonzo remained at Grand Canary by command of the Admiral, he being unable to keep the other vessels company. The Admiral afterwards returned to Grand Canary, and there with much labor repaired the Pinta, being assisted by Martin Alonzo and the others; finally they sailed to Gomera. They saw a great eruption of flames from the Peak of Teneriffe; which is a lofty mountain. The Pinta, which before had carried latine sails, they altered and made her square-rigged. Returned to Gomera, Sunday, Sept. 2d, with the Pinta repaired.

The Admiral says that he was assured by many respectable Spaniards, inhabitants of the island of Ferro, who were at Gomera with Doña Inez Peraza, mother of Guillen Peraza, afterwards first Count of Gomera, that they every year saw land to the west of the Canaries; and others of Gomera affirmed the same with the like assurances. The Admiral here says that he remembers, while he was in Portugal, in 1484, there came a person to the King from the island of Madeira, soliciting for a vessel to go in quest of land, which he affirmed he saw every year, and always of the same appearance. He also says that he remembers the same was said by the inhabitants of the Azores and described as in a similar direction, and of the same shape and size. Having taken in wood, water, meat and other provisions, which had been provided by the men which he left ashore on departing for Grand Canary to repair the Pinta, the Admiral took his final departure from Gomera with the three vessels on Thursday, Sept. 6th.

Thursday, Sept. 6th. Set sail from the harbour of Gomera this morning and shaped their course for the voyage. The Admiral learnt by a vessel from the island of Ferro that there were three Portuguese caravels cruising about there in search of him. This circumstance probably originated in the envy of the King of Portugal, as the Admiral had left him to resort to Castile. It was calm the whole day and night; in the morning they found themselves between Gomera and Teneriffe.

Monday, Oct. 1st. Continued their course W. and sailed twenty-five leagues; reckoned to the crew twenty. Experienced a heavy shower. The pilot of the Admiral began to fear this morning that they were five hundred and seventy-eight leagues West of the island of Ferro. The short reckoning which the Admiral showed his crew gave five hundred and eighty-four, but the true one which he kept to himself was seven hundred and seven leagues.

Tuesday, Oct. 2d. Continued their course W. day and night, thirty-nine leagues; reckoned to the crew thirty; the sea ever smooth and favourable. *"Many thanks be to God,"* says the Admiral here. Weeds came from the E. towards the W., the contrary to what they had before observed. Saw many fish and took one. A white bird, which appeared to be a gull, was seen.

Wednesday, Oct. 3d. Continued their accustomed course, and sailed forty-seven leagues; reckoned to the crew forty. Many *pardelas* appeared, and great quantities of weed, some of it old, and some very fresh, which appeared to contain fruit. Saw no other birds. The Admiral believed they had passed the islands contained in his chart. Here the Admiral says that he was unwilling to stay beating up and down as the week before, when they had so many signs of land, though he knew there were islands in that quarter, because his wish was to proceed onward to the Indies, and to linger on the way he thought would be unwise.

Thursday, Oct. 4th. Contained their course W. Sailed day and night, sixty-three leagues, and reckoned to the crew forty-six. There came to the ship above forty *pardelas* in a flock, with two pelicans; a boy on board the caravel hit one of them with a stone. A *rabihorcado* came to the ship, and a white bird like a gull.

Friday, Oct. 5th. Continued their course and sailed eleven miles an hour; day and night; fifty-seven leagues, the wind abating in the night, reckoned to the crew forty-five. Fine weather and the sea smooth. *"Many thanks to God,"* says the Admiral. The air soft and temperate; no weeds; many *pardelas* were seen, and swallow-fishes in great numbers came on board.

Saturday, Oct. 6th. Continued their course W. and sailed forty leagues day and night; reckoned to the crew thirty-three. This night Martin Alonzo gave it as his opinion that they had better steer from W. to S.W. The Admiral thought from this that Martin Alonzo did not wish to proceed onward to *Cipango;* but he considered it best to keep on his course, as he should probably reach the land sooner in that direction, preferring to visit the continent first, and then the islands.

Sunday, Oct. 7th. Continued their course W. and sailed twelve miles an hour, for two hours, then eight miles an hour. Sailed till an hour after sunrise, twenty-three leagues; reckoned to the crew eighteen. At sunrise the caravel Nina, who kept ahead on account of her swiftness in sailing; while all the vessels were striving to outsail one another, and gain the reward promised by the King and Queen by first discovering land—hoisted a flag at her mast head, and fired a *lombarda*, as a signal that she had discovered land, for the Admiral had given orders to that effect. He had also ordered that the ships should keep in close company at sunrise and sunset, as the air was more favourable at those times for seeing at a distance. Towards evening seeing nothing of the land which the Nina had made signals for, and observing large flocks of birds coming from the N. and making for the SW., whereby it was rendered probable that they were either going to land to pass the night, or abandoning the countries of the North, on account of the approaching winter, he determined to alter his course, knowing also that the Portuguese had discovered most of the islands they possessed by attending to the flight of birds. The Admiral accordingly shifted his course from W. to W.S.W. with a resolution to continue two days in that direction. This was done about an hour after sunset. Sailed in the night nearly five leagues, and twenty-three in the day. In all twenty-eight.

Monday, Oct. 8th. Steered W.S.W. and sailed day and night eleven or twelve leagues; at times during the night, fifteen miles an hour, if the account can be depended upon. Found the sea like the river at Seville, *"thanks to God,"* says the Admiral. The air soft as that of Seville in April, and so fragrant that it was delicious to breathe it. The weeds appeared very fresh. Many land birds, one of which they took, flying towards the S.W.; also *grajaos*, ducks, and a pelican were seen.

Tuesday, Oct. 9th. Sailed S.W. five leagues, when the wind changed, and they stood W. by N. four leagues. Sailed in the whole day and night, twenty leagues and a half; reckoned to the crew seventeen. All night heard birds passing.

Wednesday, Oct. 10th. Steered W.S.W. and sailed at times ten miles an hour, at others twelve, and at others, seven; day and night made fifty-nine leagues' progress; reckoned to the crew but forty-four. Here the men lost all patience, and complained of the length of the voyage, but the Admiral encouraged them in the best manner he could, representing the profits they were about to acquire, and adding that it was to no purpose to complain, having come so far, they had nothing to do but continue on to the Indies, till with the help of our Lord, they should arrive there.

Thursday, Oct. 11th. Steered W.S.W.; and encountered a heavier sea than they had met with before in the whole voyage. Saw *pardelas* and a green rush near the vessel. The crew of the Pinta saw a cane and a log; they also picked up a stick which appeared to have been carved with an iron tool, a piece of cane, a plant which grows on land, and a board. The crew of the Nina saw other signs of land, and a stalk loaded with roseberries. These signs encouraged them, and they all grew cheerful. Sailed this day till sunset, twenty-seven leagues.

After sunset steered their original course W. and sailed twelve miles an hour till two hours after midnight, going ninety miles, which are twenty-two leagues and a half; and as the Pinta was the swiftest sailer, and kept ahead of the Admiral, she discovered land and made the signals which had been ordered. The land was first seen by a sailor called Rodrigo de Triana, although the Admiral at ten o'clock that evening standing on the quarter-deck saw a light, but so small a body that he could not affirm it to be land; calling to Pero Gutierrez, groom of the King's wardrobe, he told him he saw a light, and bid him look that way, which he did and saw it; he did the same to Rodrigo Sanchez of Segovia, whom the King and Queen had sent with the squadron as comptroller, but he was unable to see it from his situation. The Admiral again perceived it once or twice, appearing like the light of a wax candle moving up and down, which some thought an indication of land. But the Admiral held it for certain that land was near; for which reason, after they had said the *Salve* which the seamen are accustomed to repeat and chant after their fashion, the Admiral directed them to keep a strict watch upon the forecastle and look out diligently for land, and to him who should first discover it he promised a silken jacket, besides the reward which the King and Queen had offered, which was an annuity of ten thousand maravedis.

At two o'clock in the morning the land was discovered, at two leagues' distance; they took in sail and remained under the square-sail lying to till day, which was Friday, when they found themselves near a small island, one of the Lucayos, called in the Indian language Guanahani. Presently they descried people, naked, and the Admiral landed in the boat, which was armed, along with Martin Alonzo Pinzon, and Vincent Yanez his brother, captain of the Nina. The Admiral bore the royal standard, and the two captains each a banner of the Green Cross, which all the ships had carried; this contained the initials of the names of the King and Queen each side of the cross, and a crown over each letter. Arrived on shore, they saw trees very green, many streams of water, and diverse sorts of fruits. The Admiral called upon the two Captains, and the rest of the crew who landed, as also to Rodrigo de Escovedo notary of the fleet, and Rodrigo Sanchez, of Segovia, to bear witness that he before all others took possession (as in fact he did) of that island for the King and Queen his sovereigns, making the requisite declarations, which are more at large set down here in writing. Numbers of the people of the island straightway collected together. Here follow the precise words of the Admiral: "As I saw that they were very friendly to us, and perceived that they could be much more easily converted to our holy faith by gentle means than by force, I presented them with some red caps, and strings of beads to wear upon the neck, and many other trifles of small value, wherewith they were much delighted, and became wonderfully attached to us. Afterwards they came swimming to the boats, bringing parrots, balls of cotton thread, javelins and many other things which they exchanged for articles we gave them, such as glass beads, and hawk's bells; which trade was carried on with the utmost good will. But they seemed on the whole to me, to be a very poor people. They all go completely naked, even the women, though I saw but one girl. All whom I saw were young, not above thirty years of age, well made, with fine shapes and faces; their hair short, and coarse like that of a horse's tail, combed toward the forehead, except a small portion which they suffer to hang down behind, and never cut. Some

paint themselves with black, which makes them appear like those of the Canaries, neither black nor white; others with white, others with red, and others with such colours as they can find. Some paint the face, and some the whole body; others only the eyes, and others the nose. Weapons they have none, nor are acquainted with them, for I showed them swords which they grasped by the blades, and cut themselves through ignorance. They have no iron, their javelins being without it, and nothing more than sticks, though some have fish-bones or other things at the ends. They are all of a good size and stature, and handsomely formed. I saw some with scars of wounds upon their bodies, and demanded by signs the cause of them; they answered me in the same way, that there came people from the other islands in the neighbourhood who endeavoured to make prisoners of them, and they defended themselves. I thought then, and still believe, that these were from the continent. It appears to me, that the people are ingenious, and would be good servants; and I am of opinion that they would very readily become Christians, as they appear to have no religion. They very quickly learn such words as are spoken to them. If it please our Lord, I intend at my return to carry home six of them to your Highnesses, that they may learn our language. I saw no beasts in the island, nor any sort of animals except parrots." These are the words of the Admiral.

Saturday, Oct. 13th. "At daybreak great multitudes of men came to the shore, all young and of fine shapes, very handsome; their hair, not curled but straight and coarse like horse-hair, and all with foreheads and heads much broader than any people I had hitherto seen; their eyes were large and very beautiful; they were not black, but the colour of the inhabitants of the Canaries, which is a very natural circumstance, they being in the same latitude with the island of Ferro in the Canaries. They were straight-limbed without exception, and not with prominent bellies but handsomely shaped. They came to the ship in canoes, made of a single trunk of a tree, wrought in a wonderful manner considering the country; some of them large enough to contain forty or forty-five men, others of different sizes down to those fitted to hold but a single person. They rowed with an oar like a baker's peel, and wonderfully swift. If they happen to upset, they all jump into the sea, and swim till they have righted their canoe and emptied it with the calabashes they carry with them. They came loaded with balls of cotton, parrots, javelins, and other things too numerous to mention; these they exchanged for whatever we chose to give them. I was very attentive to them, and strove to learn if they had any gold. Seeing some of them with little bits of this metal hanging at their noses, I gathered from them by signs that by going southward or steering round the island in that direction, there would be found a king who posessed large vessels of gold, and in great quantities. I endeavoured to procure them to lead the way thither, but found they were unacquainted with the route. I determined to stay here till the evening of the next day, and then sail for the S.W.; for according to what I could learn from them, there was land at the S. as well as at the S.W. and N.W. and those from the N.W. came many times and fought with them and proceeded on to the S.W. in search of gold and precious stones. This is a large and level island, with trees extremely flourishing, and streams of water; there is a large lake in the middle of the island, but no mountains: the whole is completely covered with verdure and delightful to behold. The natives are an inoffensive people, and so desirous to possess any thing they saw with us, that they kept swimming off to the ships with whatever they could find, and readily bartered for any article we saw fit to give them in return, even such as broken platters and fragments of glass. I saw in this manner sixteen balls of cotton thread which weighed above twenty-five pounds, given for three Portuguese *ceutis*. This traffic I forbade, and suffered no one to take their cotton from them, unless I should order it to be procured for your Highnesses, if proper quantities could be met with. It grows in this island, but from my short stay here I could not satisfy myself fully concerning it; the gold, also, which they wear in their noses, is found here, but not to lose time, I am determined to proceed onward and

ascertain whether I can reach Cipango. At night they all went on shore with their canoes.

Sunday, Oct. 14th. In the morning, I ordered the boats to be got ready, and coasted along the island toward the N.N.E. to examine that part of it, we having landed first at the eastern part. Presently we discovered two or three villages, and the people all came down to the shore, calling out to us, and giving thanks to God. Some brought us water, and others victuals: others seeing that I was not disposed to land, plunged into the sea and swam out to us, and we perceived that they interrogated us if we had come from heaven. An old man came on board my boat; the others, both men and women cried with loud voices— "*Come and see the men who have come from heaven. Bring them victuals and drink.*" There came many of both sexes, every one bringing something, giving thanks to God, prostrating themselves on the earth, and lifting up their hands to heaven. They called out to us loudly to come to land, but I was apprehensive on account of a reef of rocks, which surrounds the whole island, although within there is depth of water and room sufficient for all the ships of Christendom, with a very narrow entrance. There are some shoals withinside, but the water is as smooth as a pond. It was to view these parts that I set out in the morning, for I wished to give a complete relation to your Highnesses, as also to find where a fort might be built. I discovered a tongue of land which appeared like an island though it was not, but might be cut through and made so in two days; it contained six houses. I do not, however, see the necessity of fortifying the place, as the people here are simple in war-like matters, as your Highnesses will see by those seven which I have ordered to be taken and carried to Spain in order to learn our language and return, unless your Highnesses should choose to have them all transported to Castile, or held captive in the island. I could conquer the whole of them with fifty men, and govern them as I pleased. Near the islet I have mentioned were groves of trees, the most beautiful I have ever seen, with their foliage as verdant as we see in Castile in April and May. There were also many streams. After having taken a survey of these parts, I returned to the ship, and setting sail, discovered such a number of islands that I knew not which first to visit; the natives whom I had taken on board informed me by signs that there were so many of them that they could not be numbered; they repeated the names of more than a hundred. I determined to steer for the largest, which is about five leagues from San Salvador; the others were some at a greater, and some at a less distance from that island. They are all very level, without mountains, exceedingly fertile and populous, the inhabitants living at war with one another, although a simple race, and with delicate bodies.

Monday, Oct. 15th. Stood off and on during the night, determining not to come to anchor till morning, fearing to meet with shoals; continued our course in the morning; and as the island was found to be six or seven leagues distant, and the tide was against us, it was noon when we arrived there. I found that part of it towards San Salvador extending from N. to S. five leagues, and the other side which we coasted along, ran from E. to W. more than ten leagues. From this island espying a still larger one to the W. I set sail in that direction and kept on till night without reaching the western extremity of the island, where I gave it the name of *Santa Maria de la Concepcion*. About sunset we anchored near the cape which terminates the island towards the W. to enquire for gold, for the natives we had taken from San Salvador told me that the people here wore golden bracelets upon their arms and legs. I believed pretty confidently that they had invented this story in order to find means to escape from us, still I determined to pass none of these islands without taking possession, because being once taken, it would answer for all times. We anchored and remained till Tuesday, when at daybreak I went ashore with the boats armed. The people we found naked like those of San Salvador, and of the same disposition. They suffered us to traverse the island, and gave us what we asked of them. As the wind blew S.E. upon the shore where the vessels lay, I determined not to remain, and set out for the ship. A large canoe being near the caravel Nina, one of the San Salvador natives leaped overboard and swam to her; (another had made his escape the night before,) the canoe being reached by the fugitive, the natives rowed for the land too swiftly to be overtaken; having landed, some of my men went ashore in pursuit of them, when they abandoned the canoe and fled with precipitation; the canoe which they had left was brought on board the Nina, where from another quarter had arrived a small canoe with a single man, who came to barter some cotton; some of the sailors finding him unwilling to go on board the vessel, jumped into the sea and took him. I was upon the quarter deck of my ship, and seeing the whole, sent for him, and gave him a red cap, put some glass beads upon his arms, and two hawk's bells upon his ears. I then ordered his canoe to be returned to him, and despatched him back to land.

I now set sail for the other large island to the W. and gave orders for the canoe which the Nina had in tow to be set adrift. I had refused to receive the cotton from the native whom I sent on shore, although he pressed it upon me. I looked out after him and saw upon his landing that the others all ran to meet him with much wonder. It appeared to them that we were honest people, and that the man who had escaped from us had done us some injury, for which we kept him in custody. It was in order to favour this notion that I ordered the canoe to be set adrift, and gave the man the presents above mentioned, that when your Highnesses send another expedition to these parts it may meet with a friendly reception. All I gave the man was not worth four maravedis.

Terms

Cipango—Japan
lombardo—a cannon

Questions

1. Why does Columbus begin his account by noting Spain's victory over the Muslims at Grenada and mentioning reports of a great king in "India" called Can (Kahn)?

2. How did Columbus secure the cooperation of his ships' crews on their long and uncertain voyage?

3. Columbus formally took possession of the first island on which he landed. What function did this ceremony serve?
4. How did Columbus view the Indians he encountered? What do you think they thought of him?
5. How did Columbus and the Indians communicate? How much do you think they understood one another?
6. What do Columbus's descriptions of the New World suggest he wanted from it? What might a European reading them conclude about the desirability of future trans-Atlantic voyages?
7. Where did Columbus think he was? How did this belief influence his behavior?

2.3   William Bradford Describes an Outbreak of Smallpox*

William Bradford (1590–1657) served as governor of the Plymouth Colony for thirty years and wrote a classic History of Plymouth Plantation. *European colonists such as Bradford's Pilgrims brought Old World diseases with them to the New. In the following passage, Bradford describes the devastating effects of a smallpox epidemic that struck southern New England Algonquians in 1633.*

This spring, also, those Indeans that lived aboute their trading house there fell sick of the small poxe, and dyed most miserably; for a sorer disease cannot befall them; they fear it more then the plague; for usualy they that have this disease have them in abundance, and for wante of bedding and linning and other helps, they fall into a lamentable condition, as they lye on their hard matts, the poxe breaking and mattering, and runing one into another, their skin cleaving (by reason therof) to the matts they lye on; when they turne them, a whole side will flea of at once, (as it were,) and they will be all of a gore blood, most fearfull to behold; and then being very sore, what with could and other distempers, they dye like rotten sheep. The condition of this people was so lamentable, and they fell downe so generally of this diseas, as they were (in the end) not able to help on another; no, not to make a fire, nor to fetch a litle water to drinke, nor any to burie the dead; but would strivie as long as they could, and when they could procure no other means to make fire, they would burne the woden trayes and dishes they ate their

meate in, and their very bowes and arrowes; and some would crawle out on all foure to gett a litle water, and some times dye by the way, and not be able to gett in againe. But those of the English house, (though at first they were afraid of the infection,) yet seeing their woefull and sadd condition, and hearing their pitifull cries and lamentations, they had compastion of them, and dayly fetched them wood and water, and made them Fires, gott them virtualls whilst they lived, and buried them when they dyed. For very few of them escaped, notwithstanding they did what they could for them, to the haszard of them selvs. The cheefe Sachem him selfe now dyed, and allmost all his friends and kinred. But by the marvelous goodnes and providens of God not one of the English was so much as sicke, or in the least measure tainted with this disease, though they dayly did these offices for them for many weeks togeather. And this mercie which they shewed them was kindly taken, and thankfully acknowledged of all the Indeans that knew or heard of the same; and their m^{rs} here did much comend and reward them for the same.

Questions

1. How did smallpox make its way into the Indian population described by Bradford?
2. Describe the physical, emotional, and cultural effects of smallpox in Indian communities.
3. What made the disease especially lethal among the Indians Bradford observed?
4. What conclusions did he reach concerning the larger meaning of the disease?

---

*William Bradford, *Bradford's History of Plymouth Plantation* (New York: Barnes & Noble, 1908), 312–313.

3 New Spain

The Spanish invasion of the New World brought wealth and power to Spain, but at a high price to many Amerindians. The violence of Spanish conquest touched off a firestorm of debate in Spain and the rest of Europe about the legal and moral dimensions of colonialism, raising issues from the justice of armed conquest to the ethics of Christian proselytizing. The following documents, three Spanish and one Aztec, present varying interpretations of this early moment in North American colonial history.

3.1   The Requerimiento

Trying to reconcile the moral and material impulses driving its colonial enterprises, the Spanish crown sought the advice of religious and legal scholars. The following document, written between 1510 and 1512 by renowned Castilian jurist Juan López de Palacios Rubios, articulated a legal doctrine justifying the violent conquest of New World peoples. It was read aloud in Spanish, with the occasional help of an interpreter, to Native Americans encountered by Spanish explorers and conquerors. The Requerimiento remained in force throughout the sixteenth century despite copious criticism from within and outside the Spanish empire.

On the part of the King, Don Fernando, and of Doña Juana, his daughter, Queen of Castille and Leon, subduers of the barbarous nations, we their servants notify and make known to you, as best we can, that the Lord our God, Living and Eternal, created the Heaven and the Earth, and one man and one woman, of whom you and we, and all the

men of the world, were and are descendants, and all those who come after us. But, on account of the multitude which has sprung from this man and woman in the five thousand years since the world was created, it was necessary that some men should go one way and some another, and that they should be divided into many kingdoms and provinces, for in one alone they could not be sustained.

Of all these nations God our Lord gave charge to one man, called St. Peter, that he should be Lord and Superior of all the men in the world, that all should obey him, and that he should be the head of the whole human race, wherever men should live, and under whatever law, sect, or belief they should be; and he gave him the world for his kingdom and jurisdiction.

And he commanded him to place his seat in Rome, as the spot most fitting to rule the world from; but also he permitted him to have his seat in any other part of the world, and to judge and govern all Christians, Moors, Jews, Gentiles, and all

*Arthur Helps, *The Spanish Conquest in America* (New York: John Lane, 1900), 264–267.

31

other sects. This man was called Pope, as if to say, Admirable Great Father and Governor of men. The men who lived in that time obeyed that St. Peter, and took him for Lord, King, and Superior of the universe so also they have regarded the others who after him have been elected to the pontificate, and so has it been continued even till now, and will continue till the end of the world.

One of these Pontiffs, who succeeded that St. Peter as Lord of the world, in the dignity and seat which I have before mentioned, made donation of these isles and Tierra-firme to the aforesaid King and Queen and to their successors, our lords with all that there are in these territories, as is contained in certain writings which passed upon the subject as aforesaid, which you can see if you wish.

So their Highnesses are kings and lords of these islands and land of Tierra-firme by virtue of this donation: and some islands, and indeed almost all those to whom this has been notified, have received and served their Highnesses, as lords and kings, in the way that subjects ought to do, with good will, without any resistance, immediately, without delay, when they were informed of the aforesaid facts. And also they received and obeyed the priests whom their Highnesses sent to preach to them and to teach them our Holy Faith; and all these, of their own free will, without any reward or condition, have become Christians, and are so, and their Highnesses have joyfully and benignantly received them, and also have commanded them to be treated as their subjects and vassals; and you too are held and obliged to do the same. Wherefore, as best we can, we ask and require you that you consider what we have said to you, and that you take the time that shall be necessary to understand and deliberate upon it, and that you acknowledge the Church as the Ruler and Supervisor of the whole world and the high priest called Pope, and in his name the King and Queen Doña Juana and lords, in his place, as superiors and lords and kings of these islands and this Tierra-firme by virtue of the said donation, and that you consent and give place that these religious fathers should declare and preach to you the aforesaid.

If you do so, you will do well, and that which you are obliged to do to their Highnesses, and we in their name shall receive you in all love and charity, and shall leave you your wives, and your children, and your lands, free without servitude, that you may do with them and with yourselves freely that which you like and think best, and they shall not compel you to turn Christians, unless you yourselves, when informed of the truth, should wish to be converted to our Holy Catholic Faith, as almost all the inhabitants of the rest of the islands have done. And, besides this, their Highnesses award you many privileges and exemptions and will grant you many benefits.

But, if you do not do this, and maliciously make delay in it, I certify to you that, with the help of God, we shall powerfully enter into your country, and shall make war against you in all ways and manners that we can, and shall subject you to the yoke and obedience of the Church and of their Highnesses; we shall take you and your wives and your children, and shall make slaves of them, and as such shall sell and dispose of them as their Highnesses may command; and we shall take away your goods, and shall do you all the mischief and damage that we can, as to vassals who do not obey, and refuse to receive their lord, and resist and contradict him; and we protest that the deaths and losses which shall accrue from this are your fault, and not that of their Highnesses, or ours, nor of these cavaliers who come with us. And that we have said this to you and made this Requisition, we request the notary here present to give us his testimony in writing, and we ask the rest who are present that they should be witnesses of this Requisition.

Questions

1. On what grounds do the Spanish claim authority over Native Americans?
2. What choices did this document present to the Indians, and what were the consequences of each choice?
3. How do you think the Indians to whom the Requerimiento was read interpreted it?
4. Why would the Spanish create such a document? Why would they go to the trouble of

having a notary certify that it was read properly?

5. What does the Requerimiento suggest about the relationship between state and church authority in early modern Europe? How did this connection affect New World colonization?

3.2 A Soldier Recalls the Spanish Entrance into Tenochtitlán (Mexico City)*

Bernal Díaz del Castillo, who fought as a soldier in the conquest of Mexico City (1519–1521), recorded his recollection of that momentous period in 1568, when he was eighty-four years old. Although time surely altered some of his memories, his narrative remains one of the fullest and most reliable Spanish accounts of the conquest of the Aztecs. The selection here follows Cortés and his party from their arrival at Tenochtitlán to their decision to capture Montezuma.

I Bernal Díaz Del Castillo, citizen and Regidor of the most loyal city of Santiago de Guatemala, one of the first discoverers and conquerors of New Spain and its provinces, and the Cape of Honduras and all that lies within that land, a Native of the very noble and distinguished town of Medina del Campo, and the son of its former *Regidor*, Francisco Díaz del Castillo, who was also called "The graceful," (may his soul rest in glory), speak about that which concerns myself and all the true conquerors my companions who served His Majesty by discovering, conquering, pacifying and settling most of the provinces of New Spain, and that it is one of the best countries yet discovered in the New World, we found out by our own efforts without His Majesty knowing anything about it.

I also speak here in reply to all that has been said and written by persons who themselves knowing nothing, have received no true account from others of what really took place, but who nevertheless now put forward any statements that happen to suit their fancy. As there is no account of our many and remarkable services such as their merits deserve these indifferent story-tellers are now unwilling that we should receive the recompense and which His Majesty has ordered his Governors and Viceroys to afford us.

Apart from these, reasons such deeds as those I am going on to describe, cannot be forgotten, and the truth about them will be proved afresh, but, as in the books which have been written on the subject the truth has so often been perverted, [I write this history] so that when tales are told of daring deeds our fame shall not suffer, and that on account of such brilliant adventures our names may be placed among the most famous, for we have run the risk of death and wounds, and have suffered a thousand other miseries, venturing our lives in discovering lands about which nothing whatever was known, battling by day and by night with a host of doughty warriors, at so great a distance from Castille that no aid or assistance could reach us, save the only true help, namely the loving kindness of our Lord God whom it has pleased that we should conquer New Spain and the far-famed city of Tenochtitlan, Mexico, for so it is called, and many other cities and provinces which are too numerous for me to name. As soon as we had the country pacified and settled by Spaniards, we thought it to be our duty as good and loyal subjects of His Majesty, with much respect for our King and natural Lord, to hand the country over to him. With that intent we sent our Ambassadors to Castille and thence to Flanders where his Majesty at that time held his Court. I shall also tell about all the good results that came of it, and about the large number of souls which have been saved, and are daily being saved, by conversion to the faith, all of which souls were formerly lost in Hell. In addition to this holy work, attention will be called to the great treasure which we sent as a present to his Majesty, and that which has been sent and is being

*Alfred Percival Maudslay, ed. and trans., *The True History of the Conquest of New Spain, by Bernal Díaz del Castillo, One of Its Conquerors* (London: Hakluyt Society, 1910), vol. 1: 5–7, vol. 2: 39–44, 54–60, 69–75, 84–88.

sent daily and is in the form of the Royal Fifths, as well as in the large amounts carried off by many persons of all classes. I shall tell in this story who was the first discoverer of the province of Yucatan, and how we went to the discovery of New Spain and who were the Captains and soldiers who conquered and settled it and many other things which happened during the conquest, which are worth knowing and should not be forgotten; all this I shall relate as briefly as possible, and above all with the assured truth of an eye witness.

. . .

About the great and solemn reception which the Great Montezuma gave Cortés and all of us at the entering of the great City of Mexico.

Early next day we left Iztapalapa with a large escort of those great Caciques whom I have already mentioned. We proceeded along the Causeway which is here eight paces in width and runs so straight to the City of Mexico that it does not seem to me to turn either much or little, but, broad as it is, it was so crowded with people that there was hardly room for them all, some of them going to and others returning from Mexico, besides those who had come out to see us, so that we were hardly able to pass by the crowds of them that came; and the towers and cues were full of people as well as the canoes from all parts of the lake. It was not to be wondered at, for they had never before seen horses or men such as we are.

Gazing on such wonderful sights, we did not know what to say, or whether what appeared before us was real, for on one side, on the land, there were great cities, and in the lake ever so many more, and the lake itself was crowded with canoes, and in the Causeway were many bridges at intervals, and in front of us stood the great City of Mexico, and we, we did not even number four hundred soldiers! And we well remembered the words and warnings given us by the people of Huexotzingo and Tlaxcala and Tlamanalco, and the many other warnings that had been given that we should beware of entering Mexico, where they would kill us, as soon as they had us inside.

Let the curious readers consider whether there is not much to ponder over in this that I am writing. What men have there been in the world who have shown such daring? But let us get on, and march along the Causeway. When we arrived where another small causeway branches off (leading to Coyoacan, which is another city) where there were some buildings like towers, which are their oratories, many more chieftains and Caciques approached clad in very rich mantles, the brilliant liveries of one chieftain differing from those of another, and the causeways were crowded with them. The Great Montezuma had sent these great Caciques in advance to receive us, and when they came before Cortés they bade us welcome in their language, and as a sign of peace, they touched their hands against the ground, and kissed the ground with the hand.

There we halted for a good while, and Cacamatzin, the Lord of Texcoco, and the Lord of Iztapalapa and the Lord of Tacuba and the Lord of Coyoacan went on the advance to meet the Great Montezuma, who was approaching in a rich litter accompanied by other great Lords and Caciques, who owned vassals. When we arrived near to Mexico, where there were some other small towers, the Great Montezuma got down from his litter, and those great Caciques supported him with their arms beneath a marvellously rich canopy of green coloured feathers with much gold and silver embroidery and with pearls and chalchihuites suspended from a sort of bordering, which was wonderful to look at. The Great Montezuma was richly attired according to his usage, and he was shod with sandals, for so they call what they wear on their feet, the soles were of gold and the upper part adorned with precious stones. The four Chieftains who supported his arms were also richly clothed according to their usage, in garments which were apparently held ready for them on the road to enable them to accompany their prince, for they did not appear in such attire when they came to receive us. Besides these four Chieftains, there were four other great Caciques, who supported the canopy over their heads, and many other Lords who walked before the Great Montezuma, sweeping the ground where he would tread and spreading cloths on it, so that he should not tread on the earth. Not one of these chieftains dared even to think of looking him in the face, but kept their eyes lowered with great reverence, except those four relations, his nephews, who supported him with their arms.

When Cortés was told that the Great Montezuma was approaching, and he saw him coming, he dismounted from his horse, and when he was near Montezuma, they simultaneously paid great reverence to one another. Montezuma bade him welcome and our Cortés replied through Doña Marina wishing him very good health. And it seems to me that Cortés, through Doña Marina, offered him his right hand, and Montezuma did not wish to take it, but he did give his hand to Cortés and then Cortés brought out a necklace which he had ready at hand, made of glass stones, which I have already said are called Margaritas, which have within them many patterns of diverse colours, these were strung on a cord of gold and with musk so that it should have a sweet scent, and he placed it round the neck of the Great Montezuma and when he had so placed it he was going to embrace him, and those great Princes who accompanied Montezuma held back Cortés by the arm so that he should not embrace him, for they considered it an indignity.

Then Cortés through the month of Doña Marina told him that now his heart rejoiced at having seen such a great Prince, and that he took it as a great honour that he had come in person to meet him and had frequently shown him such favour.

Then Montezuma spoke other words of politeness to him, and told two of his nephews who supported his arms, the Lord of Texcoco and the Lord of Coyoacan, to go with us and show us to our quarters, and Montezuma with his other two relations, the Lord of Cuitlahuac and the Lord of Tacuba who accompanied him, returned to the city, and all those grand companies of Caciques and chieftains who had come with him returned in his train. As they turned back after their Prince we stood watching them and observed how they all marched with their eyes fixed on the ground without looking at him, keeping close to the wall, following him with great reverence. Thus space was made for us to enter the streets of Mexico, without being so much crowded. But who could

now court the multitude of men and women and boys who were in the streets and on the azoteas, and in canoes on the canals, who had come out to see us. It was indeed wonderful, and, now that I am writing about it, it all comes before my eyes as though it had happened but yesterday. Coming to think it over it seems to be a great mercy that our Lord Jesus Christ was pleased to give us grace and courage to dare to enter into such a city; and for the many times He has saved me from danger of death, as will be seen later on, I give Him sincere thanks, and in that He had preserved me to write about it, although I cannot do it as fully as is fitting or the subject needs. Let us make no words about it, for deeds are the best witnesses to what I say here and elsewhere.

Let us return to our entry to Mexico. They took us to lodge in some large houses, where there were apartments for all of us, for they had belonged to the father of the Great Montezuma, who was named Axayaca, and at that time Montezuma kept there the great oratories for his idols, and a secret chamber where he kept bars and jewels of gold, which was the treasure that he had inherited from his father Axayaca, and he never disturbed it. They took us to lodge in that house, because they called us Teules, and took us for such, so that we should be with the Idols or Teules which were kept there. However, for one reason or another, it was there they took us, where there were great halls and chambers canopied with the cloth of the country for our Captain, and for every one of us beds of matting with canopies above, and no better bed is given, however great the chief may be, for they are not used. And all these palaces were [coated] with shining cement and swept and garlanded.

As soon as we arrived and entered into the great court, the Great Montezuma took our Captain by the hand, for he was there awaiting him, and led him to the apartment and salon where he was to lodge, which was very richly adorned according to their usage, and he had at hand a very rich necklace made of golden crabs, a marvellous piece of work, and Montezuma himself placed it round the neck of our Captain Cortés, and greatly astonished his [own] Captains by the great honour that he was bestowing on him. When the necklace had been fastened, Cortés thanked Montezuma through our interpreters, and Montezuma replied—"Malinche you and your brethren are in your own house, rest awhile," and then he went to his palaces which were not far away, and we divided our lodgings by companies, and placed the artillery pointing in a convenient direction, and the order which we had to keep was clearly explained to us, and that we were to be much on the alert, both the cavalry and all of us soldiers. A sumptuous dinner was provided for us according to their use and custom, and we ate it at once. So this was our lucky and daring entry into the great city of Tenochtitlan Mexico on the 8th day of November the year of our Saviour Jesus Christ 1519.

Thanks to our Lord Jesus Christ for it all. And if I have not said anything that I ought to have said, may your honours pardon me, for I do not know now even at the present time how better to express it.

Let us leave this talk and go back to our story of what else happened to us, which I will go on to relate.

. . .

How on the following day our Captain Cortés went to see the Great Montezuma, and about a certain conversation that took place.

The next day Cortés decided to go to Montezuma's palace, and he first sent to find out what he intended doing and to let him know that we were coming. He took with him four captains, namely Pedro de Alvarado, Juan Velásquez de Leon, Diego de Ordás, and Gonzalo de Sandoval, and five of us soldiers also went with him.

When Montezuma knew of our coming he advanced to the middle of the hall to receive us, accompanied by many of his nephews, for no other chiefs were permitted to enter or hold communication with Montezuma where he then was, unless it were on important business. Cortés and he paid the greatest reverence to each other and then they took one another by the hand and Montezuma made him sit down on his couch on his right hand, and he also bade all of us to be seated on seats which he ordered to be brought.

Then Cortés began to make an explanation through our interpreters Doña Marina and Aguilar, and said that he and all of us were rested, and that in coming to see and converse with such a great Prince as he was, we had completed the journey and fulfilled the command which our great King and Prince had laid on us. But what he chiefly came to say on behalf of our Lord God had already been brought to his [Montezuma's] knowledge through his ambassadors, Tendile, Pitalpitoque and Quintalbor, at the time when he did us the favour to send the golden sun and moon to the sand dunes; for we told them then that we were Christians and worshipped one true and only God, named Jesus Christ, who suffered death and passion to save us, and we told them that a cross (when they asked us why we worshipped it) was a sign of the other Cross on which our Lord God was crucified for our salvation, and that the death and passion which He suffered was for the salvation of the whole human race, which was lost, and that this our God rose on the third day and is now in heaven, and it is He who made the heavens and the earth, the sea and the sands, and created all the things there are in the world, and He sends the rain and the dew, and nothing happens in the world without His holy will. That we believe in Him and worship Him, but that those whom they look upon as gods are not so, but are devils, which are evil things, and if their looks are bad their deeds are worse, and they could see that they were evil and of little worth, for where we had set up crosses such as those his ambassadors had seen, they dared not appear before them, through fear of them, and that as time went on they would notice this.

The favour he now begged of him was his attention to the words that he now wished to tell him; then he explained to him very clearly about the creation of the world, and how we are all brothers, sons of one father and one mother who were called Adam and Eve, and how such a brother as our Emperor, grieving for the perdition of so many souls, such as those which their idols were leading to Hell, where they burn in living flames, had sent us, so that after what he [Montezuma] had now heard he would put a stop to it and they would no longer adore these Idols or sacrifice Indian men and women to them, for we were all brethren, nor should they commit sodomy or thefts. He also told them that, in course of time, our Lord and King would send some men who among us lead very holy lives, much better than we do, who will explain to them all about it, for at present we merely came to give them due warning, and so he prayed him to do what he was asked and carry it into effect.

As Montezuma appeared to wish to reply, Cortés broke off his argument, and to all of us who were with him he said: "with this we have done our duty considering it is the first attempt."

Montezuma replied—"Señor Malinche, I have understood your words and arguments very well before now, from what you said to my servants at the sand dunes, this about three Gods and the Cross, and all those things that you have preached in the towns through which you have come. We have not made any answer to it because here throughout all time we have worshipped our own gods, and thought they were good, as no doubt yours are, so do not trouble to speak to us any more about them at present. Regarding the creation of the world, we have held the same belief for ages past, and for this reason we take it for certain that you are those whom our ancestors predicted would come from the direction of the sunrise. As for your great King, I feel that I am indebted to him, and I will give him of what I possess, for as I have already said, two years ago I heard of the Captains who came in ships from the direction in which you came, and they said that they were the servants of this your great King, and I wish to know if you are all one and the same.

Cortés replied, Yes, that we were all brethren and servants of our Emperor, and that those men came to examine the way and the seas and the ports so as to know them well in order that we might follow as we had done. Montezuma was referring to the expeditions of Francisco Hernández de Córdova and Grijalva, when we first came on voyages of discovery, and he said that ever since that time he had wished to capture some of those men who had come so as to keep them in his kingdoms and cities and to do them honour, and

his gods had now fulfilled his desires, for now that we were in his home, which we might call our own, we should rejoice and take our rest for there we should be well treated. And if he had on other occasions sent to say that we should not enter his city, it was not of his free will, but because his vassals were afraid, for they said that we shot out flashes of lightning, and killed many Indians with our horses, and that we were angry Teules, and other childish stories, and now that he had seen our persons and knew we were of flesh and bone, and had sound sense, and that we were very valiant, for these reasons he held us in much higher regard than he did from their reports, and he would share his possessions with us. Then Cortés and all of us answered that we thanked him sincerely for such signal good will, and Montezuma said, laughing, for he was very merry in his princely way of speaking: "Malinche, I know very well that these people of Tlaxcala with whom you are such good friends have told you that I am a sort of God of Teul, and that everything in my houses is made of gold and silver and precious stones, I know well enough that you are wise and did not believe it but took it as a joke. Behold now, Señor Malinche, my body is of flesh and bone like yours, my houses and palaces of stone and wood and lime; that I am a great king and inherit the riches of my ancestors is true, but not all the nonsense and lies that they have told you about me, although of course you treated it as a joke, as I did your thunder and lightning."

Cortés answered him, also laughing, and said that opponents and enemies always say evil things, without truth in them, of those whom they hate, and that he well knew that he could not hope to find another Prince more magnificent in these countries, and that not without reason had he been so vaunted to our Emperor.

While this conversation was going on, Montezuma secretly sent a great Cacique, one of his nephews who was in his company, to order his stewards to bring certain pieces of gold, which it seems must have been put apart to give to Cortés, and ten loads of fine cloth, which he apportioned, the gold and mantles between Cortés and the four captains, and to each of us soldiers he gave two golden necklaces, each necklace being worth ten pesos, and two loads of mantles. The gold that he then gave us was worth in all more than a thousand pesos and he gave it all cheerfully and with the air of a great and valiant prince. As it was now past midday, so as not to appear importunate, Cortés said to him: "Señor Montezuma, you always have the habit of heaping load upon load in every day conferring favours on us, and it is already your dinner time." Montezuma replied that he thanked us for coming to see him, and then we took our leave with the greatest courtesy and we went to our lodgings.

And as we went along we spoke of the good manners and breeding which he showed in everything, and that we should show him in all ways the greatest respect, doffing our quilted caps when we passed before him, and this we always did, but let us leave this subject here, and pass on.

How our Captain went out to see the City of Mexico and Tlaltelolco, which is the great market place and the great Cue of Huichilobos, and what else happened.

As we had already been four days in Mexico and neither the Captain nor any of us had left our lodgings except to go to the houses and gardens, Cortés said to us that it would be well to go to the great Plaza and see the great Temple of Huichilobos, and that he wished to consult the Great Montezuma and have his approval. For this purpose he sent Jerónimo de Aguilar and the Doña Marina as messengers, and with them went our Captain's small page named Orteguilla, who already understood something of the language. When Montezuma knew his wishes he sent to say that we were welcome to go; on the other hand, as he was afraid that we might do some dishonour to his Idols, he determined to go with us himself with many of his chieftains. He came out from his Palace in his rich litter, but when half the distance had been traversed and he was near some oratories, he stepped out of the litter, for he thought it a great affront to his idols to go to their house and temple in that manner. Some of the great chieftains supported him with their arms, and the tribal lords went in front of him carrying two staves like sceptres held on high, which was the sign that the Great Montezuma was coming. (When he went in his litter he carried a wand half of gold and half of wood, which was held up like a wand of justice). So he went on and ascended the great Cue accompanied by many priests, and he began to burn incense and perform other ceremonies to Huichilobos.

Let us leave Montezuma, who had gone ahead as I have said, and return to Cortés and our captains and soldiers, who according to our custom both night and day were armed, and as Montezuma was used to see us so armed when we went to visit him, he did not look upon it as anything new. I say this because our Captain and all those who had horses went to Tlaltelolco on horseback, and nearly all of us soldiers were fully equipped, and many Caciques whom Montezuma had sent for that purpose went in our company. When we arrived at the great market place, called Tlaltelolco, we were astounded at the number of people and the quantity of merchandise that it contained, and at the good order and control that was maintained, for we had never seen such a thing before. The chieftains who accompanied us acted as guides. Each kind of merchandise was kept by itself and had its fixed place marked out. Let us begin with the dealers in gold, silver, and precious stones, feathers, mantles, and embroidered goods. Then there were other wares consisting of Indian slaves both men and women; and I say that they bring as many of them to that great market for sale as the Portuguese bring negroes from Guinea; and they brought them along tied to long poles, with collars round their necks so that they could not escape, and others they left free. Next there were other traders who sold great pieces of cloth and cotton, and articles of twisted thread, and there were *cacahuateros* who sold cacao. In this way one could see every sort of merchandise that is to be found in the whole of New Spain, placed in arrangement in the same manner as they do in my own country, which is Medina del Campo, where they hold the fairs, where each line of booths has its particular kind of merchandise, and so it is in this great market. There were those who sold cloths of henequen and ropes and the *cotaras* with which they are shod, which are made from the same plant, and sweet cooked roots, and other tubers which they get from this plant, all were kept in one part of the market in the place assigned to them. In another part there were skins of tigers and lions, of otters and jackals, deer and other animals and badgers and mountain cats, some tanned and others untanned, and other classes of merchandise.

Let us go on and speak of those who sold beans and sage and other vegetables and herbs in another part, and to those who sold fowls, cocks with wattles, rabbits, hares, deer, mallards, young dogs and other things of that sort in their part of the market, and let us also mention the fruiterers, and the women who sold cooked food, dough and tripe in their own part of the market; then every sort of pottery made in a thousand different forms from great water jars to little jugs, these also had a place to themselves; then those who sold honey and honey paste and other dainties like nut paste, and those who sold lumber, boards, cradles, beams, blocks and benches, each article by itself, and the vendors of *ocote* firewood, and other things of a similar nature. I must furthermore mention, asking your pardon, that they also sold many canoes full of human excrement, and these were kept in the creeks near the market, and this they use to make salt or for tanning skins, for without it they say that they cannot be well prepared. I know well that some gentlemen laugh at this, but I say that it is so, and I may add that on all the roads it is a usual thing to have places made of reeds or straw or grass, so that they may be screened from the passers by, into these they retire when they wish to purge their bowels so that even that filth should not be lost. But why do I waste so many words in recounting what they sell in that great market, for I shall never finish if I tell it all in detail. Paper, which in this country is called *Amal*, and reeds scented with *liquidambar*, and full of tobacco, and yellow ointments and things of that sort are sold by themselves, and much cochineal is sold under the arcades which are in that great market place, and there are many vendors of herbs and other sorts of trades. There are also buildings where three magistrates sit in

judgment, and there are executive officers like *Alguacils* who inspect the merchandise. I am forgetting those who sell salt, and those who make the stone knives, and how they split them off the stone itself; and the fisherwomen and others who sell some small cakes made from a sort of ooze which they get out of the great lake, which curdles, and from this they make a bread having a flavour something like cheese. There are for sale axes of brass and copper and tin, and gourds and gaily painted jars made of wood. I could wish that I had finished telling of all the things which are sold there, but they are so numerous and of such different quality and the great market place with its surrounding arcades was so crowded with people, that one would not have been able to see and inquire about it all in two days.

Then we went to the great Cue, and when we were already approaching its great courts, before leaving the market place itself, there were many more merchants, who, as I was told, brought gold for sale in grains, just as it is taken from the mines. The gold is placed in thin quills of the geese of the country, white quills, so that the gold can be seen through, and according to the length and thickness of the quills they arrange their accounts with one another, how much so many mantles or so many gourds full of cacao were worth, or how many slaves, or whatever other thing they were exchanging.

Now let us leave the great market place, and not look at it again, and arrive at the great courts and walls where the great Cue stands. Before reaching the great Cue there is a great enclosure of courts, it seems to me larger than the plaza of Salamanca, with two walls of masonry surrounding it and the court itself all paved with very smooth great white flagstones. And where there were not these stones it was cemented and burnished and all very clean, so that one could not find any dust or a straw in the whole place.

When we arrived near the great Cue and before we had ascended a single step of it, the Great Montezuma sent down from above, where he was making his sacrifices, six priests and two chieftains to accompany our Captain. On ascending the steps, which are one hundred and fourteen in number, they attempted to take him by the arms so as to help him to ascend, (thinking that he would get tired,) as they were accustomed to assist their lord Montezuma, but Cortés would not allow them to come near him. When we got to the top of the great Cue, on a small plaza which has been made on the top where there was a space like a platform with some large stones placed on it, on which they put the poor Indians for sacrifice, there was a bulky image like a dragon and other evil figures and much blood shed that very day.

When we arrived there Montezuma came out of an oratory where his cursed idols were, at the summit of the great Cue, and two priests came with him, and after paying great reverence to Cortés and to all of us he said; "You must be tired, Señor Malinche, from ascending this our great Cue," and Cortés replied through our interpreters who were with us that he and his companions were never tired by anything. Then Montezuma took him by the hand and told him to look at his great city and all the other cities that were standing in the water, and the many other towns on the land round the lake, and that if he had not seen the great market place well, that from where they were they could see it better.

So we stood looking about us, for that huge and cursed temple stood so high that from it one could see over everything very well, and we saw the three causeways which led into Mexico, that is the causeway of Iztapalapa by which we had entered four days before, and that of Tacuba, along which later on we fled on the night of our great defeat, when Cuitlahuac the new prince drove us out of the city, as I shall tell later on, and that of Tepeaquilla, and we saw the fresh water that comes from Chapultepec which supplies the city, and we saw the bridges on the three causeways which were built at certain distances apart through which the water of the lake flowed in and out from one side to the other, and we beheld on that great lake a great multitude of canoes, some coming with supplies of food and others returning loaded with cargoes of merchandise; and we saw that from every house of that great city and of all the other cities that were built in the water it was impossible to pass from house to house, except by drawbridges which were made of wood or in canoes; and we saw in those cities Cues and oratories like towers and fortresses and all gleaming white, and it was a wonderful thing to behold; then the houses with flat roofs, and on the causeways other small towers and oratories which were like fortresses.

After having examined and considered all that we had seen we turned to look at the great market place and the crowds of people that were in it, some buying and others selling, so that the murmur and hum of their voices and words that they used could be heard more than a league off. Some of the soldiers among us who had been in many parts of the world, in Constantinople, and all over Italy, and in Rome, said that so large a market place and so full of people, and so well regulated and arranged, they had never beheld before.

Let us leave this, and return to our Captain, who said to Fray Bartolomé de Olmedo, who has often been mentioned by me, and who happened to be near by him; "It seems to me, Señor Padre, that it would be a good thing to throw out a feeler to Montezuma, as to whether he would allow us to build our church here"; . . .

When we were all assembled in those chambers, as it was our habit to inquire into and want to know everything, while we were looking for the best and most convenient site to place the altar, two of our soldiers, one of whom was a carpenter, named Alonzo Yañes, noticed on one of the walls marks showing that there had been a door there, and that it had been closed up and carefully plastered over and burnished. Now as there was a rumour and we had heard the story that Montezuma kept the treasure of his father Axayaca in that building, it was suspected that it might be in this chamber which had been closed up and cemented only a few days before. Yañes spoke about it to Juan Velásquez de Leon and Francisco de Lugo, who were Captains and relations of mine, and Alonzo Yañes had attached himself to their company as a servant, and those Captains told the story to Cortés, and the door was secretly opened. When it was open Cortés and some of his Captains went in first, and they saw such a number of jewels and slabs and plates of gold and chalchihuites and other great riches, that they were quite carried away and did not know what to say about such wealth. The news soon spread among all the other Captains and soldiers, and very secretly we went in to see it. When I saw it I marvelled, and as at that time I was a youth and had never seen such riches as those in my life before, I took it for certain that there could not be another such store of wealth in the whole world. It was decided by all our captains and soldiers, that we should not dream of touching a particle of it, but that the stones should immediately be put back in the doorway and it should be sealed up and cemented just as we found it, and that it should not be spoken about, lest it should reach Montezuma's ears, until times should alter.

Let us leave this about the riches, and say that as we had such valiant captains and soldiers of good counsel and judgment, (and first of all we all believed for certain that our Lord Jesus Christ held His Divine hand over all our affairs,) four of our captains took Cortés aside in the church, with a dozen soldiers in whom he trusted and confided, and I was one of them, and we asked him to look at the net and trap in which we found ourselves, and to consider the great strength of that city, and observe the causeways and bridges, and to think over the words of warning that we had been given in all the towns we had passed through, that Montezuma had been advised by his Huichilobos to allow us to enter into the city, and when we were there, to kill us. That he [Cortés] should remember that the hearts of the men are very changeable, especially those of Indians, and he should not repose trust in the good will and affection that Montezuma was showing us, for at some time or other, when the wish occurred to him, he would order us to be attacked, and by the stoppage of our supplies of food or of water, or by the raising of any of the bridges, we should be rendered helpless. Then, considering the great multitude of Indian warriors that Montezuma had as his guard, what should we be able to do either in offence or defence? and as all the houses were

built in the water, how could our friends the Tlaxcalans enter and come to our aid? He should think over all this that we had said, and if we wished to safeguard our lives, that we should at once, without further delay, seize Montezuma and should not wait until next day to do it. He should also remember that all the gold that Montezuma had given us and all that we had seen in the treasury of his father Axayaca, and all the food which we ate, all would be turned to arsenic poison in our bodies, for we could neither sleep by night nor day nor rest ourselves while these thoughts were in our minds, and that if any of our soldiers should give him other advice short of this, they would be senseless beasts who were dazed by the gold, incapable of looking death in the face.

When Cortés heard this he replied: "Don't you imagine, gentlemen, that I am asleep, or that I am free from the same anxiety, you must have felt that it is so with me; but what possibility is there of our doing a deed of such great daring as to seize such a great prince in his own palace, surrounded as he is by his own guards and warriors, by what scheme or artifice can we carry it out, so that he should not call on his warriors to attack us at once?" Our Captains replied, (that is Juan Velásquez de Leon and Diego de Ordás, Gonzalo de Sandoval and Pedro de Alvarado,) that with smooth speeches he should be got out of his halls and brought to our quarters, and should be told that he must remain a prisoner, and if he made a disturbance or cried out, that he would pay for it with his life; that if Cortés did not want to do this at once, he should give them permission to do it, as they were ready for the work, for, between the two great dangers in which we found ourselves, it was better and more to the purpose to seize Montezuma than to wait until he attacked us; for if he began the attack, what chance should we have? Some of us soldiers also told Cortés that it seemed to us that Montezuma's stewards, who were employed in providing us with food, were insolent and did not bring it courteously as during the first days. Also two of our Allies the Tlaxcalan Indians said secretly to Jerónimo de

Aguilar, our interpreter, that the Mexicans had not appeared to be well disposed towards us during the last two days. So we stayed a good hour discussing the question whether or not we should take Montezuma prisoner, and how it was to be done, and to our Captain this last advice seemed opportune, that in any case we should take him prisoner, and we left it until the next day. All that night we were praying to God that our plan might tend to His Holy service.

The next morning after these consultations, there arrived, very secretly, two Tlaxcalan Indians with letters from Villa Rica and what they contained was the news that Juan de Escalante, who had remained there as Chief Alguacil, and six of our soldiers had been killed in a battle against the Mexicans, that his horse had also been slain, and many Totonacs who were in his company. Moreover, all the towns of the Sierra and Cempoala and its subject towns were in revolt, and refused to bring food or serve in the fort. They [the Spaniards] did not know what to do, for as formerly they had been taken to be Teules, that now after this disaster, both the Totonacs and Mexicans were like wild animals, and they could hold them to nothing, and did not know what steps to take.

When we heard this news, God knows what sorrow affected us all, for this was the first disaster we had suffered in New Spain. The interested reader may see how evil fortune came rolling on us. No one who had seen us enter into that city with such a solemn and triumphant reception, and had seen us in possession of riches which Montezuma gave every day both to our Captain and to us, and had seen the house that I have described full of gold, and how the people took us for Teules, that is for Idols, and that we were conquerors in all our battles, would have thought that now such a great disaster could have befallen us, namely that they no longer attributed to us our former repute, but looked upon us as men liable to be conquered, and that we should have to feel their growing insolence towards us.

As the upshot of much argument it was agreed that, by one means or another, we should seize Montezuma that very day, or we would all die in the attempt.

Terms

cue—temple
chalchihuites—jade
cacique—chieftain or local political leader
teules—gods or powerful spirit beings
henequen—a coarse fiber, similar to hemp, made from the leaves of agaves
cotaras—sandals
ocote—pitch pine, used for torches
alguacil—sheriff
azotea—terrace

Questions

1. What motivated Díaz to write this account? How do those motives affect how you read the document?

2. In another part of the narrative, Díaz says that some of the soldiers with him "asked whether the things that we saw were not a dream." What did they see in the Aztec cities that made them react this way? To what did they compare these cities? How does Díaz's account of Tenochtitlán compare with Marco Polo's description of Kinsai?

3. Describe the marketplace of Tlatelolco. What can it tell you about the Aztec economy?

4. How did Cortés and his soldiers enter Tenochtitlán, and how were they treated by Montezuma and his people?

5. How did the Aztecs respond to Spanish religion? Why?

6. Why did the Spanish decide to capture Montezuma? Do you think they had other motives omitted by Díaz?

7. Does reading this document change your interpretation of Castañeda's and Ranjel's narratives of the Coronado and de Soto expeditions? How might familiarity with Mexico have influenced the conquistadors' reactions to the Indian cultures of the Southwest and Southeast?

3.3   An Aztec Account of the Conquest of Mexico*

*This document, written in the Aztec language, Nahu-
atl, contains the earliest known account of the conquest
of Mexico from an Aztec perspective. The Aztecs originally wrote in a pictorial, rather than an alphabetic,
language; but after the conquest, Spanish priests devised
a system of representing Nahuatl in letters. They taught
this system to Aztec nobles, and a group of them from the
district of Tlatelolco used it to write this narrative in
1528, forty years before Díaz published his history.*

THE ARRIVAL OF CORTES

Year 13—Rabbit. The Spaniards were sighted off
the coast.

Year 1—Canestalk. The Spaniards came to
the palace at Tlayacac. When the Captain arrived
at the palace, Motecuhzoma sent the Cuetlaxteca
to greet him and to bring him two suns as gifts.
One of these suns was made of the yellow metal,
the other of the white. The Cuetlaxteca also
brought him a mirror to be hung on his person, a
gold collar, a great gold pitcher, fans and ornaments of quetzal feathers and a shield inlaid with
mother-of-pearl.

The envoys made sacrifices in front of the
Captain. At this, he grew very angry. When they
offered him blood in an "eagle dish," he shouted
at the man who offered it and struck him with his
sword. The envoys departed at once.

All the gifts which the Cuetlaxteca brought to
the Captain were sent by Motecuhzoma. That is
why the Cuetlaxteca went to meet the Captain at
Tlayacac: he was only performing his duties as a
royal envoy.

Then the Captain marched to Tenochtitlan.
He arrived here during the month called Bird,
under the sign of the day 8—Wind. When he
entered the city, we gave him chickens, eggs, corn,
tortillas and drink. We also gave him firewood,
and fodder for his "deer." Some of these gifts were

sent by the lord of Tenochtitlan, the rest by the
lord of Tlatelolco.

Later the Captain marched back to the coast,
leaving Don Pedro de Alvarado—The Sun—in
command.

THE MASSACRE IN
THE MAIN TEMPLE

During this time, the people asked Motecuhzoma
how they should celebrate their god's fiesta. He
said: "Dress him in all his finery, in all his sacred
ornaments."

During this same time, The Sun commanded
that Motecuhzoma and Itzcohuatzin, the military
chief of Tlatelolco, be made prisoners. The
Spaniards hanged a chief from Acolhuacan named
Nezahualquentzin. They also murdered the king
of Nauhtla, Cohualpopocatzin, by wounding him
with arrows and then burning him alive.

For this reason, our warriors were on guard
at the Eagle Gate. The sentries from Tenochtitlan stood at one side of the gate, and the sentries
from Tlatelolco at the other. But messengers
came to tell them to dress the figure of
Huitzilopochtli. They left their posts and went to
dress him in his sacred finery: his ornaments and
his paper clothing.

When this had been done, the celebrants
began to sing their songs. That is how they celebrated the first day of the fiesta. On the second
day they began to sing again, but without warning they were all put to death. The dancers
and singers were completely unarmed. They
brought only their embroidered cloaks, their
turquoises, their lip plugs, their necklaces, their
clusters of heron feathers, their trinkets made of
deer hooves. Those who played the drums, the
old men, had brought their gourds of snuff and
their timbrels.

The Spaniards attacked the musicians first,
slashing at their hands and faces until they had
killed all of them. The singers—and even the
spectators—were also killed. This slaughter in the

---

*Miguel Leon-Portilla, ed. and trans., *The Broken Spears: The
Aztec Account of the Conquest of Mexico* (Boston: Beacon Press,
1992), 128–144.

Sacred Patio went on for three hours. Then the Spaniards burst into the rooms of the temple to kill the others: those who were carrying water, or bringing fodder for the horses, or grinding meal, or sweeping, or standing watch over this work.

The king Motecuhzoma, who was accompanied by Itzcohuatzin and by those who had brought food for the Spaniards, protested: "Our lords, that is enough! What are you doing? These people are not carrying shields or *macanas*. Our lords, they are completely unarmed!"

The Sun treacherously murdered our people on the twentieth day after the Captain left for the coast. We allowed the Captain to return to the city in peace. But on the following day we attacked him with all our might, and that was the beginning of the war.

THE NIGHT OF SORROWS

The Spaniards attempted to slip out of the city at night, but we attacked furiously at the Canal of the Toltecs, and many of them died. This took place during the fiesta of Tecuilhuitl. The survivors gathered first at Mazatzintamalco and waited for the stragglers to come up.

Year 2—Flint. This was the year in which Motecuhzoma died. Itzcohuatzin of Tlatelolco died at the same time.

The Spaniards took refuge in Acueco, but they were driven out by our warriors. They fled to Teuhcalhueyacan and from there to Zoltepec. Then they marched through Citlaltepec and camped in Temazcalapan, where the people gave them hens, eggs and corn. They rested for a short while and marched on to Tlaxcala.

Soon after, an epidemic broke out in Tenochtitlan. Almost the whole population suffered from racking coughs and painful, burning sores.

THE SPANIARDS RETURN

When the epidemic had subsided a little, the Spaniards marched out of Tlaxcala. The first place they attacked and conquered was Tepeyacac. They departed from there during the fiesta of Tlahuano, and they arrived in Tlapechhuan during the fiesta of Izcalli. Twenty days later they marched to Tezcoco, where they remained for forty days. Then they reached Tlacopan and established themselves in the palace.

There was no fighting of any kind while they were in Tlacopan. At the end of a week they all marched back to Tezcoco.

Eighty days later they went to Huaxtepec and Cuauhnahuac, and from there they attacked Xochimilco. A great many Tlatelolcas died in that battle. Then the Spaniards returned to Tezcoco again.

Year 3—House. The Aztecs began to fight among themselves. The princes Tzihuacpopocatzin and Cicpatzin Tecuecuenotzin were put to death, as were Axayaca and Xoxopehualoc, the sons of Motecuhzoma. These princes were killed because they tried to persuade the people to bring corn, hens and eggs to the Spaniards. They were killed by the priests, captains and elder brothers.

But the great chiefs were angry at these executions. They said to the murderers: "Have we ourselves become assassins? Only sixty days ago, our people were slaughtered at the fiesta of Toxcatl!"

THE SIEGE OF TENOCHTITLAN

Now the Spaniards began to wage war against us. They attacked us by land for ten days, and then their ships appeared. Twenty days later, they gathered all their ships together near Nonohualco, off the place called Mazatzintamalco. The allies from Tlaxcala and Huexotzinco set up camp on either side of the road.

Our warriors from Tlatelolco immediately leaped into their canoes and set out for Mazatzintamalco and the Nonohualco road. But no one set out from Tenochtitlan to assist us: only the Tlatelolcas were ready when the Spaniards arrived in their ships. On the following day, the ships sailed to Xoloco.

The fighting at Xoloco and Huitzillan lasted for two days. While the battle was under way, the warriors from Tenochtitlan began to mutiny. They said: "Where are our chiefs? They have fired scarcely a single arrow! Do they think they have fought like men?" Then they seized four of their own leaders and put them to death. They victims were two captains, Cuauhnochtli and Cuapan, and the priests of Amantlan and Tlalocan. This was the second time that the people of Tenochtitlan killed their own leaders.

THE FLIGHT TO TLATELOLCO

The Spaniards set up two cannons in the middle of the road and aimed them at the city. When they fired them, one of the shots struck the Eagle Gate. The people of the city were so terrified that they began to flee to Tlatelolco. They brought their idol Huitzilopochtli with them, setting it up in the House of the Young Men. Their king Cuauhtemoc also abandoned Tenochtitlan. Their chiefs said: "Mexicanos! Tlatelolcas! All is not lost! We can still defend our houses. We can prevent them from capturing our storehouses and the produce of our lands. We can save the sustenance of life, our stores of corn. We can also save our weapons and insignia, our clusters of rich feathers, our gold earrings, and precious stones. Do not be discouraged; do not lose heart. We are Mexicanos! We are Tlatelolcas!"

During the whole time we were fighting, the warriors of Tenochtitlan were nowhere to be seen. The battles at Yacacolco, Atezcapan, Coatlan, Nonohualco, Xoxohuitlan, Tepeyacac and elsewhere were all fought by ourselves, by Tlatelolcas. In the same way, the canals were defended solely by Tlatelolcas.

The captains from Tenochtitlan cut their hair short, and so did those of lesser rank. The Otomies and the other ranks that usually wore headdresses did not wear them during all the time we were fighting. The Tlatelolcas surrounded the most important captains and their women taunted them: "Why are you hanging back? Have you no shame? No woman will ever paint her face for you again!" The wives of the men from Tenochtitlan wept and begged for pity.

When the warriors of Tlatelolco heard what was happening, they began to shout, but still the brave captains of Tenochtitlan hung back. As for the Tletelolcas, their humblest warriors died fighting as bravely as their captains.

THE TLATELOLCAS ARE INVITED TO MAKE A TREATY

A Spaniard named Castaneda approached us in Yauhtenco. He was accompanied by a group of Tlaxcaltecas, who shouted at the guards on the watchtower near the breakwater. These guards were Itzpalanqui, the captian of Chapultepec; two captains from Tlapala; and Cuexacaltzin. Castaneda shouted to them: "Come here!"

"What do you want?" they asked him. "We will come closer." They got into a boat and approached to within speaking distance. "Now, what have you to say to us?"

The Tlaxcaltecas asked: "Where are you from?" And when they learned that the guards were from Tlatelolco, they said: "Good, you are the men we are looking for. Come with us. The 'god' has sent for you."

The guards went with Castaneda to Nonohualco. The Captain was in the House of the Mist there, along with La Malinche, The Sun (Alvarado) and Sandoval. A number of the native lords were also present and they told the Captain: "The Tlatelolcas have arrived. We sent for them to come here."

La Malinche said to the guards: "Come forward! The Captain wants to know: what can the chiefs of Tenochtitlan be thinking of? Is Cuauhtemoc a stupid, willful little boy? Has he no mercy on the women and children of his city? Must even the old men perish? See, the kings of Tlaxcala, Huexotzinco, Cholula, Chalco, Acolhuacan, Cuauhnahuac, Xochimilco, Mizquic, Cuitlahuac and Culhuacan are all here with me."

One of the kings said: "Do the people of Tenochtitlan think they are playing a game? Already their hearts are grieving for the city in which they were born. If they will not surrender, we should abandon them and let them perish by themselves. Why should the Tlatelolcas feel sorry when the people of Tenochtitlan bring a senseless destruction on themselves?"

The guards from Tlatelolco said: "Our lords, it may be as you say."

The "god" said: "Tell Cuauhtemoc that the other kings have all abandoned him. I will go to

Teocalhueyacan, where his forces are gathered, and I will send the ships to Coyoacan."

The guards returned to speak with the followers of Cuauhtemoc. They shouted the message to them from their boats. But the Tlatelolcas would not abandon the people of Tenochtitlan.

THE FIGHTING IS RENEWED

The Spaniards made ready to attack us, and the war broke out again. They assembled their forces in Cuepopan and Cozcacuahco. A vast number of our warriors were killed by their metal darts. Their ships sailed to Texopan, and the battle there lasted three days. When they had forced us to retreat, they entered the Sacred Patio, where there was a four-day battle. Then they reached Yacacolco.

The Tlatelolcas set up three racks of heads in three different places. The first rack was in the Sacred Patio of Tlilancalco [Black House], where we strung up the heads of our lords the Spaniards. The second was in Acacolco, where we strung up Spanish heads and the heads of two of their horses. The third was in Zacatla, in front of the temple of the earth-goddess Cihuacoatl, where we strung up the heads of Tlaxcaltecas.

The women of Tlatelolco joined in the fighting. They struck at the enemy and shot arrows at them; they tucked up their skirts and dressed in the regalia of war.

The Spaniards forced us to retreat. Then they occupied the market place. The Tlatelolcas—the Jaguar Knights, the Eagle Knights, the great warriors—were defeated, and this was the end of the battle. It had lasted five days, and two thousand Tlatelolcas were killed in action. During the battle, the Spaniards set up a canopy for the Captain in the market place. They also mounted a catapult on the temple platform.

EPIC DESCRIPTION OF THE BESIEGED CITY

And all these misfortunes befell us. We saw them and wondered at them; we suffered this unhappy fate.

Broken spears lie in the roads;
we have torn our hair in our grief.
The houses are roofless now, and their walls
are red with blood.

Worms are swarming in the streets and plazas,
and the walls are splattered with gore.
The water has turned red, as if it were dyed,
and when we drink it,
it has the taste of brine.

We have pounded our hands in despair
against the adobe walls,
for our inheritance, our city, is lost and dead.
The shields of our warriors were its defense,
but they could not save it.

We have chewed dry twigs and salt grasses;
we have filled our mouths with dust and bits of
adobe;
we have eaten lizards, rats and worms. . . .

When we had meat, we ate it almost raw. It was scarcely on the fire before we snatched it and gobbled it down.

They set a price on all of us: on the young men, the priests, the boys and girls. The price of a poor man was only two handfuls of corn, or ten cakes made from mosses or twenty cakes of salty couch-grass. Gold, jade, rich cloths, quetzal feathers—everything that once was precious was now considered worthless.

The captains delivered several prisoners of war to Cuauhtemoc to be sacrificed. He performed the sacrifices in person, cutting them open with a stone knife.

THE MESSAGE FROM CORTES

Soon after this, the Spaniards brought Xochitl the Acolnahuacatl, whose house was in Tenochtitlan, to the market place in Tlatelolco. They gripped him by both arms as they brought him there. They kept him with them for twenty days and then let him go. They also brought in a cannon, which they set up in the place where incense was sold.

The Tlatelolcas ran forward to surround Xochitl. They were led by the captain from Huitznahuac, who was a Huasteco. Xochitl was placed under guard in the Temple of the woman in Axocotzinco.

As soon as the Spaniards had set Xochitl loose in the market place, they stopped attacking us. There was no more fighting, and no prisoners were taken.

Three of the great chiefs said to Cuauhtemoc: "Our prince, the Spaniards have sent us one of the magistrates, Xochitl the Acolnahuacatl. It is said that he has a message for you."

Cuauhtemoc asked them: "What is your advice?"

The chiefs all began to shout at once: "Let the message be brought here! We have made auguries with paper and with incense! The captain who seized Xochitl should bring us the message!"

The captain was sent to question Xochitl in the Temple of the Woman. Xochitl said: "The 'god' and La Malinche send word to Cuauhtemoc and the other princes that there is no hope for them. Have they no pity on the little children, the old men, the old women? What more can they do? Everything is settled.

"You are to deliver women with light skins, corn, chickens, eggs and tortillas. This is your last chance. The people of Tenochtitlan must choose whether to surrender or be destroyed."

The captain reported this message to Cuauhtemoc and the lords of Tlatelolco. The lords deliberated among themselves: "What do you think about this? What are we to do?"

THE CITY FALLS

Cuauhtemoc said to the fortune tellers: "Please come forward. What do you see in your books?"

One of the priests replied: "My prince, hear the truth that we tell you. In only four days we shall have completed the period of eighty days. It may be the will of Huitzilopochtli that nothing further shall happen to us. Let us wait until these four days have passed."

But then the fighting broke out again. The captain of Huitzahuac—the same Huasteco who had brought in Xochitl—renewed the struggle. The enemy forced us to retreat to Amaxac. When they also attacked us there, the general flight began. The lake was full of people, and the roads leading to the mainland were all crowded.

Thus the people of Tenochtitlan and Tlatelolco gave up the struggle and abandoned the city. We all gathered in Amaxac. We had no shields and no *macanas*, we had nothing to eat and no shelter. And it rained all night.

THE PEOPLE FLEE THE CITY

Cuauhtemoc was taken to Cortes along with three other princes. The Captain was accompanied by Pedro de Alvarado and La Malinche.

When the princes were made captives, the people began to leave, searching for a place to stay. Everyone was in tatters, and the women's thighs were almost naked. The Christians searched all the refugees. They even opened the women's skirts and blouses and felt everywhere: their ears, their breasts, their hair. Our people scattered in all directions. They went to neighboring villages and huddled in corners in the houses of strangers.

The city was conquered in the year 3—House. The date on which we departed was the day 1—Serpent in the ninth month.

The lords of Tlatelolco went to Cuauhtitlan. Even the greatest captains and warriors left in tatters. The women had only old rags to cover their heads, and they had patched together their blouses out of many-colored scraps. The chiefs were grief-stricken and mourned to one another: "We have been defeated a second time!"

THE OFFERING OF GOLD

A poor man was treacherously killed in Otontlan as he was seeking refuge. The other refugees were shaken by his death and began to discuss what they could do. They said: "Let us beg mercy of our lord the Captain."

First the leaders of Tlatelolco demanded gold objects from everyone. They collected many lip rings, lip plugs, nose plugs and other ornaments. They searched anyone who might be hiding objects of gold behind his shield or under his clothing.

When they had gathered everything they could find, they sent the treasure to Coyoacan in the custody of several chiefs. The chiefs said to the Captain: "Our lord and master, please hear us. Your vassals, the great lords of Tlatelolco, beg you to have mercy. Your vassals and their people are being mistreated by the inhabitants of the villages where they have taken refuge. They scorn us and treacherously kill us.

"We have brought you these objects of gold, and we beg you to hear our pleas."

Then they set the baskets of gold objects before him.

When the Captain and La Malinche saw the gold, they grew very angry and said: "Is this what you have been wasting your time on? You should have been looking for the treasure that fell into the Canal of the Toltecs! Where is it? We must have it!"

The chiefs said: "Cuauhtemoc gave it to the Cihuacoatl and the Huiznahuacatl. They know where it is. Ask them."

When the Captain heard this, he ordered that the chiefs be placed in chains. La Malinche came to them later and said: "The Captain says that you may leave and speak with your leaders. He is very grateful to you. It may be true that your people are being mistreated. Tell them to return. Tell your people to come back to their houses in Tlatelolco. The Captain wants all the Tlatelolcas to reoccupy their quarter of the city. But tell your leaders that no one is to settle in Tenochtitlan itself, for that is the property of the 'gods.' You may leave now."

CUAUHTEMOC IS TORTURED

When the envoys from Tlatelolco had departed, the leaders of Tenochtitlan were brought before the Captain, who wished to make them talk. This was when Cuauhtemoc's feet were burned. They brought him in at daybreak and tied him to a stake.

They found the gold in Cuitlahuactonco, in the house of a chief named Itzpotonqui. As soon as they had seized it, they brought our princes—all of them bound—to Coyoacan.

About this same time, the priest in charge of the temple of Huitzilopochtli was put to death.

The Spaniards had tried to learn from him where the god's finery and that of the high priests was kept. Later they were informed that it was being guarded by certain chiefs in Cuauhchichilco and Xaltocan. They seized it and then hanged two of the chiefs in the middle of the Mazatlan road.

THE RETURN TO TLATELOLCO

The common people began to return to their houses in Tlatelolco. This was in the year 4—Rabbit. Then Temilotzin and Don Juan Huehuetzin came back, but Coyohuehuetzin and Tepantemoctzin both died in Cuauhtitlan.

We were left entirely alone when we reoccupied Tlatelolco. Our masters, the Spaniards, did not seize any of our houses. They remained in Coyoacan and let us live in peace.

They hanged Macuilxochitl, the king of Huitzilopochco, in Coyoacan. They also hanged Pizotzin, the king of Culhuacan. And they fed the Keeper of the Black House, along with several others, to their dogs.

And three wise men of Ehecatl, from Tezcoco, were devoured by the dogs. They had come only to surrender; no one brought them or sent them there. They arrived bearing their painted sheets of paper. There were four of them, and only one escaped; the other three were overtaken, there in Coyoacan.

Questions

1. Compare this document with the one written by Díaz. How are they similar? Where do they disagree? What can you learn from one that you cannot learn from another?
2. According to this document, what role did disease play in the conquest? What might have been different in the absence of an epidemic?
3. Who helped the Spanish take Tenochtitlán? Why?
4. Díaz described the conquistadors' actions as "daring deeds" and "brilliant adventures," lauding the "good results" of the Spanish conquest. How do the Aztec authors interpret these actions? How do you see them?

3.4 Spanish Priest Bartolomé de Las Casas Condemns Cruelty Toward the Indians*

Because the Spanish invasion of the Americas proved so destructive to Indians, it prompted strident debates about the morality of Europeans' conduct. The most vocal and effective critic of Spain's conquest was the Dominican priest, and later bishop, Bartolomé de Las Casas. Las Casas traveled to the New World in 1502, and within a decade became convinced of the injustice of Spanish treatment of Native Americans. Returning to Spain in 1547, Las Casas continued to defend Indian rights, engaging in a famous series of debates in the city of Valladolid in 1550 and 1551. His chief opponent, Juan Ginés de Sepúlveda, defended the justice of violent conquest, while Las Casas argued that civil and Christian law forbade it. The following passage, written by Las Casas in 1552 or 1553, offers a summary of this debate from Las Casas's perspective. After a reasonably fair synopsis of Sepúlveda's position, Las Casas briefly introduces his own argument.

SUMMARY OF SEPÚLVEDA'S POSITION

The work that Sepúlveda, the theologian and royal historian, wrote against the Indians can be summarized in the following arguments by which he defended armed expeditions against the Indians as justified so long as the war is carried on lawfully and according to rules, as the Kings of Spain have thus far commanded that it be waged.

He argues first that those people are barbaric, uninstructed in letters and the art of government, and completely ignorant, unreasoning, and totally incapable of learning anything but the mechanical arts; that they are sunk in vice, are cruel, and are of such character that, as nature teaches, they are to be governed by the will of others. This, at various times, many reliable men who have [known] them and lived in close association with them have asserted under oath. This is clear also from the sixth chapter of the third book of [Oviedo's] *General History of the Indies*, which was examined and approved by the Supreme Council of the Indies.

But, for their own welfare, people of this kind are held by natural law to submit to the control of those who are wiser and superior in virtue and learning, as are the Spaniards (especially the nobility), the learned, the clergy, the religious, and, finally, all those who have been properly educated and trained. Such persons must be considered when a judgment is to be made about the morals and character of any people, for in them especially shine forth natural ability, uprightness, training, and the best morals of any nation. Both in Spain and among the Indians, spiritual and temporal government is entrusted to these people rather than to soldiers, who, for the most part, are unprincipled and, under cover of military license, inflict many injuries.

The conclusion drawn from this is that the Indians are obliged by the natural law to obey those who are outstanding in virtue and character in the same way that matter yields to form, body to soul, sense to reason, animals to human beings, women to men, children to adults, and, finally, the imperfect to the more perfect, the worse to the better, the cheaper to the more precious and excellent, to the advantage of both. This is the natural order, which the eternal and divine law commands be observed, according to Augustine.

Therefore, if the Indians, once warned, refuse to obey this legitimate sovereignty, they can be forced to do so for their own welfare by recourse to the terrors of war. And this war will be just both by civil and natural law, according to the second, third, and fifth chapters of the *Politics* of Aristotle, the most perceptive commentator on justice and the wisest interpreter of the other moral virtues, as well as of nature and nature's laws. Philosophers and great theologians alike follow him as a master. The wise man in the book of Proverbs approves Aristotle's teaching that the fool ought to be slave to the wise. Saint Thomas, too, teaches the same thing, and Thomas holds first place among scholastic theologians, always following as he does, Aristotle's opinion in the explanation of natural laws. Finally, all political

---

*Stafford Poole, ed. and trans., *In Defense of the Indians* (DeKalb: Northern Illinois University Press, 1974), 11–22.

philosophers, basing themselves on this reason alone, teach that in cities, kingdoms, and states those who excel in prudence and virtue should preside with sovereignty over the government so that government may be just according to the natural law.

Everywhere in the world we see that the best kings and rightly organized states appoint their wiser and more excellent men for the administration of the government. This universal custom is considered to be a law of nature, and all natural laws are divine inasmuch as they flow from the eternal law. Saint Augustine considers this to be God's will, determining that the natural order be observed and forbidding it to be overturned. Hence Augustine often says that if someone is unwilling to do what is good for himself and he is obliged to act for his own welfare, it is just to force him to do it even though he is unwilling and resists. This agrees with what Augustine teaches in different parts of *The City of God*, which Saint Thomas cites when he upholds the same opinion that the Romans justly subjugated the other nations of the world. God wanted the greater part of the world to come under their dominion so that it might be ruled more justly under the government of a wise people who cherished justice. But even if these barbarians (that is, the Indians) do not lack capacity, with still more reason they must obey and heed the commands of those who can teach them to live like human beings and do the things that are beneficial for both their present and future life.

In the second place, Sepúlveda proves that the Indians, even though unwilling, must accept the Spanish yoke so that they may be corrected and be punished for the sins and crimes against the divine and natural laws by which they have been contaminated, especially their idolatry and the impious custom of human sacrifice. Indeed, it is proved in various passages of Holy Scripture that the Amorites and the Perizzites and other inhabitants of the Promised Land were exterminated by the Children of Israel because of these two sins, and also that the Hebrews themselves were punished for the same sins by the destruction of large numbers of their people and by the enslavement of their nation and exile from the Promised Land, their fatherland. From this it is evident that the law by which both the former and the latter were condemned is natural and divine and, as a consequence, is to be observed always. This is what that learned bishop and holy martyr Cyprian teaches. Further, it is the more common opinion among all the doctors that pagans who do no observe the natural law may be punished by Christians. Those people are considered not to be keeping the natural law among whom some mortal sins go unpunished or are not judged to be against the natural law. Thus Cajetan's tenet that war cannot be waged against a nation by reason of its lack of faith is to be understood of those who are guilty of unbelief alone. The case is different when the sins about which we spoke above accompany the unbelief.

Thirdly, Sepúlveda argues that the injuries and extreme misery which the Indians used to inflict and which those who have not yet been subdued still inflict today on a great number of innocent persons, whom they used to sacrifice each year to the evil spirit, should be stopped. All who can do so are held by the natural and divine law to defend any and all persons from such injuries, for all men are neighbors to one another and brothers, as the theologians teach, That all, if they can, are bound to ward off danger from their neighbor is proved from these words of the wise man: "Rescue those being led away to death," and again, in the same book: God "gave each one a commandment concerning his neighbor." The above-mentioned evil, however, cannot be avoided unless these barbarians are tamed and subjugated.

Fourthly, he advances the gain in bringing about the spread and growth of the Christian religion. This will be accomplished if, once those regions have been brought under control, the gospel of Christ can be preached by consecrated men safely and without any danger, so that they will not be massacred by either [pagan] rulers or priests, as they have already done three or four times. He supports this by the authority of Augustine, who writes that Christ wanted men to be drawn to the faith by meekness and gentleness during the first period of the infant Church. However, after the Church grew in power and numbers, Christ wanted men to be compelled, even when unwilling, to accept the Christian religion. This he shows in the parable of the banquet to which the first persons were invited, whereas the rest were compelled and forced. Violence was resorted to in order to bring them to the banquet because, as Augustine says, the following prophecy had not yet been fulfilled: "All kings will do him homage; all nations become his servants!" The more this is realized, the more the Church uses its powers, not only by inviting but also by compelling [unbelievers] to the faith.

Lest anyone think that the arguments Augustine uses against heretics do not apply to pagans, Sepulveda strengthens [the arguments] by citing the law of the God-fearing Emperor Constantine against the pagans. Having closed the pagan temples and prohibited shameful auguries, immolations, and sacrifices, Constantine forbade the worship of idols under penalty of death and confiscation of property. The holy Fathers Ambrose and Augustine, as well as other Christian men, praised this law as fair and just. Nevertheless, Sepúlveda declares that he does not want the unwilling to be baptized. This is forbidden by divine law, and no law can oblige anyone to be baptized against his will. But he says that violent measures and whatever is probably helpful should be tried, so that heretics and pagans may acknowledge their error, come to their senses, and thus ask for baptism of their own accord, as many of these Indians did when moved by violence and force of war.

This is similar to the methods used by Constantine and employed also by Genandius, Exarch of Africa, whom Saint Gregory praised exceedingly for waging war on the pagans to extend the limits of the Christian religion. Nor is it valid, says Sepúlveda, for someone to object that this can be admitted only when the war is waged on subjects, because those against whom Genandius drew the sword were not subjects of the Roman people, for had they been subjects of the Roman people he would not have waged war on them.

Sepúlveda concludes his work by saying that it is totally just, as well as most beneficial to these barbarians, that they be conquered and brought under the rule of the Spaniards, who are worshipers of Christ. This is the easiest way for them to embrace the Christian religion, as experience has clearly taught. This is especially true when this can be accomplished with minimum bloodshed. In fact, every year they used to sacrifice many more men to their gods than will perish when the terrors of warfare are launched against them, to the immeasurable benefit of both the living and those who will come after them.

Furthermore, he asserts that the Roman Pontiff, Alexander VI, in a decree to the College of Cardinals declared armed expeditions against the Indians to be just, that he allowed the Kings of Castile the right to conquer them and add them to their empire, and expressly forbade, for just reasons, other rulers to take up arms against them. Therefore, just as no one can deny that wars undertaken by God's command are just, no one will deny that a war is just that God's Vicar, after mature deliberation and in the exercise of his pontifical authority, declares to be justified.

Everything in his little work, says Sepúlveda, is proved most thoroughly by various citations from the sacred books of the Old and New Testaments, from the natural law, and also from the authority of theologians who teach that when war is just (that is, when it is carried on against those upon whom it has been declared, as this one was), soldiers are not bound to make restitution of things acquired by right of war. This is true even though they may have taken up arms not so much from a love of establishing truth and justice as from greed to despoil the enemy and gain possessions, although, if they wage war in this spirit, they sin gravely. However, those who inflict injuries and steal property contrary to the laws of war and justice, as many have done, are held to restitution and commit a very serious crime, and the ruler who tolerates such actions, or does not forbid them when he can, is guilty of the same crime and is held to give an account to God.

Preface to the Defense of the
Most Reverend Fray Bartolomé
de Las Casas, of the Order of
Saint Dominic, Late Bishop of
Chiapa, to Philip, Great Prince
of Spain

Fray Bartolomé de Las Casas,
of the Order of Saint Dominic,
Late Bishop of Chiapa, to
Philip, Great Prince of Spain

Illustrious Prince:

It is right that matters which concern the safety and peace of the great empire placed in your keeping by the divine goodness be reported to you, for you rule Spain and that marvelous New World in the name of the great Charles, your father, and you strive for immortal glory, not just with the imperial power but especially with the generous spirit and with the wisdom implanted in you by Christ. Therefore I have thought it advisable to bring to the attention of Your Highness that there has come into my hands a certain brief synopsis in Spanish of a work that Ginés de Sepúlveda is reported to have written in Latin. In it he gives four reasons, each of which, in his opinion, proves beyond refutation that war against the Indians is justified, provided that it be waged properly and the laws of war be observed, just as, up to the present, the kings of Spain have commanded that it be waged and carried out.

I hear that it is this man's intention to demonstrate the title by which the Kings of Spain possess the empire of the Indies and to bolster his position with arguments and laws, so that from now on no one will be able to slander you even tacitly on this point. I have read and reread this work carefully. And it is said that Sepúlveda drives home various other points at greater length in his Latin work (which I have not yet had the chance to see). What impression it has made on others I do not know. I certainly have detected in it poisons disguised with honey. Under pretext of pleasing his prince, a man who is a theologian offers honey-coated poison. In place of bread, he offers a stone. Great Prince, unless this deadly poison is stopped by your wisdom, so that it will not become widespread, it will infect the minds of readers, deceive the unwary, and arm and incite tyrants to injustice. Believe me, that little book will bring ruin to the minds of many.

In the first place, while claiming that he wants to vindicate your jurisdiction over the Indies, he tears to pieces and reduces your rights by presenting arguments that are partly foolish, partly false, partly of the kind that have the least force. Furthermore, if this man's judgment in this matter should be printed, [and] sanctioned with the royal license and privilege, there can be no doubt that within a short time the empire of the Indies will be entirely overthrown and destroyed.

Indeed, if so many laws already issued, so many decrees, so many harsh threats, and so many statutes conscientiously enacted by the Emperor Charles and his predecessors have been ineffective in preventing so many thousands of innocent men from perishing by sword, hunger, and all the misfortunes of total war, and extensive areas of their highly civilized kingdoms and most fertile provinces from being savagely devastated; if the fear of God and the dread of hell have not even moderated (I shall not say curbed) the utterly ruthless and cruel spirits of the Spaniards; if the outcries of preachers and holy men that they were barred from the sacraments of the Church and were not forgiven in sacramental confession were of no avail, what will happen when evil men (for whom, according to the old proverb, nothing is wanting except the opportunity) read that a scholar, a doctor of theology, and the royal historian has published books approving those criminal wars and hellish campaigns and, by supporting arguments, confirms and defends the unheard-of crime whereby Christian men, forgetting Christian virtue, hold in slavery those people, the most unfortunate of all, who appear to have escaped the ferocity of that most cruel race by chance rather than by the mercy of the Spaniards? Furthermore, [what will happen when they read] that he teaches that soldiers may lawfully keep everything they take in these wars, even though they undertook the campaign with the evil intention of looting, that is, of pillaging by fire, sword, murder, plunder and violence, upsetting, overturning, and throwing into confusion all laws, divine and human, and that they are not bound to restore such goods because the Spaniards who do these things and shed the blood of the innocent consecrate their hands to God (as I hear Sepúlveda has written) and merit Christ's grace because they prevent the worship of idols?

Whom will they spare? What blood will they not shed? What cruelty will they not commit, these brutal men who are hardened to seeing fields bathed in human blood, who make no distinction of sex or age, who do not spare infants at their mothers' breasts, pregnant women, the great, the lowly, or even men of feeble and gray old age for whom the weight of years usually awakens reverence or mercy? What will they not do if they hear that there is a man teaching that they are consecrating their hands to God when they crush the Indians with massacres, pillaging, and tyranny—that they are doing the same as those who killed the Children of Israel who were adoring the calf? They will give more trust to him, as to someone who tells them what they want to hear, than they would to the son of God himself if he were face to face before us and teaching something different.

If, then, the Indians are being brought to the point of extermination, if as many peoples are being destroyed as widespread kingdoms are being overthrown, what sane man would doubt that the most flourishing empire of the New World, once its native inhabitants have been destroyed, will become a wilderness, and nothing but dominion over tigers, lions, and wild beasts for the Kings of Spain? When the all-wise God commanded certain nations to be overthrown, he did not want them completely destroyed at once, lest the empty lands without human beings become the lair of wild animals which might harm the few Jews who were the new inhabitants.

Therefore when Sepúlveda, by word or in his published works, teaches that campaigns against the Indians are lawful, what does he do except encourage oppressors and provide an opportunity for as many crimes and lamentable evils as these [men] commit, more than anyone would find it possible to believe? In the meantime, with most certain harm to his own soul, he is the reason why countless human beings, suffering brutal massacres, perish forever, that it, men who, through the inhuman brutality of the Spaniards, breathe their last before they hear the word of God, [or] are fed by Christ's gentle doctrine, [or] are strengthened by the Christian sacraments. What more horrible or unjust occurrence can be imagined than this?

Therefore, if Sepúlveda's opinion (that campaigns against the Indians are lawful) is approved, the most holy faith of Christ, to the reproach of the name Christian, will be hateful and detestable to all the peoples of that world to whom to word will come of the inhuman crimes that the Spaniards inflict on that unhappy race, so that neither in our lifetime nor in the future will they want to accept our faith under any condition, for they see that its first heralds are not pastors but plunderers, not fathers but tyrants, and that those who profess it are ungodly, cruel, and without pity in their merciless savagery.

Furthermore, since Sepúlveda's book is polished, painstaking, persuasive, and carefully built up throughout with many tricky kinds of argument, it will permanently deceive these thieves, these enemies of the human race, so that they will never come to their senses nor, admitting their crimes, flee to the mercy of God, who, in his unutterable love, is perhaps calling them to penance, nor will they implore his help. Under the pretext of religion, [Sepúlveda] excuses the criminal wickedness of these men, which carries with it all the evils to be found anywhere in the lives of mortal men. He praises with lofty language these plunderers who loot with utmost savagery, and he commends their warlike virtue.

Finally, it is intolerable that a man to whom has been entrusted the duty of writing the imperial history should publish a destructive error that is in total disagreement with the words of the gospel and the meekness and kindness of which all Christ's teaching is redolent and which the Church, imitating its master, exercises toward those who do not know Christ. For men of the future will, with good reason, decide that a man who has gone wrong so disgracefully in a matter so clear has taken no account of the truth when writing history, a fact that, no matter how learnedly and gracefully that history will have been written, will tarnish the most celebrated victories of the Emperor.

Therefore I considered the many misfortunes, the great harvest of evils so deserving of rebuke, and the severest punishment which will arise from his teaching: offense against God, ill repute and hatred for our most holy religion, irreparable damage, the loss of so many believing souls, and the loss of the right of the kings of Spain to the empire of the New World. I considered also that these opinions of his will spread through all the nations of the world the savage and firmly rooted practice of seizing what belongs to others and increasing one's property by shedding human blood (an evil reproach under which the Spanish people have labored for so long), which, Sepúlveda claims, are for the power and glory of Spain.

I could not contain myself. Mindful that I am a Christian, a religious, a bishop, a Spaniard, and a subject of the King of Spain, I cannot but unsheathe the sword of my pen for the defense of the truth, the honor of God's house, and the spreading of the revered gospel of Our Lord Jesus Christ so that, according to the measure of the grace given to me, I might wipe the stain from the Christian name, take away the obstacles and stumbling blocks hindering the spread of belief in the gospel, and proclaim the truth which I have vowed in baptism, have learned in the religious life, and finally, however unworthy, have professed when consecrated bishop. For by all these titles I am bound to set myself up as a wall against the wicked for the defense of a completely innocent people, soon to be grafted onto the true house of Israel, whom the ravening wolves unceasingly pursue. I am also obliged to block the

road along which so many thousands of men are lured to their eternal destruction and to defend with my life my sheep, whom I promised by a solemn oath to protect against every wolf, ecclesiastical or lay, who breaks into my sheepfold.

Finally, I want to set forth the true right of my prince, that is, the title by which he may possess the New World, and to hide [*sic*] the frightful and disgraceful crimes that my own people, the Spaniards, have inflicted in violation of justice and right during these last few years on the Indians, who have been ruined by terrible butchery, and to wash away the shame brought upon that name among all the nations.

Four things, therefore, that I must give a full account of are to be treated here.

First, I shall refute Sepúlveda's opinion claiming that war against the Indians is justified because they are barbarous, uncivilized, unteachable, and lacking civil government.

Second, I shall show that, to the most definite ruin of his own soul, Sepúlveda is wrong when he teaches that war against the Indians is justified as punishment for their crimes against the natural law, especially the crimes of idolatry and human sacrifice.

Third, we shall attack his third argument, on the basis of which Sepúlveda teaches that war can be waged unconditionally and indiscriminately against those people in order to free the innocent.

Fourth, I shall discuss how foreign to the teaching of the gospel and Christian mercy is his fourth proposition, maintaining that war against the Indians is justified as a means of extending the boundaries of the Christian religion and of opening the way for those who proclaim and preach the gospel.

When I have finished, the truth of this case and the magnitude of the crime committed by those who have maltreated the Indians by robberies, massacres, and other incredible misfortunes of war, and continue to do so, will be clear; and at the same time how groundless are the arguments of a man who is wrong both in law and in fact, by what design he was led to write that dangerous book, in what way he has distorted the teachings of philosophers and theologians, falsified the words of Sacred Scripture, of divine and human laws, and how no less destructively he has quoted statements of Pope Alexander VI to favor the success of his wicked cause. Finally, the true title by which the Kings of Spain hold their rule over the New World will be shown.

For this reason, Most Excellent Prince, I beg Your Highness to order this work, which I have written at the cost of much sweat and [many] sleepless nights, to be weighed and examined by learned men. If anything is found to be stated improperly or badly, I shall be most pleased to have my sleepless nights perfected by their charity. If, however, anything is found to be expressed well, I look for no other human reward except that Your Highness command Sepúlveda to give me a copy of the Latin work he wrote on this subject so that, when I have refuted his falsehoods more completely, the truth many shine forth and rule the consciences of all men.

Farewell!

Questions

1. According to Las Casas, what principles did Sepúlveda use to justify the violent conquest of Indians? How did Sepúlveda defend these principles?
2. What are Las Casas's primary arguments against armed conquest? What evidence does he employ to support his claims?
3. How does Christianity figure in these discussions?
4. Las Casas claims that Sepúlveda's arguments "encourage oppressors." How? What solution does Las Casas offer to the problem of Spanish violence?
5. How are these debates similar to modern discussions about human rights? How are they different?

4

The Spanish Frontier

Hoping to emulate Spanish successes in Mexico, aspiring conquistadors quickly moved north into other regions of the continent. They failed to locate the riches they coveted, but they did encounter a breathtaking array of indigenous peoples, whom later missionaries and colonizers considered suitable for subjugation and conversion. We have already read, in the documents for Chapter 1, descriptions of parts of the Southwest and Southeast traversed by the Coronado and De Soto expeditions. In the documents that follow, we see Spanish colonization from the very different perspectives of a Spanish castaway and New Mexican Indians.

4.1   Cabeza de Vaca's Southwestern Odyssey*

Alvar Núñez Cabeza de Vaca (c. 1490–c. 1557) was second-in-command on the disastrous 1528 Panfilo de Narváez expedition to Florida and the Gulf Coast. That venture disintegrated amid hostile Indians, harsh terrain, and difficult waters. Cabeza de Vaca survived, however, and lived for eight years among the Indian peoples of the Texas coast and the Southwest. After returning to Spain, he published his Chronicle of the Narváez Expedition *in 1542. Our reading begins with Cabeza de Vaca and his Spanish companions struggling and failing to escape the Texas coast. After tracing Cabeza de Vaca's adaptation to life among the Indians of the region, the reading moves to the 1534–1536 journey of Cabeza de Vaca and three other survivors of the Narváez expedition—Andrés* Dorantes, Alfonso de Castillo, and Esteban (a black slave from Morocco)—from Texas to northwestern Mexico.

CHAPTER XII. THE INDIANS BRING US FOOD

At sunrise the next day, the time the Indians appointed, they came according to their promise, and brought us a large quantity of fish with certain roots, some a little larger than walnuts, others a trifle smaller, the greater part got from under the water and with much labor. In the evening they returned and brought us more fish and roots. They sent their women and children to look at us, who went back rich with the hawk-bells and beads given them, and they came afterwards on other days, returning as before. Finding that we had provision, fish, roots, water and other things we asked for, we determined to embark again and pursue our course. Having dug out our boat from the sand in which it was buried, it became necessary that we should strip, and go through great exertion to launch her, we being in such a state that

---

*Alvar Nuñez Cabeça de Vaca, *Relation of Alvar Nuñez Cabeça de Vaca*, trans. Buckingham Smith (New York: J. Munsell, 1871), 67–71, 74–77, 80–82, 84–88, 111–113, 115–116, 166–169, 172–177, 185–188.

things very much lighter sufficed to make us great labor.

Thus embarked, at the distance of two cross-bow shots in the sea we shipped a wave that entirely wet us. As we were naked, and the cold was very great, the oars loosened in our hands, and the next blow the sea struck us capsized the boat. The Assessor and two others held fast to her for preservation, but it happened to be far otherwise; the boat carried them over, and they were drowned under her. As the surf near the shore was very high, a single roll of the sea threw the rest into the waves and half drowned upon the shore of the island, without our losing any more than those the boat took down. The survivors escaped naked as they were born, with the loss of all they had; and although the whole was of little value, at that time it was worth much, as we were then in November, the cold was severe, and our bodies were so emaciated the bones might be counted with little difficulty, having become the perfect figures of death. For myself I can say that from the month of May passed, I had eaten no other thing than maize, and sometimes I found myself obliged to eat it unparched: for although the beasts were slaughtered while the boats were building, I could never eat their flesh, and I did not eat fish ten times. I state this to avoid giving excuses, and that every one may judge in what condition we were. Besides all these misfortunes, came a north wind upon us, from which we were nearer to death than life. Thanks be to our Lord that in looking among the brands we had used there, we found sparks from which we made great fires. And thus were we asking mercy of Him and pardon for our transgressions, shedding many tears, and each regretting not his own fate alone, but that of his comrades about him.

At sunset, the Indians thinking that we had not gone, came to seek us and bring us food; but when they saw us thus, in a plight so different from what it was before, and so extraordinary, they were alarmed and turned back. I went toward them and called, when they returned much frightened. I gave them to understand by signs that our boat had sunk and three of our number had been drowned. There, before then, they saw

two of the departed, and we who remained were near joining them. The Indians, at sight of what had befallen us, and our state of suffering and melancholy destitution, sat down among us, and from the sorrow and pity they felt, they all began to lament so earnestly that they might have been heard at a distance, and continued so doing more than half an hour. It was strange to see these men, wild and untaught, howling like brutes over our misfortunes. It caused in me as in others, an increase of feeling and a livelier sense of our calamity.

The cries having ceased, I talked with the Christians, and said that if it appeared well to them, I would beg these Indians to take us to their houses. Some, who had been in New Spain, replied that we ought not to think of it: for if they should do so, they would sacrifice us to their idols. But seeing no better course, and that any other led to a nearer and more certain death, I disregarded what was said, and besought the Indians to take us to their dwellings, and that we should tarry a little, that they might do what we asked. Presently thirty men loaded themselves with wood and started for their houses, which were far off, and we remained with the others until night, when, holding us up, they carried us with all haste. Because of the extreme coldness of the weather, lest any one should die or fail by the way, they caused four or five very large fires to be placed at intervals, and at each they warmed us; and when they saw that we had regained some heat and strength, they took us to the next so swiftly that they hardly let us touch our feet to the ground. In this manner, we went as far as their habitations, where we found that they had made a house for us with many fires in it. An hour after our arrival, they began to dance and hold great rejoicing, which lasted all night, although for us there was no joy, festivity nor sleep, awaiting the hour they should make us victims. In the morning, they again gave us fish and roots, showing us such hospitality that we were re-assured, and lost somewhat the fear of sacrifice.

CHAPTER XIV. THE DEPARTURE OF FOUR CHRISTIANS

The four Christians being gone, after a few days such cold and tempestuous weather succeeded that the Indians could not pull up roots, the cane wears in which they took fish no longer yielded any thing, and the houses being very open, our people began to die. Five Christians, of a mess on the coast, came to such extremity that they ate their dead; the body of the last one only was found unconsumed. Their names were Sierra, Diego Lopez, Corral, Palacios and Gonçalo Ruiz. This produced great commotion among the Indians, giving rise to so much censure that had they know it in season to have done so, doubtless they would have destroyed any survivor, and we should have found ourselves in the utmost perplexity. Finally, of eighty men who arrived in the two instances, fifteen only remained alive.

After this, the natives were visited by a disease of the bowels, of which half their number died. They conceived that we had destroyed them, and believing it firmly, they concerted among themselves to dispatch those of us who survived. When they were about to execute their purpose, an Indian who had charge of me, told them not to believe we were the cause of those deaths, since if we had such power we should also have averted the fatality from so many of our people, whom they had seen die without our being able to minister relief; already very few of us remaining, and none doing hurt or wrong, and that it would be better to leave us unharmed. God our Lord willed that the others should heed this opinion and counsel, and be hindered in their design.

To this island we gave the name Malhado. The people we found there are large and well formed: they have no other arms than bows and arrows, in the use of which they are very dexterous. The men have one of their nipples bored from side to side, and some have both, wearing a cane in each, the length of two palms and a half, and the thickness of two fingers. They have the under lip also bored, and wear in it a piece of cane the breadth of half a finger. Their women are accustomed to great toil. The stay they make on the island is from October to the end of February. Their subsistence then is the root I have spoken of, got from under the water in November and December. They have wears of cane and take fish only in this season: afterwards they live on the roots. At the end of February, they go into other parts to seek food: for then the root is beginning to grow and is not good.

These people love their offspring the most of any in the world, and treat them with the greatest mildness. When it occurs that a son dies, the parents and kindred weep as does every body; the wailing continuing for him a whole year. They begin before dawn every day, the parents first and after them the whole town. They do the same at noon and at sunset. After a year of mourning has passed, the rites of the dead are performed; then they wash and purify themselves from the stain of smoke. They lament all the deceased in this manner, except the aged, for whom they show no regret, as they saw that their season has passed, they having no enjoyment, and that living they would occupy the earth and take aliment from the young. Their custom is to bury the dead, unless it be those among them who have been physicians. These they burn. While the fire kindles they are all dancing and making high festivity, until the bones become powder. After the lapse of a year the funeral honors are celebrated, every one taking part in them, when that dust is presented in water for the relatives to drink.

Every man has an acknowledged wife. The physicians are allowed more freedom: they may have two or three wives, among who exist the greatest friendship and harmony. From the time a daughter marries, all that he who takes her to wive kills in hunting or catches in fishing, the woman brings to the house of her father, without daring to eat or take any part of it, and thence victuals are taken to the husband. From that time neither her father nor mother enter his house, nor can he enter theirs, nor the houses of their children; and if by chance they are in the direction of meeting, they turn aside, and pass the distance of a crossbow shot from each other, carrying the head low the while, the eyes cast on the ground; for they hold it improper to see or to speak to each other. But the woman has liberty to converse and communicate with the parents and relatives of her husband. The custom exists from this island the distance of more than fifty leagues inland.

There is another custom, which is, when a son or brother dies, at the house where the death takes place, they do not go after food for three months, but sooner famish, their relatives and neighbors providing what they eat. As in the time we were there a great number of the natives died, in most houses there was very great hunger, because of the keeping of this their custom and observance; for although they who sought after food worked hard, yet from the severity of the season they could get but little; in consequence, the Indians who kept me, left the island, and passed over in canoes to the main, into some bays where are many oysters. For three months in the year they eat nothing besides these, and drink very bad water. There is great want of wood: mosquitos are in great plenty. The houses are of mats, set up on masses of oyster shells, which they sleep upon, and is skins, should they accidentally possess them. In this way we lived until April, when we went to the sea shore, where we ate blackberries all the month, during which time the Indians did not omit to observe their areitos and festivities.

CHAPTER XV. WHAT BEFEL US AMONG THE PEOPLE OF MALHADO

On an Island of which I have spoken, they wished to make us physicians without examination or inquiring for displomas. They cure by blowing upon the sick, and with that breath and the imposing of hands they cast out infirmity. They ordered that we also should do this, and be of use to them in some way. We laughed at what they did, telling them it was folly, that we knew not how to heal. In consequence, they withheld food from us until we should practice what they required. Seeing our persistence, an Indian told me I knew not what I uttered, in saying that what he knew availed nothing; for stones and other matters growing about in the fields, have virtue, and that passing a pebble along the stomach would take away pain and restore health, and certainly then we who were extraordinary men must posses power and efficacy over all other things. At last, finding ourselves in great want we were constrained to obey; but without fear lest we should be blamed for any failure or success.

Their custom is, on finding themselves sick to send for a physician, and after he has applied the cure, they give him not only all they have, but seek among their relatives for more to give. The practitioner scarifies over the seat of pain, and then sucks about the wound. They make cauteries with fire, a remedy among them in high repute, which I have tried on myself and found benefit from it. They afterwards blow on the spot, and having finished, the patient considers that he is relieved.

Our method was to bless the sick, breathing upon them, and recite a Pater-noster and an Ave-Maria, praying with all earnestness to God our Lord that he would give health and influence them to make us some good return. In his clemency he willed that all those for whom we supplicated, should tell the others that they were sound and in health, directly after we made the sign of the blessed cross over them. For this the Indians treated us kindly: they deprived themselves of food that they might give to us, and presented us with skins and some trifles.

So protracted was the hunger we there experienced, that many times I was three days without eating. The natives also endured as much: and it appeared to me a thing impossible that life could be so prolonged, although afterwards I found myself in greater hunger and necessity, which I shall speak of farther on.

The Indians who had Alonzo del Castillo, Andrés Dorantes, and the others that remained alive, were of a different tongue and ancestry from these, and went to the opposite shore of the main to eat oysters, where they staid until the first day of April, when they returned. The distance is two leagues in the widest part. The island is half a league in breadth and five leagues in length.

The inhabitants of all this region go naked. The women alone have any part of their persons covered, and it is with a wool that grows on trees. The damsels dress themselves in deerskin. The people are generous to each other of what they possess. They have no chief. All that are of a lineage keep together. They speak two languages; those of one are called Capoques, those of the other, Han. They have a custom when they meet, or from time to time when they visit, of remaining half an hour before they speak, weeping; and, this over, he that is visited first rises and gives the other all he has, which is received, and after a little while he carries it away, and often goes without saying a word. They have other strange customs; but I have told the principal of them, and the most remarkable, that I may pass on and further relate what befell us.

CHAPTER XVI. THE CHRISTIANS LEAVE THE ISLAND OF MALHADO

After Dorantes and Castillo returned to the Island, they brought together the Christians, who were somewhat separated, and found them in all to be fourteen. As I have said, I was opposite on the main, where my Indians had taken me, and where so great sickness had come upon me, that if anything before had given me hopes of life, this were enough to have entirely bereft me of them.

When the Christians heard of my condition, they gave an Indian the cloak of marten skins we had taken from the cacique, as before related, to pass them over to where I was that they might visit me. Twelve of them crossed; for two were so feeble that their comrades could not venture to bring them. The names of those who came were Alonzo del Castillo, Andrés Dorantes, Diego Dorantes, Valdevieso, Estrada, Tostado, Chaves, Gutierrez, Asturiano a clergyman, Diego de Huelva, Estevarico a black, and Benitez; and when they reached the main land, they found another, who was one of our company, named Francisco de Leon. The thirteen together followed along the coast. So soon as they had come over, my Indians informed me of it, and that Hieronymo de Alvaniz and Lope de Oviedo remained on the island. But sickness prevented me from going with my companions or even seeing them.

I was obliged to remain with the people belonging to the island more than a year, and because of the hard work they put upon me and the harsh treatment, I resolved to flee from them and go to those of Charruco, who inhabit the forests and country of the main, the life I led being insupportable. Besides much other labor, I had to get out roots from below the water, and from among the cane where they grew in the ground. From this employment I had my fingers so worn that did a straw but touch them they would bleed. Many of the canes are broken, so they often tore my flesh, and I had to go in the midst of them with only the clothing on I have mentioned.

Accordingly, I put myself to contriving how I might get over to the other Indians, among whom matters turned somewhat more favorably for me. I set to trafficking, and strove to make my employment profitable in the ways I could best contrive, and by that means I got food and good treatment. The Indians would beg me to go from one quarter to another for things of which they have need: for in consequence of incessant hostilities, they cannot traverse the country, nor make many exchanges. With my merchandise and trade I went into the interior as far as I pleased, and traveled along the coast forty or fifty leagues. The principal wares were cones and other pieces of sea-snail, conches used for cutting, and fruit like a bean of the highest value among them, which they use as a medicine and employ in their dances and festivities. Among other matters were sea-beads. Such were what I carried into the interior; and in barter I got and brought back skins, ochre with which they rub and color the face, hard canes of which to make arrows, sinews, cement and flint for the heads, and tassels of the hair of deer that by dyeing they make red. This occupation suited me well; for the travel allowed me liberty to go where I wished, I was not obliged to work, and was not a slave. Wherever I went I received fair treatment, and the Indians gave me to eat out of regard to my commodities. My leading object, while journeying in this business, was to find out the way by which I should go forward, and I became well known. The inhabitants were pleased when they saw me, and I had brought them what they wanted; and those who did not know me sought and desired the acquaintance, for my reputation. The hardships that I underwent in this were long to tell, as well of peril and privation as of storms and cold. Oftentimes they overtook me alone and in the wilderness; but I came forth from them all by the great mercy of God, our Lord. Because of them

I avoided pursuing the business in winter, a season in which the natives themselves retire to their huts and ranches, torpid and incapable of exertion.

I was in this country nearly six years, alone among the Indians, and naked like them. The reason why I remained so long, was that I might take with me the Christian, Lope de Oviedo, from the island; Alaniz, his companion, who had been left with him by Alonzo del Castillo, Andrés Dorantes and the rest, died soon after their departure; and to get the survivor out from there, I went over to the island every year, and entreated him that we should go, in the best way we could contrive, in quest of Christians. He put me off every year, saying in the next coming we would start. At last I got him off, crossing him over the bay, and over four rivers in the coast, as he could not swim. In this way we went on with some Indians, until coming to a bay a league in width, and everywhere deep. From the appearance we supposed it to be that which is called Espiritu Sancto. We met some Indians on the other side of it, coming to visit ours, who told us that beyond them were three men like us, and gave their names. We asked for the others, and were told that they were all dead of cold and hunger; that the Indians farther on, of whom they were, for their diversion had killed Diego Dorantes, Valdevieso, and Diego de Huelva, because they left one house for another; and that other Indians, their neighbors with whom Captain Dorantes now was, had in consequence of a dream, killed Esquivel and Mendez. We asked how the living were situated, and they answered that they were very ill used, the boys and some of the Indian men being very idle, out of cruelty gave them many kicks, cuffs and blows with sticks: that such was the life they led.

We desired to be informed of the country ahead, and of the subsistence: they said there was nothing to eat, and that it was thin of people, who suffered of cold, having no skins or other things to cover them. They told us also if we wished to see those three Christians, two days from that time the Indians who had them would come to eat walnuts a league from there on the margin of that river; and that we might know what they told us of the ill usage to be true, they slapped my companion and beat him with a stick, and I was not left without my portion. Many times they threw lumps of mud at us, and every day they put their arrows to our hearts, saying that they were inclined to kill us in the way that they had destroyed our friends. Lope Oviedo, my comrade, in fear said that he wished to go back with the women of those who had crossed the bay with us, the men having remained some distance behind. I contended strongly against his returning, and urged my objections; but in no way could I keep him. So he went back, and I remained alone with those savages. They are called Quevenes, and those with whom he returned, Deaguanes.

CHAPTER XIX. OUR SEPARATION BY THE INDIANS

When the six months were over, I had to spend with the Christians to put in execution the plan we had concerted, the Indians went after prickly pears, the place at which they grew being thirty leagues off; and when we approached the point of flight, those among whom we were, quarreled about a woman. After striking with fists, beating with sticks and bruising heads in great anger, each took his lodge and went his way, whence it became necessary that the Christians should also separate, and in no way could we come together until another year.

In this time I passed a hard life, caused as much by hunger as ill usage. Three times I was obliged to run from my masters, and each time they went in pursuit and endeavored to slay me: but God our Lord in his mercy chose to protect and preserve me: and when the season of prickly pears returned, we again came together in the same place. After we had arranged our escape, and appointed a time, that very day the Indians separated and all went back. I told my comrades I would wait for them among the prickly pear plants until the moon should be full. This day was the first of September, and the first of the moon; and I said that if in this time they did not come as we had agreed, I would leave and go alone. So we parted, each going with his Indians. I remained with mine until the thirteenth day of the moon, having determined to flee to others when it should be full.

At this time Andrés Dorantes arrived with Estevanico and informed me that they had left Castillo with other Indians near by, called Lanegados; that they had encountered great obstacles and wandered about lost; that the next day the Indians, among whom we were, would move to where Castillo was, and were going to unite with those who held him and become friends, having been at war until then, and that in this way we should recover Castillo.

We had thirst all the time we ate the pears, which we quenched with juice. We caught it in a hole in the earth, and when it was full we drank until satisfied. It is sweet, and the color of must. In this manner they collect it for lack of vessels. There are many kinds of prickly pears, among them some very good, although they all appeared to me to be so, hunger never having given me leisure to choose, nor to reflect upon which were the best.

Nearly all these people drink rain-water, which lies about in spots. Although there are rivers, as the Indians never have fixed habitations, there are no familiar or known places for getting water. Throughout the country are extensive and beautiful plains with good pasturage; and I think it would be a very fruitful region were it worked and inhabited by civilized men. We nowhere saw mountains.

These Indians told us that there was another people next in advance of us, called Camones, living towards the coast, and that they had killed the people who came in the boat of Peñalosa and Tellez, who arrived so feeble that even while being slain they could offer no resistance, and were all destroyed. We were shown their clothes and arms, and were told that the boat lay there stranded. This, the fifth boat, had remained till then unaccounted for. We have already stated how the boat of the Governor had been carried out to sea, and the one of the Comptroller and the Friars had been cast away on the coast, of which Esquevel narrated the fate of the men. We have once told how the two boats in which Castillo, I and Dorantes came, foundered near the Island of Malhado.

CHAPTER XX. OF OUR ESCAPE

The second day after we had moved, we commended ourselves to God and set forth with speed, trusting, for all the lateness of the season and that the prickly pears were about ending, with the must which remained in the woods, we might still be enabled to travel over a large territory. Hurrying on that day in great dread lest the Indians should overtake us, we saw some smokes, and going in the direction of them we arrived there after vespers, and found an Indian. He ran as he discovered us coming, not being willing to wait for us. We sent the negro after him, when he stopped, seeing him alone. The negro told him we were seeking the people who made those fires. He answered that their houses were near by, and he would guide us to them. So we followed him. He ran to make known our approach, and at sunset we saw the houses. Before our arrival, at the distance of two cross-bow shots from them, we found four Indians, who waited for us and received us well. We said in the language of the Mariannes, that we were coming to look for them. They were evidently pleased with our company, and took us to their dwellings. Dorantes and the negro were lodged in the house of a physician, Castillo and myself in that of another.

These people speak a different language, and are called Avavares. They are the same that carried bows to those with whom we formerly lived, going to traffic with them, and although they are of a different nation and tongue, they understand the other language. They arrived that day with their lodges, at the place where we found them. The community directly brought us a great many prickly pears, having heard of us before, of our cures, and of the wonders our Lord worked by us, which, although there had been no others, were adequate to open ways for us through a country poor like this, to afford us people where oftentimes there are none, and to lead us through imminent dangers, not permitting us to be killed, sustaining us under great want, and putting into those nations the heart of kindness, as we shall relate hereafter . . .

CHAPTER XXXI. OF OUR TAKING THE WAY TO THE MAIZE

Two days being spent while we tarried, we resolved to go in search of the maize. We did not wish to follow the path leading to where the cattle are, because it is towards the north, and for us very circuitous, since we ever held it certain, that going towards the sunset we must find what we desired.

Thus we took our way, and traversed all the country until coming out at the South sea. Nor was the dread we had of the sharp hunger through which we should have to pass, (as in verity we did, throughout the seventeen days' journey of which the natives spoke,) sufficient to hinder us. During all that time, in ascending by the river, they gave us many coverings of cowhide; but we did not eat of the fruit. Our sustenance each day was about a handful of deer-suet, which we had a long time been used to saving for such trials. Thus we passed the entire journey of seventeen days, and at the close we crossed the river and traveled other seventeen days.

As the sun went down, upon some plains that lie between chains of very great mountains, we found a people who for the third part of the year eat nothing but the powder of straw, and that being the season when we passed, we also had to eat of it, until reaching permanent habitations, where was abundance of maize brought together. They gave us a large quantity in grain and flour, pumpkins, beans and shawls of cotton. With all these we loaded our guides, who went back the happiest creatures on earth. We gave thanks to God, our Lord, for having brought us where we had found so much food.

Some houses are of earth, the rest all of cane mats. From this point we marched through more than a hundred leagues of country, and continually found settled domicils with plenty of maize and beans. The people gave us many deer and cotton shawls better than those of New Spain, many beads and certain corals found on the South sea, and fine turquoises that come from the North. Indeed they gave us every thing they had. To me they gave five emeralds made into arrow-heads,

which they use at their singing and dancing. They appeared to be very precious. I asked whence they got these: and they said the stones were brought from some lofty mountains that stand towards the north, where were populous towns and very large houses, and that they were purchased with plumes and the feathers of parrots.

Among this people the women are treated with more decorum than in any part of the Indias we had visited. They wear a shirt of cotton that falls as low as the knee, and over it half sleeves with skirts reaching to the ground, made of dressed deer skin. It opens in front and is brought close with straps of leather. They soap this with a certain root that cleanses well, by which they are enabled to keep it becomingly. Shoes are worn. The people all came to us that we should touch and bless them, they being very urgent, which we could accomplish only with great labor, for sick and well all wished to go with a benediction. Many times it occurred that some of the women who accompanied us gave birth; and so soon as the children were born the mothers would bring them to us that we should touch and bless them.

These Indians ever accompanied us until they delivered us to others: and all held full faith in our coming from heaven. While traveling we went without food all day until night, and we ate so little as to astonish them. We never felt exhaustion, neither were we in fact at all weary, so inured were we to hardship. We possessed great influence and authority: to preserve both we seldom talked with them. The negro was in constant conversation; he informed himself about the ways we wished to take, of the towns there were, and the matters we desired to know.

We passed through many and dissimilar tongues. Our Lord granted us favor with the people who spoke them, for they always understood us, and we them. We questioned them and received their answers by signs, just as if they spoke our language and we theirs; for although we knew six languages, we could not everywhere avail ourselves of them, there being a thousand differences.

Throughout all these countries the people who were at war immediately made friends, that

spread religion

they might come to meet us, and bring what they possessed. In this way we left all the land at peace, and we taught all the inhabitants by signs, which they understood, that in heaven was a Man we called God, who had created the sky and the earth; him we worshiped and had for our master; that we did what he commanded and from his hand came all good; and would they do as we did, all would be well with them. So ready of apprehension we found them, that could we have had the use of language by which to make ourselves perfectly understood, we should have left them all Christians. Thus much we gave them to understand the best we could. And afterward, when the sun rose, they opened their hands together with loud shouting towards the heavens, and then drew them down all over their bodies. They did the same again when the sun went down. They are a people of good condition and substance, capable in any pursuit.

CHAPTER XXXII. THE INDIANS GIVE US THE HEARTS OF DEER

In the town where the emeralds were presented to us, the people gave Dorantes over six hundred open hearts of deer. They ever keep a good supply of them for food, and we called the place Pueblo de los Corazones. It is the entrance into many provinces on the South sea. They who go to look for them and do not enter there, will be lost. On the coast is no maize: the inhabitants eat the powder of rush and of straw, and fish that is caught in the sea from rafts not having canoes. With grass and straw the women cover their nudity. They are a timid and dejected people.

We think that near the coast by way of those towns through which we came, are more than a thousand leagues of inhabited country, plentiful of subsistence. Three times the year it is planted with maize and beans. Deer are of three kinds; one the size of the young steer of Spain. There are innumerable houses, such as are called bahíos. They have poison from a certain tree the size of the apple. For effect, no more is necessary than to pluck the fruit and moisten the arrow with it, or if there be no fruit, to break a twig and with the milk

do the like. The tree is abundant and so deadly that if the leaves be bruised and steeped in some neighboring water, the deer and other animals drinking it soon burst.

We were in this town three days. A day's journey farther was another town, at which the rain fell heavily while we were there, and the river became so swollen we could not cross it, which detained us fifteen days. In this time Castillo saw the buckle of a sword-belt on the neck of an Indian and stitched to it the nail of a horse shoe. He took them, and we asked the native what they were: he answered that they came from heaven. We questioned him further, as to who had brought them thence: they all responded, that certain men who wore beards like us, had come from heaven and arrived at that river; bringing horses, lances, and swords, and that they had lanced two Indians. In a manner of the utmost indifference we could feign, we asked them what had become of those men: they answered us that they had gone to sea, putting their lances beneath the water, and going themselves also under the water; afterwards that they were seen on the surface going towards the sunset. For this we gave many thanks to God our Lord. We had before despaired of ever hearing more of Christians. Even yet we were left in great doubt and anxiety, thinking those people were merely persons who had come by sea on discoveries. However, as we had now such exact information, we made greater speed, and as we advanced on our way, the news of the Christians continually grew. We told the natives that we were going in search of that people, to order them not to kill nor make slaves of them, nor take them from their lands, nor do other injustice. Of this the Indians were very glad.

We passed through many territories and found them all vacant: their inhabitants wandered fleeing among the mountains, without daring to have houses or till the earth for fear of Christians. The sight was one of infinite pain to us, a land very fertile and beautiful, abounding in springs and streams, the hamlets deserted and burned, the people thin and weak, all fleeing or in concealment. As they did not plant, they appeased their keen hunger by eating roots, and the bark of trees. We bore a share in the famine along the whole way; for poorly could these unfortunates provide for us, themselves being so reduced they looked as though they would willingly die. They brought shawls of those they had concealed because of the Christians, presenting them to us; and they related how the Christians, at other times had come through the land destroying and burning the towns, carrying away half the men, and all the women and the boys, while those who had been able to escape were wandering about fugitives. We found them so alarmed they dared not remain anywhere. They would not, nor could they till the earth; but preferred to die rather than live in dread of such cruel usage as they received. Although these showed themselves greatly delighted with us, we feared that on our arrival among those who held the frontier and fought against the Christians, they would treat us badly, and revenge upon us the conduct of their enemies; but when God our Lord was pleased to bring us there, they began to dread and respect us as the others had done, and even somewhat more, at which we no little wondered. Thence it may at once be seen, that to bring all these people to be Christians and to the obedience of the Imperial Majesty, they must be won by kindness, which is a way certain, and no other is.

They took us to a town on the edge of a range of mountains, to which the ascent is over difficult crags. We found many people there collected out of fear of the Christians. They received us well and presented us all they had. They gave us more than two thousand back-loads of maize, which we gave to the distressed and hungered beings who guided us to that place. The next day we dispatched four messengers through the country, as we were accustomed to do, that they should call together all the rest of the Indians at a town distant three days' march. We set out the day after with all the people. The tracks of the Christians and marks where they slept were continually seen. At midday we met our messengers, who told us they had found no Indians, that they were roving and hiding in the forests, fleeing that the Christians might not kill nor make them slaves: the night before, they had observed the Christians

from behind trees, and discovered what they were about, carrying away many people in chains.

Those who came with us were alarmed at this intelligence: some returned to spread the news over the land that the Christians were coming; and many more would have followed, had we not forbidden it and told them to cast aside their fear, when they reassured themselves and were well content. At the time, we had Indians with us belonging a hundred leagues behind, and we were in no condition to discharge them, that they might return to their homes. To encourage them, we staid there that night; the day after we marched and slept on the road. The following day, those whom we had sent forward as messengers, guided us to the place where they had seen Christians. We arrived in the afternoon, and saw at once that they told the truth. We perceived that the persons were mounted, by the stakes to which the horses had been tied.

From this spot, called the river Petutan, to the river to which Diego de Guzmán came, where we heard of Christians, may be as many as eighty leagues; thence to the town, where the rains overtook us, twelve leagues, and that is twelve leagues from the South sea. Throughout this region, wheresoever the mountains extend, we saw clear traces of gold and lead, iron, copper, and other metals. Where the settled habitations are, the climate is hot; even in January, the weather is very warm. Thence toward the meridian, the country unoccupied to the North sea, is unhappy and sterile. There we underwent great and incredible hunger. Those who inhabit and wander over it, are a race of evil inclination and most cruel customs. The people of the fixed residences and those beyond, regard silver and gold with indifference, nor can they conceive of any use for them.

CHAPTER XXXIV. OF SENDING FOR THE CHRISTIANS

Five days having elapsed, Andrés Dorantes and Alonzo del Castillo arrived with those who had been sent after them. They brought more than six hundred persons of that community, whom the

Christians had driven into the forests, and who had wandered in concealment over the land. Those who accompanied us so far, had drawn them out, and given them to the Christians, who thereupon dismissed all the others they had brought with them. Upon their coming to where I was, Alearaz begged that we would summon the people of the towns on the margin of the river, who straggled about under cover of the woods, and order them to fetch us something to eat. This last was unnecessary, the Indians being ever diligent to bring us all they could. Directly we sent our messengers to call them, when there came six hundred souls, bringing us all the maize in their possession. They fetched it in certain pots, closed with clay, which they had concealed in the earth. They brought us whatever else they had; but we, wishing only to have the provision, gave the rest to the Christians, that they might divide among themselves. After this we had many high words with them; for they wished to make slaves of the Indians we brought.

In consequence of the dispute, we left at our departure many bows of Turkish shape we had along with us and many pouches. The five arrows with the points of emerald were forgotten among others, and we lost them. We gave the Christians a store of robes of cowhide and other things we brought. We found it difficult to induce the Indians to return to their dwellings, to feel no apprehension and plant maize. They were willing to do nothing until they had gone with us and delivered us into the hands of other Indians, as had been the custom; for if they returned without doing so, they were afraid they should die, and going with us, they feared neither Christians nor lances. Our countrymen became jealous at this, and caused their interpreter to tell the Indians that we were of them, and for a long time we had been lost; that they were the lords of the land who must be obeyed and served, while we were persons of mean condition and small force. The Indians cared little or nothing for what was told them; and conversing among themselves said the Christians lied: that we had come whence the sun rises, and they whence it goes down: we healed the sick, they killed the sound; that we had come naked and

barefooted, while they had arrived in clothing and on horses with lances; that we were not covetous of anything, but all that was given to us, we directly turned to give, remaining with nothing; that the others had the only purpose to rob whomsoever they found, bestowing nothing on any one.

In this way they spoke of all matters respecting us, which they enhanced by contrast with matters concerning the others, delivering their response through the interpreter of the Spaniards. To other Indians they made this known by means of one among them through whom they understood us. Those who speak that tongue we discriminately call Primahaitu, which is like saying Vasconyados. We found it in use over more than four hundred leagues of our travel, without another over that whole extent. Even to the last, I could not convince the Indians that we were of the Christians; and only with great effort and solicitation we got them to go back to their residences. We ordered them to put away apprehension, establish their towns, plant and cultivate the soil.

From abandonment the country had already grown up thickly in trees. It is, no doubt, the best in all these Indias, the most prolific and plenteous in provisions. Three times in the year it is planted. It produces great variety of fruit, has beautiful rivers, with many other good waters. There are ores with clear traces of gold and silver. The people are well disposed: they serve such Christians as are their friends, with great good will. They are comely, much more so than the Mexicans. Indeed, the land needs no circumstance to make it blessed.

The Indians, at taking their leave told us they would do what we commanded, and would build their towns, if the Christians would suffer them; and this I say and affirm most positively, that if they have not done so, it is the fault of the Christians.

After we had dismissed the Indians in peace, and thanked them for the toil they had supported with us, the Christians with subtlety sent us on our way under charge of Zeburos, an Alcalde, attended by two men. They took us through forests and solitudes, to hinder us from intercourse with the natives, that we might neither witness nor have knowledge of the act they would commit. It is but an instance of how frequently men are mistaken in their aims; we set about to preserve the liberty of the Indians and thought we had secured it, but the contrary appeared; for the Christians had arranged to go and spring upon those we had sent away in peace and confidence. They executed their plan as they had designed, taking us through the woods, wherein for two days we were lost, without water and without way. Seven of our men died of thirst, and we all thought to have perished. Many friendly to the Christians in their company, were unable to reach the place where we got water the second night, until the noon of next day. We traveled twenty-five leagues, little more or less, and reached a town of friendly Indians. The Alcalde left us there, and went on three leagues farther to a town called Culiaçan where was Melchior Diaz, principal Alcalde and Captain of the Province.

Questions

1. How might the intended audience of Cabeza de Vaca's narrative have influenced its composition? To what extent do you think the characters in Cabeza de Vaca's story conformed to the expectations of his European Christian audience?
2. How much did Cabeza de Vaca change during his time among the Indians?
3. How did Cabeza de Vaca find a place among the Indian communities he encountered? What made him useful? What explains his success as a healer?
4. How did the Indian communities visited by Cabeza de Vaca differ? Characterize the relations among them.
5. Imagine what Cabeza de Vaca might have said if asked to comment on the Las Casas–Sepúlveda debate we read in Chapter 3.

4.2   Pueblo Indians Discuss the Pueblo Revolt*

After the 1680 Pueblo Revolt, Spanish officials questioned New Mexican Indians in an effort to understand what had happened. We can use records of these interrogations in an attempt to do the same. The testimony of three Indians, Don Pedro Nanboa, Juan, and Josephe, follows.

Declaration of one of the rebellious Christian Indians who was captured on the road. [Place of El Alamillo, September 6, 1680.]

In the place of El Alamillo, jurisdiction of El Socorro, on the 6th day of the month of September, 1680, for the prosecution of this case, and so that an Indian who was captured on the road as the camp was marching may be examined, in order to ascertain the plans, designs, and motives of the rebellious enemy, his lordship, the señor governor and captain-general, caused the said Indian to appear before him. He received the oath from him in due legal form, in the name of God, our Lord, and on a sign of the cross, under charge of which he promised to tell the truth concerning what he might know and as he might be questioned. Having been asked his name and of what place he is a native, his condition, and age, he said that his name is Don Pedro Nanboa, that he is a native of the pueblo of Alameda, a widower, and somewhat more than eighty years of age. Asked for what reason the Indians of this kingdom have rebelled, forsaking their obedience to his Majesty and failing in their obligation as Christians, he said that for a long time, because the Spaniards punished sorcerers and idolaters, the nations of the Teguas, Taos, Pecuries, Pecos, and Jemez had been plotting to rebel and kill the Spaniards and the religious, and that they had been planning constantly to carry it out, down to the present occasion. Asked what he learned, saw and heard in the juntas and parleys that the Indians have held, what they have plotted among themselves, and why

---

*Charles Wilson Hackett, ed., *Revolt of the Pueblo Indians of New Mexico and Otermín's Attempted Reconquest, 1680–1682*, trans. Charmion Clair Shelby (Albuquerque: University of New Mexico Press, 1942), 60–62, 232–242.

the Indians have burned the church and profaned the images of the pueblo of Sandia, he said that he has not taken part in any junta, nor has he harmed any one; that what he has heard is that the Indians do not want religious or Spaniards. Because he is so old, he was in the cornfield when he learned from the Indian rebels who came from the sierra that they had killed the Spaniards of the jurisdiction and robbed all their haciendas, sacking their houses. Asked whether he knows about the Spaniards and religious who were gathered in the pueblo of La Isleta, he said that it is true that some days ago there assembled in the said pueblo of La Isleta the religious of Sandia, Jemez, and Zia, and that they set out to leave the kingdom with those of the said pueblo of La Isleta and the Spaniards— not one of whom remained—taking along their property. The Indians did not fight with them because all the men had gone with the other nations to fight at the villa and destroy the governor and captain-general and all the people who were with him. He declared that the resentment which all the Indians have in their hearts has been so strong, from the time this kingdom was discovered, because the religious and the Spaniards took away their idols and forbade their sorceries and idolatries; that they have inherited successively from their old men the things pertaining to their ancient customs; and that he has heard this resentment spoken of since he was of an age to understand. What he has said is the truth and what he knows, under the oath taken, and he signs and ratifies it, it being read and explained to him in his language through the interpretation of Captain Sebastián Montaño, who signed it with his lordship, as the said Indian does not know how, before me, the present secretary. ANTONIO DE OTERMIN (rubric); SEBASTIÁN MONTAÑO (rubric); JUAN LUCERO DE GODOY (rubric); LUIS DE QUINTANA (rubric). Before me, FRANCISCO XAVIER, secretary of government and war (rubric) . . .

Declaration [of the Indian, Juan. Place on the Río del Norte, December 18, 1681]. . . .

Having been questioned according to the tenor of the case, and asked for what reasons and causes all the Indians of the kingdom in general rebelled, returning to idolatry, forsaking the law of God and obedience to his Majesty, burning images and temples, and committing the other crimes which they did, he said that what he knows concerning this question is that not all of them joined the said rebellion willingly; that the chief mover of it is an Indian who is a native of the pueblo of San Juan, named El Popé, and that from fear of this Indian all of them joined in the plot that he made. Thus he replied.

Asked why they held the said Popé in such fear and obeyed him, and whether he was the chief man of the pueblo, or a good Christian, or a sorcerer, he said that the common report that circulated and still is current among all the natives is that the said Indian Popé talks with the devil, and for this reason all held him in terror, obeying his commands although they were contrary to the orders of the señores governors, the prelate and the religious, and the Spaniards, he giving them to understand that the word which he spoke was better than that of all the rest; and he states that it was a matter of common knowledge that the Indian Popé, talking with the devil, killed in his own house a son-in-law of his named Nicolás Bua, the governor of the pueblo of San Juan. On being asked why he killed him, he said that it was so that he might not warn the Spaniards of the rebellion, as he intended to do. And he said that after the rebellion was over, and the señor governor and captain-general had left, defeated, the said Indian Popé went in company with another native of the pueblo of Taos named Saca through all the pueblos of the kingdom, being very well pleased, saying and giving the people to understand that he had carried out the said uprising, and that because of his wish and desire the things that had happened had been done, the religious and the people who died had been killed, and those who remained alive had been driven out. He [the deponent] said that the time when he learned of the rebellion was three days before it was carried out.

Asked how the said Indian, Popé, convoked all the people of the kingdom so that they obeyed him in the treason, he said that he took a cord made of maguey fiber and tied some knots in it which indicated the number of days until the perpetration of the treason. He sent it through all the pueblos as far as that of La Isleta, there remaining in the whole kingdom only the nation of the Piros who did not receive it; and the order which the said Popé gave when he sent the said cord was under strict charge of secrecy, commanding that the war captains take it from pueblo to pueblo. He [the deponent] learned of this circumstance after the kingdom was depopulated.

Asked to state and declare what things occurred after they found themselves without religious or Spaniards, he said that what he, the declarant, knows concerning this question is that following the departure of the señor governor and captain-general, the religious, and the Spaniards who were left alive, the said Indian, Popé, came down in person with all the war captains and many other Indians, proclaiming through the pueblos that the devil was very strong and much better than God, and that they should burn all the images and temples, rosaries and crosses, and that all the people should discard the names given them in holy baptism and call themselves whatever they liked. They should leave the wives whom they had taken in holy matrimony and take any one whom they might wish, and they were not to mention in any manner the name of God, of the most holy Virgin, or of the Saints, on pain of severe punishment, particularly that of lashing, saying that the commands of the devil were better than that which they taught them of the law of God. They were ordered likewise not to teach the Castilian language in any pueblo and to burn the seeds which the Spaniards sowed and to plant only maize and beans, which were the crops of their ancestors. And he said that all the nations obeyed in everything except in the command concerning Spanish seeds, which some of them sowed because of their fondness for the Spaniards. Thus he replied.

Asked whether they thought that perhaps the Spaniards would never return to this kingdom at any time, or that they would have to return as their ancestors did, and in this case what plans or dispositions they would make, and what else he knew about this matter, he said that they were of different minds regarding it, because some said that if the Spaniards should come they would have to fight to the death, and others said that in the end they must come and gain the kingdom because they were sons of the land and had grown up with the natives. Thus he replies.

Asked to state and declare what Indians those are who say that they must die fighting, he said that they are the chief Indians of the pueblos and the aggressors in crime. Thus he replies.

Asked how they received notice of our coming and who advised them of it, he said that on the day that the pueblo of La Isleta was surrounded, two Indian natives of the pueblo of Puaray were wandering on this side of the Río del Norte, and, as soon as they saw the Spaniards, they came to notify their pueblo and the others, and the news spread from pueblo to pueblo, it being said that the Spaniards had killed all the natives of the pueblo of La Isleta and had captured all the outsiders from other pueblos who had come to seek maize. As a result of this the pueblos of Alameda, Puaray, and Sandia were emptied of people, who went to the sierra; and those of San Felipe, Santo Domingo, and Cochití went to the sierra of La Gieneguilla; and those of Santana [Santa Ana], Zia, and Jemez to a high mesa which is near the pueblo of Los Jemez; and all the men from these pueblos and from many others, except those from the province of Moqui, had assembled in the sierra of La Gieneguilla. Thus he replies.

Asked whether it had come to the notice of the people who had assembled that no one had been killed nor a single person harmed in the said pueblo of La Isleta, he said that they had learned of this at the said post of La Gieneguilla, where the men are assembled, before the arrival of the Spaniards, the news having reached them from these pueblos; and that for this reason they were discussing it among themselves, saying, "What do these Spaniards want, and why are they coming?" They communicated it to one another, saying, "What do these Spaniards want, since they are passing on without doing any harm? Perhaps they are coming in peace." Others said, "Perhaps they are deceiving us in order to take us peacefully and kill us." He said that the latter are the ones who desire war, there being among them twenty-two Indians who are the leaders, war captains of the Teguas nation which is the one to which this declarant belongs, and also a coyote of the Queres nation named Alonso Catití, he being the one whom many have obeyed since the rebellion. He knows that the head of Pecuries is a brother-in-law of Don Luis, called Tupatú in his language, present governor in the said pueblo. He does not know who are the heads of the other nations. Thus he replies.

Asked what led him to come among the Spaniards, he said that it was because when the Spaniards arrived and communicated with the Indians with some demonstrations of desiring to establish peace, he, among others, came down, and finding Sargento Mayor Luis de Quintana, whom he had served, and Juan Ruiz de Casares, who acted as interpreter, he communicated with them privately. The said persons asking him what he thought about the actions of the Indians and whether their peaceful actions were sincere, he told them, "I do not know what to say to you. If there should be any treason, I will warn you." And in virtue of what they had communicated, he asked the said Luis de Quintana for the loan of a horse, saying to him, "Lend me a horse to bring you pinole." He gave him the horse, and while he was among the other Indians he saw that they were sending spies to reconnoiter the Spanish camp in order to attack and drive off the horses if there should be any carelessness. The declarant stated that in virtue of his agreement with the said Luis de Quintana and Juan Ruiz de Casares he invited himself to come with the said spies, and running away from them, he came to the Spanish camp and advised the said Luis de Quintana, telling him, "Mount your horse at once; there come the men who wish to surround you." Whereupon all the Spaniards armed themselves, standing guard throughout the night. He declared also that the plan of the coyote Alonso Catití was to order all the Indian girls to wash themselves and put on their mantas and induce the Spaniards to sleep with them; that then the Pecuríes and Teguas would come to take off the horses while the Queres and other nations would kill the Spaniards. For this purpose he had notified the said Pecuríes and the other nations who were above the river. Thus he replies.

Asked how it happened that they left off arranging a peace with the Spaniards after the arrival of Don Luis Tupatú, governor of the Pecuríes, an Indian respected among all the nations, he said that what he knows about this is, that as soon as the said Don Luis arrived he asked the people if anything new had occurred and they replied to him, "We have already made peace with the Spaniards and have gone down to talk with them;" and he replied, "You have done very well." Thus he responds.

Being asked repeatedly, as a person who had been among the said rebels, if he knew, saw, or there had come to his notice anything else, and why they did not conclude peace, he said that all he knows and saw and heard, he had declared, and he knows nothing else, under charge of the oath he has taken which he affirms and ratifies, this, his declaration, being read to him. He did not know his age nor how to sign; apparently he is about twenty-eight years old. The señor governor and captain-general signed it with the witnesses and the interpreters, all of whom were present, before me, the said secretary. ANTONIO DE OTERMÍN (rubric); JUAN LUCERO DE GODOY (rubric); JUAN RUIZ DE CASARES (rubric); PEDRO DE LEIVA (rubric); NICOLÁS RODRÍGUEZ REY (rubric); SEBASTIÁN DE HERRERA (rubric); LUIS DE GRANILLO (rubric); JUAN DE NORIEGA (rubric). Before me, FRANCISCO XAVIER, secretary of government and war (rubric).

Declaration of Josephe, Spanish-speaking Indian. [Place of the Río del Norte, December 19, 1681.]

In this said place and plaza de armas of this army on the 19th day of the month of December, 1681, for the said judicial proceedings of this case, his lordship caused to appear before him an Indian prisoner named Josephe, able to speak the Castilian language, a servant of Sargento Mayor Sebastián de Herrera who fled from him and went among the apostates. The interpreters and assisting witnesses being present, his lordship received from the said Indian the oath in due legal form, in the name of God, our Lord, and a sign of the cross, under charge of which and having been absolved, he promised to tell the truth as to what he might know and as he might be questioned, he having been given to understand the seriousness of the oath. Being asked why he fled from his master, the said

Sargento Mayor Sebastián de Herrera, and went to live with the treacherous Indian apostates of New Mexico, where he has been until he came among us on the present occasion, he said that the reason why he left was that he was suffering hunger in the plaza de armas of La Toma [del Río del Norte], and a companion of his named Domingo urged this declarant to go to New Mexico for a while, so as to find out how matters stood with the Indians and to give warning to the Spaniards of any treason. They did not come with the intention of remaining always with the apostate traitors and rebels, and after they arrived they [the Indians] killed the said Domingo, his companion, because of the Pecos Indians having seen him fighting in the villa along with the Spaniards. He said that because his comrade was gone he had remained until now, when he saw the Spaniards and came to them, warning them not to be careless with the horses, because he had heard the traitors say that although the Spaniards might conclude peace with them, they would come to attack them by night and take away the horses. Thus he responds to this question.

Asked what causes or motives the said Indian rebels had for renouncing the law of God and obedience to his Majesty, and for committing so many kinds of crimes, and who were the instigators of the rebellion, and what he had heard while he was among the apostates, he said that the prime movers of the rebellion were two Indians of San Juan, one named El Popé and the other El Taqu, and another from Taos named Saca, and another from San Ildefonso named Francisco. He knows that these were the principals, and the causes they gave were alleged ill treatment and injuries received from the present secretary, Francisco Xavier, and the maestre de campo, Alonso García, and from the sargentos mayors, Luis de Quintana and Diego López, because they beat them, took away what they had, and made them work without pay. Thus he replies.

Asked if he had learned or it has come to his notice during the time that he had been here the reason why the apostates burned the images, churches, and things pertaining to divine worship, making a mockery and a trophy of them, killing the priests and doing the other things they did, he said that he knows and has heard it generally stated that

while they were besieging the villa the rebellious traitors burned the church and shouted in loud voices, "Now the God of the Spaniards, who was their father, is dead, and Santa Maria, who was their mother, and the saints, who were pieces of rotten wood," saying that only their own god lived. Thus they ordered all the temples and images, crosses and rosaries burned, and this function being over, they all went to bathe in the rivers, saying that they thereby washed away the water of baptism. For their churches, they placed on the four sides and in the center of the plaza some small circular enclosures of stone where they went to offer flour, feathers, and the seed of maguey, maize, and tobacco, and performed other superstitious rites, giving the children to understand that they must all do this in the future. The captains and chiefs ordered that the names of Jesus and of Mary should nowhere be uttered, and that they should discard their baptismal names, and abandon the wives whom God had given them in matrimony, and take the ones that they pleased. He saw that as soon as the remaining Spaniards had left, they ordered all the estufas erected, which are their houses of idolatry, and danced throughout the kingdom the dance of the cazina, making many masks for it in the image of the devil. Thus he replied to this question.

Asked what plans or information the said apostates communicated with regard to the possible return of the Spaniards and how they got along in the life they were living, he said that it is true that there were various opinions among them, most of them believing that they would have to fight to the death with the said Spaniards, keeping them out. Others, who were not so guilty, said, "We are not to blame, and we must await them [the Spaniards] in our pueblos." And he said that when the hostile Apaches came they denounced the leaders of the rebellion, saying that when the Spaniards were among them they lived in security and quiet, and afterwards with much uneasiness. Thus he replied to the question.

Asked how it was that if some wished to fight and others to give themselves up, all had retired to the sierra, leaving the pueblos deserted and depopulated, and why none of them had come to our camp, he said that all of them have fled because they had been so ordered by the Indian leaders, of whom they stood in very great fear. Thus he replied to the question.

Asked why, since the said rebels had been of different minds, some believing that they should give themselves up peacefully and others opposing it, when the Spaniards arrived at the sierra of La Cieneguilla de Cochití, where the leaders of the uprising and people from all the nations were assembled, they had not attempted to give themselves up and return to the holy faith and to obedience to his Majesty—for while they had made some signs, they had done nothing definite—he said that although it is true that as soon as the Spaniards arrived some said that it was better to give up peaceably than to have war, the young men were unwilling to agree, saying that they wished to fight. In particular one Spanish-speaking Indian or coyote named Francisco, commonly called El Ollita, said that no one should surrender in peace, that all must fight, and that although some of his brothers were coming with the Spaniards, if they fought on the side of the Spaniards he would kill them, and if they came over to the side of the Indians he would not harm them. Whereupon everyone was disturbed, and there having arrived at this juncture Don Luis Tupatú, governor of the pueblo of Los Pecuries, while they were thus consulting, news came to the place where the junta was being held from another Indian named Alonso Catití, a leader of the uprising, believed to be a coyote, in which he sent to notify the people that he had already planned to deceive the Spaniards with feigned peace. He had arranged to send to the pueblo of Cochití all the prettiest, most pleasing, and neatest Indian women so that, under pretense of coming down to prepare food for the Spaniards, they could provoke them to lewdness, and that night while they were with them, the said coyote Catití would come down with all the men of the Queres and Jemez nations, only the said Catití attempting to speak with the said Spaniards, and at a shout from him they would all rush down to kill the said Spaniards; and he gave orders that all the rest who were in the other junta where the said Don Luis and El Ollita were present, should at the same time attack the horse drove, so as to finish that too. This declarant being present during all these proceedings, and feeling compassion because of the treason they were plotting, he determined to come to warn the Spaniards, as he did, whereupon they put themselves under arms and the said Indians again went up to the heights of the sierra, and the Spaniards withdrew. Thus he replies to the question.

Having been asked repeated questions touching on the matter, he said that he has already told all he knows; that what he might say further is that they should be constantly on the alert, because the traitors have all planned to join together and follow the Spaniards as far as the pueblo of La Isleta, so as to fall upon them by night and take away the horses, for on being left afoot they could do nothing and they would like them. He said that what he has stated in his declaration is the truth and what he knows, under charge of his oath, which he affirms and ratifies, this, his said declaration, being read to him. He did not sign because of not knowing how, nor does he know his age. Apparently he is about twenty years old. His lordship signed it with the interpreters and assisting witnesses, before me, the present secretary. ANTONIO DE OTERMÍN (rubric); JUAN LUCERO DE GODOY (rubric); JUAN RUIZ DE CASARES (rubric); PEDRO DE LEIVA (rubric); NICOLÁS RODRÍGUEZ REY (rubric); SEBASTIÁN DE HERRERA (rubric); LUIS GRANILLO (rubric); JUAN DE LUNA Y PADILLA (rubric); JUNA DE NORIEGA (rubric). Before me, FRANCISCO XAVIER, secretary of government and war (rubric).

Questions

1. Using this testimony as evidence, explain why the Pueblo Revolt occurred.
2. Did the Pueblos view the Spanish in New Mexico as a single, unified entity? How unified were the Pueblos?
3. What kind of future did the leaders of the revolt envision for the Pueblos?
4. How distinct were the Indian and Spanish populations of New Mexico in 1680?
5. On what points do Pedro Nanboa, Juan, and Josephe concur and differ? Why? How credible do you find their testimony? How might the context in which they were questioned have influenced what they said?

5

Canada and Iroquoia

France turned its attention to the Americas shortly after news of Columbus's discoveries reached Europe. By the early 1500s, French vessels had reached Newfoundland and Brazil, concentrating on harvesting the rich natural resources of those regions. Following Spain's spectacular conquests of Mexico and Peru, French ships began to explore the North American mainland, hoping to replicate Iberia's newfound wealth and prestige. But the primary goal of French mariners remained that of Columbus: to find an oceanic route to Asia. Failing to find such a passage, or another Tenochtitlán or Cuzco to conquer, the French instead established an empire of trade in North America, centered on the St. Lawrence River. The following documents trace three phases in the early development of France's North American colonization: exploration and early trade (Cartier), settlement and the establishment of alliances (Champlain), and sustained colonial interaction (Brébeuf).

5.1 French Explorer Jacques Cartier Encounters an Iroquoian Village*

The St. Lawrence River proved an important discovery for the French, giving them access to a network of rivers and lakes linking the Atlantic to the continental interior and the Native people controlling it. In this passage, Jacques Cartier, who made crown-sponsored voyages to North America in 1534, 1535, and 1541, describes his initial encounter with an Iroquoian village occupying an island in the St. Lawrence River. Hochelaga, as the village and sometimes the people were called, occupied the site of present-day Montreal. This account is drawn from a report of Cartier's second voyage, first published in Paris in 1545.

———————

*H. P. Biggar, ed. and trans., *The Voyages of Jacques Cartier: Published from the Originals with Translations, Notes and Appendices* (Ottawa: F. A. Acland, 1924), 148–173.

How the Captain gave orders for the long-boats to be fitted out for the voyage to Hochelaga; and for the Bark to be left behind, on account of the difficult passage; and how we reached Hochelaga; and of the reception the people gave us on our arrival.

On the morrow our Captain, seeing it was impossible to get the bark past this spot at that season, ordered the long-boats to be fitted out and provisioned, and stores to be put into them for as long a period as possible and as the long-boats would hold. And he set out in them accompanied by a few of the gentlemen, to wit: Claude du Pontbriant, cup-bearer to his Royal Highness the Dauphin, Charles de La Pommeraye, John Guyon, John Poullet, with twenty-eight sailors including Macé Jalobert and William Le Breton, who had command, under Cartier, of the other two vessels, in order to make our way up the river as far as we possibly could. And we sailed on in as fine weather as one could wish until [Saturday] October 2, when we arrived at Hochelaga, which is about forty-five leagues from the spot where we had left our bark. During this interval we came across on the way many of the people of the country, who brought us fish and other provisions, at the same time dancing and showing great joy at our coming. And in order to win and keep their friendship, the Captain made them a present of some knives, beads and other small trifles, where-at they were greatly pleased. And on reaching Hochelaga, there came to meet us more than a thousand persons, both men, women and children, who gave us as good a welcome as ever father gave to his son, making great signs of joy; for the men danced in one ring, the women in another and the children also apart by themselves. After this they brought us quantities of fish, and of their bread which is made of Indian corn, throwing so much of it into our long-boats that it seemed to rain bread. Seeing this the Captain, accompanied by several of his men, went on shore; and no sooner had he landed than they all crowded about him and about the others, giving them a wonderful reception. And the women brought their babies in their arms to have the Captain and his companions touch them, while all held a merry-making which lasted more than half an hour. Seeing their generosity and friendliness, the Captain had the women all sit down in a row and gave them some tin beads and other trifles; and to some of the men he gave knives. Then he returned on board the long-boats to sup and pass the night, throughout which the Indians remained on the bank of the river, as near the long-boats as they could get, keeping many fires burning all night, and dancing and calling out every moment *aguyase* which is their term of salutation and joy.

How the Captain and the Gentlemen, accompanied by twenty-five well-armed and marshalled sailors, went to visit the village of Hochelaga; and of the situation of the place.

At daybreak the next day, the Captain, having put on his armour, had his men marshalled for the purpose of paying a visit to the village and home of these people, and to a mountain which lies near the town. The Captain was accompanied by the gentlemen and by twenty sailors, the remainder having been left behind to guard the long-boats. And he took three Indians of the village as guides to conduct them thither. When we had got under way, we discovered that the path was as well-trodden as it is possible to see, and that the country was the finest and most excellent one could find anywhere, being everywhere full of oaks, as beautiful as in any forest in France, underneath which the ground lay covered with acorns. And after marching about a league and a half, we met on the trail one of the headmen of the village of Hochelaga, accompanied by several Indians, who made signs to us that we should rest at that spot near a fire they had lighted on the path; which we did. Thereupon this headman began to make a speech and to harangue us, which, as before mentioned, is their way of showing joy and friendliness, welcoming in this way the Captain and his company. The Captain presented him with a couple of hatchets and a couple of knives, as well as with a cross and a crucifix, which he made him kiss and then hung it about his neck. For these the headman thanked the Captain. When this was done we marched on, and about half a league thence, found that the land began to be cultivated. It was fine land with large fields covered with the corn of the country, which resembles Brazil millet, and is about as large or larger than a pea. They live on this as we do on wheat. And in the middle of these fields is situated and stands the village of Hochelaga, near and adjacent to a mountain, the slopes of which are fertile and are cultivated, and from the top of which one can see for a long distance. We named this mountain "Mount Royal". The village is circular and is completely enclosed by a wooden palisade in three tiers like a pyramid. The top one is built crosswise, the middle one perpendicular and the lowest one of strips of wood placed lengthwise. The whole is well joined and lashed after their manner, and is some two lances in height. There is only one gate and entrance to this village, and that can be barred up. Over this gate and in many places about the enclosure are species of galleries with ladders for mounting to them, which galleries are provided with rocks and stones for the defence and protection of the place. There are some fifty houses in this village, each about fifty or more paces in length, and twelve or fifteen in width, built completely of wood and covered in and bordered up with large pieces of the bark and rind of trees, as broad as a table, which are well and cunningly lashed after their manner. And inside these houses are many rooms and chambers; and in the middle is a large space without a floor, where they light their fire and live together in common. Afterwards the men retire to the above-mentioned quarters with their wives and children. And furthermore there are lofts in the upper part of their houses, where they store the corn of which they make their bread. This they call *carraconny*, and they make it in the following manner. They have wooden mortars, like those used [in France] for braying hemp, and in these with wooden pestles they pound the corn into flour. This they knead into dough, of which they make small loaves, which they set on a broad hot stone and then cover them with hot pebbles. In this way they bake their bread for want of an oven.

They make also many kinds of soup with this corn, as well as with beans and with pease, of which they have a considerable supply, and again with large cucumbers and other fruits. They have in their houses also large vessels like puncheons, in which they place their fish, such as eels and others, that are smoked during the summer, and on these they live during the winter. They make great store of these as we ourselves saw. All their food is eaten without salt. They sleep on the bark of trees, spread out upon the ground, with old furs of wild animals over them; and of these, to wit, otters, beavers, martens, foxes, wildcats, deer, stags and others, they make their clothing

and blankets, but the greater portion of them go almost stark naked. The most precious article they possess in this world is *esnoguy*, which is as white as snow. They procure it from shells in the river in the following manner. When an Indian has incurred the death-penalty or they have taken some prisoners in war, they kill one and make great incisions in his buttocks and thighs, and about his legs, arms and shoulders. Then at the spot where this *esnoguy* is found, they sink the body to the bottom and leave it there for ten or twelve hours. It is then brought to the surface; and in the above-mentioned cuts and incisions they find these shells, of which they make a sort of bead, which has the same use among them as gold and silver with us; for they consider it the most valuable article in the world. It has the virtue of stopping nose-bleeding; for we tried it. This whole tribe gives itself to manual labour and to fishing merely to obtain the necessities of life; for they place no value upon the goods of this world, both because they are unacquainted with them, and because they do not move from home and are not nomads like those of Canada and of the Saguenay, notwithstanding that the Canadians and some eight or nine other tribes along this river are subjects of theirs.

How we arrived at the village and the reception we met with; and how the Captain gave them presents and other things the Captain did, as will be seen in this chapter.

As we drew near to their village, great numbers of the inhabitants came out to meet us and gave us a hearty welcome, according to the custom of the country. And we were led by our guides and those who were conducting us into the middle of the village, where there was an open square between the houses, about a stone's throw or thereabouts in width each way. They signed to us that we should come to a halt here, which we did. And at once all the girls and women of the village, some of whom had children in their arms, crowded about us, rubbing our faces, arms and other parts of the upper portions of our bodies which they could touch, weeping for joy at the sight of us and giving us the best welcome they could. They made signs to us also to be good enough to put our hands upon their babies. After this the men made the women retire, and themselves sat down upon the ground round about us, as if we had been going to perform a miracle play. And at once several of the women came back, each with a four-cornered mat, woven like tapestry, and these they spread upon the ground in the middle of the square, and made us place ourselves upon them. When this had been done, the ruler and chief of this tribe, whom in their language they call *Agouhanna*, was carried in, seated on a large deer-skin, by nine or ten Indians, who came and set him down upon the mats near the Captain, making signs to us that this was their ruler and chief. This *Agouhanna*, who was some fifty years of age, was in no way better dressed than the other Indians except that he wore about his head for a crown a sort of red band made of hedgehog's skin. This chief was completely paralyzed and deprived of the use of his limbs. When he had saluted the Captain and his men, by making signs which clearly meant that they were very welcome, he showed his arms and his legs to the Captain motioning to him to be good enough to touch them, as if he thereby expected to be cured and healed. On this the Captain set about rubbing his arms and legs with his hands. Thereupon this *Agouhanna* took the band of cloth he was wearing as a crown and presented it to the Captain. And at once many sick persons, some blind, others with but one eye, others lame or impotent and others again so extremely old that their eyelids hung down to their cheeks, were brought in and set down or laid out near the Captain, in order that he might lay his hands upon them, so that one would have thought Christ had come down to earth to heal them.

Seeing the suffering of these people and their faith, the Captain read aloud the Gospel of St. John, namely, "In the beginning", etc. making the sign of the cross over the poor sick people, praying God to give them knowledge of our holy faith and of our Saviour's passion, and grace to obtain baptism and redemption. Then the Captain took a prayer-book and read out, word for word, the Passion of our Lord, that all who were present could hear it, during which all these poor people maintained great silence and were wonderfully attentive, looking up to heaven and going through the same ceremonies they saw us do. After this the Captain had all the men range themselves on one side, the women on another and the children on another, and to the headmen he gave hatchets, to the others knives, and to the women, beads and other small trinkets. He then made the children scramble for little rings and tin *agnus Dei*, which afforded them great amusement. The Captain next ordered the trumpets and other musical instruments to be sounded, whereat the Indians were much delighted. We then took leave of them and proceeded to set out upon our return. Seeing this the squaws placed themselves in our way to prevent us, and brought us some of their provisions, which they had made ready for us, to wit: fish, soups, beans, bread and other dishes, in the hope of inducing us to partake of some refreshment and to eat with them. But as these provisions were not to our taste and had no savour of salt, we thanked them, making signs that we were in no need of refreshment.

On issuing forth from the village we were conducted by several of the men and women of the place up the above-mentioned mountain, lying a quarter of a league away, which was named by us "Mount Royal". On reaching the summit we had a view of the land for more than thirty leagues round about. Towards the north there is a range of mountains, running east and west, and another range to the south. Between these ranges lies the finest land it is possible to see, being arable, level and flat. And in the midst of this flat region one saw the river [St. Lawrence] extending beyond the spot where we had left our long-boats. At that point there is the most violent rapid it is possible to see, which we were unable to pass. And as far as the eye can reach, one sees that river, large, wide and broad, which came from the south-west and flowed near three fine conical mountains, which we estimated to be some fifteen leagues away. And it was told us and made clear by signs by our three local Indian guides, that there were three more such rapids in that river, like the one where lay our long-boats; but through lack of an interpreter we could not make out what the distance was from one to the other. They then explained to us by signs that after passing these rapids, one could navigate along that river for more than three moons. And they showed us furthermore that along the mountains to the north, there is a large river, which comes from the west like the said river [St. Lawrence]. We thought this river [Ottawa] must be the one that flows past the kingdom and province of the Saguenay; and without our asking any questions or making any sign, they seized the chain of the Captain's whistle, which was made of silver, and a dagger-handle of yellow copper-gilt like gold, that hung at the side of one of the sailors, and gave us to understand that these came from up that river [Ottawa], where lived *Agojuda*, which means bad people, who were armed to the teeth, showing us the style of their armour, which is made with cords and wood, laced and plaited together. They also seemed to say that these *Agojuda* waged war continually, one tribe against the other, but through not under-standing their language, we could not make out what the distance was to that country. The Captain showed them some copper, which they call *caignetdazé*, and pointing towards the said region, asked by signs if it came thence? They shook their heads to say no, showing us that it came from the Saguenay, which lies in the opposite direction. Having seen and learned these things, we returned to our long-boats, accompanied by a large number of these Indians, some of whom, when they saw that our people were tired, took them upon their shoulders, as on horseback and carried them. And on our arrival at the long-boats, we at once set sail to return to the bark, for fear of any misadventure. Such a departure did not fail to cause the Indians great regret; for so long as they could follow us down the river, they did so. And we made such good headway that we reached our bark on Monday, October 4.

On Tuesday, the fifth of that month, we hoisted sail and set forth with our bark and the long-boats to return to the province of Canada and to Ste. Croix harbour, where our ships had been left. And on [Thursday] the seventh we came to anchor opposite a stream which enters the river [St. Lawrence] from the north and at the mouth of which lie four small islands covered with trees. We named this stream "Lashing river". And as one of these islands [St. Quentin] stretches out into the river [St. Lawrence], and can be seen from a distance, the Captain had a fine large cross erected upon the point of it. He then commanded the long-boats to be made ready to go up that river [St. Maurice] at high tide to find out the depth and nature of the same. These orders were carried out; and they rowed up the river that day; but when it was discovered to be of no importance and shallow, they came back. We then made sail to continue our way down the river [St. Lawrence].

Questions

1. Describe Hochelaga, including topography, houses, population, and economy. What was the relationship between these and other St. Lawrence Indians?

2. How were the French received in Hochelaga? How did they respond to their reception? How did each side communicate its intentions?

3. Why was Cartier so interested in continuing upstream? What was he looking for? Did he find it?

4. How does the author describe male and female roles in Iroquoian society? Which of Cartier's actions reflect his own ideas about the appropriate roles of men and women, and which do you think reflect Iroquoian practices?

5.2   Champlain Describes the Introduction of Firearms into Indian Warfare*

The French quickly learned that trade with their Indian neighbors went hand-in-hand with military alliance, and they soon began to engage in warfare with their allies' enemies. In the following passage, Samuel de Champlain describes a 1609 battle on Lake Champlain in which the French sided with their Montagnais, Algonkin, and Huron allies against a group of 200 Mohawk (Iroquois) warriors.

Continuing our course in this lake on the west side I saw, as I was observing the country, some very high mountains on the east side, with snow on the top of them. I inquired of the savages if these places were inhabited. They told me that they were—by the Iroquois—and that in these places there were beautiful valleys and open stretches fertile in grain, such as I had eaten in this country, with a great many other fruits; and that the lake went near some mountains, which were perhaps, as it seemed to me, about fifteen leagues from us. I saw on the south others not less high than the first, but they had no snow at all. The savages told me that it was there that we were to go to find their enemies, and that these mountains were thickly peopled. They also said it was necessary to pass a rapid, which I saw afterward, and from there to enter another lake, three or four leagues long; and that when we had reached the end of that it would be necessary to follow a trail for four leagues, and to pass over a river which empties on the coast of the Almouch-iquois, near the coast of Norumbegue; and that it was only two days' journey by their canoes, as I have [also] learned since from some prisoners that we took, who described to me very much in detail all that they had found out themselves about the matter through some Algonquin interpreters who knew the Iroquois language.

Now, as we began to approach within two or three days' journey of the home of their enemies,

we did not advance more, except at night, and by day we rested. Nevertheless, they did not omit, at any time, the practice of their customary superstitions, to find out how much of their undertakings would succeed, and they often came to me to ask if I had dreamed, and if I had seen their enemies. I answered them "no," and told them to be of good courage and to keep up hope. When night came we pursued our journey until daylight, when we withdrew into the thickest part of the woods and passed the rest of the day there. About ten or eleven o'clock, after having taken a little walk around our encampment, I went to rest; and I dreamed that I saw the Iroquois, our enemies, in the lake, near a mountain, drowning within our sight; and when I wished to help them our savage allies told me that we must let them all die, and that they were worthless. When I woke up they did not fail to ask me, as is their custom, if I had dreamed anything. I told them the substance of what I had dreamed. This gave them so much faith that they no longer doubted that good was to befall them.

When evening came we embarked in our canoes to continue on our way; and, as we were going along very quietly, and without making any noise, on the twenty-ninth of the month, we met the Iroquois at ten o'clock at night at the end of a cape that projects into the lake on the west side, and they were coming to war. We both began to make loud cries, each getting his arms ready. We withdrew toward the water and the Iroquois went ashore and arranged their canoes in line, and began to cut down trees with poor axes, which they get in war sometimes, and also with others of stone; and they barricaded themselves very well.

Our men also passed the whole night with their canoes drawn up close together, fastened to poles, so that they might not get scattered, and might fight all together, if there were need of it; we were on the water within arrow range of the side where their barricades were.

When they were armed and in array, they sent two canoes set apart from the others to learn from their enemies if they wanted to fight. They

*Edward Gaylord Bourne, ed., *The Voyages and Explorations of Samuel de Champlain (1604–1616) Narrated by Himself*, trans. Annie Nettleton Bourne (Toronto: The Courier Press, Ltd., 1911), 207–213.

replied that they desired nothing else; but that, at the moment, there was not much light and that they must wait for the daylight to recognize each other, and that as soon as the sun rose they would open the battle. This was accepted by our men; and while we waited, the whole night was passed in dances and songs, as much on one side as on the other, with endless insults, and other talk, such as the little courage they had, their feebleness and inability to make resistance against their arms, and that when day came they should feel it to their ruin. Our men also were not lacking in retort, telling them that they should see such power of arms as never before; and much other talk, as is customary in the siege of a city. After plenty of singing, dancing, and parleying with one another, daylight came. My companions and I remained concealed for fear that the enemy should see us, preparing our arms the best that we could, separated, however, each in one of the canoes of the Montagnais savages. After arming ourselves with light armor, each of us took an arquebuse and went ashore. I saw the enemy come out of their barricade, nearly 200 men, strong and robust to look at, coming slowly toward us with a dignity and assurance that pleased me very much. At their head there were three chiefs. Our men also went forth in the same order, and they told me that those who wore three large plumes were the chiefs; and that there were only three of them; and that they were recognizable by these plumes, which were a great deal larger than those of their companions; and that I should do all I could to kill them. I promised them to do all in my power, and said that I was very sorry that they could not understand me well, so that I might give order and system to their attack of the enemy, in which case we should undoubtedly destroy them all; but that this could not be remedied; that I was very glad to encourage them and to show them the good-will that I felt, when we should engage in battle.

As soon as we were ashore they began to run about 200 paces toward their enemy, who were standing firmly and had not yet noticed my companions, who went into the woods with some savages. Our men began to call me with loud cries; and, to give me a passageway, they divided into two parts and put me at their head, where I marched about twenty paces in front of them until I was thirty paces from the enemy. They at once saw me and halted, looking at me, and I at them. When I saw them making a move to shoot at us, I rested my arquebuse against my cheek and aimed directly at one of the three chiefs. With the same shot two of them fell to the ground, and one of their companions, who was wounded and afterward died. I put four balls into my arquebuse. When our men saw this shot so favorable for them, they began to make cries so loud that one could not have heard it thunder. Meanwhile the arrows did not fail to fly from both sides. The Iroquois were much astonished that two men had been so quickly killed, although they were provided with armor woven from cotton thread and from wood, proof against their arrows. This alarmed them greatly. As I was loading again, one of my companions fired a shot from the woods, which astonished them again to such a degree that, seeing their chiefs dead, they lost courage, took to flight and abandoned the field and their fort, fleeing into the depths of the woods. Pursuing them thither I killed some more of them. Our savages also killed several of them and took ten or twelve of them prisoners. The rest escaped with the wounded. There were fifteen or sixteen of our men wounded by arrow shots, who were soon healed.

After we had gained the victory they amused themselves by taking a great quantity of Indian corn and meal from their enemies, and also their arms, which they had left in order to run better. And having made good cheer, danced and sung, we returned three hours afterward with the prisoners.

Questions

1. What can we learn from Champlain's depiction of this region and its inhabitants? Who lived there, and in what numbers? What are the "open stretches fertile in grain" that he describes?
2. Discuss the role of dreams in Algonquian and Huron culture. What effect did Champlain's dream have on his allies? Why?
3. Describe the effects of French firearms on this battle. What were the larger implications of this new technology for Native warfare?

5.3 Jesuit Jean de Brébeuf Discusses Life Among the Hurons*

Between 1632 and 1673, French Catholic missionaries from the Jesuit order published reports—called Relations—*of their activities in North America, including many detailed descriptions of the Indians with whom they lived. Despite their cultural biases, these accounts remain the most important sources of information on many aspects of northeastern Indians' historical practices. In the first selection in this section, from the* Relation *of 1635, Jesuit missionary Jean de Brébeuf relates his understanding of some Huron beliefs and religious practices. In the second selection, written in 1637, Brébeuf offers advice to new missionaries about how to adapt to Huron culture.*

It remains now to say something of the country, of the manners and customs of the Hurons, of the inclination they have to the Faith, and of our insignificant labors.

As to the first, the little paper and leisure we have compels me to say in a few words what might justly fill a volume. The Huron country is not large, its greatest extent can be traversed in three or four days. Its situation is fine, the greater part of it consisting of plains. It is surrounded and intersected by a number of very beautiful lakes or rather seas, whence it comes that the one to the North and to the North-northwest is called "fresh-water sea" [mer douce]. We pass through it in coming from the Bissiriniens. The soil of this country is quite sandy, although not equally so. However, it produces a quantity of very good Indian corn, and one may say that it is the granary of most of the Algonquains. There are twenty Towns, which indicate about 30,000 souls speaking the same tongue, which is not difficult to one who has a master. It has distinction of genders, number, tense, person, moods; and, in short, it is very complete and very regular, contrary to the opinion of many. I am rejoiced to find that this language is common to some twelve other Nations, all settled and numerous;

these are, the *Conkhandeen-rhonons, khionontaterrhonons, Atiouandaronks, Sonontoerrhonons, Onontaerrhonons, Oüioeurhonons, Onoiochrhonons, Aguniierrhonons, Andastoerrhonons, Scahentoarrhonons, Rhiierrhonons,* and *Ahouenrochrhonons.* The Hurons are friends of all these people, except the *Souontoërrhonons, Onontaerrhonons Oüioenrhonons, Onoiochrhonons* and *Agnierrhonons,* all of whom we comprise under the name Hiroquois. But they have already made peace with the *Sonontoerrhonons,* since they were defeated by them a year past in the Spring.

The deputies of the whole Country have gone to *Sonontoen* to confirm this peace, and it is said that the *Onontaerhonons, Ouioeurhonons, Ouiochrhonons* and *Agnierrhonons* wish to become parties to it. But that is not certain; if it were, a noble door would be open to the Gospel. They wanted me to go to this *Sonontoen,* but I did not judge it wise to go yet into any other part, until we have better established here the foundation of the Gospel Law, and until we have drawn a line by which the other Nations that shall be converted may guide themselves. Indeed, I would not go to any place where we would not be immediately recognized as Preachers of Jesus Christ.

It is so clear, so evident that there is a Divinity who has made Heaven and earth, that our Hurons cannot entirely ignore it. And although the eyes of their minds are very much obscured by the darkness of a long ignorance, by their vices and sins, they still see something of it. But they misapprehend him grossly, and, having the knowledge of God, they do not render him the honor, the love, nor the service which is his due. For they have neither Temples, nor Priests, nor Feasts, nor any ceremonies.

They say that a certain woman named *Eataentsic* is the one who made earth and men. They give her an assistant, one named *Jouskeha,* whom they declare to be her little son, with whom she governs the world. This *Jouskeha* has care of the living, and of the things that concern life, and consequently they say that he is good. *Eataentsic* has care of souls; and, because they believe that

*Reuben Gold Thwaites, ed. and trans., *The Jesuit Relations and Allied Documents* (Cleveland: The Burrows Brothers Company, 1896–1901), vol. 8: 113–129, vol. 12: 117–123.

she makes men die, they say that she is wicked. And there are among them mysteries so hidden that only the old men, who can speak with credit and authority about them, are believed. Whence it comes that a certain young man, who was talking to me about this, said boastingly, "Am I not very learned?" Some told me that the house of these two Divinities is at the end of the world to the East. Now with them the world does not pass beyond their Country, that is, America. Others place their abode in the middle.

This God and Goddess live like themselves, but without famine; make feasts as they do, are lustful as they; in short, they imagine them exactly like themselves. And still, though they make them human and corporeal, they seem nevertheless to attribute to them a certain immensity in all places. They say that this *Eataentsic* fell from the Sky, where there are inhabitants as on earth; and, when she fell, she was with child. If you ask them who made the Sky and its inhabitants, they have no other reply than that they know nothing about it. And we preach to them of one God, Creator of Heaven and earth, and of all things, and even when we talk to them of Hell and Paradise and of our other mysteries, the headstrong savages reply that this is good for our Country and not for theirs; that every Country has its own fashions. But having pointed out to them, by means of a little globe that we had brought, that there is only one world, they remain without reply. I find in their marriage customs two things that greatly please me; the first, that they have only one wife; the second, that they do not marry their relatives in a direct or collateral line, however distant they may be. There is, on the other hand, sufficient to censure, were it only the frequent changes the men make of their wives, and the women of their husbands. They believe in the immortality of the soul, which they believe to be corporeal. The greatest part of their Religion consists in this point. There are, besides, only superstitions, which we hope by the grace of God to change into true Religion, and, like spoils carried off from the enemy, to consecrate them to the honor of our Lord, and to profit by them for their special advantage. Certainly, if, should they some day be Christians,

these superstitions help them in proportion to what they do for them now in vain, it will be necessary that we yield to them, or that we imitate them; for they spare nothing, not even the most avaricious. We have seen several stripped, or almost so, of all their goods, because several of their friends were dead, to whose souls they had made presents. Moreover, dogs, deer, fish, and other animals have, in their opinion, immortal and reasonable souls. In proof of this, the old men relate certain fables, which they represent as true; they make no mention either of punishment or reward, in the place to which souls go after death. And so they do not make any distinction between the good and the bad, the virtuous and the vicious; and they honor equally the interment of both, even as we have seen in the case of a young man who had poisoned himself from the grief he felt because his wife had been taken away from him. Their superstitions are infinite; their feasts, their medicines, their fishing, their hunting, their wars,—in short, almost their whole life turns upon this pivot; dreams, above all, have here great credit.

This whole country, and I believe it is the same elsewhere, is not lacking in wicked men, who, from motives of envy or vengeance, or from other cause, poison or bewitch, and, in short, put to death sooner or later those whom they wish to injure. When such people are caught, they are put to death on the spot, without any form of trial, and there is no disturbance about it. As to other murders, they are avenged upon the whole Nation of the murderer; so that is the only class I know about that they put to death with impunity. I knew indeed a girl that stole, who was at once killed without any inquiry, but it was by her own brother. If some traitor appears, who is planning the ruin of the Country, they endeavor in common to get rid of him as soon as possible; but these accidents are very rare.

They say that the Sorcerers ruin them; for if any one has succeeded in an enterprise, if his trading or hunting is successful, immediately these wicked men bewitch him, or some member of his family, so that they have to spend it all in Doctors and Medicines. Hence, to cure these and other diseases, there are a large number of Doctors whom they call *Arendiouane*. These persons, in my opinion, are true Sorcerers, who have access to the Devil. Some only judge of the evil, and that in divers ways, namely, by Pyromancy, by Hydromancy, Necromancy, by feasts, dances, and songs; the others endeavor to cure the disease by blowing, by potions, and by other ridiculous tricks, which have neither any virtue nor natural efficacy. But neither class do anything without generous presents and good pay.

There are here some Soothsayers, whom they call also *Arendiouane* and who undertake to cause the rain to fall or to cease, and to predict future events. The Devil reveals to them some secrets, but with so much obscurity that one is unable to accuse them of falsehood; witness one of the village of *Scanonaenrat* who, a little while before the burning of the villages before mentioned, had seen in a dream three flames falling from the Sky on those villages. But the Devil had not declared to him the meaning of this enigma; for, having obtained from the village a white dog, to make a feast with it and to seek information by it, he remained as ignorant afterward as before.

Lastly, when I was in the house of Louys de saincte Foy, an old woman, a sorceress, or female soothsayer of that village, said she had seen those who had gone to the war, and that they were bringing back a prisoner. We shall see if she has spoken the truth. Her method is by pyromancy. She draws for you in her hut the lake of the Hiroquois; then on one side she makes as many fires as there are persons who have gone on the expedition, and on the other as many fires as they have enemies to fight. Then, if her spell succeeds, she lets it be understood that the fires from this side have run over, and that signifies that the warriors have already crossed the lake. One fire extinguishing another marks an enemy defeated; but if it attracts it to itself without extinguishing it, that is a prisoner taken at mercy. It is thus,—to finish my discourse, which would be too long if I tried to say everything,—that the Devil amuses this poor people, substituting his impieties and superstitions in place of the compliance they ought to have with the providence of God, and the worship they ought to render him.

As regards morals, the Hurons are lascivious, although in two leading points less so than many Christians, who will blush some day in their presence. You will see no kissing nor immodest caressing; and in marriage a man will remain two or three years apart from his wife, while she is nursing. They are gluttons, even to disgorging; it is true, that does not happen often, but only in some superstitious feasts,—these, however, they do not attend willingly. Besides, they endure hunger much better than we,—so well that after having fasted two or three entire days you will see them still paddling, carrying loads, singing, laughing, bantering, as if they had dined well. They are very lazy, are liars, thieves, pertinacious beggars. Some consider them vindictive; but, in my opinion, this vice is more noticeable elsewhere than here. We see shining among them some rather noble moral virtues. You note, in the first place, a great love and union, which they are careful to cultivate by means of their marriages, of their presents, of their feasts, and of their frequent visits. On returning from their fishing, their hunting, and their trading, they exchange many gifts; if they have thus obtained something unusually good, even if they have bought it, or if it has been given to them, they make a feast to the whole village with it. Their hospitality towards all sorts of strangers is remarkable; they present to them in their feasts the best of what they have prepared, and, as I have already said, I do not know if anything similar, in this regard, is to be found elsewhere. I think I have read, in the lives of the Fathers, that a Pagan army was converted on seeing the charity and hospitality of a Christian town, the inhabitants of which vied with each other in caressing and feasting the Strangers,— judging well that those must profess the true Religion and worship the true God, the common Father of all, who had hearts so benign and who did so much good to all sorts of persons, without distinction. We have also hope that our Lord will give at last the light of his knowledge, and will communicate the fire of his graces, to this Nation, which he seems to have disposed thereto by the practice of this noble virtue. They never close the door upon a Stranger, and, once having received him into their houses, they share with him the best they have; they never send him away, and, when he goes away of his own accord, he repays them by a simple "thank you." This makes me hope that, if once it pleases God to illumine them, they will respond perfectly to the grace and inspiration of his Son. And, since he has come as a Stranger into his own house, I promise myself that these good people will receive him at all hours into their hearts without making him wait too long on account of their hardness, without withholding from him anything in the whole range of their affections, without betraying him or driving him outside by any serious fault, and without claiming anything in his service other than his honor and glory; which is all the fidelity one can ask in a soul for the good use and holy employment of the favors of Heaven . . .

Instructions for the fathers of our society who shall be sent to the Hurons.

The Fathers and Brethren whom God shall call to the Holy Mission of the Hurons ought to exercise careful foresight in regard to all the hardships, annoyances, and perils that must be encountered in making this journey, in order to be prepared betimes for all emergencies that may arise.

You must have sincere affection for the Savages,—looking upon them as ransomed by the blood of the son of God, and as our brethren, with whom we are to pass the rest of our lives.

To conciliate the Savages, you must be careful never to make them wait for you in embarking.

You must provide yourself with a tinder box or with a burning mirror, or with both, to furnish them fire in the daytime to light their pipes, and in the evening when they have to encamp; these little services win their hearts.

You should try to eat their sagamité or salmagundi in the way they prepare it, although it may be dirty, half-cooked, and very tasteless. As to the other numerous things which may be unpleasant, they must be endured for the love of God, without saying anything or appearing to notice them.

It is well at first to take everything they offer, although you may not be able to eat it all; for,

when one becomes somewhat accustomed to it, there is not too much.

You must try and eat at daybreak unless you can take your meal with you in the canoe; for the day is very long, if you have to pass it without eating. The Barbarians eat only at Sunrise and Sunset, when they are on their journeys.

You must be prompt in embarking and disembarking; and tuck up your gowns so that they will not get wet, and so that you will not carry either water or sand into the canoe. To be properly dressed, you must have your feet and legs bare; while crossing the rapids, you can wear your shoes, and, in the long portages, even your leggings.

You must so conduct yourself as not to be at all troublesome to even one of these Barbarians.

It is not well to ask many questions, nor should you yield to your desire to learn the language and to make observations on the way; this may be carried too far. You must relieve those in your canoe of this annoyance, especially as you cannot profit much by it during the work. Silence is a good equipment at such a time.

You must bear with their imperfections without saying a word, yes, even without seeming to notice them. Even if it be necessary to criticise anything, it must be done modestly, and with words and signs which evince love and not aversion. In short, you must try to be, and to appear, always cheerful.

Each one should be provided with half a gross of awls, two or three dozen little knives called jambettes [pocket-knives], a hundred fishhooks, with some beads of plain and colored glass, with which to buy fish or other articles when the tribes meet each other, so as to feast the Savages; and it would be well to say to them in the beginning, "Here is something with which to buy fish." Each one will try, at the portages, to carry some little thing, according to his strength; however little one carries, it greatly pleases the Savages, if it be only a kettle.

You must not be ceremonious with the Savages, but accept the comforts they offer you, such as a good place in the cabin. The greatest conveniences are attended with very great inconvenience, and these ceremonies offend them.

Be careful not to annoy any one in the canoe with your hat; it would be better to take your nightcap. There is no impropriety among the Savages.

Do not undertake anything unless you desire to continue it; for example, do not begin to paddle unless you are inclined to continue paddling. Take from the start the place in the canoe that you wish to keep; do not lend them your garments, unless you are willing to surrender them during the whole journey. It is easier to refuse at first than to ask them back, to change, or to desist afterwards.

Finally, understand that the Savages will retain the same opinion of you in their own country that they will have formed on the way; and one who has passed for an irritable and troublesome person will have considerable difficulty afterwards in removing this opinion. You have to do not only with those of your own canoe, but also (if it must be so stated) with all those of the country; you meet some to-day and others to-morrow, who do not fail to inquire, from those who brought you, what sort of man you are. It is almost incredible, how they observe and remember even to the slightest fault. When you meet Savages on the way, as you cannot yet greet them with kind words, at least show them a cheerful face, and thus prove that you endure gayly the fatigues of the voyage. You will thus have put to good use the hardships of the way, and have already advanced considerably in gaining the affection of the Savages.

This is a lesson which is easy enough to learn, but very difficult to put into practice; for, leaving a highly civilized community, you fall into the hands of barbarous people who care but little for your Philosophy or your Theology. All the fine qualities which might make you loved and respected in France are like pearls trampled under the feet of swine, or rather of mules, which utterly despise you when they see that you are not as good pack animals as they are. If you could go naked, and carry the load of a horse upon your back, as they do, then you would be wise according to their doctrine, and would be recognized as a great man, otherwise not. Jesus Christ is our true greatness; it is he alone and his cross that should be sought in running after these people, for, if you strive for anything else, you will find naught but bodily and spiritual affliction. But having found Jesus Christ in his cross, you have found the roses in the thorns, sweetness in bitterness, all in nothing.

Questions

1. Given the Jesuits' negative assessment of Indian cultures, why do historians use these documents to reconstruct Indian history? What are the potential benefits and pitfalls of using these sources?

2. Compare and contrast Catholic and Huron beliefs about deities, the creation of the world, and the afterlife. How does Brébeuf account for differences between these two belief systems?

3. How did the Hurons respond to Jesuit teachings? Why? How did Brébeuf react to Huron culture?

4. Brébeuf advises fellow missionaries that they "must have sincere affection for the savages." Does he follow his own counsel?

5. Jesuit priest François le Mercier wrote in 1667, "As God made himself man in order to make men gods, a missionary does not fear to make himself a savage, so to speak, with them, in order to make them Christians." How does Brébeuf suggest that this be done? What are the limits of Jesuit adaptation?

6

Virginia

Envious of Spain's American wealth, and fearful that growing Spanish power would jeopardize English security, the English crown started in the 1580s to support American colonial ventures. Beginning with a failed attempt on Roanoke Island, off the coast of present-day North Carolina, the English eventually established their first permanent settlement at Jamestown, Virginia, in 1607. The documents in this chapter discuss the origins of English colonial settlement in North America, concentrating on Virginia's tumultuous early years.

6.1   A Plan for English Colonization of North America*

Written in 1584 to convince Queen Elizabeth I to support North American colonization, Richard Hakluyt's "Discourse on Western Planting" represents one of the earliest and most coherent expressions of England's New World ambitions. The following selection is an extended table of contents serving as a summary of the book's major points. Hakluyt, an elder cousin who shared his name, and a small group of wealthy investors that included Sir Walter Raleigh, hoped to profit both from English trade and from anti-Spanish piracy conducted from England's new American colonies. Shortly after Hakluyt's work was published, the queen granted Raleigh the first English license to settle in North America.

[Heads of Chapters.]

I. That this westerne discoverie will be greately for thinlargemente of the gospell of Christe, whereunto the princes of

Protestant - Anglican

the refourmed relligion are chefely bounde, amongest whome her Majestie ys principall.

II. That all other Englishe trades are growen beggerly or daungerous, especially in all the Kinge of Spayne his domynions, where our men are dryven to flinge their bibles and prayer bookes into the sea, and to forsweare and renounce their relligion and conscience and consequently theyr obedience to her Majestie.

III. That this westerne voyadge will yelde unto us all the comodities of Europe, Affrica, and Asia, as farr as wee were wonte to travell, and supply the wantes of all our decayed trades.

IV. That this enterprise will be for the manifolde imploymente of nombers of idle men, and for bredinge of many sufficient, and for utteraunce of the great quantitie of the comodities of our realme.

V. That this voyadge will be a great bridle to the Indies of the Kinge of Spaine, and

---

*Richard Hakluyt, "Discourse on Western Planting, Written in the Year 1584" in *Documentary History of the State of Maine*, ed. Charles Deane (Cambridge, 1877), vol. 2: 3–5.

a meane that wee may arreste at our pleasure for the space of tenne weekes or three monethes every yere, one or twoo hundred saile of his subjectes shippes at the fysshinge in Newfounde lande.

VI. That the mischefe that the Indian threasure wroughte in time of Charles the late Emperor, father to the Spanishe kinge, is to be had in consideration of the Queens moste excellent Majestie, leaste the contynuall cõmynge of the like threasure from thence to his sonne, worke the unrecoverable annoye of this realme, whereof already wee have had very dangerous experience.

VII. What speciall meanes may bringe Kinge Phillippe from his highe throne, and make him equall to the princes his neighbours, wherewithall is shewed his weakenes in the West Indies.

VII. That the lymites of the Kinge of Spaines domynions in the West Indies be nothinge so large as ys generally ymagined and surmised, neither those partes which he holdeth be of any suche forces as ys falsly geven oute by the popishe clergye and others his fautors, to terrifie the princes of the relligion and to abuse and blynde them.

IX. The names of the riche townes lienge alonge the sea coaste on the northe side from the equinocticall of the mayne lande of AMERICA under the kinge of Spayne.

X. A brefe declaration of the chefe ilandes in the bay of MEXICO beinge under the Kinge of Spaine, with their havens and fortes, and what comodities they yelde.

XI. That the Spainardes have executed moste outragious and more then Turkishe crueltes in all the West Indies, whereby they are everywhere there become moste odious unto them, whoe woulde joyne with us or any other moste willingly to shake of their moste intollerable yoke, and have begonne to doe it already in dyvers places where they were lordes heretofore.

XII. That the passage in this voyadge is easie and shorte, that it cutteth not nere the trade of any other mightie princes, nor nere their contries, that it is to be perfourmed at all tymes of the yere, and nedeth but one kinde of winde, that Ireland beinge full of goodd havens on the southe and west sides, is the nerest parte of Europe to yt, which by this trade shall be in more securitie, and the sooner drawen to more civilitie.

XIII. That hereby the revenewes and customes of her Majestie, bothe outwardes and inwardes, shall mightely be inlarged by the toll, excises and other dueties, which withoute oppression may be raised.

XIV. That this action will be greately for the increase, mayneteynaunce and safetie of our navye, and especially of great shippinge, which is the strengthe of our realme, and for the supportation of all those occupations that depende upon the same.

XV. That spedie plantinge in divers fitt places is moste necessarie upon those luckye westerne discoveries, for feare of the daunger of being prevented by other nations which have the like intentions, with the order thereof, and other reasons therewithall alleaged.

XVI. Meanes to kepe this enterprise from overthrowe, and the enterprisers from shame and dishonour.

XVII. That by these colonies the Northwest Passage to CATHAIA and CHINA may easely quickly and perfectly be searched oute, as well by river and overlande as by sea, for proofe whereof here are quoted and alleaged divers rare testymonies oute of three volumes of voyadges gathered by Ramusius and other grave authors.

XVIII. That the Queene of Englands title to all the West Indies, or at the leaste to as moche as is from FLORIDA to the circle articke, is more lawfull and righte then the Spaniardes, or any other Christian Princes.

XIX. An aunswer to the Bull of the Donation of all the West Indies graunted to the Kinges of Spaine by Pope Alexander the VIth, who was himselfe a Spaniarde borne.

XX. A brefe collection of certaine reasons to induce her Majestie and the state to take in hande the westerne voyadge and the plantinge there.

XXI. A note of some thinges to be prepared for the voyadge, which is sett downe rather to drawe the takers of the voyadge in hande to the presente consideration then for any other reason, for that divers thinges require preparation longe before the voyadge, withoute which the voyadge ys maymed.

Terms

Cathaia—China

Ramusius—Giovanni Battista Ramusio, Italian compiler of travel narratives, including the writings of Marco Polo

Bull of Donation of all the West Indies—Called *Inter Caetera*, the 1493 proclamation by Pope Alexander VI that divided control of the New World between Spain and Portugal

Questions

1. Hakluyt lists the spread of Protestant Christianity as the first reason for England's colonization of the Americas. In comparison to the other reasons Hakluyt mentions, how important do you think religious considerations were as motives for English colonization?

2. How do the Spanish figure in Hakluyt's rationale for colonization? What, in Hakluyt's view, made English challenges to the Spanish New World empire desirable? What made this defiance feasible?

3. What kinds of commercial enterprises does Hakluyt propose for the colonies? Why?

4. Hakluyt writes that colonies could employ "numbers of idle men." To what is he referring? What was happening in England that made this a particularly important benefit?

6.2   The First Colonists Arrive at Jamestown*

George Percy, who traveled to Virginia with the first group of English settlers in 1606–1607, served as president of the Jamestown colony's council during the settlement's perilous early years. In the following document, Percy offers one of the few surviving accounts of the founding of the Jamestown colony. Percy's history was first published in London in 1625.

ON Saturday the twentieth of December in the yeere 1606, the fleet fell from London, and the fifth of January we anchored in the Downes: but the winds continued contrarie so long, that we were forced to stay there some time, where wee suffered great stormes, but by the skilfulnesse of the Captaine wee suffered no great losse or danger.

The twelfth day of February at night we saw a blazing Starre, and presently a storme.

The three and twentieth day we fell with the Iland of Mattanenio, in the West Indies. The foure and twentieth day we anchored at Dominico, within fourteene degrees of the Line, a very faire Iland, the Trees full of sweet and good smels; inhabited by many Savage Indians. They were at first very scrupulous to come aboord us. . . .

The tenth day we set saile, and disimboged out of the West Indies, and bare oure course Northerly. The fourteenth day we passed the Tropicke of Cancer. The one and twentieth day, about five a clocke at night there began a vehement tempest, which lasted all the night, with winds, raine, and thunders, in a terrible manner. Wee were forced to lie at Hull that night, because we thought wee had beene neerer land then wee were.

---

*Lyon Gardiner Tyler, *Narratives of Early Virginia, 1606–1625* (New York: Barnes & Noble, 1907), 5, 9–11, 14–22.

The next morning, being the two and twentieth day, wee sounded; and the three and twentieth, and foure and twenteth day; but we could find no ground. The five and twentieth day, we sounded, and had no ground at an hundred fathom. The six and twentieth day of Aprill, about foure a clocke in the morning, wee descried the Land of Virginia. The same day wee entred into the Bay of Chesupioc directly, without any let or hinderance. There wee landed and discovered a little way, but wee could find nothing worth the speaking of, but faire meddowes and goodly tall Trees, with such Freshwaters running through the woods, as I was almost ravished at the first sight thereof.

At night, when wee were going aboard, there came the Savages creeping upon all foure, from the Hills, like Beares, with their Bowes in their mouthes, charged us very desperately in the faces, hurt Captaine Gabrill Archer in both his hands, and a sayler in two places of the body very dangerous. After they had spent their Arrowes, and felt the sharpnesse of our shot, they retired into the Woods with a great noise, and so left us.

The seven and twentieth day we began to build up our Shallop. The Gentlemen and Souldiers marched eight miles up into the land. We could not see a Savage in all that march. We came to a place where they had made a great fire, and had beene newly a rosting Oysters. When they perceived our comming, they fled away to the mountaines, and left many of the Oysters in the fire. We eat some of the Oysters, which were very large and delicate in taste.

The eighteenth day we lanched our Shallop. The Captaine and some Gentlemen went in her, and discovered up the Bay. We found a River on the Southside running into the Maine; we entered it and found it very shoald water, not for any Boats to swim. Wee went further into the Bay, and saw a plaine plot of ground where we went on Land, and found the place five mile in compasse, without either Bush or Tree. We saw nothing there but a Cannow, which was made out of the whole tree, which was five and fortie foot long by the Rule. Upon this plot of ground we got good store of Mussels and Oysters, which lay on the ground as thicke as stones. We opened some, and found

in many of them Pearles. Wee marched some three or foure miles further into the woods, where we saw great smoakes of fire. Wee marched to those smoakes and found that the Savages had beene there burning downe the grasse, as wee thought either to make their plantation there, or else to give signes to bring their forces together, and so to give us battell. We past through excellent ground full of Flowers of divers kinds and colours, and as goodly trees as I have seene, as Cedar, Cipresse, and other kindes. Going a little further we came into a little plat of ground full of fine and beautifull Strawberries, foure times bigger and better then ours in England. All this march we could neither see Savage nor Towne. When it grew to be towards night, we stood backe to our Ships, we sounded and found it shallow water for a great way, which put us out of all hopes for getting any higher with our Ships, which road at the mouth of the River. Wee rowed over to a point of Land, where wee found a channell, and sounded six, eight, ten, or twelve fathom: which put us in good comfort. Therefore wee named that point of Land, Cape Comfort.

The nine and twentieth day we set up a Crosse at Chesupioc Bay, and named that place Cape Henry. Thirtieth day, we came with our ships to Cape Comfort; where we saw five Savages running on the shoare. Presently the Captaine caused the shallop to be manned; so rowing to the shoare, the Captaine called to them in signe of friendship, but they were at first very timersome, until they saw the Captain lay his hand on his heart; upon that they laid downe their Bowes and Arrowes, and came very boldly to us, making signes to come a shoare to their Towne, which is called by the Savages Kecoughtan. Wee coasted to their Towne, rowing over a River running into the Maine, where these Savages swam over with their Bowes and Arrowes in their mouthes. . . .

The twelfth day [of May] we went backe to our ships, and discovered a point of Land, called Archers Hope, which was sufficient with a little labour to defend our selves against any Enemy. The soile was good and fruitfull, with excellent good Timber. There are also great store of Vines in bignesse of a mans thigh, running up to the

nature

abundance a sign from God?

tops of the Trees in great abundance. We also did see many Squirels, Conies, Black Birds with crimson wings, and divers other Fowles and Birds of divers and sundrie collours of crimson, Watchet, Yellow, Greene, Murry, and of divers other hewes naturally without any art using.

We found store of Turkie nests and many Egges. If it had not beene disliked, because the ship could not ride neere the shoare, we had setled there to all the Collonies contentment.

The thirteenth day, we came to our seating place in Paspihas Countrey, some eight miles from the point of Land, which I made mention before: where our shippes doe lie so neere the shoare that they are moored to the Trees in six fathom water.

The fourteenth day, we landed all our men, which were set to worke about the fortification, and others some to watch and ward as it was convenient. The first night of our landing, about midnight, there came some Savages sayling close to our quarter. Presently there was an alarum given; upon that the Savages ran away, and we [were] not troubled any more by them that night. Not long after there came two Savages that seemed to be Commanders, bravely drest, with Crownes of coloured haire upon their heads, which came as Messengers from the Werowance of Paspihæ, telling us that their Werowance was comming and would be merry with us with a fat Deare. . . .

The nineteenth day, my selfe and three or foure more walking into the Woods by chance wee espied a pathway like to an Irish pace: wee were desirous to knowe whither it would bring us. Wee traced along some foure miles, all the way as wee went, having the pleasantest Suckles, the ground all flowing over with faire flowers of sundry colours and kindes, as though it had been in any Garden or Orchard in England. There be many Strawberries, and other fruits unknowne. Wee saw the Woods full of Cedar and Cypresse trees, with other trees, which issues out sweet Gummes like to Balsam. . . .

At Port Cotage in our Voyage up the River, we saw a Savage Boy about the age of ten yeeres, which had a head of haire of a perfect yellow and a reasonable white skinne, which is a Miracle amongst all Savages.

This River which wee have discovered is one of the famousest Rivers that ever was found by any Christian. It ebbs and flowes a hundred and threescore miles, where ships of great burthen may harbour in safetie. Wheresoever we landed upon this River, wee saw the goodliest Woods as Beech, Oke, Cedar, Cypresse, Wal-nuts, Sassafras, and Vines in great abundance, which hang in great clusters on many Trees, and other Trees unknowne; and all the grounds bespred with many sweet and delicate flowres of divers colours and kindes. There are also many fruites as Strawberries, Mulberries, Rasberries, and Fruites unknowne. There are many branches of this River, which runne flowing through the Woods with great plentie of fish of all kindes; as for Sturgeon, all the World cannot be compared to it. In this Countrey I have seene many great and large Medowes having excellent good pasture for any Cattle. There is also great store of Deere both Red and Fallow. There are Beares, Foxes, Otters, Bevers, Muskats, and wild beasts unknowne.

The foure and twentieth day wee set up a Crosse at the head of this River, naming it Kings River, where we proclaimed James King of England to have the most right unto it. When wee had finished and set up our Crosse, we shipt our men and made for James Fort. By the way, wee came to Pohatans Towre, where the Captaine went on shore suffering none to goe with him. Hee presented the Commander of this place, with a Hatchet which hee tooke joyfully, and was well pleased.

But yet the Savages murmured at our planting in the Countrie, whereupon this Werowance made answere againe very wisely of a Savage, Why should you bee offended with them as long as they hurt you not, nor take any thing away by force. They take but a litle waste ground, which doth you nor any of us any good. . . .

The fifteenth of June we had built and finished our Fort, which was triangle wise, having three Bulwarkes, at every corner, like a halfe Moone, and foure or five pieces of Artillerie mounted in them. We had made our selves sufficiently strong for these Savages. We had also sowne most of our Corne on two Mountaines. It sprang a mans height from the ground. This Countrey is a fruitfull soile, bearing many goodly and fruitfull Trees, as Mulberries, Cherries, Wal-nuts, Cedars, Cypresse, Sassafras, and Vines in great abundance.

Munday the two and twentieth of June, in the morning, Captaine Newport in the Admirall departed from James Port for England.

Captaine Newport being gone for England, leaving us (one hundred and foure persons) verie bare and scantie of victualls, furthermore in warres and in danger of the Savages, we hoped after a supply which Captaine Newport promised within twentie weekes. But if the beginners of this action doe carefully further us, the Country being so fruitfull, it would be as great a profit to the Realme of England, as the Indies to the King of Spaine. If this River which wee have found had been discovered in the time of warre with Spaine, it would have beene a commoditie to our Realme, and a great annoyance to our enemies. . . .

The sixt of August there died John Asbie of the bloudie Flixe. The ninth day died George Flowre of the swelling. The tenth day died William Bruster Gentleman, of a wound given by the Savages, and was buried the eleventh day.

The fourteenth day, Jerome Alikock, Ancient, died of a wound, the same day, Francis Midwinter, Edward Moris Corporall died suddenly.

The fifteenth day, their died Edward Browne and Stephen Galthorpe. The sixteenth day, their died Thomas Gower Gentleman. The seventeenth day, their died Thomas Mounslic. The eighteenth day, there died Robert Pennington, and John Martine Gentleman. The nineteenth day, died Drue Piggase Gentleman. The two and twentieth day of August, there died Captaine Bartholomew Gosnold, one of our Councell: he was honourably buried, having all the Ordnance in the Fort shot off, with many vollies of small shot. . . .

The foure and twentieth day, died Edward Harington and George Walker, and were buried the same day. The six and twentieth day, died Kenelme Throgmortine. The seven and twentieth day died William Roods. The eight and twentieth day died Thomas Stoodie, Cape Merchant.

The fourth day of September died Thomas Jacob Sergeant. The fift day, there died Benjamin

Beast. Our men were destroyed with cruell diseases, as Swellings, Flixes, Burning Fevers, and by warres, and some departed suddenly, but for the most part they died of meere famine. There were never Englishmen left in a forreigne Countrey in such miserie as wee were in this new discovered Virginia. Wee watched every three nights, lying on the bare cold ground, what weather soever came, [and] warded all the next day, which brought our men to bee most feeble wretches. Our food was but a small Can of Barlie sod in water, to five men a day, our drinke cold water taken out of the River, which was at a floud verie salt, at a low tide full of slime and filth, which was the destruction of many of our men. Thus we lived for the space of five moneths in this miserable distresse, not having five able men to man our Bulwarkes upon any occasion. If it had not pleased God to have put a terrour in the Savages hearts, we had all perished by those wild and cruell Pagans, being in that weake estate as we were; our men night and day groaning in every corner of the Fort most pittifull to heare. If there were any conscience in men, it would make their harts to bleed to heare the pitifull murmurings and out-cries of our sick men without reliefe, every night and day, for the space of sixe weekes, some departing out of the World, many times three or foure in a night; in the morning, their bodies trailed out of their Cabines like Dogges to be buried. In this sort did I see the mortalitie of divers of our people.

It pleased God, after a while, to send those people which were our mortail enemies to releeve us with victuals, as Bread, Corne, Fish, and Flesh in great plentie, which was the setting up of our feeble men, otherwise wee had all perished. Also we were frequented by divers Kings in the Countrie, bringing us store of provision to our great comfort.

Terms

Mattanenio—Martinique
Bay of Chesupioc—Chesapeake Bay
shallop—a small ship
shoald—shallow
Kecoughtan—Powhatan Indian town at the mouth of the Hampton River

werowance—headman, village leader, chief
Kings River—James River
bloudie flixe—bloody flux, or severe dysentery

Questions

1. What were Percy's first impressions of Virginia? What did he notice and why?

2. How does Percy describe the Indians who first discovered the English entering their lands? How does this encounter compare with those you have read earlier?

3. Why did so many English settlers die during their first year in Virginia? What saved them from total destruction? How does Percy explain their deliverance?

6.3   Captain John Smith Describes Virginia Indian Society*

John Smith traveled with Percy on the first voyage to Virginia. Although often out of favor with his fellow colonists, he became one of the most important traders, diplomats, and administrators during the first years at Jamestown. Captured by Powhatan Indians, and later deeply involved in trade with them, Smith gained a thorough, if still imperfect, understanding of their society. The following passage is drawn from Smith's pamphlet, titled A Map of Virginia, *written in 1608 and published in 1612.*

OF THE NATURALL INHABITANTS OF VIRGINIA

The land is not populous, for the men be fewe; their far greater number is of women and children. Within 60 miles of James Towne there are about some 5000 people, but of able men fit for their warres scarse 1500. To nourish so many together they have yet no means, because they make so smal a benefit of their land, be it never so fertill. 6 or 700 have beene the most [that] hath beene seene together, when they gathered themselves to have surprised Captaine Smyth at Pamaunke, having but 15 to withstand the worst of their furie. As small as the proportion of ground that hath yet beene discovered, is in comparison of that yet unknowne. The people differ very much

in stature, especially in language, as before is expressed. Some being very great as the Sesquesahamocks, others very little as the Ighcocomocoes: but generally tall and straight, of a comely proportion, and of a colour browne, when they are of any age, but they are borne white. Their haire is generally black; but few have any beards. The men weare halfe their heads shaven, the other halfe long. For Barbers they use their women, who with 2 shels will grate away the haire, of any fashion they please. The women are cut in many fashions agreeable to their yeares, but ever some part remaineth long. They are very strong, of an able body and full of agilitie, able to endure to lie in the woods under a tree by the fire, in the worst of winter, or in the weedes and grasse, in Ambuscado in the Sommer. They are inconstant in everie thing, but what feare constraineth them to keepe. Craftie, timerous, quicke of apprehension and very ingenuous. Some are of disposition fearefull, some bold, most cautelous, all Savage. Generally covetous of copper, beads, and such like trash. They are soone moved to anger, and so malitious, that they seldome forget an injury: they seldome steale one from another, least their conjurors should reveale it, and so they be pursued and punished. That they are thus feared is certaine, but that any can reveale their offences by conjuration I am doubtfull. Their women are carefull not to bee suspected of dishonesty without the leave of their husbands. Each houshold

*Tyler, *Narratives of Early Virginia*, 98–118.

knoweth their owne lands and gardens, and most live of their owne labours. For their apparell, they are some time covered with the skinnes of wilde beasts, which in winter are dressed with the haire, but in sommer without. The better sort use large mantels of deare skins not much differing in fashion from the Irish mantels. Some imbrodered with white beads, some with copper, other painted after their manner. But the common sort have scarce to cover their nakednesse but with grasse, the leaves of trees, or such like. We have seen some use mantels made of Turky feathers, so prettily wrought and woven with threeds that nothing could bee discerned but the feathers, that was exceeding warme and very handsome. But the women are alwaies covered about their midles with a skin and very shamefast to be seene bare. They adorne themselves most with copper beads and paintings. Their women some have their legs, hands, brests and face cunningly imbrodered with diverse workes, as beasts, serpentes, artificially wrought into their flesh with blacke spots. In each eare commonly they have 3 great holes, whereat they hange chaines, bracelets, or copper. Some of their men weare in those holes, a smal greene and yellow coloured snake, neare halfe a yard in length, which crawling and lapping her selfe about his necke often times familiarly would kiss his lips. Others wear a dead Rat tied by the tail. Some on their heads weare the wing of a bird or some large feather, with a Rattell. Those Rattels are somewhat like the chape of a Rapier but lesse, which they take from the taile of a snake. Many have the whole skinne of a hawke or some strange fowle, stuffed with the wings abroad. Others a broad peece of copper, and some the hand of their enemy dryed. Their heads and shoulders are painted red with the roote *Pocone* braied to powder mixed with oyle; this they hold in somer to preserve them from the heate, and in winter from the cold. Many other formes of paintings they use, but he is the most gallant that is the most monstrous to behould.

Their buildings and habitations are for the most part by the rivers or not farre distant from some fresh spring. Their houses are built like our Arbors of small young springs bowed and tyed; and, so close covered with mats or the barkes of trees very handsomely, that notwithstanding either winde raine or weather, they are as warme as stooves, but very smoaky, yet at the toppe of the house there is a hole made for the smoake to goe into right over the fire.

Against the fire they lie on little hurdles of Reedes covered with a mat, borne from the ground a foote and more by a hurdle of wood. On these round about the house, they lie heads and points one by thother against the fire: some covered with mats, some with skins, and some starke naked lie on the ground, from 6 to 20 in a house. Their houses are in the midst of their fields or gardens; which are smal plots of ground, some 20, some 40, some 100. some 200. some more, some lesse. Some times from 2 to 100 of these houses togither, or but a little separated by groves of trees. Neare their habitations is little small wood, or old trees on the ground, by reason of their burning of them for fire. So that a man may gallop a horse amongst these woods any waie, but where the creekes or Rivers shall hinder.

Men women and children have their severall names according to the severall humor of their Parents. Their women (they say) are easilie delivered of childe, yet doe they love children verie dearly. To make them hardy, in the coldest mornings they wash them in the rivers, and by painting and ointments so tanne their skins, that after year or two, no weather will hurt them.

The men bestowe their times in fishing, hunting, wars, and such manlike exercises, scorning to be seene in any woman like exercise, which is the cause that the women be verie paine-full and the men often idle. The women and children do the rest of the worke. They make mats, baskets, pots, morters, pound their corne, make their bread, prepare their victuals, plant their corne, gather their corne, beare al kind of burdens, and such like.

Their fire they kindle presently by chafing a dry pointed sticke in a hole of a little square peece of wood, that firing it selfe, will so fire mosse, leaves, or anie such like drie thing that will quickly burne. In March and Aprill they live much upon their fishing weares, and feed on fish, Turkies and squirrels. In May and June they plant their fieldes, and live most of Acornes, walnuts, and fish. But to mend their diet, some disperse themselves in small companies, and live upon fish, beasts, crabs, oysters, land Torteyses, strawberries, mulberries, and such like. In June, Julie, and August, they feed upon the rootes of *Tocknough*, berries, fish, and greene wheat. It is strange to see how their bodies alter with their diet; even as the deare and wild beastes, they seeme fat and leane, strong and weak. Powhatan their great king and some others that are provident, rost their fish and flesh upon hurdles as before is expressed, and keepe it till scarce times.

For fishing and hunting and warres they use much their bow and arrowes. They bring their bowes to the forme of ours by the scraping of a shell. Their arrowes are made, some of straight young sprigs, which they head with bone some 2 or 3 inches long. These they use to shoot at squirrels on trees. An other sort of arrowes they use, made of reeds. These are peeced with wood, headed with splinters of christall or some sharpe stone, the spurres of a Turkey, or the bill of some bird. For his knife, he hath the splinter of a reed to cut his feathers in forme. With this knife also, he will joint a Deare or any beast, shape his shooes, buskins, mantels, &c. To make the noch of his arrow hee hath the tooth of a Bever set in a sticke, wherewith he grateth it by degrees. His arrow head he quickly maketh with a little bone, which he ever weareth at his bracer, of any splint of a stone, or glasse in the forme of a hart, and these they glew to the end of their arrowes. With the sinewes of Deare, and the tops of Deares hornes boiled to a jelly, they make a glew that will not dissolve in cold water.

For their wars also they use Targets that are round and made of the barkes of trees, and a sworde of wood at their backs, but oftentimes they use for swords the horne of a Deare put through a peece of wood in forme of a Pickaxe. Some, a long stone sharpened at both ends used in the same manner. This they were wont to use also for hatchets, but now by trucking they have plenty of the same forme, of yron. And those are their chiefe instruments and armes.

Their fishing is much in Boats. These they make of one tree by bowing and scratching away the coles with stone and shels till they have made it in forme of a Trough. Some of them are an elne deepe, and 40 or 50 foot in length, and some will beare 40 men, but the most ordinary are smaller, and will beare 10, 20, or 30, according to their bignes. Instead of oares, they use paddles and sticks, with which they will row faster then our Barges. Betwixt their hands and thighes, their women use to spin the barks of trees, deare sinews, or a kind of grasse they call *Pemmenaw*; of these they make a thred very even and readily. This thred serveth for many uses, as about their housing, apparell, as also they make nets for fishing, for the quantity as formally braded as ours. They make also with it lines for angles. Their hookes are either a bone grated, as they nock their arrows, in the forme of a crooked pinne or fishhook or of the splinter of a bone tied to the clift of a litle stick, and with the ende of the line, they tie on the bate. They use also long arrowes tyed in a line wherewith they shoote at fish in the rivers. But they of Accawmack use staves like unto Javelins headed with bone. With these they dart fish swimming in the water. They have also many artificiall weares in which they get abundance of fish.

In their hunting and fishing they take extreame paines; yet it being their ordinary exercise from their infancy, they esteeme it a pleasure and are very proud to be expert therein. And by their continuall ranging, and travel, they know all the advantages and places most frequented with Deare, Beasts, Fish, Foule, Rootes, and Berries. At their huntings they leave their habitations, and reduce themselves into companies, as the Tartars doe, and goe to the most desert places with their families, where they spend their time in hunting and fowling up towards the mountaines, by the heads of their rivers, where there is plentie of game. For betwixt the rivers, the grounds are so narrowe, that little commeth there which they devoure not. It is a marvel they can so directly passe these deserts some 3 or 4 daies journey without habitation. Their hunting houses are like unto Arbours covered with mats. These their women beare after them, with Corne, Acornes, Morters, and all bag and baggage they use. When they come to the place of exercise, every man doth his best to shew his dexteritie, for by their excelling in those quallities, they get their wives. Forty yards will they shoot levell, or very neare the mark, and 120 is their best at Random. At their huntings in the deserts they are commonly 2 or 300 together. Having found the Deare, they environ them with many fires, and betwixt the fires they place themselves. And some take their stands in the midst. The Deare being thus feared by the fires and their voices, they chace them so long within that circle, that many times they kill 6, 8, 10, or 15 at a hunting. They use also to drive them into some narrowe point of land, when they find that advantage, and so force them into the river, where with their boats they have Ambuscadoes to kill them. When they have shot a Deare by land, they follow him like blood hounds by the blood and straine, and oftentimes so take them. Hares, Pattridges, Turkies, or Egges, fat or leane, young or old, they devoure all they can catch in their power. In one of these huntings, they found Captaine Smith in the discoverie of the head of the river of Chickahamania, where they slew his men, and tooke him prisoner in a Bogmire; where he saw those exercises, and gathered these observations.

One Savage hunting alone, useth the skinne of a Deare slit on the one side, and so put on his arme, through the neck, so that his hand comes to the head which is stuffed, and the hornes, head, eies, eares, and every part as arteficially counterfeited as they can devise. Thus shrowding his body in the skinne, by stalking he approacheth the Deare, creeping on the ground from one tree to another. If the Deare chance to find fault, or stande at gaze, hee turneth the head with his hand to his best advantage to seeme like a Deare, also gazing and licking himselfe. So watching his best advantage to approach, having shot him, hee chaseth him by his blood and straine till he get him.

When they intend any warres, the Werowances usually have the advice of their Priests and Conjurors, and their Allies and ancient friends, but chiefely the Priestes determine their resolution. Every Werowance, or some lustie fellow, they appoint Captaine over every nation. They seldome make warre for lands or goods, but for women and children, and principally for revenge. They have

many enimies, namely all their westernely Countries beyond the mountaines, and the heads of the rivers. Upon the head of the Powhatans are the Monacans, whose chiefe habitation is at Russawmeake, unto whome the Mouhemenchughes, the Massinnacacks, the Monahassanuggs, and other nations, pay tributs. Upon the head of the river of Toppahanock is a people called Mannahoacks. To these are contributers the Tauxsnitanias, the Shackaconias, the Outponcas, the Tegoneaes, the Whonkentyaes, the Stegarakes, the Hassinnungas, and diverse others, all confederats with the Monacans, though many different in language, and be very barbarous, living for most part of wild beasts and fruits. Beyond the mountaines from whence is the head of the river Patawomeke, the Savages report, inhabit their most mortall enimies, the Massawomekes upon a great salt water, which by all likelyhood is either some part of Commada, some great lake, or some inlet of some sea that falleth into the South sea. These Massawomekes are a great nation and very populous. For the heads of all those rivers, especially the Pattawomekes, the Pautuxuntes, the Sasquesahanocks, the Tockwoughes, are continually tormented by them: of whose crueltie, they generally complained, and very importunate they were with Captaine Smith and his company, to free them from these tormentors. To this purpose, they offered food, conduct, assistance, and continuall subjection. To which he concluded to effect. But the counsell then present, emulating his successe, would not thinke it fit to spare him 40 men to be hazarded in those unknowne regions, having passed (as before was spoken of) but with 12, and so was lost that opportunitie. Seaven boats full of these Massawomeks the discoverers encountred at the head of the Bay; whose Targets, Baskets, Swords, Tobaccopipes, Platters, Bowes and Arrowes, and every thing shewed, they much exceeded them of our parts: and their dexteritie in their small boats made of the barkes of trees sowed with barke, and well luted with gumme, argueth that they are seated upon some great water.

Against all these enimies the Powhatans are constrained sometimes to fight. Their chiefe attempts are by Stratagems, trecheries, or surprisals. Yet the Werowances, women and children, they put not to death, but keepe them Captives. They have a method in warre, and for our pleasures, they shewd it us, and it was in this manner performed at Mattapanient.

Having painted and disguised themselves in the fiercest manner they could devise, they divided themselves into two Companies, neare a 100 in a company. The one company called Monacans, the other Powhatans. Either army had their Captaine. These as enimies tooke their stands a musket shot one from another; ranked themselves 15 abreast, and each ranke from another 4 or 5 yards, not in fyle, but in the opening betwixt their fyles, so as the Reare could shoot as conveniently as the Front. Having thus pitched the fields; from either part went a Messenger with these conditions, that whosoever were vanquished, such as escape, upon their submission in 2 daies after, should live, but their wives and children should be prize for the Conquerers. The messengers were no sooner returned, but they approached in their orders. On each flanke a Sarjeant, and in the Reare an office for leuitenant, all duly keeping their orders, yet leaping and singing after their accustomed tune, which they use only in warres. Upon the first flight of arrowes, they gave such horrible shouts and screeches, as though so many infernall helhounds could not have made them more terrible. When they had spent their arrowes, they joined together prettily, charging and retiring, every ranke seconding other. As they got advantage, they catched their enimies by the haire of the head, and downe he came that was taken. His enimie with his wooden sword seemed to beat out his braines, and still they crept to the Reare, to maintaine the skirmish. The Monacans decreasing, the Powhatans charged them in the forme of a halfe moone: they unwilling to be inclosed, fled all in a troope to their Ambuscadoes, on whome they led them very cunningly. The Monacans disperse themselves among the fresh men, whereupon the Powhatans retired with al speed to their seconds; which the Monacans seeing, took that advantage to retire againe to their owne battell, and so each returned to their owne quarter. All their actions, voices and gestures, both in charging and retiring, were so strained to the hight of their quallitie and nature, that the strangenes thereof made it seem very delightfull.

For their musicke they use a thicke cane, on which they pipe as on a Recorder. For their warres, they have a great deepe platter of wood. They cover the mouth thereof with a skin, at each corner they tie a walnut, which meeting on the backside neere the bottome, with a small rope they twitch them togither till it be so tought and stiffe, that they may beat upon it as upon a drumme. But their chiefe instruments are Rattels made of small gourds or Pumpion shels. Of these they have Base, Tenor, Counter-tenor, Meane and Trible. These mingled with their voices sometimes 20 or 30 togither, make such a terrible noise as would rather affright then delight any man. If any great commander arrive at the habitation of a Werowance, they spread a mat as the Turkes do a carpet, for him to sit upon. Upon an other right opposite they sit themselves. Then doe all with a tunable voice of showting bid him welcome. After this, doe 2, or more of their chiefest men make an oration, testifying their love. Which they do with such vehemency and so great passions, that they sweate till they drop, and are so out of breath they can scarce speake. So that a man would take them to be exceeding angry or starke mad. Such victuall as they have, they spend freely, and at night where his lodging is appointed, they set a woman fresh painted red with *Pocones* and oile, to be his bedfellow.

Their manner of trading is for copper, beades, and such like; for which they give such commodities as they have, as skins, fowle, fish, flesh, and their country corne. But their victuall is their chiefest riches.

Every spring they make themselves sicke with drinking the juice of a root they call *wighsacan*, and water, whereof they powre so great a quantity, that it purgeth them in a very violent maner; so that in 3 or 4 daies after, they scarce recover their former health. Sometimes they are troubled with dropsies, swellings, aches, and such like diseases; for cure wherof they build a stove in the form of a dovehouse with mats, so close that a fewe coales therein covered with a pot, will make the pacient sweate extreamely. For swellings also they use smal peeces of touchwood, in the forme of cloves, which pricking on the griefe, they burne close to the flesh, and from thence draw the corruption with their mouth. With this root *wighsacan* they ordinarily heal greene wounds: but to scarrifie a swelling or make incision, their best instruments are some splinted stone. Old ulcers or putrified hurtes are seldome seene cured amongst them. They have many professed Phisitions, who with their charmes and Rattels, with an infernall rowt of words and actions, will seeme to sucke their inwarde griefe from their navels or their grieved places; but of our Chirurgians they were so conceipted, that they beleeved any Plaister would heale any hurt.

OF THEIR RELIGION

There is yet in Virginia no place discovered to bee so Savage in which the Savages have not a religion, Deare, and Bow and Arrowes. All thinges that were able to do them hurt beyond their prevention, they adore with their kinde of divine worship; as the fire, water, lightning, thunder, our ordinance, peeces, horses, &c. But their chiefe God they worship is the Divell. Him they call *Oke* and serve him more of feare than love. They say they have conference with him, and fashion themselves as neare to his shape as they can imagine. In their temples, they have his image evill favouredly carved, and then painted and adorned with chaines, copper, and beades, and covered with a skin, in such manner as the deformity may well suit with such a God. By him is commonly the sepulcher of their kings. Their bodies are first bowelled, then dryed upon hurdles till they bee verie dry, and so about the most of their jointes and necke they hang bracelets or chaines of copper, pearle, and such like, as they use to weare: their inwards they stuffe with copper beads and cover with a skin, hatchets, and such trash. Then lappe they them very carefully in white skins, and so rowle them in mats for their winding sheetes. And in the Tombe, which is an arch made of mats, they lay them orderly. What remaineth of this kinde of wealth their kings have, they set at their feet in baskets. These Temples and bodies are kept by their Priests.

For their ordinary burials, they digge a deep hole in the earth with sharpe stakes, and the corp[s]es being lapped in skins and mats with their jewels, they lay them upon sticks in the ground, and so cover them with earth. The buriall ended, the women being painted all their faces with black cole and oile, doe sit 24 howers in the houses mourning and lamenting by turnes, with such yelling and howling as may expresse their great passions.

In every Territory of a werowance is a Temple and a Priest 2 or 3 or more. Their principall Temple or place of superstition is at Uttamussack at Pamaunke, neare unto which is a house Temple or place of Powhatans.

Upon the top of certaine redde sandy hils in the woods, there are 3 great houses filled with images of their kings and Divels and Tombes of their Predecessors. Those houses are neare 60 foot in length, built arbor wise, after their building. This place they count so holy as that [none] but the Priestes and kings dare come into them: nor the Savages dare not go up the river in boats by it, but that they solemnly cast some peece of copper, white beads, or Pocones, into the river, for feare their *Oke* should be offended and revenged of them.

In this place commonly is resident 7 Priests. The chiefe differed from the rest in his ornaments: but inferior Priests could hardly be knowne from the common people, but that they had not so many holes in their eares to hang their jewels at. The ornaments of the chiefe Priest was certain attires for his head made thus. They tooke a dosen or 16 or more snake skins, and stuffed them with mosse; and of weesels and other vermine skins, a good many. All these they tie by their tailes, so as all their tailes meete in the toppe of their head, like a great Tassell. Round about this Tassell is as it were a crown of feathers; the skins hang round about his head necke and shoulders, and in a manner cover his face. The faces of all their Priests are painted as ugly as they can devise. In their hands, they had every one his Rattell, some base, some smaller. Their devotion was most in songs which the chiefe Priest beginneth and the rest followed him: sometimes he maketh invocations with broken sentences, by starts and strange passions, and at every pause, the rest give a short groane.

It could not bee perceived that they keepe any day as more holy then other: but only in some great distresse, of want, feare of enimies, times of triumph and gathering togither their fruits, the whole country of men women and children come togither to solemnities. The manner of their devotion is sometimes to make a great fire in the house or fields, and all to sing and dance about it, with rattles and shouts togither, 4 or 5 houres. Sometimes they set a man in the midst, and about him they dancc and sing, he all the while clapping his hands as if he would keepe time. And after their songs and dauncings ended, they goe to their Feasts.

They have also divers conjurations. One they made when Captaine Smith was their prisoner (as they reported) to know if any more of his countrymen would arive there, and what he there intended. The manner of it was thus. First they made a faire fire in a house. About this fire set 7 Priests setting him by them, and about the fire, they made a circle of meale. That done, the chiefe Priest attired as is expressed, began to shake his rattle, and the rest followed him in his song. At the end of the song, he laid downe 5 or 3 graines of wheat, and so continued counting his songs by the graines, till 3 times they incirculed the fire. Then they divide the graines by certaine numbers with little stickes, laying downe at the ende of every song a little sticke. In this manner, they sat 8, 10, or 12 houres without cease, with such strange stretching of their armes, and violent passions and gestures as might well seeme strange to him they so conjured, who but every houre expected his end. Not any meat they did eat till, late in the evening, they had finished this worke: and then they feasted him and themselves with much mirth. But 3 or 4 daies they continued this ceremony.

They have also certaine Altar stones they call *Pawcorances*: but these stand from their Temples, some by their houses, other in the woodes and wildernesses. Upon these, they offer blood, deare suet, and Tobacco. These they doe when they returne from the warres, from hunting, and upon many other occasions. They have also another superstition that they use in stormes, when the waters are rough in the rivers and sea coasts. Their Conjurers runne to the water sides, or passing in their boats, after many hellish outcries and invocations, they cast Tobacco, Copper, *Pocones*, and such trash into the water, to pacifie that God whome they thinke to be very angry in those stormes. Before their dinners and suppers, the better sort will take the first bit, and cast it in the fire, which is all the grace they are known to use.

In some part of the Country, they have yearely a sacrifice of children. Such a one was at Quiyoughcohanock, some 10 miles from James Towne, and thus performed. Fifteene of the properest young boyes, betweene 10 and 15 yeares of age, they painted white. Having brought them forth, the people spent the forenoone in dancing and singing about them with rattles. In the afternoone, they put those children to the roote of a tree. By them, all the men stood in a guard, every one having a Bastinado in his hand, made of reeds bound together. This made a lane betweene them all along, through which there were appointed 5 young men to fetch these children. So every one of the five went through the guard, to fetch a child, each after other by turnes: the guard fearelessly beating them with their Bastinadoes, and they patiently enduring and receiving all, defending the children with their naked bodies from the unmercifull blowes they pay them soundly, though the children escape. All this while, the women weepe and crie out very passionately, providing mats, skinnes, mosse, and drie wood, as things fitting their childrens funerals. After the children were thus passed the guard, the guard tore down the tree, branches and boughs, with such violence, that they rent the body, and made wreathes for their heads, or bedecked their haire with the leaves. What else was done with the children was not seene; but they were all cast on a heape in a valley, as dead where they made a great feast for al the company. The Werowance being demanded the meaning of this sacrifice, answered that the children were not al dead, but that the *Oke* or Divell did sucke the blood from their left breast, who chanced to be his by lot, till they were dead. But the rest were kept in the wildernesse by the yong men till nine moneths were expired, during which time they must not converse with any: and of these, were made their Priests and Conjurers. This sacrifice they held to bee so necessarie, that if they should omit it, their *Oke* or Divel and all their other *Quiyoughcosughes* (which are their other Gods) would let them have no Deare, Turkies, Corne nor fish: and yet besides, hee would make great slaughter amongst them.

They thinke that their Werowances and Priestes, which they also esteeme *Quiyoughcosughes*, when they are dead, doe goe beyond the mountaines towards the setting of the sun, and ever remaine there in forme of their Oke, with their heads painted with oile and *Pocones*, finely trimmed with feathers, and shal have beades, hatchets, copper, and tobacco, doing nothing but dance and sing with all their Predecessors. But the common people, they suppose shall not live after death.

To divert them from this blind idolatrie, many used their best indeavours, chiefly with the Werowances of Quiyoughcohanock, whose devotion, apprehension, and good disposition much exceeded any in those Countries: who though we could not as yet prevaile withall to forsake his false Gods, yet this he did beleeve, that our God as much exceeded theirs, as our Gunnes did their Bowes and Arrows, and many times did send to the President, at James towne, men with presents, intreating them to pray to his God for raine, for his Gods would not send him any. And in this lamentable ignorance doe these poore soules sacrifice themselves to the Divell, not knowing their Creator.

OF THE MANNER OF THE VIRGINIANS GOVERNEMENT

Although the countrie people be very barbarous; yet have they amongst them such governement, as that their Magistrats for good commanding, and their people for due subjection and obeying, excell many places that would be counted very civill.

The forme of their Common wealth is a monarchicall governement. One as Emperour ruleth over many kings or governours. Their chiefe ruler is called Powhatan, and taketh his name of the principall place of dwelling called Powhatan. But his proper name is Wahunsonacock. Some countries

he hath, which have been his ancestors, and came unto him by inheritance, as the countrie called Powhatan, Arrohateck, Appamatuke, Pamaunke, Youghtanud, and Mattapanient. All the rest of his Territories expressed in the Map, they report have beene his severall conquests. In all his ancient inheritances, hee hath houses built after their manner like arbours, some 30, some 40 yardes long, and at every house, provision for his entertainement, according to the time. At Werowcomoco, he was seated upon the North side of the river Pamaunke, some 14 miles from James Towne, where for the most part, hee was resident, but he tooke so little pleasure in our neare neighbourhood, that were able to visit him against his will in 6 or 7 houres, that he retired himself to a place in the deserts at the top of the river Chickahamania betweene Youghtanund and Powhatan. His habitation there is called Orapacks, where he ordinarily now resideth. He is of parsonage a tall well proportioned man, with a sower looke, his head somwhat gray, his beard so thinne that it seemeth none at al. His age neare 60; of a very able and hardy body to endure any labour. About his person ordinarily attendeth a guard of 40 or 50 of the tallest men his Country doth afford. Every night upon the 4 quarters of his house are 4 Sentinels, each standing from other a flight shoot: and at every halfe houre, one from the Corps du guard doth hollowe, unto whom every Sentinell doth answer round from his stand. If any faile, they presently send forth an officer that beateth him extreamely.

A mile from Orapakes in a thicket of wood, hee hath a house, in which he keepeth his kind of Treasure, as skinnes, copper, pearle, and beades, which he storeth up against the time of his death and buriall. Here also is his store of red paint for ointment, and bowes and arrowes. This house is 50 or 60 yards in length, frequented only by Priestes. At the 4 corners of this house stand 4 Images as Sentinels, one of a Dragon, another a Beare, the 3 like a Leopard, and the fourth like a giantlike man: all made evill favordly, according to their best workmanship.

He hath as many women as he will: whereof when hee lieth on his bed, one sitteth at his head, and another at his feet, but when he sitteth, one sitteth on his right hand, and another on his left. As he is wearie of his women, hee bestoweth them on those that best deserve them at his hands. When he dineth or suppeth, one of his women, before and after meat, bringeth him water in a wo[o]den platter to wash his hands. Another waiteth with a bunch of feathers to wipe them insteed of a Towell, and the feathers when he hath wiped are dryed againe. His kingdome descendeth not to his sonnes nor children: but first to his brethren, whereof he hath 3. namely Opitchapan, Opechancanough, and Catataugh, and after their decease to his sisters. First to the eldest sister, then to the rest: and after them to the heires male and female of the eldest sister, but never to the heires of the males.

He nor any of his people understand any letters wherby to write or read, only the lawes whereby he ruleth is custome. Yet when he listeth, his will is a law and must bee obeyed: not only as a king, but as halfe a God they esteeme him. His inferiour kings whom they cal werowances are tyed to rule by customes, and have power of life and death as their command in that nature. But this word Werowance which we call and conster for a king, is a common worde whereby they call all commanders: for they have but fewe words in their language and but few occasions to use anie officers more then one commander, which commonly they call werowances. They all knowe their severall landes, and habitations, and limits to fish, fowle, or hunt in, but they hold all of their great Werowances Powhatan, unto whome they pay tribute of skinnes, beades, copper, pearle, deare, turkies, wild beasts, and corne. What he commandeth they dare not disobey in the least thing. It is strange to see with what great feare and adoration all these people doe obay this Powhatan. For at his feet, they present whatsoever he commandeth, and at the least frowne of his browe, their greatest spirits will tremble with feare: and no marvell, for he is very terrible and tyrannous in punishing such as offend him. For example, hee caused certaine malefactors to be bound hand and foot, then having of many fires gathered great store of burning coles, they rake these coles round in the forme of a cockpit, and in the midst they cast the offenders to broyle to death. Sometimes he causeth the heads of them that offend him, to be laid upon the altar or sacrificing stone, and one with clubbes beates out their braines. When he would punish any notorious enimie or malefactor, he causeth him to be tied to a tree, and, with muscle shels or reeds, the executioner cutteth of[f] his joints one after another, ever casting what they cut of[f] into the fire; then doth he proceed with shels and reeds to case the skinne from his head and face; then doe they rip his belly, and so burne him with the tree and all. Thus themselves reported they executed George Cassen. Their ordinary correction is to beate them with cudgels. Wee have seene a man kneeling on his knees, and at Powhatans command, two men have beat him on the bare skin, till he hath fallen senselesse in a s[w]ound, and yet never cry nor complained.

In the yeare 1608, hee surprised the people of Payankatank, his neare neighbours and subjects. The occasion was to us unknowne, but the manner was thus. First he sent diverse of his men as to lodge amongst them that night, then the Ambuscadoes invironed al their houses, and at the houre appointed, they all fell to the spoile; 24 men they slewe, the long haire of the one side of their heades with the skinne cased off with shels or reeds, they brought away. They surprised also the women and the children and the Werowance. All these they present to Powhatan. The Werowance, women and children became his prisoners, and doe him service. The lockes of haire with their skinnes he hanged on a line unto two trees. And thus he made ostentation as of a great triumph at Werowocomoco, shewing them to the English men that then came unto him, at his appointment: they expecting provision; he, to betray them, supposed to halfe conquer them, by this spectacle of his terrible crueltie.

And this is as much as my memory can call to mind worthie of note; which I have purposely collected, to satisfie my friends of the true worth and qualitie of Virginia. Yet some bad natures will not sticke to slander the Countrey, that will slovenly spit at all things, especially in company where they can find none to contradict them. Who though they were scarse ever 10 miles from James Town, or at the most but at the falles; yet holding it a great disgrace that amongst so much action, their actions were nothing, exclaime of all things, though they never adventured to knowe any thing; nor ever did any thing but devoure the fruits of other mens labours. Being for most part of such tender educations and small experience in martiall accidents: because they found not English cities, nor such faire houses, nor at their owne wishes any of their accustomed dainties, with feather beds and downe pillowes, Tavernes and alehouses in every breathing place, neither such plenty of gold and silver and dissolute liberty as they expected, had little or no care of any thing, but to pamper their bellies, to fly away with our Pinnaces, or procure their means to returne for England. For the Country was to them a miserie, a ruine, a death, a hell, and their reports here, and their owne actions there according

Some other there were that had yearely stipends to pass to and againe for transportation: who to keepe the mystery of the businesse in themselves, though they had neither time nor meanes to knowe much of themselves; yet al mens actions or relations they so formally tuned to the temporizing times simplicitie, as they could make their ignorances seeme much more then al the true actors could by their experience. And those with their great words deluded the world with such strange promises as abused the businesse much worse then the rest. For the business being builded upon the foundation of their fained experience, the planters, the mony, tinne [time], and meanes have still miscaried: yet they ever returning, and the Planters so farre absent, who could contradict their excuses? which, stil to maintain their vaineglory and estimation, from time to time they have used such diligence as made them passe for truthes, though nothing more false. And that the adventurers might be thus abused, let no man wonder; for the wisest living is soonest abused by him that hath a faire tongue and a dissembling heart.

There were many in Virginia meerely projecting verbal and idle contemplatours, and those so devoted to pure idlenesse that though they had lived two or three yeares in Virginia lordly, necessitie it selfe could not compell them to passe the Peninsula, or Pallisadoes of James Towne; and those wittie spirits, what would they not affirme in the behalfe of our transporters, to get victuall from their ships, or obtaine their good words in England to get their passes? Thus from the clamors and the ignorance of false informers are sprung those disasters that spring in Virginia, and our ingenious

verbalists were no lesse plague to us in Virginia, then the Locusts to the Egyptians. For the labour of 30 of the best only, preserved in Christianitie, by their industrie, the idle livers of neare 200 of the rest: who lived neer 10 months of such naturall meanes, as the Country naturally of it selfe afforded. Notwithstanding all this, and the worst furie of the Savages, the extremitie of sicknesse, mutinies, faction, ignorances, and want of victuall; in all that time I lost but 7 or 8 men: yet subjected the Savages to our desired obedience, and receaved contribution from 35 of their kings, to protect and assist them against any that should assalt them, in which order they continued true and faithful, and as subjects to his Majestie, so long after as I did govern there, untill I left the Country: Since, how they have revolted, the Countrie lost, and againe replanted, and the businesses hath succeeded from time to time, I referre you to the relations of them returned from Virginia, that have bin more diligent in such observations.

Questions

1. What aspects of Indian society seem to interest Smith the most? Why?
2. How does this account compare with popular images of Smith's relationship with Indians?
3. Describe Powhatan society. Do you feel that Smith paints a fair portrait of this people? Do you think that they would agree with his assessment of their culture?
4. Smith claims that "their Chiefe God they worship is the Divell." How does this fit with the rest of his description of Powhatan religion?
5. Smith describes Powhatan government as "mōnarchical," and Powhatan himself as an "Emperour." Why does he use these terms? How did Powhatan government compare with English government?
6. How does the Indian society described by Smith compare with those encountered by the de Soto expedition? To the Hurons described by Brébeuf?
7. What, in Smith's view, explains the early English difficulties in Virginia?

CHAPTER

7

Chesapeake Colonies

Much of the seventeenth-century Chesapeake's history revolved around interrelated questions of power, land, and labor. As English settlers moved to the region, an ocean away from long-established political institutions and social hierarchies, they would have to determine who would rule. Those who obtained power in this unstable environment would have to devise ways to retain it. Moreover, wealth for Virginians would come not from finding gold or silver, or from controlling Indian labor, but rather from acquiring land and importing workers whose drudgery could make it profitable. But who would be fortunate enough to own, and who could be made to toil? The documents that follow display the struggles arising from efforts to resolve these issues.

7.1   Frontier Planters Appeal for Protection from Indian Attacks*

Seeking new land to accommodate a growing population, English settlers expanded rapidly into Indian territory in the mid-seventeenth century. As the Virginians pressed in, some Indians responded with violence. In this document, written in spring 1676, a group of English settlers appeal to the governor of Virginia for protection against these Indian attacks. His unresponsiveness eventually sparked a frontier rebellion that threatened to overthrow Virginia's government.

5. THE CAUSES OF DISCONTENT

A. Frontier Planters Petition Governor Berkeley to Commission Volunteers against the Indians, ca. Spring 1676

To the Right Honorable Sir William Barkly Knight governour and Capt. Generall of verginia: The Humble petition of the poore distressed subjects in the upper parts of James River in verginia Humbly Complain that the Indians hath allready most barberously and Inhumanly taken and Murdered severall of our bretheren and put them to most cruell torture by burning of them alive and by cruell torturing of them which makes our harts Ready to bleed to heare and wee the poore subjects are in dayly dandger of loosing our lives by the Heathen in soe much that wee are all afraid of

---

*"Frontier Planters to Governor William Berkeley, Spring 1676," in *The Old Dominion in the Seventeenth Century: A Documentary History of Virginia, 1606–1689,* ed. Warren M. Billings (Chapel Hill, NC: Institute of Early American History and Culture, 1975), 267.

101

goeing about our demesticall affaires. Wherefore we Most Humbly request that your gratious Honor would be pleased to grant us a Committion and to make choice of Commitioned Officers to lead this party now redy to take armes in defence of our lives and estates which without speedy prevention lie liable to the Injury of such insulting enimmies not that your petitioners desires to make any disturbance or put the Country to any charge wherefore we Humbly implead your Honnours speedy answer for we are informed that the Indians dayly approach our habitations and we your petitioners as in duty bound shall ever pray.

Questions

1. How do these settlers describe the Indians' motives for the attacks? How do they describe the Indians' behavior?
2. Why would the authors stress their inability to carry out their "domesticall affaires?"
3. What is the tone of the letter? How does this reflect the social and political structure of seventeenth-century Virginia?

7.2 Virginia's Governor Accuses His Enemies of Treason*

This document is a "Declaration and Remonstrance" by Governor William Berkeley, governor of Virginia from 1642 to 1652 and 1660 to 1677. Berkeley wrote the proclamation to condemn a group of renegades, led by his wife's cousin Nathaniel Bacon, who had defied his authority by raising an independent army against local Indians.

Sheweth that about the Yeare 1660 Col. [Samuel] Mathewes the then Governor Died and then in Consideration of the service I had donne the Country in defending them from and destroying great numbers of the Indians without the losse of theire men in al the time that warr lasted and in contemplation of the Equal and uncorrupt Justice I had distributed to al men not only the Assembly but the unanimous Votes of al the Country Concurred to make me Governor in a time when if the Rebels in England had prevailed I had certainly died for accepting of it and was there an unfortunate love shewed to me for to shew my selfe grateful for this I was willing to accept of this Goverment againe when by my Gracious Kings favour I might have had other places much more profitable and lesse toylesome then this has beene since that time I returned into the Country I cal the Great God Judge of al things in heaven and Earth to Witnesse that I doe not know of any thing Relative to this country wherein I have acted unjustly corruptly or neglegently in distributing Equal Justice to al men and taking al possible care to preserve their properties and to defend them from their Barbarous Enimies

But for al this perhaps I have Erred in things I know not of if I have I am so conscious of humane fraylty and my owne defects that I wil not only acknowledge them but repent of them and amend them and not like that Rebel Bacon persist in an Error only because I have Committed it and tells me in Divers of his letters that tis not for his honor to Acknowledge a fault But I am of opinion it is only for Divels to be incorrigeable and men of Principles like the worst of Divels and these if truth be reported to me of divers of his Expressions of Atheisme, tending to take away al Religion and lawes

And NOW loving frends I wil State the Question betweene me as Governor and Mr. Bacon and Say that if any Ennimies should envade England any councelor Justice of the peace or other superior Officer might rayse what forces they could to protect his majesties subjects But I say againe if after the Kings knowledge of this invasion any the greatest Peare of England should rayse forces against the Kings prohibition this would be now and was ever in al Ages and nations accounted Treason Nay I wil goe farther (and it shal be printed) that though this Peere were truly sealous [i.e., zealous] for the preservation of his

*"Declaration and Remonstrance," in *The Old Dominion on the Seventeenth Century,* 270–272.

King and subjects to doe his King and Country service Yet if the King though by false information should suspect the contrary it were treason in this Noble Peere to proceed after the Kings prohibition and for the Truth of this I appeale to al the lawes of England and the lawes and constitutions of al other nations in the World and yet further it is declared by this Parliament that the taking up Armes for the King and Parliament is declared Treason for the Event shewed that what ever the Pretence was to seduce Ignorant and wel affected people yet the end was such as told to King and People as this wil bc if not prevented I doe therefore againe declare that Bacon proceeding against al lawes of al nations modern and ancient is a Rebel to his Sacred majestie and the country nor will I insist uppon his swearing of men to live and dye together which is Treason by the very words of the law

Now my friends I have liv'd amongst you fower and thirty years as uncorrupt and diligent as ever governor was: Bacon is a man of two years amongst you his person and qualities unknown to most of you and to al men Its by any vertuous action that ever I heard of, and this very action wherein he so much boasted was fully foolishly and as I am informed Treacherously carried to the dishonor of the English nation. Yet in it he lost more men then I did in three wars and by the Grace of god wil put myselfe to the same dangers and troubles again when I have brought Bacon to acknowledge the lawes are above him and I doubt not by the assistance of god to have better successe than Mr. Bacon has had the reason of my hopes are that I wil take councel of wiser men then my selfe But Mr. Bacon has none aboute him but the lowest of the people.

Yet I must farther enlarge that I can not without your helpe doe anything in this but Dye in the defence of my King his lawes and subjects which I wil cherfully doe though alone I doe it: and considering my poore fortunes I cannot leave my poore wife and frends a better legacy then by diyng for the King and you for his sacred majestie wil easily distinguish betweene Mr. Bacons actions and mine and Kings long hands either to reward or punish.

Now after al this if Mr. Bacon can shew me presedent or example where such actings in any nation what soever was approved of I wil mediate with the King and you for a pardon and excuse for him, But I can shew him an hundred examples where brave and greate men have ben put to death for gaining victories against the command of their superiors.

Lastly my most assured frends I would have preserved those Indians that I knew were hourely at our mercy to have beene our spies and intelligence that they also were also treacherous Ennimies I have given out commissions to destroy them al as the commissions wil speake it to conclude I have donne what was possible both to frend and Ennimies have granted Mr. Bacon Pardons which he has scornfully rejected supposing himselfe stronger to [subvert?] then I and you to maintaine the lawes by which only and [good?] assisting grace and mercy al men must hope for Peace and safety I wil add no more thoughe much more is yet remaining to justifye me and condemne Mr. Bacon but to desire that this Declaration may be made in every county court in the country and that a court be presently cald to doe it before the Assembly meet that your approbation or dissatisfaction of this Declaration may be knowne to al the country and to the Kings Councel to whose most revered judgements it is submitted. Given this 29 of May a happy day in the 28 yeare of his most sacred majesties Raigne Charles the Second whome god grant long and prosperously to reing [sic] and let al his good subjects say amen Amen

Your incessant Servant
William Berkeley

Questions

1. Describe the contrast Berkeley draws between himself and Bacon. What does this comparison reveal about Berkeley's view of society?
2. Berkeley accuses Bacon of professing atheism. Why? Who would find this accusation most damning?
3. What is the tone of Berkeley's declaration? What does that reveal about his strategy for maintaining power?

7.3   Nathaniel Bacon Justifies Rebellion*

In this letter, Nathaniel Bacon responds to Berkeley's charges of treason, summarizing his reasons for acting against the governor's orders. In June 1676, Bacon led a body of about 500 armed men into Jamestown, driving Berkeley from power and burning much of the colonial capital to the ground. After Bacon's death a few months later, however, the rebellion disintegrated, and Brekeley resumed power.

If vertue be a sin, if Piety be giult, all the Principles of morality goodness and Justice be perverted, Wee must confesse That those who are now called Rebells may be in danger of those high imputations, Those loud and severall Bulls would affright Innocents and render the defence of our Brethren and the enquiry into our sad and heavy oppressions, Treason. But if there bee as sure there is, a just God to appeal too, if Religion and Justice be a sanctuary here, If to plead the cause of the oppressed, If sincerely to aime at his Majesties Honour and the Publick good without any reservation or by Interest, If to stand in the Gap after soe much blood of our dear Brethren bought and sold, If after the losse of a great part of his Majesties Colony deserted and dispeopled, freely with our lives and estates to indeavor to save the remaynders bee Treason God Almighty Judge and lett guilty dye, But since wee cannot in our hearts find one single spott of Rebellion or Treason or that wee have in any manner aimed at subverting the setled Government or attempting of the Person of any either magistrate or private man not with standing the severall Reproaches and Threats of some who for sinister ends were disaffected to us and censured our ino[cent] and honest designes, and since all people in all places where wee have yet bin can attest our civill quiet peaseable behaviour farre different from that of Rebellion and tumultuous persons let Trueth be bold and all the world know the real Foundations of pretended giult, Wee appeale to the Country itselfe what and of what nature their Oppressions have bin or by what Caball and mistery the designes of many of those whom

*"Bacon's Manifesto," in *The Old Dominion in the Seventeenth Century*, 277–279.

wee call great men have bin transacted and caryed on, but let us trace these men in Authority and Favour to whose hands the dispensation of the Countries wealth has been commited; let us observe the sudden Rise of their Estates composed with the Quality in which they first entered this Country Or the Reputation they have held here amongst wise and discerning men, And let us see wither their extractions and Education have not bin vile, And by what pretence of learninig and vertue they could soe soon into Imployments of so great Trust and consequence, let us consider their sudden advancement and let us also consider wither any Publick work for our safety and defence or for the Advancement and propogation of Trade, liberall Arts or sciences is here Extant in any [way] adaquate to our vast chardg, now let us compare these things togit[her] and see what spounges have suckt up the Publique Treasure and wither it hath not bin privately contrived away by unworthy Favourites and juggling Parasites whose tottering Fortunes have bin repaired and supported at the Publique chardg, now if it be so Judg what greater giult can bee then to offer to pry into these and to unriddle the misterious wiles of a powerfull Cabal let all people Judge what can be of more dangerous Import then to suspect the soe long Safe proceedings of Some of our Grandees and wither People may with safety open their Eyes in soe nice a Concerne.

Another main article of our Giult is our open and manifest aversion of all, not onely the Foreign but the protected and Darling Indians, this wee are informed is Rebellion of a deep dye For that both the Governour and Councell are by Colonell Coales Assertion bound to defend the Queen and Appamatocks with their blood Now whereas we doe declare and can prove that they have bin for these Many years enemies to the King and Country, Robbers and Theeves and Invaders of his Majesties' Right and our Interest and Estates, but yet have by persons in Authority bin defended and protected even against His Majesties loyall Subjects and that in soe high a Nature that even the Complaints and oaths of his Majesties Most loyall Subjects in a lawfull Manner proffered by them against those barborous Out-lawes have bin by the right honourable Governour rejected and the Delinquents from his presence dismissed not only with pardon and indemnitye but with all incouragement and favour, Their Fire Arms soe destructfull to us and by our lawes prohibited, Commanded to be restored them, and open Declaration before Witness made That they must have Ammunition although directly contrary to our law, Now what greater giult can be then to oppose and indeavour the destruction of these Honest quiet neighbours of ours.

Another main article of our Giult is our Design not only to ruine and extirpate all Indians in Generall but all Manner of Trade and Commerce with them, Judge who can be innocent that strike at this tender Eye of Interest; Since the Right honourable the Governour hath bin pleased by his Commission to warrant this trade who dare oppose it, or opposing it can be innocent. Although Plantations be deserted, the blood of our dear Brethren Spilt, on all Sides our complaints, continually Murder upon Murder renewed upon us, who may or dare think of the generall Subversion of all Mannor of Trade and Commerce with our enemies who can or dare impeach any of [word missing] Traders at the Heades of the Rivers if contrary to the wholesome provision made by lawes for the countries safety, they dare continue their illegall practises and dare asperse the right honourable Governours wisdom and Justice soe highly to pretend to have his warrant to break that law which himself made, who dare say That these Men at the Heades of the Rivers buy and sell our blood, and doe still notwithstanding the late Act made to the contrary, admit Indians painted and continue to Commerce, although these things can be proved yet who dare bee soe guilty as to doe it.

Another Article of our Guilt is To Assert all those neighbour Indians as well as others to be outlawed, wholly unqualified for the benefitt and Protection of the law, For that the law does reciprocally protect and punish, and that all people offending must either in person or Estate make equivalent satisfaction or Restitution according to the manner and merit of the Offences Debts or Trespasses; Now since the Indians cannot according to the tenure and forme of any law to us known be prosecuted, Seised or Complained against, Their Persons being difficulty distinguished or known, Their many nations languages, and their subterfuges such as makes them incapeable to make us Restitution or satisfaction would it not be very giulty to say They have bin unjustly defended and protected these many years.

If it should be said that the very foundation of all these disasters the Grant of the Beaver trade to the Right Honourable Governour was illegall and not granteable by any power here present as being a monopoly, were not this to deserve the name of Rebell and Traytor.

Judge therefore all wise and unprejudiced men who may or can faithfully or truely with an honest heart attempt the country's good, their vindication and libertie without the aspersion of Traitor and Rebell, since as soe doing they must of necessity gall such tender and dear concernes, But to manifest Sincerity and loyalty to the World, and how much wee abhorre those bitter names, may all the world know that we doe unanimously desire to represent our sad and heavy grievances to his most sacred Majesty as our Refuge and Sanctuary, where wee doe well know that all our Causes will be impartially heard and Equall Justice administred to all men.

Questions

1. Summarize Bacon's complaints against Virginia's ruling elites? Which of these does he find most important?
2. Identify the words that Bacon used to describe Indians. Why does he use these terms? Would Berkeley disagree?
3. How does Bacon defend his actions against Berkeley's accusation of treason? Who is more persuasive?
4. What remedy does Bacon propose for the injustices he enumerates? By what authority?
5. Were the Anglo-Indian tensions Berkeley and Bacon were arguing about the inevitable result of two different types of society coming into contact or the preventable consequence of particular incidents and policies?

7.4   The Virginia Slave Code of 1705*

During the last quarter of the seventeenth century, white Virginians increasingly relied on enslaved Africans to produce export crops. Because slaves frequently challenged their bondage, masters made repeated appeals to colonial authorities for new powers to control their workers. A patchwork of legislation emerged during these years to define the nature of slavery in Virginia. The following document, written in 1705, represents the efforts of Virginia lawmakers to synthesize and systematize the large body of slave law already in place. Officially titled "An act concerning Servants and Slaves," this slave code became a model for slave law in many other colonies, including South Carolina and Georgia.

An act concerning Servants and Slaves.

I. *Be it enacted, by the governor, council, and burgesses, of this present general assembly, and it is hereby enacted, by the authority of the same,* That all servants brought into this country without indenture, if the said servants be christians, and of christian parentage, and above nineteen years of age, shall serve but five years; and if under nineteen years of age, 'till they shall become twenty-four years of age, and no longer.

How long servant shall serve.

II. *Provided always,* That every such servant be carried to the county court, within six months after his or her arrival into this colony, to have his or her age adjudged by the court, otherwise shall be a servant no longer than the accustomary five years, although much under the age of nineteen years; and the age of such servant being adjudged

To have their age adjudged by the court.

by the court, within the limitation aforesaid, shall be entered upon the records of the said court, and be accounted, deemed, and taken, for the true age of the said servant, in relation to the time of service aforesaid.

III. *And also be it enacted, by the authority aforesaid, and it is hereby enacted,* That when any servant sold for the custom, shall pretend to have indentures, the master or owner of such servant, for discovery of the truth thereof, may bring the said servant before a justice of the peace; and if the said servant cannot produce the indenture then, but shall still pretend to have one, the said justice shall assign two months time for the doing thereof; in which time, if the said servant shall not produce his or her indenture, it shall be taken for granted that there never was one, and shall be a bar to his or her claim of making use of one afterwards, or taking any advantage by one.

When to produce their indentures.

IV. *And also be it enacted, by the authority aforesaid, and it is hereby enacted,* That all servants imported and brought into this country, by sea or land, who were not christians in their native country, (except Turks and Moors in amity with her majesty, and others that can make due proof of their being free in England, or any other christian country, before they were shipped, in order to transportation hither) shall be accounted and be slaves, and as such be here bought and sold notwithstanding a conversion to christianity afterwards.

Who shall be slaves.

V. *And be it enacted, by the authority aforesaid, and it is hereby enacted,* That if any person or persons shall hereafter import into this colony, and here sell as a slave, any person or persons that shall have been a freeman in any christian country, island, on plantation, such

Penalty for importing and selling free persons as slaves.

*William Waller Hening, ed., *Statutes at Large, Being a Collection of All the Laws of Virginia, from the First Session of the Legislature, in the Year 1619* (Philadelphia: Thomas Desilver, 1828), vol. 3: 447–462.

importer and seller as aforesaid, shall forfeit and pay, to the party from whom the said freeman shall recover his freedom, double the sum for which the said freeman was sold. To be recovered, in any court of record within this colony, according to the course of the common law, wherein the defendant shall not be admitted to plead in bar, any act or statute for limitation of actions.

VI. *Provided always*, That a slave's being in England, shall not be sufficient to discharge him of his slavery, without other proof of his being manumitted there.

VII. *And also be it enacted, by the authority aforesaid, and it is hereby enacted*, That all masters and owners of servants, shall find and provide for their servants, wholesome and competent diet, clothing, and lodging, by the discretion of the county court; and shall not, at any time, give immoderate correction; neither shall, at any time, whip a christian white servant naked, without an order from a justice of the peace: And if any, notwithstanding this act, shall presume to whip a christian white servant naked, without such order, the person so offending, shall forfeit and pay for the same, forty shillings sterling, to the party injured: To be recovered, with costs, upon petition, without the formal process of an action, as in and by this act is provided for servants complaints to be heard; provided complaint be made within six months after such whipping.

VIII. *And also be it enacted, by the authority aforesaid, and it is hereby enacted*, That all servants, (not being slaves,) whether imported, or become servants of their own accord here, or bound by any court or church-wardens, shall have their complaints received by a justice of the peace, who, if he find cause, shall bind the master over to answer the complaint at court; and it shall be there determined: And all complaints of servants, shall and may, by virtue hereof, be received at any time, upon petition, in the court of the county wherein they reside, without the formal process of an action; and also full power and authority is hereby given to the said court, by their discretion, (having first summoned the masters or owners to justify themselves, if they think fit,) to adjudge, order, and appoint what shall be necessary, as to diet, lodging, clothing, and correction: And if any master or owner shall not thereupon comply with the said court's order, the said court is hereby authorised and impowered, upon a second just complaint, to order such servant to be immediately sold at an outery, by the sheriff, and after charges deducted, the remainder of what the said servant shall be sold for, to be paid and satisfied to such owner.

IX. *Provided always, and be it enacted*, That if such servant be so sick or lame, or otherwise rendered so encapable, that he or she cannot be sold for such a value, at least, as shall satisfy the fees, and other incident charges accrued, the said court shall then order the church-wardens of the parish to take care of and provide for the said servant, until such servant's time, due by law to the said master, or owner, shall be expired, or until such servant, shall be so recovered, as to be sold for defraying the said fees and charges: And further, the said court, from time to time, shall order the charges of keeping the said servant, to be levied upon the goods and chattels of the master or owner of the said servant, by distress.

X. *And be it also enacted*, That all servants, whether, by importation, indenture, or hire here, as well feme coverts, as others, shall, in like manner, as is provided,

Marginal notes:

Being in England no discharge from slavery.

Duty of masters to servants.

Restriction as to correction.

Complaints of servants, how redressed.

Remedy on second complaint.

Sick and disabled servants, how provided for.

Servants wages, how recovered.

upon complaints of misusage, have their petitions received in court, for their wages and freedom, without the formal process of an action; and proceedings, and judgment, shall, in like manner, also, be had thereupon.

Negroes, &c. disabled from purchasing servants.

XI. And for a further christian care and usage of all christian servants, *Be it also enacted, by the authority aforesaid, and it is hereby enacted,* That no negros, mulattos, or Indians, although christians, or Jews, Moors, Mahometans, or other infidels, shall, at any time, purchase any christian servant, nor any other, except of their own complexion, or such as are declared slaves by this act: And if any negro, mulatto, or Indian, Jew, Moor, Mahometan, or other infidel, or such as are declared slaves by this act, shall, notwithstanding, purchase any christian white servant, the said servant shall, *ipso facto,* become free and acquit from any service then due, and shall be so held, deemed, and taken: And if any person, having such christian servant, shall intermarry with any such negro, mulatto, or Indian, Jew, Moor, Mahometan, or other infidel, every christian white servant of every such person so intermarrying, shall *ipso facto,* become free and acquit from any service then due to such master or mistress so intermarrying, as aforesaid.

Inter-marrying with such.

Contracts of masters with their servants void unless approved in court.

XII. *And also be it enacted, by the authority aforesaid, and it is hereby enacted,* That no master or owner of any servant shall during the time of such servant's servitude, make any bargain with his or her said servant for further service, or other matter or thing relating to liberty, or personal profit, unless the same be made in the presence, and with the approbation, of the court of that county where the master or owner resides: And if any servants shall, at any time bring in goods or money, or during the time of their service, by

gift, or any other lawful ways or means, come to have any goods or money, they shall enjoy the propriety thereof, and have the sole use and benefit thereof to themselves. And if any servant shall happen to fall sick or lame, during the time of service, so that he or she becomes of little or no use to his or her master or owner, but rather a charge, the said master or owner shall not put away the said servant, but shall maintain him or her, during the whole time he or she was before obliged to serve, by indenture, custom, or order of court: And if any master or owner, shall put away any such sick or lame servant, upon pretence of freedom, and that servant shall become chargeable to the parish, the said master or owner shall forfeit and pay ten pounds current money of Virginia, to the church-wardens of the parish where such offence shall be committed, for the use of the said parish: To be recovered by action of debt, in any court of record in this her majesty's colony and dominion, in which no essoin, protection, or wager of law, shall be allowed.

Property in goods.

Sick, not to be discharged.

XIII. And whereas there has been a good and laudable custom of allowing servants corn and cloaths for their present support, upon their freedom; but nothing in that nature ever made certain, *Be it also enacted, by the authority aforesaid, and it is hereby enacted,* That there shall be paid and allowed to every imported servant, not having yearly wages, at the time of service ended, by the master or owner of such servant, viz: To every male servant, ten bushels of indian corn, thirty shillings in money, or the value thereof, in goods, and one well fixed musket or fuzee, of the value of twenty shillings, at least: and to every woman servant, fifteen bushels of indian corn, and

Freedom dues.

forty shillings in money, or the value thereof, in goods: Which, upon refusal, shall be ordered, with costs, upon petition to the county court, in manner as is herein before directed, for servants complaints to be heard.

Penalty on servants resisting their masters.

XIV. *And also be it enacted, by the authority aforesaid, and it is hereby enacted,* That all servants shall faithfully and obediently, all the whole time of their service, do all their masters or owners just and lawful commands. And if any servant shall resist the master, or mistress, or overseer, or offer violence to any of them, the said servant shall, for every such offence, be adjudged to serve his or her said master or owner, one whole year after the time, by indenture, custom, or former order of court, shall be expired.

Penalty for dealing with servants, or slaves, without leave of their owners.

XV. *And also be it enacted, by the authority aforesaid, and it is hereby enacted,* That no person whatsoever shall buy, sell, or receive of, to, or from, any servant, or slave, any coin or commodity whatsoever, without the leave, licence, or consent of the master or owner of the said servant, or slave: And if any person shall, contrary hereunto, without the leave or licence aforesaid, deal with any servant, or slave, he or she so offending, shall be imprisoned one calender month, without bail or mainprize; and then, also continue in prison, until he or she shall find good security, in the sum of ten pounds current money of Virginia, for the good behaviour for one year following; wherein, a second offence shall be a breach of the bond; and moreover shall forfeit and pay four times the value of the things so bought, sold, or received, to the master or owner of such servant, or slave: To be recovered, with costs, by action upon the case, in any court of record in this her majesty's colony and dominion,

wherein no essoin, protection, or wager of law, or other than one imparlance, shall be allowed.

Punishment by stripes.

XVI. *Provided always and be it enacted,* That when any person or persons convict for dealing with a servant, or slave, contrary to this act, shall not immediately give good and sufficient security for his or her good behaviour, as aforesaid: then, in such case, the court shall order thirty-nine lashes, well laid on, upon the bare back of such offender, at the common whipping-post of the county, and the said offender to be thence discharged of giving such bond and security.

Servants may be whipped, in lieu of fines, for a breach of penal laws.

XVII. *And also be it enacted, by the authority aforesaid, and it is hereby enacted, and declared,* That in all cases of penal laws, whereby persons free are punishable by fine, servants shall be punished by whipping, after the rate of twenty lashes for every five hundred pounds of tobacco, or fifty shillings current money, unless the servant so culpable, can and will procure some person or persons to pay the fine; in which case, the said servant shall be adjudged to serve such benefactor, after the time by indenture, custom, or order of court, to his or her then present master or owner, shall be expired, after the rate of one month and a half for every hundred pounds of tobacco; any thing in this act contained, to the contrary, in any-wise, notwithstanding.

Women servants having bastards.

XVIII. And if any women servant shall be delivered of a bastard child within the time of her service aforesaid, *Be it enacted, by the authority aforesaid, and it is hereby enacted,* That in recompence of the loss and trouble occasioned her master or mistress thereby, she shall for every such offence, serve her said master or owner one whole year after her time by indenture, custom, and former order of court, shall be expired; or pay

Duty of reputed father.

her said master or owner, one thousand pounds of tobacco; and the reputed father, if free, shall give security to the church-wardens of the parish where that child shall be, to maintain the child, and keep the parish indemnified; or be compelled thereto by order of the county court, upon the said church-wardens complaint: But if a servant, he shall make satisfaction to the parish, for keeping the said child, after his time by indenture, custom, or order of court, to his then present master or owner, shall be expired; or be compelled thereto, by order of the county court, upon complaint of the church-wardens of the said parish, for the time being. And if any

Master getting his servant with child.

woman servant shall be got with child by her master, neither the said master, nor his executors administrators, nor assigns, shall have any claim of service against her, for or by reason of such child; but she shall, when her time due to her said master, by indenture, custom or order of court, shall be expired, be sold by the church-wardens, for the time being, of the parish wherein such child shall be born, for one year, or pay one thousand pounds of tobacco; and the said one thousand pounds of tobacco, or whatever she shall be sold for, shall be emploied, by the vestry, to the use of the said parish. And if any woman servant shall have a bastard child by a negro, or mulatto,

Women servants having bastards by negroes.

over and above the years service due to her master or owner, she shall immediately, upon the expiration of her time to her then present master or owner, pay down to the church-wardens of the parish wherein such child shall be born, for the use of the said parish, fifteen pounds current money of Virginia, or be by them sold for five years, to the use aforesaid: And if a free christian white woman shall have such bastard child, by a negro, or mulatto, for every such

offence, she shall, within one month after her delivery of such bastard child, pay to the church-wardens for the time being, of the parish wherein such child shall be born, for the use of the said parish fifteen pounds current money of Virginia, or be by them sold for five years to the use aforesaid: And in both the said cases, the church-wardens shall bind the said child to be a servant, until it shall be of thirty one years of age.

Or free women.

How long the child to be bound.

XIX. And for a further prevention of that abominable mixture and spurious issue, which hereafter may increase in this her majesty's colony and dominion, as well by English, and other white men and women intermarrying with negros or mulattos, as by their unlawful coition with them, *Be it enacted, by the authority aforesaid, and it is hereby enacted*, That whatsoever English, or other white man or woman, being free, shall intermarry with a negro or mulatto man or woman, bond or free, shall, by judgment of the county court, be committed to prison, and there remain, during the space of six months, without bail or mainprize; and shall forfeit and pay ten pounds current money of Virginia, to the use of the parish, as aforesaid.

Penalty on white persons marrying with negroes.

XX. *And be it further enacted*, That no minister of the church of England, or other minister, or person whatsoever, within this colony and dominion, shall hereafter wittingly presume to marry a white man with a negro or mulatto woman; or to marry a white woman with a negro or mulatto man, upon pain of forfeiting and paying, for every such marriage the sum of ten thousand pounds of tobacco; one half to our sovereign lady the Queen, her heirs and successors, for and towards the support of the government, and the contingent charges thereof; and the other half to the informer; To be

On ministers marrying them.

recovered, with costs, by action of debt, bill, plaint, or information, in any court of record within this her majesty's colony and dominion, wherein no essoin, protection, or wager of law, shall be allowed.

XXI. And because poor people may not be destitute of emploiment, upon suspicion of being servants, and servants also kept from running away, *Be it enacted, by the authority aforesaid, and it is hereby enacted,* That every servant, when his or her time of service shall be expired, shall repair to the court of the county where he or she served the last of his or her time, and there, upon sufficient testimony, have his or her freedom entered; and a certificate thereof from the clerk of the said court, shall be sufficient to authorise any person to entertain or hire such servant, without any danger of this law. And if it shall at any time happen, that such certificate is worn out, or lost, the said clerk shall grant a new one, and therein also recite the accident happened to the old one. And whoever shall hire such servant, shall take his or her certificate, and keep it, 'till the contracted time shall be expired. And if any person whatsoever, shall harbour or entertain any servant by importation, or by contract, or indenture made here, not having such certificate, he or she so offending, shall pay to the master or owner of such servant, sixty pounds of tobacco for every natural day he or she shall so harbour or entertain such runaway: To be recovered, with costs, by action of debt, in any court of record within this her majesty's colony and dominion, wherein no essoin, protection, or wager of law, shall be allowed. And also, if any runaway shall make use of a forged certificate, or after the same shall be delivered to any master or mistress, upon being hired, shall

Freedom of servants to be recorded.

Penalty for entertaining them without certificate.

Runaways forging or stealing certificates.

steal the same away, and thereby procure entertainment, the person entertaining such servant, upon such forged or stolen certificate, shall not be culpable by this law: But the said runaway, besides making reparation for the loss of time, and charges in recovery, and other penalties by this law directed, shall, for making use of such forged or stolen certificate, or for such theft aforesaid, stand two hours in the pillory, upon a court day: And the person forging such certificate, shall forfeit and pay ten pounds current money; one half thereof to be to her majesty, her heirs and successors, for and towards the support of this government, and the contingent charges thereof; and the other half to the master or owner of such servant, if he or she will inform or sue for the same, otherwise to the informer: To be recovered, with costs, by action of debt, bill, plaint or information, in any court of record in this her majesty's colony and dominion, wherein no essoin, protection, or wager of law, shall be allowed. And if any person or persons convict of forging such certificate, shall not immediately pay the said ten pounds, and costs, or give security to do the same within six months, he or she so convict, shall receive, on his or her bare back, thirty-nine lashes, well laid on, at the common whipping post of the county; and shall be thence discharged of paying the said ten pounds, and costs, and either of them.

XXII. *Provided,* That when any master or mistress shall happen to hire a runaway, upon a forged certificate, and a servant deny that he delivered any such certificate, the *Onus Probandi* shall lie upon the person hiring, who upon failure therein, shall be liable to the fines and penalties, for entertaining runaway servants, without certificate.

Runaways hired on a forged certificate.

XXIII. And for encouragement of all persons to take up runaways, *Be it enacted, by the authority aforesaid, and it is hereby enacted,* That for the taking up of every servant, or slave, if ten miles, or above, from the house or quarter where such servant, or slave was kept, there shall be allowed by the public, as a reward to the taker-up, two hundred pounds of tobacco; and if above five miles, and under ten, one hundred pounds of tobacco; Which said several rewards of two hundred, and one hundred pounds of tobacco, shall also be paid in the county where such taker-up shall reside, and shall be again levied by the public upon the master or owner of such runaway, for re-imbursement of the same to the public. And for the greater certainty in paying the said rewards and re-imbursement of the public, every justice of the peace before whom such runaway shall be brought, upon the taking up, shall mention the proper name and sur-name of the taker-up, and the county of his or her residence, together with the time and place of taking up the said runaway; and shall also mention the name of the said runaway, and the proper-name and sur-name of the master or owner of such runaway, and the county of his or herresidence, together with the distance of miles, in the said justice's judgment, from the place of taking up the said runaway, to the house or quarter where such runaway was kept.

XXIV. *Provided,* That when any negro, or other runaway, that doth not speak English, and cannot, or through obstinacy will not, declare the name of his or her masters or owner, that then it shall be sufficient for the said justice to certify the same, instead of the name of such runaway, and the proper name and sur-name of his or her master or owner, and the county of his or her residence and distance of miles, as aforesaid; and in such case, shall, by his warrant, order the said runaway to be conveyed to the public gaol, of this country, there to be continued prisoner until the master or owner shall be known; who, upon paying the charges of the imprisonment, or giving caution to the prison-keeper for the same, together with the reward of two hundred or one hundred pounds of tobacco, as the case shall be, shall have the said runaway restored.

XXV. And further, the said justice of the peace, when such runaway shall be brought before him, shall by his warrant commit the said runaway to the next constable, and therein also order him to give the said runaway so many lashes as the said justice shall think fit, not exceeding the number of thirty-nine; and then to be conveyed from constable to constable, until the said runaway shall be carried home, or to the country gaol, as aforesaid, every constable through whose hands the said runaway shall pass, giving a receipt at the delivery; and every constable failing to execute such warrant according to the tenor thereof, or refusing to give such receipt, shall forfeit and pay two hundred pounds of tobacco to the church-wardens of the parish wherein such failure shall be, for the use of the poor of the said parish: To be recovered, with costs, by action of debt, in any court of record in this her majesty's colony and dominion, wherein no essoin, protection or wager of law, shall be allowed. And such corporal punishment shall not deprive the master or owner of such runaway of the other satisfaction here in this act appointed to be made upon such servant's running away.

XXVI. *Provided always, and be it further enacted,* That when any servant or

over the bay.

slave, in his or her running away, shall have crossed the great bay of Chesapeak, and shall be brought before a justice of the peace, the said justice shall, instead of committing such runaway to the constable, commit him or her to the sheriff, who is hereby required to receive every such runaway, according to such warrant, and to cause him, her, or them, to be transported again across the bay, and delivered to a constable there; and shall have, for all his trouble and charge herein, for every such servant or slave, five hundred pounds of tobacco, paid by the public; which shall be re-imbursed again by the master or owner of such runaway, as aforesaid, in manner aforesaid.

Sheriff's fee.

XXVII. *Provided also*, That when any runaway servant that shall have crossed the said bay, shall get up into the country, in any county distant from the bay, that then, in such case, the said runaway shall be committed to a constable, to be conveyed from constable to constable, until he shall be brought to a sheriff of some county adjoining to the said bay of Chesapeak, which sheriff is also hereby required, upon such warrant, to receive such runaway, under the rules and conditions aforesaid; and cause him or her to be conveyed as aforesaid; and shall have the reward, as aforesaid.

Run-aways crossing the bay.

XXVIII. And for the better preventing of delays in returning of such runaways, *Be it enacted*, That if any sheriff, under sheriff, or other officer of, or belonging to the sheriffs, shall cause or suffer any such runaway (so committed for passage over the bay) to work, the said sheriff, to whom such runaway shall be so committed shall forfeit and pay to the master or owner, of every such servant or slave, so put to work, one thousand pounds of tobacco; To be recovered, with costs, by action of debt, bill,

Penalty on sheriff's suffering run-aways to work.

plaint, or information, in any court of record within this her majesty's colony and dominion, wherein no essoin, protection, or wager of law, shall be allowed.

XXIX. *And be it enacted, by the authority aforesaid and it is hereby enacted*, That if any constable, or sheriff, into whose hands a runaway servant or slave shall be committed, by virtue of this act, shall suffer such runaway to escape, the said constable or sheriff shall be liable to the action of the party grieved, for recovery of his damages, at the common law with costs.

Suffering to escape.

XXX. *And also be it enacted, by the authority aforesaid, and it is hereby enacted*, That every runaway servant, upon whose account, either of the rewards aforementioned shall be paid, for taking up, shall for every hundred pounds of tobacco so paid by the master or owner, serve his or her said master or owner, after his or her time by indenture, custom, or former order of court, shall be expired, one calendar month and an half, and moreover, shall serve double the time such servant shall be absent in such running away; and shall also make reparation, by service, to the said master or owner, for all necessary disbursements and charges, in pursuit and recovery of the said runaway; to be adjudged and allowed in the county court, after the rate of one year for eight hundred pounds of tobacco, and so proportion ably for a greater or lesser quantity.

Run-aways to repay all ex-pences.

To be allowed by county court.

XXXI. *Provided*, That the masters or owners of such runaways, shall carry them to court the next court held for the said county, after the recovery of such runaway, otherwise it shall be in the breast of the court to consider the occasion of delay, and to hear, or refuse the claim, according to their discretion, without appeal, for the refusal.

Proviso.

XXXII. *And also be it enacted, by the authority aforesaid, and it is hereby enacted,* That no master, mistress, or overseer of a family, shall knowingly permit any slave, not belonging to him or her, to be and remain upon his or her plantation, above four hours at any one time, without the leave of such slave's master, mistress, or overseer, on penalty of one hundred and fifty pounds of tobacco to the informer; cognizable by a justice of the peace of the county wherein such offence shall be committed.

Penalty for permitting slaves of others to remain on a plantation.

XXXIII. *Provided also,* That if any runaway servant, adjudged to serve for the charges of his or her pursuit and recovery, shall, at the time, he or she is so adjudged, repay and satisfy, or give good security before the court, for repaiment and satisfaction of the same, to his or her master or owner, within six months after, such master or owner shall be obliged to accept thereof, in lieu of the service given and allowed for such charges and disbursements.

Runaway servants may give security to repay expenses.

XXXIV. And if any slave resist his master, or owner, or other person, by his, or her order, correcting such slave, and shall happen to be killed in such correction, it shall not be accounted felony; but the master, owner, and every such other person so giving correction, shall be free and acquit of all punishment and accusation for the same, as if such accident had never happened: And also, if any negro, mulatto, or Indian, bond or free, shall at any time, lift his or her hand, in opposition against any christian, not being negro, mulatto, or Indian, he or she so offending, shall, for every such offence, proved by the oath of the party, receive on his or her bare back, thirty lashes, well laid on; cognizable by a justice of the peace for that county wherein such offence shall be committed.

Killing slaves, under correction, no felony.

Penalty on slave resisting a white person.

XXXV. *And also be it enacted, by the authority aforesaid, and it is hereby enacted,* That no slave go armed with gun, sword, club, staff, or other weapon, nor go from off the plantation and seat of land where such slave shall be appointed to live, without a certificate of leave in writing, for so doing, from his or her master, mistress, or overseer; And if any slave shall be found offending herein, it shall be lawful for any person or persons to apprehend and deliver such slave to the next constable or head-borough, who is hereby enjoined and required, without further order or warrant, to give such slave twenty lashes on his or her bare back, well laid on, and so send him or her home: And all horses, cattle, and hogs, now belonging, or that hereafter shall be long to any slave, or of any slaves mark in this her majesty's colony and dominion, shall be seised and sold by the church-wardens of the parish, wherein such horses, cattle, or hogs shall be, and the profit thereof applied to the use of the poor of the said parish: And also, if any damage shall be hereafter committed by any slave living at a quarter where there is no christian overscer, the master or owner of such slave shall liable to action for the trespass and damage, as if the same had been done by him or herself.

Guns, &c. found in possession of slaves.

Horses, &c. belonging to slaves may be seized.

Owners of slaves, at a quarter, without an overseer liable for their trespasses.

XXXVI. *And also it is hereby enacted and declared,* That baptism of slaves doth not exempt them from bondage; and that all children shall be bond or free, according to the condition of their mothers, and the particular directions of this act.

Baptism of slaves. Children bond, or free, according to condition of their mothers.

XXXVII. And whereas, many times, slaves run away and lie out, hid and lurking in swamps, woods, and other obscure places, killing hogs, and committing other injuries to the inhabitants of this her majesty's colony and dominion, *Be it therefore enacted, by the authority*

Outlying slaves how apprehended.

aforesaid, *and it is hereby enacted,* That in all such cases, upon intelligence given of any slaves lying out, as aforesaid, any two justices (*Quorum unus*) of the peace of the county wherein such slave is supposed to lurk or do mischief, shall be and are impowered and required to issue proclamation against all such slaves, reciting their names, and owners names, if they are known, and thereby requiring them, and every of them, forthwith to surrender themselves; and also impowering the sheriff of the said county, to take such power with him, as he shall think fit and necessary, for the effectual apprehending such out-lying slave or slaves, and go in search of them: Which proclamation shall be published on a Sabbath day, at the door of every church and chapel, in the said county, by the parish clerk, or reader, of the church, immediately after divine worship: And in case any slave, against whom proclamation hath been thus issued, and once published at any church or chapel, as aforesaid, stay out, and do not immediately return home, it shall be lawful for any person or persons whatsoever, to kill and destroy such slaves by such ways and means as he, she, or they shall think fit, without accusation or impeachment of and crime for the same: And if any slave, that hath run away and lain out as aforesaid, shall be apprehended by the sheriff, or any other person, upon the application of the owner of the said slave, it shall and may be lawful for the county court, to order such punishment to the said slave, either by dismembring, or any other way, not touching his life, as they in their discretion shall think fit, for the reclaiming any such incorrigible slave, and terrifying others from the like practices.

When they may be killed.

When may be dismembered.

XXXVIII. *Provided always, and it is further enacted,* That for every slave killed, in pursuance of this act, or put to death by law, the master or owner of such slave shall be paid by the public:

XXXIX. And to the end, the true value of every slave killed, or put to death, as aforesaid, may be the better known; and by that means, the assembly the better enabled, to make a suitable allowance thereupon, *Be it enacted,* That upon application of the master or owner of any such slave, to the court appointed for proof of public claims, the said court shall value the slave in money, and the clerk of the court shall return a certificate thereof to the assembly, with the rest of the public claims.

XL. And for the better putting this act in due execution, and that no servants or slaves may have pretense of ignorance hereof, *Be it also enacted,* That the church-wardens of each parish in this her majesty's colony and dominion, at the charge of the parish, shall provide a true copy of this act, and cause entry thereof to be made in the register book of each parish respectively; and that the parish clerk, or reader of each parish, shall, on the first sermon Sundays in September and March, annually, after sermon or divine service is ended, at the door of every church and chapel in their parish, publish the same; and the sheriff of each county shall, at the next court held for the county, after the last day of February, yearly, publish this act, at the door of the court-house: And every sheriff making default herein, shall forfeit and pay six hundred pounds of tobacco; one half to her majesty, her hens, and successors, for and towards the support of the government; and the other half to the informer. And every parish clerk, or reader, making default herein, shall, for each time so offending, forfeit and pay

Value of slaves killed, to be repaid by the public.

Court of claims to certify the value.

This act to be registered in each parish, and read.

six hundred pounds of tobacco; one half whereof to be to the informer; and the other half to the poor of the parish, wherein such omission shall be: To be recovered, with costs, by action of debt, bill, plaint, or information, in any court of record in this her majesty's colony and dominion, wherein no essoin, protection, or wager of law, shall be allowed.

Repealing clause.

XLI. *And be it further enacted,* That all and every other act and acts, and every clause and article thereof, heretofore made, for so much thereof as relates to servants and slaves, or to any other matter or thing whatsoever, within the purview of this act, is and are hereby repealed, and made void, to all intents and purposes, as if the same had never been made.

Questions

1. How does this law define the status of servants and slaves? Who can and cannot be enslaved? How are servants and slaves to be treated differently?
2. What powers does the law give to masters to control and punish slaves? Why would masters feel they needed such powers?
3. How does the law limit slaveholders' authority? Why?
4. When the law states the need to prevent "that abominable mixture and spurious issue," what does it mean? What role did race play in the larger story of slavery in late seventeenth- and early eighteenth-century Virginia?
5. What measures did Virginia's planters take to prevent slaves from running away? What other prohibitions limited slaves' ability to resist their enslavement?

7.5   The Diary of Virginia Planter William Byrd II

Among the wealthiest and most influential planters in eighteenth-century Virginia, William Byrd II controlled tobacco plantations, mills, and trade operations across a wide swath of Virginia's tidewater region. His plantation at Westover, about twenty-five miles west of Williamsburg, was one of the largest and most profitable in the region. Byrd also occupied important political offices in Virginia, including a place on the Council of State and a term as the receiver-general. For more than thiry years, Byrd kept a daily journal written in a secret code, pieces of which were discovered and translated in the twentieth century. This selection contains passages from years 1709–1712, tracing the relationship between Byrd and two people he considered his dependents: his wife, Lucy Parke Byrd, and his personal slave, Eugene.

1709

FEBRUARY

8. I rose at 5 o'clock this morning and read a chapter in Hebrew and 200 verses in Homer's *Odyssey*. I ate milk for breakfast. I said my prayers. Jenny and Eugene were whipped. I danced my dance. I read law in the morning and Italian in the afternoon. I ate tough chicken for dinner. The boat came with the pork from Appomattox and was cut. In the evening I walked about the plantation. I said my prayers. I had good thoughts, good health, and good humor this day, thanks be to God Almighty.

APRIL

6. I rose before 6 o'clock and read two chapters in Hebrew and 200 verses in Homer's *Odyssey*. I said my prayers devoutly. My wife and I disagreed about employing a gardener. I ate milk for breakfast. John made an end of [trimming] the boat, which he performed very well. I settled my

*Louis B. Wright and Marion Tinling, eds., *The Secret Diary of William Byrd of Westover, 1709–1712* (Richmond, VA: Dietz Press, 1941).

accounts and read Italian. I ate nothing but fish for dinner and a little asparagus. We played at billiards. I read more Italian. In the evening we walked about the plantation after I read in Dr. Lister's book to the ladies. My wife and I continued very cool. I said my prayers, and had good health, good thoughts and good humor, thanks be to God Almighty.

7. I rose before 6 o'clock and read two chapters in Hebrew and 250 verses in Homer's *Odyssey* and made an end of it. I said my prayers devoutly. I ate milk for breakfast. I danced my dance. The men began to work this day to dig for brick. I settled my accounts and read Italian. I reproached my wife with ordering the old beef to be kept and the fresh beef used first, contrary to good management, on which she was pleased to be very angry and this put me out of humor. I ate nothing but boiled beef for dinner. I went away presently after dinner to look after my people. When I returned I read more Italian and then my wife came and begged my pardon and we were friends again. I read in Dr. Lister again very late. I said my prayers. I had good health, good thoughts, and bad humor, unlike a philosopher.

8. I rose after 6 o'clock this morning and read a chapter in Hebrew and 150 verses in Homer's last work. I said my prayers and ate milk for breakfast. I danced my dance. My wife and I had another foolish quarrel about my saying she listened on the top of the stairs, which I suspected, in jest. However, I bore it with patience and she came soon after and begged my pardon. I settled my accounts and read some Dutch. Just before dinner Mr. Custis came and dined with us. He told us that my father Parke instead of being killed was married to his housekeeper which is more improbable. He told us that the distemper continued to rage extremely on the other side the Bay and had destroyed abundance of people. I did not keep to my rule of eating but the one dish. We played at billiards and walked about the plantation. I said my prayers and had good humor, good health, and good thoughts, thanks be to God Almighty. The Indian woman died this evening, according to a dream I had last night about her.

9. I rose at 5 o'clock and read a chapter in Hebrew and 150 verses in Homer. I said my prayers

devoutly and ate milk for breakfast. My wife and I had another scold about mending my shoes but it was soon over by her submission. I settled my accounts and read Dutch. I ate nothing but cold roast beef and asparagus for dinner. In the afternoon Mr. Custis complained of a pain in his side for which he took a sweat of snakeroot. I read more Dutch and took a little nap. In the evening we took a walk about the plantation. My people made an end of planting the corn field. I had an account from Rappahannock that the same distemper began to rage there that had been so fatal on the Eastern Shore. I had good health, good thoughts and good humor, thanks be to God Almighty. I said my prayers.

17. I rose at 5 o'clock and read a chapter in Hebrew and 150 verses in homer. I said my prayers, and ate milk for breakfast. I danced my dance. The child had her fever again last night for which I gave her a vomit this morning, which worked very well. Anaka was whipped yesterday for stealing the rum and filling the bottle up with water. I went to church, where were abundance of people, among whom was Mrs. H-m-l-n, a very handsome woman. Colonel Eppes and his wife, with Captain Worsham came to dine with me, who told me that Tom Haynes as gone out of his wits. I sent Tom and Eugene to Mr. Harvey's to meet me tomorrow morning. I took a walk about the plantation. I said my prayers. I had good health, good thoughts, and good humor, thanks be to God Almighty.

JUNE

9. I rose at 5 o'clock and read two chapters in Hebrew and some Greek in Josephus. I neglected to say my prayers, for which God forgive me. I ate milk for breakfast. I received a very foolish letter from Robin Bolling which contained many ridiculous arguments to justify his late foolish proceedings, to which I sent him a full answer. I ate mutton and sallet for dinner. My Eugene ran away this morning for no reason but because he had not done anything yesterday. I sent my people after him but in vain. The sloop came from Falling Creek with copper, timber, and planks.

In the evening Captain Keeling came to see us to account with me for the quitrents of New Kent. I ate some supper with him, contrary to custom. I neglected to say my prayers, for which God forgive me. I had good health, good thoughts, and good humor, thanks be to God Almighty. I danced my dance.

10. I rose at 5 o'clock this morning but could not read anything because of Captain Keeling, but I played at billiards with him and won half a crown of him and the Doctor. George B-th brought home my boy Eugene. I ate milk for breakfast, but neglected to say my prayers, for which God forgive me. The Captain and I had some discourse about the philosopher's stone which he [is following with great diligence]. He stayed to dinner. I ate mutton for dinner. In the afternoon he went away. I read some Greek in Homer. In the evening I took a walk about the plantation. Eugene was whipped for running away and had the [bit] put on him. I said my prayers and had good health, good thoughts, and good humor, thanks be to God Almighty.

NOVEMBER

2. I rose at 6 o'clock and read a chapter in Hebrew and some Greek in Lucian. I said my prayers and ate milk for breakfast, and settled some accounts, and then went to court where we made an end of the business. We went to dinner about 4 o'clock and I ate boiled beef again. In the evening I went to Dr. [Barret's] where my wife came this afternoon. Here I found Mrs. Chiswell, my sister Custis, and other ladies. We sat and talked till about 11 o'clock and then retired to our chambers. I played at [r-m] with Mrs. Chiswell and kissed her on the bed till she was angry and my wife also was uneasy about it, and cried as soon as the company was gone. I neglected to say my prayers, which I should not have done, because I ought to beg pardon for the lust I had for another man's wife. However I had good health, good thoughts, and good humor, thanks be to God Almighty.

30. I rose at 3 o'clock and read two chapters in Hebrew and some Greek in Cassius. I went to

bed again and lay till 7. I said my prayers, danced my dance, and ate milk for breakfast. Eugene was whipped for pissing in bed and Jenny for concealing it. I settled several accounts. I ate boiled beef for dinner. In the afternoon I played at billiards with my wife and then took a walk about the plantation to look over my affairs. I said my prayers. In the evening I read some Italian. About 8 o'clock we went to bed and I had good health, good thoughts, and good humor, thanks be to God Almighty.

DECEMBER

1. I rose at 4 o'clock and read two chapters in Hebrew and some Greek in Cassius. I said my prayers and ate milk for breakfast. I danced my dance. Eugene was whipped again for pissing in bed and Jenny for concealing it. About 11 o'clock came Captain Stith and his wife, not on a visit but Mrs. Stith came to desire me justify her to Mrs. Harrison that she had not told me that Mrs. Harrison was delivered of two children before her time. I wrote to Mrs. Harrison to assure her that Mrs. Stith had never told me any such thing. But my wife could not deny but she had told that Mrs. Stith told her so. Thus women will be [p-r-t]. I denied her and so did Mrs. Mallory and Bannister's sister. In the afternoon the company went away. I took a walk [about] the plantation. In the evening I read Italian. I said my prayers and had good health, good thoughts, and good humor, thanks be to God Almighty.

3. I rose at 5 o'clock and read two chapters in Hebrew and some Greek in Cassius. I said my prayers and ate milk for breakfast. I danced my dance. Eugene pissed abed again for which I made him drink a pint of piss. I settled some accounts and read some news. About 12 o'clock I went to court where I found little good company. However I persuaded Mr. Anderson and Colonel Eppes to come and dine with me. I ate a venison pasty for dinner. In the evening Mr. Anderson and I walked to Mr. Harrison's where we found Frank W-l-s and James Burwell and Isham Randolph. Here I ate custard and was merry. I stayed till 9 o'clock and when I came home my wife was in bed. I neglected

to say my prayers and had good health, good thoughts, and good humor, thanks be to God Almighty.

10. I rose at 7 o'clock and said a short prayer. Then I walked with my brother to see the dam he was making for a mill. I ate milk for breakfast. About 10 o'clock I took my leave and Colonel Duke was so complaisant that he came about three miles with me. About 1 o'clock I got home, where I found all well, thanks be to God. Eugene had pissed in bed for which I gave him a pint of piss to drink. I ate fish for dinner. In the afternoon Mr. C-s came to visit me. We played at billiards and then took a walk. In the afternoon I read a little Italian and said a short prayer. I had good health; good thoughts, and good humor, thanks be to God Almighty.

13. I rose at 5 o'clock and read a chapter in Hebrew and some Greek in Cassius. I said my prayers and ate milk for breakfast. I danced my dance. Last night I gave my wife a flourish and this morning I quarreled with her about her neglect of the family. I settled some accounts. About 12 o'clock Mr. J—[Gee ?] came and dined with me. He told me the Doctor was extremely ill, which made me resolve to go there in the afternoon. I ate fish for dinner and as soon as I had dined I rode with Mr. J—to Captain Stith's where I found the Doctor in a very weak condition. We prayed by him and I took my leave, committing him to God, before whom he was likely to appear very soon. Then I returned home with Mr. Harrison, and Mr. Anderson, and Mr. Cocke who had all been to take leave of the poor Doctor. In the evening I read some Latin. I neglected to say my prayers, but had good health, good thoughts, and good humor, thanks be to God Almighty.

16. I rose at 5 o'clock and read a chapter in Hebrew and some Greek in Cassius. I said my prayers and ate [milk for] breakfast. My wife had a great pain in her belly and so took a purge which worked very well. Eugene was whipped for doing nothing yesterday. I danced my dance. I settled several accounts. I ate roast mutton for dinner. My [wife] was better after her physic, which worked 12 times. In the afternoon I played at piquet with my wife to divert her. Peter Hamlin came over. In the evening I took a walk about the plantation and

found things in good order. I read some Latin. I said my prayers and had good thoughts, good humor, and good health, thanks be to God Almighty.

1710

APRIL

21. I rose at 5 o'clock and read two chapters in Hebrew and some Greek in Homer. I said my prayers and ate milk for breakfast. I had abundance of people come to see me. About 8 o'clock I went to see the President and then went to court. I settled some accounts first. Two of the negroes were tried and convicted for treason. I wrote a letter to England and then went to court again. About 3 o'clock I returned to my chambers again and found above a girl who I persuaded to go with me into my chambers but she would not. I ate some cake and cheese and then went to Mr. Bland's where I ate some boiled beef. Then I went to the President's where we were merry till 11 o'clock. Then I stole away. I said a short prayer but notwithstanding committed uncleanness in bed. I had good health, bad thoughts, and good humor, thanks be to God Almighty.

MAY

4. I rose at 6 o'clock and read a chapter in Hebrew and some Greek in Anacreon. I said my prayers and ate milk for breakfast. Eugene and another boy were sick and my wife was not well. I danced my dance. My sloop came from Falling Creek, where she left all well, thank God. I settled some accounts and then took a walk before dinner. I ate hashed mutton. In the afternoon my wife and I played at billiards and then took a nap. I settled more accounts and then took another walk about the plantation. The two boys grew better. In the evening I read some French. I said my prayers and had good health, good thoughts, and good humor, thank God Almighty. My sloop went this night to Appomattox for tobacco.

JUNE

1. I rose at 6 o'clock and because I was not easy in my belly I took some [purge 1-p of scurvy grass].

They worked but little. I read a chapter in Hebrew and some Greek in Anacreon. I said my prayers and drank some broth for breakfast. The child was a little better. Colonel Hill and Mr. Anderson called to see us on their way over the river. I wrote a letter to England. My purge worked but a little. I ate some boiled chicken for dinner. In the afternoon we played at billiards and then cut some [sage]. Then I set my closet in order. In the evening I took a walk and met the new negroes which Mr. Bland had bought for me to the number of 26 for £23 apiece. This evening the sloop likewise came from above where all was well. I said my prayers and had good health, good thoughts, and good humor, thanks be to God Almighty.

2. I rose at 6 o'clock and read a chapter in Hebrew and some Greek in Pindar. I said my prayers and ate bread and butter for breakfast. I sent away the sloop to Appomattox. The child was worse and his nurse was very ill. I gave her a vomit which worked very well. Colonel Eppes called here. I ate cold mutton for dinner. In the afternoon I read some English. About 5 o'clock Robin Hix and Robin Mumford came to discourse about the skin trade. We gave them some mutton and sallet for supper. In the evening I did not walk because of my company. Robin Hix asked me to pay £70 for two negroes which he intended to buy of John [Evans] which I agreed to in hope of gaining the trade. I neglected to say my prayers but was griped in my belly and had indifferent bad humor.

3. I rose at 6 o'clock and as soon as I came out news was brought that the child was very ill. We went out and found him just ready to die and he died about 8 o'clock in the morning. God gives and God takes away; blessed be the name of God. Mrs. Harrison and Mr. Anderson and his wife and some other company came to see us in our affliction. My wife was much afflicted but I submitted to His judgment better, notwithstanding I was very sensible of my loss, but God's will be done. Mr. Anderson and his wife with Mrs. B-k-r dined here. I ate roast mutton. In the afternoon I was griped in my belly very much but it grew better towards the night. In the afternoon it rained and was fair again in the evening. My poor wife and I walked in the garden. In the evening I neglected

to say my prayers, had indifferent health, good thoughts, and good humor, thanks be to God Almighty.

4. I rose at 6 o'clock and read nothing because I took physic which did not work. I said my prayers and ate water gruel. I had no more than two stools but was a little griped. I was so indisposed that I could not settle to anything. My wife had several fits of tears for our dear son but kept within the bounds of submission. I ate hashed mutton for dinner. In the afternoon we walked a little abroad but it was so hot we soon returned. My dinner griped me again but not so much as it did. My man Tom returned from Williamsburg and brought me letters from Green Springs and Queen's Creek. Jimmy brought a coffin from Falling Creek made of walnut tree. In the evening we took a walk. I said my prayers and had good thoughts, good humor, and indifferent good health, thank God Almighty.

5. I rose at 6 o'clock and read a chapter in Hebrew and some Greek in Pindar. I said my prayers and ate water gruel for breakfast. Mrs. Ann B-k-r came to assist my wife. I gave John W-l-r-c a note to Colonel Digges for a negro. My gripes continued still, and made me uneasy. About 12 o'clock my brother Custis came without my sister who could not come because she was big with child. He could tell no news. I ate roast veal for breakfast [*sic*]. In the afternoon I was worse of my gripes. My wife continued very melancholy, notwithstanding I comforted her as well as I could. I took a glyster in the evening which worked a I little. Then we walked in the garden. I said my prayers. and had good thoughts, good humor, but indifferent health, thank God Almighty.

6. I rose at 6 o'clock and read two chapters in Hebrew and no Greek because we prepared to receive company for the funeral. I said my prayers and ate cake and water gruel for breakfast. About 10 o'clock Colonel Hill, Mr. Anderson and his wife came. Half an hour after my sister Duke came without my brother who could not leave his business, and about 11 came my cousin Harrison with her son and daughter, Mr. C-s and Mr. Doyley. We gave them burnt claret and cake. About 2 o'clock we went with the corpse to the churchyard and as soon as the service was begun it rained very hard so

that we were forced to leave the parson and go into the church porch but Mr. Anderson stayed till the service was finished. About 3 o'clock we went to dinner and I ate boiled beef for dinner. The company stayed till the evening and then went away. Mr. Custis and I took a walk about the plantation. Two of the new negroes were taken sick and I gave each of them a vomit which worked well. I said my prayers and had good health, good thoughts, and better health [*sic*], thank God Almighty.

AUGUST

31. I rose at 5 o'clock and read two chapters in Hebrew, some Greek in Lucian. I said my prayers and ate milk for breakfast. I danced my dance. The sick people were better, thank God. Eugene was whipped for cheating in his work and so was little Jenny. About 11 o'clock I went to see Colonel Hill to condole him over the death of his wife, who died in England. I found him in great concern; however he came out to me and talked a little. Mr. Drury Stith came [there] likewise on the same errand. About 3 o'clock we went to dinner and I ate boiled pork for dinner. I stayed there till about 6 o'clock and then rode home, where I found all well and the sick people better. In the evening I said my prayers and read some news. I had good health, good thoughts, and good humor, thanks be to God Almighty.

1711

JANUARY

31. I rose at 5 o'clock and read two chapters in Hebrew and some Greek in Lucian. I said my prayers and ate boiled milk for breakfast. My wife quarreled with me about not sending for Mrs. Dunn when it rained to [lend her John]. She threatened to kill herself but had more discretion. I danced my dance and then read some English about [love]. It rained again all the morning. I ate some roast shoat for dinner. In the afternoon Nurse was taken sick of a [purging]. I took a walk to see the boatwright at work. My wife came into good humor again and we resolved to live for the future in love and peace. At night I ate some bat-

tered eggs with her and drank some cider. I said my prayers and had good health, good thoughts, and good humor, thank God Almighty. The wind was still northeast as it was when the moon was at full and since that a good deal of rain has fallen. The boy whose thigh was swollen grew worse.

FEBRUARY

2. I rose at 5 o'clock and read a chapter in Hebrew and some Greek in Lucian. I said my prayers and ate boiled milk for breakfast. I danced my dance. I chastised Moll and Eugene for not doing their business on pretence of sickness. It was very fine weather and warm, thank God. I settled some accounts and then wrote a letter to Falling Creek. Then I read a little English. Then Mr. Dunn and I played at billiards and I gave him three and a go and beat him. I ate some boiled beef for dinner. In the afternoon Mr. Dunn and I went to Mrs. Harrison's where we found Colonel Hill and Mr. Gee and Mrs. Anderson. I bought two negroes of Mrs. Harrison for the Governor for £63. She was out of humor about her accounts. In the evening we returned home where we found all well. We drank some cider. I said my prayers and had good health, good thoughts, and good humor, thank God Almighty.

5. I rose about 8 o'clock and found my cold still worse. I said my prayers and ate milk and potatoes for breakfast. My wife and I quarreled about her pulling her brows. She threatened she would not go to Williamsburg if she might not pull them; I refused, however, and got the better of her, and maintained my authority. About 10 o'clock we went over the river and got to Colonel Duke's about 11. There I ate some toast and canary. Then we proceeded to Queen's Creek, where we found all well, thank God. We ate roast goose for supper. The women prepared to go to the Governor's the next day and my brother and I talked of old stories. My cold grew exceedingly bad so that I thought I should be sick. My sister gave me some sage tea and leaves of [s-m-n-k] which made me mad all night so that I could not sleep but was much disordered by it. I neglected to say my prayers in form but had good thoughts, good humor, and indifferent health, thank God Almighty.

APRIL

14. I rose at 6 o'clock and read nothing because of the company. I neglected to say my prayers and ate boiled milk for breakfast. Then I played at billiards with Mr. Mumford. I settled some accounts. About 11 o'clock Frank Eppes and Mr. Kennon went away but Mr. Mumford stayed. John Randolph called here on his way to Williamsburg. Captain Posford sent his boat to fetch Eugene and my trunk to carry them to Williamsburg. Mr. Mumford and I took a walk about the plantation till dinner. I ate some roast mutton for dinner. In the afternoon Mr. Mumford went away and Mr. Gee came and I gave him some seeds of the [u-n-y] tree. He stayed about an hour and then went away. Then came Captain L-th-m for some planks and drank some strong beer. In the evening it rained and hindered me from walking. Mr. G-r-1 came and told me all was well. I ate some supper with him and gave him some strong beer. I neglected to say my prayers but had good health, good thoughts, and good humor, thank God Almighty.

SEPTEMBER

28. I rose about 6 o'clock and read a chapter in Hebrew and some Greek in Lucian. I said my prayers and ate milk and rhubarb for breakfast. I danced my dance. The young ladies went away after breakfast. The weather was hot and fair. Eugene was whipped for neglecting his business when the company was here yesterday. I read some Latin in Terence till dinner and then I ate some boiled beef. In the afternoon we cleaned the new knives, forks, and spoons. Then I read some Latin again till the evening and then took a walk about the plantation. The weather continued fair and warm. I gave a vomit to a woman that came over to be cured of obstruction. At night I read more Latin in Terence.

OCTOBER

21. I rose about 6 o'clock and we began to pack up our paggage in order to return. We drank chocolate with the Governor and about 10 o'clock we took leave of the Nottoway town and the Indian boys went away with us that were designed for the College. The Governor made three proposals to the Tuscaroras: that they would join with the English to cut off those Indians that had killed the people of Carolina, that they should have 40 shillings for every head they brought in of those guilty Indians and be paid the price of a slave for all they brought in alive, and that they should send one of the chief men's sons out of every town to the College. I waited on the Governor about ten miles and then took leave of him and he went to Mr. Cargill's and I with Colonel Hill, Mr. Platt, and John Hardiman went to Colonel Harrison's where we got about 3 o'clock in the afternoon. About 4 we dined and I ate some boiled beef. My man's horse was lame for which he was let blood. At night I asked a negro girl to kiss me, and when I went to bed I was very cold because I pulled off my clothes after lying in them so long. I neglected to say my prayers but had good health, good thoughts, and good humor, thank God Almighty.

23. I rose about 7 o'clock and got ready for my journey, notwithstanding it rained. I said my prayers and ate boiled milk for breakfast. About 9 o'clock I took leave of my wife and daughter and was set over the creek and was angry with Tom for forgetting the strap of my portmantle and I was displeased with Eugene for forgetting his cape. It rained all the way I rode to Williamsburg, where I got about 3 o'clock pretty wet. Then I got ready to go to court that I might not lose my day and accordingly did save it. I made my honors to the Governor and to the gentlemen of the council and took my place. We sat in court till about 5 o'clock and then the Governor took me home to dinner and there I found Mrs. Russell returned from her travels. I ate boiled beef for dinner. The Governor told me that our design upon Canada had miscarried by the fault of the Admiral. About 8 o'clock we went to the coffeehouse where I played and won 50 shillings. About 10 I went to my lodgings and wrote a letter to my wife. I said my prayers and had good health, good thoughts, and good humor, thank God Almighty.

31. I rose about 7 o'clock and found it very cold. I read a chapter in Hebrew and some Greek

in Homer. I neglected to say my prayers but had chocolate for breakfast. About 10 o'clock I went to court where I sat till about 3 and then I went up stairs and danced my dance and wrote a letter to England. About 4 I returned to court and we sat till past 5. Then we went to dine at Marot's and I ate roast veal for dinner. About 8 o'clock we went to the coffeehouse and I had not been there half an hour before Eugene came and told me that my wife was at my lodgings. I instantly went home and found her there. She told me all was well at home, thank God, this morning. I neglected to say my prayers but had good health, good thoughts, and good humor, thank God Almighty. I rogered my wife. The weather was very cold.

DECEMBER

14. I rose about 7 o'clock and read a chapter in Hebrew and some Greek in Homer. I said my prayers and ate boiled milk for breakfast. It threatened rain; however I wrote a letter and sent Eugene home with it to let my wife know why I could not come. Several gentlemen came to my lodgings but about 10 o'clock I went to see Colonel Carter and found him better. Then I walked to the capitol where I danced my dance; then we went to Council and read some bills the third time and particularly Mr. Custis his bill. Then we examined Mr. Cary's accounts and found several articles wrongly charged. It rained very hard almost all day. About 4 o'clock we went to dinner and I ate a fricassee of turkey. Then we went to the coffeehouse and I won £5. About 11 o'clock I went home, where I said my prayers and had good health, good thoughts, and good humor, thank God Almighty.

31. I rose about 7 o'clock and read a chapter in Hebrew and six leaves in Lucian. I said my prayers and ate boiled milk for breakfast. The weather continued warm and clear. I settled my accounts and wrote several things till dinner. I danced my dance. I ate some turkey and chine for dinner. In the afternoon I weighed some money and then read some Latin in Terence and then Mr. Mumford came and told me my man Tony had been very sick but he was recovered

again, thank God. He told me Robin Bolling had been like to die and that he denied that he was the first to mention the imposition on skins which he certainly did. Then he and I took a walk about the plantation. When I returned I was out of humor to find the negroes all at work in our chambers. At night I ate some broiled turkey with Mr. Mumford and we talked and were merry all the evening. I said my prayers and had good health, good thoughts, and good humor, thank God Almighty. My wife and I had a terrible quarrel about whipping Eugene while Mr. Mumford was there but she had a mind to show her authority before company but I would not suffer it, which she took very ill; however for peace sake I made the first advance towards a reconciliation which I obtained with some difficulty and after abundance of crying. However it spoiled the mirth of the evening, but I was not conscious that I was to blame in that quarrel.

1712

JANUARY

1. I lay abed till 9 o'clock this morning to bring my wife into temper again and rogered her by way of reconciliation. I read nothing because Mr. Mumford was here, nor did I say my prayers, for the same reason. However I ate boiled milk for breakfast, and after my wife tempted me to eat some pancakes with her. Mr. Mumford and I went to shoot with our bows and arrows but shot nothing, and afterwards we played at billiards till dinner, and when we came we found Ben Harrison there, who dined with us. I ate some partridge for dinner. In the afternoon we played at billiards again and I won two bits. I had a letter from Colonel Duke by H-1 the bricklayer who came to offer his services to work for me. Mr. Mumford went away in the evening and John Bannister with him to see his mother. I took a walk about the plantation and at night we drank some mead of my wife's making which was very good. I gave the people some cider and a dram to the negroes. I read some Latin in Terence and had good health, good thoughts, and good humor, thank God Almighty. I said my prayers.

SEPTEMBER

18. I rose about 6 and had a sore throat; however I rose and read a chapter in Hebrew and some Greek in Herodian. I said my prayers and ate boiled milk for breakfast. The weather was very cool. I wrote three letters, two to Williamsburg, and one to Appomattox. My wife was disordered with her [m-d]. My man John was incommoded still with the piles. Mr. Catesby and I took a walk and I found Eugene asleep instead of being at work, for which I beat him severely. This is the first day we had a fire in the hall. I settled several accounts and then ate some hog's haslet. In the afternoon came Sam Good and bought two negroes of me for £60 towards paying for the land which I had of him. Then I settled more accounts till the evening and then took a walk about the plantation. At night I ate some milk and roast apples for my sore throat. I neglected to say my prayers but had good health, good thoughts, and good humor, thank God Almighty. My wife began this morning to take the bark again.

Questions

1. Describe a typical day for William Byrd. How would his day differ from that of others within his household?
2. How would you characterize the relationship between William and Lucy Byrd? What do these passages reveal about relationships between men and women in early eighteenth-century Virginia?
3. Discuss the relationship between Byrd and his slave Eugene. How can this document provide insight into master-slave relations more generally?
4. Discuss the relationship between high culture and base behavior, between Christian piety and patriarchal authority. Do you consider Byrd a hypocrite? Did he consider himself one?
5. What can these passages tell us about the economy of colonial Virginia? About politics?
6. Byrd wrote his diary in coded shorthand so that only he could read it. How does this influence your interpretation of his writings?

8

New England

Originating from the same country as their Virginia counterparts, New Englanders nonetheless produced a very different colonial society. Compared with the ships sailing to the Chesapeake, those bound for New England carried more Puritans and fewer Anglicans, more families and fewer single men, more "middling sorts" and fewer "sturdy beggars," more who would be free and fewer who would be slaves. Blessed and cursed with a colder climate and less yielding soil, and animated by an ethos of industry and entrepreneurialism, New Englanders farmed, fished, and logged; built and sailed ships—and prospered. In their houses and churches, they pored over scripture and prayed, examined themselves for signs of salvation, and as the generations passed, asked themselves from time to time if they had quite lived up to the expectations of those idealized early emigrants.

8.1   Winthrop's Vision of New England*

In the following sermon, John Winthrop expresses the ideals he hoped would shape New England society in New England. A lawyer, government official, and member of the English gentry, Winthrop (1588–1649) was also a devout and learned Puritan. He was a leading figure of Massachusetts's first decades, his fellow Puritans electing him governor twelve times. He wrote the sermon that follows in 1630 on the transatlantic crossing to America. Known as "A Modell of Christian Charity," it became one of the most influential sermons in American history. The selection here presents pages from its opening and closing sections.

A Modell of Christian Charity. Written on board the Arbella, on the Atlantic Ocean

By the Hon. John Winthrop Esqr. In his passage (with a great company of Religious people, of which Christian tribes he was the Brave Leader and famous Governor;) from the Island of Great Brittaine to New-England in the North America. Anno 1630.

CHRISTIAN CHARITIE

A Modell hereof

God Almighty in his most holy and wise providence, hath soe disposed of the condition of mankind, as in all times some must be rich, some

---

*John Winthrop, "A Modell of Christian Charity," in *Collections of the Massachusetts Historical Society*, 3d ser. (Boston: Charles C. Little and James Brown, 1838), vol. 1: 33–35, 44–48.

poore, some high and eminent in power and dignitie; others mean and in submission.

The Reason hereof.

1. *Reas.* First to hold conformity with the rest of his world, being delighted to show forth the glory of his wisdom in the variety and difference of the creatures, and the glory of his power in ordering all these differences for the preservation and good of the whole; and the glory of his greatness, that as it is the glory of princes to have many officers, soe this great king will have many stewards, counting himself more honoured in dispensing his gifts to man by man; than if he did it by his owne immediate hands.

2. *Reas.* Secondly that he might have the more occasion to manifest the work of his Spirit: first upon the wicked in moderating and restraining them: soe that the riche and mighty should not eate upp the poore nor the poore and dispised rise upp against and shake off theire yoake. 21y In the regenerate, in exerciseing his graces in them, as in the grate ones, theire love, mercy, gentleness, temperance &c., in the poore and inferior sorte, theire faithe, patience, obedience &c.

3. *Reas.* Thirdly, that every man might have need of others, and from hence they might be all knitt more nearly together in the Bonds of brotherly affection. From hence it appears plainly that noe man is made more honourable than another or more wealthy &c., out of any particular and singular respect to himselfe, but for the glory of his creator and the common good of the creature, man. Therefore, God still reserves the propperty of these gifts to himself as Ezek. 16. 17. he there calls wealthe, *his gold and his silver*, and Prov. 3. 9. he claims theire service as his due, *honor the Lord with thy riches* &c.—All men being thus (by divine providence) ranked into two sorts, riche and poore; under the first are comprehended all such as are able to live comfortably by their own meanes duely improved; and all others are poore according to the former distribution. There are two rules whereby we are to walk one towards another: Justice and Mercy. These are always distinguished in their act and in their object, yet may they both concurre in the same subject in eache respect; as sometimes there may be an occasion of showing

mercy to a rich man in some sudden danger or distresse, and alsoe doeing of meere justice to a poor man in regard of some perticular contract &c. There is likewise a double Lawe by which wee are regulated in our conversation towardes another; in both the former respects, the lawe of nature and the lawe of grace, or the morrall lawe or the lawe of the gospell, to omitt the rule of justice as not propperly belonging to this purpose otherwise than it may fall into consideration in some perticular eases. By the first of these lawes man as he was enabled soe withall is commanded to love his neighbour as himself. Upon this ground stands all the precepts of the morrall lawe, which concernes our dealings with men. To apply this to the works of mercy; this lawe requires two things. First that every man afford his help to another in every want or distresse. Secondly, that hee performe this out of the same affection which makes him carefull of his owne goods, according to that of our Savior, (Math.) *Whatsoever ye would that men should do to you.* This was practised by Abraham and Lot in entertaining the angells and the old man of Gibea. The lawe of Grace or of the Gospell hath some difference from the former; as in these respects, First the lawe of nature was given to man in the estate of innocency; this of the Gospell in the estate of regeneracy. 21y, the former propounds one man to another, as the same flesh and image of God; this as a brother in Christ allsoe, and in the communion of the same Spirit, and soe teacheth to put a difference betweene christians and others. *Doe good to all, especially to the household of faith*; upon this ground the Israelites were to putt a difference betweene the brethren of such as were strangers though not of the Canaanites.

31y. The Lawe of nature would give no rules for dealing with enemies, for all are to be considered as friends in the state of innocency, but the Gospell commands love to an enemy. Proofe. *If thine Enemy hunger, feed him; Love your Enemies, doe good to them that hate you.* Math. 5. 44.

This lawe of the Gospell propounds likewise a difference of seasons and occasions. There is a time when a christian must sell all and give to the poor, as they did in the Apostles times. There is a time allsoe when christians (though they give not all yet) must give beyond their abillity, as they of

Macedonia, Cor. 2, 6. Likewise community of perills calls for extraordinary liberality, and soe doth community in some speciall service for the churche. Lastly, when there is no other means whereby our christian brother may be relieved in his distress, we must help him beyond our ability rather than tempt God in putting him upon help by miraculous or extra ordinary meanes.

This duty of mercy is exercised in the kinds, Giving lending and forgiving.—. . .

It, rests now to make some application of this discourse, by the present designe, which gave the occasion of writing of it. Herein are 4 things to be propounded; *first* the persons, 21y the worke, 31y the end, 4thly the meanes.

1. *For the persons.* Wee are a company professing ourselves fellow members of Christ, in which respect onely though wee were absent from each other many miles, and had our imployments as farre distant, yet wee ought to account ourselves knitt together by this bond of love, and, live in the exercise of it, if wee would have comforte of our being in Christ. This was notorious in the practise of the Christians in former times; as is testified of the Waldenses, from the mouth of one of the adversaries *Æneas Sylvius* "mutuo ament pere antequam norunt," they use to love any of theire owne religion even before they were acquainted with them. 2nly for the *worke* wee have in hand. It is by a mutuall consent, through a speciall overvaluing providence and a more than an ordinary approbation of the Churches of Christ, to seeke out a place of cohabitation and Consorteshipp under a due forme of Government both ciuill and ecclesiasticall. In such cases as this, the care of the publique must oversway all private respects, by which, not only conscience, but meare civill pollicy, dothe binde us. For it is a true rule that particular Estates cannot subsist in the ruin of the publique. 31y The *end* is to improve our lives to doe more service to the Lord; the comforte and encrease of the body of Christe, whereof we are members; that ourselves and posterity may be the better preserved from the common corruptions of this evill world, to serve the Lord and worke out our Salvation under the power and purity of his holy ordinances. 4thly for the *meanes* whereby this must be effected. They are twofold, a conformity with the worke and end wee aime at. These wee see are extraordinary, therefore wee must not content ourselves with usuall ordinary meanes. Whatsoever wee did, or ought to have done, when wee liued in England, the same must wee doe, and more allsoe, where wee goe. That which the most in theire churches mainetaine as truthe in profession onely, wee must bring into familiar and constant practise; as in this duty of love, wee must love brotherly without dissimulation, wee must love one another with a pure hearte servently. Wee must beare one anothers burthens. We must not looke onely on our owne things, but allsoe on the things of our brethren. Neither must wee thinke that the Lord will beare with such faileings at our hands as he dothe from those among whome wee have lived; and that for these 3 Reasons; 1. In regard of the more neare bond of mariage between him and us, wherein hee hath taken us to be his, after a most strickt and peculiar manner, which will make them the more jealous of our love and obedience. Soe he tells the people of Israell, *you onely have I knowne of all the families of the Earthe, therefore will I punishe you for your Transgressions.* 21y, because *the Lord will be sanctified in them that come neare him.* We know that there were many that corrupted the service of the Lord; some setting upp altars before his owne; others offering both strange fire and strange sacrifices allsoe; yet there came noe fire from heaven, or other sudden judgement upon them, as did upon Nadab and Abihu, whoe yet wee may think did not sinne presumptuously. 31y When God gives a speciall commission he lookes to have it strictly observed in every article. When he gave Saule a commission to destroy Amaleck, Hee indented with him upon certain articles, and because hee failed in one of the least, and that upon a faire pretense, it lost him the kingdom, which should have beene his reward, if hee had observed his commission. Thus stands the cause betweene God and us. We are entered into Covenant with Him for this worke. Wee have taken out a commission. The Lord hath given us leave to drawe our own

articles. Wee have professed to enterprise these and those accounts, upon these and those ends. Wee have hereupon besought Him of favour and blessing. Now if the Lord shall please to heare us, and bring us in peace to the place we desire, then hath hee ratified this covenant and sealed our Commission, and will expect a strict performance of the articles contained in it; but if wee shall neglect the observation of these articles which are the ends wee have propounded, and, dissembling with our God, shall fall to embrace this present world and prosecute our carnall intentions, seeking great things for ourselves and our posterity, the Lord will surely breake out in wrathe against us; be revenged of such a [sinful] people and make us knowe the price of the breache of such a covenant.

Now the onely way to avoyde this shipwracke, and to provide for our posterity, is to followe the counsell of Micah, *to doe justly, to love mercy, to walk humbly with our God.* For this end, wee must be knitt together, in this worke, as one man. Wee must entertaine each other in brotherly affection. Wee must be willing to abridge ourselves of our superfluities, for the supply of other's necessities. Wee must uphold a familiar commerce together in all meekeness, gentlenes, patience and liberality. Wee must delight in eache other; make other's conditions our oune; rejoice together, mourne together, labour and suffer together, allwayes having before our eyes our commission and community in the worke, as members of the same body. Soe shall wee *keepe the unitie of the spirit in the bond of peace.* The Lord will be our God, and delight to dwell among us, as his oune people, and will command a blessing upon us in all our wayes. Soe that wee shall see much more of his wisdome, power, goodness and truthe, than formerly wee have been acquainted with. Wee shall finde that the God of Israell is among us, when ten of us shall be able to resist a thousand of our enemies; when hee shall make us a prayse and glory that men shall say of succeeding plantations, "the Lord make it likely that of *New England.*" For wee must consider that wee shall be as a citty upon a hill. The eies of all people are uppon us. Soe that if wee shall deale falsely with our God in this worke wee have

undertaken, and soe cause him to withdrawe his present help from us, wee shall be made a story and a by-word through the world. Wee shall open the mouthes of enemies to speake evill of the wayes of God, and all professors for God's sake. Wee shall shame the faces of many of God's worthy servants, and cause theire prayers to be turned into curses upon us till wee be consumed out of the good land whither wee are a goeing.

I shall shutt upp this discourse with that exhortation of Moses, that faithfull servant of the Lord, in his last farewell to Israell, Deut. 30. *Beloved there is now sett before us life and good, Death and evill, in that wee are commanded this day to love the Lord our God, and to love one another, to walke in his wayes and to keepe his Commandements and his, Ordinance and his lawes,* and the articles of our Covenant with him, that *wee may live and be multiplied, and that the Lord our God may blesse us in the land whither wee goe to possesse it. But if our heartes shall turne away, soe that wee will not obey, but shall be seduced, and worshipp and serve other Gods,* our pleasure and proffitts, *and serve, them;* it is propounded unto us this day, *wee shall surely perishe out of the good land whither wee passe over this vast sea to possesse it;*

> Therefore lett us choose life
> that wee, and our seede
> may liue, by obeyeing His
> voyce and cleaveing to Him,
> for Hee is our life and
> our prosperity.

Questions

1. How would you characterize Winthrop's conceptions of hierarchy, community, and charity?
2. How did Winthrop define the relationship between the New England Puritans and God? What benefits would New Englanders derive from this relationship? What burdens would it impose on them?
3. How did the society Winthrop envisioned compare with the one taking shape in the Chesapeake? To the actual development of New England?
4. What role was Massachusetts to play in the larger world?

8.2   Anne Hutchinson Challenges Massachusetts Orthodoxy*

Vigorous critics of the Church of England, Massachusetts ministers and magistrates quickly found themselves the targets of criticism in New England. Among the most prominent of those challenging the ideas of Massachusetts's leading figures was Anne Hutchinson (1591–1643), an archetypal American dissenter. Brilliant, articulate, and magnetic, Hutchinson conducted popular prayer meetings in her home, during which she discussed Christian doctrine and impugned Massachu- *setts's clergy and officials. In the document that follows, the Massachusetts General Court questions Hutchinson about her beliefs and behavior. Banished from Massachusetts in 1637, Hutchinson eventually made her way to Long Island Sound, where she was killed in a 1643 Indian raid. This account of her examination appeared in an appendix to a history of Massachusetts written by her great-great-grandson, Thomas Hutchinson (governor of Massachusetts, 1771–1774).*

November 1637

The Examination of Mrs. Ann Hutchinson at the court at Newtown.

Mr. Winthrop governor. Mrs. Hutchinson, you are called here as one of those that have troubled the peace of the commonwealth and the churches here; you are known to be a woman that hath had a great share in the promoting and divulging of those opinions that are causes of this trouble, and to be nearly joined not only in affinity and affection with some of those the court hath taken notice of and passed censure upon, but you have spoken divers things as we have been informed very prejudicial to the honour of the churches and ministers thereof, and you have maintained a meeting and an assembly in your house that hath been condemned by the general assembly as a thing not tolerable nor comely in the sight of God nor fitting for your sex, and notwithstanding that was cried down you have continued the same, therefore we have thought good to send for you to understand how things are, that if you be in an erroneous way we may reduce you that so you may become a profitable member here among us,

otherwise if you be obstinate in your course that then the court may take such course that you may trouble us no further, therefore I would intreat you to express whether you do not hold and assent in practice to those opinions and factions that have been handled in court already, that is to lay whether you do not justify Mr. Wheelwright's sermon and the petition.

Mrs. Hutchinson. I am called here to answer before you but I hear no things laid to my charge.

Gov.   I have told you some already and more I can tell you. (Mrs. H.) Name one Sir.

Gov.   Have I not named some already?

Mrs. H.   What have I said or done?

Gov.   Why for your doings, this you did harbour and countenance those that are parties in this faction that you have heard of. (Mrs. H.) That's matter of conscience, Sir.

Gov.   Your conscience you must keep or it must be kept for you.

Mrs. H. Must not I then entertain the saints because I must keep my conscience,

Gov.   Say that one brother should commit felony or treason and come to his other brother's house, if he knows him guilty and conceals him he is guilty of the same. It is his conscience to entertain him, but if his conscience comes into act in giving countenance and entertainment to him that hath broken the law he is guilty too. So if you do countenance those that are trans-gressors of the law you are in the same fact.

*"The Examination of Mrs. Ann Hutchinson at the court at Newtown," in Thomas Hutchinson, *The History of the Province of Massachusets-Bay* (Boston: 1767), 482–490, 495–497, 507–509, 513–515, 519–520.

Mrs. H.   What law do they transgress?

Gov.   The law of God and of the state;

Mrs. H.   In what particular?

Gov.   Why in this among the rest, whereas the Lord doth say honour thy father and thy mother.

Mrs. H.   Ey Sir in the Lord. (Gov.) This honour you have broke in giving countenance to them.

Mrs. H.   In entertaining those did I entertain them against any act (for there is the thing) or what God hath appointed?

Gov.   You knew that Mr. Wheelwright did preach this sermon and those that countenance him in this do break a law.

Mrs. H.   What law have I broken?

Gov.   Why the fifth commandment.

Mrs. H.   I deny that for he saith in the Lord.

Gov.   You have joined with them in the faction.

Mrs. H.   In what faction have I joined with them?

Gov. In presenting the petition.

Mrs. H.   Suppose I had set my hand to the petition what then? (Gov.) You saw that case tried before.

Mrs. H. But I had not my hand to the petition.

Gov.   You have councelled them. (Mrs. H.) Wherein?

Gov.   Why in entertaining them.

Mrs. H.   What breach of law is that Sir?

Gov. Why dishonouring of parents.

Mrs. H.   But put the case Sir that I do fear the Lord and my parents, may not I entertain them that fear the Lord because my parents will not give the leave?

Gov.   If they be the fathers of the commonwealth, and they of another religion, if you entertain them then you dishonour your parents and are justly punishable.

Mrs. H.   If I entertain them, as they have dishonoured their parents I do.

Gov.   No but you by countenancing them above others put honor upon them.

Mrs. H.   I may put honor upon them as the children of God and as they do honor the Lord.

Gov.   We do not mean to discourse with those of your sex but only this; you do adhere unto them and do endeavour to set forward this faction and so you do dishonour us.

Mrs. H.   I do acknowledge no such thing neither do I think that I ever put any dishonour upon you.

Gov. Why do you keep such a meeting at your house as you do every week upon a set day?

Mrs. H.   It is lawful for me so to do, as it is all your practices and can you find a warrant for yourself and condemn me for the same thing? The ground of my taking it up was, when I first came to this land because I did not go to such meetings as those were, it was presently reported that I did not allow of such meetings but held them unlawful and therefore in that regard they said I was proud and did despite all ordinances, upon that a friend came unto me and told me of it and I to prevent such aspersions took it up, but it was in practice before I came therefore I was not the first.

Gov.   For this, that you appeal to our practice you need no confutation. If your meeting had answered to the former it had not been offensive, but I will say that there was no meeting of women alone, but your meeting is of another sort for there are sometimes men among you.

Mrs. H.   There was never any man with us.

Gov.   Well, admit there was no man at your meeting and that you was sorry for it, there is no warrant for your doings, and by what warrant do you continue such a course?

Mrs. H.   I conceive there lyes a clear rule in Titus, that the elder women should instruct the younger and then I must have a time wherein I must do it.

Gov.   All this I grant you, I grant you a time for it, but what is this to the purpose that you Mrs. Hutchinson must call a company together from their callings to come to be taught of you?

Mrs. H.   Will it please you to answer me this and to give me a rule for then I will willingly submit to any truth. If any come to my house to be instructed in the ways of God what rule have I to put them away?

Gov.   But suppose that a hundred men come unto you to be instructed will you forbear to instruct them?

Mrs. H.   As far as I conceive I cross a rule in it.

Gov.   Very well and do you not so here?

Mrs. H.   No Sir for my ground is they are men.

Gov. Men and women all is one for that, but suppose that a man should come and say Mrs. Hutchinson I hear that you are a woman that God hath given his grace unto and you have knowledge in the word of God I pray instruct me a little, ought you not to instruct this man?

Mrs. H.   I think I may.—Do you think it not lawful for me to teach women and why do you call me to teach the court?

Gov.   We do not call you to teach the court but to lay open yourself.

Mrs. H.   I desire you that you would then set me down a rule by which I may put them away that come unto me and so have peace in so doing.

Gov.   You must shew your rule to receive them.

Mrs. H.   I have done it.

Gov.   I deny it because I have brought more arguments than you have.

Mrs. H.   I say, to me it is a rule.

Mr. Endicot.   You say there are some rules unto you. I think there is a contradiction in your own words. What rule for your practice do you bring, only a custom in Boston.

Mrs. H.   No Sir that was no rule to me but if you look upon the rule in Titus it is a rule to me. If you convince me that it is no rule I shall yield.

Gov.   You know that there is no rule that crosses another, but this rule crosses that in the Corinthians. But you must take it in this sense that elder women must instruct the younger about their business and to love their husbands and not make them to clash.

Mrs. H.   I do not conceive but that it is meant for some publick times.

Gov.   Well, have you no more to say but this?

Mrs. H.   I have said sufficient for my practice.

Gov.   Your course is not to be suffered for, besides that we find such a course as this to be greatly prejudicial to the state, besides the occasion that it is to reduce many honest persons that are called to those meetings and your opinions being known to be different from the word of God may reduce many simple souls that resort unto you, besides that the occasion which hath come of late hath come from none but such as have frequented your meetings, so that now they are shown off from magistrates and ministers and this since they have come to you, and besides that it will not well stand with the commonwealth that families should be neglected for so many neighbours and dames and so much time spent, we see no rule of God for this, we see not that any should have authority to set up any other exercises besides what authority hath already set up and so what hurt comes of this you will be guilty of and we for suffering you.

Mrs. H.   Sir I do not believe that to be so.

Gov.   Well, we see how it is we must therefore put it away from you or restrain you from maintaining this course.

Mrs. H.   If you have a rule for it from God's word you may.

Gov.   We are your judges, and not you ours and we must compel you to it.

Mrs. H.   If it please you by authority to put it down I will freely let you for I am subject to your authority.

Mr. Bradstreet.   I would ask this question of Mrs. Hutchinson, whether you do think this is lawful? for then this will follow that all other women that do not are in a sin.

Mrs. H.   I conceive this is a free will offering.

Bradst.   If it be a free will offering you ought to forbear it because it gives offence.

Mrs. H.   Sir, in regard of myself I could, but for others I do not yet see light but shall further consider of it.

Bradst.   I am not against all women's meetings but do think them to be lawful.

Mr. Dudley, dep. gov. Here hath been much spoken concerning Mrs. Hutchinson's meetings and among other answers she saith that men come not there, I would ask you this one question then, whether never any man was at your meeting?

Gov. There are two meetings kept at their house.

Dep. gov. How; is there two meetings?

Mrs. H.   Ey Sir, I shall not equivocate, there is a meeting of men and women and there is a meeting only for women.

Dep. gov.   Are they both constant?

Mrs. H.   No, but upon occasions they are deferred.

Mr. Endicot.   Who teaches in the men's meetings none but men, do not women sometimes?

Mrs. H.   Never as I heard, not one.

Dep. gov.   I would go a little higher with Mrs. Hutchinson. About three years ago we were all in peace. Mrs. Hutchinson from that time she came hath made a disturbance, and some that came over with her in the ship did inform me what she was as soon as she was landed. I being then in place dealt with the pastor and teacher of Boston and desired them to enquire of her, and then I was satisfied that she held nothing different from us, but within half a year after, she had vented divers of her strange opinions and had made parties in the country, and at length it comes that Mr. Cotton and Mr. Vane were of her judgment, but Mr. Cotton hath cleared himself that he was not of that mind, but now it appears by this woman's meeting that Mrs. Hutchinson hath so forestalled the minds of many by their resort to her meeting that now she hath a potent party in the country. Now if all these things have endangered us as from that foundation and if she in particular hath disparaged all our ministers in the land that they have preached a covenant of works, and only Mr. Cotton a covenant of grace, why this is not to be suffered, and therefore being driven to the foundation and it being found that Mrs. Hutchinson is she that hath depraved all the ministers and hath been the cause of what is fallen out, why we must take away the foundation and the building will fall.

Mrs. H.   I pray Sir prove it that I said they preached nothing but a covenant of works.

Dep. Gov.   Nothing but a covenant of works, why a Jesuit may preach truth sometimes.

Mrs. H.   Did I ever say they preached a covenant of works then?

Dep. Gov.   If they do not preach a covenant of grace clearly, then they preach a covenant of works.

Mrs. H.   No Sir, one may preach a covenant of grace more clearly than another, so I said.

D. Gov.   We are not upon that now but upon position,

Mrs. H.   Prove this then Sir that you say I said.

D. Gov.   When they do preach a covenant of works do they preach truth?

Mrs. H.   Yes Sir, but when they preach a covenant of works for salvation, that is not truth.

D. Gov.   I do but ask you this, when the ministers do preach a covenant of works do they preach a way of salvation?

Mrs. H.   I did not come hither to answer to questions of that sort.

D. Gov.   Because you will deny the thing.

Mrs. H.   Ey, but that is to be proved first.

D. Gov.   I will make it plain that you did say that the ministers did preach a covenant of works.

Mrs. H.   I deny that.

D. Gov.   And that you said they were not able ministers of the new testament, but Mr. Cotton only.

Mrs. H.   If ever I spake that I proved it by God's word.

Court.   Very well, very well.

Mrs. H.   If one shall come unto me in private, and desire me seriously to tell them what I thought of such an one. I must either speak false or true in my answer.

D. Gov.   Likewise I will prove this that you said the gospel in the letter and words holds forth nothing but a covenant of works and that all that do not hold as you do are in a covenant of works.

Mrs. H.   I deny this for if I should so say I should speak against my own judgment.

Mr. Endicot.   I desire to speak seeing Mrs. Hutchinson seems to say something against them that are to witness against her.

Gover.   Only I would add this. It is well discerned to the court that Mrs. Hutchinson can tell when to speak and when to hold her tongue. Upon the answering of a question which we desire her to tell her thought . . . of she desires to be pardoned.

Mrs. H.   It is one thing for me to come before a public magistracy and there to speak what they would have me to speak and another when a man comes to me in a way of friendship privately there is difference in that.

Gov.   What if the matter be all one?

Mr. Hugh Peters.   That which concerns us to speak unto as yet we are sparing in unless the court command us to speak, then we shall answer to Mrs. Hutchinson notwithstanding our brethren are very unwilling to answer.

Govern.   This speech was not spoken in a corner but in a public assembly, and though things were spoken in private yet now coming to us, we are to deal with them as public. . . .

Gov.   Here are six undeniable ministers who say it is true and yet you deny that you did say that they did preach a covenant of works and that they were not able ministers of the gospel, and it appears plainly that you have spoken it, and whereas you say that it was drawn from you in a way of friendship, you did profess then that it was out of conscience that you spake and said The fear of man is a snare wherefore should I be afraid, I will speak plainly and freely.

Mrs. H.   That I absolutely deny, for the first questions was thus answered by me to them. They thought that I did conceive there was a difference between them and Mr. Cotton. At the first I was somewhat reserved, then said Mr. Peters I pray answer the question directly as fully and as plainly as you desire we should tell you our minds. Mrs. Hutchinson we come for plain dealing and telling you our hearts. Then I said I would deal as plainly as I could, and whereas they say I said they were under a covenant of works and in the state of the apostles why there two speeches cross one another. I might say they might preach a covenant of works as did the apostles, but to preach a convenant of works and to be under a convenant of works is another business.

Dep. Gov.   There have been six witnesses to prove this and yet you deny it.

Mrs. H.   I deny that these were the first words that were spoken.

Gov.   You make the case worse, for you clearly shew that the ground of your opening your mind was not to satisfy them but to satisfy your own conscience.

Mr. Peters.   We do not desire to be so narrow to the court and the gentlewoman about times and seasons, whether first or after, but said it was.

Dep. Gov.   For that other thing I mentioned for the letter of the scripture that it held forth nothing but a covenant of works, and for the latter that we are in a state of damnation, being under a convenant of works, or to that effect, these two things you also deny. Now the case stands thus. About three quarters of a year ago I heard of it, and speaking of it there came one to me who is not here, but will affirm it if need be, as he did to me that he did hear you say in so many words. He set it down under his hand and I can bring it forth when the court pleases. His name is subscribed to both these things, and upon my peril be it if I bring you not in the paper and bring the minister (meaning Mr. Ward) to be deposed.

Gov.   What say you to this, though nothing be directly proved yet you hear it may be.

Mrs. H.   I acknowledge using the words of the apostle to the Corinthians unto him, that they that were ministers of the letter and not the spirit did preach a covenant of works. Upon his saying there was no such scripture, then I fetched the bible and shewed him this place 2 Cor. iii. 6. He said that was the letter of the law. No said I it is the letter of the gospel.

Gov.   You have spoken this more than once then.

Mrs. H.   Then upon further discourse about proving a good estate and holding it out by the manifestation of the spirit he did acknowledge that to be the nearest way, but yet said he, will you not acknowledge that which, we hold forth to be a way too wherein we may have hope; no truly if that be a way it is a way to hell.

Gov. Mrs. Hutchinson, the court you see hath laboured to bring you to acknowledge the error of your way that so you might be reduced, the time now grows late, we shall therefore give you a little more time to consider of it and therefore desire that you attend the court again in the morning.

The next morning.

Gov.   We proceeded the last night as far as we could in hearing of this cause of Mrs. Hutchinson.

There were divers things laid to her charge, her ordinary meetings about religious exercises, her speeches in derogation of the ministers among us, and the weakning of the hands and hearts of the people towards them. Here was sufficient proof made of that which she was accused of in that point concerning the ministers and their ministry, as that they did preach a covenant of works when others did preach a covenant of grace, and that they were not able ministers of the new testament, and that they had not the seal of the spirit, and this was spoken not as was pretended out of private conference, but out of conscience and warrant from scripture alledged the fear of man is a snare and seeing God had given her a calling to it she would freely speak. Some other speeches she used, as that the letter of the scripture held forth a covenant of works, and this is offered to be proved by probable grounds. If there be any thing else that the court hath to say they may speak. . . .

Mrs. H.   If you please to give me leave I shall give you the ground of what I know to be true. Being much troubled to see the falseness of the constitution of the church of England, I had like to have turned separatist; whereupon I kept a day of solemn humiliation and pondering of the thing; this scripture was brought unto me—he that denies Jesus Christ to be come in the flesh is antichrist—this I considered of and in considering found that the papists did not deny him to be come in the flesh, nor we did not deny him—who then was antichrist? Was the Turk antichrist only? The Lord knows that I could not open scripture; he must by his prophetical office open it unto me. So after that being unsatisfied in the thing, the Lord was pleased to bring this scripture out of the Hebrews. He that denies the testament denies the testator, and in this did open unto me and give me to see that those which did not teach the new covenant had the spirit of antichrist, and upon this he did discover the ministry unto me and ever since, I bless the Lord, he hath let me see which was the clear ministry and which the wrong. Since that time I confess I have been more choice and he hath let me to distinguish between the voice of my beloved and the voice of Moses, the voice of John Baptist and the voice of antichrist, for all those voices are spoken of in scrip-ture. Now if you do condemn me for speaking what in my conscience I know to be truth I must commit myself unto the Lord.

Mr. Nowell.   How do you know that that was the spirit?

Mrs. H.   How did Abraham know that it was God that bid him offer his son, being a breach of the sixth commandment?

Dep. Gov.   By an immediate voice.

Mrs. H.   So to me by an immediate revelation.

Dep. Gov.   How! an immediate revelation.

Mrs. H.   By the voice of his own spirit to my soul, I will give you another scripture, Jer. 46. 27, 28—out of which the Lord shewed me what he would do for me and the rest of his servants.—But after he was pleased to reveal himself to me I did presently like Abraham run to Hagar. And after that he did let me see the atheism of my own heart, for which I begged of the Lord that it might not remain in my heart, and being thus, he did shew me this (a twelvemonth after) which I told you of before. Ever since that time I have been confident of what he hath revealed unto me.

Obliterated: another place out of Daniel chap. 7, and he and for us all, wherein he shewed me the sitting of the judgment and the standing of all high and low before the Lord and how thrones and kingdoms were cast down before him. When our teacher came to New-England it was a great trouble unto me, my brother Wheelwright being put by also. I was then much troubled concerning the ministry under which I lived, and then that place in the 30th of Isaiah was brought to my mind. Though the Lord give thee bread of adversity and water of affliction yet shall not thy teachers be removed into corners any more, but thine eyes shall see thy teachers. The Lord giving me this promise and they being gone there was none then left that I was able to hear, and I could not be rest but I must come hither. Yet that place of Isaiah did much follow me, though the Lord give thee the bread of adversity and water of affliction. This place lying I say upon me then this place in Daniel was brought unto me and did shew me that though I should meet with affliction yet I am the same God that delivered Daniel out of the lion's den, I will also deliver thee.——

Therefore I desire you to look to it, for you see this scripture fulfilled this day and therefore I desire you that as you tender the Lord and the church and commonwealth to consider and look what you do. You have power over my body but the Lord Jesus hath power over my body and soul, and assure yourselves thus much, you do as much as in you lies to put the Lord Jesus Christ from you, and if you go on in this course you begin you will bring a curse upon you and your posterity, and the mouth of the Lord hath spoken it.

Dep. Gov.   What is the scripture she brings?

Mr. Stoughton.   Behold I turn away from you.

Mrs. H.   But now having seen him which is invisible I fear not what man can do unto me.

Gov.   Daniel was delivered by miracle do you think to be deliver'd so too?

Mrs. H.   I do here speak it before the court. I look that the Lord should deliver me by his providence.

Mr. Harlakenden.   I may read scripture and the most glorious hypocrite may read them and yet go down to hell.

Mrs. H.   It may be so. . . .

Gover.   The case is altered and will not stand with us now, but I see a marvellous providence of God to bring things to this . . . . that they are. We have been hearkening about the trial of this thing and now the mercy of God by a providence hath answered our desires and made her to lay open her self and the ground of all these disturbances to be by revelations, for we receive no such . . . made out of the ministry of the word . . . and so one scripture after another, but all this while there is no use of the ministry of the word nor of any clear call of God by his word, but the ground work of her revelations is the immediate revelation of the spirit and not by the ministry of the word, and that is the means by which she hath very much abused the country that they shall look for revelations and are not bound to the ministry of the word, but God will teach them by immediate revelations and this hath been the ground of all these tumults and troubles, and I would that those were all cut off from us that trouble us, for this is the thing that hath been the root of all the mischief.

Court. We all consent with you.

Gov.   Ey it is the most desperate enthusiasm in the world, for nothing but a word comes to her mind and then an application is made which is nothing to the purpose, and this is her revelations when as it is impossible but that the word and spirit should speak the same thing.

Mr. Endicot.   I speak in reference to Mr. Cotton I am tender of you Sir and there lies much upon you in this particular, for the answer of Mr. Cotton doth not free him from that way which his last answer did bring upon him, therefore I beseech you that you'd be pleased to speak a word to that which Mrs. Hutchinson hath spoken of her revelations as you have heard the manner of it. Whether do you witness for her or against her.

Mr. Cotton.   This is that I said Sir, and my answer is plain that if she doth look for deliverance from the hand of God by his providence, and the revelation be in a word or according to a word, that I cannot deny.

Mr. Endicot.   You give me satisfaction.

Dep. Gov.   No, no, he gives me none at all.

Mr. Cotton. But if it be in a way of miracle or a revelation without the word that I do not assent to, but look at it as a delusion, and I think so doth she too as I understand her.

Dep. Gov.   Sir, you weary me and do not satisfy me.

Mr. Cotton.   I pray Sir give me leave to express my self. In that sense that she speaks I dare not bear witness against it.

Mr. Nowell.   I think it is a devilish delusion.

Gover.   Of all the revelations that ever I read of I never read the like ground laid as is for this. The Enthusiasts and Anabaptists had never the like.

Mr. Cotton.   You know Sir, that their revelations broach new matters of faith and doctrine.

Gover.   So do these and what may they breed more if they be let alone. I do acknowledge that there are such revelations as do concur with the word but there hath not been any of this nature.

Dep. Gov.   I never saw such revelations as these among the Anabaptists, therefore am sorry that Mr. Cotton should stand to justify her.

Mr. Peters.   I can say the same and this runs to enthusiasm, and I think that is very disputable which our brother Cotton hath Spoken [*wanting*] an immediate promise that he will deliver them [*wanting*] in a day of trouble.

Gover.   It overthrows all.

Dep. Gov.   These disturbances that have come among the Germans have been all grounded upon revelations, and so they that have vented them have stirred up their hearers to take up arms against their prince and to cut the throate one of another, and these have been the fruits of them, and whether the devil may inspire the same into their hearts here I know not, for I am fully persuaded that Mrs. Hutchinson is deluded by the devil, because the spirit of God speaks truth in all his servants.

Gov.   I am persuaded that the revelation she brings forth is delusion.

All the court but some two or three ministers cry out we all believe it—we all believe it.

Mr. Endicot.   I suppose all the world may see where the foundation of all these troubles among us lies.

Mr. Eliot.   I say there is an expectation of things promised, but to have a particular revelation of things that shall fall out, there is no such thing in the scripture.

Gov.   We will not limit the word of God. . . .

Gov.   The court hath already declared themselves satisfied concerning the things you hear, and concerning the troublesomness of her spirit and the danger of her course among us, which is not to be suffered. Therefore if it be the mind of the court that Mrs. Hutchinson for these things that appear before us is unfit for our society, and if it be the mind of the court that she shall be banished out of our liberties and imprisoned till she be sent away, let them hold up their hands.

All but three.

Those that are contrary minded hold up yours.

Mr. Coddington and Mr. Colborn, only.

Mr. Jennison.   I cannot hold up my hand one way or the other, and I shall give my reason if the court require it.

Gov.   Mrs. Hutchinson, the sentence of the court you hear is that you are banished from out of our jurisdiction as being a woman not fit for our society, and are to be imprisoned till the court shall send you away.

Mrs. H.   I desire to know wherefore I am banished?

Gov.   Say no more, the court knows wherefore and is satisfied.

Terms

John Wheelwright (c. 1592–1679)—Puritan clergyman; exiled from Massachusetts for defending Hutchinson's beliefs

Henry Vane (1613–1662)—Governor of Massachusetts in 1636, supporter of Hutchinson; returned to England in 1637

John Cotton (1584–1652)—influential Massachusetts Puritan clergyman; advocated Hutchinson's exile.

Questions

1. What was it about Anne Hutchinson that the Massachusetts authorities found so troubling? Her ideas? Her behavior? Her sex? Why were the meetings at her house problematic? Did her conduct and thinking challenge Winthrop's "Modell of Christian Charity"?

2. What does Hutchinson's examination tell you about early New English notions of the proper role for women?

3. To what extent did Hutchinson's conflict with colonial authorities represent a singular incident, a confluence of particular individuals and circumstances? To what extent was it an example of a more general characteristic of the New England colonies?

4. What did Hutchinson and her examiners mean by a "covenant of grace" and a "covenant of works"? Why did the distinction matter? Why was her claim of "immediate revelation" so significant?

5. What were the limits of tolerance and intolerance in the 1630s Massachusetts?

8.3   Cotton Mather Wrestles with Witchcraft*

The 1692 Salem witch trials demonstrated the danger that witchcraft accusations could spin out of control, and suggested the desirability of reconsidering the nature of and evidence for witchcraft. One of the most thoughtful treatments of the subject came from Boston minister and author Cotton Mather (1663–1728). The son and *grandson of New England ministers, Cotton Mather became an accomplished scientist, well known for promoting inoculation against smallpox and writing about American natural phenomena. The document that follows, "Enchantments Encounter'd," was first published in 1693.*

Enchantments Encounter'd.

I. It was as long ago, as the Year 1637, that a Faithful Minister of the Church of *England*, whose Name was Mr. *Edward Symons*, did in a Sermon afterwards Printed, thus express himself; 'At *New-England*' now the Sun of Comfort begins to appear, and the glorious Day-Star to slow it self;—*Sed Venient Annis Sæculæ Seris*, there will come Times in after Ages, when the *Clouds will overshadow and darken the Sky there.* Many now promise to themselves nothing but successive Happiness there, which for a time through God's Mercy they may enjoy; and I pray God, they may a long time; but in this World there is no Happiness perpetual.' An *Observation*, or I had almost said, an *Inspiration*, very dismally now verify'd upon us! It has been affirm'd by some who best knew *New-England*, That the World will do *New-England* a great piece of Injustice, if it acknowledge not a measure of Religion, Loyalty, Honesty, and Industry, in the People there, beyond what is to be found with any other People for the Number of them. When I did a few years ago, publish a Book, which mentioned a few memorable Witchcrafts, committed in this Country; the excellent *Baxter*, graced the Second Edition of that Book, with a kind Preface, wherein he sees cause to say, If any are Scandalized, that New-England, *a place of as serious Piety, as any I can hear of, under Heaven, should be troubled so much with*

Witches; I think, 'tis no wonder: *Where will the Devil show most Malice, but where he is hated, and hateth most:* And I hope, the Country will still deserve and answer the Charity so expressed by that Reverend Man of God. Whosoever travels over this Wilderness, will see it richly bespangled with Evangelical Churches, whose Pastors are holy, able, and painful Overseers of their Flocks, lively Preachers, and vertuous Livers; and such as in their several Neighbourly Associations, have had their Meetings whereat Ecclesiastical Matters of common Concernment are considered: *Churches*, whose Communicants have been seriously examined about their Experiences of Regeneration, as well as about their Knowledge, and Belief, and blameless Conversation, before their Admission to the Sacred Communion; although others of less but hopeful Attainments in Christianity are not ordinarily deny'd Baptism for themselves and theirs; Churches, which are shye of using any thing in the Worship of God, for which they cannot see a Warrant of God; but with whom yet the Names of *Congregational, Presbyterian, Episcopalian,* or *Antipædobaptist,* are swallowed up in that of *Christian;* Persons of all those Perswasions being taken into our Fellowship, when visible Goodliness has recommended them: Churches, which usually do within themselves manage their own Discipline, under the Conduct of their Elders; but yet call in the help of *Synods* upon Emergencies, or Aggrievances; *Churches*, Lastly, wherein Multitudes are growing ripe for Heaven every day; and as fast as there are taken off, others are daily rising up. And by the Presence and

---

*Cotton Mather, "Enchantments Encounter'd," in Samuel G. Drake, ed., *The Witchcraft Delusion in New England* (Roxbury, Mass., 1866), 9–36.

Power of the Divine Institutions thus maintained in the Country. We are still so happy, that I suppose there is no Land in the Universe more free from the debauching, and the debasing Vices of Ungodliness. The Body of the People are hitherto so disposed, that *Swearing, Sabbath-breaking, Whoring, Drunkenness*, and the like, do not make a Gentleman, but a Monster, or a Goblin, in the vulgar Estimation. All this notwithstanding, we must humbly confess to our God, that we are miserably degenerated from the first Love of our Predecessors; however we boast our selves a little, when Men would go to trample upon us, and we venture to say, *Wherein Soever any is bold (we speak foolishly) we are bold also.* The first Planters of these Colonies were a chosen Generation of Men, who were first so pure, as to disrelish many things which they thought wanted Reformation elsewhere; and yet withal so peaceable, that they embraced a voluntary Exile in a squalid, horrid, *American* DESART, rather than to live in Contentions with their Brethren. Those good Men imagined that they should leave their Posterity in a place, where they should never see the Inroads of Profanity, or Superstition: And a famous Person returning hence, could in a Sermon before the Parliament profess, *I have been Seven Years in a Country, where I never Saw one Man drunk, or heard one Oath sworn, or beheld one Beggar in the Streets all the while.* Such great Persons as *Budæus*, and others, who mistook Sir *Thomas Moor's* UTOPIA, for a Country really existent, and stirr'd up some Divines charitably to undertake a Voyage thither, might now have certainly found a Truth in their Mistake; *New-England* was a true *Utopia*. But, alas, the Children and Servants of those old Planters must needs afford many degenerate Plants, and there is now risen up a Number of People, otherwise inclined than our *Joshua's*, and the Elders that out-liv'd them. Those two things our holy Progenitors, and our happy Advantages make Omissions of Duty, and such Spiritual Disorders as the whole World abroad is overwhelmed with, to be as provoking in us, as the most flagitious Wickednesses committed in other places; and the Ministers of God are accordingly severe in their Testimonies: But in short, those Interests of the Gospel, which were the Errand of our Fathers into these Ends of the Earth, have been too much neglected and postponed, and the Attainments of an handsome Education, have been too much undervalued, by Multitudes that have not fallen into Exorbitances of Wickedness; and some, especially of our young Ones, when they have got abroad from under the Restraints here laid upon them, have become extravagantly and abominably Vicious. Hence 'tis, that the Happiness of *New-England* has been but for a time, as it was foretold, and not for a long time, as has been desir'd for us. A Variety of Calamity has long follow'd this Plantation; and we have all the Reason imaginable to ascribe it unto the Rebuke of Heaven upon us for our manifold *Apostasies*; we make no right use of our Disasters: If we do not, *Remember whence we are fallen, and repent, and do the first Works.* But yet our Afflictions may come under a further Consideration with us: There is a further Cause of our Afflictions, whose due must be given him.

II. The *New-Englanders* are a People of God settled in those, which were once the *Devil's* Territories; and it may easily be supposed that the *Devil* was exceedingly disturbed, when he perceived such a People here accomplishing the Promise of old made unto our Blessed Jesus, *That He should have the Utmost parts of the Earth for his Possession.* There was not a greater Uproar among the *Ephesians*, when the Gospel was first brought among them, than there was among, *The Powers of the Air* (after whom those *Ephesians* walked) when first the *Silver Trumpets* of the Gospel here made the *Joyful Sound.* The Devil thus Irritated, immediately try'd all sorts of Methods to overturn this poor Plantation: and so much of the Church, as was *Fled into this Wilderness*, immediately found, *The Serpent cast out of his Mouth a Flood for the carrying of it away.* I believe, that never were more *Satanical Devices* used for the Unsetling of any People under the Sun, than what have been Employ'd for the Extirpation of the *Vine* which God has here *Planted, Casting out the Heathen, and preparing a Room before it, and causing it to take deep Root, and fill the Land, so that it sent its Boughs unto the* Atlantic *Sea* Eastward, *and its Branches unto the* Connecticut *River* Westward, *and the Hills were covered with the shadow thereof.* But, All those Attempts of Hell, have hitherto been Abortive, many an *Ebenezer* has been Erected unto the Praise of God, by his Poor People here; and, *Having obtained Help from God, we continue to this Day.* Wherefore the Devil is now making one Attempt more upon us; an Attempt more Difficult, more Surprizing, more snarl'd with unintelligible Circumstances than any that we have hitherto Encountred; an Attempt so *Critical*, that if we get well through, we shall soon Enjoy *Halcyon* Days with all the *Vultures* of Hell *Trodden under our Feet.* He has wanted his *Incarnate Legions* to Persecute us, as the People of God have in the other Hemisphere been Persecuted: he has therefore drawn forth his more *Spiritual* ones to make an Attacque upon us. We have been advised by some Credible Christians yet alive, that a Malefactor, accused of *Witchcraft* as well as *Murder*, and Executed in this place more than Forty Years ago, did then give Notice of, *An Horrible* PLOT *against the Country* by WITCHCRAFT, *and a Foundation of* WITCHCRAFT *then laid, which if it were not seasonably discovered, would probably Blow up, and pull down all the Churches in the Country.* And we have now with Horror seen the *Discovery* of such a *Witchcraft!* An Army of *Devils* is horribly broke in upon the place which is the *Center*, and after a sort, the *First-born* of our *English* Settlements: and the Houses of the Good People there are fill'd with the doleful Shrieks of their Children and Servants, Tormented by Invisible Hands, with Tortures altogether preternatural. After the Mischiefs there Endeavoured, and since in part Conquered, the terrible Plague, of *Evil Angels*, hath made its Progress into some other places, where other Persons have been in like manner Diabolically handled. These our poor Afflicted Neighbours, quickly after they become *Infected* and *Infested* with these *Dæmons*, arrive to a Capacity of Discerning those which they conceive the *Shapes* of their Troublers; and notwithstanding the Great and Just Suspicion, that the *Dæmons* might Impose the *Shapes* of Innocent Persons in their *Spectral Exhibitions* upon the Sufferers, (which may perhaps prove no small part of the *Witch-Plot* in the issue) yet many of the Persons

thus Represented, being Examined, several of them have been Convicted of a very Damnable *Witchcraft:* yea, more than One *Twenty* have *Confessed*, that they have Signed unto a *Book*, which the Devil show'd them, and Engaged in his Hellish Design of *Bewitching*, and *Ruining* our Land. *We* know not, at least *I* know not, how far the *Delusions* of Satan may be Interwoven into some Circumstances of the *Confessions;* but one would think, all the Rules of Understanding Humane Affairs are at an end, if after so many most Voluntary Harmonious *Confessions*, made by Intelligent Persons of all Ages, in sundry Towns, at several Times, we must not Believe the *main strokes* wherein those *Confessions* all agree: especially when we have a thousand preternatural Things every day before our eyes, wherein the *Confessors* do acknowledge their Concernment, and give Demonstration of their being so Concerned. If the Devils now can strike the minds of men with any *Poisons* of so fine a Composition and Operation, that Scores of Innocent People shall Unite, in *Confessions* of a Crime, which we see actually committed, it is a thing prodigious, beyond the Wonders of the former Ages, and it threatens no less than a sort of a Dissolution upon the World. Now, by these *Confessions* 'tis Agreed, *That* the Devil has made a dreadful Knot of *Witches* in the Country, and by the help of *Witches* has dreadfully increased that Knot: *That* these *Witches* have driven a Trade of Commissioning their *Confederate Spirits*, to do all sorts of Mischiefs to the Neighbours, whereupon there have ensued such Mischievous consequences upon the Bodies and Estates of the Neighbourhood, as could not otherwise be accounted for: yea, *That* at prodigious *Witch-Meetings*, the Wretches have proceeded so far, as to Concert and Consult the Methods of Rooting out the Christian Religion from this Country, and setting up instead of it, perhaps a more gross *Diabolism*, than ever the World saw before. And yet it will be a thing little short of *Miracle*, if in so *spread* a Business as this, the Devil should not get in some of his Juggles, to confound the Discovery of all the rest.

III. Doubtless, the Thoughts of many will receive a great Scandal against *New-England*, from the Number of Persons that have been Accused, or Suspected, for *Witchcraft*, in this Country: But it were easie to offer many things, that may Answer and Abate the Scandal. If the Holy God should any where permit the Devils to hook two or three wicked *Scholars* into *Witchcraft*, and then by their Assistance to Range with their *Poisonous Insinuations* among Ignorant, Envious, Discontented People, till they have cunningly decoy'd them into some sudden *Act*, whereby the Toyls of Hell shall be perhaps inextricably cast over them: what Country in the World would not afford *Witches*, numerous to a Prodigy? Accordingly, The Kingdoms of *Sweden*, *Denmark*, *Scotland*, yea, and *England* it self, as well as the Province of *New-England*, have had their Storms of *Witchcrafts* breaking upon them, which have made most Lamentable Devastations: which also I wish, may be *The Last*. And it is not uneasie to be imagined, that God has not brought out all the *Witchcrafts* in many other Lands with such a speedy, dreadful, destroying *Jealousie*, as burns forth upon such *High Treasons*, committed here in *A Land of Uprightness:* Transgressors may more quickly here than elsewhere become a Prey to the Vengeance of Him, *Who has Eyes like a Flame of Fire*, and, *who walks in the midst of the Golden Candlesticks.* Moreover, There are many parts of the World, who if they do upon this Occassion insult over this People of God; need only to be told the Story of what happened at *Loim*, in the Dutchy of *Gulic*, where a Popish Curate having ineffectually try'd many Charms to Eject the Devil out of a Damsel there possessed, he passionately bid the Devil come out of her into himself; but the Devil answered him, *Quid mihi Opus, est eum tentare, quem Novissimo die, Jure Optimo, sum possessurus?* That is, *What need I meddle with one whom I am sure to have, and hold at the Last-day as my own for ever!*

But besides all this, give me leave to add, it is to be hoped, That among the Persons represented by the *Spectres* which now afflict our Neighbours, there will be found *some* that never explicitly contracted with any of the *Evil Angels.*

The Witches have not only intimated, but some of them acknowledged, That they have plotted the Representations of *Innocent Persons*, to cover and shelter themselves in their Witchcrafts; now, altho' our good God has hitherto generally preserved us from the Abuse therein design'd by the Devils for us, yet who of us can exactly state, *How far our God may for our Chastisement permit the Devil to proceed in such an Abuse?* It was the Result of a Discourse, lately held at a Meeting of some very Pious and Learned Ministers among us, *That the Devils may sometimes have a permission to Represent an Innocent Person, as Tormenting such as are under Diabolical Molestations: But that such things are Rare and Extraordinary; especially when such matters come before Civil Judicature.* The Opinion expressed with so much Caution and Judgment, seems to be the prevailing Sense of many others, who are men Eminently Cautious and Judicious; and have both *Argument* and *History* to Countenance them in it. It is *Rare and Extraordinary*, for an Honest *Naboth* to have his Life it self Sworn away by two *Children of Belial*, and yet no Infringement hereby made on the Rectoral Righteousness of our Eternal Soveraign, whose *Judgments are a Great Deep*, and who *gives none Account of His matters.* Thus, although the Appearance of Innocent Persons in *Spectral Exhibitions* afflicting the Neighbourhood, be a thing *Rare and Extraordinary*; yet who can be sure, that the great *Belial* of Hell must needs be always *Yoked* up from this piece of Mischief? The best man that ever lived has been called a *Witch:* and why may not this too usual and unhappy Symptom of A *Witch*, even a Spectral Representation, befall a person that shall be none of the worst? Is it not possible? The *Laplanders* will tell us 'tis possible: for Persons to be unwittingly attended with officious *Dæmons*, bequeathed unto them, and impos'd upon them, by Relations that have been *Witches. Quæry*, also, Whether at a Time, when the Devil with his Witches are engag'd in a War upon a people, some certain steps of ours, in such a War, may not be follow'd with our appearing so and so for a while among them in the Visions of our afflicted *Forlorns!* And, Who can certainly say, what other Degrees or Methods of sinning, besides that of a *Diabolical Compact*, may give the Devils advantage to act in the Shape of them that have miscarried? Besides what may happen for a while, to try the *Patience* of the Vertuous. May not some that have been ready upon feeble grounds uncharitably to Censure and Reproach other people, be punished for it by *Spectres* for a while exposing them to Censure and Reproach? And furthermore, I pray, that it may be considered, Whether a World of Magical Tricks often used in the World, may not insensibly oblige *Devils* to wait upon the Superstitious Users of them. A Witty Writer against *Sadducism* has this Observation, That persons who never made any express Contract with *Apostate Spirits*, yet may Act strange Things by *Diabolick Aids*, which they procure by the use of those wicked *Forms* and *Arts*, that the Devil first imparted unto his Confederates. And he adds, *We know not but the Laws of the Dark Kingdom may Enjoyn a particular Attendance upon all those that practice their Mysteries, whether they know them to be theirs or no.* Some of them that have been cry'd out upon as *Employing Evil Spirits* to hurt our Land, have been known to be most bloody *Fortune-Tellers;* and some of them have confessed, That when they told *Fortunes*, they would pretend the Rules of *Chiromancy* and the like Ignorant Sciences, but indeed they had no Rule (they said) but this, *The things were then Darted into their minds. Darted!* Ye Wretches; By whom I pray? Surely by none but the *Devils;* who, tho' perhaps they did not exactly *Foreknow* all the thus Predicted Contingencies; yet having once *Foretold* them, they Stood bound in Honour now to use their Interest, which alas, in *This World*, is very great, for the Accomplishment of their own Predictions. There are others, that have used most wicked *Sorceries* to gratifie their unlawful Curiosities, or to prevent Inconveniencies in Man and Beast; *Sorceries*, which I will not *Name*, lest I should by Naming, *Teach them*. Now, some *Devil* is evermore Invited into the Service of the Person that shall Practise these *Witchcrafts;* and if they have gone on Impenitently in these Communions with any *Devil*, the *Devil* may perhaps become at last a *Familiar* to them, and so assume their *Livery*, that they cannot shake him off in any way, but that

One, which I would most heartily prescribe unto them, Namely, That of a deep and long *Repentance*. Should these *Impieties* have been committed in such a place as *New-England*, for my part I should not wonder, if when *Devils* are Exposing the *Grosser* Witches among us, God permit them to bring in these *Lesser* ones with the rest for their perpetual Humiliation. In the Issue therefore, may it not be found, that *New-England* is not so stock'd with *Rattle Snakes*, as was imagined.

IV. But I do not believe, that the progress of *Witchcraft* among us, is all the Plot which the Devil is managing in the *Witchcraft* now upon us. It is judged, That the Devil rais'd the Storm, whereof we read in the Eighth Chapter of *Matthew*, on purpose to over-set the little Vessel wherein the Disciples of Our Lord were Embarqued with Him. And it may be fear'd, that in the *Horrible Tempest* which is now upon ourselves, the design of the Devil is to sink that Happy Settlement of Government, wherewith Almighty God has graciously enclined Their Majesties to favour us. We are blessed with a GOVERNOUR, than whom no man can be more willing to serve Their Majesties, or this their Province: He is continually venturing his *All* to do it: and were not the Interests of his Prince dearer to him than his own, he could not but soon be weary of the *Helm*, whereat he sits. We are under the Influence of a LIEUTENANT GOVERNOUR, who not only by being admirably accomplished both with Natural and Acquired Endowments, is fitted for the Service of Their Majesties, but also with an unspotted Fidelity applies himself to that Service. Our COUNCELLOURS are some of our most Eminent Persons, and as Loyal Subjects to the Crown, as hearty lovers of their Country. Our Constitution also is attended with singular Priviledges; All which Things are by the Devil exceedingly *Envy'd* unto us. And the Devil will doubtless take this occasion for the raising of such complaints and clamours, as may be of pernicious consequence unto some part of our present Settlement, if he can so far *Impose*. But that which most of all Threatens us, in our present Circumstances, is the *Misunderstanding*, and so the *Animosity*, whereunto the *Witchcraft* now Raging, has

Enchanted us. The Embroiling, first, of our *Spirits*, and then of our *Affairs*, is evidently as considerable a Branch of the Hellish Intrigue which now vexes us as any one Thing what so ever. The Devil has made us like a *Troubled Sea*, and the *Mire* and *Mud* begins now also to heave up apace. Even Good and Wise Men suffer themselves to fall into their *Paroxysms;* and the Shake which the Devil is now giving us, fetches up the *Dirt* which before lay still at the bottom of our sinful Hearts. If we allow the Mad Dogs of Hell to poyson us by biting us, we shall imagine that we see nothing but such things about us, and like such things fly upon all that we see. Were it not for what is IN US, for my part, I should not fear a thousand Legions of Devils: 'tis by our Quarrels that we spoil our Prayers; and if our humble, zealous, and united Prayers are once hindred; Alas, the *Philistines* of Hell have cut our Locks for us; they will then blind us, mock us, ruine us: In truth, I cannot altogether blame it, if People are a little transported, when they conceive all the secular Interests of themselves and their Families at the Stake; and yet at the sight of these Heartburnings, I cannot forbear the Exclamation of the Sweet-spirited *Austin*, in his Pacificatory Epistle to *Jerom*, on the Contest with *Ruffin, O misera & miseranda Conditio!* O Condition, truly miserably! But what shall be done to cure these Distractions? It is wonderfully necessary, that some healing Attempts be made at this time: And I must needs contest (if I may speak so much) like a *Nazianzen*, I am so desirous of a share in them, that if, being thrown overboard, were needful to allay the *Storm*, I should think Dying, a Trifle to be undergone, for so great a Blessedness.

V. I would most importunately in the first place, entreat every Man to maintain an holy Jealousie over his own Soul at this time, and think; May not the Devil make me, though ignorantly and unwillingly, to be an instrument of doing something that he would have to be done? For my part, I freely own my Suspicion, left something of Enchantment, have reach'd more Persons and Spirits among us, than we are well aware of. But then, let us more generally agree to maintain a kind Opinion one of another. That Charity without which, even our giving our Bodies to be burned would profit nothing, uses to proceed by this Rule; It is kind, it is not easily provok'd, it thinks no Evil, it believes all things, hopes all things. But if we disregard this Rule of Charity, we shall indeed give our Body Politick to be burned. I have heard it affirmed, That in the late great Flood upon *Connecticut*, those Creatures which could not but have quarreled at another time, yet now being driven together very agreeably flood by one another. I am sure we shall be worse than *Brutes* if we fly upon one another at a time when the Floods of Belial make us afraid. On the one side; [Alas, my Pen, must thou write the word, *Side* in the Business?] There are very worthy Men, who having been call'd by God, when and where this Witchcraft first appeared upon the Stage to encounter it, are earnestly desirous to have it sifted unto the bottom of it. And I pray, which of us all that should live under the continual impressions of the Tortures, Outcries, and Havocks which Devils confessedly Commissioned by Witches make among their distressed Neighbours, would not have a Biass that way beyond other Men? Persons this way disposed have been Men eminent for Wisdom and Vertue, and Men acted by a noble Principle of Conscience. Had not Conscience (of Duty to God) prevailed above other Considerations with them, they would not for all they are worth in the World have medled in this Thorny business. Have there been any disputed Methods used in discovering the Works of Darkness? It may be none but what have had great Precedents in other parts of the World; which may, though not altogether justifie, yet much alleviate a mistake in us if there should happen to be found any such mistake in so dark a Matter. They have done what they have done, with multiplied Addresses to God for his Guidance, and have not been insensible how much they have exposed themselves in what they have done. Yea, they would gladly contrive and receive an expedient, how the shedding of Blood, might be spared, by the Recovery of Witches, not gone beyond the Reach of Pardon. And after all, they invite all good Men, in Terms to this purpose, 'Being amazed at the Number and Quality of those accused of late, we do not know but Satan by his Wiles may have enwrapped some innocent Persons; and therefore should earnestly and humbly desire the most Critical Enquiry upon the place, to find out the Falacy; that there may be none of the Servants of the Lord, with the worshippers of *Baal*. I may also add, That whereas, if once a Witch do ingeniously confess among us, no more *Spectres* do in their Shapes after this, trouble the Vicinage; if any guilty Creatures will accordingly to so good purpose confess their Crime to any Minister of God, and get out of the Snare of the Devil, as no Minister will discover such a Conscientious Confession, so I believe none in the Authority will press him to discover it; but rejoyc'd in a Soul sav'd from Death. On the other side [if I must again use the word *Side*, which yet I hope to live to blot out] there are very worthy Men, who are not a little dissatisfied at the Proceedings in the Prosecution of this Witchcraft. And why? Not because they would have any such abominable thing, defended from the Stokes of Impartial Justice. No, those Reverend Persons who gave in the Advice unto the Honourable Council; 'That Presumptions, whereupon Persons may be 'Committed, and much more Convicitions, whereupon Persons may be Condemned, as guilty of 'Witchcrafts, ought certainly to be more considerable than barely the Accused Persons being represented by a *Spectre* unto the Afflicted; Nor are Alterations made in the Sufferers, by a Look or Touch of the Accused, to be esteemed an infallible Evidence of Guilt; but frequently liable to be abused by the Devils Legerdemains: I say, those very Men of God most conscientiously Subjoined this Article to that Advice, —Nevertheless we cannot but humbly recommend unto the Government, the speedy and vigorous Prosection of such as have rendred themselves Obnoxious; according to the best Directions given in the Laws of God, and the wholesome Statues of the *English* Nation for the Detection of Witchcraft. Only 'tis a most commendable Cautiousness, in those gracious Men, to be very shye lest the Devil get so far into our Faith, as that for the sake of many Truths which we find he tells us, we come at length to believe any Lyes, wherewith he may abuse us: whereupon, what a Desolation of Names would soon ensue, besides a thousand other pernicious Consequences? and lest there should be any such Principles taken up, as when put into Practice must unavoidably cause the *Righteous to perish with the Wicked;* or procure the Bloodshed of any Persons, like the *Gibeonites,* whom some learned Men suppose to be under a false Notion of Witches, by *Saul* exterminated.

They would have all due steps taken for the Extinction of Witches; but they would fain have them to be sure ones; nor is it from any thing, but the real and hearty goodness of such Men, that they are loth to surmise ill of other Men, till there be the fullest Evidence for the surmises. As for the Honourable Judges that have been hitherto in the Commission, they are above my Consideration: wherefore I will only say thus much of them, That such of them as I have the Honour of a Personal Acquaintance with, are Men of an excellent Spirit; and as at first they went about the work for which they were Commission'd, with a very great aversion, so they have still been under Heart-breaking Sollicitudes, how they might therein best serve both God and Man? In fine, Have there been faults on any side fallen into? Surely, they have at worst been but the faults of a well-meaning Ignorance. On every side then, why should not we endeavour with amicable Correspondencies, to help one another out of the Snares wherein the Devil would involve us? To wrangle the Devil out of the Country, will be truly a New Experiment: Alas! we are not aware of the Devil, if we do not think, that he aims at inflaming us one against another; and shall we suffer our selves to be Devilridden? or by any unadvisableness contribute unto the Widening of our Breaches?

To say no more, there is a published and credible Relation; which affirms, That very lately in a part of *England*, where some of the Neighbourhood were quarrelling, a *Raven* from the Top of a Tree very articulately and unaccountably cry'd out, *Read the Third of Collossians and the Fifteenth!* Were I my self to chuse what sort of Bird I would be transformed into, I would say, *O that I had wings like a Dove!* Nevertheless, I will for once do the Office, which as it seems, Heaven sent that *Raven* upon; even to beg, *That the Peace of God may Rule in our Hearts.*

VI. 'Tis necessary that we unite in every thing: but there are especially two Things wherein our Union must carry us along together. We are to unite in our Endeavours to deliver our distressed Neighbours, from the horrible Annoyances and Molestations with which a dreadful Witchcraft is now persecuting of them. To have an hand in any thing, that may stifle or obstruct a Regular Detection of that Witchcraft, is what we may well with an holy fear avoid. Their Majesties good Subjects must not every day be torn to pieces by horrid Witches, and those bloody Felons, be lest wholly unprosecuted. The Witchcraft is a business that will not be sham'd, without plunging us into sore plagues, and of long continuance. But then we are to unite in such Methods for this deliverance, as may be unquestionably safe, lest *the latter end be worse than the beginning.* And here, what shall I say? I will venture to say thus much, That we are safe, when we make just as much use of all Advice from the invisible World, as God sends it for. It is a safe Principle, That when God Almighty permits any Spirits from the unseen Regions, to visit us with surprizing Informations, there is then something to be enquired after; we are then to enquire of one another, What Cause there is for such things? The peculiar Government of God, over the unbodied Intelligences, is a sufficient Foundation for this Principle. When there has been a Murder committed, an Apparition of the slain Party accusing of any Man, altho' such Apparitions have oftner spoke true than false, is not enough to Convict the Man as guilty of that Murder; but yet it is a sufficient occasion for Magistrates to make a particular Enquiry, whether such a Man have afforded any ground for such an Accusation. Even so a Spectre exactly resembling such or such a Person, when the Neighbourhood are tormented by such Spectres, may reasonably make Magistrates inquisitive whether the Person so represented have done or said any thing that may argue their confederacy with Evil Spirits, altho' it may be defective enough in point of Conviction; especially at a time, when 'tis possible, some over-powerful Conjurer may have got the shill of thus exhibiting the Shapes of all sorts of Persons, on purpose to stop the Prosecution of the Wretches, whom due Enquiries thus provoked, might have made obnoxious unto Justice.

Quære, Whether if God would have us to proceed any further than bare *Enquiry,* upon what Reports there may come against any Man, from the World of *Spirits,* he will not by his Providence at the same time have brought into our hands, these more evident and sensible things, whereupon a man is to be esteemed a Criminal. But I will venture to say this further, that it will be safe to account the Names as well as the Lives of our Neighbors; two considerable things to be brought under a Judicial Process, until it be found by Humane Observations that the Peace of Mankind is thereby disturbed. We are Humane Creatures, and we are safe while we say, they must be Humane Witnesses, who also have in the particular Act of Seeing, or Hearing, which enables them to be Witnesses, had no more than Humane Assistances, that are to turn the Scale when Laws are to be executed. And upon this Head I will further add: A wise and a just Magistrate, may so far give way to a common Stream of Dissatisfaction, as to forbear acting up to the heighth of his own Perswasion, about what may be judged convictive of a Crime, whose Nature shall be so abstruse and obscure, as to raise much Disputation. Tho' he may not do what he should leave undone, yet he may leave undone something that else he could do, when the Publick Safety makes an *Exigency.*

Questions

1. Why, in Mather's view, was New England plagued by witchcraft? Were New Englanders being punished for their virtues or vices? Why did Mather try to establish that New England's travails had been predicted decades before?
2. How did Mather think that those guilty and innocent of witchcraft could be distinguished? What constituted reliable evidence?

3. What problems were witchcraft accusations creating for New Englanders? How did Mather think New England should respond to such accusations of witchcraft ?

4. How did Mather explain events? What was the relation between phenomena of the visible and "invisible" worlds? Does this text represent a transitional moment between two ways of understanding the world?

5. Does Mather furnish evidence supporting or undermining the idea of New England "declension"?

Puritans and Indians

The relationship between English immigrants and New England's Indians varied widely over time. After establishing an alliance in the early 1620s, the English alternately fought alongside and against their Indian neighbors for the next three generations. The documents in this chapter highlight the complexities of English-Indian relations in New England, running from early peaceful encounters to accounts of a bloody war, known as King Philip's War, that wreaked havoc throughout the region on natives and newcomers alike.

9.1   English and Indians Establish an Alliance*

The following passage is drawn from a 1622 pamphlet of uncertain authorship, but evidence suggests that it was the work of Edward Winslow in collaboration with William Bradford and possibly others. Winslow and Bradford were among the religious separatists, popularly known as "Pilgrims," who settled at Plymouth, Massachusetts, in 1620. Both men played important roles in negotiating early relations with their Indian hosts, including the establishment of an alliance between the English and their closest Indian neighbors. This selection recounts the circumstances and terms of their mutual agreement, reached in 1621.

Friday, the 16th, a fair warm day towards; this morning we determined to conclude of the military orders, which we had begun to consider of before but were interrupted by the savages, as we mentioned formerly. And whilst we were busied hereabout, we were interrupted again, for there

presented himself a savage, which caused an alarm. He very boldly came all alone and along the houses straight to the rendezvous, where we intercepted him, not suffering him to go in, as undoubtedly he would, out of his boldness. He saluted us in English, and bade us welcome, for he had learned some broken English among the Englishmen that came to fish at Monchiggon, and knew by name the most of the captains, commanders, and masters that usually come. He was a man free in speech, so far as he could express his mind, and of a seemly carriage. We questioned him of many things; he was the first savage we could meet withal. He said he was not of these parts, but of Morattiggon, and one of the sagamores or lords thereof, and had been eight months in these parts, it lying hence a day's sail with a great wind, and five days by land. He discoursed of the whole country, and of every province, and of their sagamores, and their number of men, and strength. The wind beginning to rise a little, we cast a horseman's coat about him,

---

*Dwight B. Heath, ed., *A Journal of the Pilgrims at Plymouth* (New York: Corinth Books, 1963), 50–57.

for he was stark naked, only a leather about his waist, with a fringe about a span long, or little more; he had a bow and two arrows, the one headed, and the other unheaded. He was a tall straight man, the hair of his head black, long behind, only short before, none on his face at all; he asked some beer, but we gave him strong water and biscuit, and butter, and cheese, and pudding, and a piece of mallard, all which he liked well, and had been acquainted with such amongst the English. He told us the place where we now live is called Patuxet, and that about four years ago all the inhabitants died of an extraordinary plague, and there is neither man, woman, nor child remaining, as indeed we have found none, so as there is none to hinder our possession, or to lay claim unto it. All the afternoon we spent in communication with him; we would gladly have been rid of him at night, but he was not willing to go this night. Then we thought to carry him on shipboard, wherewith he was well content, and went into the shallop, but the wind was high and the water scant, that it could not return back. We lodged him that night at Stephen Hopkin's house, and watched him.

The next day he went away back to the Massasoits, from whence he said he came, who are our next bordering neighbors. They are sixty strong, as he saith. The Nausets are as near southeast of them, and are a hundred strong, and those were they of whom our people were encountered, as we before related. They are much incensed and provoked against the English, and about eight months ago slew three Englishmen, and two more hardly escaped by flight to Monchiggon; they were Sir Ferdinando Gorges his men, as this savage told us, as he did likewise of the *huggery*, that is, fight, that our discoverers had with the Nausets, and of our tools that were taken out of the woods, which we willed him should be brought again, otherwise, we would right ourselves. These people are ill affected towards the English, by reason of one Hunt, a master of a ship, who deceived the people, and got them under color of trucking with them, twenty out of this very place where we inhabit, and seven men from the Nausets, and carried them away, and sold them for slaves like a wretched man (for twenty pound a man) that cares not what mischief he doth for his profit.

Saturday, in the morning we dismissed the savage, and gave him a knife, a bracelet, and a ring; he promised within a night or two to come again, and to bring with him some of the Massasoits, our neighbors, with such beavers' skins as they had to truck with us.

Saturday and Sunday, reasonable fair days. On this day came again the savage, and brought with him five other tall proper men; they had every man a deer's skin on him, and the principal of them had a wild cat's skin, or such like on the one arm. They had most of them long hosen up to their groins, close made; and above their groins to their waist another leather, they were altogether like the Irish-trousers. They are of complexion like our English gypsies, no hair or very little on their faces, on their heads long hair to their shoulders, only cut before, some trussed up before with a feather, broad-wise, like a fan, another a fox tail hanging out. These left (according to our charge given him before) their bows and arrows a quarter of a mile from our town. We gave them entertainment as we thought was fitting them; they did eat liberally of our English victuals. They made semblance unto us of friendship and amity; they sang and danced after their manner, like antics. They brought with them in a thing like a bow-case (which the principal of them had about his waist) a little of their corn pounded to powder, which, put to a little water, they eat. He had a little tobacco in a bag, but none of them drank but when he listed. Some of them had their faces painted black, from the forehead to the chin, four or five fingers broad; others after other fashions, as they liked. They brought three or four skins, but we would not truck with them at all that day, but wished them to bring more, and we would truck for all, which they promised within a night or two, and would leave these behind them, though we were not willing they should, and they brought us all our tools again which were taken in the woods, in our men's absence. So because of the day we dismissed them so soon as we could. But Samoset, our first acquaintance, either was sick, or feigned himself so, and would not go with them, and stayed with us till Wednesday morning. Then we sent him to them, to know the reason they came not according to their words, and we gave him a hat, a pair of stockings and shoes, a shirt, and a piece of cloth to tie about his waist.

The Sabbath day, when we sent them from us, we gave every one of them some trifles, especially the principal of them. We carried them along with our arms to the place where they left their bows and arrows, whereat they were amazed, and two of them began to slink away, but that the other called them. When they took their arrows, we bade them farewell, and they were glad, and so with many thanks given us they departed, with promise they would come again.

Monday and Tuesday proved fair days; we digged our grounds, and sowed our garden seeds.

Wednesday a fine warm day, we sent away Samoset.

That day we had again a meeting to conclude of laws and orders for ourselves, and to confirm those military orders that were formerly propounded and twice broken off by the savages' coming, but so we were again the third time, for after we had been an hour together on the top of the hill over against us two or three savages presented themselves, that made semblance of daring us, as we thought. So Captain Standish with another, with their muskets went over to them, with two of the master's mates that follow them without arms, having two muskets with them. They whetted and rubbed their arrows and strings, and made show of defiance, but when our men drew near them, they ran away; thus were we again interrupted by them. This day with much ado we got our carpenter that had been long sick of the scurvy, to fit our shallop, to fetch all from aboard.

Thursday, the 22nd of March, was a very fair warm day. About noon we met again about our public business, but we had scarce been an hour together, but Samoset came again, and Squanto, the only native of Patuxet, where we now inhabit, who was one of the twenty captives that by Hunt were carried away, and had been in England, and dwelt in Cornhill with Master John Slanie, a merchant, and could speak a little English, with three

others, and they brought with them some few skins to truck, and some red herrings newly taken and dried, but not salted, and signified unto us, that their great sagamore Massasoit was hard by, with Quadequina his brother, and all their men. They could not well express in English what they would, but after an hour the king came to the top of a hill over against us, and had in his train sixty men, that we could well behold them and they us. We were not willing to send our governor to them, and they unwilling to come to us, so Squanto went again unto him, who brought word that we should send one to parley with him, which we did, which was Edward Winslow, to know his mind, and to signify the mind and will of our governor, which was to have trading and peace with him. We sent to the king a pair of knives, and a copper chain with a jewel at it. To Quadequina we sent likewise a knife and a jewel to hang in his ear, and withal a pot of strong water, a good quantity of biscuit, and some butter, which were all willingly accepted.

Our messenger made a speech unto him, that King James saluted him with words of love and peace, and did accept of him as his friend and ally, and that our governor desired to see him and to truck with him, and to confirm a peace with him, as his next neighbor. He liked well of the speech and heard it attentively, though the interpreters did not well express it. After he had eaten and drunk himself, and given the rest to his company, he looked upon our messenger's sword and armor which he had on, with intimation of his desire to buy it, but on the other side, our messenger showed his unwillingness to part with it. In the end he left him in the custody of Quadequina his brother, and came over the brook, and some twenty men following him, leaving all their bows and arrows behind them. We kept six or seven as hostages for our messenger; Captain Standish and Master Williamson met the king at the brook, with half a dozen musketeers. They saluted him and he them, so one going over, the one on the one side, and the other on the other, conducted him to a house then in building, where we placed a green rug and three or four cushions. Then instantly came our governor with drum and trumpet after him, and some few musketeers. After salutations, our governor kissing his hand, the king kissed him, and so they sat down. The governor called for some strong water, and drunk to him, and he drunk a great draught that made him sweat all the while after; he called for a little fresh meat, which the king did eat willingly, and did give his followers. Then they treated of peace, which was:

1. That neither he nor any of his should injure or do hurt to any of our people.
2. And if any of his did hurt to any of ours, he should send the offender, that we might punish him.
3. That if any of our tools were taken away when our people were at work, he should cause them to be restored, and if ours did any harm to any of his, we would do the like to them.
4. If any did unjustly war against him, we would aid him; if any did war against us, he should aid us.
5. He should send to his neighbor confederates, to certify them of this, that they might not wrong us, but might be likewise comprised in the conditions of peace.
6. That when their men came to us, they should leave their bows and arrows behind them, as we should do our pieces when we came to them.

Lastly, that doing thus, King James would esteem of him as his friend and ally.

Terms

Monchiggon, Morattiggon—Monhegan Island, off the Maine coast
Massasoits—Wampanoags, mistakenly named after one of their headmen, Massasoit
antics—clowns
strong water—liquor

Questions

1. Samoset, the first Indian described in this passage, speaks English. How did he learn the language? Besides their language what else did he know of the English?
2. What happened to the Indians who used to live near Plymouth?
3. Discuss the role of "trucking," or trade, in these negotitations.
4. Outline the provisions of the treaty concluded between the English and the Indians. Is the agreement equally beneficial to both sides, or does it favor one over the other?
5. How clearly do you think both sides understood the provisions of this agreement? How were the provisions communicated and approved?
6. How could Massasoit secure the compliance of his people and neighbors with the terms of the treaty?

9.2   Minister Daniel Gookin Discusses the Dilemmas Confronting Christian Indians*

As English-Indian relations deteriorated in the 1660s and 1670s, those Indians who had embraced certain aspects of European culture found themselves in a difficult position, not fully trusted by either Indians or English. The following document discusses the difficulties faced by Christian Indians who remained loyal to the English even during the violence of King Philip's War (1675–1676) but were nevertheless mistrusted by their New English allies. It was published in 1677 by Daniel Gookin a missionary who championed the cause of Christianizing New England Indians.

HISTORY OF THE CHRISTIAN INDIANS

A true and impartial narrative of the doings and sufferings of the Christian or praying Indians, in New England, in the time of the war between the English and barbarous heathen, which began the 20th of June, 1675.

*Daniel Gookin, *An Account of the Doing and Sufferings of the Christians Indians in New England, in the Years 1675, 1676, 1677* (Cambridge MA: American Antiquarian Society, 1836, reprint), Vol. 2: 433–437, 449–450.

Forasmuch as sundry persons have taken pains to write and publish historical narratives of the war; between the English and Indians in New England, but very little hath been hitherto declared (that I have seen) concerning the Christian Indians, who, in reality, may be judged to have no small share in the effects and consequences of this war; I thought it might have a tendency to God's glory, and to give satisfaction to such worthy and good persons as have been benefactors and well-willers to that pious work of Gospelizing the poor Indians in New England, to give them right information how these Christian natives have demeaned themselves in this hour of tribulation. And therefore (through divine assistance) I shall endeavour to give a particular and real account of this affair. Before I come to declare matter of fact, I shall premise some things necessary to be understood for the better clearing of our ensuing discourse.

The Christian Indians in New England have their dwellings in sundry Jurisdictions of the English Colonies, and that at a considerable distance from each other; more particularly,

1st. Upon the Islands of Nantucket and Martha's Vineyard, in which two Islands there inhabit many hundreds of them that visibly profess the Gospel. These Indians have felt very little of this war comparatively; for the English that dwell upon those Islands have held a good correspondency with those Indians all the time of the war, as they did before the war began. The only sufferings of these Christian Indians was of their coming up in the summer, during the war, to work for the English in the Massachusetts Colony, whither many scores of them did usually repair to work, whereby they and their families were accommodated with necessary clothing, which is scarce and dear upon those Islands. Besides, several of those Indians belonging to the Islands, being at work at some of the English towns when the war began in the summer, 1675, were not permitted to stay in the Colonies, but were forced to pack away to their own habitations to their great loss, because the English were so jealous, and filled with animosity against all Indians without exception.

Hereby they tasted but little of the effects of the war, and therefore they will not so properly fall under our consideration.

2dly. Another considerable number of Christian Indians live within the Jurisdiction of New Plymouth, called the Cape Indians; these also (through God's favor) have enjoyed much peace and quiet by their English neighbours, and several of them have served the English in the war, especially in the heat of the war, and did acquit themselves courageously and faithfully. Indeed, at the beginning of the war, the English of that colony were suspicious of them, and slow to improve any of them in the war, though divers of those Christian Indians manifested themselves ready and willing to engage with the English against their enemies; and this is so much the more remarkable that those Indians proved so faithful to the English interest, considering the war first began in the Colony of Plymouth, by the rashness and folly of Philip, Chief Sachem of the Indians in those parts, unto whom, or to some of his people doubtless, these praying Indians were allied by affinity or consanguinity. Therefore good reason it is, to attribute it to the grace and favor of God, and to the efficacy of religion upon their hearts, that they carried it so well in this war; the greatest sufferings these underwent was, being impeded by the war to come and work in harvest among the English, whereby they had a good helper to get apparel. These also do not fall so properly under consideration in this narrative.

3dly. There were a few other praying Indians, about 40 persons, that began to embrace the Christian religion, who lived near to New Norwich, in Connecticut Colony, who were taught by that worthy and reverend minister, Mr. James Fitch, pastor at Norwich, who had taken much pains to declare the Gospel to the Indians in those parts. But the chief Sachem; Uncas, and his eldest son, Oineko, not being encouragers of the Christian religion, (though otherwise they and their people have joined with the English in the war, and proved faithful, especially against their ancient and implacable enemies, the Narragansetts,)

I say, this Sachem and people being generally averse to entertain Christian religion, or countenance any such as did among his people incline to it, hence it came to pass, that those few in those parts that prayed to God are not distinguishable from the rest, and so nothing of remark is spoken of any of them, and hence will not be subjects of this discourse.

4thly. The fourth and not the least company of Christian Indians, are those that inhabit the Jurisdiction or Colony of Massachusets, who were taught and instructed in the Christian faith by that indefatigable servant of God and minister of Christ, Mr. John Eliot, (who hath also labored among all the praying Indians in New England, more or less, for about 30 years,) but more especially among those of Massachusetts Colony. And of these Indians, it is, I shall principally speak, who have felt more of the effects of this war than all the rest of the Christian Indians, as may appear in that which ensues.

For the better understanding of the following discourse, we are to know that all these praying Indians dwelt upon the south side of Merrimack river, and inhabited seven villages, viz. Wamesit, Nashobah, Okkokonimesit, alias Marlborough, Hassannamesit, Makunkokoag, Natick, and Punkapog, alias Pakomit. These were for distinction's sake called the *old* praying Indian towns, for there were five or six small villages of the Nipmuck Indians that had some people in them inclining to entertain the Gospel, therefore were called, the *new* praying towns. But those latter being but raw and lately initiated into the Christian profession, most of them fell off from the English and joined the enemy in the war, some few excepted, whose hearts God had turned, that came in to Okkokonimesit, or Marlborough, and lived among the praying Indians; they were drawn together there until such time as the one and other were driven and drawn away among the enemy, as shall afterward (God willing) be declared. I am therefore principally to speak of the Christian Indians belonging to the old praying towns above mentioned.

The situation of those towns was such, that the Indians in them might have been improved as a wall of defence about the greatest part of the colony of Massachusetts; for the first named of those villages bordered upon the Merrimack river, and the rest in order about twelve or fourteen miles asunder, including most of the frontiers. And had the suggestions and importunate solicitations of some persons, who had knowledge and experience of the fidelity and integrity of the praying Indians been attended and practised in the beginning of the war, many and great mischiefs might have been (according to reason) prevented; for most of the praying towns, in the beginning of the war, had put themselves into a posture of defence, and had made forts for their security against the common enemy; and it was suggested and proposed to the authority of the country, that some English men, about one third part, might have been joined with those Christian Indians in each fort, which the praying Indians greatly desired, that thereby their fidelity might have been better demonstrated, and that with the assistance and company of some of those English soldiers, they might daily scout or range the woods from town to town, in their several assigned stations, and hereby might have been as a living wall to guard the English frontiers, and consequently the greatest part of the Jurisdiction, which, with the blessing of God, might have prevented the desolations and devastations that afterward ensued. This was not only the suggestion of some English, but the earnest desire of some of the most prudent of the Christian Indians, who in all the actions declared that they were greatly ambitious to give demonstration to the English of their fidelity and good affection to them and the interest of the Christian religion, and to endeavour all that in them lay to abate and take off the animosity and displeasure that they perceived was enkindled in some English against them; and hence it was that they were always found ready to comply cheerfully with all commands of the English authority. But such was the unhappiness of their affairs, or rather the displeasure of God in the case, that those counsels were rejected, and on the contrary a spirit of enmity and hatred conceived by many against those poor Christian Indians, as I apprehend without cause, so far as I could ever understand, which was, according to the operation of second causes, a very great occasion of many distressing calamities that befell both one and the other . . .

But, notwithstanding those signal and faithful services done by those Christian Indians, and divers others not here related, yet the animosity and rage of the common people increased against them, that the very name of a praying Indian was spoken against, in so much, that some wise and principal men did advise some that were concerned with them, to forbear giving that epithet of praying. This rage of the people, as I contend, was occasioned from hence. Because much mischief being done and English blood shed by the brutish enemy, and because some neighbour Indians to the English at Quabage, Hadley, and Springfield (though none of those were praying Indians) had proved perfidious and were become enemies, hence it was that all the Indians are reckoned to be false and perfidious. Things growing to this height among the English, the Governor and Council, against their own reason and inclination, were put upon a kind of necessity, for gratifying the people, to disband all the praying Indians, and to make and publish an order to confine them to five of their own villages, and not to stir above one mile from the centre of such place, upon perril of their lives.

Questions

1. Gookin suggests that the English were "filled with animosity against all Indians without exception." Why?
2. Which "praying Indians" does Gookin think suffered the most during the war? What did they suffer? Why?
3. Gookin believes that the English could have avoided much of the war's destruction had they trusted the Christian Indians to defend them. Why were the English reluctant to do so?

9.3 Mary Rowlandson Recounts Her Captivity*

Mary Rowlandson, an English resident of Lancaster, Massachusetts, spent nearly three months as a captive of the Wampanoag Indians in the winter and spring of 1676. Lancaster lay near the western edge of English settlement and, until the outbreak of war the previous summer, had enjoyed an amicable relationship with its Indian neighbors. Captured in a February raid on her town, Rowlandson was separated from her family, with the exception of one child, who died during their forced retreat into Indian territory. After Rowlandson was "redeemed," or ransomed, she composed this account, first published in Cambridge, Massachusetts, in 1682.

A NARRATIVE OF THE CAPTIVITY AND RESTAURATION OF MRS. MARY ROWLANDSON

On the tenth of February 1675 [1676]. Came the Indians with great numbers upon Lancaster: Their first coming was about Sun-rising; hearing the noise of some Guns, we looked out; several Houses were burning, and the Smoke ascending to Heaven. There were five persons taken in one house, the Father, and the Mother and a sucking Child, they knockt on the head; the other two they took and carried away alive. Their were two others, who being out of their Garison upon some occasion were set upon; one was knockt on the head, the other escaped: Another there was who running along was shot and wounded, and fell down; he begged of them his life, promising them Money (as they told me) but they would not hearken to him but knockt him in head, and stript him naked, and split open his Bowels. Another seeing many of the Indians about his Barn, ventured and went out, but was quickly shot down. There were three others belonging to the same Garison who were killed; the Indians getting up upon the roof of the Barn, had advantage to shoot down upon them over their Fortification. Thus these murtherous wretches went on, burning, and destroying before them.

*Charles H. Lincoln ed., *Narratives of the Indian Wars, 1675–1699* (New York: Barnes & Noble, 1952), 118–131, 149–167.

At length they came and beset our own house, and quickly it was the dolefullest day that ever mine eyes saw. The House stood upon the edg of a hill; some of the Indians got behind the hill, others into the Barn, and others behind any thing that could shelter them; from all which places they shot against the House, so that the Bullets seemed to fly like hail; and quickly they wounded one man among us, then another, and then a third, About two hours (according to my observation, in that amazing time) they had been about the house before they prevailed to fire it (which they did with Flax and Hemp, which they brought out of the Barn, and there being no defence about the House, only two Flankers at two opposite corners and one of them not finished) they fired it once and one ventured out and quenched it, but they quickly fired it again, and that took. Now is the dreadfull hour come, that I have often heard of (in time of War, as it was the case of others) but now mine eyes see it. Some in our house were fighting for their lives, others wallowing in their blood, the House on fire over our heads, and the bloody Heathen ready to knock us on the head, if we stirred out. Now might we hear Mothers and Children crying out for themselves, and one another, Lord, What shall we do? Then I took my Children (and one of my sisters, hers) to go forth and leave the house: but as soon as we came to the dore and appeared, the Indians shot so thick that the bulletts rattled against the House, as if one had taken an handfull of stones and threw them, so that we were fain to give back. We had six stout Dogs belonging to our Garrison, but none of them would stir, though another time, if any Indian had come to the door, they were ready to fly upon him and tear him down. The Lord hereby would make us the more to acknowledge his hand, and to see that our help is always in him. But out we must go, the fire increasing, and coming along behind us, roaring, and the Indians gaping before us with their Guns, Spears and Hatchets to devour us. No sooner were we out of the House, but my Brother in Law (being before wounded, in defending the house, in or near the throat) fell down dead, wherat the Indians scornfully shouted, and hallowed, and were presently upon him, stripping off his cloaths, the bulletts flying thick, one went through my side, and the same (as would seem) through the bowels and hand of my dear Child in my arms. One of my elder Sisters Children, named William, had then his Leg broken, which the Indians perceiving, they knockt him on head. Thus were we butchered by those merciless Heathen, standing amazed, with the blood running down to our heels. My eldest Sister being yet in the House, and seeing those wofull sights, the Infidels haling Mothers one way, and Children another, and some wallowing in their blood: and her elder Son telling her that her Son William was dead, and my self was wounded, she said, And, Lord, let me dy with them; which was no sooner said, but she was struck with a Bullet, and fell down dead over the threshold. I hope she is reaping the fruit of her good labours, being faithfull to the service of God in her place. In her younger years she lay under much trouble upon spiritual accounts, till it pleased God to make that precious Scripture take hold of her heart, 2 Cor. 12. 9. *And he said unto me, my Grace is sufficient for thee.* More then twenty years after I have heard her tell how sweet and comfortable that place was to her. But to return: The Indians laid hold of us, pulling me one way, and the Children another, and said, Come go along with us; I told them they would kill me: they answered, If I were willing to go along with them, they would not hurt me.

Oh the dolefull sight that now was to behold at this House! *Come, behold the works of the Lord, what dissolations he has made in the Earth.* Of thirty seven persons who were in this one House, none escaped either present death, or a bitter captivity, save only one, who might say as he, Job 1. 15, *And I only am escaped alone to tell the News.* There were twelve killed, some shot, some stab'd with their Spears, some knock'd down with their Hatchets. When we are in prosperity, Oh the little that we think of such dreadfull sights, and to see our dear Friends, and Relations ly bleeding out their heart-blood upon the ground. There was one who was chopt into the head with a Hatchet, and stript naked, and yet was crawling up and down. It is a solemn sight to see so many Christians lying in their blood, some here, and some there, like a company of Sheep torn by Wolves, All of them stript naked by a company of hell-hounds, roaring, singing, ranting and insulting, as if they would have torn our very hearts out; yet the Lord by his Almighty power preserved a number of us from death, for there were twenty-four of us taken alive and carried Captive.

I had often before this said, that if the Indians should come, I should chuse rather to be killed by them then taken alive but when it came to the tryal my mind changed; their glittering weapons so daunted my spirit, that I chose rather to go along with those (as I may say) ravenous Beasts, then that moment to end my dayes; and that I may the better declare what happened to me during that grievous Captivity, I shall particularly speak of the severall Removes we had up and down the Wilderness.

The First Remove

Now away we must go with those Barbarous Creatures, with our bodies wounded and bleeding, and our hearts no less than our bodies. About a mile we went that night, up upon a hill within sight of the Town, where they intended to lodge. There was hard by a vacant house (deserted by the English before, for fear of the Indians). I asked them whither I might not lodge in the house that night to which they answered, what will you love English men still? This was the dolefullest night that ever my eyes saw. Oh the roaring, and singing and dancing, and yelling of those black creatures in the night, which made the place a lively resemblance of hell. And as miserable was the wast that was there made, of Horses, Cattle, Sheep, Swine, Calves, Lambs, Roasting Pigs, and Fowl (which they had plundered in the Town) some roasting, some lying and burning, and some boyling to feed our merciless Enemies; who were joyful enough though we were disconsolate. To add to the dolefulness of the former day, and the dismalness of the present night: my thoughts ran upon my losses and sad bereaved condition. All was gone, my Husband gone (at least separated from me, he being in the Bay; and to add to my grief, the Indi-

ans told me they would kill him as he came homeward) my Children gone, my Relations and Friends gone, our House and home and all our comforts within door, and without, all was gone, (except my life) and I knew not but the next moment that might go too. There remained nothing to me but one poor wounded Babe, and it seemed at present worse than death that it was in such a pitiful condition, bespeaking Compassion, and I had no refreshing for it, nor suitable things to revive it. Little do many think what is the savageness and bruitishness of this barbarous Enemy, I even those that seem to profess more than others among them, when the English have fallen into their hands.

Those seven that were killed at Lancaster the summer before upon a Sabbath day, and the one that was afterward killed upon a week day, were slain and mangled in a barbarous manner, by one-ey'd John, and Marlborough's Praying Indians, which Capt. Mosely brought to Boston, as the Indians told me.

The Second Remove

But now, the next morning, I must turn my back upon the Town, and travel with them into the vast and desolate Wilderness, I knew not whither. It is not my tongue, or pen can express the sorrows of my heart, and bitterness of my spirit, that I had at this departure: but God was with me, in a wonderfull manner, carrying me along, and bearing up my spirit, that it did not quite fail. One of the Indians carried my poor wounded Babe upon a horse, it went moaning all along, I shall dy, I shall dy. I went on foot after it, with sorrow that cannot be exprest. At length I took it off the horse, and carried it in my armes till my strength failed, and I fell down with it: Then they set me upon a horse with my wounded Child in my lap, and there being no furniture upon the horse back, as we were going down a steep hill, we both fell over the horses head, at which they like inhumane creatures laught, and rejoyced to see it, though I thought we should there have ended our dayes, as overcome with so many difficulties. But the Lord renewed my strength still, and carried me along, that I might see more of his Power; yea, so much that I could never have thought of, had I not experienced it.

After this it quickly began to snow, and when night came on, they stopt: and now down I must sit in the snow, by a little fire, and a few boughs behind me, with my sick Child in my lap; and calling much for water, being now (through the wound) fallen into a violent Fever. My own wound also growing so stiff, that I could scarce sit down or rise up; yet so it must be, that I must sit all this cold winter night upon the cold snowy ground, with my sick Child in my armes, looking that every hour would be the last of its life; and having no Christian friend near me, either to comfort or help me. Oh, I may see the wonderfull power of God, that my Spirit did not utterly sink under my affliction: still the Lord upheld me with his gracious and mercifull Spirit, and we were both alive to see the light of the next morning.

The Third Remove

The morning being come, they prepared to go on their way. One of the Indians got up upon a horse, and they set me up behind him, with my poor sick Babe in my lap. A very wearisome and tedious day I had of it; what with my own wound, and my Childs being so exceeding sick, and in a lamentable condition with her wound. It may be easily judged what a poor feeble condition we were in, there being not the least crumb of refreshing that came within either of our mouths, from Wednesday night to Saturday night, except only a little cold water. This day in the afternoon, about an hour by Sun, we came to the place where they intended, *viz.* an Indian Town, called Wenimesset, Norward of Quabaug. When we were come, Oh the number of Pagans (now merciless enemies) that there came about me, that I may say as David, Psal. 27. 13, *I had fainted, unless I had believed*, etc. The next day was the Sabbath: I then remembered how careless I had been of Gods holy time, how many Sabbaths I had lost and mispent, and how evily I had walked in Gods sight; which lay so close unto my spirit, that it was easie for me to see how righteous it was with God to cut off the thread of my life, and cast me out of his

presence for ever. Yet the Lord still shewed mercy to me, and upheld me; and as he wounded me with one hand, so he healed me with the other. This day there came to me one Robbert Pepper (a man belonging to Roxbury) who was taken in Captain Beers his Fight, and had been now a considerable time with the Indians; and up with them almost as far as Albany, to see king Philip, as he told me, and was now very lately come into these parts. Hearing, I say, that I was in this Indian Town, he obtained leave to come and see me. He told me, he himself was wounded in the leg at Captain Beers his Fight; and was not able some time to go, but as they carried him, and as he took Oaken leaves and laid to his wound, and through the blessing of God he was able to travel again. Then I took Oaken leaves and laid to my side, and with the blessing of God it cured me also; yet before the cure was wrought, I may say, as it is in Psal. 38. 5, 6. *My wounds stink and are corrupt, I am troubled, I am bowed down greatly, I go mourning all the day long.* I sat much alone with a poor wounded Child in my lap, which moaned night and day, having nothing to revive the body, or cheer the spirits of her, but in stead of that, sometimes one Indian would come and tell me one hour, that your Master will knock your Child in the head, and then a second, and then a third, your Master will quickly knock your Child in the head.

This was the comfort I had from them, miserable comforters are ye all, as he said. Thus nine dayes I sat upon my knees, with my Babe in my lap, till my flesh was raw again; my Child being even ready to depart this sorrowfull world, they bade me carry it out to another Wigwam (I suppose because they would not be troubled with such spectacles) Whither I went with a very heavy heart, and down I sat with the picture of death in my lap. About two houres in the night, my sweet Babe like a Lambe departed this life, on Feb. 18, 1675. It being about six yeares, and five months old. It was nine dayes from the first wounding, in this miserable condition, without any refreshing of one nature or other, except a little cold water. I cannot, but take notice, how at another time I could not bear to be in the room where any dead person was, but now the case is changed; I must and could ly down by my dead Babe, side by side all the night after. I have thought since of the wonderfull goodness of God to me, in preserving me in the use of my reason and senses, in that distressed time, that I did not use wicked and violent means to end my own miserable life. In the morning, when they understood that my child was dead they sent for me home to my Masters Wigwam: (by my Master in this writing, must be understood Quanopin, who was a Saggamore, and married King Phillips wives Sister; not that he first took me, but I was sold to him by another Narrhaganset Indian, who took me when first I came out of the Garison). I went to take up my dead child in my arms to carry it with me, but they bid me let it alone: there was no resisting, but goe I must and leave it. When I had been at my masters wigwam, I took the first opportunity I could get, to go look after my dead child: when I came I askt them what they had done with it? then they told me it was upon the hill: then they went and shewed me where it was, where I saw the ground was newly digged, and there they told me they had buried it: There I left that Child in the Wilderness, and must commit it, and my self also in this Wilderness-condition, to him who is above all. God having taken away this dear Child, I went to see my daughter Mary, who was at this same Indian Town, at a Wigwam not very far off, though we had little liberty or opportunity to see one another. She was about ten years old, and taken from the door at first by a Praying Ind and afterward sold for a gun. When I came in sight, she would fall a weeping; at which they were provoked, and would not let me come near her, but bade me be gone; which was a heart-cutting word to me. I had one Child dead, another in the Wilderness, I knew not where, the third they would not let me come near to: *Me* (as he said) *have ye bereaved of my Children, Joseph is not, and Simeon is not, and ye will take Benjamin also, all these things are against me*. I could not sit still in this condition, but kept walking from one place to another. And as I was going along, my heart was even overwhelm'd with the thoughts of my condition, and that I should have Children, and a Nation which I knew not ruled over them.

Whereupon I earnestly entreated the Lord, that he would consider my low estate, and shew me a token for good, and if it were his blessed will, some sign and hope of some relief. And indeed quickly the Lord answered, in some measure, my poor prayers: for as I was going up and down mourning and lamenting my condition, my Son came to me, and asked me how I did; I had not seen him before, since the destruction of the Town, and I knew not where he was, till I was informed by himself, that he was amongst a smaller percel of Indians, whose place was about six miles off; with tears in his eyes, he asked me whether his Sister Sarah was dead; and told me he had seen his Sister Mary; and prayed me, that I would not be troubled in reference to himself. The occasion of his coming to see me at this time, was this: There was, as I said, about six miles from us, a smal Plantation of Indians, where it seems he had been during his Captivity: and at this time, there were some Forces of the Ind. gathered out of our company, and some also from them (among whom was my Sons master) to go to assault and burn Medfield: In this time of the absence of his master, his dame brought him to see me. I took this to be some gracious answer to my earnest and unfeigned desire. The next day, *viz.* to this, the Indians returned from Medfield, all the company, for those that belonged to the other smal company, came thorough the Town that now we were at. But before they came to us, Oh! the outragious roaring and hooping that there was: They began their din about a mile before they came to us. By their noise and hooping they signified how many they had destroyed (which was at that time twenty three.) Those that were with us at home, were gathered together as soon as they heard the hooping, and every time that the other went over their number, these at home gave a shout, that the very Earth rung again: And thus they continued till those that had been upon the expedition were come up to the Sagamores Wigwam; and then, Oh, the hideous insulting and triumphing that there was over some Englishmens scalps that they had taken (as their manner is) and brought with them. I cannot but take notice of the wonderfull mercy of God to me in those afflictions, in sending me a Bible. One of the Indians that came from Medfield fight, had brought some plunder, came to me, and asked me, if I would have a Bible, he had got one in his Basket. I was glad of it, and asked him, whether he thought the Indians would let me read? he answered, yes: So I took the Bible, and in that melancholy time, it came into my mind to read first the 28. Chap. of Deut., which I did, and when I had read it, my dark heart wrought on this manner, That there was no mercy for me, that the blessings were gone, and the curses come in their room, and that I had lost my opportunity. But the Lord helped me still to go on reading till I came to Chap. 30 the seven first verses, where I found, There was mercy promised again, if we would return to him by repentance; and though we were scatered from one end of the Earth to the other, yet the Lord would gather us together, and turn all those curses upon our Enemies. I do not desire to live to forget this Scripture, and what comfort it was to me.

Now the Ind. began to talk of removing from this place, some one way, and some another. There were now besides my self nine English Captives in this place (all of them Children, except one Woman). I got an opportunity to go and take my leave of them; they being to go one way, and I another, I asked them whether they were earnest with God for deliverance, they told me, they did as they were able, and it was some comfort to me, that the Lord stirred up Children to look to him. The Woman *viz.* Goodwife Joslin told me, she should never see me again, and that she could find in her heart to run away; I wisht her not to run away by any means, for we were near thirty miles from any English Town, and she very big with Child, and had but one week to reckon; and another Child in her Arms, two years old, and bad Rivers there were to go over, and we were feeble, with our poor and course entertainment. I had my Bible with me, I pulled it out, and asked her whether she would read; we opened the Bible and lighted on Psal. 27, in which Psalm we especially took notice of that, *ver. ult., Wait on the Lord, Be of good courage, and he shall strengthen thine Heart, wait I say on the Lord.*

The Fourth Remove

And now I must part with that little Company I had. Here I parted from my Daughter Mary, (whom I never saw again till I saw her in Dorchester, returned from Captivity), and from four little Cousins and Neighbours, some of which I never saw afterward: the Lord only knows the end of them. Amongst them also was that poor Woman before mentioned, who came to a sad end, as some of the company told me in my travel: She having much grief upon her Spirit, about her miserable condition, being so near her time, she would be often asking the Indians to let her go home; they not being willing to that, and yet vexed with her importunity, gathered a great company together about her, and stript her naked, and set her in the midst of them; and when they had sung and danced about her (in their hellish manner) as long as they pleased, they knockt her on head, and the child in her arms with her: when they had done that, they made a fire and put them both into it, and told the other Children that were with them, that if they attempted to go home, they would serve them in like manner: The Children said, she did not shed one tear, but prayed all the while. But to return to my own Journey; we travelled about half a day or little more, and came to a desolate place in the Wilderness, where there were no Wigwams or Inhabitants before; we came about the middle of the afternoon to this place, cold and wet, and snowy, and hungry, and weary, and no refreshing, for man, but the cold ground to sit on, and our poor Indian cheer.

Heart-aking thoughts here I had about my poor Children, who were scattered up and down among the wild beasts of the forrest: My head was light and dissey (either through hunger or hard lodging, or trouble or altogether) my knees feeble my body raw by sitting double night and day, that I cannot express to man the affliction that lay upon my Spirit, but the Lord helped me at that time to express it to himself. I opened my Bible to read, and the Lord brought that precious Scripture to me, Jer. 31. 16. *Thus saith the Lord, refrain thy voice from weeping, and thine eyes from tears, for thy work shall be rewarded, and they shall come again from the land of the Enemy*. This was a sweet Cordial to me, when I was ready to faint, many and many a time have I sat down, and weept sweetly over this Scripture. At this place we continued about four dayes.

The Fifth Remove

The occasion (as I thought) of their moving at this time, was, the English Army, it being near and following them: For they went, as if they had gone for their lives, for some considerable way, and then they made a stop, and chose some of their stoutest men, and sent them back to hold the English Army in play whilst the rest escaped: And then, like Jehu, they marched on furiously, with their old, and with their young: some carried their old decrepit mothers, some carried one, and some another. Four of them carried a great Indian upon a Bier; but going through a thick Wood with him, they were hindered, and could make no hast; whereupon they took him upon their backs, and carried him, one at a time, till they came to Bacquaug River. Upon a Friday, a little after noon we came to this River. When all the company was come up, and were gathered together, I thought to count the number of them, but they were so many, and being somewhat in motion, it was beyond my skil. In this travel, because of my wound, I was somewhat favoured in my load; I carried only my knitting work and two quarts of parched meal: Being very faint I asked my mistriss to give me one spoonfull of the meal, but she would not give me a taste. They quickly fell to cutting dry trees, to make Rafts to carry them over the river: and soon my turn came to go over: By the advantage of some brush which they had laid upon the Raft to sit upon, I did not wet my foot (which many of themselves at the other end were mid-leg deep) which cannot but be acknowledged as a favour of God to my weakned body, it being a very cold time. I was not before acquainted with such kind of doings or dangers. *When thou passeth through the waters I will be with thee, and through the Rivers they shall not overflow thee*, Isai. 43. 2. A certain number of us got over the River that night, but it was the night after the Sabbath before all the company was got over. On the Saturday they

boyled an old Horses leg which they had got, and so we drank of the broth, as soon as they thought it was ready, and when it was almost all gone, they filled it up again.

The first week of my being among them, I hardly ate any thing; the second week, I found my stomach grow very faint for want of something; and yet it was very hard to get down their filthy trash: but the third week, though I could think how formerly my stomach would turn against this or that, and I could starve and dy before I could eat such things, yet they were sweet and savoury to my taste. I was at this time knitting a pair of white cotton stockins for my mistriss; and had not yet wrought upon a Sabbath day; when the Sabbath came they bade me go to work; I told them it was the Sabbath day, and desired them to let me rest, and told them I would do as much more tomorrow; to which they answered me, they would break my face. And here I cannot but take notice of the strange providence of God in preserving the heathen: They were many hundreds, old and young, some sick, and some lame, many had Papooses at their backs, the greatest number at this time with us, were Squaws, and they travelled with all they had, bag and baggage, and yet they got over this River aforesaid; and on Munday they set their Wigwams on fire, and away they went: On that very day came the English Army after them to this River, and saw the smoak of their Wigwams, and yet this River put a stop to them. God did not give them courage or activity to go over after us; we were not ready for so great a mercy as victory and deliverance; if we had been, God would have found out a way for the English to have passed this River, as well as for the Indians with their Squaws and Children, and all their Luggage. *Oh that my People had hearkened to me, and Israel had walked in my ways, I should soon have subdued their Enemies, and turned my hand against their Adversaries*, Psal. 81: 13. 14. . . .

The Sixth Remove

On Munday (as I said) they set their Wigwams on fire, and went away. It was a cold morning, and before us there was a great Brook with ice on it;

some waded through it, up to the knees and higher, but others went till they came to a Beaver-dam, and I amongst them, where through the good providence of God, I did not wet my foot. I went along that day mourning and lamenting, leaving farther my own Country, and travelling into the vast and howling Wilderness, and I understood something of Lot's Wife's Temptation, when she looked back: we came that day to a great Swamp, by the side of which we took up our lodging that night. When I came to the brow of the hil, that looked toward the Swamp, I thought we had been come to a great Indian Town (though there were none but our own Company) The Indians were as thick as the trees: it seemed as if there had been a thousand Hatchets going at once: if one looked before one, there was nothing but Indians, and behind one, nothing but Indians, and so on either hand, I my self in the midst, and no Christian soul near me, and yet how hath the Lord preserved me in safety? Oh the experience that I have had of the goodness of God, to me and mine!

The Seventh Remove

After a restless and hungry night there, we had a wearisome time of it the next day. The Swamp by which we lay, was, as it were, a deep Dungeon, and an exceeding high and steep hill before it. Before I got to the top of the hill, I thought my heart and legs, and all would have broken, and failed me. What through faintness, and soreness of body, it was a grievous day of travel to me. As we went along, I saw a place where English Cattle had been: that was comfort to me, such as it was: quickly after that we came to an English Path, which so took with me, that I thought I could have freely lyen down and dyed. That day, a little after noon, we came to Squaukhcag, where the Indians quickly spread themselves over the deserted English Fields, gleaning what they could find; some pickt up cars of Wheat that were crickled down, some found ears of Indian Corn, some found Ground-nuts, and others sheaves of Wheat that were frozen together in the shock, and went to threshing of them out. My self got two ears of

Indian Corn, and whilst I did but turn my back, one of them was stolen from me, which much troubled me. There came an Indian to them at that time, with a basket of Horse-liver. I asked him to give me a piece: What, sayes he, can you eat Horse-liver? I told him, I would try, if he would give a piece, which he did, and I laid it on the coals to rost; but before it was half ready they got half of it away from me, so that I was fain to take the rest and eat it as it was, with the blood about my mouth, and yet a savoury bit it was to me: *For to the hungry Soul every bitter thing is sweet.* A solemn sight methought it was, to see Fields of wheat and Indian Corn forsaken and spoiled: and the remainders of them to be food for our merciless Enemies. That night we had a mess of wheat for our Supper.

The Eighth Remove

On the morrow morning we must go over the River, *i. e.* Connecticot, to meet with King Philip; two Cannoos full, they had carried over, the next Turn I my self was to go; but as my foot was upon the Cannoo to step in, there was a sudden out-cry among them, and I must step back; and instead of going over the River, I must go four or five miles up the River farther Northward. Some of the Indians ran one way, and some another. The cause of this rout was, as I thought, their espying some English Scouts, who were thereabout. In this travel up the River, about noon the Company made a stop, and sate down; some to eat, and others to rest them. As I sate amongst them, musing of things past, my Son Joseph unexpectedly came to me: we asked of each others welfare, bemoaning our dolefull condition, and the change that had come upon uss. We had Husband and Father; and Children, and Sisters, and Friends, and Relations, and House, and Home, and many Comforts of this Life: but now we may say as Job, *Naked came I out of my Mothers Womb, and naked shall I return: The Lord gave, and the Lord hath taken away, Blessed be the Name of the Lord.* I asked him whither he would read; he told me, he earnestly desired it, I gave him my Bible, and he lighted upon that comfortable Scripture, Psal. 118. 17, 18. *I shall not dy but live, and declare the works of the Lord: the Lord hath chastened me sore, yet he hath not given me over to death.* Look here, Mother (sayes he) did you read this? And here I may take occasion to mention one principall ground of my setting forth these Lines: even as the Psalmist sayes, To declare the Works of the Lord, and his wonderfull Power in carrying us along, preserving us in the Wilderness, while under the Enemies hand, and returning of us in safety again, And His goodness in bringing to my hand so many comfortable and suitable Scriptures in my distress. But to Return, We travelled on till night; and in the morning, we must go over the River to Philip's Crew. When I was in the Cannoo, I could not but be amazed at the numerous crew of Pagans that were on the Bank on the other side. When I came ashore, they gathered all about me, I sitting alone in the midst: I observed they asked one another questions, and laughed, and rejoyced over their Gains and Victories. Then my heart began to fail: and I fell a weeping which was the first time to my remembrance, that I wept before them. Although I had met with so much Affliction, and my heart was many times ready to break, yet could I not shed one tear in their sight: but rather had been all this while in a maze, and like one astonished: but now I may say as, Psal. 137. 1. *By the Rivers of Babylon, there we sate down: yea, we wept when we remembered Zion.* There one of them asked me, why I wept, I could hardly tell what to say: yet I answered, they would kill me: No, said he, none will hurt you. Then came one of them and gave me two spoon-fulls of Meal to comfort me, and another gave me half a pint of Pease; which was more worth than many Bushels at another time. Then I went to see King Philip, he bade me come in and sit down, and asked me whether I woold smoke it (a usual Complement nowadayes amongst Saints and Sinners) but this no way suited me. For though I had formerly used Tobacco, yet I had left it ever since I was first taken. It seems to be a Bait, the Devil layes to make men loose their precious time: I remember with shame, how formerly, when I had taken two or three pipes, I was presently ready for another, such a bewitching thing it is: But I thank God, he has now given me power over it; surely there are many who may be better imployed than to ly sucking a stinking Tobacco-pipe.

Now the Indians gather their Forces to go against North Hampton: over-night one went about yelling and hooting to give notice of the design. Whereupon they fell to boyling of Ground-nuts, and parching of Corn (as many as had it) for their Provision: and in the morning away they went. During my abode in this place, Philip spake to me to make a shirt for his boy, which I did, for which he gave me a shilling: I offered the mony to my master, but he bade me keep it: and with it I bought a piece of Horse flesh. Afterwards he asked me to make a Cap for his boy, for which he invited me to Dinner. I went, and he gave me a Pancake, about as big as two fingers; it was made of parched wheat, beaten, and fryed in Bears grease, but I thought I never tasted pleasanter meat in my life. There was a Squaw who spake to me to make a shirt for her *Sannup*, for which she gave me a piece of Bear. Another asked me to knit a pair of Stockins, for which she gave me a quart of Pease: I boyled my Pease and Bear together, and invited my master and mistriss to dinner, but the proud Gossip, because I served them both in one Dish, would eat nothing, except one bit that he gave her upon the point of his knife. Hearing that my son was come to this place, I went to see him, and found him lying flat upon the ground: I asked him how he could sleep so? he answered me, That he was not asleep, but at Prayer; and lay so, that they might not observe what he was doing. I pray God he may remember these things now he is returned in safety. At this Place (the Sun now getting higher) what with the beams and heat of the Sun, and the smoak of the Wigwams, I thought I should have been blind. I could scarce discern one Wigwam from another. There was here one Mary Thurston of Medfield, who seeing how it was with me, lent me a Hat to wear: but as soon as I was gone, the Squaw (who owned that Mary Thurston) came running after me, and got it away again. Here was the Squaw that gave me one spoonfull of Meal. I put it in my Pocket to keep it safe: yet notwithstanding some body stole it, but put five. Indian Corns in the room of it: which Corns were the greatest Provisions I had in my travel for one day.

The Indians returning from North-Hampton, brought with them some Horses, and Sheep, and other things which they had taken: I desired them, that they would carry me to Albany, upon one of those Horses, and sell me for Powder: for so they had sometimes discoursed. I was utterly hopless of getting home on foot, the way that I came. I could hardly bear to think of the many weary steps I had taken, to come to this place.

The Ninth Remove

But in stead of going either to Albany or homeward, we must go five miles up the River, and then go over it. Here we abode a while. Here lived a sorry Indian, who spoke to me to make him a shirt. When I had done it, he would pay me nothing. But he living by the River side, where I often went to fetch water, I would often be putting of him in mind, and calling for my pay: at last he told me if I would make another shirt, for a Papoos not yet born, he would give me a knife, which he did when I had done it. I carried the knife in, and my master asked me to give it him, and I was not a little glad that I had any thing that they would accept of, and be pleased with. When we were at this place, my Masters maid came home, she had been gone three weeks into the Narrhaganset Country, to fetch Corn, where they had stored up some in the ground: she brought home about a peck and half of Corn. This was about the time that their great Captain, Naananto, was killed in the Narrhaganset Countrey. My Son being now about a mile from me, I asked liberty to go and see him, they bade me go, and away I went: but quickly lost my self, travelling over Hills and thorough Swamps, and could not find the way to him. And I cannot but admire at the wonderfull power and goodness of God to me, in that, though I was gone from home, and met with all sorts of Indians, and those I had no knowledge of, and there being no Christian soul near me; yet not one of them offered the least imaginable miscarriage to me. I turned homeward again, and met with my master, he shewed me the way to my Son: When I came to him I found him not well: and withall he had a boyl on his side, which much troubled him: We bemoaned one another awhile, as the Lord helped us, and then I returned again. When I was returned, I found my self as unsatisfied as I was before. I went up and down mourning and lamenting: and my spirit was ready to sink, with the thoughts of my poor Children: my Son was ill, and I could not but think of his mournfull looks, and no Christian Friend was near him, to do any office of love for him, either for Soul or Body. And my poor Girl, I knew not where she was, nor whither she was sick, or well, or alive, or dead. I repaired under these thoughts to my Bible (my great comfort in that time) and that Scripture came to my hand, *Cast thy burden upon the Lord, and He shall sustain thee*, Psal. 55. 22.

But I was fain to go and look after something to satisfie my hunger, and going among the Wigwams, I went into one, and there found a Squaw who shewed, her self very kind to me, and gave me a piece of Bear. I put it into my pocket, and came home, but could not find an opportunity to broil it, for fear they would get it from me, and there it lay all that day and night in my stinking pocket. In the morning I went to the same Squaw, who had a Kettle of Ground nuts boyling; I asked her to let me boyle my piece of Bear in her Kettle, which she did, and gave me some Ground-nuts to eat with it: and I cannot but think how pleasant it was to me. I have sometime seen Bear baked very handsomly among the English, and some like it, but the thoughts that it was Bear, made me tremble: but now that was savoury to me that one would think was enough to turn the stomach of a bruit Creature.

One bitter cold day, I could find no room to sit down before the fire: I went out, and could not tell what to do, but I went in to another Wigwam, where they were also sitting round the fire, but the Squaw laid a skin for me, and bid me sit down, and gave me some Ground-nuts, and bade me come again: and told me they would buy me, if they were able, and yet these were strangers to me that I never saw before.

The Tenth Remove

That day a small part of the Company removed about three quarters of a mile, intending further the next day. When they came to the place where they intended to lodge, and had pitched their wigwams, being hungry I went again back to the place we were before at, to get something to eat: being encouraged by the Squaws kindness, who bade me come again; when I was there, there came an Indian to look after me, who when he had found me, kickt me all along: I went home and found Venison roasting that night, but they would not give me one bit of it. Sometimes I met with favour, and sometimes with nothing but frowns. . . .

The Nineteenth Remove

They said, when we went out, that we must travel to Wachuset this day. But a bitter weary day I had of it, travelling now three dayes together, without resting any day between. At last, after many weary steps, I saw Wachuset hills, but many miles off. Then we came to a great Swamp, through which we travelled, up to the knees in mud and water, which was heavy going to one tyred before. Being almost spent, I thought I should have sunk down at last, and never gat out; but I may say, as in Psal. 94.18, *When my foot slipped, thy mercy, O Lord, held me up*. Going along, having indeed my life, but little spirit, Philip, who was in the Company, came up and took me by the hand, and said, Two weeks more and you shal be Mistress again. I asked him, if he spake true? he answered, Yes, and quickly you shal come to your master again; who had been gone from us three weeks. After many weary steps we came to Wachuset, where he was: and glad I was to see him. He asked me, When I washt me? I told him not this month, then he fetcht me some water himself, and bid me wash, and gave me the Glass to see how I lookt; and bid his Squaw give me something to eat: so she gave me a mess of Beans and meat, and a little Ground-nut Cake. I was wonderfully revived with this favour shewed me, Psal. 106. 46, *He made them also to be pittied, of all those that carried them Captives*.

My master had three Squaws, living sometimes with one, and sometimes with another one, this old Squaw, at whose Wigwam I was, and with whom my Master had been those three weeks. Another was Wattimore, with whom I had lived and served all this while: A severe and proud Dame she was, bestowing every day in dressing her self neat as much time as any of the Gentry of the land: powdering her hair, and painting her face, going with Neck-laces, with Jewels in her ears, and Bracelets upon her hands: When she had dressed her self, her work was to make Girdles of Wampom and Beads. The third Squaw was a younger one, by whom he had two Papooses. By that time I was refresht by the old Squaw, with whom my master was, Wettimores Maid came to call me home, at which I fell a weeping. Then the old Squaw told me, to encourage me, that if I wanted victuals, I should come to her, and that I should ly there in her Wigwam. Then I went with the maid, and quickly came again and lodged there. The Squaw laid a Mat under me, and a good Rugg over me; the first time I had any such kindness shewed me. I understood that Wettimore thought, that if she should let me go and serve with the old Squaw, she would be in danger to loose, not only my service, but the redemption-pay also. And I was not a little glad to hear this; being by it raised in my hopes, that in Gods due time there would be an end of this sorrowfull hour. Then came an Indian, and asked me to knit him three pair of Stockins, for which I had a Hat, and a silk Handkerchief. Then another asked me to make her a shift, for which she gave me an Apron.

Then came Tom and Peter, with the second Letter from the Council, about the Captives. Though they were Indians, I gat them by the hand, and burst out into tears; my heart was so full that I could not speak to them; but recovering my self, I asked them how my husband did, and all my friends and acquaintance? they said, They are all very well but melancholy. They brought me two Biskets, and a pound of Tobacco. The Tobacco I quickly gave away; when it was all gone; one asked me to give him a pipe of Tobacco, I told him it was all gone; then began he to rant and threaten. I told him when my Husband came I would give him some: Hang him Rogue (sayes he) I will knock out his brains, if he comes here. And then again, in the same breath they would say, That if there should come an hundred without Guns, they would do them no hurt. So unstable and like mad men they were. So that fearing the worst, I durst not send to my Husband, though there were some thoughts of his coming to Redeem and fetch me, not knowing what might follow. For there was little more trust to them then to the master they served. When the Letter was come, the

Saggamores met to consult about the Captives, and called me to them to enquire how much my husband would give to redeem me, when I came I sate down among them, as I was wont to do, as their manner is: Then they bade me stand up, and said, they were the General Court. They bid me speak what I thought he would give. Now knowing that all we had was destroyed by the Indians, I was in a great strait: I thought if I should speak of but a little, it would be slighted, and hinder the matter; if of a great sum, I knew not where it would be procured: yet at a venture, I said Twenty pounds, yet desired them to take less; but they would not hear of that, but sent that message to Boston, that for Twenty pounds I should be redeemed. It was a Praying-Indian that wrote their Letter for them. There was another Praying Indian, who told me, that he had a brother, that would not eat Horse; his conscience was so tender and scrupulous (though as large as hell, for the destruction of poor Christians). Then he said, he read that Scripture to him, 2 Kings, 6.25. *There was a famine in Samaria, and behold they besieged it, untill an Asses head was sold for fourscore pieces of silver, and the fourth part of a Kab of Doves dung, for five pieces of silver.* He expounded this place to his brother, and shewed him that it was lawfull to eat that in a Famine which is not at another time. And now, says he, he will eat Horse with any Indian of them all. There was another Praying-Indian, who when he had done all the mischief that he could, betrayed his own Father into the English hands, thereby to purchase his own life. Another Praying-Indian was at Sudbury-fight, Though, as he deserved, he was afterward hanged for it. There was another Praying Indian, so wicked and cruel, as to wear a string about his neck, strung with Christians fingers. Another Praying-Indian, when they went to Sudbury-fight, went with them, and his Squaw also with him, with her Papoos at her back: Before they went to that fight, they got a company together to *Powaw*; the manner was as followeth. There was one that kneeled upon a Deerskin, with the company round him in a ring who kneeled, and striking upon the ground with their hands, and with sticks, and muttering or humming with their mouths; besides him who kneeled in the ring, there also stood one with a Gun in his hand: Then he on the Deer-skin made a speech, and all manifested assent to it: and so they did many times

together. Then they bade him with the Gun go out of the ring, which he did, but when he was out, they called him in again; but he seemed to make a stand, then they called the more earnestly, till he returned again: Then they all sang. Then they gave him two Guns, in either hand one: And so he on the Deer-skin began again; and at the end of every sentence in his speaking, they all assented, humming or muttering with their mouthes, and striking upon the ground with their hands. Then they bade him with the two Guns go out of the ring again; which he did, a little way. Then they called him in again, but he made a stand; so they called him with greater earnestness; but he stood reeling and wavering as if he knew not whither he should stand or fall, or which way to go. Then they called him with exceeding great vehemency, all of them, one and another: after a little while he turned in, staggering as he went, with his Armes stretched out, in either hand a Gun. As soon as he came in, they all sang and rejoyced exceedingly a while. And then he upon the Deer-skin, made another speech unto which they all assented in a rejoicing manner: and so they ended their business, and forthwith went to Sudbury-fight. To my thinking they went without any scruple, but that they should prosper, and gain the victory. And they went out not so rejoycing, but they came home with as great a Victory. For they said they had killed two Captains, and almost an hundred men. One English-man they brought along with them: and he said, it was too true, for they had made sad work at Sudbury, as indeed it proved. Yet they came home without that rejoycing and triumphing over their victory, which they were wont to shew at other times, but rather like Dogs (as they say) which have lost their ears. Yet I could not perceive that it was for their own loss of men: They said, they had not lost above five or six: and I missed none, except in one Wigwam. When they went, they acted as if the Devil had told them that they should gain the victory: and now they acted, as if the Devil had told them they should have a fall. Whither it were so or no, I cannot tell, but so it proved, for quickly they began to fall, and so held on that Summer, till they came to utter ruine. They came home on a Sabbath day, and the *Powaw* that kneeled upon the Deerskin came home (I may say, without abuse) as black as the

Devil. When my master came home, he came to me and bid me make a shirt for his Papoos, of a holland-laced Pillowbeer. About that time there came an Indian to me and bid me come to his Wigwam, at night, and he would give me some Pork and Ground-nuts. Which I did, and as I was eating, another Indian said to me, he seems to be your good Friend, but he killed two Englishmen at Sudbury, and there ly their Cloaths behind you: I looked behind me, and there I saw bloody Cloaths, with Bullet-holes in them; yet the Lord suffered not this wretch to do me any hurt; Yea, instead of that, he many times refresht me: five or six times did he and his Squaw refresh my feeble carcass. If I went to their Wigwam at any time, they would always give me something, and yet they were strangers that I never saw before. Another Squaw gave me a piece of fresh Pork, and a little Salt with it, and lent me her Pan to Fry it in; and I cannot but remember what a sweet, pleasant and delightfull relish that bit had to me, to this day. So little do we prize common mercies when we have them to the full.

The Twentieth Remove

It was their usual manner to remove, when they had done any mischief, lest they should be found out: and so they did at this time. We went about three or four miles, and there they built a great Wigwam, big enough to hold an hundred Indians, which they did in preparation to a great day of Dancing. They would say now amongst themselves, that the Governour would be so angry for his loss at Sudbury, that he would send no more about the Captives, which made me grieve and tremble. My Sister being not far from the place where we now were, and hearing that I was here, desired her master to let her come and see me, and he was willing to it, and would go with her: but she being ready before him, told him she would go before, and was come within a Mile or two of the place; Then he overtook her, and began to rant as if he had been mad; and made her go back again in the Rain; so that I never saw her till I saw her in Charlestown. But the Lord requited many of their ill doings, for this Indian her Master, was hanged afterward at Boston. The Indians now began to come from all quarters, against their merry

dancing day. Among some of them came one Goodwife Kettle. I told her my heart was so heavy that it was ready to break: so is mine too said she, but yet said, I hope we shall hear some good news shortly. I could hear how earnestly my Sister desired to see me, and I as earnestly desired to see her: and yet neither of us could get an opportunity. My Daughter was also now about a mile off, and I had not seen her in nine or ten weeks, as I had not seen my Sister since our first taking. I earnestly desired them to let me go and see them: yea, I intreated, begged, and perswaded them, but to let me see my Daughter; and yet so hard hearted were they, that they would not suffer it. They made use of their tyrannical power whilst they had it: but through the Lords wonderfull mercy, their time was now but short.

On a Sabbath day, the Sun being about an hour high in the afternoon, came Mr. John Hoar (the Council permitting him, and his own foreward spirit inclining him) together with the two forementioned Indians, Tom and Peter, with their third Letter from the Council. When they came near, I was abroad: though I saw them not, they presently called me in, and bade me sit down and not stir. Then they catched up their Guns, and away they ran, as if an Enemy had been at hand; and the Guns went off apace. I manifested some great trouble, and they asked me what was the matter? I told them, I thought they had killed the English-man (for they had in the mean time informed me that an Englishman was come) they said, No; They shot over his Horse and under, and before his Horse; and they pusht him this way and that way, at their pleasure: shewing what they could do: Then they let them come to their Wigwams. I begged of them to let me see the English-man, but they would not. But there was I fain to sit their pleasure. When they had talked their fill with him, they suffered me to go to him. We asked each other of our welfare, and how my Husband did, and all my Friends? He told me they were all well, and would be glad to see me. Amongst other things which my Husband sent me, there came a pound of Tobacco: which I sold for nine shillings in Money: for many of the Indians for want of Tobacco, smoaked Hemlock, and Ground-Ivy. It was a great mistake in any, who thought I sent for Tobacco: for through the favour of God, that desire was overcome. I now asked them, whither I should go home with Mr. Hoar? They answered No, one and another of them: and it being night, we lay down with that answer; in the morning, Mr Hoar invited the Saggamores to Dinner; but when we went to get it ready, we found that they had stollen the greatest part of the Provision Mr. Hoar had brought, out of his Bags, in the night. And we may see the wonderfull power of God, in that one passage, in that when there was such a great number of the Indians together, and so greedy of a little good food; and no English there, but Mr. Hoar and my self: that there they did not knock us in the head, and take what we had: there being not only some Provision, but also Trading-cloth, a part of the twenty pounds agreed upon: But instead of doing us any mischief, they seemed to be ashamed of the fact, and said, it were some Matchit Indian that did it. Oh, that we could believe that there is no thing too hard for God! God shewed his Power over the Heathen in this, as he did over the hungry Lyons when Daniel was cast into the Den. Mr. Hoar called them betime to Dinner, but they ate very little, they being so busie in dressing themselves, and getting ready for their Dance: which was carried on by eight of them, four Men and four Squaws: My master and mistress being two. He was dressed in his Holland shirt, with great Laces sewed at the tail of it, he had his silver Buttons, his white Stockins, his Garters were hung round with Shillings, and he had Girdles of Wampom upon his head and shoulders. She had a Kersey Coat, and covered with Girdles of Wampom from the Loins upward: her armes from her elbows to her hands were covered with Bracelets; there were handfulls of Necklaces about her neck, and severall sorts of Jewels in her ears. She had fine red Stokins, and white Shoos, her hair powdered and face painted Red, that was alwayes before Black. And all the Dancers were after the same manner. There were two other singing and knocking on a Kettle for their musick. They keept hopping up and down one after another, with a Kettle of water in the midst, standing warm upon some Embers, to drink of when they were dry. They held on till it was almost night, throwing out Wampom to the standers by. At night I asked them again, if I should go home? They all as one said No, except my Husband would come for me. When we were lain down, my Master went out of the Wigwam, and by and by sent in an Indian

called James the Printer, who told Mr. Hoar, that my Master would let me go home to morrow, if he would let him have one pint of Liquors. Then Mr. Hoar called his own Indians, Tom and Peter, and bid them go and see whither he would promise it before them three: and if he would, he should have it; which he did, and he had it. Then Philip smeling the business cal'd me to him, and asked me what I would give him, to tell me some good news, and speak a good word for me. I told him, I could not tell what to give him, I would any thing I had, and asked him what he would have? He said, two Coats and twenty shillings in Mony, and half a bushel of seed Corn, and some Tobacco. I thanked him for his love: but I knew the good news as well as the crafty Fox. My Master after he had had his drink, quickly came ranting into the Wigwam again, and called for Mr. Hoar, drinking to him, and saying, He was a good man: and then again he would say, Hang him Rogue: Being almost drunk, he would drink to him, and yet presently say he should be hanged. Then he called for me. I trembled to hear him, yet I was fain to go to him, and he drank to me, shewing no incivility. He was the first Indian I saw drunk all the while that I was amongst them. At last his Squaw ran out, and he after her, round the Wigwam, with his mony jingling at his knees: But she escaped him: But having an old Squaw he ran to her: and so through the Lords mercy, we were no more troubled that night. Yet I had not a comfortable nights rest: for I think I can say, I did not sleep for three nights together. The night before the Letter came from the Council, I could not rest, I was so full of feares and troubles, God many times leaving us most in the dark, when deliverance is nearest: yea, at this time I could not rest night nor day. The next night I was overjoyed, Mr. Hoar being come, and that with such good tidings. The third night I was even swallowed up with the thoughts of things, *viz.* that ever I should go home again; and that I must go, leaving my Children behind me in the Wilderness; so that sleep was now almost departed from mine eyes.

On Tuesday morning they called their General Court (as they call it) to consult and determine, whether I should go home or no: And they all as one man did seemingly consent to it, that I should go home; except Philip, who would not come among them.

But before I go any further, I would take leave to mention a few remarkable passages of providence, which I took special notice of in my afflicted time.

1. Of the fair opportunity lost in the long March, a little after the Fort-fight, when our English Army was so numerous, and in pursuit of the Enemy, and so near as to take several and destroy them: and the Enemy in such distress for food, that our men might track them by their rooting in the earth for Ground-nuts, whilest they were flying for their lives. I say, that then our Army should want Provision, and be forced to leave their pursuit and return homeward: and the very next week the Enemy came upon our Town, like Bears bereft of their whelps, or so many ravenous Wolves, rending us and our Lambs to death. But what shall I say? God seemed to leave his People to themselves, and order all things for his own holy ends. *Shal there be evil in the City and the Lord hath not done it? They are not grieved for the affliction of Joseph, therefore shal they go Captive, with the first that go Captive.* It is the Lords doing, and it should be marvelous in our eyes.

2. I cannot but remember how the Indians derided the slowness, and dulness of the English Army, in its setting out. For after the desolations at Lancaster and Medfield, as I went along with them, they asked me when I thought the English Army would come after them? I told them I could not tell: It may be they will come in May, said they. Thus did they scoffe at us, as if the English would be a quarter of a year getting ready.

3. Which also I have hinted before, when the English Army with new supplies were sent forth to pursue after the enemy, and they understanding it, fled before them till they came to Baquaug River, where they forthwith went over safely: that that River should be impassable to the English. I can but admire to see the wonderfull providence of God in preserving the heathen for farther affliction to our poor Countrey. They could go in great numbers over, but the English must stop: God had an over-ruling hand in all those things.

4. It was thought, if their Corn were cut down, they would starve and dy with hunger: and all their Corn that could be found, was destroyed, and they driven from that little they had in store, into the Woods in the midst of Winter; and yet how to admiration did the Lord preserve them for his holy ends, and the destruction of many still amongst the English! strangely did the Lord provide for them; that I did not see (all the time I was among them) one Man, Woman, or Child, die with hunger.

Though many times they would eat that, that a Hog or a Dog would hardly touch; yet by that God strengthned them to be a scourge to his People.

The chief and commonest food was Ground-nuts: They eat also Nuts and Acorns, Harty-choaks, Lilly roots, Groundbeans, and several other weeds and roots, that I know not.

They would pick up old bones, and cut them to pieces at the joynts, and if they were full of wormes and magots, they would scald them over the fire to make the vermine come out, and then boile them, and drink up the Liquor, and then beat the great ends of them in a Morter, and so eat them. They would eat Horses guts, and ears, and all sorts of wild Birds which they could catch: also Bear, Vennison, Beaver, Tortois, Frogs, Squirrels, Dogs, Skunks, Rattle-snakes; yea, the very Bark of Trees; besides all sorts of creatures, and provision which they plundered from the English. I can but stand in admiration to see the wonderful power of God, in providing for such a vast number of our Enemies in the Wilderness, where there was nothing to be seen, but from hand to mouth. Many times in a morning, the generality of them would eat up all they had, and yet have some forther supply against they wanted. It is said, Psal. 81. 13, 14. *Oh, that my People had hearkned to me, and Israel had walked in my wayes, I should soon have subdued their Enemies, and turned my hand against their Adversaries.* But now our perverse and evil carriages in the sight of the Lord, have so offended him, that instead of turning his hand against them, the Lord feeds and nour-ishes them up to be a scourge to the whole Land.

5. Another thing that I would observe is, the strange providence of God, in turning things about when the Indians was at the highest, and the English at the lowest. I was with the Enemy eleven weeks and five dayes, and not one Week passed without the fury of the Enemy, and some desola-tion by fire and sword upon one place or other. They mourned (with their black faces) for their own lossess, yet triumphed and rejoyced in their inhumane, and many times devilish cruelty to the

English. They would boast much of their Victories; saying, that in two hours time they had destroyed such a Captain, and his Company at such a place; and such a Captain and his Company in such a place; and such a Captain and his Company in such a place: and boast how many Towns they had destroyed, and then scoffe, and say, They had done them a good turn, to send them to Heaven so soon. Again, they would say, This Summer that they would knock all the Rogues in the head, or drive them into the Sea, or make them flie the Countrey: thinking surely, Agag-like, *The bitterness of Death is past.* Now the Heathen begins to think all is their own, and the poor Christians hopes to fail (as to man) and now their eyes are more to God, and their hearts sigh heaven-ward: and to say in good earnest, *Help Lord, or we perish:* When the Lord had brought his people to this, that they saw no help in any thing but himself: then he takes the quarrel into his own hand: and though they had made a pit, in their own imaginations, as deep as hell for the Christians that Summer, yet the Lord hurll'd them selves into it. And the Lord had not so many wayes before to preserve them, but now he hath as many to destroy them.

But to return again to my going home, where we may see a remarkable change of Providence: At first they were all against it, except my Husband would come for me; but afterwards they assented to it, and seemed much to rejoyce in it; some askt me to send them some Bread, others some Tobacco, others shaking me by the hand, offering me a Hood and Scarfe to ride in; not one moving hand or tongue against it. Thus hath the Lord answered my poor desire, and the many earnest requests of others put up unto God for me. In my travels an Indian came to me, and told me, if I were willing, he and his Squaw would run away, and go home along with me: I told him No: I was not willing to run away, but desired to wait Gods time, that I might go home quietly, and without fear. And now God hath granted me my desire. O the wonderfull power of God that I have seen, and the experience that I have had: I have been in the midst of those roaring Lyons, and Salvage Bears, that feared neither God, nor Man, nor the Devil, by night and day, alone and in company: sleeping all sorts together, and yet not

one of them ever offered me the least abuse of unchastity to me, in word or action. Though some are ready to say, I speak it for my own credit; But I speak it in the presence of God, and to his Glory. Gods Power is as great now, and as sufficient to save, as when he preserved Daniel in the Lions Den; or the three Children in the fiery Furnace. I may well say as his Psal. 107. 12, *Oh give thanks unto the Lord for he is good, for his mercy endureth for ever.* Let the Redeemed of the Lord say so, whom he hath redeemed from the hand of the Enemy, especially that I should come away in the midst of so many hundreds of Enemies quietly and peacably, and not a Dog moving his tongue. So I took my leave of them, and in coming along my heart melted into tears, more then all the while I was with them, and I was almost swallowed up with the thoughts that ever I should go home again. About the Sun going down, Mr. Hoar, and my self, and the two Indians came to Lancaster, and a solemn sight it was to me. There had I lived many comfortable years amongst my Relations and Neighbours, and now not one Christian to be seen, nor one house left standing. We went on to a Farm house that was yet standing, where we lay all night: and a comfortable lodging we had, though nothing but straw to ly on. The Lord preserved us in safety that night, and raised us up again in the morning, and carried us along, that before noon, we came to Concord. Now was I full of joy, and yet not without sorrow: joy to see such a lovely sight, so many Christians together, and some of them my Neighbours: There I met with my Brother, and my Brother in Law, who asked me, if I knew where his Wife was? Poor heart! he had helped to bury her, and knew it not; she being shot down by the house was partly burnt: so that those who were at Boston at the desolation of the Town, and came back afterward, and buried the dead, did not know her. Yet I was not without sorrow, to think how many were looking and longing, and my own Children amongst the rest, to enjoy that deliverance that I had now received, and I did not know whither ever I should see them again. Being recruited with food and raiment we went to Boston that day, where I met with my dear Husband, but the thoughts of our dear Children, one being dead, and the other we could not tell where, abated our comfort each to other. I was not before so much hem'd in with the merciless and cruel Heathen, but now as much with pittiful, tender-hearted and compassionate Christians. In that poor, and destressed, and beggerly condition I was received in, I was kindly entertained in severall Houses: so much love I received from several (some of whom I knew, and others I knew not) that I am not capable to declare it. But the Lord knows them all by name: The Lord reward them seven fold into their bosoms of his spirituals, for their temporals. The twenty pounds the price of my redemption was raised by some Boston Gentlemen, and Mrs. Usher, whose bounty and religious charity, I would not forget to make mention of. Then Mr. Thomas Shepard of Charlstown received us into his House, where we continued eleven weeks; and a Father and Mother they were to us. And many more tender-hearted Friends we met with in that place. We were now in the midst of love, yet not without much and frequent heaviness of heart for our poor Children, and other Relations, who were still in affliction. The week following, after my coming in, the Governour and Council sent forth to the Indians again; and that not without success; for they brought in my Sister, and Good-wife Kettle: Their not knowing where our Children were, was a sore tryal to us still, and yet we were not without secret hopes that we should see them again. That which was dead lay heavier upon my spirit, than those which were alive and amongst the Heathen; thinking how it suffered with its wounds, and I was no way able to relieve it; and how it was buried by the Heathen in the Wilderness from among all Christians. We were hurried up and down in our thoughts, sometime we should hear a report that they were gone this way, and sometimes that; and that they were come in, in this place or that: We kept enquiring and listning to hear concerning them, but no certain news as yet. About this time the Council had ordered a day of publick Thanks-giving though I thought I had still cause of mourning, and being unsettled in our minds, we thought we would ride toward the Eastward, to see if we could hear any thing concerning our Children. And as we were riding along (God is the wise disposer of all things) between Ipswich and Rowly we met with Mr. William Hubbard, who told us that

our Son Joseph was come in to Major Waldrens, and another with him, which was my Sisters Son. I asked him how he knew it? He said, the Major himself told him so. So along we went till we came to Newbury; and their Minister being absent, they desired my Husband to Preach the Thanks giving for them; but he was not willing to stay there that night, but would go over to Salisbury, to hear further, and come again in the morning; which he did, and Preached there that day. At night, when he had done, one came and told him that his Daughter was come in at Providence: Here was mercy on both hands: Now hath God fulfiled that precious Scripture which was such a comfort to me in my distressed condition. When my heart was ready to sink into the Earth (my Children being gone I could not tell whither) and my knees trembled under me, And I was walking through the valley of the shadow of Death: Then the Lord brought, and now has fulfilled that reviving word unto me: *Thus saith the Lord, Refrain thy voice from weeping, and thine eyes from tears, for thy Work shall be rewarded, saith the Lord, and they shall come again from the Land of the Enemy.* Now we were between them, the one on the East, and the other on the West: Our Son being nearest, we went to him first, to Portsmouth, where we met with him, and with the Major also: who told us he had done what he could, but could not redeem him under seven pounds; which the good People thereabouts were pleased to pay. The Lord reward the Major, and all the rest, though unknown to me, for their labour of Love. My Sisters Son was redeemed for four pounds, which the Council gave order for the payment of. Having now received one of our Children, we hastened toward the other; going back through Newbury, my Husband preached there on the Sabbath-day: for which they rewarded him many fold.

On Munday we came to Charlstown, where we heard that the Governour of Road-Island had sent over for our Daughter, to take care of her, being now within his Jurisdiction: which should not pass without our acknowledgments. But she being nearer Rehoboth than Road-Island, Mr. Newman went over, and took care of her, and brought her to his own House. And the goodness of God was admirable to us in our low estate, in that he raised up passionate

Friends on every side to us, when we had nothing to recompance any for their love. The Indians were now gone that way, that it was apprehended dangerous to go to her: But the Carts which carried Provision to the English Army, being guarded, brought her with them to Dorchester, where we received her safe: blessed be the Lord for it, For great is his Power, and he can do whatsoever seemeth him good. Her coming in was after this manner: She was travelling one day with the Indians, with her basket at her back; the company of Indians were got before her, and gone out of sight, all except one Squaw; she followed the Squaw till night, and then both of them lay down, having nothing over them but the heavens, and under them but the earth. Thus she travelled three dayes together, not knowing whither she was going: having nothing to eat or drink but water, and green Hirtle-berries. At last they came into Providence, where she was kindly entertained by several of that Town. The Indians often said, that I should never have her under twenty pounds: But now the Lord hath brought her in upon free-cost, and given her to me the second time. The Lord make us a blessing indeed, each to others. Now have I seen that Scripture also fulfilled, Deut. 30: 4, 7. *If any of thine be driven out to the outmost parts of heaven, from thence will the Lord thy God gather thee, and from thence will he fetch thee. And the Lord thy God will put all these curses upon thine enemies, and on them which hate thee, which persecuted thee.* Thus hath the Lord brought me and mine out of that horrible pit, and hath set us in the midst of tender-hearted and compassionate Christians. It is the desire of my soul, that we may walk worthy of the mercies received, and which we are receiving.

Our Family being now gathered together (those of us that were living) the South Church in Boston hired an House for us: Then we removed from Mr. Shepards, those cordial Friends, and went to Boston, where we continued about three quarters of a year: Still the Lord went along with us, and provided graciously for us. I thought it somewhat strange to set up House-keeping with bare walls; but as Solomon sayes, *Mony answers all things*, and that we had through the benevolence of Christian-friends, some in this Town, and some in that, and others: And some from England, that in a little time we might look, and see the House furnished with love. The Lord hath been exceeding good to us in our low estate, in that when we had neither house nor home, nor other necessaries; the Lord so moved the hearts of these and those towards us, that we wanted neither food, nor raiment for our selves or ours, Prov. 18. 24. *There is a Friend which sticketh closer than a Brother.* And how many such Friends have we found, and now living amongst? And truly such a Friend have we found him to be unto us, in whose house we lived, *viz.* Mr. James Whitcomb, a Friend unto us near hand, and afar off.

I can remember the time, when I used to sleep quietly without workings in my thoughts, whole nights together, but now it is other wayes with me. When all are fast about me, and no eye open, but his who ever waketh, my thoughts are upon things past, upon the awfull dispensation of the Lord towards us; upon his wonderfull power and might, in carrying of us through so many difficulties, in returning us in safety, and suffering none to hurt us. I remember in the night season, how the other day I was in the midst of thousands of enemies, and nothing but death before me: It is then hard work to perswade my self, that ever I should be satisfied with bread again. But now we are fed with the finest of the Wheat, and, as I may say, With honey out of the rock: In stead of the Husk, we have the fatted Calf: The thoughts of these things in the particulars of them, and of the love and goodness of God towards us, make it true of me, what David said of himself, Psal. 6. 5. *I watered my Couch with my tears.* Oh! the wonderfull power of God that mine eyes have seen, affording matter enough for my thoughts to run in, that when others are sleeping mine eyes are weeping.

I have seen the extrem vanity of this World: One hour I have been in health, and wealth, wanting nothing: But the next hour in sickness and wounds, and death, having nothing but sorrow and affliction.

Before I knew what affliction meant, I was ready sometimes to wish for it. When I lived in prosperity, having the comforts of the World about me, my relations by me, my Heart chearfull, and taking little care for any thing; and yet seeing many, whom I preferred before my self, under many tryals and afflictions, in sickness, weakness, poverty, losses, crosses, and cares of the World, I should be sometimes jealous least I should have my portion in this life, and that Scripture would come to my mind, Heb. 12. 6. *For whom the Lord loveth he chasteneth, and scourgeth every Son whom he receiveth.* But now I see the Lord had his time to scourge and chasten me. The portion of some is to have their afflictions by drops, now one drop and then another; but the dregs of the Cup, the Wine of astonishment, like a sweeping rain that leaveth no food, did the Lord prepare to be my portion. Affliction I wanted, and affliction I had, full measure (I thought) pressed down and running over; yet I see, when God calls a Person to any thing, and through never so many difficulties, yet he is fully able to carry them through and make them see, and say they have been gainers thereby. And I hope I can say in some measure, As David did, *It is good for me that I have been afflicted.* The Lord hath shewed me the vanity of these outward things. That they are the Vanity of vanities, and vexation of spirit; that they are but a shadow, a blast, a bubble, and things of no continuance. That we must rely on God himself, and our whole dependance must be upon him. If trouble from smaller matters begin to arise in me, I have something at hand to check my self with, and say, why am I troubled? It was but the other day that if I had had the world, I would have given it for my freedom, or to have been a Servant to a Christian. I have learned to look beyond present and smaller troubles, and to be quieted under them, as Moses said, Exod. 14. 13. *Stand still and see the salvation of the Lord.*

Finis.

Questions

1. Using Rowlandson's narrative for evidence, how distinct were the English and Indian populations of New England in the 1670s?
2. Characterize Wampanoag military techniques and technologies. What advantages did the Wampanoags have over English in the early phase of King Philip's War? From what disadvantages would they suffer in a longer confict?
3. Whom did the Wampanoags kill, and whom did they spare? When and to whom were they cruel or kind? Why?
4. How did Rowlandson feel about praying Indians? Why?
5. How does Rowlandson captivity narrative compare with Cabeza de Vaca's? How much did she change over the course of her captivity? What role did she find among the Wampanoags?
6. What larger meaning did Rowlandson find in her travails? How does her fashion of interpreting events compare with John Winthrop's and Cotton Mather's? Are there episode in her narrative which seem to undercut her main points?
7. Imagine reading an account of the war from an Indian's perspective. How might it differ from Rowlandson's? What would be similar?

10

The West Indies

Columbus failed to locate Japan or the Great Khan in what turned out to be the islands of the West rather than the East Indies, but later European colonists would find a different foundation for fortunes there: tropical crops worked by bound labor. Their tropical island geography and export-oriented economies pushed the colonies of the West Indies to extremes, and splendid mansions and raucous port cities arose alongside fields worked first by indentured Englishmen and then by enslaved Africans. Cultivation and commerce were not, however, the only routes to riches in the Caribbean, and the sea's famous pirates quickly found that cannon and cutlass could extort from ship and town what the whip had extracted from soil and servant.

10.1 A Portrait of Barbados*

An impoverished Royalist fleeing the turmoil of the English civil war, Richard Ligon visited Barbados from 1647 to 1650. He had hoped to find a new fortune, but instead contracted a near-fatal fever. He returned to England and soon landed in debtor's prison. While incarcerated, he wrote A True and Exact History of the Island of Barbados, *first published in 1657. The portion that follows offers a firsthand account of a developing tropical plantation society.*

It were somewhat difficult, to give you an exact account, of the number of persons upon the Island; there being such store of shipping that brings passengers daily to the place, but it has been conjectur'd, by those that are long acquainted, and best seen in the knowledge of the Island, that there are not less than 50 thousand souls, besides *Negroes*;

and some of them who began upon small fortunes, are now risen to very great and vast estates.

The Island is divided into three sorts of men, *viz*: Masters, Servants, and Slaves. The slaves and their posterity, being subject to their Masters for ever, are kept and preserv'd with greater care than the servants, who are theirs but for five years, according to the law of the Island. So that for the time, the servants have the worser lives, for they are put to very hard labour, ill lodging, and their dyet very sleight. When we came first on the Island, some Planters themselves did not eat bone meat, above twice a week: the rest of the seven dayes, Potatoes, Loblolly, and Bonavist. But the servants no bone meat at all, unless an Oxe dyed: and then they were feasted, as long as that lasted. And till they had planted good store of Plantines, the *Negroes* were fed with this kind of food; but most of it Bonavist, and Loblolly, with some ears of Mayes toasted, which food (especially Loblolly,) gave

*Richard Ligon, A *True and Exact History of the Island of Barbados* (London: 1657), 43–54.

them much discontent: But when they had Plantines enough to serve them, they were heard no more to complain; for 'tis a food they take great delight in, and their manner of dressing, and eating it, is this: 'tis gathered for them (somewhat before it be ripe, for so they desire to have it,) upon *Saturday*, by the keeper of the Plantine grove; who is an able *Negro*, and knowes well the number of those that are to be fed with this fruit; and as he gathers, layes them all together, till they fetch them away, which is about five a clock in the afternoon, for that day they break off work sooner by an hour: partly for this purpose, and partly for that the fire in the furnaces is to be put out, and the Ingenio and the rooms made clean; besides they are to wash, shave and trim themselves against *Sunday*. But 'tis a lovely sight to see a hundred handsom *Negroes*, men and women, with every one a grasse-green bunch of these fruits on their heads, every bunch twice as big as their heads, all coming in a train one after another, the black and green so well becoming one another. Having brought this fruit home to their own houses, and pilling off the skin of so much as they will use, they boyl it in water, making it into balls, and so they eat it. One bunch a week is a *Negroe's* allowance. To this, no bread nor drink, but water. Their lodging at night a board, with nothing under, nor any thing a top of them. They are happy people, whom so little contents. Very good servants, if they be not spoyled by the *English*. But more of them hereafter.

As for the usage of the Servants, it is much as the Master is, merciful or cruel; Those that are merciful, treat their Servants well, both in their meat, drink, and lodging, and give them such work, as is not unfit for Christians to do. But if the Masters be cruel, the Servants have very wearisome and miserable lives. Upon the arrival of any ship, that brings servants to the Island, the Planters go aboard; and having bought such of them as they like, send them with a guid to his Plantation; and being come, commands them instantly to make their Cabins, which they not knowing how to do, are to be advised by other of their servants, that are their Seniors; but, if they be churlish, and will not show them, or if materials

be wanting, to make them Cabins, then they are to lye on the ground that night. These Cabins are to be made of sticks, withs, and Plantine leaves, under some little shade that may keep the rain off; Their suppers being a few Potatoes for meat, and water or Mobbie for drink. The next day they are rung out with a Bell to work, at six a clock in the morning, with a severe Overseer to command them, till the Bell ring again, which is at eleven a clock; and then they return, and are set to dinner, either with a mess of Lob-lolly, Bonavist, or Potatoes. At one a clock, they are rung out again to the field, there to work till six, and then home again, to a supper of the same. And if it chance to rain, and wet them through, they have no shift, but must lye so all night. If they put off their cloaths, the cold of the night will strike into them; and if they be not strong men, this ill lodging will put them into a sickness: if they complain, they are beaten by the Overseer; if they resist, their time is doubled, I have seen an Overseer beat a Servant with a cane about the head, till the blood has followed, for a fault that is not worth the speaking of; and yet he must have patience, or worse will follow. Truly, I have seen such cruelty there done to Servants, as I did not think one Christian could have done to another. But, as discreeter and better natur'd men have come to rule there, the servants lives have been much bettered; for now, most of the servants lie in Hamocks, and in warm rooms, and when they come in wet, have shift of shirts and drawers, which is all the cloths they wear, and are fed with *bone meat* twice or thrice a week. Collonel *Walrond* seeing his servants when they came home, toyled with their labour, and wet through with their sweating, thought that shifting of their linnen not sufficient refreshing, nor warmth for their bodies, their pores being much opened by their sweating; and therefore resolved to send into *England* for rug Gowns, such as poor people wear in Hospitals, that so when they had shifted themselves, they might put on those Gowns, and lye down and rest them in their Hamocks; For the Hamocks being but thin, and they having nothing on but Shirts and Drawers, when they awak'd out of their sleeps, they found themselves very cold; and a cold taken there, is harder to be recovered, than in *England*, by how much the body is infeebled by the great toyl, and the Sun's heat, which cannot but very much exhaust the spirits of bodies unaccustomed to it. But this care and charity of Collonel *Walrond's*, lost him nothing in the conclusion; for, he got such love of his servants, as they thought all too little they could do for him; and the love of the servants there, is of much concernment to the Masters, not only in their diligent and painful labour, but in foreseeing and preventing mischiefs that often happen, by the carclessness and sloth-fulness of retchlesse servants; sometimes by laying fire so negligently, as whole lands of Canes and Houses too, are burnt down and consumed, to the utter ruine and undoing of their Masters: For, the materials there being all combustible, and apt to take fire, a little oversight, as the fire of a Tobacco-pipe, being knockt out against a dry stump of a tree, has set it on fire, and the wind fanning that fire, if a land of Canes be but near, and they once take fire, all that are down the wind will be burnt up. Water there is none to quench it, or if it were, a hundred *Negroes* with buckets were not able to do it; so violent and spreading a fire this is, and such a noise it makes, as if two Armies, with a thousand shot of either side, were continually giving fire, every knot of every Cane, giving as great a report as a Pistol. So that there is no way to stop the going on of this flame, but by cutting down and removing all the Canes that grow before it, for the breadth of twenty or thirty footdown the wind, and there the *Negroes* to stand and beat out the fire, as it creeps upon the ground, where the Canes are cut down. And I have seen some *Negroes* so earnest to stop this fire, as with their naked feet to tread, and with their naked bodies to tumble, and roll upon it; so little they regard their own smart or safety, in respect of their Masters benefit. The year before I came away, there were two eminent Planters in the Island, that with such an accident as this, lost at least 10000 J. Sterling, in the value of the Canes that were burnt; the one, Mr. *James Holduppe*, the other, Mr. *Constantine Silvester*: And the latter had not only his Canes, but his house burnt down to the ground. This, and much more mischief has been done, by the negligence and willfulness of servants. And yet some cruel Masters will provoke their Servants so, by extream ill usage, and often and cruel beating them, as they grow desperate, and so joyn together to revenge themselves upon them.

A little before I came from thence, there was such a combination amongst them, as the like was never seen there before. Their sufferings being grown to a great height, and their daily complainings to one another (of the intolerable burdens they labour'd under) being spread throughout the Island; at the last, some amongst them, whose spirits were not able to endure such slavery, resolved to break through it, or dye in the act; and so conspired with some others of their acquaintance, whose sufferings were equal, if not above theirs; and their spirits no way inferiour, resolved to draw as many of the discontented party into this plot, as possibly they could; and those of this perswasion, were the greatest numbers of Servants in the Island. So that a day was appointed to fall upon their Masters, and cut all their throats, and by that means, to make themselves only freemen, but Masters of the Island. And so closely was this plot carried, as no discovery was made, till the day before they were to put it in act: And then one of them, either by the failing of his courage, or some new obligation from the love of his Master, revealed this long plotted conspiracy; and so by this timely advertisement, the Masters were saved: Justice *Hethersall* (whose servant this was) sending Letters to all his friends, and they to theirs, and so one to another, till they were all secured; and, by examination, found out the greatest part of them; whereof eighteen of the principal men in the conspiracy, and they the first leaders and contrivers of the plot, were put to death, for example to the rest. And the reason why they made examples of so many, was, they found these so haughty in their resolutions, and so incorrigible, as they were like enough to become Actors in a second plot, and so they thought good to secure them; and for therest, to have a special eye over them.

It has been accounted a strange thing, that the *Negroes*, being more than double the numbers of the Christians that are there, and they accounted a bloody people, where they think they have power or advantages; and the more bloody, by how much they are more fearful than others: that these should not commit some horrid massacre upon the Christians, thereby to enfranchise themselves, and become Masters of the Island. But there are three reasons that take away this wonder; the one is, They are not suffered to touch or handle any weapons: The other, That they are held in such awe and slavery, as they are fearful to appear in any daring act; and seeing the mustering of our men, and hearing their Gun-shot, (than which nothing is more terrible to them) their spirits are subjugated to so low a condition, as they dare not look up to any bold attempt. Besides these, there is a third reason, which stops all designs of that kind, and that is, They are fetch'd from several parts of *Africa*, who speak several languages, and by that means, one of them understands not another: For, some of them are fetch'd from *Guinny* and *Binny*, some from *Cutchem*, some from *Angela*, and some from the River of *Gambia*. And in some of these places where petty Kingdomes are, they sell their Subjects, and such as they take in Battle, whom they make slaves; and some mean men sell their Servants, their Children, and sometimes their Wives; and think all good traffick, for such commodities as our Merchants send them.

When they are brought to us, the Planters buy them out of the Ship, where they find them stark naked, and therefore cannot be deceived in any outward infirmity. They choose them as they do Horses in a Market; the strongest, youth fullest, and most beautiful, yield the greatest prices. Thirty pound sterling is a price for the best man *Negroe*; and twenty five, twenty fix, or twenty seven pound for a Woman; the Children are at easier rates. And we buy them so, as the sexes may be equal; for, if they have more Men than Women, the men who are unmarried will come to their Masters, and complain, that they cannot live without Wives, and desire him, they may have Wives. And he tells them, that the next ship that comes, he will buy them Wives, which satisfies them for the present; and so they expect the good time: which the Master performing with them, the bravest fellow is to choose first, and so in order, as they are in place, and every one of them knows his better, and gives him the precedence, as Cows do one another, in passing through a narrow gate; for, the most of them are as near beasts as may be, setting their souls aside. Religion they know none; yet most of them acknowledge a God, as appears by their motions and gestures: For, if one of them do another wrong, and he cannot revenge himself, he looks up to Heaven for vengeance, and holds up both his hands, as if the power must come from thence, that must do him right. Chast they are as any people under the Sun; for, when the men and women are together naked, they never cast their eyes towards the parts that ought to be covered; and those amongst us, that have Breeches and Petticoats, I never saw so much as a kiss, or embrace, or a wanton glance with their eyes between them. Jealous they are of their Wives, and hold it for a great injury and scorn, if another man make the least courtship to his Wife. And if any of their Wives have two Children at a birth, they conclude her false to his Bed, and so no more adoe but hang her. We had an excellent *Negro* in the Plantation, whose name was *Macow*, and was our chief Musician; a very valiant man, and was keeper of our Plantine-Grove. This *Negroe's* Wife was brought to bed of two Children, and her Husband, as their manner is; had provided a cord to hang her. But the Overseer finding what he was about to do, enformed the Master of it, who sent for *Macow*, to disswade him from this cruel act, of murdering his Wife, and used all perswasions that possibly he could, to let him see, that such double births are in Nature, and that divers presidents were to be found amongst us of the like; so that we rather praised our Wives, for their fertility, than blamed them for their falseness. But this prevailed little with him, upon whom custom had taken so deep an impression; but resolved, the next thing he did, should be to hang her. Which when the Master perceived, and that the ignorance of the man, should take away the life of the woman, who was innocent of the crime her Husband condemned her for, told him plainly, that if he hang'd her, he himself should be hang'd by her, upon the same bough; and therefore wish'd him to consider what he did. This threatning wrought more with him than all the reasons of Philosophy that could be given him; and so let her alone; but he never car'd much for her afterward, but chose another which he lik'd better. For the Planters there deny not a slave, that is a brave fellow, and one that has extraordinary qualities, two or three Wives, and above that number they seldom go: But no woman is allowed above one Husband.

At the time the wife is to be brought a bed, her Husband removes his board, (which is his bed) to another room (for many several divisions they have, in their little houses,) and none above fix foot square) And leaves his wife to God, and her good fortune, in the room, and upon the board alone, and calls a neighbour to come to her, who gives little help to her delivery, but when the child is born, (which she calls her Pickaninny) she helps to make a little fire near her feet, and that serves instead of Possets, Broaths, and Caudles. In a fortnight, this woman is at work with her Pickaninny at her back, as merry a soul as any is there: If the Overseer be discreet, she is suffer'd to rest her self a little more than ordinary; but if not, she is compelled to do as others do. Times they have of suckling their Children in the fields, and refreshing themselves; and good reason, for they carry burthens on their backs; and yet work too. Some women, whose Pickaninnies are three years old, will, as they work at weeding, which is a stooping work, suffer the hee Pickaninny, to sit astride upon their backs, like St.*George* a Horseback; and there Spur his mother with his heels, and sings and crows on her back, clapping his hands, as if he meant to flye; which the mother is so pleas'd with, as she continues her painful stooping posture, longer than she would do, rather than discompose her. Jovial Pickaninny of his pleasure, so glad she is to see him merry; The work which the women do, is most of it weeding, a stooping and painful work; at noon and night they are call'd home by the ring of a Bell, where they have two hours time for their repast at noon; and at night, they rest from six, till six a Clock next morning.

On *Sunday* they rest, and have the whole day at their pleasure; and the most of them use it as a day of rest and pleasure; but some of them who will make benefit of that dayes liberty, go where the Mangrave trees grow, and gather the bark, of which they make ropes, which they truck away for other Commodities, as Shirts and Drawers.

In the afternoons on *Sundayes*, they have their, Musick, which is of kettle drums, and those of several sizes; upon the smalleft the best Musitian playes, and the other come in as Chorasses: the drum all men know, has but one tone; and therefore variety of tunes have little to do in this musick; and yet so strangely they varie their time, as 'tis a pleasure to the most curious ears, and it was to me one of the strangest noises that ever I heard made of one tone; and if they had the variety of tune, which gives the greater scope in Musick, as they have of time, they would do wonders in that Art. And if I had not faln sick before my coming away, at least seven months in one sickness, I had given them some hints of tunes, which being understood, would have serv'd as a great addition to their harmony; for time without tune, is not an eighth part of the Science of Musick.

I found *Macow* very apt for it of himself, and one day coming into the house, (which none of the *Negroes* use to do, unless an Officer, as he was,) he found me playing on a Theorbo, and singing to it, which he hearkened very attentively to; and when I had done, he took the Theorbo in his hand, and strook one string, stopping it by degrees upon every fret, and finding the notes to varie, till it came to the body of the instrument; and that the nearer the body of the instrument he stopt, the smaller or higher the sound was, which he found was be the shortning of the string, considered with himself, how he might make some tryal of this experiment upon such an instrument as he could come by; having no hope ever to have any instrument of this kind to practice on: In a day or two after, walking in the Plantine grove, to refresh me in that cool shade, and to delight my self with the sight of those plants, which are so beautiful, as though they left a fresh impression in me when I parted with them, yet upon a review, something is discern'd in their beauty more than I remembered at parting: which caused me to make often repair thither, I found this *Negro* (whose office it was to attend there) being the keeper of that grove, sitting on the ground, and before him a piece of large timber, upon which he had laid cross, six Billets, and having a handsaw and a hatchet by him, would cut the billets by little and little, till he had brought them to the tunes, he would sit them to; for the shorter they were, the higher the Notes, which he tryed by knocking upon the ends of them with a stick, which he had in his hand. When I sound him at it, I took the stick out of his hand, and tryed the sound, finding the six billets to have six distinct notes, one above another, which put me in a wonder, how he of himself, should without teaching do so much. I then shewed him the difference between flats and sharps, which he prefently apprehended, as between *Fa*, and *Mi:* and he would have cut two more billets to those tunes, but I had then no time to see it done, and so left him to his own enquiries. I say thus much to let you see that some of these people are capable of learning Arts.

Another, of another kind of speculation I found; but more ingenious than he: and this man with three or four more, were to attend me into the woods, to cut Church wayes, for I was employed sometimes upon publick works; and those men were excellent Axe-men, and because there were many gullies in the way, which were impassable, and by that means I was compell'd to make traverses, up and down in the wood; and was by that in danger to miss of the point, to which I was to make my passage to the Church, and therefore was fain to take a Compass with me, which was a Circumferenter, to make my traverses the more exact, and indeed without which, it could not be done, setting up the Circumferenter, and observing the Needle: This *Negre Sambo* comes to me, and seeing the needle wag, desired to know the reason of its stirring, and whether it were alive: I told him no, but it stood upon a point, and for a while it would stir, but by and by stand still, which he observ'd and found it to be true.

The next question was, why it stood one way, and would not remove to any other point, I told him that it would stand no way but North and South, any upon that shew'd him the four

Cardinal points of the compass, East, West, North, South, which he presently learnt by heart, and promis'd me never to forget it. His last question was, why it would stand North, I gave this reason, because of the huge Rocks of Loadstone that were in the North part of the world, which had a quality to draw Iron to it; and this Needle being of Iron, and touch'd with a Loadstone, it would always stand that way.

This point of Philosophy was a little too hard for him, and so he stood in a strange muse; which to put him out of, I bad him reach his axe, and put it near to the Compass, and remove it about; and as he did so, the Needle turned with it, which put him in the greatest admiration that ever I saw a man, and so quite gave over his questions, and desired me, that he might be made a Christian; for, he thought to be a Christian, was to be endued with all those knowledges he wanted.

I promised to do my best endeavour; and when I came home, spoke to the Master of the Plantation, and told him, that poor *Sambo* desired much to be a Christian. But his answer was, That the people of that Island were governed by the Lawes of *England*, and by those Lawes, we could not make a Christian a Slave. I told him, my request was far different from that, for I desired him to make a Slave a Christian. His answer was, That it was true, there was a great difference in that: But, being once a Christian, he could no more account him a Slave, and so lose the hold they had of them as Slaves, by making them Christians; and by that means should open such a gap, as all the Planters in the Island would curse him. So I was struck mute, and poor *Sambo* kept out of the Church; as ingenious, as honest, and as good a natur'd poor soul, as ever wore black, or eat green.

On *Sundayes* in the afternoon, their Musick playes, and to dancing they go, the men by themselves, and the women by themselves, no mixt dancing. Their motions are rather what they aim at, than what they do; and by that means, transgress the less upon the *Sunday*; their hands having more of motion than their feet, and their heads more than then hands. They may dance a whole day, and ne'r heat themselves; yet, now and then, one of the activest amongst them will leap bolt upright, and fall in his place again, but without cutting a capre. When they have danc'd an hour or two, the men fall to wrestle, (the Musick playing all the while) and their manner of wrestling is, to stand like two Cocks, with heads as low as their hips; and thrusting their heads one against another, hoping to catch one another by the leg, which sometimes they do: But if both parties be weary, and that they cannot get that advantage, then they raise their heads, by pressing hard one against another, and so having nothing to take hold of but their bare flesh, they close, and grasp one another about the middle, and have one another in the hug, and then a fair fall is given on the back. And thus two or three couples of them are engaged at once, for an hour together, the women looking on: for when the men begin to wrestle, the women leave off their dancing, and come to be spectators of the sport.

When any of them dye, they dig a grave, and at evening they bury him, clapping and wringing their hands, and making a doleful sound with their voices. They are a people of a timerous and fearful disposition, and consequently bloody, when they find advantages. If any of them commit a fault, give him present punishment, but do not threaten him; for if you do, it is an even lay, he will go and hang himself, to avoid the punishment.

What their other opinions are in matter of Religion, I know not; but certainly, they are not altogether of the sect of the *Sadduces:* For, they believe a Resurrection, and that they shall go into their own Countrey again, and have their youth renewed. And lodging this opinion in their hearts, they make it an ordinary practice, upon any great fright, or threatning of their Masters, to hang themselves.

But Collonel *Walrond* having lost three or four of his best *Negroes* this way, and in a very little time, caused one of their heads to be cut off, and set upon a pole a dozen foot high; and having done that, caused all his *Negroes* to come forth, and march round about this head, and bid them look on it, whether this were not the head of such an one that hang'd himself. Which they acknowledging, he then told them, That they were in a main errour, in thinking they went into their own Countreys, after they were dead; for, this mans head was here, as they all were witnesses of; and how was it possible, the body could go without a head. Being convinc'd by this sad, yet lively spectacle, they changed their opinions; and after that, no more hanged themselves.

When they are sick, there are two remedies that cure them; the one, an outward, the other, an inward medicine. The outward medicine is a thing they call *Negro-oyle*, and 'tis made in *Barbary*, yellow it is as Beeswax, but soft as butter. When they feel themselves ill, they call for some of that, and annoint their bodies, as their breasts, bellies, and sides, and in two dayes they are perfectly well. But this does the greatest cures upon such, as have bruises or strains in their bodies. The inward medicine is taken, when they find any weakness or decay in their spirits and stomachs, and then a dram or two of *kill-devil* revives and comforts them much.

I have been very strict, in observing the shapes of these people; and for the men, they are very well timber'd, that is, broad between the shoulders, full breasted, well filletted, and clean leg'd and may hold good with *Albert Durers* rules, who allowes *twice the length of the head*, to the breadth of the shoulders, and twice the *length of the face*, to the breadth of the hips, and according to this rule these men are shap'd. But the women not; for the fame great Master of Proportions, allowes to each woman, twice the length of the face to the breadth of the shoulders, and twice the length of her own head to the breadth of the hips. And in that, these women are faulty; for I have seen very few of them, whose hips have been broader than their shoulders, unless they have been very fat. The young Maids have ordinarily very large breasts, which stand strutting out so hard and firm, as no leaping, jumping, or stirring, will cause them to shake any more, than the brawns of their arms. But when they come to be old, and have had five or six Children, their breasts hang down below their Navels, so that when they stoop at their common work of weeding, they hang almost down to the ground, that at a distance, you would think they had six legs: And the reason of this is, they tye the cloaths about their Children's backs, which comes upon their breasts, which by pressing very hard, causes them to heng down to that length. Their Children, when they are first born, have the palms of their hands and the soles of their feet, of a whitish colour, and the sight of their eyes of a blewish colour, not unlike the eyes of a young Kitling; but, as they grow older, they become black.

Their way of reckoning their ages, or any other notable accident they would remember, is by the Moon; and so accounting from the time of their Childrens births, the time they were brought out of their own Countrey, or the time of their being taken Prisoners, by some Prince or Potentate of their own Country, or any other notorious accidents, that they are resolved to remember, they account by the Moon; as, so many Moons since one of these, and so many Moons since another; and this account they keep as long as they can: But if any of them live long, their Arithmetick fails them, and then they are, at a dead fault, and forgive over the chafe, wanting the skill to hunt counter. For what can poor people do, that are without Letters and Numbers, which is the soul of all business that is acted by Mortals, upon the Globe of this World.

Some of them, who have been bred up amongst the *Portugals* have some extraordinary qualities, which the others have not; as singing and fencing. I have seen some of these *Portugals Negres*, at Collonel *James Draxes*; play at Rapier and Dagger very skilfully, with their Stookados, their Imbrocados, and their Passes: And at single Rapier too, after the manner of *Charanza*, with such comeliness; as, if the skill had been wanting, the motions would have pleased you; but they were skilful too, which I perceived by their binding with their points, and nimble and subtle avoidings with their bodies, and the advantages the strongest man had in the close, which the other avoided by the nimbleness and skilfulness of his motion. For, in this Science, I had been so well vers'd in my youth, as I was now able to be a competent Judge. Upon their first appearance upon the Stage, they march towards one another, with a slow majestick pace, and a bold commanding look, as if they meant both to conquer; and coming near together, they shake hands, and embrace one another, with a chearful look. But their retreat is much quicker than their advance, and, being at

first distance change their countenance, and put themselves into their posture; and so after a pass or two, retire, and then to't again: And when they have done their play, they embrace, shake hands, and putting on their smoother countenances, give their respects to their Master, and so go off. For their Singing, I cannot much commend that, having heard so good in *Europe*; but for their voices, I have heard many of them very loud and sweet.

Excellent Swimmers and Divers they are, both men and women. Collonel *Drax (who was not so strict an observer of* Sundayes, as to deny himself lawful recreations) would sometimes, to shew me sport, upon that day in the afternoon, send for one of the *Muscovia* Ducks, and have her put into his largest Pond, and calling for some of his best-swimming *Negroes*, commanded them to swim and take this Duck; but forbad them to dive, for if they were not bar'd that play, they would rise up under the Duck, and take her as she swome, or meet her in her diving, and so the sport would have too quick an end. But that play being forbidden, the duck would make them good sport, for they are stronger Ducks, and better Divers by far than ours: and in this chase, there was much of pleasure, to see the various swimmings of the *Negroes*; some the ordinary wayes, upon their bellies, some on their backs, some by striking out their right leg and left arm, and then turning on the other side, and changing both their leg and arm, which is a stronger and swifter way of swimming, than any of the others: and while we were-seeing this sport, and observing the diversities, of their swimmings, a *Negro* maid, who was not there at the beginning of the sport, and therefore heard nothing of the forbidding them to dive, put off her peticoat behind a bush, that was at one end of the Pond, and closely sunk down into the water, and at one diving got to the Duck, pull'd her under water, and went back again the same way she came to the bush, all at one dive. We all thought the Duck had div'd: and expected her appearance above water, but nothing could be seen, till the subtilty was discovered, by a Christian that saw her go in, and so the duck was taken from her. But the trick being so finely and so closely done, I beg'd that the Duck might be given her again, which was granted, and the young girle much pleased.

Though there be a mark set upon these people, which will hardly ever be wip'd off, as of their cruelties when they have advantages, and of their fearfulness and falseness; yet no rule so general but hath his acception: for I believe, and I have strong motives to cause me to be of that perswasion, that there are as honest, faithful, and conscionable people amongst them, as amongst those of *Europe*, or any other part of the world.

A hint of this, I will give you in a lively example; and it was in a time when Victuals were scarce, and Plantins were not then so frequently planted, as to afford them enough. So that some of the high spirited and turbulent amongst them, began to mutiny, and had a plot, secretly to be reveng'd on their Master; and one or two of these were Firemen that made the fires in the furnaces, who were never without store of dry wood by them. These villains, were resolved to make fire to such part of the boyling-house, as they were sure would fire the rest, and so burn all, and yet seem ignorant of the fact, as a thing done by accident. But this plot was discovered, by some of the others who hated mischief, as much as they lov'd it; and so traduc'd them to their Master, and brought in so many witnesses against them, as they were forc'd to confess, what they meant should have been put in act the next night: so giving them condign punishment, the Master gave order to the overseer that the rest should have a dayes liberty to themselves and their wives, to do what they would; and withall to allow them a double proportion of victual for three dayes, both which they refus'd: which we all wonder'd at, knowing well how much they lov'd their liberties, and their meat, having been lately pinch'd of the one, and not having overmuch of the other; and therefore being doubtful what their meaning was in this, suspecting some discontent amongst them, sent for three or four of the best of them, and desir'd to know why they refus'd this favour that was offer'd them, but receiv'd such an answer: as we little expected; for they told us it was not sullenness, or slighting the gratuity their Master bestow'd on them, but they would not accept any thing as a recompence for doing that which became them in their duties to do, nor would they have him think, it was hope of reward, that made them to accuse their fellow servants, but an act of justice, which they thought themselves bound in duty to do, and they thought themselves sufficiently rewarded in the Act. The substance of this, in such language as they had, they delivered, and poor *Sambo* was the Orator; by whose example the others were led both in the discovery of the Plot, and refusal of the gratuity. And withall they said, that if it pleas'd their Master, at any time, to bestow a voluntary boon upon them, be it never so sleight, they would willingly and thankfully accept it: and this act might have beseem'd the best Christians, though some of them were denyed Christianity, when they earnestly sought it. Let others have what opinion they please, yet I am of this belief; that there are to be found amongst them, some who are as morally honest, as Conscionable, as humble, as loving to their friends, and as loyal to their Masters, as any that live under the Sun; and one reason they have to be so, is, they set no great value up on their lives: And this is all I can remember concerning the *Negroes*; except of their games, which I could never learn, because they wanted language to teach me.

Questions

1. In Ligon's view, who on Barbados was worse off, servants or slaves? Do you agree? Does the evidence he offers uniformly support his position?

2. What means were available to servants and slaves wishing to protest ill treatment?

3. What, according to Ligon, impeded slave revolts?

4. How committed were Barbados slave owners to spreading Christianity among their bondsmen?

5. Using Ligon's *History* for evidence, characterize English ideas about race in the years around 1657. Do we observe deeply rooted racism? Nascent prejudice? A rigid or flexible fashion of thinking about the diverse peoples of the Atlantic world? Does Ligon's account undermine the English rationale for race-based slavery?

10.2 Pirates of the Caribbean*

Having endured the travails of servitude on the island of Tortuga, French surgeon John Esquemeling (also known as Alexander Oliver Exquemelin) tried a pirate's life beginning around 1669. After returning to Europe in 1674, his used his experiences as the basis for his Buccaneers of America, *first published in Dutch in 1678.*

CHAP. VII

After what manner the Pirates arm their Vessels, and how they regulate their Voyages.

Before the Pirates go out to Sea, they give notice unto every one, that goeth upon the voyage, of the day on which they ought precisely to imbarque. Intimating also unto them, their obligation of bringing each man in particular, so many pound of powder, and bullet, as they think necessary for that expedition. Being all come on board, they joyn together in Council, concerning what place they ought first to go unto, wherein to get provisions? Especially of flesh: seeing they scarce eat any thing else. And of this the most common fort among them is Pork. The next food is Tortoises, which they use to salt a little. Sometimes they resolve to rob such, or such *Hog-yards*; wherein the Spaniards often have a thousand heads of Swine together. They come unto these places in the dark of the night, and having beset the Keepers lodge, they force him to rise, and give them as many heads as they desire; threatning withal to kill him in case he disobeyeth their commands, or maketh any noise. Yea, these menaces are oftentimes, put in execution, without giving any quarter unto the miserable Swine keepers, or any other person, that endeavoureth to hinder their Robberies.

Having gotten provisions of flesh, sufficient for their Voyage, they return unto their Ship. Here their allowance, twice a day, unto every one,

is as much as he can eat; without either weight, or measure. Neither doth the Steward of the Vessel give any greater proportion of flesh, or any thing else unto the Captain, then unto the meanest Mariner. The ship being well victuall'd, they call another Council, to deliberate, towards what place they shall go, to seek their desperate fortunes? In this Council, likewise they agree upon certain Articles, which are put in writing, by way of bond, or obligation, the which every one is bound to observe, and all of them, or the chiefest, do set their hands unto. Herein they specifie, and set down very distinctly, what sums of Mony each particular person ought to have for that voyage. The fond, of all the payments, being the common stock, of what is gotten, by the whole expedition; for otherwise it is the same law, among these people, as with other Pirates, *no prey, no pay*. In the first place, therefore they mention, how much the Captain ought to have for his Ship. Next the salary of the Carpenter, or Shipwright, who careen'd, mended, and rigg'd the vessel. This commonly, amounteth unto one hundred or an hundred and fifty pieces of eight; being according to the agreement, more or less. Afterwards for provisions and victualling, they draw out of the same common stock, about two hundred pieces of eight. Also a competent salary for the Chyrurgeon, and his Chest of Medicaments, which usually is rated at two hundred, or two hundred and fifty pieces of eight. Lastly they stipulate in writing, what recompence or reward each one ought to have, that is either wounded, or maimed in his body, suffering the loss of any Limb, by that voyage. Thus they order for the loss of a right Arm, six hundred pieces of eight, or six slaves: For the loss of a left Arm, five hundred pieces of eight, or five slaves: For a right leg, five hundred pieces of eight, or five slaves: For the left leg, four hundred pieces of eight, or four slaves: For an eye, one hundred pieces of eight, or one slave: For a Finger of the hand, the same reward, as for the eye. All which sums of Mony, as I have said before, are taken out of the capital sum, or common stock, of what is gotten by their Piracy. For a very exact,

_____
*John Esquemeling, *The Buccaneers of America* (London: Swan Sonnenschein & Co., 1898), 58–60, 62–76.

and equal, dividend, is made of the remainder, among them all. Yet herein they have also regard unto qualities, and places. Thus the Captain, or chief Commander, is allotted five, or six portions to what the ordinary Seamen have. The Masters-Mate, only two: And other Officers proportionable to their employ. After whom they draw equal parts from the highest, even to the lowest Mariner; the boys not being omitted. For even these draw half a share; by reason, that when they happen to take a better Vessel, than their own, it is the duty of the Boys, to set fire unto the Ship or boat, wherein they are, and then retire unto the prize, which they have taken.

They observe among themselves, very good orders. For in the prizes they take, it is severely prohibited, unto every one to usurp any thing in particular, unto themselves. Hence all they take, is equally divided, according to what hath been said before. Yea, they make a solemn Oath to each other, not to abscond, or conceal the least thing they find amongst the prey. If afterwards any one is found unfaithful, and that hath contraven'd the said oath, immediately he is separated, and turned out of the society. Among themselves they are very civil and charitable to each other. Insomuch, that if any wanteth what another hath, with great liberality, they give it one to another. As soon as these Pirates have taken any Prize of Ship, or Boat, the first thing they endeavour is to set on shore the prisoners; detaining only some few for their own help, and service. Unto whom also they give their liberty, after the space of two or three years. They put in very frequently for refreshment, at one Island, or another. But more especially into those which lie on the Southern side of the Isle of *Cuba*. Here they careen their vessels, and in the mean while, some of them go to hunt, others to cruze upon the Seas, in Canows, seeking their fortune. Many times they take the poor Fishermen of Tortoises, and carrying them to their habitations, they make them work so long, as the Pirates are pleased. . . .

The Inhabitants of *New-Spain*, and *Campeche*, lade their principal sorts of Merchandises, in Ships of great bulk; and with these they exercise their commerce to and fro. The vessels from *Campeche* in winter time, set out towards *Caracas, Trinity Isles*, and that of *Margarita*. For in Summer the winds are contrary; though very favourable to return unto *Campeche*; as they use to do, at the beginning of that season. The Pirates are not ignorant of these times; as being very dextrous in searching out all places, and circumstances, most suitable to their designs. Hence in the places, and seasons aforementioned, they cruze upon the said Ships, for some while. But in case they can perform nothing, and that fortune doth not favour them with some prize, or other, after holding a Council thereupon, they commonly enterprize things very desperate. Of these their resolutions I shall give you one instance very remarkable. One certain Pirate, whose name was *Pierre Francois*, or *Peter Francis*, happened to be a long time at Sea with his boat, and six and twenty persons, waiting for the Ships that were to return from *Maracaibo* towards *Campeche*. Not being able to find any thing, nor get any prey, at last he resolved to direct his course to *Rancherias*, which is nigh unto the River, called *de la Plata*, in the altitude of twelve degrees, and a half Northern latitude. In this place lieth a rich *Bank of Pearl*, to the fishery whereof they yearly send from *Cartagena*, a Fleet of a dozen vessels with a man of war, for their defence. Every Vessel hath at least a couple of *Negros* in it, who are very dextrous in diving, even to the depth of six fathoms, within the Sea; whereabouts they find good store of Pearls. Upon this Fleet of Vessels though small, called the *Pearl Fleet; Pierre Francois* resolved to adventure; rather then go home with empty hands. They rid at Anchor, at that time, at the mouth of the River *de la Hacha*; the Man of War being scarce half a league distant, from the small. Ships; and the wind very calm. Having espyed them in this posture, he presently pull'd down his fails, and rowed along the coast, dissembling to be a spanish Vessel, that came from *Maracaibo*, and only passed that way. But no sooner was he come unto the *Pearl-bank*, when suddainly he assaulted the Vice-admiral of the said Fleet, mounted with eight Guns, and three-score men well arm'd, commanding them to surrender. But the Spaniards running to their arms, did to what they could to defend themselves, fighting for some while; till at last they were constrained to submit unto the Pirate. Being thus possessed of the Vice-Admiral, he resolved next to adventure with some other stratagem, upon the Man of War; thinking thereby to get strength sufficient, to master the rest of the Fleet. With this intent he presently sunk his own Boat in the River, and putting forth the Spanish Colours, weighed Anchor, with a little wind, which then began to stir; having with promises, and menaces, compelled most of the Spaniards; to assist him in his design. But no sooner did the Man of War perceive one of his Fleet to set fail, when he did so too; fearing lest, the Mariners should have any design to run away, with the Vessel, and riches they had on board. This caused the Pirates, immediately to give over that dangerous enterprize, as thinking themselves unable to encounter force to force, with the said Man of War, that now came against them. Hereupon, they attempted to get out of the River, and gain the open Seas, with the riches they had taken; by making as much sail, as possibly the vessel would bear. This being perceived, by the Man of War, he presently gave them chace. But the Pirates, having laid on too much sail, and a gust of wind suddainly arising, had their Mainmast blown down by the board, which disabled them from prosecuting their escape.

This unhappy event much encouraged those that were in the Man of War; they advancing, and gaining upon the Pirates every moment. By which means at last they were overtaken. But these notwithstanding, finding themselves still with two and twenty persons sound, the rest being either killed or wounded, resolved to defend themselves so long as it were possible. This they performed very couragiously for some while, until being thereunto forced by the Man of War, they were compelled to surrender. Yet was not this done without Articles, which the Spaniards were glad to allow them, as followeth. That they should not use them as slaves, forcing them to carry or bring stones, or employing them in other labours, for three or four years, as they commonly employ their Negros. But that they should set them on shore, upon free land; without doing them any harm in their bodies. Upon these Articles they deliver'd

themselves, with all that they had taken; which was worth only in Pearls, to the value of above one hundred thousand peices of eight, besides the vessel, provision goods, and other things. All which being put together, would have made unto this Pirate, one of the greatest prizes, he could desire. Which he had certainly obtained, had it not been for the lost of his Main-mast, as was said before.

Another bold attempt, not unlike unto that which I have related, nor less remarkable; I shall also give you at present. A certain Pirate, born in *Portugal*, and from the name of his Country, called *Bartholomew Portugues*, was cruzing in his Boat from *Jamaica* (wherein he had only thirty men, and four small guns) upon the Cape *de Corriente*, in the Island of *Cuba*. In this place he met with a great ship, that came from *Maracaibo*, and *Cartagena*, bound for the *Havana*, well provided, with twenty great guns, and threescore and ten Men, between passengers and Mariners. This ship he presently assaulted, but found as strongly defended by them that were on board. The Pirate escaped the first encounter, resolving to attacque her more vigorously then before, seeing he had sustained no great damage hitherto. This resolution of his, he boldly performed, renewing his assaults so often, till that after a long and dangerous fight, he became Master of the great Vessel. The Potugues lost only ten men, and had four wounded, so that he had still remaining twenty fighting men, whereas the Spaniards had double the same number. Having possessed themselves of such a Ship, and the wind being contrary to return unto *Jamaica*, they resolved to steer their course towards the Cape of *Saint Antony*, (which lieth on the Western side of the isle of *Cuba*) there to repair themselves, and take in fresh water, of which they had great necessity, at that time.

Being now very near unto the *Cape* abovementioned, they unexpectedly met with three great Ships, that were coming from *New-Spain*, and bound for the *Havana*. By these as not being able to escape, they were easily retaken both Ship, and Pirates. Thus they were all made prisoners, through the suddain change of fortune, and found themselves poor, oppress'd, and stript of all the riches they had purchased so little before. The *Cargo* of this Ship consisted in one hundred, and twenty thousand weight of *Cacao-nuts*, the cheifest ingredient of that rich liquor called *Chocolate*, and threescore and ten thousand peices of eight. Two days after this misfortune, there happened to arise an huge and dangerous tempest, which largely separated the Ships from one another. The great Vessel, wherein the Pirates were, arrived at *Campeche*; where many considerable Merchants came to salute, and welcom the Captain thereof. These presently knew the *Portugues* Pirate, as being him who had committed innumerable excessive insolences upon those coasts, not only infinite Murthers and Robberies, but also lamentable *incendiums*, which those of *Campeche*, still preserved very fresh in their memory.

Hereupon the next day after their arrival, the Magistrates of the City sent several of their Officers, to demand and take into custody, the criminal prisoners, from on board the ship, with intent to punish them, according to their deserts. Yet fearing least the Captain of those Pirates should escape out of their hands on those (as he had formerly done, being once their prisoner in the City before,) they judg'd it more convenient to leave him safely guarded on board the Ship, for that present. In the mean while they caused a Gibbet to be erected, whereupon to hang him the very next day, without any other form of process, then to lead him from the Ship, unto the place of punishment. The rumour of this future tragedy, was presently brought unto *Bartholomew Portugues* his ears, whereby he sought all the means he could to escape that night. With this design he took two earthen Jars, wherein the Spaniards usually carry wine from *Spain* unto the West-Indies, and stopp'd them very well; intending to use them for swimming, as those, who are unskilful in that art, do *calabacas*, a sort of pumkins in *Spain*; and in other places empty bladders. Having made this necessary preparation, he waited for the night, when all should be at sleep; even the Centry that guarded him. But seeing he could not escape his vigilancy, he secretly purchased a knife, and with the same gave him such a mortal stab, as suddainly depriv'd him of life, and the possibility of making any noise. At that instant, he committed himself to Sea, with those two earthen jarrs aforemen-

tioned, and by their help and support, though never having learn'd to swim, he reached, the shore. Being arrived upon land, without any delay, he took his refuge in the Woods, where he hid himself for three days, without daring to appear, nor eating any other food then wild herbs.

Those of the City failed not the next day, to make a diligent search for him in the woods, where they concluded him to be. This strict enquiry *Portugues* had the convenience to espy from the hallow of a Tree, wherein he lay absconded. Hence perceiving them to return without finding, what they sought for, he adventur'd to sally forth towards the coasts, called *del Golfo triste*, forty leagues distant from the City of *Campeche*. Hither he arrived within a fortnight after his escape from the Ship. In which space of time, as also afterwards, he endured extream hunger, thirst, and fears, of falling again into the hands of the Spaniards. For during all this journy he had no other provision with him, then a small *Calabaca*, with a little water: Neither did he eat any thing else, then a few shell fish, which he found among the Rocks, nigh the Seashore. Besides that, he was compell'd to pass as yet some Rivers, not knowing well to swim. Being in this distress, he found an old board, which the waves had thrown upon the shore, wherein did stick a few great nailes. These he took and with no small labour, whetted against a stone, until that he had made them capable of cutting like unto knives, tho very imperfectly. With these, and no better instruments, he cut down some branches of Trees, the which with twigs, and Osiers he joyn'd together, and made as well as he could, a boat, or rather a waste, wherewith he wasted over the Rivers. Thus he arrived finally at the Cape of *Golfo triste*, as was said before; where he happened to find a certain Vessel of Pirates, who were great Comrades of his own, and were lately come from *Jamaica*.

Unto these Pirates, he instantly related all his adversities, and misfortunes. And withal demanded of them, they would fit him with a boat, and twenty men. With which company alone, he promised to return unto *Campeche*, and assault the Ship, that was in the River, by which he had been taken, and escaped fourteen days before. They easily granted his request, and equipped him a boat, with the said number of Men. With this small company he set forth towards the execution of his design; which he bravely performed eight days after he separated from his Comrades at the Cape of *Golfo triste*. For being arrived at the River of *Campeche*, with an undaunted courage, and without any rumour of noise, he assaulted the Ship aforementioned. Those that were on board, were perswaded, this was a boat from land, that came to bring *contra bands* goods; and hereupon were not in any posture of defence. Thus the Pirates laying hold on this occasion, assaulted them without any fear of ill success, and in short space of time, compelled the Spaniards to surrender.

Being now Masters of the Ship, they immediately weighed Anchor, and set sail, determining to fly from the Port, least they should be pursued by other Vessels. This they did with extremity of joy, seeing themselves possessours of such a brave Ship. Especially *Portugues*, their Captain, who now by a second turn of fortunes wheel, was become rich, and powerful again, who had been so lately in that same Vessel, a poor miserable prisoner, and condemned to the Gallows. With this great purchase he designed in his mind greater things; which he might well hope to obtain, seeing he had found in the Vessel great quantity of rich Merchandise, still remaining on board, although the plate had been transported into the City. Thus he continued his Voyage towards *Jamaica* for some days. But coming nigh unto the Isle of *Pinos* on the South-side of the Island of *Cuba*, fortune suddainly turned her back unto him once more, never to shew him her countenance again. For a horrible storm arising at Sea occasion'd the Ship to split against the Rocks or Banks called *Jardines*. Insomuch that the Vessel was totally lost, and *Portugues*, with his Companions, escaped in a Canow. After this manner he arrived at *Jamaica*, where he remained no long time. Being only there, till he could prepare himself to seek his fortune anew, which from that time proved always adverse unto him.

Nothing less rare and admirable than the precedent, are the Actions of another Pirate;

who at present liveth at *Jamaica*, and who hath, on sundry occasions, enterprized and acheived, things very strange. The place of his birth was the City of *Groningen*, in the *United Provinces*; but his own proper Name is not known: The Pirates, his Companions, having only given him that of *Roche Brasiliano*, by reason of his long residence in the Country of *Brasil*. From whence he was forced to flie, when the *Portuguises* retook those Countries, from the West India Company of *Amsterdam*; several Nations then inhabiting at *Brasil* (as English, French, Dutch, and others) being constrained to seck new Fortunes.

This Fellow at that conjuncture of time retired unto *Jamaica*. Where being at a stand how to get a livelyhood, he entred himself into the Society of Pirates. Under these, he served in quality of a private Mariner for some while. In which degree he behaved himself so well, as made him both beloved and respected by all; as one that deserved to be their Commander for the future. One day certain Mariners happen'd to engage in a dissention with their Captain; the effect whereof was that they left the Boat. *Brasiliano* followed the rest, and by these was chosen for their Conductor and Leader; who also fitted him out a Boat, or small Vessel, wherein he received the Title of Captain.

Few days were past, from his being chosen Captain, when he took a great Ship, that was coming from *New-Spain*. On board of which he found great quantity of plate; and both one and the other, he carried unto *Jamaica*. This action gave him renown, and caused him to be both esteemed and feared; every one apprehending him much abroad. Howbeit, in his domestick, and private affairs, he had no good behaviour, nor government, over himself; for in these he would oftentimes shew himself either brutish, or foolish. Many times being in drink, he would run up and down the streets, beating or wounding whom he met; no person daring to oppose him, or make any resistance.

Unto the Spaniards he always shewed himself very barbarous, and cruel; only out of an inveterate hatred, he had against that Nation. Of these he commanded several to be rosted alive upon wooden spits; for no other crime, than that they would not shew him the places, or *Hog-yards*, where he might steal Swine. After many of these cruelties, it happened as he was cruzing upon the coasts of *Campeche*, that a dismal tempest suddainly surprized him. This proved to be so violent, that at last his Ship was wrackt, upon the coasts; the Mariners only escaping with their Musquets, and some few bullets, and powder, which were the only things they could save, of all that was in the Vessel. The place where the Ship was lost, was precisely between *Campeche*, and the *Golfo triste*. Here they got on shore in a *Canow*, and marching along the coast, with all the speed they could, they directed their course towards *Golfo triste*; as being a place where the Pirates commonly use to repair, and refresh themselves. Being upon this Journy, and all very hungry, and thirsty, as is usual in desert places, they were pursued by some Spaniards; being a whole troop of an hundred horsemen. *Brasiliano* no sooner perceived this imminent danger, then he animated his companions, telling them: *We had better fellow Soldiers, choose to die under our arms fighting, as it become the men of courage, then surrender unto the Spaniards; who in case they overcome us, will take away our lives with cruel torments.* The Pirates were no more then thirty in number; who notwithstanding, seeing their brave Commander oppose himself with courage, unto the enemy, resolved to do the like. Hereupon they faced the troop of Spaniards, and discharged their Musquets against them; with such dexterity, as they almost kill'd one horseman with every shot. The fight continued for the space of an hour, till at last the Spaniards were put to flight, by the Pirates. They stripp'd the dead, and took from them what they thought most convenient for their use. But such as were not already dead; they helped to quit the miseries of life, with the ends of their Musquets.

Having vanquished the Enemy, they all mounted on several horses, they found in the field, and continued the Journy aforementioned; *Brasiliano* having lost but two of his Companions in this bloody fight, and had two other wounded. As they prosecuted their way, before they came unto the Port, they espyed a boat from *Campeche*, well

man'd, that rid at anchor, protecting a small number of Canows, that were lading wood. Hereupon, they sent a detachment of six of their Men, to watch them; and these the next morning by a wild possessed themselves of the Canows. Having given notice unto their Companions, they went all on board, and with no great difficulty, took also the Boat, or little Man of War, their Convoy. Thus having rendred themselves Masters of the whole Fleet, they wanted only provisions, which they found but very small aboard those Vessels. But this defect was supplied by the horses, which they instantly killed, and salted; with Salt, which, by good fortune, the Wood-cutters had brought with them. Upon which virtuals they made shift to keep themselves, until such time, as they could purchase better.

These very same Pirates, I mean *Brasiliano*, and his companions, took also another Ship, that was going from *New-Spain* unto *Maracaibo*; laden with divers sorts of Merchandize, and a very considerable number of peices of eight, which were design'd to buy *Cacao-nuts*, for their lading home. All these prizes they carried into *Jamaica*, where they safely arrived, and according to their custom, wasted in a few days, in Taverns and Stews, all they had gotten, by giving themselves to all manner of debauchery, with Strumpets, and Wine. Such of these Pirates are found who will spend two or three thousand peices of eight, in one night, not leaving themselves peradventure a good shirt to wear, on their backs, in the morning. Thus upon a certain time, I saw one of them give unto a common. Strumpet, five hundred peices of eight, only that he might see her naked. My own Master would buy, in like occasions, a whole pipe of wine, and placing it in the street, would force every one, that passed by to drink with him; threatning also to Pistol them, in case they would not do it. At other times he would do the same, with Barrels of Ale, or Beer. And very often, with both his hands, he would throw these liquors about the streets, and wet the cloathes of such as walked by, without regarding, whether he spoil'd their Apparrel, or not, were they Men, or Women.

Among themselves, and to each other, these Pirates are extreamly liberal, and free. If any one of them hath lost all his goods, which often happeneth in their manner of life, they freely give him, and make him partaker of what they have. In Taverns, and Ale houses, they always have great credit; but in such houses at *Jamaica*, they ought not to run very deep in debt, seeing the inhabitants of that Island, do easily sell one another for debt. Thus it happened unto my *Patron*, or Master, to be sold for a debt of a Tavern, wherein he had spent the greatest part of his mony. This Man had within the space of three months before, three thousand peices of eight in ready cash; all which he wasted in that short space of time, and became so poor, as I have told you.

But now to return unto our discourse, I must let my Reader know, that *Brasiliano*, after having spent all that he had robb'd, was constrained to go to Sea again, to seek his fortune once more. Thus he set forth towards the coast of *Campeche*, his common place of rendezvous. Fifteen days after his arrival there, he put himself into a *Canow*, with intent to espy the Port of that City, and see if he could rob any Spanish Vessel. But his fortune was so bad, that both he and all his Men, were taken prisoners, and carried unto the presence of the Governour. This Man immediately, cast them into a dungeon, with full intention to hang them every person. And doubtless he had performed his intent, were it not for a Stratagem, that *Brasiliano* used, which proved sufficient to save their lives. He writ therefore a Letter unto the Governour, making him believe it came from other Pirates, that were abroad, at Sea; and withal telling him: *He should have a care, how be used those persons be had in his custedy. For in case be caused them any harm, they did Swear unto him, they would never give quarter, unto any person of the Spanish Nation, that should fall into their hands.*

Because these Pirates had been many times at *Campeche*, and in many other Towns and Villages, of the West-Indies, belonging to the Spanish dominions, the Governour began to fear, what mischeif they might cause by the means of their companions abroad, in case he should punish them. Hereupon he released them out of prison, exacting only an Oath of them, before hand, that they would leave their exercise of Piracy for ever. And withal he

sent them as common Mariners, or Passengers, in the *Galoon's*, to *Spain*. They got in this Voyage all together five hundred peices of eight; whereby they tarried not long there, after their arrival. But providing themselves with some few necessaries, they all returned unto *Jamaica*, within a little while. From whence they set forth again to Sea, committing greater Robberies and cruelties, then ever they had done before. But more especially, abusing the poor Spaniards, that happened to fall into their hands, with all sorts of cruelty imaginable.

The Spaniards perceiving they could gain nothing upon this sort of people, nor diminish their number, which rather increased dayly, resolved to diminish the number of their Ships, wherein they exercised trading to and fro. But neither this resolution was of any effect, or did them any good service. For the Pirates finding not so many Ships at Sea, as before, began to gather into greater Companies, and land upon the Spanish Dominions, ruining whole Cities, Towns, and Villages; and withal pillaging, burning, and carrying away, as much as they could possible.

The first Pirate, who gave a beginning unto there invasions by Land, was named *Lewis Scot*, who Sack't and Pillag'd the City of *Campeche*. He almost ruin'd the Town, Robbing and destroying all he could; and after he had put it to the ransome of an excessive summ of mony, he left it. After *Scot*, came another named *Mansvelt*, who enterprised to set footing in *Granada*, and penetrate with his Piracies, even unto the South Sea. Both which things he effected, till that at last for want of provision, he was constrained to go back. He assaulted Isle of *Saint Catherine*, which was the first land he took, and upon it some few prisoners. These shewed him the way towards *Cartagena*, which is a principal City, situate in the Kingdom of *Nueva Granada*. But the bold attempts and actions, of *John Davis*, born at *Jamaica*, ought not to be forgotten in this History, as being some of the most remarkable thereof. Especially his rare prudence and valour, wherewith he behaved himself in the aforementioned Kingdom of *Granada*. This Pirate having cruzed a long time in the *Gulf* of *Pocatauro*, upon the Ships, that were expected from *Cartagena*, bound for *Nicaragua*, and not being able to meet any of the said Ships, resolved at last, to land in *Nicaragua*, leaving his Ship concealed about the coast.

This design he presently put in execution. For taking fourscore men, out of fourscore and ten, which he had in all, (the rest being left to keep the Ship) he divided them equally into three Canows. His intent was to Rob the Churches, and rifle the Houses of the chiefest Citizens of the aforesaid Town of *Nicaragua*. Thus in the obscurity of the night, they mounted the River, which leadeth to that City, Rowing with Oars in their Canows. By day they concealed themselves, and boats, under the branches of Trees, that were upon the banks. These grow very thick, and intricate, along the sides of the Rivers, in those Countries, as also along the Sea coast. Under which likewise those, who remained behind, absconded their Vessel, least they should be seen, either by Fishermen, or Indians. After this manner, they arrived at the City the third night, where the Centry, who kept the post of the River, thought them to be Fishermen that had been fishing in the Lake. And as the greatest part of the Pirates are skilful in the Spanish Tongue, so he never doubted thereof, as soon as he heard them speak. They had in their Company an Indian, who was run away from his Master, because he would make him a slave, after having served him a long time. This Indian went the first on shore, and rushing at the Centry, he instantly killed him. Being animated with this success, they entred into the City, and went directly unto three or four Houses of the chiefest Citizens, where they knocked with dissimulation. These beleiving them to be friends, opened the doors, and the Pirates suddainly possessing themselves of the Houses, robb'd all the mony and plate, they could find. Neither did they spare the Churches, and most sacred things, all which were pillaged and prophan'd, without any respect, or veneration.

In the mean while great cries and lamentation were heard about the Town, of some, who had escaped their hands; by which means the whole City was brought into an uproar, and alarm. From hence the whole number of Citizens rallied together, intending to put themselves in defence. This being perceived by the Pirates, they, instantly, put themselves to flight, carrying with them all that they had robb'd, and likewise some Prisoners. These they led away; to the intent, that if any of them should happen to be taken by the Spaniards, they might make use of them for ransom. Thus they got unto their Ship, and with all speed imaginable put out to Sea; forcing the Prisoners, before they would let them go, to procure them as much flesh, as they thought necessary, for their Voyage to *Jamaica*. But no sooner had they weighed Anchor, when they saw on shore a Troop of about five hundred Spaniards, all being very well armed, at the Seaside. Against these, they let lie several Guns, wherewith they forced them to quit the sands, and retire towards home, with no small regret, to see those Pirates carry away so much plate of their Churches, and Houses, tho distant at least forty leagues from the Sea.

These Pirates Robb'd in this occasion, above four thousand peices of eight in ready mony. Besides great quantity of plate uncoyned, and many Jewels. All which was computed to be worth the sum of fifty thousand peices of eight, or more. With this great purchase, they arrived a *Jamaica*, soon after the exploit. But as this sort of people, are never Masters of their mony, but a very little while, so were they soon constrained to seek more, by the same means, they had used before. This adventure, caused Captain *John Davis*, presently after his return, to be chosen Admiral of seven or eight Boats of Pirates; he being now esteemed by common consent, an able Conductor for such enterprizes as these were. He began the exercise of this new Command by directing his Fleet towards the coasts of the North of *Cuba*, there to wait for the Fleet, which was to pass from *New-Spain*. But, not being able to find any thing by this design, they determined to go towards the coasts of *Florida*. Being arrived there, they landed part of their Men, and Sacked a small City, named Saint *Augustine* of *Florida*. The Castle of which place, had a Garrison of two hundred Men. The which notwithstanding, could not prevent the pillage of the City; they effecting it without receiving the least damage from either Soldiers, or Townsmen.

Questions

1. Why did Esquemeling devote so much attention to the pirates' diet?
2. Did pirate communities represent a challenge to conventional European societies in the Americas, or a variant of them?
3. What circumstances facilitated New World piracy?
4. What sorts of people became buccaneers? Why?
5. In Ligon, Esquemeling, and the Virginia Slave Code, what was the relation between the status of African slaves and that of lower-class Europeans?

11 Carolina

Hoping to imitate the success of Caribbean plantation economies, in the 1660s a group of wealthy investors proposed a new colony on the mainland between Virginia and Spanish-controlled Florida. Called Carolina in honor of King Charles II, the colony developed an economy divided between Indian trade and plantation agriculture. Early in the eighteenth century, Carolina became the only society on mainland North America with a slave majority. The documents in this chapter discuss Indian trade, slavery, and the relationship between the two.

11.1 Colonial Leader Thomas Nairne Discusses Carolina's Wartime Geopolitics*

In the following passage, Thomas Nairne, an Indian agent, trader, political leader, and planter, explains the importance of Carolina to English interests in North America. Nairne, who had traveled extensively in the Carolina backcountry as an Indian trader, government agent, and wartime spy, wrote this report in 1708 to Charles Spencer, Earl of Sunderland, who was among a handful of powerful men then controlling English overseas policy. Nairne wrote during the War of the Spanish Succession (1702–1713), which pitted England against France and Spain. As we will see in a later chapter, by this time France had begun efforts to establish a colony in the Mississippi Valley and along the Gulf of Mexico.

May it please Your Lordship,

Having been Imployed by the Generall Assembly, of This Province in the quality of an Agent, and Itenerary Justice, among the Indians, Subject to our government among other things usefull, to be known for the Safety, and Interest, of this Colony, I aplyed my self, in particular, to have a very minute account, of all people as well Europeans, as Salvages, from Virginia to the mouth of the Mississippi. I have had a personall View off most of These parts, Either formerly when a Commander in the warrs, or This year by Travelling. Altho my Inquiries & Searches of This kind are not Finished and perfect, yett Considering, the Juncture, that peace must of necessity in some small time be concluded, I could not dispense with my self from Laying before your Lordship a map of Such Travells & observations as I have already taken, to

*Alexander Moore, ed., *Nairne's Muskhogean Journals: The 1708 Expedition to the Mississippi River* (Jackson: University Press of Mississippi, 1988), 73–78.

the End your noble Lordship may at one View perceive what part of the Continent we are now possest off, and what not, and procure the articles of peace, to be formed in such a manner that the English American Empire may not be unreasonably Crampt up. Your Lordships may depend on the Inland Topography to be Exact as any Thing of That Kind, can well be. The Numbers of The Inhabitant[s] I took with The greatest Care.

Your Lordship upon View of the Map will presently conclude that If the french now Setled at Mobile were possest of all the Indians subject to the government of Carolina, and had united them to Those of the Mississipi, they wold be in Circumstances to draw from among them such bodies of forces as wold be Intollerably Troublesom Either to the English Colonies or the Naked unarmed Country of New Mexico, and That this Province, only by trading and other mannagement can put a Check to Them. A Consequence of this is That This province being a frontier, both against The French and Spaniards, ought not to be Neglected.

I have represented this matter in such a true light to the generall Assembly, that They resolved to raise some forces, to reduce Either the French fort at Mobile, or at Least all the Indians Betwixt us and the Mississipi, now in their alliance. Accordingly I was Busy providing every thing for my voyage. I entertained Intelligence among the yassas, Tassas, and Nochess, Inviteing them to Setle up Cussate river. I ventured my Life, and made peace with the Chactas. In short I designed to Incite by fair means all that wold accept of our friendship, upon the Terms of Subjecting themselves, to our government and removeing into our territory, and quite to ruine Such as wold not, soe that the french might never be in a Capacity to raise an Indian Army to Disturb us or our allies, & that the Lower parts of the Mississipi, being left Desolate, the trade of the uper might fall to this province by means of factories, Setled on Cussate river for the French from Mobile wold find it Extreme Difficult, to carry on that Commerce, unless had releif and defence, from the Indian towns, on the Lower parts. But as I was Imploying myself in Concerting measures for The Intended Expedition, The Intelligence of the french &

Spaniards Designing to Invade Carolina put a full stop to it. Only I continue to Invite over by fair means all that I can, which I hope will not be altogether In Vain. My Design was to fall down from the Talapoosies against the french with a fleet of Eighty Canoes manned with 500 Indians & 1000 By land 15 English on the one part and 30 with the other. With These forces I pretended Either to destroy or remove into our Territory all the Salvages from Mobile to the Mississipi, & up the river to 36 Degrees of Latitude.

The French of Mobile have their Support by the furr trade from the head of the Mississipi & a good underhand trade with the Spaniards of La vera Cruz by way of Pansacola. That small garrison depends on Vera Cruz and Live in Extream good terms with Mobile being both afraid of our Subjects the Talapoosies who Last year burnt Pansacola town. Tho the French at Mobile be now weak yett they are well Scituated for Indian trade. I have fixed a red Cross to these places now Subject to Carolina and a Triangle at these in amity with Mobile.

May it Please Your Lordship the English trade for Cloath alwayes atracts and maintains the obedience and friendship of the Indians. They Effect them most who sell best cheap. This makes it necessary that the trade with them should in England lye under as small duties and Embarrassment as may be. Sixpence Custom for such dear skins as are small and not worth 12d. seems unreasonable.

Your Lordship may perceive by the map that the garrison of St. Augustine is by this warr Reduced to the bare walls their Catle and Indian towns all Consumed Either by us In our Invasion, of that place or by our Indian Subjects Since who in quest of Booty are now obliged to goe down as farr on the point of Florida as the firm land will permitt. They have drove the Floridians to the Islands of the Cape, have brought in and sold many Hundreds of them, and Dayly now Continue that Trade so that in some few years they'le Reduce these Barbarians to a farr less number. There is not one Indian Town betwixt Charles Town and Mowila Bay Except what are prickt, in the mapp, only am uncertain of the numbers of the Floridians.

Our friend the Talapoosies and Chicasas Imploy themselves in making Slaves of such

Indians about the Lower parts of the Mississipi as are now Subject to the french. The good prices The English Traders give them for slaves Encourages them to this trade Extreamly and some men think that it both serves to Lessen their numbers before the french can arm them and it is a more Effectuall way of Civilising and Instructing, Then all the Efforts used by the french Missionaries.

May it please your Lordship the English in next Treaty of Peace have Just reason to Insist upon the French quitting that Settlement on the Bay of Mowila because they Setled it in prejudice to and Dispight of the Just Title the English had to that Bay and the Rivers of it. It Seem they found the Mississipi unfitt to Setle on, and not willing to give any umbrage at that time to the Spaniards by going to The westward of it, made bold (Tho in time of Peace) with the English of Carolina, and Setled on the bay of Mowila 150 miles to the East of the Mississipi all the Inhabitants whereof had for 10 years before Submitted themselves and Country to the government of Carolina, and then actually Traded with us. The french upon their first arrivall were so liberall of their Presents that they Entirely decoyed the People of the Lower parts from their duty and Endeavouring to doe the Same with the Talapoosies that live Higher up 5 of them were killed in the attempt as they were coming up by an Indian Called Dearsfoot. This has made them desist ever since, and the English are now in possession of the greatest part of the People of That River.

Your Lordship by a view of the map will perceive that If the English think fitt to use any Efforts to make themselves masters of the furr trade from the head of the Mississipi, it must be done by drawing up the Yassas &c to Setle on Cussate river and making small forts to defend the Traders merchantdise where the places are marked.

Your Lordship will likewise see that the Cherickee nation now Entirely Subject to us are Extreamly well Scituate to Keep of any Incursions which Either the Illinois or any other french Indians may think of making into Carolina and in Effect So it is, they are now our only defence on the Back parts But are themselves miserably harrassed by the Iroquis. Your Lordship may please

to write to the governours of Maryland and New York to Interpose as much with the Iroquois in their behalf as possible. All parts of the English Dominions ought mutually to Espouse one anothers interest in Every thing that relates to the Common defence against the French and their party.

May it Please your Lordship I have Considered this Coast what parts may be any way usefull to the Brittish nation in order to Setle Colonies. It is Certain we have firm Possession by means of our Indians, from Charles Town to Mowila Bay, Excepting only the garrison of St. Augustine and the Island of Cape Florida. If the English could spare people it Seems fitter to Strengthen this Province then Setle any New, But If an Inclination to Setle any Place to the East ward of the Mississipi, Should prevaile, the old Country of the Apalachias is the only best, Being for 40 miles Long and 20 wide Clear feild fitt for the plough, formerly mannured by the Indians who were four year agoe Subdued and the remaining part of them removed to Carolina. This place wold be proper for the Seat of a government to take in the Neck of florida, and 100 miles to the westward along the Bay. That Country is full of Catle and horses which before the war Belonged to the Spaniard and Apalachia Indians but are now all wild.

But if your Lordship please to have laid before you all the Printed mapps, and Descriptions that are in England of the Country to the westward of the Mississipi and Thoroughly Consider all Circumstances you will Incline to beleive that the English Nation can Setle a Colony no where to greater purpose then upon some Convenient place any where 60 or 80 miles to the westward of the mouth of the Mississipi. It is Certain there are Considerable numbers of Indians there, so farr from being Subject, that are at Constant warrs with the Spaniards of new Mexico. It is certain the French could not persue La Salle's design formed against the mine Country, by reason of their Present Circumstances with Spain, So that It seems If the English put in and gett the Indians of Their Side, it may be a means of at Least Enjoying a good Share of the trade Both with the Spaniards and their Indian Subjects, of that part of New Spain. The example of Queriaso[?] Shows us that neither galleys[,] men of warr nor garrisons can prevent a trade of that nature and no man Can foretell how favourable some revolutions of Time might prove, in affording oppertunities worth Catching att, to gain Some of the mines. The Bay of Campeche Lying not farr of[f] the Baymen might be Invited to Setle in the new Colony & make it The port of Cutting Logwood from that port, above all things arming the Indians, purchasing their Commodities[,] making Discoveries and sending Youths to Learn their Language, to ship home their wood, from, and occasionally Exercise the trade wold be of the utmost Consequence to the firm Establishing the Colony for of them might be had men ready at any time to help oppose the Spaniards. A thing of this nature must be done with great Secrecy, and first Setled with Considerable strength and fortified with the utmost Celerity. If the Spaniard patiently suffer the French to goe Sharers with them in the Peruvian trade Its equally Reasonable that the English, should aim at gaining some of the Mexican. Its easy to make the peace and Inland Discoveries from Carolina, from whence we are already well acquainted as farr as the Missisipi. 2 or 300 lbs. Sterlings worth of goods proper will be Sufficient & for discovering the Coast and finding a fitt River to Setle on a Sloop may be sent from hence privately. 1 Remain Your Lordships most obedient Humble Servant, Thomas Nairne.

[P.S.] Your Lordship I hope will please to pardon Defect of Title whereof I am Ignorant. [Endorsement:] So. Carolina. 10 July 1708. Mr. Tho[ma]s Nairne with a Map and account of those parts.

Questions

1. How does Nairne propose to check the expansion of the French and Spanish colonies in North America? What evidence does he present that this effort would succeed?
2. Speaking of Indians, Nairne writes that "they effect them most who sell best cheap." What does he mean? What does he hope to accomplish by pointing this out?
3. Discuss the role of the Indian slave trade in Southeastern geopolitics. Who is involved and why?
4. Describe Nairne's proposal for an English colony west of the Mississippi. How does this fit into his larger vision of British empire in America?

11.2 Missionary Francis LeJau Discusses Christianity and Slavery*

Francis LeJau, an Anglican missionary, came to Carolina from England in the early eighteenth century to preach Protestant Christianity to the young colony's inhabitants. Unlike previous missionaries, LeJau concentrated on converting Africans and Indians, both enslaved and free. Frustrated with what he viewed as a lack of support for his missionary efforts, Le Jau wrote a series of letters to authorities both within the colony and in London. The selection here is drawn from letters written between 1712 and 1714.

[LeJau to the Secretary, February 20, 1712]

South Carolina Parish of St. James Goose Creek
Feby. 20th 1711/12

Sr.

As I had no Convenient opportunity to Write to you directly from this place since Capt. Thomas went off, in September last, I thought it was my duty to give my selfe that Honr. by the way of Barbados my Lre was dated January the 4th last past and I hope that way will prove as safe as at other times I repeat here the Principal matters—

*Frank J. Klingberg, ed., *The Carolina Chronicle of Dr. Francis Le Jau, 1706–1717* (Berkeley: University of California Press, 1956), 107–110, 128–138.

The State of my Parish relateing to Spiritual things for the last halfe year ending upon new Yeares day was as follows—

2 Marriages. . *12* Children Baptised. 2 Adults. 4 Buryals *36* Communicants at Xtmas last among whome 5 new Communicants, and near 60 in the Parish, Children Catechised at a time *10* or *12* in all above 20 Negroes Catechised 40. or *50*. The Mortality that begun to rage in Augt. is not yet over, especialy in Towne where the Commissary has attended with much zeal, and I thank God he has been preserved from dangerous sickness, the number of the White People dead of late in the Province is near *200*, and the slaves as many again, which is a Considble loss for a place, so thin Inhabited we have allso wanted Salt, and Provisions are very scarce chiefly in the Towne where no Body durst go from the Country. The Surgeons are of opinion that the Aire has been infected these 14 Yeares. I look upon a more immediat Cause that is the Irreligion and Lewdness of too many Persons, but chiefly the Barberous usage of the poor Slaves. I endeavour to urge the dutyes of mercy towards them as much as I am able, and I bless God things are upon a better foot in that respect about me— but still I am Contradicted by several Masters, but I trust in God these visitations will serve to make them mind better things than worldly advantages—

I have had of late an opportunity to oppose with all my might the putting of a very unhumane Law and in my Judgmt. very unjust it is in Execution, in Relation to run away Negroes, by a Law Enacted in this Province some years before I came; such an Negroe must be mutilated by amputation of Testicles if it be a man. and of Ears if a Woman. I have openly declared against such punishment grounded upon the Law of God, which setts a slave at liberty if he should loose an Eye or a tooth when he is Corrected. Exod. 21. and some good Planters are of my opinion. I must Informe you of a most Cruel Contrivance a man has Invented to punish small faults in slaves. he puts them in a Coffin where they are crushed almost to death, and he keeps them in that hellish Machine for 24 hours commonly with their feet Chained out, and a Lid pressing upon their stomack,

this is a matter of fact universally knowen, when I look upon the ordinary cause that makes those poor Souls run away, and almost dispaire I find it is imoderate labour and want of Victualls and rest. God Alm: inspire the Honourable Society my most Illustrious Patrons to Consider those things so that they may be remedyed for the Encouragemt. of those poor Creatures, I will allso transmit to you what I observe Concerning our Indians, when I am Informed yt. you have received my Lres, and the papers I sent by Mrs Johnston, it is now 8 Months since I heard from any friend in Europe the last orders of the Society are of 18 Months date, the last Lre I had the Honour to receive from you was dated last Octobr. was twelve month. I take pains to do my duty as diligently as I am able, and wait with patience for further Instructions and Commands from my Honrd. Superiours which I will ever receive with respect and obey with all Submission. I gave you an account in my last of the desolate Condition of Renoque. it was in Octobr. or the latter End of September that the Tuscararo's Indians liveing near Cape fair Cutt off *137* of our people, most of them Palatines and some Switzers. I am not able to declare whether they were sett on by some of the partys that have been long at variance in that place or whether they were provoked by some great Injustice & taking their Land by force, it is so reported among us. our forces are Actualy marched to Suppress those Murderers. Vizt. a Generall Called Barnewell and 16 White men, whome 6 or 700 Indians have Joined and they are to meet the Virginians many wise men in this Province doubt of the Success it is evident that our Traders have promoted Bloody Warrs this last Year to get slaves and one of them brought lately *100* of those poor Souls. It do's not belong to me to say any more upon those Melaneholy Affaires I submit as to the Justice of those Proceedings to Your Wisdom. When I am asked how we are to deal with those unfortunate slaves, I content my selfe to Exhort that they be used with Xtian Charity and yt. we render their Condition as tollerable as we can. I don't know where the fault lyes but I see 30 Negroes at Church for an Indian slave, and as for our free Indians—they goe their own way and bring their Children like themselves with little Conversation among us but when they want something from us, I generaly Pceive something Cloudy in their looks, An argumt. I fear, of discontent. I am allso Informed yt. our Indian Allyes are grown haughty of late—

We long very much to see the Governmt. of this Province Settled things are quiet Eno among us by Divine Grace. We are 4 of the Clergy doing as well as we can Mr. Maule, and Mr. Hazel are very well for the present so is Mr Comissary. I allso here that Monsr L Pierre is well in his little Settlement—Monsr. Gignilliat has been this pritty while one of my Parishioners. Some Body has reported that there was a Minister in Bermudas who intended to come here. I did not hear from Mr. Auchinleck nor Mr. Dun these 6 months this last I am told is Marryed and Settled in Virginia.

Relateing to my Pticular affaires God has Graciously preserved me and mine in this sickly time. I am very well as to matter of health. So is my Familly. I have been forced to pass my own word for the payment of things necessary for the finishing my Church and house, else we were like never to see the End of that tedious work,—I hope the Parishioners will not suffer me to loose too much, and I trust above all in the mighty Providence and to the favour of the Illustrious Society my ever respected Superiours and Benefactors. Give me leave to assure his Grace, My Lord President, My Ld. of London, My Lords and the Honourable Members of that Noble Body of my most humble respect duty and obedience. I humbly crave the Blessing of my Lords, and the Prayers of the Members whome I daily pray to Alm: God to Bless and preserve.

I have mentioned our Schoolmaster in my 3 last Lres he is pretty well recovered of a fall, and we have great reason to be well Sattisfied with his Behavour & qualifications, I only doubt whether we shall be able to Encourage him as he deserves. his Familly is not Come yet from Virginia. I Recommend myselfe and my small Concerns to your goodness, and begg the Continuation of yr Prayers, Your good offices, and Esteem being with due Respect and Pfect Gratitude—

Sr

Your most humble and Obedt Servant
Francis Le Jau . . .

Addressed To
The Right Honourable
and the Right Reverend
Henry Lord Bishop of London
Endorsed S. Carolina
Mr Le Jau Jan 1712/13

[*Le Jau to the Secretary, February 23, 1713*]

So Carolina Parish of St. James near Goose Creek
February 23th 1712/13

Sr.

I had the Honour to write to you Deer. 11 last past, and to desire you to desire the Society my much honoured Superiors & Benefactors of my humble Respects & Obedience, Permitt me to Acquit my Self again of my Duty to that Illustrious Body, and to beg the Continuance of their favour & Goodness to me, I dayly Pray for their Prosperity and take All the Paines I am able to Exercise my function of Missionary with faithfullness & Diligence & through Divine Blessing I have the Comfort to See my Small Endeavours are not altogether fruitless, for beside the 3 Adults that received lately the holy Baptism, as I mentioned in my last, I baptized a fortnight agoe a Negro Woman being Presented by her own Mistress, And, God Willing, other Negroe women shall be Baptized against this next Easter with the Consent of their Master Here is the Account of the Spiritual State of my Parish from July 1st 1712 to the last day of December

Baptized 8, Among whom 3 Adults
Marriages 4, Burials 2 Actual Comunicants
at Xmas day 36 Among whom 3 New
Comunicants & 5 Negroes—
Comunicants in the whole Parish
above 55

Mr. Osborne arrived here about a Month or 5 Weeks ago and makes the Number of the

Clergy to be at Present, Eleaven, But it Seems Mr. Comissary Johnston has taken a Resolution to go for England, if he continues in that Mind We will Write by him to the Honrble Society And as he is very well Acquainted with our present State and what the Clergy thinks the Society is to be Informed of, I do not Question but the Relation he will give of All things concerning this Province will Prove Satisfactory, I beg leave to referr my Self to it, But if he should either break of[f] or defer his Intended Voyage I will not fail to Acquaint the Society with Some Particular Things wch I think it is my Duty to lay before them And I Submit to their wise Consideration & Judgemt. what Afflicts and Discourages me beyond Expression is to see the pious Designes of the Honrble Society very much Obstructed by the rash Conduct of Some of our Inhabitants. I humbly Apprehend That it is Expected the Missionaries should Endeavour to Promote the knowledge of Christ among the Ignorant Heathens begining with the Poor Negroe & Indian Slaves that live in our families, and Seeking all Opportunites to do good to the free Indians Scattered in the Province till God Gives us meanes to Instruct those Indian Nations that are our Neighbours, Which I firmly hope shall be Accomplished in his own time, But indeed few Masters appear Zealous or even pleased with what the Missionaries try to do for the Good of their Slaves, they are more Cruel Some of them of late Dayes than before, They hamstring main & unlimb those poor Creatures for Small faults, A man within this Month had a very fine Negroe batized, Sensible Carefull & good in all Respects who being wearyed with Labour & fallen asleep had the Mischance to loose a parcell of Rice weh by the Oversetting of a Periogua fell into a River. The man tho Intreated by the Minister of the Parish, who is Brother Maule and some Persons of the best Consideration among us to forgive the Negroe, who had Offended only through Neglect without Malice, thought fit to keep him for several Dayes in Chains, & I am told muffled up that he might not Eat, & Scourge him twice a Day, and at Night to put him into a hellish Machine contrived by him into the Shape of a Coffin where could not Stirr, The punishmt having continued Several Dayes & Nights and there being no Appearance when it should End, the poor Negroe through Despair Ask't one of his Children for a knife & manacled as he was Stabb'd himself with it; I am told this is the 5th Slave that Same man has destroyed by his Cruelty within 2 or 3 Yeares, but he is onely an hired Overseer the Owner of the Slaves lives out of this Province, I own I See everybody almost angry at So much Barbarity, Yet he pretends to go to Church, and they look upon the Man as Guilty of Murder, and So do great many of my Acquaintance who tho not So Barbarous take no Care at all of the Souls of their Slaves, and as little as the[y] can of their bodies I am at a loss when I see them in a praying posture knowing that at the same time they do not love their Neighbour, and what is most Amazeing I cannot make them Comprehend that their Neglect is an habitual state of Sin, I have Seen very Severe Judgemts. Since I came, Nothing Else almost but Judgemts and I don't admire at it I am mighty desirous to Receive the Comands & Instructions of the Society, I am told Coll Nicholson will bring them when he comes, he is Expected every day. I will Obey by the Grace of God as Exactly as I can the Orders you'l transmit to me I beg the Continuation of your friendship and the Assistance of your Good Offices, I Do not hear that any of the Missionaries be Sick, This Province is very happy to have such a Number of worthy & pious men as my Bretheren are, God Give me Grace to imitate their Vertues, The Countrey is healthy enough & at peace among our Selves through Gods Mercy, Our forces have done but Litle Yet, That we can hear against the Tuscaroras Indians That Warr is not to be concluded without much Trouble & Cost,

I am with due Respect
Sr

Your most humble &
Obedient Servant
ffrancis Le Jau. . . .

[Le Jau to the Secretary, August 10, 1713]

South Carolina Parish of St. James near
Goose Creek Augt. 10th 1713

Sr

I am in hope that by this time The Illustrious Society my most Honoured Superiours & Patrons have recd. full Information concerning the State of the Clergy of this Province from our Revd. Mr Commry Johnston and that my last Letter sent by Mr Guy dated April [11?] 13 last past is Come to your hands.

The chief matter I humbly presume to offer to the Consideration of the Honble Society is the Earnest Desire of all my Bretheren with myself that we may soon possess our Dear Mr Commissary. We Endeavour to serve his Cure in our Turns as diligently as possibily we can, and are unanimously resolved to continue cheerfully to do it. Yet I perceive the Inhabitants of Charles Town would be much better pleased if their own Pastor did reside among them.

Here is an Account of the Spiritual State of my Parish from January to June last inclusive.

Baptized 11 among whom 4 honest and pious Negroe women and a Gentleman called Mr Th: Barker with a Kinswoman of his Mrs Jane Barker, it is Imposible to relate all the Arts the Anabaptists of this Province have used to delude these two persons. But God Almighty by his Grace has Supported them and they prove faithfull children of his Holy Church, to my Incredible Comfort.

I had no burials this last half year, and onely 2 mariages Communicants upon Easter Sunday 36 or 38 upon Whitesunday 32 among whom 3 new Communicants.

Communicants in all near 60. among whom 5 Negroe men and 2 Negro women.

With the Blessing of God I hope to Administer in a short time the holy Sacrament of Baptism to 2 Negroe men, and receive the abjuration of a Negroe woman that had been bred in Guadalupe, but now Expresses a great desire to serve God according to his Word. The Honble Society will I am persuaded, be very well pleased to hear that among many of our Inhabitants that are remiss in promoting the Instruction of their Slaves, and some who shew an absolute unwillingness that they should hear any thing of God and Jesus our Saviour, yet there is a good number of Honest Masters and Mistresses Sincerely zealous in that Important point. I hear that upon all occasions they defend wth vigour the Cause of the Holy Gospel, and answer very well the objections of those uncharitable persons, who will not suffer their slaves to come to Church to Learn their Prayers, because, say they, knowledge makes them worse, this is now their main Argument.

If the Society thinks fit to print anything by way of Admonition to the Masters that have Slaves I humbly ask a Sufficient Number to be distributed in our 11 Parishes.

I have mentioned something in Relation to our Cunning and Artfull Anabaptists, I thank God there is no danger they should do harm to any person of sense but the Simple and Ignorant are sometimes ensnared by their tricks, I look upon them with whom I may be somewhat acquainted to be very obstinate, and hardly capable to form a right Judgment of things for being Illiterate. Yet they stirr and are Active beyond expression to increase the Number of their Sectaryes, there came lately a tradesman of their faction from Philadelphia there was two teachers before here among them.

I distributed the Abridgements of Mr Wall which I had the Honour to receive from the Society; and offered to one of their chief men in the Civilest Manner I could that if they would take the trouble to set down in writing their difficulties and objections, and the Answer I would give shou'd not be satisfactory I would Communicate the matter to the Honble Society, they made slight of my proposal; and go on their own way without giving any tollerable acct of themselves.

Permit me to ask a number of Walls Abridgment I am not Inform'd whether there be any short Acct of the rise and Progress of Anabaptism in English fit to be distributed, if there be any such thing, I humbly ask that a sufficient Number be sent to me about three or four dozens will be sufficient, I believe: some time agoe I gave my selfe the Honour to represent to the Society my humble opinion relating to the Promoting of the Instruction of our Yamoussee Indians, I have lately been informd of some Circumstances which I know it is my duty to declare, that my Hond Superiours may consider what is best to be done. That Nation was formerly very numerous but by degrees they are come to very little they could muster 800 fighting men and now they are hardly 400. I am possitively told also the rest of our Indian Allies and Neighbours are in the like case, they decrease apace, the Reason of it is the continual Warr they all make against their Indian Neighbours subject either to the french or Spaniards, as I asked whether upon the Conclusion of Peace those Indian warrs were like to continue: I was answered it would be almost Impossible to break the Indians of their Practice I suspect there is no other Necessity for those Nations to Warr against their Neighbours but that of making slaves to pay for the goods the traders Sell them, for the Skins trade do's not flourish as formerly.

Having often spoken of our Expedition against the Tuscaroras I may now presume to say that we look upon that Business as Ended, Since my Parishioner and friend Coll. Moore went against them by the Authority of our Government he has destroyed above 800 of that Nation it was lately reported he had received them that remained upon terms, but it seems those Indians broke the Articles they had accepted which Occasioned the destruction of some more of their People, I believe some means shall be found to keep them that are alive from doing any more harm. we Expect Col. Moore back in two Months or Sooner.

The Clergy of this Province is very loving towards one another and in perfect Union God be praised. I don't hear of any of us thats sick at present, we design to meet as usually we do in October next.

We had lately a Ship from London, one Capt Taylour I did not hear that any of the Clergy had any letter from the Society we have been waiting this half year for the arrival of Coll. Nicholson. As soon as I have the happiness to receive the Particular Commands and Directions of the Honble Society I will not fail to pay to them the Obedience I owe.

I take the Liberty to Assure His Grace my Lord President, My Lords, and the Honble Members of that Illustrious Body of my most humble respects & duty I ever pray to God Alm: to Bless their Persons to prosper their designs and Reward their Zeal, I humbly crave my Lords Blessing and the Charitable Prayers of the Members begging the continuation of their favour & Protection I subscribe myself

Sir
Your most humble and obedient Servant
Francis Le Jau . . .

[Le Jau to the Secretary, January 22, 1714]

*South Carolina Parish of St James
near Goose Creek January 22th 1713/4*

Sr

The last Letter I had the Honour to write to you was dated Augt 10th last past, since which time I could not hear of any vessel bound for London, else I would not have failed to acquaint myself of my duty to the Illustrious Society, my much respected Superiors and Benefactors.

The Spiritual state of my Parish from July 1st 1713 to the 1st of this instant is as follows, baptized 11 among whom three Adult Negro's, one burial, three Marriages at Christmas last. I had 5 new communicants, 31 Actual Communicants among whome 5 Negroe men & 2 women in my Parish about 65 Communicants.

Being uncertain whether my last Letter came to your hands I take this Liberty to insert in this that the number of the Baptized in this Parish from Janry to July 1713 was 11 among whom a Gentleman and Gentlewoman & four Negroe Women, 2 Marriages no Burial, 3 new Communicants, actual Communicants on whitesunday 32 Communicants in all 60.

Since the first of this month I baptized an old Sensible Negroe Man upon his death bed, and three Negroe children, and all of them with their masters consent some more come to me, Shewing an Earnest desire to receive that holy Sacrament. I Encourage them and instruct them the best I can by Divine Grace

It is a singular comfort to me to see that while so many professed Christians appear but Lukewarm, it pleases God to raise to himself faithfull and devout Servts from among the heathens, who are very zealous in the Practice of our Christian dutyes. I hear no Complaining of our Proselytes, their masters commend them for their faithfullness, and from what I am going to relate, the Honble Society shall have a satisfactory Instance that their Pious designs are not fruitless, as Irreligious men would insinuate, when they pretend That the knowledge of the true God and Jesus his Son renders our Slaves worse.

About Christmas last past there was a rumour spread of an Intended Conspiracy of the Negro's against us all like that of New York. I was told that the Plot had been form'd in Goose Creek where there is a good number of fine Negro's. This News made me Inquire and observe being resolved to find out how true the thing might be. The matter has been examined very diligently by our Government this very week. 12 or 15 Negroes living on the North side of Cooper River, having been apprehended under suspicion it has appeared upon good evidence that a Negroe fellow brought hither some years ago from Martineco, and of a very stubborn temper, had Inticed some Slaves to joyn with him that they might get their liberty by force. the thing being proved against him he has been put to death for it, two more Slaves have been very severely chastis'd for hearkening to him, but there was not any sufficient proof to take their life and all denied the Crime, the other prisoners have been acquited but what I consider as a singular Providence there has not been so much as one of our Goose Creek Negroes accused of having knowledge of the Plot, far from having consented to so great a Crime. The most sensible of our Slaves whom I have admitted to the holy Sacrament have solemnly protested to me that if ever they hear of any Ill design of the Slaves I shall know it from them that it may be prevented, and I can't but depend upon the truth of their words, knowing them to be Exemplarily Pious and Honest.

I wish I could prevail upon the Inhabitants of this Place to make serious Reflexions upon the Judgments wch our Sins and in particular the want of Charity and the Love of this World bring down upon our heads from time to time. It is Miraculous how any of us came to escape from the great Hurricane we felt Sept 5th last past it continued for 12 hours, had the two rivers on both sides of Charles Town been joyned for some time that place would now be destroyed. there has been 70 persons drowned in the Province, and much damage to our Fortifications, houses, barns, & Plantations. God of his Goodness has Preserved us. The Clergy has suffered but little we all enjoy our Health only Brother Maule has been of late much indisposed wth a running distemper that has seized several Persons just above the Eye. Our Schoolmaster Mr B. Dennis does very well We endeavour all of us through Divine blessing to discharge our duty in our Mission, but we have Enemys who would discourage us. a spirit of faction continues still, more sectaryes with Teachers are come of late and more are expected. We trust in God for our support and hope the Illustrious Society will Protect us. We have been deprived of a Tender Father when we lost our Good Lord Bp of London, but we hope for our Comfort that his Worthy Sucessor so famous by his eminent Vertues will extend his Charitable Care over us that are settled in this remote Place.

We assure ourselves that Mr Comissary Johnston has done Justice to us, and represented to the Honble Board of the Society what we had desired him to do I cannot forbear adding that his Parishioners want very much his presence. The Clergy do what they can but the People is not satisfied. I hope when he comes he will bring the Societys Commands for us which in my Brothers and my own name I presume to promise we will obey with all the diligence we are capable of.

I beg leave to Assure his Grace my Lord President, My Lords, and the Honble Members of the Society of my humble duty, respects, obedience, and gratitude. I ask with all humility their blessing and Prayers, with the favour of their Protection and subscribe myself with all Veneration.

Sr
Your most humble and
obedient Servant
Francis Le Jau

Terms

Palatines—Germans from the Rhineland Palatinate
Switzers—Swiss

Questions

1. Le Jau writes that he wants to remind masters of their "dutyes of mercy" toward their slaves. What specifically does he want to change?
2. How does Le Jau view the Africans and Indians he is trying to convert?
3. What does Le Jau write about the Indian slave trade in Carolina? Why did it begin, and why did he think it would continue?
4. Is Le Jau an abolitionist? Why or why not?
5. What benefits does Le Jau suggest the spread of Christianity among South Carolina's slaves might bring to their masters?

11.3 A Description of Eighteenth-Century South Carolina*

The following description of South Carolina was published anonymously in London in 1763. According to the author, it "was first written for the information and private use of a gentleman in England, without any intention of its being ever exposed to the public view."

OF THE INHABITANTS AND THEIR FOOD

The inhabitants are either white or black; the white are between thirty and forty thousand; all the males, from sixteen years of age to sixty, are mustered, and carry arms in the militia regiments, and form together a body of about seven thousand: Their complexion is little different from the inhabitants of Britain, and they are generally of a good stature and well-made, with lively and agreeable countenances; sensible, spirited, and open-hearted, and exceed most people in acts of benevolence, hospitality, and charity. The men and women who have a right to the class of gentry (who are more numerous here than in any other colony in North America) dress with elegance and neatness: The personal qualities of the ladies are much to their credit and advantage; they are generally of a middling stature, genteel and slender; they have fair complexions, without the help of art, and regular features; their air is easy and natural; their manner free and unaffected; their eyes sparkling, penetrating, and inchantingly sweet: They are fond of dancing, an exercise they perform very gracefully; and many sing well, and play upon the harpsicord and guitar with great skill; nor are they less remarkable for goodness of heart, sweetness of disposition, and that charming modesty and diffidence, which command respect

*R. R. Carroll, ed., *Historical Collections of South Carolina* (New York: Harper & Brothers, 1836), vol. 2: 478–488.

whilst they invite love, and equally distinguish and adorn the sex—in short, all who have the happiness of their acquaintance, will acquit me of partiality, when I say they are excelled by none in the practice of all the social virtues, necessary for the happiness of the other sex, as daughters, wives, or mothers.

The weather is much too hot in summer, for any kind of diversion or exercise, except riding on horseback, or in chaises, (which few are without) in the evenings and mornings; and this is much practised. In the autumn, winter, and spring, there is variety and plenty of game for the gun or dogs; the gentlemen are not backward in the chase. During this season there is once in two weeks a dancing-assembly in Charles-town, where is always a brilliant appearance of lovely, well-dress'd women: We have likewise a genteel playhouse, where a very tolerable set of actors, called the American company of comedians, frequently exhibit; and often concerts of vocal and instrumental music, generally performed by gentlemen.

The Negro slaves are about seventy thousand; they, with a few exceptions, do all the labour or hard work in the country, and are a considerable part of the riches of the province; they are supposed worth, upon an average, about forty pounds sterling each; And the annual labour of the working slaves, who may be about forty thousand, is valued at ten pounds sterling each. They are in this climate necessary, but very dangerous domestics, their number so much exceeding the whites; a natural dislike and antipathy, that subsists between them and our Indian neighbours, is a very lucky circumstance, and for this reason: In our quarrels with the Indians however proper and necessary it may be to give them correction, it can never be our interest to extirpate them, or to force them from their lands; their ground would be soon taken up by runaway Negroes from our settlements, whose numbers would daily increase, and quickly become more formidable enemies than Indians can ever be, as they speak our language, and would never be at a loss for intelligence.

The general assembly, about two years ago, (understanding that there was in the treasury a considerable sum of that money appropriated by the general duty act, for the encouragement of poor protestants, to become settlers in the province) passed an act to increase the bounty to be given to each; which is now four pounds sterling to all above the age of twelve years, and two pounds to those who are between two years and twelve, and one pound to all under two years; besides this, his majesty's bounty is one hundred acres of land, wherever they chuse it, provided it has not been granted before, to the head of every family, male or female; and fifty acres for every child, indented servant, or slave, the family consists of. If this act has the desired effect, the security and opulence of the province will be increased, and the adventurers will be pleased to find a change from poverty and distress to ease and plenty; they are invited to a country not yet half settled, where the rivers are crouded with fish, and the forests with game: and no game-act to restrain them from enjoying those bounties of providence, no heavy taxes to impoverish them, nor oppressive landlords to snatch the hard-earned morsel from the mouth of indigence, and where industry will certainly inrich them.

There is both great plenty and variety of food, for the subsistence of the inhabitants, at reasonable prices. I shall here only name the different sorts, as it will be sufficient for my present purpose; and begin with the vegetables: Of these the Indian corn, or maize, is of general use, being the chief subsistence of the plantation slaves. Rice, which is produced here in great quantity and perfection; upwards of one hundred thousand barrels of it are now exported annually to Europe, to the Northern colonies, and to the West-Indies, each barrel containing between five and six hundred weight. Wheat is cultivated, with much success, by the German protestants, who are settled on the interior parts of the province; they would have been able to supply the province with all the flour we consume, by this time, had they not been interrupted by the Cherokee war. These industrious people distil a palatable brandy from peaches, which they have in great plenty; likewise from potatoes, Indian corn, and rye: But to return to our vegetable food: We have plenty of potatoes, both Irish and Spanish; pompions, pease, and beans, of different kinds; apples, pears, nectarines, peaches, plums of several sorts, chesnuts, walnuts, olives, pomegranates, oranges, lemons, figs, citrons, melons, with a great variety of other fruits, and many of the European pot-herbs, as cabbages, brocoli, colliflower, &c. &c. In enumerating the animal part of our food, I begin with the fish: Mullet, whiting, black-fish, rock-fish, sturgeon, porgys, trout, bream, and many other sorts of flat fish; likewise oisters, crabs, shrimps, and sometimes turtle. Black cattle are extremely plentiful, many gentlemen owning from five hundred to fifteen hundred head; the beef is best about Christmas, the stall-fed cattle being then brought to market; the sheep are numerous; poultry and pork we have in plenty, and very good, though I cannot agree with the inhabitants, who believe they have both these of a kind superior to the rest of the world: In the woods and fields are plenty of wild turkeys of a large size, geese, ducks, doves, pigeons, partridges, hares, rabbits, racoons, possums, &c. likewise a beautiful species of deer: The hunting of them is a healthy exercise, and a very entertaining diversion; they are the principal animal food of our back settlers, and of the Indians; and likewise a considerable branch of trade, great quantities of their skins being yearly exported; a small duty laid on them is appropriated for the support and maintenance of the clergy. The buffalo's are sometimes found in the woods near the mountains; but they are not near so numerous as they were a few years ago; they are used as food, though their beef is hard and disagreeable to the palate.

Madeira wine and punch are the common drinks of the inhabitants; yet, few gentlemen are without claret, port, lisbon, and other wines, of the French, Spanish, or Portugal vintages. The ladies, I mention it to their credit, are extremely temperate, and generally drink water; which, in Charles-town, and all places near the sea, is very unwholesome; as the soil is not solid enough to strain it sufficiently, it has always a mixture of sand or earth in it.

Before I finish this chapter, it may not be improper to add, that Indigo is cultivated here with much success; between four and five hundred thousand weight of it is yearly exported; and that the soil, in many parts of the province, is very proper for the cultivation of olive-trees and vines, articles that have been hitherto almost totally neglected; a little attention to them would save much money expended on oil and wine, which we now import. The cotton-tree likewise grows naturally in this province, and might be of great use in cloathing the poorer sort of white inhabitants and the Negroes, if any pains were taken to cultivate it. The honourable society for the propagation of arts, manufactures, and commerce, may be assured, that their most sanguine expectations would be gratified in the culture of many other useful commodities, native and exotic, if pursued here with vigour and perseverance; the situation and climate of the colony, and of all other places about the same distance from the equator in both hemispheres. being universally allowed to be the best for the production of all the necessaries and conveniencies of life.

Of Charles Town, and the other Towns and Garrisons.

The province is divided into four counties and nineteen parishes. Charles-town is the metropolis, which is happily situated on a neck of land, or peninsula, formed by two navigable rivers, where they mix their streams, and present us with a large commodious harbour; Ashley-river washes the town on the west and south, and Cooper-river on the east; these rivers run parallel to one another, at about a mile's distance, for a considerable way into the country, gradually separating to their sources. The streets are broad, straight, and uniform, intersecting one another at right angles; those that run east and west extend from one river to the other; the Bay-street which fronts Cooper-river and the ocean, is really handsome, and must delight the stranger who approacheth it from the sea.

There are about eleven hundred dwelling-houses in the town, built with wood or brick; many of them have a genteel appearance, though generally incumbered with balconies or piazzas; and are always decently, and often elegantly, furnished; the apartments are contrived for coolness, a very necessary consideration.

The white inhabitants are about four thousand, and the Negro servants near the same number. I have examined a pretty exact register of the births and burials for fifteen years, and find them, excepting when the small-pox prevailed, nearly equal; the advantage, though small, is in favour of the births; though to the burials are added all transient people who die here, as sailors, soldiers, or the inhabitants of the country, whose business or pleasure bring them frequently to this Metropolis. The south-east part of the town fronts the sea, from which it is about three leagues distant, and from whence, in the hot season, we have refreshing breezes, which the flood-tide always brings or increases.

The town is divided into two parishes, St. Philip's and St. Michael's; St. Philip's church is one of the handsomest buildings in America: It is of brick plaistered, and well enlightened on the inside; the roof is arched except over the galleries; two rows of Tuscan pillars support the galleries and arch that extend over the body of the church; the pillars ornamented, on the inside, with fluted Corinthian pilasters, whose capitals are as high as the cherubims over the center of each arch, supporting their proper cornice: The west end of the church is adorned with four Tuscan columns, supporting a double pediment, which has an agreeable effect; the two side doors, which enter into the belfry, are ornamented with round columns of the same order, which support angular pediments that project a considerable way, and give the church some resemblance of a cross: Pilasters of the same order with the columns are continued round the body of the church; over the double pediment is a gallery with banisters; from this the steeple rises octogonal, with windows in each face of the second course, ornamented with Ionic pilasters, whose intablature supports a balustrade; from this the tower still rises octogonal, with sashed windows on every other face, till it is terminated by a dome, upon which stands a lanthorn for the bells, and from which rises a vane in the form of a cock.

St. Michael's church is built of brick; it is not yet quite finished. It consists of a body of a regular shape, and a lofty and well-proportioned steeple, formed of a tower and spire; the tower is square from the ground, and in this form rises to a considerable height: the principal decoration of the lower part is a handsome portico, with Doric columns, supporting a large angular pediment, with a modilion cornice; over this rises two square rustic courses; in the lower one are small round windows, on the North and South; in the other, small square ones: On the East and West from this the steeple rises octangular, having windows on each face, with Ionic pilasters between each, whose cornice supports a balustrade; the next course is likewise octogonal, has sashed windows and festoons alternately on each face, with pilasters and a cornice, upon which rises a circular range of Corinthian pillars, with a balustrade connecting them; from whence is a beautiful and extensive prospect over the town and harbour, along the coast, and into the sea, as far as the eye can carry one; this charming prospect is frequently heightened by the appearance of ships, at a distance, sailing towards the port. The body of the steeple is carried up octangular within the pillars, on whose intablature the spire rises, and is terminated by a gilt globe, from which rises a vane, in the form of a dragon: This steeple is one hundred and ninety-two feet in height, and is very useful to the shipping, who see it long before they make any other part of the land; which eminently distinguishes this place from the rest of the coast, where there is a sameness very dangerous to mariners. The church is eighty feet in length, without including the tower and retired place for the altar, and fifty-eight feet wide.

Besides the churches, there are meeting-houses for the members of the church of Scotland, for those called Independents, two for Baptists, one for French, and one for German protestants: Though all of them are neat, large, and convenient, they are too plain to merit particular descriptions.

Near the center of the town is the state-house, a large, commodious brick building; the south front is decorated with four $\frac{2}{3}$ columns of the composite order, whose capitals are highly finished, supporting a large angular pediment and cornice; it consists of two stories besides the roof; on the lower are the court-room, the secretary's office, and apartments for the house-keeper; on the upper story are two large, handsome rooms; one is for the Governour and Council, the other for the Representatives of the people, with lobbies and rooms for their clerks: The room, called the council-chamber, appears rather crouded and disgusting, than ornamented and pleasing, by the great profusion of carved work in it; in the upper part of the house or roof is a large room for the provincial armory: Near the state-house is a very neat market-place, well-regulated and plentifully supplied with provisions.

Above three hundred top-sail vessels enter and clear at this port, annually, bringing us necessaries and luxuries from every quarter of the globe, and carrying our produce to Europe, the northern colonies, and the West-Indies.

About ten years ago, a plan was approved of for fortifying Charles-town in a very respectable manner, and soon after began to be put in execution, on the south and south-east of the town, but was discontinued without finishing any part of it, though much money had been laid out for that purpose; the town is at present defended, towards the water, by seven batteries or bastions, of which three are considerable ones,

connected by courtine lines, having platforms with about one hundred heavy cannon mounted. The old fortification, on the land side, is in ruins; a new work was begun in 1757, a little without the other; the plan was a horn-work, to be built with tappy, and flanked with little batteries and redoubts, at proper distances; the whole to extend from one river to the other, but a stop was put to this likewise, after a considerable progress was made in it, either for want of money, which is probable; or from an opinion, that it was unnecessary: Besides these works, the harbour is defended by Fort-Johnson, about two miles distant from Charles-town, on a sea island, which forms one side of the harbour: It is placed within point-blank shot of the channel, through which the ships must pass in their way to town: The lower battery is on a level with the water, and has fifteen eighteen-pounders, and five nine-pounders, mounted *en Barbette;* the upper part of this fort is old and very irregular; it has two demi-bastions towards the water, and a third projection in the form of a swallow's tail, all of them having platforms and cannon mounted. Towards the land is a gate with a ravelin, two ditches, two bridges, and a glacis, with the beginning of a new work built with tappy, on the north-west, left unfinished. The captain of this fort is commissioned by the King. There are barracks in it for fifty men; but, on the approach of an enemy, the militia of the island march into it for its defence.

There are several charitable societies in the town; the principal of them is called the Carolina Society, which, by an easy subscription, maintains many decayed families, and educates many orphans; I must not forget to mention the St. Andrew's Club, which is chiefly composed of Scotsmen, but whose charitable donations are confined to no country. There is a society calculated for the promotion of literature, named the Library Society, at present in a flourishing state, and through whose means many useful and valuable books have been already introduced into the province, which probably would not otherwise have soon found their way here, private fortunes not being equal to the expence.

Questions

1. The author calls slaves "necessary, but very dangerous domestics." Explain.
2. What is the author's position on Indian policy? Why?
3. If you lived in London or Bristol and read this pamphlet, would you want to move to South Carolina? How would your sex and social status affect your answer to this question?
4. Describe the subsistence and export economies of South Carolina. How and by whom were commodities produced?

CHAPTER

12 *Middle Colonies*

Between Virginia and New England lay temperate, fertile, and well-watered lands that attracted European settlers from a wide variety of national, ethnic, and religious backgrounds. With the most diverse population of North America's colonial regions, the "Middle Colonies," as they came to be known, embodied the unprecedented connections among European, African, and American lands that characterized the colonial period.

12.1 Dutch Ministers Discuss New Netherland*

In the letters that follow, three Dutch Reformed ministers in New Netherland, Johannes Megapolensis (1603–1670), Samuel Drisius (1620–1673), and Henricus Selyns (1636–1701), report on conditions in the young, multiethnic, and multidenominational colony of New Netherland in the decade before English conquest.

Letters of the Dutch Ministers to the classis of Amsterdam, 1655–1664

Rev. Johannes Megapolensis to the Classis of Amsterdam (March 18, 1655).

Reverendissimi Domini, Fratres in Christo, Synergi observandi:

---

*Johannes Megapolensis, Samuel Drisius, and Henricus Selyns, "Letters of the Dutch Ministers to the Classis of Amsterdam, 1655–1664," in *Narratives of New Netherland, 1609–1664*, ed. J. Franklin Jameson, (New York: Barnes & Noble, 1909), 391–393, 396–402, 408–411.*

I feel it my duty, to answer the letter of your Reverences, dated the 11th of November, [1654].

We have cause to be grateful to the Messrs. Directors and to your Reverences for the care and trouble taken to procure for the Dutch on Long Island a good clergyman, even though it has not yet resulted in anything. Meanwhile, God has led Domine Joannes Polhemius from Brazil, by way of the Caribbean Islands, to this place. He has for the present gone to Long Island, to a village called Midwout, which is somewhat the *meditullium* of the other villages, to wit, Breuckelen, Amersfoort and Gravesande. There he has preached for the accommodation of the inhabitants on Sundays during the winter, and has administered the sacraments, to the satisfaction of all, as Director Stuyvesant has undoubtedly informed the Messrs. Directors.

As to William Vestiens, who has been schoolmaster and sexton here, I could neither do much, nor say much, in his favor, to the Council, because for some years past they were not satisfied or pleased with his services. Thereupon when he asked for an increase of salary last year, he

205

received the answer, that if the service did not suit him, he might ask for his discharge. Only lately I have been before the Council on his account, and spoken about it, in consequence of your letter, but they told me that he had fulfilled his duties only so-so and that he did little enough for his salary.

Some Jews came from Holland last summer, in order to trade. Later some Jews came upon the same ship as D: Polheymius; they were healthy, but poor. It would have been proper, that they should have been supported by their own people, but they have been at our charge, so that we have had to spend several hundred guilders for their support. They came several times to my house, weeping and bemoaning their misery. When I directed them to the Jewish merchant, they said, that he would not lend them a single stiver. Some more have come from Holland this spring. They report that many more of the same lot would follow, and then they would build here a synagogue. This causes among the congregation here a great deal of complaint and murmuring. These people have no other God than the Mammon of unrighteousness, and no other aim than to get possession of Christian property, and to overcome all other merchants by drawing all trade towards themselves. Therefore we request your Reverences to obtain from the Messrs. Directors, that these godless rascals, who are of no benefit to the country, but look at everything for their own profit, may be sent away from here. For as we have here Papists, Mennonites and Lutherans among the Dutch; also many Puritans or Independents, and many atheists and various other servants of Baal among the English under this Government, who conceal themselves under the name of Christians; it would create a still greater confusion, if the obstinate and immovable Jews came to settle here.

In closing I commend your Reverences with your families to the protection of God, who will bless us and all of you in the service of the divine word.

Your obedient
Johan. Megapolensis.
Amsterdam in New Netherland the 18th of March, 1655.

Addressed to the Reverend, Pious and very Learned Deputies ad res Ecclesiasticas Indicas, in the Classis of Amsterdam.

Revs. J. Megapolensis and S. Drisius to the Classis of Amsterdam (August 5, 1657).

Reverend, Pious and Learned Gentlemen, Fathers and Brethren in Christ Jesus: . . .

On Long Island there are seven villages belonging to this province, of which three, Breuckelen, Amersfoort and Midwout, are inhabited by Dutch people, who formerly used to come here to communion and other services to their great inconvenience. Some had to travel for three hours to reach this place. Therefore, when Domine Polheymus arrived here from Brazil, they called him as preacher, which the Director-General and Council confirmed.

The four other villages on Long Island, viz., Gravensand, Middelburgh, Vlissingen, and Heemstede are inhabited by Englishmen. The people of Gravensand are considered Mennonites. The majority of them reject the baptism of infants, the observance of the Sabbath, the office of preacher, and any teachers of God's word. They say that thereby all sorts of contentions have come into the world. Whenever they meet, one or the other reads something to them. At Vlissingen, they formerly had a Presbyterian minister who was in agreement with our own church. But at present, many of them have become imbued with divers opinions and it is with them *quot homines tot sententiae.* They began to absent themselves from the sermon and would not pay the preacher the salary promised to him. He was therefore obliged to leave the place and go to the English Virginias. They have now been without a preacher for several years. Last year a troublesome fellow, a cobbler from Rhode Island in New England, came there saying, he had a commission from Christ. He began to preach at Vlissingen and then went with the people into the river and baptized them. When this became known here, the *fiscaal* went there, brought him to this place, and he was banished from the province.

At Middelburgh, alias Newtown, they are mostly Independents and have a man called Joannes Moor, of the same way of thinking, who preaches there, but does not serve the sacraments. He says he was licensed in New England to preach, but not authorized to administer the sacraments. He has thus continued for some years. Some of the inhabitants of this village are Presbyterians, but they cannot be supplied by a Presbyterian preacher. Indeed, we do not know that there are any preachers of this denomination to be found among any of the English of New England.

At Heemstede, about seven leagues from here, there live some Independents. There are also many of our own church, and some Presbyterians. They have a Presbyterian preacher, Richard Denton, a pious, godly and learned man, who is in agreement with our church in everything. The Independents of the place listen attentively to his sermons; but when he began to baptize the children of parents who are not members of the church, they rushed out of the church.

On the west shore of the East River, about one mile beyond Hellgate, as we call it, and opposite Flushing, is another English village, called Oostdorp, which was begun two years ago. The inhabitants of this place are also Puritans or Independents. Neither have they a preacher, but they hold meetings on Sunday, and read a sermon of some English writer, and have a prayer.

About eighteen leagues up the North River, half way between the Manhattans and Rensselaer or Beverwyck, lies a place, called by the Dutch Esopus or Sypous, and by the Indians Atharhacton. It is an exceedingly fine country there. Thereupon some Dutch families settled there who are doing very well. They hold Sunday meetings and then one or the other of them reads from the Postilla.

Such is the condition of the church in our province. To this we must add that, as far as we know, not one of all these places, Dutch or English, has a schoolmaster, except the Manhattans, Beverwyck, and now also Fort Casimir on the South River. And although some parents try to give their children some instruction, the success is far from satisfactory, and we can expect nothing else than young men of foolish and undisciplined minds. We see at present no way of improving this state of affairs; first, because some of the villages are just starting, and have no means, the people having come half naked and poor from Holland, to pay a preacher and schoolmaster; secondly, because there are few qualified persons here who can or will teach.

We can say but little of the conversion of the heathens or Indians here, and see no way to accomplish it, until they are subdued by the numbers and power of our people, and reduced to some sort of civilization; and also unless our people set them a better example, than they have done heretofore.

We have had an Indian here with us for about two years. He can read and write Dutch very well. We have instructed him in the fundamental principles of our religion, and he answers publicly in church, and can repeat the Commandments. We have given him a Bible, hoping he might do some good among the Indians, but it all resulted in nothing. He took to drinking brandy, he pawned the Bible, and turned into a regular beast, doing more harm than good among the Indians.

Closing we commend your Reverences to the gracious protection of the Almighty, whom we pray to bless you in the Sacred Ministry.

Vestri et officio et effectu,
Johannes Megapolensis.
Samuel Drissius.
Amsterdam, in New Netherland,
the 5th of August, 1657.

Revs. Megapolensis and Drisius to the Classis of Amsterdam (October 25, 1657).

Brethren in Christ:

Since our last letter, which we hope you are receiving about this time, we have sent in a petition in relation to the Lutheran minister, Joannes Ernestus Gutwasser. Having marked this on its margin, we have sent it to the Rev. Brethren of the Classis. We hope that the Classis will take care that, if possible, no other be sent over, as it is easier to send out an enemy than afterward to thrust him out. We have the promise that the magistrates here will compel him to leave with the ship *De Wage*. It is said that there has been collected for him at Fort Orange a hundred beaver skins, which are valued here at eight hundred guilders, and which is the surest pay in this country. What has been collected here, we cannot tell. Our magistrates have forbidden him to preach, as he has received no authority from the Directors for that purpose. Yet we hear that the Hon. Directors at Amsterdam gave him permission to come over. We have stated in a previous letter the injurious tendency of this with reference to the prosperity of our church.

Lately we have been troubled by others. Some time since, a shoemaker, leaving his wife and children, came here and preached in conventicles. He was fined, and not being able to pay, was sent away. Again a little while ago there arrived here a ship with Quakers, as they are called. They went away to New England, or more particularly, to Rhode Island, a place of errorists and enthusiasts. It is called by the English themselves the *latrina* of New England. They left several behind them here, who labored to create excitement and tumult among the people—particularly two women, the one about twenty, and the other about twenty-eight. These were quite outrageous. After being examined and placed in prison, they were sent away. Subsequently a young man at Hempstead, an English town under the government, aged about twenty-three or twenty-four years, was arrested, and brought thence, seven leagues. He had pursued a similar course and brought several under his influence. The magistrate, in order to repress the evil in the beginning, after he had kept him in confinement for several days, adjudged that he should either pay one hundred guilders or work at the wheelbarrow two years with the negroes. This he obstinately refused to do, though whipped on his back. After two or three days he was whipped in private on his bare back, with threats that the whipping would be repeated again after two or three days, if he should refuse to labor. Upon this a letter was brought by an unknown messenger from a person unknown to the Director-General. The import of this, (written in English), was, Think, my Lord-Director, whether it be not best to send him to Rhode Island, as his labor is hardly worth the cost.

Since the arrival of *De Wage* from the South River [the Director?] has again written to Joannes Ernestus Gutwasser to go away. On this he presented a petition, a copy of which is herewith transmitted, as also a copy signed by several of the Lutheran denomination. We observe that it is signed by the least respectable of that body, and that the most influential among them were unwilling to trouble themselves with it. Some assert that he has brought with him authority from the West India Company to act as minister. Whether dismission and return will take place without trouble remains to be seen.

We are at this time in great want of English ministers. It is more than two years since Mr. Doughty, of Flushing which is a town here, went to Virginia, where he is now a preacher. He left because he was not well supported. On October 13, Mr. Moore, of Middelburg, which is another town here, died of a pestilential disease, which prevailed in several of our English towns and in New England. He left a widow with seven or eight children. A year before, being dissatisfied with the meagre and irregular payments from his hearers, he went to Barbadoes, to seek another place. Mr. Richard Denton, who is sound in faith, of a friendly disposition, and beloved by all, cannot be induced by us to remain, although we have earnestly tried to do this in various ways. He first went to Virginia to seek a situation, complaining of lack of salary, and that he was getting in debt, but he has returned thence. He is now fully resolved to go to old England, because his wife, who is sickly, will not go without him, and there is need of their going there, on account of a legacy of four hundred pounds sterling, lately left by a deceased friend, and which they cannot obtain except by their personal presence. At Gravesend there never has been a minister. Other settlements, yet in their infancy, as Aernem, have no minister. It is therefore to be feared that errorists and fanatics may find opportunity to gain strength. We therefore request you, Rev. Brethren, to solicit the

Hon. Directors of the West India Company, to send over one or two English preachers, and that directions may be given to the magistracy that the money paid by the English be paid to the magistrate, and not to the preacher, which gives rise to dissatisfaction, and that at the proper time any existing deficiency may be supplied by the Hon. Directors. Otherwise we do not see how the towns will be able to obtain ministers, or if they obtain them, how they will be able to retain them. Complaints continually reach us about the payment of ministers. Nevertheless in New England there are few places without a preacher, although there are many towns, stretching for more than one hundred leagues along the coast. Hoping that by God's blessing and your care something may be effected in this matter, we remain,

Your friends and fellow laborers,
Johannes Megapolensis.
Samuel Drisius. . . .
Manhattans, Oct. 22, 1657.

Rev. Henricus Selyns to the Classis of Amsterdam (June 9, 1664).

Very Reverend, Pious and Learned Brethren in Christ:

With Christian salutations of grace and peace, this is to inform you, that with proper submission, we take the liberty of reporting to the Very Rev. Classis the condition and welfare of the Church of Jesus Christ, to which your Reverences called me, as well as my request and friendly prayer for an honorable dismission.

As for me, your Rev. Assembly sent me to the congregation at Breuckelen to preach the Gospel there, and administer the sacraments. This we have done to the best of our ability; and according to the size of the place with a considerable increase of members. There were only a few members there on my arrival; but these have with God's help and grace increased fourfold.

Trusting that it would not displease your Reverences, and would also be very profitable to the Church of Christ, we found it easy to do what might seem troublesome; for we have also taken charge of the congregation at the General's Bouwery in the evening, as we have told you before. An exception to this arrangement is made in regard to the administration of the Lord's Supper. As it is not customary with your Reverences to administer it in the evening, we thought, after conference with our Reverend Brethren of the New Amsterdam congregation, and mature deliberation, that it would be more edifying to preach at the Bouwery, on such occasions, in the morning, and then have the communion, after the Christian custom of our Fatherland.

As to baptisms, the negroes occasionally request that we should baptize their children, but we have refused to do so, partly on account of their lack of knowledge and of faith, and partly because of the worldly and perverse aims on the part of said negroes. They wanted nothing else than to deliver their children from bodily slavery, without striving for piety and Christian virtues. Nevertheless when it was seemly to do so, we have, to the best of our ability, taken much trouble in private and public catechizing. This has borne but little fruit among the elder people who have no faculty of comprehension; but there is some hope for the youth who have improved reasonably well. Not to administer baptism among them for the reasons given, is also the custom among our colleagues. But the most important thing is, that the Father of Grace and God of Peace has blessed our two congregations with quietness and harmony, out of the treasury of his graciousness; so that we have had no reason to complain to the Rev. Classis, which takes such things, however, in good part; or to trouble you, as we might have anticipated.

Meanwhile, the stipulated number of years, pledged to the West India Company, is diminishing; although the obligation we owe to them who recommended us naturally continues. Also, on account of their old age, we would love to see again our parents, and therefore we desire to return home. On revolving the matter in my mind, and not to be lacking in filial duty, I felt it to be proper to refer the subject to God and my greatly beloved parents who call for me, whether I should remain or return home at the expiration of my contract.

As we understand, they are, next to myself, most anxious for my return, and have received my discharge from the Hon. Directors, and have notified the Deputies ad Causas Indicas thereof, which has pleased us. We trust that we shall receive also from your Reverences a favorable reply, relying upon your usual kindness. Yet it is far from us to seem to pass by your Reverences, and give the least cause for dissatisfaction. I have endeavored to deserve the favor of the Rev. Classis by the most arduous services for the welfare of Christ's church, and am always ready to serve your Reverences.

It is my purpose when I return home, when my stipulated time is fulfilled, to give a verbal account of my ministry here, and the state of the church, that you may be assured that any omissions in duty have been through ignorance.

Domine Samuel Megapolensis has safely arrived, but Domine Warnerus Hadson, whom you had sent as preacher to the South River, died on the passage over. It is very necessary to supply his place, partly on account of the children who have not been baptized since the death of Domine Wely, and partly on account of the abominable sentiments of various persons there, who speak very disrespectfully of the Holy Scriptures.

In addition there is among the Swedes a certain Lutheran preacher, who does not lead a Christian life. There is also another person, who has exchanged the Lutheran pulpit for a schoolmaster's place. This undoubtedly has done great damage among the sheep, who have so long wandered about without a shepherd except the forementioned pastor, who leads such an unchristian life. God grant that no damage be done to Christ's church, and that your Reverences may provide a blessed instrument for good.

In view of the deplorable condition of New Netherland, for the savages have killed, wounded and captured some of our people, and have burnt several houses at the Esopus, and the English, with flying banners, have declared our village and the whole of Long Island to belong to the King: therefore the first Wednesday of each month since last July has been observed as a day of fasting and prayer, in order to ask God for his fatherly compassion and pity. The good God, praise be to him, has brought about everything for the best, by the arrival of the last ships. The English are quiet, the savages peaceful; our lamentations have been turned into songs of praise, and the monthly day of fasting into a day of thanksgiving. Thus we spent last Wednesday, the last of the days of prayer. Blessed be God who causes wars to cease to the ends of the earth, and breaks the bow and spear asunder. Herewith, Very Reverend, Pious, and Learned Brethren in Christ, be commended to God for the perfecting of the saints and the edification of the body of Christ. *Vale.*

Your Reverences' humble servant in Christ Jesus, Henricus Selyns.
Breuckelen, in New Netherland,
June 9, 1664.

Terms

classis—a governing body within the Dutch Reformed Church
meditullium—middle place
quot homines tot sententiae—"as many opinions as men"
fiscal—a kind of Dutch judicial officer

Questions

1. Define the limits of religious tolerance and intolerance in New Netherland.
2. In the eyes of Dutch ministers, what challenges did the New Netherland's religious diversity present?
3. Characterize attitudes concerning race in New Netherland.
4. What strategies could African slaves in New Netherland employ to better their condition?
5. Compare the relation between religion and the developing systems of race-based slavery in New Netherland, Virginia, the West Indies, and South Carolina.

12.2 Stuyvesant Explains the Fall of New Netherland*

In 1664, during one of three seventeenth-century Anglo-Dutch wars, an English expeditionary force secured the surrender of New Netherland. In a letter to the directors of the Dutch West India Company, *New Netherland Governor Peter Stuyvesant (governor 1647 to 1664) offers his interpretation of what happened.*

Report of the Honble Peter Stuyvesant, late Director-General of New Netherland, on the Causes which led to the Surrender of that Country to the English, 1665.

Illustrious, High and Mighty Lords:

Whilst I, your Illustrious High Mightinesses' humble servant, was still in New Netherland I was informed, verbally and in writing, that the unfortunate loss and reduction of New Netherland were, in consequence of ignorance of the facts, spoken of and judged in this country by many variously, and by most people not consistently with the truth, according to the appetite and leaning of each. Therefore your Illustrious High Mightinesses' servant, sustained by the tranquillity of an upright and loyal heart, was moved to abandon all, even his most beloved wife, to inform you, Illustrious, High and Mighty, of the true state of the case, that you, when so informed, may decide according to your profound wisdom;

Not doubting that you, Illustrious, High and Mighty, will judge therefrom that this loss could not be avoided by human means, nor be imputed to me, your Illustrious High Mightinesses' humble servant.

I dare not interrupt your Illustrious High Mightinesses' most important business by a lengthy narrative of the poor condition in which I found New Netherland on my assuming its government. The open country was stripped of inhabitants to such a degree that, with the exception of the three English villages of Heemstede, New Flushing and Gravesend, there were not fifty bouweries and plantations on it, and the whole province could not muster 250, at most 300 men capable of bearing arms.

Which was caused, first, (in default of a settlement of the boundary so repeatedly requested) by the troublesome neighbors of New England, who numbered full fifty to our one, continually encroaching on lands within established bounds, possessed and cultivated in fact by your Illustrious High Mightinesses' subjects.

Secondly, by the exceedingly detrimental, land-destroying and people-expelling wars with the cruel barbarians, which endured two years before my arrival there, whereby many subjects who possessed means were necessitated to depart, others to retreat under the crumbling fortress of New Amsterdam, which, on my arrival, I found resembling more a molehill than a fortress, without gates, the walls and bastions trodden under foot by men and cattle.

Less dare I, to avoid self-glorification, encumber your weighty occupations, Illustrious, High and Mighty, with the trouble, care, solicitude and continual zeal with which I have endeavored to promote the increase of population, agriculture and commerce; the flourishing condition whereunto they were brought, not through any wisdom of mine, but through God's special blessing, and which might have been more flourishing if your formerly dutiful, but now afflicted, inhabitants of that conquest had been, Illustrious, High and Mighty, protected and remained protected by a suitable garrison, as necessity demanded, against the deplorable and tragical massacres by the barbarians, whereby (in addition to ten private murders) we were plunged three times

---

*Peter Stuyvesant, "Report on the Surrender of New Netherland," in *Narratives of New Netherland*, 458–466.

into perilous wars, through want of sufficient garrisons; especially had they, on the supplicatory remonstrances of the people and our own so iterated entreaties, which must be considered almost innumerable, been helped with the long sought for settlement of the boundary, or in default thereof had they been seconded with the oft besought reinforcement of men and ships against the continual troubles, threats, encroachments and invasions of the English neighbors and government of Hartford Colony, our too powerful enemies.

That assistance, nevertheless, appears to have been retarded so long (wherefore and by what unpropitious circumstances the Honble Directors best know) that our abovementioned too powerful neighbors and enemies found themselves reinforced by four royal ships, crammed full with an extraordinary amount of men and warlike stores. Our ancient enemies throughout the whole of Long Island, both from the east end and from the villages belonging to us united with them, hemmed us by water and by land, and cut off all supplies. Powder and provisions failing, and no relief nor reinforcement being expected, we were necessitated to come to terms with the enemy, not through neglect of duty or cowardice, as many, more from passion than knowledge of the facts, have decided, but in consequence of an absolute impossibility to defend the fort, much less the city of New Amsterdam, and still less the country. As you, Illustrious, High and Mighty, in your more profound and more discreet wisdom, will be able to judge from the following:

First, in regard to want of powder: The annexed account shows what had been received during the last four years and what was left over, from which it appears that there were not 2000 pounds in store in the city and fort; of that quantity there were not 600 pounds good and fit for muskets; the remainder damaged by age, so that when used for artillery, the cannon required a double charge or weight.

If necessary and you, Illustrious High and Mighty, demand it, the truth hereof can be sought from the gunner, who accompanies me hither, and who will not deny having said in the presence of divers persons and at various times: "What can my lord do? he knows well that there is no powder,

and that the most of it is good for nothing; there is powder enough to do harm to the enemy, but 'tis no good; were I to commence firing in the morning, I should have all used up by noon."

What efforts we have employed to receive this and some other reinforcements and assistance may appear from the copies of two letters sent to the colonie of Renselaerswyck and village of Beverwyck, marked N° A.

Whose answers intimate, that we could not be assisted by either the one or the other, because of the difficulties into which they had just then fallen with the northern Indians owing to the killing of three or four Christians and some cows, whether urged to do so by evil disposed neighbors, I submit to wiser opinions.

In regard to provisions: Although our stores were reasonably well supplied with them the whole fore part of the summer, even more than ever heretofore, the falling off being commonly caused by the want of credit or ready money to lay up an abundant stock of provisions;

Nevertheless our supplies became, from various accidents, so much diminished that on capitulating to the enemy, not 120 *skepels* of breadstuffs, and much less of peas and meat were remaining in store,

This scarcity being caused by the exportation of a large quantity of provisions to the island of Curaçao, in the little craft *De Musch*, dispatched thither three weeks previous to the arrival of the frigates, without any apprehension or suspicion of experiencing a want of provisions, as the good wheat harvest was not only at hand, but between the barn and the field.

In addition to this favorable prospect, we were relieved from all fear of any approaching enemy or imminent danger from Old England, by the last letters from the Honble Directors, dated 21 April, and received one month before the arrival of the frigates; in the words following:

On the other hand, according to the intelligence we receive from England, His Royal Majesty of Great Britain, being disposed to bring all his kingdoms under one form of government, both in church and state, hath taken care that commissioners are ready at present to repair to New England, and there to install the Episcopal government as in Old England; wherefore we are in hopes that as the English at the North have removed mostly from Old England for the causes aforesaid, they will not give us henceforth so much trouble, but prefer to live free under us at peace with their consciences, than to risk getting rid of our authority and then falling again under a government from which they had formerly fled.

Two reasons which will serve you for speculation, in order to make a disposition of our force, and assist considerably the execution of our intentions and maintenance of our conquest by that means without difficulty, until a final agreement shall be concluded.

The settlement of the boundary now begins to assume a different aspect from that it formerly wore, partly in consequence of our efforts, partly from other circumstances.

Placed by the aforesaid advices beyond all apprehension, we felt no difficulty in letting the aforesaid little vessel, *De Musch*, go with the loaded provisions; indeed we would have sent off more if we could have procured them anywhere.

The asserted scarcity of provisions is proved by the annexed declaration of the commissary himself, and of Sergeant Harmen Martensen, and moreover by the efforts we employed to obtain a greater quantity of these, were that possible. N° B.

Provisions were likewise so few and scarce in the city, in consequence of the approaching harvest, for the inhabitants are not in the habit of laying up more provisions than they have need of, that about eight days after the surrender of the place, there was not in the city of New Amsterdam enough of provisions, beef, pork and peas, to be obtained for the transportation of the military, about ninety strong, and the new grain had to be thrashed.

In addition to the want of the abovementioned necessaries, and many other minor articles, a general discontent and unwillingness to assist in defending the place became manifest among the people,

Which unwillingness was occasioned and caused in no small degree, first among the people living out of the city, and next among the burghers, by the attempts and encroachments experienced at the hands of the English in the preceding year, 1663.

First, through Captain John Talcot's reducing Eastdorp, situate on the main, not two leagues from New Amsterdam, by order and commission of the government of Hartford.

Next, through Captain Co's later invasion and subjugation of all the English villages and plantations on Long Island, which were under oath and obedience to you, Illustrious, High and Mighty, and the Honble Company, with an armed troop of about 150 to 160 of John Schott's horse and foot. That this was done also by the order of Hartford's Colony appears from the fact that in the following year, 1664, Governor Winthrop himself came with two commissioners from Hartford, and one from the east end of Long Island, with a considerable number of people on foot and on horseback, to the reduced English towns, in order to get the inhabitants to take the oath of allegiance in the King's name.

Owing to the very serious war with the Esopus Indians and their confederates, in consequence of a third deplorable massacre perpetrated there on the good inhabitants, we could not at the time do anything against such violent attempts and encroachments, except to protest against them verbally and in writing.

All this, recorded fully in the form of a journal, was, on November 10, 1663, and last of February, 1664, transmitted to the Honorable Directors, together with our, and the entire commonalty's grievances, remonstrances and humble petitions for redress, either by means of a settlement of the boundary, or else by an effective reinforcement of men and ships.

I could and should lay the authenticated copies before you, Illustrious, High and Mighty, were it not that I am apprehensive of incumbering thereby your present much more important business. On that account, therefore, in verification of what is set forth, are most humbly submitted to you, Illustrious, High and Mighty, only

No. 1. An humble remonstrance of the country people on Long Island, whereof the original was sent on the last of February to the Honorable Directors, setting forth the threats and importunity made use of towards them by the English troop aforesaid, with a request for redress; otherwise, in default thereof, they shall be under the necessity of abandoning their lands or submitting to another government.

No. 2 is a copy of a letter sent to all the Dutch villages for a reinforcement, whence can be inferred our good inclination to defend the city and fort as long as possible. The answer thereto intimates their refusal, as they, living in the open country unprotected, could not abandon their lands, wives and children.

No. 3. The burghers' petition and protest exhibits their uneasiness; wherein they set forth at length the very urgent necessity to which they were reduced in consequence of the overwhelming power of the enemy; the impossibility, owing to want of provisions and munitions of war, especially powder, of defending the city one, and the fort three, days; and the absence of any relief to be expected or reinforcement to be secured, certainly not within six months; whereas by effective resistance everything would be ruined and plundered, and themselves, with wives and children, more than 1,500 in number, reduced to the direst poverty.

This dissatisfaction and unwillingness on the part of burgher and farmer were called forth by the abovementioned and other frequently bruited threats, by the hostile invasions and encroachments that had been experienced and the inability to oppose them for want of power and reinforcements; but mainly by the sending of proclamations and open letters containing promises, in the King's name, to burgher and farmer, of free and peaceable possession of their property, unobstructed trade and navigation, not only to the King's dominions, but also to the Netherlands with their own ships and people.

Besides the abovementioned reasons for dissatisfaction and unwillingness, the former as well as the ruling burgomasters and schepens, and principal citizens, complained that their iterated remonstrances, letters and petitions, especially the last, of the 10th of November, wherein they had informed the Honble Directors of the dire extremity of the country both in regard to the war with the barbarians and to the hostile attacks of the English, had not been deemed worthy of any answer; publicly declaring, "If the Honble Company give themselves so little concern about the safety of the country and its inhabitants as not to be willing to send a ship of war to its succor in such pressing necessity, nor even a letter of advice as to what we may depend on and what succor we have to expect, we are utterly powerless, and, therefore, not bound to defend the city, to imperil our lives, property, wives and children without hope of any succor or relief, and to lose all after two or three days' resistance."

Your patience would fail you, Illustrious, High and Mighty, if I should continue to relate all the disrespectful speeches and treatment which, Illustrious, High and Mighty, your servants of the Superior Government have been obliged to listen to and patiently to bear, during the approach of the frigates, whenever they sought to encourage the burghers and inhabitants to their duty, as could be verified by credible witnesses.

This further difficulty was made by the burghers that they were not certain of their lives and properties on account of the threats of plundering heard from some of the soldiers, who had their minds fixed more on plunder than on defence; giving utterance, among other things, to the following: We now hope to find an opportunity to pepper the devilish Chinese, who have made us smart so much; we know well where booty is to be got and where the young ladies reside who wear chains of gold. In verification whereof, it was alleged and proved, that a troop of soldiers had collected in front of one Nicolaus Meyer's house in order to plunder it, which was prevented by the burghers.

In addition to the preceding, many verbal warnings came from divers country people on Long Island, who daily noticed the growing and increasing strength of the English, and gathered from their talk that their business was not only with New Netherland but with the booty and plunder, and for these were they called out and enrolled. Which was afterwards confirmed not only by the dissolute English soldiery, but even by the most steady officers and by a striking example exhibited to the colonists of New Amstel on the South River, who, notwithstanding they had offered no resistance, but requested good terms, could not obtain them, but were invaded, stripped, utterly plundered and many of them sold as slaves to Virginia.

To prevent these and many other misfortunes, calamities and mischiefs overtaking evidently and assuredly the honest inhabitants, owing to the aforesaid untenableness of the place and fort without assistance from Fatherland, which was not to be expected for six months, we and the Council, on the presentation of so many remonstrances, complaints and warnings, were under the necessity, God and the entire community know without any other object than the welfare of the public and the Company, to come to terms with the enemy and neighbors whose previous hostile invasions and encroachments neither we nor our predecessors have been able to oppose or prevent.

And, even if the good God had, for the moment, been pleased to avert the misfortune from us, to delay or prevent the arrival of those frigates, yet had we, through want of the reinforcements of men and ships from Fatherland so repeatedly demanded but not come, shortly after fallen, by this war with England, into a worse state and condition, in consequence of the overpowering might of the neighbors. This is sufficiently evident and plain from their hostile acts and encroachments against the inhabitants in a season of profound peace; being, as already stated, fifty to our one, they would afterwards, *jure belli*, have attacked, overwhelmed, plundered us and the good inhabitants whom they would have utterly expelled out of the country.

Many more reasons and circumstances could be adduced, Illustrious, High and Mighty, for your greater satisfaction and my vindication, if your occupations, Illustrious, High and Mighty, permitted you to cast your eyes over, or allow others to take cognizance of, the continual remonstrances, applications and petitions for a settlement of the boundary or a reinforcement, particularly of the latest of the years 1663 and 1664, and of the daily entries in the minutes bearing thereupon.

But fearing that your patience, Illustrious, High and Mighty, will be exhausted by this too long and unpalatable relation, I shall break off here and submit myself, Illustrious, High and Mighty, to your most wise and discreet opinion, command and order—with this prayer, that you, Illustrious, High and Mighty, would please to dispatch me, your humble servant, as quickly as your more important occupations will possibly allow; meanwhile praying that God will temper this loss with other more notable successes and prosper your government.

Illustrious, High and Mighty,
Your most humble servant,
P. Stuyvesant.
Exhibited 16th October, 1665.

Questions

1. Why did New Netherland succumb so easily to English conquest?
2. Why might Stuyvesant think it wise to emphasize the colony's indefensibility?

12.3 William Penn Promotes Pennsylvania*

In addition to being a wealthy proprietor and an able colonial administrator, William Penn (1644–1718) was also an accomplished author. In the 1681 document that follows, Penn introduces his new colony to the European world in an effort to lure investors and settlers to Pennsylvania.

SOME ACCOUNT OF THE PROVINCE OF PENNSILVANIA, BY WILLIAM PENN, 1681

Some account of the province of Pennsilvania in America; Lately Granted under the Great Seal of England to William Penn, etc. Together with Priviledges and Powers necessary to the well-governing thereof. Made publick for the Information of such as are or may be disposed to Transport themselves or Servants into those Parts.
London: Printed, and Sold by Benjamin Clark Bookseller in George-Yard, Lombard-street, 1681.

---

*William Penn, "Some Account of the Province of Pennsilvania," in *Narratives of Early Pennsylvania, West New Jersey, and Delaware, 1630–1707*, ed. Albert Cook Myers (New York: Barnes & Noble, 1912), 202, 207–211, 215.

Since (by the good providence of God) a Country in America is fallen to my lot, I thought it not less my Duty than my honest Interest to give some publick notice of it to the World, that those of our own, or other Nations, that are inclin'd to Transport themselves or Families beyond the Seas, may find another Country added to their choice, that if they shall happen to like the Place, Conditions and Constitutions, (so far as the present Infancy of things will allow us any prospect) they may, if they please, fix with me in the Province hereafter describ'd. . . .

I. SOMETHING OF THE PLACE

The Place lies 600 miles nearer the Sun than England; for England begins at the 50th Degree and ten minutes of North Latitude, and this Place begins at fourty, which is about the Latitude of Naples in Italy, or Mompellier in France. I shall say little in its praise, to excite desires in any, whatever I could truly write as to the Soil, Air and Water: This shall satisfie me, that by the Blessing of God, and the honesty and industry of Man, it may be a good and fruitful Land.

For Navigation it is said to have two conveniencies; the one by lying Ninescore miles upon Delaware River; that is to say, about three-score and ten miles, before we come to the Falls, where a Vessel of Two hundred Tuns may Sail, (and some Creeks and small Harbours in that distance, where Ships may come nearer than the River into the Country) and above the Falls, for Sloops and Boats, as I am informed, to the extent of the Patent. The other convenience is through Chesapeak-Bay.

For Timber and other Wood there is variety for the use of man.

For Fowl, Fish, and Wild-Deer, they are reported to be plentiful in those Parts. Our English Provision is likewise now to be had there at reasonable Rates. The Commodities that the Country is thought to be capable of, are Silk, Flax, Hemp, Wine, Sider, Woad, Madder, Liquorish, Tobacco, Potashes, and Iron, and it does actually produce Hides, Tallow, Pipe-staves, Beef, Pork, Sheep, Wool, Corn, as Wheat, Barly, Ry, and also Furs, as your Peltree, Mincks, Racoons, Martins, and such

like; store of Furs which is to be found among the Indians, that are profitable Commodities in Europe.

The way of trading in those Countries is thus: they send to the Southern Plantations Corn, Beef, Pork, Fish and Pipestaves, and take their Growth and bring for England, and return with English Goods to their own Country. Their Furs they bring for England, and either sell them here, or carry them out again to other parts of Europe, where they will yield a better price: And for those that will follow Merchandize and Navigation there is conveniency, and Timber sufficient for Shipping.

II. THE CONSTITUTIONS

For the Constitutions of the Country, the Patent shows, first, That the People and Governour have a Legislative Power, so that no Law can be made, nor Money raised, but by the Peoples Consent.

2dly. That the Rights and Freedoms of England (the best and largest in Europe) shall be in force there.

3dly. That making no Law against Allegiance (which should we, 'twere by the Law of England void of it self that moment) we may Enact what Laws we please for the good prosperity and security of the said Province.

4thly. That so soon as any are ingaged with me, we shall begin a Scheam or Draught together, such as shall give ample Testimony of my sincere Inclinations to encourage Planters, and settle a free, just and industrious Colony there.

III. THE CONDITIONS

My Conditions will relate to three sorts of People: 1st. Those that will buy: 2dly. Those that take up Land upon Rent: 3dly. Servants. To the first, the Shares I sell shall be certain as to number of Acres; that is to say, every one shall contain Five thousand Acres, free from any Indian incumbrance, the price a hundred pounds, and for the Quit-rent but one English shilling or the value of it yearly for a hundred Acres; and the said Quit-Rent not to begin to be paid till 1684. To the second sort, that take up Land upon Rent, they shall have liberty so to do, paying yearly one peny per Acre, not exceeding Two hundred Acres. To the third sort, to wit, Servants that are carried over, Fifty Acres shall be allowed to the Master for every Head, and Fifty Acres to every Servant when their time is expired. And because some engage with me that may not be disposed to go, it were very advisable for every three Adventurers to send an Overseer with their Servants, which would well pay the Cost.

The Divident may be thus; if the persons concern'd please, a Tract of Land shall be survey'd; say Fifty thousand Acres to a hundred Adventurers; in which some of the best shall be set out for Towns or Cities; and there shall be so much Ground allotted to each in those Towns as may maintain some Cattel and produce some Corn; then the remainder of the fifty thousand Acres shall be shar'd among the said Adventurers (casting up the Barren for Commons, and allowing for the same) whereby every Adventurer will have a considerable quantity of Land together; likewise every one a proportion by a Navigable River, and then backward into the Country. The manner of divident I shall not be strict in; we can but speak roughly of the matter here; but let men skilful in Plantations be consulted, and I shall leave it to the majority of votes among the Adventurers when it shall please God we come there, how to fix it to their own content.

IV. THESE PERSONS THAT PROVIDENCE SEEMS TO HAVE MOST FITTED FOR PLANTATIONS ARE

1st. Industrious Husbandmen and Day-Labourers, that are hardly able (with extreme Labour) to maintain their Families and portion their Children.

2dly. Laborious Handicrafts, especially Carpenters, Masons, Smiths, Weavers, Taylors, Tanners, Shoemakers, Shipwrights, etc. where they may be spared or are low in the World: And as they shall want no encouragement, so their Labour is worth more there than here, and there provision cheaper.

3dly. A Plantation seems a fit place for those Ingenious Spirits that being low in the World, are much clogg'd and oppress'd about a Livelyhood, for the means of subsisting being easie there, they may have time and opportunity to gratify their inclinations, and thereby improve Science and help Nurseries of people.

4thly. A fourth sort of men to whom a Plantation would be proper, takes in those that are younger Brothers of small Inheritances; yet because they would live in sight of their Kindred in some proportion to their Quality, and can't do it without a labour that looks like Farming, their condition is too strait for them; and if married, their Children are often too numerous for the Estate, and are frequently bred up to no Trades, but are a kind of Hangers on or Retainers to the elder Brothers Table and Charity: which is a mischief, as in it self to be lamented, so here to be remedied; For Land they have for next to nothing, which with moderate Labour produces plenty of all things necessary for Life, and such an increase as by Traffique may supply them with all conveniencies.

Lastly, There are another sort of persons, not only fit for, but necessary in Plantations, and that is, Men of universal Spirits, that have an eye to the Good of Posterity, and that both understand and delight to promote good Discipline and just Government among a plain and well intending people; such persons may find Room in Colonies for their good Counsel and Contrivance, who are shut out from being of much use or service to great Nations under settl'd Customs: These men deserve much esteem, and would be harken'd to. Doubtless 'twas this (as I observ'd before) that put some of the famous Greeks and Romans upon Transplanting and Regulating Colonies of People in divers parts of the World; whose Names, for giving so great proof of their Wisdom, Virtue, Labour and Constancy, are with Justice honourably delivered down by story to the praise of our own times; though the World, after all its higher pretences of Religion, barbarously errs from their excellent Example.

V. THE JOURNEY AND IT'S APPURTENANCES, AND WHAT IS TO BE DONE THERE AT FIRST COMING

Next let us see, What is fit for the Journey and Place, when there, and also what may be the Charge of the Voyage, and what is to be expected and done there at first. That such as incline to go, may not be to seek here, or brought under any disappointments there. The Goods fit to take with them for use, or sell for profit, are all sorts of Apparel and Utensils for Husbandry and Building and Household Stuff. And because I know how much People are apt to fancy things beyond what they are, and that Immaginations are great flatterers of the minds of Men; To the end that none may delude themselves, with an expectation of an Immediate Amendment of their Conditions, so soon as it shall please God they Arrive there; I would have them understand, That they must look for a Winter before a Summer comes; and they must be willing to be two or three years without some of the conveniences they enjoy at home; And yet I must needs say that America is another thing then it was at the first Plantation of Virginia and New-England: For there is better Accommodation, and English Provisions are to be had at easier rates: However, I am inclin'd to set down particulars, as near as those inform me, that know the Place, and have been Planters both in that and in the Neighbouring Colonys.

1st. The passage will come for Masters and Mistresses at most to 6 Pounds a Head, for Servants Five Pounds a Head, and for Children under Seven years of Age Fifty Shillings, except they Suck, then nothing.

Next being by the mercy of God, safely Arrived in September or October, two Men may clear as much Ground by Spring (when they set the Corn of that Country) as will bring in that time twelve month Forty Barrels, which amounts to two Hundred Bushels, which makes Twenty Five quarters of Corn. So that the first year they must buy Corn, which is usually very plentiful. They may so soon as they come, buy Cows, more or less, as they want, or are able, which are to be had at easy rates. For Swine, they are plentiful and cheap; these will quickly Increase to a Stock. So that after the first year, what with the Poorer sort, sometimes labouring to others, and the more able Fishing, Fowling, and sometime Buying; They may do very well, till their own Stocks are sufficient to supply them, and

their Families, which will quickly be and to spare, if they follow the English Husbandry, as they do in New-England, and New-York; and get Winter Fodder for their Stock. . . .

To conclude, I desire all my dear Country-Folks, who may be inclin'd to go into those Parts, to consider seriously the premises, as well the present inconveniences, as future ease and Plenty, that so none may move rashly or from a fickle but solid mind, having above all things, an Eye to the providence of God, in the disposal of themselves. And I would further advise all such at least, to have the permission, if not the good liking of their near Relations, for that is both Natural, and a Duty Incumbent upon all; and by this means will natural affection be preserved, and a friendly and profitable correspondence be maintained between them. In all which I beseech Almighty God to direct us, that his blessing may attend our honest endeavour, and then the Consequence of all our undertaking will turn to the Glory of his great Name, and the true happiness of us and our Posterity.

Amen.

William Penn.

Questions

1. At whom was this description directed? To what end?
2. What did Penn offer to prospective colonists? Why?
3. Why didn't Penn emphasize Quakerism?
4. What had Penn learned from previous colonial ventures?
5. What kind of colony did Penn envisage? How did this compare with the colonies that had already taken shape in other parts of North America?

12.4 Welsh Immigrant Life in Pennsylvania*

Colonial promoters had much of interest to tell prospective voyagers to North America. The following letter from John Jones, the child of Welsh immigrants to Penn's colony, affords insight into the way settlers themselves perceived the process of founding a new colony.

---

*John Jones, "Letter of John Jones, 1725," in *Narratives of Early Pennsylvania*, 454–459.

Letter of John Jones, 1725

My Kinsman, Hugh Jones:

I received a letter from you, dated May 8 last [1725]; and I was glad to find that one of my relatives, in the old land of which I have heard so much, was pleased to recollect me. I have heard my father speak much about old Wales; but I was born in this woody region, this new world.

I remember him frequently mentioning such places as Llanycil, Llanuwchllyn, Llanfor, Llangwm, Bala, Llangower, Llyn Tegid, Arenig Fawr, Fron Dderw, Brynllysg, Phenbryn, Cyffdy, Glanllafar, Fron Goch, Llaethgwm, Hafodfadog, Cwm Tir y Mynach, Cwm Glan Lleidiog, Trawsfynydd, Tài Hirion yn Mignaint, and many others. It is probably uninteresting to you to hear these names of places; but it affords me great delight even to think of them, although I do not know what kind of places they are; and indeed I long much to see them, having heard my father and mother so often speak in the most affectionate manner of the kind-hearted and innocent old people who lived in them, most of whom are now gone to their long home. Frequently, during long winter evenings, would they in merry mood prolong their conversation about their native land till midnight; and even after they had retired to rest, they would sometimes fondly recall to each other's recollection some man, or hill, house, or rock. Really I can scarcely express in words how delighted this harmless old couple were to talk of their old habitations, their fathers and mothers, brothers and sisters, having been now twenty-four years in a distant and foreign land, without even the hope of seeing them more. I fear this narrative will be irksome to you; but I cannot forbear when I think of these innocent artless old people.

And now, my kinsman, I will give you an account of the life and fortunes of my dear father, from the time when he left Wales to the day of his death. Three weeks to the time when he first heard tell of Pennsylvania, at St. Peter's Fair in Bala he took leave of his neighbors and relatives, who were taking account of his departure for London. He was waiting three months for a ship; after boarding the first ship he set out from England by [or upon] the name of William Penn. He had a very tempestuous passage for several weeks; and when in sight of the river [Delaware], owing to adverse winds and a boisterous sea, the sails were torn, and the rudder injured. By this disaster they were greatly disheartened, and were obliged to go back to Barbadoes, where they continued three weeks, expending much money in refitting their ship. Being now ready for a second attempt, they easily accomplished their voyage, and arrived safely in the river [Delaware] on the 16th of April, being thirty weeks from the time they left London. During this long voyage he learned to speak and read English tolerably well.

They now came up the river a hundred and twenty miles, to the place where Philadelphia is at present situated. At that time there was, as the Welsh say, *na thŷ nac ymogor* (neither house nor shelter), but the wild woods; nor any one to welcome them to land. A poor outlook, this, for persons who had been so long at sea, many of whom had spent their little all. This was not the place for remaining stationary. My father therefore went alone where chance led him, to endeavor to obtain the means of subsistence. He longed very much at this time for milk. During his wanderings he met with a drunken old man, who understood neither Welsh nor English, and who, noticing the stranger, invited him to his dwelling, where he was received by the old man's wife and several sons in the most hospitable manner. They were Swedes. Here he made his home, till he had a habitation of his own.

As you shall hear, during this summer (1682) our governor, William Penn, Esquire, arrived here, together with several from England, having bought lands here. They now began to divide the country into allotments, and to plan the city of Philadelphia, (which was to be more than two miles in length), laying it out in streets and squares, etc., with portions of land assigned to several of the houses. He also bought the freehold of the soil from the Indians, a savage race of men, who have lived here from time immemorial, as far as I am able to understand. They can give no account of themselves, not knowing when or whence they came here; an irrational set, I should imagine; but they have some kind of reason, too, and extraordinary natural endowments in their peculiar way; they are very observant of their customs, and more unblamable, in many respects, than we are. They had neither towns nor villages, but lived in booths or tents.

In the autumn of this year several from Wales arrived here: Edward ab Rhys, Edward Jones of Bala, William ab Edward, and many others. By this time there was a kind of neighborhood here, although as neighbors they could little benefit each other. They were sometimes employed in making huts beneath some cliff, or under the hollow banks of rivulets, thus sheltering themselves where their fancy dictated. There were neither cows nor horses to be had at any price. "If we have bread, we will drink water, and be content," they said; yet no one was in want, and all were much attached to each other; indeed much more so, perhaps, than many who have every outward comfort this world can afford.

During this eventful period, our governor began to build mansion-houses at different intervals, to the distance of fifty miles from the city, although the country appeared a complete wilderness.

The governor was a clever intelligent man, possessing great penetration, affable in discourse, and a pleasant orator; a man of rank, no doubt, but he did not succeed according to his merit; the words of the bard Edward Morys might be applied to him:

> The old person did not keep a fragment of his sense; He fell away to the pursuit of wealth.

At this time my father, Thomas Sion Evan, was living with the Swedes, as I mentioned before, and intending daily to return to Wales; but as time advanced, the country improved. In the course of three years several were beginning to obtain a pretty good livelihood, and my father determined to remain with them. There was by this time no land to be bought within twelve miles of the city; and my father, having purchased a small tract of land, married the widow of Thomas Llwyd of Penmaen.

> You have heard tell in Dyffryn Clwyd
> Of Thomas Lloyd of Penmaen.

He now went to live near the woods. It was a very rare but pleasing thing to hear a neighbor's cock crow. My father had now only one small horse; and his wife was much afflicted with the tertian ague. We might suppose that many things would be revolved in the mind of a man in such a situation as this; but I never heard him complain of the difficulties under which he labored. Everything was agreeable to these innocent people; although in want of some present necessaries, yet they were peaceable and friendly to each other. In process of time, however, the little which he had prospered, so that he became possessed of horses, cows, and everything else that was necessary for him, or even that he wished; indeed he never coveted much. During the latter years of his life, he kept twelve good milch cows. He had eight children, but I was the eldest. Having lived in this manner twenty-four years, he now became helpless and infirm, and very subject to difficulty of breathing at the close of his day's labor. He was a muscular man, very careful and attentive to his worldly occupations. About the end of July [1707], eighteen years to last July, he became sick, and much enfeebled by a severe fever; but asthma was his chief complaint. Having been thus five weeks indisposed, he departed this life, leaving a small farm each for my brother and myself, a corresponding portion for my sister, and a fair dower for my mother. My sister married Rhisiart ab Tomas ab Rhys, a man whom I much respected prior to his marriage, and still regard. My brother and I continue to live with my mother, as before, endeavoring to imitate our father in the management of his affairs; but we are in many respects unequal to him. Our mother is seventy-three years old, somewhat infirm, but enjoying pretty good health, considering her age.

And now, my kind kinsman, I have given you the history of my father and myself, and I hope you will be pleased with it. Do send me some news; if you should have anything remarkable to mention I should be glad to hear it.—I must conclude my letter.

Your kinsman,
Hugh Jones.

Questions

1. How did the early days of Pennsylvania compare with those of other colonies?
2. What about Pennsylvania might have attracted immigrants from places like Wales?
3. How does Jones's description of what his family found in Pennsylvania compare with what Penn said they would find there?

13

Atlantic Revolutions

The English Empire in North America formed in a rather haphazard fashion, the product of diverse initiatives and multiple improvisations rather than centralized and careful design. In the latter decades of the seventeenth and the early decades of the eighteenth centuries, the pressures of war, commerce, and government finance pushed figures on both sides of the Atlantic to try and define more clearly the relationships among the different parts of the empire. Did English laws and liberties extend across the ocean? Would the empire remain English or become British? Who would govern the colonies, and to whom would these governors be accountable? How would the colonies be defended? Who would benefit from their growing prosperity? Would colonial income derive from cultivation, licit commerce, and customs duties? Or from pirate raids and rapine? The resolution of such questions proved neither straightforward nor complete.

13.1   Rebellion in Boston*

New Englanders had chafed under the Dominion of New England. News of the Glorious Revolution in England gave them an opportunity to translate their discontent into action. In the two documents that follow, New England merchant Nathanael Byfield (1653–1733) describes the events of 1689, and the Boston rebels explain themselves.

*"Byfield's Account of the Late Revolution" and "The Declaration of the Gentlemen, Merchants and Inhabitants of Boston, and the Country Adjacent," in *Narratives of the Insurrections, 1675–1690*, ed. Charles M. Andrews (New York: Barnes & Noble, 1915), 170–182.

BYFIELD'S ACCOUNT OF THE LATE REVOLUTION, 1689

Gentlemen,

Here being an opportunity of sending for London, by a Vessel that loaded at Long-Island, and for want of a Wind put in here; and not knowing that there will be the like from this Country suddenly, I am willing to give you some brief Account of the most remarkable Things that have hapned here within this Fortnight last past; concluding that till about that time, you will have received *per*

Carter, a full Account of the management of Affairs here. Upon the Eighteenth Instant, about Eight of the Clock in the Morning, in Boston, it was reported at the South end of the Town, That at the North end they were all in Arms; and the like Report was at the North end, respecting the South end: Whereupon Captain John George was immediately seized, and about Nine of the Clock the Drums beat thorough the Town; and an Ensign was set up upon the Beacon. Then Mr. Bradstreet, Mr. Dantforth, Major Richards, Dr. Cooke, and Mr. Addington, etc. were brought to the Council-house by a Company of Soldiers under the Command of Captain Hill. The mean while the People in Arms did take up and put into Goal Justice Bullivant, Justice Foxcroft, Mr. Randolf, Sheriff Sherlock, Captain Ravenscroft, Captain White, Farewel, Broadbent, Crafford, Larkin, Smith, and many more, as also Mercey the then Goal-keeper, and put Scates the Bricklayer in his place. About Noon, in the Gallery at the Council-house, was read the Declaration here inclosed. Then a Message was sent to the Fort to Sir Edmund Andross, by Mr. Oliver and Mr. Eyres, signed by the Gentlemen then in the Council-Chamber, (which is here also inclosed); to inform him how unsafe he was like to be if he did not deliver up himself, and Fort and Government forthwith, which he was loath to do. By this time, being about two of the Clock (the Lecture being put by) the Town was generally in Arms, and so many of the Countrey came in, that there was twenty Companies in Boston, besides a great many that appeared at Charles Town that could not get over (some say fifteen hundred). There then came Information to the Soldiers, That a Boat was come from the Frigat that made towards the Fort, which made them haste thither, and come to the Sconce soon after the Boat got thither; and 'tis said that Governor Andross, and about half a score Gentlemen, were coming down out of the Fort; but the Boat being seized, wherein were small Arms, Hand-Granadoes, and a quantity of Match, the Governour and the rest went in again; whereupon Mr. John Nelson, who was at the head of the Soldiers, did demand the Fort and the Governor, who was loath to submit to them; but at length did come down, and was, with the Gentlemen that were with him, conveyed to the Council-house, where Mr. Bradstreet and the rest of the Gentlemen waited to receive him; to whom Mr. Stoughton first spake, telling him, He might thank himself for the present Disaster that had befallen him, etc. He was then confined for that Night to Mr. John Usher's House under strong Guards, and the next Day conveyed to the Fort, (where he yet remains, and with him Lieutenant Collonel Ledget) which is under the command of Mr. John Nelson; and at the Castle, which is under the Command of Mr. John Fairweather, is Mr. West, Mr. Graham, Mr. Palmer, and Captain Tryfroye. At that time Mr. Dudley was out upon the Circuit, and was holding a Court at Southold on Long-Island. And on the 21st Instant he arrived at Newport, where he heard the News. The next Day Letters came to him, advising him not to come home; he thereupon went over privately to Major Smith's at Naraganzett, and Advice is this Day come hither, that yesterday about a dozen young Men, most of their own Heads, went thither to demand him; and are gone with him down to Boston. We have also Advice, that on Fryday last towards Evening, Sir Edmond Andross did attempt to make an Escape in Woman's Apparel, and pass'd two Guards, and was stopped at the third, being discovered by his Shoes, not having changed them. We are here ready to blame you sometimes, that we have not to this Day received advice concerning the great Changes in England, and in particular how it is like to fair with us here; who do hope and believe that all these Things will work for our Good; and that you will not be wanting to promote the Good of a Country that stands in such need as New England does at this Day. The first Day of May, according to former Usage, is the Election Day at Road Island; and many do say they intend their Choice there then. I have not farther to trouble you with at present, but recommending you, and all our Affairs with you, to the

Direction and Blessing of our most Gracious God, I remain

Gentlemen,

> Your most Humble
> Servant at Command,
> Nathanael Byfield.

> Bristol, *April 29, 1689.*
> *Through the Goodness of God, there hath*
> *been no Blood shed. Nath. Clark is in*
> *Plymouth Gaol, and John Smith in Gaol*
> *here, all waiting for News from England.*

THE DECLARATION OF THE GENTLEMEN, MERCHANTS AND INHABITANTS OF BOSTON, AND THE COUNTRY ADJACENT. APRIL 18, 1689.

§ I. We have seen more than a decad of Years rolled away since the English World had the Discovery of an horrid Popish Plot; wherein the bloody Devotoes of Rome had in their Design and Prospect no less than the Extinction of the Protestant Religion: which mighty Work they called the utter subduing of a Pestilent Heresy; wherein (they said) there never were such Hopes of Success since the Death of Queen Mary, as now in our Days. And we were of all Men the most insensible, if we should apprehend a Countrey so remarkable for the true Profession and pure Exercise of the Protestant Religion as New-England is, wholly unconcerned in the Infamous Plot. To crush and break a Countrey so entirely and signally made up of Reformed Churches, and at length to involve it in the miseries of an utter Extirpation, must needs carry even a Supererogation of Merit with it among such as were intoxicated with a Bigotry inspired into them by the great Scarlet Whore.

§ II. To get us within the reach of the Desolation desired for us, it was no improper thing that we should first have our Charter vacated, and the Hedge which kept us from the wild Beasts of the Field, effectually broken down. The Accomplishment of this was hastned by the unwearied Sollicitations and slanderous Accusations of a Man, for

his Malice and Falshood well known unto us all. Our Charter was with a most injurious Pretence (and scarce that) of Law, condemned before it was possible for us to appear at Westminster in the legal Defence of it; and without a fair leave to answer for our selves, concerning the Crimes falsly laid to our Charge, we were put under a President and Council, without any liberty for an Assembly, which the other American Plantations have, by a Commission from his Majesty.

§ III. The Commission was as Illegal for the Form of it, as the Way of obtaining it was Malicious and Unreasonable: yet we made no Resistance thereunto as we could easily have done; but chose to give all Mankind a Demonstration of our being a People sufficiently dutiful and loyal to our King: and this with yet more Satisfaction, because we took Pains to make our selves believe as much as ever we could of the Whedle then offer'd unto us; That his Magesty's Desire was no other then the happy Encrease and Advance of these Provinces by their more immediate Dependance on the Crown of England. And we were convinced of it by the Courses immediately taken to damp and spoyl our Trade; whereof Decayes and Complaints presently filled all the Country; while in the mean time neither the Honour nor the Treasure of the King was at all advanced by this new Model of our Affairs, but a considerable Charge added unto the Crown.

§ IV. In little more than half a Year we saw this Commission superseded by another yet more absolute and Arbitrary, with which Sir Edmond Andross arrived as our Governour: who besides his Power, with the Advice and Consent of his Council, to make Laws and raise Taxes as he pleased, had also Authority by himself to Muster and Imploy all Persons residing in the Territory as occasion shall serve; and to transfer such Forces to any English Plantation in America, as occasion shall require. And several Companies of Souldiers were now brought from Europe, to support what was to be imposed upon us, not without repeated Menaces that some hundreds more were intended for us.

§ V. The Government was no sooner in these Hands, but Care was taken to load Preferments principally upon such Men as were Strangers to and Haters of the People: and every ones Observation hath noted, what Qualifications recommended a Man to publick Offices and Employments, only here and there a good Man was used, where others could not easily be had; the Governour himself, with Assertions now and then falling from him, made us jealous that it would be thought for his Majesties Interest, if this People were removed and another succeeded in their room: And his far-fetch'd Instruments that were growing rich among us, would gravely inform us, that it was not for his Majesties Interest that we should thrive. But of all our Oppressors we were chiefly squeez'd by a Crew of abject Persons fetched from New York, to be the Tools of the Adversary, standing at our right Hand; by these were extraordinary and intollerable Fees extorted from every one upon all Occasions, without any Rules but those of their own insatiable Avarice and Beggary; and even the probate of a Will must now cost as many Pounds perhaps as it did Shillings heretofore; nor could a small Volume contain the other Illegalities done by these Horse-leeches in the two or three Years that they have been sucking of us; and what Laws they made it was as impossible for us to know, as dangerous for us to break;* but we shall leave the Men of Ipswich or Plimouth (among others) to tell the Story of the Kindness which has been shown them upon this Account. Doubtless a Land so ruled as once New-England was, has not without many Fears and Sighs beheld the wicked walking on every Side, and the vilest Men exalted.

§ VI. It was now plainly affirmed, both by some in open Council, and by the same in private Converse, that the People in New-England were all Slaves, and the only difference between them and Slaves is their not being bought and sold; and it was a Maxim delivered in open Court unto us by one of the Council, that we must not think the Priviledges of English men would follow us to the End of the World: Accordingly we have been treated with multiplied Contradictions to Magna Charta, the Rights of which we laid claim unto. Persons who

did but peaceably object against the raising of Taxes without an Assembly, have been for it fined, some twenty, some thirty, and others fifty Pounds. Packt and pickt Juries have been very common things among us, when, under a pretended Form of Law, the Trouble of some honest and worthy Men has been aimed at: but when some of this Gang have been brought upon the Stage, for the most detestable Enormities that ever the Sun beheld, all Men have with Admiration seen what Methods have been taken that they might not be treated according to their Crimes. Without a Verdict, yea, without a Jury sometimes have People been fined most unrighteously; and some not of the meanest Quality have been kept in long and close Imprisonment without any the least Information appearing against them, or an Habeas Corpus allowed unto them. In short, when our Oppressors have been a little out of Mony, 'twas but pretending some. Offence to be enquired into, and the most innocent of Men were continually put into no small Expence to answer the Demands of the Officers, who must have Mony of them, or a Prison for them, tho none could accuse them of any Misdemeanour.

§ VII. To plunge the poor People every where into deeper Incapacities, there was one very comprehensive Abuse given to us; Multitudes of pious and sober Men through the Land scrupled the Mode of Swearing on the Book, desiring that they might Swear with an uplifted Hand, agreeable to the ancient Custom of the Colony; and though we think we can prove that the Common Law amongst us (as well as in some other places under the English Crown) not only indulges, but even commands and enjoins the Rite of lifting the Hand in Swearing; yet they that had this Doubt, were still put by from serving upon any Juries; and many of them were most unaccountably Fined and Imprisoned. Thus one Grievance is a Trojan Horse, in the Belly of which it is not easy to recount how many insufferable Vexations have been contained.

§ VIII. Because these Things could not make us miserable fast enough, there was a notable Discovery made of we know not what flaw in all our Titles to our Lands; and tho, besides our purchase of them from the Natives, and besides our actual peaceable unquestioned Possession of them for

---

*He would neither suffer them to be printed nor fairly published. (Note in margin of original.)

near threescore Years, and besides the Promise of K. Charles II. in his Proclamation sent over to us in the Year 1683, That no Man here shall receive any Prejudice in his Free-hold or Estate, We had the Grant of our Lands, under the Seal of the Council of Plimouth: which Grant was Renewed and Confirmed unto us by King Charles I. under the Great Seal of England; and the General Court which consisted of the Patentees and their Associates, had made particular Grants hereof to the several Towns (though 'twas now deny'd by the Governour, that there was any such Thing as a Town) among us; to all which Grants the General Court annexed for the further securing of them, A General Act, published under the Seal of the Colony, in the Year 1684. Yet we were every day told, That no Man was owner of a Foot of Land in all the Colony. Accordingly, Writs of Intrusion began every where to be served on People, that after all their Sweat and their Cost upon their formerly purchased Lands, thought themselves Freeholders of what they had. And the Governor caused the Lands pertaining to these and those particular Men, to be measured out for his Creatures to take possession of; and the Right Owners, for pulling up the Stakes, have passed through Molestations enough to tire all the Patience in the World. They are more than a few, that were by Terrors driven to take Patents for their Lands at excessive rates, to save them from the next that might petition for them: and we fear that the forcing of the People at the Eastward hereunto, gave too much Rise to the late unhappy Invasion made by the Indians on them. Blanck Patents were got ready for the rest of us, to be sold at a Price, that all the Mony and Moveables in the Territory could scarce have paid. And several Towns in the Country had their Commons begg'd by Persons (even by some of the Council themselves) who have been privately encouraged thereunto, by those that sought for Occasions to impoverish a Land already Peeled, Meeted out and Trodden down.

§ IX. All the Council were not ingaged in these ill Actions, but those of them which were true Lovers of their Country were seldom admitted to, and seldomer consulted at the Debates which produced these unrighteous Things: Care

was taken to keep them under Disadvantages; and the Governor, with five or six more, did what they would. We bore all these, and many more such Things, without making any attempt for any Relief; only Mr. Mather, purely out of respect unto the Good of his Afflicted Country, undertook a Voyage into England; which when these Men suspected him to be preparing for, they used all manner of Craft and Rage, not only to interrupt his Voyage, but to ruin his Person too. God having through many Difficulties given him to arrive at White-hall, the King, more than once or twice, promised him a certain Magna Charta for a speedy Redress of many Things which we were groaning under: and in the mean time said, That our Governor should be written unto, to forbear the Measures that he was upon. However, after this, we were injured in those very Things which were complained of; and besides what Wrong hath been done in our Civil Concerns, we suppose the Ministers and the Churches every where have seen our Sacred Concerns apace going after them: How they have been Discountenanced, has had a room in the Reflection of every Man, that is not a Stranger in our Israel.

§ X. And yet that our Calamity might not be terminated here, we are again Briar'd in the Perplexities of another Indian War; how, or why, is a mystery too deep for us to unfold. And tho' 'tis judged that our Indian Enemies are not above 100 in Number, yet an Army of One thousand English hath been raised for the Conquering of them; which Army of our poor Friends and Brethren now under Popish Commanders (for in the Army as well as in the Council, Papists are in Commission) has been under such a Conduct, that not one Indian hath been kill'd, but more English are supposed to have died through sickness and hardship, than we have Adversaries there alive; and the whole War hath been so managed, that we cannot but suspect in it a Branch of the Plot to bring us low; which we leave to be further enquir'd into in due time.

§ XI. We did nothing against these Proceedings, but only cry to our God; they have caused the cry of the Poor to come unto him, and he hears the cry of the Afflicted. We have been quiet hitherto, and so still we should have been, had not the Great God at this time laid us under a double engagement to do something for our Security: besides what we have in the strangely unanimous Inclination which our Countrymen by extreamest necessities are driven unto. For first, we are informed that the rest of the English America is alarmed with just and great Fears, that they may be attaqu'd by the French, who have lately ('tis said) already treated many of the English with worse then Turkish Cruelties; and while we are in equal Danger of being surprised by them, it is high time we should be better guarded, than we are like to be while the Government remains in the hands by which it hath been held of late. Moreover, we have understood, (though the Governour has taken all imaginable care to keep us all ignorant thereof) that the Almighty God hath been pleased to prosper the noble Undertaking of the Prince of Orange, to preserve the three Kingdoms from the horrible brinks of Popery and Slavery, and to bring to a condign Punishment those worst of Men, by whom English Liberties have been destroy'd; in compliance with which glorious Action we ought surely to follow the Patterns which the Nobility, Gentry and Commonalty in several parts of those Kingdoms have set before us, though they therein chiefly proposed to prevent what we already endure.

§ XII. We do therefore seize upon the Persons of those few ill Men which have been (next to our Sins) the grand Authors of our Miseries; resolving to secure them, for what Justice, Orders from his Highness with the English Parliament shall direct, lest, ere we are aware, we find (what we may fear, being on all sides in Danger) our selves to be by them given away to a Forreign Power, before such Orders can reach unto us; for which Orders we now humbly wait. In the mean time firmly believing, that we have endeavoured nothing but what meer Duty to God and our Country calls for at our Hands: We commit our Enterprise unto the Blessing of Him, who hears the cry of the Oppressed, and advise all our Neighbours, for whom we have thus ventured our selves, to joyn with us in Prayers and all just Actions, for the Defence of the Land.

At the Town-House in Boston, April 18, 1689.

Sir,

Our Selves and many others the Inhabitants of this Town, and the Places adjacent, being surprized with the Peoples sudden taking of Arms; in the first motion whereof we were wholly ignorant, being driven by the present Accident, are necessitated to acquaint your Excellency, that for the quieting and securing of the People inhabiting in this Country from the imminent Dangers they many ways lie open and exposed to, and tendring your own Safety, We judge it necessary you forthwith surrender and deliver up the Government and Fortification, to be preserved and disposed according to Order and Direction from the Crown of England, which suddenly is expected may arrive; promising all security from violence to your Self or any of your Gentlemen or Souldiers in Person and Estate: Otherwise we are assured they will endeavour the taking of the Fortification by Storm, if any Opposition be made.

To Sir Edmond Andross Kt.

Waite Winthrop.	Elisha Cook.
Simon Bradstreet.	Isaac Addington.
William Stoughton.	John Nelson.
Samuel Shrimpton.	Adam Winthrop.
Bartholomew Gidney.	Peter Sergeant.
William Brown.	John Foster.
Thomas Danforth.	David Waterhouse.
John Richards.	

Finis.

Questions

1. What kind of "revolution" does Byfield describe? Spontaneous or planned? Chaotic or directed? The work of a few or a multitude? Violent or peaceable? Were the signatories really "surprized with the Peoples sudden taking of Arms"?

2. Explain the significance of the rumor about Andros's fashion of escape.

3. What were the rebels' grievances? Which do you think were most important to them?
4. How did the Boston rebels justify their conduct?
5. What assumptions concerning New England's place in the world appear in the Declaration? How do these compare with the views John Winthrop and Cotton Mather expressed in the documents from earlier chapters?
6. How does the Declaration compare with "Bacon's Manifesto"?

13.2   Rebellion in New York*

News of the Glorious Revolution also triggered unrest in the much more ethnically diverse colony of New York. The tumult lasted for two years, and the tensions causing and caused by it continued for decades more. The anonymous 1698 letter that follows presents one interpretation of events. The probable author was David Jamison, who had served as secretary of the colony and as a clerk for the Council of New York Governor Benjamin Fletcher (who served from 1692 to 1697).

A LETTER FROM A GENTLEMAN OF THE CITY OF NEW YORK, 1698

A Letter From A Gentleman of the City of New-York To Another, Concerning the Troubles which happen'd in That Province in the Time of the late Happy Revolution.

Printed and Sold by William Bradford at the Sign of the Bible in New-York, 1698.

Sir;

I cannot but admire to hear that some Gentlemen still have a good Opinion of the late Disorders committed by Capt. Jacob Leysler, and his Accomplices, in New-York, as if they had been for His Majesties Service, and the Security of that Province; and that such Monstrous Falshoods do find Credit, That the Persons before in Commission, and did labour to oppose and prevent those Disorders, were Jacobites, or Persons ill affected to the Happy Revolution in England. But it has been often the Calamity of all Ages to palliate Vice with false Glosses, and to criminate the best Actions of the most Virtuous and most Pious Men. So that Truth and Innocency, without some Defence, has not proved at all times a sufficient Bullwork against malitious Falshoods and Calumnies. Wherefore I shall endeavour to give you a true and brief Account of that matter, as I my self have been a Personal Witness to most of them.

It was about the beginning of April, 1689, when the first Reports arrived at New-York, that the Prince of Orange, now his present Majesty, was arrived in England with considerable Forces, and that the late King James was fled into France, and that it was expected War would be soon proclaimed between England and France.

The Leiut. Governour, Francis Nicholson, and the Council, being Protestants, resolved thereupon to suspend all Roman Catholicks from Command and Places of Trust in the Government, and accordingly suspended Major Baxter from being a Member of Council and Captain of a Company at Albany, and Bartholomew Russel from being Ensign in the Fort at New-York, they both being Papists, who forth-with left their Command, and departed the Province.

And because but three Members of the Council were residing in New-York, *viz.* Mr. Frederick Phillips, Coll. Stephanus Cortlandt, and Coll. Nicholas Bayard, all of Dutch Birth, all Members, and the two last, for the space of near thirty Years past, Elders and Deacons of the Dutch Protestant Church in New-York, and most affectionate to the Royal House of Orange, It was

---

*"A Letter from a Gentleman of the City of New York," in *Narratives of the Insurrections*, 360–371.

Resolved by the said Lieut. Governor and Council, to call and conveen to their Assistance all the Justices of the Peace, and other civil Magistrates, and the Commission Officers in the Province, for to consult and advise with them what might be proper for the Preservation of the Peace, and the Safety of said Province in that Conjuncture, till Orders should arrive from England.

Whereupon the said Justices, Magistrates and Officers were accordingly convened, and stiled by the Name of The General Convention for the Province of New-York; and all matters of Government were carried on and managed by the major Vote of that Convention.

And in the first place it was by them agreed and ordered, Forth-with to fortifie the City of New-York.

And that for the better Security of the Fort (since the Garrison was weak, and to prevent all manner of Doubts and Jealousies) a competent Number of the City Militia should keep Guard in said Fort, and Nicholas Bayard, Coll. of said Militia, recommended to give suitable Orders accordingly.

And that the Revenue should be continued and received by some Gentlemen appointed by that Convention, for Repairing the Fort, and Fortifying of the City; but against this Order Capt. Leysler (who as a Captain was a Member of that Convention) did enter his dissent, with some few others.

It was also recommended to said Coll. Bayard to hasten to fortifie the City with all possible speed, who upon the Credit of the Revenue did advance what Money was needful for Materials, And by the Assistance of the Militia Officers, and daily Labour of the Inhabitants, had the same finish't before the end of May, excepting Capt. Leysler's Quota.

About the middle of May the Ship *Beaver*, John Corbit Master, being ready to sail for England, the Lieut. Governour and Council sent in her by Mr. John Riggs, and in several other Ships that soon followed, Letters to the Earl, now Duke, of Shrewsbury, then Principal Secretary of State, and to the Lords of the Committee for Trade and Plantations, wherein they signified their rejoycing at

the News of his Royal Highness the Prince of Orange, now his present Majesties, arrival in England, in order to Redress the Grievances of the Nation, and giving a particular Account of the state of Affairs of this Province, and that they would endeavour to preserve its Peace and Security till Orders should arrive from England, which they humbly prayed might be hastened with all possible speed. Which said Letters were most graciously received, and answered by his Majesties Letter, bearing date the 30th of July, 1689.

But against Expectation it soon happened, that on the last day of said Moneth of May, Capt. Leysler having a Vessel with some Wines in the Road, for which he refused to pay the Duty, did in a Seditious manner stir up the meanest sort of the Inhabitants (affirming, That King James being fled the Kingdom, all manner of Government was fallen in this Province) to rise in Arms, and forcibly possess themselves of the Fort and Stores, which accordingly was effected whilest the Lieut. Governour and Council, with the Convention, were met at the City Hall to consult what might be proper for the common Good and Safety; where a party of Armed Men came from the Fort, and forced the Lieut. Governour to deliver them the Keys; and seized also in his Chamber a Chest with Seven Hundred Seventy Three Pounds, Twelve Shillings, in Money of the Government. And though Coll. Bayard, with some others appointed by the Convention, used all endeavours to prevent those Disorders, all proved vain; for most of those that appeared in Arms were Drunk, and cryed out, They disown'd all manner of Government. Whereupon, by Capt. Leysler's perswasion, they proclaimed him to be their Commander, there being then no other Commission Officer amongst them.

Capt. Leysler being in this manner possest of the Fort, took some Persons to his Assistance, which he call'd, The Committee of Safety. And the Lieut. Governour, Francis Nicollson, being in this manner forced out of his Command, for the safety of his Person, which was daily threatned, withdrew out of the Province.

About a week after, Reports came from Boston, That their Royal Highnesses, the Prince and Princes of Orange were proclaimed King and Queen of England. Whereupon the Council and Convention were very desirous to get that Proclamation, and not only wrote for it, but some of them hearing that two Gentlemen were coming from Connecticut with a Copy of said Proclamation, went out two days to meet them, in expectation of having the Happiness to proclaim it; but Major Gold and Mr. Fitz, missing them, having put the Proclamation into Capt. Leysler's hands, he, without taking any Notice of the Council or Convention, did proclaim the same, though very disorderly, after which he went with his Accomplices to the Fort, and the Gentlemen of the Council and Magistrates, and most of the principal Inhabitants and Merchants, went to Coll. Bayards House and drank the Health and Prosperity of King William and Queen Mary with great Expressions of Joy.

Two days after, a printed Proclamation was procured by some of the Council, dated the 14th of February, 1688, whereby their Majesties confirmed all Sheriffs, Justices of the Peace, Collectors and Receivers of the Revenues, etc., being Protestants; which was forth-with published at the City Hall by the Mayor and Alder-men, accompanyed with the Council, and most of the chief Citizens and Merchants. And pursuant thereunto the Collector, Mat. Plowman, being a Papist, was forth-with suspended by the Convention; and Coll. Bayard, Alder-man, Paul Richards, Capt. Thomas Winham, and Lieut. John Haynes, Merchants, were by them commissionated and appointed to collect the Revenue until Orders should arrive from England. Whereupon those Gentlemen were sworn by Coll. Cortland, then Major of the City, they being the first in this Province that took the Oathes to their Majesties appointed by Act of Parliament, instead of the Oathes of Allegiance and Supreamacy.

But as soon as those Gentlemen entered upon the Office, Capt. Leysler with a party of his Men in Arms, and Drink, fell upon them at the Custom-House, and with Naked Swords beat them thence, endeavouring to Massacree some of them, which were Rescued by Providence. Whereupon said Leysler beat an Alarm, crying about the City, "Treason, Treason," and made a strict search to seize Coll. Bayard, who made his escape, and departed for Albany, where he staid all Summer, in hopes that Orders might arrive from England to settle those Disorders.

The said Capt. Leysler, finding almost every man of Sence, Reputation, or Estate in the place to oppose and discourage his Irregularities, caused frequent false Alarms to be made, and sent several parties of his armed Men out of the Fort, drag'd into nasty Goals within said Fort several of the principal Magistrates, Officers and Gentlemen, and others, that would not own his Power to be lawful, which he kept in close Prison during Will and Pleasure, without any Process, or allowing them to Bail. And he further publish't several times, by beat of Drums, That all those who would not come into the Fort and sign their hands, and so thereby to own his Power to be lawful, should be deemed and esteemed as Enemies to his Majesty and the Country, and be by him treated accordingly. By which means many of the Inhabitants, tho' they abhor'd his Actions, only to escape a nasty Goal and to secure their Estates were by fear and compulsion drove to comply, submit and sign to whatever he commanded.

And though Capt. Leysler had at first so violently opposed the collecting of the Revenue, alledging it unlawful, as soon as his Wines were landed, and that he got into some Power, he forth-with set up for himself the collecting of said Revenue by Peter d' Lanoy, allowing him a great Sallary, and all the Perquisits of that Office.

Upon the 10th of December following returned the said Mr. John Riggs from England, with Letters from his Majesty and the Lords, in answer to the Letters sent by the Lieut. Governour and Council above recited, Directed, "To Our Trusty and Well-beloved Francis Nicholson, Esq; Our Lieutenant Governour and Commander in chief of Our Province of New-York in America, and in his absence To such as for the time being, take care for the Preservation of the Peace, and administring the Laws in Our said Province." Whereby his Majesty approved of the Proceedings and Care that had been taken by said Lieut. Governour and Council for the Peace and

Safety of the Province, with further Power and Directions to continue therein till further Orders. Which said Letters the said Mr. Riggs designed to deliver on the following Morning to the Gentlemen of the Council, to whom they properly did belong, being an answer to their said Letter; but was obstructed therein by said Leysler, who sent a party of his Men in Arms, and brought said Riggs to the Fort, where he forced said Letters from him, though some Gentlemen of the Council, that went the same time to the Fort, protested against it, but he drove them out of the Fort, calling them Rogues, Papists, and other opprobious Names.

Soon after the Receipt of said Letters, said Capt. Leysler stiled himself Lieutenant Governour, appointed a Council, and presumed further to call a select Number of his own Party, who called themselves The General Assembly of the Province, and by their advice and assistance raised several Taxes and great Sums of Money from their Majesties good Subjects within this Province. Which Taxes, together with that 773*l*. 12*s*. in Money, which he had seized from the Government, and the whole Revenue, he applyed to his own use, and to maintain said Disorders, allowing his private men 18*d. per* Day, and to others proportionably.

On the 20th of January following Coll. Bayard and Mr. Nicolls had the ill fortune to fall into his hands, and were in a barbarous manner, by a party in Arms, drag'd into the Fort, and there put into a Nasty place, without any manner of Process, or being allowed to bayl, though the same was offered for said Coll. Bayard, by some of the ablest and richest Inhabitants, to the Sum of Twenty Thousand Pounds, either for his appearance to answer, or depart the Province, or to go for England; but without any Cause given, or Reasons assigned, laid said Coll. Bayard in Irons, and kept him and Mr. Nicolls close Prisoners for the space of fourteen Moneths, where they, with several others, that had been long detained Prisoners, were set at Liberty by Governour Slaughter.

And whilest he kept those Gentlemen in Prison, he quartered his armed Men in their Houses, where they committed all manner of Outrages; And to give one Instance of many others, A Party of twelve Men were quartered at the House of Coll. Bayard, with directions to pillage and plunder at discretion, which was bought off with Money and plentiful Entertainment. But the same day, when that party had received their Money, another party came in with Naked Swords, opened several Chambers and Chests in said House, and did Rob and carry away what Money and other Goods they found.

At the same time Coll. Bayard and Mr. Nicolls were taken, strict search was made for Coll. Cortlandt, but he, with several other Gentlemen, having made their escape, were forced to leave their Families and Concerns, and remain in Exile, till relieved by the arrival of Governour Slaughter.

It is hardly to be exprest what Cruelties Capt. Leysler and his Accomplices imposed upon the said Prisoners, and all others that would not own his Power to be lawful. Neither could the Protestant Ministers in the Province escape their Malice and Cruelty; for Mr. Selyns, Minister of New-York, was most grosly abused by Leysler himself in the Church at the time of Divine Service, and threatned to be silenced, etc. Mr. Dellius, Minister at Albany, to escape a nasty Goal, was forced to leave his Flock, and fly for shelter into New-England. Mr. Varick, Minister of the Dutch Towns on Nassaw-Island, was by armed men drag'd out of his House to the Fort, then imprisoned without bayl, for speaking (as was pretended) Treasonable words against Capt. Leysler and the Fort; then prosecuted, and decreed by Peter d' Lanoy, pretended Judge, without any Commission or Authority, To be deprived from his Ministerial Function, amerced in a Fine of 80*l*. and to remain in close Prison till that Fine should be paid; yea, he was so tormented, that in all likelyhood it occasioned and hastened the suddain Death of that most Reverend and Religious Man. The French Ministers, Mr. Perret and Mr. Dellie, had some better Quarters, but were often threatned to be prosecuted in like manner, because they would not approve of his Power and disorderly proceedings.

None in the Province, but those of his Faction, had any safety in their Estates; for said Capt. Leysler, at will and pleasure, sent to those who disapproved of his Actions, to furnish him with Money, Provisions, and what else he wanted, and upon denyal sent armed men out of the Fort, and forcibly broke open several Houses, Shops, Cellars, Vessels, and other places where they expected to be supplied, and without any the least payment or satisfaction, carried their Plunder to the Fort; all which was extreamly approved of by those poor Fellows which he had about him, and was forced to feed and maintain; and so he stiled those his Robberies with the gilded Name and Pretence, That it was for their Majesties King William and Queen Mary's special Service, though it was after found out, that whole Cargo's of those stolen goods were sold to his Friends in the City, and Shipt off for the West Indies and else where.

In this manner he the said Leysler, with his Accomplices, did force, pillage, rob and steal from their Majesties good Subjects within this Province, almost to their utter Ruin, vast Sums of Money, and other Effects, the estimation of the Damages done only within this City of New-York amounting, as by Account may appear, to the Sum of Thirteen Thousand Nine Hundred and Fifty Nine Pounds, besides the Rapines, Spoils and Violences done at Coll. Willets on Nassaw-Island, and to many others in several parts of the Province.

And thus you may see how he used and exercised an Exorbitant, Arbitrary and Unlawful Power over the Persons and Estates of his Majesties good Subjects here, against the known and Fundamental Laws of the Land, and in subvertion of the same, to the great Oppression of his Majesties Subjects, and to the apparent decay of Trade and Commerce.

In this Calamity, Misery and Confusion was this Province, by those Disorders, enthrawled near the space of two years, until the arrival of his Majesties Forces, under the command of Major Ingoldsby, who, with several Gentlemen of the Council, arrived about the last day of January, 1690/1, which said Gentlemen of the Council, for the Preservation of the Peace, sent and offered to said Leysler, That he might stay and continue his Command in the Fort, only desiring for themselves and the Kings Forces quietly to quarter and refresh themselves in the City, till Governour Slaughter should arrive; but the said Leysler, instead of complying, asked Mr. Brooke, one of his Majesties Council, Who were appointed of the Council in this Province? and Mr. Brooke having named Mr. Phillips, Coll. Cortland and Coll. Bayard, he fell into a Passion and cry'd, "What! those Papist Dogs, Rogues! Sacrament! if the King should send Three Thousand such I would cut them all off"; And without any cause given, he proclaimed open War against them. Whereupon they, for Self-preservation, protection of the Kings Forces and Stores, and the safety of the City, were necessitated to perswade to their assistance several of their Majesties good Subjects then in Opposition against the said Leysler, with no other intent, as they signified to him by several Letters and Messages, but only for self-security and Defence; yet notwithstanding, the said Leysler proceeded to make War against them and the Kings Forces, and fired a vast Number of great and small Shot in the City, whereby several of his Majesties Subjects were killed and wounded as they passed in the streets upon their lawful Occasions, tho' no Opposition was made on the other side.

At this height of Extremity was it when Governour Slaughter arrived on the 19th of March, 1691, who having publish't his Commission from the City Hall, with great signs of Joy, by firing all the Artillary within and round the City, sent thrice to demand the surrender of the Fort from Capt. Leysler and his Accomplices, which was thrice denyed, but upon great Threatnings, the following Day surrendered to Governor Slaughter, who forth-with caused the said Capt. Leysler, with some of the chief Malefactors, to be bound over to answer their Crimes at the next Supream Court of Judicature, where the said Leysler and his pretended Secretary Millborn did appear, but refused to plead to the Indictment of the grand Jury, or to own the Jurisdiction of that Court; and so after several hearings, as Mutes, were found guilty of High Treason and Murder, and executed accordingly.

Several of the other Malefactors that pleaded were also found Guilty, and particularly one Abraham Governeer for Murdering of an Old Man peaceably passing along the Street, but were Reprieved by Governour Sloughter, and upon Coll. Fletcher's arrival by him set at liberty, upon their Submission and promise of good Behaviour.

Sir, All what is here set down is True, and can be proved and justified by the Men of greatest Probity and best Figure amongst us. If I were to give a particular Narrative of all the Cruelties and Robberies perpetrated upon their Majesties most affectionate Subjects in this Province, they would fill a Volumn: There was no need of any Revolution here; there were not ten Jacobites in the whole; they were all well known, and the strictest Protestants, and men of best Figure, Reputation and Estates were at the Helm, it may plainly be perceived by the several steps and measures were followed at that time, and by their Letters to the then Earl, now Duke of Shrewsbury, and to the Lords, and the Kings Answer thereunto. The Copy of which Answer, and some other Papers worthy of your perusal, are inclosed.

So soon as Governour Sloughter arrived, an Assembly was called, which upon the 18th of April, 1691, did present an Address to his Excellency, signed by their Speaker, together with the Resolves of that House, which when you are pleased to read, gives the Conclusive Opinion and Judgment of the General Assembly of this Province, of all those disorderly Proceedings, for which those two have suffered Death, and their Sentence was since approved by Her Majesty, of ever blessed Memory, in Council.

Many worthy Protestants in England, and other parts of the world, being sincerely devoted to his Majesties Interest, have yet notwithstanding (unacquainted with our Circumstances, and not duely apprized of the truth) been more easily induced to give credit to the false Glosses and Calumnies of byassed and disaffected Persons from this Province. But in my Observation, most Gentlemen that have come hither so prepossessed, after some time spent here have been thorowly convinced of their Mistake, and that those men who suffered Death, did not from pure zeal for their Majesties Interest, and the Protestant Religion, but being of desperate Fortune, thrust themselves into Power, of purpose to make up their wants by the Ruin and Plunder of his Majesties Loyal Subjects, and were so far engaged in their repeated Crimes, that they were driven to that height of Desperation, had not the Providence of Almighty God prevented it, the whole Province had been Ruined and Destroyed.

I have put this in writing at your Request, to assist your Memory, and leave it to his Excellency Coll. Fletcher, and your own Observations, to enlarge upon the Characters of those Persons who have been the greatest Sufferers in the time of those Disorders, and of their Patience and Moderation since your arrival; also, of the Disaffected, and the Causes which you have frequently observed to hold this Province in Disquiet and Trouble. Notwithstanding all which, and the frequent Attachs of the French and Indians upon our Fronteers, this Province has not lost one foot of ground during the War, but have had considerable Advantages upon the Enemy, which, under God, is due to the prudent and steady Conduct and great Care and Diligence of Coll. Fletcher, our present Governour.

You have been an Eye Witness, and have had Time and Experience enough to enable you to inform others in England, which if you will please to do, I doubt not but it will gain Credit, and be an extraordinary piece of Service to this Province. I am,

Sir,

Your Most Humble Servant.
New-York, December 31, 1697.

Terms

Jacobite—a supporter of James II

Questions

1. How does the "Gentleman" characterize the parties in conflict? In his view, why did Leisler incite rebellion? What sort of men followed Leisler? Whose side is the Gentleman on? What did he most fear?

2. Using the Gentleman's letter for evidence, discuss the roles of religion, ethnicity, and social class in Leisler's rebellion.

3. How do events in New York compare with the 1689 rebellion in Boston? To Bacon's Rebellion?

13.3 Captive Hannah Dustan Strikes Back*

We are already familiar with the story of the captive Mary Rowlandson and with New England minister and author Cotton Mather. In this selection from Mather's ecclesiastical history of New England, Magnalia Christi Americana *(1702), he presents the tale of captive Hannah Dustan, whose method of escape was altogether different from Rowlandson's.*

ARTICLE XXV.

A Notable Exploit; *Dux Fæmina Facti.*

On March 15, 1697, the salvages made a descent upon the skirts of Haverhill, murdering and captivating about thirty-nine persons, and burning about half a dozen houses. In this broil, one Hannah Dustan, having lain in about a week, attended with her nurse, Mary Neff, a body of terrible Indians drew near unto the house where she lay, with designs to carry on their bloody devastations. Her husband hastened from his employments abroad unto the relief of his distressed family; and first bidding *seven* of his *eight* children (which were from *two* to *seventeen* years of age) to get away as fast as they could unto some garrison in the town, he went in to inform his wife of the horrible distress come upon them. Ere she could get up, the fierce Indians were got so near, that, utterly desparing to do her any service, he ran out after his children; resolving that on the horse which he had

with him, he would ride away with *that* which he should in this extremity find his affections to pitch most upon, and leave the rest unto the care of the Divine Providence. He overtook his children, about forty rod from his door; but then such was the *agony* of his parental affections, that he found it impossible for him to distinguish any one of them from the rest; wherefore he took up a courageous resolution to live and die with them all. A party of Indians came up with him; and now, though they fired at him, and he fired at them, yet he manfully kept at the reer of his *little army* of unarmed children, while they marched off with the pace of a child of five years old; until, by the singular providence of God, he arrived safe with them all unto a place of safety about a mile or two from his house. But his house must in the mean time have more dismal *tragedies* acted at it. The nurse, trying to escape with the new-born infant, fell into the hands of the formidable salvages; and those furious tawnies coming into the house, bid poor Dustan to rise immediately. Full of astonishment, she did so; and sitting down in the chimney with an heart full of most fearful *expectation*, she saw the raging dragons rifle all that they could carry away, and set the house on fire. About nineteen or twenty Indians now led these away, with about half a score other English captives; but ere they had gone many steps, they dash'd out the brains of the infant against a tree; and several of the other captives, as they began to tire in the sad journey, were soon sent unto their long home; the salvages would presently bury their hatchets in their brains, and leave their carcases on the ground

*Cotton Mather, "A Notable Exploit," in *Magnalia Christi Americana* (Hartford, CT: Silas Andrus & Son, 1853), 634–636.

for birds and beasts to feed upon. However, Dustan (with her nurse) notwithstanding her present condition, travelled that night about a dozen miles, and then kept up with their new masters in a long travel of an hundred and fifty miles, more or less, within a few days ensuing, without any sensible damage in their health, from the hardships of their *travel*, their *lodging*, their *diet*, and their many other difficulties.

These two poor women were now in the hands of those whose "tender mercies are cruelties;" but the good God, who hath all "hearts in his own hands," heard the sighs of these prisoners, and gave them to find unexpected favour from the master who hath laid claim unto them. That Indian family consisted of twelve persons; two stout men, three women, and seven children; and for the shame of many an English family, that has the character of *prayerless* upon it, I must now publish what these poor women assure me. 'Tis this: in obedience to the instructions which the French have given them, they would have *prayers* in their family no less than thrice every day; in the morning, at noon, and in the evening; nor would they ordinarily let their children *eat* or *sleep*, without first saying their prayers. Indeed, these *idolaters* were, like the rest of their whiter brethren, *persecutors*, and would not endure that these poor women should retire to their English prayers, if they could hinder them. Nevertheless, the poor women had nothing but fervent prayers to make their lives comfortable or tolerable; and by being daily sent out upon business, they had opportunities, together and asunder, to do like another Hannah, in "pouring out their souls before the Lord." Nor did their praying friends among our selves forbear to "pour out" supplications for them. Now, they could not observe it without some wonder, that their Indian master sometimes when he saw them dejected, would say unto them, "What need you trouble your self? If your God will have you delivered, you shall be so!" And it seems our God would have it so to be. This Indian family was now travelling with these

two captive women, (and an English youth taken from Worcester, a year and a half before,) unto a rendezvouz of salvages, which they call a *town*, some where beyond Penacook; and they still told these poor women that when they came to this town, they must be stript, and scourg'd, and run the *gantlet* through the whole army of Indians. They said this was the *fashion* when the captives first came to a town; and they derided some of the faint-hearted English, which, they said, fainted and swoon'd away under the *torments* of this discipline. But on April 30, while they were yet, it may be, about an hundred and fifty miles from the Indian town, a little before break of day, when the whole crew was in a *dead sleep*, (reader, see if it prove not so!) one of these women took up a resolution to imitate the action of Jael upon Sisera; and being where she had not her own *life* secured by any *law* unto her, she thought she was not forbidden by any *law* to take away the *life* of the *murderers* by whom her child had been butchered. She heartened the nurse and the youth to assist her in this enterprize; and all furnishing themselves with hatchets for the purpose, they struck such home blows upon the heads of their sleeping oppressors, that ere they could any of them struggle into any effectual resistance, "at the feet of these poor prisoners, they bow'd, they fell, they lay down; at their feet they bow'd, they fell; where they bow'd, there they fell down dead." Only one squaw escaped, sorely wounded, from them in the dark; and one boy, whom they reserved asleep, intending to bring him away with them, suddenly waked, and scuttled away from this desolation. But cutting off the scalps of the ten wretches, they came off, and received *fifty pounds* from the General Assembly of the province, as a recompence of their action; besides which, they received many "presents of congratulation" from their more private friends: but none gave 'em a greater taste of bounty than Colonel Nicholson, the Governour of Maryland, who, hearing of their action, sent 'em a very generous token of his favour.

Questions

1. Whom did Dustan kill? How old were they? What sex? What were their religious practices? In what kind of community did they live?

2. What is Mather's attitude toward Dustan's actions? Does he consider them justified? If so, on what grounds?

3. How can we ascertain the veracity of the events described? If one of Dustan's victims were to tell the story, how might it differ?

4. Were Dustan's actions unique? Or were they representative of some more general tendency?

5. Were New England colonists rendered brutal by American circumstances? Were American circumstances rendered brutal by the New England colonies?

13.4 The Trial of William Kidd*

In the late seventeenth century, the English Empire began a concerted effort to regulate Atlantic commerce. Although the English crown had relied extensively on privateers, or licensed pirates, to harass their Spanish and French competitors, they feared that pirates had grown too numerous and powerful, threatening the security of English commerce and undermining imperial authority. William Kidd, previously supported as an official privateer, found himself a target of England's antipiracy campaign in 1701, when he was brought to trial for seizing a ship off the southwest coast of India. The following two documents present the prosecution's case against Kidd and his protestation of innocence to the House of Commons.

L. C. B. *Ward.* Gentlemen of the Jury, the Prisoners at the Bar, *W. Kidd, N. Churchill, J. Howe, R. Lamley, Will. Jenkins, Gabriel Loff, Hugh Parrot, Rich. Barlicorn, Abel Owens,* and *Darby Mullins,* in Number Ten; stand all here Indicated for the Crime of Piracy, charged to be committed by them. And the Instance of the Crime, is for Feloniously and Piratcally Seizing and Taking the Ship called the *Quedagh* Merchant, with the Apparel and Tackling thereof, to the value of 400£ and divers Goods mentioned in the Indict-to the value of 4500£ the Goods of the several Persons unknown, from the Mariners of the said Ship, and this at High Sea, within the Jurisdiction of the Court of Admiralty, about ten Leagues from *Cutsheen* in the *East-Indies* the 30th of *January,* 1697, and in the 9th Year of his Majesty's Reign. Now whether all, or any, and which if these Prisoners are guilty of this Crime of Piracy laid in this Indictment, or not guilty, it is your Part to determine according to the Evidence that has been given on both Sides. The Crime charged on them is Piracy, that is, Seizing and Taking this Ship and Goods in it Piratically and Feloniously, the Time and Place is laid also in the Indictment. To make good this Accusation, the King's Council have produced their Evidence; and two Witnesses have been examined in this Cafe, each of them were in the Ship which took the *Quedagh Merchant,* and very well acquainted with all the Proceedings, that is, *Robert Bradinham,* and *Joseph Palmer.* The first has given you an Historical Account of the whole Proceedings of Captain *Kidd,* from his first going out of *England* in the *Adventure Galley,* to the Time of this Fact charged on them. They tell you, that about *May* 1696, the King instructed this Captain *Kidd* with two Commissions, and they were both read to you. By one of them, under the Admiralty Seal, he was Authorized to set

---

*Don C. Seitz, ed., *The Tryal of Capt. William Kidd* (New York: Rufus Rockwell Wilson, 1936), 150–156, 158; "William Kidd to the Speaker of the House of Commons," in *Privateering and Piracy in the Colonial Period: Illustrative Documents,* ed., John Franklin Jameson (New York: Macmillan Company, 1923), 250–252

out as a Privateer the *Adventure Galley*, and therewith to Take and Seize the Ships and Goods belonging to the *French* King, or his Subjects, and such other as were liable to Confiscation. And by the other Commission under the Broad Seal of *England*, Authority was given for the taking of some Pirates by Name, and all other Pirates in the several Places therein mentioned. But in no sort to offend or molest any of the King's Friends or Allies, their Ships or Subjects by Colour thereof. And by both Commissions command was given to bring all such Ships and Goods, as should be taken to legal Trials and Condemnations. They tell us, that this Ship set out from *Plymouth* about *May*, 1696, and that in their Passage, they did take a *French* Ship, and they did condemn that Ship. Now Gentlemen, you must bear this in your Minds, that to make it Piracy, it must be the taking Piratically and Feloniously upon the High Seas, within the Jurisdiction of the Admiralty of *England*, the Goods of a Friend, that is such as are in Amity with the King. Now you fee what Way they went to work, and what Measures they took. Captain *Kidd* goes out, and goes to *New-York*; and when he was there, he has a Project in his Head of setting up Articles between himself and the People that were willing to be concerned with him: For now whether it seems more probable from what followed that Captain *Kidd* designed to manage himself according to the Measures given him, and the Powers of his Commissions, or another Way, you must consider; for it is told you that between 150, and 160 Men came in under those Articles, whereof the other Prisoners were part and concerned in them. And as to those Articles, the Import of them was, that whatever should be taken by these People in their Expeditions, should be divided into 160 Parts, whereof Captain *Kidd* was to have 40 Shares for his Part, and the rest were to have according to the Merit of each Party, some whole Shares, and some half Shares.

Now after these Articles, you perceive what Progress they made, and what Course they took. They went from one place to another, and used a pretty deal of Severity where ever they came. A design they had to go into the Red-Sea, and they had expectations of the *Moco* Fleet that lay at *Moco*, and they sent their Spies three times to get Intelligence. The two times they could make no Discovery; but the third time they made an effectual Discovery that the Fleet was ready to Sail; and in the mean time Capt. *Kidd* lay there in expectation of this Fleet; and as the first Witness tells you, Capt. *Kidd* said he intended to make a Voyage out of this Fleet. Well, he had a Discovery of this Fleet, and they came accordingly, and they tell you, that he and his Men in the Ship did attack one of the Ships: But these Ships being guarded by two Men of War, he could make nothing of them, however he shewed what his intention and design was. Could he have proved that what he did was in pursuance of his Commissions, it had been something: But what had he to do to make an attack on these Ships, the Owners and Freighters whereof, were in Amity with the King; this does not appear to be an action suitable to his Commission. After he had done this, he came to Land, and there, and afterwards at Sea, pursued strange Methods, as you have heard. The seeming justification he depends on, is his Commissions; now it must be observed how he acted with relation to them, and what irregularities he went by. He came to a place in the Indies, and sent his Cooper ashore, and that Cooper was killed by Natives; and he uses Barbarity, and ties an *Indian* to a Tree, and shoots him to death. Now he went from place to place and committed Hostilities upon several Ships, dealing very severely with the People.

But this being something foreign to the Indictment, and not the Facts for which the Prisoners at Bar are Indicted, we are confined to the *Quedagh Merchant*; but what he did before shews his Mind and Intentions not to act by his Commissions, which warrant no such things. Gentlemen, you have an account that he met with this Ship the *Quedagh Merchant* at Sea, and took her; that this Ship belonged to People in Amity with the King of *England*; that he seized this Ship, and divers Goods were taken out of her, and sold, and the Money divided pursuant to the heads contained in those Articles set up at *New York*. The Witnesses that speak to that, come home to every one of the Prisoners: They tell you that this Dividend was made, that Capt. *Kidd* had 40 Shares of the Money, and the rest of the Prisoners had their proportions according to the Articles, some whole Shares, and some a half Share of that Money. After they had seized on the Ship, you hear of a certain sort of project, that a *French* Man should come and pretend himself the Master, and produce, or pretend to produce a *French* Pass, under a colour that these Peoples Ship and Goods, who were Moors, should be *French* Men's Ship and Goods, or Sailed under a *French* Pass, and so justify what they did under the colour of his Commission from the King. Now no Man knows the Mind and Intention of another, but as it may be discovered by his Actions. If he would have this to be understood to be his Intention, or that it was a reality, that he took this as a *French* Ship, or under a *French* Pass, then he ought to have had the Ship and Goods inventoried, and Condemned, according to Law, that he might have had what proportion belonged to him, and that the King might have had what belonged to him, as his Commissions directed. But here was nothing of that done, but the Money and Goods that were taken were shared; and you have an account likewise how some of the Goods were sold and the Money disposed of, and how the remaining Goods were disposed of; and one Witness speaks positively of the distribution of the Goods that remained unsold, that they were divided according to the same proportions as the Articles mentioned, and every one of the Prisoners had his Share. There belonged 40 Shares to Capt. *Kidd*, and Shares and half Shares to the rest.

Now this is the great Case that is before you on which the Indictment turns. The Ships and Goods, as you have heard, are said by the Witnesses, to be the Goods of the Armenians, and other People that were in Amity with the King; and Capt. *Kidd* would have them to be the Goods of *French* Men, or at least that the Ship was Sailed under *French* Passes. Now if it were so, as Capt. *Kidd* says, it was a lawful Prize, and liable to Confiscation, but if they were the Goods of Persons in Amity with the King, and the Ship was not Navigated under *French* Passes, it was very plain it was a Piratical taking of them. Gentlemen, it is to be considered what Evidence Capt. *Kidd*. hath given to prove that Ship and

Goods to belong to the *French* King, or his Subjects, or that the Ship was Failed under a *French* Pass, or indeed that ever there was a *French* Pass shewn or seen. He appeals indeed to the Witnesses over and over again, Did you never see it? No, say they: Nor did not you, saith he, say you saw it? No. saith the Witness, I said that Capt. *Kidd* said he had a *French* Pass, but I never saw it. Now after all, the taking of the *Quedagh Merchant* is brought down to Mr. *Kidd*, and the Prisoners with others, and the distribution of the Money produced by the Sale of the Goods among Mr. *Kidd*, and his Crew, whereof every one of these Prisoners were present at the same time, and had Proportions.

Now Gentlemen, this must be observed, if this was a Capture on the High Sea, and these were the Goods of Persons in Amity with the King, and had no *French* Pass, then it is a plain Piracy. And if you believe the Witnesses, here is a taking of the Goods and Ship of Persons in Amity, and converting them to their own Use. Such a taking at Land as this would be Felony, and being at Sea it will be Piracy: For this is a taking the Ship from the right Owners, and turning it to their own use. So that you have Evidence as to the Seizing of the Ship, and dividing the Money rising from the Goods sold, and sharing the remainder according to the Articles.

Now, what does Capt. *Kidd* say to all this? He has told you he acted pursuant to his Commission; but that cannot be, unless he gives you satisfaction that the Ship and Goods belonged to the *French* King, or his Subjects, or that the Ship had a *French* Pass, otherwise neither of them will excuse him from being a Pirate; for if he takes the Goods of Friends he is a pirate, he had no Authority for that: There is no colour from either of his Commissions for him to take them. And as to the *French* Passes, there is nothing of that appears by any Proof, and for ought I can see, none saw them but himself, if there were ever any. It is proved that the People that were Owners of the Goods, made him very large Offers to redeem the Ship (Twenty Thousand Ruppees, as I remember) but he would not accept their Proposal; but said, That is a small Summ, the Cargo is worth a great deal more, or to that effect: And further said, he must answer these People, that his Men will not part with it. And a *French* Man was to be set up for a Mock business, as you have heard; and if the Witnesses say true, they were said by the Captain of the Ship to be, and were reputed to be, the Ship and Goods of Friends, and not of Enemies; and if they were so, and had no *French* Pass, then is he, and those that were concerned with him, guilty of Piratically taking this Ship, and of Piratically seizing the Goods in the Ship; and neither of his Commissions will justify such an Action as this. If he had acted pursuant to his Commission, he ought to have condemned the Ship and Goods, if they were a *French* Interest, or Sailed under a *French* Pass; but by his not condemning them, he seems to shew his Aim, Mind and Intention, that he did not act in that Case by virtue of his Commission, but quite contrary to it; for he takes the Ship, and shares the Money and Goods, and is taken in that very Ship by my Lord *Bellamont*, and he had continued in that Ship till that time, so that there is no colour or pretence appears, that he intended to bring this Ship to *England*, to be condemned, or to have condemned it in any of the English Plantations, having disposed of the whole Cargo, as aforesaid. Here I must leave it to you, to consider whether, according to the Evidence that appears, there is any Ground for him to say, he has acted by his Commission in taking the *Quedagh Merchant* and Goods in her, or whether he has not acted contrary thereunto.

Now for himself he has called some Persons here, to give an account of his Reputation, and of his Services done in the *West-Indies;* and one of them says, about 10 to 12 Years, he did good Service there. Why so he might, and might have, and 'tis very like he had such Reputation, when the King trusted him with these Commissions, else I believe he had never had them; so what thatever he might be so many Years ago, that is not a matter to be insisted on now, but what he hath been since, and how he hath acted in this matter charged against him. So that, Gentlemen, as to Mr. *Kidd*, I must leave it to you, whether he is Guilty of Piracy, or no, and if you believe him Guilty upon the Evidence, you will find him so, if not you will acquit him. . . .

Then the Jury withdrew, and *after half an hour's stay, brought in their Verdict.*

Cl. of *Arr.* Gentlemen of the Jury, Answer to your Names, *John Cooper*, &c.

J. Cooper. Here, &c.

Cl. of *Arr*. Are you agreed of your verdict? *Omnes*. Yes.

Cl. of *Arr.* Who shall say for you? *Omnes*. Foreman.

Cl. of *Arr. Will. Kidd*, hold up thy Hand, (which he did.) How say you, Is he Guilty of the Piracy whereof he stands Indicted, or not Guilty? And so of the rest.

Foreman. Guilty.

87. William Kidd to the Speaker of the House of Commons (Robert Harley). April (?), 1701.

May it please Y'r Hon'r

The long Imprisonment I have undergone, or the tryall I am to undergoe, are not soe great an affliction to me, as my not being able to give your Hon'ble House of Commons such satisfaction as was Expected from me. I hope I have not offended against the Law, but if I have, It was the fault of others who knew better, and made me the Tool of their Ambition and Avarice, and who now perhaps think it their Interest that I should be removed out of the world.

I did not seek the Commission I undertook, but was partly Cajold, and partly menac'd into it by the Lord Bellomont, and one Robert Livingston of New York, who was the projector, promoter, and Chief Manager of that designe, and who only can give your House a satisfactory account of all the Transactions of my Owners. He was the man admitted into their Closets, and received their private Instructions, which he kept in his own hands, and who encouraged me in their names to doe more than I ever did, and to act without regard to my Commission. I would not Exceed my Authority, and took noe other ships than such as had French passes, which I brought with me to New England, and relyed upon for my Justification. But my Lord Bellomont seized upon them together with my Cargoe, and tho he promised to send them into England, yet has he detained part of the effects, kept these passes wholly from me, and has stript me of all the Defence I have to make, which is such Barbarous, as well as dishonorable usage, as I hope Your Hon'ble House will not let an Englishman suffer, how unfortunate soever his Circumstances are; but will intercede with his Maj'ty to defer my tryall till I can have those passes, and that Livingston may be brought under Your Examination, and Confronted by me.

I cannot be so unjust to my selfe, as to plead to an Indictment till the French passes are restored to me, unlesse I would be accessary to my own destruction, for though I can make proof that the ships I took had such passes, I am advised by Council, that It will little avail me without producing the passes themselves. I was in great Consternation when I was before that great Assembly, Your Hon'ble House, which with the disadvantages of a mean Capacity, want of Education, and a Spirit Cramped by Long Confinem't, made me Uncapable of representing my Case; and I have therefore presumed to send your Honor a short and true state of It, which I humbly beg Your Honors perusall, and Communication of to the House, if you think it worthy their Notice.

I humbly crave leave to acquaint Your Honor that I was not privy to my being sent for up to Your House the second time, nor to the paper lately printed in my name (both which may justly give Offence to the House) but I owe the first to a Coffeeman in the Court of Wards who designed to make a shew of me, for his profit; and the latter was done by one Newy a prisoner in Newgate to get money for his support, at the hazard of my safety.

I humbly beg the Compassion and protection of the Hon'ble House of Commons, and Your Honors intercession with them on behalfe of

Your Honors
Most Dutifull and Distressed Serv't
Wm. Kidd.

Questions

1. What, precisely, was Kidd's crime? What distinguished the legal from the illegal seizure of goods? On what did Kidd's guilt or innocence depend?
2. What was the role of New York and its governor in this affair?
3. What does Kidd's case suggest about the nature of late seventeenth- and early eighteenth-century war?
4. How does this discussion of piracy compare with Esquemeling's?
5. How did pirates differ from conquistadors?

Atlantic Worlds

During the late seventeenth and throughout the eighteenth century, an unprecedented volume of people and goods circulated among Europe, Africa, and the Americas. The populations and economies of these regions became so enmeshed that historians now frequently speak of an early modern "Atlantic World." The documents in this chapter illustrate some of the forces that created this world, focusing on human migration, popular consumption, and the flow of information.

14.1 German Immigrant Gottlieb Mittelberger's Journey to America*

Responding to extensive promotional efforts by Pennsylvania and other colonies, about one hundred thousand Germans migrated to North America during the eighteenth century. Many, like Gottlieb Mittelberger, came with high expectations only to find themselves disappointed. A relatively well-educated schoolteacher and organist, Mittelberger published the following account of his experience in 1756, two years after his return to Germany. The first English edition did not appear until 1898.

JOURNEY TO PENNSYLVANIA IN AMERICA

In the month of May, 1750, I departed from Enzweihingen, Vaihingen County, my native place, for Heilbronn, where an organ stood ready to be shipped and sent to Pennsylvania. With this organ, I sailed the usual way, down the Neckar and Rhine to Rotterdam in Holland. From Rotterdam I sailed with a transport of about 400 souls, Würtembergers, Durlachers, Palatines and Swiss, etc., across the North Sea to Kaupp [Cowes] in England, and after a sojourn of 9 days there, across the great ocean, until I landed in Philadelphia, the capital of Pennsylvania, Oct. 10, 1750.* From home to Rotterdam, including my sojourn there, I spent 7 weeks, caused by the many stoppages down the Rhine and in Holland, whereas this journey could otherwise be made swifter; but from Rotterdam to Philadelphia the voyage lasted 15 weeks. I was nearly 4 years in that country, engaged, as my testimonials show, as organist and schoolmaster with the German St. Augustine's Church in Providence, having besides given private instruction in music and in the German language, as the following certificate will show, at the house of Captain Diemer.

_____

*In the list of names of Foreigners arriving in the ship "Osgood," William Wilkie, Captain, from Rotterdam, and taking the oath of allegiance Sept. 29th, 1750 [O.S.], is that of Gottlieb Mittelberger.—Penna. Archives, 2nd Series, Vol. XVII., p. 324.

_____

*Carl Theo. Eben, ed. and trans., *Gottlieb Mittelberger's Journey to Pennsylvania in the Year 1750 and Return to Germany in the Year 1754* (Philadelphia: John Jos. McVey, 1898), 13–32.

Whereas the Bearer, Mr. Mittelberger, Music Master, has resolved to return from this Province, to his native Land, which is in the Dukedom of Würtemberg in High Germany; I have at his Request granted these Lines to certify that ye above nam'd Mr. Mittelberger has behaved himself honestly, diligently, and faithfully in ye Offices of Schoolmaster and Organist, during ye Space of three Years; in ye Township of New-Providence, County of Philadelphia and Province of Pennsylvania, etc. So that I and all his Employers were entirely satisfied, and would willingly have him to remain with us. But as his Call obliges him to proceed on his long Journey; we would recommend ye s'd Mr. Mittelberger to all Persons of Dignity and Character; and beg their Assistance, so that he may pass and repass untill he arrives at his Respective Abode which may God grant, and may ye Benediction of Heaven accompany him in his Journey. Deus benedicat susceptis ejus & ferat eum ad amicos suos maxima prosperitate.

Dabam, Providentiæ Philadelphiæ. Comitatu Pennsylvania in America, die 25. Apr. A. D. 1754.

John Diemer, Cap.Sam. Kennedy, M. D.Henery Pawling, Esqr.

T. Henry Marsteiler. Matthias Gmelin.

I have carefully inquired into the condition of the country; and what I describe here, I have partly experienced myself, and partly heard from trustworthy people who were familiar with the circumstances. I might possibly be able to relate a great deal more, if I had thought that I should ever publish something about Pennsylvania. For I always considered myself far too weak for such an undertaking. But the fatalities which I suffered on my journey to and fro (for in the country itself I fared well, because I immediately found good support and could get along well), and the evil tricks of the newlanders, which they intended to play me and my family, as I shall relate hereafter, have awakened the first impulse in me not to keep concealed what I knew. But the most important occasion for publishing this little book was the wretched and grievous condition of those who travel from Germany to this new land, and the outrageous and merciless proceeding of the Dutch man-dealers and their man-stealing emissaries; I mean the so-called newlanders, for they steal, as it were, German people under all manner of false pretenses, and deliver them into the hands of the great Dutch traffickers in human souls. These derive a large, and the newlanders a smaller profit from this traffic. This, I say, is the main cause why I publish this book. I had to bind myself even by a vow to do so. For before I left Pennsylvania, when it became known that I was about to return to Würtemberg, many Würtembergers, Durlachers and Palatines, of whom there are a great number there who repent and regret it while they live that they left their native country, implored me with tears and uplifted hands, and even in the name of God, to make this misery and sorrow known in Germany, so that not only the common people, but even princes and lords, might learn how they had fared, to prevent other innocent souls from leaving their fatherland, persuaded thereto by the newlanders, and from being sold into a like slavery. And so I vowed to the great God, and promised those people, to reveal to the people of Germany the pure truth about it, to the best of my knowledge and ability. I hope, therefore, that my beloved countrymen and all Germany will care no less to obtain accurate information as to how far it is to Pennsylvania, how long it takes to get there; what the journey costs, and besides, what hardships and dangers one has to pass through; what takes place when the people arrive well or ill in the country; how they are sold and dispersed; and finally, the nature and condition of the whole land. I relate both what is good and what is evil, and I hope, therefore, to be considered impartial and truthful by an honor-loving world.

When all this will have been read, I do not doubt that those who may still desire to go there will remain in their fatherland, and carefully avoid this long and tedious journey and the fatalities connected with it; as such a journey involves with most a loss of their property, liberty and peace; with not a few even a loss of life, and I may well say, of the salvation of their souls.

From Würtemberg or Durlach to Holland and the open sea we count about 200 hours; from there across the sea to Old England as far as Kaupp, [Cowes] where the ships generally cast anchor before they start on the great sea-voyage, 150 hours; from there, till England is entirely lost sight of, above 100 hours; and then across the great ocean, that is from land to land, 1200 hours according to the statements of mariners; at length from the first land in Pennsylvania to Philadelphia over 40 hours. Which makes together a journey of 1700 hours or 1700 French miles.

This journey lasts from the beginning of May to the end of October, fully half a year, amid such hardships as no one is able to describe adequately with their misery.

The cause is because the Rhine-boats from Heilbronn to Holland have to pass by 36 custom-houses, at all of which the ships are examined, which is done when it suits the convenience of the custom-house officials. In the meantime the ships with the people are detained long, so that the passengers have to spend much money. The trip down the Rhine alone lasts therefore 4, 5 and even 6 weeks.

When the ships with the people come to Holland, they are detained there likewise 5 or 6 weeks. Because things are very dear there, the poor people have to spend nearly all they have during that time. Not to mention many sad accidents which occur here; having seen with my own eyes how a man, as he was about to board the ship near Rotterdam, lost two children at once by drowning.

Both in Rotterdam and in Amsterdam the people are packed densely, like herrings so to say, in the large sea vessels. One person receives a place of scarcely 2 feet width and 6 feet length in the bedstead, while many a ship carries four to six hundred souls; not to mention the innumerable implements, tools, provisions, water-barrels and other things which likewise occupy much space.

On account of contrary winds it takes the ships sometimes 2, 3 and 4 weeks to make the trip from Holland to Kaupp [Cowes] in England. But when the wind is good, they get there in 8 days or even sooner. Everything is examined there and the custom-duties paid, whence it comes that the ships ride there 8, 10 to 14 days and even longer at anchor, till they have taken in their full cargoes. During that time every one is compelled to spend his last remaining money and to consume his little stock of provisions which had been reserved for the sea; so that most passengers, finding themselves on the ocean where they would be in greater need of them, must greatly suffer from hunger and want. Many suffer want already on the water between Holland and Old England.

When the ships have for the last time weighed their anchors near the city of Kaupp [Cowes] in Old England, the real misery begins with the long voyage. For from there the ships, unless they have good wind, must often sail 8, 9, 10 to 12 weeks before they reach Philadelphia. But even with the best wind the voyage lasts 7 weeks.

But during the voyage there is on board these ships terrible misery, stench, fumes, horror, vomiting, many kinds of sea-sickness, fever, dysentery, headache, heat, constipation, boils, scurvy, cancer, mouth-rot, and the like, all of which come from old and sharply salted food and meat, also from very bad and foul water, so that many die miserably.

Add to this want of provisions, hunger, thirst, frost, heat, dampness, anxiety, want, afflictions and lamentations, together with other trouble, as *c. v.* the lice abound so frightfully, especially on sick people, that they can be scraped off the body. The misery reaches the climax when a gale rages for 2 or 3 nights and days, so that every one believes that the ship will go to the bottom with all human beings on board. In such a visitation the people cry and pray most piteously.

When in such a gale the sea rages and surges, so that the waves rise often like high mountains one above the other, and often tumble over the ship, so that one fears to go down with the ship;

when the ship is constantly tossed from side to side by the storm and waves, so that no one can either walk, or sit, or lie, and the closely packed people in the berths are thereby tumbled over each other, both the sick and the well—it will be readily understood that many of these people, none of whom had been prepared for hardships suffer so terribly from them that they do not survive it.

I myself had to pass through a severe illness at sea, and I best know how I felt at the time. These poor people often long for consolation, and I often entertained and comforted them with singing, praying and exhorting; and whenever it was possible and the winds and waves permitted it, I kept daily prayer-meetings with them on deck. Besides, I baptized five children in distress, because we had no ordained minister on board. I also held divine service every Sunday by reading sermons to the people; and when the dead were sunk in the water, I commended them and our souls to the mercy of God.

Among the healthy, impatience sometimes grows so great and cruel that one curses the other, or himself and the day of his birth, and sometimes come near killing each other. Misery and malice join each other, so that they cheat and rob one another. One always reproaches the other with having persuaded him to undertake the journey. Frequently children cry out against their parents, husbands against their wives and wives against their husbands, brothers and sisters, friends and acquaintaces against each other. But most against the soul-traffickers.

Many sigh and cry: "Oh, that I were at home again, and if I had to lie in my pig-sty!" Or they say: O God, if I only had a piece of good bread, or a good fresh drop of water." Many people whimper, sigh and cry piteously for their homes; most of them get home-sick. Many hundred people necessarily die and perish in such misery, and must be cast into the sea, which drives their relatives, or those who persuaded them to undertake the journey, to such despair that it is almost impossible to pacify and console them. In a word, the sighing and crying and lamenting on board the ship continues night and day, so as to cause the hearts even of the most hardened to bleed when they hear it.

No one can have an idea of the sufferings which women in confinement have to bear with their innocent children on board these ships. Few of this class escape with their lives; many a mother is cast into the water with her child as soon as she is dead. One day, just as we had a heavy gale, a woman in our ship, who was to give birth and could not give birth under the circumstances, was pushed through a loop-hole [port-hole] in the ship and dropped into the sea, because she was far in the rear of the ship and could not be brought forward.

Children from 1 to 7 years rarely survive the voyage; and many a time parents are compelled to see their children miserably suffer and die from hunger, thirst and sickness, and then to see them cast into the water. I witnessed such misery in no less than 32 children in our ship, all of whom were thrown into the sea. The parents grieve all the more since their children find no resting-place in the earth, but are devoured by the monsters of the sea. It is a notable fact that children, who have not yet had the measles or small-pocks, generally get them on board the ship, and mostly die of them.

Often a father is separated by death from his wife and children, or mothers from their little children, or even both parents from their children; and sometimes whole families die in quick succession; so that often many dead persons lie in the berths beside the living ones, especially when contagious diseases have broken out on board the ship.

Many other accidents happen on board these ships, especially by falling, whereby people are often made cripples and can never be set right again. Some have also fallen into the ocean.

That most of the people get sick is not surprising, because, in addition to all other trials and hardships, warm food is served only three times a week, the rations being very poor and very little. Such meals can hardly be eaten, on account of being so unclean. The water which is served out on the ships is often very black, thick and full of worms, so that one cannot drink it without loathing, even with the greatest thirst. O surely, one would often give much money at sea for a piece of good bread, or a drink of good water, not to say a drink of good wine, if it were only to be had. I myself experienced that sufficiently, I am sorry to say. Toward the end we were compelled to eat the ship's biscuit which had been spoiled long ago; though in a whole biscuit there was scarcely a piece the size of a dollar that had not been full of red worms and spiders nests. Great hunger and thirst force us to eat and drink everything; but many a one does so at the risk of his life. The sea water cannot be drunk, because it is salt and bitter as gall. If this were not so, such a voyage could be made with less expense and without so many hardships.

At length, when, after a long and tedious voyage, the ships come in sight of land, so that the promontories can be seen, which the people were so eager and anxious to see, all creep from below on deck to see the land from afar, and they weep for joy, and pray and sing, thanking and praising God. The sight of the land makes the people on board the ship, especially the sick and the half dead, alive again, so that their hearts leap within them; they shout and rejoice, and are content to bear their misery in patience, in the hope that they may soon reach the land in safety. But alas!

When the ships have landed at Philadelphia after their long voyage, no one is permitted to leave them except those who pay for their passage or can give good security; the others, who cannot pay, must remain on board the ships till they are purchased, and are released from the ships by their purchasers. The sick always fare the worst, for the healthy are naturally preferred and purchased first; and so the sick and wretched must often remain on board in front of the city for 2 or 3 weeks, and frequently die, whereas many a one, if he could pay his debt and were permitted to leave the ship immediately, might recover and remain alive.

Before I describe how this traffic in human flesh is conducted, I must mention how much the journey to Philadelphia or Pennsylvania costs.

A person over 10 years pays for the passage from Rotterdam to Philadelphia 10 pounds, or 60 florins. Children from 5 to 10 years pay half price, 5 pounds or 30 florins. All children under 5 years are free. For these prices the passengers are conveyed to Philadelphia, and, as long as they are at sea, provided with food, though with very poor, as has been shown above.

But this is only the sea-passage; the other costs on land, from home to Rotterdam, including the passage on the Rhine, are at least 40 florins, no matter how economically one may live. No account is here taken of extraordinary contingencies. I may safely assert that, with the greatest economy, many passengers have spent 200 florins from home to Philadelphia.

The sale of human beings in the market on board the ship is carried on thus: Every day Englishmen, Dutchmen and High-German people come from the city of Philadelphia and other places, in part from a great distance, say 20, 30, or 40 hours away, and go on board the newly arrived ship that has brought and offers for sale passengers from Europe, and select among the healthy persons such as they deem suitable for their business, and bargain with them how long they will serve for their passage money, which most of them are still in debt for. When they have come to an agreement, it happens that adult persons bind themselves in writing to serve 3, 4, 5 or 6 years for the amount due by them, according to their age and strength. But very young people, from 10 to 15 years, must serve till they are 21 years old.

Many parents must sell and trade away their children like so many head of cattle; for if their children take the debt upon themselves, the parents can leave the ship free and unrestrained; but as the parents often do not know where and to what people their children are going, it often happens that such parents and children, after leaving the ship, do not see each other again for many years, perhaps no more in all their lives.

When people arrive who cannot make themselves free, but have children under 5 years, the parents cannot free themselves by them; for such children must be given to somebody without compensation to be brought up and they must serve for their bringing up till they are 27 years old. Children from 5 to 10 years, who pay half price for their passage. viz. 30 florins, must likewise serve for it till they are 21 years of age; they cannot, therefore, redeem their parents by taking the debt of the latter upon themselves. But children above 10 years can take part of their parents' debt upon themselves.

A woman must stand for her husband if he arrives sick and in like manner a man for his sick wife, and take the debt upon herself or himself, and thus serve 5 to 6 years not alone for his or her own debt, but also for that of the sick husband or wife. But if both are sick, such persons are sent from the ship to the sick-house [hospital], but not until it appears probable that they will find no purchasers. As soon as they are well again they must serve for their passage, or pay it they have means.

It often happens that whole families, husband, wife, and children, are separated by being sold to different purchasers, especially when they have not paid any part of their passage money.

When a husband or wife has died at sea, when the ship has made more than half of her trip, the survivor must pay or serve not only for himself or herself, but also for the deceased.

When both parents have died over half-way at sea, their children, especially when they are young and have nothing to pawn or to pay, must stand for their own and their parents' passage, and serve till they are 21 years old. When one has served his or her term, he or she is entitled to a new suit of clothes at parting; and if it has been so stipulated, a man gets in addition a horse, a woman, a cow.

When a serf has an opportunity to marry in this country; he or she must pay for each year which he or she would have yet to serve, 5 to 6 pounds. But many a one who has thus purchased and paid for his bride, has subsequently repented his bargain, so that he would gladly have returned his exorbitantly dear ware, and lost the money besides.

If some one in this country runs away from his master, who has treated him harshly, he cannot get far. Good provision has been made for such cases, so that a runaway is soon recovered. He who detains or returns a deserter receives a good reward.

If such a runaway has been away from his master one day, he must serve for it as a punishment a week, for a week a month, and for a month half a year. But if the master will not keep the runaway

after he has got him back, he may sell him for so many years as he would have to serve him yet.

Work and labor in this new and wild land are very hard and manifold, and many a one who came there in his old age must work very hard to his end for his bread. I will not speak of young people. Work mostly consists in cutting wood, felling oak-trees, rooting out, or as they say there, clearing large tracts of forest. Such forests, being cleared, are then laid out for fields and meadows. From the best hewn wood, fences are made around the new fields; for there all meadows, orchards and fruit fields, are surrounded and fenced in with planks made of thickly-split wood, laid one above the other, as in zigzag lines, and within such enclosures, horses, cattle, and sheep, are permitted to graze. Our Europeans, who are purchased, must always work hard, for new fields are constantly laid out; and so they learn that stumps of oak-trees are in America certainly as hard as in Germany. In this hot land they fully experience in their own persons what God has imposed on man for his sin and disobedience; for in Genesis we read the words: In the sweat of thy brow shalt thou eat bread. Who therefore wishes to earn his bread in a Christian and honest way, and cannot earn it in his fatherland otherwise than by the work of his hands, let him do so in his own country, and not in America; for he will not fare better in America. However hard he may be compelled to work in his fatherland, he will surely find it quite as hard, if not harder, in the new country. Besides, there is not only the long and arduous journey lasting half a year, during which he has to suffer, more than with the hardest work; he has also spent about 200 florins which no one will refund to him. If he has so much money, it will slip out of his hands; if he has it not, he must work his debt off as a slave and poor serf. Therefore let every one stay in his own country and support himself and his family honestly. Besides I say that those who suffer themselves to be persuaded and enticed away by the man-thieves, are very foolish if they believe that roasted pigeons will fly into their mouths in America or Pennsylvania without their working for them.

How miserably and wretchedly so many thousand German families have fared, 1) since they lost all their cash means in consequence of the long and tedious journey; 2) because many of them died miserably and were thrown into the water; 3) because, on account of their great poverty, most of these families after reaching the land are separated from each other and sold far away from each other, the young and the old. And the saddest of all this is that parents must generally give away their minor children without receiving a compensation for them; inasmuch as such children never see or meet their fathers, mothers, brothers or sisters again, and as many of them are not raised in any Christian faith by the people to whom they are given.

For there are many doctrines of faith and sects in Pennsylvania which cannot all be enumerated, because many a one will not confess to what faith he belongs.

Besides, there are many hundreds of adult persons who have not been and do not even wish to be baptized. There are many who think nothing of the sacraments and the Holy Bible, nor even of God and his word. Many do not even believe that there is a true God and devil, a heaven and a hell, salvation and damnation, a resurrection of the dead, a judgment and an eternal life; they believe that all one can see is natural. For in Pennsylvania every one may not only believe what he will, but he may even say it freely and openly.

Consequently, when young persons, not yet grounded in religion, come to serve for many years with such free-thinkers and infidels, and are not sent to any church or school by such people, especially when they live far from any school or church. Thus it happens that such innocent souls come to no true divine recognition, and grow up like heathens and Indians.

A voyage is sometimes dangerous to people, who bring money or goods away with them from home, because much is spoiled at sea by entering sea water: sometimes they are even robbed on board the ship by dishonest people; so that such formerly opulent persons find themselves in a most deplorable condition.

Questions

1. What motivated the author to write this account?
2. Mittleberger describes the "misery and sorrow" of many Germans who went to America. What does he say they suffered? How common were these hardships? If conditions were so bad, why did they keep coming?
3. The author compares many aspects of German immigration with the slave trade. Identify and evaluate his comparisons in light of the Equiano document that follows.
4. What does Mittelberger think of Pennsylvania's religious landscape? What opportunities and dangers did Pennsylvania's religious tolerance present for pious immigrants?

14.2   Former Slave Olaudah Equiano Describes His Capture and the Middle Passage*

In 1789, Olaudah Equiano, also known as Gustavus Vassa, published an account of his experience as a slave from his capture in the African interior in the 1750s until he purchased his own freedom in 1766. Although some documents suggest that Equiano might have been born in South Carolina rather than Africa, most historians still accept the value of the following account of his enslavement.†

*Olaudah Equiano, *The Interesting Narrative of the Life of Olaudah Equiano, or Gustavus Vassa, the African* (New York: W. Durell, 1791), 32–36, 47–62.

†For two different perspectives on Equiano's African or North American birth, see Vincent Carretta, *Equiano the African: Biography of a Self-Made Man* (Athens, GA: University of Georgia Press, 2005); and Alexander X. Byrd, "Eboe, Country, Nation, and Gustavus Vassa's *Interesting Narrative,*" *William and Mary Quarterly* 63 (January 2006), 123–148.

The Author's birth and parentage—His being kidnapped with his sister—Their separation—Surprise at meeting again—Are finally separated—Account of the different places and incidents the Author met with till his arrival on the coast—The effect the sight of a slave-ship had on him—He sails for the West-Indies—Horrors of a slave-ship—Arrives at Barbadoes, where the cargo is sold and dispersed.

I hope the reader will not think I have trespassed on his patience in introducing myself to him with some account of the manners and customs of my country. They had been implanted in me with great care, and made an impression on my mind, which time could not erase, and which all the adversity and variety of fortune I have since experienced served only to rivet and record: for, whether the love of one's country be real or imaginary, or a lesson of reason, or an instinct of nature, I still look back with pleasure on the first scenes of my life, though that pleasure has been for the most part mingled with sorrow.

I have already acquainted the reader with the time and place of my birth. My father, besides many slaves, had a numerous family, of which seven lived to grow up, including myself and a sister, who was the only daughter. As I was the youngest of the sons, I became, of course, the greatest favourite with my mother, and was always with her; and she used to take particular pains to form my mind. I was trained up from my earliest years in the arts of agriculture and war: my daily exercise was shooting and throwing javelins; and my mother adorned me with emblems, after the manner of our greatest warriors. In this way I grew up till I was turned the age of eleven, when an end was put to my happiness in the following manner:—Generally, when the grown people in the neighbourhood were gone far in the fields to labour, the children assembled together in some of the neighbours' premises to play; and commonly some of us used to get up a tree to look out for any assailant, or kidnapper, that might come upon us; for they sometimes took those opportunities of our parents' absence, to attack and carry off as many as they could seize. One day, as I was watching at the top of a tree in our yard, I saw one of those people come into the yard of our next neighbour but one, to kidnap, there being many stout young people in it. Immediately, on this, I gave the alarm of the rogue, and he was surrounded by the stoutest of them, who entangled him with cords, so that he could not escape till some of the grown people came and secured him. But, alas! ere long it was my fate to be thus attacked, and to be carried off, when none of the grown people were nigh. One day, when all our people were gone out to their works as usual, and only I and my dear sister were left to mind the house, two men and a woman got over our walls, and in a moment seized us both; and, without giving us time to cry out, or make resistance, they stopped our mouths, tied our hands, and ran off with us into the nearest wood: and continued to carry us as far as they could, till night came on, when we reached a small house, where the robbers halted for refreshment, and spent the night. We were then unbound, but were unable to take any food; and, being quite overpowered by fatigue and grief, our only relief was some sleep, which allayed our misfortune for a short time. The next morning we left the house, and continued travelling all the day. For a long time we had kept the woods, but at last we came into a road which I believed I knew. I had now some hopes of being delivered; for we had advanced but a little way before I discovered some people at a distance, on which I began to cry out for their assistance; but my cries had no other effect than to make them tie me faster, and stop my mouth, and then they put me into a large sack. They also stopped my sister's mouth, and tied her hands; and in this manner we proceeded till we were out of the sight of these people.—When we went to rest the following night they offered us some victuals; but we refused them; and the only comfort we had was in being in one another's arms all that night, and bathing each other with our tears. But, alas! we were soon deprived of even the smallest comfort of weeping together. The next day proved a day of greater sorrow than I had yet experienced; for my sister and I were then separated, while we lay clasped in each other's arms. It was in vain that we besought them not to part us: she was torn from me, and immediately carried away, while I was left in a state of distraction not to be described. I cried and grieved continually; and for several days I did not eat any thing but what they forced into my mouth. . . .

All the nations and people I had hitherto passed through resembled our own in their manners, customs and language: but I came at length to a country, the inhabitants of which differed from us in all those particulars. I was very much struck with this difference, especially when I came among a people who did not circumcise, and eat without washing their hands. They cooked also in iron pots, and had European cutlasses and cross bows, which were unknown to us, and fought with their fists among themselves. Their women were not so modest as ours, for they eat, and drank, and slept with their men. But, above all, I was amazed to see no sacrifices or offerings among them. In some of those places the people ornamented themselves with scars, and likewise filed their teeth very sharp. They wanted sometimes to ornament me in the same manner, but I would not suffer them; hoping that I might some time be among a people who did not thus disfigure themselves, as I thought they did. At last, I came to the banks of a large river, which was covered with canoes, in which the people appeared to live with their household utensils and provisions of all kinds. I was beyond measure astonished at this, as I had never before seen any water larger than a pond or a rivulet; and my surprise was mingled with no small fear when I was put into one of these canoes, and we began to paddle and move along the river. We continued going on thus till night; and when we came to land, and made fires on the banks, each family by themselves, some dragged their canoes on shore, others staid and cooked in theirs, and laid in them all night. Those on the land had mats, of which they made tents, some in the shape of little houses: In these we slept; and after the morning meal we embarked again, and proceeded as before. I was often very much astonished to see some of the women, as well as the men, jump into the water, dive to the bottom, come up again, and swim about. Thus I continued to travel, sometimes by land, sometimes by water, through different countries, and various nations, till, at the end of six or seven months after I had been kidnapped, I arrived at the sea coast. It would be tedious and uninteresting to relate all the incidents which befel me during this journey, and which I have not yet forgotten; of the various hands I passed through, and the manners and customs of all the different people among whom I lived: I shall therefore only observe, that, in all the places where I was, the soil was exceedingly rich; the pomkins, eadas, plantains, yams, &c. &c. were in great abundance, and of incredible size. There were also vast quantities of different gums, though not used for any purpose; and every where a great deal of tobacco. The cotton even grew quite wild; and there was plenty of red wood. I saw no mechanics whatever in all the way, except such as I have mentioned. The chief employment in all these countries was agriculture, and both the males and females, as with us, were brought up to it, and trained in the arts of war.

The first object which saluted my eyes when I arrived on the coast was the sea, and a slave-ship, which was then riding at anchor, and waiting for its cargo. These filled me with astonishment, which was soon converted into terror, which I am yet at a loss to describe, nor the then feelings of my mind. When I was carried on board I was immediately handled, and tossed up, to see if I were sound, by some of the crew; and I was now persuaded that I had gotten into a world of bad spirits, and that they were going to kill me. Their complexions too differing so much from ours, their long hair, and the language they spoke, which was very different from any I had ever heard, united to confirm me in this belief. Indeed, such were the horrors of my views and fears at the moment, that, if ten thousand worlds had been my own, I would have freely parted with them all to have exchanged my condition with that of the meanest slave in my own country. When I looked round the ship too, and saw a large furnace of copper boiling, and a multitude of black people of every description chained together, every one of their countenances expressing dejection and sorrow, I no longer doubted of my fate, and, quite over-powered with horror and anguish, I fell motionless on the deck and fainted. When I recovered a little, I found some black people about me, who I believed were some of those who brought me on board, and had been receiving their pay; they talked to me in order to cheer me, but all in vain. I asked them if we were not to be eaten by those white men with horrible looks, red faces, and long hair? They told me I was not; and one of the crew brought me a small portion of spirituous liquor in a wine glass; but, being afraid of him, I would not take it out of his hand. One of the blacks therefore took it from him and gave it to me, and I took a little down my palate, which, instead of reviving me, as they thought it would, threw me into the greatest consternation at the strange feeling it produced, having never tasted any such liquor before. Soon after this, the blacks who brought me on board went off, and left me abandoned to despair. I now saw myself deprived of all chance of returning to my native country, or even the least glimpse of hope of gaining the shore, which I now considered as friendly: and I even wished for my former slavery in preference to my present situation, which was filled with horrors of every kind, still heightened by my ignorance of what I was to undergo. I was not long suffered to indulge my grief; I was soon put down under the decks, and there I received such a salutation in my nostrils as I had never experienced in my life; so that with the loathsomeness of the stench, and crying together, I became so sick and low that I was not able to eat, nor had I the least desire to taste any thing. I now wished for the last friend, Death, to relieve me; but soon, to my grief, two of the white men offered me eatables; and, on my refusing to eat, one of them held me fast by the hands, and laid me across, I think, the windlass, and tied my feet, while the other flogged me severely. I had never experienced any thing of this kind before; and although, not being used to the water, I naturally feared that element the first time I saw it; yet, nevertheless, could I have got over the nettings,

I would have jumped over the side, but I could not; and, besides, the crew used to watch us very closely who were not chained down to the decks, lest we should leap into the water; and I have seen some of these poor African prisoners most severely cut for attempting to do so, and hourly whipped for not eating. This indeed was often the case with myself. In a little time after, amongst the poor chained men, I found some of my own nation, which in a small degree gave ease to my mind. I inquired of these what was to be done with us? they gave me to understand we were to be carried to these white people's country to work for them. I then was a little revived, and thought, if it were no worse than working, my situation was not so desperate: but still I feared I should be put to death, the white people looked and acted, as I thought, in so savage a manner; for I had never seen among any people such instances of brutal cruelty; and this not only shewn towards us blacks, but also to some of the whites themselves. One white man in particular I saw, when we were permitted to be on deck, flogged so unmercifully with a large rope near the foremast, that he died in consequence of it; and they tossed him over the side as they would have done a brute. This made me fear these people the more; and I expected nothing less than to be treated in the same manner. I could not help expressing my fears and apprehensions to some of my countrymen: I asked them if these people had no country, but lived in this hollow place the ship? they told me they did not, but came from a distant one. "Then," said I, "how comes it in all our country we never heard of them?" They told me, because they lived so very far off. I then asked where were their women? had they any like themselves! I was told they had: "And why," said I, "do we not see them?" they answered, because they were left behind. I asked how the vessel could go? they told me they could not tell; but that there were cloths put upon the masts by the help of the ropes I saw, and then the vessel went on; and the white men had some spell or magic they put in the water when they liked in order to stop the vessel. I was exceedingly amazed at this account, and really thought they were spirits. I therefore wished much to be from amongst them, for I expected they would sacrifice me: but my wishes were vain; for we were so quartered that it was impossible for any of us to make our escape. While we staid on the coast I was mostly on deck; and one day, to my great astonishment, I saw one of these vessels coming in with the sails up. As soon as the whites saw it, they gave a great shout, at which we were amazed; and the more so as the vessel appeared larger by approaching nearer. At last she came to an anchor in my sight, and when the anchor was let go, I and my countrymen who saw it were lost in astonishment to observe the vessel stop; and were now convinced it was done by magic. Soon after this the other ship got her boats out, and they came on board of us, and the people of both ships seemed very glad to see each other. Several of the strangers also shook hands with us black people, and made motions with their hands, signifying, I suppose, we were to go to their country; but we did not understand them. At last, when the ship we were in had got in all her cargo, they made ready with many fearful noises, and we were all put under deck, so that we could not see how they managed the vessel. But this disappointment was the least of my sorrow. The stench of the hold while we were on the coast was so intolerably loathsome, that it was dangerous to remain there for any time, and some of us had been permitted to stay on the deck for the fresh air; but now that the whole ship's cargo were confined together, it became absolutely pestilential. The closeness of the place, and the heat of the climate, added to the number in the ship, which was so crowded that each had scarcely room to turn himself, almost suffocated us. This produced copious perspirations, so that the air soon became unfit for respiration, from a variety of loathsome smells, and brought on a sickness among the slaves, of which many died, thus falling victims to the improvident avarice, as I may call it, of their purchasers. This wretched situation was again aggravated by the galling of the chains, now

become insupportable; and the filth of the necessary tubs, into which the children often fell, and were almost suffocated. The shrieks of the women, and the groans of the dying, rendered the whole a scene of horror almost inconceiveable. Happily perhaps for myself I was soon reduced so low here that it was thought necessary to keep me almost always on deck; and from my extreme youth I was not put in fetters. In this situation I expected every hour to share the fate of my companions, some of whom were almost daily brought upon deck at the point of death, which I began to hope would soon put an end to my miseries. Often did I think many of the inhabitants of the deep much more happy than myself; I envied them the freedom they enjoyed, and as often wished I could change my condition for theirs. Every circumstance I met with served only to render my state more painful, and heighten my apprehensions, and my opinion of the cruelty of the whites. One day they had taken a number of fishes; and when they had killed and satisfied themselves with as many as they thought fit, to our astonishment who were on the deck, rather than give any of them to us to eat, as we expected, they tossed the remaining fish into the sea again, although we begged and prayed for some as well as we could, but in vain; and some of my countrymen, being pressed by hunger, took an opportunity, when they thought no one saw them, of trying to get a little privately; but they were discovered, and the attempt procured them some very severe floggings.

One day, when we had a smooth sea, and moderate wind, two of my wearied countrymen, who were chained together (I was near them at the time), preferring death to such a life of misery, somehow made through the nettings, and jumped into the sea: immediately another quite dejected fellow, who, on account of his illness, was suffered to be out of irons, also followed their example; and I believe many more would very soon have done the same, if they had not been prevented by the ship's crew, who were instantly alarmed. Those of us that were the most active were, in a moment, put down under the deck; and there was such a noise and confusion amongst the people of the ship as I never heard before, to stop her, and get the boat out to go after the slaves. However, two of the wretches were drowned, but they got the other, and afterwards flogged him unmercifully, for thus attempting to prefer death to slavery. In this manner we continued to undergo more hardships than I can now relate; hardships which are inseparable from this accursed trade.—Many a time we were near suffocation, from the want of fresh air, which we were often without for whole days together. This, and the stench of the necessary tubs, carried off many. During our passage I first saw flying fishes, which surprised me very much: they used frequently to fly across the ship, and many of them fell on the deck. I also now first saw the use of the quadrant. I had often with astonishment seen the mariners make observations with it, and I could not think what it meant. They at last took notice of my surprise; and one of them, willing to increase it, as well as to gratify my curiosity, made me one day look through it. The clouds appeared to me to be land, which disappeared as they passed along. This heightened my wonder: and I was now more persuaded than ever that I was in another world, and that every thing about me was magic. At last we came in sight of the island of Barbadoes, at which the whites on board gave a great shout, and made many signs of joy to us. We did not know what to think of this; but as the vessel drew nearer we plainly saw the harbour, and other ships of different kinds and sizes: and we soon anchored amongst them off Bridge Town. Many merchants and planters now came on board, though it was in the evening. They put us in separate parcels, and examined us attentively. They also made us jump, and pointed to the land, signifying we were to go there. We thought by this we should be eaten by these ugly men, as they appeared to us; and, when soon after we were all put down under the deck again, there was much dread and trembling among us, and nothing but bitter cries to be heard all the

night from these apprehensions, insomuch that at last the white people got some old slaves from the land to pacify us. They told us we were not to be eaten, but to work, and were soon to go on land, where we should see many of our country people. This report eased us much; and sure enough, soon after we were landed, there came to us Africans of all languages. We were conducted immediately to the merchant's yard, where we were all pent up together like so many sheep in a fold, without regard to sex or age. As every object was new to me, every thing I saw filled me with surprise. What struck me first was, that the houses were built with bricks, in stories, and in every other respect different from those in I have seen in Africa: but I was still more astonished on seeing people on horseback. I did not know what this could mean; and indeed I thought these people were full of nothing but magical arts. While I was in this astonishment, one of my fellow prisoners spoke to a countryman of his about the horses, who said they were the same kind they had in their country. I understood them, though they were from a distant part of Africa, and I thought it odd I had not seen any horses there; but afterwards, when I came to converse with different Africans, I found they had many horses amongst them, and much larger than those I then saw. We were not many days in the merchant's custody before we were sold after their usual manner, which is this:—On a signal given, (as the beat of a drum), the buyers rush at once into the yard where the slaves are confined, and make choice of that parcel they like best. The noise and clamour with which this is attended, and the eagerness visible in the countenances of the buyers, serve not a little to increase the apprehensions of the terrified Africans, who may well be supposed to consider them as the ministers of that destruction to which they think themselves devoted. In this manner, without scruple, are relations and friends separated, most of them never to see each other again. I remember in the vessel in which I was brought over, in the men's apartment, there were several brothers, who, in the sale, were sold in different lots; and it was very moving on this occasion to see and hear their cries at parting. O, ye nominal Christians! might not an African ask you, learned you this from your God? who says unto you, Do unto all men as you would men should do unto you? Is it not enough that we are torn from our country and friends to toil for your luxury and lust of gain? Must every tender feeling be likewise sacrificed to your avarice? Are the dearest friends and relations, now rendered more dear by their separation from their kindred, still to be parted from each other, and thus prevented from cheering the gloom of slavery with the small comfort of being together and mingling their sufferings and sorrows? Why are parents to lose their children, brothers their sisters, or husbands their wives? Surely this is a new refinement in cruelty, which, while it has no advantage to atone for it, thus aggravates distress, and adds fresh horrors even to the wretchedness of slavery.

Questions

1. Discuss Equiano's experience as a slave in Africa from the time of his capture until he reached the Atlantic.
2. How would Equiano's experience have been different had he been born in 1445 rather than 1745? What does this tell us about the development of the Atlantic slave trade? About the Atlantic World more generally?
3. Describe Equiano's experience on the slave ship during the "middle passage." Do you think his experience was typical or exceptional? In what ways?
4. Equiano wrote that the suffering of the middle passage was "inseparable from this accursed trade." What does he mean? Do you agree or disagree?
5. If Equiano was in fact born in South Carolina rather than in Africa, what might make his account historically valuable nonetheless?

14.3 Benjamin Franklin Reflects on His Life and Times*

The following passage from Benjamin Franklin's Autobiography *suggests some of the changes occurring in eighteenth-century North America, including a growing impulse for consumption and the increasing importance of print media.*

We have an English proverb that says, *"He that would thrive, must ask his wife."* It was lucky for me that I had one as much dispos'd to industry and frugality as myself. She assisted me cheerfully in my business, folding and stitching pamphlets, tending shop, purchasing old linen rags for the papermakers, etc., etc. We kept no idle servants, our table was plain and simple, our furniture of the cheapest. For instance, my breakfast was a long time bread and milk (no tea), and I ate it out of a twopenny earthen porringer, with a pewter spoon. But mark how luxury will enter families, and make a progress, in spite of principle: being call'd one morning to breakfast, I found it in a China bowl, with a spoon of silver! They had been bought for me without my knowledge by my wife, and had cost her the enormous sum of three-and-twenty shillings, for which she had no other excuse or apology to make, but that she thought *her* husband deserv'd a silver spoon and China bowl as well as any of his neighbors. This was the first appearance of plate and China in our house, which afterward, in a course of years, as our wealth increas'd, augmented gradually to several hundred pounds in value. . . .

In 1732 I first publish'd my Almanack, under the name of *Richard Saunders;* it was continu'd by me about twenty-five years, commonly call'd *Poor Richard's Almanac.* I endeavor'd to make it both entertaining and useful, and it accordingly came to be in such demand, that I reap'd considerable profit from it, vending annually near ten thousand. And

*John Bigelow, ed., *Autobiography of Benjamin Franklin* (Philadelphia: J. B. Lippincott & Co., 1868), 210, 235–239.

observing that it was generally read, scarce any neighborhood in the province being without it, I consider'd it as a proper vehicle for conveying instruction among the common people, who bought scarcely any other books; I therefore filled all the little spaces that occurr'd between the remarkable days in the calendar with proverbial sentences, chiefly such as inculcated industry and frugality, as the means of procuring wealth, and thereby securing virtue; it being more difficult for a man in want, to act always honestly, as, to use here one of those proverbs, *it is hard for an empty sack to stand upright.*

These proverbs, which contained the wisdom of many ages and nations, I assembled and form'd into a connected discourse prefix'd to the Almanack of 1757, as the harangue of a wise old man to the people attending an auction. The bringing all these scatter'd counsels thus into a focus enabled them to make greater impression. The piece, being universally approved, was copied in all the newspapers of the Continent; reprinted in Britain on a broad side, to be stuck up in houses; two translations were made of it in French, and great numbers bought by the clergy and gentry, to distribute gratis among their poor parishioners and tenants. In Pennsylvania, as it discouraged useless expense in foreign superfluities, some thought it had its share of influence in producing that growing plenty of money which was observable for several years after its publication.

I considered my newspaper, also, as another means of communicating instruction, and in that view frequently reprinted in it extracts from the Spectator, and other moral writers; and sometimes publish'd little pieces of my own, which had been first compos'd for reading in our Junto. Of these are a Socratic dialogue, tending to prove that, whatever might be his parts and abilities, a vicious man could not properly be called a man of sense; and a discourse on self-denial, showing that virtue was not secure till its practice became a habitude, and was free from the opposition of contrary inclinations. These may be found in the papers about the beginning of 1735.

In the conduct of my newspaper, I carefully excluded all libelling and personal abuse, which is of late years become so disgraceful to our country. Whenever I was solicited to insert any thing of that kind, and the writers pleaded, as they generally did, the liberty of the press, and that a newspaper was like a stage-coach, in which any one who would pay had a right to a place, my answer was, that I would print the piece separately if desired, and the author might have as many copies as he pleased to distribute himself, but that I would not take upon me to spread his detraction; and that, having contracted with my subscribers to furnish them with what might be either useful or entertaining, I could not fill their papers with private altercation, in which they had no concern, without doing them manifest injustice. Now, many of our printers make no scruple of gratifying the malice of individuals by false accusations of the fairest characters among ourselves, augmenting animosity even to the producing of duels; and are, moreover, so indiscreet as to print scurrilous reflections on the government of neighboring states, and even on the conduct of our best national allies, which may be attended with the most pernicious consequences. These things I mention as a caution to young printers, and that they may be encouraged not to pollute their presses and disgrace their profession by such infamous practices, but refuse steadily, as they may see by my example that such a course of conduct will not, on the whole, be injurious to their interests.

In 1733 I sent one of my journeymen to Charleston, South Carolina, where a printer was wanting. I furnish'd him with a press and letters, on an agreement of partnership, by which I was to receive one-third of the profits of the business, paying one-third of the expense. He was a man of learning, and honest but ignorant in matters of account; and, tho' he sometimes made me remittances, I could get no account from him, nor any satisfactory state of our partnership while he lived. On his decease, the business was continued by his widow, who, being born and bred in Holland, where, as I have been inform'd, the knowledge of accounts makes a part of female education, she not only sent me as clear a state as she could find of the transactions past, but continued to account with the greatest regularity and exactness every quarter afterwards, and managed the business with such success, that she not only brought up reputably a family of children, but, at the expiration of the term, was able to purchase of me the printing-house, and establish her son in it.

I mention this affair chiefly for the sake of recommending that branch of education for our young females, as likely to be of more use to them and their children, in case of widowhood, than either music or dancing, by preserving them from losses by imposition of crafty men, and enabling them to continue, perhaps, a profitable mercantile house, with establish'd correspondence, till a son is grown up fit to undertake and go on with it, to the lasting advantage and enriching of the family.

Questions

1. Discuss Franklin's observation about the rise of consumption in his own household. How does this reflect trends in eighteenth-century British America? What does it say about Franklin's understanding of the roles of men and women?
2. Franklin touts the virtue of "industry and frugality." To what end? How does this relate to his earlier remarks about china and silverware?
3. When Franklin advises young printers "not to pollute their presses," what does he mean? What role does he believe printers play in the communities in which they live?

14.4 Slave Advertisements from the *Pennsylvania Gazette*

The Pennsylvania Gazette was published in Philadelphia from 1728 to 1800, flourishing under the ownership of Benjamin Franklin, who bought the paper in 1729. The following three advertisements, published in the Gazette in the 1750s and 1760s, offer African men, women, and children for sale and promise rewards to those who help masters recover escaped slaves.

PENNSYLVANIA GAZETTE, MAY 4, 1758

On Saturday next will be sold at publick Vendue, at the London Coffee house, about Noon, A very strong likely Negroe Boy, about 17 Years old, has had the small pox, understands taking Care of Horses perfectly, can lay Cloth, and wait on Table for a Gentleman Family, and can do every Part of hard Labour. He will be put up at Fifty Pounds, and not under. Enquire of Mr. JUDAH FOULKE.

PENNSYLVANIA GAZETTE, JUNE 14, 1759

Run away from John Lloyd, of Stanford, in the Colony of Connecticut, on the 26th of May last, a Negroe Man Servant, named Cyrus, about Five Feet Nine Inches high, well built, but rather slim waisted, Legs and Feet somewhat large, has lost one or more of his fore Teeth, about 28 or 30 Years of Age, long visaged, very black, active and ingenious in all Sorts of Country business, and is a good Butcher; bred in the Country, speaks good English, and a little French, but stammers when frighted or confused: Carried off with him a brown Irish Camblet Coat, a brown Fustian Vest, one of white Flannel, and one of Calicoe; one Pair of blue Cloth Breeches, one of brown Thickset, one of good Buckskin, and about 30 or 40 Dollars in Money: 'Tis imagined he went off with some Soldiers who deserted from the 48th Regiment, just before they embarked at Boston, as some of them have lately been discovered lurking in these Parts, and are possibly gone to the Westward or Northward. Whoever secures said Negroe in any of his Majesty's Goals, and sends me Word, so that I may have him again, or brings him to me, shall have FIVE POUNDS New-York Money Reward, and all reasonable Charges, paid by JOHN LLOYD, or RICHARD SMITH, in Philadelphia.

N.B. Whoever takes up said Negroe is desired to put him in Irons, and not to trust him out of Sight, unless in a strong Goal; and all Masters of Vessels and others, are cautioned against harbouring or carrying him off, as they will answer it at their Peril. It is supposed said Negroe has a Counterfeit Pass with him.

PENNSYLVANIA GAZETTE, MAY 6, 1762

Just imported from the Coast of Africa, in the Brig Nancy, and to be sold at Wilmington, in New Castle County (where Attendance is given) by Willing, Morris, and Company, OF PHILADELPHIA, ONE Hundred and Seventy fine Gold Coast NEGROES.

N.B. In the West India Islands, where Slaves are best known, those of the Gold Coast are in much greater Esteem, and higher valued, than any others, on Account of their natural good Dispositions, and being better capable of hard Labour.

Questions

1. What role did these advertisements play in the perpetuation of slavery? Why would people pay Franklin and his successors to print these ads?
2. Were publishers like Franklin partly responsible for the suffering of people like Olaudah Equiano? Why or why not?
3. What skills did the advertised slaves possess? It was obviously in a seller's interest to tout the qualities of the people he was selling, but why mention the skills of a runaway slave?
4. From the description in the second advertisement, what tasks do you think the slave named Cyrus performed for John Lloyd or previous masters? How might this description be different if Cyrus had worked in rural Virginia, Carolina, or the Caribbean?

CHAPTER

15

Religion and Society

The British colonies witnessed a series of religious revivals in the middle decades of the eighteenth century. This Great Awakening roiled congregations from New England to Georgia and stirred powerful emotions from the shores of the Atlantic to the far side of the Appalachians. Itinerant preachers traveled throughout an increasingly integrated Anglo-America, filling listeners with fears of damnation and hopes of salvation and antagonizing ministers accused of spiritual inertness. These challenges disrupted habits of deference and obedience that structured colonial social relations. In the aftermath of this period of revival and reaction, early Americans would be left with both a wider array of spiritual choices and a diminished sense of religious unity.

15.1 Jonathan Edwards Speaks of Sin and Salvation*

Minister, theologian, and later president of what would become Princeton University, Jonathan Edwards (1703–1758) was one of the great figures associated with the Great Awakening. His preaching stimulated mid-1730s revivals in Northampton, Massachusetts, and other towns in the Connecticut River Valley, and his written account of events there encouraged revivals elsewhere. His 1741 sermon, "Sinners in the Hands of an Angry God," provides a famous example of the kind of fiery preaching associated with the Awakening.

SINNERS IN THE HANDS OF AN ANGRY GOD.

DEUT. xxxii. 35.

—Their foot shall slide in due time.—

In this verse is threatened the vengeance of God on the wicked unbelieving Israelites, who were

---

*Jonathan Edwards, "Sinners in the Hands of an Angry God," in The Works of President Edwards *(New York: G. & C. & H. Carvill, 1830), vol. 7: 163–164, 168–171, 175–177.*

God's visible people, and who lived under the means of grace; but who, notwithstanding all God's wonderful works towards them, remained (as ver. 28.) void of counsel, having no understanding in them. Under all the cultivations of heaven, they brought forth bitter and poisonous fruit; as in the two verses next preceding the text.—The expression I have chosen for my text, *Their foot shall slide in due time.* . . .

The observation from the words that I would now insist upon is this.—"There is nothing that keeps wicked men at any one moment out of hell, but the mere pleasure of God"—By the *mere* pleasure of God, I mean his *sovereign* pleasure, his arbitrary will, restrained by no obligation, hindered by no manner of difficulty, any more than if nothing else but God's mere will had in the least degree, or in any respect whatsoever, any hand in the preservation of wicked men one moment.— . . .

So that, whatever some have imagined and pretended about promises made to natural men's earnest seeking and knocking, it is plain and manifest, that whatever pains a natural man takes in religion, whatever prayers he makes, till he believes in Christ, God is under no manner of obligation to keep him a moment from eternal destruction.

So that, thus it is that natural men are held in the hand of God, over the pit of hell; they have deserved the fiery pit, and are already sentenced to it; and God is dreadfully provoked, his anger is as great towards them as to those that are actually suffering the executions of the fierceness of his wrath in hell, and they have done nothing in the least to appease or abate that anger, neither is God in the least bound by any promise to hold them up one moment; the devil is waiting for them, hell is gaping for them, the flames gather and flash about them, and would fain lay hold on them, and swallow them up; the fire bent up in their own hearts is struggling to break out: and they have no interest in any Mediator, there are no means within reach that can be any security to them. In short, they have no refuge, nothing to take hold of; all that preserves them every moment is the mere arbitrary will, and uncovenanted, unobliged forbearance of an incensed God.

APPLICATION

The use of this awful subject may be for awakening unconverted persons in this congregation. This that you have heard is the ease of every one of you that are out of Christ.—That world of misery, that lake of burning brimstone, is extended abroad under you. There is the dreadful pit of the glowing flames of the wrath of God; there is hell's wide gaping mouth open; and you have nothing to stand upon, nor any thing to take hold of: there is nothing between you and hell but the air; it is only the power and mere pleasure of God that holds you up:

You probably are not sensible of this; you find you are kept out of hell, but do not see the hand of God in it; but look at other things, as the good state of your bodily constitution, your care of your own life, and the means you use for your own preservation. But indeed these things are nothing; if God should withdraw his hand, they would avail no more to keep you from falling, than the thin air to hold up a person that is suspended in it.

Your wickedness makes you as it were heavy as lead, and to tend downwards with great weight and pressure towards hell; and if God should let you go, you would immediately sink and swiftly descend and plunge into the bottomless gulf, and your healthy constitution, and your own care and prudence, and best contrivance, and all your righteousness, would have no more influence to uphold you and keep you out of hell, than a spider's web would have to stop a fallen rock. Were it not for the sovereign pleasure of God, the earth would not bear you one moment; for you are a burden to it; the creation groans with you; the creature is made subject to the bondage of your corruption, not willingly; the sun does not willingly shine upon you to give you light to serve sin and Satan; the earth does not willingly yield her increase to satisfy your lusts; nor is it willingly a stage for your wickedness to be acted upon; the air does not willingly serve you for breath to maintain the flame of life in your vitals, while you spend your life in the service of God's enemies, God's creatures are good, and were made for men to serve God with, and do not willingly subserve to any other purpose, and groan when they are abused to purposes so directly contrary to their nature and end. And the world would spew you out, were it not for the sovereign hand of him who hath subjected it in hope. There are black clouds of God's wrath now hanging directly over your heads full of the dreadful storm, and big with thunder; and were it not for the restraining hand of God, it would immediately burst forth upon you. The sovereign pleasure of God, for the present, stays his rough wind; otherwise it would come with fury, and your destruction would come like a whirlwind, and you would be like the chaff of the summer threshing floor.

The wrath of God is like great waters that are dammed for the present; they increase more and more, and rise higher and higher, till an outlet is given; and the longer the stream is stopped, the more rapid and mighty is its course, when once it is let looose. It is true, that judgment against your evil works has not been executed hitherto; the floods of God's vengeance have been withheld; but your guilt in the mean time is constantly increasing, and you are every day treasuring up more wrath; the waters are constantly rising, and waxing more and more mighty; and there is nothing but the mere pleasure of God, that holds the waters back, that are unwilling to be stopped, and press hard to go forward. If God should only withdraw his hand from the flood-gate, it would immediately fly open, and the fiery floods of the fierceness and wrath of God, would rush forth with inconceivable fury, and would come upon you with omnipotent power; and if your strength were ten thousand times greater than it is, yea, ten thousand times greater than the strength of the stoutest, sturdiest devil in hell, it would be nothing to withstand or endure it.

The bow of God's wrath is bent, and the arrow made ready on the string, and justice bends the arrow at your heart, and strains the bow, and it is nothing but the mere pleasure of God, and that of an angry God, without any promise or obligation at all, that keeps the arrow one moment from being made drunk with your blood. Thus all you that never passed under a great change of heart, by the mighty power of the Spirit of God upon your souls; all you that were never born again, and made new creatures, and raised from being dead in sin, to a state of new, and before altogether unexperienced light and life, are in the hands of an angry God. However you may have reformed your life in many things, and may have had religious affections, and may keep up a form of religion in your families and closets, and in the house of God, it is nothing but his mere pleasure that keeps you from being this moment swallowed up in everlasting destruction. However unconvinced you may now be of the truth of what you hear, by and by you will be fully convinced of it. Those that are gone from being in the like circumstances with you, see that it was so with them; for destruction came suddenly upon most of them; when they expected nothing of it, and while they were saying, Peace and safety: now they see,

that those things on which they depended for peace and safety, were nothing but thin air and empty shadows.

The God that holds you over the pit of hell, much as one holds a spider, or some loathsome insect over the fire, abhors you, and is dreadfully provoked: his wrath towards you burns like fire; he looks upon you as worthy of nothing else, but to be cast into the fire; he is of purer eyes than to bear to have you in his sight; you are ten thousand times more abominable in his eyes, than the most hateful venomous serpent is in ours. You have offended him infinitely more than ever a stubborn rebel did his prince; and yet it is nothing but his hand that holds you from falling into the fire every moment. It is to be ascribed to nothing else, that you did not go to hell the last night; that you was suffered to awake again in this world, after you closed your eyes to sleep. And there is no other reason to be given, why you have not dropped into hell since you arose in the morning, but that God's hand has held you up. There is no other reason to be given why you have not gone to hell, since you have sat here in the house of God, provoking his pure eyes by your sinful wicked manner of attending his solemn worship. Yea there is nothing else that is to be given as a reason why you do not this very moment drop down into hell.

O sinner! Consider the fearful danger you are in: it is a great furance of wrath, a wide and bottomless pit, full of the fire of wrath, that you are held over in the hand of that God, whose wrath is provoked and incensed as much against you, as against many of the damned in hell. You hang by a slender thread, with the flames of divine wrath flashing about it, and ready every moment to singe it, and burn it asunder; and you have no interest in any Mediator, and nothing to lay hold of to save yourself, nothing to keep off the flames of wrath, nothing of your own, nothing that you ever have done, nothing that you can do, to induce God to spare you one moment. . . .

And now you have an extraordinary opportunity, a day wherein Christ has thrown the door of mercy wide open, and stands in calling and crying with a loud voice to poor sinners; a day wherein many are flocking to him, and pressing into the kingdom of God. Many are daily coming from the east, west, north and south; many that were very lately in the same miserable condition that you are in, are now in a happy state, with their hearts filled with love to him who has loved them, and washed them from their sins in his own blood, and rejoicing in hope of the glory of God. How awful is it to be left behind at such a day! To see so many others feasting, while you are pining and perishing! To see so many rejoicing and singing for joy of heart, while you have cause to mourn for sorrow of heart, and howl for vexation of spirit! How can you rest one moment in such a condition? Are not your souls as precious as the souls of the people at Suffield, where they are flocking from day to day to Christ?

Are there not many here who have lived long in the world, and are not to this day born again? and so are aliens from the commonwealth of Israel, and have done nothing ever since they have lived, but treasure up wrath against the day of wrath? Oh, sirs, your case, in an especial manner, is extremely dangerous. Your guilt and hardness of heart is extremely great. Do you not see how generally persons of your years are passed over and left, (in the present remarkable and wonderful dispensation of God's mercy?) You had need to consider yourselves, and awake thoroughly out of sleep. You cannot bear the fierceness and wrath of the infinite God.—And you; young men, and young women, will you neglect this precious season which you now enjoy, (when so many others of your age are renouncing all youthful vanities, and flocking to Christ?) You especially have now an extraordinary opportunity; but if you neglect it, it will soon be with you as with those persons who spent all the precious days of youth in sin, and are now come to such a dreadful pass in blindness and hardness.—And you, children, who are unconverted, do not you know that you are going down to hell, to bear the dreadful wrath of that God, who is now angry with you every day and every night? Will you be content to be the children of the devil, when so many other children in the land are converted, and are become the holy and happy children of the King of kings?

And let every one that is yet of Christ, and hanging over the pit of hell, whether they be old men and women, or middle aged, or young people, or little children, now hearken to the loud calls of God's word and providence. This acceptable year of the Lord, a day of such great favours to some, will doubtless be a day of as remarkable vengeance to others. Men's hearts harden, and their guilt increases apace at such a day as this, if they neglect their souls; and never was there so great danger of such persons being given up to hardness of heart and blindness of mind. God seems now to be hastily gathering in his elect in all parts of the land; and probably the greater part of adult persons that ever shall be saved, will be brought in now in a little time, and that it will be as it was on the great out-pouring of the Spirit upon the Jews in the apostles' days; the election will obtain, and the rest will be blinded. If this should be the case with you, you will eternally curse this day, and will curse the day that ever you was born, to see such a season of the pouring out of God's Spirit, and will wish that you had died and gone to hell before you had seen it. Now undoubtedly it is, as it was in the days of John the Baptist, the axe is in an extraordinary manner laid at the root of the trees, that every tree which brings not forth good fruit, may be hewn down and cast into the fire.

Therefore, let every one that is out of Christ, now awake and fly from the wrath to come. The wrath of Almighty God is now undoubtedly hanging over a great part of this congregation: Let every one fly out of Sodom: "Haste and escape for your lives, look not behind you, escape to the mountain, lest you be consumed."

Questions

1. Characterize Edwards's view of human nature. What fate could most people expect?
2. What route away from damnation did Edwards offer? What opportunity did the revivals offer? How much control over their own destiny did Edwards think individuals had?
3. What made this sermon so effective?
4. How does the sermon compare with Winthrop's "Modell of Christian Charity"?

15.2   Franklin Contemplates Whitefield*

From reading one famous sermon, we move to reading one reaction to a famous preacher. Historians sometimes speak of George Whitefield as a kind of Elvis Presley of the Great Awakening. In the following passage from Franklin's autobiography, Franklin considers the Whitefield phenomenon.

In 1739 arrived among us from Ireland the Reverend Mr. Whitefield, who had made himself remarkable there as an itinerant preacher. He was at first permitted to preach in some of our churches; but the clergy, taking a dislike to him, soon refus'd him their pulpits, and he was oblig'd to preach in the fields. The multitudes of all sects and denominations that attended his sermons were enormous, and it was matter of speculation to me, who was one of the number, to observe the extraordinary influence of his oratory on his hearers, and how much they admir'd and respected him, notwithstanding his common abuse of them, by assuring them they were naturally *half beasts and half devils*. It was wonderful to see the change soon made in the manners of our inhabitants. From being thoughtless or indifferent about religion, it seem'd as if all the world were growing religious, so that one could not walk thro' the town in an evening without hearing psalms sung in different families of every street.

And it being found inconvenient to assemble in the open air, subject to its inclemencies, the building of a house to meet in was no sooner propos'd, and persons appointed to receive contributions, but sufficient sums were soon receiv'd to procure the ground and erect the building, which was one hundred feet long and seventy broad, about the size of Westminster Hall; and the work was carried on with such spirit as to be finished in a much shorter time than could have been expected. Both house and ground were vested in trustees, expressly for the use of any preacher of any religious persuasion who might desire to say some-

thing to the people at Philadelphia; the design in building not being to accommodate any particular sect, but the inhabitants in general; so that even if the Mufti of Constantinople were to send a missionary to preach Mohammdanism to us, he would find a pulpit at his service.

Mr. Whitefield, in leaving us, went preaching all the way thro' the colonies to Georgia. The settlement of that province had lately been begun, but, instead of being made with hardy, industrious husbandmen, accustomed to labor, the only people fit for such an enterprise, it was with families of broken shop-keepers and other insolvent debtors, many of indolent and idle habits, taken out of the jails, who, being set down in the woods, unqualified for clearing land, and unable to endure the hardships of a new settlement, perished in numbers, leaving many helpless children unprovided for. The sight of their miserable situation inspir'd the benevolent heart of Mr. Whitefield with the idea of building an Orphan House there, in which they might be supported and educated. Returning northward, he preach'd up this charity, and made large collections, for his eloquence had a wonderful power over the hearts and purses of his hearers, of which I myself was an instance.

I did not disapprove of the design, but, as Georgia was then destitute of materials and workmen, and it was proposed to send them from Philadelphia at a great expense, I thought it would have been better to have built the house here, and brought the children to it. This I advis'd; but he was resolute in his first project, rejected my counsel, and I therefore refus'd to contribute. I happened soon after to attend one of his sermons, in the course of which I perceived he intended to finish with a collection, and I silently resolved he should get nothing from me. I had in my pocket a handful of copper money, three or four silver dollars, and five pistoles in gold. As he proceeded I began to soften, and concluded to give the coppers. Another stroke of his oratory made me asham'd of that, and determin'd me to give the silver; and he finish'd so admirably, that I empty'd my pocket wholly into the collector's dish, gold and all. At this sermon there was also one

---

*Bigelow, ed., *Autobiography of Benjamin Franklin*, 251–258. John Bigelow, ed., *Autobiography of Benjamin Franklin*, (Philadelphia: J. B. Lippincott & Co., 1868), 251–239.

of our club, who, being of my sentiments respecting the building in Georgia, and suspecting a collection might be intended, had, by precaution, emptied his pockets before he came from home. Towards the conclusion of the discourse, however, he felt a strong desire to give, and apply'd to a neighbour, who stood near him, to borrow some money for the purpose. The application was unfortunately [made] to perhaps the only man in the company who had the firmness not to be affected by the preacher. His answer was, "*At any other time, Friend Hopkinson, I would lend to thee freely; but not now, for thee seems to be out of thy right senses.*"

Some of Mr. Whitefield's enemies affected to suppose that he would apply these collections to his own private emolument; but I, who was intimately acquainted with him (being employed in printing his Sermons and Journals, etc.), never had the least suspicion of his integrity, but am to this day decidedly of opinion that he was in all his conduct a perfectly *honest man;* and methinks my testimony in his favour ought to have the more weight, as we had no religious connection. He us'd, indeed, sometimes to pray for my conversion, but never had the satisfaction of believing that his prayers were heard. Ours was a mere civil friendship, sincere on both sides, and lasted to his death.

The following instance will show something of the terms on which we stood. Upon one of his arrivals from England at Boston, he wrote to me that he should come soon to Philadelphia, but knew not where he could lodge when there, as he understood his old friend and host, Mr. Benezet, was removed to Germantown. My answer was, "You know my house; if you can make shift with its scanty accommodations, you will be most heartily welcome." He reply'd, that if I made that kind offer for Christ's sake, I should not miss of a reward. And I returned, "*Don't let me be mistaken; it was not for Christ's sake, but for your sake.*" One of our common acquaintance jocosely remark'd, that, knowing it to be the custom of the saints, when they received any favour, to shift the burden of the obligation from off their own shoulders, and place it in heaven, I had contriv'd to fix it on earth.

The last time I saw Mr. Whitefield was in London, when he consulted me about his Orphan House concern, and his purpose of appropriating it to the establishment of a college.

He had a loud and clear voice, and articulated his words and sentences so perfectly, that he might be heard and understood at a great distance, especially as his auditories, however numerous, observ'd the most exact silence. He preach'd one evening from the top of the Court-house steps, which are in the middle of Market-street, and on the west side of Second-street, which crosses it at right angles. Both streets were fill'd with his hearers to a considerable distance. Being among the hindmost in Market-street, I had the curiosity to learn how far he could be heard, by retiring backwards down the street towards the river; and I found his voice distinct till I came near Front-street, when some noise in that street obscur'd it. Imagining then a semicircle, of which my distance should be the radius, and that it were fill'd with auditors, to each of whom I allow'd two square feet, I computed that he might well be heard by more than thirty thousand. This reconcil'd me to the newspaper accounts of his having preach'd to twenty-five thousand people in the fields, and to the antient histories of generals haranguing whole armies, of which I had sometimes doubted.

By hearing him often, I came to distinguish easily between sermons newly compos'd, and those which he had often preach'd in the course of his travels. His delivery of the latter was so improv'd by frequent repetitions that every accent, every emphasis, every modulation of voice, was so perfectly well turn'd and well plac'd, that, without being interested in the subject, one could not help being pleas'd with the discourse; a pleasure of much the same kind with that receiv'd from an excellent piece of musick. This is an advantage itinerant preachers have over those who are stationary, as the latter can not well improve their delivery of a sermon by so many rehearsals.

His writing and printing from time to time gave great advantage to his enemies; unguarded expressions, and even erroneous opinions, deliver'd in preaching, might have been afterwards explain'd or qualifi'd by supposing others that might have accompani'd them, or they might have been deny'd; but *litera scripta manet.* Critics attack'd his writings violently, and with so much appearance of reason as to diminish the number of his votaries and prevent their encrease; so that I am of opinion if he had never written any thing, he would have left behind him a much more numerous and important sect, and his reputation might in that case have been still growing, even after his death, as there being nothing of his writing on which to found a censure and give him a lower character, his proselytes would be left at liberty to feign for him as great a variety of excellences as their enthusiastic admiration might wish him to have possessed.

Questions

1. Why did other preachers dislike Whitefield?
2. Why did so many people attend Whitefield's sermons? What made his preaching so captivating?
3. What made it possible for Whitefield to preach in so many places? For his writings to circulate?
4. What attitude does Franklin evince concerning religious revivalism? Concerning Whitefield?

15.3 Hannah Heaton's Conversion Experience*

The learned eloquence of Edwards and Franklin was unrepresentative of most eighteenth-century Americans. The comparatively unrefined diary of "Connecticut farm woman" Hannah Heaton (1721–1793) provides a rare but invaluable window into how ordinary people experienced events such as the Great Awakening.

Now after a while i went over to new haven in the fall just before that great work of god began which was in the year 1741. There i heard mr tennant and mr whitefeild preach which awakened me much. Mr whitefeild laid down the marks of an unconverted person. O strange it was such preaching as i never heard before. Dont you said he when you are at the house of god long service should be over that your minds may be about your worldly conserns and pleasures. Is it not a wearines to you said he if one days serving god is so wearisom to you. How could you endure to be in heaven with him forever where nothing but praises are. He said if you was carried to heaven in this condition the first prayer you would make would be that yould might go into hell for that would be more agreeable to your natures. O thot i i have found it a wearines to me many a time over and over again. Then i began to think my nature must be changed but how to attain it i knew not. When i was coming from meeting to my quarters

which was about 6 miles my company began to worry me to sing. I put them of till i feard they would be offended. At last i sang some verses about a contented mi[]. I thot that was better than to sing a song but o they little thot how i felt. It was hard work for me to sing i felt in such distress in my mind but i went to frollicks all winter and stifeld the conviction i had of its being a soul ruining sin. I was much for fine cloaths and fashons. In the spring in may i went to middletown to keep election. One of the days while i was there i was at a tavern in a frolic. Then there come in a young man from long island belonging to the society that i did and told me how the work of god was carried on there and of several of my mates that was converted. My sister elisabeth also sent a letter. I trembled when i read it. She said her soul magnifyed the lord her spirit rejoysed in god her saviour. Her sighs was turned into songs the comforter is come. I had a strong impression upon my mind to go home which i did in a few days. As soon as i got into my fathers house young people come in and began to talk. Sister elisabeth began to cry over me because i had no intrest in christ. That i wonderd at but the next morning father examined me and i was forst to tell

[p. 4]

my experiences as wel as i could. He told me when i had done what a dreadful condition i was in. It took hold of my heart. I kept going to the meetings and was more and more concerned. And o what

---

*Barbara E. Lacey, ed., *The World of Hannah Heaton: The Diary of an Eighteenth-Century New England Farm Woman* (DeKalb: Northern Illinois University Press, 2003), 6–14.

crying out there was among the people what shall i do to be saved. Now it began to be whispered in my ear it is too late too late you had better hang your self. And when i see a convenient place o how it would strike me. I was afraid to go alone to pray for fear i should see the devil. Once when i was on the ground away alone at prayer trying to give up all to christ in great distres of soul i thot i felt the devil twitch my cloaths. I jumpt up and run in fixed with terror and o how did i look at the winders in the night to see if christ was not coming to judgment. O how i did invi toads or any creature that had no souls to perish eternally. Many a time i kneeled down to pray and my mouth was as it were stopt and i did vent out my anguish with tears and groans and a few broken speches. Now it cut me to think how i had spent my precious time in vanity and sin against god. My not regarding the sabbath no more was bitter to me now. I thot sometime i could be willing to burn in the flames of fire if i could be delivered from the anger of god or appease his wrath that was out against me. Now my heart and soul and all nature was set against nay loathed the way of salvation by christ. And it seemed to me if i should give up all to christ he would send me directly to hell. Sometimes my heart would quarrel with god thus why he knows i cant convert myself why then dont he convert me. Now i thot if i knew of any place on earth where i could hide from god o how would i run to it. But them words was terrible to me. In amos 9 chap read to the 5th verce— tho they dig into hell tho they climb up to heaven tho they hide in the top of carmel tho they be hid in the bottom of the sea &. O how it cut me to think i could not get away from god but appear before him i must and i lived in daily expectation of it. Now sometimes it would be cast into my mind thus you need not be so conserned you are not so great a sinner as some are some have murdered and done dreadful things but you pray and go to meeting and god will not have a heart to send you to hell. This i thot was the devil trying to beat me of. True i had no sence of the justice of god all this while nor could i think what conversion was unles it was this & i fancied it was. I thot a person must be in a sort of trance and be carried to heaven and see wonders there and then be brought back again—but now them words was terror to me

[p. 5]

where it says god is angry with the wicked every day and the day cometh that shall burn as an oven and all the proud & them that do wickedly shall be stubble and the day cometh that shall burn them up saith the lord of hosts that it shall leave them neither root nor branch. Some years back i use to pray for many things that i was afraid god would hear and answer them but now i cryed for mercy mercy mercy lord o save me from thy wrath o save me from hell. This my soul wanted. I did not want to go to heaven. I thot i should be tired of singing praises nay i felt a hatred against it and it seemd impossible to me that christ was willing to save me that i could not believe. I was such a loathsome sinner and he such a holy god sometimes i thot i was willing but he was not. I could hear of others finding mercy but o how it would strike me for i feard greatly that while others was taken i should be left. Now the promises in the scriptures was terror to me for i thot they belonged to the children of god. I had no part in them and i felt such an enmity against the way of salvation by christ. I could see no way to escape damnation. Now i began to feel like one lost in the woods. I knew not what to do nor what course to take for my heart began to grow hard. Now i could not cry and pray as before when i thot of hell. It did not terrify me as before it use to. Me thot i envied the very devils for they believed and trembled but i did not. Nothing now semd to help me. I grew worse and worse. I thot it must be a gone case with me and i thot so the more because father never spoke one word to me about my soul in particular as i remember after he first examined me till after i had found comfort which was about three weeaks after. It being in the year 1741 june 20 i was then i suppose in my twentieth year. It was the lord's day. I went to our separate meeting in the school house. They i think read a book of joseph allins but i felt so stupid and hardned and shut up that i could not hear nor keep my mind upon anything. I thot if i could have purchased a world by it i could not shed a tear. Now i feard i was hardend & seald down to damnation with a witnes (jarico was straitly shut up when the walls fell).

[p. 6]

for i had lost all my consern and felt a heart of stone. Meeting being done i got away to go home. I thot i would not go to the night meeting which was to be at thomas sanfords for it would do me no good. I remember in the lot as i went i see strawberries and these thots past through my mind. I may as wel go to picking strawberries now as not its no matter what i do its a gone case with me. I fear i have committed the unpardonable sin and now herdned but as i was going home i considered at last. I turned and went to meeting. Soon after meeting began the power of god come down. Many were crying out the other side of the room what shall i do to be saved. I was immediately moved to pres through the multitude and went to them. A great melting of soul come up on me. I wept bitterly and pleaded hard for mercy mercy. Now i was brought to vew the justice of god due to me for my sin. It made me tremble my knees smote together then i thot of belshezer when he see the hand writing against him. It seemd to me i was a sinking down into hell. I thot the flor i stood on gave way and i was just a going but then i began to resign and as i resind my distres began to go of till i was perfectly easy quiet and calm. I could say lord it is just if i sink in to hell. I felt for a few moments like a creature dead, I was nothing i could do nothing nor i desired nothing. I had not so much as one desire for mercy left me but presently i heard one in the room say seek and you shall find come to me all you that are weary and heavy laden and i will give you rest. I began to feel a thirsting after christ and began to beg for mercy free mercy for jesus sake. Me thot i see jesus with the eyes of my soul stand up in heaven. A lovely god man with his arms open ready to receive me his face was full of smiles he lookt white and ruddy and was just such a saviour as my soul wanted every way suitable for me. O how it melted my heart to think he had been willing all this while to save me but i was not willing which i never believed before now. I cryed from the very heart to think what a tender herted savior i had been refusing how often i turned a deaf ear to his gracious calls and invitations. All that had kept me from him was my will. Jesus appeared altogether lovely to me now.

[p. 7]

My heart went out with love and thankfulness and admiration. I cryed why me lord and leave so many. O what a fulnes was their in christ for others if they would come and give up their all to him. I went about the room and invited people to come to him.

June 20 1741. About nine oclock in the evening in the twentyeth year of my age. I got a way to go home from meeting. It was about a mile but o me thot the moon and stars seemd as if they praisd god with me. It seemd as if i had a new soul & body both. I felt a love to gods children. I thot that night that jesus was a precious jesus. It being late our famile went to bed but i sat up and walked about the chamber. It seemd as if i could not sleep while the heavens was fild with praises and singing. That night i was brought into the lords prayr. Before i was afraid to say it but now it seemd sweet to call god father. Yea my heart could say every word in it. Ah what sweet peace i felt while my mind was swallowed up in that scripture matthew 5 from 9 to the 14. And now methinks i must stop & offer a song of praise and admiration to that god that has done great things for me.

1. The soul that doth a jesus seek; his cries & groans he heard; hagers son cried under a shrub; and water did appear
2. He hears the ravens when they cry; & will he not hear me for whom he shed his own hearts blood: & love beyond degree
3. Does god the little sparrows feed: my soul heel feast much more because for me he suffered all in his purple gore
4. May i now with hannah of old: her soul was in distres god gave her what she did desire: and what she did request
5. Abide my jesus now with me: and let me feel thy love; my soul then like a minadab: with swift delight shall move

[p. 8]

6. My soul now longs to be with thee: o let me see my christ my soul shall then be free from sin: when i am in paradise

7. O when shall i eat of those grapes: that grow on ashcols hill

8. O come my jesus take me up that i may have my fill

9. My jesus he is cald a rock: on which my soul does rest; hees cald the blest emanuel: which my soul does feast

10. Hosanna to the sacred three: with praises singing loud to him who sits upon the throne: beyond the sterry clouds

11. O land me on the eternal shores: my jesus to behold those crowned heads that dazel bright: beyond the shining gold

12. O there they are quite free from sin: thave got the victory ore death and hell ore sorrow sin; triumphing gloriously

13. O the sweet musick that is heard: in heavens courts above
O there they sing most gloriously: of jesus dying love

14. Blest saints do there see eye to eye: in glorious liberty there i shall be from sinning free: to all eternity

15. Sorrow for sin here almost makes:my heart to rend asunder there i shall have nothing to do: but praise & love & wonder

16. O there they sing to christ their king; while i sit mourning here there they rejoyce with heart & voice: while i am prest with fear

17. O glorious jesus how i long: to get fast hold of thee to twine my heart & never part: threw a vast eternity

[p. 9]

18. O love amazing love indeed: o soul aluring love o love is heaven fild with love: o lovely place indeed

19. O how i long to wing away: to that supernal throng who swim in seas of boundles joys eternity along

20. O what a blessed happy place: are saints in glory crownd o there they sing to christ their king: with one eternal sound

21. The wicked there from troubling cease: the weary are at rest o there they swim in seas of love: and lean on jesus breast

22. Oppression there cant never come: to trouble or molest there i shall see my jesus dear: and be forever blest

23. There cherubims and ceraphims: stretch forth their charming wings o there they talk of nothing else: but lovely glorious things

24. In thee i trust & come i must: i long to be with thee and there to sing to christ my king: to all eternitee

25. behold behold our jesus comes; with beauty in his eyes to bless his saints here on this earth: and sinners to surprise

26. I long to have an angels tongue: that i might sing aloud to him who shines upon a throne: above the starry cloud

27. When i lay open to gods wrath he said peace and be still the blessed dove comes from above: the ollive in her bill

28. Wonder of wonders lovely lord: to set thy love on me i know the only reason was: thy love alone was free

29. Halaluiah halaluiah: to christ who come to dye for sinful me to set me free: from sin and misery

Hannah Heaton

[p. 10]

Now when i first found comfort i felt as if all my sins was gone. It seemd as if i had not one left and who could have made me believe but that i should feel so always. But o in a short time i began to feel a wicked heart and it was cast into my mind that if i went to heaven i should certainly commit sin and be sent down to hell like the fallen angels. I was in sore distres not being acquainted with those scriptures that proves the perceverance of the saints. Wel i knew not what to do. At last i told my father what distressing thots i had. His answer was: child he whom christ loves he loves to the end. Here the lord helpt me i was distrest with it no more. Soon after i had a sweet time of refreshing come from the presence of the lord. About this time i heard mr pasons of lime preach from them words—i am the way the truth and the life. I was fild with the love of christ. Then i heard young mr jud preach my soul travelled for sinners. In the meantime we believed there was one converted. Then i heard mr youngs of southold preach. I believe the house was fild with the power of god. My heart rejoyced in god my saviour but not long after i got into the dark so that i hated prayer. I felt enmity in my heart against the dealings of god. Now i began to think i was not converted. These thots was cast into my mind that if god would keep in the dark not to pray to him but o free mercy brought me near again to god. I had many sweet revivals but after a while my soul was dejected again and i was talking with some christians about my stupidity. I said i wanted to see hell and see if it would not move me to praise the lord and that night i had a vew in my sleep of hell. Me thot i was by the side of a great mountain and there was a hollow or cave in the mountain. Me thot i see it full of burning flames like a gloing oven. Me thot i see a man in it which i very well knew and the devil in the shape of a great snake all on a

[p. 11]

flame with his sting out ran violently at the man and seemd to aim at the mans mouth. I knew he was a wicked prophane man so i awoke with a great sence of the dreadful state of the wicked and wrasled with god in prayer and felt distrest for them that their souls might be converted. O the condecention of the great god towards dust & ashes. Them words was imprest upon my mind behold i come quickly even so come lord jesus. Now I heard mr deavenport of southold preach II sermons. I felt the power of gods spirit almost all the while. I believe also the power of god was visible in the assemblyes sinners crying out for mercy for their souls some saints a praising god some exorting and praying over poor sinners. Sometimes mr deavenport would cry out with a great voice above the multitude and say come away come away to the lord jesus. One night after meeting mr deavenport come to me and warned me not to marry an unconverted man and told me them schriptures that speakes against it. Oh poor me here i rebelled as i shall shew by and by (now i began to see more and more that the world flesh

and devil was against me) I remember one night i sat by the fire my mother and sister was with me. These words come with power to me—i will shew thee how great things thou shalt suffer for my name sake. I spoke and told them of it that i must suffer for christ. I had sweet vews of the love of god. My heart burnt with love to christ. I felt resind to suffer for jesus. Ah what a glory and lovelynes i see in it. If he stands by to suffer for him me thot was the sweetest of all. The most contrary to nature of all duties so brings more honour to the lord than other graces. They that suffer with him shall rein with him but after a while i got something dejected in my mind. O my cruel sins that pull me from my god. I went mourning till one day i was at meeting and there was some christian indians wonderfully fild. It affected my heart to think the set time to favour the poor heathen was come. O how wofully have they been neglected by us that had the byble but o what have we been better than christian heathen. It made me weep till my bodily strength was weakned. O to vew the condecention of god.

[p. 12]

About this time i had many sweet manifestations of the love of god in christ which i thot i should never forget. Now after a while i felt sin'rage i felt a wicked proud heart which made me loath myself and weep bitterly. Methinks i was now like the disciples that did not know jesus when he walked on the water to them but thot it was a spirit and cryed out. My soul thirsted for the sweet love of god. I went to a night meting the power of god come down. A great number was struck sinners crying out saints praising and praying. I hant skill nor time to write what a meeting that was. My soul seemd on the mount. I vewd the promist land. Them works was sweet to me—the winter is past the rain is over and gone the flowers appear the time of the singing of birds is come the voice of the turtle is heard in the land. Also this was a good word to me—they that trust in the lord shall be as mount zion which cannot be moved. Glory to my god bless his name o my soul o let me live to thy glory. One day i saw some indians who was under concern my heart was moved for them. Those words come with power to me—behold the fig tree and all the trees when they shoot forth ye know that summer is nigh. Me thot i see the signs of the lovely day of judgment approaching the heathen coming into the kingdom i prayed hard for christles souls. O why me why me lord and leave so many. O vile me and lovely jesus. This lasted not a great while before i was troubled again with sin. It seemd as if i had nothing nor was nothing but sin from the crown of my head to the soles of my feet no clean part in me. I felt a body of death. I would say to myself o my sins that naild jesus to the cursed tree and o my sins that peirce him still my heart was ready to burst with grief. O how many times did i plead and weep before the lord. This grieving and mourning for sin and for the want of a new pardon seald by the comforter lasted a considerable time till one night i had given to me a spirit of prayr for the comfortable presence

[p. 13]

of god. I went to bed. I had vews that night of christs coming to judgment a glorious day a dreadful day. Next day i felt a calm serene mind. Glory to god in the highest for peace on earth and good will towards men.

Questions

1. How does Heaton's reaction to charismatic preachers compare with Franklin's?
2. What does Heaton's diary suggest about the way audiences received sermons such as Edwards's "Sinners in the Hands of an Angry God"?
3. Describe the stages of Heaton's conversion.
4. What was the place of Indians in her theological worldview? How does her view compare with Rowlandson's and Dustan's? If it differs, why?
5. How could critics or supporters of the revivals have used Heaton's diary to support their positions?
6. How might this diary differ if Heaton were older? Male? An African-American slave? A praying Indian?

15.4 Itinerant Preacher James Davenport Provokes the Wrath of Established Clergy*

If Edwards and Whitefield were among the stars of the Great Awakening, James Davenport (1716–1757) was one of its incendiaries. Like Edwards a brilliant student at Yale, Davenport was ordained the minister of the Southold, Long Island Congregational Church in 1738. Davenport later felt inspired to try to emulate the achievements of figures like Whitefield, and he began his own itinerant preaching in 1740. His conduct sparked controversy, inciting the anger of established traditionalists who condemned his itinerancy, his accusations against other clergymen, and his highly emotional method of preaching. In the following document, a chastised Davenport apologizes for his "misguided Zeal."

THE REV. MR. *DAVENPORT'S* RETRACTIONS

Altho' I don't question at all, but there is great Reason to bless God for a *glorious and wonderful Work of his Power and Grace* in the *Edification* of his Children, and the *Conviction* and *Conversion* of Numbers in *New-England*, in the *neighbouring Governments* and *several other Parts*, within a few Years past; and believe that the Lord hath favoured me, tho' most unworthy, with several others of his Servants, in granting special Assistance and Success; the Glory of all which be given to JEHOVAH, to whom alone it belongs:

Yet after frequent Meditation and Desires that I might be enabled to apprehend Things

---

*James Davenport, *The Reverend Mr. James Davenport's Consession & Retractions* (Boston: 1744), 3–8.

justly, and, I hope I may say, mature Consideration I am now fully convinced and persuaded that
several Appendages to *this glorious Work* are no
essential Parts thereof, but of a *different* and
contrary Nature and Tendency; *which Appendages* I
have been in the Time of the Work very industrious in and instrumental of promoting, by a misguided Zeal: being further much influenced in the
Affair by the *false Spirit*; which, un observed by
me, did (as I have been brought to see since)
prompt me to *unjust Apprebensions* and *Misconduct*
in *several Articles*; which have been great Blem-
ishes to the Work of God, very grievous to some
of God's Children, no less ensnaring and corrupting to others of them, a sad Means of many Persons questioning the Work of God, concluding
and appearing against it, and of the hardening of
Multitudes in their Sins, and an awful Occasion of
the Enemies blaspheming the right Ways of the
Lord; and withal very offensive to that God,
before whom I would lie in the Dust, prostrate in
deep Humility and Repentance on this Account,
imploring Pardon for the Mediator's Sake, and
thankfully accepting the Tokens thereof.

The *Articles*, which I especially refer to, and
would in the most public Manner *retract*, and
warn others against, are these which follow, *viz.*

I. The Method I us'd for a considerable
Time, with Respect to some yea many *Ministers* in
several Parts, in openly *exposing such as I fear'd or
thought unconverted, in public Prayer or otherwise*:
herein making my private Judgment, (in which
also I much suspect I was mistaken in several
Instances, and I believe also that my Judgment
concerning several, was formed rashly and upon
very slender Grounds.) I say making my private
Judgment, the Ground of public Actions or Conduct; offending, as I apprehend (altho' in the
Time of it ignorantly) against the *ninth Commandment*, and such other Passages of Scripture, as are
similar; yea, I may say, offending against the Laws
both of Justice and Charity: Which Laws were
further broken,

II. By my *advising and urging to such Separations* from *those Ministers*, whom I treated as above,
as I believe may justly be called rash, unwar-

rantable, and of sad and awful Tendency and Consequence. And here I would ask the Forgiveness
of those Ministers, whom I have injured in both
these Articles.

III. I confess I have been much led astray by
following Impulses or Impressions as a Rule of Conduct, whether they came with or without a Text of
Scripture; and my neglecting also duly to observe
the Analog of Scripture: I am persuaded this was
a great Means of corrupting my Experiences and
carrying me off from the Word of God, and a
great Handle, which the false *Spirit* has made use
of with Respect to a Number, and me especially.

IV. I believe further that I have done much
Hurt to Religion by *encouraging private Persons to
a ministerial and authoritative* Kind or *Method of
exhorting*; which is particularly observable in
many such being much puft up and *falling into the
Snare of the Devil*, while many others are thus
directly prejudic'd against the Work.

V. I have Reason to be deeply humbled that I
have not been duly careful to endeavour to
remove or prevent Prejudice, (where I now
believe I might then have done it consistently
with Duty) which appear'd remarkable in the
Method I practis'd, of *singing with others in the
Streets* in Societies frequently.

I would also penitently confess and bewail my
great Stiffness in retaining these *aforesaid Errors* a
great while, and Unwillingness to examine into
them with any Jealousy of their being Errors, not
withstanding the friendly Counsels and Cautions
of real Friends, especially in the Ministry.

Here may properly be added a Paragraph or
two, taken out of a *Letter from me* to Mr. *Barber*
at *Georgia*; a *true Copy* of which I gave Consent
should be publish'd lately at *Philadelphia*; "——I
would add to what Brother *T*——hath "written
on the awful Affair of Books and "Cloaths at *New-
London*, which affords Grounds "of deep and lasting Humiliation; I was to "my Shame be it
spoken, the Ringleader in "*that horrid Action*; I
was, my dear Brother, "under the powerful Influence of the "*false Spirit* almost one whole Day
together, and Part "of several Days. The Lord
shewed me after "wards that the Spirit I was then

acted by was "in it's Operations void of true inward Peace, "laying the greatest Stress on Externals, neglect- "ing the Heart, full of Impatience, Pride and "Arrogance; altho' I thought in the Time of "it, that 'twas the Spirit of God in an high "Degree; awful indeed! my Body especially "my Leg much disorder'd at the same Time, "which Satan and my evil Heart might make "some Handle of.———"

And now may the holy wise and good God, be pleas'd to guard and secure me against *such Errors* for the future, and stop the Progress of those, whether Ministers or People, who have been corrupted by my Words or *Example* in any of the above mention'd Particulars; and if it be his holy Will, bless *this public Recantation* to this Purpose. And Oh! may he grant withal, that such as by Reason of the aforesaid *Errors and Misconduct* have entertained unhappy Prejudices against Christianity in general, or the late glorious Work of God in particular, may by this Account learn to distinguish the *Appendage* from the *Substance or Essence*, that which is *vile* and *odious* from that which is *precious, glorious* and *divine* and thus be entirely and happily freed from all those Prejudices refer'd to, and this in infinite Mercy through Jesus Christ: and to these Requests may all God's Children, whether Ministers or others say, *Amen*.

July 28. 1744.

James Davenport.

P.S. In as much as a Number, who have fallen in with and promoted the *aforesaid Errors* and *Misconduct*, and are not alter'd in their Minds, may be prejudic'd against this *Recantation*, by a Supposition or Belief, that I came into it by Reason of Desertion or Dulness and Deadness in Religion: It seems needful therefore to signify, what I hope I may say without boasting, and what I am able thro' pure rich Grace to speak with Truth and Freedom; that for *some Months* in the Time of my coming to the *abovesaid Conclusions* and *Retractations*, and since I have come through Grace to them; I have been favoured a great Part of the Time, with a sweet *Calm and Serenity of Soul and Rest in God*, and sometimes with special and remarkable Refreshments of Soul, and these more free from corrupt Mixtures than formerly: *Glory to God alone.*
J. D.

Questions

1. Why did Davenport's conduct trouble the Boston and Charles-Town pastors? How did their reaction to his preaching compare with Heaton's?
2. How did the reactions of leading figures in New England to the excesses of the Great Awakening compare with the reactions of their predecessors to the Salem witch trials and Anne Hutchinson's prayer meetings? Had he still been alive, what might Cotton Mather have said about Heaton's visions of Satan and Davenport's ruminations about the role of the "false Spirit"?
3. What did the pastors mean by "Enthusiasm"?
4. What caused Davenport to concede and retract?
5. What constituted legitimate and reliable religious authority in mid-eighteenth-century Anglo-America?

15.5 Whitefield Reproves and Exhorts Slaveholders*

The Great Awakening raised again the question of masters' religious responsibilities toward their slaves.

*George Whitefield, "To the Inhabitants of Maryland, Virginia, North and South-Carolina, Concerning Their Negroes," in *Three Letters from the Reverend Mr. G. Whitefield* (Philadelphia, 1740), 13–16.

In the following document, published in 1740, George Whitefield condemns masters who do not teach Christianity to their slaves and warns them of the consequences should they fail to take this responsibility seriously.

LETTER III.

To the Inhabitants of Maryland, Virginia, North *and* South-Carolina.

As I lately passed through your Provinces in my Way hither, I was sensible touched with a Fellow-feeling of the Miseries of the poor Negroes. Could I have preached more frequently amongst you, I should have delivered my Thoughts in my publick Discourses; but as my Business here required me to stop as little as possible on the Road, I have no other Way to discharge the Concern which at present lies upon my Heart, than by sending you this Letter: How you will receive it I know not; whether you will accept it in Love, or be offended with me, as the Master of the Damsel was with *Paul*, for casting the Evil Spirit out of her, when he saw the Hope of his Gain was gone; I am uncertain. Whatever be the Event, I must inform you in the Meekness and Gentleness of *Christ*, that I think God has a Quarrel with you for your Abuse of and Cruelty to the poor Negroes. Whether it be lawful for Christians to buy Slaves, and thereby encourage the Nations from whom they are bought, to be at perpetual War with each other, I shall not take upon me to determine; sure I am, it is sinful, when bought, to use them as bad, nay worse, than as though they were Brutes; and whatever particular Exceptions there may be (as I would charitably hope there are some) I fear the Generality of you that own Negroes, are liable to such a Charge; for your Slaves, I believe, work as hard if not harder than the Horses whereon you ride.

These, after they have done their Work, are fed and taken proper Care of; but many Negroes when wearied with Labour in your Plantations, have been obliged to grind their own Corn after they return home.

Your Dogs are caress'd and fondled at your Tables: But your Slaves, who are frequently stiled Dogs or Beasts, have not an equal Privilege. They are scarce permitted to pick up the Crumbs which fall from their Masters Tables. Nay, some, as I have been informed by an Eye-Witness, have been, upon the most trifling Provocation, cut with Knives, and had Forks thrown into their Flesh— Not to mention what Numbers have been given up to the inhuman Usage of cruel Task Masters, who by their unrelenting Scourges have ploughed upon their Backs, and made long Furrows, and at length brought them even to Death itself.

It's true, I hope there are but few such Monsters of Barbarity suffered to subsist amongst you. Some, I hear, have been lately executed in *Virginia* for killing Slaves, and the Laws are very severe against such who at any Time murder them.

And perhaps it might be better for the poor Creatures themselves, to be hurried out of Life, than to be made so miserable, as they generally are in it. And indeed, considering what Usage they commonly meet with, I have wondered, that we have not more Instances of Self-Murder among the Negroes, or that they have not more frequently rose up in Arms against their Owners. *Virginia* has once, and *Charlestown* more than once been threatned in this Way.

And tho' I heartily pray God they may never be permitted to get the upper Hand; yet should such a Thing be permitted by Providence, all good Men must acknowlege the Judgment would be just.—For is it not the highest Ingratitude, as well as Cruelty, not to let your poor Slaves enjoy some Fruits of their Labour?

When, passing along, I have viewed your Plantations cleared and cultivated, many spacious Houses built, and the Owners of them faring sumptuously every Day, my Blood has frequently almost run cold within me, to consider how many of your Slaves had neither convenient Food to eat or proper Raiment to put on, notwithstanding most of the Comforts you enjoy were solely owing to their indefatigable Labours.—The Scripture says, *Thou shalt not muzzle the Ox that treadeth out the Corn.* Does God take Care of Oxen? And will he not take care of the Negroes also? Undoubtedly he will.—Go to now, ye rich Men, weep and howl for your Miseries that shall come upon you! Behold the Provision of the poor Negroes, which have reaped down your Fields, which is by you denied them, crieth; and the Cries of them which reaped, are entered into the Ears of the Lord of *Sabaoth*! We have a remarkable Instance of God's taking cognizance of, and avenging the Quarrel of poor Slaves, 2 *Sam*. 21. 1. *Then there was a Famine in the Days of David, three Years, Year after Year;* and David *enquired of the Lord. And the Lord answered, it is for* Saul *and his bloody House, because he slew the* Gibeonites."—Two Things are here very remarkable.—First, that these *Gibeonites* were only Hewers of Wood and Drawers of Water, or in other Words, Slaves like yours. Secondly, That this Plague was sent by God many Years after the Injury, the Cause of the Plague, was committed.—And for what End was this and such like Examples recorded in Holy Scripture? Without doubt, for our Learning, upon whom the Ends of the World are come—For God is the same to Day as he was Yesterday, and will continue the same forever. He does not reject the Prayer of the poor and destitute, nor disregard the Cry of the meanest Negroes! The Blood of them spilt for these many Years in your respective Provinces, will ascend up to Heaven against you. I wish I could say, it would speak better Things than the Blood of *Abel*. But this is not all—Enslaving or misusing their Bodies would, comparatively speaking, be an inconsiderable Evil, was proper Care taken of their Souls. But I have great reason to believe, that most of you, on Purpose, keep your Negroes ignorant of Christianity; or otherwise, why are they permitted thro' your Provinces, openly to prophane the Lord's Day, by their Dancing, Piping and such like? I know the general Pretence for this Neglect of their Souls is, That teaching them Christianity would make them proud and consequently unwilling to submit to Slavery: But what a dreadful Reflection is this on your Holy Religion? What blasphemous Notions must those that make such an Objection have of the Precept of Christianity? Do you find any one Command in the Gospel, that has the least Tendency to make People forget their relative Duties? Do you not read that Servants, and as many as are under the Yoke of Bondage, are required to be subject, in all

lawful Things, to their Masters; and that not only to the good and gentle, but also to the froward? Nay, may I not appeal to your own Hearts, whether deviating from the Laws of Jesus Christ, is not the Cause of all the Evils and Miseries Mankind now universally groan under, and of all the Vices we find both in ourselves and others? Certainly it is.—And therefore, the Reason why Servants generally prove so bad is, because so little Care is taken to breed them up in the Nurture and Admonition of the Lord.—But some will be so bold perhaps as to reply, *That a few of the Negroes have been taught Christianity, and, notwithstanding, have been remarkably worse than others.* But what Christianity were they taught? They were baptized and taught to read and write: and this they may do, and much more, and and yet be far from the Kingdom of God; for there is a vast Difference between civilizing and christianizing an Negroe. A Black as well as a white Man may be civilized by outward Restraints, and afterwards break thro' those Restraints again. But I challenge the whole World to produce a single Instance of a Negroe's being made a thorough Christain, and thereby made a worse Servant. It cannot be.—But farther, if teaching Slaves Christianity has such a bad Influence upon their Lives, why are you generally desirous of having your Children taught? Think you they are any way better by Nature than the poor Negroes? No, in no wise. Blacks are just as much, and no more, conceived and born in Sin, as White Men are. Both, if born and bred up here, I am persuaded, are naturally capable of the same Improvement.—And as for the grown Negroes, I am apt to think, whenever the Gospel is preach'd with Power amongst them, that many will be brought effectually home to God. Your present and past bad Usage of them, however ill-designed, may thus far do them good, as to break their Wills, increase the Sense of their natural Misery, and consequently better dispose their Minds to accept the Redemption wrought out for them, by the Death and Obedience of Jesus Christ. God has, not long since, been pleased to make some of the Negroes in *New-England*, Vessels of Mercy; and some of them, I hear, have been brought to cry out, *What shall we do to be saved?* in the Province of *Pennsylvania*. Doubtless there is a Time, when the Fullness of the Gentiles will come in: And then I believe, if not before, these despised Slaves will find the Gospel of Christ to be the Power of God to their Salvation, as well as we.—But I know all Arguments to prove the Necessity of taking Care of your Negroes Souls, though never so conclusive, will prove ineffectual, till you are convinced of the Necessity of securing the Salvation of your own. That you yourselves are not effectually convinced of this, I think is too notorious to want Evidence.—A general Deadness as to divine Things, and not to say a general Prophaneness, is discernible both in Pastors and People.

Most of you are without any teaching Priest.—And whatever Quantity of Rum there may be, yet I fear but very few Bibles are annually imported into your different Provinces.—God has already began to visit for this as well as other wicked Things.—For near this two Years last past, he has been in a remarkable Manner contending with the People of *South-Carolina*. Their Houses have been depopulated with the Small Pox and Fever, and their own Slaves have rose up in Arms against them.—These Judgments are undoubtedly sent abroad, not only that the Inhabitants of that, but of other Provinces, should learn Righteousness: And unless you all repent, you all must in like Manner expect to perish.—God first generally corrects us with Whips; if that will not do, he must chastize us with Scorpions.—A foreign Enemy is now threatning to invade you, and nothing will more provoke God, to give you up as a Prey into their Teeth, than Impentience and Unbelief,—Let these be removed, and the Sons of Violence shall not be able to hurt you:—No; your

Oxen shall be strong to labour; there shall be no Decay of your People by epidemical Sickness; no Leading away into Captivity from abroad, and no Complaining in your Streets at Home:—Your Sons shall grow up as young Plants, and your Daughters be as the polished Corners of the Temple; and to sum up all Blessings in one,—Then shall the LORD be your GOD.—That you may be the People who are in such a happy Case, is the earnest Prayer of

Your Sincere Well-Wisher and Servant in Christ, *Savannah*,
Jan. 23, 1739, 40.

G. WHITEFIELD

Questions:

1. Was Whitefield arguing against slavery or merely against the mistreatment of slaves? Characterize his ideas about race and about the relation between race and Christianity.

2. What reasons did Whitefield offer slave owners for why they should mend their ways and teach Christianity to their slaves? What temporal benefits did he hold out to them? What punishments if they continued as before?

3. Imagine Whitefield reading the Chapter 7 selections from William Byrd's *Secret Diary*, Byrd reading Whitefield's letter, and the two of them having a chat. How might the conversation go?

4. Whitefield used income from a slave-worked plantation to sustain an orphanage in Georgia. How does this knowledge affect your interpretation of this document?

16 French North America

Although relatively few in number, French colonists claimed large portions of North America against the pretensions of competing European empires. Supported by an extensive network of Indian alliances, French settlements stretched from the St. Lawrence River, through the Great Lakes, and down the Mississippi River to Louisiana. Building on the work of seventeenth-century traders and missionaries, and relying on shared interests with Indian peoples, the French established a viable (if never very profitable) colonial enterprise in North America, with furs and fish driving the Canadian economy and plantation agriculture struggling to flower in Louisiana. The following documents reflect the diversity of settlement patterns and survival strategies found in eighteenth-century French North America.

16.1 Indian Diplomacy in New France*

Following the brutal warfare of the 1680s and 1690s, French and Algonquian diplomats arranged a conference to secure existing French-Indian alliances and to establish peace with the Iroquois. During the deliberations, which occurred in the summer of 1701 in Montreal, French and Indian representatives articulated a wide range of interests using the symbolic diplomacy that had come to dominate intercultural relations in New France and its borderlands. The following account of these negotiations, drawn from the report of a French participant, was first published by the Jesuit historian Pierre de Charlevoix in 1744.

On the following days there were several private councils, in which the Iroquois complained of the distrust shown of their sincerity, and they added

that if their prisoners were restored, there should be no reason to repent confiding in their word. The Chevalier de Callieres showed them the injustice of their complaints, and detailed all the grounds for being uneasy in regard to them. Still, as he wished to put them entirely in the wrong, he promised to lay their request before the interested nations, and to support it. He did so in fact, and as he had already discussed this question with the Rat, who advised satisfying them, and as many others left it to his prudence, he resolved to run the risk, and the event justified him.

Disease had from the first prevailed among the Indians, and many of the most important men had already died.

The Hurons had suffered most severely, and imagined it was the effect of witchcraft thrown on them to destroy them all. Some even went to Father Anjelran to beg him to induce the priests of the Seminary, to remove the pretended spell.

---

*Pierre de Charlevoix, *History and General Description of New France* (New York, 1870), vol. 5: 148–154.

On this occasion God showed in a striking manner that he is Lord of men's hearts. In spite of the rumor spread by evil-minded men, that the French had gathered so many nations among them only for their ruin, there was not a pagan who did not desire baptism before he died, nor a Christian who did not die in sentiments worthy of Christianity.

This affliction however obliged the Governor-General to hasten the conclusion of the treaty. All had been agreed upon in the private audiences, and it only remained to sign the articles and proclaim Peace. He appointed the 4th of August for the last general assembly, and wished nothing omitted to give the transaction all possible celebrity. A great plain without the city was selected: a double fence one hundred and twenty-eight feet long by seventy-two wide was erected, the space between being six feet. At one end there was a covered hall, twenty-nine feet long and almost square, for the ladies and all the fashion of the town. The soldiers were drawn up around, and within the enclosure thirteen hundred Indians were arranged in fine order.

De Champigny, the Chevalier de Vaudreuil and the principal officers surrounded the Governor-General, who occupied a position so as to be seen and heard by all. He spoke first, and stated briefly, that he had the preceding year established peace among all the nations; but that as of all those of the north and west, only some Hurons and Ottawas appeared at Montreal, he had notified the others that he wished them to send him deputies, so that when all were assembled he might solemnly take the hatchet from their hands, and declare to all who recognized him as their Father, that henceforward he wished to be sole arbiter of their disputes; that they should then forget all the past, and place all their interests in his hands: that he would always render them exact justice; that they must be wearied enough of war which had been of no advantage to them, and when once they had tasted the delights of peace, they would thank him infinitely for all he had done to secure it for them.

When he had ceased speaking, one of the Fathers Bigot repeated to the Abénaquis in their language what he had just said; Nicholas Perrot did the same to the Miamis, Illinois and other Western Indians; Father Garnier to the Hurons, Father Bruyas to the Iroquois and Father Anjelran to the Ottawas and Algonquins. All applauded with great acclamations, making the air echo far and wide; belts were then distributed to all the chiefs, who rose in succession, and, with a grave step, attired in their long fur robes, went up and presented their slaves to the Governor-General, with belts of which they explained the tenor.

All spoke with much intelligence, and some even with greater politeness than was expected from Indian orators; but they took great care to explain above all that they were sacrificing their private interests to a desire for peace, and that this desire was induced only by their extreme anxiety to gratify their Father; that they should therefore be regarded with the greater consideration, as they stood in no dread of the Iroquois, and relied less on any sincere return from them. There was not one to whom the Governor-General did not make some graceful remarks, and as they presented the captives to him, he placed them in the hands of the Iroquois.

But this ceremony, serious as it was to the Indians, was a kind of comedy to the French, who were greatly entertained. Most of the deputies, especially those of the more remote tribes, were dressed and adorned in a manner quite grotesque, contrasting curiously with the grave and serious demeanor they affected.

The Algonquin chief was dressed as a Canadian voyageur, and had his hair put up as a cock's head, with a red feather forming the crest and hanging down behind. He was a tall young man, perfect in form, the same who, at the head of thirty warriors of his tribe, of his own age or younger, had defeated the Iroquois party near Catarocouy, when Black Kettle, the great Onondaga war-chief, was killed, a vigorous action, which, more than any other, drove the cantons to seek peace with the French and their allies. This brave advanced towards de Callieres with a noble and unembarrassed air, and said: "Father, I am not a man of council; but I always hear your voice; you have made peace, and I forget the past."

Onanguicé, the Pottowatamie chief, wore the skin of the head of a young bull, the horns hanging over his ears. He was regarded as a man of much sense and mildness, and strongly attached to the French. Indeed he spoke very well and courteously.

The Fox had his face painted red, and wore on his head an old rusty wig, profusely powdered and ill combed, which gave him an air at once frightful and ridiculous. As he had neither hat nor cap, and wished to salute the Governor-General in French style, he took off his wig. A great outburst of laughter followed, which did not disconcert him, for he doubtless took it as applause. He said that he had brought no prisoners, because those whom he had taken, had all escaped. "Moreover," he added, "I have never had any great quarrel with the Iroquois, though I am much involved with the Sioux."

The chief of the Sault Indians had a plume like a kind of band around his head in the shape of a halo; he said that he had already set his prisoners at liberty, and he begged his Father to grant him his friendship. The domiciliated Iroquois and the Abénaquis spoke last, evincing great zeal for the increase of the French colony. They more easily carried persuasion, as during the whole war they had proved by their actions, what they then attested in words.

The other deputies having ended their compliments, all eyes turned to the orator of the Cantons, who had not yet spoken. He said only two words, to the purport that those whose word he bore, would soon convince all the nations of their injustice in distrusting them; that they would convince the most incredulous of their fidelity, sincerity and respect for their common Father.

The treaty of peace was then brought, which was signed by thirty-eight deputies, then the great calumet of peace. The Chevalier de Callieres smoked it first, de Champigny after him, then de Vaudreuil, and all the chiefs and deputies, each in turn. The *Te Deum* was then chanted. Last of all appeared great kettles, in which three oxen had had been boiled; each one was served in his place without noise or confusion, and all passed gaily. It ended with the firing of squibs and cannon, and in the evening with an illumination and feux de joie.

On the 6th de Callieres assembled the deputies of the upper tribes and told them that though he had grounds for not being entirely satisfied with some of them, he would, in consideration of peace, overlook the irregularity of their conduct; that he pardoned the Sacs for the death of the Frenchman whom they had killed, because they had agreed to surrender the murderer to Mr. de Courtemanche, and their deputy had offered satisfactory reparation.

The Illinois deputies had died on the way, and in their last moments had confided the interests of their nation to Onanguicé. The Governor-General ordered this chief to notify the Illinois that if they should again plunder the French, he would not be satisfied as now with the restitution of the goods taken by the robbers. He spoke in the same tone to some others, who were subject to the same fault, and gave them all to understand that they should find him a Father, but a Father no longer disposed to allow them to swerve from the path of duty, as heretofore.

He then distributed to them the King's presents. The Ottawas asked for Father Anjelran and Nicholas Perrot, and he told them that he would willingly accede to it; that the missionary was disposed to follow them; but on condition that they should correspond with greater docility to his instructions. Their deputy also conjured him not to permit brandy to be carried anywhere, because that liquor troubled the mind, and could only lead the young men to excesses, which would infallibly entail deplorable results; all present applauded this request, except a Huron chief, who was a great drunkard, and had already taken steps to carry home a supply of liquor.

The next day the Governor-General gave audience to the deputies of the cantons. After impressing on them that they would be inexcusable and deserving of all his anger, if they refused to set their prisoners free, he ordered them to deliver these captives to Joncaire, who was to set out with them, pledging his word, that if some of these prisoners then wished to return to their country, they should be free to do so, as had just happened with the prisoners whom the Hurons had brought to him.

He also recommended them to remain neutral between the French and English, should war be renewed between those two nations, as would apparently soon be the case. He showed them that it was utterly contrary to their interests to allow the English to build forts in their towns and on their rivers, and he assured them that he would never permit it. He was very anxious that they should ask him for Jesuit missionaries, convinced that their presence was the most effectual means of retaining them in a strict neutrality; but he deemed it inexpedient to allude to it, the Court having given him no instructions on the point, and the indirect means which he employed to bring them to it, succeeding to his desire.

He last of all gave them explanations in regard to the post he wished to found at Detroit, whither, in June, he had sent the Sieur de la Motte Cadillac with about one hundred men and a Jesuit, in order to attract the Indians there. He had used all expedition to get this convoy off before the Iroquois deputies came, lest, in case they begged him to defer the execution of his project, his refusal should prove an obstacle to the peace; whereas, the thing done, he would be more justified in not yielding. They in fact adduced difficulties enough to embarrass him, had he not gone so far, but he made them relish his reasons, the chief being, that the English, had he not anticipated them, would undoubtedly have attempted to settle there, and thus drawn the war into the heart of the country.

The Mohawks had not sent deputies to the Congress as they had promised, and the General expressed his resentment to the deputies of the other cantons; but the latter had scarcely left Montreal before the Mohawks arrived. They made their excuses and signed the treaty. Some time after, Joncaire arrived with very few prisoners, the others absolutely refusing to follow him. It was believed, or the authorities chose to pretend to believe, that this was no fault of the Iroquois, and there the matter rested.

Questions

1. What are the key issues at this conference? Whose interests are addressed most directly and whose are ignored?

2. Discuss the importance of French-English relations to these deliberations. What did the French want from the Iroquois with respect to the English? Why?

3. What role did the French governor wish to play in relations among various Indian peoples? What metaphors did he use to evoke the relationship he favored? How did the Indians respond?

4. Identify examples of symbolic diplomacy in these negotiations. What items were exchanged, and what was their meaning? What were the roles of symbolic language, gestures, and costume? Did French or Indian culture dominate the proceedings?

5. Discuss the impact of disease on these deliberations. How did the French and Indians perceive its effects?

6. Describe the audience at the peace conference. How did French spectators view the events? Why?

16.2 Traveler Pehr Kalm Describes French Society in the St. Lawrence Valley*

Swedish-born naturalist Pehr (or Peter) Kalm traveled thousands of miles through British and French North America from 1748 to 1751. The following selection from his published account of these journeys contains his observations of French society along the St. Lawrence River in Canada, where he spent several months in the summer and fall of 1749.

August the 1st. THE governor-general of *Canada* commonly resides at *Quebec*; but he frequently goes to *Montreal*, and generally spends the winter there. In summer he chiefly resides at *Quebec*, on account of the king's ships, which arrive there

---

*Peter Kalm, *Travels into North America* trans. John Reinold Forster (London, 1771). vol. 3:68, 70–75, 77–82, 90–92, 97–108, 153–154, 162–164, 178–185.

during that season, and bring him letters, which he must answer; besides other business which comes in about that time. During his residence in *Montreal* he lives in the castle, as it is called, which is a large house of stone, built by governor-general *Vaudreuil*, and still belonging to his family, who hire it to the king. The governor-general *de la Galissoniere* is said to like *Montreal* better than *Quebec*, and indeed the situation of the former is by far the more ageeable one. . . .

They commonly give one hundred and fifty livres a year to a faithful and diligent footman, and to a maid-servant of the same character one hundred livres. A journeymen to an artist gets three or four livres a day, and a common labouring man gets thirty or forty sols a day. The scarcity of labouring people occasions the wages to be so high; for almost every body finds it so easy to set up as a farmer in this uncultivated country, where he can live well, and at a small expence, that he does not care to serve and work for others.

Montreal is the second town in *Canada*, in regard to size and wealth; but it is the first on account of its fine situation, and mild climate. Somewhat above the town, the river St. *Lawrence* divides into several branches, and by that means forms several islands, among which the isle of *Montreal* is the greatest. It is ten *French* miles long, and near four broad, in its broadest part. The town of *Montreal* is built on the eastern side of the island, and close to one of the most considerable branches of the river St. *Lawrence*; and thus it receives a very pleasant, and advantageous situation. The town has a quadrangular form, or rather it is a rectangular parallelogram, the long and eastern side of which extends along the great branch of the river. On the other side it is surrounded with excellent corn-fields, charming meadows, and delightful woods. It has got the name of *Montreal* from a great mountain, about half a mile westwards of the town, and lifting its head far above the woods. Mons. *Cartier*, one of the first *Frenchmen* who surveyed *Canada* more accurately, called this mountain so, on his arrival in this island, in the year 1535, when he visited the mountain, and the *Indian* town *Hoshelaga* near it. The priests who, according to the Roman catholic way, would call every place in this country after

some saint or other, called *Montreal, Ville Marie*, but they have not been able to make this name general, for it has always kept its first name. It is pretty well fortified, and surrounded with a high and thick wall. On the east side it has the river St. *Lawrence*, and on all the other sides a deep ditch filled with water, which secures the inhabitants against all danger from the sudden incursions of the enemy's troops. However, it cannot long stand a regular siege, because it requires a great garrison, on account of its extent; and because it consists chiefly of wooden houses. Here are several churches, of which I shall only mention that belonging to the friars of the order of St. *Sulpitius*, that of the Jesuits, that of the *Franciscan* friars, that belonging to the nunnery, and that of the hospital; of which the first is however by far the finest, both in regard to its outward and inward ornaments, not only in this place, but in all *Canada*. The priests of the seminary of St. *Sulpitius* have a fine large house, where they live together. The college of the *Franciscan* friars is likewise spacious, and has good walls, but it is not so magnificent as the former. The college of the Jesuits is small, but well built. To each of these three buildings are annexed fine large gardens, for the amusement, health, and use of the communities to which they belong. Some of the houses in the town are built of stone, but most of them are of timber, though very neatly built. Each of the better sort of houses has a door towards the street with a seat on each side of it, for amusement and recreation in the morning and evening. The long streets are broad and strait, and divided at right angles by the short ones: some are paved, but most of them very uneven. The gates of the town are numerous; on the east side of the town towards the river are five, two great and three lesser ones; and on the other side are likewise several. The governor-general of *Canada*, when he is at *Montreal*, resides in the castle, which the government hires for that purpose of the family of *Vaudreuil*; but the governor of *Montreal* is obliged to buy or hire a house in town; though I was told, that the government contributed towards paying the rents.

In the town is a *Nunnery*, and without its walls half a one; for though the last was quite ready, however, it had not yet been confirmed by the pope. In the first they do not receive every girl that offers herself; for their parents must pay about five hundred *ecus*, or crowns, for them. Some indeed are admitted for three hundred ecus, but they are obliged to serve those who pay more than they. No poor girls are taken in.

The king has erected a hospital for sick soldiers here. The sick person there is provided with every thing he wants, and the king pays twelve sols every day for his stay, attendance, &*C.* The surgeons are paid by the king. When an officer is brought to this hospital; who is fallen sick in the service of the crown, he receives victuals and attendance gratis: but if he has got a sickness in the execution of his private concerns, and comes to be cured here, he must pay it out of his own purse. When there is room enough in the hospital, they likewise take in some of the sick inhabitants of the town and country. They have the medicines, and the attendance of the surgeons, gratis, but must pay twelve sols per day for meat, &*C.*

Every Friday is a market-day, when the country people come to the town with provisions, and those who want them must supply themselves on that day, because it is the only market-day in the whole week. On that day likewise a number of *Indians* come to town, to sell their goods, and buy others. . . .

August the 2d. Early this morning we left *Montreal*, and went in a *bateau* on our journey to *Quebec*, in company with the second major of *Montreal*, M. *de Sermonville*. We fell down the river St. *Lawrence*, which was here pretty broad on our left; on the north-west side was the isle of *Montreal*, and on the right a number of other isles, and the shore. The isle of *Montreal* was closely inhabited along the river; and it was very plain, and the rising land near the shore consisted of pure mould, and was between three or four yards high. The woods were cut down along the river-side, for the distance of an *English* mile. The dwelling-houses were built of wood, or stone, indiscriminately, and white-washed on the out-side. The other buildings, such as barns, stables, &*C.* were all of wood. The ground next to the river was turned either into corn-fields, or meadows. Now and then we perceived churches on both sides of the river, the steeples of which were generally on that side of the church, which looked towards the river, because they are not obliged here to put the steeples on the west end of the churches. Within six *French* miles of *Montreal* we saw several islands of different sizes on the river, and most of them were inhabited; and if some of them were without houses on them, they were sometimes turned into corn-fields, but generally into meadows. We saw no mountains, hills, rocks, or stones to-day, the country being flat throughout, and consisting of pure mould.

All the farms in *Canada* stand separate from each other, so that each farmer has his possessions entirely distinct from those of his neighbour. Each church, it is true, has a little village near it; but that consists chiefly of the parsonage, a school for the boys and girls of the place, and of the houses of tradesmen, but rarely of farm-houses; and if that was the case, yet their fields were separated. The farm-houses hereabouts are generally built all along the rising banks of the river, either close to the water or at some distance from it, and about three or four *arpens* from each other. To some farms are annexed small orchards; but they are in general without them; however, almost every farmer has a kitchen-garden.

I have been told by all those who have made journies to the southern parts of *Canada*, and to the river *Missisippi*, that the woods there abound with peach-trees, which bear excellent fruit, and that the *Indians* of those parts say, that those trees have been there since times immemorial.

The farm-houses are generally built of stone, but sometimes of timber, and have three or four rooms. The windows are seldom of glass, but most frequently of paper. They have iron stoves in one of the rooms, and chimnies in the rest. The roofs are covered with boards. The crevices and chinks are filled up with clay. The other buildings are covered with straw.

There are several *Crosses* put up with the road side, which is parallel to the shores of the river. These crosses are very common in *Canada*, and are put up to excite devotion in the travellers. They are made of wood, five or six yards high, and proportionally broad. In that side which looks towards the road is a square hole, in which they place an image of our Saviour, the cross, or of the holy Virgin, with the child in her arms; and before that they put a piece of glass, to prevent its being spoiled by the weather. Those crosses which are not far from churches, are very much adorned, and they put up about them all the instruments which they think the *Jews* employed in crucifying our Saviour, such as a hammer, tongs, nails, a flask of vinegar, and perhaps many more than were really made use of. A figure of the cock, which crowed when *St. Peter* denied our Lord, is commonly put at the top of the cross.

The country on both sides was very delightful to day, and the fine state of its cultivation added greatly to the beauty of the scene. It could really be called a village, beginning at *Montreal*, and ending at *Quebec*, which is a distance of more than one hundred and eighty miles; for the farmhouses are never above five arpens, and sometimes but three, asunder, a few places excepted. The prospect is exceedingly beautiful, when the river goes on for some miles together in a strait line, because it then shortens the distances between the houses, and makes them form exactly one continued village.

All the women in the country, without exception, wear caps of some kind or other. Their jackets are short, and so are their petticoats, which scarce reach down to the middle of their legs; and they have a silver cross hanging down on the breast. In general they are very laborious; however, I saw some, who, like the *English* women in the colonies, did nothing but prattle all the day. When they have any thing to do within doors, they (especially the girls) commonly sing songs, in which the words *Amour* and *Cœur* are very frequent. In the country it is usual, that when the husband receives a visit from persons of rank, and dines with them, his wife stands behind and serves him; but in the towns, the ladies are more distinguished, and would willingly assume an equal, if not a superior, power to their husbands. When they go out of doors they wear long cloaks, which cover all their other clothes, and are either grey, brown, or blue. The men sometimes make use of them, when they are obliged to go into the rain.

The women have the advantage of being in a *deshabille* under these cloaks, without any body's perceiving it.

We sometimes saw wind-mills near the farms. They were generally built of stone, with a roof of boards, which, together with its flyers, could be turned to the wind occasionally. . . .

As we went on, we saw several churches of stone, and often very well built ones. The shores of the river are closely inhabited for about three quarters of an *English* mile up the country; but beyond that the woods and the wilderness encrease. All the rivulets falling into the river St. *Lawrence* are likewise well inhabited on both sides. I observed throughout *Canada*, that the cultivated lands ly only along the river St. *Lawrence*, and the other rivers in the country, the environs of towns excepted, round which the country is all cultivated and inhabited within the distance of twelve or eighteen *English* miles. The great islands in the river are likewise inhabited.

The shores of the river now became higher, more oblique and steep, however they consisted chiefly of earth. Now and then some rivers or great brooks fall into the river St. *Lawrence*, among which one of the most considerable is the *Riviere Puante*, which unites on the south-east side with the St. *Lawrence*, about two *French* miles below *Trois Rivieres*, and has on its banks, a little way from its mouth, a town called *Becancourt* which is wholly inhabited by *Abenakee Indians*, who have been converted to the *Roman catholic* religion, and have *Jesuits* among them. At a great distance, on the north-west side of the river, we saw a chain of very high mountains, running from north to south, elevated above the rest of the country, which is quite flat here without any remarkable hills.

Here were several lime-kilns along the river; and the lime-stone employed in them is broke in the neighbouring high grounds. It is compact and grey, and the lime it yield is pretty white.

The fields here are generally sown with wheat, oats, maize, and pease. Gourds and water-melons are planted in abundance near the farms. . . .

August the 6th. *Quebec*, the chief city in *Canada*, lies on the western shore of the river St. *Lawrence*, close to the water's edge, on a neck of land, bounded by that river on the east side, and by the river St. *Charles* on the north side; the mountain, on which the town is built, rises still higher on the south side, and behind it begin great pastures, and the same mountain likewise extends a good way westward. The city is distinguished into the lower and the upper. The lower lies on the river, eastward of the upper. The neck of land, I mentioned before, was formed by the dirt and filth, which had from time to time been accumulated there, and by a rock which lay that way, not by any gradual diminution of the water. The upper city lies above the other, on a high hill, and takes up five or six times the space of the lower, though it is not quite so populous. The mountain, on which the upper city is situated, reaches above the houses of the lower city, not withstanding the latter are three or four stories high, and the view, from the palace, of the lower city (part of which is immediately under it) is enough to cause a swimming of the head. There is only one easy way of getting to the upper city, and there part of the mountain has been blown up. This road is very steep, notwithstanding it is made winding and serpentine. However, they go up and down it in carriages, and with waggons. All the other roads up the mountain are so steep, that it is very difficult to climb to the top by them. Most of the merchants live in the lower city, where the houses are built very close together. The streets in it are narrow, very rugged, and almost always wet. There is likewise a church, and a small market-place. The upper city is inhabited by people of quality, by several persons belonging to the different offices, by tradesmen, and others. In this part are the chief buildings of the town, among which the following are worthy particular notice.

I. The *Palace* is situated on the west or steepest side of the mountain, just above the lower city. It is not properly a palace, but a large building of stone, two stories high, extending north and south. On the west side of it is a court-yard, surrounded partly with a wall, and partly with houses. On the east side, or towards the river, is a gallery as long as the whole building, and about two fathom broad, paved with smooth flags, and included on the outsides by iron rails, from whence the city and the river exhibit a charming prospect. This gallery serves as a very agreeable walk after dinner, and those who come to speak with the governor-general wait here till he is at leisure. The palace is the lodging of the governor-general of *Canada*, and a number of soldiers mount the guard before it, both at the gate and in the court-yard; and when the governor, or the bishop, comes in or goes out, they must all appear in arms, and beat the drum. The governor-general has his own chapel where he hears prayers; however, he often goes to mass at the church of the *Recolets*, which is very near the palace.

II. THE *Churches* in this town are seven or eight in number, and all built of stone.

1. The *Cathedral* church is on the right hand, coming from the lower to the upper city, somewhat beyond the bishop's house. The people were at present employed in ornamenting it. On its west side is a round steeple, with two divisions, in the lower of which are some bells. The pulpit, and some other parts within the church, are gilt. The seats are very fine.

2. The *Jesuits* church is built in the form of a cross, and has a round steeple. This is the only church that has a clock, and I shall mention it more particularly below.

3. The *Recolets* church is opposite the gate of the palace, on the west side, looks well, and has a pretty high pointed steeple, with a division below for the bells.

4. The church of the *Ursulines* has a round spire.

5. The church of the hospital.

6. The bishop's chapel.

7. The church in the lower city was built in 1690, after the town had been delivered from the *English*, and is called *Notre Dame de la Victoire*. It has a small steeple in the middle of the roof, square at the bottom, and round at the top.

8. The little chapel of the governor-general, may likewise be ranked amongst these churches.

III. The bishop's house is the first, on the right hand, coming from the lower to the upper town. It is a fine large building, surrounded by an extensive courtyard and kitchen-garden on one side, and by a wall on the other.

IV. The college of the Jesuits, which I will describe more particularly. It has a much more noble appearance, in regard to its size and architecture, than the palace itself, and would be proper for a palace if it had a more advantageous situation. It is about four times as large as the palace, and is the finest building in town. It stands on the north side of a market, on the south side of which is the cathedral.

V. The house of the Recolets lies to the west, near the palace and directly over against it, and consists of a spacious building, with a large orchard, and kitchen-garden. The house is two stories high. In each story is a narrow gallery with rooms and halls on one, or both sides.

VI. The *Hôtel de Dieu*, where the sick are taken care of, shall be described in the sequel. The nuns, that serve the sick, are of the *Augustine* order.

VII. The house of the clergy is a large building, on the north-east side of the cathedral. Here is on one side a spacious court, and on the other, towards the river, a great orchard, and kitchen-garden. Of all the buildings in the town none has so fine a prospect as that in the garden belonging to this house, which lies on the high shore, and looks a good way down the river. The Jesuits on the other hand have the worst, and hardly any prospect at all from their college; nor have the Recolets any fine views from their house. In this building all the clergy of *Quebec* lodge with their superior. They have large pieces of land in several parts of *Canada*, presented to them by the government, from which they derive a very plentiful income.

VIII. The convent of the *Ursuline* nuns shall be mentioned in the sequel.

These are all the chief public buildings in the town.

IX. The house of the intendant, a public building, whose size makes it fit for a palace. It is covered with tin, and stands in a second lower town, situated southward upon the river St. *Charles*. It has a large and fine garden on its north side. In this house all the deliberations concerning this province, are held; and the gentlemen who have the management of the police and the civil power meet here, and the intendant generally presides. In affairs of great consequence the governor-general is likewise here. On one side of this house is the store-house of the crown, and on the other the prison.

Most of the houses in *Quebec* are built of stone, and in the upper city they are generally but one story high, the public buildings excepted. I saw a few wooden houses in the town, but they must not be rebuilt when decayed. The houses and churches in the city are not built of bricks, but the black lime-slates of which the mountain consists, whereon *Quebec* stands. When these lime-slates are broke at a good depth in the mountain, they look very compact at first, and appear to have no shivers, or *lamellæ*, at all; but after being exposed a while to the air, they separate into thin leaves. These slates are soft, and easily cut; and the city-walls, together with the garden-walls, consist chiefly of them. The roofs of the public buildings are covered with common slates, which are brought from *France*, because there are none in *Canada*.

The slated roofs have for some years withstood the changes of air and weather, without suffering any damage. The private houses have roofs of boards, which are laid parallel to the spars, and sometimes to the eaves, or sometimes obliquely. The corners of houses are made of a grey small grained lime-stone, which has a strong smell, like the *stink-stone*, and the windows are generally enchased with it. This lime-stone is more useful in those places than the lime-slates, which always shiver in the air. The outsides of the houses are generally whitewashed. The windows are placed on the inner side of the walls; for they have sometimes double windows in winter. The middle roof has two, or at most three spars, covered with boards only. The rooms are warmed in winter by small iron stoves, which are removed in summer. The floors are very dirty in every house, and have all the appearance of being cleaned but once every year.

The *Powder magazine* stands on the summit of the mountain, on which the city is built, and southward of the palace.

The streets in the upper city have a sufficient breadth, but are very rugged, on account of the rock on which it lies; and this renders them very disagreeable and troublesome, both to foot-passengers and carriages. The black lime-slates basset out and project every where into sharp angles, which cut the shoes in pieces. The streets cross each other at all angles, and are very crooked.

The many great orchards and kitchen-gardens, near the house of the Jesuits, and other public and private buildings, make the town appear very large, though the number of houses it contains is not very considerable. Its extent from south to north is said to be about six hundred toises, and from the shore of the river along the lower town, to the western wall between three hundred and fifty, and four hundred tosies. It must be here observed, that this space is not yet wholly inhabited; for on the west and south side, along the town walls, are large pieces of land without any buildings on them, and destined to be built upon in future times, when the number of inhabitants will be encreased in *Quebec*.

The bishop, whose see is in the city, is the only bishop in *Canada*. His diocese extends to *Louisiana*, on the *Mexican* gulf southward, and to the south-seas westward.

No bishop, the pope excepted, ever had a more extensive diocese. But his spirtual flock is very inconsiderable at some distance from *Quebec*, and his sheep are often many hundred miles distant from each other.

Quebec is the only sea-port and trading town in all *Canada*, and from thence all the produce of the country is exported. The port is below the town in the river, which is there about a quarter of a *French* mile broad, twenty-five fathoms deep, and its ground is very good for anchoring. The ships are secured from all storms in this port; however, the north-east wind is the worst, because it can act more powerfully. When I arrived here, I reckoned thirteen great and small vessels, and they expected more to come in. But it is to be remarked, that no other ships than *French* ones can come into the port, though they may come from any place in *France*, and likewise from the *French* possessions in the *West-Indies*. All the foreign goods, which are found in *Montreal*, and other parts of *Canada*, must be taken from hence. The *French* merchants from *Montreal* on their side, after making a six months stay among several *Indian* nations, in order to purchase skins of beasts and furrs, return about the end of *August*, and go down to *Quebec* in *September* or *October*, in order to sell their goods there. The privilege of selling the imported goods, it is said, has vastly enriched the merchants of *Quebec*; but this is contradicted by others, who allow that there are a few in affluent circumstances, but that the generality possess no more than is absolutely necessary for their bare subsistence, and that several are very much in debt, which they say is owing to their luxury and vanity. The merchants dress very finely, and are extravagant in their repasts; and their ladies are every day in full dress, and as much adorned as if they were to go to court.

The town is surrounded on almost all sides by a high wall, and especially towards the land. It was not quite completed when I was there, and they were very busy in finishing it. It is built of the above mentioned black lime-slate, and of dark-grey sand-stone. For the corners of the gates they have employed a grey lime-stone. They have not made any walls towards the water side, but nature seems to have worked for them, by placing a rock there which it is impossible to ascend. All the rising land thereabouts is likewise so well planted with cannon, that it seems impossible for an enemy's ships or boats to come to the town without running into imminent danger of being sunk. On the land side the town is likewise guarded by high mountains so that nature and art have combined to fortify it. . . .

August the 12th. THIS afternoon I and my servant went out of town, to stay in the country for a couple of days that I might have more leisure to examine the plants which grow in the woods here, and the state of the country. In order to proceed the better, the governor-general had sent for an *Indian* from *Lorette* to shew us the way, and teach us what use they make of the spontaneous plants hereabouts. This *Indian* was an *Englishman* by birth, taken by the *Indians* thirty years ago, when he was a boy, and adopted by them, according to their custom, instead of a relation of theirs killed by the enemy. Since that time he constantly stayed with them, became a *Roman Catholic* and married an *Indian* woman: he dresses like an *Indian*, speaks *English* and *French*, and many of the *Indian* languages. In the wars between the *French* and *English*, in this country, the *French Indians* have made many prisoners of both sexes in the *English* plantations, adopted them afterwards, and they married with people of the *Indian* nations. From hence the *Indian* blood in *Canada* is very much mixed with *European* blood, and a great part of the *Indians* now living owe their origin to *Europe*. It is likewise remarkable, that a great part of the people they had taken during the war and incorporated with their nations, especially the young people, did not choose to return to their native country, though their parents and nearest relations came to them and endeavoured to persuade them to it, and though it was in their power to do it. The licentious life led by the *Indians*, pleased them better than that of their *European* relations; they dressed like the *Indians*, and regulated all their affairs in their way. It is therefore difficult to distinguish them, except by their colour, which is somewhat whiter than that of the *Indians*. There are likewise examples of some *Frenchmen* going amongst the *Indians* and following their way of life. There is on the contrary scarce one instance of an *Indian*'s adopting the *European* customs; but those who were taken prisoners in the war, have always endeavoured to come to their own people again, even after several years of captivity, and though they enjoyed all the privileges, that were ever possessed by the *Europeans* in *America*. . . .

August the 14th. *Lorette* is a village, three *French* miles to the westward of *Quebec*, Inhabited chiefly by *Indians* of the *Huron* nation, converted to the Roman catholic religion. The village lies near a little river, which falls over a rock there, with a great noise, and turns a saw-mill, and a flour-mill. When the Jesuit, who is now with them, arrived among them, they lived in their usual huts, which are made like those of the *Laplanders*. They have since laid aside this custom, and built all their houses after the *French* fashion. In each house are two rooms, *viz.* their bed-room, and the kitchen on the outside before it. In the room is a small oven of stone, covered at top with an iron plate. Their beds are near the wall, and they put no other clothes on them, than those which they are dressed in. Their other furniture and utensils, look equally wretched. Here is a fine little church, with a steeple and bell. The steeple is raised pretty high, and covered with white tin plates. They pretend, that there is some similarity between this church in its figure and disposition, and the *Santa Casa*; at *Loretto* in *Italy*, from whence this village has got its name. Close to the church is a house built of stone, for the clergymen, who are two Jesuits, that constantly live here. The divine service is as regularly attended here, as in any other Roman catholic church; and I was pleased with seeing the alacrity of the *Indians*, especially of the women, and hearing their good voices, when they sing all sorts of hymns in their own language. The *Indians* dress chiefly like the other adjacent *Indian* nations; the men, however, like to wear waistcoats, or jackets, like the *French*. The women keep exactly to the *Indian* dress. It is certain, that these *Indians* and their ancestors, long since, on being converted to the *Christian* religion, have made a vow to God, never to drink strong liquors. This vow they have kept pretty inviolable hitherto, so that one, seldom sees one of them drunk, though brandy and other strong liquors are goods, which other *Indians* would sooner be killed for, than part with them.

These *Indians* have made the *French* their patterns in several things, besides the houses. They all plant maize; and some have small fields of wheat and rye. Many of them keep cows. They plant our common sun-flower in their maize-fields, and mix the seeds of it into their *sagamite*, or maize-soup. The maize, which they plant here, is of the small sort, which ripens sooner than the other: its grains are smaller, but give more and better flour in proportion. It commonly ripens here at the middle, sometimes however, at the end of *August*.

August the 21st. To-day there were some people of three *Indian* nations in this country with the governor-general, viz. *Hurons*, *Mickmacks*, and *Anies*; the last of which are a nation of *Iroquese*, and allies of the *English*, and were taken prisoners in the last war.

The *Hurons* are some of the same *Indians* with those who live at *Lorette*, and have received the christian religion. They are tall, robust people, well shaped, and of a copper colour. They have short black hair, which is shaved on the forehead, from one ear to the other. None of them wear hats or caps. Some have ear-rings, others not. Many of them have the face painted all over with vermillion; others have only strokes of it on the forehead, and near the ears; and some paint their hair with vermillion. Red is the colour they chiefly make use of in painting themselves; but I have likewise seen some, who had daubed their face with a black colour. Many of them have figures in the face, and on the whole body, which are stained into the skin, so as to be indelible. The manner of making them shall be described in the sequel. These figures are commonly black; some have a snake painted in each cheek, some have several crosses, some an arrow, others the sun, or any thing else their imagination leads them to. They have such figures likewise on the breast, thighs, and other parts of the body; but some have no figures at all. They wear a shirt, which is either white or checked, and a shaggy piece of cloth, which is either blue or white, with a blue or red stripe below. This they always carry over their shoulders, or let it hang down, in which case they wrap it round their middle. Round their neck, they have a string of violet wampums, with little white wampums between them. These wampums are small, of the figure of oblong pearls, and made of the shells which the *English* call clams. I shall make a more particular mention of them in the sequel. At the end of the wampum strings, many of the *Indians* wear a large *French* silver coin, with the king's effigy, on their breasts. Others have a large shell on the breast, of a fine white colour, which they value very high, and is very dear; others, again, have no ornament at all round the neck. They all have their breasts uncovered. Before them hangs their tobacco-pouch, made of the skin of an animal, and the hairy side turned outwards. Their shoes are made of skins, and bear a great resemblance to the shoes without heels, which the women in *Finland* make use of. Instead of stockings, they wrap the legs in pieces of blue cloth, as I have seen the *Russian* boors do.

The *Mickmacks* are dressed like the *Hurons*, but distinguish themselves by their long strait hair, of a jetty-black colour. Almost all the *Indians* have black strait hair; however I have met with a few, whose hair was pretty much curled. But it is to be observed, that it is difficult to judge of the true complexion of the *Canada Indians*, their blood being mixed with the *Europeans*, either by the adopted prisoners of both sexes, or by the *Frenchmen*, who travel in the country, and often contribute their share towards the encrease of the *Indian* families, their women not being very shy. The *Mickmacks* are commonly not so tall as the *Hurons*. I have not seen any *Indians* whose hair was as long and strait as theirs. Their language is different from that of the *Hurons*; therefore there is an interpreter here for them on purpose. . . .

There is no printing-press in *Canada*, tho there formerly was one: but all books are brought from *France*, and all the orders made in the country are written, which extends even to the paper-currency. They pretend that the press is not yet introduced here, lest it should be the means of propagating libels against the government and religion. But the true reason seems to ly in the poorness of the country, as no printer could put off a sufficient number of books for his subsistence; and another reason may be, that *France* may have the profit arising from the exportation of books hither.

The meals here are in many respects different from those in the *English* provinces. This perhaps depends upon the difference of custom, taste, and religion, between the two nations.

They eat three meals a day, *viz.* breakfast, dinner, and supper. They breakfast commonly between seven and eight. For the *French* here rise very early, and the governor-general can be spoke to at seven o'clock, which is the time when he has his level. Some of the men dip a piece of bread in brandy, and eat it; others take a dram of brandy, and eat a piece of bread after it. Chocolate is likewise very common for breakfast, and many of the ladies drink coffee. Some eat no breakfast at all. I have never seen tea made use of; perhaps because they can get coffee and chocolate from the *French* provinces in *South-America*; but must get tea from *China*, for which it is not worth their while to send the money out of their country. Dinner is pretty exactly at noon. People of quality have a great variety of dishes, and the rest follow their example, when they invite strangers. The loaves are oval, and baked of wheat flour. For each person they put a plate, napkin, spoon, and fork. Sometimes they likewise give knives; but they are generally omitted, all the ladies and gentlemen being provided with their own knives. The spoons and forks are of silver, and the plates of *Delft* ware. The meal begins with a soup, with a good deal of bread in it. Then follow fresh meats of various kinds, boiled, and roasted, poultry, or game, fricassees, ragoos, &c. of several sorts; together with different kinds of sallads. They commonly drink red claret at dinner, mixed with water; and spruce beer is likewise much in use. The ladies drink water, and sometimes wine. After dinner the fruit and sweet-meats are served up, which are of many different kinds, *viz.* walnuts from *France*, or *Canada*, either ripe, or pickled; almonds, raisins, haselnuts, several kinds of berries, which are ripe in the summer season, such as currants, cran-berries, which are preserved in treacle; many preserves in sugar as straw-berries, raspberries, black-berries, and moss-berries. Cheese is likewise a part of the desert, and so is milk, which they eat last of all with sugar. Friday and Saturday they eat no flesh, according to the Roman catholic rites; but they well know how to guard against hunger. On those days they boil all sorts of kitchen-herbs, and fruit; fishes, eggs, and milk, prepared in various ways. They cut cucumbers into slices, and eat them with cream, which is a very good dish. Sometimes they put whole cucumbers on the table, and every body that likes them takes one, peels, and slices it, and dips the slices into salt, eating them like raddishes. Melons abound here, and are always eaten with sugar. They never put any sugar into wine, or brandy, and upon the whole, they and the *English* do not use half so much sugar, as we do in *Sweden*; though both nations have large sugar-plantations in their *West-Indian* possessions. They say no grace before, or after their meals, but only cross themselves, which is likewise omitted by some. Immediately after dinner, they drink a dish of coffee, without cream. Supper is commonly at seven o'clock, or between seven and eight at night, and the dishes the same as at dinner. Pudding and punch is not to be met with here, though the latter is well known.

Questions

1. How did the Montreal that Kalm saw compare with the Hochelaga viewed by Cartier?
2. What advantages did New France offer the ordinary French farmer or laborer? Given the long history of Iroquois and English attacks on New France, why did "all the farms in Canada stand separate from one another"? Why was all the cultivated land in New France along rivers?
3. How did religious institutions, beliefs, and practices in New France compare with those in the contemporary British colonies to the south?
4. How distinct were the Indian and European populations of New France?
5. Does Kalm's claim that many English captives chose to stay among the Indians influence your reading of Rowlandson and Dustan? How might a narrative written by someone who preferred to remain with the Indians read? What made these Indian communities appealing?

16.3 Le Page du Pratz Discusses the Natchez War*

In 1729, tiring of French demands on their goods and lands, the Natchez Indians organized war parties to drive the French from their settlements in the lower Mississippi Valley, killing nearly 150 French colonists and taking many others captive. The following account of the Natchez attacks is drawn from a history of Louisiana first published in Paris in 1758 by Antoine-Simon Le Page du Pratz, who lived in Louisiana from 1718 to 1734.

At the time the succours were expected from *France*, in order to destroy the *Natchez*, the *Negroes* formed a design to rid themselves of all the *French* at once, and to settle in their room, by making themselves masters of the Capital, and of all the property of the *French*. It was discovered in the following manner.

A female *Negro* receiving a violent blow from a *French* soldier, for refusing to obey him, said in her passion, that the *French* should not long insult *Negroes*. Some *Frenchmen*, overhearing these threats, brought her before the Governor, who sent her to prison. The Judge Criminal not being able to draw any thing out of her, I told the Governor, who seemed to pay no great regard to her threats, that I was of opinion, that a man in liquor, and a woman in passion, generally speak truth. It is therefore highly probable, said I, that there is some truth in what she said: And if so, there must be some conspiracy, ready to break out, which cannot be formed without many *Negroes* of the King's plantation being accomplices therein: And if there are any, I take upon me, said I, to find them out, and arrest them, if necessary, without any disorder or tumult.

The Governor and the whole Court approved of my reasons: I went that very evening to the camp of the *Negroes*, and from hut to hut, till I saw a light. In this hut I heard them talking together of their scheme. One of them was my first commander and my confidant, which surprized me greatly; his name was *Samba*.

I speedily retired for fear of being discovered; and in two days after, eight *Negroes*, who were at the head of the conspiracy, were separately arrested, unknown to each other, and clapt in irons without the least tumult.

The day after, they were put to the torture of burning matches; which, tho' several times repeated, could not bring them to make any confession. In the mean time I learnt, that *Samba* had, in his own country, been at the head of the revolt, by which the *French* lost Fort *Arguin*; and when it was recovered again by M. *Perier de Salvert*, one of the principal articles of the peace was, that this *Negro* should be condemned to slavery in *America*: That *Samba*, on his passage, had laid a scheme to murder the crew, in order to become master of the ship; but that being discovered, he was put in irons, in which he continued, till he landed in *Louisiana*.

I drew up a memorial of all this; which was read before *Samba* by the Judge Criminal; who, threatening him again with the torture, told him, he had ever been a seditious fellow: Upon which *Samba* directly owned all the circumstances of the conspiracy; and the rest, being confronted with him, confessed also: After which, the eight *Negroes* were condemned to be broke alive on the wheel, and the woman to be hanged before their eyes; which was accordingly done, and prevented the conspiracy from taking effect.

The War of the Natchez. Massacre of the French in 1729. Extirpation of the Natchez in 1730.

In the beginning of the month of *December* 1729, we heard at *New Orleans*, with the most affecting grief, of the massacre of the *French* at the Post of the *Natchez*, occasioned by the imprudent conduct of the Commandant. I shall trace that whole affair from its first rise.

The Sieur *de Chopart* had been Commandant of the Post of the *Natchez*, from which he was removed on account of some acts of injustice. M. *Perier*, Commandant General, but lately arrived, suffered himself to be pre-possessed in

---

*M. Le Page du Pratz, *The History of Louisiana* (London, 1763), vol. 2: 131–161.

his favour, on his telling him, that he had commanded that Post with applause: And thus he obtained the command from M. *Perier*, who was unacquainted with his character.

This new Commandant, on taking possession of his Post, projected the forming one of the most eminent settlements of the whole Colony. For this purpose he examined all the grounds, unoccupied by the *French*: But could not find any thing that came up to the grandeur of his views. Nothing but the village of the *White Apple*, a square league at least in extent, could give him satisfaction; where he immediately resolved to settle. This ground was distant from the Fort about two leagues. Conceited with the beauty of his project, the Commandant sent for the *Sun* of that village to come to the Fort.

The Commandant, upon his arrival at the Fort, told him, without further ceremony, that he must look out for another ground to build his village on, as he himself resolved, as soon as possible, to build on the village of the *Apple*; that he must directly clear the huts, and retire somewhere else. The better to cover his design, he gave out, that it was necessary for the *French* to settle on the banks of the rivulet, where stood the Great Village, and the abode of the *Grand Sun*. The Commandant, doubtless, supposed that he was speaking to a slave, whom we may command in a tone of absolute authority. But he knew not, that the natives of *Louisiana* are such enemies to a state of slavery, that they prefer death itself thereto; above all, the *Suns*, accustomed to govern despotically, have still a greater aversion to it.

The *Sun* of the *Apple* thought, that if he was talked to in a reasonable manner, he might listen to him: In this he had been right, had he to deal with a reasonable person. He therefore made answer, that his ancestors had lived in that village for as many years as there were hairs in his double cue, and therefore it was good, that they should continue there still.

Scarce had the interpreter explained this answer to the Commandant, but he fell into a passion, and threatned the *Sun*, if he did not quit his village in a few days, he might repent it. The *Sun* replied; when the *French* came to ask us for lands

to settle on, they told us, there was land enough still unoccupied, which they might take; the same sun would enlighten them all, and all would walk in the same path. He wanted to proceed farther in justification of what he alleged; but the Commandant, who was in a passion, told him, he was resolved to be obeyed, without any further reply. The *Sun*, without discovering any emotion or passion, withdrew, only saying, he was going to assemble the old men of his village, to hold a Council on this affair.

He actually assembled them: And in this Council it was resolved to represent to the Commandant, that the corn of all the people of their village was already shot a little out of the earth, and that all the hens were laying their eggs; that if they quitted their village at present, the chickens and corn would be lost both to the *French* and to themselves; as the *French* were not numerous enough to weed all the corn, they had sown in their fields.

This resolution taken, they sent to propose it to the Commandant, who rejected it with a menace to chastise them, if they did not obey in a very short time, which he prefixed.

The *Sun* reported this answer to his Council, who debated the question, which was knotty. But the policy of the old men was, that they should propose to the Commandant, to be allowed to stay in their village till harvest, and till they had time to dry their corn, and shake out the grain; on condition each hut of the village should pay him in so many Moons (months,) which they agreed on, a basket of corn and a fowl; that this Commandant appeared to be a man highly self-interested, and that this proposition would be a means of gaining time, till they should take proper measures to withdraw themselves from the tyranny of the *French*.

The *Sun* returned to the Commandant, and proposed to pay him the tribute I just mentioned, if he waited till the first colds, (winter;) that then the corn would be gathered in, and dry enough to shake out the grain; that thus, they would not be exposed to lose their corn, and die of hunger: That the Commandant himself would find his account in it, and that as soon as any corn was shaken out, they should bring him some.

The avidity of the Commandant made him accept the proposition with joy, and blinded him with regard to the consequences of his tyranny. He, however, pretended, that he agreed to the offer out of favour, to do a pleasure to a nation so beloved, and who had ever been good friends of the *French*. The *Sun* appeared highly satisfied to have obtained a delay, sufficient for taking the precautions, necessary to the security of the nation; for, he was by no means the dupe of the feigned benevolence of the Commandant.

The *Sun*, upon his return, caused the Council to be assembled; told the old men, that the *French* Commandant had acquiesced in the offers which he had made him, and granted the term of time they demanded. He then laid before them, that it was necessary, wisely to avail themselves of this time, in order to withdraw themselves from the proposed payment and tyrannic domination of the *French*, who grew dangerous in proportion as they multiplied. That the *Natchez* ought to remember the war, made upon them, in violation of the Peace concluded between them: That this war having been made upon their village alone, they ought to consider of the surest means to take a just and a bloody vengeance: That this enter-prize being of the utmost consequence, it called for much secrecy, for solid measures, and for much policy: That thus it was proper to cajole the *French* Chief more than ever: That this affair required some days to reflect on, before they came to a resolution therein, and before it should be proposed to the *Grand Sun* and his Council: That at present they had only to retire; and in a few days he would assemble them again, that they might then determine the part they were to act.

In five or six days he brought together the old men, who in that interval were consulting with each other: which was the reason, that all the suf-frages were unanimous in the same and only means of obtaining the end, they proposed to themselves, which was the entire destruction of the *French* in this province.

The *Sun*, seeing them all assembled, said: "You have had time to reflect on the proposition I "made you: and so I imagine, you will soon set "forth the best means, how to get rid of your bad "neighbours without hazard." The *Sun* having done speaking, the oldest rose up, saluted his Chief after his manner, and said to him:

"We have a long time been sensible, that the "neighbourhood of a greater preju dice than "benefit to us: we, who are old men, see "this; the young see it not. The wares of the *French* "yield pleasure to the youth; but in effect to what "purpose is all this, but to debauch the young "women, and taint the blood of the nation, and "make them vain and idle? The young men are in "the same case; and the married must work them "selves to death to maintain their families, and "please their children. Before the *French* came "amongst us, we were men, content with what we "had, and that was sufficient: we walked with "boldness every road, because we were then our "own masters: but now we go groping, afraid of "meeting thorns, we walk like slaves, which we "shall soon be, since the *French* already treat us as "if we were such. When they are sufficiently "strong, they will no longer dissemble. For the "least fault of our young people, they will tie them "to a post, and whip them, as they do their black "slaves. Have they not already done so to one of our "young men; and is not death preferable to slavery?"

"Here he paused a while, and after taking "breath, proceeded thus:

"What wait we for? Shall we suffer the *French* "to multiply, till we are no longer in a condition "to oppose their efforts? What will the other "nations say of us, who pass for the most "ingenious of all the *Red-men*? They will then say, "we have less understanding than other people. "Why then wait we any longer? Let us set "ourselves at liberty, and show we are really men, "who can be satisfied with what we have. From "this very day let us begin to set about it, order "our women to get provisions ready, without "telling them the reason; go and carry the Pipe of "Peace to all the nations of this country; make "them sensible, that the *French*, being stronger in "our neighbourhood than elsewhere, make us, "more than others, feel, that they want to enslave "us; and when become sufficiently strong, will, in "like manner, treat all the nations of the country; "that it is their interest to prevent so great a "misfortune; and for this purpose they have only "to join us, and cut off the *French* to a man, in one "day and one hour; and the time to be that, on "which the term prefixed and obtained of "the *French* Commandant, to carry him the "contribution agreed on, is expired; the hour to be "the quarter of the day (nine in the morning;) and "then several warriors to go and carry him the "corn, as the beginning of their several payments, "also carry with them their arms, as if going out to "hunt: and that to every *Frenchman* in a *French* "house, there shall be two or three *Natchez*; to ask "to borrow arms and ammunition, for a general "hunting-match, on account of a great feast, and "to promise to bring them meat; the report of the "firing at the Commandant's, to be the signal to "fall at once upon, and kill the *French*: That then "we shall be able to prevent those, who may come "from the old *French* village, *(New Orleans)* by the "great water *(Missisipi)* ever to settle here."

He added, that after apprizing the other nations of the necessity of taking that violent step, a bundle of rods, in number equal to that they should reserve for themselves, should be left with each nation, expressive of the number of days that were to precede that on which they were to strike the blow at one and the same time. And to avoid mistakes, and to be exact in pulling out a rod every day, and breaking and throwing it away, it was necessary to give this in charge to a person of prudence. Here he ceased and sat down: They all approved his counsel, and were to a man of his mind.

The project was in like manner approved of by the *Sun* of the *Apple*: The business was to bring over the *Grand Sun*, with the other Petty *Suns*, to their opinion; because all the Princes being agreed as to that point, the nation would all to a man implicitly obey. They however took the precaution to forbid apprizing the women thereof, not excepting the female *Suns*, (Princesses,) or giving them the least suspicion of their designs against the *French*.

The *Sun* of the *Apple* was a man of good abilities; by which means he easily brought over the *Grand Sun* to favour his scheme, he being a young man of no experience in the world; and having no great correspondence with the *French*: He was the

more easily gained over, as all the *Suns* were agreed, that the *Sun* of the *Apple* was a man of solidity and penetration; who having repaired to the Sovereign of the nation, apprized him of the necessity of taking that step, as in time himself would be forced to quit his own village; also of the wisdom of the measures concerted, such as even ascertained success; and of the danger to which his youth was exposed, with neighbours so enterprizing; above all, with the present *French* Commandant, of whom the inhabitants, and even the soldiers complained: That as long as the *Grand Sun*, his father, and his uncle, the *Stung Serpent*, lived, the Commandant of the Fort durst never undertake any thing to their detriment; because the Grand Chief of the *French*, who resides at their great village *(New Orleans,)* had a love for them: But that he, the *Grand Sun*, being unknown to the *French*, and but a youth, would be despised. In fine, that the only means to preserve his authority, was to rid himself of the *French*, by the method, and with the precautions, projected by the old men.

The result of this conversation was, that on the day following, when the *Suns* should in the morning come to salute the *Grand Sun*, he was to order them to repair to the *Sun* of the *Apple*, without taking notice of it to any one. This was accordingly executed, and the seducing abilities of the *Sun* of the *Apple* drew all the *Suns* into his scheme. In consequence of which they formed a Council of *Suns* and aged Nobles, who all approved of the design: And then these aged Nobles were nominated Heads of Embassies to be sent to the several Nations; had a guard of Warriors to accompany them, and on pain of death, were discharged from mentioning it to any one what ever. This resolution taken, they set out severally at the same time, unknown to the *French*.

Notwithstanding the profound secrecy observed by the *Natchez*, the Council held by the *Suns* and aged Nobles gave the people uneasiness, unable as they were to penetrate into the matter. The female *Suns* (Princesses) had alone in this Nation a right to demand, why they were kept in the dark in this affair. The young *Grand female Sun* was a Princess scarce eighteen: And none but the *Stung Arm*, a woman of great wit, and no less sensible of it, could be offended, that nothing was disclosed to her. In effect, she testified her displeasure at this reserve with respect to herself, to her son; who replied, that the several Deputations were made, in order to renew their good intelligence with the other nations, to whom they had not of a long time sent an Embassy, and who might imagine themselves slighted by such a neglect. This feigned excuse seemed to appease the Princess, but not quite to rid her of all her uneasiness; which, on the contrary, was heightened, when, on the return of the Embassies, she saw the *Suns* assemble in secret Council together with the Deputies, to learn what reception they met with; whereas ordinarily they assembled in public.

At this the female *Sun* was filled with rage, which would have openly broke out, had not her prudence set bounds to it. Happy it was for the *French*, she imagined herself neglected: For I am persuaded the Colony owes its preservation to the vexation of this woman rather than to any remains of affection she entertained for the *French*, as she was now far advanced in years, and her gallant dead some time.

In order to get to the bottom of the secret, she prevailed on her son to accompany her on a visit to a relation, that lay sick at the village of the *Meal*; and leading him the longest way about, and most retired, took occasion to reproach him with the secrecy he and the other *Suns* observed with regard to her, insisting with him on her right as a mother, and her privilege as a Princess: Adding, that tho' all the world, and herself too, had told him he was the son of a *Frenchman*, yet her own blood was much dearer to her than that of strangers; that he needed not apprehend she would ever betray him to the *French*, against whom, said she, you are plotting.

Her son, stung with these reproaches, told her, it was unusual to reveal what the old men of the Council had once resolved upon; alledging, he himself, as being *Grand Sun*, ought to set a good example in this respect: That the affair was concealed from the Princess his consort as well as from her; and that tho' he was the son of a *Frenchman*, this gave no mistrust of him to the other *Suns*. But

seeing, says he, you have guessed the whole affair, I need not inform you farther; you know as much as I do myself, only hold your tongue.

She was in no pain, she replied, to know against whom he had taken his precautions: But as it was against the *French*, this was the very thing that made her apprehensive he had not taken his measures aright in order to surpize them; as they were a people of great penetration, tho' their Commandant had none: That they were brave, and could bring over by their presents, all the Warriors of the other nations; and had resources, which the *Red-men* were without.

Her son told her, she had nothing to apprehend as to the measures taken: That all the Nations had heard and approved their project, and promised to fall upon the *French* in their neighbourhood, on the same day with the *Natchez*: That the *Chactaws* took upon them to destroy all the *French* lower down and along the *Missisipi*, up as far as the *Tonicas*; to which last people, he said, we did not send, as they and the *Oumas* are too much wedded, to the *French*; and that it was better to involve both these nations in the same general destruction with the *French*. He at last told her, the bundle of rods lay in the temple, on the flat timber.

The *Stung Arm* being informed of the whole design, pretended to approve of it, and leaving her son at ease, henceforward was only sollicitous how she might defeat this barbarous design: The time was pressing, and the term prefixed for the execution was almost expired.

This woman, unable to bear to see the *French* cut off to a man in one day by the conspiracy of the natives, sought how to save the greatest part of them: For this purpose she bethought herself of acquainting some young women therewith, who loved the *French*, enjoining them never to tell, from whom they had their information.

She herself desired a soldier she met, to go and tell the Commandant, that the *Natchez* had lost their senses, and to desire him to be upon his guard: That he need only make the smallest repairs possible on the Fort, in presence of some of them, in order to shew his mistrust; when all their resolutions and bad designs would vanish and fall to the ground.

The soldier faithfully performed his commission: But the Commandant, far from giving credit to the information, or availing himself thereof; or diving into, and informing himself of the grounds of it, treated the soldier as a coward and a visionary, caused him to be clapt in irons, and said, he would never take any step towards repairing the Fort, or putting himself on his guard, as the *Natchez* would then imagine, he was a man of no resolution, and was struck with a mere panick.

The *Stung Arm* fearing a discovery, notwithstanding her utmost precaution, and the secrecy she enjoined, repaired to the temple, and pulled some rods out of the fatal bundle: Her design was to hasten, or forward the term prefixed, to the end, that such *Frenchmen*, as escaped the massacre, might apprize their countrymen, many of whom had informed the Commandant; who clapt seven of them in irons, treating them as cowards on that account.

The female *Sun*, seeing the term approaching, and many of those punished, whom she had charged to acquaint the Governor, resolved to speak to the Under-Lieutenant; but to no better purpose, the Commandant paying no greater regard to him than to the common soldiers.

Notwithstanding all these informations, the Commandant went out the night before on a party of pleasure, with some other *Frenchmen*, to the Grand Village of the *Natchez*, without returning to the Fort till break of day; where he was no sooner come, but he had pressing advice to be upon his guard.

The Commandant, still flustered with his last night's debauch, added imprudence to his neglect of these last advices; and ordered his Interpreter instantly to repair to the Grand Village, and demand of the *Grand Sun*, whether he intended, at the head of his Warriors, to come and kill the *French*, and to bring him word directly. The *Grand Sun*, tho' but a young man, knew how to dissemble, and spoke in such a manner to the Interpreter, as to give full satisfaction to the Commandant, who valued himself on his contempt of former advices: He then repaired to his house, situate below the Fort.

The *Natchez* had too well taken their measures, to be disappointed in the success thereof. The fatal moment was at last come. The *Natchez* set out on the Eve of St. *Andrew*, 1729, taking care to bring with them one of the lower sort, armed with a wooden hatchet, in order to knock down the Commandant*: They had so high a contempt for him, that no Warrior would deign to kill him. The houses of the *French* filled with enemies, the Fort in like manner with the natives, who entered in at the gate and breaches, deprived the soldiers, without officers, or even a serjeant at their head, of the means of self-defence. In the mean time the *Grand Sun* arrived, with some Warriors loaded with corn, in appearance as the first payment of the contribution; when several shot were fired. As this firing was the signal, several shot were heard at the same instant. Then at length the Commandant saw, but too late, his folly: He ran into his garden, whither he was pursued and killed. This massacre was executed every where at the same time. Of about seven hundred persons, but few escaped to carry the dreadful news to the Capital; on receiving which the Governor and Council were sensibly affected, and orders were dispatched every where to put people on their guard.

The other *Indians* were displeased at the conduct of the *Natchez*, imagining they had forwarded the term agreed on, in order to make them ridiculous, and proposed to take vengeance the first opportunity, not knowing the true cause of the precipitation of the *Natchez*.

After they had cleared the fort, warehouse, and other houses, the *Natchez* set them all on fire, not leaving a single building standing.

The *Yazous*, who happened to be at that very time on an Embassy to the *Natchez*, were prevailed on to destroy the Post of the *Yazous*; which they failed not to effect some days after, making themselves masters of the Fort, under colour of paying a visit, as usual, and knocking all the garrison on the head.

M. *Perier*, Governor of *Louisiana*, was then taking the proper steps to be avenged: He sent M. *le Sueur* to the *Chactaws*, to engage them on

---

*Others say he was shot: But neither account can be ascertained, as no *Frenchman* present escaped.

our side against the *Natchez*; in which he succeeded without any difficulty. The reason of their readiness to enter into this design was not then understood, it being unknown that they were concerned in the plot of the *Natchez* to destroy all the *French*, and that it was only to be avenged of the *Natchez*, who had taken the start of them, and not given them a sufficient share of the booty.

M. *de Loubois*, King's Lieutenant, was nominated to be at the head of this expedition: He went up the river with a small army, and arrived at the *Tonicas*. The *Chactaws* at length arrived in the month of *February* near the *Natchez*, to the number of fifteen or sixteen hundred men, with M. *le Sueur* at their head; whither M. *de Loubois* came the *March* following.

The army encamped near the ruins of the old *French* settlement; and after resting five days there, they marched to the enemy's Fort, which was a league from thence.

After opening the trenches and firing for several days upon the fort without any great effect, the *French* at last made their approach so near as to frighten the enemy, who sent to offer to release all the *French* women and children, on the condition of obtaining a lasting peace, and of being suffered to live peaceably on their ground, without being driven from thence, or molested for the future.

M. *de Loubois* assured them of peace on their own terms, if they also gave up the *French*, who were in the fort, and all the *Negroes* they had taken belonging to the *French*; and if they agreed to destroy the fort by fire. The *Grand Sun* accepted these conditions, provided the *French* General should promise, he would neither enter the fort with the *French*, nor suffer their auxiliaries to enter; which was accepted by the General; who sent the allies to receive all the slaves.

The *Natchez*, highly pleased to have gained time, availed themselves of the following night, and went out of the fort, with their wives and children, loaded with their baggage and the *French* plunder, leaving nothing but the cannon and ball behind.

M. *de Loubois* was struck with amazement at this escape, and only thought of retreating to the landing-place, in order to build a fort there: But first is was necessary to recover the *French* out of

the hands of the *Chactaws*, who insisted on a very high ransom. The matter was compromised by means of the Grand Chief of the *Tonicas*, who prevailed on them to accept what M. *de Loubois* was constrained to offer them, to satisfy their avarice; which they accordingly accepted, and gave up the *French* slaves, on promise of being paid as soon as possible: But they kept as security a young *Frenchman* and some *Negro* slaves, whom they would never part with, till payment was made.

M. *de Loubois* gave orders to build a terrace-fort, far preferable to a stoccado; there he left M. *du Crenet*, with an hundred and twenty men in garrison, with cannon and ammunition; after which he went down the *Missisipi* to *New Orleans*. The *Chactaws*, *Tonicas*, and other allies, returned home.

After the *Natchez* had abandoned the fort, it was demolished, and its piles, or stakes, burnt. As the *Natchez* dreaded both the vengeance of the *French*, and the insolence of the *Chactaws*, that made them take the resolution of escaping in the night.

A short time after, a considerable party of the *Natchez* carried the Pipe of Peace to the Grand Chief of the *Tonicas*, under pretence of concluding a peace with him and all the *French*. The Chief sent to M. *Perier* to know his pleasure: but the *Natchez* in the mean time assassinated the *Tonicas*, beginning with their Grand Chief; and few of them escaped this treachery.

M. *Perier*, Commandant General, zealous for the service, neglected no means, whereby to discover in what part the *Natchez* had taken refuge. And after many enquiries, he was told, they had entirely quitted the East side of the *Missisipi*, doubtless to avoid the troublesome and dangerous visits of the *Chactaws*; and in order to be more concealed from the *French*, had retired to the West of the *Missisipi*, near the *Silver* Creek, about sixty leagues from the mouth of the *Red River*.

These advices were certain: But the Commandant General not thinking himself in a condition fit to attack them without succours, had applied for that purpose to the Court; and succours were accordingly sent him.

In the mean time the Company, who had been apprized of the misfortune at the Post of the

Natchez, and the losses they had sustained by the war, gave up that Colony to the King, with the privileges annexed thereto. The Company at the same time ceded to the King all that belonged to them in that Colony, as fortresses, artillery, ammunition, warehouses, and plantations, with the *Negroes* belonging thereto. In consequence of which, his Majesty sent one of his ships, commanded by M. *de Forant*, who brought with him M. *de Salmont*, Commissary-General of the Marine, and Inspector of *Louisiana*, in order to take possession of that Colony in the King's name.

I was continued in the inspection of this plantation, now become the King's in 1730, as before.

M. *Perier*, who till then had been Commandant General of *Louisiana* for the *West-India* Company, was now made Governor for the King; and had the satisfaction to see his brother arrive, in one of the King's ships, commanded by M. *Perier de Salvert*, with the succours he demanded, which were an hundred and fifty soldiers of the marine. This Officer had the title of Lieutenant General of the Colony conferred upon him.

The Messrs *Perier* set out with their army, in very favourable weather; and arrived at last, without obstruction, near to the retreat of the *Natchez*. To get to that place, they went up the *Red River*, then the *Black River*, and from thence up the *Silver Creek*, which communicates with a small Lake at no great distance from the fort, which the *Natchez* had built, in order to maintain their ground against the *French*.

The *Natchez*, struck with terror at the sight of a vigilant enemy, shut themselves up in their fort. Despair assumed the place of prudence, and they were at their wits end, on seeing the trenches gain ground on the fort: They equip themselves like Warriors, and stain their bodies with different colours, in order to make their last efforts by a sally, which resembled a transport of rage more than the calmness of valour, to the terror, at first, of the soldiers.

The reception, they met from our men, taught them, however, to keep themselves shut up in their fort; and tho' the trench was almost finished, our Generals were impatient to have the mortars put in a condition to play on the place.

At last they are set in battery; when the third bomb happened to fall in the middle of the fort, the usual place of residence of the women and children, they set up a horrible screaming and the men, seized with grief at the cries of their wives and children, made the signal to capitulate.

The *Natchez*, after demanding to capitulate, started difficulties, which occasioned messages to and fro till night, which they waited to avail themselves of, demanding till next day to settle the articles of capitulation. The night was granted them, but being narrowly watched on the side next the gate, they could not execute the same project of escape, as in the war with M. *de Loubois*. However, they attempted it, by taking advantage of the obscurity of the night, and of the apparent stillness of the *French*: But they were discovered in time, the greatest part being constrained to retire into the fort. Some of them only happened to escape, who joined those that were out a hunting, and all together retired to the *Chicasaws*. The rest surrendered at discretion, among whom was the *Grand Sun*, and the female *Suns*, with several Warriors, many women, young people, and children.

The *French* army re-embarked, and carried the *Natchez* as slaves to *New Orleans*, where they were put in prison; but afterwards, to avoid an infection, the women and children were disposed of in the King's plantation, and elsewhere; among these women was the female *Sun*, called the *Stung-Arm*, who then told me all she had done, in order to save the *French*.

Some time after, these slaves were embarked for *St. Domingo*, in order to root out that nation in the Colony; which was the only method of effecting it, as the few that escaped had not a tenth of the women necessary to recruit the nation. And thus that nation, the most conspicuous in the Colony, and most useful to the *French*, was destroyed.

Questions

1. How does the Natchez culture described by du Pratz compare with the Mississippian world glimpsed by the de Soto expedition?
2. Why did Louisiana's African slaves revolt when they did? Were the Natchez and the

African slaves allies? Did they have common interests? Which Indian nations supported the French or Natchez and why?

3. How did French relations with the Natchez compare with those with the Indian nations of the upper country? Why did French colonists treat the Natchez so differently?

4. How did the Natchez uprising compare with the Pueblo Revolt? To Opechancanough's 1622 attack on Virginia? To King Philip's War?

5. Where did du Pratz acquire the information he used for this account?

17

Indians and Empires on the Great Plains

The number of Europeans on the Great Plains in the seventeenth and eighteenth centuries was small, but the Spanish colonies in New Mexico and Texas, the French explorers and traders moving west of the Great Lakes and the Mississippi, and the British factories on Hudson Bay contributed to revolutionary changes in the region nonetheless. Horses originating in Spanish settlements dispersed east of the Rockies, and peoples who had once stalked buffalo on foot now pursued them on horseback. French traders trafficked in guns, rendering warfare more lethal. Hunters deep in the Canadian interior sent furs downstream in exchange for British cloth and metal. Some riverside farming villages prospered by continuing to exchange their crops and handicrafts for hunters' bounty; other became mounted hunters themselves. Perhaps most fatefully, as Europeans and their goods made their way onto the Plains, smallpox came with them.

17.1 A French Explorer Describes His Interactions with Plains Indians*

Between 1731 and 1743, Pierre Gaultier de Varennes et de La Vérendrye and his sons explored the lands northwest and southwest of Lake Superior in quest of new fur supplies and the long-sought water route through North America. La Vérendrye had heard intriguing tales of sophisticated, fair-skinned villagers living along a great river flowing west, and he hoped these Mandan communities could help him find a way to the Pacific. In the following passages from La Vérendrye's journal, covering the period from September to December 1738, La Vérendrye acquires Assiniboine guides and then visits the Mandan villages near present-day Bismarck, North Dakota.

I proceeded to the fork of the Assiniboine and, reaching there on the 24th, I found ten cabins of

Cree, including two war chiefs, awaiting me with a large quantity of meat, they having been notified of my coming. They begged me to stay with them for a while, so that they might have the pleasure of seeing and entertaining us. I agreed to do so, being glad of a chance of talking to them.

I got the two chiefs to come to my tent. I knew that they went every year to the English post, and that one of them, according to a report made to me, had received a collar from the English together with a present as an inducement to do some bad turn to the French. I told the one who had been accused all that had been said to me about him. I had the honour to write you last year from Michilimackinac an account of the rumours that were current on this subject.

He replied: 'My Father, I know that there are a lot of envious people who talk against me. I have not been to the English for the last six years, but in

---

*Lawrence J. Burpee, ed., *Journals of La Vérendrye* (Toronto: Champlain Society, 1927), 298-306, 318-343. Reprinted with permission from University of Toronto Press (www.utpjournals.com)

Europeans supply needs – don't care ab country

recent years when the French abandoned us I did send there: we had to have our needs supplied. Ask those who went there for me, and who are here now, if they ever heard anything like that spoken of. I assure you that the Englishman is quiet and does not talk of the Frenchman. They are liars who have set those stories afloat. You will know the truth of the matter later. As long as the Frenchman remains in our lands we promise you not to go elsewhere.'

I made them a little present to encourage them to keep their promises, and went over what I had said to the others both in regard to your orders and to general news. Our old man then gave them a great account of his journey which pleased them exceedingly.

The chief whom I had accused said to me: 'My Father, we thank you for having spoken well in our behalf down there to our Father. We know today that he has pity on us in sending Frenchmen into our country to bring us the things we need. We will keep quiet as he desires, and let the Sioux do the same. Our heart is still sore on account of your son, who was the first to come and build a fort on our land; we loved him deeply. I have already been once at war to avenge him. I only destroyed ten cabins, which is not enough to content us; but now our Father orders us to keep quiet and we shall do so.'

He asked me then where I was thinking of going, that the river of the Assiniboin was very low and that we ran a great risk of ruining our canoes; moreover that we were going among people who did not know how to kill beaver, and whose only clothing was buffalo skin, a thing we did not require. They were people without intelligence, who had never seen the French and would not be able to make anything of them.

I replied that I wanted to go in the autumn and visit that tribe of whites that I had heard so much about; that I would go up the river as far as I could in order to put it in my power to pursue my journey according to your orders, and that I wanted to increase the number of your children, teach the Assiniboin to hunt, and put some intelligence into them; and that next year I would take another direction.

'You are running a great risk, my Father,' he said, 'of your canoes leaving there empty. It is true

the Assiniboin are a numerous people, but they do not know how to hunt beaver; I hope you will be able to sharpen their wits.'

I left on the 26th. My old man asked to be allowed to remain a few days with the Cree who were urgently asking him to do so, saying that he would overtake me in a short time. As he had his own canoe I readily consented, and told him to encourage those people to be active in hunting, to carry provisions to the French fort, and to keep the promise he had given me not to go to the English. He assured me he would speak to them to the best of his ability and hoped I would be satisfied.

I found the water very low, as there had been no rain all the summer. The river comes from the west, winds a great deal, is wide, has a strong current and many shallows. There are fine trees along the banks, and behind these a boundless stretch of prairie in which are multitudes of buffalo and deer.

I determined to go by land across the prairie, and let the men I did not require follow in the canoes. The road is much shorter by the prairie, as you cut off several bends of the river and keep a straight road. Game is to be found along the river in great abundance. I did not walk far before meeting some Assiniboin who, having been notified that I was coming up the river, came to meet me. I pursued my way, however, deferring to speak to them till I should be on their land. The band increased in numbers day by day. I marched steadily for six days.

On the evening of October 2 the savages notified me that I could not go any higher up the river on account of the lowness of the water, that my canoes could not pass the wood; and that if it was a question of being well situated for reaching everybody, there was no better place than the portage which leads to the Lake of the Prairies, for that is the road by which the Assiniboin go to the English, and being there [they said] you will stop every one on the way; and, if you wish to go to the Mandan, you are close to the road.

I held a consultation as to what we should do, our reckoning being that we were sixty leagues from the fork by water and thirty-five or forty by land across the prairies. The general opinion was, seeing that we could not go any further, and that we ran great risk of so injuring our canoes that we should not be able to get them out, the place in which we were being one in which neither gum nor resin was to be had for mending them, that the best thing to do was to stay there, as there were good facilities for building, as it was the road to the English posts, and as we had reason to expect a great many people to pass that way, and all of them people who certainly do not go to fort Maurepas.

On the morning of the 3rd I determined to choose a good spot for building a fort, which I caused to be commenced at once. I was still hoping that M. de Lamarque would come and join me. Had I gone further up the river he could not have found me.

While the men were building as hard as they could I spoke to the Assiniboin, assembling them all near my tent. I made them a present from you of powder, ball, tobacco, axes, knives, chisels, awls, these all being things which they value highly, owing to their lack of everything. They received me with much ceremony, shedding many tears in testimony of their joy. For their trouble I received them into the number of your children, fully instructing them afterwards as to your orders, which I repeated several times so that they might fully grasp them. They seemed greatly pleased, thanked me earnestly, and promised to do wonders.

I asked them to let the Assiniboin of the Red river know that they had Frenchmen among them, and that the French would never abandon them as long as they acted sensibly; they ought to recognize, I said, our kindness towards them in sending them useful things from so great a distance; their relative, the old man I had brought with me, could tell them right off all that had happened to us.

The old man then spoke and certainly he left nothing unsaid that could instruct them, or help them to understand what it is to have to do with Frenchmen. The whole was brought to a conclusion with copious tears and thanksgivings.

A few days later I secured a guide, whom I paid with the rest to accompany me on my journey of discovery and help in carrying the baggage. . . .

On the morning of the 28th we arrived at the place indicated as a rendezvous for the Mandan, who arrived in the evening, one chief with thirty men and four Assiniboin. After the chief had studied for some time from a height the extent of our village, which certainly looked pretty large, I had him conducted into the lodge in which I was, where a place at one side had been prepared for him. He came and sat beside me and some of his people sat next. He then presented me with some Indian corn in the ear and with a roll of their tobacco, which is not good as they do not know how to prepare it as we do. It is a good deal like ours, with this difference, that they do not plant it, and that they cut it green, using the stalks and leaves together. I gave him some of mine which he found very good.

I confess I was greatly surprised, as I expected to see people quite different from the other savages according to the stories that had been told us. They do not differ from the Assiniboin, being naked except for a garment of buffalo skin carelessly worn without any breechcloth. I knew then that there was a large discount to be taken off all that had been told me. The chief spoke to me in Assiniboin testifying the joy which my arrival caused to all their people, and requesting me to receive them into the number of your children; he wished in future to make only one with us, and I might dispose of all he had; he begged me to stay at his fort, which was the nearest, a smaller one than the others but well stocked with provisions. There were six forts, he said, belonging to the same tribe; his was the only one that was a little far from the river; when I arrived he would show me two collars that he had received from me; he had always hoped to see me.

I thanked him for all his politeness and offers, saying that I came from a great distance to form a friendship with them, and that I would talk to them as soon as I had arrived at their fort. At once he played us a sharp trick. As I have already observed, he had, on his arrival, carefully noted the size of our encampment, and he saw that, if all those people arrived at his fort, there would be a vast consumption of grain, the custom being to feed without charge those who go to visit them, and only to sell such grain as is carried away. So he now gave great thanks to the Assiniboin for having brought the French to see them: they could not, he said, have arrived more apropos, because the

Sioux would soon be there having been notified of our movements; and he begged me as well as the Assiniboin to be so good as to assist them, as they hoped much from our valour and courage.

I was imposed upon as were the Assiniboin, but with this difference, that they were dismayed while I was rejoiced, hoping for a chance to avenge myself on that accursed nation. I promised the chief that, if the Sioux came while we were with him, I and all our Frenchmen would give him all the help in our power. He thanked me, and then he was summoned to the feast, when I questioned him regarding the Sioux. The Assiniboin, I learnt, though a numerous race, strong and robust, are not brave, and are greatly afraid of the Sioux, whom they consider braver than themselves. The Mandan know their weakness and on occasion profit by it.

A council was held to deliberate as to what they should do. The majority were of opinion that they should not proceed any farther, and that I ought to be warned of the risk I ran if I determined to go on. An old man then rose quickly to his feet: 'Don't think,' said he, 'that our father is a coward; I know him better than you do; I have been with him ever since he left his fort, and don't you imagine that the Sioux are able to frighten him or any of his men. What will he think of us? He has lengthened his journey in order to join us, in accordance with our request, we undertaking to accompany him to the Mandan and then conduct him back to his fort. He would be there [with the Mandan] to-day if he had not listened to us, and you would think of abandoning him and letting him go alone. That shall never be. If you are afraid of the Sioux let us leave our village here till we return, and let the men who are fit to march follow our Father.'

All fell in with the sentiment of the old man, and it was decided that only a few men should remain to protect the women, and that all the rest should accompany me. I was notified of the result of the council, and proclamation was made through the village that every one was to be in readiness to march the day after next, the 30th of the month, a stay to be made with the Mandan, who knew well how to profit by it in selling their grains, tobacco, skins and coloured plumes which they know the Assiniboin prize highly. The latter brought them in exchange guns, axes, kettles, powder, bullets, knives, awls. The Mandan are much more crafty than the Assiniboin in their commerce and in everything, and always dupe them.

We left on the morning of the 30th, about 600 men and several women without children, some of the best walkers. On the evening of the third day of our march, when we were about seven leagues from the first fort of the Mandan, I was told that an Assiniboin had taken the bag my slave was carrying on the road, under pretext of relieving him, and had returned to the village, my box, in which were my papers and many things for my own use, being in the bag. Instantly I hired two young men to run after him and paid them, making them promise to bring the bag to me at the Mandan settlement where I would await them. They left in the night and caught up with the rascal, who had already decamped from the village, made him hand everything back, and then went back to their village to keep the recovered property till my return, as they were afraid to come where I was on account of the Sioux; and so I found myself deprived of many things that I was much in need of every day.

The orator gave notice that we should have to leave before four the next morning in order to arrive in good time at the fort. At a distance of a league and a half I found towards noon, near to a small river, a number of people who had come to meet us. They had lighted a fire while waiting, and had brought along some cooked grain and flour worked into a paste with pumpkin, so as to give us all something to eat. Two chiefs had prepared me a place near the fire, but first they gave me some food and a pipe. M. de Lamarque arrived shortly after me. I begged him to sit down beside me and eat while resting. We continued resting for two full hours. Then I was notified that it was time to move on. I made one of my sons take the flag showing in colours the arms of France and march at the head, while the French were directed to follow in proper marching order. The Sieur Nolan relieved my son by taking turns with him in carrying the flag. The Mandan would not let me walk, offering to carry me, and I had to consent, the Assiniboin begging me to do so and saying that I should displease them [the Mandan] greatly if I refused.

At four arpents from the fort, on a little elevation, a party of the older men of the fort, accompanied by a great number of young men, were waiting to present me with the pipe and to show me the two collars I had sent them four or five years before. They gave seats to me and to M. de Lamarque. I received their compliments, the substance of which was that they were delighted at our arrival. I ordered my son the Chevalier to draw the French up in line with the standard four paces in front. All the Assiniboin who had guns fell into line also like our Frenchmen, and after the compliments were over I ordered a salute to the fort of three volleys. A great many people had come to meet us, but that was nothing in comparison with what we saw on the rampart and along the ditches. I marched in good order to the fort, which I entered on the 3rd December at four in the afternoon, escorted by all the French and the Assiniboin.

I was led into the lodge of the principal chief, a large one truly, but not large enough to hold all the people who wanted to enter it. The crowd was so great that Assiniboin and Mandan were all treading on one another's heels. The only free space was where we were, myself, M. de Lamarque, his brother, and my sons. I asked that most of them might be made to retire so as to give more room to our Frenchmen and enable them to put their baggage in a place of safety. I said to them that they would have plenty of time to see me. So the place was cleared, but I had not had it done soon enough; for some one had stolen my bag of merchandise in which were all my presents, and this through the serious fault of one of my hired men into whose care I had given it before arriving at the fort. He took off his load when he entered the lodge without thinking of the bag that he had put close to himself in the great crowd.

I was a little disconcerted with my box lost as well as my bag of presents, which was most necessary to us for the place we had arrived at; there were goods in it to the value of over three hundred livres. The Assiniboin appeared to be much troubled over it, and made great search immediately, but to no purpose. Their [the Mandan] fort is provided with a great many cellars, fine for storing things in. The chief of the Mandan seemed very sorry for my loss,

and told me, for my consolation, that they had a great many rascals among them; he would do his best to find out something about it. If I had cared to avail myself of the offer of the Assiniboin, I might have found it quickly by using force; but I preferred to suffer loss and keep things quiet, as I meant to pass part of the winter with them to get some information about more distant parts.

On the 4th I got together the principal Mandan and Assiniboin men in the lodge in which I was, and made them a present of powder and ball, saying that I could not give them anything else; that they knew all the things that I had had to bring in order to give as presents [had been carried off]. I stated that I felt inclined to remain some time in order to become acquainted with the country in accordance with our orders, a thing which could not be done in a day. The Mandan expressed the joy this announcement caused them, and assured me that I need not be afraid of starving because they had provisions in reserve far beyond our requirements, their whole fort being stocked with them, and that all was at my disposal as, with them, I was master.

The Assiniboin elder who was orator of the village said to me: 'My Father, we brought you here, and I don't doubt that you will be comfortable here. We were hoping to take you back to your fort; but you are free to do what you judge best; we shall come for you whenever you wish it.' Then addressing the Mandan: 'We are leaving you our Father; take great care of him and of all the French; learn to know them, for they are wise, they know how to do everything. We love our Father and we fear him; do as we do. We are leaving much distressed over the theft committed on our Father as he came in among us. What can he think of us? We cannot help considering it a shameful thing: the Frenchman comes to see you and you rob him. It was fortunate for you that our Father is kind, as otherwise the thing would have taken a different turn. I don't fear to tell you that, if he had wished, he could have made us find that bag, and there is time yet if he wishes it.' I put a stop to his speech, seeing that the old man was getting hot.

One of the Mandan chiefs replied: 'Neither I nor my people have any part in the accusations you are making: I do not answer for the others; I feel sore enough about it. I have made all enquiry in my power with the aid of my young men, and I have nothing to reproach myself with. Who knows that it was not an Assiniboin? There were men of both tribes in the crowd; you cannot answer for anything yourself. Don't be uneasy about our Father and all his men; he is master here as much as if he were at home; we beg him to admit us to the number of his children.'

This I did on the spot by placing my hands on the head of each chief, which is the usual form; and they all reply with shouts of joy and thankfulness. I then said to the Assiniboin; 'I am sending four Frenchmen to my fort to give them news of my doings, and I beg you to take them there as speedily as may be. I have left powder at the village and all else that is necessary for the accomplishment of the journey.' The council closed with great thanks from both parties.

As yet the Assiniboin were not talking of leaving, though they had completed their purchases of all the things they were to buy, such as coloured buffalo robes, deer and buck skins, carefully dressed and ornamented with fur and feathers, painted feathers and furs, worked garters, headbands, girdles. Of all the tribes they [the Mandan] are the most skilful in dressing leather, and they work very delicately in hair and feathers; the Assiniboin cannot do work of the same kind. They are sharp traders, and clean the Assiniboin out of everything they have in the way of guns, powder, ball, kettles, axes, knives and awls.

Seeing the great quantity of provisions the Assiniboin were consuming every day, and being afraid they would stay a long time, they spread the report that the Sioux were not far away; that several of their hunters had caught sight of them. The Assiniboin fell into the trap and quickly decided to decamp, not wanting to have to fight. A Mandan chief made a sign to me to wait and that the report about the Sioux was only to get the Assiniboin to go. On the morning of the 6th they all left in great haste, believing the Sioux to be at hand and fearing that they would intercept them.

The chief with whom I had lodged in the village brought me five men to stay with me saying:

'My Father, I regret to leave you. I still hope you will come and overtake us in a short time; I will move on gently. Here are five of my young men whom I give you to stay here with you; they will bring you along whenever you wish to leave.' I made him a little present to thank him, telling him that he would know in a short time that I was the right kind of man, my intention being to make him some due recompense for his attention. He left with great protestations of friendship.

Shortly afterwards I was informed that my interpreter, whom I had paid well to make sure of him, had decamped, in spite of all the offers my son the Chevalier could make him, in order to follow an Assiniboin woman of whom he was enamoured, but who had refused to remain with him. He was a young man, a Cree by nationality, who spoke good Assiniboin, and as there are several Mandan who speak it pretty well I made myself perfectly understood. My son spoke in Cree, and the Cree interpreted it into Assiniboin; but now, to crown our misfortunes, we were reduced to trying to make ourselves understood by signs and gestures. If I had distrusted my interpreter, who every day assured me that he would always stay with me and never abandon me, I would have taken advantage of the time he was with me to ask the questions that I wished to ask the Mandan; but, flattering myself that I had a man whom I could depend on, I had put off doing so till after the departure of the Assiniboin.

All day long I was greatly perplexed. All that I succeeded in learning in the evening, after all the people had gone, in reply to any questions that I asked, such as whether there was much population along the river banks farther down, and of what nations it consisted, and whether they had any knowledge of a country far beyond, was that there were five forts of their own people on the two sides of the river much larger than the one we were in; that at a day's journey from the last of their forts were the Panaux, who had several forts, and beyond them the Pananis; that these two tribes occupied a large territory, and that at present they were at war with the Mandan and had been for the last four years. Formerly they had always been their close allies, and I should hear later what had caused the falling out.

The Panana and the Pananis built their forts and lodges in the same way in which they themselves did. In the summer corn and tobacco grew lower down the river, which was very wide so that you could not see the land on the other side. The water was not drinkable; all the land there was inhabited by people white like ourselves who worked in iron. Among all the tribes of this region the word iron seems to be applied indiscriminately to all metals. Those people, I was told, never went on foot, but always on horseback, both when they hunted and when they went to war. You could not kill any of these men with arrow or gun as they had iron armour, but that by killing a horse you could capture the man easily enough as he could not run. They had iron bucklers, very bright, and fought with lances and sabres, which they handled with great skill. You never saw a woman in their fields; their fort and houses were of stone.

I asked if the country was well wooded, and if the prairies continued to be marked by risings and depressions. They said that wood was found along the river in places, and also in clumps through the prairies; the further you went down, the higher the hills became, and that there were many that were bare rocks of fine stone, especially along the river. I asked if it took a long time to go to the country where the whites, the men who rode horses, were. They replied that the Panana and Pananis had horses like the whites; it took them a whole summer to make the journey with men alone; but since they had been at war with the Panana they did not venture to go very far. The roads were blocked so far as they were concerned. Buffaloes abounded in the prairies, much larger and heavier beasts than those we see in the prairies here, their hides white and of several colours. They showed us some horns cut across the middle which hold nearly three pints, their colour being greenish. There are some in all the lodges which are used as ladles, a proof that they killed a great many of them when the road was open.

That was all I was able to learn, and even so there was a good deal of chance about it. I had counted fully on my interpreter and expected to have plenty of time to inform myself thoroughly and at my leisure. On the sixth day after the departure of the Assiniboin I sent my son the Chevalier with the Sieur Nolan, six Frenchmen, and several Mandan, to the nearest fort, which is on the bank of the river. If they were well received they were to stay there over night and get as much information as they could as to the further course of the river on which those people dwell; and, if they have any knowledge of the lower portion of it, according to what has been told to us, to get as many facts from them as possible, all of which would have to be done by signs and gestures.

After their departure M. de Lamarque and I took a walk to examine the extent of their fortifications. I gave orders to count the cabins, and we found that there were about one hundred and thirty. All the streets, squares and cabins are uniform in appearance; often our Frenchmen would lose their way in going about. They keep the streets and open spaces very clean; the ramparts are smooth and wide; the palisade is supported on cross pieces mortised into posts fifteen feet apart with a lining. For this purpose they use green hides fastened only at the top in places where they are needed. As to the bastions, there are four of them at each curtain well flanked. The fort is built on an elevation in mid-prairie with a ditch over fifteen feet deep and from fifteen to eighteen wide. Entrance to the fort can only be obtained by steps or pieces [of wood] which they remove when threatened by the enemy. If all their forts are similar you may say that they are impregnable to savages. Their fortification, indeed, has nothing savage about it.

This tribe is of mixed blood, white and black. The women are rather handsome, particularly the light-coloured ones; they have an abundance of fair hair. The whole tribe, men and women, is very industrious. Their dwellings are large and spacious, divided into several apartments by wide planks. Nothing is lying about: all their belongings are placed in large bags hung on posts; their beds are made in the form of tombs and are surrounded by skins. They all go to bed naked, both men and women. The men go naked all the time, being covered only by a buffalo robe. Many of the women go naked like the men, with this difference, that they wear a small loin-cloth about a hand wide and a foot long sewed to a girdle in front only. All the women wear this kind of protection even when they wear a petticoat, so that they are not embarrassed when they sit down and do not have to keep the thighs closed like other Indian women. Some wear a kind of jacket of very soft buckskin.

The roebuck is abundant in the region and is of a very small variety. Their fort is very well provided with cellars, where they store all they have in the way of grains, meat, fat, dressed skins and bearskins. They have a great stock of these things, which form the money of the country. The more they have the richer they consider themselves. They are very fond of tattooing, but neither men nor women ever have more than half the body tattooed. They do very fine wicker work, both flat and in basket form. They use earthen vessels, which they make like many other tribes, for cooking their victuals.

For the most part they are great eaters and are strong on feasts. Every day more than twenty dishes were brought to me, corn, beechnuts, pumpkin, and always cooked. M. de Lamarque, who had no repugnance to feasts, went continually to them with my sons. As I did not go, they sent me my dish. The men are big and tall, very active and, for the most part, good-looking, fine physiognomies, and affable. The women generally have not a savage cast of features. The men play at a kind of ball game on the open spaces and the ramparts.

Terms

English post—York Factory at the mouth of the Hayes River, on Hudson Bay

river of the Assiniboin—Assiniboine River of southern Manitoba and Saskatchewan

Questions

1. What factors facilitated the westward extension of French influence? What factors complicated it? What did the French and Indians offer each other?
2. Characterize relations among the Mandan, Cree, Assiniboine, Sioux, Panaux, and Pananis? Were these people culturally uniform or varied? What factors brought them together and pushed them apart?
3. What role did the Mandan play in the Plains trading networks?
4. La Vérendrye wrote that there "was nothing savage" about the Mandan village. What did he mean? How did he evaluate Mandan culture overall?
5. How did the French communicate with the Cree, Assiniboine, and Mandan?
6. How did the Mandan communities visited by La Vérendrye compare with the Pueblo peoples portrayed by Castañeda? To the Mississippians described by Ranjel?

17.2 New Mexico Governor Vélez Cachupín Discusses Spanish-Indian Relations on the Southern Plains*

New Mexico narrowly survived the internal Indian assaults of the 1680 Pueblo Revolt, but the colony remained vulnerable to Indian attacks from outside, especially from increasingly formidable Great Plains peoples like the Comanches. In 1754, outgoing New Mexico Governor Thomas Vélez Cachupín left advice for his successor on how best to manage relations with the Indian peoples around the colony.

My desires and zeal for the success of your grace in these offices and the love I contracted for them during the time of my government by faithful endeavor to satisfy the confidence which my person and conduct were directed to merit, and the exact fulfillment of what had been ordered of

---

*"Instruction of Don Thomas Vélez Cachupín, 1754," in *The Plains Indians and New Mexico, 1751–1778: A Collection of Documents Illustrative of the History of the Eastern Frontier of New Mexico*, ed. Alfred Barnaby Thomas (Albuquerque: University of New Mexico Press, 1940), 129–143.

me, which your grace by your conscientiousness knows how to merit, can not excuse me from giving your grace an impression of the experiences I have acquired in the five years during which, with careful attention and application, I have managed these duties, and communicating to you the rules I have followed. These guided me in reëstablishing in this government the peace and tranquility which its inhabitants enjoy today with the barbarous tribes of Apaches, Carlanas, and the rest they speak of on the plains, and with the Comanches, Utes, Chaguaguas, and Muaches. Because of this peace it has been possible in the period of my rule to repopulate and extend the settlements of this province on the north which, because of war with the Utes, had been destroyed and its population driven out, with the loss of all their possessions and many of their lives.

The conservation of the friendship of this Ute nation and the rest of its allied tribes is of the greatest consideration because of the favorable results which their trade and good relations bring to this province. This is especially true of those settlements dependent upon the villa of La Cañada, which, without peace, can not conserve themselves or their neighborhoods, or increase their haciendas engaged in raising cattle, sheep, and horses. Besides, this nation with its trade in deerskins benefits the province in such a way that it stimulates in its settlers the disposition to go to La Vizcaya and Sonora to purchase whatever effects they may need for their subsistence and for their families. Without this trade they could not provide for themselves, for they have no other commerce than that of these skins. Invariably when, because of war, the trade with the Utes ceases, that of these neighborhoods also ends. They are without the possibility of clothing themselves and existing. Whatever they possess in wealth from the land may also become the spoil of the Utes.

It is extremely easy for this numerous nation to consort with the other two, Chaguaguas and Moaches, to commit upon this province the greatest hostilities because of their proximity and because the extremely rough terrain which shelters them makes it difficult to attack them on the north

and northeast. They are a bold, warlike nation, skillful in the management of arms. As valorous as they are, they watch suspiciously our friendship, because lack of faith, in former times, was on our part characterized by little religiosity and by a violation of the laws of the king which charge so strongly the winning and conversion of the Indians to vassalage and the Catholic religion. Thus, because of inconsequential and badly supported suspicions, without the necessary investigation and mature consideration of the consequences, this [Ute] nation, counting upon peace and support against another tribe, the Comanches, was with the greatest error surprised by the armed forces of this province, which captured and put to the sword a ranchería of more than one hundred tipis. This occurred at a time when the Utes were doing their best to advance their good relations in the court of the Spaniards and were repaid with a sharp sword. Because of this scandalous indignity, they summoned their power, took note of the justice of their arms, and attacked this province, so that everything lay in lamentable ruin, the victim of their just indignation, without their being defeated or restrained.

With the government in this condition, I took charge. Applying myself completely to its pacification, I extended to the Utes the satisfaction necessary to secure their peace, tranquility, and trade. During the last four years, this has been maintained. Their love and confidence being won in so far as I have been able, they have put aside their old grudges, but a very bad example is not easy for them to forget. For these reasons it is necessary that the zeal of your grace be completely applied to maintain with these four nations of Utes, Chaguaguas, and Payuches [and Moaches] the best friendship and good relations, treating them with generosity and simpleness of spirit, with some show of pleasure, and be very humane in your contacts with them. You should show the greatest kindness without revealing fastidiousness or repugnance at their rude clownishness and manners. Protect them in their commerce and do them justice whenever advantage may be taken of them by these settlers. Thus the person and office of your lordship may be made pleasing to the Utes and not inspire a lack

take adv of native hostilities.

of confidence in your actions. To their captain, named Thomas, show all courteousness, great friendship, and love. Impress upon him that you look upon his tribe with entire good faith and friendship and urge that they forget their fears which make them circumspect. If because of strange conduct, they again become ill humored, it will not be very easy to reduce them to the tranquility and peace which today they observe. I recommend this matter so strongly to your grace because of the especial charges which the most excellent viceroy has made concerning this affair.

Your grace ought also to note that even when a Ute displeases by stealing some horses, a general threat should not be made against the whole tribe, nor their chiefs advised of the fact with harshness. Give them notice of it as I have done so that they may punish the culprit and return the property. I have succeeded in securing peacefully the return of some horse herds which were carried off, without their republic being held culpable. The chiefs have been exact in giving satisfaction in such thefts, for out of harshness in persuading and treating with them originates their dissatisfaction and ends their docility. There is not a nation among the numerous ones which live around this government in which a kind word does not have more effect than the execution of the sword. This fact I have observed and acted upon it accordingly. It is the policy which your grace should follow in your conduct, unless your understanding persuades you to other means, the more so because of the stupidity of the country. There are few here who will not accept a discreet, reasonable word of advice.

The Comanche tribe is equally pacific and maintains an attitude of unexampled good faith since I punished them with the rigor of the armed forces. I have observed with them the greatest equity and kindness and have made them understand the authority of our arms, which they did not believe in, for they were excessively arrogant from dominating the rest of the tribes. Thus the encounters which they had had in the past with us had always left their vanity and pride confident of overcoming our arms. Because of this attitude, they frequently attacked these settlements and committed robberies in the province. But, having been decisively defeated in a pitched battle I had with them, they are entirely persuaded and have maintained up to now perfect and faithful friendship with complete confidence in us. This is what your grace must try to maintain. Use the greatest efforts and observe faithfully whatever conduces to pleasing their spirits without permitting, on the occasions when they come to trade at the pueblo of Taos, the settlers and Pueblo Indians, who also attend, to do them the slightest injury. They suffer from many extortions, such as robbing them of their skins or some horses or other priceless possession, which for them is very serious and stirs their animosity. To remedy this practice, I published the edict which is on record for your grace. As already noted, to secure its complete observance, I had it approved by the most excellent sir, the viceroy, with previous opinions submitted by the fiscal and auditor.

The attendance of your grace at all the fairs, to which this tribe and others come, is necessary, as I have done, for there is no subject to delegate this duty to who would discharge the trust with the zeal equal to that of the governor himself. The Comanches find much satisfaction in observing that any appeal for justice is met at once and that the governor goes about their rancherías, fulfilling his duties with care and seeing that they are not molested in their possessions. They are always attentive to the governor's actions and decisions, from which they draw inferences. Being left unmolested in their selling, so that, with no prohibited goods for sale, they may purchase to their satisfaction, they can not draw a mistaken inference by being denied such goods which, after buying, they may not esteem. In order not to find yourself forced to condescend to permit them to buy mares and studs, you must prohibit these animals in the vicinity, as I have had to order done, in order to avoid Comanche petitions and the evil practices of some of the settlers.

Naturally, with your coming, understanding that there is to be a new administration, the Indians will test out (as they are very shrewd) the qualities of the new governor. They will observe in your grace on their visit even your most accidental actions to conclude whether the new governor is vigorous, strong for war, and capable of putting up with the inconveniences of it, especially in these countries. At the same time they will learn whether they will have in their trade the protection and security which they have had up to the present, because the manner in which it used to be carried on caused resentment. There even occurred the case in which, during the fair in the time of my predecessor, they picked up their weapons and left with grudges which inspired them to vengeance. For these reasons, it is necessary, when the Comanches come to Taos to trade, that your grace present yourself in that pueblo surrounded with a suitable guard and your person adorned with all splendor possible. The first measures your grace must take must be to provide security and protection for their ranchería. Prohibit any one from entering it when the fair is not open and your excellency not present. Place in the ranchería a garrison from the presidio, under the command of an officer, to look after and guard their horse herd to prevent it from being stolen. The Comanches have such confidence in this action that, with their horse herd under the vigilance of the soldiers, they feel themselves completely relieved from responsibility, a condition they appreciate in the highest degree. At the moment of your arrival at the fair, if the rancherías have already entered, your grace will have the chiefs called and receive them with every kindness and affection. Sit down with them and command tobacco for them so that they may smoke, as is their custom. Afterwards your grace will make them understand that they are welcome, using various expressions of friendship and confidence which discretion and wisdom suggest to learn their desires and give them a favorable opinion of the advisability of continuing their tranquility and to inspire affection for the person of your grace. This should always be done with an appearance of pleasure and agreeableness, which they also esteem highly. Exterior acts and circumstances of one's looks influence considerably the idea that they ought to form. You should introduce yourself with skill and with expressive words, maintain in your looks a mien, grave and serene, which they may observe and thus continue the faithful

friendship they have at present. With these necessary exaggerations which are required to make them cling to peace, without using threats, for as yet the Comanches do not warrant them, permit their familiarities and take part in their fun at suitable times, all of which is necessary with this kind of people. I have done so and have been able to win the love they profess for me.

If this tribe should change its idea and declare war, your grace may fear the complete ruin of this government. The armed forces of this government, especially if they were not managed with skill and valor, would not be able to resist, in continuous action, their great numbers and ferocious attacks, supported by their allies, the Pawnees and Jumanos, all warlike and equipped with guns. Although perhaps some successes might be achieved, the inconvenience of this war would be extremely prejudicial to this jurisdiction, which could not support it. An extremely useful branch of trade would be lost and the French of New Orleans would acquire it in toto. For this purpose, I have learned, the French have influenced the Comanches to alienate them from our friendship and trade. Because of these suspicious and sound reasons, your grace ought to conduct yourself with the greatest energy and precaution to prevent this tribe from withdrawing from its dependence upon us. Out of such an action would originate the most pernicious evils.

The Carlanas, with their other subordinate groups, Cuartelejos, Chilpaines, and the rest of those on the plains who live to the east of this province as far as the boundaries of Texas, also maintain peaceful relations and trade with this government. I found them, on my arrival here, with little communication with the province and with not a few indications of enmity. But, having taken advantage of an opportune occasion in those early years, I insured the friendships which they profess today. A large part of this nation is at present in the neighborhood of Pecos with such confidence in us that they have lived among these dispersed settlements except during the times when it is necessary for them to hunt buffalo or when some groups go back and forth to the plains to see their relatives. It is also extremely important to the security of this province to conserve their friendship and hold it without force. Positive friendship should be maintained with the Natageses and Faraones, and care should be taken that the latter do not associate with the Carlanas, who should be urged to remain independent, as I have done. I have always tried to keep them under my eye. Because of the trade which the Natageses carry on with the Carlanas on the plains, the first seeking buffalo meat, which resembles elk, and buffalo skins, which the Carlanas make into tents to trade for horses and mules, it is impossible to prevent the trade based upon their respective needs. One wants horses, which they lack, and the other, skins for shelter. These horses of the Natageses are those which they steal in company with the Sumas and Faraones in La Vizcaya and Sonora. While their exchanges can not be completely prevented, at least let it not be frequent with the Natageses and let it be only trade, not union and alliance against this province and La Vizcaya. In such case, the Natageses, strengthened by the support and cunning of the Plains Apaches, would develop among the Sumas the greatest boldness, which would result in the total ruin of the frontiers of La Vizcaya and the Real of Chihuahua. Thus, for these reasons, if a change should come over the Comanches, the Apaches' chief enemy, the greatest consideration becomes keeping the Carlanas and the rest of the Plains Indians at peace, always sympathetic and linked to our interests.

If by accident the three nations, Comanches, Utes, and Apaches, should come at the same time to Taos (as has happened in my time), your grace should prevent the two latter tribes from doing any injury to the Comanches, their chief enemy. Protect and ward off any annoyance which the two confederates might attempt toward the Comanches. I have always kept between them in this meeting as much harmony as if they were friends. They have exchanged their horses and arms without the least altercation in my presence and I have helped the Apaches ransom their relatives from the possession of the Comanches. I was constantly present so that by my intervening as much as was necessary in regard to prices, the two tribes might not encounter the least difficulty or become disgusted. In this case it is necessary for you to conduct yourself with

much skill and discretion and maintain respect for your person. This is the proper spirit to adopt for the treatment of these tribes; show yourself indifferent in general, but, in particular cases, persuade each one for his best interest.

The condition of this government and its circumstances, due to its organization and the diversity of the nations which surround it, must be ruled more with the skillful measures and policies of peace than those which provoke incidents of war; the latter is never favorable and may be calamitous. The small forces which this province has would be crushed by tribes of their size if they conspired against it. As the province, the bulwark of La Vizcaya and Sonora, is remote from the rest, support for it is the most precarious task that the king has in New Spain.

The domestic tribes, with their missionaries and pueblos, are subject to the vassalage of the king and to the Catholic religion. They are to be given the greatest consideration under the laws for their protection, which provide in detail for their indemnity in case of injury. In this way they may live contentedly and enjoy all possible comforts so that the example of their well-being and freedom from want may be an attraction for converting the heathen. These pueblos I have also administered with the greatest humanity and loving treatment. I have extended to them executive protection and rendered justice, so that, in the five years of my government, there has not been the slightest suspicion of subversiveness. They have always been very prompt to serve the king in war at the opportunities offered. With regard to the province of Moqui, your grace will be pleased to be guided by the representation and report which I made to his most excellent sir, the viceroy, and the opinion given as a consequence by the auditor general of war and which his excellency agreed with in the file of papers sent me, which are to be delivered to your grace.

The Apache natives of the province of Navajo to the west have in the larger part abandoned it and taken shelter in La Cebolleta near the pueblo and mission of Laguna and along the sierra and neighborhood of Zuñi. They have fled from the war with which the Utes satisfied the injury done to them by the Navajos when the latter failed to keep faith in the friendship which my good offices concerted between them. The Navajos took advantage of the simpleness and confidence of the Utes, killed a ranchería of this tribe, and stole everything they had. For this evil and traitorous action, the Utes have been frequent in making war and punishing the Navajos, whom they have forced to abandon the province. In this war I have been swayed by the very just cause of the Utes and, taking advantage of the opportunity, I sent the alcalde mayor of Santa Ana, Sía, and Jemes, Don Antonio Vaca, to persuade the Navajos to come and occupy the old missions of the Rio del Norte from Fonclara to Socorro along the El Paso road, where I would provide them with all possible conveniences and care and where they would be considerably distant from their enemies, the Utes. But on that occasion they did not wish to agree to the proposal. It will be very appropriate to hint again of a greater persecution by the Utes because fear would make the Navajos agree. Notwithstanding that I lack confidence in their wild, brute spirit, untamed and free, their congregation and establishment in those old abandoned pueblos would be extremely useful.

Satisfied that the three nations of the plains, Utes, Comanches, and Apaches, will continue in the future the firm friendship they have at present, and not noticing any disturbing actions among them, your grace can with ease, when an opportune moment makes it possible, turn the arms of this presidio and the settlers against the Faraone Apaches. Attack them and raid them in their own territories; instill fear of the rigor of the armed forces in them so that they may not provoke our military power by their thefts. While they live in fear of the armed forces, because of the punishments they have suffered, they invade La Vizcaya and Sonora. As this governor does not have any duties other than those of attending to the Faraones, your grace can humble their pride with more facility, supported by the presidio of El Paso, than can La Vizcaya, for they are within the jurisdiction of your grace. Besides, the soldiers, settlers, and warlike Indians, whose courage and valor reinforces the *gente de cuera*, have more

understanding of their terrain and the advantage of greater proximity [than La Vizcaya].

Your excellency must take care and maintain the military discipline of the soldiers and the militia by frequent exercises afoot and mounted or they will become inefficient in the use of arms. By having the troop of this presidio well instructed by officers who have sufficient intelligence to command them, your grace will not be disappointed in such necessary qualities in the soldiers. The ignorance which the presidios in this interior country suffer from in regard to what are the military regulations and discipline is extremely sad.

The lieutenant of this royal presidio, D. Nicolás Ortiz, is an officer in whom the confidence of your grace can well be placed to command any expedition because of his experience, valor, and good conduct. He has great strength for the demands of war, is a moderate soul, and without vanity. At the moment there is no other subject in the whole province suitable for this office who will give equal satisfaction and success in the royal service. Although Don Manuel Sáenz de Garbizu has been an officer of all honor and conduct and worthy of the greatest consideration because of his merit, he is at present thinking of retiring. The ensign-bearer, Don Juan Philipe de Ribera, also an officer of honor and zeal with many years of service, although elderly, is still robust. The first sergeant, Francisco Esquibel, is a man of honor and known valor. I have seen him perform with gallantry and to my satisfaction against the enemy, and at the same time with thought and astuteness in this kind of war. He is the one who frequently instructs the soldiers in the management of arms. The second sergeant, Christóbal Martín, is also very experienced and old in the service and of sufficient valor and understanding. Thus these two officers and sergeants, being worthy of every consideration, should be continued in the discharge of their offices by your grace, since the greater part of the success of the undertakings depends upon officers who are apt, capable from experience, and of known valor.

I have also instructed and drilled the militias of the country in the use of arms, having them do so together at times in their respective districts and individually, in order to teach them the exercises afoot and mounted. It is extremely convenient to the royal service to continue them in this military schooling, for, with their good will and valor, although they are few in number, they are capable of resisting many enemies among these barbarous nations. The commandant, Thomas Madrid, who has already been appointed to command them on a campaign under the orders of the lieutenant of the presidio, is a subject of much valor and honor, whose robust presence inspires respect, which also is necessary. Accordingly, it is convenient to continue him in the command of the militias when they are called upon and when it may be necessary to make a campaign or sallies.

The present alcalde mayores who were selected by me in this whole province for their duties have served to my satisfaction and with great dispatch and zeal on the occasions which the war has demanded, an understanding of which is necessary here and which they have. In La Cañada, Don Juan Joseph Lobato is one of the most capable, a man of much zeal in the fulfillment of his obligations and greatly esteemed by the Utes. He is one whose opinion may be considered judicial and of substance. In my opinion, your grace should continue him in his office, as there is no one else to look for. In Albuquerque, Luzero is a vigorous soldier, needed in that jurisdiction to oppose the Faraone Apache. In the past year he made an advance into the neighborhood of El Paso with his militia, who attacked these Indians well. He made a considerable capture and punished them for killing an Indian of Isleta and their attempt to steal the horse herd of that pueblo. He is a trifle defective in spirit because of his asperity, but he knows how to restrain himself. He is also useful in the prosecution of the duties of his office.

At Pecos and Galisteo is Thomas de Sena, who, because of his kindness, is greatly loved by the Indians. If he should be separated from them, you could not find any one who would wish to serve in that office. At Taos, Don Juan Joseph Moreno, because of accidental illness, is not in service, although he is a man of merit and has served as an officer in the presidio. Antonio Vaca of the three pueblos, Sía, Santa Ana, and Jemes, is also very suitable for those

pueblos. He is an accommodating man, and, with his charity, attends to the building of the church at Sía. He has well-known valor and merit in the service. At Acoma, Laguna, and Zuñi, the most distant ones from this capital, Don Manuel Barreras also has the necessary qualities for that office. He is the son of Ignacio Barreras, who died at the hands of the Apaches in the defense of those pueblos, because of whose merits and those of his son, who was his lieutenant, I kept him as the major justice. On those occasions which he has offered himself against the Apaches, he has conducted himself with much valor. His brother, Marcial, is the lieutenant in the pueblo of Zuñi. Both are of high spirit, goodness, and experience. With the Indians of the three pueblos, they pursue the Gila and Mescalero enemies, and at present have my orders for a campaign to carry out whatever measures are necessary in persecution and punishment of those Apaches. Because of these considerations, I hold most suitable their continuance in office. In Cochití, San Phelipe, and Santo Domingo, Juan Montes Vigil, although he is very competent, is old and ill, which makes work for him impossible.

The people of the country are perverse, poor, and lazy. Accordingly, one finds in them many irregularities which makes rigorous justice necessary and a corresponding zeal in putting down vulgar demonstrations. The omission in the execution of justice or softness on the part of the judge are consequent reasons for irregularity and lack of respect. At the same time, however, because of their extreme poverty, they are worthy of compassion. Their small haciendas, which consist of a few horses, cattle, and sheep, are exposed to the attacks of the barbarians.

To free the settlements from robberies and enemy attacks, I have ordered the regions and terrains through which the enemy can enter to be guarded by scouts continually and in necessary numbers to impede the enemy from gaining access to rob. The enemy never comes in large numbers but in small parties to hide their trail and prevent their discovery. When the scouts see them in such number that they cannot defeat them, they promptly advise the pueblos to gather forces to drive them out and pursue them. To impede the entrance of the Faraones and Natagés into the villa of Alburquerque and the neighborhood of the arroyo called Maragua, and in Santo Domingo and San Phelipe, I have continually maintained, in the summer, forty Indians from the six pueblos of Los Queres and two squads of soldiers, while the presidio has been able to operate in the spot of Coara, or Tajique, of the old missions, along the cordillera of the sierra of Sandía and the route to the south of this villa. Through these precise spots the Apaches must enter. The scouts take care to examine the hidden paths and the one which comes through the Bocas de Abó. This activity the officers of the presidio and the Queres Indians engage in by making an examination of all these terrains and entrances. In this manner the jurisdictions remain free from thefts. Although in Alburquerque the Gilas can invade along the Rio de Puerco, the sierra de Los Ladrones is at such a great distance that they rarely try to come in from that direction. They always seek the shelter of the sierra de Sandía. The troops which occupy this area are posted in the spot of Coara, or Tafique, and make the entry of the Apaches impossible. The settlers of Alburquerque, however, wish to have a soldier for every cow and horse they pasture so that they would have nothing to worry about and could live in slovenly indifference. I have tried to accustom them to the idea that each one should take care of the defense of his own hacienda. The number of settlers in that area is sufficient to do so; besides, they are well trained and experienced in war. I wished them to do this because of the great difficulty the presidio meets in providing the escorts which each jurisdiction wishes. One should always keep the presidio as a unit, otherwise its strength, which is the main thing, is weakened when it is necessary to attend immediately to any area threatened. When such a threat occurs, one can quickly oppose the enemy by calling the militia together until the troops arrive.

At the entrances through Mora, which is to the northeast of this villa on the flank of the pueblo of Picuríes and through which the Comanches can enter, notwithstanding it has been three years since they did so, it is necessary that Picuríes scouts should be placed. Those of Taos should examine the slope as far as the Rio Colorado, for, notwithstanding security, one must not forget the use of care. When intelligence is necessary, it is always those of Pecos and Galisteo of all regions who show themselves most capable and swift in action. These Indians also guard the approaches to their pueblos. In these duties one must always take care, since the effect of carelessness produces the consequences of a defeat for us and an enemy victory.

My zealous desire is to put the understanding of your grace upon the right road and make your conduct suitable and well directed for whatever may occur in this government. But there are circumstances in which only discretion and lively understanding at the precise moment of the event can discern what to do. I shall always be occupied with earnest desires for your success. I shall praise those which your grace may have, and which I sincerely desire for you, in the service of both Majesties and for the public benefit for this government. May God guard you many years, as I desire, for this, your home. August 12, 1754. It is a copy of the original.

Questions

1. How do the Plains peoples described by Vélez Cachupín compare with those portrayed by Castañeda? What explains the differences?
2. Characterize relations between the Spanish and Indian populations of New Mexico and the Indian peoples to its north and west. Were these relations hostile? Profitable?
3. What was the tenor of relations among the Indians in the regions around New Mexico? What divided or linked them?
4. What strategies did Vélez Cachupín find effective in securing and maintaining good relations with New Mexico's Indian neighbors?
5. What effect did the French presence in Louisiana have on the security of New Mexico?

18 Imperial Wars and Crisis

In a series of conflicts between 1689 and 1763, the French and British Empires fought to deter-mine who would be the dominant European presence north of Mexico, and perhaps who would pose the greatest danger to the Spanish colony. The stakes were high. As the British and French colonies in North America and the West Indies developed, and as trade between them and Europe increased, their economic and strategic value mushroomed. Like Spain in the sixteenth century, France and Britain were deriving wealth and power from American possessions, and they were increasingly threatening one another as Spain had once threatened them. So long as this vigorous Anglo-French rivalry subsisted, the Indian nations of the continent could exploit it, demanding recognition, presents, trade goods, and military support as the price of alliance. And so long as the French Empire remained formidable in North America, the British colonies would remain dependent on the British Empire for defense. With the French defeat in the Seven Years' War, North America's Indians would suddenly find themselves facing Britain and its colonists alone, and these same colonists would increasingly contemplate striking out on their own.

18.1 La Galissonière Explains the Value of France's American Colonies*

We have already met the Marquis de al Galissonière, who was serving as governor-general of New France when Peter Kalm visited it in 1749. In this 1751 memoir, La Galissonière asserts the strategic impor-tance of the French North American colonies.

MEMOIR

On the colonies of France in North America

By M. le Marquis de la Galissonière

The claims set forth by the commissaries of His Britannic Majesty as to the extent of Acadia, and the measures pursued by England to establish herself in that part of the American Continent are of a nature to require the most serious attention of the government.

---

*"Memoir of La Galissonière," in *Anglo-French Boundary Dis-putes in the West, 1749–1763*, ed., *Theodore Calvin Pease* (Springfield: Illinos State Historical Library, *1936*), 5–22.

Just when the peace appeared to have lulled the jealousy of the English in Europe, it breaks forth in full force in America; and if barriers are not immediately opposed to it capable of checking its results, England will have prepared herself to invade the French colonies throughout at the beginning of the first war.

It is with that view that they seek to make sure of all the approaches to Canada. To demonstrate how important the matter is, it will be necessary to go into detail on that colony and on the neighboring regions.

First, though briefly, the usefulness of the colonies in general will be demonstrated. What can in particular be alleged against Canada will not be concealed; but it will be shown that there are essential and capital reasons for looking to its preservation, and for fortifying and enlarging it.

The description will begin with the north and Hudson Bay, which bounds it on that side; then the settlements of the Gulf of St. Lawrence, Isle Royale, and Acadia will be successively reviewed; next will be considered the heart of the colony along the river St. Lawrence; the importance of the posts of Oswego, Niagara, Detroit, and the Illinois will be examined. It will be demonstrated how necessary it is to maintain the communication by the Ohio River with Louisiana. And from this various information will be deduced the means that are indispensable to bring to pass the failure of the ambitious designs of England, and to save to France, countries which have become one of the most important portions of the domain of the crown. All these different subjects will be treated by as many separate articles.

ARTICLE 2

Of the importance and the necessity of preserving Canada and Louisiana:

It may be objected that colonies like San Domingo, Martinique, and the other tropical islands which produce a revenue to the state and wealth to the realm may well be preserved; but that colonies which, far from producing revenue or wealth, are an expense, like Canada and Louisiana, should be abandoned to their own resources; that, otherwise, their vast extent prevents their affording mutual assistance; that they can be communicated with only by the mouths of two rivers more than nine hundred leagues apart; that the length and difficulty of navigation always makes their goods dearer than those coming from New England; that moreover since it is easy for enemies superior in naval strength to interrupt their communication with Europe, it is always necessary to keep them provisioned a year in advance; finally that the expenses of those colonies far exceed their produce. Despite all these disadvantages the motives of honor, glory, and religion do not permit the abandonment of an established colony; or giving up to themselves (or rather to a nation hostile by taste, education, and religious principle) the Frenchmen who have gone thither at the solicitation of the government in the hope of its protection, and who peculiarly merit it by their fidelity and devotion; or, finally, abandoning so salutary a task as the conversion of the heathen who dwell in this vast continent.

These motives however will not be urged. However great the disadvantages of these colonies the uncertain future products both of Canada and Louisiana will not be adduced as arguments, although the expectation of them is based on an immense country, a great people, fertile lands, forests, quarries, and mines already discovered. Here Canada will be regarded only as a barren frontier, such as the Alps are to Piedmont, or as Luxemburg would be to France, and as it is perhaps to the Queen of Hungary.

The question is if it is possible to abandon a country, however ill-favored, and however great the expense of maintaining it, when by its position it affords great advantages against its neighbors.

This is precisely the case of Canada; it cannot be denied that this colony has always been an expense to France, and that there is every appearance that it will long remain on the same footing; but it is at the same time the strongest bulwark that can be opposed to the ambition of the English.

We should not flatter ourselves that we shall long be able to maintain the expense of a navy equal to theirs [the English]; there remains then only the expedient of attacking them in their possessions; that cannot be done by forces sent from Europe save with little hope of success and with great expense. On the contrary, by fortifying ourselves in America and husbanding the resources of our colonies, we can retain the advantages we now have and even increase them at an expense very moderate in comparison with the cost of armaments equipped in Europe.

The utility of Canada does not end with preserving the French colonies and making the English fear for their own. That colony is not less essential for the preservation of the Spanish possessions in America, and above all of Mexico.

As long as that barrier is so well guarded that the English cannot penetrate it, as long as care is taken to fortify it more and more, it will serve as the outwork of Louisiana, which up to now has only maintained itself under the protection of Canada, and by the alliance of the Canadians with the Indians.

All that has been set forth sufficiently proves that it is of the last importance and an absolute necessity to omit no means, and to spare no expense, to assure the preservation of Canada, since only through it can America be enslaved to English ambition; and the progress of their empire in that part of the world is what is most likely to give them the upper hand in Europe.

Here the point of right will not be further discussed, but it must be observed that this post [Oswego], which has always been regarded as an object of small importance, is capable of causing the complete ruin of Canada and has already dealt the colony some rude blows. It is there that the French often carry on an illicit trade which transfers to England clear profits that Canada should afford to France. It is there that the English lavish brandy on the Indians, the use of which had been forbidden them by the ordinances of our kings, because it makes them madmen. Finally it is thither that the English draw all the Indian tribes, and try by means of presents, not only to win them over, but even to induce them to assassinate the French traders scattered throughout the vast extent of the forests of New France.

So long as the English retain Oswego, we can only be in perpetual distrust of those Indians who till now have been the most faithful to the French; in the most profound peace we shall have to maintain twice the troops the state of the colony requires or permits, to build and guard forts in numberless places, and to send nearly every year numerous and expensive detachments to control the various Indian tribes.

The navigation of the lakes will always be in danger of being disturbed; the cultivation of the soil will progress only by halves and can be carried on only in the center of the colony. Finally we shall always be in a situation that has all the inconveniences and none of the advantages of a state of war. Nothing therefore must be omitted for the destruction of this dangerous post, on the first occasion for reprisals that the English afford us from the hostilities they are only too used to committing in time of peace; always supposing that it is not possible to get them to give it up of good will for some equivalent.

What has already been said in the course of this memoir of the utility of Canada with respect to the preservation of Mexico, makes it evident that the free and sure communication of Canada with the Mississippi is absolutely necessary. That chain broken, would leave a gap by which the English would doubtless profit to reach the silver mines. Many of their books enlarge on this project, which will never be carried out if France maintains its possession of Canada.

What is most important to this end is the Ohio River, sometimes called the Beautiful River. It rises near the country occupied in part by the Iroquois, flows to the south, empties into the Wabash, and goes with it to the Mississippi. The Ohio was discovered by the Sieur de la Salle, who took possession of it in the name of the king. The region might today be filled with French settlements if the governors of Canada had not been deterred from establishing strong posts there by the fear that they might be the scene of a contraband trade between the English and French traders.

The English have no posts there, and only came secretly to trade until the last war, when the revolt of some neighboring tribes against the French encouraged them to come more boldly. Since the peace they have been summoned to withdraw, and if they do not, no doubt the governor of Canada will force them to do so. Otherwise it would be the same as at Oswego, and the evil would be even worse; for a settlement on the Ohio River would put the English in a much better position to do harm than at Oswego.

1. They would have even more than at Oswego the opportunity of seducing the Indians.

2. They could with greater ease interrupt the communication of Canada and Louisiana since it is almost solely by the Ohio River that detachments from Canada can be carried to the Mississippi, that are of sufficient size to secure that colony, still feeble, against the enterprises of the Indians bordering on Carolina whom the English ceaselessly incite against the French.

3. If ever the English became strong enough in America to venture on the conquest of Mexico, they must necessarily descend upon it by the Ohio River.

4. Only by that river can they attack in considerable force, and with prospects of success, the posts of the Illinois and those which are or may be established along the St. Louis River, otherwise called the Mississippi.

5. By this river also they can attack the post of Miamis, which would destroy one of our best communications with the Mississippi River, and would entail the loss of Detroit, an important post which will be dealt with later.

It is thought therefore that one of the outlays most urgently needed is for the establishment of posts on the Ohio River; but it also appears that those posts will not acquire solidity until the strength of both Niagara and Detroit has been increased.

It is to this last post especially that we must cling today. If there were once a thousand farmer inhabitants in that region, it would feed and defend all the others. In the whole interior of Canada, it is the fittest site for a city where all the commerce of the lakes would center and which, furnished with a good garrison and surrounded with a good number of inhabitants, would overawe all the Indians of the continent. To see its position on the map is enough to perceive its usefulness. Situated on the St. Lawrence River, close to the Ohio, the Illinois, and the Mississippi River, it is in a position to protect all these places, and even the posts north of the lakes.

Following nearly the same route, as well as the same line of reasoning, the post meriting most attention after Detroit, or perhaps concurrently with it, is that of the Illinois.

There the climate is almost completely different: no longer is one exposed to the hardship of a seven months' winter; not as in the neighborhood of Quebec is one forced to clearing the forest at ruinous expense to put to use land that is of quite indifferent quality: away from the banks of the rivers all the country is open, and only awaits the plow. There are already some inhabitants who possess a good number of cattle, but nothing in comparison with what could be done there.

Furthermore these vast plains that by different extents reach for several hundred leagues beyond Lake Superior are covered with an innumerable multitude of cattle of a species that presumably will not be destroyed for some centuries, both because the country is not sufficiently peopled for their consumption to be noticeable, and because, the leather being unfit for the same uses as that from the European species, it will never happen as in the case of the Spaniards on the La Plata, that the cattle will be killed solely for their hides.

If the Illinois cattle cannot supply much in the future for the tanneries, advantages at least equivalent may be expected from them over which we may pause a moment.

1. They are covered with a kind of wool fine enough to be used for various purposes: trials have been made of it.

2. It cannot be doubted that by catching them young and splaying them, they would be fit for draft; perhaps they would have the same advantages

over domestic oxen as horses, being much quicker. They also appear more vigorous, but perhaps it is their wild upbringing which contributes to that: it does not appear that they would be hard to tame. Bulls and cows that were very gentle have been noticed at four to five years of age.

3. If the Illinois country were sufficiently settled so that the inhabitants could enclose a large number of the cattle in parks, the beef could be salted. This could be carried very far without a large population in the Illinois. This trade might enable one to do without Irish beef for Martinique and even to furnish the Spanish colonies in competition with the English and at a lower price.

It will without doubt be objected that these profits are very remote, and that there may be unforeseen obstacles; but postpone them as long as you will, one question always remains; not if the post should be abandoned, but if it should be given up to England, who would make it a solidly established depot for undertaking the conquest of Mexico.

Nothing is said of the mines that it is claimed have been discovered in this district. Independently of the fact that we are not sufficiently informed, we should not think of them until the district has been sufficiently developed in men, wheat, and cattle.

ARTICLE 6

Of Louisiana:

We will not enlarge on what regards Louisiana, which, weak as it is today, can only sustain itself under the shadow of the strength of Canada.

Louisiana is a country very susceptible to useful cultivation, in which inhabitants are not lacking. It can be peopled on the lower or upper course of the river; neither should be neglected. The progress of commerce would be more rapid if the portion close to the sea were settled: it may none the less be doubted if it is this side that should receive the chief attention of the government. Independent of the fact that it is the portion most capable of exciting the envy and clamor of neighboring colonies, it is also the portion which will best fill itself with inhabitants without the government's interfering.

If only the strength and solidity of settlements are considered, the decision should be to people Louisiana on the upper river. It should draw its chief strength and its principal resources from the post of the Illinois, mentioned in the preceding article. This post, as was just indicated, is not nearly so attractive as the lower river. In some sort it is a lost land where for a long time to come commerce will not be lucrative, nor fortunes quickly made; but on the other hand they may be more permanent, than in any other place in the colonies. It should further be considered that the difficulties of ascending the river are such that the lower part of the colony can never feed the Illinois. The post of the Illinois on the contrary seems placed where it can always, despite all the navies of the world, export grain and meat.

There are some things to say of the posts near Georgia and Carolina, but since they are immediately subordinate to the government of Louisiana, and since we have but an imperfect knowledge of them, we will refrain from speaking of them, the more since this memoir is already long, and since to these posts may be applied what has already been said of the Ohio River and of Oswego.

Questions

1. What, in La Galissonière's view, makes Canada and Louisiana so important?
2. How does he understand the intentions of the British?
3. According to La Galissonière, what role did Indians play in the geopolitics of North America?
4. Explain the importance of the Ohio Valley to French and British interests.
5. In La Galissonière's view, what future benefits might North America offer France?

18.2 Disaster in the Forest*

In 1755, General Edwards Braddock famously led a British army to a costly and humiliating defeat about eight miles form the junction of the Ohio and Monongahela Rivers (the site of modern Pittsburgh). In a passage from his autobiography, Benjamin Franklin offers his one explanation of what happened.

This general was, I think, a brave man, and might probably have made a figure as a good officer in some European war. But he had too much self-confidence, too high an opinion of the validity of regular troops, and too mean a one of both Americans and Indians. George Croghan, our Indian interpreter, join'd him on his march with one hundred of those people, who might have been of great use to his army as guides, scouts, etc., if he had treated them kindly; but he slighted and neglected them, and they gradually left him.

In conversation with him one day, he was giving me some account of his intended progress. "After taking Fort Duquesne," says he, "I am to proceed to Niagara; and, having taken that, to Frontenac, if the season will allow time; and I suppose it will, for Duquesne can hardly detain me above three or four days; and then I see nothing that can obstruct my march to Niagara." Having before revolv'd in my mind the long line his army must make in their march by a very narrow road, to be cut for them thro' the woods and bushes, and also what I had read of a former defeat of fifteen hundred French, who invaded the Iroquois country, I had conceiv'd some doubts and some fears for the event of the campaign. But I ventur'd only to say, "To be sure, sir, if you arrive well before Duquesne, with these fine troops, so well provided with artillery, that place not yet compleatly fortified, and as we hear with no very strong garrison, can probably make but a short resistance. The only danger I apprehend of obstruction to your march is from

ambuscades of Indians, who, by constant practice, are dexterous in laying and executing them; and the slender line, near four miles long, which your army must make, may expose it to be attack'd by surprise in its flanks, and to be cut like a thread into several pieces, which, from their distance, can not come up in time to support each other."

He smil'd at my ignorance, and reply'd, "These savages may, indeed, be a formidable enemy to your raw American militia, but upon the king's regular and disciplin'd troops, sir, it is impossible they should make any impression." I was conscious of an impropriety in my disputing with a military man in matters of his profession, and said no more. The enemy, however, did not take the advantage of his army which I apprehended its long line of march expos'd it to, but let it advance without interruption till within nine miles of the place; and then, when more in a body (for it had just passed a river, where the front had halted till all were come over), and in a more open part of the woods than any it had pass'd, attack'd its advanced guard by a heavy fire from behind trees and bushes, which was the first intelligence the general had of an enemy's being near him. This guard being disordered, the general hurried the troops up to their assistance, which was done in great confusion, thro' waggons, baggage, and cattle; and presently the fire came upon their flank: the officers, being on horseback, were more easily distinguish'd, pick'd out as marks, and fell very fast; and the soldiers were crowded together in a huddle, having or hearing no orders, and standing to be shot at till two-thirds of them were killed; and then, being seiz'd with a panick, the whole fled with precipitation.

The waggoners took each a horse out of his team and scamper'd; their example was immediately followed by others; so that all the waggons, provisions, artillery, and stores were left to the enemy. The general, being wounded, was brought off with difficulty; his secretary, Mr. Shirley, was killed by his side; and out of eighty-six officers,

*John Bigelow, ed., *Autobiography of Benjamin Franklin* (Philadelphia: J. B. Lippincott & Co., 1868), 309–313.

sixty-three were killed or wounded, and seven hundred and fourteen men killed out of eleven hundred. These eleven hundred had been picked men from the whole army; the rest had been left behind with Colonel Dunbar, who was to follow with the heavier part of the stores, provisions, and baggage. The flyers, not being pursu'd, arriv'd at Dunbar's camp, and the panick they brought with them instantly seiz'd him and all his people; and, tho' he had now above one thousand men, and the enemy who had beaten Braddock did not at most exceed four hundred Indians and French together, instead of proceeding, and endeavoring to recover some of the lost honour, he ordered all the stores, ammunition, etc., to be destroy'd, that he might have more horses to assist his flight towards the settlements, and less lumber to remove. He was there met with requests from the governors of Virginia, Maryland, and Pennsylvania, that he would post his troops on the frontiers, so as to afford some protection to the inhabitants; but he continu'd his hasty march thro' all the country, not thinking himself safe till he arriv'd at Philadelphia, where the inhabitants could protect him. This whole transaction gave us Americans the first suspicion that our exalted ideas of the prowess of British regulars had not been well founded.

Questions

1. What did Franklin see as the main reason for Braddock's defeat?
2. What was Franklin's assessment of the Indians' martial skills? What was Braddock's view? Who was more accurate?
3. How reliable is Franklin's account of events? Do you think Franklin really predicted what would happen to Braddock's army, or simply claimed that he did after the fact?
4. How might European strategists use Franklin's discussion of Braddock's defeat to plan future operations in America?

18.3   Frenchmen, Indians, and Prisoners at Fort William Henry*

On August 9, 1757 British Fort William Henry (on the southern end of Lake George in northeastern New York) surrendered to a besieging Franco-Indian army led by the Marquis de Montcalm. Under the terms of the surrender, British forces were to be escorted safely to another British position. The events that followed are difficult to reconstruct and have been the source of controversy for more than two centuries, but it appears that Indian allies of the French assaulted first the British sick and wounded within the fort and then the British column marching away from it. The event was made famous in part because of James Fenimore Cooper's fictionalized account of it in The Last of the Mohicans. *In the document that follows, French officer Louis-Antoine de Bougainville offers one version of events surrounding the "massacre."*

[1757]

August 9:

Two hundred workers were ordered to improve the work during the night. At seven in the morning the fort raised a white flag and asked to capitulate. Colonel Young came to propose articles of capitulation to the Marquis de Montcalm. I was sent to draw them up and to take the first steps in putting them in operation.

In substance the capitulation provided that the troops, both of the fort and of the entrenched camp, to the number of two thousand men, should depart with the honors of war with the baggage of the officers and of the soldiers, that they should be conducted to Fort Lydius escorted by a detachment of our troops and by the principal officers and interpreters attached to the Indians, that until the return of this escort an officer should remain in our hands as a hostage, that the troops would not serve for eighteen months against His Most Catholic Majesty nor against his allies, that within

*Louis Antoine de Bougainville, *Adventure in the Wilderness: The American Journals of Louis Antoine de Bougainville, 1756–1760,* trans. and ed. Edward P. Hamilton (Norman: University of Oklahoma Press, 1964), 169–175.

three months all French, Canadian, and Indian prisoners taken on land in North America since the commencement of the war should be returned to French forts, that the artillery, vessels, and all the munitions and provisions would belong to His Most Catholic Majesty, except one six pounder cannon which the Marquis de Montcalm granted Colonel Monro and the garrison to witness his esteem for the fine defense they had made.

Before signing the capitulation the Marquis de Montcalm assembled a council to which the chiefs of all the nations had been summoned. He informed them of the articles granted the besieged, the motives which determined his according them, asked their consent and their promise that their young men would not commit any disorder. The chiefs agreed to everything and promised to restrain their young men.

One sees by this action of the Marquis de Montcalm to what point one is a slave to Indians in this country. They are a necessary evil.

I think that we could have had these troops as prisoners at discretion, but in the first case there would have been two thousand more men to feed, and in the second one could not have restrained the barbarity of the Indians, and it is never permitted to sacrifice humanity to what is only the shadow of glory.

At noon the fort was turned over to our troops from the trenches, and, the garrison leaving with its baggage, it was necessary to let the Indians and Canadians in to pillage all the remaining effects. Only with the greatest trouble could the provisions and munitions be saved. The English troops were to remain in their entrenched camp until the next day. Despite a guard from our troops that we had put on it, the Indians could not be stopped from entering and pillaging. Everything was done to stop them, consultation with the chiefs, wheedling on our part, authority that the officers and interpreters attached to them possessed. We will be most fortunate if we can avoid a massacre. Detestable position of which those who are not here can have no idea, and one which makes the victory painful to the conquerors.

The Marquis de Montcalm went himself to the entrenched camp. He there made the greatest efforts to prevent the greed of the Indians and, I will say it here, [also] of certain people attached to them from being the cause of misfortunes far greater than pillage.

At last by nine in the evening it appeared that order had been re-established in the camp. The Marquis de Montcalm even was able to arrange that, beyond the escort agreed upon by the capitulation, two chiefs from each nation should escort the English as far as the vicinity of Fort Edward. I had taken care upon going into the English camp to advise the officers and soldiers to throw away all wine, brandy, and intoxicating liquors; they themselves had realized of what consequence it was for them to take this precaution.

At ten in the evening I was sent by order of the Marquis de Montcalm to carry to the Marquis de Vaudreuil the news of the surrender of Fort William Henry and the capitulation.

I reached Montreal the eleventh at four in the afternoon. The news I brought caused a sensation, all the more agreeable because a courier who left Fort William Henry thirty-six hours before me and had arrived only three hours previously had caused uneasiness there, saying that the enemy still held out, something which to the Canadians appeared extraordinary and disturbing. Several, however, were not pleased by the news because the English were not taken prisoners and we had not at once marched against Fort Lydius. These same people had always advised against taking prisoners, the colony not being in condition to feed them. Doubtless blood was necessary to content them, but pray God that the French be not inclined to such wishes. In regard to the enterprise against Fort Lydius, invincible obstacles prevented us from thinking of it, the lack of munitions, and provisions, the difficulty of a portage of six leagues without oxen or horses, with an army worn out by fatigue and bad food, the departure of all the Indians of the Far West who have five hundred leagues to go over lakes and rivers which freeze and prevent them remaining longer, the flight of almost all the domesticated Indians, the necessity of sending back the Canadians for the harvests already ripe, sixteen hundred men assembled at the fort whose capture they think so easy, these then are the reasons which stopped the further advance of the King's army.

If the wheat survey successfully made in July had been ordered in April, as the welfare of the colony demanded, our campaign would have started six weeks earlier, the enemy would not have had time to render his defense so strong, the difficulties outlined above would not have existed, and I dare say that today we would have had Fort Lydius. But this wheat survey was against the interest of the Commissary of Stores, and this Commissary of Stores is only the dummy of the great society to which the Governor General himself belongs. It is thus that they serve the King in the colonies.

August 12–31:

A great misfortune which we dreaded has happened. Apparently the capitulation is violated and all Europe will oblige us to justify ourselves.

During the night of the ninth to tenth the guard we placed in the entrenched camp of the English did everything it could to prevent disorder. They had decided to have the garrison march out during the night, because it was known that the Indians almost never acted during the night. But the warning that was given that six hundred of these barbarians were in ambush at the moment caused a contrary order to be sent. This warning, however, was false. At daybreak the English, who were inconceivably frightened by the sight of the Indians, wished to leave before our escort was all assembled and in place. They abandoned their trunks and other heavy baggage that the lack of wagons prevented their carrying away, and started to march. The Indians had already butchered a few sick in the tents which served as a hospital. The [domesticated] Abnakis of Panaomeska, who pretend to have recently suffered from some bad behavior on the part of the English, commenced the riot. They shouted the death cry and hurled themselves on the tail of the column which started to march out.

The English, instead of showing resolution, were seized with fear and fled in confusion, throwing away their arms, baggage, and even their coats. Their fear emboldened the Indians of all the nations who started pillaging, killed some dozen soldiers, and took away five or six hundred. Our escort did what it could. A few grenadiers were wounded. The Marquis de Montcalm rushed up at the noise; M. de Bourlamaque and several French officers risked their lives in tearing the English from the hands of the Indians. For in a case like this the Indians respect nothing. Add to that, that a great number of English soldiers, hoping to put them in a good humor, had given them rum which, despite all our warnings, they had kept in their flasks. Finally the disorder quieted down and the Marquis de Montcalm at once took away from the Indians four hundred of these unfortunate men and had them clothed. The French officers divided with the English officers the few spare clothes they had and the Indians, loaded with booty, disappeared that same day. Only a few domesticated ones remained.

The same day the army moved its camp to a place in front of the entrenched camp facing the road from Lydius. The demolition was started.

August 11–13:

They continued the demolition with much difficulty, the fort having been solidly built.

August 14:

The Marquis de Montcalm sent Sieur Hamilton, English officer, with Sieur Savournin, lieutenant in La Sarre regiment, and an escort of thirty men to Fort Edward, charged with carrying two letters addressed, one to General Webb, the other to Milord Loudoun. In the first he explained to General Webb how the tumult had occurred and advised him that the next day he would send back all the English that he could gather together half way on the road to Fort Lydius, where he prayed him to come and look for them. In the same way he told Milord Loudoun the details of the disorder occasioned by the Indians, of his attempt to stop it and to carry out [the provisions of] the capitulation; that he, [acting] in good faith on his part expected that he [Loudoun] would observe it scrupulously, adding that the least infraction on the part of the English would bring unpleasant consequences.

August 15:

In the morning the Marquis de Montcalm sent off with an escort of three hundred men four hundred English ransomed from the Indians. Halfway to Fort Edward they found a like detachment of their [British] nation, to whom our escort delivered them. They had with them the cannon accorded Lieutenant Colonel Monro by the capitulation. This same day the demolition was completed.

August 17:

Madness and indecent folly on the part of the Canadians. Officers and men leave without permission. It was necessary to fire over their heads to stop them. La Sarre brigade camped at the Falls under orders of the Chevalier. The rest of the army at the head of the Portage with the Marquis de Montcalm. Portaging was started on the seventeenth and pushed along with great vigor.

August 19:

Béarn goes to take up again its former camp and the work at the fort. The same day all the army sang a *Te Deum*.

Meanwhile, the Indians arrived at Montreal in a crowd with about two hundred English. M. de Vaudreuil scolded them for having violated the capitulation. They excused themselves and put the blame on the domesticated Indians. They were told that they must give up these English, who were captured unfairly, and that they would be paid for them, two kegs of brandy apiece. But this ransom was not greeted with enthusiasm. The Canadians bought the English plunder from them.

They did not spare the brandy, and this liquor, the god of the Indians, abounds in their camp. They get drunk, and the English die a hundred deaths from fear every day.

August 15:

At two o'clock in the presence of the entire town they killed one of them, put him in a kettle, and forced his unfortunate compatriots to eat him.

I would believe that if immediately upon their arrival, the Governor had stated to them that until all the English were given up, there would be no presents, nor even any food, that under the most severe penalties he had forbidden the citizens either to sell or to give them brandy, that he himself could have gone to their cabins and snatched the English away from them. I believe it, accustomed as I am to think like a European. I have seen just the opposite, and my soul has several times shuddered at spectacles my eyes have witnessed.

Will they in Europe believe that the Indians alone have been guilty of this horrible violation of the capitulation, that desire for the Negroes and other spoils of the English has not caused the people who are at the head of these nations to loosen the curb, perhaps to go even farther? The more so since one today may see one of these leaders, unworthy of the name of officer and Frenchman, leading in his train a Negro kidnapped from the English commander under the pretext of appeasing the shades of a dead Indian, giving his family flesh for flesh. That is enough of the horror, the memory of which I would hope could be effaced from the minds of men. *Heu fuge crudeles terras fuge littus iniquum.*

On the twentieth I finished the dispatches reporting our expedition to the court. The Marquis de Montcalm, busy with other matters, had charged me with writing the details to the ministers. The courier left on the twenty-first to carry these dispatches to Quebec and the flute *Fortune* is ordered to sail at once.

Questions

1. How reliable is Bougainville's account? What motives might influence his portrayal of events?
2. Who controlled Montcalm's Indian allies?
3. Why, in Bougainville's view, was the French army "a slave to Indians"? What made the

Indians "necessary" for the French? If the Indians were so necessary, why did Montcalm take the chance of antagonizing them by depriving them of their British prisoners?

4. What prevented the French forces from following up their victory at Fort William Henry? How would such considerations affect French fortunes in the war as a whole?

5. How many British prisoners did the Indians actually kill? What did they intend to do with the rest? What did France's Indian allies expect in exchange for their assistance? In an earlier war, what secured the release of Mary Rowlandson?

18.4 Pontiac's Forces Surprise and Are Surprised*

With French defeat in the Seven Years' War, the Indians of the Ohio Valley and the Great Lakes found themselves deprived of a useful trading partner and an effective restraint on the expansion and arrogance of the British Empire. In 1763, hoping to chasten British subjects and draw France back to the continent, an array of Indian nations attacked British forts and settlements throughout the Great Lakes Ohio Valley. In the following selection, explorer Jonathan Carver recounts the very different course of events at Michilimackinac and Detroit, two former French strongholds recently taken over by the British.

Michillimackinac, from whence I began my travels, is a fort composed of a strong stockade, and is usually defended by a garrison of one hundred men. It contains about thirty houses, one of which belongs to the governor, and another to the commissary. Several traders also dwell within its fortifications, who find it a convenient situation to traffic with the neighbouring nations. Michillimackinac, in the language of the Chipeway Indians, signifies a Tortoise; and the place is supposed to receive its name from an island, lying about six or seven miles to north-east, within sight of the fort, which has the appearance of that animal.

During the Indian war that followed soon after the conquest of Canada in the year 1763, and which was carried on by an army of confederate nations, composed of the Hurons, Miamies,

Chipeways, Ottowaws, Pontowattimies, Missis-sauges, and some other tribes, under the direction of Pontiac, a celebrated Indian warrior, who had always been in the French interest, it was taken by surprize in the following manner: The Indians having settled their plan, drew near the fort, and began a game at ball, a pastime much used among them, and not unlike tennis. In the height of their game, at which some of the English officers, not suspecting any deceit, stood looking on, they struck the ball, as if by accident, over the stockade; this they repeated two or three time, to make the deception more complete; till at length, having by this means lulled every suspicion of the centry at the south gate, a party rushed by him; and the rest soon following, they took possession of the fort, without meeting with any opposition. Having accomplished their design, the Indians had the humanity to spare the lives of the greatest part of the garrison and traders, but they made them all prisoners, and carried them off. However, some time after they took them to Montreal, where they were redeemed at a good price. The fort also was given up again to the English at the peace made with Pontiac, by the commander of Detroit the year following. . . .

How well the party he detached to take Fort Michillimackinac succeeded, the reader already knows. To get into his hands Detroit, a place of greater consequence, and much better guarded, required greater resolution, and more consummate art. He of course took the management of this expedition on himself, and drew near it with the principal body of his troops. He was, however, prevented from carrying his designs into

---

*Jonathan Carver, *Three Years Travels through the Interior Parts of North America* (Philadelphia, 1789), 77–82.

execution, by an apparently trivial and unforeseen circumstance. On such does the fate of mighty empires frequently depend!

The town of Detroit, when Pontiac formed his plan, was garrisoned by about three hundred men, commanded by Major Gladwyn, a gallant officer. As at that time every appearance of war was at an end, and the Indians seemed to be on a friendly footing, Pontiac approached the Fort, without exciting any suspicions in the breast of the governor or the inhabitants. He encamped at a little distance from it, and sent to let the commandant know that he was come to trade; and being desirous of brightening the chain of peace between the English and his nation, desired that he and his chiefs might be admitted to hold a council with him. The governor still unsuspicious, and not in the least doubting the sincerity of the Indians, granted their general's request, and fixed on the next morning for their reception.

The evening of that day, an Indian woman who had been employed by Major Gladwyn, to make him a pair of Indian shoes, out of curious elk-skin, brought them home. The Major was so pleased with them, that, intending these as a present for a friend, he ordered her to take the remainder back, and make it into others for himself. He then directed his servant to pay her for those she had done, and dismissed her. The woman went to the door that led to the street, but no further; she there loitered about as if she had not finished the business on which she came. A servant at length observed her, and asked her why the staid there; she gave him, however, no answer.

Some short time after, the governor himself saw her; and enquired of his servant what occasioned her stay. Not being able to get a satisfactory answer, he ordered the woman to be called in. When she came into his presence he desired to know what was the reason of her loitering about, and not hastening home before the gates were shut, that she might complete in due time the work he had given her to do. She told him, after much hesitation, that as he had always behaved with great goodness towards her, she was unwilling

to take away the remainder of the skin, because he put so great a value upon it; and yet had not been able to prevail upon herself to tell him so. He then asked her, why she was more reluctant to do so now, than she had been when she made the former pair. With encreased reluctance she answered, that she never should be able to bring them back.

His curiosity being now excited, he insisted on her disclosing to him the secret that seemed to be struggling in her bosom for utterance. At last on receiving a promise that the intelligence she was about to give him should not turn to her prejudice, and that if it appeared to be beneficial, she should be rewarded for it, she informed him, that at the council to be held with the Indians the following day, Pontiac and his chiefs intended to murder him; and, after having massacred the garrison and inhabitants, to plunder the town. That for this purpose all the chiefs who were to be admitted into the council-room, had cut their guns short, so that they could conceal them under their blankets; with which, at a signal given by their general, on delivering the belt, they were all to rise up, and instantly to fire on him and his attendants. Having effected this, they were immediately to rush into the town, where they would find themselves supported by a great number of their warriors, that were to come into it during the sitting of the council, under pretence of trading, but privately armed in the same manner. Having gained from the women every necessary particular relative to the plot, and also of the means by which she acquired a knowledge of them, he dismissed her with injunctions of secrecy, and a promise of fulfilling on his part with punctuality, the engagements he had entered into.

The intelligence the governor had just received, gave him great uneasiness; and he immediately consulted the officer who was not next to him in command, on the subject. But that gentleman considering the information as a story invented for some artful purposes, advised him to pay no attention to it. This conclusion, however, had happily no weight with him. He thought it prudent to conclude it to be true, till he was convinced that it was not so; and therefore, without revealing his suspicions to any other person, he took every needful precaution that the time would admit of. He walked round the fort during the whole night, and saw himself that every centinel was on duty, and every weapon of defence in proper order.

As we traversed the ramparts, which lay nearest to the Indian camp, he heard them in high festivity, and, little imagining that their plot was discovered, probably pleasing themselves with the anticipation of their success. As soon as the morning dawned, he ordered all the garrison under arms; and then imparting his apprehensions to a few of the principal officers, gave them such directions as he thought necessary. At the same time he sent round to all the traders, to inform them, that as it was expected a great number of Indians would enter the town that day, who might be inclined to plunder, he desired they would have their arms ready, and repel every attempt of that kind.

About ten o'clock, Pontiac and his chiefs arrived; and were conducted to the council-chamber, where the governor and his principal officers, each with pistols in their belts, awaited his arrival. As the Indians passed on, they could not help observing that a greater number of troops than usual were drawn up on the parade, or marching about. No sooner were they entered, and seated on the skins Prepared for them, than Pontiac asked the governor on what occasion his young men, meaning the soldiers, were thus drawn up, and parading the streets. He received for answer, that it was only intended to keep them perfect in their exercise.

The Indian chief-warrior now began his speech, which contained the strongest professions of friendship and good-will towards the English; and when he came to the delivery of the belt of wampum, the particular mode of which, according to the woman's information, was to be the signal for his chiefs to fire, the governor and all his attendants drew their swords halfway out of their scabbards; and the soldiers at the same instant made a clattering with their arms before the doors, which had been purposely left open. Pontiac, though one of the boldest of men, immediately turned pale, and trembled; and instead of giving the belt in the manner proposed, delivered it according to the usual way. His chiefs, who had impatiently expected the signal, looked at each other with astonishment, but continued quiet, waiting the result.

The governor in his turn made a speech; but instead of thanking the great warrior for the professions of friendship he had just uttered, he accused him of being a traitor. He told him that the English, who knew every thing, were convinced of his treachery and villainous designs; and as a proof that they were well acquainted with his most secret thoughts and intentions, he stepped towards the Indian chief that sat nearest to him, and drawing aside his blanket, discovered the shortened firelock. This entirely disconcerted the Indians, and frustrated their design.

He then continued to tell them, that as he had given his word at the time they desired an audience, that their persons should be safe, he would hold his promise inviolable, though they so little desorved it. However, he advised them to make the best of their way out of the fort, lest his young men on being acquainted with their treacherous purposes, should cut every one of them to pieces.

Pontiac endeavoured to contradict the accusation, and to make excuses for his suspicious conduct; but the governor, satisfied of the falsity of his protestation, would not listen to him. The Indians immediately left the fort, but instead of being sensible of the governor's generous behaviour, they threw off the mask, and the next day made a regular attack upon it.

Major Gladwyn has not escaped censure for this mistaken lenity; for probably had he kept a few of the principal chiefs prisoners, whilst he had them in his power, he might have been able to have brought the whole confederacy to terms, and have prevented a war. But he atoned for this oversight, by the gallant defence he made for more than a year, amidst a variety of discouragements.

Questions

1. How did the Indians gain access to the fort at Michilimackinac?
2. What did the Indians intend to do with the captives taken there? How does this affect your interpretation of what happened at Fort William Henry?
3. Discuss the differences between events at Detroit and Michilimackinac. What happened at Detroit to foil the Indians' original plans? How does this compare with du Pratz's discussion of the Natchez uprising? What element do the two stories have in common? Why?
4. How does Carver portray Pontiac's motivations? His character? His power over other Indians? Is this portrayal consistent with the course of events?
5. What can you infer from Carver's description of events regarding the military tactics and capabilities of the Great Lakes and Ohio Indians? What were the Indians' military strengths and limitations?

19

Pacific Worlds

The Pacific shores of North America stood as far from New England and the Chesapeake as Massachusetts and Virginia did from Europe and Africa, and in the absence of a Northwest Passage or Panama Canal, reaching California from New York was considerably more difficult than reaching Boston from London. It was only in the latter third of the eighteenth century that the European presence north of Baja California begun to become significant. Russian fur traders moved east across the North Pacific from Siberia, Spanish missionaries moved north from Mexico, and British and American ships began rounding Cape Horn en route to the waters of the Pacific Northwest. A staggering diversity of Native peoples inhabited North America's western slope, ensuring a wide range of colonial experiences in the lands occupied by European newcomers.

19.1 Salvador Palma Asks for Missons*

To sustain the chain of presidios and missions in upper California, the Spanish Empire sought to secure both water and land routes to them. The arid and mountainous terrain of the Southwest made land travel particularly difficult and the assistance of strategically located Native peoples especially important. Of particular significance was the Yuma crossing of the Colorado River. Spanish army officer Juan Bautista de Anza led parties across the river there in 1774 and 1775; and in 1776 he brought Olleyquotequiebe, a prominent chief of the Quechan Indian living around the crossing, to Mexico City. In the following 1776 letter, Olleyquotequiebe, known to the Spanish as Salvador Palma, asks that missions be established among the Quechans.

---

*"Petition of Salvador Palma," in Correspondence, *vol. 5 of* Anza's California Expeditions, *ed. and trans. Herbert Eugene Bolton (Berkeley: University of California Press, 1930), 365–376.*

Mexico, November 11, 1776

Petition of Salvador Palma, Captain of the Yuma tribe, requesting that missions be established in his territory on the margins of the Colorado and Gila rivers, where they live.

Most Excellent and Dear Sir:

It will not seem strange that, animated by the charitable generosity with which your Excellency has received me, and by the great advantages which I am able to promise myself from so noble a nature, I should set forth simply the object of my pretension and the lively anxiety with which I come for a distance of more than seven hundred leagues to implore the assistance of your Excellency. And, persuaded that the only obstacle which might retard the satisfaction of my desires would be an unjust distrust concerning my constancy, it appears to be necessary at the outset to give a brief account of myself, for perhaps this alone will suffice to persuade you of my good faith and of the sincerity with which I request holy baptism for myself, my children, my brothers, my relatives, and my subjects.

My tribe, Sir, lives in several regular settlements situated in the most advantageous locations on the banks of the Gila and Colorado rivers, with whose benefit we enjoy abundant harvests which put us in a position of not needing outside aid in order to live commodiously. I enjoy in it the supreme rule, which, by right of primogeniture inherited from my fathers and by these from my grandfathers, descended as far as myself from one to the other from time immemorial, and upon their death I entered into the command with the universal applause of my subjects.

My first care was to preserve for them the rights of my tribe over my neighbors and to promote the quietude of families and pueblos, and make us respectable to the other tribes. To accomplish this I established new laws and gave force to others already recognized. I considered witchcraft as the greatest of crimes, and so I imposed the death penalty upon witches. Other misdemeanors I punished with blows and beating in proportion to their apparent gravity. I have always regarded polygamy with horror, and although, on account of finding it generally accepted, I did not condemn it in others, yet I did not accept it for myself, for I have never recognized as legitimate any other wife than the one which I have at present, and who has given me six children, five girls and one boy. With regard to the external as well as to the internal government of my state, I saw myself under the necessity of making war on all my neighbors, with the sole exception of the Pápagos, with whom I have always been allied in arms and in commerce. But I have been so successful with the rest that I have almost always vanquished them, for which reason I have made peace with them when I have wished, and have never abused my victories.

In these cares I have been occupied all my life, having no other knowledge of the deity than that which was given me by a confused idea, representing him to me as a being superior to all others whom I knew, who lived above the clouds, Creator of all things, and whom I called *Duchi* and *Pá*, and whose favor I implored in all my necessities and perils. Here ended all my light, and doubtless I should have died in this unhappy state if providence had not afforded me other light when least I merited and hoped for it.

In the year '74 it was rumored through the tribe that Captain Ansa was directing his way toward it with men-at-arms. This rumor greatly disturbed the people, and, fearful of some attack, they resolved to receive him with weapons in their hands, and to risk their lives rather than permit themselves to be trodden under foot. I pondered the case carefully. I reflected that I had never done any injury to the Spaniards, neither had I received any from them, and that consequently there was not the least reason why I should fear their arms. Moreover, I reflected that they were at peace with the Pápagos, and that these were our friends and relatives; and it appeared to me unjust to receive with hostility the friends of my allies, when I had no reason for distrusting them. I set forth these reasons to my people. When I found them intractable I saw myself under the necessity of declaring that in spite of them I should defend the Spaniards with only those who might remain obedient to me; and though not a soul should follow me I alone would place myself at their side, even if it cost me my life. This threat had the desired effect, and not a single one disobeyed my orders.

In a few days I received a message from Captain Ansa, inviting me to come and talk with him on the banks of the river. I went promptly with sixty men and found him at the place indicated. He told me that he had heard about the commotion of the people, but I made him understand that all were now in a different frame of mind. I promised him all the assistance and the services within my limited faculties, and received from him in return all manner of thanks and hospitality, which I have continued to receive down to the present, bestowed with all the love which a father could show for his own son. That same night, which I spent with him, he told me the story, although briefly, of the Supreme Being, and of the laws which He imposes upon men and of the worship which He exacts of them. This so filled my heart, and I found it so in keeping with my own way of thinking, that from that very moment I resolved to be a Christian, even if it should be at the cost of my life. He told me likewise of the existence of the king and of his dominions, and of the obedience which is owed to him.

I listened with attention to everything he said to me, and, although in my heart I was convinced, I wished nevertheless to talk it over with my people, not so much in order to obtain approval as to win them over to the same view. I asked permission to tell it to them, and having obtained it I went apart with them. I explained briefly what the Captain had told me, adding that I was resolved to be a Christian and to obey the king, and that, considering these two things to be the greatest happiness with respect to this and the other life, and loving them with the tenderness which I had shown them in continuous experiences, I desired that they likewise should embrace this opportunity. And I found them so well disposed that they agreed unanimously to anything I might do.

With this announcement I went immediately to give a report of everything to the Captain, begging him to receive me as a vassal of the king and treat me as such, imposing any commands that he might wish in order to prove my obedience, my sincerity, and my good faith. Thereupon, to honor me, in the name of his Majesty he gave me a bastón and made me a present of the king's portrait. From this moment I have considered myself honored by the noble status of subject of the greatest of kings.

Next day he began the crossing of the river. In this undertaking we served him, I and my people, with all the zeal and energy to which the Captain himself will testify; indeed, without this opportune aid of ours perhaps the expedition would have been frustrated. At this same time he gave me the name of Salvador Palma, in which I gloried to the extent of rejecting the name I enjoyed in my own country, which was Olley quotequiebe, which they say is the equivalent of

Wheezy, changing likewise the title of Cofot, expressive of the supreme rule which I had among my people, to that of Capitán.

After I had received these favors from Ansa, they continued on their way. But, a few days later he found himself under the necessity of returning to the same river to recuperate himself, where I had the pleasure of dealing with him a second time, and the satisfaction that he should entrust to my honesty the care of seven men and a considerable portion of provisions and stock. They, disregarding the interests of their country, fled to it; nevertheless they testified that I treated them as brothers, and as vassals all of the same king. The stock and provisions I preserved with greatest scruple, so that on his return he found them intact, and they were very useful to him.

I learned then that he was coming to Mexico, and desiring to unite the quality of Christian with that of vassal of the king, which I already had, I affectionately begged him to urge upon your Excellency the establishment of the Catholic religion in my country. He gave me his word that he would do so, assuring me that he would not be more than a year at the longest in bringing it about. Trusting in his promise I was satisfied. But, seeing that the period had passed without his fulfilling it, I undertook at great risk a journey to Sonora to remind him of his word. Arriving at the presidio of San Miguel de Horcasitas, and learning that he was absent, occupied in matters of the royal service, I directed myself to the military governor of those provinces, in order through him to repeat my petition to your Excellency, and he dismissed me consoled with new hopes.

With these hopes I remained until at the end of ten months I suddenly found myself again with my Captain Ansa and many people. At first sight I thought he was about to give fulfillment to his word and success to my desires, and this conviction filled me with inexplicable joy. But I very soon learned that he was bound for another destination. I begged him with the greatest urgency to remain with me and plant the establishment in my country. But he lovingly undeceived me, making me see that he had no authority to do this, that he must carry out the orders given him, and that only in your Excellency resided the necessary faculty to satisfy my just pretensions. I begged him then, and he agreed, that if at the time of his return his promises to me had not been fulfilled, he would bring me with him to this city, where, placed at the feet of your Excellency, I might unburden my heart and personally make known my desires.

Well, he returned, and on that very day I presented myself before him, accompanied by two hundred men, who were to make known the permission of my people that I might go to Mexico to procure what I desired in the name of the tribe. He asked them if what I was saying was true, and he found that they unanimously agreed, even though I might be detained in the journey two years, nor am I unaware that the Captain, afraid to implicate himself in this matter, secretly inquired into my conduct.

But I have the satisfaction that he did not find anything to cause him distrust of my fidelity. On the contrary, he could see many things which attest my good faith and which ought to convince him of the sincerity of my desires. For example, the first time we met he instructed me that neighborly peace and love were ordered as a precept of the Christian religion; and since the establishment of it depended upon my authority, because my victories put me in a position to give the law, as soon as I departed from his side I gave the appropriate orders to terminate war, and when he returned he found me without enemies. He told me likewise that polygamy was condemned by the Catholic Church, and immediately I banished it from my country, and today there is not a single example of it, for I did not exempt my own brother, from whom I took away seven of the wives which he had.

This, Sir, is a most brief resumé of my life, of the fatigues and cares with which I have come to beg your Excellency that I be given baptism, and that, extending your liberality to my country, you may afford equal benefits for my children, brothers, relatives, and countrymen, by means of missionaries or settlements. To this pretension of mine I am not moved by any human interest or consideration. The only self interest which might induce me would be the desire to acquire Spanish arms to defend myself against my enemies, as I learn other nations have done. But with only the forces of my own tribe I have always chastised all who have tried to do me injury. I have made myself feared by my neighbors and respected by those more distant. No other impulse, indeed, moves me with such anxiety to become one of the faithful as the desire to obtain eternal happiness, which I cannot acquire in any other way.

I know that the religion to which I aspire is all founded in what has been taught me, and that one of the sublimest acts of this religion is to labor for the conversion of the heathen. I know that nothing is more in keeping with the most beneficent spirit of our Catholic Monarch than my conversion to Christianity. Indeed, I have seen in my journey many missions and presidios, and when I have asked the reason for their existence I have been told that the king paid for it all with no other purpose than the spread of the gospel. I know that the pious inclination of your Excellency toward me will support my pretension. For, if the religion commands it, and the king is pleased to make it possible even to ungrateful and rebellious tribes who have not known how to appreciate the motive of his benefactions, what can cause it to be denied to me? The charge of inconstancy? I think, Sir, that what I have set forth is proof of my firmness. But if this is not enough, your Excellency may order any proofs which you may think necessary, and prompt I am to give any satisfaction which may be asked of me. I am not so infamous as to have the audacity to fail in the obligation which I contract with God and with the king, with your Excellency, with my Captain Ansa, and with all the Spaniards. I love them too much to be ungrateful toward them. I know too well the extent of their power to hope to be able to escape from the full punishment which I should deserve for my perfidy. I should be an object of execration to my people. I should find no one to accept me if they should see me fail in promises so solemn that they are confirmed by the ratification of all my nation. For my part, I do not need to give any other proof than to reaffirm the renunciation which I have made of the supreme rule of my tribe, gladly remaining in the class of vassal, with that rank to which the charity of the king may be pleased to assign me.

My country is abundant in wheat, maize, beans, cotton, tobacco, watermelons, calabashes, and cantaloupes, and is capable, as I see it, of producing many other products, with which the settlements would be able to sustain themselves in plenty. My people number more than three thousand, with whom I obligate myself to defend the missionaries and Spaniards from every insult. I believe that my neighbors will follow my example; and, in case of necessity, I have no doubt I could draw into a general alliance in the services of his Majesty the Galchedunes, Jamajá, or Soyopas, Pimas, Opas, Cocomaricopas, Cajuenes, Jaliquamas, Cucupas, Comeiás, Pápagos, and part of the Apaches who live on the opposite bank of the Colorado River and who do not communicate with those of this other bank, some because of enmity, and others for the fear which my victories have inspired in them. This alliance, together with the establishments in my country, would not only keep the roads secure for the Spaniards, and keep free mutual communication between California and Sonora, San Francisco and New Mexico, because they will be situated in the center of these provinces, but also, aided by the arms of the Spaniards, we could serve to advantage in the pacification of the neighboring kingdoms.

Finally, most Excellent Sir, for the greater assurance and verification of what I have hereinbefore set forth to your Excellency, I present to you this respectful petition by the hand of my Captain Ansa, as an ocular witness of my deeds, in order that from him your Excellency may inform yourself how better you may be served, and I have begged him to sign this for me, notwithstanding that in default of signatures I and two of my followers set down with our own hands the holy cross, with the counsel and instruction of my Captain, and for greater justification of what I have set forth and promise to fulfill. Mexico, November 11, 1776.

+
+ +

Most Excellent Sir, at the request of the Yuma captain, Salvador Palma.

Juan Bap.ta de Anza

Questions

1. Why did Palma ask for Spanish missionaries and settlements? What did he hope to gain by becoming a "vassal" of the Spanish King?
2. What did Palma's letter offer the Spanish government? How did it appeal to Spanish sentiments? What did the Spanish need from him?
3. How can we discern whether we are hearing the voice of Palma or Anza here? What do you think Anza contributed to this letter? What represents Palma's own agenda?
4. How does the knowledge that Palma would lead his Quechan people in rebellion against the Spanish in 1781 affect your interpretation of this document?

19.2 Lasuén and the "Denaturalizing" of California's Indians*

The California missions were controversial in their own time, and they remain a topic of dispute today. In the following selection from an 1801 letter responding to criticisms of the missions, Fray Fermín Francisco de Lasuén, who served as president of the California missions from 1785 to 1803, discusses the challenges of converting California's Indians.

They appreciate, of course, the fruits from the forest; but in addition to the fact that they are given plenty of time to gather them, they know quite well the superiority of those we supply. Among all our Indians, ours are worth double the price of theirs. Our neophytes sell one measure of wheat, or corn, etc., (it is true; they sell them, and they even keep them in order to sell them) for four strings of beads. They can buy a like quantity of forest seeds for just two. The Indians themselves have established this rate of exchange; and they

*Finbar Kenneally, ed. and trans., *Writings of Fermín Francisco de Lasuén* (Washington, DC: Academy of American Franciscan History, 1965), 201–205.

are in the habit of saying that among all the seeds of the forest, there are none to equal our barley.

The effort entailed in procuring a sustenance from the open spaces is incomparably greater than what is now enjoined on them so that they can sustain themselves; but the former is free and according to their liking, and the latter prescribed, and not according to their liking.

Here, then, (and it cannot be otherwise) lies all the loss and harm which can be imagined or said to have befallen these natives through Christianity.

In their pagan state it is quite certain that they disregard the law of self preservation which nature implants in us, a law which binds under penalty of the total destruction of the human race. Hence, as a rule, they live without providing for what is indispensably necessary for existence; they know nothing of comforts; and they enjoy life as long as they can sustain it with ease, and without having recourse to what they regard as work.

The bow and arrow, which they fashion without much effort, by and large are their only instruments of industry. The uncultivated soil supports their manner of life, which differs little from that of the lower animals. They live on herbs while they are in season, and then gather the seeds for the winter, and as a rule they celebrate the end of it by holding a feast or a dance. They satiate themselves today, and give little thought to tomorrow.

Here then we have the greatest problem of the missionary: how to transform a savage race such as these into a society that is human, Christian, civil, and industrious. This can be accomplished only by "denaturalizing" them. It is easy to see what an arduous task this is, for it requires them to act against nature. But it is being done successfully by means of patience, and by an unrelenting effort to make them realize that they are men. They are treated with tolerance, or dealt with more or less firmly, depending on the longer or shorter time that has elepased since their conversion, while awaiting the time when they will gently submit themselves to rational restraint, something they had not known before. At the same time they can see that those who are ill and those who are well receive what is necessary for their daily needs without too much effort on their part, and that they are sure of daily sustenance when before they lived from hand to mouth.

Among the more pressing problems that can arise in any mission is that of not having food for the workers. This supplies a good excuse for a trip to the mountains; but no one is forced to go. Instead, for such emergencies a sufficient supply of food is purchased and brought from some other place so as to maintain all who remain at the mission, both the healthy and the sick.

In addition to the three meals—morning, noon, and evening—they are seldom refused if they come to ask for something to eat, and on each of these occasions it is customary to give the Indians what they would not get perhaps in a week in the mountains. This, and the distribution of meat, fruits, and raw grain are made in accordance with the capacity of each mission. The capacity varies; but what there is, is distributed among the neophytes of each respective mission.

Furthermore, it cannot be denied that among missionaries some are more generous and liberal in meeting the needs of their wards, just as in the case of good parents in a family. If some are poor, as they are here, they cannot but act accordingly.

A hospital is not the same as a palace. The missions are communities whose resources have to come from the labor of individuals; and of the three groups that make up [a mission], one group, the aged, the retired, the children, and the sick, contribute only to the consumption.

They are helped to the best of our ability. Nothing is kept back from them, and despite that, they run away. They know very well how greatly improved is their condition as compared with that of the pagans—a condition in which many perish through want of care, and many die of hunger. Despite that, because of their untrained nature they recognize an affinity for the mountains that more than offsets this obvious truth. I have seen Indians run away although they were on the sick list and excused even from Sunday Mass, individuals who at the same time, in addition to the three customary rations, were being given morning and evening atole made from corn specially prepared for the sick, a good meat stew at midday, more than two pints of milk each day, and a good dish from the Fathers' table with a piece of bread (this is the way we do it when it appears that they have taken a fancy for something from the Fathers' table). And when such persons are returned from their flight, they intimate that they are hungry. This they have told me—I have discussed with them what they have been given—they have told me (after having eaten all or maybe most of what they had been served) that they cannot swallow atole made from corn or flour, that what they need is fish. And if we have it we give it to them; and if we do not have it we go and look for it, so that we may have it for them.

On an occasion like that, when some one asked permission for some of this group who get "hungry" to go to the mountains for a week, I said to them with some annoyance: "Why, you make me think that if one were to give you a young bull, a sheep, and a fanega of grain every day you would still be yearning for your mountains and your beaches." Then the brightest of the Indians who were listening to me said, smiling and half ashamed of himself, "What you say is true, Father. It's the truth."

In the light of this, anyone can see whether or not complaints of this kind made by the Indians have a right to be considered by the authorities as accusations against the missionaries. And if the mere hearing of them, without taking the trouble of verifying them, suffices to affirm that the Indians could not have a stronger motive for robbing the missions or taking to flight, then it is my firm belief that these flights will cost the Indians many a fast, for when they get to the mountains they will not find something to eat—if that is what they are in search of. And if some expression like this by one of the commandants is not satire, it can have no other meaning, for fasting, or a reduced ration, has never been imposed as a punishment on any Indian anywhere for any crime.

Finally, I point as tangible proof to the fact that among our neophytes the most robust, the healthiest, and the stoutest are those who absent themselves the least from the mission. I pointed out to the San Diego Indians that the occasion when vast numbers of pagans died of hunger coincided with the two years, and especially the one, when there were no seeds from the soil to give them; and I told them this, for with a horrible catastrophe such as that before their eyes, they asked permission to go to the mountains.

We must not fail to note here how different women are in this respect. In their native state they are slaves to the men, obliged to maintain them with the sweat of their brow. They are ill-treated, trampled on by them even to the point of death if, on returning to their huts after spending the entire night in raids or in dancing, the entire morning in play, and the entire evening in sleeping they find that the women have made no provision for food for them. They never object or show any dislike for the work we assign. They are not so much given to running away. And if it were not for their husbands, if they are married; or their fathers, if they are not; or for their sons and grandsons, if they are aged, they would perhaps never leave the mission. I add the word "perhaps", for the majority of them, whether because of the example of their elders, or the force of habit, often fall like the Israelites into the weakness of ingratitude. For them, not even food from heaven, enjoyed in liberty and accompanied only by work that was pleasing, could suffice to overcome the longing for grosser foods purchased at the price of cruel labor in the heartless slavery of Egypt. What food, then, will be able to overcome in these men the hankering after the brutal life they knew? It was free and it was lazy. Who can keep them from murmuring after it?

Questions

1. Why might Indians choose to come to the California missions? Why might they wish to avoid them?
2. What did the Franciscans do to make the missions more attractive?
3. What did Lasuén means by terms such as "savage," "nature," "human," and "civil"?
4. How does Lasuén's discussion of the conversion process compare with Brébeuf's?

19.3 Cook and Anderson Contemplate the Moachat*

In 1778, on his third Pacific voyage, British explorer Captain James Cook reached North America's Northwest Coast and spent a month trading with and observing the Moachat peoples living around Nootka Sound on the west coast of Vancouver Island. The passage that follows comes from a 1784 edition of Cook's journal, and includes material from both Cook and a member of his crew named William Anderson. Both men died on the voyage. The passage begins with the British expedition having just anchored in the sound.

A great many canoes, filled with the natives, were about the ships all day; and a trade commenced betwixt us and them, which was carried on with the strictest honesty on both sides. The articles which they offered to sale were skins of various animals, such as bears, wolves, foxes, deer, rackoons, polecats, martins; and, in particular, of the sea otters, which are found at the islands East of Kamtschatka. Besides the skins in their native shape, they also brought garments made of them, and another sort of clothing made of the bark of a tree, or some plant like hemp; weapons, such as bows, arrows, and spears; fish-hooks, and instruments of various kinds; wooden vizors of many different monstrous figures; a sort of woollen stuff, or blanketing; bags filled with red ochre; pieces of carved work; beads; and several other little ornaments of thin brass and iron, shaped like a horse-shoe, which they hang at their noses; and several chissels, or pieces of iron, fixed to handles. From their possessing which metals, we could infer that they had either been visited before by some civilized nation, or had connections with tribes on their continent, who had communication with them. But the most extraordinary of all the articles which they brought to the ships for sale, were human skulls, and hands not yet quite stripped of the flesh, which they made our people plainly understand they had eaten; and, indeed, some of them had evident marks that they had been upon the fire. We had but too much reason to

suspect, from this circumstance, that the horrid practice of feeding on their enemies is as prevalent here, as we had found it to be at New Zealand and other South Sea islands. For the various articles which they brought, they took in exchange knives, chissels, pieces of iron and tin, nails, looking-glasses, buttons, or any kind of metal. Glass beads they were not fond of; and cloth of every sort they rejected. . . .

The fame of our arrival brought a great concourse of the natives to our ships in the course of this day. We counted above a hundred canoes at one time, which might be supposed to contain, at an average, five persons each; for few of them had less than three on board; great numbers had seven, eight, or nine; and one was manned with no less than seventeen. Amongst these visiters, many now favoured us with their company for the first time, which we could guess, from their approaching the ships with their orations and other ceremonies. If they had any distrust or fear of us at first, they now appeared to have laid it aside; for they came on board the ships, and mixed with our people with the greatest freedom. We soon discovered, by this nearer intercourse, that they were as light-fingered as any of our friends in the islands we had visited in the course of the voyage. And they were far more dangerous thieves; for, possessing sharp iron instruments, they could cut a hook from a tackle, or any other piece of iron from a rope, the instant that our backs were turned. A large hook, weighing between twenty and thirty pounds, several smaller ones, and other articles of iron, were lost in this manner. And, as to our boats, they stripped them of every bit of iron that was worth carrying away, though we had always men left in them as a guard. They were dextrous enough in effecting their purposes; for one fellow would contrive to amuse the boat-keeper, at one end of a boat, while another was pulling out the iron work at the other. If we missed a thing immediately after it had been stolen, we found little difficulty in detecting the thief, as they were ready enough to impeach one another. But the guilty person generally

*James Cook, *A Voyage to the Pacific Ocean* (London, 1784), vol. 2: 270–275, 277–278, 279–287, 313–318, 326–327.

relinquished his prize with reluctance; and some-times we found it necessary to have recourse to force. . . .

A considerable number of the natives visited us daily; and, every now and then, we saw new faces. On their first coming, they generally went through a singular mode of introducing them-selves. They would paddle, with all their strength, quite round both ships, a Chief, or other principal person in the canoe, standing up with a spear, or some other weapon, in his hand, and speaking, or rather hollowing, all the time. Sometimes the ora-tor of the canoe would have his face covered with a mask, representing either a human visage, or that of some animal; and, instead of a weapon, would hold a rattle in his hand, as before described. After making this circuit round the ships, they would come along-side, and begin to trade without further ceremony. Very often, indeed, they would first give us a song, in which all in the canoe joined, with a very pleasing harmony.

During these visits, they gave us no other trouble, than to guard against their thievish tricks. But, in the morning of the 4th, we had a serious alarm. Our party on shore, who were employed in cutting wood, and filling water, observed, that the natives all around them were arming themselves in the best manner they could; those, who were not possessed of proper weapons, preparing sticks, and collecting stones. On hearing this, I thought it prudent to arm also; but, being determined to act upon the defensive, I ordered all our workmen to retreat to the rock, upon which we had placed our observatories; leaving the natives in quiet posses-sion of the ground where they had assembled, which was within a stone's throw of the Resolu-tion's stern. Our fears were ill-grounded: these hostile preparations were not directed against us, but against a body of their own countrymen, who were coming to fight them; and our friends of the Sound, on observing our apprehensions, used their best endeavours to convince us that this was the case. We could see, that they had people look-ing out, on each point of the cove, and canoes fre-quently passed between them and the main body assembled near the ships. At length, the adverse party, in about a dozen, large canoes, appeared off the South point of the cove, where they stopped, and lay drawn up in line of battle, a negociation having commenced. Some people in canoes, in conducting the treaty, passed between the two par-ties, and there was some speaking on both sides. At length, the difference, whatever it was, seemed to be compromised; but the strangers were not allowed to come along-side the ships, nor to have any trade or intercourse with us. Probably we were the cause of the quarrel; the strangers, perhaps, being desirous to share in the advantages of a trade with us; and our first friends, the inhabitants of the Sound, being determined to engross us entirely to themselves. We had proofs of this on several other occasions; nay, it appeared, that even those who lived in the Sound were not united in the same cause; for the weaker were frequently obliged to give way to the stronger party, and plundered of every thing, without attempting to make the least resistance. . . .

The bad weather which now came on, did not, however, hinder the natives from visiting us daily; and, in such circumstances, their visits were very advantageous to us. For they frequently brought us a tolerable supply of fish, when we could not catch any ourselves with hook and line; and there was not a proper place near us where we could draw a net. The fish which they brought us were either sardines; or what resembled them much, a small kind of bream; and sometimes small cod.

On the 11th, notwithstanding the rainy weather, the main-rigging was fixed and got over head; and our employment, the day after, was to take down the mizen-mast, the head of which proved to be so rotten, that it dropped off while in the slings. In the evening we were visited by a tribe of natives whom we had never seen before; and who, in general, were better looking people than most of our old friends, some of whom attended them. I prevailed upon these visiters to go down into the cabin for the first time; and observed, that there was not a single object that fixed the attention of most of them for a moment; their countenances marking, that they looked upon all our novelties with the utmost indiffer-ence. This, however, was not without exception;

for a few of the company shewed a certain degree of curiosity. . . .

The fore-mast being, by this time, finished, we hauled it along-side; but the bad weather prevented our getting it in till the afternoon; and we set about rigging it with the greatest expedition, while the carpenters were going on with the mizen-mast on shore. They had made very considerable progress in it on the 16th; when they discovered, that the stick upon which they were at work was sprung, or wounded; owing, as supposed, to some accident in cutting it down. So that all their labour was thrown away; and it became necessary to get another tree out of the woods, which employed all hands above half a day. During these various operations, several of the natives, who were about the ships, looked on with an expressive silent surprize, which we did not expect, from their general indifference and inattention.

On the 18th, a party of strangers, in six or eight canoes, came into the cove, where they remained, looking at us, for some time; and then retired, without coming along-side either ship. We supposed, that our old friends, who were more numerous, at this time, about us, than these new visiters, would not permit them to have any intercourse with us. It was evident, upon this and several other occasions, that the inhabitants of the adjoining parts of the Sound engrossed us entirely to themselves; or if, at any time, they did not hinder strangers from trading with us, they contrived to manage the trade for them in such a manner, that the price of their commodities was always kept up, while, the value of ours was lessening every day. We also found, that many of the principal natives, who lived near us, carried on a trade with more distant tribes, in the articles they had procured from us. For we observed, that they would frequently disappear for four or five days at a time, and then return with fresh cargoes of skins and curiosities, which our people were so passionately fond of, that they always came to a good market. But we received most benefit from such of the natives as visited us daily. These, after disposing of all their little trifles, turned their attention to fishing; and we never failed to partake of what they caught. We also got from these people a considerable quantity of very good animal oil, which they had reserved in bladders. In this traffic some would attempt to cheat us, by mixing water with the oil; and, once or twice, they had the address to carry their imposition so far, as to fill their bladders with mere water, without a single drop of oil. It was always better to bear with these tricks, than to make them the foundation of a quarrel; for our articles of traffic consisted, for the most part, of mere trifles; and yet we were put to our shifts to find a constant supply even of these. Beads, and such other toys, of which I had still some left, were in little estimation. Nothing would go down with our visiters but metal; and brass had, by this time, supplanted iron; being so eagerly sought after, that before we left this place, hardly a bit of it was left in the ships, except what belonged to our necessary instruments. Whole suits of clothes were stripped of every button; bureaus of their furniture; and copper kettles, tin cannisters, candlesticks, and the like, all went to wreck; so that our American friends here got a greater medley and variety of things from us, than any other nation whom we had visited in the course of the voyage.

After a fortnight's bad weather, the 19th proving a fair day, we availed ourselves of it, to get up the top masts and yards, and to fix up the rigging. And, having now finished most of our heavy work, I set out the next morning to take a view of the Sound. I first went to the West point, where I found a large village, and, before it, a very snug harbour, in which was from nine to four fathoms water, over a bottom of fine sand. The people of this village, who were numerous, and to most of whom I was well known, received me very courteously; every one pressing me to go into his house, or rather his apartment; for several families live under the same roof. I did not decline the invitations; and my hospitable friends, whom I visited, spread a mat for me to fit down upon, and shewed me every other mark of civility. In most of the houses were women at work, making dresses of the plant or bark before mentioned, which they executed exactly in the same manner that the New Zealanders manufacture their cloth. Others were occupied in opening sardines. I had seen a large quantity of them brought on shore from canoes, and divided by measure amongst several people, who carried them up to their houses, where the operation of curing them by smoke-drying is performed. They hang them on small rods; at first, about a foot from the fire; afterward they remove them higher and higher, to make room for others, till the rods, on which the fish hang, reach the top of the house. When they are completely dried, they are taken down and packed close in bales, which they cover with mats. Thus they are kept till wanted; and they are not a disagreeable article of food. Cod, and other large fish, are also cured in the same manner by them; though they sometimes dry these in the open air, without fire.

From this village I proceeded up the West side of the Sound. For about three miles, I found the shore covered with small islands, which are so situated as to form several convenient harbours, having various depths of water, from thirty to seven fathoms, with a good bottom. Two leagues within the Sound, on this West side, there runs in an arm in the direction of North North West; and two miles farther, is another nearly in the same direction, with a pretty large island before it. I had no time to examine either of these arms; but have reason to believe, that they do not extend far inland, as the water was no more than brackish at their entrances. A mile above the second arm, I found the remains of a village. The logs or framings of the houses were standing; but the boards that had composed their sides and roofs did not exist. Before this village were some large fishing wears; but I faw nobody attending them. These wears were composed of pieces of wicker-work made of small rods, some closer than others, according to the size of the fish intended to be caught in them. These pieces of wicker-work (some of whose *superficies* are, at least, twenty feet by twelve), are fixed up edgewise in shallow water, by strong poles or pickets, that stand firm in the ground. Behind this ruined village is a plain of a few acres extent, covered with the largest pine-trees that I ever saw. This was more remarkable, as the elevated ground, on most other parts of this West side, was rather naked.

From this place, I crossed over to the other, or East side of the Sound, passing an arm of it that runs in North North East, to appearance not far. I now found, what I had before conjectured, that the land, under which the ships lay, was an island; and that there were many smaller ones lying scattered in the Sound on the West side of it. Opposite the North end of our large island, upon the main land, I observed a village, and there I landed. The inhabitants of it were not so polite as those of the other I had just visited. But this cold reception seemed, in a great measure, if not entirely, owing to one surly Chief, who would not let me enter their houses, following me wherever I went; and several times, by expressive signs, marking his impatience that I should be gone. I attempted in vain to sooth him by presents; but though he did not refuse them, they did not alter his behaviour. Some of the young women, better pleased with us than was their inhospitable Chief, dressed themselves expeditiously in their best apparel, and, assembling in a body, welcomed us to their village, by joining in a song, which was far from harsh or disagreeable.

The day being now far spent, I proceeded for the ships, round the North end of the large island; meeting, in my way, with several canoes laden with sardines, which had been just caught, somewhere in the East corner of the Sound. When I got on board, I was informed, that, while I was absent, the ships had been visited by some strangers, in two or three large canoes, who, by signs, made our people understand that they had come from the South East, beyond the bay. They brought several skins, garments, and other articles, which they bartered. But what was most singular, two silver table spoons were purchased from them, which, from their peculiar shape, we supposed to be of Spanish manufacture. One of these strangers wore them round his neck, by way of ornament. These visiters also appeared to be more plentifully supplied with iron than the inhabitants of the Sound. . . .

Next morning, about eight o'clock, we were visited by a number of strangers, in twelve or fourteen cannoes. They came into the cove from the Southward; and as soon as they had turned the point of it, they stopped, and lay drawn up in a body above half an hour, about two or three hundred yards from the ships. At first, we thought, that they were afraid to come nearer; but we were mistaken in this, and they were only preparing an introductory ceremony. On advancing toward the ships, they all stood up in their canoes, and began to sing. Some of their songs, in which the whole body joined, were in a slow, and others in in quicker time; and they accompanied their notes with the most regular motions of their hands; or beating in concert, with their paddles, on the sides of the canoes; and making other very expressive gestures. At the end of each song, they remained silent a few seconds, and then began again, sometimes pronouncing the word *hooee!* forcibly, as a chorus. After entertaining us with this specimen of their music, which we listened to with admiration, for above half an hour, they came along side the ships, and bartered what they had to dispose of. Some of our old friends of the Sound, were now found to be amongst them; and they took the whole management of the traffic between us and the strangers, much to the advantage of the latter.

Our attendance on these visiters being finished, Captain Clerke and I went, in the forenoon, with two boats, to the village at the West point of the Sound. When I was there the day before, I had observed, that plenty of grass grew near it; and it was necessary to lay in a quantity of this, as food for the few goats and sheep which were still left on board. The inhabitants received us with the same demonstrations of friendship which I had experienced before; and the moment we landed, I ordered some of my people to begin their operation of cutting. I had not the least imagination, that the natives could make any objection to our furnithing ourselves with what seemed to be of no use to them, but was necessary for us. However, I was mistaken; for the moment that our men began to cut, some of the inhabitants interposed, and would not permit them to proceed, saying they must "*makook;*" that is, must first buy it. I was now in one of the houses; but as soon as I heard of this, I went to the field, where I found about a dozen of the natives, each of whom laid claim to some part of the grass that grew in this place. I bargained with them for it, and having completed the purchase, thought that we were now at liberty to cut wherever we pleased. But here, again, it appeared, that I was under a mistake; for the liberal manner in which I had paid the first pretended proprietors, brought fresh demands upon me from others; so that there did not seem to be a single blade of grass, that had not a separate owner; and so many of them were to be satisfied, that I very soon emptied my pockets. When they found, that I really had nothing more to give, their importunities ceased, and we were permitted to cut wherever we pleased, and as much as we chose to carry away.

Here I must observe, that I have no where, in my several voyages, met with any uncivilized nation, or tribe, who had such strict notions of their having a right to the exclusive property of every thing that their country produces, as the inhabitants of this Sound. At first, they wanted our people to pay for the wood and water that they carried on board; and had I been upon the spot, when these demands were made, I should certainly have complied with them. Our workmen, in my absence, thought differently for they took but little notice of such claims; and the natives, when they found that we were determined to pay nothing, at last ceased to apply. But they made a merit of necessity; and frequently afterward, took occasion to remind us, that they had given us wood and water out of friendship.

During the time I was at this village, Mr. Webber, who had attended me thither, made drawings of every thing that was curious, both within and without doors. I had also an opportunity of inspecting, more narrowly, the construction of the houses, household furniture, and utensils, and the striking peculiarities of the customs and modes of living of the inhabitants. These shall be described in another place, in the best manner I can, calling in to my assistance the observations of Mr. Anderson. When we had completed all our operations at this village, the natives and we parted very good friends; and we got back to the ships in the afternoon.

The three following days were employed in getting ready to put to sea; the fails were bent; the observatories and instruments, brewing vessels, and other things, were moved from the shore; some small spars, for different uses, and pieces of timber, which might be occasionally sawn into boards, were prepared and put on board; and both ships were cleared, and put into a sailing condition.

Every thing being now ready, in the morning of the 26th, I intended to have put to sea; but both wind and tide being against us, was obliged to wait till noon, when the South West wind was succeeded by a calm; and the tide turning in our favour, we cast off the moorings, and with our boats towed the ships out of the cove. After this, we had variable light airs and calms, till four in the afternoon, when a breeze sprung up Northerly, with very thick, hazy weather. The mercury in the barometer fell unusually low; and we had every other fore-runner of an approaching storm, which we had reason to expect would be from the Southward. This made me hesitate a little, as night was at hand, whether I should venture to fail, or wait till the next morning. But my anxious impatience to proceed upon the voyage, and the fear of losing this opportunity of getting out of the Sound, making a greater impression on my mind, than any apprehension of immediate danger, I determined to put to sea at all events.

Our friends, the natives, attended us, till we were almost out of the Sound; some on board the ships, and others in their canoes. One of their Chiefs, who had, some time before, attached himself to me, was amongst the last who left us. Having, before he went, bestowed upon him a small present, I received in return, a beaver-skin, of much greater value. This called upon me to make some addition to my present, which pleased him so much, that he insisted upon my acceptance of the beaver-skin cloak which he then wore; and of which I knew he was particularly fond. Struck with this instance of generosity, and desirous that he should be no sufferer by his friendship to me, I presented to him a new broad-sword, with a brass hilt; the possession of which made him completely happy. He, and also many others of his countrymen, importuned us much to pay them another visit; and, by way of encouragement, promised to lay in a good stock of skins. I make no doubt, that whoever comes after me to this place, will find the natives prepared accordingly, with no inconsiderable supply of an article of trade, which, they could observe, we were eager to possess; and which we found could be purchased to great advantage.

Such particulars about the country, and its inhabitants, as came to our knowledge, during our short stay, and have not been mentioned in the course of the narrative, will furnish materials for the two following Chapters.

The two towns or villages, mentioned in the course of my Journal, seem to be the only inhabited parts of the Sound. The number of inhabitants in both might be prettry exactly computed from the canoes that were about the ships the second day after our arrival. They amounted to about a hundred; which, at a very moderate allowance, must, upon an average, have held five persons each. But as there were scarcely any women, very old men, children, or youths amongst them at that time, I think it will rather be rating the number of the inhabitants of the two towns too low, if we suppose they could be less than four times the number of our visiters; that is, two thousand in the whole.

The village at the entrance of the Sound stands on the side of a rising ground, which has a pretty steep afcent from the beach to the verge of the wood, in which space it is situated.

The houses are disposed in three ranges or rows rising gradually behind each other; the largest being that in front, and the others less; besides a few straggling, or single ones, at each end. These ranges are interrupted or disjoined at irregular distances, by narrow paths, or lanes, that pass upward; but those which run in the direction of the houses, between the rows, are much broader. Though there be some appearance of regularity in this disposition, there is none in the single houses; for each of the divisions, made by the paths, may be considered either as one house, or as many; there being no regular or complete separation, either without or within, to distinguish them by. They are built of very long and broad planks, resting upon the edges of each other, fastened or tied by withes of pine bark, here and there; and have only slender posts, or rather poles, at considerable distances, on the outside, to which they also are tied; but within are some larger poles placed aslant. The height of the sides and ends of these habitations, is seven or eight feet; but the back part is a little higher, by which means the planks, that compose the roof, slant forward, and are laid on loose, so as to be moved about; either to be put close, to exclude the rain; or, in fair weather, to be separated, to let in the light, and carry out the smoke. They are, however, upon the whole, miserable dwellings, and constructed with little care or ingenuity. For, though the side-planks be made to fit pretty closely in some places, in others they are quite open; and there are no regular doors into them; the only way of entrance being either by a hole, where the unequal length of the planks has accidentally left an opening; or, in some cases, the planks are made to pass a little beyond each other, or overlap, about two feet asunder; and the entrance is in this space. There are also holes, or windows, in the sides of the houses to look out at; but without any regularity of shape or disposition; and these have bits of mat hung before them, to prevent the rain getting in.

On the inside, one may frequently see from one end to the other of these ranges of building without interruption. For though, in general, there be the rudiments, or rather vestiges, of separations on each side, for the accommodation of different families, they are such as do not intercept the sight; and often consist of no more than pieces of plank, running from the side toward the middle of the house; so that, if they were complete, the whole might be compared to a long stable, with a double range of stalls, and a broad passage in the middle. Close to the sides, in each of these parts, is a little bench of boards, raised five or six inches higher than the rest of the floor, and covered with mats, on which the family fit and sleep. These benches are commonly seven or eight feet long, and four or five broad. In the middle of the floor, between them, is the fire-place, which has neither hearth nor chimney. In one house, which was in the end of a middle range, almost quite separated from the rest by a high close partition, and the most regular, as to design, of any that I faw, there were four of these benches; each of which held a single family, at a corner, but

without any separation by boards; and the middle part of the house appeared common to them all.

Their furniture consists chiefly of a great number of chests and boxes of all sizes, which are generally piled upon each other, close to the sides or ends of the house; and contain their spare garments, skins, masks, and other things which they set a value upon. Some of these are double, or one covers the other as a lid; others have a lid fastened with thongs; and some of the very large ones have a square hole, or scuttle, cut in the upper part; by which the things are put in and taken out. They are often painted black, studded with the teeth of different animals, or carved with a kind of freeze-work, and figures of birds or animals, as decorations. Their other domestic utensils are mostly square and oblong pails or buckets to hold water and other things; round wooden cups and bowls; and small shallow wooden troughs, about two feet long, out of which they eat their food; and baskets of twigs, bags of matting, &c. Their fishing implements, and other things also, lie or hang up in different parts of the house, but without the least order; so that the whole is a complete scene of confusion; and the only places that do not partake of this confusion are the sleeping-benches, that have nothing on them but the mats; which are also cleaner, or of a finer fort, than those they commonly have to sit on in their boats.

The nastiness and stench of their houses are, however, at least equal to the confusion. For, as they dry their fish within doors, they also gut them there, which, with their bones and fragments thrown down at meals, and the addition of other sorts of filth, lie every where in heaps, and are, I believe, never carried away, till it becomes troublesome, from their size, to walk over them. In a word, their houses are as filthy as hog-sties; every thing in and about them stinking of fish, train-oil, and smoke.

But, amidst all the filth and confusion that are found in the houses, many of them are decorated with images. These are nothing more than the trunks of very large trees, four or five feet high, set up singly, or by pairs, at the upper end of the apartment, with the front carved into a human face; the arms and hands cut out upon the sides, and variously painted; so that the whole is a truly monstrous figure. The general name of these images is *Klumma*; and the names of two particular ones, which stood abreast of each other, three or four feet asunder, in one of the houses, were *Natchkon* and *Matfeeta*. Mr. Webber's view of the inside of a Nootka house, in which these images are represented, will convey a more perfect idea of them than any description. A mat, by way of curtain, for the most part hung before them, which the natives were not willing, at all times, to remove; and when they did unveil them, they seemed to speak of them in a very mysterious manner. It should seem that they are, at times, accustomed to make offerings to them; if we can draw this inference from their desiring us, as we interpreted their signs, to give sometimes to these images, when they drew aside the mats that covered them. It was natural, from these circumstances, for us to think that they were representatives of their gods, or symbols of some religious or superstitious object: and yet we had proofs of the little real estimation they were in; for with a small quantity of iron or brass, I could have purchased all the gods (if their images were such) in the place. I did not see one that was not offered to me; and I actually got two or three of the very smallest sort. . . .

To their taste or design in working figures upon their garments, corresponds their fondness for carving, in every thing they make of wood. Nothing is without a kind of freeze-work, or the figure of some animal upon it; but the most general representation is that of the human face, which is often cut out upon birds, and the other monstrous figures mentioned before; and even upon their stone and their bone weapons. The general design of all these things is perfectly sufficient to convey a knowledge of the object they are intended to represent; but the carving is not executed with the nicety that a dexterous artist would bestow even upon an indifferent design. The same, however, cannot be said of many of the human masks and heads; where they shew themselves to be ingenious sculptors. They not only preserve, with great exactness, the general charac-

ter of their own faces, but finish the more minute parts, with a degree of accuracy in proportion, and neatness in execution. The strong propensity of this people to works of this sort, is remarkable, in a vast variety of particulars. Small whole human figures; representations of birds, fish, and land and sea animals; models of their household utensils and of their canoes, were found amongst them in great abundance.

The imitative arts being nearly allied, no wonder that, to their skill in working figures in their garments, and carving them in wood, they should add that of drawing them in colours. We have sometimes seen the whole process of their whale-fishery painted on the caps they wear. This, though rudely executed, serves, at least, to shew, that though there be no appearance of the knowledge of letters amongst them, they have some notion of a method of commemorating and representing actions, in a lasting way, independently of what may be recorded in their songs and traditions. They have also other figures painted on some of their things; but it is doubtful if they ought to be considered as symbols, that have certain established significations, or only the mere creation of fancy and caprice.

Questions

1. Characterize the Moachat approach to commerce. What did they want from the British? What did they offer? With whom did they trade more generally? To whom did they grant trading access? Where did they get metal? From answering these questions, what larger conclusions can you draw about the nature of Moachat society?
2. What item the Moachat provided would be of greatest interest to Cook's successors in the region? Why?
3. Why did Cook and Anderson consider the Moachat "uncivilized"?
4. We have seen mentions of cannibalism or human sacrifice in sources such as Castañeda, Bernal Díaz, Cabeza de Vaca, Brébeuf, Equiano, Bougainville, and Cook. In what kinds of circumstances did such suspicions

arise and in what kinds of texts did such references occur? Were these suspicions and references more likely the expression of insecurities inherent in encounters with unfamiliar peoples, slander employed to justify conquest, or an indication of actual practices?

5. In his second inaugural address, Thomas Jefferson lamented that Indians were "now reduced within limits too narrow for the hunter's state," urging that "humanity enjoins us to teach them agriculture and the domestic arts." Using Cook and Anderson's description of the Moachat, Salvador Palma's of the Quechans, La Vérendrye's of the Mandan, Du Pratz's of the Natchez, Smith's of the Powhatans, Cartier's of the Iroquois, Rangel's of the Mississippians, and Castañeda's of the Pueblos, evaluate Jefferson's statement. Was North America predominantly a continent of unsettled hunter-gatherers?

6. Observing the Moachat use of "figures," Cook and Anderson surmised "that though there be no appearance of the knowledge of letters amongst them, they have some notion of a method of commemorating and representing actions, in a lasting way, independently of what may be recorded in their songs and traditions." If we had more access to such "methods," how might our understanding of early American history differ?

THE
Art of
ROMAN
BRITAIN

Frontispiece: *Bronze figurine of a muse or temple musician from Silchester, Hampshire. H.11.5cm. (Photo: Professor Michael Fulford, Department of Archaeology, University of Reading.)*

THE
Art of
ROMAN
BRITAIN

Martin Henig

B.T. Batsford Ltd, London

For Ben Pomerance and in memory of
Professor Jocelyn Toynbee

First published 1995

Typeset by Graphicraft Typesetters Ltd.,
Hong Kong
and printed in Great Britain by
Bath Press, Bath

Published by B. T. Batsford Ltd.
4, Fitzhardinge Street, London W1H OAH

A CIP catalogue record for this book is
available from the British Library

ISBN 0-415-15136-8

Reprinted 1996

Contents

Illustrations

COLOUR PLATES

Between pages 96 and 97

Introduction

O, patience!
The statue is but newly fix'd, the colour's
Not dry.

In his essay, *The Romanization of Roman Britain*, read to the British Academy in 1905 (and revised twice in the next ten years), Francis Haverfield wrote:

> When the Romans spread their dominion over the island [Celtic art] almost wholly vanished. For that we are not to blame any evil influence of this particular Empire. All native arts, however beautiful tend to disappear before the more even technique and the neater finish of town manufactures (p.48).

Later, when discussing the Celtic artist in Roman society, Haverfield concluded that 'his Celtic art lost its power and approximated to the conventionalism of Samian ware' (p.51). When he writes of 'the heavy inevitable atmosphere of the Roman material civilisation', it is hard not to conclude that his bias is formed by Late Victorian society and those values which Morris and Burne-Jones assailed so passionately. Clearly complex societies, whatever their undoubted virtues, were no good for art.

In the next generation, R.G. Collingwood's assessment of Romano-British art was still more damning. Haverfield's essay belongs to the confident Edwardian age. Collingwood's has the experience of the First World War, of the rise of fascist tyranny exemplified by the Italian invasion of Abyssinia, and the menace of Nazi Germany behind it. Native cultures were being trodden underfoot by 'Imperial' powers which were anything but benificent. Of course Collingwood was too good a philosopher, Classicist and historian to make a direct comparison between the Empire of Rome and the Empire of Mussolini, but the chapter on art in *Roman Britain and the English Settlements* first published in 1936 and revised in the following year contains telling remarks:

> At its lowest terms, the history of Romano-British art can be told in a couple of sentences. Before the Roman conquest the Britons were a race of gifted and brilliant artists: the conquest, forcing them into the mould of Roman life *with its vulgar efficiency and lack of taste*, destroyed that gift and reduced their arts to the level of mere manufactures (p.247; author's italics).

Remember that in Italy this was the fascist era, where Mussolini dreamed of a refounded Roman Empire and where the trains ran on time into tasteless and grandiose railway stations.

9

Rome taught the Britons to carve stone, to paint wall-plaster, to decorate floors in mosaic. But, of all the results, there is hardly anything that rises above the level of dull, mechanical imitation to that of even third-rate artistic achievement. The Roman models themselves were poor enough; the empire was not an age of good taste; but there is perhaps no province where local attempts to reproduce them failed so dismally as they failed in Britain . . . On any Romano-British site the impression that constantly haunts the archaeologist, like a bad smell or a stickiness on the fingers, is that of an ugliness which pervades the place like a London fog: not merely the common vulgar ugliness of the Roman empire, but a blundering, stupid ugliness that cannot even rise to the level of that vulgarity (pp.249–50).

Collingwood said in his autobiography (*An Autobiography*, Oxford 1939, 144) how proud he was of this chapter 'which', he wrote, 'I would gladly leave as the sole memorial of my Romano-British studies, and the best example I can give to posterity of how to solve a much-debated problem in history, not by discovering fresh evidence, but by reconsidering questions of principle'. Unfortunately Collingwood's logic is hopelessly flawed by passion and false premises, which are surprising faults to find in a philosopher. His dismissal of 'the naturalistic and merely amusing character of the "Woolworth art" of the Roman empire', means that for him the Bath Gorgon *has* to be Celtic. He claims to have proved this, but in fact he does no more than state his prejudice. Few would deny the beauties of Celtic art, and it is very likely that it often had a symbolic character, but Celtic society and culture were far too limited to merit the term 'civilization' (ibid. p.137). The power and seductiveness of Collingwood lies in the beauty of his prose, for except for the Gorgon (which he admires) examples do not come into his argument. One wonders where he would have placed the Woodchester pavement.

Collingwood's book is hardly read now, because several decades of archaeological research have inevitably rendered it out of date. Indeed, with a single exception, the factual aspects of the volume have been replaced by Peter Salway's splendid volume in the same *Oxford History of England* (1981). However, Salway decided not to include a chapter on art. Despite Jocelyn Toynbee's superb *Art in Britain under the Romans* (1964) which attempts to analyse and catalogue the art existing in the island in Roman times and so provides a solid corpus of evidence on which all future study has to be based, and even despite Sheppard Frere's short corrective section in his *Britannia*, the 'official' or at least the generally-held view of British art and of Rome's effect on it remains for many people very much as Collingwood wrote it fifty years ago.

Although Anglo-Saxon art finds a place in most courses on art in the British Isles, Roman Britain has until now been beneath the notice of professional art historians. Even though Toynbee revised Collingwood's extremely negative approach and demonstrated that there are many items worth looking at – as a Roman art historian she does not start with the premise that Roman art was a bad thing in itself – the achievements of British artists under Rome are seen as modest. The best works of art were imports. More recently John Phillips and Claire Lindgren have made a virtue of necessity. The awkward figure modelling and stylization of certain sculptures, the very 'ugliness' despised by Collingwood are selected as distinctive features of a legitimate provincial style. The influence of modern art, such as the sculpture of Henry Moore and Elizabeth Frink may be important here.

Other specialist studies have not attempted to preach on such large issues, although David Neal's book on mosaics in Britain (1981) tries to show, as only a practising artist can, how mosaics were composed. In doing so, he proves (as Collingwood did not) the living power of artistic imagination. Another rather 'quiet' book which is of similar importance is the volume on wall-painting by Norman Davey and Roger Ling, published in the same year. It needs to be supplemented by a short book (1985) and various papers by the second author. The evidence is more fragmentary than it is for mosaic, but what is revealed is, once again, living art which could on occasion rise to distinction.

If I had thought that Collingwood or Haverfield were right or even half right it is doubtful whether I would have bothered to embark on this book. Instead, I believe that Roman art has for too long been underrated and that the art of Roman Britain, a very interesting provincial version of it, reaches surprising heights of excellence. Of Roman art in its wider context we now know and appreciate much more.

The *Ara Pacis* must here stand for a cornucopia of works ranging in size from exquisitely cut gems and masterpieces of silver plate to paintings such as those in the Villa of the Mysteries, outside Pompeii, instinct with religious fervour, and the shady grove of Livia's garden room at Prima Porta. Roman mosaic displays the same discipline in design found in Celtic art; softness in modelling appears on stucco vaults and in sculpture, whose themes include portraiture and historical relief. Roman art encompasses daily life and nature, splendour, colour and intimacy. Recent studies have brought out the magnitude of an achievement to which the epithet 'vulgar ugliness' scarcely seems appropriate.

The genesis of the present work lies in the period when I was editing a handbook on the art of the Empire (cf. M. Henig (ed.), *A Handbook of Roman Art* (Oxford 1983)), and realized that almost every theme could be addressed from the standpoint of this one province. However, as I was working on *Religion in Roman Britain* (1984) at the time I was very aware that art is created to meet specific needs; the patron is as important as the sculptor or mosaicist. I intend this book to be a companion to *Religion* and a modest contribution towards understanding society in a Roman province.

It is a number of years since I first raised the standard for the better understanding of Romano-British art (M. Henig, 'Graeco-Roman Art and Romano-British Imagination', *JBAA* cxxxviii, 1985, 1–22) and I apologize for the delay in turning the many thoughts circulating in my mind into a manuscript. Unlike Collingwood, I am no philosopher and I offer no theory of historical processes. I would hope that this book will occasion debate and encourage visitors to museums to use their eyes and aesthetic senses in the same way in the archaeology gallery as they do when confronted by paintings.

I have attempted to present, in seven chapters, how art was practised and what it meant in Roman Britain. The technicalities of craftsmanship are not, however, discussed. Other specialist writers have done this better, and the reader will find an excellent introduction to many of the arts in the book edited by the late Donald Strong and by David Brown, *Roman Crafts* (1976). The final chapter here is intended to suggest that we can only approach the aesthetic world of the past through our own experience. Sometimes such experience is personal; but other shifts in attitude,

towards the Romans for example, tell us a great deal about the period in which a scholar worked: I am still thankful that I studied Modern History both at school and at Cambridge. Why, for instance, with its long history of publication in the field of English art (see H. Bolitho (ed.), *A Batsford Century, 1843–1943* (1943)), is this the first book on the art of Roman Britain to be published by Batsford? Surely it is because the Arts and Crafts movement rather distrusted a civilization deemed to be mechanical, and preferred church architecture and rural customs? We are back to Haverfield and his world once again.

The illustrations in this book can only reveal a small part of the large and rich corpus of Romano-British art. In making a selection I have aimed to exclude the examples figured in my *Religion in Roman Britain*, which I regard as a companion to the present volume – the more so as a large percentage of artworks came into being in the service of the gods, and it is never possible to keep the two themes distinct. The photographs and drawings in the two books will at least show that, despite Collingwood's diatribe, the inhabitants of *Britannia* were far from blind to beautiful things. The reader should have no difficulty in finding additional illustrations by following up references in the notes. I have included a number of engravings and drawings made in the late eighteenth, nineteenth and early twentieth centuries, for where they are accurate they often bring out the quality of the pieces better than the 'objective' modern photograph. Moreover, they provide a vital visual commentary to chapter 8. In recent years, there has been a marked revival in archaeological draughtsmanship, as examples of the work of Margaret Darling, Nick Griffiths and David Neal all testify.

A large number of people have helped me in my studies, in discussions on art (most of it non-Roman) and by taking me to sites or providing that atmosphere of *otium* which has aided relaxation. My debt to my mother and to my brother, Stephen, is immense. I also wish to thank Elisabeth de Bièvre, Tom Blagg, Richard and Katherine Bradley, Marian Campbell, Derek Content, Audrey Cruse, Barry Cunliffe, Kenneth Dark, Graham Davies, Sheppard Frere, Brian and Lauren Gilmour, Catherine Johns, Laurence Keen, Marianne Maaskant-Kleibrink, Julian Munby, David Neal, Ann, Ian and Margaret Nimmo-Smith, John Onians, June Osborne, Ben Pomerance, Nigel Ramsay, Philip Redpath, David Richards,

Gertrud Seidmann, Grahame Soffe, Jack and Jenny Stringer, Alison and Robin Taylor, Percival Turnbull, Julian Ward, Graham Webster and Robert Wilkins. Like Thomas Morgan (1886), I acknowledge a very warm debt to the *British Archaeological Association* for keeping me amused and stimulated over the years I have spent as Hon. Editor and for its wonderful conferences; it is very inspiring to be in an atmosphere where art is of such passionate concern to so many people. The Institute of Archaeology, Oxford, has provided a very agreeable base in a University not always noted for its friendliness and the free run of its photo-archive from which the unacknowledged illustrations have been taken. In particular I must thank Robert Wilkins and Jenny Lowe, without whom I could not have illustrated the book. Tim Potter and John Cherry and Catherine Johns obtained many photos from the British Museum for me, and the Trustees kindly gave me permission to publish. John Coulston, John Davies (Norfolk Museums Service), Margaret Darling, Sheppard Frere, Mike Fulford, George Gray, Tony Giles, Francis Grew, Nick Griffiths, Jenny Hall (Museum of London), Mark Hassall, the late R.A. Hattatt, Christine Insley-Green, Christine Jones (Colchester Museums); Keith Knowles, Arthur Macgregor (Ashmolean Museum), Julian Munby, Lynn Pitts, Jude Plouviez, Grahame Soffe, Bryn Walters, Graham Webster, David Wicks (Norfolk Landscape Archaeology) were also helpful in supplying photos or drawings. Above all, I am most grateful to Robert Kiln FSA, the British Academy, the Marc Fitch Fund and Sheppard Frere FSA for grants towards the cost of colour plates, which I judged to be essential to this project.

Without all the recent monographs on art, for instance the British fascicules of the *Corpus Signorum Imperii Romani* (sculpture), works by Roger Ling (wall-painting and mosaics), David Smith, David Neal and Peter Johnson (mosaics), Catherine Johns and Kenneth Painter (jewellery and minor arts), I don't think I would have had the confidence to start. I am sure that some – perhaps all – will disagree with aspects, at least, of the present work. As when I was writing *Religion in Roman Britain* (1984), I am still conscious of the debt I owe to Professor Peter Brown, whose seminars, now two decades ago, helped to shape my approach to the past. It has been a privilege to share my enthusiasm for Roman archaeology with students of the University of East Anglia, Queen's University, Belfast and Oxford University (both within and outside its walls). Finally I must thank Peter Kemmis Betty of Batsford for commissioning the book and for his subsequent patience, and also two successive archaeological editors, Graham Webster and Mike Fulford as well as Sarah Vernon-Hunt who helped to discipline an unruly manuscript and Charlotte Kilenyi who saw it through the press.

Oxford, 1994
Translation of King Edward the Martyr

CHAPTER ONE

The Art of the Celts

Sometime we see a cloud that's dragonish;
A vapour sometime like a bear or lion, . . .
That which is now a horse, even with a thought
The rock dislimns, and makes it indistinct
As water is in water.

For anyone accustomed to the traditions of Classical and Hellenistic art, the dissolution of natural forms must imply a retreat from reality. The Celtic artist thrived on those very ambiguities evoked by Mark Antony in his final despair. We have only to look at the bird heads incorporated in the fleshy leaf forms derived from Greek acanthus ornament upon the circular shield-boss from Wandsworth, or the reinterpretation of the head of Apollo and the biga respectively on the obverse and the reverse of Gaulish and British copies of the gold staters of Philip II of Macedon to see what was involved.[1]

Nevertheless, the art of Mediterranean lands was a constant stimulus to the Celtic craftsman in the lowland zone of mainland Britain until the Roman Conquest. Thereafter, the disciplines of classicism appear generally to have been paramount, although Celtic inspiration can be seen behind a continued liking for line and pattern as well as in certain specific forms and motifs. Indeed, a considerable quantity of metalwork, mainly brooches, pins, studs and other such trinkets, were still ornamented in the traditional style and embellished with enamel. Celtic-derived ornament is even to be found on thoroughly Roman items such as the *trullae* used in Roman houses and at religious shrines for the service of food

and libations, and seal-boxes which protected wax impressions made with signet rings. Ireland, never incorporated in the Roman Empire, and most of Scotland, only part of which was occupied for about a century, remained thoroughly Celtic in culture, and any art practised there was in the La Tène style throughout the Roman Iron Age; so much so that the main problem, in Ireland at any rate, is to date it.[2] The continuity of native art through large parts of Britain led to a reflorescence of high-quality metalwork during the Dark Ages. The apogee of late Celtic achievement, manuscripts and associated ecclesiastical metalwork, was compared by Giraldus Cambrensis in the twelfth century to 'the work of angels', but this art was itself a fusion between native and Roman ideas as its literate Latin and Christian context testifies, and it could not have come into being but for Rome.[3]

Earlier attempts at such fusion between two very different artistic cultures can be seen in the Roman province of Britain. Although purely Celtic art was confined to comparatively unimportant items of dress and the style was otherwise only manifested directly in a few motifs, notably S-scrolls and the almond-shaped eyes on some human figures even in major sculpture, other far deeper influences illustrate the debt. With regard to the Roman mainstream of artistic development, which is the chief theme of this book, it was the qualities of the Celtic imagination in terms of pattern, design and colour which gave distinction to the art of the north-western provinces in general, and especially that of Britain. One of the aims of this book will be to suggest that the strength of Insular and Gaulish art lay in a constant tension between the Graeco-Roman prototype and a native interpretation of it.

To many enthusiasts for Celtic culture the advent of Rome was a disaster, a classic case of a colonial power destroying a refined and delicate local civilization. The best-formulated expression of this idea, as noted in the introduction, is that of Collingwood when he writes that the Britons had been brilliant artists until the brutality and 'vulgar efficiency' of the conquest had 'destroyed that gift and reduced their arts to the level of mere manufactures'.[4] The concept of the Celt as a victim doubtless appealed to Collingwood in the era of rampant fascism, but it ignores the fact that the Romans were normally very careful not to attack native identity, but rather to encourage it and thereby help it to conform to their own ideals. The process is most familiar in the case of religion, where it is called syncretism, but the equation of Sulis with Minerva, for example, not only created a new language for religion but, at the same time, new means of artistic expression. It has not only been the specialist in Celtic culture who has judged the results harshly. The dedicated classical archaeologist has seen the standards of Graeco-Roman civilization swamped by barbarism, although on the whole such an attitude has been expressed either as a result of ignoring Romano-British (or Gallo-Roman) art or at best by relegating it to a footnote in wide surveys of the Roman achievement; after all there is a great deal to survey and is it not a perverse desire to survey Roman art through the medium of a remote provincial culture?

In order to understand the art of Roman Britain it is vital to come to an appreciation of both Celtic design and Graeco-Roman art. Those who have written seriously and sympathetically on Celtic art, such as Paul Jacobsthal in his great work *Early Celtic Art*, have indeed explored the debt of the Celts to the Greek world in the early period.[5] The most characteristic fleshy lobes and sweeping free-flowing curves derive from palmettes and vegetal friezes.

Satyr-heads become fantastic masks; naturalistic lions, curious half-abstract beasts. Masterpieces such as the Lorraine flagons in the British Museum could not have existed without Greek and Etruscan metalwork and the wine trade, but they required smiths of enormous skill and artistic flair for their realization. However, most students have seen the coming of the Romans to Gaul and Britain in the first centuries BC and AD as having had a very different effect, as though classicism was like medicine, a little being beneficial and a lot being poison. Admittedly, apart from the present writer, this has been questioned explicitly by Professor E.M. Jope and implicitly by others writing on provincial culture.[6] We can be certain that, if a change occurred, it did so because patrons and artists willed it and that there was a good reason for a change of direction, lying in the nature and limitations of Celtic art.

Surviving examples of Celtic art, established in the British Isles from about the fourth century BC, are largely confined to metalwork, although wood-carving may well have had considerable importance and patterned textiles, too, probably had cultural significance. There are a few carved stones in Ireland, notably the Turoe Stone, which perhaps had a religious or commemorative significance, but there was no major tradition even here, and it may be assumed that large-scale sculpture as well as painting were unknown. Art was thus used in a fairly narrow range of circumstances and, as far as our knowledge of it is concerned, it was largely synonymous with the craft of the iron-, bronze- and gold-smiths who produced weapons, armour, horsegear, fire-dogs, buckets and cauldrons, drinking vessels, torques and other jewellery and mirrors. It was a means of display at the feast and in battle, and was thus central to the rather limited requirements of a tribal society. The major pieces belonged to chieftains and their wives, who could only establish their rank in society either by the intrinsic worth of their possessions or by the virtuosity of workmanship displayed by the craftsman in their employ.

As far as I know, no major item of Celtic art in Britain actually comes from the battlefield or from the feasting hall where it was displayed. The preservation of so much art is the result of secondary use. In some instances, these objects accompanied their owners to the grave. One important area for such finds lies in eastern Yorkshire and north Lincolnshire

(Humberside) where they are associated with the so-called Arras culture of the second century BC.[7] Grave goods include swords with decorated scabbards for men and brooches and mirrors for women. A small canister with engraved curvilinear ornament from a grave at Wetwang Slack is an example of a more unusual item; perhaps containing either some precious commodity or an amulet.[8] A century and more later, the graves of the chieftain class of the Aylesford–Swarling culture of Kent and the Welwyn culture of Hertfordshire, Essex and contiguous counties contain a more luxurious range of treasures, many of them influenced by Rome if not actual Roman imports, associated with the drinking of wine – such as the Aylesford bucket itself.[9] The iron fire-dogs from several of the Welwyn culture graves demonstrate the skills of a local blacksmithing tradition, which could also be used in constructing a stand for Italian amphorae.[10] Almost half of the fine series of some 36 recognized British mirrors with decorated backs are known to have come from burials of women, and range from Essex in the east to Cornwall and Gloucestershire in the west.[11] However, weapons were not generally thought appropriate in male burials by this period and perhaps this indicates a change in custom towards the consumerism prevalent in Roman times. Certainly, art-objects continued to be placed in graves long after the Conquest, and although the practice was universal in the ancient world, it is tempting to see many of the insular examples, such as the Bartlow barrows on the Cambridgeshire–Essex border, as marking the final Romanization of a native rite, even though by the second century none of the art was truly Celtic.[12] Whatever the exact form of the objects, they established the status of the deceased in the other world, and incidentally provide us with a showpiece of their cultural and artistic aspirations.

The other way in which objects have been preserved was their deliberate deposition in rivers or lakes, or in pits on dry land. Posidonius quoted by Strabo tells us of the gold ornaments deposited in sacred lakes near Toulouse (Strabo iv, i, 13). The caches of gold torques from Snettisham, Norfolk, seem to mark a similar series of votive deposits within a sacred area on land, and the Ipswich torques may be part of another such deposit.[13] The cache of bronze objects, armour and horse- and chariot-fittings from Llyn Cerrig Bach in Anglesey, many of which are decorated, indeed came from a lake, and the vast majority of single finds of metalwork in Britain were dredged from rivers, and are likewise votive offerings.[14] To some degree this is equivalent to the gift of a precious object to a Roman temple, but a prestige item such as the Battersea shield (1), once it was thrown into the Thames, was no longer available to advertise its original owner's greatness, unlike a piece of plate deposited in a temple during Roman times, which continued to be used in temple ritual or at least shown to worshippers on feast days. In human terms the only moment at which the former could serve such a purpose was at the very moment of the sacrifice when it was removed from circulation for ever.[15] Of course the intricate artistry could hardly be admired in such circumstances, again unlike the treasures in Greek and Roman temples which frequently served as museums. For us it seems odd that art should be destroyed in this way; part of the answer must be that the lost objects continued to have a real life in the hands of the unseen powers (like the sword Excalibur in Arthurian myth). The practice may also have helped to preserve the owners of great wealth from envy, both human and divine, and, after all, goldsmiths and bronzesmiths were at hand to replace what was lost. Most surviving Celtic art has thus been found in special contexts where it had been discarded.

Some art does come from settlement sites of high status, such as hillforts, albeit mainly as fragments or else as small items such as brooches. Coins, too, deserve a mention here as decorated objects of wide circulation. Such material enables us to relate Celtic art to daily life. The workshop debris found at Gussage All Saints, Dorset, dating from the first century BC is of particular importance.[16] The site lay close to the perimeter, at the main entrance of the fort, which makes sense considering the danger of fire. Over 7000 fragments of moulds for the manufacture of horse trappings were found, as well as some discarded scrap-metal, a small billet of tin bronze, modelling tools of bone and fragmentary crucibles.

As far as we can tell from the designs on the moulds, which include leaf-like ornament for a terret identical to one from Mill Plain, Suffolk, and a triskele for a lynchpin like an example found at Owlesbury, Hampshire, the style drew on a repertoire common throughout southern Britain. It can be argued that the workshop only flourished for a brief period and that the smith was itinerant. Clearly, the existence of

1 *The Battersea shield. L.77.5cm.* (Photo: British Museum.)

a *koiné* without pronounced regional variation suggests smiths travelling from patron to patron. On the other hand it has been pointed out that a bronze-casting workshop demanded organization, with supplies of oak-charcoal, beeswax, levigated clay, sand and metals being available. Smiths moved from court to court and doubtless they could be sought out by other patrons and might expect to find facilities in which to practise their craft elsewhere. The appearance of smiths on coins of Cunobelin (2) and Dubnovellaunus, of course, demonstrate their assured status in Iron Age society. Even more significant than the existence of a couple of coin-types depicting smiths is the fact of coinage itself, struck by the ruling powers of the Celtic world. This demonstrated the importance of the courts of tribal chieftains in patronage, either simply as providers of largesse in the form of gold coins and torques and similar items, or, later, when a sophisticated monetary system came into existence, as the authorities which guaranteed the exchange system.[17] Clearly the smith had a major function in society throughout the Iron Age.

If casting requires a good knowledge of technique which can only have been acquired through rigorous apprenticeship, designing patterns whether with bone tools for casting, with graver, or with hammer and punches, required a strong sense of design. As has been demonstrated in studying the layout of the patterns on the backs of the Holcombe and Mayer mirrors, there was nothing fay or wayward here. It required skill with compasses, in laying out arcs, conceptualizing finished results, and an instinctive feeling for harmony.[18] There is no doubt that the technical problems of casting metals or producing attractive designs were taxing ones, but they touch only one aspect of artistic creativity. What did the decoration of metalwork mean to those who commissioned it? Before attempting to address this question, it is a good idea to take some representative masterworks; even though none is well dated they allow us to appreciate this art at its best and to assess the taste prevalent in Britain before the Conquest.

Sword scabbards are perhaps the quintessential items of Celtic metalwork, clearly being designed as protectors of the iron swords which rendered Celtic warriors so formidable to their enemies. Even so they are less typical of the last phase of Celtic art in the south-east than they were earlier and as they perhaps continued to be in more distant regions. As we know,

2 *Iron Age coins: smith (bronze, Cunobelin); boar (silver, Epaticcus); Pegasus wearing chamfrein (silver, Tasciovanus). (All x3.)*

3 *Sword scabbards from Lisnacroghera, Co. Antrim (1 and 3): lengths 54 and 42 cm; Bugthorpe, Yorkshire (2), 51cm. (After Déchelette, Manuel d'archéologie II.3, p.1122.)*

the similar early Germanic peoples named their swords, and they assumed personalities of their own. Celtic warriors certainly took enormous trouble to beautify their swords with *repoussé*, engraving, open-work and enamel. It is difficult to select a single representative scabbard, though several from Northern Ireland, mainly from the river Bann, and others from the area of the Arras culture in east Yorkshire/Humberside (e.g. Bugthorpe, Kirkburn and Wetwang Slack), with virtually repeating patterns of curves and tendrils down their length, are especially harmonious (**3**).[19] Other scabbards have their main decoration confined to the tops and bottoms, including an early example (c.300 BC) from Standlake, Oxfordshire, and a much later one from Little Wittenham in the same county, with a motif of three roundels in a design similar to those on the British series of mirrors (see below).[20] These employ *repoussé* ornament, as does the curious non-symmetrical, engraved mount at the top of the sword scabbard from the river Witham, Lincolnshire, which seems to combine both vegetal and zoomorphic elements.[21] Occasionally the hilts of the swords themselves survive and bear elaborate ornament such as the enamelled studs upon the Kirkburn sword.

Shields are another typical category of Celtic metalwork, though the extent to which the highly ornamented examples were actually used in battle may be disputed. Unlike scabbards they could not hang relatively safely by the side at such a time but would have been required to parry blows from swords and spears and, in use, could hardly have escaped considerable damage. However, if they were simply flourished before battle, or flaunted in contexts of ritual display and the ceremonial disposal of wealth, they would have been highly satisfactory as large and brilliantly crafted objects. The Battersea shield in the British Museum, perhaps the most famous item in its Celtic collections (see **1**), is the subject of an excellent monograph by Dr Ian Stead.[22] Opinions

1   2   3

as to its date have ranged from the fourth century BC to the first century AD. The apparently symmetrical arrangement of the curvilinear scrollwork on the roundels reminds some of Augustan art, while the inset enamelled bosses recall enamelwork from the Lexden tumulus which certainly dates to the decade or so before the Roman Conquest. Against this, however, is the similarity of the *repoussé* work on the roundels to that of the circular boss from Wandsworth while enamelling occurs on the Basse-Yutz flagons. Undoubtedly there are Classical elements here as there are in all Celtic art but these could have been disseminated from the Greek world or from northern Italy long before Augustus. It seems best to date the Battersea shield to the third century BC, a little later than the Witham and Wandsworth shields. Not the least interesting aspect of such shields is that they reflect an ancient European warrior-tradition. The Battersea shield, with its concave sides, is very like the *ancilla* carried by the Salian priests of Mars at Rome, shown on the well-known intaglio in Florence.[23]

Related to these shields by its *repoussé* technique is another famous and controversial work, the Torrs chamfrein, now in Edinburgh but once in the collection of Sir Walter Scott. It consists of two elements: a cap of sheet metal and two horns terminating in bird heads; these horns bear some engraved ornament. Until Professors Atkinson and Piggott reinterpreted the find as a pony-cap and two drinking-horn terminals,[24] the object was seen as a unitary piece, doubtless both protecting the horse's head and making it look fiercer. The most telling argument against this explanation is that the horse would have had to be a very small one, but the Atkinson/Piggott assumption that there were no ancient holes for attaching the horns to the cap seems to be wrong. The original reconstruction may in fact be the true one and is supported by the representation of a horned chamfrein on a coin of Tasciovanus (see **2**); opinion has swung back in this direction.[25] As a small object, which would not stand up to hard use, it is allowable to see the object as having been worn by a model horse (perhaps of wood) in some native shrine or else, as has also been proposed, as the headdress of a hobby-horse employed in some ritual; indeed such mummery is suggested by the confronted men wearing animal-skins upon the Aylesford bucket. The Torrs chamfrein, which came from a votive deposit in water,

would in that case testify to religious imagery rather than to secular ornament. Another horned headdress, though this time a helmet for a human from the Thames at Waterloo, is possibly not so very different in its function as a religious or ceremonial object.[26] The horns are symbols of power and vitality – in the Celtic world bulls were of paramount importance, their horns were often knobbed as on the terminals of iron fire-dogs and on bronze bucket-escutcheons. The Waterloo helmet's horns are likewise knobbed but the Torrs headdress terminates in bird-heads. Avian imagery is also widespread in the Celtic world, including heads on the round shield-boss from Wandsworth, probably because for the Celts as for the Romans birds occupied the sky and could act as intermediaries between the gods and man.[27] The image of a horse at a shrine would not be inappropriate, given the great importance of horsemanship to the Celts, attested in art by splendid horse-furniture such as linchpins and harness-mounts, often enamelled, and by the ubiquity of equine images on coins. Moreover, the Uffington White Horse (**4**), which has recently been examined by the Oxford Archaeological Unit, is now known to have been excavated and built-up of chalk in the Iron Age, in approximately the same form as that in which it is now preserved. It is thus the largest work of art to be mentioned in these pages, a religious image on a vast scale, intended to be seen from afar.[28]

Neck-torques were typical Celtic accoutrements, as much in the days of the Celtic ascendancy, as portrayed on the Attalid memorials,[29] as at the time of Boudica's last stand (Dio lxii, 2, 4). There are stylistic differences between examples judged to belong to the early Celtic period such as the fine examples from the grave of a princess excavated at Waldalgesheim in Germany and its analogues, such as the torque from Clonmacnois, Co. Offaly, Ireland, dated to the third century BC, and those made in Britain in the decades prior to the Roman Conquest, notably the gold torques from Snettisham, Norfolk (**5**) and Ipswich, Suffolk. Fleshy leaf-like shapes have given way to much tighter curls, loops and spirals. The archaeological associations of the Waldalgesheim grave and of the Snettisham cache do suggest that the three centuries' gap is valid.[30] However, save by invoking a Darwinian or Montelian concept of evolution, it is not possible to give a valid reason why such a development should have occurred. Torques

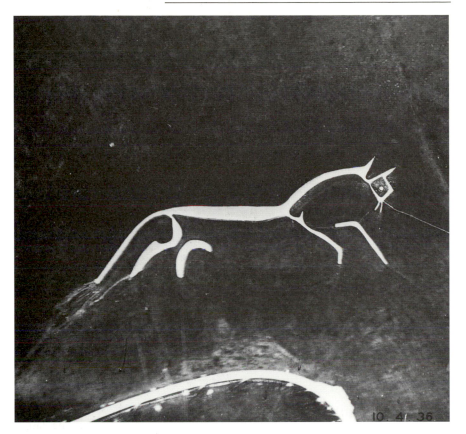

4 *The White Horse,*
Uffington, Oxfordshire
(formerly Berkshire).
L.110m. (Air Photo by
Major Allen, Ashmolean
Museum.)

5 *Gold torque from cache*
found in 1990, Hoard L.
Snettisham, Suffolk. D.
20cm (Photo: British
Museum.)

6 *Bronze mirror from Desborough, Northamptonshire. L.36cm. (Photo: British Museum.)*

appear in anthropomorphic art and seem to be associated with deities as well as with rulers; once again we see that an object of apparently abstract form is an image of rank and power with religious overtones.

The finest examples of late Insular design are surely the mirrors (see above) whose general shapes were based on Classical prototypes but whose backs were engraved with balanced if not symmetrical curvilinear compositions as meticulously planned as any medieval manuscript or, to take near contemporary metalwork, first-century silver plate from Hildesheim and Hockwold.[31] The best example is probably the mirror from Desborough, Northamptonshire (6). The fact that so many have been found in graves implies that they were associated with the status and the daily life of women, who would require them in the other world. Fragments of Roman mirror from Iron Age levels at the Hayling Island temple suggest that the introduction of mirrors came from the Roman Empire. Indeed, the actual forms of the British decorated mirrors, as distinct from their decoration, is very similar to that of the more elaborate Greek, Etruscan and Roman mirrors, though their manufacture was handled expertly and with ease by British craftsmen.[32] It is of interest that in Pictish Scotland, after the Roman period, one of the elusive symbols on the memorial stones is a mirror with a handle.[33]

In matters of technique the Greek or Roman smith had little to teach the Iron Age master craftsmen who made the objects mentioned above. *Repoussé*, casting and engraving were practised with consummate skill. The Celts also mastered the technique of using glass fluxes (enamelling). Gold, bronze and wrought-iron were handled with expert authority, though silverwork of high quality is rare and its presence, together with certain techniques such as mercury gilding, is indicative of Classical influence. Whether or not the beautiful parcel-gilt silver trumpet brooch from Carmarthen really dates to the 30s AD, it belongs technically at least to a Romano-Celtic milieu.[34] The Celts never had to face the problems of making large castings for they had no tradition of statuary in metal. Almost every item of Celtic art challenges the beholder to admire the virtuosity of the creator in organizing a pattern, but like a kaleidoscope such pattern-forming has no potential to lead on to other developments.

By definition the Celts were practitioners of *ars*, which has more to do with the mastery of a skill than with what we would describe as 'art'; the famous maxim '*Ars longa vita brevis*' is attributed in its original Greek to Hippocrates and describes a craft, that of medicine. The Celtic smith ornamented a narrow range of objects connected with warfare and the feast. He did not, and was not expected to, comment on that life. The zoomorphic masks and leafy tendrils which ornament the shield bosses from Wandsworth and Witham, for example, may have endowed the shield with protective power, and they might even allude to myths, for the later Christian Celts had stories of shape-changing creatures, but it is, nevertheless, unsafe for us to interpret them. In this period Celtic mythology was possibly even more local and inchoate than it was later, in Ireland and Wales. At any rate, naturalistic representations were confined to a few animal figurines and stylized portrayals of humans, in very few of which is it possible to see the forebears of Romano-Celtic deities, though an antlered head on a coin found in Hampshire is a convincing representative of the Cernunnos type.[35]

Is the abstraction of Celtic art overstressed and were myths inherent in it – do the masks, animal-images, even tendrils correspond to elements in mythology? Vincent Megaw, one of the best commentators on Celtic art in our time, writes of the 'elusive image', and this seems to me a very fair evaluation of what is involved.[36] If pattern and animal and plant elements meant anything in terms of myth, religion or even status, there is no way of our recovering their significance. If they still inspire some people, such a reaction is subjective, depending on ideas of Celts as 'noble savages' or as precursors of modern Celtic nations (Ireland, Wales and Scotland). It is, however, likely that a particularly fine object would have suggested the owner as a man able to employ the best craftsmen, though it would be anachronistic to call him 'a man of taste'. We can guess that the beauty of armour directly equals nobility, an equation which is by no means foreign to Homeric Greece (though the society recorded by Homer is already being seen through the more sophisticated eyes of the early Archaic period) or to other heroic societies, such as that of the early Anglo-Saxons, though the world of *Beowulf* is in the process of becoming civilized and Christian. In truth Celtic art was far too limited in scope and so the naturalism offered by Classical, humanist art would not have been something to avoid but something to master.

7 *Bronze bucket from grave at Aylesford, Kent. D.26.7cm; H.28cm (escutcheon c.4cm). (Photo: British Museum.)*

Realistic elements in Celtic art – animal figurines and even attempts to render the human figure – were parts of a natural process of advance, not of decline. There is, however, nothing to compare in sophistication and use of emotion with the group including the 'dying Gaul' and the defeated Gaul who has just killed his wife, derived from the Victory Monument of Attalos I; nor, like Eumenes II, did any Celt think of figuring a military victory symbolically by the use of myth as on the Great Altar of Zeus at Pergamum.

The possession of such a fine and distinctive tradition of ornament, albeit associated with a narrow group in their society (the warriors and their women), was a notable achievement. Furthermore, there is nothing to prevent us from enjoying Celtic curvilinear scrollwork today, above all in the British Isles where its supreme manifestations are to be found. However, when all is said in its praise, it remains simply pattern. As art it lacks the essential human dimension of sympathy, commentary and sometimes struggle, which inform the great artistic traditions of Europe

(including – significantly – the best post-Roman Celtic art of Ireland). The relatively impoverished nature of the early Celtic tradition when viewed from this standpoint is not unexpected for it would be surprising if such a tribal and pre-urban society had given birth to a major art. Pre-Roman Britain can show us many striking objects with a figural element but they are almost all subordinated to decoration; even the masks and animals on the Marlborough and Aylesford buckets (**7**) have still not broken away from the common Celtic use of animal forms in pattern-making. There was no stone statuary though there is some evidence for simple wooden images, represented by a few undated figures from Britain and many more from the continent of Europe at sites such as the Source of the Seine; and a number of small bronze figures are known, influenced by Etruscan and north Italian figurines.[37] The more sophisticated the piece of figural art, the stronger is the Roman influence and, in lamenting the loss of most of the products of what must have been a widespread craft, we must suspect that its real development lay in the future with the Celtic artists of Roman times. Coins sometimes take us further in the field of naturalistic representation, but these are late issues in Gaul and Britain, where for propaganda purposes Roman or Roman trained die-cutters, or more probably gem-engravers were being used (see Chapter 2).[38] The 'advanced' coins of Cunobelin and Verica cannot be called Celtic in an artistic sense, though they suggest directions in which art was to develop. We cannot tell why coin-devices such as Jupiter Ammon or Apollo were chosen; it is equally hard to see what the sphinx, centaur or lion (**8**) meant to the Britons. Horses and boars, warriors, priests and smiths which also appear as coin-devices were of course, another matter. But even here, except in the purely chronological sense, we are no longer dealing with the Celtic tradition of decorative art.

As stated above, we cannot lightly dismiss the possibility that the patterns of Celtic art had detailed meaning for both practitioners and patrons. To take an anthropological analogy, modern Australian aborigine art, much of it apparently non-figurative, has meanings in terms of myth and geography. Such meanings can be attributed to bark paintings, for example, through questioning the artists who create them. Nearer home, untrained but often artistically talented children will explain their paintings to parents.

'Primitive' cultures, ancient and modern, are valuable because they tell us about ourselves, the more primitive side of our natures and about untutored talent and imagination. To cling to the primitive, as for instance so many 'modern' artists have done, or to abstraction over representation, has an element of clinging to the nursery. Celtic art, for all its admirable qualities, had weaknesses. It was narrowly based both socially and in its repertoire of forms and would surely have become ever more repetitive if it had continued without new influences, until it became moribund. For the uncritical admirer of all things Celtic, the Romans are denigrated as cruel destroyers, but they can also be seen very differently – as most useful nurses helping to lead a culture in an adolescent state of development (epitomized by Tacitus in the comment that the Britons were hitherto 'scattered, uncouth and therefore likely to fight') towards the adult world of urban amenities, literacy and the arts of civilization.

8 *Iron Age coins: Top Sow, lion (bronze, Cunobelin); horse (bronze, Tasciovanus). Middle Sphinx and sleeping hound (silver minim of Verica). Bottom Two griffins (bronze and silver, Cunobelin); centaur (bronze, Tasciovanus). (All x2.)*

Art in the Era of the Conquest

. . . the Roman eagle,
From south to west on wing soaring aloft,
Lessen'd herself and in the beams o' th' sun
So vanish'd; which foreshadow'd our princely eagle,
Th' imperial Caesar, should again unite
His favour with the radiant Cymbeline,
Which shines here in the west.

THE NATURE OF ROMAN ART

The *Ara Pacis* in the Campus Martius at Rome dates from between 13 and 9 BC.[1] It is not an advertisement for the brash strength of the Empire but proclaims the piety of the Roman people and of its *Princeps*, Augustus. Above all it is concerned with that love of peace which was central to Roman propaganda. Rome's enemies would undoubtedly have rejected such claims, and in the words that Tacitus put into the mouth of Calgacus as the Britons prepared to take their stand against the forces of Agricola at Mons Graupius in AD 83 or 84 made the following accusation:

> Brigands of the world, they have exhausted the land by their indiscriminate plunder, and now they ransack the sea. The wealth of an enemy excites their cupidity, his poverty their lust for power. East and West have failed to satisfy them. They stand alone in being as violently disposed to attack the poor as the rich. Robbery, murder and rape, the liars call Empire; they create a desolation and call it peace (Tacitus, *Agricola*, 30).

Colonial powers by their very nature encourage this sort of response and, as will be made clear later in this chapter, some of the works of art and of architecture set up in Roman Britain were those of an occupying power. Tacitus again finds the right words: the Temple of Divus Claudius at Colchester was *Arx Aeternae Dominationis*, 'the Citadel of Eternal Servitude' (*Annals*, xiv, 31). But even here there is another point of view. Tacitus belonged to the ruling class; his father-in-law was Agricola, whose achievements in Britain certainly shed lustre on his family. Under such circumstances it says much for his sensitivity, a sensitivity not rare among educated Romans, that he could look with sympathy at the defeated Britons. Had not the Emperor Claudius been similarly compassionate when he had spared the life of Caratacus (*Annals*, xii, 36 and 37)?

Vergil, the greatest poet and probably the most subtle artist Rome ever produced, makes the shade of Anchises speak the following words to his son Aeneas when he goes down to the Underworld:

> *Excudent alii spirantia mollius aera,*
> *(credo equidem), vivos ducent de marmore voltus;*
> *orabunt causas melius, caelique meatus*
> *describent radio et surgentia sidera dicent:*
> *tu regere imperio populos, Romane, memento*
> *(hae tibi erunt artes) pacique imponere morem,*
> *parcere subiectis et debellare superbos.*

Others will be better sculptors in bronze and marble, better orators, better astronomers. The specifically Roman mission is 'to rule the nations under your sway, to impose peace with law, to spare the vanquished and to put down the proud' (*Aeneid* vi, 847–53).

The context of the poem, certainly does *not* allow us to use the passage as a disparagement of Roman art. The culture of Augustan Rome was probably the richest and most assured before the Renaissance, not excluding Classical Athens. However it does reveal how the Roman achievement is to be measured. Both the *Aeneid* and the *Ara Pacis* are more than beautiful human creations; they are vessels for the Roman Mission. Returning to the sculptured monument we note that *Ara Pacis* is not simply a magnificent accomplishment of designers and sculptors but a sermon in stone; like Vergil and Tacitus it proclaims the manner in which humane Romans should think of themselves, though it is much closer to the energy and confidence of the poet than the bleak pessimism of the historian. It shows us both how art was used and also the relationship between private thought and public act.

The first observation which should be made is that a high degree of organization was needed to create the structure, starting with the quarrying of the marble at Carrara, continuing with the transport and preparation of the blocks and concluding with their assembly and carving. Secondly the sculpture evokes a long tradition of relief going back through the Hellenistic world to Classical Athens. The processional friezes on the screen wall first bring to mind the frieze on the Parthenon, although the Roman work, with its crowd of men, women and children in contemporary dress, all trying but not quite all succeeding in living up to the solemnity of a great religious occasion, is undoubtedly more human and intimate. The panels on either side of the west entrance hark back to early Rome. On the right is Aeneas, about to sacrifice the white sow he found on the site of Lavinium, and on the left the suckling of Romulus and Remus by the *Lupa Romana*, both foundation-myths which recall those of Greek cities – it will be remembered that the Telephos myth, including Herakles finding the infant Telephos suckled

by a wild beast, is shown on the Great Altar of Zeus at Pergamum.[2]

It will be noted that the use of personifications came to Rome from the Hellenistic world and *Ara Pacis* figures *Dea Roma*, on the right side of the east entrance through the screen wall, the goddess that the whole world would learn to love and to venerate. On the left is another female figure, not martial but a suckling mother, watching over a cow and a sheep, the pastoral world of Vergil's *Georgics*. Is she mother Italy or *Tellus*, the earth? She sits between a maiden seated on the back of a flying swan, representing the air (though we are also to remember that the swan is Apollo's bird and thus represents Augustus' tutelary deity who brought him victory at Actium), and another maiden on a *ketos* or sea-monster, figuring the sea (and again we are not to forget Actium). There is great subtlety of association here. Thirdly it should be noted that these relief panels were very like genre and mythological sculptures (the so-called Neo-Attic reliefs) and paintings with which wealthy people adorned their houses, while the lower part of the screen, ornamented with a rich and wonderful acanthus scroll (9) in which nesting birds, insects and lizards had their homes was the sort of decorative art with which the rich embellished urns and other ornaments in their gardens. All the decoration of the monument proclaims the fecundity of the Empire and the blessings of peace brought about by Augustus.[3]

What did the word '*pax*', peace, mean to the Romans? It was not simply the absence of conflict. The purpose of peace, secured by the army, was to allow the inhabitants of the Empire to do other things. A fifth-century Athenian was never able to forget war, and the possibility of violent death or slavery for himself and his family was ever on his mind. Romans, on the other hand, were able to devote themselves to other concerns, to selling goods, writing poems to their mistresses, studying philosophy or making works of art (the subject of this book). War was sometimes necessary, sometimes a lust for acts of valour impelled even the most rational of men, but it always brought affliction to both sides. Not all war was waged against enemies without: Civil War such as that which had broken out between Caesar and Pompey, and again after Caesar's murder in 44 BC, between the Tyrannicides and the Dictator's heirs was long, bitter and horrifying. Ovid's response to the Altar of Peace was heartfelt:

9 Ara Pacis, *Rome.*
Detail of acanthus ornament
of screen wall. (Photo:
author.)

Frondibus Actiacis comptos redimita capillos,
    Pax, ades et toto mitis in orbe mane.
dum desint hostes, desit quoque causa triumphi:
    tu ducibus bello gloria maior eris.
sola gerat miles, quibus arma coerceat, arma,
    canteturque fera nil nisi pompa tuba.
Horreat Aeneadas et primus et ultimus orbis:
    si qua parum Romam terra timebat, amet.
Tura, sacerdotes, pacalibus addite flammis,
    albaque percussa victima fronte cadat,
utque domus, quae praestat eam, cum pace perennet
    ad pia propensos vota rogate deos.

Come, Peace, thy dainty tresses wreathed with
Actian laurels, and let thy gentle presence abide in
the whole world. So but there be nor foes nor food
for triumphs, thou shalt be unto our chiefs a glory
greater than war. May the soldier bear arms only to
check the armed aggressor, and may the fierce
trumpet blare for naught but solemn pomp! May the
world near and far dread the sons of Aeneas, and if
there by any land that feared not Rome, may it love
Rome instead! Add incense, ye priests, to the flames
that burn on the Altar of Peace, let a white victim
fall with cloven brow, and ask of the gods, who lend
a favouring ear to pious prayers, that the house,
which is the warranty of peace, with peace may last
for ever) (Ovid, *Fasti,* i, 711–22 trans. Sir George
Frazer).

Men never live up to their ideals but it is a sign of
moral greatness to have them. Roman art in its widest
sense, with its tradition, subtlety and use of symbol,
reflected a complex, intelligent and fundamentally
magnanimous society. This book is concerned with
that art in one province, one which many scholars
have wrongly dismissed as lacking interest in cultural
matters, but at no time should we forget that we are
studying aspects of that same culture which produced
Latin literature and the famous monuments of Imperial
Rome.

The myth that the simpler peoples of the world
are superior to the civilized is a very ancient one. It
influenced writers in antiquity such as Tacitus as much
as the eighteenth-century *Philosophes,* though Tacitus
(in writing of the rebellion of Boudica for example)
could see the gory savagery inherent in barbarian
behaviour. Unfortunately he does not give us any
real impression of Boudica's personal appearance but
Dio Cassius, evidently drawing on a genuine tradition, does provide a glimpse:

> Around her neck was a large golden torque; and she
> wore a tunic of divers colours over which a thick
> mantle was fastened with a brooch. This was her
> invariable attire (Dio, *Ept.,* lxii, 2).

It is clear, as we saw in Chapter 1, that Celtic art
was virtually always portable. It was employed in

enhancing the prestige of the fighting man and helped to establish the authority of the rulers of tribes in their dealings one with another and with their tribesmen, notably at social occasions of feasting and sacrifice. However, the forms were, for the most part, aniconic, and it is hard to see how they could have had the same depth of symbolic meaning as Roman art, whose characteristics have been briefly set out above, even if some of the patterns and their hidden anthropomorphic and zoomorphic elements did have a significance now lost to us. That is no reason to disparage the lovely objects produced by Celtic smiths (and there were no Celtic painters, mosaicists or architects and the evidence for sculpture is minimal) but equally it is very hard to see why the coming of Rome should have been regarded as a cultural disaster. The Celts had no cities, no community organization and thus no public art. There was never any such thing as a Celtic *Civilization* in its literal sense, denoting the sort of culture and community life to be found in cities.

Our first task is to describe the art imported from the Mediterranean world to Britain or copied in the island in more or less Roman style both before and after AD 43. This will help to establish the nature of the Roman contribution. Our second need is to demonstrate how Britons responded to this Imperial art in the generation or so after the Conquest.

ROMAN ART IN BRITAIN BEFORE THE CONQUEST

Roman art was very far from being rejected as an unpopular 'foreign' intrusion by the chieftain class in late Iron Age Britain. Modern apologists for Celtic culture have good reason to feel distressed by the lack of loyalty and tribal pride displayed by Cunobelin and his like to native art as such. As we would expect from Iron Age society, imports were largely of items connected with display and feasting, prestige items which served *precisely* the same purpose as the Greek imports to Mt Lassois and Vix on the upper Seine half a millennium earlier. Thus they include the silver cups of kylix form from two burials at Welwyn. One of the graves, excavated in 1906, contained alongside two cups (see **16**), wine amphorae and a bronze jug and pan; the other, found in 1965, also contained Roman vessels comprising a silver cup, a bronze dish

and a bowl, which had been adapted as a strainer and which had an applied zoomorphic spout in native style, but of assured classical prototype.[4] These burials are tentatively dated to the end of the first century BC, though perhaps the 1965 grave at any rate is a little later, as the spout of the strainer appears rather debased compared with the example from a probable burial at Felmersham, Bedfordshire, which is normally ascribed to the early first century AD.[5] However, as we shall see below, there is reason to suppose that such strainers continued to be used until well after the Conquest. Even more remarkable was the tumulus at Lexden, *Camulodunum*, which likewise seems to date from the end of the first century BC or the very beginning of the first century AD. Leaving aside the 'architectural' form of the tumulus which may ultimately come from Italy via the tumulus-cemeteries of Belgium, it contains a remarkable assortment of Roman objects, and presumably contained many more before it was robbed (in antiquity). There were remnants of a folding-chair made of iron with anthropomorphic feet, a bronze stand, perhaps for a candelabrum, escutcheons from a bronze bowl and the handle of a jug, a small bronze cupid with a goose (a stock rendering of a genre subject), a griffin protome, a realistically modelled boar which would have appealed to any Celt but is not here related to any Celtic portrayal of the animal, fragments from textiles including gold tissue, and two mounts in the form of barley stems. Most remarkable of all is a silver medallion containing a portrait of Augustus, not cut down from a coin as was once thought but moulded from it. The only native element among these finds is a bull, naturalistically modelled but with knobbed horns, a local feature.[6]

It is clear that these graves represent romanized taste, with the native tradition relegated to a subsidiary place. *Negotiatores* were evidently busy at the courts of leading chieftains, supplying their needs for wine from the south and for other luxuries.[7] Insofar as native craftsmen were employed, they were trying to adapt to a new aesthetic. This is certainly the case with the famous bucket from a rich grave at Aylesford in Kent (see **7**), a burial which also contained imported bronzes (a jug and a pan). The bucket's escutcheons are often seen as quintessentially Celtic but the plumed helmets, albeit stylistically treated, derive from the Italic bronzeworking tradition and it is not unlikely that the bucket's owner associated them with what to us are more convincing Roman imports; at any rate the bucket was doubtless used to hold imported wine from the south.[8]

The classicizing preferences of the highest levels of society, in south-eastern Britain at any rate, is reflected in the coinage. The most widespread and best-known coin-type, with its hackneyed and degenerate renderings of Philip II of Macedon's gold stater, no longer pleased the most culturally advanced rulers of late Iron Age Britain, among the Atrebates, Trinovantes and Catuvellauni. They had been taught the propaganda possibilities of coins and they used them, sometimes getting their die-engravers to strike what are virtually copies of Roman coins, sometimes more interestingly to use devices drawn from glyptic art (see 2 and 8). Were these connected with sealings on letters arriving at the courts or with the prized possessions of British nobles? It is hard to believe that a ruler such as Cunobelin would have lacked a signet, or indeed a secretary to conduct diplomacy with the powerful, and literate, Empire on the other side of the Channel.[9]

The iconography of coins reflects the same mixture found in the chieftain graves; some are entirely Roman, others effect to create a symbiosis between the Roman and Celtic worlds. Exotic elements include lions, sphinxes, griffins and centaurs, the gods Apollo and Neptune, symbols of prosperity such as cornucopia and cantharus and portraits copied from coin issues of Augustus and Tiberius. Famously Verica shows a vine leaf on his gold staters, and Cunobelin a corn-ear. Archaeological finds do not suggest that Britons *preferred* beer to wine; drink of any sort had an evident appeal within the culture, as did horses, boars and the hunting dog shown sleeping on a few of Verica's minims. Smiths, priests with severed human heads and Pegasus wearing a horned chamfrein reminiscent of the famous Torrs chamfrein (see above, Chapter 1) represent fusion between Roman and native iconography. The rich variety of these fascinating coins has not been fully assessed as art, though Jocelyn Toynbee has rightly brought them to our attention from this point of view in her great corpus of Roman-period art from Britain.[10] Since then other types have become known, including more that appear to have been derived from seal devices, and we are in a better position to appraise the society which produced them.[11]

It was certainly not a society in decline, but rather one which was responding to the Roman world across the sea, although the full implications of these contacts in terms of society, religion and art could only come after the events of AD 43. The Claudian Conquest can be seen not as break but as the beginning of an intensification of what had gone before. Indeed, as will be discussed in the examination of the native response to Roman art, there is sometimes considerable difficulty in establishing dates within the first century, and both the Icenian and Brigantian client kingdoms offer real problems in trying to marry cultural and political developments.

BRITAIN AFTER THE CONQUEST

The art of the Roman invaders

The fact of the Roman Conquest should be viewed apart from moral consideration or prejudice, if only because we know all too little of the detailed political situation in Britain at the time. There were losers – the sons of Cunobelin, the Trinovantes who lost land at Camulodunum to a legionary fortress and then to its successor, a *colonia* with its *territorium*, and we may be sure that many individual Britons from hostile tribes were captured and sold into slavery. But there were also many gainers, first the Atrebates-Regni, on whose behalf the invasion had ostensibly been mounted, recovered their freedom from their oppressors and were able to embark on impressive developments in their territories – developments which were Roman rather than Celtic. Then Verulamium, the old capital of the Catuvellauni, was made a *municipium*: there is a strong suggestion that all or part of the Catuvellauni, in contradistinction to the Trinovantes, took the Roman side in the conflict, whose politics were inevitably highly confused. For the sons of friendly chiefs there was education as there had been, no doubt, for a few favoured clients who went to Rome before 43 – including probably Cogidubnus of the Regni (see below). Now the Britons who welcomed the Romans found their living standards greatly enhanced. For those who aspired to supply the material needs of these people as well as those of the soldiers and administrators stationed in Britain, this was a time of opportunity.

We must return to the theme of mainstream Roman art which began this chapter and relate it directly to the Romans in Britain – the soldiers, administrators and traders from the Continent mentioned above – from the Conquest to about the end of the first century. The most direct approach is through the tombstones of soldiers, both legionary and civilian, which comprise the pre-eminent artworks of the Conquest era together with contemporary and near-contemporary examples of arms and armour. They will be more fully discussed in Chapter 3; here it is sufficient to record their initial impact and probable effect on well-disposed Britons. The scabbard of the sword, of Tiberian date, found in the river Thames at Fulham (10) is ornamented *en repoussé* with that same acanthus ornament seen on the screen wall of *Ara Pacis* (see 9) together with the *Lupa Romana*, the She-wolf suckling Romulus and Remus, which is likewise found on that monument. The tombstones, too, are fully in Roman style (though they differ in quality) but made use of British limestone. Although they were executed by sculptors travelling with the army and probably originating in Gaul, the two Colchester *stelae* of the centurion M. Favonius Facilis (11), depicted wearing his splendid mail cuirass and holding his *vitis* as a badge of office, and of the Thracian cavalryman Longinus, son of Sdapezematygus, who is dressed in scale armour and seated upon a horse, demonstrate a new method of commemoration by word and image that would become normal among the upper classes in Roman Britain as elsewhere in the Empire.[12]

Their inscriptions should also not be forgotten, for the Romans had a passion for epigraphy, something for which their (and our) alphabet unlike that of the Greeks is pre-eminently suitable. Unfortunately it has far too seldom been considered as art in its own right, but art it certainly is.[13] The finest inscriptions, of course, were those on great public monuments. It is very likely that there would have been some equivalent in Britain to the Victory arch set up in Rome to celebrate Claudius' Triumph in AD 44, part of whose inscription can be admired in the courtyard of the Conservatori palace. The letters, finely graded and meticulously cut, the entire panel set in a rich vegetal frame, provided a very handsome centrepiece to the arch. Fragmentary inscriptions which aim at this standard are, indeed, known from southern Britain. For instance, from the end of our period, some of the marble casing and inscription of the late Flavian *quadrifrons* at Richborough is extant. Even more

10 *Scabbard of a sword from the Thames at Fulham. L.50cm. (Photo: British Museum.)*

11 Tombstone of M. Favonius Facilis from Colchester. Limestone. H.1.83m. Colchester and Essex Museum. (After J.E. Price, A bastion of London Wall, 1880, pl.vi.)

evocative is part of a monumental letter A from the area of the temple of Divus Claudius, Colchester, cut on a slab of Caen limestone, which must have graced the façade of the temple or the architrave of its surrounding court.[14] It very probably belongs to the post-Boudican reconstruction, but the style of the letter and the use of an imported material point to an early date. We can guess at the language of the inscription, possibly, like the arch, commemorating the prowess of the Emperor in adding Britain to the Empire. Colchester must have been full of enormous monumental inscriptions from which the Britons would learn to read – and at the same time to read of the triumph of the Roman legions. But that is not the whole story, for some of the earliest inscriptions from Britain, complete enough to be interpreted, speak of compromise and even consensus.

The monumental tomb of the procurator Caius Julius Classicianus, which dates to the period after the Boudican revolt (Tacitus, *Ann.* xiv, 38), was a dignified, if severe, structure which owes its beauty (and that is not too strong a word) to the boldness and balance of its lettering.[15] As a major official who died in office and was buried at London, in the province where he served, Classicianus' tomb was clearly exceptional and the inscription is much closer in quality to a public monument than it is to those on the soldiers' tombstones mentioned above. It informs us that his wife Iulia Pacata, named no doubt after the Roman Peace (the same *pax* as that celebrated in *Ara Pacis*), set it up. She was herself the daughter of the great Treviran nobleman Iulius Indus who had helped the Romans to suppress a revolt in the reign of Tiberius and had founded a cavalry regiment called the *Ala Indiana* (Tacitus, *Ann.* iii, 40). Experts on Roman names are not slow to point out that Classicianus was himself of Gaulish origin. This highly romanized Gaul is best known as the leading advocate of clemency after Suetonius Paullinus' suppression of the Boudican revolt, which ended with overmuch severity, according perhaps with the governor's feelings but hardly providing a basis for a resumption of settled life in the province.

Agricola did not make Paullinus' mistake of neglecting the legitimate needs of the Britons, and thanks to the *topoi* introduced in the twenty-first book of Tacitus' *Agricola*, the famous governor has good cause to appear in a book concerned with art in Britain. The '*templa, fora, domos*' whose construction he encouraged were in every way incentives for artists; the dedicatory inscription of the forum at Verulamium, again with highly accomplished lettering, shows the town council of that *municipium* at work beautifying the city.[16] The Latin culture imparted to the leading men of the Britons and their adoption of Roman habits of dress and behaviour were far from being signs of servitude as Tacitus disingenuously states. They were, in fact, the paths of cultural freedom. Which of us would really like to spend a year in an Iron Age hut? But most visitors to a Roman villa can imagine what it was like to dwell in such a place, and imagination can here be fleshed out with contemporary descriptions of country house life, like those of the Younger Pliny.

Some of the best evidence for early romanization comes from the client kingdom of the Regni based on Chichester, the domain of Tiberius Claudius Cogidubnus. He is mentioned by Tacitus (*Agricola* 14) as having been loyal to Rome down to living memory and is recorded, with the grandiose title of *Rex Magnus Britannorum*, 'Great King of Britain', on a monumental inscription from his presumed capital, Chichester, as the patron of the temple of Neptune and Minerva. Cogidubnus was probably a Briton and a relative of the last recorded Atrebatan ruler, Verica, who had fled to Claudius and provided the occasion of Roman intervention in Britain. It is possible that Verica was restored by the Romans and also just possible that he resumed minting; but before long his successor was in position. Cogidubnus had almost certainly been fully educated in Rome and his culture would have been Roman rather than native. He appears on the inscription as a Roman citizen with the *nomen* of Claudius and the *praenomen* Tiberius, having in all probability been so honoured by Claudius. Little is known of the temple of Neptune and Minerva save that it was probably of Classical style, flanking North Street, towards the centre of the town. Presumably it contained two cult images, one of each deity. The quality of the lettering is high but neither as good nor as large as a base from the same city with a dedication 'To Jupiter Greatest and Best (*Optimus Maximus*), in honour of the Imperial family (*Domus Divina*)' (**12**a). This is part of a monument comparable with the monument of the *Nautae Parisiaci* at Paris, and is surely not so very much later in date.

The *pilier des nautes* is dedicated to Tiberius; the

12 *Monument dedicated to Iuppiter Optimus Maximus and the Domus Divina. a inscription; b water nymphs. Limestone. W.1.05m. Chichester District Museum.* (Photo: Grahame Soffe.)

Chichester stone is probably Neronian or early Flavian to judge from the style of inscription and relief-carving. One of the sides shows two nymphs amidst reeds – carved in the pictorial tradition of the mythological scenes on the *Ara Pacis* although executed in British limestone (**12**b). The two other sides are too battered to elucidate their subjects with certainty but a deity holding a sceptre could be Minerva.[17] A mile or so from Chichester lay the *domus* of Fishbourne, a great house of the type that Tacitus tells us the native aristocracy was building, and surely to be connected with Cogidubnus himself.[18] First constructed in the reign of Nero, and even in its earliest stage a fine building embellished with wall-paintings, it was reconstructed on a more lavish scale early in the Flavian period and was provided, not only with frescoes but with wall-veneers (*opus sectile*), mosaics, marble, sculpture and formal gardens. The life of this impressive palace, which can be reconstructed from excavations by Barry Cunliffe and others, is a valuable commentary on what romanization could mean at a formative stage. If it is not breathtakingly original (for all that the interior decorators used local stones as well as imported marble, and the gardeners had to contend with the British climate), we are a long way from the tasteless vulgarity of which Collingwood complains.[19]

The early floors, largely monochrome, are, in fact, outliers of a style widespread in southern Gaul and in Italy. For example the mosaic in the sanctuary of the goddess Minerva at Breno, Valcamonica, in northern Italy probably of Neronian date (c.50–60) and so a few years anterior to the Fishbourne mosaic, is very similar in design to those of rooms W8 and N12 (**colour plate V**) at Fishbourne. Comparison has also been made between mosaics at Fishbourne and those of Besançon. The mosaic discovered in 1980 below the second-century Cupid and Dolphin mosaic has a border representing a city wall; similar representations are, once again, known in southern Europe, and there is an especially splendid example from Orange, laid in the first half of the century.[20]

It is not surprising that the palace in London likewise appears to have had early (Flavian) mosaics, though all too little is known about them. The governor could, no doubt, bring in from outside whatever artisans were required and were not to be found locally for such a work, but it is not likely that Cerialis, Frontinus or Agricola would need to have gone far. Indeed excavations of private houses at Watling Court, London, have revealed equally early mosaics and we may assume that at least one *officina* of Italian or Gaulish mosaicists existed in London to serve the needs of officials, *negotiatores*, and romanized Britons. It is unfortunate that the Watling Court mosaics are so fragmentary; among them and of especial interest are mosaic roundels set in a floor of *opus signinum*, certainly an Italian technique.[21] Equally emphasizing *romanitas* early mosaics have also been found at the second legion fortress at Exeter and from the very end of the century at Caerleon.[22]

Portable objects came to Britain in much greater quantity than before the Conquest. As already seen some red-gloss pottery and silver had been treasured by Iron Age chieftains but now a great deal more tableware came in. The factories of southern Gaul replaced those of Italy for pottery; later in the Roman period the style and quality of samian ware deteriorated and can hardly be regarded as art, but in the first century it was often very handsome, especially vessels with moulded decoration of scrollwork looping around the circumference. This is in the same taste as that found on first-century silver cups including those from Hockwold, Norfolk (either belonging to the Icenian client kingdom or looted during the Boudican revolt), and the handles of bronze vessels such as an *askos* from Fishbourne.[23]

Naturalism is also to be found on engraved gems. Evidence for the use of sealstones in the Iron Age is confined to the devices on some coins (see above, Chapter 1), and may indicate that the secretariats of the kings in south-eastern Britain used such objects in diplomatic correspondence with the Roman Empire. Or perhaps we should take it no further than to say that gem-engravers from the Continent were employed to cut coin dies, using their own familiar repertory.[24] Numbers of gemstones were imported (and lost) after the Conquest, as befits a society fully dependent on literacy and bureaucracy. Many have been found in military contexts as well as at Colchester and at centres of romanization such as London and Chichester.

Gems generally have a protective or apotropaic significance. Thus Roman soldiers quite often wore intaglios showing one or other of the heroes of myth such as Achilles, Ajax (**13a**), Diomedes or Hercules. Sometimes these seals were clearly old – heirlooms deliberately selected from family possessions. Here we may compare the wearing as amulets of Italo-Greek figurines of the Dioscuri, of which examples have been found at Colchester, Canterbury and Wroxeter.[25] Devices signifying prosperity were widespread in the Invasion period and representations of horns of plenty, parrots, dolphins, wine-cups and other lucky symbols were clearly both used and understood. Some had, indeed, occurred on pre-Conquest coins as we have seen, like the sphinx which is figured on a sard from Chichester. The legionary 'eagle and standards', or in the case of an intaglio from Verulamium (**13b**) an eagle on a war-galley with a standard and a trophy, had specifically military application. Deities too were popular: we may note a gem from Colchester, probably belonging to a settler in the early *colonia*, who presumably possessed equestrian rank for it is set in a gold ring which was the especial privilege of this order. It depicts Mars descending from the sky as though to

impregnate the sleeping Rhea Silvia.[26] A figure of Mercury on an amethyst from Fishbourne was found in a later layer associated with the palace, and its high quality may suggest it belonged to a member of the owner's family or to one of his clients.[27] Mercury was to become a very popular deity in Britain, portrayed in many media, notably stone and bronze.

The existence of a market and possibly even of manufacture is demonstrated by a small cache of four unset intaglios from a Neronian pit in Eastcheap, London, which are in perfect condition and must be part of the stock of a *gemmarius*.[28] It should be noted that an attempt to cut the name ALBA on one of them has not been fully executed. The subject of this stone was a pair of clasped hands (**14**a) and so the gem was intended as a betrothal gift; the others show Pegasus (**14**b), a discobolus and a head of Dea Roma. Study of the gems from the main drain at Bath, whether thrown into the spring or washed out from the great bath, shows enough stylistic similarities to suggest that

13 Intaglios. a Ajax with body of Achilles, Waddon Hill, Dorset. Cornelian. b Galley with trophy, eagle and standard, Verulamium. Sardonyx. (Both x4.) (Photos: Graham Webster; Robert Wilkins.)

14 Intaglios from Eastcheap, City of London. a Clasped hands in wreath of olive. Onyx. b Pegasus. Banded agate. (Photos: J. Bailey, Museum of London.)

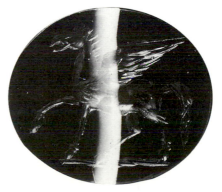

a gem-cutter was working here too.[29] However, it should be emphasized that the style and taste informing glyptic art never deviated from the Classical.

Gold jewellery could be equally uncompromisingly Roman. This is shown by gold finger rings from London and Colchester, which would have been equally at home in Pompeii.[30] However, the intriguing possibility of manufacture in Britain to fully Classical standards is raised by the workshop of another jeweller living behind the riverside quays of London (on the site of the Flavian palace, Bush Lane). Remains of two crucibles used for refining gold, together with three lids, have been found. Pieces of clay luting used to seal the crucibles employ stamps which the goldsmith evidently used in his work and which depict in all but one instance a lion and a boar confronted (15); the exception shows a sea creature, possibly a hippocamp.[31] However, goldworking, unlike gem-cutting, had flourished in the Iron Age and the story here is not one simply of copying imported forms as we shall see in discussing the Rhayader bracelet.

Native art and response

The response of native artists to the challenge of Roman art will be discussed in Chapters 5 to 7 and this section is limited to the immediate impact of Mediterranean culture in Britain. Dating is often difficult and some of the items mentioned may conceivably be later than I believe, but all have been selected because they appear to reveal the direct influence of Roman art on native craftsmanship. This was largely limited to metalwork, for the obvious reason that only here was there a strong tradition already in existence. Metalworkers did not change their styles overnight and some examples of curvilinear metalwork, even in southern Britain, are probably post-Conquest in date. On the other hand, as noted above, some earlier British metalwork was influenced by Roman example. Examples would include such items as the escutcheons of the Aylesford bucket (see 7), the *repoussé* masks on the Marlborough bucket, the figure of a bull with knobbed horns from the Lexden Tumulus, and more distantly the forms (though not the ornament) of the splendid series of British mirrors (see 6).

As we have seen, Roman vessels connected with the service of wine, fashioned from silver (such as the Welwyn cups, 16) and from bronze, are well known

15 *Clay luting from crucible, jeweller's workshop, Bush Lane, City of London. L. of stamp 5.4cm.* (Photo: R. Merrifield, Museum of London.)

from pre-Conquest burials. This process did not stop and indeed such items are likely to have become commoner. The client kingdom of the Iceni provides some interesting examples. A cache of vessels discovered at Crownthorpe, Norfolk, in 1982 and now in the Castle Museum, Norwich, contains a *patera* with a ram-handle and a small *trulla*, both characteristic Roman imports.[32] However, there is also a wine-strainer with a zoomorphic spout comparable with others from the area, including caches from Brandon, Suffolk, and 'Santon' (Santon Downham, Suffolk, or Santon, Norfolk).[33] Such strainers certainly go back to before the Conquest and an example of the same type was present in the Welwyn burial discovered in 1965. Evidently made in south-eastern Britain, the spouts of the best of them, such as the masterpieces from Felmersham, Bedfordshire, and from far away at Łęg Piekarski in Poland, are superb examples of insular art. There is no reason why their manufacture should have been brought to an end by the events of 43, least of all in the client kingdom. Indeed an Italian prototype lies behind all such strainers.[34]

The most remarkable items at Crownthorpe, however, are two bronze cups (**17**a) clearly modelled on Roman silver cups such as those from Welwyn (see **16**) and Hockwold. Their shapes are almost, but not quite, of classical form and the mouldings around the rims and the tops of the pedestals of the feet display a Roman restraint without being Roman. In addition, the handles are rivetted on, unlike Roman examples where the handles are soldered. While no comparanda come to mind from Britain, silver cups from the Sîncrăieni treasure in Romania dated to the first century BC are reminiscent for the same reason – they were made by craftsmen on the edge of the Empire intent on copying prestige Roman luxury goods.[35] The use of base metal for the Crownthorpe cups distances them further from their prototypes than the Romanian copies. Even more eccentric are the birds sitting upon the handles, their eyes inlaid with red enamel (**17**b). These are native features, and perhaps we can see their remote descendant in the woodpeckers flanking a vase on one of the fourth-century gold rings from Thetford or even the birds on the Sarre brooch (see **100**).[36]

It is tempting to ascribe these cups to the period of the Icenian client kingdom which flourished from the Conquest down to AD 60. During this period northern East Anglia would have provided a ready market for Roman merchants, but clearly native craftsmen were also active in the area. The strainer in the contemporary 'Santon' cache carries two birds on its lid. The 'Santon' find like that at Crownthorpe contains a mixture of Roman imports and items of native fabrication. The Roman items include a jug and *patera*; the Roman-influenced native pieces include, besides the strainer, a disk worked with a *repoussé* griffin, evidently from a disk-brooch. South of the Thames, in Cogidubnus' client kingdom of the southern Atrebates, the Regni ('the people of the kingdom') – a similar use of Classical iconography is to be seen on a disk-brooch from Lancing, Sussex, showing a hippocamp.[37] However, traditional ornament also survives on such brooches and a disk-brooch of late first-century date from Silchester is decorated with a curvilinear design arranged as a *triskele* device. The *repoussé* plaque from Dowgate in London displays analogous ornament.[38] It is of some interest that the 'Santon' cache contains two enamelled harness mounts in a native style, and we must bear in mind Boudica's golden torque in Dio's narrative as exemplifying Celtic continuity in its most distinctive form outside the direct ambit of Rome. What is the date of the last of the Snettisham torques or, in Ireland, of the 'Petrie crown'?[39]

There is in fact quite a large quantity of Celtic metalwork which could have been made after the formal date of the Roman Conquest, but it is only when it embellishes objects of a form associated with the incoming Romans that we can be certain of this. Several of the best examples are from the north or west of Britain and are Flavian rather than Claudian. Among brooches the Aesica brooch of gilt-bronze is pre-eminent and Sir Arthur Evans in a bout of hyperbole wrote that it is 'of its kind probably the most fantastically beautiful creation that has come to us from antiquity'.[40] The form is a derivative of the thistle-brooch, introduced from the Rhineland with the Roman army and the brooch is generally regarded as having been cast in a north British workshop in early Flavian times, that is probably during the existence of the Brigantian client kingdom which flourished under Roman protection. A more modest example of the type from Hook Norton, Oxfordshire, also bears Celtic ornament on its tail and, although it is very much inferior to the masterpiece from Great Chesters, it demonstrates that Romano-Celtic art was not confined to the periphery of the province.[41]

The trumpet-brooches, with their central 'acanthus' mouldings and expanded heads, include some splendid examples of craftsmanship. The best is a silver-gilt example from Carmarthen, which has been dated to about the time of the Conquest or even before. The mercury-gilding, like that on the Aesica brooch, shows familiarity with (and skill in using) a Roman technique, while the rosette on the headloop which linked the brooch to its pair has a naturalistic, Roman appearance. The scroll-work, however, is executed with confidence and a Claudio-Neronian date is reasonable.[42]

A bracelet from Rhayader (see 58) has a close analogy with a late Hellenistic or Augustan example from Egypt, though its decoration of two registers of knotted wires is simpler than the vine-scrolls of its Alexandrian analogue. However, at each end there are plates of Celtic ornament inset with enamel. It has been associated with other items of gold jewellery, including plates set with gems, from the same site and ornaments from Southfleet, Kent, as the products of a single workshop of the second century. It is true that they can be seen as belonging to the same tradition, although in every way the bracelet with Celtic ornament looks earlier than its fellows, still preserving distinct and unmixed traditions of classicism

and celticity.[43] The same could be said of a bronze mount from Elmswell, Yorkshire. The larger part of this is worked *en repoussé* with a symmetrical design of scrolls, reminiscent on the layout of some mirror backs, although the detail is closer to the Dowgate plaque. The inclusion of rosettes, like that on the headloop of the Carmarthen brooch, suggests that the smith was equating the design with the sort of acanthus ornament to be seen on Roman metalwork, like the scabbard of the Fulham sword which includes similar flowers (see 10).[44] A plate of enamel along the top of the Elmswell mount demonstrates skill with a native technique but the scroll shown is thoroughly Roman, being in the form of a leafy tendril. Such romanization of enamelwork is likewise to be seen in similar scrolls, together with two pairs of griffins each confronted across a cantharus, ornamenting a plaque from the Thames at London.[45]

Naturalistic portrayal of animals and of human beings began, in a tentative manner, before the Conquest. Metalworkers made further headway afterwards. A statuette in the form of a stag, found to the north of Brighton, Sussex, is particularly impressive (18). It is relatively large, standing 16.4cm (6½ in) in height and, despite damage to three of its legs, is still in excellent condition. The modelling is surprisingly

16 *Two silver cups from a grave. Welwyn, Hertfordshire. H. of both cups, c.11cm.* (Photo: British Museum.)

17 a *Two bronze cups from Crownthorpe, Norfolk. H. of both cups, c.8cm; b Detail of bird on handle of one cup. Castle Museum, Norwich.* (Photos: David Wicks, Norfolk Landscape Archaeology.)

18 *Bronze statuette of stag, found near Brighton, Sussex. H.16.4cm. Brighton Museum.* (Photo: Christie's.)

androphage' could be fully Romano-British, but there is something about the stag, its fresh, clean lines and its stylized eyes which suggest that it was cast as early as about AD 50.[46]

Boar figurines have been well studied by Jennifer Foster and span the Conquest period, with some animals, like those from Hounslow, certainly early and fully Iron Age. The boar from Muntham Court, Findon, Sussex, rendered in high relief and probably employed as a furniture mount, is strongly influenced by Roman naturalism, and is probably later (although the imported Roman boar from the Lexden tumulus demonstrates that such influence could well be prior to 43).[47] Its stylized outline recalls two near identical lions from Capel St Mary, Suffolk, which are clearly mounts of the same type. They are naturalistically modelled in Graeco-Roman fashion, with delicately hatched fur and rugged manes but their lentoid eyes, like the outline of their bodies, betray a native hand. Although they have been dated as late as the second century, a date in the first century AD is far more likely. Indeed, it is possible that the boar is a product of the kingdom of the Regni while the lions come from the ill-fated Icenian client kingdom.[48]

Rendition of the human form was much less well developed than animal art in the Iron Age, but the skill of the smiths could be turned towards this subject. Inevitably the main strength in native production lay in the dramatic, often scowling, mask which was present in the Iron Age repertoire. That the line of development followed by the smiths of Britain was not broken by the Conquest is also demonstrated by a number of small cast-bronze human heads which can be compared with the escutcheons on the Aylesford bucket. Most 'Celtic' are the head from Holme Hale, Norfolk, in the Icenian client kingdom, and the sceptre-head from Chalton, Hampshire, whose simplified physiognomies display hair brushed well forward and almond-shaped eyes in thoroughly native style. It would be possible to argue about the date of these, but a sceptre-head from Kirmington, Lincolnshire, with a helmeted 'Mars' head is probably Roman (**20**), and can be associated with the type of sceptre recovered from the Roman priest's grave at Brough-on-Humber.[49]

The same continuity is visible in *repoussé* work. For instance, the mask from the South Cadbury excavations, which, although recognizably Julio-Claudian, is a descendant of pre-Roman masks such

assured, but the smith was not constrained by the demands of naturalism. Large recessed eye-sockets were probably intended to take glass settings, as in the cases of other early bronzes including the Duncliffe Hill (Dorset) boar and the Aust-by-Severn and Henley Wood 'Venus' figurines (**19**), all assuredly of Iron Age date. The stag has a shaggy mane, allowing full scope for the smith to explore pattern and texture. This mannerism has more to do with artistic caprice than with study of an actual animal; it is a feature the stag shares with a very different beast: a terrifying ithyphallic, wolf-like monster engaged in eating a man, found near Oxford (perhaps at the temple site of Woodeaton) where a prominent mane runs the length of the creature's spine. There is no dating evidence for either bronze although both show familiarity with Roman naturalism. The '*carnassier*

as those on the Marlborough bucket, as is, again, especially manifest in the treatment of hair. Such pieces as the clean-shaven head with spirally curled hair, now in Copenhagen, the Jupiter mask from Felmingham Hall, Norfolk, the female head with almond-shaped eyes probably from Silkstead near Otterbourne in Hampshire and the masks found in the Icklingham cache (**21**a and b), confirm the continuity of skill in this kind of work through the Roman period.[50]

Figures in the round were rarer but the Aust-by-Severn and Henley Wood (see **19**) figurines gave rise to the likes of the deities in the Southbroom (Devizes) cache, at least those figurines of deities which survive and are preserved in the British Museum. As explained in *Religion in Roman Britain*, these are important for the story of the romanization of cult.[51] The simple depressions for glass insets in some instances provide a formal link with the two bronzes mentioned above, but the very schematized garments and misunderstood attributes also suggest an early date. The association with coins down to the third century does not date the individual items in the deposit which were varied in character and may well have been derived from a temple repository or *favissa*. A boldly rendered figure of Vulcan from North Bradley, likewise in Wiltshire, shows affinities with the Southbroom pieces but is possibly not so early; stylistically, at least, it is more advanced.[52] The male figure from Earith, shown making an offering (see **61**), is a splendid work of art. His hair and physiognomy are close to the native tradition of the masks mentioned above, especially those from South Cadbury and in Copenhagen, while the flexible modelling of the folds of his garments displays Celtic linearity very well. However, the dress does bring to mind that of natives of north-western Europe shown on stone sculpture of the Middle Empire.[53] This small selection of pieces, if I am right, leads us from native craft to classic Romano-British artistry.

Mention of masks is a reminder that the Roman Conquest provided enormous opportunities for artists to learn new skills. The famous Bath Gorgon with its richly curling tresses sculpted on the central shield, in the pediment of the Temple of Sulis Minerva at Bath, can be seen as a much enlarged version of a Celtic or Romano-Celtic mask in metal (**22**). Certainly the treatment of the eyes, which are lentoid in form with circular pupils, confirms a British (or

19 *Bronze Venus figurine from the temple at Henley Wood, Yatton, Somerset. H.7.5cm. (Photo: Robert Wilkins, Institute of Archaeology, Oxford.)*

20 *Bronze sceptre with helmeted ('Mars') head from Kirmington, Lincolnshire. Front and side views. H.6.6cm. (Photo: Robert Wilkins, Institute of Archaeology, Oxford.)*

Gaulish) hand at work. Collingwood was wrong, however, to see this as symbolizing the last flicker of Celtic originality before it was suppressed by Rome. The pediment is fundamentally Roman in design. Not only is its central motif, the male Gorgon itself, comparable with others, for instance that on a pediment from a second-century tomb at Chester, but the particular hairiness of the Bath example can be proved on examination to spring from conflation with an Oceanus or Neptune mask, a highly sophisticated concept. The shield on which it is set is a Roman motif and is surrounded by a vegetal wreath in disciplined Roman style. Victories support it and tritons flank it.[54] The Gorgon cannot be separated from the cornice and Corinthian capitals of the temple, both emphatically Roman, yet clearly part of the same programme of work dating from Neronian or early Flavian times.

The sanctuary was full of other sculpture, some, like the altar with its figures of deities, probably quite early; much of it was very good. Britons seem to have taken to sculpture with alacrity as the not infrequent inclusion of Celtic traits, especially in the coiffure, confirms. In this respect we may note a mask from a tomb at Towcester, Northamptonshire (see **65**), and the head of Mercury from Uley, Gloucestershire.[55]

Despite the setback of the Boudican Revolt, the process of romanization was not long drawn out. For the artist, as for the potential barrister (Tacitus, *Agricola* 21), it provided opportunities for the display of skills never possible before. This chapter has shown some examples of continuity from Iron Age craft, notably in metalwork. Nobody doubts Tacitus that Celtic eloquence survived the Conquest; albeit, as far as the leading classes of society were concerned, this ability was to be expressed in Latin. Art too changed, but did not, as generations of students of Roman Britain have been taught, decline. However, as later chapters of this book will demonstrate, the skills of British artists were most fully exercised not in keeping alive the almost exhausted tradition of native metalwork but mainly in interpreting the varied styles and media of Graeco-Roman art. In short there is a parallel with religious developments whereby the Roman Conquest brought radical changes of outlook and at the same time a symbiosis between native and Roman beliefs; the term *interpretatio romana* is an appropriate description of what happened in art too.[56]

21 *Hollow bronze votive heads or masks from Icklingham, Suffolk. Scale not known.*

22 *Sculptured pediment of the Temple of Sulis Minerva, Bath. Limestone. L.8.03m; H.2.46m. Roman Bath Museum.* (Photo: Robert Wilkins, Institute of Archaeology, Oxford.)

CHAPTER THREE

Art and the Roman Army

An eye like Mars, to threaten and command;
A station like the herald Mercury
New lighted on a heaven-kissing hill –
A combination and a form indeed
Where every god did seem to set his seal,
To give the world assurance of a man.

Roman soldiers and the Roman army appear fairly frequently in these pages. The legions stationed in Britain, comprised a fully romanized nucleus of people whose manner of life was to a large degree Mediterranean. The objects used by members of the army in the course of duty or at their leisure, in the baths or when dining, were often decorated in a Roman manner. As comparison of the small finds from a fortress, such as Caerleon, with those from an Italian city (for example Pompeii) reveals, cultural rubbish is similar, though the world of women, the *mundus muliebris*, is less in evidence in the military camp and decorated arms and armour more so.[1] Alongside imports from elsewhere, such as bronze drinking vessels and signet rings, there are works commissioned by the legion or members of it, notably sculpture, which was employed for both official and unofficial purposes and executed either by members of the regiment or by civilians living in close proximity.

At least half the army of Britain – and probably more than half – consisted of auxiliary troops. Although not a citizen, the premise of the career of an auxiliary in the first and second centuries AD was that he would obtain that coveted honour. Every such regiment had a prefect as commanding officer, a man of equestrian rank who was allowed to live with his family in a house of standard Italian style at the centre of the fort. Inscriptions on stone, letters written on wooden tablets (found at Vindolanda) and objects from forts assignable to the commander and his wife reveal the nature of that life. For instance, a gold ring set with a garnet intaglio cut with the representation of a dramatic mask from the commandant's latrine at Housesteads is comparable with many similar rings from Italy; the material of the ring is an indication of the wearer's status as the *annulus aureus* was the badge of members of the equestrian order.[2] A Vindolanda letter shows that a prefect's wife was important enough to be escorted many miles to a party at a friend's house, just as wealthy and well-connected women were able to do in Italy. The prefect's children would be educated by a tutor and studied the classics, notably Vergil.[3] Some of this culture and way of life percolated through to the men and to the inhabitants of the *vicus*, as has been well shown by the Vindolanda excavations. Again, both imported works of art and locally-made items attest a Roman culture in both language and art, instanced by a bronze figurine of a man wearing a *pallium*, a vehicle fitting surmounted by the figure of a horse, many gems from finger rings and other items of jewellery.[4]

The influence of the army on art as on other aspects of daily life, for instance religion, is hard to over-stress. The legions and the colonies of veterans provided encouragement and example for the economically active societies of the province, to the south and east of them. The auxiliaries were the primary agents of romanization on the northern frontier and in Wales, and Roman art, such as it is in these regions, largely owes its existence to these regiments. I have tried to pay due attention to the influence of the army elsewhere in this book, but in this chapter the aim is to concentrate on the soldiers themselves (together with their immediate dependants), for they were after all an important element in the population of Britain and, initially at any rate, the largest pool of foreigners.

We are not accustomed to think of armies today in connection with art: the images conjured up by the dress, arms and living-quarters of the modern soldier – khaki, barbed wire, ugly barracks and uglier weapons – repel anyone with aesthetic sense. Only the work of 'war artists' who record and comment upon battles and the silver plate and pictures in an Officers' Mess belong to the cultural sphere. Mention, however, the armies of the Middle Ages, with gorgeously apparelled knights, swords with personal names, brightly-coloured tents, and the myths of chivalry, and military life assumes a certain romance. Even much later, indeed until the nineteenth century, brightly-coloured clothes and beautiful weapons maintained a tradition of display. The Roman army was disciplined like the early modern armies but in other respects the soldier was closer to the knightly ideals of the Middle Ages. Of course, like all armies, it aimed to subdue its enemies – though, in theory at least, it was supposed to spare the suppliant (*parcere subiectis*). Soldiers were trained to kill but they were driven by a thirst for glory in the steps of Greek and Roman heroes of the legendary past (Tacitus, *Agricola* 5).

The legionary fortress, and indeed the auxiliary fort, was not normally a grim and soulless place but the most rational expression of Classical (Hippodamian) town planning to be found anywhere in the Empire. A legionary fortress in particular would have had its headquarters building, baths, officers' houses and barracks given appropriate architectural expression, enlivened with colour, sculptured fountains (see **54**) and impressively cut inscriptions. Much of this reflected contemporary taste and *romanitas*, though reminders of the soldier's calling in the form of figures of military virtues, such as Virtus and Victoria, of protective deities, notably Jupiter, Best and Greatest, Father Mars, Minerva and Hercules, occurred with greater frequency than they did in civil settlements.[5]

We lack any example of the battle paintings carried in Roman triumphs, although we should not overlook their existence and influence. It is very likely that paintings of this sort were treasured by army units, just as they have been in the officers' messes of more recent times.[6] Military historians can only regret that no large easel paintings entitled 'The final defeat of Boudica' and 'The Battle of Mons Graupius' have come down to us. Records of battles are now best known from the famous state reliefs in Rome, notably the columns of Trajan and of Marcus Aurelius and the arches of Titus and Severus. The episodes are standardized and, if they are related to campaign paintings, they suggest that they too would have been largely conventional, made up of stock themes. Indeed that is the implication of sculpture from the Antonine Wall, the battle and sacrifice of boar, ram and bull (*suovetaurilia*) on the Bridgeness distance slab, Britannia (or Roma) presenting a wreath to a legionary *aquila* on the relief from Hutcheson Hill (**23**), and the representations of soldiers, notably auxiliary cavalrymen riding down their foes (see **70, 71**), on tomb *stelae* throughout the province.[7]

The arms and armour of the soldiers have been the subject of detailed studies and it is not my aim here to vie with these. It is simply that in the equipment of the Roman soldier, above all in the early Imperial period, we can find an expression of Roman culture and art as impressive in its way as the sculptural monuments of Rome. Because the Roman army was stationed on the frontiers it is to the outlying provinces that we must look for the material, and because one of these provinces was Britannia, there is ample material for study here. In considering many of these items, we should realize that we are dealing essentially with the mainstream of Roman art, and it is regrettable that Classical archaeologists have so seldom given it due attention. Alongside purely Roman decoration, there was also some use of Celtic motifs and techniques, notably enamel work and *repoussé*, to embellish the armour of men and horses; these too add a dimension to the understanding of Roman military art and of taste in ornament.

23 *Antonine Wall distance slab from Hutcheson Hill, Dunbartonshire. Centre panel showing Britannia(?) and signifer. Sandstone. H.74.5cm.* (Photo by courtesy of Hunterian Museum and University Court, University of Glasgow.)

Apart from the physical remains of camps themselves, scholars have paid most attention to lapidary work. From this source comes much of our knowledge of how the army in Britain operated, its personnel and recruitment. Frequently there is a sculptural element embellishing official inscriptions, altars and tombstones and these too have been studied, though more often with an eye to content than to style and quality. It is clear that legionary commanders and their men aimed to have the most 'Roman' work available to them. This is clearly seen in the case of an imported commemorative slab of Tuscan marble set up on a building in Caerleon with Trajan's titles and the name of the Second Legion on it.[8] It must have looked exceedingly fine with its well-spaced letters tastefully graded so that the first two lines with the name of Trajan and the last with that of the legion show up especially well. Traces of red colouring remain in the letters, which would have stood out boldly against the white of the marble, and the panel has been further embellished with an ansate frame and rosettes.

The panel was evidently drafted as early as AD 99, but it must have taken a number of months before the finished plaque reached Caerleon. By then Trajan had entered his third consulate (AD 100), which necessitated the addition of one character to the inscription. It is surely not likely that the craftsman assigned to do this was totally unskilled, though he may have been new to marble carving. On an ordinary inscribed building stone, of which a number have been found at Caerleon, his effort would have passed without comment, but it is clear that the final I of COS ▼ III on this formal masterpiece is not straight. Despite this qualification, good lapidary work was carried out in a legionary ambience in Britain, and the south-east gate of the fortress of the Ninth Legion at York carries a long commemoration cut in local magnesian limestone. Neither the spacing nor the letter forms display quite the skill of the Italian expert, but there is no doubting its *romanitas*. Examples of inscriptions cut on slate from north Wales from the fortress of the Twentieth Legion at Chester are also well done and visually must have been a good substitute for the coloured marbles used for inscriptions in Mediterranean lands.[9] These lapidary skills would have been passed on to civilian centres. Indeed it is probable that the Hadrianic carver of that masterpiece of epigraphy from Britain, the sandstone

dedication of the Forum at Wroxeter,[10] was more regularly employed by the Twentieth Legion, though whether he was a soldier himself or a civilian resident in the *canabae* is uncertain (see below).

At this official level we must remember that Imperial statues were to be seen in fortresses and forts. Most were cast in bronze, like those of which we have fragments from Caerleon, consisting of small parts of a cuirassed figure including a *pteryx* from an armoured skirt, found close to the statue pedestals which stood near the north-west side of the *basilica principiorum* at Caerleon. A finger from this or another statue was found nearby and another finger came from the site of the barracks of the first cohort. Presumably, similar bronze statues stood in the other fortresses. A *pteryx* from Caernarfon shows that similar statues stood in auxiliary forts. Bronze statuary in the *coloniae* and other towns will be discussed elsewhere. The headquarters building at York has yielded the head of an emperor carved from the local limestone. Despite its classicizing features, its general physiognomy is Tetrarchic rather than Trajanic, and it has been generally accepted as a very early image of Constantine who was proclaimed at York on the death of his father in 306 (see Chapter 7). Like the York inscription mentioned above, it may well have been cut by a craftsman in the employ of the legion (now the Sixth), although in both cases the exemplar will have been an official model (in the case of portraits, plaster casts could have been employed).[11]

In considering the three long-term legionary bases of Britain, there is no reason to think that there was any differential where such major, official commissions are concerned. The situation appears rather different when ordinary dedications and tombstones commissioned by soldiers are considered, and fortunately here evidence is plentiful.[12] This is especially so in the case of Chester, where the north wall had been repaired in Late Roman times and, when investigated in the nineteenth century, was found to incorporate a great many reused tombstones. These, along with the other sculpture and inscriptions from Chester, have been fully published by R.P. Wright and I.A. Richmond who have rightly declared that they 'form one of the most individual and important collections in Britain'. Sculpture from Caerleon and York has been fully published in relevant fascicules of the *Corpus Signorum Imperii Romani*. The sculpture from Chester amounts to over 70 items, excluding architectural ornament. Figured sculpture from the Caerleon fortress and from Bulmore nearby comprises some 27 items, while York yields 62 pieces, although many of them must belong to the *colonia*. The sample from each fortress is thus a reasonably good one.

The introductory section of the Chester catalogue does not say a great deal about the quality of the sculpture but includes the following revealing comment in connection with the tombstones:

> The artistic standard of these panels is often crude if they are judged as formal sculpture. When, however, it is realized that most of them will have been coated with gesso and painted, their character, as the mere groundwork for a painted picture, becomes more in keeping with their purpose. To estimate their original poster-like effect is now almost beyond our power.[13]

The remarks about gesso and paint would apply equally to the best legionary sculpture in Britain, such as the first-century tombstone of Facilis at Colchester or the Trajanic monument of a *beneficiarius consularis* from London (24), as they do to the Chester sculpture.[14] It would not have been possible to make much improvement to poor work with the liberal addition of paint. Fortunately we are not left with surmise, but can parallel many of the tombstones of Chester with those from other fortresses. The commonest type is a figure or a pair of figures standing within a recess. For the former the stele of the *optio* Caecilius Avitus and that of the *imaginifer* Aurelius Diogenes may be taken as typical. These were important members of the legion, but their images are distinctly lumpy, with thick legs and arms protruding from thick garments. Nor do the frames bear any ornament.[15]

Turning to York, the *signifer* of the Ninth Legion, Lucius Duccius Rufinus, stands within a deeper recess. Although the representation has been called 'dry and simplified', it is markedly more competent than most of the Chester tombstones; the subject's legs and arms are more in scale with his body and the sculptor has been successful in suggesting the folds of the *paenula* which he wears over his tunic. Its style is similar to that of the tombstone of a man, likewise from York and of Trajanic date, as indeed his hair style suggests. He wears a torque and holds a spray of flowers in his right hand and a scroll in his left; he is housed in a handsome surround with Corinthian

24 *Tombstone of a* beneficiarius consularis *from Camomile Street bastion, City of London. Limestone. H.1.32m. Museum of London. (After J.E. Price, A bastion of London Wall, 1880, pl.iv.)*

pilasters ornamented with leaves and above them rosettes, while at the apex of the arch is a *bucranium*.

Another York tombstone, probably a century later, shows a man and a boy; again the adult is well rendered – indeed Sergio Tufi describes the execution of the body and of the clothing as 'perhaps more careful than in other tombstones from York'.[16] It is not certain whether he is a legionary or a veteran but the former is likely. Certainly the gravestone from near Caerleon (Little Bulmore) with the same subject must show a legionary to judge from his military cloak (*sagum*). His left arm is slightly raised so that the folds create a rippling effect where the fabric hangs slackly above that point. The turn of the head, the shaping of the arms, bare on the right and enveloped in drapery on the left, and the tender gesture towards his child as he places his right hand upon the infant's head, almost give the viewer the illusion of life, despite the very grievous damage the stone has received – and the lack of gesso and paint! Here the niche is a deep one and embellished with a shell canopy and the flanking Corinthian pilasters are enriched with fine acanthus scrollwork. The monument, carved in oolitic limestone, was surely created by a Cotswold sculptor of the first rank.[17]

A number of tombstones from Chester show a husband and wife or a family group. Some exhibit the same visual coarseness as the single figures, for instance the stele of the centurion, Marcus Aurelius Nepos, set up by his wife (**25**). He is crudely carved, although the vigorous grooving of the front of his cloak and of the kilt of his tunic below the belt breaks the monotony of the form. His wife, who is shown with little pin-legs below a flounced skirt, also well grooved, has to be given a pedestal to bring her up to his level. The stone has the charm and child-like quality of some seventeenth- and eighteenth-century village tombstones but is hardly the 'high Roman manner'. There is better work from Chester such as the well-known relief of a woman holding a mirror with her maid, and several related stones which must have been carved by the same sculptor. Although the clothing forms are comparatively simple and the relief is not very high, this is sculpture of acceptable quality. It is, however, outclassed by the memorial of Flavia Augustina, the wife of a veteran of the Sixth Legion at York, which shows a whole family standing within a double-headed niche with an elaborate frame.[18]

25 *Tombstone of M. Aurelius Nepos and his wife from Chester. Sandstone. H.1.85m. Grosvenor Museum. (After Journal of the Chester Archaeological and Historic Society. N.S. ii, 1888, pl.1.)*

York has yielded three examples of the banquet tombstone, all dedicated to women, probably the dependants of veterans. The concept is a very wide-spread one in Graeco-Roman art; those under discussion here follow the local Eboracan style of deep niches, bold framing and an attractive use of pattern. The tombstone of Julia Velva is perhaps the best, crisply carved in three planes of relief. The woman reclines on a well-padded couch. In front stands her husband, Lucius Aurelius Mercurialis, and a son, and on the other side of a table is their daughter, seated in a basket chair. Once again the Chester comparisons are far inferior in standard, although no less than eight such stele survive at the fortress; the best-known is per-haps that of Curatia Dinysia whose tombstone is more elaborate than usual for Chester, with trumpet-blowing tritons in the spandrels and birds standing on garlands within a rather shallow niche. The deceased, who rests on her couch with a singularly ill-executed table beside her, is very badly modelled. The stock nature of the figure is apparent when it is compared with an almost identical carvings on other stones including those of Aurelius Lucianus and Caecilius Donatus, serving soldiers. Presumably they are all products of the same workshop. Although as yet no banquet-tombstone is known from Caerleon, the theme of the feast of the dead is brought out by a sepulchral *mensa* with a central hole, allowing wine to be poured down to the ashes of the dead. This is now lost but it is clear from the eighteenth-century illustration that the form of the *mensa* (a Doric capital), its accomplished rendering of Venus and the surrounding myrtle sprays mark a very high level of classicism, which would have been at home in the Mediterranean world.[19]

With regard to other sculpture of high quality or iconographic interest the following finds connected with the three fortresses are illuminating. A fine Purbeck marble *labrum* with a Medusa-mask in the centre comes from the Castle Baths at Caerleon. The use of this material (also employed for wall veneers at Caerleon) is perhaps evidence that the Second Legion retained some control of the quarries on the Isle of Purbeck. The 'marble' had been used in the earlier fortress at Exeter, notably for a noble rendering of an eagle but also for another *labrum*, mouldings and plaques for inlay. It is also found at Fishbourne where the Legion may have helped supply materials to Cogidubnus or whoever built the palace. The Caerleon *labrum* is a splendid translation into British

stone of an essential item of equipment for Roman-style bathing. Also at the Castle Baths was found an excellent relief of Fortuna and Bonus Eventus, given by Cornelius Castus and his wife in the third century, by which time soldiers were allowed to marry. This can be regarded as a public benefaction, for these deities would have protected the baths. A statue of a Genius in oolitic limestone and a spirited piece of work by a Cotswold carver probably came from a *schola* within the headquarters building.[20]

An almost complete statue of Mars from York, carved with considerable dexterity in the local sand-stone, may have come from the fortress, and certainly looks like an expression of formal state religion. There are also some good private votive sculptures, such as a figure of Mercury and an altar to the *matres*, who are depicted on its main face set in a deep niche, like those found on the tombstones. A statue of the Mithraic deity, Arimanes, is also very well carved, but Mithraists in the army seem to have had access to sculptors of above average quality.[21]

Chester's contribution lies in some stones prob-ably from a tomb or tombs, showing mythological themes, including the deaths of Adonis and Actaeon, and Hercules rescuing Hesione, atrociously carved though of great interest on account of their subject matter, expressing as they do some knowledge of Greek mythology. However, there is also a powerful-looking male gorgon on a tomb-pediment, the work of a carver of superior skill. Even if, in absolute terms, it falls below the level of the Bath Gorgon, the presence of something so good here demands explanation.[22]

The reason for the marked differences in quality lies in the relation of each legion to its hinterland and to the province in general. Caerleon is only just beyond the limestone belt and sculptors from this region were at hand to execute commissions. The Purbeck marble *labrum* and two wall-veneers from baths, as we have seen, suggest that the legion may have maintained links with the south of the prov-ince. Outside the fortress was a flourishing civilian settlement and the cantonal capital of the Silures was only a few miles away at Caerwent. York was also favoured and, although at first it must have been in a military zone, the vale of York was fertile and soon became civilized. The civilian settlement which grew up on the other side of the Ouse quickly became urban in the true sense and was honoured with the title of *colonia* in about 200. The situation at Chester was different. Here there was no comparable civil city in the hinterland (though there was the usual *canabae*, of course, now known to be quite extensive in area) and the sculpture has a much more provincial appearance. First-rate sculptors were far less likely to be attracted here than to the more civilized ambience of the other fortresses, which had close contacts with civilian culture. The quality of work associated with the legions along the Rhine and Danube is also higher than that prevailing at Chester, because here again fortresses were not far distant from the towns.[23]

However, the Roman military ethos, which saw the legionary camp as a microcosm of Rome itself, provided a standard to which art should aspire, even though in practice it often fell short of this ideal, as at Chester. The legate of a legion could do a very great deal as a patron, collecting sculptors and setting them to work. Roman art under these conditions could

26 *Altar of Flavius Longus, dedicated to the Genius Loci at Chester. Sandstone. H.81cm. Grosvenor Museum. (After W. Thompson Watkin, Roman Cheshire, 1886, pl.op.p.170.)*

flourish, as a measure of *romanitas*, as two lovely altars from Chester demonstrate. The first is the altar dedicated to Fortuna Redux, Aesculapius and Salus by the freedmen of the legionary legate early in the second century. Both sides are carved with appropriate sacrificial symbols and emblems of the deities honoured. Equally ambitious is the other altar (**26**), dedicated in the early third century to the Genius Loci by a military tribune of the Twentieth Legion, called Flavius Longus, and his son, natives of Samosata, which had also nurtured Lucian and his sculptor uncle before him. One side depicts a statue of the Genius, the other an acanthus in a vase, and the back a draped cloth, as it were hanging from an offering table, surmounted by fruit. The crisp carving of the leaves of the acanthus and the rippling folds of the cloth are excellent.

Flavius Longus must have known what sculptors were capable of producing and would not have found the average quality of Chester work to his liking. Clearly, as an important officer of the legion, he was able to call upon the legate's best sculptor. The sculptor of the Chester Gorgon (see above) may well have been introduced to do important work for the legion or the legate; indeed it has to be said that the pediment comes from a very large tomb. Another example of patronage at this level from the fortresses comes from Caerleon. A contemporary altar dedicated by a prefect of the Second Legion to Salus has a well-lettered inscription and a small bust in a shell-niche stood between the bolsters. It is not, however, exceptional for Caerleon, where good sculptors were probably easier to find as explained above. Likewise of Severan date is the dedicatory tablet of a temple to Serapis at York, built by the legate Claudius Hieronymianus. The inscription is set within a cabled frame with *peltae*, all fine and dignified despite the religious standards which seem to have been added by a different and inferior hand, somewhat spoiling the effect.[24]

It is likely that some sculpture at this level was the work of serving soldiers with privileges, *immunes* (meaning that they were exempt from certain routine duties), and whose tasks would have been to work with carvers of official inscriptions to celebrate the prowess of the emperor, as well as those of the particular military unit to which they belonged. Often, indeed, inscription and sculpture may have been the work of the same artist. An important source of

work for official legionary sculptors in the second century lay in commemorative slabs, above all the distance slabs from the Antonine Wall. All three legions there are represented in works of varying quality, though it can be argued that the two best are Twentieth Legion stones, regardless of the general level of Chester's sculpture. In particular the Hutcheson Hill slab (see **23**) has none of the gaucheness of the Chester sculpture. The frame is a triumphal arch with fluted pilasters; before the two side openings kneel captives; in the centre an *à la mode* Britannia, attractively clad and coiffured, offers a wreath to the *aquila* held by a standard bearer. From Old Kilpatrick comes another panel, again with fluted pilasters but this time just a single pediment, below which Victory, holding a palm and a massive wreath, reclines on a globe. Her drapery is richly vibrant and the modelling of her body a world away from the depressing banquet tombstones.

The Second Legion does not do badly with the Bridgeness distance slab but the frames of the figure panels lack the grace of those just mentioned. The *suovetaurilia*, with its out-of-scale animals and the figures, with nicely patterned (but not well modelled), garments looks like local sculpture. The Braidfield slab set up by the Sixth Legion shows diminutive figures of Mars and Virtus and two victories reaching up to hold a panel that appears to be too heavy for them; it is devoid of framing. It is clear that these slabs are individual works and there was no overall quality control. The Twentieth Legion used a better sculptor than the other two legions on this occasion, perhaps the man who produced major dedications for the legion and privately for the legate. The Second Legion's dedications on the Antonine Wall look much more like the work of masons familiar with tombstone-cutting. On the other hand, peltate dedication slabs from Corbridge, Shirva in Dunbartonshire and Castell Collen in Wales have a richness and monumental grandeur which the Antonine Wall memorials lack, so perhaps the best *lapidarius* was being employed elsewhere.[25]

On the whole the position with regard to auxiliary units was comparable to the situation of the legionaries at Chester, if anything to a greater degree. They were in distant stations which did not help to draw in the talent to establish viable artistic schools in their hinterland; moreover, the troops and their dependants were less well off and on the whole less

27 *Relief of Ceres and Persephone(?) from Housesteads, Northumberland. H.66.5cm. Sandstone. Destroyed.* (Photo: Museum of Antiquities, Newcastle upon Tyne.)

educated than legionaries. These generalizations did not apply to auxiliaries everywhere and the distinguished class of cavalry tombstones showing horsemen riding down their foes – a device going back to Classical Greek times – provides a notable exception, which is partially explained by the better pay and greater prestige of these mounted regiments.[26] Another important factor lay in the fact that the commanding officers of the auxiliary units were of equestrian rank and had the money to patronize sculptors when they could be found.

The sculpture from the region of Hadrian's Wall, now fully published in two fascicules of CSIR, is very revealing; at its best, the carving can stand comparison with Romano-British work anywhere (see Chapter 6). There were evidently some very accomplished artists at Housesteads for instance. Especially distinctive are two gravestones showing men dressed in long-sleeved tunics, a relief of two goddesses – perhaps Ceres and Persephone (27) – and four statues of mother goddesses, which stand out by virtue of their excellent modelling and the liveliness of their draperies – when painted, they would have created a very rich effect. From Housesteads, too, comes the amazing representation of the birth of Mithras from an egg, carved in the round within a frame bearing the signs of the zodiac in relief. These are clearly

private commissions, as in all probability are two reliefs depicting Neptune, very much in the Classical tradition. Elsewhere, the superb handling of drapery of a river-god from the bath-house at Chesters and a figure of Fortuna from the commandant's own bath-house at Birdoswald (28) betray the hands of skilled Romano-British carvers. The latter may be attributed to the notable school of sculptors based at Carlisle, though the most distinctive surviving products of this studio appear to be tombstones of women. Carlisle was effectively a town, although its economy was linked to the military markets of the western Wall region. It thus offered a limited base for the arts to flourish in – although there were limitations: nobody, so far as I know, attempted to establish a mosaic studio here.[27]

Most of the sculpture from the Wall is, however, of very poor quality, with lumpy and ill-proportioned figures which cannot simply be defended as representing a popular tradition. It results from the lack of skill and expertise among the dwellers in the *vici* outside the forts. For example, there are a number of reliefs of Mars from Housesteads, ranging from good official work down to some very clumsily modelled representations indeed. The gravestone of a soldier from Castlesteads, although it clearly shows a man of some rank (his case of writing-tablets reveals him to have been a clerk with *immunis* status), is child-like in its bungling execution – the neck is tubular, the body virtually rectangular beneath a shapeless coat and the legs stumpy. There is also the tombstone of a woman from Vindolanda, depicted in low relief with no attempt at modelling. Her body is encased in a shift in the form of a truncated cone, she has

*28   Statue of Fortuna from
Birdoswald, Cumberland.
Sandstone. H.1.05m.*
(Photo: City Museum,
Carlisle.)

a triangular neck and a schematized face. This low quality extends to art which must have been intended to be official. A stone from the fort wall of Vindolanda shows a figure of Victory standing stiffly in profile, her skirt split on the right side to reveal a fat thigh and both arms rigidly bent at the elbows.[28]

Official sculpture certainly or possibly attributed to auxiliary units includes the dedication to the Imperial Numina by the Fourth Cohort of Gauls from Risingham, Northumberland. This is a richly-patterned panel, whose ornamentation figures cranes (possibly the emblem of the unit) as well as apotropaic heads, one of them a *tricephale*, which hints at 'native' beliefs. Nonetheless the Victory in a niche on the left, and Mars in an even deeper *aedicula* on the right, express the language of *romanitas*. There are also two large renderings of Victory in high relief from Housesteads, one of which may have come from the Severan reconstruction of the east gateway of the fort (**29**); even more beautiful by virtue of her billowing *chiton* is the relief of Victory from Stanwix (**30**), which once flanked an inscription. These, however, may well have been the work of legionary sculptors. There are, of course, many altars dedicated by auxiliary units in which a certain skill with letter forms and some use of framing ornament create a powerful impression. Exceptional here are the Antonine altars of the Second Cohort of Tungrians from Birrens in south Scotland, dedicated in excellent epigraphy to Disciplina, to Mars and Victory and to Minerva. The first of these altars has been described as 'one of the most highly decorated and accomplished known in Britain', but the embellishment consists of no more than simple cult implements on the sides and a shrine with doors above the inscription, just below the *focus*; the ends and sides of the bolsters are decorated with rosettes. The other two altars are distinguished by almost identical ivy-leaf tendrils and must be from the same hand; indeed all three altars were surely produced by the unit's official *lapidarius*.[29]

A small but special category of work linked to Roman soldiers in the legions and to the officer-class of the auxiliaries is that composed of the sculptures and dedications attributed to the cult of Mithras. In London there are imported marbles, one of them, a votive tauroctony, dedicated by a veteran of the Second Legion. In all probability most of the votaries were associated with the legionary guard of the gov-

ernor. There are remains of high-quality limestone sculpture too, presumably from one of the London workshops staffed by craftsmen from the limestone belt. The York Mithraeum was probably used largely by soldiers of the Sixth Legion, but of course there again sculptors were easy to find. The Housesteads relief of Mithras Saecularis (mentioned above) and other carvings from the Wall region are more impressive in that they were probably carved more or less *in situ* without a local workshop tradition to back them. They are testimony to the devoted piety and patron-

VICTORY
HOLDING A PALM-BRANCH.
[BORCOVICUS: EASTERN GATEWAY, 1852.]

[200]

29 Relief of Victory from Housesteads, Northumberland. Sandstone. H.1.035m. Chesters Museum. (Photo: J.C. Coulston.)

30 *Relief of Victory from Stanwix, Cumberland. Sandstone. H.67cm.* (Photo: Museum of Antiquities Newcastle upon Tyne.)

age of the officer class, prepared to bring in sculptors from afar if necessary.[30]

With regard to other large-scale art, evidence is very limited and evidently confined to the legions. The Second Legion certainly seems to have been in the vanguard with very early (Neronian) mosaics in the Exeter baths and high-quality floors in the Fortress Baths at Caerleon as soon as they were built. Elsewhere the military camps of the province have provided little. Leaving sculpture aside, northern Britain certainly had no mosaic studios north of York and the mosaics from the *colonia* at York found so far are not very interesting. There are a few mosaics from

the Fortress Baths at Chester which are rather arresting in appearance but unrelated to other mosaic schools.

Evidence for wall-painting is also apparently somewhat lacking, though there were ambitious schemes of decoration in the Fortress Baths at Caerleon during the late first and second centuries, including a painted ceiling in the *frigidarium* imitating a coffered vault and vegetal ornament on the walls both here and in the basilica-vestibule. A fresco from the headquarters building at York, dated to the fourth century, depicts a rather garish architectural screen with columns rising from ill-drawn double-torus bases; additional elements include birds and a hideous theatrical mask but it is not possible to make full sense of the ensemble. Frescoed walls are known in auxiliary forts on the Continent, perhaps most notably the Hadrianic mythological paintings from the fort at Echzell in Germany, and small fragments are recorded from forts in Britain, including Chesters on the Wall. Perhaps something like the Echzell paintings will be found in the Wall region, although even here we must keep in mind the remoteness of soldiers on the British frontiers from the urban amenities which produced such luxuries as firms of interior decorators.[31]

Pottery importers and *negotiatores* in wine knew that there was a ready market on the Wall for portable objects and comestibles. On the whole, lapidary artists did not. The taste for gaudy enamels was widespread, ranging from souvenirs of the Wall, which even reached Amiens in Gaul and Rudge in Wiltshire (see **41**), to studs and belt-fittings. Soldiers in the Roman army had always been good patrons of the metalworker. Although basic armour was provided from military *fabrica*, there was nothing to prevent a man having his equipment embellished with silver, niello, tin or enamel, even though Pliny clearly disapproved of soldiers 'whose scabbards jingle with little silver chains and their belts with silver tabs' (*NH* xxxiii, 152). Horsemen had even more opportunity for display, as numerous trappings, pendants and junction-fittings attest. Tombstones, especially in the first century, show all this equipage being used, although, alas, the colour has gone from these reliefs. The love of colour attested later by enamels was surely no new taste. The reason for this lies in human nature. In this, the 'disciplined' legionary was no different from the 'bragging' Celt. Bright shining armour and intricate workmanship were a source of pride to all ancient warriors, as authors as diverse as Homer, Josephus and Tacitus suggest. Ironically, a very fine set of silvered horse-fittings in the British Museum, but found at Xanten, was owned by a member of the regiment Pliny commanded in Germany. None of this magnificence made the Roman soldier less tough.[32]

A recent study of pre-Flavian belts from Britain provides a good starting point.[33] The belt was an essential part of military dress for it carried the sword and dagger. In fact two belts were thought necessary in order to distribute the weight of these items. From a purely functional standpoint leather strips strengthened with metal plates would have been sufficient, but both sculpture and actual remains show that rich decoration was normally applied, decoration which complemented that of the sword- and dagger-scabbards attached to the belt. *Repoussé* decoration, punched into a mould, includes a plate from Chichester showing the *Lupa Romana* suckling Romulus and Remus, a device also to be seen on the sword-sheath from Fulham, likewise of the Conquest period. Other mounts from Colchester, Hod Hill and Waddon Hill are decorated with acanthus as, indeed, is the body of the Fulham scabbard. Beyond military art, as Grew indeed points out, such motifs bring to mind the decor of the screen wall of *Ara Pacis*.[34]

Another technique is inlay, normally with *niello* (silver sulphide) in the form of vegetal devices. On the better plates the designs were cut into the metal. The finest example, from Sheepen, Colchester, displays two identical motifs consisting of four corn-ears arranged diagonally (**31**), well paralleled in stucco from the Farnesina House. There are many examples of a simplified form of the motif. Niello was used on silver plate, for instance in two vessels from the Hildesheim Treasure and also on high-quality bronze-work such as the statuette of Nero from Baylham Mill, Coddenham, Suffolk (see **108**), where it ornaments the emperor's cuirass. Incidentally, as Graham Webster has suggested to me, it is quite probable that this object stood in the *sacellum* of a fort until the rebellion of Boudica, and thus is itself of military significance.[35]

Repoussé technique was used to ornament sword scabbards and especially armour of both men and horses and these items are, in consequence, an important source of figural art. Such work was doubtless valued for itself, because it impressed others and because the deities and other motifs (for instance the

Roman she-wolf and twins on the Fulham sword **10**) which were portrayed in the medium gave protection to the wearer. For some reason the richest decoration is associated with auxiliary cavalrymen who wore special helmets with face-mask visors on parade and in skilfully orchestrated manoeuvres. However, other helmets, scarcely less ornamental, were used by cavalrymen on service and even in battle.

The parade helmets divide into two categories, one with idealized classical features and the other with those of barbarians, thus allowing the military exercise to take the form of a legendary battle, such as the Greeks fighting Trojans or Amazons. Only the idealized type has so far been found in Britain, at Ribchester, Lancashire (**32** and see **107**) and at Newstead, Roxburghshire. Sir James Curle wrote of the finest of the Newstead helmets, made from beaten iron and originally silvered, that 'even in its present mutilated condition', it 'must rank as one of the most beautiful things that the receding tide of Roman conquest has left behind it'.[36] It was found in a Flavian-period pit in the south annexe of the fort and depicts a head with rich S-curved hair bound with a wreath of laurel. The hair hints at Celtic influence and presumably the piece was made in the north-west provinces. In the same pit was another sports helmet, though of bronze, of which the mask is now lost. The back of this helmet shows Cupid in a *biga* pulled by leopards. Such a combination of figural scene and mask survives almost complete on the Ribchester helmet, which Jocelyn Toynbee assessed as 'the most impressive face-mask visor-helmet so far found in Britain'.[37] Surmounting the brows runs a mural crown and above that a fanciful scene including sea-monsters. There are battle-scenes on the crown of the head, a direct relation to the life of the wearer. Cheek pieces from helmets used in the field include one from Kingsholm, Gloucester, depicting a seated Jupiter. This was made of very thin sheet worked into a mould and would have been backed with iron. An example from Leicester shows a cupid with a parrot, alluding to the god Bacchus. Although published as part of a parade helmet, Graham Webster (in an appended note) points out that such separate cheek-pieces should come from fighting helmets. Another such cheek-piece from Brough, Nottinghamshire, showed a Dioscurus, an appropriate deity for a cavalryman.[38] As a possible example of horse-armour, its suggested use being as the frontal of a

31 *Bronze*, nielloed *belt-mount from Sheepen, Colchester. L.7cm.* (Drawing by N. Griffiths, Grew and Griffiths 1991, fig.5 no.A.1.

32 *Bronze parade helmet from Ribchester, Lancashire. H.28cm. British Museum.* (Engraving by J. Basire in Vet. Mon. iv, 1815 (Townley 1799), pl.1.) (See also fig.107.)

chamfrein, the exquisite plate showing a trophy-bearing Victory from Caerleon is surely among the masterpieces of military art from Britain. It was found in a mid-second-century context but both technique and style suggest it was made in the first or early second century.[39]

It is not known where such attractive examples of figured armour were actually made, though a stamp from Sheepen perhaps used for belt plates shows that the work could have been done in some instances by military *fabricae* in Britain.[40] There are very few concessions to provincial style, however, apart from the highly individual working of the hair on the Newstead helmet mentioned above. Early Roman military art may be individual in its lack of uniformity but each piece, whether a harness-fitting or an important item of armour, stresses *romanitas*. Legionaries were Romans and auxiliaries strived to end their careers with the all important *diplomata* giving them citizenship.

From the second century onwards a change is perceptible, though of course Classical elements are still easy to find. Thus, for instance, a Dioscurus is the subject of the cheek-piece from South Shields; however, the subject was simply drawn on to the metal and presumably picked out as it is now by filling the fine lines so made. This dates to the end of the second century at earliest. The same use of incision is to be seen on the helmet from Guisborough. Yorkshire, where figures of Victory, Minerva and Mars are portrayed.[41] A much stronger impression is achieved by the use of openwork and above all by enamel to give texture and colour to belts and other items of dress. The use of enamel was quintessentially Celtic and to find it used not only on the brooches worn by native women but on armour and equipment worn by soldiers (**33**) suggests a change in attitude. Many of the fittings found at forts such as Newstead in its Antonine phase, at Vindolanda and the forts along the Wall are likely to have been made locally. Indeed, the Hadrian's Wall souvenirs such as the Rudge cup must have been manufactured in its vicinity, by craftsmen working for a largely military

clientele. The quantity and often the very real quality of these enamels do not (*pace* Collingwood) give the impression of native art *in extremis*, but rather show that the Empire-wide shift in taste towards abstraction and texture had been able to make use of a living native art even within the confines of the fort, the microcosm of Rome.[42] Outside the fort, as the Vindolanda excavations reveal, was a mixed population including many women whose jewellery was enamelled just like their husbands' belt-studs and slides. As even the traditional and old-fashioned tombstones of soldiers suggest, the auxiliary, and even the legionary, was becoming part of local society and adopting local tastes rather than continuing to maintain the attitudes of a superior class, whose reality had, in all probability, ceased within little more than a generation of the Conquest. Art is a most valuable indicator of this shift in values.

33 *Bronze enamelled belt-plate from South Shields, Co.Durham. L.8.3cm. (After Arch Ael² x, 1885, p.262 (fig).)*

CHAPTER FOUR

The Uses of Art in Roman Britain

Thou art a lady;
If only to go warm were gorgeous,
Why, nature needs not what thou gorgeous wear'st,
Which scarcely keeps thee warm.

Nowadays the practice of art is often regarded as a precious activity, largely divorced from daily life. An artist is defined as someone who works on expensive commissions for members of an educated and wealthy élite, or at least that is the impression given by the expensive, glossy art journals, bulging with sale-room advertising. The daily visual experience of the majority of people is limited to prints and photographs and to low-quality ornaments in the home, all of them mass-produced. Public art today consists on the one hand of 'commercial art' and on the other of the occasional self-conscious statue set up by an industrialist outside a factory or by a benefactor, or even a municipality, in an open space within a town. The current split between 'high art' and popular experience owes much to the results of the Industrial Revolution. The creation of new towns broke up traditional societies with their folk crafts. In place of the latter came cheap, mass-produced substitutes. This appalled sensitive artists and critics, first and foremost in nineteenth-century England, the pre-Raphaelites and John Ruskin. However, the very nature of nineteenth-century life meant, ironically, that it was the educated élite and not the masses who responded to their call. High art could not be other than *Salon* art, offering an escape into fantasy for those who could afford

to ignore the appalling results of capitalism. What was lost in the Victorian Age was not artistic commissions, but the continuity of more humble crafts, for example the traditions of the woodcarver and the blacksmith, the skills of the village stone mason carving tombstones and those of the vernacular builder and decorator. It was now much cheaper to buy in quantity from a factory, but a glance at Victorian and post-Victorian mass-produced ornament at once reveals how much was lost.

It should be noted that the situation in Roman Britain was very different, for the simple reason that the Conquest had not ushered in an Industrial Revolution. When Francis Haverfield wrote of 'monotonous Roman culture' and announced that 'to pass from Glastonbury to Woodcutts is like passing from some old timbered village of Kent or Sussex to the uniform streets of a modern city suburb',[1] we read the words of a near-contemporary of William Morris. Haverfield makes much of the vast import of mass-produced samian ware, but this is not really typical. Pottery has always been produced in quantity, though that has not necessarily meant low quality, as wares as various as Attic figured pottery of the sixth and fifth century BC or Chinese and later European porcelains attest. Indeed, first-century samian vessels, especially many of the south Gaulish products, provide admirable specimens of contemporary taste, especially cups and bowls embellished with running scrolls of vines and other plants. There are also splendid examples of later (second-century) samian, such as the vase from Southwark, imported from central Gaul, which is decorated with moulded appliqué ornament of cupids and animals (boars, deer, hares).[2] This represents a resilience in taste, and even the aesthetic failure of the Gaulish kilns in the case of other products only encouraged the development of new industries, such as those in the Rhineland and Britain responsible for a distinctive style of beaker. These too are ornamented in high relief, but free-hand, *en barbotine*, often with hunting scenes (Hunt cups) which clearly attest to the interests of the potters' patrons.[3]

Haverfield does not describe the real culture of Roman Britain, which nurtured in large part the very skills whose loss the Victorians lamented. In almost every respect the categories of art, types of patronage and the uses to which craftsmanship were put, can be compared with the position in the Middle Ages, which no Victorian would have criticized, though as in medieval times some production was organized in highly complex ways.[4] The idea that there was once a time when the simple craftsman operated for himself in a beautiful rustic environment belongs to the world of utopian myth.

This chapter is not concerned with the subjective concept of quality as such, beyond noting that, for the most part, art in its widest sense (that is including decorated, functional items) could not be bought off-the-peg in Roman Britain as it can today. There are a few exceptions such as the pottery mentioned above, clay figurines from the Allier valley and Cologne and low-quality jewellery, but generally art had to be commissioned by the purchaser (or patron) and, when acquired, it presumably meant something to him or her. This concern was, of course, more marked in the case of expensive luxuries such as mosaic pavements, or items intimately connected with the owner's life and persona, such as a seal-ring. Of course, aesthetic taste played a part in all such commissions, but almost always other factors, such as prestige or religion, were involved in some way with the choice of theme and style of presentation. Even élite art in the Roman world was very seldom, if ever, a matter of simple hedonism or 'art for art's sake'. Indeed, it is

doubtful whether art can ever exist in a social vacuum, and Nero, who acted as though art was all in all (and is so often regarded merely as an irresponsible aesthete), used it ruthlessly in an attempt to bolster his power and prestige.

Luxuria was certainly to be condemned, but the reason why Nero commissioned Famulus to paint the Golden House and the reason why the owners of houses in second-century Britain had their much more modest dwellings decorated with similar fanciful designs do not differ in essentials. 'Living like a human being', Nero's own description of his day-to-day existence in the Golden House, evidently meant living in a wonderland, owing more to the theatre than to reality. However, there is a competitive element in human nature which means that, even when living in a fantasy world, people are not content unless their environment is superior to that of their neighbours. As Tacitus tells us (*Agricola* 21), the various public amenities and private mansions had everything to do with prestige and emulation: romanization implies competition, the striving literally to get out of the Iron Age. As we have seen, the urge to do so goes back even before 43 with the well-designed 'Classical' coinages of Cunobelin and Verica and the cherishing of Roman imports (see Chapter 2). Emulation and competitiveness have been seen in Verica's vine-leaf answering Cunobelin's head of barley. Probably art served the same purpose in the curious Romano-Celtic hybrid metalwork of the Iceni, and the luxury imports both here and among the Brigantes. We should not, however, overemphasize native acceptance of Roman ways, and the Boudican revolt demonstrates how terrible the clash of cultures could be.

ART FOR THE STATE

The official use of art to bolster Imperial prestige is best known from famous monuments in Rome, such as the Arch of Titus and Trajan's Column. There would have been provincial examples of 'State Art' in all provinces, including Britain, but unfortunately little remains of the sculptural decoration of such structures as the altar of the Imperial Cult at Colchester, the *quadrifons* at Richborough and the arch which apparently provided a monumental entrance to the governor's palace at London and may have been remembered in ruin as the 'London Stone'.[5] Analogy helps a little: the Colchester altar was presumably a monument similar to that at Lyon for the Three Gauls, which is figured on coins and had a decorative screen wall embellished with acanthus ornament, like that of *Ara Pacis* in Rome. It also had standing victories at the corners. The massive Temple of Divus Claudius at Colchester was certainly embellished with rich marbles and perhaps had a sculpted pediment like some of the grander temples in Rome. Undoubtedly it would have contained a splendid statue of the deceased emperor, and very probably other sculpture.[6] The Richborough arch was a Victory monument, probably erected by Domitian to mark the pacification of the entire province, and this has preserved some of its marble facing in the form of fragments of inscription and architectural ornament as well as two small pieces of sculpture. In addition, a number of fragments of a gilded cast bronze statue, mainly consisting of hair and drapery, could well have come from an Imperial statue, presumably of Domitian, possibly part of an equestrian group surmounting the arch. Such arches with their statuary are well attested in Roman art, notably on coins, including for example the Claudian arch in Rome marking the Conquest of Britain.[7]

Thus, although no officially-inspired artistic programme survives from first-century Britain to compare with the reliefs recovered from the *Sebasteion* of Aphrodisias (which include a tableau of Claudius vanquishing Britannia), it is highly probable that some such works would have existed.[8] Certainly, examples of what can be described as minor examples of state art can be seen in forts and fortresses, and especially on the mid-second-century distance slabs from the Antonine Wall mentioned above.[9] Although modest in comparison with the Aphrodisias slabs or the famous State reliefs of Rome, these do demonstrate that sculptors working for the legions were able to rise to the stock themes of battle, sacrifice and triumph. The best of these stones may have been the work of craftsmen kept busy with commemorative plaques and official altars for the unit, together with private commissions for the officer class, but many of them were the production of sculptors more used to turning out modest tombstones for soldiers and their dependants (Chapter 3). Whether they were soldiers or, more probably, civilians settled in the *canabae* outside the fortress walls and following their units

on campaign by way of trade, is unknown. Among examples of the genre are the slab from Bridgeness, West Lothian, portraying on the left side a mounted soldier riding down barbarians and on the right a group of men under a *vexillum* of the Second Legion offering the sacrifice of a *suovetaurilia* to the gods, the source of Roman power. Another slab already mentioned, that from Hutcheson Hill, Dunbartonshire, displays a triumphal arch beneath which Britannia (or Roma) places a laurel wreath in the beak of an eagle on top of a standard (see **23**). On either side is a bound captive. Here the legend identifies the dedicators as a vexillation of the Twentieth Legion. A Sixth-Legion slab found at Braidfield, Dunbartonshire (see above), portrays Mars and Virtus and two victories. 'Roman' art of this sort was by no means the monopoly of the legions, for instance the Fourth Cohort of Gauls set up a dedication to the Imperial *numina* at Risingham, in which the *aediculae* flanking the dedication panel were occupied respectively by Victory and Mars. The headquarters buildings of both legionary fortresses and auxiliary forts would have been embellished with such reliefs as well as with statuary in stone (of which the limestone head of Constantine from York is a surviving example) and especially in bronze. Fragments of Imperial statuary in bronze have come from the fortress of Caerleon and the forts of Caernarfon and Carmarthen. In addition, the leg of an equestrian statue from Milsington, Roxburghshire is likely to be an Imperial image, probably from a fort. Such works may be donations by private individuals, such as the silver statue of the Victory of *Legio* VI whose arm was found at Tunshill, Lancashire, together with a label saying that Valerius Rufus presented it in fulfilment of a vow. It is presumed that it was placed in the *sacellum* of the York fortress.[10]

Analogous to such commissions were those of established communities, notably *coloniae, municipia* and the *civitates*, and by guilds. The Forum dedications at Verulamium (either by the *Civitas Catuvellaunum* or the *Municipium* of Verulamium) and Wroxeter (by the *Civitas Cornoviorum*; **34**) are not directly associated with surviving sculpture, save that it seems that the Verulamium inscription may have been held in place by clamps in the form of four giant fingers of which one remains, telling the viewer to mark the message expressed.[11] The beauty of the lettering of these monuments, especially of the Wroxeter inscription, commands attention. As they

record the Imperial names and titulature they can be regarded as State monuments as well as demonstrations of local pride.

The same community of purpose was surely manifest in many of the statues in bronze which stood in major cities. Some may have been set up by agencies of central administration, but most will have been presented by town councils, guilds or even private individuals. The head of Claudius from the river Alde (perhaps Boudican loot from Colchester), and the head of Hadrian from London (35) are the only fully preserved Imperial bronze heads from Britain. It is just possible that the former can be associated with a fragment of an equestrian statue (a hock from a horse's leg) from Ashill, Norfolk, surely also Boudican loot. If so, it must represent an equestrian statue of Claudius like the one figured on coins showing his triumphal arch. Other fragments of Imperial statues cast in bronze include a number of fragments of a Julio-Claudian head from Billingford, Norfolk – again probably Claudius – and pieces of an equestrian statue from Gloucester (could it have shown the founder, the emperor Nerva?), a horse's foreleg from Lincoln and small fragments of a cuirassed statue with inlay of different alloys from Cirencester. There must have been many more. Indeed, Suetonius (*Divus Titus* iv, 1) writes that Titus served as a military tribune in Germany and Britain and that as a result of his popularity many statues and busts were set up in these provinces with laudatory inscriptions. A statue base from Wroxeter with the legend, often used on inscriptions honouring the Emperor, BONO REIPUBLICAE NATUS was probably the base of an Imperial statue but if connected with the *civitas* must be Hadrianic at earliest.[12]

34 Commemorative dedication of the forum at Wroxeter, Shropshire. Sandstone. L.3.70m. H.1.24m. Rowley's House Museum, Shrewsbury. (After RIB i.288. Administrators of the Haverfield Bequest.)

35 *Hollow cast bronze head of Hadrian from the Thames at London.* H.42cm. (Photo: British Museum.)

ART FOR THE COMMUNITY

Most of the great public buildings of the Roman world in the early and middle Empire were the result of benefactions by individuals and corporations in a seemingly never-ending struggle for prestige and influence. The evidence for Britain, which is comparable with that from other Western provinces, has been collected by Dr Blagg (and will be further discussed in a companion volume to this one). There are many simple building inscriptions, though it is worth emphasizing that the majority of architectural projects would have required sculptural embellishments. For example, the dedication slab of the *proscaenium* of M. Ulpius Januarius, aedile of Petuaria, which apparently only had the status of *vicus* within the *civitas* of the Parisii, was flanked by pelta-ornament, and the stage very likely carried vegetal or even figural sculpture as well.[13] This was certainly the case with the excellently carved 'Façade of the Four Seasons' at Bath. The inscription on it proclaims that it was repaired and painted by a guild. This screen was presumably a religious monument and it is in this context that we should also think of the arches dedicated by L. Viducius Placidus, a *sevir* of York to the Genius of the Place and the Imperial Numina, by Q. Neratius Proxsimus, a citizen of Lincoln, to Mars Rigonemetos at Nettleham and by Trenico to a god called Viridius at Ancaster, Lincolnshire. No sculpture survives in any of these instances, but such arches recorded elsewhere in the Empire could be highly decorated, like the Arch of Dativius Victor at Mainz.

Many of the sculptured blocks which were found at Blackfriars, London, reused in the fourth-century Riverside Wall can be reconstructed as just such an arch, although unfortunately there is no accompanying inscription in this case. Other blocks from here, depicting figures of deities, have been reconstructed as a screen like the one from Bath mentioned above. Monumental city gateways, too, may often have carried sculpture, and the large block found near the Bath Gate at Cirencester, deeply cut with a very fine representation of Mercury wearing a floppy *petasos*, is likely to have been paid for by an important citizen. Other occasions for patronage would have included public fountains, such as the beautiful example said to have been seen by St Cuthbert at Carlisle, and wayside altars like the one dedicated to the Genius Loci at Cirencester, which carries a figure of the deity in relief.[14]

Imperial statues have been discussed above, but individual citizens and benefactors were also honoured by communities, though only one example is to my knowledge attested in Britain. This is at Caerwent where a statue base was set up by the *Civitas Silurum* to its patron Tiberius Claudius Paulinus, one-time legate of *Legio* II *Augusta*, and at the time the image was commissioned governor of Gallia Lugdunensis (36). It may be regarded both as a simple act of gratitude to a benefactor and as an example of civic munificence.[15]

PRIVATE COMPETITIVENESS

Competitive giving in public life (for which the Greeks had the word *philotimia*) is merely the counterpart to private competitiveness. The world of Trimalchio, as satirized by Petronius, cannot have been totally foreign to the experience of towns in Britain. Here the descendants of British notables, successful businessmen and merchants who were often freedmen, and retired soldiers attempted to cut a figure in society by living in a more opulent state than their neighbours. Art was a visible sign of Roman life and this is one reason why the *Satyricon* tells us so much about the decoration of Trimalchio's house. The modern visitor to Pompeii comes away marvelling at the richness of the painting and perhaps thinking, in the House of the Vettii at least, that it is all rather overdone. Archaeological evidence suggests that the best rooms of houses in Britain, with their rich, patterned mosaic floors and both ceilings and walls painted with bold architectural or decorative designs, were, likewise, hardly restful on the eye. The present imaginative display of wall-painting and mosaic at the Verulamium Museum offers a bold assault on the viewer's senses. These frescoes were not designed to accord with modern notions of good taste.[16]

Other more sophisticated, and intellectually respectable, reasons for the lavish use of art in the home will be discussed below. Personal aesthetic choice and, in the case of figural schemes, religious and cultural interests were surely involved, but at the crudest level fashion and keeping up with neighbours must have provided the impetus to call in the house-decorators. The one-mosaic house, such as the Sparsholt farmhouse, Hampshire, was better than the house with none, but the truly wealthy would demand numerous mosaics. Sometimes the spirit of emulation actually shows in the choice of scheme, such as imitation marbling as a substitute for real marble. It is also significant that the most lavish mosaic decoration is to be found in dining rooms (*triclinia*) and in baths, where other people were entertained; such a use of private art is no different in essence from the way an Iron Age chieftain displayed his dominance at the feast with his swords and drinking cups or his wife's mirror (Chapter 1). Indeed Roman women were often notorious for wearing quantities of jewellery and at times (in the Flavian age for example) outlandish coiffures.

36 Base of statue of Tiberius Claudius Paulinus at Caerwent, Gwent. Limestone. H.1.19m. (After RIB i. 311. Administrators of the Haverfield Bequest.)

COMMEMORATION

The erection of tombs was intended to emphasize the status of the deceased and hence of his or her surviving family. It also had a more personal meaning, aiding the memory of those who grieved and hence, in a sense, ensuring that something tangible survived death. The sepulchral *mensa* from Caerleon, carved with an image of Venus and pierced by a tube down which wine could be poured, is a graphic example of this.[17] Normally the tombstone was a sort of religious image, to be decked with flowers on appropriate festivals such as the *rosalia* and on the birthday of the dead person. In the house, portrait busts might serve the same purpose. All the certain examples known to me are of marble and thus imports.[18] Commemoration on tombs was often achieved by means of images combined with an inscription.

Trimalchio's fictional tomb provides a starting point (*Sat* 71). Petronius brings in Trimalchio's architect to discuss his tomb. The directions given include scenes of his commercial life, benefactions to the people and statues of himself and his wife, Fortunata. The inscription confirms the sculptured image, that this was a very rich, self-made freedman. The type of character he desires to be shown as is made clear by the sentence that 'he never heard a philosopher'. Elaborate tombs like this are well known in Italy and were widespread in the provinces. Assertive mausolea were evidently a feature of the landowning class in the Moselle Valley and indeed elsewhere in Belgica. Sculptures from Arlon and Neumagen survive in some numbers and the Igel monument of the Secundinii remains intact.

There is not much evidence of monumental competitiveness on this scale in Britain though it doubtless did exist. Fragmentary relief sculpture from Stanwick, Northamptonshire, carved with images of deities and the deeds of heroes may have come from a similar tomb or tombs. The Bartlow Barrows on the Cambridgeshire–Essex border are impressive but there are no features, at least none remaining, on their exteriors to engage the art historian. The rich finds within presumably attest more private artistic and religious tastes. A twice-life size portrait of a woman wearing an elaborate Flavian-style hair-do, found at Walcot, Bath, is likely to come from a tomb as the features do not match any contemporary Imperial portrait; if so the structure must have been in scale with the head, large and perhaps rather vulgar.[19]

That is not a description to use of the tomb of Classicianus from London, of which much of the inscription and one of the decorative bolsters remains. It has a severity and good taste that reminds us of Tacitus' comment about the tomb of the Emperor Otho: 'modest and therefore likely to endure' (Hist. ii, 49). The monumental character of the lettering is very impressive, but the tomb is in no way boastful. Another early tombstone, this time from Wroxeter, depicted a legionary. The well-cut legend gives his name, Titus Flaminius, his legion (XIV Gemina), his origo, Faventia in Italy, age and length of service, respectively 45 and 22 years. Three lines of verse in an Epicurean vein remind the beholder that there is no drinking after death and that he should live honourably while he has time. To judge from this brief epitaph, Titus Flaminius was a far worthier individual than Trimalchio and it is a pity that of his image only the feet are now preserved.[20]

If competitiveness in death does not seem to have been especially pronounced in Britain from the surviving evidence, at least those who could afford it did their best to set up decent-looking stelae which would show them and their families as they were in life. The best tombstones commemorating men found in Britain are of serving and retired members of the army. Thus when viewing the image carved on the magnificent mid-first-century gravestone of the centurion, M. Favonius Facilis from Colchester, we can feel that we are especially meant to admire his armour, with its elaborate cingulum, and his vitis, the emblem of his rank (see 11). A later stele, probably Trajanic or early Hadrianic, from Gloucester depicts L. Valerius Aurelius, a veteran of the same Twentieth Legion still wearing his military-style cloak with pride. This style of commemoration established a norm which kept sculptors in business well into the third century. Civilians too, men, women and children, were shown looking as they were in life. We do not know what Philus the Sequanian who died at Cirencester did for a living, though his full-length, birrus-enveloped image suggests that he must have been fairly prosperous. The inscription, apart from giving his origo, informs us that like Titus Flaminius he achieved the age of 45 years.[21]

On Trimalchio's tomb, his wife Fortunata was to have been shown holding a dove, as is the anonymous woman seated comfortably in her basket-chair on the fine early second-century tombstone from Murrell Hill (37), Carlisle – a product of the Carlisle school which has been well-studied by John Phillips. Most of the reliefs attributed to this workshop are of women, a circumstance which is probably simply chance, but makes comparison easy. The subject is either shown at home, as a mother and domina of the household, or, as with Aurelia Aureliana, dressed in good-quality outdoor clothes as though going on a journey. Traditional female display in the form of a mirror and jewellery is figured on a fragmentary relief from Chester depicting a woman holding a mirror, while her maid is shown holding her jewel-box. Regina, the Catuvellaunian wife of the Palmyrene Barates, died and was buried at South Shields with a highly decorative stele showing her clad in fine garments, wearing a necklace and bracelets, and with her jewel-box beside her (38). A common subject is the feast, of which the stones of Curatia Dinysia at Chester and of Julia Velva at York are good examples. The types are formal: women sitting or reclining in the cubiculum or triclinium with their possessions, clad in Roman clothes or at least the provincial equivalent. They remind us in a direct manner of the sort of life which went on in the Roman-style houses of Britain and attempt to make good their subjects' claims to be members of polite Roman society.[22]

COMFORT: 'MAKING VICE AGREEABLE'

The title of this section is of course Tacitean, even though British examples of comfort are often later than the first century; from the second century town houses were often embellished with wall-paintings and mosaics. Although, as discussed above, there was an element of keeping up with the neighbours – and this was inevitably a major factor when art was intended to be seen by the public – most works of art were acquired because the purchaser liked them. The Roman way of life presupposed all the assumptions that civilized people take for granted – warmth and comfort, good food, eaten in style, and entertainment. In all these activities the craftsmen has (or had until recently) a part to play.

Only the wealthy could furnish their houses with marble statuary, such as the collection from Woodchester, with bronze statuettes, like the Cupid from a house in Cirencester (see **105**), evidently a lamp-holder, and have fine vessels of copper alloy or even silver-plate displayed on their sideboards. Most such items (though not all) were imported.[23] Mosaic floors are not portable in the same way and were laid either by entrepreneurs, immigrant mosaicists (especially in the first century) or later by the employees of workshops established in the towns of Roman Britain. However, the taste for such floors as well as the settings in which they are so often found – bath-houses and dining rooms – expresses a Roman manner of life. Wall-paintings of reasonably high quality would likewise have graced only the better houses, though the evidence of archaeology suggests that plastered and painted walls with simple red and/or white ground colour were fairly widespread. Evidence for artistic taste is also to be found in furnishings, ornamental fittings used in the home and in jewellery. Some is of high quality, but many of the decorative objects found on excavations in Britain belonged to fairly humble people and show how Roman fashions infiltrated the whole of society.

Then as now there were doubtless many people whose attitudes were formed by others, and who simply wanted to own what their social superiors have declared to be in good taste. In so far as there is truth in the widely held assumption that the art of Roman Britain was a pale imitation of Roman art elsewhere, it lies in the pull that the fashionable art of Rome had in the provinces. Trimalchio is presented by

37   Tombstone of a woman, from Murrell Hill, Carlisle. Sandstone. H.1.285m. (Photo: City Museum, Carlisle.)

38 *Tombstone of Regina, wife of the Palmyrene, Barates. South Shields, Co.Durham. Sandstone. H.1.255m. (After Arch. Ael*[2] *x, 1885, p.238 (fig).)*

Petronius as a boor who had mythological paintings in the house which he did not understand and to which he awarded no more significance than representations of gladiatorial fights, and who valued silver by its weight. In sculpture he was ignorant and tasteless enough to be fobbed off with fakes and copies, but it is likely that most objects he owned were of excellent quality and simply in the wrong hands. Of course, his main motive was to impress his guests and it has already been suggested that this was a motive in Britain too. It is, however, possible to overstate the case; as at other periods the majority of owners appreciated the works of art surrounding them and found them meaningful. Not only were they influenced by aesthetic considerations and religious interests but even by intellectual and literary culture.

Provincial preference cannot be defined as an absolute quality, but a surprising number of works of art in various media have shared features. Influenced as I was long ago by the late Sir Niklaus Pevsner's 1955 Reith Lectures, *The Englishness of English Art*, I have already attempted to look at Romano-British Art in the same manner.[24] Large works of art were performing functions which Celtic art had never done, but there does seem to have been an inheritance from the pre-Roman world of a *liking* for marked linear design and bold patterning. A visitor from Italy to second-century Verulamium would not have been surprised by the geometric and figured content of the mosaics laid by the local mosaicists, but might have commented on the strong linear detail and the bold use of shading. Turning from the lion mosaic in Verulamium (**colour plate VIII**), Insula XXI, Building 2, Room 4, to the peopled scroll, painted as a frieze in the north-west of the courtyard, it can be seen that the taste for pattern was not confined to mosaics. In wall-painting, indeed, there are numerous examples of schemes incorporating vegetal ornament, sometimes in the form of simplified candelabra and hanging swags (**colour plates II and III**), serving as formal elements in 'wallpaper' patterns. Such decor derives from the late Second Style and especially from Third Style decoration in the first century BC and early first century AD; the effect of so much rich painting around the walls of a comparatively small and fairly dark room, typical of town-houses in Britain, especially when it was accompanied by an equally restless ceiling design and a polychrome mosaic floor must have been quite startling. This would even have been

so when large areas of colour were used without further embellishment, as in the case of the room with the lion pavement mentioned above, where the walls of the room consisted of a dark red dado with emerald green panels above. As soon as such thoroughly Roman decoration began to appear there would have been competition between neighbours to emulate and surpass.[25]

However, in some ways decor of this sort is far from being out of sympathy with the tastes of the Britons as we can reconstruct them in earlier times. It is true that mosaics and wall-paintings do not seem to owe anything, as such, to pre-Roman Celtic art but it is easy to see that the 'sons of tribal chiefs' or at least their descendants responded to the rich geometry of, say, the Leicester Blackfriars pavement or of the Bucklersbury pavement, now in the Museum of London. Indeed the mosaicists themselves were very much at their ease in this kind of work as the excellence of their designs makes clear, and in almost all instances they must have come of 'Celtic' stock from the north-western provinces; some, if not the majority, were probably British. In place of the large round hut of pre-Conquest times, where burnished and enamelled shields glinted in the firelight as the chief held court over a feast, his descendant presided in a still more splendid room where civilized dining took place against a background of permanent pattern. The artistic revolution followed the same pattern as that of rhetoric. Taste and natural ability were able to make the transition from one culture to another because there were positive links between them.

The patron's deliberate selection of those facets of Roman art which were in accord with Celtic aesthetics is not, however, the whole story. Many aspects of decor were not only new, but must have jolted traditional assumptions about the function of art very considerably. The use of architectural illusion in wall-painting seems especially revolutionary, in that the owners of Building XXVIII, 3 at Verulamium (already mentioned), where Room 3 carried an arcade of reticulated columns, and of a house in Leicester, Insula XVI, where architecture unites with caprice, were indulging in the popular Roman fantasy of living in a Hellenistic palace (**colour plate I**). There are even finer examples of fanciful architecture from a bath-house on the site of Winchester Palace, Southwark, and at the third-century 'Painted House' at Dover but these may well have ornamented official buildings, and thus represent patronage at a higher level.

Brian Philp, the excavator, mentions the possibility that Olus Cordius Candidus, a government transport officer, may have lived in the Painted House, in which case the relatively high quality of the artistic decor establishes him as a man of refined, metropolitan tastes. The Southwark painting, to judge from an inscription found in the same building, though of later (third century) date, may have belonged to a military guild. Presumably all towns contained trabeated buildings by the end of the first century, at least in *fora*, temples and major public monuments. Outside Chichester, the client king Cogidubnus (if he was the owner of the Fishbourne complex) indeed lived in such a palace, where marble and coloured stones were used for real. His wealth and good fortune were exceptional, but that his taste was shared in the area is shown by *opus sectile* from Angmering, Sussex, and Buriton, Hampshire, as well as by much later ornamental wall-panelling from the villa at Bignor; it is also demonstrated by imitation marbling in wall-painting at Verulamium and elsewhere.[26]

The use of representational figure scenes was clearly one result of romanization: the lion carrying the head of a stag in its mouth, portrayed on a mosaic at Verulamium (**colour plate VIII**) and other naturalistic depictions on mosaics and wall-paintings demonstrate profound changes in taste and attitude. Some, of course, were connected with Italian and southern Gaulish settlers, and in *coloniae* such as Camulodunum the presence of this élite minority-group is very much in evidence. A minor but nevertheless interesting example is the gladiator *emblema*, painted in the centre of a panel of a wall in a house dating to the late first century, which is perhaps no more than a provincial equivalent of 'the gladiatorial show given by Laenas' (*Sat.* 29). The Middleborough pavement of the second century, with its wrestling cupids (**colour plate VII**), refers ultimately to the Greek *gymnasium*, a theme also attested by a signet-ring from Colchester showing a cupid with a herm.

By the second century there would also have been a widespread taste for and enjoyment of figural art among the landowners and the prosperous citizens of the other towns. For example, the bust of Neptune or Oceanus in the centre of a mosaic floor from Verulamium is a simplified, linear rendering of the god but nevertheless one of the most attractive and striking floors from the city. Almost geometric in its composition is an apsidal pavement in the form of a sea-shell, no doubt alluding to the birth of Venus from the sea. Marine themes are also found at Dorchester, Dorset, with another head of Neptune, and at Fishbourne in the north wing of the former palace, now truncated in size but still luxurious. It shows Cupid riding a dolphin, surrounded by sea-beasts (**colour plate VI**). The most ambitious of the second-century floors from Britain are those from Dyer Street, Cirencester. One, now lost, portrayed a marine *thiasos*, again including a cupid on a dolphin, together with another cupid, perhaps holding the wheel of Neptune's chariot, a nereid and a wide range of marine life. Jocelyn Toynbee rightly comments that 'the original would appear to have been one of the best-drawn and most classical in style of all the British figured mosaics'. The other mosaic, fortunately still extant in Corinium Museum, depicts personified Seasons in their proper Mediterranean guise, as well as scenes of myth (Bacchus, a centaur, Silenus and the death of Actaeon). It is likely to have belonged to a member of the curial class of the Dobunni.

Even more remarkable, as revealing a taste for Latin literature, is the wall-painting from a villa at Otford, Kent, painted with a scene or scenes from the *Aeneid*, accompanied by an inscription; this too is second century. It is a pity that we cannot be certain that the owner was a Briton. There are, in fact, hints (in the form of portrait busts of Greek marble) that the owner of another Kentish villa, Lullingstone, was a settler from the Mediterranean world though the surviving paintings dating to this time, two water-nymphs in a niche in the cellar-shrine, show that he venerated the local deities. Much later, in the fourth century, a large number of myths appear in mosaic, and this is also the time to which most of the recognizable figural mural scenes belong. At this period, in particular, subjects seem to have been chosen with care, but for reasons as much religious and philosophical as aesthetic (see Chapter 7).[27]

THE ART OF THE FEAST

Evidence for furniture, so closely connected with the 'elegant banquets' of Tacitus, was collected together by Joan Liversidge in a monograph published in 1955 and can be augmented through more recent finds.

Actual feasting is a *topos* of a category of tombstones and is also represented at Colchester by little pipe-clay figures, imported from Gaul, of diners and of a man reciting a literary work found in a child's tomb. The furniture which remains demonstrates romanizing taste. This is especially apparent in the circular side tables, traditionally of marble and resting on feet with panther-protomes in reference to the god Bacchus. An example of just such a leg, carved from Parian marble and evidently an import, was found in Colchester recently. Other table legs were carved in Britain from shale, including examples from Dorchester, Frampton and Preston in Dorset, Rothley in Leicestershire and Verulamium. The features of these beasts are very simplified (in part because shale laminates easily and will not take complex detail); they are shown with forward-pointing ears like griffins, though the Rothley lion has a mane.

A large class of rectangular table or sideboard carved from stone and ornamented with chip-carved decoration on front and sides is found particularly in the south and west of Britain, and frequently in villas, such as Rockbourne, Hampshire, Keynsham, Avon and Chedworth, Gloucestershire. Like other tables these could have been used for the service of food or drink, but their elaborate sides, perhaps enriched with paint, would have rendered them suitable for the display of plate, in silver or pewter, and of other objects valued by the owner.[29]

Wine was sometimes served from a bowl mounted on a tripod. Examples of Bacchic heads from such tripods are known from Britain, for instance at London, Lincoln and Old Harlow, as well as the feline feet upon which they stood. Attachments from chests and perhaps couches, in the form of human busts, are also known, ranging from the very fine imported casting of Bacchus Zagraeus/Antinoos from Littlecote, Wiltshire (**39**), to local work – a female bust, perhaps Venus from Cirencester and a satyr from the villa of Tarrant Hinton, Dorset (**40**). Both of these display markedly Insular idiosyncracies in their stylized physiognomies and the patterned textures of their hair, and in the case of the satyr his *nebris* as well.[30]

Cups and jugs for the consumption of wine, as well as the plates and spoons employed for eating, are the objects which bring us closest to the Roman banquet. Such feasts were normally leisurely affairs (even Petronius's account of Trimalchio's ghastly party testifies as much); this meant that the guests had

plenty of time to study the decorations on the varied items of the *ministerium* from which they were dining as well as those of the surrounding room. Among the wealthy, such services were always of silver. Pliny the Elder, whose moral purpose in writing his *Natural History* has recently been well explored by Jacob Isager: mentions Pompeius Paulinus, propraetor in Lower Germany in 55–7, as 'the son of a knight from Arles, descended on his father's side from a tribe that went around wearing skins' (in other words he was of Gaulish origin) who took twelve thousand pounds weight of silver with him on campaign (*NH* xxxiii, 143). There are no early Roman finds from Britain which compare with this luxury, though the massive treasure from Hildersheim in Germany shows that Pliny was not exaggerating. In fact, very little early silverware has been found in the province, and none in a domestic context, though presumably the Hockwold cups represent the sort of drinking equipment which people wanted to own.[31]

Decorated samian pottery provides further evidence for contemporary taste in tableware. The vegetal ornament imitates the *repoussé* designs on silver. Thus, although not rare and costly as is popularly supposed, it is nevertheless worth far more attention from art historians than it has ever received because of what it can tell us about the tastes and aspirations of its owners.

Among the many examples of bronze jugs known from British sites, the very highest quality is represented by a silvered *askos* handle from the palace at Fishbourne, Sussex, embellished with vegetal ornament and the head of a young satyr as an escutcheon. *Askoi* were employed for the serving of water to mix with wine. Many jugs come from burials; of these, an example (now destroyed) from one of the Bartlow Barrows on the Cambridgeshire/Essex border was especially fine (see **109**). The neck had a moulding, part silvered, and the handle carried a sphinx on top and a *bucranium* escutcheon below. Objects from the tomb, including a folding stool, a *patera* and a lamp as well as other vessels, were clearly designed to make the dead person thoroughly at home. Another fine and complete bronze jug, with a theatrical mask in the same position, was found with a glass jug, plain samian cups and plates and a rectangular shale trencher in a Flavian grave at Winchester. As a dining-service this is rather a motley collection, but presumably the heir did not want to inter his best

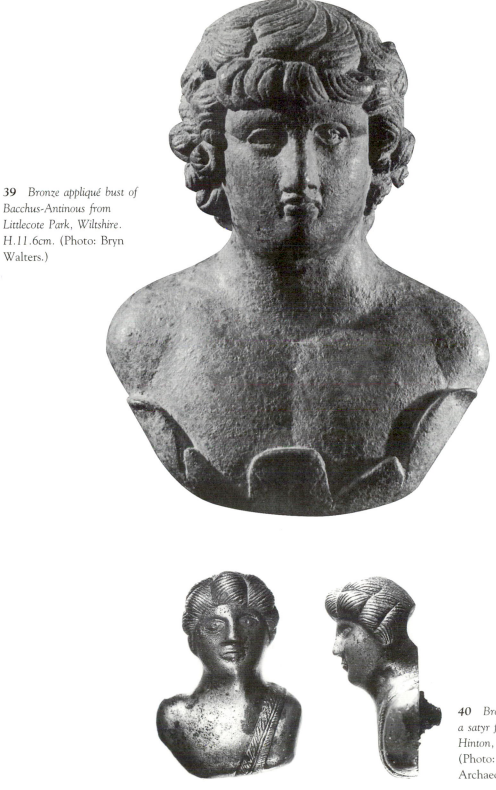

39 *Bronze appliqué bust of Bacchus-Antinous from Littlecote Park, Wiltshire. H.11.6cm.* (Photo: Bryn Walters.)

40 *Bronze appliqué bust of a satyr from Tarrant Hinton, Dorset. H. 5.5cm.* (Photo: Wimbourne Archaeological Group.)

plate in his father's grave! Religious (frequently Bacchic) imagery, scenes of myth and theatre, protective lions and sphinxes and naturalistic vegetation are all to be seen on these elegant objects as on grave monuments. Their exact counterparts are also found in domestic wall-paintings and mosaics – there are motifs such as as panther heads and birds in an inhabited scroll from Verulamium and a theatre-mask and swags at Leicester. Linked as they were to the complementary designs on the plate or its samian ware substitutes, these provided a permanent festive decor, and perhaps a perpetual reminder of death.[32]

There is more evidence for polite dining on a lavish scale much later, in the fourth century, such as the important silver *ministerium* from Mildenhall, Suffolk, and also the British-made pewter services like the Appleford hoard, Oxfordshire, and these will be discussed below, in Chapter 7.

DRESS AND JEWELLERY

The transformation of life would have extended to portable art, including dress and jewellery. The purpose of personal adornment is very often the same, whatever the culture: it is designed to impress the man or woman in the street. If we were to take the words of Tacitus literally we would imagine the major difference in daily life was that, in place of Celtic plaids, men began to wear togas. Insofar as this was true in the forum or at the dinner-party, it was a manifestation of *romanitas* which separated the *togatus* from his unregenerate countrymen. However, John Peter Wild has suggested, on the basis of sculpture and other evidence, that clothing fashion even among the upper classes was largely resistant to change and on all but the most formal occasions, the Gallic coat with accompanying fringed scarf seems to have been worn by men, while women wore a longer coat. It is tempting to see clothing as patterned or highly coloured, as it certainly was in the Late Empire. The fragmentary mosaic of two huntsmen carrying a deer from East Coker, Somerset, and the Orantes painting at Lullingstone, Kent, exemplify this, as does the tantalizing reference to the *curiales* of Verulamium in Constantius' life of St Germanus (*Vita S. Germani* iii, 14). Even though this style was to be found throughout the Empire, and was not simply a British or north-west European fashion, it is possible that its

emergence is to be explained by the widespread influence of provincial taste for the bold use of colour and texture.[33]

As far as female adornment was concerned, the continuing employment of Celtic motifs was largely confined to brooches, which were often enamelled. The liking for pattern and texture also manifested itself in other ways, especially in the third century, in jet pendants cut at York and gold openwork jewellery. It is interesting to observe that the metalwork fittings worn by auxiliary soldiers in the Middle Empire likewise included enamelled studs and belt-slides and openwork, sometimes with Celtic motifs. This sort of display is reminiscent of Iron Age times, but in the Roman period various subtleties and ambiguities are to be found. For example, enamelling came to be used for the lids of seal-boxes which accompanied letters and packages and were thus intended to be given away. These 'Celtic'-style objects protected figurative sealings made with Roman intaglios which, through their several iconographies, made some religious or intellectual statement about the ring-wearer's Roman credentials. Bronze vessels, too, were sometimes also enamelled, and in the case of the cup from Rudge, Wiltshire (**41**), whose mural design is essentially Classical, we have a souvenir commemorating a visit to Hadrian's Wall![34]

Jewellery and jet pendants were not always intended for public display and were often highly personal in nature, as presents from lovers to their girls. An iron ring of second-century date found in London is inlaid with crossed strips of copper-alloy inscribed in nielloed letters DA MI VITA with the evident meaning of 'Give me life!' or 'You give me life!' (**42**). Such intimate messages are also to be found on cameos and in openwork (*opus interrasile*) rings. A gold ring from Bedford has the legend EVSEBIA VITA carefully cut out and a similar ring from Corbridge is inscribed AEMILIA ZESES, the second word transliterated Greek for 'Life'. Greek, like French in the eighteenth century, was the language of love and another similar Corbridge ring has the Greek legend ΠΟΛΕΜΙΟΥ ΦΙΛΤΡΟΝ, which can be interpreted as the love token of Polemion, presumably his present to his girl (**43**). Greek is still the language on a precious third-century ring from Stonham Aspal, Suffolk, its shoulders inscribed ΟΛΥΜΠΕΙ ΖΗϹΑΙϹ. 'Life to Olympis!', and set with a sapphire in its bezel (**44**). Jewellery could, however, be presented in a more public way in order

41 *Enamelled bronze cup from a villa at Rudge, Wiltshire. H.4.45cm. (After: J. Horsley, Britannia Romana (1732), p.192 N.74.)*

42 *Iron ring with copper-alloy inlaid inscription. New Fresh Wharf, City of London. D.2cm. (Photo: J. Bailey, Museum of London.)*

43 *Inscribed openwork gold ring from Corbridge, Northumberland. D.2.7cm. (Photo: British Museum.)*

44 *Inscribed gold ring containing an uncut sapphire, from Stonham Aspal, Suffolk. D.2.5cm. Ashmolean Museum. (Photo: Robert Wilkins, Institute of Archaeology, Oxford.)*

to reward a client or to secure the loyalty of a subject. Evidence is sparse from Britain but Claudius Paulinus, governor of Lower Britain in the third century, sent 'a gold brooch set with gems' to Sennius Sollemnis, a friend and dependant in Gaul, while an openwork cross-bow brooch from Erickstanebrae, Dumfriesshire, with its legends IOVIAVG and VOTXX celebrates the *vicennalia* of Diocletian's accession (AD 303) and seems from a graffito to have been bestowed on a soldier or official called Fortunatus.[35]

Engraved gemstones, cut both in intaglio and cameo, provide a remarkable conspectus of how art was seen and used. Clearly a coloured stone set in a gold ring is an object which has the potential of impressing the neighbours, for, although much less showy than the Iron Age torque, the gold ring was supposed to be the jealously-guarded privilege of the Roman aristocracy, especially the *equites*. However, the owner of a signet especially if it was old or very well engraved, would have influenced his more discriminating friends by the artistry of the gem's device, which was laid before them every time they received a sealed letter from him.[36]

In detail intaglios belonged to the new literate world, and in assessing them we can forget the Iron Age past of the province. Most of the gems from Britain can be paralleled in Gaul and Dalmatia, Pompeii and Aquileia in Italy, Gadara in Jordan and Caesarea in Israel, to take the subjects of recent site-catalogues.[37] Neither in Gaul nor in Britain do Celtic themes occur, though the old civilizations of Egypt and the Levant provide a few oriental deities such as Isis and Zeus Heliopolitanus, which demonstrate the presence of easterners. Deities were always popular for their protective powers. A particularly fine seal-stone of blue onyx (nicolo) set in a second-century silver ring from Colchester shows Jupiter feeding the Cretan goat, Amaltheia, who nurtured him in his youth (**45a**); here is sophisticated knowledge of mythology as well as piety. Another Colchester gem, a garnet, is set in a gold ring of early Roman form, when the sumptuary laws were operative. The owner, of equestrian rank, chose an erotic theme: Cupid with a goose, standing by a herm (**45b**). A red jasper depicting Victory driving a quadriga, found in a small villa at Sandy Lodge in south Hertfordshire, presumably evoked success in life (**45d**); the younger Pliny also had a quadriga device, though whether with a Victory driving it we are not told (*Ep* x, 74). An in-

taglio on a green chrome-rich chalcedony ('plasma'), with the device of a lion devouring its prey (**45c**), demonstrates the same morbidity as revealed by the Verulamium lion mosaic. Other animals such as cattle, horses (see **48**) and the winged Pegasus (see **14b**) referred to prosperity and fecundity, also demonstrated by a host of symbols such as horns of plenty, drinking-cups and masks.

Although they register personal taste and religious belief, we can see how various groups in society were led to adopt particular subjects. For instance, legionaries certainly found such deities as Mars, Minerva, the Dioscuri, Victory and Fortune appropriate, as well as the legionary eagle and standards (see **13b**) and such heroes as Hercules, Achilles (see **13a**) and his historical avatar Alexander the Great. The fine collection of sealstones recovered from the fortress baths of the Second Legion at Caerleon provides a good selection of soldiers' seal-rings.[38] As the stock in trade of the Snettisham jeweller demonstrates, the second-century farmers of East Anglia were especially inclined to purchase representations of Ceres, Bonus Eventus and Fortune, all of whom would have been especially relevant to farming.[39] We know other factors also played a part, such as the use of ancestral family devices or ones which had a particular significance to the wearer, such as clasped hands for a lover (see **14a**), a theme which appears at its most poignant in an uncut cornelian from the grave of a girl at Skeleton Green, Puckeridge, Hertfordshire.[40]

Love tokens are better represented in cameos, not so common in Britain, including the clasped hands, and as with gold jewellery sometimes cut with messages wishing good fortune to the wearer in both Greek and Latin.[41] Portrait cameos depicting women are another common category of love-token, although only one example in onyx has been found in Britain, the bust of a young lady from Silchester (**46**).[42] However, it was a favourite theme of the York jet industry, which exported its wares as far as southern Britain and the Rhineland and perhaps even to Rome. One medallion from Vindolanda is double, with portraits of the two lovers on one side and clasped hands on the other. A unique jet medallion from Colchester (see **83**) depicts two cupids, an amorous or perhaps protective theme if they are regarded as genii.[43] By far the commonest subject on cameos are Medusa heads – protective charms against the Evil Eye – a theme likewise ubiquitous on jet pendants.[44]

45 *Intaglios. a Jupiter with Cretan goat. Nicolo in silver ring, from Colchester. b Cupid with goose. Garnet in gold ring, from Colchester. c Lion with prey. High chrome chalcedony (plasma), from Wroxeter. d Victory in quadriga. Red Jasper, from Sandy Lodge near Moor Park, Hertfordshire. (a and b × 3; c and d × 4 a: Colchester and Essex Museum; b and d: British Museum; c: Rowley's House Museum, Shrewsbury.) (Photos: a, b, d author; c Robert Wilkins, Institute of Archaeology, Oxford.)*

RELIGION IN THE HOME

The one area where not even the least art-conscious patron would have been indifferent was in the sphere of religion, defined in its widest sense to include superstition. A very high proportion of the devices on gemstones are religious, and the wearing of a deity ensured that the god was with the wearer always. The art found in the Roman house, ranging from masks of Silenus and Attis on bronze tableware to the figures and symbols on painted walls and mosaic floors, had religious overtones. The world of the gods was all-pervasive.[45] Thus, while it would be absurd to invest every symbol, even every deity, portrayed in a Roman house with overmuch significance, the Other World inhabited by powerful protectors as well as malignant spirits would not have been ignored. The obvious centre for religious activity, certainly in

46 *Cameo depicting a female portrait-bust, from Silchester, Hampshire. Onyx. H.2.4cm. (Photo: Mike Fulford, Dept. of Archaeology, University of Reading.)*

romanized houses, would have been the *lararium* containing figures of the lares and other deities such as Venus (see Petronius, *Sat.* 29). Evidence for such little shrines in Britain is elusive, because the remains of houses seldom survive far above floor level. Sometimes, however, cellars were used as shrines and here interesting evidence of cult has been found, for instance niches and apses which could have held figures, and votive deposits. The best evidence for the employment of art comes from the cellar at Lullingstone, where the niche contained a late second-century painting of three water-nymphs. This is, or was when the colour was fresh, a most attractive and colourful painting which, as Ling points out, deserves a footnote in art history for the central nymph has water-spouting breasts, an attribute only otherwise attested in art by Philostratus the Elder (*Imagines* ii, 4, 3).

No figurines have been recovered *in situ*, but the bronze Venus from the cellar of a house (XIV, 5) in Verulamium, discovered with various other bronzes, is more likely to be part of a votive deposit than scrap-metal belonging to a dealer as proposed by Sheppard Frere in the excavation report. However, there is no proof that this was its original location (any more than the two marble busts at Lullingstone which were venerated at a later phase in the villa's cellar). It is more likely that it originally stood in a house-shrine. Although most of the figurines from well-excavated contexts come from temple sites, others were used to guard the home. Several sculptures of Fortuna from private houses express a widespread belief in her power. At Llantwit Major villa, South Glamorgan, figures of Fortuna and of a Genius (or Bonus Eventus) seem to have stood in shrines on either side of the doorway into the best room. Two such deities appear on the same stone on a relief from the Stonesfield villa, Oxfordshire, doubtless likewise from a house-shrine. However, other statues of Fortuna, including a very fine and large one from Cirencester, come from baths. Here not only were the perils of fire greatest but the bathers were unclothed and thus vulnerable.[46]

The dividing line between real religious sculpture, regarded by the pious at least as a vital source of protection and divine succour, and genre decoration such as the cupid lamp-stand from Cirencester or even the Cupid and Psyche marble-group from Woodchester (which on analogy with the complete Ostian example of the group in its courtyard setting could simply have been intended to give a romantic ambience to a room or small garden) is impossible to establish. It is likely that the Spoonley Wood marble of Bacchus was originally acquired to preside over an elegant *triclinium* in the villa, but when it was buried with the villa-owner it assumed a secondary role as a protector of the deceased; it thus became a symbol of the real faith which was never far away from that powerful and unpredictable saviour-god. In any case, as stated above, the personal selection of decorative schemes would generally have taken belief into account. Even at a fairly popular level, the other-worldly symbolism of several Verulamium mosaics – Neptune, dolphins, cantharus, lion devouring its prey (**colour plate VIII**) and sea-shell, so easy to parallel on tombstones – is part of that superstitious and morbid culture so brilliantly lampooned by Petronius. More significant are the two rooms frescoed with Bacchic decoration from the Painted House at Dover, possibly indicating the residence of a real votary of the god, as well as a number of schemas in late Roman mosaic, such as those of Brading and Frampton where the purposes of (private) cult seem uppermost (see Chapter 7).[47]

COMMISSIONING ART FOR TEMPLES

The main outlet for religious patronage lay, of course, in the shrines and sanctuaries, such as that at Bath. Here it is possible to demonstrate the major difference between pre-Roman patronage and that which appertained under the Empire. In the Iron Age offerings consisted of war gear and rich ornaments. The majority of items of Iron Age art from Britain were deposited in rivers. While the giving of objects of daily use continued in the Roman period, and silverware and other rich gifts were bestowed on temples, there were now other alternatives, such as the actual presentation of buildings (for instance arches) or of sculpture which was especially appropriate to the god.

The patron would not order the same type of work which he might need in his house. Instead he was guided by the priests towards what the deity was supposed to want. The archaeologist finding a number of images of, and altars carrying dedications to, Mercury, for example, will know that the findspot is likely to be religious rather than domestic. Art from Roman temples was in the first place a means of prayer, supplication or, more usually, thank offering for favours received. It was doubtless a means of achieving definite material results, such as wealth and health, although in the final analysis it depended on the existence of a system of belief which was widely accepted.

Patronage brought prestige, just as it had done in pre-Roman times, although now there was far more choice involved. Presumably temples themselves, including their ornamentation such as the pediment of the temple of Sulis Minerva at Bath – and their cult images upon which veneration was centred – the gilt bronze head of Sulis fom the same sanctuary and the head of Mercury from Uley – were originally presented as votive gifts. The striking bronze statuette of Mercury from a temple at Gosbecks, Colchester (see 60) and many lesser figurines were likewise intended to attest piety. The reason for major donations would have been made clear by means of an inscription. Thus Quintus Neratius Proxsimus, presumably a citizen of the *colonia* of Lincoln, dedicated an arch to Mars Rigonemetos from his own resources at Nettleham, Lincolnshire. Even more informative is the sandstone statue of 'Mars Lenus or Ocelus Vellaunus' set up by Marcus Nonius Romanus at Caerwent in return for freedom from liability to the *collegium* of the god. In this respect there was a very close similarity to private patronage directed at the secular community as discussed earlier in this chapter.

Art was commissioned for urban settings such as the Forum as well as for temples, with the same range of motives in play, from genuine philanthropy and piety on the one hand to cynical self-promotion on the other. At the basest level the provision of public art and architecture was a good way to bribe the gods as well as one's fellow men! It was, in any case, hardly possible to keep secular and sacred art apart, for there was generally a religious aspect to public works, ranging from the figures of such deities as Venus or the water-nymphs shown on fountains, to the *numina* of Emperors mentioned on inscriptions and inherent wherever their images were displayed. We can compare the nature of patronage in Roman times with that found in the Middle Ages where royal and aristocratic building and the embellishment of major churches were both a means of obtaining God's favour and also a way of advertising the donor's secular importance. At a more humble level the dedication of silver leaves with the images of deities on them, the Matres at London, Mars and Vulcan at Barkway, Hertfordshire as well as the Christian chi-rho at Water Newton, are part of a continuing tradition of popular devotional patronage which runs from antiquity until our own day.[48]

An interesting category is temple paraphernalia, including plate dedicated to the service of the gods, though only the elegant *trulla* with acanthus ornament on its handle, dedicated in letters of gold to the Matres by Fabius Dubitatus, and plain silver vessels from the Christian church at Water Newton, have primary dedications. A number of cast-bronze sceptres are recorded from Britain and it is virtually certain that these were made specifically for particular shrines. Three are in the form of heads of Mars, two from a priestly grave at Brough-on-Humber and a third, very much of native Celtic appearance, from Kirmington, also Lincolnshire (see 20). There is an attractive bust of Minerva from Stonea, Cambridgeshire, whose bold massing of hair and stylized drapery emphasize its local character (47), while a Venus from Ludford Magna, Lincolnshire, although now headless, is given distinction by two little doves, one on each shoulder. Perhaps the most interesting of all these sceptre-heads carrying divine images is one recently found in the parish of Aldworth, Berkshire, in the form of a spear-head with three 'fins', with a young, female bust between each. The spear-head rests upon three consols of acanthus and all in all is a casting of very high quality, virtually certainly used in the north-west European cult of the three Matres.

Other heads or busts from Cambridgeshire and Northamptonshire, in the form of Imperial busts, likewise display a regional character and are presumably to be connected with the Imperial *numina*, venerated alongside the gods. The most valuable group of religious objects consists of the silver spoons and gold jewellery of late fourth-century date from Thetford, Norfolk, dedicated to Faunus, though it is not certain that by this time they were connected with a thriving public cult.[49]

47 *Bronze sceptre in form of a bust of Minerva from Stonea, Cambridgeshire. H.8cm. Wisbech Museum. (Photo: British Museum.)*

CHAPTER FIVE

Natives and Strangers in Roman Britain

*. . . a piece many years in doing and now newly perform'd
by that rare Italian master, Julio Romano, who, had he himself eternity and
could put breath into his work, would beguile nature of her custom, so
perfectly he is her ape.*

Most previous attempts at understanding Insular art have concentrated on sculpture, and have taken either a condemnatory or, at best, an apologetic tone. In her great compilation of all the material known to her at the time, Professor Jocelyn Toynbee rationalizes her value judgements by defining three basic categories of finds from Britain.[1] First there is art imported from the Mediterranean area, obeying classical canons of proportion. The marble busts from the villa at Lullingstone, Kent, for example, are of great interest in the social context and these, or similar sculptures, could conceivably have acted as models for local lapidaries but are irrelevant to actual artistic production in Britain. The second category is high-quality provincial work, normally attributed to Gaulish artists, such as the bronze statuette of Mercury from Gosbecks, Colchester (see 60). Finally there is a residue of low-quality art, much of it produced by British craftsmen (though including some imports such as samian ware); some of it may be interesting, but it cannot be regarded as good, let alone great, art.

This model necessitates complex explanations of the total non-receptiveness of the Britons to Classical culture, an interpretation contradicted not only by the findings of archaeology but also by our one relevant literary source, Tacitus' *Agricola*.[2] It does not account either for the sudden transformation of the artistic expression of the late Iron Age which had depended on the art of the bronzesmith. What happened to such people? In fact it is quite unhistorical to think of Gaul and Britain as nation states, though regrettably scholars on both sides of the Channel have tended to do so. The almost universal dismissal of a possible British contribution to the more accomplished work made in the province is patently a result of the long-established but irrational modern English feelings of cultural dependency on France as the European nation of 'culture'. There is, of course, truth in the premise that in antiquity the neighbouring provinces of Gaul played an important part in the story of art in Roman Britain. For a period of less than a century, between Caesar and Claudius, political control of northern Gaul was with Rome, and it was only after AD 43 that the same held true of Britain. However, during that century artistic ability in Britain was far from stagnant and soon after the Conquest the same romanization of art that had occurred in Gaul happened in Britain. In cultural terms Romano-Celtic is a more accurate description than Romano-British for much of what is found in Britain, and the same sorts of production are to be found on both sides of the Channel. It is only as a temporary phase – with the introduction of Roman art to the Britons – that the Gallic style need be regarded as a distinct phenomenon.

There is one great qualification to be made: most production in the ancient world was regional. The English Channel did provide a barrier, and Insular Roman art does sometimes seem to display greater distinctiveness from the Classical norm than that of Gaul. That, however, is not a value judgement of the traditional sort, for such characteristics are more obvious in the better items and less clear in the mediocre. We do not know whether the early fourth-century Corinian mosaicists were natives of the Cotswolds, the sons of Gaulish immigrants or immigrants from Gaul themselves, but they worked in a style which is not directly matched elsewhere in the Empire and we may call it British or, more properly, Dobunnic. Without a doubt they were also Roman in their sophisticated choice of pattern and image, and if the Woodchester villa was indeed the palace of the governor of *Britannia Prima* (and its size and luxury certainly support this interpretation) they worked for some of the most important people in Roman Britain.

In place of Professor Toynbee's categories a slightly different scheme is proposed here. First there are imports, which were certainly influential in a number of ways, for example in the consideration of artistic influences and of how art was used (Chapter 4), but are not of great concern in this chapter. These are items such as marble statuary and the silver plates in the Mildenhall treasure. Secondly, there is art which it is fair to assume was made by foreigners from outside Britain, especially by artists from the Mediterranean area and which is strongly Classical in its character. Thirdly, there is art which was probably created by Britons or Gauls which approximates in quality to the previous group, but where various (mainly stylistic) indications suggest that the work was done by natives. Fourthly, there are objects where Celtic influences are so strong, that the anti-naturalistic trends of treating the natural world in terms of pattern are very much to the fore. Finally, there is a very small and discrete group of sculptures carved by artists from the Orient. With the exception of the first and last groups these categories shade off one into the other and there will frequently be differences of opinion. When looking at art, we will not go far wrong if we see the major distinction as being between 'Roman'

work and the results of 'Romano-Celtic' production. In academic terms, the distinction to be drawn is whether any particular work of art should be the province of 'Classical Archaeology' or 'European Archaeology'.

The second and third categories are especially interesting because they help us to examine the dynamics of change; without so strong and continuous a Classical influence there would not have been a provincial Roman art at all but simply a slightly adapted Celtic art. Unfortunately there has been more interest in anti-Classical trends, largely because of another modern bias, misplaced Celtic nationalism. The following brief survey begins with a selection of items which may have been made by foreigners (Italians, Greeks, southern Gauls and Easterners), then continues with Classical works probably made by Celts and which may also be regarded as Roman without too much serious qualification. It ends with a brief discussion of traditional Celtic style in the Roman period. In each section I begin with the so-called minor arts where evidence is often richest and progress on to sculpture, wall-painting and mosaic.

FOREIGN ARTISTS IN ROMAN BRITAIN

Positive romanization began in the pre-Roman Iron Age with a few exotic imports and more significantly with native coins which have the same idiosyncracies, such as detailing with small round pellets, that we see on coins and gems dating to the late Republic (see **2** and **8**); I suspect that a gem-engraver was responsible for the Insular dies.[3] Such a craftsman could well have come from north Italy, where Aquileia appears to have been a leading centre of gem production. His bow drill would have been very easily portable, and the cutting of metal dies can have caused little difficulty to an artist already skilled in glyptics. Not long after the Conquest a gem-engraver seems to have been operating at Eastcheap in London (**14**). The evidence here consists of four gems, unset and in very fresh condition, found together in a pit. One of them portrays a pair of clasped hands (see **14a**) and was unfinished: two attempts had been made to cut the name 'Alba' on it, but even the better one had not got beyond the primary tracing of the word. The other intaglios included a head of Roma which was used widely on intaglios in the Empire and it can, indeed, be closely matched by an example from Jordan.[4] Gems recovered at Bath (**48**b and c) from the main drain taking water away from the sacred spring as well as from the great bath were again in large part the work of one gem-cutter, who also seems to have cut intaglios found at Tiverton, Devon (**48**a), Sea Mills, near Bristol, Caerwent and Wroxeter. Records of finding are not good enough to tell whether the gems were a votive offering thrown into the spring or whether they were the casual losses of bathers which had been sucked into the drain lower down. They are all in the current Flavio-Trajanic style.[5]

The same area of London where the Eastcheap gems were found has revealed a goldsmith's workshop in operation before the construction of the Flavian palace which later occupied the site. Although we cannot know the range of his production, this goldsmith used stamps showing a lion, a boar and a sea-creature, perhaps a hippocamp, to seal the luting of his crucibles during the cupelation process (see **15**). These stamps would normally have been used to make plaques for his jewellery, probably by means of the *repoussé* technique, with thin sheets of gold being hammered into a mould.[6]

With regard to bronze figurines and statuettes, there are some imported examples of excellent Classical workmanship. These include the splendid statuette of Nero in the character of Alexander from Baylham Mill, Suffolk, with his inlaid cuirass (see **108**); a vigorous Hercules shooting his bow (perhaps at the Stymphalian birds) found in London (**49**); a figurine of Vulcan seated at his anvil from Richborough (**50**); an image of Jupiter from Colchester; the Cupid lamp-stand from Cirencester (see **105**); and a recently revealed masterpiece: a lithe and dangerous leopard with spotted coat, evidently inlaid with silver, from the Icklingham cache. The workmanship of all of these may be described as 'metropolitan' and consequently none is likely to have been cast in the province.[7] However, the mould for a statuette from Gestingthorpe, Essex, which would have yielded a chubby, nude figure, almost certainly Bacchus, shows that at least lower-quality figures of Classical type were made in Britain; the Gestingthorpe mould could have been the work of an immigrant. The figurine of Apollo from the Thames at London Bridge (**51**) exemplifies this class; Toynbee says it is '*undoubtedly* [my italics] the product of a Mediterranean workshop', but the existence of the Gestingthorpe

48 Intaglios showing horses. a Bloodstone from Tiverton, Devon; b pale cornelian from Bath; c bloodstone from Bath. (× 4.) (Photos: Robert Wilkins, Institute of Archaeology, Oxford.)

49 *Bronze statuette of Hercules shooting the Stymphalian birds(?), from Cheapside, City of London. H.27.7cm. (Photo: British Museum.)*

50 *Bronze figurine of Vulcan from Richborough, Kent. H.14.5cm. Ashmolean Museum. (Photo: Robert Wilkins, Institute of Archaeology, Oxford.)*

51 *Bronze figurine of Apollo from the Thames at London Bridge. H.10.75cm. British Museum.* (Photos: Lynn F. Pitts.)

mould provides grounds for the student to question her certainty.[8]

Another more surprising example is an image of Mars from Martlesham, Suffolk, in which he is shown as a native rider god with the epithet Corotiacus, riding down his foe, borrowed from the repertoire of Hellenistic triumphal art, gigantomachies and celtomachies. The bronzesmith who made it for a British woman called Simplicia signed its base, using the Greek name Glaucus. Was he really a Greek, a humbler counterpart of the great Zenodoros who came from Greece to produce a statue of the local conception of Mercury for the Arverni in the time of Nero (Pliny, *NH* xxxiv, 45)? Zenodoros cannot have been the only Greek plying his trade in the West.[9] The problem of assigning bronzes to particular national groups unless there is clear evidence will be taken up below.

For large bronzes, relative lack of portability means that it may have been easier to 'import' a living bronzesmith (as was the case of Zenodoros among the Arverni in Gaul) than the statue itself. Unfortunately,

52 Funerary statue of a sphinx from Colchester.
Limestone. H.84cm. (Colchester Museums.)

full-size bronze statues do not survive well as they had such value as scrap, but as we have seen there are a number of fragments, including the head of Claudius from the river Alde in Suffolk. Some at least of the triumphal statues of the Emperor set up after 43 were presumably equestrian and the hock of a horse from Ashill, Norfolk, is surely another example of Boudican loot. Hardly enough remains to make any comment about the later equestrian statue from the Forum at Gloucester and perhaps representing Nerva, the founder of the *colonia*, or his successor Trajan. This was, however, a statue of importance, not so unlike the Marcus Aurelius from the Roman Capitol in scale.[10] Despite the close reliance on a Roman model, the head of Hadrian found in the Thames at London (see **35**) seems to me to exhibit local features and thus was almost certainly made in Britain. So too was the head of Sulis Minerva from Bath and, in all likelihood, the eagle from the Basilica at Silchester (see **64**) which was an attribute of a statue of Jupiter, or possibly of an emperor (see below).

Imports of sculpture in stone are confined to marbles (such as the first-century portraits from Fishbourne and Exeter, the second-century Lullingstone busts and the second–fourth-century sculptures from the London Mithraeum and the Woodchester villa

and a third-century sarcophagus from Welwyn, Hertfordshire). However, it is clear that Britain lay beyond the general area of the marble trade. Although a few small, high-quality figures in limestone could also have been brought across the Channel, such as a statuette of Fortuna from Chilgrove, West Sussex, which was carved in Caen stone, this might equally well have been cut in Britain from an imported block.[11] Sculpture was carved in local stone throughout Britain from Dover to the forts of Scotland and provides important evidence of local workshops (see Chapter 6); discernible regional idiosyncrasies belonging to the mixed Romano-Celtic tradition will be discussed in the second part of this chapter. But there are certainly examples of Roman art in British stone, denoting the presence of foreign sculptors. Some of the early military tombstones, notably the fine *stele* of the legionary centurion, Marcus Facilis at Colchester, come into this class (see **11**): as does the memorial to a *beneficiarius consularis* from London (see **24**). I would also guess that some early auxiliary tombstones, notably that of the Thracian Longinus, son of Sdapezematygus, likewise from Colchester and Genialis' memorial from Cirencester (see **170**) were the work of Gaulish sculptors. Not surprisingly, it has been suggested that the two Colchester *stelae* have their closest affinities with military tombstones in the Rhineland.[12]

In all probability the slightly later Colchester Sphinx (**52**) was carved by a resident of the *colonia*, thus perhaps an Italian by descent. The statue is of thoroughly Roman standard, though worked in British limestone and was, indeed, surmised by Toynbee to have been carved by a very good continental sculptor. The boldly-cut wing-feathers may be compared with those of Minerva Victrix from the Porta Marina at Ostia (**53**) and the character of the head between the creature's paws suggests a Flavian or a Trajanic date.[13] A Purbeck marble eagle from Exeter and a fountain figure representing a nymph, or perhaps Venus, carved in the local sandstone from the fortress at Wroxeter demonstrate the wide-ranging artistic patronage of the army (**54**). The latter evidently follows a Hellenistic prototype.[14] Bath provides us with a version of another interesting Greek statue, a figure of a seated boar, cornered in a hunt, which is carved in the excellent local Bath limestone (**55**).

53 Statue of a winged Minerva from Porta Marina, Ostia. Marble. H.2.40m. (Photo: author.)

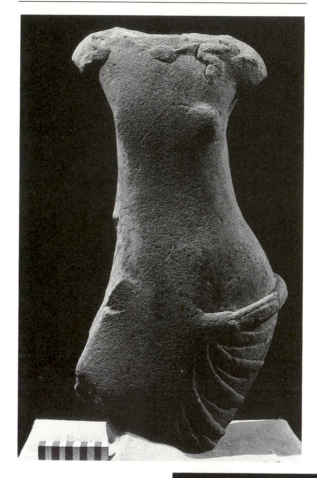

54 a *Statue of Venus or nymph from a fountain, Wroxeter, Shropshire. Sandstone. H.62cm. b The water jug held in the right hand of the nymph.* (Graham Webster, Fortress into City, p.142, pls 6.18 and 6.19.)

There is a version in marble in the Uffizi Museum, Florence, which has been well-known since the sixteenth century.[15] From Walcot, near Bath, comes a female portrait of Flavian type, twice life size and very much in contemporary Roman tradition, save for the material which is again local limestone.[16] There was evidently at least one sculptor from the Mediterranean area at Silchester. A head of a city goddess (*Tyche*) and a head of Serapis, both carved in Portland stone, are highly competent examples of the work of a late second-century sculptor. Jocelyn Toynbee and George Boon agree that the sculptor came from the Continent and Boon reminds us that Silchester had a *collegium peregrinorum*, a guild of resident foreigners, which was involved in the dedication of a statue of Victory to the Numen of the Emperor.[17]

Two statues of Minerva may be by Mediterranean sculptors and, if not, are certainly close to Roman

55 *Statue of a seated boar, from Bath. Limestone. H.44cm.*

work. One, from near Water Newton, at Sibson, Huntingdonshire (56) is described by Toynbee as having been carved by 'an immigrant provincial . . . well schooled in the classical tradition'. It is certainly very fine considering that here the material is Barnack ragstone. The Sibson Minerva is headless, but a limestone head of the goddess has recently been found in a temple at Harlow, Essex, where it may have come from the cult image. Although rather sadly battered, this would have looked splendid when new and decked out with a separately-made metal helmet, just like the gilt bronze head of Minerva from Bath (see above) or the marble head of the goddess from the Walbrook Mithraeum. Indeed, this practice of decking statuary with detachable fittings, sometimes in precious metal, was normal in the ancient world the best known example being Pheidias' *Athena Parthenos*. The type to which the Sibson statue belongs

56 *Statue of Minerva from Sibson, Huntingdonshire. H.1.27m. Woburn Abbey.*
(After, Archaeologia xxxii, 1847, pl.iv.)

approximates to that great statue and this was surely also the prototype of the Harlow head.[18] A pair of very neatly carved charioteers, likewise in the local Barnack limestone, were found not far away at Bedford Purlieus (**57**). Not only are they among the most accomplished studies in Roman Britain but the subject is connected with the Circus, in general an obsession of the Romans, but not well attested in Britain.[19]

In Britain, as elsewhere in the European provinces, wall-painting in the Mediterranean tradition was practised with very few concessions being made to native artistic mannerisms.[20] Leaving aside some very early fragments, notably at Fishbourne, Sussex, what remains lies outside the classic 'Four Styles', although reminiscences of these are frequent. There are also many compositions in which relatively small areas of wall carry figural or decorative devices displayed against a plain ground, a schema which is so

57 *Statues of two charioteers from Bedford Purlieus, Northamptonshire. H.61cm and 76cm. Woburn Abbey. J. Basire (iii), (Engraving by J. Basire (iii) in Archaeologia xxxii, 1847, pl.1.)*

characteristic of second-century Ostia. While it is often impossible to tell whether the painters were Italians (or came from southern Gaul), the accomplished architectural composition from the Roman building on the site of Winchester Palace, Southwark, with its exotic materials (cinnabar and gold leaf) and deft approximation to the Second (theatrical) Style of two centuries earlier, looks like thoroughly Metropolitan work. Although there may be a few local idiosyncrasies, suggestive of developments in the province and probably, therefore, of local recruitment (see below), there is not much reason to think about this art in other than Roman terms.

Remains of wall-painting are especially important because they provide evidence of the background against which the art-owning classes in both town and country lived their lives. Paintings of columnar architecture, sometimes employing perspective and imitation panels of marble, breccia and alabaster, suggests much more palatial housing than was normally to be found in Britain. Conceits incorporating hanging swags, which appear to be suspended in mid-air (colour plate II), canopies supported on volutes and peopled scrolls express desires to escape from reality into fantasy, which is why Vitruvius had so strongly disapproved of them in late Second Style and Third Style paintings.

Figural painting throughout reflects Roman life, myth and religion. Examples include the gladiators panel at Colchester, a theatrical mask on a small panel in the frieze of a room at Leicester (colour plate I), a Vergilian scene from a villa at Otford, Kent, complete with literary inscription, a series of Bacchic figures at Dover in the same house as the room with the perspective architecture, Venus and Mars from Kingscote and a dreamy-looking youth, probably Narcissus, from the Tarrant Hinton villa, Dorset (colour plate IV). A very interesting painting still *in situ* at Lullingstone, Kent, depicts nymphs, one of them, as already mentioned, with water-pouring breasts as described by Philostratus the Elder (*Imagines* ii, 4, 3). The villa's house church is painted in the style of late antiquity with *orantes* and chi-rhos, but nothing gives it away specifically as the product of a British workshop. Even though it seems likely that local workshops were set up, probably manned by British painters, there are no easily identifiable schools with their own traditions and idiosyncrasies as there are with mosaics.[21]

The supreme manifestation of Roman art is the mosaic pavement which, although originally a Greek and essentially a Hellenistic invention, was only brought to perfection under the Empire. Here, as with painting, it is likely that the first-century mosaics were laid by craftsmen from the Continent. Workshops were set up in British cities in the second century and different traditions are represented at Verulamium and Colchester on the one side and those in western Britain on the other.[22] These differences, however, must derive in the first instance from different repertoires (and 'pattern books') employed, although the individuality of the different circles of craftsmen which constitute a 'school' must also be taken into account. It seems that both Roman artists and their native pupils are represented. The best examples, such as the Middleborough Mosaic at Colchester (Eastern group) (colour plate VII) and the Dyer Street mosaic, Cirencester (Western group), are very Classical in composition and execution. Doubtless the attractive designs of the geometric mosaics would have appealed to members of the British gentry who had not lost their taste for abstract Celtic art, now mainly represented by small dress items such as coloured enamel brooches. However, Romano-British mosaics never include Celtic features and are comparable with mosaics from other parts of the Roman world in quality and technique.

The fourth-century revival almost certainly began with mosaicists arriving in Britain in the wake of Constantius Chlorus' conquest, encouraged by the wealth of the island and the lack of established mosaicists. Certainly, the magnificent and detailed mosaic floors at Bignor, a villa which achieved its apogee in the reign of Constantine, are very much in the classicizing style of figured mosaics executed in Gaul during the third century.[23] The famous bust of Venus, her hair cascading over her shoulders, is entirely Hellenistic in conception (colour plate XII); the frieze of cupid-gladiators below her is Graeco-Roman and finds a parallel in such conceits as the little putti at work and play painted on the walls of the House of the Vettii at Pompeii. The Romano-British schools which eventually emerged in the fourth century, all of which probably comprised several distinct, possibly independent workshops, produced startlingly different work one from the other. Local elements in design and choice of colour come to the fore, and these will be discussed in Chapters 6 and 7.

PROVINCIAL ART IN ROMAN BRITAIN: ROMANO-GAULISH AND ROMANO-BRITISH

This section lies at the heart of any study of art in Roman Britain, but the distinction between art produced in Britain and what was made outside, in Gaul, is not an easy one to define, as a glance at any catalogue of such material from the north-western provinces will show. In the first century continental artists taught their British pupils and the resultant work was virtually indistinguishable from that of their mentors. In a few cases a work of art is placed in this section rather than in the previous one simply because of some evidence that its creator was of Celtic origin (and it is not at all unlikely that some of the material in the first section should also be relocated here), but generally there is some telltale sign, such as the influence of local Gaulish or British style which differentiates provincial Roman art from the products of continental craftsmen working in a Mediterranean tradition. Although this book is basically concerned with Britain, it is important not to consider Insular art in isolation and, in the examples that follow, a few will be included from Gaul. The review begins with the minor arts for the good reason that many of the technologies existed in the Iron Age, and goes on to review provincial elements in other arts.

Jewellery

A number of pieces of gold jewellery, published by Hilary Cool and ascribed to a British workshop, take an important place among works of art from the province. They include Hercules' club pendants from Ashstead, Kent, and from Birdoswald, as well as a possible hair-ornament from Southfleet, Kent. The best and most distinctive item is a bracelet from Rhayader, Powys (**58**). The use of Celtic curvilinear ornament in two panels of the Rhayader bracelet, as well as the use of enamel in much of the other ornament produced by the workshop, demonstrates its local origin, but Dr Cool is quite right in seeing the jewellery as belonging essentially to the Hellenistic Roman tradition. The smith was a Briton who certainly did not eschew his past, though he clearly understood the spirit of the best ornament of the time in the Roman world, and this goldwork is properly considered as Roman. The same may be said of the

58 *Gold bracelet from Rhayader, Powys. The two pieces are respectively 9.8 and 9cm in length. (Photo: British Museum.)*

two necklaces and the bracelet with attached wheel-ornaments from the Backworth treasure. It has been claimed that this might relate to a widespread Celtic cult, but although the type was certainly made in Britain, as examples in the Snettisham cache attest, it is also very familiar from Italy and indeed beyond; this demonstrates that the taste (and I suggest the symbolism) here was more Roman than native.

The second-century cache of rings, bracelets, gems and coins found at Snettisham, Norfolk, is of exceptional importance. It certainly belonged to a Romano-British jeweller and, apart from his stock-in-trade, contained one of his tools, a burnisher made from a piece of chalcedony. The serpent-bracelets are of Insular type, paralleled by the well-known pair from Castlethorpe, Buckinghamshire. So too are the rings with bezels, each consisting of three flower-like bosses around which a pair of serpents is symmetrically disposed, one head on each side. The type is paralleled by examples, for instance from the Backworth hoard (made of gold) and a house in Caerwent (silver). Both bracelets and rings are once again of Hellenistic inspiration.[24] Such a mixed pedigree is also to be found in certain brooches made of bronze, such as the one from Bignor which has a plate portraying an ecstatic maenad in a style familiar from Augustan and Julio-Claudian art, on its foot, though the general form of the brooch is provincial, albeit continental rather than British. It is possible that the craftsman who made the brooch applied a stamp with a classical device made by another jeweller and the same might be true of the London goldsmith mentioned above – but we cannot take that for granted: normally artisans in the ancient world made their own tools and fashioned all their own materials.[25]

The Snettisham jeweller both set and, in all probability, made signet-rings. This is certain because many of the rings are unfinished, including 17 signet-rings, of standard early Imperial form, set with cornelian intaglios, and 110 intaglios, likewise cornelians, as yet unset. The stones are of somewhat mediocre work compared with the earlier Bath gems mentioned above, though they too are engraved in the manner standard throughout the Empire; their subjects are very much related to rural prosperity being for the most part portrayals of Bonus Eventus, Ceres and Fortuna.[26] A long-recognized example of a Romano-British craft is the jet industry, probably centred on the York colonia, which flourished in the third and fourth centuries, producing pins and bracelets as well as small figurines and cameo medallions (see **83**). There was an export industry to the Rhineland and, indeed, there is a jet Medusa amulet in the Vatican collection at Rome. Many of the Medusa heads and portraits are virtually identical to cameos cut in onyx, and certainly belong to the Roman tradition, but others are decidedly strange, for example on a pendant from Strood, Kent, Medusa is shown in profile while the serpents still appear as though the image was frontal. The medallions display a rich use of texture which we will see again and again in the work of British artists.[27]

The Late Roman Thetford treasure will be considered in Chapter 7; here it is sufficient to note the flair and imagination of the jeweller who designed such a little masterpiece as the Woodpecker ring; there are 21 others in the hoard and his output includes at least one ring found on another site. All are characterized by considerable inventiveness in design, as is the belt-buckle and other items of jewellery, all made for the god Faunus.

Silversmithing

Silver vessels were likewise made in Britain. While the province may never have been a major centre of silver manufacture, the recent discovery that mercury-gilding was applied to a silver trumpet-brooch from Carmarthen, dating to the Conquest period, shows that technical competence was present from the beginning. The Crownthorpe cups (see **17**), although made of bronze, and above all the discovery of a bronze mould in Kent used in the casting of foot-rings, means that nothing technical stood in the way of silver plate being produced from the middle of the first century onwards. The second-century Backworth cache, a mixed collection of jewellery and plate, appears to have been dedicated to the local mother goddesses. One of the gold rings carries an inscription on its bezel to this effect, as does the handle of a silver *trulla*. As we have seen, some of the jewellery at least was Romano-British and it is logical to think that the dedicator, Fabius Dubitatus, had this item of plate made at the same time for presentation to this particular shrine. It is, nevertheless, a thoroughly Roman-looking piece of second-century plate, confidently ornamented with an acanthus design in high relief. Comparison has been made with the handle of a *trulla* from the Chatuzange treasure, probably made in Gaul.

There is some reason to ascribe the *trullae* in another northern British hoard, the Capheaton treasure, of the late second or early third century, to a workshop in the province. The reasoning here depends on subject matter rather than technique or style. One of the handles portrays an offering at a temple and spring presided over by Minerva. Could this be Sulis Minerva, patron goddess of Bath, as I have suggested? Another handle shows a female personification holding a maniple standard, so presumably the object was meant to be identified with the Imperial army, and of course that army was very prominent in Britain, especially in northern Britain. Again there are good analogues in treasures from Gaul, including Chatuzange and the temple treasure of Berthouville.

It is possible, too, that the splendid late third-century mirror from Wroxeter, its back ornamented with a Hercules-knot handle, was made in Britain. This type is widespread in the north-western provinces at the time, although it is more likely that it was imported from the Rhineland. One, which must have been of similar size and weight, is shown on a well-known sculpture from Neumagen, being held by a maid for her mistress' contemplation, while smaller examples are commonly found in excavations. If the form is regional, the general character of the decoration, notably the handle with its rosettes, and the surrounding vegetal frieze, is completely Graeco-Roman in spirit.

In late Roman Britain, as Esmonde Cleary rightly comments, there must have been some very wealthy people. Much of their silverware, such as the picture plates in the Mildenhall treasure (see **86**), the Corbridge lanx (see **93**) and the Ulysses flagon (see **96**) from the large cache of *Hacksilber* discovered north of the fourth-century frontier at Traprain Law, Scotland, came from the Mediterranean world, but some is more local. The evidence will be fully considered in Chapter 7 but it is convenient to mention here some items which may well have been manufactured in Britain. They certainly include the simpler Water Newton vessels, with their Christian inscriptions engraved for the votaries who presented them to the local church. The square dish from Mileham, Norfolk (**59**) with its stylized leafy ornament, could

also be Romano-British, as Jocelyn Toynbee hinted. It is paralleled in the Traprain Law and Balline treasures, from Scotland and southern Ireland (Co. Limerick) respectively, which were probably assembled in an orderly fashion within the province of Britain as bullion payment to mercenaries rather than as 'loot' grabbed by pirate raiders; the distinctive form is also found in British pewter. The original casting of the Risley Park lanx (see **94**) appears to show some knowledge of pewter manufacture, and is likely to have been made in Britain – certainly the secondary dedicatory inscription on the base was added on behalf of a bishop who donated it to a (nearby?) church. A very strong candidate for local manufacture is a bowl from another *Hacksilber* hoard from Ballinrees, near Coleraine in Northern Ireland, whose engraved ornament is analogous to that of Romano-British buckles (see Chapter 7). Finally the swan-necked spoons with elegantly coiled handles from the Thetford treasure, Canterbury and Hoxne, are likely to be a Romano-British speciality.[28] To sum up, if this evidence is accepted, we can see strong grounds for proposing a considerable quantity of manufacture, at least in Late Roman Britain, to match the undoubted spending power evinced both by hoards of late Roman silver coins and the large number of high-quality mosaics (see below) in the province.

Bronze statuary and figurines

The range of bronze statuettes found in Britain extends from completely Mediterranean work, mainly imported but probably including a few pieces made here by foreign artists – even executing commissions for British clients – to purely native work. The high degree of competence exhibited by the Romano-British smith Celatus in creating the figure of Mars found in the Foss Dyke, Lincolnshire, for the Colasuni brothers shows that the distinction is not one of ability. The Foss Dyke Mars has sufficient local characteristics in terms of patterning to be considered as in part representative of Romano-Celtic work, but the understanding of physiognomy in the basic structure of the body and the selection of a type of nude based, in all probability, on a statue of Alexander the Great by Lyssipos demands explanation. All the more so as the type is not common in Italy but is well represented in Britain and is especially widely disseminated in Gallia Belgica. While the native features

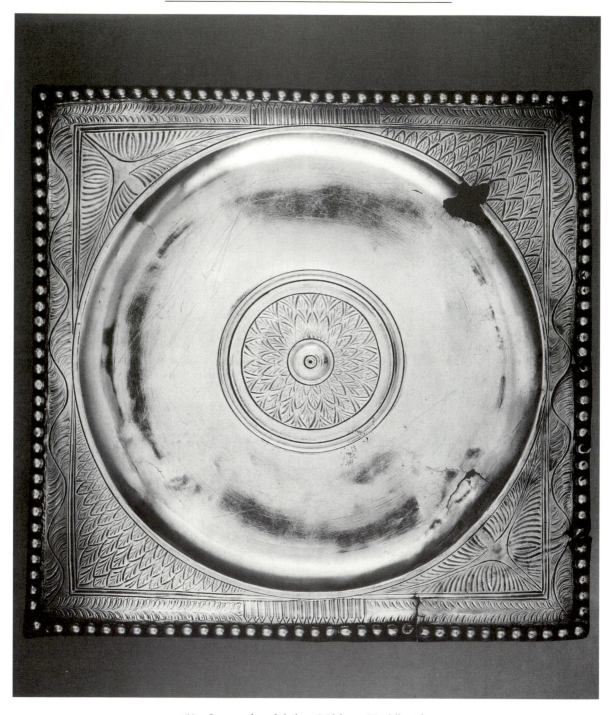

59 *Square silver dish from Mileham, Norfolk. sides
each 37.5cm.* (Photo: British Museum.)

here are obvious, an appliqué bust of the same general type, found in Cirencester, is almost Hellenistic in its ideal beauty and sensuousness, accentuated by its copper nipples. Despite its very Roman appearance, a British origin is not totally impossible even here. It is likely that this specific Mars-type, with its dreamy beauty had been selected by some powerful individual in Rome for the benefit of the Celts, an image as distant as possible from their harsh and warlike traditions.[29]

Mercury was pre-eminent among the deities venerated in Britain. The largest and best bronze is the statuette of Mercury, shown at the moment of alighting, from Gosbecks near Colchester (**60**). The image is a very lively one and Toynbee calls it 'wholly Classical', though the bold texture of the hair and overemphasized eyelids do suggest provincial subtleties as she recognized. Nevertheless there is no reason whatsoever why it should have been cast in Gaul rather than Britain especially in the territory of a *Colonia*.[30] The castings of most Roman-period figurines of Mercury from Britain are in fact iconographically Classical. One type in which the god holds his purse on the palm of his hand has a largely Gaulish distribution and Boucher has proposed that it is derived from the statue which Zenodoros produced for the Arverni. An excellent example comes from Manea Fen, Cambridgeshire. Lynn Pitts suggests that it is local work because its eyes are rather large, but it is undoubtedly Classical in spirit. Another example came from a probable temple-site at Great Walsingham, Norfolk, together with two much more obviously local images, one of which had a thoroughly Celtic patterned treatment of the hair.[31]

The 'Verulamium Venus' found in a cellar (which may have served as a storage place for scrap of a metalworker or, more plausibly, as a shrine) represents yet another Hellenistic statuary type, though Toynbee accepts that the best parallels are from southern Gaul. The smith has not quite understood the physical anatomy, and the body is somewhat pear-shaped, as are several other Gaulish figurines, such as a silvered statuette of Fortuna from Sainpuits, Yonne.[32] Provincial Roman figurines of high quality and showing yet more native features, such as accentuation of texture in the clothing and patterned hair, include a priestess, temple-musician or, more probably, the muse Euterpe, from Silchester (**frontispiece**), and a male votary or possibly a Genius from Earith, Cambridge-

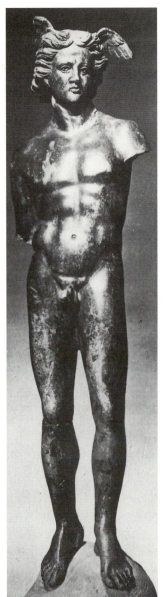

60 *Bronze statuette of Mercury from Gosbecks Farm, near Colchester. H.53cm. (Photo: Colchester Museums.)*

shire (**61**) and a figure of Vulcan from Catterick, Yorkshire (see **78**), both of which combine accurate modelling with a harmonious use of line. They were probably all commissioned for dedication at local shrines, as the Foss Dyke Mars certainly was. Two identical heads of Jupiter found near Amersham, Buckinghamshire, perhaps tripod mounts rather than sceptre-heads (as was thought when only one had been found), display a similar frame of hair and beard to the Catterick Vulcan. They may also be compared

61 *Bronze figurine of a
votary from Earith,
Cambridgeshire. H.14.7cm.
Museum of Archaeology and
Anthropology, Cambridge.*

I Second-century fresco with an architectural schema and theatrical mask, from Leicester.

II Detail of a second-century fresco from Verulamium showing a hanging swag.

III (Left) Detail of a second-century fresco from Verulamium showing a candelabrum.

IV (Below) Fourth-century fresco from Tarrant Hinton, Dorset showing Narcissus and a satyr(?).

V (Right) First-century geometric mosaic at Fishbourne, Sussex (Room N12).

VI (Left) Second-century mosaic at Fishbourne. Cupid on a dolphin (Room N7).

VII (Left) Second-century mosaic at Colchester depicting two wrestling cupids (the Middleborough Pavement).

VIII (Below) Second-century mosaic at Verulamium showing a lion.

IX (Right) Fourth-century mosaic from Low Ham, Somerset (detail). Aeneas and Ascanius with Dido – and Venus.

X (Below right) Fourth-century mosaic from Low Ham, Somerset (detail). Dido and Aeneas make love after the hunt.

XIII (Left) Fourth-century mosaic with vault-design from
Horkstow, Lincolnshire. (S. Lysons, Reliquiae Britannico
Romanae i, pl. iv.)

XIV (Below) Fourth-century mosaic from Thruxton,
Hampshire depicting Bacchus (detail). (Coloured drawing by
John Lickman, now in Saffron Walden Museum. Photo:
Grahame Soffe.)

XV Fourth-century geometric
mosaic from Mill Hill,
Castor. (From E. T. Artis,
The Durobrivae of
Antoninus, 1828, pl. xix.)

XVI Fourth-century
geometric mosaic from Roxby,
Lincolnshire, engraved by
William Fowler.

with a silver bust of Jupiter from a shrine on the Little St Bernard pass in south-eastern Gaul.[33]

Figures of animals include the hounds dedicated to Nodens at his temple at Lydney Park, Gloucestershire, of which the finest is shown seated. It has a long muzzle and delicately patterned hair. Although the type is to be found elsewhere, as for instance at Voorburg in the Netherlands, this example, with its attractively textured hair, is the best. A protome of a stag from Brampton near Norwich (**62**), Norfolk with its stylized facial musculature, rather glaring, elongated eyes and textured hair on its breast, is a masterpiece hardly less interesting than the very early stag-statuette found near Brighton (see **18**). Incidentally, it is thought that the post-Roman stag on the Sutton Hoo sceptre (see **104**) is 'strongly influenced by the Romano-British tradition' (see Chapter 8). Other mammals include boars, like the spirited late first-century figure from Camerton, Somerset, with its stiff crest and short-hatched pelt. Here, close examination has revealed casting flashes on the insides of the legs and even traces of tooling of the wax original inside the ears. Lions, like boars, range from fully Roman renditions to the patently native version, but especially formidable is the monster, more wolf than lion, from Oxfordshire (Woodeaton?), shown devouring a human victim. This is certainly more frighteningly effective than the unintentionally comic key-handle (presumably an import), once again from Brampton, which shows an unfortunate man being mauled by a lion in some amphitheatre. Finally it is appropriate to mention figures of birds such as eagles, found at various sites, for instance Woodeaton, Oxfordshire, and cockerels (**63**), associated with Mercury, which allowed their creators great scope in the rendition of plumage.[34]

There are only a few large-scale bronze sculptures remaining, a tiny percentage of what must at one time have existed. The head of Hadrian from London (see **35**) is of excellent technical quality, and but for the decorative hair-treatment could have been ascribed to a Metropolitan workshop. The local bronzesmith added a patterned treatment of the hair to his otherwise carefully observed model, and the head retains its classical gravity, a quality that Hadrian so carefully fostered. The Bath Minerva is another very fine work of local classicism, the modelling skilful and the expression suitably benign. Its proportions (the head seems a little too wide) and the heavy

modelling of the eyelids suggest the work of a Gaul or a Briton, and Toynbee opts for the former. There is no cause to doubt that a shrine of international repute like that of Bath could have attracted bronzesmiths just as it did sculptors, but equally there is no good reason to rule out a local hand, even though the head is indeed more lifelike than the (clearly imported) marble head from the Walbrook Mithraeum.

There must have been many figures of Jupiter in Britain. It has been suggested that the very well-known eagle from the basilica of Silchester (**64**) accompanied the god, who presided over justice here; the slight curvature of the bird's talons made it suitable for standing on a globe, which the god might have held in his hand. Alternatively it could have accompanied a statue of the emperor, Jupiter's representative on earth. It is unfortunately not an *aquila* from a legionary standard, though generations of readers of Rosemary Sutcliff's inspiring *The Eagle of the Ninth* (1954) will find it hard to reject that idea, so basic to the novel. Now wingless, the eagle's textured plumage creates a bold effect, although there is admittedly a certain gaucheness in the actual modelling of the bird. Jocelyn Toynbee believed it to be 'undoubtedly an import from some central Mediterranean area, perhaps from Italy', but this seems to me unlikely. On the one hand the dominance of a rich, patterned, textured effect over the mechanical restrictions of form is a hallmark of local Romano-British work; on the other, although the eagle is fairly small in itself, the statue which accompanies it would have been reasonably grand and thus not very likely to have been transported over a long distance.

A lappet with lion and *pelta* on it was also found in the Basilica. It could have come from the same statue, or more probably another of an emperor, but it is too small a piece on which to base deductions as to provenance. A head of Jupiter from Felmingham Hall, Norfolk, is certainly British though it is not part of a fully-modelled image but was probably a votive of a type also represented in the Icklingham treasure (see **21**), an assemblage of masks and statuettes found in Suffolk and subsequently smuggled out of England to the United States. The Felmingham Hall mask has the dignity of the usual Capitoline type, but the hair-textures are linear designs, the curls above the brow marking a further stage in abstraction from that observed in the image of Hadrian.[35]

63 *Bronze figurine of cockerel from Aston, Hertfordshire. H.6.2cm.* (Photo: British Museum.)

62 *Bronze appliqué protome of stag from Brampton, Norfolk. H.14cm. Castle Museum, Norwich.* (Photo: Hallam Ashley, by courtesy of Dr A.K. Knowles.)

64 *Bronze statuette of eagle (probably part of Jupiter statue) from Silchester, Hampshire. H.15cm.* (Photo: Michael Fulford, Department of Archaeology, University of Reading.)

Sculpture in stone

Most stone sculpture from Britain was carved by native sculptors, although initially 'foreigners' associated with the army must have opened up the quarries, as noted earlier in connection with early military tombstones. The materials are local, much of the best work being in limestone. The carvers of the Cotswold region and the further extension of the jurassic ridge north into Lincolnshire and south to Dorset, could count many notable achievements to their credit. Sculptors from this region seem to have set up studios in London, and others may have worked at the legionary fortress of Caerleon. Two examples of sculpture in the round have been selected here to emphasize that quality and classicism are not necessarily the preserve of continental craftsmen. A female mask with high coif of hair (*onkos*) and fierce expression, ornamented a monumental tomb at Towcester, Northamptonshire (**65**). The conception is Mediterranean, but not the bold outlining of the bulging eyes or the long curling lock of hair in front of each ear. The statue of Mercury from Uley, carved in the local oolitic limestone, is clearly based on a prototype by Praxiteles and seems to be especially close to the Hermes of Andros. The modelling of the face and the legs are entirely in the Roman tradition, but the treatment of the hair in terms of a pattern of S-scrolls clearly betrays the hand of a Celtic, and almost certainly a British, artist.[36]

Relief sculpture sometimes comes into the same high class as the Uley Mercury. A figure of the same deity was set in a niche of the Bath gate at Cirencester or else it came from a nearby building. Body modelling is well understood here and the sculptor has managed to convey the texture of the floppy *petasos*. The best of the Gloucester reliefs of Mercury and Rosmerta shows how well local artists could adapt the Classical repertoire, and this can also be seen with the conflation of local hunter-god and Attis from Bevis Marks, London. Although only fragments remain, it is clear that at least one Cotswold artist was prepared to cope with the Mithraic repertoire. The most harmonious and ambitious composition in the region is the scheme of the Bath pediment (see **22**). The design of the vegetal wreath and the supporting victories and the tritons in the spandrels convey the visual order of Classical art. The male Medusa or rather the Neptune–Medusa conflation is an original creation, with strong Celtic idiosyncrasies in the treatment of the eyes and the luxuriance of the hair, but it is fully integrated into the design and, I would argue, was always intended to be read in the Roman way as alluding to Neptune as Minerva's companion. There is some similarity between the style of the Bath pediment and sculpture from south-eastern Gaul, for instance Avenches and Nyon in Switzerland as well as Arles, where an especially fine mask of a sea-god in a clipeate roundel is recorded. Perhaps the Bath sculptor originated in that region.

There were accomplished workshops elsewhere in Britain, for instance at Lincoln, York and Carlisle. Again and again we see how British sculptors were able to breathe new life into Classical models, especially by a lively response to form, vigorous patterning of hair and draperies, sometimes even by changing proportions and concentrating on linear effects.[37]

Wall-painting

Painting was widespread but because of the fragmentary nature of survivals and the closeness between provincial work and its prototype, it is more than usually difficult to isolate the home-produced work. Candelabra, as in the Third Style, were common in provincial art but those in paintings from Britain (**colour plate III**) are rather simpler than those found in paintings in Gaul and Germany. On a more positive note a wall in a house in Insula xxi at Verulamium has a frieze containing a 'peopled scroll'; the calyx ornament in the forks of the scroll with its richly toned crests, is reminiscent of the taste for bold colour contrasts exhibited in the scrolls of the Corinian mosaicists at Woodchester, Chedworth and Stonesfield, but that was well over a century later, in another place and another medium.[38]

Mosaics

There are hints in second-century pavements, at Verulamium in particular, of a local attitude towards representing figural subject-matter by breaking the forms down into areas of pattern: the Neptune pavement and the lion (**colour plate VIII**) show this best.[39] The latter, indeed, prefigures the treatment of animals on the Corinian Orpheus pavements. It is almost

65 *Female mask from a funerary monument, Towcester, Northamptonshire. Limestone. H.56cm.* (Photo: British Museum.)

certain that the majority of mosaicists came from a Gaulish or British milieu and their workshops were, of course, locally based, and yet it is still best to see the work as essentially Roman. This is true throughout the second century and indeed later.

There are few third-century mosaics, at least after the Severan period, and D.J. Smith has recently suggested that the 'Venus pavement' at Rudston, which was formerly ascribed to the mid-late fourth century, should be placed among them, reflecting 'an acute dearth of trained mosaicists in Britain in the second half of the third century and, in the north, possibly also the early fourth'. This mosaic is a world away from the style and quality of the Venus mosaic (**colour plate XII**) and the other major floors at Bignor, for example, and is sometimes wrongly regarded as showing strong native features, though in fact its iconography is clearly derived from the North African tradition. It was laid by a mosaicist who was simply a bungling and incompetent draughtsman. The curiously mis-shapen figures and animals fit in well with misconceived notions of Romano-British art, but it could have been laid by an entrepreneur whose art was too poor to secure him a living in his homeland. It should be noted that at Bignor, too, there is a crude mosaic of a Medusa in the middle of a circular design, including ill-rendered peacocks, a dolphin and a fish, and with busts of seasons in the spandrels, likewise of amateurish quality. Such childlike work is found throughout the Empire, and at every period; it is a reminder that quality is not always constant.[40]

Only in the fourth century does British mosaic art again come into its own (Chapter 7), but then it does so in a decidedly ambitious manner, at least in Cirencester, Dorchester and Aldborough/Brough-on-Humber and the schools associated with them. The subject matter is Roman and sometimes even esoteric. The circles of animals and plants on the Corinian Orpheus floors hint at a knowledge of Neo-Platonism, but the bold linear details, use of pattern and shading, and strongly contrasting tones are almost reminiscent of a carpet. Indeed, the use of pattern on such pavements as that of Stonesfield which is only partly figurative bring to mind the much later Carpet pages of Hiberno-Northumbrian art. I do not see how there can be any real link, unless it was through surviving Roman manuscripts and the British (or West Gaulish) *Vergilius Romanus* (**76, 92**) suggests how such a style might be passed on, but

there is certainly a community of taste. The common denominator is that both have strongly linear elements, regularized and put to the service of civilization by the culture of the Roman Empire in the one case and of Christianity in the other (see Chapter 8).

Strong patterns, distinctive fleshy vegetation and figures marked out by bold outlining help to define the *oeuvre* of the Durnovarian school, with its extraordinary eclecticism in myth types evidently based on the mosaicists' abilities in copying manuscripts in the libraries of their patrons. A chi-rho at Frampton is not so surprising given that the device was widely used as the Emperor's *labarum* and even occupied the entire reverse of bronze coins of Magnentius which were more or less contemporary. The Hinton St Mary pavement with a chi-rho behind the fleshy bust in the centre of the main floor (see **85**) is reminiscent of vault-design but, despite the advocacy of Painter, no evidence of a fourth-century church or baptistery, sparkling with mosaics such as we find in Rome and Naples is known, and I am not convinced that any such existed. The design is eclectic and the Christian device is ill-matched with the 'Pagan' theme of Bellerophon slaying the chimaera in the other section. The odd juxtaposition of subjects suggests that the patron had his own meaning for what was shown. Was he a Christian using Pagan imagery or a Pagan employing contemporary Christian language? The iconography is as odd as the style. However it is visually stunning, and I have never understood why the great fourth-century mosaics of Britain have not been the general starting point for an exposition of Romano-British art.

Pottery

In following a sequence from small objects (minor art) to large ones (major art), I have omitted what must have been the most frequent contact most people had with art, so unselfconscious that it can scarcely have been regarded as art at all. Pottery was essentially utilitarian but there was a considerable quantity of so-called 'fine wares', the most ubiquitous being samian ware, mostly imported from Gaul, though a small quantity was also made in kilns in Britain – at Colchester and London. The figured vessels were surely helpful in spreading a taste for representational art, but they do not play a very important part in the

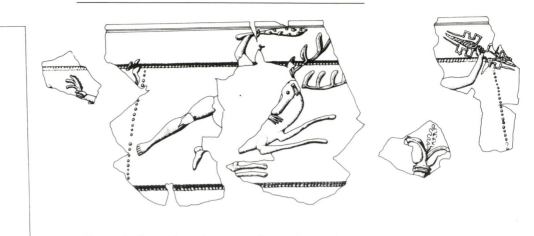

66 *Pottery beaker made in the Nene Valley, with figured barbotine decoration including Hercules and the Cerneian hind and Jupiter. From Lincoln. Diameter of pot 23cm. (Drawing by Margaret J. Darling (Darling 1989, fig.1).)*

history of the arts and crafts of Britain. It was different with the products of some of the native potters of Colchester, the Nene Valley and elsewhere, who decorated drinking cups with figural scenes *en barbotine*, depicting hunting and amphitheatre scenes, myths – especially the labours of Hercules, erotic-fertility scenes and festivals. The subject has now been explored by Graham Webster who has revealed the potters' astonishing fecundity of imagination and deftness of hand. Their products do not seem to have been intended for everyday use but were perhaps given at seasonal festivals, like the New Year, or sold at fairs held at religious sanctuaries.[41]

The circumstances of creation were very different from those of the mosaics discussed above, which are also earlier, so there is no direct link between them. They have in common the melding of native sense of line and Roman content. Sherds from a vessel from Lincoln figure Hercules capturing the Cerneian Hind (**66**) and I agree with Dr Webster that the vigour and panache of this representation is unsurpassed in more carefully finished, Classical portrayals of the scene; it cannot have taken the potter many minutes to make. The elongated creature which matches the hares, deer and hounds on the hunt cups is reminiscent of the hunt-scenes on the Hinton St Mary mosaic. The hunting of *cucullati* in a *venatio* scene from Colchester and of the woman driving a phallic chariot on a beaker from Great Chesterton have an

earthy vigour which makes us laugh, at the same time as realizing that here art has been placed at the service of man's most important instincts. The humour hides the anxieties all must have in dealing with the great powers of fertility and procreation. Similar barbotine ware is known from Central Gaul and elsewhere, but the British products are often distinctive.[42]

OTHER PROVINCIAL STYLES IN ROMAN BRITAIN

In theory the Roman Empire could have seen the sort of blending of cultures current today. However, most art was very local and, as I have already explained in my book on religion, there was no widespread dissemination even of the attractive saviour cults among the native population. There do, however, appear to have been a few Eastern sculptors at work in north Britain, relying in large part on patronage from their countrymen.

In Palmyra, tomb-sculpture is largely situated within built structures; it does not ornament *stelae*. Barates, a native of Palmyra, employed one of his countrymen to produce a gravestone for his British wife when she died at South Shields (see **38**). The design on the stone is one found widely in Britain, with the woman sitting with her jewel-box beside her, but the style is not British. The same hand is at work in the case of another *stele* from South Shields, but this time of a North African called Victor, apparently with no link with Syria; his heirs must have liked the Palmyrene's style. Victor reclines in just the fashion shown on so much Palmyrene sculpture. A Syrian hand is also to be seen in the case of a free-standing statue from Chesters, depicting Juno Regina wearing a garment ornamented with rich draperies with borders ornamented with wave designs (**67**). Finally the facing radiate bust of Sol (or should we rather call him Helios here) from Corbridge may well be associated with an oriental cult, perhaps Jupiter Dolichenus. Indeed the other sculptures from the putative temple, such as the fragments of pediment, one of which has a distinctive *bucranium*, look provincial and yet decidedly non-British. The *bucranium* mentioned is comparable to one on the side of an altar, the front of which is dedicated in Greek to Herakles of Tyre.[43]

NATIVE BRITISH ART OF THE ROMAN PERIOD

The final category of art to be found in Britain is in some ways the most intriguing, for it provides a link between the high-quality Celtic art which resulted in the weapons, armour, torques and mirrors of the pre-Conquest period and the Celtic revival. There used to be an idea that Celtic art somehow went underground and re-emerged in the fifth and sixth centuries, or that it died and was re-imported from Ireland. Neither simple explanation entirely fits the facts.

As we have seen, pre-Roman Iron Age ornament had a limited range of uses. After the Conquest, Celtic weaponry was redundant and with it went much characteristic Celtic art. The wearing of large gold neck torques would hardly have been acceptable in good Roman society for which blatant *luxuria* was anathema, and in any case the upper classes had the many attractions of wall-painting, sculpture, glass and silver plate to provide fresh fields for emulation. That left minor trinkets such as studs, horse-trappings and, above all, brooches. These all had practical functions and were cheap. Did those who owned them regard them as art at all? It is doubtful that they did. Nevertheless I know of few objects so aesthetically pleasing

67 *Statue of Juno Regina, standing on heifer, from Chesters, Northumberland. Sandstone. H.1.6m. (Photo: J.C. Coulston.)*

as the so-called dragonesque brooch with its two zoomorphic terminals.[44] Its rigid symmetry may owe something to Roman example but enamelling was a native craft and the brooch is basically an embellished S-scroll. Other enamelled brooches are circular in shape, ornamented with circles and segments or, sometimes, simple linear features such as *triskele* forms. While these items presumably did not appeal to the highest levels of society, they tended to be used by women who could afford to buy them and they are frequently found on Roman sites.[45] They were in no way alternatives to Roman art but adjuncts to it.

The army provided considerable patronage, and enamelled metalwork was used to embellish military equipment such as scabbards and belt slides (see **33**). The craft also overlaps into areas of provincial Roman interest in the decoration of Roman-style bronze vessels. Thus a cup from Rudge, Wiltshire (see **41**), and a *patera* from Amiens in France record the names of the forts on Hadrian's Wall, of which they were surely tourist souvenirs. Representations of human figures and notably of horsemen (rider-gods?), mammals, birds and fish, even of capricorns, on figured brooches likewise show significant Roman influence, though it was never dominant in objects of this sort.[46] The splendid fourth-century penannular brooch from Bath (**68**) which I previously published as being of Irish type, more probably belongs on this side of the water, in south-western Britain. The earliest example, of third- or fourth-century date, of a form of pin known as a 'hand pin', which continues to develop throughout the so-called Dark Ages, comes from Oldcroft, Lydney, Gloucestershire.[47]

During the Roman centuries it was only in Ireland and Scotland that there were still societies with warrior leaders who continued to exercise patronage in a fully Celtic manner and context. Although the Celtic tradition here provides artistic continuity at a high level between the pre- and post-Roman periods, it does so as an outsider to the Roman provincial system. The headdress known as the 'Petrie Crown' and similar horns from Cork probably date to the Roman Iron Age, as does the enigmatic Monasterevan disc and others like it, which look like Celtic versions of *paterae* (hence the designation 'offering bowls' though nobody knows how they were used). In Scotland the virility of the Celtic tradition of art in the first and second centuries is demonstrated by the Stichill collar, from Roxburghshire, and by a number of massive enamelled armlets from various sites in north-east Scotland, such as those from Pitkelloney,

68 *Enamelled bronze penannular brooch from Bath. a brooch; b detail of terminals. D.6.5cm; each terminal L.1cm.* (Photos: Robert Wilkins, Institute of Archaeology, Oxford.)

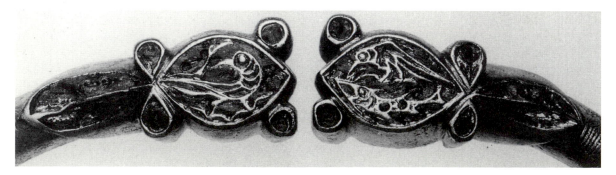

69 *Large bronze hanging bowl with enamelled fittings and central fish escutcheon from the ship burial at Sutton Hoo, Suffolk. D.29.8cm; depth 13.5cm.* (Photo: British Museum.)

Perthshire. The problem in the lands beyond Roman control is to document the tradition between this early Celtic art and Pictish metalwork of the sixth and seventh centuries, such as the enamelled silver plaques from the Norrie's Law hoard, Fife.[48]

While Classical art was dominant, enamelled objects were generally regarded as of relatively low status, as noted above, but after the disruption of Roman power in late antiquity, they appear to have assumed their old prestige in Celtic society, a prestige that may never have been lost in Ireland and Scotland. This is demonstrated above all by the splendid series of bronze hanging bowls with their enamelled escutcheons, the quintessential valuable of the British Dark Ages, not of Anglo-Saxon manufacture. The

greatest of them all, not surprisingly, comes from the Sutton Hoo ship burial (**69**). Despite possible, but tenuous, links with Roman hanging bowls made of silver, like that from Water Newton, and the employment of Classical motifs such as the *pelta* or, in one case, crosses flanked by dolphins, renewed contacts between Anglo-Saxons and Celts and the Mediterranean world in the sixth and seventh centuries must not be ignored either. There is assuredly Classicism here, but is it Romano-British, Roman or even early Byzantine? In any case such special objects do not belong to a surviving Roman culture of polite dinner-parties but to a tribal world re-established, whether Celtic or Anglo-Saxon, of warrior-feasts and epic tales sung around the hearth.[49]

CHAPTER SIX

Artists and their Patrons

Mine eye hath play'd the painter and hath stell'd
Thy beauty's form in table of my heart;
My body is the frame wherein 'tis held,
And perspective it is best painter's art.
For through the painter must you see his skill
To find where your true image pictur'd lies,
Which in my bosom's shop is hanging still,
That hath his windows glazed with thine eyes.

Most of the artists working in Britain are anonymous; at least they remain anonymous to us. It is important to remember that behind the creation of every work of art lay a transaction between the creator and the customer. That was as true of the enamelled fairing bought at a country market as it was of the architectural complex or a suite of mosaic floors for which the rich patron must have signed an elaborate and legally-binding contract. In the former case it was simply a matter of purchase; in the latter, however, precise instructions would have been given by the patron as to subject matter, size and materials, limited only by the availability of skill and stone, while the artist for his part needed to secure his fee. Where the contract was expensive or complicated, the artist was anything but an unknown background figure. This chapter will emphasize the fact that whatever else art history encompasses, it is above all concerned with human relationships. This is what archaeologists and historians mean, or should mean, when they describe their professions as bringing empathy with the people of antiquity.

Naturally, the written word adds a further dimension. A pitifully few signed works from Britain tell us a little about patronage in the province, but they are not widely informative about workshop practice. Thus

the relationship between the artist and his patron has to be explored, to a considerable extent, by examining the works of art themselves. Their architectural settings, whether in sanctuaries, public buildings in towns or even private dwellings, provide vital clues; so does comparative material from other provinces and ancient literary sources relating to art in general.[1]

As is often the case, in attempting to reconstruct the cultural climate of Roman Britain, we find a natural point of departure in Tacitus' all too brief description of the mechanics of romanization (*Agricola*, 21). This certainly leaves a great many questions unanswered, for the great historian is presenting an idealized sketch of a conscientious governor as a *topos*, not writing a government report, even if he had access to factual information denied to us. Of what did the 'private encouragement and public assistance' which Agricola provided as governor consist? Were any of the early public buildings (excluding military forts) commissioned by the State, or were they undertaken by private enterprise coupled with liberal support from the authorities, such as the use of surplus raw materials, from State holdings? Above all, were there any official inducements to encourage sculptors, mosaicists and painters to come to Britain from the Continent?

Frankly we do not know how most of the major

works of art were financed, although we have the evidence that the Temple of Divus Claudius at Colchester was voted by Decree of the Senate in AD 54, and certainly the priests, leading men chosen by the tribes to serve there, were obliged to be more generous than their finances permitted (Tacitus, *Ann.* xiv, 31).[2] The governor's palace in London is of Flavian date and it is probable that the similar, but rather better known, complex at Fishbourne was the official residence either of a client-king, Cogidubnus, or else of a major official in the province. In a sense these would have been State works, though discontent over the construction of the Temple of Claudius perhaps suggests that the funding even of such large projects was more local. Pliny the Younger, when he was governing Bithynia, asked Trajan for a surveyor, and although the appeal was refused we may presume that similar requests were sometimes successful (*Ep.* x, 17b, 18).

The three buildings mentioned would have been richly embellished with marble, and the two palaces had many mosaic floors. Doubtless there were Imperial statues in all three. Here was patronage on a large scale, undoubtedly patronage highly approved by the State, but nevertheless essentially private. Pliny (*Ep.* III, 4; IV, 1 and x, 8) gave a temple with many Imperial statues to Tifurnum, of which he was patron, and this must indicate the normal situation. Large-scale patronage relied on very wealthy private individuals, sometimes acting in concert as a corporation or guild and sometimes individually.[3] Britain never had the same wealth of patronage as some other provinces, for instance those of North Africa and the Gauls. It is significant, for example, how little marble statuary, sarcophagi or architectural elements were imported into Britain. Also, while many high-quality buildings south of York had mosaics, no mosaics are known in the Wall region, even though it might have been expected that there were sufficient people of consequence and culture, in the forts and at Corbridge and Carlisle, to have demanded the Roman equivalent of a 'regulation carpet' if such things had been in the gift of the government. Large-scale State involvement, as we understand it, would probably have ironed out differences and anomalies in supply but such involvement simply did not exist.

THE BEGINNINGS OF PATRONAGE IN ROMAN BRITAIN

From the first, artists had to be opportunists in finding employment, either from communities or individuals, as can be seen very clearly in the carving of first-century military tombstones. The soldier's need for art was largely confined to the provision of a memorial for himself, and perhaps also for religious dedications (see Chapter 3). Major concentrations of troops could support workshops although even they could not ensure quality and there is no direct indication as to whether the sculptors responsible for these were themselves serving soldiers (*immunes*), though probably, in most instances, not. The early exploitation of good-quality stone, however, implies military involvement in the extraction of raw materials and the production of monumental inscriptions recording legionary projects seems to confirm the existence of at least a few such specialists in the army. The wording of the tombstones says nothing of this directly, but is more informative about how grave-stele were financed — largely by money left in the deceased person's will, or a direct benefaction by his heirs. Does this explain their variable quality, well demonstrated by the contrast between two cavalry *stelae* from Cirencester — the accomplished tombstone of Genialis (**70**) and the much less skilled memorial of Dannicus (**71**)? To these can be added the tombstone of Rufus Sita at Gloucester which, in point of artistic quality, falls somewhere between them. Nothing in the rank of these three riders explains the discrepancy. Two explanations spring to mind, one or both of which may have been relevant. First, it is tempting simply to invoke market forces and put the differences down to the fact that the heir of Genialis was richer, or spent more on a better sculptor, than did the heirs of Rufus Sita or than did Fulvius Natalis and Flavius Bitucus in commemorating Dannicus. Secondly, it is well to remember that, unlike cheese, art cannot be had on demand. There were better sculptors available at one particular moment or place than at another, and the patron commissioning a tombstone could not simply wait for service, or travel to secure a more skilled artist.

It seems likely that, with regard to military tombstones, the craftsmen were often civilians, belonging outside the fort and the disciplines of military life, and thus in no way constrained to provide their

70 *Tombstone of Sextus Valerius Genialis from Cirencester. Limestone. H.2.1m. Corinium Museum. (Photo: The late M.B. Cookson, Institute of Archaeology, Oxford archive.)*

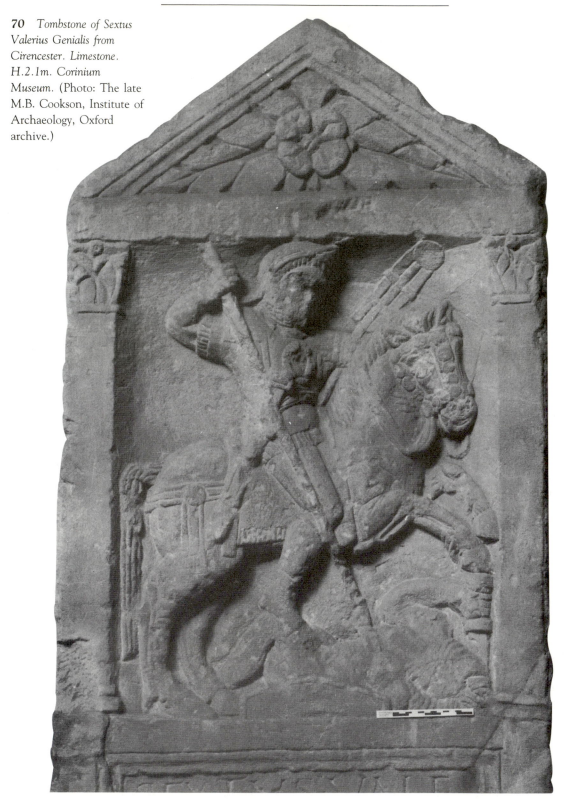

services; while the money for the tombstones is unlikely to have been provided simply as part of the compulsory burial club contributions. Admittedly Dannicus, with 16 years' service, would have paid in least, but Rufus Sita had paid for 22 years and got a monument that was only somewhat better, while Genialis, with his outstanding memorial, served only for 20 years. In Chapter 3 it was suggested that the Middle Empire tombstones from Chester were often inferior to those from other fortresses and the discrepancy was put down to Chester's relative remoteness from any town.[4]

If civilian artisans were involved in production from the beginning, commissions for army personnel would have led on to a wider range of contracts for people resident in the vicinity of forts, especially the *vicus* which often continued to thrive, eventually to become a town after the troops themselves had moved on to other postings. There is no direct proof that the sculptors of the early military tombstones were producing other kinds of work, though this is highly likely. The most that can be said is that it is probable that the stele of Philus, a Gaulish (Sequanian) civilian, discovered in the same cemetery as the memorial stones of Dannicus and Genialis, is nearly contemporary with them.[5] It is not possible to date the religious sculpture from Cirencester and Gloucester at all closely, although most surviving pieces probably date to the later civilian use of the sites; but judging from what we know of the religiosity of Roman soldiers the tradition surely goes back to the military phase when the Graeco-Roman deities and even the Celtic (but Rhenish) cult of the Matres were doubtless imported.

Sculpture workshops

One place in Britain, the spa of Aquae Sulis (Bath) certainly does provide evidence of early romanization and commissions, from soldiers and civilians, for both tombstones and religious sculpture. Here we can clearly appreciate how the wealth and patronage brought to the sanctuary by soldiers helped to promote civilian patronage too. Among military sculptures there is a tombstone of a cavalryman called Lucius Vitellius Tancinus who had served 26 years and, as far as can be seen from the damaged relief, had a stele rather similar in quality to that of Rufus Sita. A second cavalry *stele* is of slightly better

71 *Tombstone of Dannicus from Cirencester. Limestone. H.1.08m. Corinium Museum.* (Photo: The late M.B. Cookson, Institute of Archaeology, Oxford archive.)

72   *Relief of the three Matres from Ashcroft, Cirencester. Limestone. H.78cm. Corinium Museum.*
(Photo: The late M.B. Cookson, Institute of Archaeology, Oxford archive.)

craftsmanship, though only the upper part of the stone remains and the inscription is lost. Other military tombstones here are legionary and attest to the continuing interest of soldiers in the spa, as do a number of votive altars. Among civilian dedications to Sulis we may note those of two craftsmen. Priscus son of Toutius was a *lapidarius* (a stonemason or perhaps a sculptor, carving dedications and tombstones) from near Chartres. He exemplifies the Gallic influence seen, for instance, in the Neptune/Medusa pediment of the temple which, as mentioned in Chapter 5, has affinities with work in Gaul, specifically south-eastern Gaul rather than Priscus' own region.[6] Sulinus, son of Brucetus, who calls himself a *scultor*, is more interesting. He was presumably born at Bath as implied by his theophoric name, and we know that he sought his clientele over a fairly wide region as we have a dedication from the same man at Cirencester. In both inscriptions Sulinus venerates the Suleviae, who seem to have been mother goddesses (though perhaps the sculptor himself associated them with his patron goddess Sulis, who presided over his presumed birthplace and home). The altar from Ashcroft, Cirencester was found with two representations of the three mother goddesses as well as with a single Mater and a statue of Diana. They are clearly all by different hands and so it is not possible to say whether any one of them is by Sulinus himself. The cache, in fact, is suggestive of a shrine rather than a workshop. Nevertheless all the sculpture must have been carved at Corinium and, even if all the pieces fall short of Classical canons of modelling, several have qualities which show their creators to have been artists of no mean distinction. Perhaps the best is the relief shown here (**72**). The hair and especially the clothing of the three women have a graphic quality, effective in terms of two-dimensional design. There is no doubt that the image is a very powerful one, even if these goddesses lack the soft motherly appearance of some other Matres.

All the sculpture of any accomplishment in the Cotswold region will have depended on artists fully committed to their craft, not to part-time peasants, and their studios are likely to have been in the towns – Gloucester, Cirencester and Bath – in this respect the great sanctuary of Bath being regarded as urban. The very best work was correspondingly expensive and marks important patronage. The pedimental sculptures of the Temple of Sulis Minerva at Bath were surely ordered by someone of the highest standing in the province, such as King Cogidubnus, and the screen of the Four Seasons in the same sanctuary was possibly erected at the behest of a guild and certainly at some later period repaired and repainted at the expense of a guild member Claudius Ligur(ius?). A large *antefix* found north-east of Gloucester Cathedral, depicting a tragic mask backed by a honeysuckle palmette, is also of superb quality and must have adorned a major public building in the *colonia*, perhaps provided by members of the city council (*ordo*).[8] The Bath gate at Cirencester, with its niche containing the upper part of a well-modelled figure of Mercury, and the Bacchic figures of the well-known Jupiter Column are likewise candidates for having been provided by the public generosity of *curiales*, though we know that in the fourth century a Jupiter Column in Cirencester was restored by a governor of *Britannia Prima*.[9]

The fine-quality sculpture – the cult image and the altars – from the temple at Uley was almost certainly ordered from Cirencester workshops by patrons who had surplus cash to spend on benefactions. The cult image of Mercury is a measure of the high standard of skill available, and must have been given by an important patron of the sanctuary, possibly a landowner or the official in charge of what seems to have been an Imperial Estate at Kingscote, lying just below the ridge upon which the Uley temple stands. In one respect, however, the votive altars are even more informative in establishing a link with Cirencester, as they each have a relief of Mercury standing within niche like that on a relief depicting the god, from Corinium. One of the Uley altars bears an inscription, not very well preserved, which gives the name of the sculptor as Searigillus son of Searix, and that of the dedicator as Lovernius. These were Britons; Lovernius was perhaps a local peasant farmer making a good living out of his flocks – with the aid of Mercury. It is worth mentioning that there are other votive reliefs from the *colonia* at Gloucester depicting Mercury with a female consort, a different conception of the deity, implying the presence of a workshop here as well.[10]

Another Cotswold speciality consisted of altars depicting Mars, similarly esconced within a niche. These were mainly found around Stroud, notably at King's Stanley and at Bisley (**73**), but it is tempting to ascribe these to sculptors trained in Corinium because

73 *Altar with a relief of Mars from Bisley Common, Chalford, Gloucestershire. Limestone. H.59cm. Stroud District Museum.* (Photo: Robert Wilkins, Institute of Archaeology, Oxford.)

the general approach to composition, the *aediculae* and even the naturalistic manner of showing the deity recall the Mercury figures of Cirencester and Uley; they too are likely to have been dedicated by peasant farmers rather than by villa-owning gentry.[11] Some sculpture in the Cotswolds was far less skilled than this, for example some of the miniature altars and reliefs from Chedworth, Wycomb and Lower Slaughter, but these are surely the work of rustic craftsmen, perhaps even revealing the hands of the dedicators themselves, rather than of full-time professional sculptors. There is a stage at which art ceases to be a specialized activity and simply reflects the abilities of the ordinary countryman. Oolitic limestone is fairly soft and is quite easy for the lay hand to make some sort of impression on.[12]

Another distinctive school is to be found in the *colonia* of Lincoln and in the vicinity of the small town of Ancaster to its south. The votive reliefs of Vulcan from Keisby (**74**) and of another deity from nearby Wilsford show figures far more stiffly posed than the gods on the Cotswold altars and set in shallower niches. However, the Lincolnshire sculptors seem to have an excellent sense of composition and of line. This is also to be seen on the Stragglethorpe relief of a rider-god, perhaps Mars, spearing a monster. From Ancaster comes a group of Matres seated in a compact group, effectively in relief, with only their heads free of the surrounding stone matrix. The anatomy of the figures is fairly crude, but the patterning of the garments and hair is excellent. Two fragmentary reliefs, likewise from Ancaster, may also show mother-goddess groups.[13] A clue as to the sort of people who commissioned this sculpture is provided by an inscription, not well cut but evidently in a carved frame. It reads: DEO VIRIDIO TRENICO ARCUM FECIT DE SUO DONAVIT.

In other words Trenico commissioned an arch in honour of a local deity – the word *fecit* does not mean he erected it himself; though *de suo donavit* certainly implies that he paid for it.[14] Sheppard Frere has written of the Ancaster sculpture that 'though not of the highest art, the achievement certainly ranks far above the flat and often grotesque efforts of Romano-British sculptors in other parts of the limestone belt, and is one further indication of the strength of Roman influence emanating from the *colonia* of Lincoln'.[15] In fact that influence is to be seen even more strongly in the battered torso, likewise from Ancaster,

of a male figure wearing a mantle. It is not necessary to go along with Jocelyn Toynbee's suggestion that it was possibly the work of 'a Gaulish sculptor, working in the local medium'.[16]

Lincoln has recently yielded a group probably of Venus and Adonis (**75**). It is fascinating from the point of view of iconography, with its allusion to Classical mythology, but despite attractive patterning on Venus' gown and a brave attempt at rendering a male nude, this seems to be from the same school as the majority of the Ancaster sculptures.[17] It was clearly possible for those with money to commission better work, equalling the quality of the best that the Cotswold school could offer. Direct demonstration of this can be seen from a tombstone carved with two half-length figures. The woman (to the left) identified by her necklace is Volusia Faustina, wife of the decurion Aurelius Senecio. The man was presumably intended for Senecio, but the right-hand side of the panel has been taken over by a stranger, Claudius Catiotus, with a less well-cut inscription. This demonstrates that the normal patron–client relationship between creator and owner could be totally disrupted when a third party purloins the goods. This second- or third-century *stele* with its richly dressed subjects is a highly accomplished work.[18] It is surpassed, however, by the relief of boy holding a hare which recalls the naturalism of the art displayed on the rich funerary monuments in the Trier region.

It is possible, of course, that sculptors were attracted to important cities such as Lincoln from the Moselle valley. This is clearly a portrait of a young member of the curial class, as is a fragmentary relief showing a boy-charioteer, possibly part of an ambitious monument such as is, again, familiar from Belgica.[19] The top class of the colony also set up representations of deities. In Lincoln itself most notable is a high-relief figure of a city Tyche, her clothing a symphony of curves. On the sides is some rich, boldly vegetal ornament. The Ancaster torso to which reference has been made can be related to the Lincoln Tyche in terms of style, and demonstrates the fact that high-quality work was commissioned in an important city to be set some distance away from it, just as as the cult image of Mercury from Uley represents Corinian art outside Corinium.[20]

Another example of high art in a rural setting, but within the *territorium* of Lincoln, is implied by Q. Neratius Proxsimus' dedication of an arch at

74 *Relief of Vulcan from Keisby, Lincolnshire. Limestone. H.49cm, In Lenton church, near Grantham.* (Photo: The late M.B. Cookson, Institute of Archaeology, Oxford archive.)

Nettleham. The letters are cut in the best Roman style and the panel is flanked by *peltae*. It is probable that sculpture was associated with this arch. No greater contrast could be imagined than with Trenico's Ancaster arch found at the same time.[21] Of course there were various gradations between the rough but vigorous work of the countryside and the best urban work. Two mother-goddess groups from Lincoln demonstrate careful modelling and correct physiognomy on a comparatively modest scale. The more ornamental of the two shows the goddesses in fairly low relief in an *aedicula*, with a pediment embellished with leaf moulding and pilasters with Corinthian capitals at the side. We can follow Blagg in describing the sculptor as 'a competent worker in an established local tradition', though it is possible to go beyond it

75 *Relief of Venus and Adonis(?), Lincoln. Limestone. H.35cm.*
(Photo: Trust for Lincolnshire Archaeology.)

to note that the 'tradition' included workshops of degrees of skill, probably catering for people of different classes or at least of different degrees of wealth.[22]

Both the Cotswolds and the oolitic belt further north in Northamptonshire and Lincolnshire produced skilled stonemasons and sculptors whose work is to be seen in London too. The London Arch and the screen of gods, parts of which were found reused in the riverside wall of London, exemplify major commissions, but we also find individual sculptures such as the hunter-gods carved in the round (from Southwark and Bevis Marks) as well as in relief (Goldsmiths' Hall altar), Mercury (Moorgate) and the mother-goddesses (Riverside Wall) which are comparable in style as well as subject matter with statuary and reliefs from the limestone belt.[23] It may be possible in one or two cases to localize the connection; thus the hunter-god, leaving aside the London examples, is a specifically Cotswold-region phenomenon.[24] However, the London studios may well have recruited workers from different places. The sculptors responsible for major commissions will often have moved to their work because large monuments had of necessity, to be carved *in situ*; smaller, and theoretically more portable, pieces, will also have been carved away from the limestone hills because the patron, a citizen of London, could not travel many miles to a distant town every time he wanted to order an altar or a tombstone. In the case of the provincial capital, we are surely dealing with limestone-sculptors operating from *officinae* in the city and permanently resident, importing large blocks of stone from the upper Thames, making use of the river, or having them brought by wagon from the East Midlands.

Only the marble trade demanded the import of ready-made work (from the Mediterranean world), though the quantity of marble from London as from elsewhere in Britain is so low that it is clear this trade cannot have been very extensive. It is true that there are a number of carvings in marble from the Walbrook Mithraeum, though as far as the major pieces are concerned only the heads were of marble, the bodies being provided in some other material, presumably limestone. There are actually several Mithraic sculptures from this temple in oolitic limestone, clearly special commissions executed for the soldiers and merchants who patronized the shrine, and by no means the stock-in-trade of an itinerant Cotswold or Lincolnshire sculptor.[25] The only other

surviving images of an oriental deity depicted by such sculptors are two renderings of Attis, one in the round and the other in relief, from the *colonia* of Gloucester, another city where, as noted above, at least one group of Cotswold sculptors must have had an *officina*.[26]

All towns in Britain will have had monumental sculptors based within them. To take a final example from the north of the country, the Carlisle workshop has been the subject of special study by John Phillips. It seems to have been in operation during the second and third centuries and to have concentrated on the production of tombstones, the finest being the mother and child from Murrell Hill, Carlisle (see **37**) which has been dated to the second century. The most distinctive feature is a rich pattern of folds composing the dress of the two figures and the equally bold rendition of the fan held by the woman. Unfortunately there is no surviving inscription, but a tombstone of third-century date ascribed to the same school from Gallows Hill, Carlisle, which shows a woman wearing a Gallic gown, gives the name of the deceased as Aurelia Aureliana who died aged 41, and tells us that the stone was set up (and thus commissioned) by her husband Ulpius Apolinaris. Did he select the attribute held by his wife, here a bunch of poppies symbolizing death as a sleep, from the various possibilities on offer? A small girl, Vacia, shown on a stone from Lowther Street, Carlisle, holds a bunch of grapes, as does a woman on a *stele* from Bowness-on-Solway. This figure and the woman from Murrell Hill, Carlisle, both hold doves. A relief showing the god Mercury standing within an *aedicula* with striking barley-sugar columns is funerary, since not only was it found in a cemetery but it was ornamented with pine-cones in the surviving spandrel, as on Aurelia Aureliana's stone. However, the type and the style of the cutting matches that of Mercury on a Carlisle altar, which is more probably votive though here there is no *aedicula* nor any pine-cones. A more recent find of votive sculpture from Carlisle and attributable to the school is a fragmentary relief of Minerva with her owl shown perched on a column.[27]

In view of the rich drapery, similar in style to that of the Murrell Hill woman, I would attribute the fine statue of Fortuna from Birdoswald (see **28**) to the same Carlisle workshop. This figure was found in the commandant's bath-house and presumably he commissioned the piece in order to provide protection for himself and his family in a place where men and women, being naked, are vulnerable. The Carlisle workshop is not the only one that can be recognized in the region. As we saw in Chapter 3, there is some outstanding work from Housesteads (see **27**), though this is unusual for ordinary forts with their little *vici* outside them and may merely represent the temporary presence of a trained sculptor or two. The sculpture from most of the Wall forts, however, is admittedly of rather amateur standard. Only in Carlisle can we see sculptors regularly meeting the demands of Roman provincial society, in a way essentially no different from that prevailing in the south of the province.[28]

I know of only one instance of a foreign sculptor partly, at least, catering for an immigrant community and unfortunately only two tombstones from South Shields can be attributed to him with certainty. As stated in Chapter 5, he was certainly a Palmyrene because both *stelae* show many of the stylistic traits typical of the Palmyrene school, though the subjects have been adapted to the conventional form of the western gravestone. One of them was actually commissioned by a fellow Palmyrene called Barates, and shows his wife, a Catuvellaunian freedwoman called Regina, seated frontally within a very ornate architectural setting, so popular in the Eastern provinces (see **38**). The stone carries a short inscription in Palmyrene Aramaic as well as one in Latin, and is certainly an example of members of national communities staying together and patronizing each other. But there cannot have been many Palmyrenes at South Shields and the sculptor clearly had commissions from others. We have the *stele* of a Moorish freedman of a trooper of the first *ala* of Asturians, reclining on a couch and partaking of a banquet. In detail, the type comes from the Palmyrene repertory although the funerary banquet was a popular subject throughout the Empire. In addition a statue of Juno Regina from Chesters (see **67**) looks, from the form and patterning of the drapery, to be the work of a Syrian, though not necessarily the same man as the author of the South Shields gravestones. Here the high quality of the image and the subject matter may suggest a sculptor in the entourage of Julia Domna, at the end of the first decade of the third century.[29]

Lucian of Samosata wrote a lecture or story (*Somnium sive Vita Luciani*) contrasting *techne* (craft) with *paideia* (culture). As Lucian came from a family of sculptors on his mother's side, sculpture represents craft in this lecture and offers Lucian the respect of the local community and even fame if he is lucky. The representative of culture, however, points out that he will only be an ordinary workman if he follows this trade and at the mercy of his superiors. Fame will pass him by and he will be quite unknown. We do know of famous sculptors in the Roman period, such as Zenodoros who lived in the reign of Nero and was commissioned by the Arverni to cast a colossal bronze statue of Mercury for them, at the fantastic cost of forty million sesterces (Pliny, *NH* xxxiv, 45), but essentially Lucian is right.

The best examples of cast-bronze heads from Britain, both double life-size – the gilded head of Minerva at Bath and the head of Hadrian from London (see **35**) – are anonymous though the latter in particular, with its distinctive, celticized hair and powerfully expressive face, might be considered as the product of a sculptor, possibly a Briton, whose name deserves to have come down to us.[30] However, Imperial portraits were adapted to order from copies sent out from Rome to every province in the Empire. This one, gracing the bridge or some public building (the *forum* or basilica?) and perhaps marking Hadrian's presence in Britain, is likely to have had an accompanying inscription naming the donor and giving the Emperor's official titulature. The Bath statue probably stood on a plinth in the *cella* of the temple, again with an inscription naming the donor (who may have been a very important person in the province especially if this masterpiece is, indeed, the cult image as we believe). The identity of the actual creator was not of much account in either case and it is most unlikely that the names of the sculptors were recorded (but see below for a few small bronzes bearing the names of smiths).

Another complete but smaller head, of the Emperor Claudius, was found in the river Alde in Suffolk, and probably represents Boudican loot from Colchester. While it is tempting to associate it with the Temple of Divus Claudius this should probably be resisted. If it came from a standing figure the statue would have been comparatively modest but it could have come from an equestrian figure, in which case it would have been a fairly prominent and important image. Incidentally, another piece of Boudican spoil, a horse's hock from Ashill, Norfolk, has a similar analysis.

Other fragments of what are probably Imperial

images, including equestrian statues, are known from elsewhere in Britain, including the *coloniae* of Gloucester and Lincoln, as well as the great cities of Cirencester and London, further emphasizing the probability of large-scale casting in the province. In addition there would have been bronzes of deities, not only in temples like the Bath Minerva, but standing in public places like the statue of Jupiter from the basilica at Silchester of which only his eagle remains, now wingless but still attractive thanks to the artist's ability in rendering plumage.[31] There is no major surviving bronze sculpture commissioned by a tribe or community, though doubtless the Silchester Jupiter – with his eagle – came into that class. There are other fragments from Silchester and Cirencester, both from major figures of emperors and a stone base from an Imperial statue at Wroxeter. In addition there is the pedestal of the statue set up by the *ordo* of the canton of the Silures at Caerwent to their patron, Tiberius Claudius Paulinus (see **36**). Both served the same purpose, to elevate an honorific statue above the level of the onlooker.[32]

Two splendid specimens of inscriptions recording the completion of *fora* commissioned by *civitates* survive; one is the Domitianic dedication from Verulamium, set up in Agricola's governorship, for the Catuvellauni, and the other the Hadrianic dedication from Wroxeter for the Cornovii (see **34**).[33] Robert Ireland has rightly written: 'The inscription is a fact of Roman civilization; and at its best, its masters raised it to the level of the highest and most exacting art.'[34] Epigraphy 'at its best' certainly includes the *forum* inscription of Wroxeter which was carved in the local sandstone and is thus not an import, even though the *lapidarius* may have came from the Mediterranean world (and could have been chiefly in the employ of *Legio XX* at Chester, not far to the north). His identity, as opposed to those who commissioned his work, was naturally regarded as being of no account to posterity.

INTERIOR DECORATION

Wall-painting

Among the other arts of Roman Britain, wall-painting should take pride of place, for it was ubiquitous and must have been thoroughly familiar to the romanized inhabitants of Britain. Almost everyone

who could afford a votive relief or a tombstone will have employed a house-painter at some time in his life. Indeed, if we follow Trimalchio, his contemporaries thought far more about lavishly embellishing their houses than their tombs, in which they would reside for far longer. Even where designs were simple the skills involved were considerably above those which we would expect from an interior decorator today. Roger Ling points out that painting was far more widespread than mosaic, and there must have been workshops in every town throughout Roman times. The main factor inhibiting study of schools is the fragmentary nature of the bulk of the remains.[35]

What the patron required was something that would turn the bare wall into a setting that would express status, often a status higher than the owner actually had, but to which he aspired. Thus we find reminiscences of the 'Pompeian First (masonry) Style' in second-century Verulamium. The use of slabs of exotic marble as well as veneers of shaped and cut stone (*opus sectile*) is associated with Hellenistic luxury but it continued in the houses of the very wealthy under the Empire and examples have even been found in Britain, at Fishbourne.[36] The opening out of the wall, often accompanied by a rich architectural framework, associated with the Second Style, is likewise an evocation of palace architecture. Examples are still to be seen in the *in situ* paintings of the Dover Painted House and most magnificently in a second-century building at Southwark.[37] A painting in a house at Leicester presents the illusion of a projecting podium but this is combined with delicate, linear ornament in the manner of the Pompeian Fourth Style, more artificial and playful but equally luxurious (**colour plate I**).[38] The eclecticism of wall-painting in the second and third centuries is not confined to Britain but is a feature of Middle-Empire fresco elsewhere in the Empire, for instance at Ostia.[39] Wall-painting seems to have been more conservative in its style than mosaic (see below) and sculpture, and it is possible that the same conditions applied in Roman Britain as in eighteenth-century England when Swiss Italians were predominant in plasterwork. It would be interesting to know to what extent, if at all, Continental painters were employed in, or even monopolized, the workshops set up in British cities.

Figural subjects will have been chosen by the clients. A small panel containing a gladiatorial fight is set in the midst of a post-Boudican Third Style schema on the wall of a room in a house at Colchester. Roger Ling rightly comments that 'it is unlikely that a house-owner would have commissioned a wall-decoration involving gladiatorial scenes unless he had some personal familiarity with, or enthusiasm for, the entertainments of the amphitheatre'. A gladiatorial scene formed the central *emblema* of a late first-century mosaic from the *frigidarium* of the villa at Eccles, Kent, which significantly was destroyed in Roman times and has been reconstructed from loose debris. The subject represents a mass entertainment whose popularity is also attested on glassware and pottery, most notably from the *colonia* of Colchester. The absence to date of major gladiatorial compositions in wall-painting and mosaic (see below) suggests that the theme did not appeal greatly to the British gentry.[40] Much more well-attested, and an obvious choice in the context, are the aquatic decorations of swimming cupids, fish etc. in villa bath-houses, including the Fishbourne protopalace, Sparsholt, Hampshire, Lullingstone, Kent, Winterton, Lincolnshire, and Southwell, Nottinghamshire.[41]

Other choices show the owner displaying culture or, at least cultural pretensions. Such was the Vergilian scene which graced a wall of the villa at Otford, Kent, probably painted as early as the late first or early second century. An inscription in bold rustic capitals, BINA MANV L[*ato crispans hastilia ferro*], alongside the figure-scene, could suggest that the villa owner produced the copy from his own library to illustrate either Aeneas at Carthage (*Aeneid* i, 313) or Turnus' final fight with Aeneas (xii, 165). Was the book, presumably a scroll, itself an illuminated one? There is clear evidence for such manuscripts in late antiquity (see Chapter 7).[42] Another instance of a programme, here applied to paintings in several rooms and including both figures and still-life, is to be found in the 'Painted House' at Dover dated to *c.* AD 200. The paintings refer to Bacchus who, as Brian Philp points out in his report, had a universal appeal: 'The very strong Bacchic theme would have been recognized and appreciated by both occupants and visitors and this must have been a deliberate conception agreed and planned in advance.'[43]

Two other mythological scenes, both dating to the fourth century, are of excellent quality but to some degree less personalized and both might well have originated in the repertory of their respective workshops. It is a fair assumption that there was a constant demand for amorous and erotic scenes among villa-owners, and both scenes are fairly well-known episodes. The painting from Tarrant Hinton, Dorset, evidently shows Narcissus looking down at his own reflection (**colour plate IV**). The very high quality of the work, reminiscent in the facial modelling and the deeply shadowed eyes of the ceiling paintings from the Imperial palace at Trier, could suggest a decorator from Gaul with a good supply of sketches taken from well-known masterpieces which he could use or embellish to the taste of his client.[44] The same is true of the painting from a building at Kingscote, Gloucestershire. Here the mythological episode, first identified as Achilles on Skyros, is more likely to be a simple love scene as the cupid between the two protagonists implies. The affair depicted is probably that of Mars and Venus; the figure seated on the ground in that case is Venus with Mars' shield. It is of the greatest interest that the mosaic floor of the room figures a bust of Venus. The patron had not just commissioned random decoration for his chief room but had attempted to get both wall and floor to express amorous themes. As the building here is no ordinary villa but probably the centre of an Imperial estate, it seems to give us a very human view of the civil servant off duty.[45]

Finally religious patronage is likely to have required special commissions. The villa at Lullingstone has yielded a little painted niche depicting nymphs, dated to the second century. The motivation here was clearly similar to that of the villa owner who commissioned a votive altar or a relief to be set up at or near his house. Such paintings were surely quite common in houses. It would be interesting to know whether the well-known painting of Priapus, at the entrance to the House of the Vettii, had counterparts in Britain. Temples too would have been painted. A geometric scheme was noted at Nettleton, Wiltshire, though, despite the excavator's attempts to ascribe a Christian significance to it, it was probably simply geometric. It is a pity that there are no painted *mithraea* in Britain, and we can only speculate that the Walbrook *Mithraeum* could have been as splendidly painted as that at Capua. The fourth-century house church at Lullingstone, Kent, with its rows of *orantes*, probable biblical scenes and chi-rhos was surely decorated as an aid to worship. It bears comparison with painting in the Roman catacombs. It is possible that the artist was a member of the congregation who worshipped there, but whether this was so or not, as always the scheme was one over which the patron had ultimate control. It should be emphasized that the literary or religious interests were always those of the patron rather than of the artist.[46]

Mosaics

Despite many losses over the centuries, mosaics have survived better than wall-paintings, often in a complete or near-complete state. Those from Britain have been the subject of considerable study by David Smith and others, with especial attention being given to identifying individual schools of mosaicists.[47] As a result they now provide some of the best evidence for the existence of craft workshops in the province. Moreover, they are remarkably revealing as to the power of patronage. This is despite the relative paucity of epigraphic evidence within them. In fact only a single mosaicist is known to us by name, from an inscription on a floor at Bignor, TER(*entius*) – or perhaps Tertius or Tertullus – and the signature looks too modest to be that of the master-mosaicist.[48] Unfortunately there is no floor in Britain like that from Lillebonne, which was signed by a master mosaicist, Titus Sennius Felix from Puteoli, together with his assistant (*discipulus*), by name of Amor whose position in the workshop was possibly analogous with that of Terentius at Bignor.[49] The Lillebonne inscription is a reminder that master mosaicists could have travelled from the Mediterranean area. Although the Lillebonne mosaic is not related in style to floors from Britain, the subject matter combining mythology (the myth of Apollo and Daphne) and hunting scenes was designed, like so many of the mosaics of late Roman Britain (for example floors from East Coker, Somerset, and Frampton, Dorset), to appeal to the culture of the romanized gentry.

As for villa owners named on mosaics as commissioning floors, there is only the prominent inscription surviving in a panel on the upper border of a mosaic from Thruxton, Hampshire, reading QUINTUS NATALIUS NATALINUS ET BODENI. Below it is a representation of Bacchus with his panther, and there was once another line of inscription under this (**colour plate XIV**). The legend introduces us to a country landowner with typically Romano-Celtic *nomen* and manufactured *cognomen* and two other, related people who could well have been his clients and were

perhaps tenants on the estate; a reasonable conjecture is that all were members of a private pagan group, certainly so if the inscription continues as I have surmised '*promiserunt ex voto*' (see Chapter 7). The very large lettering renders it virtually impossible that they made the pavement except in the sense that the patron was regarded, ultimately, as the creator, the 'onlie begetter' of a work of art. The mosaic from the *cella* of the temple of Nodens at Lydney is interesting as an example of what appears to be a late Roman mosaic in a public pagan building. The only real difference between the commission here and that of Thruxton is the source of the commissioning patron's funds. The mosaic was laid '*ex stipibus*' (from offerings) under the general control of Titus Flavius Senilis who was in charge of religious rites at the site, with Victorinus the dream-interpreter taking detailed care of the work. It may be assumed that when most mosaics were laid the patron would have kept away from the dust and noise, leaving his steward to pay the workman and make sure that the job was done to his satisfaction.[50]

The reasons for choosing specific themes for floor-mosaics would have been as various as those conditioning the choice of wall-paintings. The display element was always important; a mosaic was much more expensive to lay than was the frescoing of a wall and consequently it made a bolder statement of the owner's wealth and influence. Most mosaics are simply geometric but many, especially in the fourth century, carry figure scenes. Two mosaics, at Lullingstone and the anomalous villa-cum-cult-house at Frampton, actually include samples of home-produced Latin verse which confirm the learning (or at least the pretension to possess it) of the owners of these 'villas'.[51] To them may be added a fragmentary floor of a late third-century town house at Aldborough, Yorkshire, depicting the Muses, with the Greek name ΕΛΗΚΩΝ (Helicon), remaining beside one of them, another display of higher culture.[52]

A rather refined and literary aspect can be seen on other British mosaics, especially in the fourth century (Chapter 7), expressed in purely visual terms. Most notably this occurs in an example from Low Ham, Somerset, with scenes of Dido and Aeneas (**colour plates IX** and **X**), reflecting a manuscript tradition close to – but different from – the *Vergilius Romanus* in the Vatican (**76** and see **92**), and probably derived from the villa owner's own copy of

Vergil.[53] I argue that religious and philosophical ideas also have a place in a number of mosaics, for instance in the Orpheus pavements, especially the example rediscovered at Littlecote, and in the richly iconographic complexes of Frampton and Brading, though this has not been appreciated by every critic.[54] The Hinton St Mary pavement with its clean-shaven male bust set against a chi-rho (see **85**) is a good candidate for a Christian mosaic, though scholars continue to be troubled as to why the patron chose to juxtapose this with a scene from pagan myth, Bellerophon slaying the chimaera. It just might represent local Christian heterodoxy for a chi-rho also occurs in mosaic at Frampton associated with a veritable gallery of pagan myths.[55]

What is not found in British mosaics, strangely enough, is much reflection of popular culture. In North Africa and Germany a great many fine examples of gladiatorial scenes and beast-fights on mosaics can be seen but the upper classes of Britain seem to have eschewed the theme. The first-century gladiatorial mosaic from the villa at Eccles, Kent, had been deliberately smashed, just as a modern house-owner might take a sledgehammer to a garish 1950s' tiled fireplace. A mosaic from Rudston, now regarded as dating from the later third century, is another exception which proves the rule. It was made by very unskilled (local?) mosaicists but appears to follow North African tradition. The central subject is Venus and she is surrounded by *bestiarii* and circus-animals including two labelled as LEO FRAMMEFER and TAURUS OMICIDA. Here neither theme nor latinity have anything in common with the tastes in mosaic of most British villa owners, to judge from their pavements. Where gladiatorial themes occur, at Bignor and Brading, for example, they seem to symbolize the pains and pitfalls of life. Chariot-racing may have had a higher social cachet, but even here, at both Horkstow and Rudston, the context seems to show that they were meant more symbolically than as simply expressions of an interest in sport.[56]

The history of mosaics in Roman Britain with regard to character and organization can be reconstructed much better than it can for fresco painting, falling into four phases of differing importance: pre-Hadrianic; Hadrianic–Severan; third century; and fourth century. Each period has a different character with regard to the organization of the craft and patronage.

In the first century mosaics are very rare, as noted in Chapter 2. The most important remains are the geometric floors at the Roman palace of Fishbourne (**colour plate V**) which were probably laid by a team of craftsmen especially recruited in Gaul or Italy. Such special commissions would have been beyond the resources of the private citizen to initiate but Fishbourne, as we have seen, is likely to have been the home of the client-king Tiberius Claudius Cogidubnus who could call upon the 'private encouragement and official assistance' of the governor. There were certainly traces of similar mosaics in the governor's own palace in London but the lack of survival precludes comparison. In addition, private houses at Watling Court, London, had early mosaics, again suggesting the presence of 'Italian mosaicists, if not also Italian clients'. We also find mosaics in the bath-houses of legionary fortresses, notably at Exeter and Caerleon, both belonging to *Legio II Augusta*. Somewhat later, possibly even second century, are the few mosaics (of curiously low quality) from the Chester fortress, probably associated with *Legio XX Valeria Victrix*. Mention has already been made of sculptors following the army, if not serving in it, and it is not surprising to find a few mosaicists in the entourage of the legions, though this does not seem to have had any effect on the civil population (which was backward and poor) nor to have created schools. The craft remained entirely imported.[57]

It was only in the middle of the second century that the laying of mosaics became widespread with the establishment of urban workshops. David Smith has proposed the existence of schools both at this time and later. These are very convenient and basically his groupings work, but it is necessary to consider what exactly is meant. Evidence for craft organization is entirely derived from the works themselves, which probably represent a very small percentage of total output. Many mosaics have been destroyed without (or with very little) record and others are constantly being discovered. There can be no reliable means of establishing total numbers either of mosaics or of mosaic-workers. Fortunately, mosaics are large and fairly complex and where they survive well allow detailed comparison to be made.

Clearly where two mosaics show exactly the same nuances of style, pattern, subject and choice of colour, we may suspect the same mosaicists to be involved and we can write of a workshop. Theoretically, a large urban workshop could have employed several working groups, but it is just as likely that these were independent, in other words that the mosaicists were small men, though perhaps linked to each other through membership of the same guild. We are thus concerned with a local style, similar to the persistence over time of a Cotswold or a Carlisle style of sculpture. The term 'school' may, indeed be appropriate but we must not be surprised to find mosaicists from different schools combining together, for example the Durnovarian school adopting features from Corinium, or influencing mosaic art in Yorkshire and north Lincolnshire.[58]

In the second century, distinctive mosaic schemes are found in eastern England, often based on a lozenge pattern or on a series of nine rectangular panels. The best mosaic at Colchester, the Middleborough pavement (**colour plate VII**), evidently dates from about AD 150–75. The subject of its central panel is two wrestling cupids (or the contest of Eros and Anteros) with a lunette containing a sea-beast set at a tangent to each side; around this composition is a rich scroll. The mosaicists seem to have used a multiple of $2\frac{1}{2}$ Roman feet to lay the floor. The same general design is to be seen on a mosaic at Verulamium, with a central design of a lion with a stag's head in its jaws (**colour plate VIII**); here the lunettes do not contain figural motifs nor is there a surrounding scroll. David Smith has suggested a Camulodunum–Verulamium workshop, with the higher quality of the Middleborough mosaic pointing to its origin in Colchester. However, it may be easier, as suggested above, to see at least two distinct workshops, with certain shared designs. Perhaps the original workshop was at Colchester and a pupil set up on his own account at Verulamium. As an alternative scenario, we could posit a rich businessman (a Romano-British Trimalchio) setting up branches in at least two cities, through slaves or freedmen.[59] The farming out of labour was a very general practice in Roman times and an example will be given below in the case of a goldsmith's shop at Malton.

To the west, for instance at Cirencester and Leicester, contiguous octagons are the predominant theme used in composition. Many of the mosaics from Silchester seem to belong to that tradition too, though not all.[60] Presumably there were contacts between artists at one centre and those at another – personal as well as business links which are now lost to us.

Among other places, London had at least one workshop, as the Bucklersbury pavement and those from Leadenhall Street proclaim, and there was also an early workshop at Aldborough (Isurium Brigantium) in Yorkshire.[61] Mosaics of this date are also recorded from Chichester and Fishbourne, where the dolpin mosaic shows a more accomplished craftsman producing the sea-beasts in the side lunettes than the 'master-mosaicist' who surely laid the central cupid-on-a-dolphin (**colour plate VI**); it hardly seems likely that the most important part of a floor would be left to an apprentice.[62]

At least a few other country-house owners had mosaics laid, though the mosaicists responsible will have come from nearby towns. Verulamium mosaicists seem to have worked at Boxmoor, High Wycombe and, surprisingly, far to the west at North Leigh, Oxfordshire. Indeed a mosaic of high quality, with a design of lozenges and L-shapes has been excavated at Boughspring villa near Tidenham, not far from the Wye. It 'has affinities with pavements from Colchester, Boxmoor and Silchester' and 'might suggest craftsmen moving west'. The nearest second-century villa with a mosaic is Great Witcombe, Gloucestershire, whose floor seems to be the work of the western (Cirencester?) workshop.[63]

Individual mosaicists and workshops probably devised their own patterns, an ability easily mastered with some knowledge of simple geometry and a capacity to use a traditional grammar of ornament. David Neal has convincingly demonstrated how a craftsman set about creating such all-over carpet designs.[64] There were relatively few figured subjects at this time and these are mainly fairly traditional and uncomplicated. The most ambitious is a mosaic at Cirencester depicting the seasons and mythological scenes including the death of Actaeon, torn to pieces by his own hounds because he had seen the goddess Diana naked. We may see here, in the use of Classical mythology, a pretension to culture (as is so much commoner in the fourth century). Perhaps also visible is a morbid concern with death, so much the vogue in the private art of the early Empire that it was mercilessly ridiculed by Petronius; it may have been copied from a stock rendering of the well-known episode, preserved in portable form by either the workshop or the patron.[65] As mentioned above, one of the best Verulamium floors shows a lion with the head of a stag in its jaws. This certainly does represent the devouring jaws of death, and it hardly seems appropriate for a dining-room floor until we remember the cloying morbidity of Trimalchio's dinner party at which silver skeletons were passed around and the host discusses details of his tomb with his architect. Mosaic workshops, like monumental masons, must have been prepared to indulge the whims of their clients.

Mosaics were expensive to make and it is not surprising that the inflationary and recessionary difficulties of the third century closed down the workshops providing what was, after all, a luxury service. A very few, mainly low-quality, floors of the third century can probably be explained as the work of 'jobbing masons employed to repair existing mosaics and perhaps occasionally to try their hand at new ones'. Most are not very ambitious though a geometric and isometric floor at Rapsley, Surrey, is fairly effective. Occasionally, speculative artists may have attempted something more ambitious, such as the Rudston 'Venus' pavement or the early 'Gorgon and seasons' floor at Bignor. The results are hardly inspiring but can hardly be the work of amateurs because the skill needed to cut and lay *tesserae* to make patterns and pictures even of this standard was considerable. The idiosyncracies of the Rudston Venus pavement are peculiar and markedly non-Classical, but nevertheless the pavement seems to be based on a North African design. Its theme is largely concerned with the *venationes*, even though it appears to depend on a simple reminiscence of its prototype rather than on an accurate drawing. Although it cannot be attributed to a school, we should be on the look out for other mosaics laid by the same men. It is just possible that the childlike draughtsmanship of the wolf and twins mosaic from Aldborough, which is similarly more ambitious in iconography than technique and execution, was laid by the same studio.[66] The main problem in reviving the craft lay in lack of patrons rather than lack of skill, but the Constantinian renaissance brought in both.

According to David Smith, schools of mosaicists were once again established in Britain in the fourth century. His thesis has, in general, stood the test of time, though modifications are constantly being suggested. Clearly the relationships between teams of mosaicists, their influence upon each other and the probable movement of individual practitioners of the craft introduces complications which we are unlikely

to unravel. An account of the subject matter of the pavements is included in Chapter 7 and the following paragraphs serve only to illuminate the operation of mosaicists during this period. There seems to have been a marked shift away from the south-east to western Britain as well as north to Yorkshire and Lincolnshire; a majority of mosaics were laid where the wealth now was, that is in the villas of these regions (though there are a number of pavements in the often luxurious town-houses). Dr Smith accepts six schools in operation during the century based on Cirencester (Corinium) where there were two schools, Dorchester, Dorset (Durnovaria), Water Newton (Durobrivae) and Brough on Humber (Petuaria); Finally, as proposed by David Johnston, there is a Central-Southern school which could have originated in Winchester, Chichester or even Silchester. Martin Millett has argued that the Durobrivan school was more probably centred on Leicester, while Aldborough (Isurium Brigantium) seems a better guess than Brough for the school in the north-east. An offshoot of the Durnovarian school has been postulated at Ilchester (Lindinis) in Somerset by Peter Johnson, and this may also have operated in the area of the Corinian schools after they had ceased to exist, Perhaps there was some sort of merger here. Conversely, Stephen Cosh has suggested that a little earlier in the century mosaics attributed to the Corinian Saltire *officina* in Somerset and Dorset, for example at Hurcot, Halstock, Lufton and Ilchester itself, were in fact laid by a 'branch' of the Corinian workshop; if so we have no way of telling whether the enterprises were linked as a business venture or remained financially independent.[67]

It is important to try to understand what these schools and workshops, postulated mainly on aesthetic grounds, may have involved for individual mosaicists. Not all were necessarily the same sort of enterprise. At the minimalist extreme a school could have been the firm of a single entrepreneur, employing one or more working teams. On the other hand a school might have represented a number of independent masters linked by common membership of a craft-guild. It is very possible that a mosaicist apprenticed in a major studio at Dorchester (Durnovaria) would have set up his own independent business; yet because of his early training his work might continue to be classified as Durnovarian. Some such event might have created the Ilchester (Lindinis) 'school'.

It is only when significant differences occur that we can proclaim the existence of a new school with any confidence. The mosaics of the two Corinian schools can probably be attributed to one or two entrepreneurs while others, the Central Southern school, the Durnovarian school and the Petuarian school, may be surmised in each case as representing several workshops linked by a common tradition. The patron presumably ordered his mosaic at the nearest workshop, though it is not unlikely that there were offices at other centres (such as Gloucester for the Corinian schools). However, the patron wishing to have a new floor laid at some future time might have found that his previous supplier had ceased trading and in such an instance had to go elsewhere. This presumably explains the 'Durnovarian' additions to a Corinian Orpheus panel at the villa of Withington, Gloucestershire.[68]

The major mosaics of Bignor, attributed to the Central Southern school, are close to the mainstream mosaic tradition of Gaul which continued through the third century. It is of approximately the same date as the Lillebonne floor mentioned above, that is the very beginning of the fourth century. The magnificent bust of Venus with its frieze of cupids as gladiators below (**colour plate XII**) and the apotheosis of Ganymede mark the beginning of a new mosaic tradition imported from Gaul at this time. The school has other figured floors ascribed to it, for instance the Hercules and Antaeus floor at Bramdean, Hampshire, but many of the floors are geometric, often employing intersecting squares. A key motif is a tulip-like flower, sometimes used for a *cantharus*.[69]

The output of all six fourth-century schools does indeed suggest the limits of patronage. The villa-owner in Gloucestershire, perhaps the wealthiest area in Britain, was lucky in that mosaics were available for much of the fourth century. Nevertheless the patron's choice was limited by the skills of the mosaicists available at the time. The two Corinian schools, the 'Orpheus school' dated by Smith *c*.300–*c*.320 and the 'Saltire school', *c*.320–*c*.340/50, seem to represent two distinct enterprises in the same city without shared repertoire and, apparently, operating in successive periods; however, notionally they might represent no more than a change of designer/master mosaicist in the same business. The Corinium Orpheus school had a figural repertoire of Dionysiac themes which are conventional in iconography, if not in execution. In

addition there was the theme which gives its name to the school: the setting of Orpheus in a frame of concentric circles was a brilliant answer to the question of how that myth should best be presented in philosophical terms (see **91** and **106**). It was surely not devised by the mosaicists themselves, but perhaps by a patron of advanced neo-platonic tastes, possibly even the owner of the great Woodchester villa, where the scheme is executed with rare brilliancy despite a few minor flaws in execution. If so, we see how an important patron might influence art.

The subject clearly became popular in the area, probably less because every villa-owner was a philosopher than because 'Orpheus' was seen as the type of a local, highly revered, hunter-god widely attested in Cotswold sculpture. The Corinian schools both produced some striking geometric designs which can be recognized quite far afield – indeed the work of a mosaicist of the Orpheus school has been recognized at Trier, the Imperial capital. Mosaics of the Saltire school, distinguished as its name suggests by its frequent use of saltire crosses although interlocking squares were also highly favoured, were laid as far east as Silchester and London, typical Saltire mosaics were also laid at Halstock in Dorset to the south. It seldom used figural subjects and then rather timidly and at a small scale as central *emblemata* – Bacchus on a panther at Gloucester and probably at London, – but the masterpiece here is surely the hare mosaic from Beeches Road, Cirencester.[70]

With the advent of Durnovarian mosaicists in the area a wider figural repertoire became available once more. It is true that the Central Southern mosaicists were both competent and adaptable, but their work was only available in the Sussex and Hampshire region and did not continue after about 325. In the south-west there was no workshop until the Durnovarian mosaicists began at about this time or a little later, though they came to comprise by far the most interesting school with regard to iconography in the whole of Britain. They appear to have made a speciality of highly idiosyncratic scenes taken from the patron's prized manuscripts (Vergil or Ovid at Low Ham and Frampton) or interpreting esoteric religious beliefs (Christian or Orphic at Hinton St Mary and Littlecote), as well as having a wide repertoire of animals, hunt scenes and sea-creatures, brilliantly illuminating the culture of the age of Constantius II, Julian and Valentinian (see Chapter 7).

The Durnovarian school can at the very least be divided into two traditions. One was represented by such works as the Hinton St Mary (see **85**) and Frampton mosaics (**colour plate XI**), which were certainly the work of the same mosaic team and characterized by rather fleshy figures, animals and plants (including plant scrolls). In the other I would include floors from Low Ham, Somerset (sometimes ascribed to Ilchester) (**colour plates IX** and **X**), Littlecote, Wiltshire, Croughton, Northamptonshire and Lullingstone, Kent (see **77**) all with lither, elongated animals, sparer human figures and less luxuriant vegetation. In this regard it is instructive to compare the four Bellerophon pavements, those from Hinton St Mary and Frampton on the one hand and Croughton and Lullingstone on the other. If I am right, the later phases of the Durnovarian tradition spreads far beyond the core area of the school as far as Kent and the south Midlands. Also of interest is the way in which the Littlecote mosaic adapts the Corinian Orpheus mosaic, and there are several mosaics in Gloucestershire, for instance those at Kingscote and Lydney belonging to a late Durnovarian tradition.[71]

In the north-east, as discussed, the Petuarian school likewise pursued a catholic repertoire through the middle years of the fourth century. The range included a wide range of mythological themes, including at Horkstow an amazing recreation of a painted vault on a floor with figures from the land and sea *thiasoi* (**colour plate XIII**) and above all concentric, segmental Orpheus pavements, influenced by but certainly not copied from from the earlier Corinian and contemporary Durnovarian schools. The Durobrivan workshop in the East Midlands, however, only produced mosaics after the middle of the fourth century, and though its mosaicists had a splendid appreciation of design (**colour plates XV** and **XVI**) and represent a distinct tradition, with its own discrete pattern-books, they never attempted figural compositions.

The problem of supply and demand, not unfamiliar in the twentieth century, and so graphically shown by the history of mosaics, affected the whole Roman period not just the fourth century. From the first century when mosaicists were only lured across the Channel by large building projects in London, Fishbourne and presumably elsewhere, the would-be patron had to live in the right place at the right time to get the floor he wanted. There were no mosaics much north of York, though the commanders of forts and officials and administrators at Carlisle, for instance, or Corbridge were certainly in the right social class and a few of them must have longed for mosaic floors; most could have afforded them had there been a convenient workshop. There was simply too small a clientele to allow an enterprise to be set up and subsequently to flourish.

The *officinae* established in Britain subsequent to the time of Hadrian's visit in 122 (though whether the Emperor personally had much to do with the economic stimulation of the province at the time is disputable) must have owed their impulse to masters from the Continent seeking their fortunes in a new area where rising wealth meant buoyant patronage. Soon, local talent would have been recruited, and much of the art produced has distinct regional motifs. Moreover figure-scenes with boldly linear portrayals against plain grounds is suggestive of British taste, as is the treatment of surface in terms of boldly-contrasting pattern (for instance on the Verulamium lion and Neptune pavements). If demand had continued, there would have been the same continuity that is apparent in sculpture (for instance the Carlisle workshop) but after fifty years or so all the workshops failed. Despite spasmodic attempts to revive the art in the third century, it was only with the rising prosperity of the Tetrarchy that permanent workshops again became possible, though taken individually even these had a short life. Again, as we have seen, it is likely that entrepreneurs from outside started it.

After a period of initial influence from Gaul, well represented by the Bignor pavements, I feel certain that local taste and thus local mosaicists became involved once more. The animals on the Corinian Orpheus mosaics at Woodchester and Barton Farm, with their linear forms and strongly stylized patterned pelts, and the idiosyncratic treatment of foliage, notably the striking bi-coloured scrollwork on the Woodchester mosaic, on a floor at Chedworth and another at Stonesfield, would be distinctive anywhere and were clearly products of the same mosaicists.[72] The patterning is foreshadowed on some second-century floors, but I do not think there is a direct link. Line and texture are leitmotifs of Insular art, notable on metalwork and sculpture as well as in mosaic. The Durnovarian school does not derive its basic repertoire from Corinium and its style is very different and even more eccentric, but here too is Romano-British art at its most flagrant and brilliant.

MOSAICS AND MANUSCRIPT PAINTING

In the case of literary themes the pattern was surely likely to be the patron's very own *de luxe* manuscript. The owner of a palatial complex such as that of Woodchester could certainly have had his own private library as assuredly as the Renaissance prince. Did the Corinian Orpheus school owe its imaginative treatment of the myth to the intellectual speculations of the lord of that place? Even if the design was worked out in a mosaic studio, the original impetus behind it would have been supplied by a patron, an intellectual who wanted to use the myth in a new and powerful manner and he is likely to have depended on the book to guide the master mosaicist.

A Vergil manuscript in the Vatican (*Codex Vat. Lat. 3867* or the *Vergilius Romanus*) is strangely reminiscent of Insular mosaic art and of the Durnovarian mosaics in particular. I have suggested that this codex is actually Romano-British in origin rather than Gaulish or north Italian and consequently of earlier date than previously proposed – fourth rather than fifth century. (I am grateful to Dr Kenneth Dark for pointing out to me that the textual tradition of the manuscript descends through a Hibernian *stemma*.)[73] It is worth a brief excursus here not only because it posits the existence of another craft in Roman Britain but also because it brings to the fore the problem of the mosaicists' artistic sources. The upper classes of Roman Britain had benefited from Roman culture and education since the first century. There is no doubt that the poetry of Vergil was studied by children and read for pleasure by adults (**76**). This is reflected in the figural arts, as noted above, by a very fragmentary wall-painting from Otford, Kent, which carries a line of the Aeneid as an explanatory caption, as well as by the Lullingstone pavement with its verse reference to the same poem (see **77**) and the bath-house floor from Low Ham which tells the story of Dido and Aeneas (**colour plates IX** and **X**). The form of the elegiac couplet and the language used at Lullingstone further suggest familiarity with Ovid.[74]

Mythology (including this particular myth) was probably best known in the Latin west, through the medium of Ovid's verse. It is possible that some scenes on British mosaics, such as those in a room at Frampton (including Cadmus killing the serpent of Mars, Perseus slaying the sea-monster, Aeneas plucking the golden bough (**colour plate XI**)), are taken from the *Metamorphoses*.[75] The prototypes of these scenes are not likely to have been provided by the mosaic workshops themselves. Pattern books (so-called) would have been limited to geometric designs, copied, adapted or invented by the individual workshop plus a few stock figural themes such as Seasons, dolphins and canthari. The Low Ham pavement thus provides evidence not only of the operation of the Durnovarian school but also of a lost manuscript bearing illustrations of books two and four of the Aeneid. The bold outlining of the figures, the patterned folds of the protagonists' garments and the sparing use of extraneous material (which is, incidentally, also a feature of the Lullingstone mosaic) may have been adopted by the Durnovarian workshop from an illuminated manuscript similar to the *Romanus*. It is virtually certain that there were workshops of scribes and illuminators in Britain, the Roman equivalent of the publisher, who could have provided the aristocracy with books to read as well as drawing up formal legal documents, whether or not the *Vergilius Romanus* itself actually came from an Insular workshop.

THE MINOR ARTS

The so-called 'minor arts' provide further evidence of craft organization. One of the clearest examples of how an object was commissioned is the well-known statuette of Mars from the Foss Dyke in Lincolnshire. Its base is inscribed on two sides, telling us that it was presented to Mars and the *Numina Augustorum* by the Colasuni brothers, Bruccius and Caratius, at the cost of 100 sesterces (i.e. 25 denarii). The full cost would have been 112 sesterces (28 denarii) as Celatus the smith who made it gave a pound of bronze worth three denarii. As the figure weighs 1.8kg (3lb 10oz – say 4lb) we can estimate that the price of raw material was 48 sesterces (12 denarii) and of labour,

ETIAM·SVMMA·PROCVL·VILLARVM·CVLMIN·NA·TVMANT
MAIORESQVE·CADVNT·ALTISDEMONTIBVSVMBRAE·

POETA   CORYDON

FORMONSVM·CORYDON·PASTOR·ARDEBAT·ALEXIN·
DELICIAS·DOMINI·NECQVID·SPERARET·HABEBAT·
TANTVM·INTER·DENSASVMBROSACACVMINA·FAGOS
ADSIDVAEVENIEBAT·IBI·HAECINCONDITASOLVS·

overheads and profit 64 sesterces (18 denarii). Celatus deftly added his name to the dedication and thus obtained the favour of the god by giving a small discount to his customers.

Another signed bronze is the base of a statuette of Mars as a rider-god with the Celtic epithet Corotiacus, from Martlesham, Suffolk. It was given to his shrine by a woman called Simplicia. The smith, who had a Greek name, Glaucus, signed the base. An *aerarius* called Cintusmus made a gift to Silvanus at a rural shrine outside Colchester, perhaps a sample of his own work: a figurine of a stag was found here.[76] Temple sites were always good places for smiths to sell their wares and it is not unlikely that Gestingthorpe, where moulds for figurines have been

76 *The* Virgilius Romanus (*Ms. Vat.Lat. 3867. 3ᵛ). The poet Virgil.* (Vatican Library.)

77 *Mosaic in the* triclinium, *Lullingstone, Kent. Europa and the Bull with verse inscription.*

found, served that purpose. Unfortunately the excavation was too limited both in extent and quality to be certain. Bronzesmithing was also carried out at Woodeaton. At such places images of the deities worshipped could be made in advance for sale to votaries, just as Demetrius made his silver shrines for Diana (Artemis) at Ephesus. The existence of types of figurine particular to specific temples, horsemen from Brigstock, Northamptonshire, and Mercury from Great Walsingham, Norfolk, and Uley, Gloucestershire, as well as the hounds at Lydney strongly supports this surmise, as do sceptre-heads, specific to particular deities such as the Matres, mentioned at the end of Chapter 4.

The image of the British bronzesmith is preserved generically in representations of Vulcan cast in the province, notably in the splendid figurines from Catterick, Yorkshire (**78**) and North Bradley, Wiltshire, as well as in relief on the gold bezel of a silver finger ring from Brant Braughton, Lincolnshire (did it belong to a smith?) and on silver votive leaves from Barkway, Hertfordshire. A relief from York portraying a similar figure has often been thought to be the tombstone of a smith, but it is not inscribed and is probably a votive relief of Vulcan. The costume of hat (*pileus*) and tunic fastened over the left shoulder, leaving the right arm free, was evidently universal amongst smiths in the ancient world.[77]

There was also a ready market in metal vessels, for secular as well as religious purposes. A *trulla* from Prickwillow, Cambridgeshire is stamped '*Bodvogenus f(ecit)*' upon the handle (**79**); the stamping of makers' names was normal on such vessels from Campanian factories. The name on this example is, however, Celtic and very possibly British. If it is, then the attractive handle which terminates in a pair of dolphins flanking a shell and incorporates a vine tendril inlaid with niello, shows a high degree of skill, and Bodvogenus surely deserved any fame he had.[78] We cannot know where he practised. A few enamelled vessels depicting Hadrian's Wall – with the names of some of the forts indicated in the case of the Rudge Cup (see **41**) and Amiens *patera* – suggest souvenirs from the frontier, but we can be sure that enamelled vessels were also made elsewhere, as were brooches and other trinkets. Simple silver vessels

78 *Bronze figurine of
Vulcan from Catterick,
Yorkshire. H.14.5cm.
(Photo: English Heritage.)*

79 Bronze trulla *handle with* niello *inlay, signed by Bodvogenus from Prickwillow, Isle of Ely, Cambridgeshire. L. of handle c.14cm. (Photo: British Museum.)*

in the Water Newton treasure were very probably specially made for patrons, and thus locally, for only thus could Innocentia and Viventia in one instance and Publianus in another have had the little bowls they presented to their church so elegantly lettered. Other examples of local production such as the Thetford spoons, similarly made with specific dedicatory inscriptions, are more fully considered in Chapter 7.[79]

The Risley Park *lanx* (see **94**), which survives in a modern re-casting, also needs to be included here because of its technique; it was originally cast in Britain by someone who knew how to manufacture pewter vessels, but its prototype was not local. Its subject matter is secular, depicting a boar-hunt, although it came into the possession of a bishop called Exuperius who presented it to a church, as its inscription tells us. Pewter itself was a major industry, as the finds of moulds in the vicinity of Bath as well as in Cornwall demonstrate. Interesting finds from the sacred spring of Sulis were two ingots, each weighing 3kg ($6\frac{1}{2}$lb), presumably dedicated by manufacturers themselves. Pewter was designed to imitate silver and provide a comparable show at a fraction of the cost; many vessels exhibit not only the forms but also the geometric decoration common on such late Roman silver vessels as the large nielloed dish from Mildenhall (**80** and **81**).

Some *trullae* from the sacred spring at Bath are engraved with dedications to Sulis, and one from Cornwall was a gift to Mars. An inscription on a large pewter plate from Appleford, Oxfordshire, tells us that a man called Lovernianus gave it to a woman, his wife or girlfriend, called Pacata, while in the case of a vessel from North Oxfordshire the recipient was a man, Docilinus, Most graffiti, however, are simply the names of owners. Only one inscription is neat enough to have been executed at the factory, and here on a dish from Welney, Norfolk, the legend UTERE FELIX (badly blundered) was a generalized greeting by an illiterate pewterer. The *floruit* of the industry lies in the fourth century and it too will be more fully considered in the next chapter.[80]

Jewellers were also active in Britain. A well-known inscription from Malton, Yorkshire, reads 'Good luck to the Genius of this place. Young slave, use to your good fortune this goldsmith's shop'. This suggests that the slave was being set up in business by an enlightened master. Presumably if he succeeded he would have been able to keep some of the profit and purchase his freedom. That was a frequent occurrence in the ancient world.[81] It is a pity that the location of the goldsmith's shop at Malton is not known but we do have crucibles from such premises on the site of the later Flavian palace in London (see **15**). The crucibles had to be sealed in the process of refining; this was done with clay on which were impressed stamps normally employed as moulds for jewellery. Theft must always have been a hazard in such work and the Malton goldsmith would have needed his luck.

The Snettisham smith, represented by the treasure found there, is not known by name. He evidently worked in gold although most of his output was of silver. With the cache were coins, representing a proportion of the smith's savings, with which he doubtless hoped to purchase more bullion, which dates his activity to the middle of the second century. In addition the cache contained a burnishing tool made of chalcedony. Examination of the treasure has already indicated that he had an associate or associates, probably apprentices. The accompanying gems are engraved by at least two people, and very possibly three. Did the silversmith and his apprentice(s) also cut seals, as was the case in the Middle Ages, or was there a second master, a gem-cutter, with his own team? I prefer the former hypothesis. Among the jewellery was a distinctive Insular serpent ring with two heads curled around a central ornament, of which other examples have been found at Backworth (made of gold) as well as at Ditton, Cambridgeshire, and Caerwent. There were also serpent bracelets, the heads of which have affinity with those on the rings and are matched by the well-known pair from Castlethorpe, Buckinghamshire, which belonged to a woman called Vernico. Serpent bracelets were also made at Alchester, Oxfordshire, as a bronze mould or form in the Ashmolean Museum attests; it presents two pairs of confronted heads in intaglio and presumably the ends of the bracelet were beaten into these.[82]

A case has been made for the existence of an innovative goldsmith's workshop in Britain in the second century, but though the gold jewellery from

80 *Silver dish with geometric design inlaid with* niello, *from the Mildenhall treasure, Suffolk.* D.55.6cm. (Photo: British Museum.)

81 *Pewter dish with geometric decoration from Appleford, Oxfordshire. Detail.* (Photo: Ashmolean Museum.)

Rhayader (see **58**), Southfleet and elsewhere looks Romano-British, I suspect that more than one smith was involved. At best we can only posit the existence of a 'school'.[83] A large proportion of the trade must always have consisted of special commissions. The most convincing example of such an order is to be found in the unusual late fourth-century gold rings from the Thetford treasure (see **98**), one of which has two woodpeckers on the shoulders and another a head of the god Faunus as a bezel. The silver spoons in the treasure, though of current fourth-century types, were especially engraved with dedications to the god and were probably ordered either from the same workshop or another one in the vicinity.[84]

The enormous output of brooches of varied form and including enamelled brooches was probably carried on in many places. It is a pity that we do not know the names of the craftsmen or their organization, for while most brooches are of modest importance in themselves, they are among the most universal of art objects and are of particular interest in charting personal taste in curvilinear (Celtic) ornament and, in the case of enamels, colour sense. Only in special cases – for instance the large and anomalous brooches from Great Chesters or the 'gold brooch set with gems' mentioned on the Marble of Thorigny – were they special commissions. This last is not extant of course, but contemporary third-century gilt bronze brooches of oval form set with imitation glass jewels or even intaglios, like one from Abbots Ann, Hampshire (**82**), thought to be of British manufacture, suggest what it may have looked like.[85]

Although the best Roman gem-cutters, such as Augustus' seal-maker Dioscourides, signed their work, none has been found in Britain, where most of the evidence for the craft is inferential. The gems found in the main drain at Bath and attributed to a local workshop of the first century, and another putative workshop cutting red-jasper intaglios somewhere in north Britain a hundred years later come into this category. More specific, however, are the cornelian gems from the Snettisham cache (see above). They are cut with common subjects, notably Fortuna, Ceres and Bonus Adventus, and were certainly not made with any special order in mind. The best-attested gem-carving craft practised in Britian was the jet industry; it is actually mentioned by Solinus (*Collectanea rerum memorabilium* 22, 11) as a speciality of the province

though he does not localize it. Jet only outcrops on the Yorkshire coast, near Whitby, and finds of unworked jet, as well as unfinished pins in York, point to the centre being there. Products were exported widely in the western provinces, notably to the Rhineland. Portrait medallions might suggest special orders but, in parallel with onyx cameos carved in many parts of the Empire (see **46**), this seems unlikely. The commonest subject, as on onyx cameos, is the apotropaic Medusa head, but there are other themes, such as the two cupids on a medallion from Colchester (**83**). A substitute material was available for simpler items of jewellery, notably bracelets, from the other end of the province. Shale from the Dorset coast was worked on a lathe at a number of sites and found its central market at Dorchester. However, shale found its most important use in the manufacture of furniture.[86]

It is reasonable to suppose that all these luxury crafts were normally town-based even if their practitioners sometimes made forays into the countryside to sell their wares; we know this to have been the case in Italy, for instance jewellers and silversmiths were to be found along the Via Sacra in Rome, and there were similar quarters in Pompeii (Via della Abbondanza) and elsewhere. The existence of a guild of silversmiths at Ephesus, so well know from Acts, raises the question of trade guilds. There is evidence for guilds in Roman Britain, for instance at Lincoln, Chichester, Silchester and Bath, but none is certainly connected with the arts.[87] Workers in the minor arts could carry their tools with them, and to some extent they might remain itinerant craftsmen as they had been in the Iron Age. Temple (and church) sites not only provided patrons, as is demonstrated at Water Newton, Thetford and Risley Park, but it might be convenient to practise one's craft at certain times in the vicinity of such places when there were frequent fairs and festivals, as was noted in the case of bronzesmiths.[88]

FURNITURE DESIGN

Much Romano-British furniture was comparatively simple and, indeed, would hardly be considered as art by most people. Basket chairs are shown in reliefs and a few simple turned wooden chair- and table-legs are known from waterlogged deposits. They were presumably made everywhere. Much more localized was the shale industry. Shale outcrops on the coast of Dorset, as noted above, and recent excavation at Norden suggests that even the better items such as trenchers with their elegant engraved designs, tables and jewel-boxes would have been worked on site though they were probably marketed at Dorchester before being distributed across southern England. The black colour would have recalled ebony and made such items suitable substitutes for expensive imported furniture carved from marble and other coloured stones. The simplified chip-carved detail of the zoomorphic table-legs may have been forced on the craftsmen by the nature of the material, but it is very much in accord with provincial taste. The Cotswold stonemasons were adept at handling freestones but nevertheless used chip-carving to embellish the edges of sideboards.[89]

FIGURED POTTERY, FIGURINES AND APPLIQUÉS

Most patronage and thus most art was connected with the upper, wealthy stratum of society. Below that level, art had a more limited role; we find it applied to trinkets, as mentioned above, and also ceramics. The majority of pottery vessels were utilitarian, and although we may appreciate technique or shape, aesthetic considerations were not normally paramount. Nevertheless potters did employ a variety of simple techniques including rilling, burnishing and even painting to improve the appearance of their products, and sometimes figured decoration is used. This is, of course, the hallmark of a good proportion of the red fine-ware imported from Gaul known as samian, a term describing the technique of providing the attractive gloss of these vessels. Although some vessels are pleasant to look at and their iconography repays more study than it has received, the story of samian is essentially one of mass-production in Gaul and efficient distribution in Britain.

More interesting are the colour-coated vessels with relief decoration showing hunting and circus and gladiatorial scenes, phalli and explicitly erotic episodes and deities. Colchester and the Nene Valley were considerable centres for their production. Colchester potters specialized in hunting and circus scenes, but those of the Nene valley also made pots depicting

82 Oval gilt-bronze brooch with glass intaglio, found at Abbots Ann, Hampshire. L.2.5cm. (Photo: courtesy of the late R.A. Hattatt.)

83 Jet pendant with two cupids shown in relief, from Colchester. L.5.5cm. (Photo: British Museum.)

84 *Mask from a pottery face-flagon (front and side views) made in an Oxfordshire kiln. From Toot Baldon, Oxfordshire. H.11cm. Ashmolean Museum. (Photos: Julian Munby.)*

deities, religious scenes and the Labours of Hercules, from the late second to the fourth century. There are problems of patronage with these, for if the prototypes of the best of these vessels lay in more expensive works of art such as silver plate, as has been suggested, who owned such expensive originals? Surely not the potter. The best pots could have been special commissions like a large beaker depicting Hercules capturing the Cernean Hind, Jupiter and other figures, found in the excavation of the East Gate at Lincoln and published by Margaret Darling (see **66**). Did the patron have to go to Durobrivae and place a special order – or were pots such as this speculative ventures by the potters? There is no difficulty in seeing the majority of these beakers as having been made for

sale at festivals and fairs and as gifts for the Saturnalia and the New Year. For many people the amusing, and often erotic, themes, scenes of field sport, the circus or the arena, must have marked their main departure from purely utilitarian purchases. Some display considerable artistic dexterity. Face flagons, sometimes painted, were widespread and it is possible to distinguish the styles of different industries. Those of Oxfordshire display heads, mainly female (**84**) but occasionally male of strongly Classical appearance. Similar Face-flagons from other industries in East Anglia and the north are more stylized. An interesting discovery from one of the Oxfordshire kilns at Horspath brings us close to one of these humble artists. It is a mould yielding the impression of a male head, thoroughly Classical in type; however, the outside of the mould is in the form of a caricature. The first surely came from a carved model; the latter is a free-hand example of modelling by a workman. Another type of pot, the head pot, provides examples ranging from fully Roman craft to stylized facial features applied to the walls of the vessel. For the most part they were used for funerary purposes and must have had a religious meaning.[90]

Certainly protective are the *antefixa* from both military and civil sites including Exeter, Caerleon, Chester, York and Dorchester, Dorset. Heads and masks (often Medusa masks) were designed to keep away the Evil Eye. They were clearly made in considerable numbers, and are paralleled in function if not in style by the many *antefixa* to be seen in Pompeii. The tile-makers who produced them are again unlikely to have seen themselves as artists. It is only occasionally that real patronage can be seen among such people, but two of the most distinctive votives from Coventina's spring at Carrawburgh are the incense burners made with his own hand by Gabinius Saturninus. Although he does not tell us his profession these two objects with their architecturally-conceived forms are so accomplished that their maker must have been a professional potter.[91]

CHAPTER SEVEN

Art in Late Roman Britain

This is a most majestic vision,
and Harmonious charmingly.

Late Antique culture and society have received considerable attention in recent years. The fourth century is no longer seen as a time of decadence but rather of vitality and innovation. These are the decades in which the Roman state underwent a subtle evolution and, in the Eastern provinces, became the Byzantine Empire.[1] In the West the unity of the Roman world proved to be more fragile and during the fifth century the Empire fell apart into successor states, often dominated by Germanic ruling classes, and so the Middle Ages were born. It is too easy to view Late Antiquity retrospectively. Both in East and West men thought they were preserving the traditions of the Roman past – save perhaps the Christians who, nevertheless, based their legitimacy on history. In the West nobody imagined himself on a road to the fall of the Roman Empire; these provinces too enjoyed their Late Antique (early 'Byzantine') period. The different character of this period – even in Roman Britain – demands separate treatment as much as that of the Conquest in the first century, and it has recently received it.[2] There will naturally be some overlap in coverage with what has come before; for example we have already considered in the previous chapter the question of mosaic workshops. Here the stress will be on the content and use of art as an expression of Late Antiquity.

In its broad outlines the nature of this new age is readily apparent from literature and art. Its most visible break with the past lay in the adoption of Christianity by Constantine and most of his successors, a move which ultimately led to the displacement of the long established cults of Greece and Rome. Social distinctions were perceived more sharply than they had been, with the emperor, a monarch in name as well as in substance, at the apex of a rigid hierarchy. The economy of the cities had been failing for a century and the patronage of local magistrates could no longer be relied upon to construct and embellish public buildings. Like all such generalizations, there are major exceptions and contradictions. The ideal of public munificence was still very much alive, even if it was often applied to more private ends such as the embellishment of a church rather than to repairing the civic basilica. In the Rome of the great Imperial Christian basilicas (St John Lateran, St Peter's and the rest), a powerful and eloquent pagan aristocracy was still active and involved itself not only with contemporary politics but with scholarship and the preservation of the literary traditions of Rome.[3]

Despite divisions between classes, *romanitas* was perceived as something binding all inhabitants of the

Empire together: Rutilius Namatianus' famous lines, written in the early fifth-century, state this succinctly.

Dumque offers victis proprii consortia iuris
Urbem fecisti quod prius orbis erat. (*De Reditu Suo* i. 65–6)

Because you offered the conquered equality under your laws, you have made a City from what was once a world.

The sentiment is echoed by an episode in the history of Britain recorded by Ammianus Marcellinus. He writes of the brutality of the notorious informer and secret policeman, Paulus 'Catena' (Paul the chain), sent in 354 by the emperor Constantius II to hunt down those suspected of having supported the usurper Magnentius. Magnentius seems to have been very strongly supported in the province and many members of gentry were arrested. Eventually Martinus, the *vicarius* (governor) of Britain, attempted to remonstrate with Paulus and as a result he lost his own life, an event which, according to Ammianus cast an eternal stain on the reign of Constantius (Ammianus xiv, 5, 6–8). The episode is an eloquent reminder that Britons of the land-owning class were now clearly regarded as fellow Romans by the historian's readers in Rome. Martinus' action was surely directed at protecting friends and colleagues who were Roman citizens of rank (*honestiores*) rather than subject peoples.

Artistic style is characterized by greater abstraction, use of colour and texture and formal pattern.[4] Figural work tends to emphasize qualities such as power (religious or secular) and class. The Neo-Platonic theory that the eyes were the windows of the soul established a powerful link between the artistic image, whether deity or human, and the viewer.[5] The icons so produced are very different from the classicism of the Early Empire, being regarded as more significant and powerful. The flaunting of brightly coloured clothes and gold jewellery enhanced the wearer's prestige, while feasting off lavish silver plates dignified the owner's rank; often such objects were given as gifts by the Emperor to his supporters. The ideals of secular life, as seen on mosaics, silver-plate and manuscripts, consisted on the one side of feasting, hunting and fishing upon one's estate and on the other of literary pursuits. The world of the court, whether the court of the Emperor or of the local

notable or *dominus*, seems to have required considerable ceremony by all concerned. This often demanded that the principal actor strike a statuesque pose before the serried ranks of those paying him homage, without moving either to the right or to the left. Religion imagined the Court of Heaven as obeying the same rules, with equally static rows of adoring saints standing before the Heavenly Throne.

A very few examples of art, drawn from the wider Roman world, will suffice to define the classic characteristics of the Late Roman style, before turning in greater detail to the local evidence. The rich jewel-box effect of wall and ceiling mosaic, especially when gold tesserae were employed, as at the church of Hagios Georgios at Thessalonika, was orchestrated so as to create emotion as in a theatre.[6] Similar results could be achieved by the use of *opus sectile*. Sidonius Apollinaris in mid-fifth-century Gaul affects a self-denying simplicity when describing the baths of his own villa at Avitacum, near Clermont, to his friend Domitius:

If you want to know what marbles are employed, neither Paros nor Carystos, nor Proconesos, nor Phrygia nor Numidia, nor Sparta have contributed their diverse inlays. I had no use for stone that simulates a broken surface, with Ethiopic crags and purple precipices stained with genuine murex (*Letters* II, ii, 7, trans. O.M. Dalton).

However, he is far more enthusiastic describing the abstract splendours of the marbles of Bishop Patiens' church at Lyon as though it were a perfect country scene, Paradise in fact:

Within is shining light, and the gilding of the coffered ceiling allures the sunbeams golden as itself. The whole basilica is bright with diverse marbles, floor vaulting and windows all adorned with figures of most various colour, and mosaic green as a blooming mead shows its design of sapphire cubes winding through the ground of verdant glass . . . (*Letters* II, x, 4, trans. O.M. Dalton).

Presumably what he thought inappropriate for his own use was right for a public place. Not many aristocrats, even in Roman Britain, were so self-denying when it came to grandeur. Other writers of Late Roman and Byzantine times, for example Paul the Silentiary in the sixth century, saw the natural world in such abstract forms. The tradition that began at least as early as the third century but was by no means dead in the thirteenth when the great *opus sectile* pavement in Westminster Abbey, laid by Italian craftsmen before the high altar, was explained as nothing less than a portrayal of the whole of Creation.[7]

Many items of silver plate display similar qualities of colour and pattern through the use of chasing and sometimes openwork (*opus interrasile*), gilding and niello. A good example is to be found with the Ariadne *lanx* from the Kaiseraugst Treasure, where the interplay of colour, bold textures and openwork, gives a startling effect. Even more dramatic are the intricately cut *vasa dietrata*, perhaps the most expensive cut from semi-precious stone, like the Rubens vase, or from dichroic glass containing small quantities of gold and silver, like the Rothschild-Lycurgus cup in the British Museum. This is green by reflected light and cherry-red by transmitted light and may, perhaps, have been used in feasts and ceremonies honouring the god Bacchus.[8]

The best-known treatment of the mesmerizing portrait in Late Antique art is to be seen in the colossal head of Constantine in the Palazzo dei Conservatori in Rome, although there are many other such portraits both on a large scale and on a smaller one, coins for example. Great emphasis is placed on the eyes as windows to the soul, whether the portraits are of divine figures, such as the painted Christ upon the vault of a tomb in the catacomb of Commodilla, or of private individuals, like the *dominus* on the Great Hunt mosaic at Piazza Armerina, now believed by most scholars to be the wealthy senator who owned the property. The gorgeously coloured robes of the Piazza Armerina senator likewise emphasize his importance. The *Dominus Iulius* mosaic in Tunis depicts a similar world of noble wealth but here the lord rides towards his château amidst scenes of agricultural prosperity and hunting.[9] The great 'Sevso dish', from the treasure that bears his name, probably from northern Croatia (though this is uncertain), tells the same story. A verse inscription on the dish shows that it was given to someone called Sevso (or Seuso), though it does not reveal the name of the donor; it does, however, emphasize how this society was linked by gift-giving and consequently reveals the crucial part played by the artist in cementing bonds of friendship and loyalty.[10] At the apex of society was the Emperor,

and those scenes on the Arch of Constantine in Rome and on the base of the Obelisk of Theodosius at Constantinople, which show the Imperial family flanked by their leading subjects, demonstrated a view of society which would have been familiar even in Britain.[11]

EARLY BYZANTINE BRITAIN: RELIGIOUS AND CULTURAL FACTORS

The title of this section is intended to be arresting. It is meant to emphasise that for a hundred years Britain took a full part in the nexus of provinces which saw the beginning of the culture which would come to fruition as the Byzantine Empire with its capital at Constantinople, founded by Constantine in AD 324 and formally inaugurated in 330. During the fourth century, of course, the character of the nascent Byzantine Empire was not fully formed, and Peter Brown and others have coined the term 'Late Antiquity' for this early stage.

Britain sometimes seems to be a remote and unimportant island to modern historians of the Late Empire. However, as the Martinus episode demonstrates, it was much less remote and backward than it had been in earlier centuries. Following the decade in which first Carausius (287–93) and then Allectus (293–6) had ruled as emperors from London (and indeed struck coins there), the Caesar, Constantius Chlorus, restored Britain to the 'eternal light' of the Empire in 296, as the legend on a gold medallion struck at Trier expressed it.[12] Under the Tetrarchy the two Severan provinces of *Britannia Inferior* in the north with its capital at York and *Britannia Superior* with its centre at London were further sub-divided into four. These were *Maxima Caesariensis* with its capital at London, *Britannia Prima* which epigraphic evidence from Cirencester shows was in the west, and very possibly based on that city, *Flavia Caesariensis* which bears the family name of Constantius and *Britannia Secunda*. One of these must have had its centre at York and I opt for *Flavia Caesariensis*: here Constantius had his capital when he returned as Augustus (senior emperor) to campaign in the north and here he died and his son Constantine was proclaimed in 306.

The British provinces continued to be of concern to the central government. Issues of coins from the

London mint celebrating an Imperial *Adventus* struck in 312 and 314 suggest that Constantine returned to Britain later in his reign. Ammianus Marcellinus, in an allusion to a lost part of his history, tells us that Constantine's son, Constans, was there in the winter of 343. Further, as stated above, prominent Britons were strongly involved in the usurpation of Magnentius (350–3), and the island seems to have backed Julian in his rise to power (360–1). Magnus Maximus used Britain as a springboard in his bid for power (383), as did Constantine III at the beginning of the fifth century (407). Britain thus played a significant part in the political history of the fourth century even if it was, admittedly, less important in terms of the destiny of the Roman world than were the Gallic provinces. Neither London nor York was ever an Imperial capital as was Trier in neighbouring Belgica; but nor was either entirely lacking in prominence. At some point London was even dignified by a new and glamorous name, *Augusta*.

Conformity of local art with the aesthetics of the Empire as a whole can be seen again and again in mosaics, wall-painting and silver-plate. The tendency to present events in the form of striking tableaux, often in order to glorify a superior – God, the Emperor, a great magnate (*dominus*) on his estate – is seen, for example, in the frescoes of the *orantes* at Lullingstone and the baptism scene on the lead font from Walesby, Lincolnshire.[13] 'Waiting on the Lord' mirrors endless waits before the throne of the Emperor or the chair of some high official. Even the gods, as shown in pagan art, acquire a new hieratic solemnity. It can be seen on a Bignor mosaic where the nimbed bust of Venus stares out at the viewer like an icon in a Greek church, or at Low Ham where the same goddess is portrayed in all her glory in the central octagon, all-powerful and omnipresent, disposer of life and death. Bacchus is frequently glorified, for example at Thruxton where he is depicted encircled by eight heads representing the spirits of nature. The Brantingham mosaic presents a nimbed bust, probably Tyche but possibly a muse, with two rows of eight facing busts on each side.

A very impressive example of explicit power exhibited on a mosaic is the centre of the Hinton St Mary mosaic which shows a youthful facing bust flanked by pomegranates and backed by a chi-rho. Whether the image shows Christ or his representative, the Emperor, this is a supreme example of an icon

whose power, so the pomegranates suggest, extends even over death. It is not surprising, given the structure and design of the floor, that Kenneth Painter has suggested it was intended for a vault-mosaic, and certainly the great *Cosmocrator* images in Byzantine churches represent continuity from this type of depiction (**85**). Incidentally, this would not seem to have been the only use of a vault design on a floor mosaic in Roman Britain. At Horkstow in north Lincolnshire a series of Bacchic scenes, or perhaps, *pace* A.J. Beeson, episodes in the life of Achilles, were combined with others appertaining to the marine *thiasos*. It is tempting to relate these to the hero's mother, the nereid Thetis. The scenes are depicted against red and blue backgrounds in a great roundel which may allude to the shield brough to Achilles by Thetis, and the roundel is supported by four *gigantes* (**colour plate XIII**).

Sarah Scott has rightly pointed out how mosaics, and presumably frescoes, were used to mirror the power of an élite, generally epitomized by a magnate (*dominus*). This is very apparent in the concentric Orpheus pavements of south-western Britain, like Woodchester, set for the most part in great reception rooms where the control exercised by that divine hero over nature is equated to the power of the earthly *dominus* over his society.[14]

The use of dazzling colour to produce an impression mirroring the splendours of the Court of the Emperor or even the Court of Heaven is to be seen in both wall-painting and mosaics, figural and geometric. On the east wall of the late-fourth-century Lullingstone house-church, the *orantes* are dressed in rich Late Antique robes, which have analogies with surviving Coptic textiles, while the chi-rho on the south wall with its jewelled wreath surround and accompanying doves is a gorgeous symbol of otherworldly magnificence.[15] The brilliance and complexity of the geometric panels around the great Woodchester Orpheus-roundel (see **106**) also allude to an untouchable, and dangerous, glory. Here we should recall that the effect would have been completed by a splashing fountain in which beams of sunlight were reflected off water-droplets and the tinkling sound of the ever-flowing stream added an audible refinement.[16] Remembering Sidonius Apollinaris' praise of colour and light in Bishop Patiens' basilica at Lyon, we can see that even the products of the purely geometric floors of the Durobrivan/Rataean school probably had a

141

85   *The mosaic from
Hinton St Mary, Dorset.
Painting by Dr David Neal.*
(Photo: British Museum.)

real resonance to the highly-charged emotions of Late Antiquity.

It is within such settings that silver plate (whether we are dealing with the Mildenhall Treasure or the *Hacksilber* from Traprain) as well as high-quality glassware (*vasa diatreta*) must be placed. These are the movable components. Such vessels were used in a very public way, in dining (as shown in the miniatures of the *Vergilius Romanus*) and in religious ceremonial (made clear by dedicatory inscriptions), frequently both. On figured silver the subject-matter was surely looked at carefully and commented upon. Thus the great dish from Mildenhall (**86**) exemplifies the power of Bacchus and can be seen as equivalent to references to the power of the god on mosaic, while the Corbridge *lanx* (see **93**), which may have been made to commemorate a possible visit by the Emperor Julian to Delos in 363 prior to his ill-fated Persian expedition, is very likely to have belonged originally to a devotee of Apollo, though admittedly other vessels bearing Christian symbols may have been associated in a hoard from which it was derived. Thus it might have lost its particular nuance when its final owner buried it to keep it from some unknown harm.[17] Apart from subject matter the colour and texture of silver, whether by itself or embellished with gilding and niello, was highly valued and in Britain copied in pewter. Water or wine would have added to the effect, as Sidonius reminds us:

If water of our famous springs is served and quickly poured into the cups, one sees snowy spots and clouded patches form outside them; the sudden chill dulls the fugitive reflections of the surface almost as if it had been greased (Sidonius, *Letters* II, ii, 12, trans. O.M. Dalton).

Glass, too, would have added sparkle to the feast, especially when it was engraved, like the bowl from Wint Hill, Somerset (**87**), and similar cut-glass vessels. The Wint Hill bowl shows a hunting-scene and bears an inscription wishing the drinker long life. No complete *diatreton* has been found in Britain, but a small fragment is recorded from Silchester which may have come from a figural vessel, and there is another piece from Great Staughton, Huntingdonshire. Intricacy of work and texture, exemplified by the cut-out *interrasile* effect, also to be seen on gold jewellery, was to be found here as well as translucency and colour (sometimes provided by wine). Did anyone in Britain own a vessel of dichroic glass like the Rothschild-Lycurgus cup?[18]

Colour, light, texture and ceremony were also manifested by dress and jewellery. The well-published Thetford treasure, though made in Britain and perhaps intended from the first as a votive gift, is thoroughly Byzantine in the taste it exhibits, its use of gems for colouristic effects and, even on such small objects as rings, a desire to show as much gold as

86 *The great silver dish
with scenes from the Bacchic
and marine* thiasoi, *from
the Mildenhall treasure,
Suffolk. D.60.5cm.* (Photo:
British Museum.)

144

87 *Cut-glass bowl with
hunting scene from Wint
Hill, Somerset. D.19cm.*
(Photo: Ashmolean
Museum.)

145

88 *Gold body-chain from Hoxne, Suffolk. L. of individual chains 36cm; junction pendants c.3cm. (Photo: British Museum.)*

possible. The much more metropolitan goldwork of the Hoxne treasure contains a jewelled body-chain of a rare type, though worn by Venus in one of the scenes upon the Low Ham mosaic (**colour plate IX**) and known from later Byzantine jewellery (**88**) and *opus interrasile* bracelets, one of which was meant to read VTERE FELIX DOMINA JVLIANE (use happily, Lady Juliane) (**89**). Personal glorification is thus combined with an emphasis on the wealth of the magnate's wife – and, by implication, the power of the magnate himself.[19]

As we have seen, the world of Late Antiquity was very much influenced by Christianity, despite the fact that by no means the entire population was Christian and in some places there may have been considerable resistance to the new rites. In Britain, for the most part, the evidence points to Christians being in a minority almost everywhere, at least before the fifth century. There is, in fact, no evidence for Christianity in Britain before the third century, during which Alban was martyred at Verulamium and Julius and Aaron at Caerleon. Certainly it was established in a regular fashion by 314, when the list of bishops present at the Council of Arles included bishops from York, London and Lincoln. The early fourth-century cache of silver from Water Newton with its votive dedications probably belonged to a small Christian community in that town. In addition the recently rediscovered *lanx* from Risley Park (see **94**) was given by a bishop called Exuperius to the church at 'Bogium' (perhaps a villa estate in the immediate vicinity). These are exceedingly modest presents to churches alongside Constantine's benefactions to churches in Rome (cf. *Liber Pontificalis* 34), but they belong to the same world of ecclesiastical patronage.

At the later end of the century the paintings of the house-church at Lullingstone, Kent, are as advanced as anything elsewhere in the Empire and

89 *Openwork bracelet from Hoxne, Suffolk. L.6cm. (Photo: British Museum.)*

147

indeed look forward to Byzantine art, while the chi-rhos can be compared with the best in Catacomb art. Although only a few fragments have been recognized there were also figured (biblical?) scenes here. A powerful image, though not quite so certainly from a house-church, is the youthful bust backed by a chi-rho on the main section of a mosaic floor from Hinton St Mary (see above and **85**). Whatever its precise significance (see below) this incorporates a highly effective use of the *labarum* of Constantine, not a provincial solecism. Most Christian artefacts from Britain are fairly small items of metalwork such as spoons and finger rings, which at least point to men possessed of some wealth. There is no question that British Christians could hold their own in the wider world. In the late fourth century Pelagius and his associates were formidable and sophisticated contro-versialists, not country bumpkins, and Patrick, who seems to have come from the curial class in the Carlisle region, was an orthodox but effective mis-sionary beyond the Roman frontiers, in Ireland.[20]

BRITAIN IN ITS GOLDEN AGE

If the quantity of Christian art in Britain seems comparatively meagre, this is probably because many of the leading members of provincial society remained pagan; far from being concealed, their beliefs were flaunted upon the mosaic floors and painted walls of their villas. The art they patronized exhibits tradi-tional values, shot through with a new seriousness and religiosity, no less fervent than the Christianity manifested by the frescoes of the Lullingstone Church and just as characteristic of Late Antiquity. Here is the culture of the great Roman aristocrats Symmachus and Praetextatus rather than that of the Imperial court or the Church. Late Antique pagan images include the nimbed deities at Bignor, Sussex, and Branting-ham, Yorkshire; Saviour figures, such as Bacchus and Orpheus, for example at Littlecote, Wiltshire; and serious exegesis of Ovid and Vergil notably at Frampton, Dorset, and Low Ham, Somerset. But these deviations in subject-matter from what is often re-garded as the Christian norm will all have been to display the owner's prestige as well as his piety. Even nominal Christians were not immune. The fourth-century poet Ausonius wrote to his son Gregorius

telling him that his poem on the crucifixion of Cupid was inspired by a painting in the *triclinium* of Zoïlus in Trier (introduction to book viii). The context is always one of Late Roman ceremony and manners whether we are looking at mythological scenes in the *triclinia* at Keynsham, Somerset, or Lullingstone, the reception room at Woodchester, the putative cult-room at Littlecote, the baths at Low Ham or various other chambers and corridors.

The nature of the surviving art from Britain at this time reflects society. It is overwhelmingly private. The great villas and villa-like buildings with their ambitious array of mosaic floors and frescoes stand out as the centres of art and patronage. In many ways they took on a quasi-urban role, even if they were not as thick on the ground as along the Moselle:

> If a stranger were to arrive here from the shores of Cumae, he would believe that Euboean Baiae had bestowed on this region a miniature copy of its own delights: so great is the charm of its refinement and distinction, while its pleasures breed no excess (Ausonius, *Mosella* 11.345–8, trans. H.G. Evelyn-White).

Their owners would have used or displayed a great many portable objects. It is likely that many of the villas had imported marble statuary, the Woodchester Cupid and Psyche finding an attractive parallel in a Late Roman house at Ostia.[21] Doubtless much of the silver plate was imported but the Thetford treasure (a special order and probably made in East Anglia) in-cluded among the spoons, two with chased and gilded ornamental bowls, one showing a triton and the other a running panther. The Risley Park *lanx* (see **94**) is thought to have been cast in the province albeit from an imported model, by someone adept at producing pewter. Its central scene is a boar hunt, while the surrounding frieze shows other hunting scenes as well as pastoral life. These subjects, the realm of Bacchus (see **86**) and the hunt are well represented in the magnificent imported service of plate found at Mildenhall, Suffolk. Quite apart from figural subject matter there is a liking for abstract pattern, seen in the Mildenhall silver (see **80**) as well as on British pewter. Indeed, large *ministeria* of pewter such as those from Appleshaw, Hampshire, and Appleford, Oxford-shire (see **81**), exhibit the same taste for domestic magnificence as does silver, at a tiny fraction of the cost. In addition there were illustrated books, and a possible survival from this category of luxury art has been mentioned in Chapter 6. Finally there was the splendid dress and jewellery with which the Roman upper classes established their *personae*. Dress is mainly glimpsed through contemporary painting and mosaic. Jewellery doubtless included a wide range of gold and jewelled art though villa excavation has yielded little. However, the jewellery from the Hoxne treasure as well as the votive Thetford treasure reveal the extravagance of contemporary taste.

When it is compared with private display, patronage in the way of public monuments is notably lacking. The mosaics laid in the temple of Nodens at Lydney and its guest-house are a partial exception, although the dedication on the important mosaic laid in the temple's *cella* stated that the source of funding was the individual offerings of worshippers. If the Chedworth 'villa' is the guest-house of another sanctuary, as Graham Webster has cogently argued, its mosaics, too, will have been the gifts of worshippers. An alternative explanation is that the property belonged to an entrepreneur who found it very profitable 'farming' a sacred *locus* on his land instead of (or as well as) sheep or cereals. Like the Lydney *cella* mosaic, the Thruxton floor (**colour plate XIV**) also carries an inscription which, I believe, was rightly identified as a religious dedication in the middle of the last century. However the context here is that of a small private cult of the villa owner, Quintus Natalius Natalinus, and two clients, the Bodeni (named on the pavement) and perhaps a few others, who met to venerate Bacchus in the villa's *triclinium*.[22]

The wall-painting from the *praetorium* of the York fortress and the limestone head of Constantine which may have come from the same place reveal, however, that public commissions for major centres of power still existed. Indeed, at York the river front of the fortress was embellished with poygonal towers at this time. There is not much to report of other cities except that a Jupiter-column was restored at Cirencester. There is no indication that this involved fresh carving but, as Professor Peter Brown reminds us, 'throughout the Late Antique period to "renew" a city was the most praiseworthy achievement of the powerful'. Lucius Septimius, *praeses* of *Britannia Prima*, used hexameters to record his achievement, emphasizing that power and culture go together.[23] Cirencester, however, is chiefly notable in the fourth century for its mosaics and mosaic-workshops catering for the rich landowners of its own 'Little Baiae'. At London the evidence for public art is more negative: the smashing of Mithraic sculpture early in the fourth century may not have been officially organized, but the use of other sculptures as building-blocks in the riverside wall presumably was. Nevertheless there was a mint at London striking bronze during the reigns of Constantius Chlorus and Constantine and again, very briefly, under Magnus Maximus when it coined in precious metal.

SCULPTURE

Although sculptors were evidently still operating in the fourth century, as is shown by the York head of Constantine – which is to some extent comparable with the Conservatori portrait mentioned above – it is hard to find any other work of monumental sculpture which is truly characteristic of the age. A bronze steelyard counterweight from the Imperial Estate (?) at Kingscote, Gloucestershire, is in the form of a female bust, possibly of Fausta wearing a *stola* with a fringed neck-line (**90**). The rigid frontality of the head seems to partake of the formality of the York portrait, though the striated patterning of her garment is a Romano-British feature: it is possible that after all this is a stylized portrait of the second-century empress Faustina II by a provincial bronzesmith. There is no such uncertainty with regard to the silver gilt image of a late fourth-century empress (clearly identified as such both by her distinctive coiffure and almost hieratic appearance) recently discovered in the Hoxne treasure. This is a wonderful example of a Late Antique Imperial image, here incongruously serving as a pepper-pot. Was it part of an Imperial gift to a supporter of the dynasty?[24]

The same paucity of evidence with regard to the fourth century has long been observed with regard to monumental inscriptions. While it is true that much sculpture, such as the cult image of Mercury from Uley carved in limestone and probably the bronze of Sulis Minerva at Bath, continued to be venerated until near the end of the century, the main story is one of destruction and recycling. We are not told that the re-erection of the Cirencester Jupiter-column required any extra carving. However, it should be

150

90 *Steelyard weight of heavy leaded bronze in the form of a bust of Constantine's first wife, Fausta(?), from Kingscote, Gloucestershire. H.9cm. Corinium Museum.* (Photo: Nick Pollard, Institute of Archaeology, Oxford.)

noted that many of the imported marbles in Britain come from late contexts, especially in villas, and may have been used if not carved then. Clearly at Woodchester representations of deities and particularly the Cupid and Psyche group helped to provide a decor of ostentatious Classicism. The Spoonley Wood Bacchus belonged to a similar milieu, but although intended originally for the *triclinium* of the villa, it ended up in its owner's grave and so illustrates the inscription on the base of another, probably third- or fourth-century, statuette group from the Walbrook *Mithraeum* (now probably a shrine of Bacchus) reading HOMINIBUS BAGIS BITAM (*sic*) 'Thou givest life to wandering men'. Such statuettes could be given as votives, and one was presented to a temple at Maiden Castle, Dorset, at this time. Busts, albeit of earlier date, at Lullingstone and Woodchester, helped to add a cachet of antiquity. So far we have nothing like the limestone balustrade from around the pond at Welschbilling near Trier ornamented with contemporary busts alongside versions of portraits of the early Empire and Greek philosophers.[25]

LATE ANTIQUE MOSAICS

The most important surviving art of the period, that of the mosaicist, has been well-studied from the point of view of workshop practice (see Chapter 6). The content of the floors as an expression of society demands further consideration here. Many of the mosaics, including most attributed to the Corinian Saltire school and its possible Lindinis branch, as well as all of those of the Durobrivan or Rataean school, are in fact abstract in character. Geometric pavements and elements of pattern in pavements are of course universal, but the highly-accomplished use of simple geometry to produce dazzling pattern on British floors certainly accords with local taste going back to the Iron Age. However, as noted above, all-over designs and also strong colours are features of all manner of Late Antique art – textiles, silver-plate and *opus sectile* – as well as mosaic, and could well have been 'meaningful' to their owners. British geometric pavements (**colour plates XV** and **XVI**) have been thought (wrongly) to have influenced the 'carpet pages' of

91 *Mosaic pavement showing Orpheus from Barton Farm, Cirencester. Detail. Corinium Museum.*
(Photo: The late M.B. Cookson, Institute of Archaeology, Oxford archive.)

Hiberno-Northumbrian art.[26] This is hardly likely because there are no mosaics in the Wall region, let alone in Ireland and Scotland. There is an element of truth in this connection, however, because both mosaics and the much later manuscripts share a common Late Antique aesthetic.

As we have seen, contemporary descriptions interpret abstract art in naturalistic terms making it not impossible that the fourth-century villa-owner stepping along the varied 'carpets' of the corridor mosaic at Scampton, for example, saw these patterns as reflecting spiritual as well as aesthetic values. In the case of a geometric panel of zigzags at the threshold of the triconch of the Orpheus Hall at Littlecote, there seems to be good reason to interpret the motif as relating to Orphic beliefs, indicative of a pool of water ('The Well of Memory').[27] It seems reasonable to assume also that flower motifs, such as the example in the centre of the Sparsholt floor, represented life and stars, or swastika-*peltae*, the heavens. This would allow the purely geometric frame of the great Woodchester pavement to impart a new dimension to the floor, the whole of life and the very heavens themselves being figured here.

Indeed, literary and religious interests seem to have characterized the world of many members of the local aristocracy of Roman Britain, at least to judge from the figured mosaic pavements which survive.[28] This is hardly surprising, for the more closely the art of Late Antiquity is studied, the less likely it appears that anything was done without an intellectual reason. Without a key, it is inevitable that we should, more often than not, fail to perceive what the meaning is, but it is surely better to try to understand than to admit defeat, bearing in mind that we know a great deal about fourth-century society and possess a large number of highly relevant literary sources, such as the works of Julian and Macrobius.

Brading, on the Isle of Wight, is a good starting point. The most controversial room is very small. In the centre is a bust of Bacchus and on one side is a cock-headed figure, clearly guarding a ladder leading up to a house beset by griffins. I have previously taken the guardian to be the Gnostic deity Iao, comparing him with the cock-headed figure often found on magical amulets who, however, has snaky rather than avian legs; alternatively he could be another deity connected with the cockerel, Hermes (Mercury) in his persona as guide of souls. A fox is shown beside another building balancing this scene. Another floor at the entrance to the Brading villa shows Orpheus with the beasts, with a fox as his familiar as usual. It is reasonable to take as Orphic the fox in the little chamber as well. It is, after all, appropriate that Orpheus, who was very closely connected with Bacchus, should be shown with him on this mosaic. Finally there is a gladiatorial fight, surprisingly almost the only one in Late Roman mosaic in Britain. The theme, which together with beast fights was so popular in North Africa and elsewhere, is transmuted here and at Bignor (where the contestants are cupids) into a symbol of the hazards of life. The floors of the two main reception rooms at Brading show myths whose significance can only be fully realized by one who, like the astronomer depicted on the threshold between them, was a practitioner of theurgy, able like any Late Antique 'holy man' to raise himself to the sphere of the gods. The myths shown in the larger room include those of Lycurgus and Ambrosia and Attis and the nymph Sangaritis, possibly referring to specific mystery cults – those of Bacchus and Cybele in these cases. There were obviously splendid opportunities for exegesis here. The linked room depicts

Perseus and Andromeda and other scenes now too fragmentary for certainty, but possibly including Cadmus approaching the spring. If so, it may be a coincidence that the two myths both occur on a mosaic at Frampton, albeit in iconographically quite different versions, representing on the one hand the killing of monsters, and thus victory over evil, and on the other a familiarity with (and love of) the *Metamorphoses* of Ovid (see below).[29]

In cases such as this, we are not concerned with simple, popular paganism but with recondite knowledge. This is the sort of esoteric religion which the Emperor Julian, Symmachus, Praetextatus, Macrobius and Proclus relished. The religious thought behind these floors is probably deeper and more complex than contemporary Christianity and many of the keys to understanding it have been lost. The Dorchester school appears to have had the richest repertoire, but it is at Cirencester where the single most inventive motif first evolved, though it was later to be employed by both Durobrivan and Petuarian mosaicists. Indeed, the centralized Orpheus mosaic in which the birds and mammals ever revolve in separate registers around the central and completely still image of Orpheus is one of the high points in all mosaic art, especially as presented in its classic form at Woodchester and also in abbreviated form at Barton Farm, Cirencester (**91** and see **106**).[30] There are two reasons why the type should have come into existence. First, Orpheus could be seen as the *avatar* of both Bacchus and Apollo, thus representing the divine centre around which creation revolves. The mosaics therefore have Platonic significance. The invention of the type at Cirencester is not fortuitous, for the Cotswolds together with London had long venerated a youthful hunter-deity, perhaps syncretized with Attis and shown on a number of sculptures. He probably went under a number of epithets: Ralph Merrifield suggests that he was called Apollo among other names. At the octagonal temple on Pagans Hill in north Somerset two pieces of sculpture are recorded, a hound and the head of an Attis-like figure. A similar temple at Nettleton Shrub in Wiltshire has yielded an altar to Apollo Cunomaglus. Was the Cotswold Orpheus in part a translation of the Cotswold hunter into mosaic, and was the association of the octagonal shape with the god important? For what it is worth the centre of the great Orpheus pavement at Woodchester was of this form. The British Orpheus pavement is thus to be seen as a local contribution to Late Antique art, drawing on a local cult but syncretizing the deity and giving him a universal significance.[31]

The Corinian Orpheus pavements were not just an opportunity to display virtuosity. They meant something to their owners. The Woodchester pavement with its dazzling display of ornament was at the hub of a veritable villa-palace. It is probable that there was a fountain at its centre (the water-nymphs shown in the spandrels around the central roundel suggest as much), and plashing water and the play of light and shadow must have been part of the display. Just as Orpheus orders the birds and beasts into registers which circle around him, so does the *dominus*, the aristocrat living here, order his world. The loveliness of the design and the subtle choice of colours would not have been lost on those who saw the floor, and there must have been a demand for more compact versions, such as that at Barton Farm and at Withington, likewise in Gloucestershire, as well as at Newton St Loe near Bath. A variant on the design was even taken up to Humberside, as mosaics from Horkstow and Winterton attest. Apart from the design and display aspects of the type, it may well have had subtle religious and social significance. The design has implicit within it the idea of a still centre and a turning, changing world. It uses myth to explore the nature of the divine, in accordance with Neo-Platonic tenets, but also the place of the villa-owner himself in his society.[32]

Religious ideas were developed to a remarkable degree by Durnovarian and Ilchester mosaicists. The rediscovered and restored Littlecote pavement which floors the cult room, beside a villa which had seen better days, is some thirty years later than the great Woodchester mosaic. The mosaic marks a development from the Corinian type of Orpheus floor and has been explained by the excavator, Bryn Walters, as a monument of syncretism between the cults of Orpheus, Apollo and Bacchus. He has cited Macrobius' *Saturnalia* in support of his arguement and could have found further support for his thesis in other contemporary pagan works, notably in the writings of the Emperor Julian himself. His views were severely criticized by Roger Ling and others, but there seems little doubt to me that Walters is essentially right.

We should be cautious of calling the Littlecote room a 'temple', with the implication of public worship inherent in the name; it was clearly not a public shrine but rather marks the 'privatization' of religion. This tendency was partly a result of that general shift from public to private patronage mentioned above, and partly because under Constantius II (337–61), pagan practices were looked on with suspicion and disfavour by the very autocratic Imperial government, though it is possible that this particular building was erected under the pagan Emperor, Julian (361–3). The effect of anti-pagan legislation, while such civilized men as Martinus held sway in Britain, may be doubted, but as Graham Webster points out the effects of the Magnentian revolt were ultimately more severe than has sometimes been realized, and certainly affected the public shrines.[33] The British aristocracy were not, however, cut off from the paganism of Rome and the central Empire. Just before Julian as Caesar in Gaul raised his standard in revolt he wrote to his friend Alypius, then vicar in Britain, to invite his participation. It is easy to believe that the pagan upper classes of Britain supported Julian as they did Magnentius, and were delighted by his religious policy.

The important complex at Frampton not far from Dorchester probably dates to about this time. It is on a low-lying site beside a river and, what is most extraordinary, ancillary domestic buildings seem to be lacking. Because a chi-rho and a *cantharus* are incorporated in the design of the mosaic there, though only in an apse off the main hall, it has sometimes been considered as a Christian pavement; if so the impressive number and variety of the mythological scenes suggest rather the paganization of its owner! I have proposed, alternatively, that the presence of the chi-rho among all those scenes of myth and cult may simply be intended to paganize Christ. A simpler suggestion is that the chi-rho was chosen because it was in the Emperor's standard or *labarum* and thus provided a very powerful amulet against the demons in which everyone believed.

The arrangement of scenes on the Frampton mosaics is revealing of the ceremonial approach to art at this time. We can well imagine the feasting and rituals (the putting down and taking up of special objects) depicted upon the Trier Mysteries Mosaic taking place here; the layout of the various floors encourages us to see stately processions from room to room. The description that follows shows the richness of these mosaics, and attempts to explain their cultural significance.

154

The largest hall has a central roundel which shows Bellerophon seated upon Pegasus, slaying the Chimaera. There were four panels in the corners of the hall of which the figured scenes in three survived in part or in whole. One depicts Paris and Oenone or Attis and Sangaritis. Another shows a female figure with torch pointing downwards and a dead or sleeping youth; Selene with the eternally-sleeping Endymion has been proposed, as has Venus and Adonis but there are other possibilities. The third panel appears to show the children of Jason and Medea bringing poisoned gifts to Creusa. There is an evident contrast between the central hero, who overcame all difficulties to win the daughter of king Proteus, and the unhappy scenes surrounding it. There is a veiled allusion to death, at least at one level, in a hexameter verse set along one side referring to a head of Neptune and his flanking dolphins: it is beyond this head set upon the chord of an apse containing a *cantharus* that the chi-rho is situated.

Bellerophon is in the same plane as a figure of Cupid (who represents the young Bacchus) in the border where he is mentioned in a hexameter, with the possible implication that he is greater (than Neptune), 'and you do not perform any service, if you deem it fit'. Beyond lies a room with a figure of Bacchus in triumph, seated on a leopard flanked by two hunting scenes, one of them a lion-hunt and the other a deer-hunt. These hunts, so popular in art in Late Antiquity, symbolize the life-force. There is even room for more interpretation here: perhaps the mortal who confronts a lion symbolizes humans facing up to all difficulties, while the deer stands for the suffering which is the part of all human existence. Certainly, another hunting-scene with hounds chasing deer is found along the edge of a panel in a chamber linked to this room by a corridor, and similar scenes by the same mosaicists but in a more probably Christian context at Hinton St Mary have been explained in that way. In the centre of the larger part of that chamber, set within a roundel, Bacchus again presides; around him are four panels. One pair contains scenes of prowess – Cadmus slaying the serpent of Mars and Perseus overcoming the sea-monster – the other of prophecy – Aeneas plucking the Golden Bough (**colour plate XI**) and perhaps the head of Tages. The source may have been Ovid's *Metamorphoses*. The contiguous panel shows a female bust, possibly Venus, within a roundel. In the border around her are sea-

creatures. Here we are to think of life coming from the sea. There was one more room at the end of another corridor leading from the room with Bacchus and the leopard, depicting a head of Neptune in the centre surrounded by the winds; presumably at one level, as with the other Neptune-head, making allusion to the world of the dead.[35]

We will never understand the full implications of what is shown here. The complexities of exegesis revealed in late pagan writings such as those of Julian or Macrobius make it certain that the owner and his or her guests would have found an endless field for speculation. Life begins and ends in the sea. Venus, born from the sea-spume, symbolizes the beginning; the voyage of the soul to the Blessed Isles the end. Nevertheless, that journey leads to new life, so that reversing the progress from Bacchus to Neptune is also a path to salvation, or to rebirth. In fact both the land *thiasos* and the marine *thiasos* are a commonplace in late pagan art, not only on mosaics but note also the great silver dish from Mildenhall and various items in the Thetford treasure. Treating both visual art and literature as a quarry for religious ideas is also characteristic of Late Roman paganism. Hunting lions was outside the experience of the British gentry, but deer-hunting was an activity which many must have enjoyed. Despite the chi-rho, it is unlikely that the owner of Frampton and his friends were Christians in any positive sense. The processions which the long corridors at Frampton seem to demand, recall the public liturgies of earlier days; now aristocrats who would have held public priestly office process with circumspection at home; they do so with great magnificence but in relative privacy, passing from room to room and from god to god.

A mosaic from Thruxton, Hampshire, now preserved in a sadly damaged state (without its central *emblema*) has already been mentioned in the previous chapter as evidence for patronage. It was laid, as its inscription tells us, by order of Quintus Natalius Natalinus and the Bodeni, the latter explained as two of his clients. The end of a lower line of inscription, of which only two letters remained to be recorded, was restored as '[ex] v[ot]o', preceded by another word. 'Posuerunt' or, better, 'promiserunt', would fit. The central roundel depicted Bacchus seated on a feline (**colour plate XIV**), and presumably the dedication was to him. In the Early Empire such dedications would have been made at public temples, though not to

Bacchus. In the fourth century Bacchus was popular in private cult, as seen on the mosaics of Brading, Littlecote and Frampton. His popularity increased because he united the patronage of convivial dinner-parties with salvation. We should not forget the marble statuette of the god from the Spoonley Wood villa, which eventually came to be buried with its owner.

The significance of the Thruxton mosaic is thus to show us three members of a religious guild meeting in a private house (as at Trier in the room in which the Mysteries mosaic was laid). Their practices are unknown to us, but probably only extended to the drinking of toasts and the recital of verses. It is perhaps the place to point out that there seems to have been another guild of Bacchus meeting in the former *mithraeum* by the Walbrook in London. Associated with this phase is not only the well-known marble HOMINIBUS BAGIS BITAM statuette but a handsome silver-gilt casket cast and chased with scenes of beast fights. It seems to be of third-century date but it was old and had been repaired before its final concealment, probably well on in the fourth century. It contains a silver infusor with the base in the form of a perforated pattern. This may well have been used to lace drinks with some hallucinogenic drug.[36] The Thetford treasure which was dedicated to Faunus, a deity who was clearly regarded as analogous to Bacchus, contained both strainers for wine and spoons inscribed with the names of cult-members. This treasure will be discussed further below.

The Hinton St Mary mosaic (see **85**), unlike that at Frampton, is still extant. It may be the *only* Christian mosaic we have to set against the wealth of pagan evidence, but it is even more problematic than that at Frampton and its contradictions cannot be fully resolved. It is certainly a work of the same school, sharing very similar scenes of hounds hunting deer, to that at Frampton. Unfortunately the villa (if that was indeed the nature of the building it came from) has not been properly investigated and until it is we cannot know whether to 'read' it by itself or as part of a larger scheme. The smaller section of the mosaic, acting as a vestibule to the larger part, shows Bellerophon slaying the Chimaera, the same subject as the central *emblema* of the largest room at Frampton. Here it is flanked by two oblong panels of hounds chasing deer. Presumably these panels were intended to convey the pains of life and the heroic efforts needed to overcome them. For anyone used to

pagan mythology there would have been no difficulty.

The major part of the mosaic, which might be expected to portray Bacchus or another heroic scene, instead has a clean-shaven bust backed by a chi-rho and flanked by pomegranates. This could be one of the sons of Constantine or even Magnentius with the *labarum*, but bearing in mind vault mosaics from outside Britain, it is easier to see this as Jesus Christ, who overcomes death, as symbolized by the pomegranates. Three of the lunettes on the chords of the long sides show hounds chasing deer and one, a tree of life. In the spandrels of the square are half-length figures without attributes but flanked by rosettes. They seem to be de-mythologized attributes, but in the next room Bellerophon is far from being de-mythologized. The lack of intellectual coherence here probably owes much to the state of mind of the man commissioning the mosaic from his local workshop, perhaps for his chapel. If he was a conventional Christian it is surprising that he made the gaffes of taking a pagan theme 'off the peg', having the sacred image of Christ shown on a floor, and having to make do with neutral human images to represent the evangelists. Surely, if he had wanted to, he could have provided 'orthodox' copy for the mosaicist? A likely conclusion is that he did not want something else, was perfectly satisfied with it as it was and may well have had what, to Catholic eyes, were heterodox views. Individual Christians may have suffered from the confusion of being caught between cultures, as was the poet Ausonius in contemporary Gaul.[37] Indeed, we should remember that Pelagius, who left Britain for Rome at the end of the century, promulgated the view that man was responsible for his own actions without the need of divine grace. Essentially his emphasis on moral struggle was very much at home in traditional Graeco-Roman religion. Much as he might have winced at the analogy (and certainly at the pagan image), Bellerophon's fight with the Chimaera fitted the Pelagian view of life. It is here suggested that some 'pre-Pelagian' landowners were willing to adapt their religion and compromise with the Neo-Platonic paganism of their contemporaries.

At Frampton the visual evidence suggests a pagan gingerly approaching Christianity; the alternative is that the owner was a nominal Christian whose beliefs and emotions were fired by the old gods. Excavation of the cemetery at Poundbury near Dorchester suggests that there was an established Christian community in the town, but I do not see the evidence even here for the cultural *predominance* of Christianity in local mosaic art, or indeed anywhere else. As far as the art of Late Roman Britain is concerned, and with a few major exceptions (Lullingstone; Hinton St Mary), its history could be written without mentioning the State religion of the Empire, though one suspects that much of the exuberance of pagan imagery was a reaction to its shadow.[38]

PEOPLE OF THE BOOK

Classical literature seems to have been a mark of aristocratic worth almost as much as it was in Mandarin China. This is clear not only from the writings of pagan authors, self-evidently obsessed by religious themes, but is manifest in the work of commentators such as Servius on Vergil as well as editors, including those of the very highest social rank from the families of the Nichomachi and Symmachi.[39] We owe the preservation of the major Classics in codex form to such dedicated scholars. Some of the Frampton panels may have been abstracted not from hypothetical 'pattern books' but from the owner's *de luxe* edition of Ovid. This could possibly have been the derivation of the mythological scenes on the *triclinium* floor from Keynsham as well, for the two which can be identified (Europa and the bull, Minerva inventing the *tibia*) are in Ovid's works.[40]

The Low Ham pavement with its powerful presentation of the story of Dido and Aeneas is excerpted from books Two and Four of the *Aeneid* and is a particularly convincing example; the pictorial form is typically Late Antique in keeping detail to the minimum and using significant gesture, eye-contact between protagonists (see **colour plate IX**) or symbolism to carry the dramatic impact of the story. Thus in the hunting scene Aeneas, who is seated upon his horse, turns round to look at Dido riding behind him. This inevitably leads on to the scene in a cave within a wood, simply represented by two trees (**colour plate X**). Dido, nude apart from a scanty veil, represents the vulnerability of love, but Aeneas has acquired armour and here the artist tells us that he has chosen duty above love. The centre of the mosaic presents the moral: Venus, whose body is made especially alluring by the towel she holds behind her, is the disposer of love and death (symbolized by a cupid

holding a torch downwards) and life and power (a cupid with raised torch).[41] Two fine illustrated Vergil codices, preserved in the Vatican, point to the real source of the mosaic. Some years ago I suggested that one of them, the *Vergilius Romanus*, which is characterized by strong simple shapes and a distinctive use of pattern and line (**92** and see **76**), might be very considerably earlier than the date of *c.*500 proposed for it and, in fact, could belong to mid to late fourth-century Britain, though admittedly Gaul has to remain a possibility. Since then Dr Kenneth Dark tells me that he, too, thinks the manuscript is insular on stylistic and paleographical grounds, though he would prefer to assign it to the later fifth century. As we have seen, the mosaic evidence discussed above renders it virtually certain that members of the British aristocracy owned and treasured literary manuscripts like this.[42]

Further support for this surmise is to be found in the Lullingstone mosaics. The subject of Bellerophon and the Chimaera, the fleshy dolphins and the elongated Pegasus and the equally linear nature of the bull on the other panel (comparable with animals on the Littlecote and Low Ham pavements) suggest a Durnovarian origin; perhaps the pavement was laid by a branch workshop. The Bellerophon theme in one room makes a pendant with that of Europa and the Bull in the dining-room next door (see **77**). Here the milieu is largely literary rather than religious; it certainly should not be assumed that these pavements are of the same date or executed for the same owner as the Christian frescoes of the house-church upstairs. They are probably at least a decade earlier. What sort of conversation went on between the villa-owner and his guests as they reclined on a semicircular couch set on the floor of red *tesserae* around the apse of the *triclinium*, just as the *Vergilius Romanus* depicts Dido and Aeneas as they feast at Carthage? We may think of the dining scenes shown on many Late Antique works of art like the great dish from the Sevso treasure, where the strong suggestion is that hunting and fishing were predominant subjects. Here, at Lullingstone, conversation was encouraged at a more refined and literary level – even if it was not altogether prim and proper! The villa-owner himself may well have been the proud author of the verse above Europa and the Bull which alludes to the jealousy of Juno and the storm she stirred up to wreck Aeneas and how much more cause she had for her action in this case, when

92 *The* Virgilius Romanus *(Ms. Vat.Lat. 3867. 74ᵛ).* *Turnus and Iris.* (Vatican Library.)

her own husband had metamorphosed himself in order to have a good time with a scantily-clad young lady. The allusion is to the *Aeneid*; but the elegiac couplet is one often employed by Ovid, and analysis of the actual language used points to personal knowledge of that poet.[43] The Aldborough mosaic showing the muses on Mt Helicon (with the name ΕΛΗΚΩΝ in Greek) proves that literary themes were not confined to southern Britain.[44]

DAILY LIFE, CEREMONY AND RELIGION

Apart from religion and literature, there are some indications of the daily life of the aristocratic patrons. The theme of hunting with hounds is quite well represented and we have seen it employed as a motif in Frampton and at Hinton St Mary. In addition, a fragmentary mosaic from Cherhill, Wiltshire, laid by the same Durnovarian mosaicists, depicts a running hound. A fragment from East Coker, Somerset, portrays two huntsmen carrying a deer on a pole. One of them has distinctive coloured *orbiculi* (patches) on his tunic, as worn by huntsmen on the near-contemporary mosaics at Piazza Armerina. One of the best-known vignettes from Roman Britain is the presentation of the season of winter on the *triclinium* mosaic at Chedworth. Here the hunter is in native dress, specifically the *birrus Britannicus*, and holds a hare. Finally, a mosaic from Cirencester itself has a hare as a centrepiece, presumably as a symbol of fecundity though of course the hare was the commonest beast of the chase. The feast is not figured as such on Romano-British mosaics but the presence of Bacchus with his panther on mosaics from Gloucester, Stonesfield, Thruxton and Frampton indicates a convivial aspect. Most of these rooms were, at least on occasion, used for dining. Although women were of considerable importance in the high society of Late Antiquity, as is emphasized by the wonderful gold jewellery from Hoxne, the *mundus muliebris* as such is not much in evidence on mosaics from Britain, save perhaps in images of Venus like that from Bignor (**colour plate XII**). Also, a simple but effective device in the centre of a floor in the villa of Grateley, Hampshire, depicted a fan, identical to the one carried by a woman on the second-century relief from Murrell Hill, Carlisle (see **37**).[45]

Bacchus was far too great a deity to limit himself to the superficial delights of the *triclinium* – there were other nuances here, for instance protection from evil and above all salvation from death. It should be noted that the marble statuette of the god which was found in a burial at Spoonley Wood, Gloucestershire, was presumably intended originally as a dining-room ornament but that it came to be used with serious religious intent, protecting its former owner after death. The idea of protection is associated with certain other figures, notably Hercules whose only appearance on a mosaic in Britain seems to be a very fine example from Bramdean, Hampshire, in which the hero is shown defeating Antaeus, watched by his own protector Minerva. Belief in the Evil Eye was universal, but it could be defeated by the head of Medusa, appearing as a centrepiece on another Bramdean floor, as well as at Bignor and Brading.

As has already been suggested above, the mosaics of Frampton and Littlecote and Thruxton were commissioned to reflect the religious enthusiasms of their respective owners and the rooms in which they were set probably had cult associations. Littlecote is essentially a small hall with a triconch apse in the centre of which Orpheus, with his canine companion, is depicted surrounded by representations of the animals into which Bacchus transformed himself when fleeing from the Titans. Four female personifications probably reflect the seasons, properly the domain of Apollo, while the rayed-designs in the apses are likewise solar, though the panther heads on the chords remind us again that this is a monument to syncretism. The many mosaics of Frampton are still more complicated, involving, as we have seen, two representations of Bacchus and two of Neptune who is the subject of a verse inscription here. A chi-rho and *cantharus* may demonstrate Christian influence. The myths shown in the main hall, Selene and Endymion, Paris and Oenone, and Jason's and Medea's children before Creusa, represent unhappy love-affairs, though the centrepiece is the ever-striving Bellerophon on Pegasus. Beyond a room in which Bacchus is seated on a feline is another room, depicting a standing Bacchus surrounded by scenes of heroic striving – Cadmus slaying the serpent of Mars, Perseus slaying the sea-monster in order to rescue Andromeda and Aeneas plucking the Golden Bough. Literature and religious exegesis are inextricably bound together here.

At Brading on the Isle of Wight the same is true. Here is a holy man as astrologer, an image which may be derived from Thales or Plato, but now represents the practitioner of theurgy, who has understood the mysteries and seen God. On one side of him is a room which contains a representation of Perseus; on the other mythological scenes (grouped as pendants around a central Medusa head). These include Lycurgus and Ambrosia, Ceres and Triptolemus, Attis and the nymph Sangaritis, and another scene which I believe could be Apollo and Daphne, reflecting the mysteries of Bacchus, the Eleusinian Mysteries and the Magna Mater, according to Roger Ling (and of Apollo, if my interpretation of the final scene is right). Alternatively, as I have suggested elsewhere, the owner could have read the episodes in terms of the acceptance or rejection of the divine: Ambrosia and Triptolemus remained faithful to Bacchus and Ceres respectively; Attis rejected Cybele and Daphne fled from Apollo. Other Brading floors include one with an image of Orpheus and another containing Iao or perhaps Mercury with the head of a cockerel guarding a ladder leading up to a house against two prowling griffins. These provide very heady and exciting examples of fourth-century pagan art, which – together with those of Frampton – are scarcely matched in the Late Empire, save in Cyprus, far away in the eastern Mediterranean.

Nor are these all; other mosaics should at least be considered in the light of religious exegesis in mind. Thus the representation of the Bacchic *thiasus* portrayed on the floor of the dining-room at Chedworth, long regarded as the embellishment of a rich villa, may likewise have had a far deeper purpose than mere festivity if Dr Webster is right in seeing the excavated complex as serving as the guest-house of a sanctuary. Here, paying guests would presumably have stayed, their minds inflamed by the imminence of the divine. Indeed, the scene of feasting combined with pagan religious ceremony depicted on the Trier 'Mystery mosaic' in which a man called Andesasus offers an egg(?) to Qodvoldeus (meaning literally 'What the god wills'), while another votary, Felox (Felix) takes up some other ritual commestible, may not be irrelevant in our attempts to understand any of these mosaic floors.[46]

Marine scenes, sometimes including deities such as Neptune, are not uncommon in the fourth century. As Neptune and the dolphins at Frampton show, they could have an eschatological significance, representing the realm over which the souls of the dead had to pass to the other world, and thus indicative of Salvation. The theme and the meaning go back to much earlier mosaics in Britain, and can be see for instance on second-century mosaics at Verulamium (a sea-shell and a head of Neptune), Cirencester (a marine *thiasos* including a cupid on a dolphin, fish and sea-beasts), Fishbourne (the Cupid on a dolphin) and perhaps an early third-century apse of a floor at Dorchester, Dorset (a head of Neptune with dolphins and fish). Such traditional subject-matter continued to appeal in the

fourth century. A panel containing two dolphins and a sea-beast occupies the threshold of the one room with a mosaic at Kingscote, Gloucestershire, here alluding to Venus shown holding her mirror in the centre of the floor of the main room.

Venus born from the spume of the sea and coming ashore on a large bivalve sea-shell is the theme of a mosaic from the villa at Hemsworth, Dorset. Here she is set in an apse and surrounded by a frieze of very fleshy dolphins, together with fish and molluscs. There is, of course, the famous treatment of this subject by Botticelli, but there are many ancient versions and the Renaissance artist was clearly copying and adapting one of them. The villa is not well known, but parts of other floors have been recovered from it, including a splendid *emblema* in a circular frame depicting a bust of Neptune (or Oceanus). A very popular place for such a theme was the bath-house. This is certainly true of another fine head of the god from a late town house in Cirencester and of a rather amateurish or child-like mosaic from the *apodyterium* at Rudston, depicting a head of Neptune amidst a free composition of fish. Bathing was a quintessential part of Roman life and bath-houses were often of great splendour in Late Antiquity, as is well attested in literature. In the most interesting bath-house mosaic from Britain, discovered in the *frigidarium* at Low Ham, culture takes the place of mere convention with the treatment of the love of Dido and Aeneas. Nevertheless, the centre of the pavement depicts Venus outlined against a dark red, fringed wrap or towel, as though she has just emerged from the bath, or perhaps, like the Hemsworth Venus, representing the epiphany of the goddess. In any case it is a deft touch rendering this fine composition especially appropriate to its setting.[47]

There are some interesting and significant omissions among the mosaics of Late Roman Britain. Neither gladiatorial contests nor wild-beast fights appear to have accorded with the rather refined interests of the British aristocracy. The cupid-gladiators of Bignor (**colour plate XII**) and the two gladiators in the chamber with the cock-headed god at Brading are merely references to the uncertainties of life, and unlike the floor at Nennig in Germany do not show any enthusiasm for such degrading pastimes. The Rudston pavement, depicting beasts in the arena, appears to be a poor copy of a North African design, probably of the third century. A mosaic from Dewlish,

Dorset, shows a leopard leaping onto the back of a Dorcas gazelle and another from Verulamium depicts a lion bringing down a similar animal; there were also minor scenes of lion hunts on mosaics at Withington the Frampton. All of these are less reflections of the arena than symbols of life and death, which have to be seen in the context of the main subjects of the floors.

Horse-racing is likewise far from well represented, though it was at least more respectable to those with a cultivated turn of mind. The Rudston charioteer and the Horkstow race presumably evoke the turning seasons of the year rather than suggesting close acquaintance with the circus, which has, left little trace in Britain. The Horkstow mosaic is in fact linked to panels showing a concentric Bacchic and marine *thiasos* combined – if it is not a 'shield of Achilles' – (**colour plate XIII**), to some degree recalling the Mildenhall great dish (see **86**), and also a concentric Orpheus pavement, both wheel-like motifs suggesting an eschatological significance, the turning of time and ultimate salvation. The Rudston mosaic includes personifications of the seasons and has two linked panels, one Bacchic – two leopards and a *cantharus* – and the other an octagon whose subject matter is now lost, but which could have represented the days of the week. Here, too, symbolism must have been more important to the owner than mere sport.[48]

The hieratic character typical of so much Late Antique art, and familiar from the early Christian art of Italy (for instance the wall and vault mosaics of Rome and Ravenna), is not absent from the British mosaics, being especially evident in the facing and nimbed bust from Hinton St Mary. As stated above, this probably shows Christ, but a member of the family of Constantine, perhaps even Constantine himself who adopted the chi-rho as his emblem, remains an alternative possibility. If so it would give the floor as much a political as a religious connotation; at least there would then be no need to agonize over the significance of Bellerophon, as the emperor was always in action, travelling and fighting barbarians. The Court of the Divine Emperor was, after all, modelled on the Court of Heaven, and to him was imparted the same ethereal qualities which belonged to deities and personifications. Among these, the beautiful Venus of the Bignor mosaic comes to mind, with her nimbus, diadem (restored) and attendant long-tailed

birds. In another villa mosaic, from Brantingham, Yorkshire, a large mosaic reveals a central nimbed bust and, along each of the short sides of the mosaic, a line of four nimbed female busts. Roger Ling has recently suggested that the subject is the Nine Muses, with one given greater prominence than the rest. This is possible though, allowing for blundering, the central bust still seems to be distinguished by a mural crown (rather than feathers) and thus a Tyche, very possibly the City-goddess of York. In each of the eight lunettes radiating from the centre is a water nymph and the eight busts on either side could have represented subsidiary *tychai*. If the busts are the muses, and, as we have seen, the muses on Helicon was the theme of a mosaic at Aldborough, we have further confirmation of the importance of culture to the Late Roman aristocrat; the other explanation gives them a more overtly political significance, most fitting if someone involved in the administration of the province lived here. Remains of fresco show that the ceiling or walls also carried nimbed heads. This icon-filled hall reflects the intensity and theatricality of Late Antique art, in which every gesture had a meaning. If only we knew what ceremonies, such as levées or banquets or religious celebrations, took place here.[49]

LATE ANTIQUE FRESCOES

It is not long since a consideration of the subject matter of Late Roman wall-painting in Britain would have been regarded as an almost impossible task but, thanks to the scholarship of Joan Liversidge and Roger Ling and the reconstruction work of Norman Davey and others, just about enough is now known about provincial paintings to give us some idea of the range of figured subjects they display and to show that they accord with the much better known contemporary mosaics. This means that we can literally reconstruct something of the rich physical backdrop of daily life.

The room of the Venus pavement at the villa-like building at Kingscote, perhaps the house of a procurator of an Imperial estate, is especially interesting because there is clear evidence of correspondence between floor and walls. The theme is love, perhaps an unexpected theme in the official house of a civil servant (if that is what it is) but fully in accord with the private nature of fourth-century art. The wall-paintings were first identified as depicting the young Achilles among the daughters of King Lycomedes, but the cupid between the two protagonists makes a more obviously amorous subject such as Venus and Mars more likely. We here remember the painting of Cupid in the House of Zoïlus at Trier. Although the painting was of an impressive standard, an even more accomplished mythological painting probably portraying the Narcissus myth has been excavated from the villa at Tarrant Hinton, Dorset (**colour plate IV**). These figure-paintings are conceived on a large scale and use exaggerated shadowing and rich colours. They cannot have stood alone, and undoubtedly there was far more wall-painting of high quality in Late Antiquity than mosaic, though the degree to which a strong provincial character was manifested is questionable. These two examples of mythological painting are traditional in content and illustrate the conservatism of so much fourth-century pagan art.[50]

The nimbed bust set within a roundel from Room 1 of the villa at Brantingham, Yorkshire, is of great interest not only intrinsically but because it too shows that the decor of the whole chamber followed a carefully-planned programme; its ceiling (or walls) was designed to reflect the subject matter of the floor, though its significance remains uncertain, as does the much better preserved floor mosaic. What has been reconstructed invites comparison with the very much finer and more complete 'portraits' from the Palace of Constantine at Trier, possibly members of the *Domus Divina*, though they might be personifications.[51]

The most 'advanced' wall-paintings are, not surprisingly, those from the house-church at Lullingstone, Kent, dating from late in the fourth century and representing the single most important work of Christian art from Roman Britain. Clearly, the tradition of Christian art had to develop during the century in which it came into its own. The west wall portrays a row of six *orantes* wearing very brightly coloured and distinctive robes. They are portrayed frontally and two-dimensionally. The north and south walls were apparently painted in two zones with figure scenes. On the south wall there was certainly a chi-rho within a wreath. Although the art of the catacombs comes to mind, Christian paintings from non-funerary

contexts are not common in the fourth century, and the Lullingstone church has an interest beyond the merely local. Possibly also Christian (or at least showing Christians) is the painting of a number of figures from a mausoleum at Poundbury, Dorchester, some of them holding staves or wands. However, the most covincing explanation is that they represent local members of the curial class to which the deceased surely belonged, 'perhaps specifically those who had held office as *duoviri*, and assumed a form of dress and insignia appropriate to those in higher authority'. To an even greater degree than in the case of the brightly-clad Lullingstone *orantes*, we cannot help being reminded of the fifth-century magistrates of Verulamium in their gorgeous robes, as described by Constantius in his life of St Germanus (*Vita Germani* xiv).[52]

PLATE AND ITS SUBSTITUTES IN LATE ROMAN BRITAIN

The basic aim of these mosaics, and of the brightly-coloured wall-paintings which accompanied them, was to provide a sumptuous background for aristocratic living (to which we may add the palatial guest-house of the Lydney sanctuary, as well as that of Chedworth if it is a building of the same sort). We lack the splendid textiles to which allusion has already been made; they must often have been magnificent works of art, richly dyed and embroidered. However, there is enough in the way of plate and jewellery remaining to add to what has been discussed above. Portable objects were used as personal gifts both to gods and men, as mosaics could never be, and there is indication that silver plate, and its cheaper local substitute pewter, was so employed; the same was of course true of jewellery.

A surprising quantity of silverware has been found in Britain. Although many of the better-quality vessels appear to have been imported from workshops elsewhere in the Empire, all have something to tell us of taste in Late Roman Britain. Figures and decoration are now generally chased (worked from above) and sometimes further embellishment was provided by means of niello (silver sulphide) or gilding. Not surprisingly, the style of the ornament parallels that manifested on mosaic floors. We can easily imagine great feasts and impressive ceremonies taking place at Woodchester, employing *ministeria* of silver plate as grand as the Mildenhall treasure. Incidentally, the formal design of the great dish from Mildenhall with its two concentric registers and central device (see **88**) is close to that of the Woodchester Orpheus pavement (see **106**), though in subject matter the Dionysiac imagery of the dish and two smaller plates at Mildenhall is nearer to scenes of revelry shown, for example, in the dining-room at Chedworth and above all, as noted above, in the *thiasos* mosaic from Horkstow (**colour plate XIII**), if that is what it is.[53]

It is well to emphasize that any particular piece of plate may have been treasured in a number of different places in its lifetime; thus it is generally harder to attribute individual items to any precise social context than it is in the case of a mosaic. The figural subject matter includes many scenes from mythology in which it is tempting to see reflections of the conservative pagan tastes which seem to have prevailed in Britain. The Mildenhall vessels already referred to could well have belonged to such a context, though – originally at least – *not* in Britain, as the two small plates each bear a graffito in Greek: EYΘHPIOY, just possibly designating that Eutherios who was *praepositus sacri cubiculi* with Julian in Gaul. Most of the subjects portrayed in the treasure appear to be religiously neutral, though possibly the paired *emblemata* in two bowls showing Alexander the Great and his mother Olympias would have had a greater appeal to pagans – as indeed might the wild animals and the Bacchic-style heads on the flanges of these and two other vessels. Three spoons with the treasure bear chi-rho monograms, and so possibly the treasure did belong to a Christian – or, as with the chi-rho on the Frampton pavement (see above), were there other explanations?[54]

The same query can be made of the Corbridge *lanx* (**93**) depicting Apollo, Leto, Asteria-Ortygia. Artemis and Athena, and thus alluding to Apollo's birthplace, Delos. If, however, it was manufactured in the Eastern Empire it cannot have been in Britain until later, and in any case it was almost certainly associated with other vessels found in the North Tyne, one of them a flanged bowl ornamented with chi-rhos.[55] Mythological scenes on vessels from the *Hacksilber* hoard of Traprain Law, perhaps recycled scrap silver collected by the authorities in tax and

given to mercenaries, tell us little directly about context. They do, however, show that people elsewhere in Britain possessed such items as a flagon showing the adoration of the Magi, Adam and Eve and Moses striking the rock (**94**). Presumably the original owner here was a Christian. Another flagon depicted the Recognition of Ulysses (**95**). A plate depicted the crowning of Bacchus and there was a bowl with the head of Hercules as an *emblema* and wild beasts on the exterior frieze, as well as a very fine and virtually complete scalloped bowl portraying a nereid on a sea-panther. In addition, there are fragments from a range of plate with geometric ornament, including two square vessels which by analogy with other silver and pewter vessels could well be of British manufacture (see Chapter 5). To all this evidence we should add the fragment of a plate from the Balline treasure, Co. Limerick in the Irish Republic, showing three horsemen (one of whom seems to have an African hairstyle), presumably part of a hunt scene.[56]

Only the spoons in the Thetford treasure, made for a *collegium* of worshippers of the god Faunus and mainly inscribed with dedications to him, allow us any certainty as to the commissioning and subsequent use of plate in Britain, where it is logical to see the cache as having been made. Three of the spoons have engraved bowls, one with only a simple fish but the two others are much more interesting. A silver-gilt swan-necked spoon has a bowl engraved with a triton and a dolphin and the inscription DEI NARI, here an epithet of Faunus. The device, like the Traprain sea-panther evokes the marine *thiasos*. The other spoon with a rat-tailed handle inscribed DEI FAVNI NARI and likewise with a gilded bowl shows a panther running in front of a tree, evoking the land *thiasos* and bringing to mind the animal friezes on British Orpheus pavements. The high quality of the silver, the elegance of the swan-necked spoons, which in some cases display a pleasing native conceit in the berry which the bird carries in its bill, and the attractive linearity of the engraved bowls of the spoons, both figural and epigraphic designs, do not suggest that High Roman art, if at the end of its range, was at the end of its confidence. Still less does the associated jewellery (see below). The linear engraving is well matched on a spoon bowl from the Canterbury treasure on which a sea-stag swims towards a stylized plant. Two superimposed friezes of stylized plants are to be seen on the silver bowl from the Ballinrees treasure, which Sonia

93 *Silver lanx from Corbridge, Northumberland showing Apollo and other deities. L.48cm. (Photo: British Museum.)*

94 Biblical scenes on silver gilt flagon found at Traprain Law, East Lothian. L. of frieze 25.5cm; H. of frieze 8.5cm. Royal Museum of Scotland. (After A Curle, Treasure of Traprain, 1923, fig.2.)

95 The Recognition of Ulysses on a silver flagon found at Traprain Law, East Lothian. H.15cm. Royal Museum of Scotland. (After A Curle, Treasure of Traprain, 1923, fig.9.)

165

96 *Recast silver lanx from Risley Park, Derbyshire, with boar-hunting scene. L.49.7cm. (Photo: British Museum.)*

Hawkes rightly compares with plants shown on a distinctive type of Late Romano-British buckle. We can now see a certain similarity between the style of engraving of the creatures on the spoon bowls and that of the peacocks on the Trimontium buckle, though this last is of bronze and not quite of the same quality.[57]

The subject matter of the recently 'rediscovered' *lanx* from Risley Park, Derbyshire (**96**), with its boar-hunt and surrounding pastoral and hunting scenes, while not overtly pagan is very similar to several of the Mildenhall bowls, the bear-hunt making an especially felicitous parallel. However, an inscription on the underside of the dish shows that it eventually came into the possession of an important Christian, Bishop Exuperius, who gave it to the church of 'Bogium' (possibly a Roman estate at Risley, Derbyshire). The *lanx* as we now have it is an eighteenth- or nineteenth-century casting from the fragments of the original, using the original silver, but it is clear that the Risley Park *lanx* was itself cast in Roman Britain from a mould, presumably by a pewterer.[58]

Pewter is only occasionally figured, and an item such as the flanged polygonal pedestal-bowl from the Isle of Ely with engraved ornament including a chi-rho and a peacock is of greater iconographic interest than artistic value. However, mould-made pewter plates could provide a useful *ministerium* for a family with high social pretentions but lacking the cash and perhaps the rank to buy a *ministerium* of silver. Such a service would look very grand on the sideboard, and in the dim light of most Roman houses the difference would have been hard to tell. As noted in the last chapter, pewter plates were given as gifts, either with personal messages scratched on by the donor as at Appleford or, in one case, provided as part of the design. Certainly, the large plate from Welney, Norfolk, with its elaborate geometric ornament in the centre comparable with that in the centre of the niello dish in the Mildenhall treasure, is one of the best pewter plates from Roman Britain; though surely any moderately well-educated recipient would have winced over the blundered rendering of the words UTERE FELIX 'Use happily'.

Such geometric work is quite common, as it is on silverware. Examples include several items from the Appleshaw hoard in the British Museum and the intersecting squares and central rosette on an Appleford dish (see **81**) in the Ashmolean, as well

as the braided cross-design at the centre of a bowl from Bath. The effect is certainly attractive even where execution is not entirely accomplished. One of the most attractive pewter vessels is a fish dish from Appleshaw, with the engraved figure of a fish within a *vesica*-shaped field. It is paralleled by a rather plainer pewter dish from Alise-Sainte-Reine in the south of France, likewise with a fish on it. The material of which this collection of vessels is made very strongly suggests that it was brought from Britain, though whether as an export order or simply by the owner is not known. Another fascinating find is a pewter bowl from Bath, containing in its centre the cast of a coin of Constantine. It thus appears to imitate the silver bowls from the so-called 'Munich treasure' containing central medallions representing portraits of Licinius I and Licinius II, which were made as Imperial gifts. The Bath copy was surely made for someone who wanted to pretend to his friends that he was the recipient of similar largess.[59]

LATE ANTIQUE JEWELLERY IN BRITAIN

Jewellery was a quintessential part of Late Antique art, and at its most luxurious and impressive denoted the rank and social standing of its owner. We think of the great cross-bow brooches and heavy belt-fittings of the Ténès treasure and the parures shown on mosaics, ivory diptychs and silver plate from elsewhere in the Empire. Actual examples of such high-quality metalwork did reach Britain, as is shown by some of the astonishing objects in the Hoxne treasure, like the jewelled body-chain (see **88**) and the four *opus interrasile* bracelets (see **89**). These belonged to a very important lady indeed. Cross-bow brooches made of gold were worn on the right shoulder by men of high rank, as is shown on the dress of an official portrayed on the *Missorium* of Theodosius found at Almendralejo in the province of Badejoz, Spain; Stilicho himself sports a brooch of this type on the ivory diptych now in Monza Cathedral treasury. There are a few examples of gold brooches of this type from Britain; the most informative for the student of Late Roman history is the example found at Erickstanebrae, Dumfries and Galloway. Although its head is lost, its inscribed *opus interrasile* bow remains, with its inscription proclaiming that it was part of a

97 *Gold crossbow brooch from the Moray Firth, Scotland. L.7.9cm.* (Photo: British Museum.)

donative from the Emperor Diocletian (see chapter 4). Likewise from Scotland, the Moray Firth cross-bow brooch is embellished with engraved triangles on both bow and foot, while a cusped-motif in open-work projects on each side of the latter (**97**). There is a smaller and rather plainer brooch from Odiham, Hampshire. Other cross-bow brooches of silver and niello or gilded bronze were presumably worn by those of lower rank.[60]

Perhaps even more interesting than the standard Late Roman jewellery are the pieces from the Thetford treasure, because, although they are thoroughly Roman in technique, they all appear to have been made locally (in East Anglia) and many bear ornament in a distinctive provincial Roman style. There were no brooches here, but 22 rings, a belt-buckle, four bracelets, two pendants and a number of chains display rare virtuosity in techniques, including filigree, chasing, casting, gem-setting and inlay of gold in glass. Texture, colour and the play of light on angled surfaces are all features of Late Roman taste generally, but most of the designs here are totally unique. We also find a religious conceit in a ring whose bezel is a vase containing a blue-green glass jewel representing water, and whose shoulders are woodpeckers, thus alluding to the father of Faunus (Picus). The head of Faunus, with two inlaid garnet ears, on another ring and the belt-buckle set with an appliqué of a satyr (or is it Faunus himself?) also point to the cult. Whether the

98 *Gold, multi-jewelled ring with dolphin-hoop from the Thetford treasure, Norfolk. D.3.2cm.* (Photo: British Museum.)

jewellery comes from the same workshop as the silver is not known, but it too was surely a special order. The Thetford treasure belongs very much to its age, both generally in its deliberately antiquarian reference to an Early Roman cult, here revived, and in its cross-references to other contemporary jewellery. Filigree wires are used to produce curvilinear or plaited ornament on several rings, a technique found widely in Britain, for example on two rings from a small hoard found recently at Silchester and also on two rings from New Grange in Ireland. The type is not confined to Britain, though, as Thetford shows, such rings were certainly made here. The crested dolphins which support bezels on two of the Thetford rings (**98**) can be paralleled on a bronze ring from Canterbury. A similar dolphin comprises the bow of an unusual silver zoomorphic cross-bow brooch from Sussex (which is, incidentally, ornamented with a chi-rho on a disc at the head). Dolphins are also incorporated in the decoration of late Roman buckles, though others are embellished with confronted horse-heads – a feature also to be seen on the Thetford buckle.[61]

The belt, like the cross-bow brooch, was an important feature in Late Roman dress. As Esmonde Cleary rightly points out, it too could be worn as a symbol of rank and hence of authority, and, as with brooches, was frequently bestowed as an official gift. A well-known painting from a tomb at Silistra in Bulgaria depicts a servant about to take such a belt to his master. No high-ranking Roman would have wished to be seen in public without his belt, any more that an English gentleman would enter his club without a tie; indeed it was even more important. The gold example from Thetford is, of course, a special case, and evidently a purpose-made gift to the god Faunus who is probably depicted (as a satyr) on the plate.

More characteristic of the high-status belt are various items from the Traprain Law treasure. These include a square-ended buckle ornamented with a wave pattern and inlaid with niello. The plate exhibits an Alpha and Omega, showing that in all probability the owner was a Christian. The belt consists of segmented plates of silver, themselves with niello designs. Another belt, of leather, is partially preserved and is ornamented with lozenge-shaped studs. There is no other *cingulum* from Britain of precious metal though we can point to others of base metal which may have been official issue. Part of a buckle embellished with niello from Snodland, Kent, incorporates two portraits in its design, very possibly intended to be Imperial portraits. Similar portraits are in fact found on silver and there is an example on a vessel from Traprain Law. The plate of a buckle from Caves Inn (Tripontium), Warwickshire, has a design of peacocks flanking a tree of life (**99**), perhaps less a sign of Christianity as such than a symbol of (eternal) life, acceptable to any wearer.

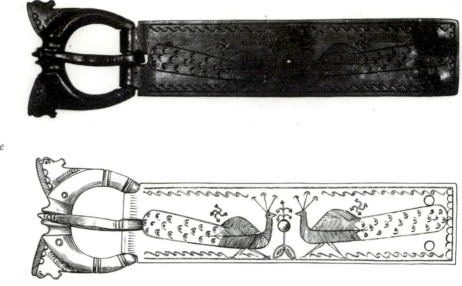

99 *Bronze horse-head buckle with plate engraved with peacocks flanking a tree of life, from Cave's Inn (Trimontium), Warwickshire. Total L.1.7cm. Warwickshire Museum (Photo: Robert Wilkins, Institute of Archaeology, Oxford; Drawing: P.A. Broxton.)*

Other buckles carry geometric ornament of various types. Many buckles bear 'chip-carved' decoration. Although originally thought to be 'Germanic' we can now see this taste as exploiting the increasing pre-occupation with texture in Late Antiquity; indeed such motifs as lozenges. S-scrolls and tendrils can observed on many items of silver plate. Indeed, there are two silver strap-ends of this characteristic style from Traprain Law, described as 'Teutonic' but very similar to silverware actually preserved in the treasure. Most examples of the style from Britain are of bronze, but they are just as Roman. Some of the wearers may have been soldiers, whatever their ethnic origin; others may have been civilians, and very possibly all served the State in some way – or fancied that they did so.[62]

A local style of art, the origins of which are disputed, is associated with flat, circular brooches (quoit brooches) and with buckles; its decorative repertoire includes stylized animals, plants and rosettes. Although it is often quite removed from Classical ornament, the relationship to Late Roman work is quite close. Thus the splendid circular silver brooch from Sarre, Thanet in Kent (**100**) has a beaded border within which are two concentric friezes of animals with circular eyes. On the plate are two confronted doves in relief, with another on the pin. The formality and discipline of the design, with its double frieze, is reminiscent of Roman silverware and

specific comparisons can be made between the animals depicted here and the deer on a silver ring from the Amesbury hoard (**101**), which has always been regarded as Roman, while the rendering of the confronted birds recalls the Thetford woodpeckers.

The formal rosettes and tendrils on the plate of a buckle from Orpington, Kent, and similar rosettes on a buckle-plate from Bishopstone, Sussex, are very like plates which are undoubtedly Roman. The most splendid examples of belt-fittings in this style come from a fifth-century grave at Mucking, Essex (**102**); this; was originally inlaid with silver, now largely missing. The buckle itself has a zoomorphic surround of two double-headed beasts; its attached plate has a scrolled border and contains a rectangular panel of chip-carved ornament. An associated plate has a circular panel of chip-carving and a zoomorphic surround. While some of the Roman analogues are Continental, for instance in the Vermand cemetery, Aisne, the style does not mark a break with the past. Belts and brooches were, after all, the prestige objects of the Late Roman world and, as Vera Evison wrote of the Mucking mounts, they 'were made for a privileged and possibly military section of the community . . . equipped partly after the Roman fashion'. Whether their taste was 'Germanic' lies in the beholder's eye.

The 'quoit-brooch style' has been associated with Germanic invaders and with Roman Britons or sub-Roman Britons. It has, however, mainly been studied

100 *Silver annular quoit brooch from Sarre, Kent. D.7.7cm. (Photo: British Museum.)*

by students of the Anglo-Saxons rather than by those interested in Late Roman and Early Byzantine art. Clearly most of the finds are from Anglo-Saxon contexts, but that does not tell us much about the nationality of the creators of the style, or for that matter what the wearers of these splendid ornaments thought about them. Three silver rings with square bezels found with a hoard of Late Roman coins at Amesbury,

101 *Three silver rings from a hoard found at Amesbury, Wiltshire, one with helmeted heads; two with animals. All have D. of c.2.5cm. British Museum. (Photo: author.)*

Wiltshire (see **101**), may cast some light on this; they have engraved designs on the bezels and were probably intended to be used as signet-rings. One depicts a stag(?) very like the beasts on the Sarre brooch in its style, another has a griffin and the third, four helmeted heads. Other 'quoit-brooch rings' include one of silver found near Wantage (**103**), portraying two sea-beasts, and a gold ring from Richborough with a single helmeted bust. These all suggest the beginning of the transformation of Roman art into something else, probably in the early fifth century rather than before. Like the belt and the brooch, the signet-ring was a sign of *romanitas*. All these objects dating to the age of the English settlements seem still to belong to the culture of the Late Roman world and they form a fitting climax to the story of art in Roman Britain.[63]

Jewellery allows us to see the beginning of the re-emergence of Celtic enamelling as a major art form, in Late Roman Britain decorating the terminals of grand penannular brooches like the example from Bath with an eagle on one terminal and an osprey catching a salmon on the other (see **68**), or the silver handpin from Oldcroft, Lydney, Gloucestershire. Both objects are ancestral to an artistic development continuing well beyond the fourth century. Although it is tempting to bring the British art of the Dark Ages into the discussion, this is seldom Roman in spirit even where there are typological links with Roman art. Late Roman art was the art of a villa-owning aristocracy (and of Roman officials) which passed away even where it left successor kingdoms (as on the Welsh Marches, in Gwent, and in the vicinity of Wroxeter). Even the art of the Christian church, which at its late stage achieves dominance, owes only a small material debt to the artistic culture of Roman Britain. Quite often 'Roman' elements such as the designs of some hanging-bowl escutcheons really derive from the early Byzantine culture of the sixth-century Mediterranean world, where of course the physical presence of Late Antiquity still survived as a living culture. The Sutton Hoo find – the grave goods of an Anglian king – with its Byzantine silverware is perhaps the supreme example of this 'revival' of interest in Rome, past and present. From now on Roman art is a matter of antiquarian interest in the widest sense although, as we shall find in the final chapter of this book, the art of Roman Britain as such is only very occasionally held up as worthy of praise and emulation.[64]

102 *Cast bronze and silvered buckle and belt mounts from Grave 117, Mucking, Essex. Buckle: L.10.1cm; counter plate: 5.8cm. Rectangular mount: 6.4cm; triangular mounts: both 4.8cm.* (Photo: British Museum.)

103 *Silver ring depicting sea-creatures, from Wantage, Oxfordshire.* (After Proc.Soc.Ant². iv, 1867, p.38.)

CHAPTER EIGHT

Attitudes to the Art of Roman Britain

How many ages hence
Shall this our lofty scene be acted over
In states unborn and accents yet unknown!

The rather negative view of Romano-British art expressed so eloquently by Haverfield and Collingwood, to which this book is inevitably an extended reply, has influenced the views of all writers on Roman Britain this century; not least those of Jocelyn Toynbee whose monumental study, discussing listing and often all items which could be described as *Art in Britain under the Romans* known to her in 1964, will not easily be superseded. While praise is sometimes generously given, the best native craftsmanship is always ascribed to Gauls. It is only very occasionally that the objects described are treated as having tremendous aesthetic merit in themselves, and it is this apologetic and muted response that coloured the linked exhibition on *Art in Roman Britain* held in 1962. This situation is very different from the enthusiasm for Celtic art, both pre- and post-Roman or for Anglo-Saxon art.

Essentially the reason for this lies in the traditions of research into Roman antiquity, especially from the sixteenth century onwards, though its roots go back to the early Middle Ages. I began my book on *Religion in Roman Britain* with a quotation from Gildas who mentions 'the devilish monstrosities of my land . . . some of which we can see today, stark as ever, inside or outside deserted city walls: outlines still ugly, faces

still grim' (*De Excid. Brit.* 4, 2). Here, of course, aesthetic judgement is coloured by ideology. The ugliest thing about them was that they were pagan. The debt to Roman art of much early 'Anglo-Saxon' art and of the Celtic ornament ascribed to the Dark Ages is debatable. The most convincing link with the Romano-British past is perhaps the late sixth- or early seventh-century Sutton Hoo whetstone-sceptre with its carved faces and head consisting of a bronze stag figurine (**104**). This is not only because sceptres were widely employed in the Roman world and, indeed, in Roman Britain, but also because the naturalistic stag itself has good Romano-British analogues. Bruce-Mitford mused in the report: '[Raedwald] sought to fuse in his *bretwalda*-ship the Roman legacy and the sacral power of Germanic kingship with the role of suzerain over Celts and Celtic lands, in a new, imaginatively conceived, expertly designed and executed symbol.' Other examples of animal art which appear Classical in their realism are the early Pictish symbolic beasts, perhaps beginning in the sixth century. Again these bulls, eagles, snakes, geese, etc., are best considered as being survival rather than revival.[1]

Certainly, the Augustinian mission in the late sixth century which reintroduced Italian Christianity also brought back Roman art – a contemporary Late

104 *Sceptre from the ship burial, Sutton Hoo, Suffolk consisting of ceremonial whetstone surmounted by iron ring and cast bronze stag. H.82cm.* (Photo: British Museum.)

Antique Roman art which is well represented by the *Gospels of St Augustine* now in Corpus Christi College, Cambridge, but also by the *Codex Amiatinus*, now in Florence but actually produced at Jarrow. The Ezra miniature in the latter shows a scribe in Classical dress, his implements beside him and a book-cupboard embellished with typical early Christian ornament, such as confronted peacocks, confronted sheep, chalices and a chi-rho as well as crosses. However, the art here is that of the central Empire just as the churches of what the late Stuart Rigold called the 'Litus Romanum' are Italian and not Romano-British. David Wilson writes of the Codex that it 'was perhaps too advanced in its stylistic approach to appeal to the taste of the English Church; its style never caught on'. The silver vessels from Sutton Hoo are no more products of Roman Britain than these manuscripts; the exceptionally large Anastasius dish, indeed, has control stamps of that East Roman emperor (AD 491–518) and no doubt came to Britain as a result of renewed contact with the Mediterranean at the end of the sixth century.[2]

However, the reinvigorated taste for antiquity meant that, potentially at least, Roman art could be admired and copied wherever it was to be found. The well-known and beautiful poem *The Ruin* can probably be localized at Bath because of its mention of hot springs, but its poignant lament for fallen grandeur is too general to form any basis for a critical assessment of Anglo-Saxon taste in such matters.[3] The best-known instance of specific interest in the artistic past is St Cuthbert's visit to Carlisle (Bede, *Vita Sancti Cuthberti*, 27) when he admired a beautiful fountain of Roman date, although there is no information that it was ornamented. Possible direct influence of Romano-British art may be seen in the inhabited vine-scrolls in eighth-century sculpture fragments from Jarrow and upon the Ruthwell and Bewcastle crosses dating to c.800, which it is tempting to compare with a Romano-British relief from Hexham depicting scrollwork. However, it is at least as likely that the inspiration here, like that on the late eighth-century Ormside bowl, comes from contemporary southern Europe, no earlier than the Augustinian mission.

The linear drapery of the figures on the Ruthwell Cross, as well as those in the Lindisfarne gospels, is certainly reminiscent of the style of the Murrell Hill tombstone (see **37**) and other examples of the

Carlisle school on the one hand, and of the *Vergilius Romanus* (see **76** and **92**) or the Low Ham mosaic (**colour plates IX, X**) on the other. However, it is quite possible to derive the influence from elsewhere – from icons or even *opus sectile*, with dates much closer to the seventh and eighth centuries.[4] I am more convinced about prototypes from Roman Britain in the case of the stacked half-length figures on the Otley Cross, Yorkshire, and on certain other Anglo-Saxon tombstones, such as the bust of Christ from Whitchurch, Hampshire, which seems to echo a type represented by *stelae* from Vindolanda, Risingham, High Rochester, York and London, although even here it has been suggested that the Roman sources used by the sculptors came from abroad.[5] A Classical source may lie behind the representation of a warrior on a mid-eighth-century cross-shaft at Repton, Derbyshire – perhaps a cavalry tombstone (which is one of the Roman prototypes canvassed in the publication) or a religious monument such as the warrior relief in Nottingham University Museum, or the much finer relief from Stragglethorpe, Lincolnshire; but once again it is impossible to be confident about the true nature of the source.[6]

Roman forms were absorbed into Romanesque art and perhaps for this reason specific local prototypes are even harder to suggest. While Roman art could be very much admired (even though misunderstood, as for instance in the case of the Great Cameo of St Albans illustrated by Matthew Paris), it is seldom that we can point to specifically Romano-British exemplars, though it is not unlikely that objects found on Roman sites provided inspiration to artists. On the whole, as much later, in the Renaissance, the twelfth century took its culture from southern Europe, and Henry of Blois evidently collected his statues in Rome. Respond capitals from Normandy and England may, nevertheless, owe something to Roman inhabited capitals which were fairly widespread in Europe. The very rich example from York is paralleled by Zarnecki with examples from the Loire Valley, but a Roman capital on an imbricated column from Catterick allows the possibility of a nearer source in Roman Britain. Also in Yorkshire, a font at Reighton of square shape and ornamented with chip-carving could well be derived from a Roman altar, while another font at Toller Porcorum, Dorset, embellished with a volute and ram's head seems to be indebted to a lost Romano-British original.[7]

During the Middle Ages actual examples of Roman sculpture, *spolia*, were visibly incorporated in buildings, such as the Great Hall of Chepstow Castle and churches at Compton Dando, Somerset, and Marlborough and Tockenham in Wiltshire; but a positive attitude to such objects had to await the new learning, at first historical and then epigraphic, in the sixteenth century. Sir Robert Cotton, who spanned the reigns of Elizabeth I and James I, visited the 'Picts Wall' in 1599 and collected some inscriptions including one set up by the Fourth Cohort of Gauls at Risingham, one of the most attractively decorated dedication slabs from northern Britain. Its central frame containing an octagonal wreath is flanked by *aediculae* in which are images of Victory and Mars respectively. Camden refers to it and the stone is still extant in Cambridge, although presumably it was preserved in the first instance for its short dedication rather than for its rich frame.[8] Nevertheless, the cenotaph erected in 1613–15 by Cotton in All Saints, Conington, Huntingdonshire, to Prince David of Scotland incorporates features of Roman art which Cotton had learned about from his northern trip. By this time Roman art was being experienced by wealthy Englishmen in Italy itself, and in any case Classical art, whether Roman or Renaissance, could be enjoyed or emulated through books, notably by Serlio and Palladio. There was no need to seek precedents in Roman Britain.[9]

The main interest in the seventeenth and eighteenth centuries was aristocratic and concerned with the marbles and gems which could be obtained in Rome and further afield. The Grand Tour travels of the *dilettanti* made this possible and left to the more humble antiquaries, whose interests were largely topographical and historical, the charting of Roman Britain. Here inscriptions, albeit often associated with sculpture, remained of primary interest. This is evident in the ambitious coverage of sculpture and inscriptions in the second book of John Horsley's *Britannia Romana* published in 1733. The author recommends them as being 'very curious' and throughout is concerned with historical rather than aesthetic considerations. When he finally comes on to the gilt-bronze head of Minerva from Bath, found in 1727, he does describe it as 'yet a very beautiful and elegant figure' but goes on to add: 'whether we should call it the head of Pallas or Apollo (though both the place where it was found, and the air of the face, seem to favour the latter) 'tis not for me to say; since that learned body, who first published it, have not thought fit to determine this.'[9]

Occasionally, the ability of a particular scholar achieved higher standards. A statuette, possibly part of a table-lamp stand, was ploughed up in the Lewses, Cirencester, in 1732 and shown to Thomas Hearne. Although suspicious of the finders, he correctly identified the subject matter as Cupid rather than Apollo. It was exhibited at the Society of Antiquaries some thirty years later and was ultimately published in *Archaeologia* in 1785 with a fine plate by the eldest James Basire (**105**). Later it came to form part of the Bodleian Collection, before being transfered to the Ashmolean in the late nineteenth century.[10] William Stukeley, too, for all his delving into the Druids, was versed in Classical scholarship and had friends in those aristocratic circles which admired it, and could afford to travel to see it. His publication of the Risley Park *lanx* in a paper read to the Society of Antiquaries on 8 April 1736 is the result of one of his forays into Roman art and its quality and scholarship makes one wish he had not been side-tracked into the insidious snares of 'British Antiquity'. Nevertheless his identification of the *Ecclesia Bogiensis* of the inscription with Bouges in Tourain, encouraged him to believe that it was brought to England from France during the French wars of the fifteenth century. Stukeley also produced a pioneering study of the interesting coin issues of Carausius; he has been criticized for wrongly identifying an unusual coin showing a female bust with Carausius' wife 'Oriuna', when in fact it shows Fortuna, but given the ubiquity of coins showing empresses, the lapse is in fact quite understandable, and the large-scale plates in the book certainly allow for the appreciation of these British-minted coins as art.[11]

Mosaics provided the best opportunity for the pursuit of Classical archaeology within Britain during the eighteenth and nineteenth centuries. At first there was little opportunity for scholarly comparison and the learned were driven back on their knowledge of ancient writers. Without any tradition of iconographical scholarship it is not surprising that a mosaic from Leicester showing Cyparissus and the stag, discovered about 1675 and published 1710–12 in the *Philosophical Transactions*, was thought to portray Actaeon. However, the fact that the fragment has been preserved shows that its merits, especially its

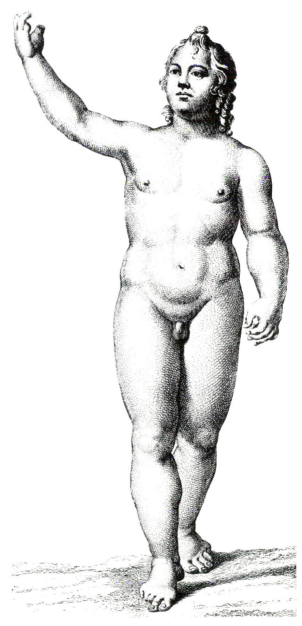

105 *Bronze statuette of Cupid from Cirencester. H.41cm. Ashmolean Museum. (After J. Basire (i), Archaeologia vii, 1785, pl.xxix.)*

iconographical interest, were appreciated at the time.[12] Unfortunately most other mosaics were allowed to deteriorate not long after discovery, although not before they had been the subject of considerable interest. The Stonesfield Pavement is perhaps the best known of these early finds. Discovered in January 1712 it was soon the talk of Oxford and was visited on five occasions by the young Hearne, who at first thought it was medieval and depicted St Michael and the dragon, though he later came to the conclusion that it was laid about 369 and depicted 'Apollo Sagitarius', the view he put forward in his *Discourse concerning the Stonesfield Tesselated Pavement*. Despite his Classical abilities and access to books in the Bodleian, he was not as clear sighted here as he was in the case of the Cirencester cupid and it was other men, including the astronomer, Edmund Halley and John Pointer, chaplain of Merton, who pointed out that the subject was Bacchus holding a *thyrsus*, seated upon a large feline.

Hearne's fervent advocacy of the Apollo hypothesis convinced Dr Woodward, though that gentleman's credulity is forever associated with his famous or infamous iron shield, which he believed to be Roman. We do at least owe it to Hearne that the mosaic was engraved after study of the original by Michael Burghers, the University of Oxford engraver. It entered European scholarship, however, through a somewhat inferior engraving which found its way to Samuel Pitiscus, who used it as a frontispiece for his *Lexicon Antiquitatum Romanorum*, published in Leeuwarden in 1713. Later, in 1725, after the pavement had been lost to sight it was re-engraved by George Vertue and the design was apparently used by a lady as a pattern for embroidering a carpet. The pavement was rediscovered in tolerable condition in 1779, by which time it could be compared with work at Herculaneum.[13] The Littlecote pavement, found in 1730 by William George of Littlecote Park, had a similar fate; it too was engraved by Vertue (this time from the life) and later embroidered in needlework by George's widow, whose enchanting and unusual recreation of one of the most interesting (and controversial) mosaics of Roman Britain was, until recently, in Littlecote House. This mosaic floor was seen as of a temple dedicated to Bacchus, which accords with the views of the excavators and the present writer more than with the more prosaic views of other recent scholars. The pavement was literally 'lost', only to be recovered in recent times by Bryn Walters and happily repaired and restored.[14]

The culmination of the interest in and investigation of mosaics came at the end of the eighteenth century and the beginning of the nineteenth, with the gentleman-scholar Samuel Lysons. His account of Woodchester was dedicated very fulsomely to George III:

> *Georgio III Britanniae Regi has Romanorum apud Britannos magnificentiae reliquias humillime d.d.d. Samuel Lysons.*

It was issued in 1797 in a giant folio volume with a French text as well as one in English, and it was clearly intended that it should find a place in noble libraries throughout Europe (106).[15] Lysons' style of excavation around this time becomes apparent in the text to the first part of his *Reliquiae Britannico-Romanae*, in connection with Frampton, where he worked in 1796 and 1797. 'After inspecting these remains', he writes:

> I proceeded to Weymouth, about twelve miles distant, where the King then was, and his Majesty understanding that I was desirous of making further discoveries, was graciously pleased to order that a party of the Royal Lancashire regiment of fencibles, then encamped in the neighbourhood, should be at my disposal for that purpose and they were shortly afterwards marched to the spot, with tents for their accommodation.

In September Lysons 'had the high gratification of shewing the whole to their Majesties, who with their Royal Highnesses the Princesses Augusta, Elizabeth and Mary, proceeded from Weymouth to Frampton with the purpose of inspecting them.' During the following year Lysons had the use of the South Gloucestershire regiment and again entertained the Royal party.[16] Lysons was always careful to depict only what was there; sometimes he conjectures missing pieces in simple line, but in one major case, even here, he used solid evidence. The first mosaic to be found at Frampton had been uncovered in 1794 by James Engleheart. However, it was already partially destroyed (by frost?) by the time Lysons first saw it two years later, and so he used the Engleheart drawing (now in the Dorset County Museum) when he

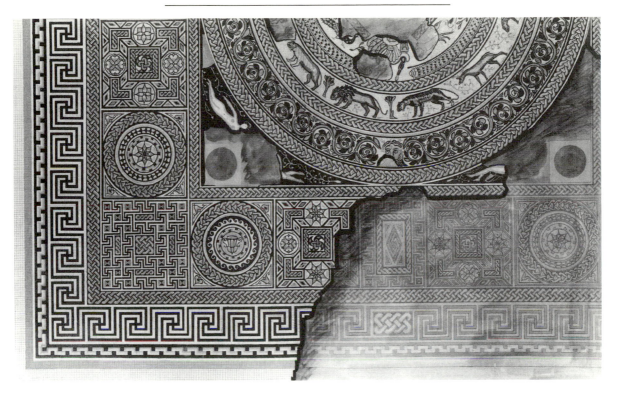

came to publish his own engraving (**colour plate XI**).[17]

The Frampton excavation seems to have had the same cachet as the contemporary Neapolitan researches in Pompeii and Herculaneum. So did the excavation of the villa at Bignor, Sussex, which Lysons supervised and published (**colour plate XII**) for John Hawkins of Bignor Park. Hawkins had travelled extensively in Europe and had just rebuilt his house in Neo-Classical style. It is clear that Bignor provided the opportunity for finding high-quality works of art, such as a man of Hawkins' taste might have expected to find in Italy. Just at this time, during the Napoleonic wars, access to the famous sites of Rome and Italy was often difficult and so the discovery of mosaics in Britain was timely. Bignor was a pioneering site in another way, for, like Pompeii and Herculaneum, albeit on a smaller scale, it has continued to be a site to visit down to the present day, thanks to the excellent *cottages ornées* provided as cover buildings.[18]

Lysons' excavations and the *Reliquiae Britannico-Romanae*, however imperfectly realized, do seem to have broken new ground in the study of the mosaic art of Roman Britain – from Horkstow, Lincolnshire (**colour plate XIII**) in volume 1, discovered in 1796

106 *South side of great Orpheus pavement, Woodchester, Gloucestershire. (After Lysons 1797, pl.vii.)*

and engraved in 1801, to Bignor, Sussex (**colour plate XII**) in volume 3, discovered in 1811, with the publication of the plates in 1814. The title page of the first volume, dedicated to the Prince Regent and issued in 1813, makes an eloquent point by including two roundels derived from coins, one showing *Roma* and the other *Britannia*: two goddesses of equal standing. The advertisement is worth quoting *in extenso*, as the sentiments, while of the Augustan age, seem to me closer to the truth of the matter than are those of most writers even of the present century:

> Although scarcely any traces exist above ground, of the buildings erected by the Romans, during the four hundred years they continued in possession of this Island, yet sufficient remains have been discovered beneath the surface of the earth to shew that they were very abundant: and perhaps it is not too much to say, that no province of the Roman Empire contained a greater number of extensive and richly-decorated villas. So much at least may be inferred from the splendid vestiges of Mosaic pavements, found in our midland and southern counties. These remains exhibit many interesting and curious examples of ancient art and magnificence; having been produced at different periods, several varieties of style, as well as gradations of excellence, may be perceived in them; but though not all equally admirable, either in design or execution, they all evince the pure sources of taste and genius from which they originated.

The noble reader is thus told that the mosaics of Roman Britain are fully as worthy of his notice as Roman art from Italy. Despite some stylistic lapses:

> There are, nevertheless, few of the figures . . . so maimed by a stubborn process, as not to preserve evident traces of the graceful originals whence they were derived; and many forms and attitudes, long known and admired in gems, in paintings, and basso-relievos, may be easily recognized in the pavements of these British-Roman edifices.

At the end of this introduction Lysons concludes by hoping that the work 'may be thought an acceptable addition to the Libraries of this and other countries'. He also apologizes for the expense of production which was necessary if quality was to be maintained.[19]

The *Reliquiae Britannico-Romanae* was not confined to mosaics though it is for these that it is best remembered. Among the rest, the drawings of the architectural sculpture discovered at Bath in 1790 are of great importance. Lysons tells us that 'several very imperfect representations' had already been published but he had been fortunate:

> to obtain most accurate drawings, in the year 1800 by the assistance of Mr Robert Smirke, jun, who from those remains restored the fronts of the two Temples, with a degree of taste and judgement, which at that early period of his life, gave an earnest of the architectural skill he has since shewn.

The elevation of the main temple has been widely accepted and the most recent study concludes that 'there is nothing among the recent discoveries to require any significant modification to be made'; the second temple is now reconstructed somewhat differently as the 'Façade of the Four Seasons', but that does not take anything away from the meticulous craftsmanship revealed here. For only the second time, the arts of Roman Britain were being recognized by a Neo-Classical architect, though it does not seem that these two structures influenced any building. How fitting if the Temple of Sulis Minerva had been allowed to influence the design of the British Museum.[20]

Lysons does not stand completely alone in work of high quality; for example his contemporary. William Fowler, engraved the mosaics of the East Midlands and especially Winterton and other sites in Lincolnshire, including Horkstow, where, however, Samuel Lysons also recorded the mosaics and produced far superior results (**colour plate XIII**). In less ambitious schemes such as at Roxby a few miles away (**colour plate XVI**) he managed to achieve almost the same standard as his great rival. E.T. Artis was another fine archaeologist of the Neo-Classical period who published excellent plates not only of mosaics (**colour plate XV**) but also of wall-paintings and barbotine pottery, all found in the vicinity of Water Newton.[21] However, the tradition of high-quality mosaic-recording and publication did not long survive and its decline is signalled by Sir Richard Colt Hoare in his treatment of the 'Roman Aera', appended in 1821 to *Auncient Wiltescire*.[22]

Colt Hoare was a great and pioneering scholar as prehistorians everywhere will testify; he also had good

Classical credentials. However, in surveying Roman remains in his own county, 110 pages are devoted to topography and a mere 15 to mosaics. Nor is it only in quantity that the treatment of art is lacking. On page 72, a bronze figurine from Folly Farm near Marlborough is mentioned and is illustrated in a plate. The comment is: 'The female figure is given of its original size, and is not devoid of elegance in proportion and design. She appears to have held a *speculum* in her hand.' Colt Hoare should surely have been able to identify the figure as Venus, even with the poor drawing by P. Crocker. In discussing mosaics Colt Hoare writes: 'The magnificent work entitled *Britannia Romana*, which Mr Lysons lived to complete, will ever reflect the greatest honour on himself, and credit to the nation.' Not only are the monochrome plates used by Colt Hoare very disappointing, but the scholarship is cursory too.[23]

Elsewhere, it is true, the polite treatment of works of art from Roman Britain continued through the first half of the nineteenth century. Colt Hoare himself was concerned with the first publication of the mosaic found at Thruxton, Hampshire, in 1823, together with his contemporary, the Revd Dr James Ingram. Ingram's own definitive and most scholarly account was not published until 1851, the year after his death, together with a hand-coloured engraving by J.H. Le Keux. Although this rather mediocre illustration has been the basis for discussion of the floor, a series of much better engravings, real works of art not unworthy of Lysons himself, had been produced by a local Hampshire schoolmaster, John Lickman (**colour plate XIV**). Colt Hoare had examples at Stourhead, but the best is arguably a reconstruction of the mosaic which came into the hands of Joseph Clarke of Saffron Walden, a close friend of Roach Smith and a member of that brilliant circle of antiquaries which remained true to the British Archaeological Association after a faction of the Association split away to form the Archaeological Institute in 1845/6. Lickman produced other engravings, notably of the Bramdean mosaics, but these too remained unpublished at Stourhead, and Lickman remains largely unknown. The reason is surely expense; the time of Stukeley's royal patronage and of *de luxe* productions had almost passed, though Henry Ecroyd Smith's *Reliquiae Isurianae*, with its archaic title and high-quality illustrations of mosaics, appeared as late as 1852.[24]

During the same period, individual objects of Roman date found in Britain sometimes caught the eye of the connoisseur, and were illustrated by three generations of engravers working for the Society of Antiquaries, all called James Basire. The Ribchester helmet (**107** and see **32**) was published in 1799 by Charles Townley, and a very detailed treatment of a statuette of inlaid bronze, portraying a cuirassed emperor, probably Nero (**108**), then in the possession of the Earl of Ashburnham whose seat was Barking Hall, Suffolk, appeared on five plates in 1807. They were bound together in the fourth volume of *Vetusta Monumenta* in 1815.[25] The same meticulous care in illustration is still to be observed by the last James Basire in John Gage's meticulous and remarkable excavation report on the Bartlow Barrows, which deserves to be far better known than it is. In *Archaeologia* for 1836, he describes a jug (**109**) in the following terms:

> The elegance in the form of the *praefericulum* may be observed, which certainly is not unworthy of Greece. . . . The inlaying of metals, as the silver cones introduced into the bronze was common to the ancients, and the Museo Borbonico possesses many examples of candelabri, and other things, in that species of work which the Italians call alla Damaschina. . . .[26]

He continues by praising an enamelled vessel as 'a most rare specimen of the encaustum of the ancients': citing both Philostratus and Pliny. In this case he is aware that the work is provincial – Gaulish or British. For the most part, however, the Roman works which were praised are those of strongly Classical character, such as a group of bronzes found in the course of railway works at Colchester, which Charles Newton, in *Archaeologia* for 1846, singled out as 'distinguished by the beauty of the art from almost all the works of Roman times hitherto discovered in this country'. They were 'tokens of a degree of social refinement beyond the general standard of civilisation in the remote and half-reclaimed province of Roman Britain'. The finds included a miniature bust of Caligula, and a figure of Jupiter, on which the sculptor Sir Richard Westmacott was called in to give an appreciation.[27]

A more remarkable report by C.H. Hartshorne on sculptures, carved from local oolitic limestone,

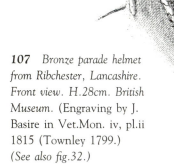

107 *Bronze parade helmet from Ribchester, Lancashire. Front view. H.28cm. British Museum.* (Engraving by J. Basire in Vet.Mon. iv, pl.ii 1815 (Townley 1799.) *(See also fig.32.)*

found upon the estates of the Duke of Bedford, was published in the following year's *Archaeologia* (see **56** and **57**). He writes that the sculptor:

> . . . used the material that was at hand; and considering its hard, uncertain, and occasionally schistous or laminated character, he has produced as fair specimens of his art as these natural circumstances would allow. Their actual merit . . . has however been thus determined by the judgement of Sir Richard Westmacott, one of your Society, who has examined them, and some of whose works, adorning the same noble collection where these are placed, whilst they will bring their own author before admiring posterity, will also be the safest test of our forming a correct judgement upon the merits of the present ones.

In other words these sculptures, for all their fragmentary condition, will compare with Westmacott's own productions.[28]

Bearing present interests in mind, the most striking book title of the middle of the nineteenth century is surely *Illustrations of the Remains of Roman Art in Cirencester, the site of Ancient Corinium* by Professor Buckman and C.H. Newmarch which appeared in 1850, the year before the Great Exhibition. The dedication still reads as though it were written in the eighteenth century, although there was admittedly more justification for the fulsome praise here than usually: 'To the Right Honourable Henry George Earl Bathurst to whose liberality the Public is indebted for the preservation of the tessellated pavements, which form so important a part of the remains of Roman art in Britain, this volume is respectfully inscribed by his Lordship's obedient, servants, the authors'. It is unfortunate that the contents do not live up to the promise of the title or the preface that the work 'by means of accurate drawings and descriptions', will 'afford to the antiquary, and the man of taste, an opportunity of forming conclusions as to the state of the people who occupied this interesting station at a period long prior to the one marked by modern civilization' and even to make these observations secondary to the 'elucidation of matters of a like character, which are continually being found in the many Roman sites in our Island'.

As in Colt Hoare's work, there is a distinct retreat from the learned and international scholarship of

108 *Bronze statuette with silver and* niello *inlay from Baylham Mill, Coddenham, Suffolk showing the emperor Nero (detail). British Museum.* (Engraving by J. Basire (1807), Vet. Mon. iv, 1815, pl.xiii.)

109 *Bronze jug from one of the Bartlow Barrows on the Essex/Cambridgeshire border. H.24.5cm. (After J. Basire (iii), Archaeologia xxvi, 1836, pl.xxxiv.)*

Lysons and other like-minded Classicists, in favour of the topographical tradition of the English antiquaries. This is shown in sections covering the site, fortifications and roads associated with the City at the front of the volume, and in those on the finds of pottery, small finds and coins which conclude it. The chapter on architecture is very thin and limited to a few conjectures, except that it gives the most accurate interpretation of the inhabited capital that was to appear until John Phillips published his paper in 1976, for all the figures were rightly recognized as Bacchic. In the description of the first figure over whose 'right shoulder rises a double faced axe (the *Bipennis*), while the elevated left hand holds a branch of the vine with a bunch of grapes upon it', one cannot help but feel that if the writers had been nurtured in eighteenth-century Classicism, the figure would have been identified as Lycurgus rather than the 'Indian Bacchus'.

The tessellated pavements are described, notably the newly-discovered floors of Dyer Street. The descriptions are accompanied by illustrations which were executed with great care and reproduced by means of a newly invented process, Talbotype, clearly very much cheaper than Lysons' great lithographs. The artistic assessment by the authors is amateur in the extreme, and for the expert view Mr Westmacott is again called in: 'Here is grandeur of form, dignity of character, and great breadth of treatment, which strongly reminds me of the finest Greek schools. I do not mean to say that of Phidias, but of subsequent masters, even of Lysippus.' He goes on to compare the treatment of the figures with that of statues and reliefs in the British Museum, and to praise the excellence of the colouring and 'the fine feeling of the picturesque confined within the limits of grand simplicity'. He concludes that 'these interesting specimens satisfy me as an artist, beyond the shadow of doubt, that such works were produced after examples of the very highest reach of Art.' Buckman and Newmarch themselves were clearly more interested in materials and methods of construction than in aesthetic questions and devote chapters to them as well as to wall decoration, of which only fragments remained.[29]

The middle of the century saw a great growth of public interest in archaeology among the new middle classes and a consequent proliferation of societies. Although the list of subscribers to Buckman and Newmarch is headed by the Prince Consort, the Archbishop of York and two dozen peers of the realm, there was also a large number of commoners, including many of the scholars of the age, notably Charles Roach Smith and his circle. The project was associated with the Archaeological Institute, which carried reports on the discovery of Roman antiquities, as did the rival *British Archaeological Association* which was especially associated with Charles Roach Smith, who published a paper on the beautiful bronze head of Hadrian from London in the first issue:

> It is our duty rather to rejoice over what has been saved from the general wreck, than to lament over what cannot be recovered; and especially when we consider how few of the many similar relics which are accidently dug up from their resting places are secured from the hand of ignorance, which unintentionally, and simply from want of knowledge of their value, consigns them to a fate from which there is no recall.

Although for the most part the new populism was inimical to Roman archaeology, it had a fervent advocate here. However, Roach Smith and his friends, such as Joseph Clarke, Thomas Wright and Joseph Mayer (all stalwarts of the British Archaeological Association), were exceptional in the catholicity of their interests; Mayer at Liverpool and Clarke at Saffron Walden were avid collectors of Classical antiquities. Clarke amassed a useful archive of drawings and engravings of Roman mosaics. Wright wrote a useful paper on engraved gems from Wroxeter.[30]

Roach Smith towers above them all. The unusual quality of his scholarship can best be seen in his *Illustrations of Roman London*, printed in 1859 but which looked back to the exacting standards of a past age. As he tells us in the Preface, his own great collection was acquired in London from excavations made for sewers as well as dredging to deepen the bed of the Thames. He also roundly condemns the Corporation of the City of London for not founding a museum of antiquities which, in the context, would have been largely Roman. Thus, indirectly, he reveals a decline, or at least a shift, in taste, to which Roach Smith himself was immune. In writing of Christian iconoclasm as a result of 'the exuberance of religious zeal, which aimed at the annihilation of every object of pagan worship, or which was likely to perpetuate or recall tendencies to paganism', we find in him a spiritual heir to Edward Gibbon and the Enlightenment:

> When we consider . . . the total absence, in the
> middle ages, of that feeling for the remains of
> antiquity which prevails among the better educated
> of the present day, the general indifference with
> which they are still regarded, and the natural
> consequence of this apathy, we have reviewed the
> main causes which have combined to efface in so
> many towns all vestiges of the grander works of
> antiquity; vestiges which serve to create, when they
> do exist, an impression of their entirety, and permit
> the mind to renovate monuments from their ruins
> and picture them in their days of youth and glory.[31]

In this book sculptures and mosaics are discussed with wide-ranging scholarship and are meticulously illustrated by F.W. Fairholt and others. Thus a group of *matres* discovered at Crutched Friars is compared with similar groups from the Rhineland, while the great head of Hadrian from the Thames provides the excuse for an encomium on the arts of that Emperor's day.[32] He continues with a sensitive account of the figurines also found in the Thames, with pertinent quotations from Tibullus and Ovid. How many modern excavators would do the same? He is most interested by the Atys which, although inferior as art, afforded 'a representation of a mythological personage whose effigies are somewhat uncommon'. He rightly compares the figure with a relief on the side of a [Jupiter] column found at Wroxeter.[33] The section on tessellated pavements begins with a short but masterly account of mosaic-work in Classical sources and remains, at home and abroad. He then turns to those of Bishopsgate Street, Theadneedle Street, Leadenhall Street and Fenchurch Street in London, noting that those he is about to describe 'cannot be considered as constituting, upon the most moderate calculation, the tenth part of the number destroyed during the present century, or, perhaps, during the last twenty or thirty years'.

His account is marked by an intelligent appreciation of workmanship and an instinctive feel for iconography. Although his identification of the *emblema* on the Bishopsgate Street mosaic as Europa and the Bull may be wrong, he rightly compares the Bacchic pavement of Leadenhall Street with that from Thruxton.[34] When he turns to wall-painting, he illustrates a grave-relief from Sens and discusses technique. If this section is brief and the full designs could not be recovered, the reason is 'the fractured condition in which these paintings were excavated, and the total want of any provision for extricating them with care'. Nevertheless, in his two-coloured plates he shows that imitation marbling as well as figural subjects were employed.[35] Meticulous care was also taken with samian and other pottery, glass and small finds, so much so that this is still a book which can be used by the scholar when many much more recent books are forgotten.

As has already been hinted, the taste of the second half of the nineteenth century was predominantly for the work of the Middle Ages rather than that of Ancient Rome. Medieval art was relatively abundant, spoke for the new religiosity of the High Victorian Age and was above all English. There was a medieval church in almost every village. Thus although, even in 1886, Thomas Morgan's *Romano-British Mosaic Pavements* still pays lip service to the aristocratic traditions represented by Lysons, he finds it necessary to apologise for the pagan nature of the subject matter! Another sign of the times is an attempt to show that the designs of mosaics influenced those employed by medieval sculptors, presumably thus giving the material enhanced value. Morgan is explicit that he is writing for the newly educated middle class, specifically 'the whole body of Associates of the British Archaeological Association' to whom, alongside the noble president of the Association, the Right Hon. the Earl Granville K.G. and other members of the council, the work is dedicated. The book is curiously discursive, with chapters on the Roman topography of Britain, Greek astronomy and philosophy interrupting the flow of the narrative. The plates 'plain and coloured' are a sad disappointment and do not suggest the artistic qualities of their originals.

Archaeological discoveries were made at an increasing rate but those from Britain were for the most part discussed by local antiquaries and seldom illustrated by draughtsmen of merit. Collingwood Bruce's work on Hadrian's Wall (published in 1867) and W.T. Watkin's on Cheshire (1886) admittedly contain pleasing woodcuts (see **26**) but the authors were not art historians nor, admittedly, can a great percentage of their material be claimed as work of great artistic value. There were exceptions to this general neglect, most notably the excavation of the Bucklersbury pavement in the heart of the City of London in 1869. It was visited by more than 50,000 people, and so engaged the enthusiasm of the Lord Mayor and the Corporation that it was lifted for the new Guildhall Museum. The 1870 publication by J.E. Price, entitled *A Description of the Roman Tessellated Pavement found in Bucklersbury with observations on analogous discoveries*, aims to put mosaics into context for the Victorian Londoner. Ten years later Price, together with F.G. Hilton Price, published a guide to the newly discovered remains at Brading on the Isle of Wight.[36]

By now photography could have provided a new tool for the study of ancient art but its potential was not realized in relation to the present subject until this century. James Curle's meticulous report on Newstead (1911) included many items of artistic value, such as the parade helmets, and photographs of these duly appear in this splendid volume. Then, in 1914, Haverfield published the Corbridge *lanx* properly for the first time, with a photograph. However, the first monograph to publish a large assemblage of art objects from a site in Britain using this valuable medium was Alexander Curle's book on the Traprain Law treasure (1923). Its coverage is exceptional and its splendid photographs and careful drawings (see **95** and **96**) show how such works should be viewed; it was not until the Thetford treasure was published in 1983 that we had any other project on the same scale. It might be assumed that special treatment was accorded the silver because it was essentially 'High art', Classical rather than British, but the fact that both Curles were Scots, living in a country where Classical taste flourished strongly through the nineteenth century, is illuminating.[37]

However, Classicism increasingly meant Ancient Greece, whose discovery and archaeological and touristic exploitation led to a general undervaluing of Roman art in general, which lasted through the first three quarters of the twentieth century. Provincial art was especially scorned, for surely here were copies of copies that had lost all contact with original ideas. The standard statements on art in Roman Britain used by the author of this work when studying for his Ancient History A-Level in the late 1950s were those of Haverfield and especially Collingwood, though by then they were beginning to appear inadequate. Indeed, a first hint of a new understanding was published at about the same time that Collingwood wrote his famous chapter. It is an altogether more

detailed account by Thomas Kendrick, but as it was buried in a book about the succeeding period not a great deal of notice was taken of it.[38] Kendrick's Roman Britain, like Haverfield's and Collingwood's, comprised on the one side the Romans whose art 'is not very much more than an unequivocal statement . . . of the majestic fact of the Roman world-empire. It is revealed to us at once as something foreign and imposed'. On the other hand there is barbarian art. Unlike Haverfield and Collingwood this is not epitomized by the Bath Gorgon save in its expression – 'an un-Roman quality of menacing divinity' – though on the whole Kendrick does not see sufficient here to ascribe the work to a Briton. The sculpture which Kendrick really admires are coarsely cut heads such as:

> . . . the magnificent horned head of red sandstone in the Carlisle Museum, which I am inclined to honour as the finest piece of native carving in the whole length of Roman Britain. It is a relentless and implacable Celtic wonder, terrifying in its grimly supernatural power. There is nothing here that is just decadent or unskilled classicism; on the contrary, the work is conspicuously brilliant in its unimpaired native vigour, and, in fact, gains strength from a courageous and downright renunciation of the classical method.[39]

With this build up we expect something truly remarkable. Instead Kendrick illustrates a very incompetently carved, block-like head, certainly not from a regular sculptural workshop, and to my eyes totally without merit. He goes on to praise one of the more inept and child-like gravestones from Chester, figuring the centurion Marcus Aurelius Nepos and his wife (see **25**) '. . . it is genuine, and is barbarously strong and truthful, instead of being a poor classical fake'.[40]

If his treatment of sculpture appears perverse, there was still no objective criterion on which he could base his assessment of provincial art. Although he got closer to identifying the subjects of the great Cirencester Jupiter-column capital, 'busts of Zeus with the bipennis, of Silvanus, and of Bacchus and of an Amazon', it is seen as official Roman art, 'probably the work of an Asiatic of the Constantine Age'.[41]

Kendrick saw the characteristics of Romano-British art as low relief and linearity, anticipating later Celtic and Anglo-Saxon work. He explores

Insular vine-scrolls in sculpture and metalwork (though he does not think it likely that it was 'in any way connected with the Saxon version of the same theme . . . of the second half of the seventh century'), but he compares the figured friezes of mosaics in southwest Britain to the carpet-like pages of early Irish manuscripts, seeing them as a possible prototype. I believe that is most unlikely, but it says much that Kendrick was willing to address the problems of artistic influence.[42]

Kendrick certainly tried to get at the spirit of things. In a discussion of colour, notably in enamel, he includes a paragraph on colour which cannot be bettered even today:

> The daily life of the richer sections of the Romano-British community was passed amid surroundings in which colour played a considerable part, and to appreciate this we have only to think of the brilliant polychrome appearance of many mosaics, of the elaborately painted walls, the wide range of colours in the finer ceramic wares, the sumptuous mottled glasses, and the fine enamels. Even sculpture was often painted and there must have been an air of chromatic cheerfulness about Roman Britain that the drab and corroded surviving antiquities do not adequately reflect.[43]

After the Second World War, knowledge of Roman Britain grew very fast. The Mildenhall treasure came to light, though nothing like an adequate publication was to appear until 1977. Archaeology, some of it consequent on war damage, also increased knowledge, for example when a Temple of Mithras was discovered in London in 1954. Most, though not all, of the sculptures were marble imports, but for the crowds which visited the excavation what mattered was the revelation of an exotic religion and its art. The development in art-historical understanding since the war also making progress, and in the field of Roman art this was associated with a major authority on the art of the Roman world. Professor Jocelyn Toynbee wrote the catalogue for an exhibition mounted in 1960–61 at Goldsmiths Hall by the Society for the Promotion of Roman Studies in celebration of its Jubilee year (though due to industrial action the book did not appear until after the exhibition had closed). Although Toynbee's claims for local originality were over-cautious, *Art in Roman Britain* was, after all, an

'art-book' in an age of 'art-books', illustrated with wonderful photographs by Otto Fein. All it lacked was the colour plates which could have shown mosaics to better effect. It was a revelation to me when I visited the exhibition and it can certainly be said to have changed thinking about the subject; it helped to develop my own attitudes and I am very pleased to use a similar title for this book. It was followed a couple of years later by a very large and exhaustive catalogue, *Art in Britain under the Romans*, which has remained the starting point for all further study.

An increasing number of scholars worked on Roman Britain and its art. Three years after Toynbee's great corpus, Sheppard Frere published his *Britannia*, in its way no less epoch-making than its sixteenth-century namesake. Only seven pages are devoted to art, though there are a number of plates. However, Frere had already written perceptive papers on sculpture, and could dismiss Collingwood's brilliantly written nonsense from a position of personal knowledge. For Frere Roman art was a vital new force, admittedly introduced from the Continent, though in time finding skilled practitioners among native craftsmen. Much of what was produced, the sculpture of the Cotswolds for example and fourth-century mosaics, is singled out for its merit. Re-reading Frere's brief account, I realize how important it has been for my own perception of the subject. The art of Roman Britain by now had its own specialists. There were, for instance, the pioneering efforts of David Smith in distinguishing mosaic workshops and of Joan Liversidge in studying the fragmentary remains of wall-painting. From 1970, Roman Britain had its own journal *Britannia*, which included articles and notes on artistic production from its very first issue. Two notable monographs published by the Roman Society, David Neal's book on mosaics and Norman Davey and Roger Ling's work on fresco, both published in 1981, advanced studies considerably. In David Neal we once again have an artist of the stature of Lysons himself, in illustrating mosaic art. Commencing in 1977 the British fascicules of the great international project the *Corpus Signorum Imperii Romani* began to appear. Not only was it now possible to begin working on schools of sculpture systematically, but the very nature of the project transcended national frontiers. In the field of minor arts I conducted doctoral research on engraved gems, publishing my dissertation in 1974, and Catherine Johns and

Timothy Potter's monograph on the Thetford treasure (1983) set a new standard in the publication of jewellery and silver.

There was, indeed, so much new work that when, in 1989, the time came to publish a retrospective volume, *Research on Roman Britain 1960–89*, it was natural to include a chapter on art and architecture, written with authority by T.F.C. Blagg. The position now is that the way we study Roman Britain has been transformed. Only the occasional reminiscence of the old attitudes remain; in a forthcoming and long-delayed fascicule of *Aufstieg und Niedergang*, we are to be offered an article by Richard Reece with the perverse title 'The Badness of British Art under the Romans'. The latest textbook on Roman Britain by Potter and Johns (issued in 1992), however, devotes at least a third of its length to architecture and art, personal possessions and pagan gods and goddesses, and many of its plates are of works of art. The 'captains and the kings' have not departed but they have faded into the background.[44]

That so many projects concerned with art should have been undertaken in Britain, shows that Roman art in general is now being taken much more seriously. This is demonstrated in the wider Roman context, by work progressively stressing the originality of the Romans in matters artistic. We can instance books by art historians as various as Donald Strong, Paul Zanker, Niels Hannestad, John Onians and Roger Ling, and exhibitions both temporary and permanent – for instance the current presentation of the Roman world by Susan Walker at the British Museum. Roman art is no longer the poor relation of Greek art, nor is there any longer a gulf between this province and others. Perhaps, in British terms, it has taken such discoveries as the painted house-church at Lullingstone, Kent, the Hinton St Mary mosaic, the London *Mithraeum*, and the Mildenhall, Thetford and Hoxne treasures to demonstrate this obvious fact.

It is still difficult to view these changed attitudes objectively, but I suspect that this new enthusiasm, especially in more recent years, is conditioned in part by the importance that the European Community is assuming in the lives of Europe's inhabitants. The Roman Empire was an institution which covered many (though by no means all) of the countries in the new association of states. It is thus reassuring to look back to a common culture, albeit almost two millennia ago. Whether such a curiosity has any real bearing on modern problems is, of course, another matter, but at least we Europeans will add to our aesthetic enjoyment by once more being fully alive to the beauties of Roman art, within the borders of Europe's respective countries.

Abbreviations

ANRW   *Aufstieg und Niedergang der Römischen Welt*
Ant. J.   *The Antiquaries Journal*
Arch. Ael.   *Archaeologia Aeliana*
Arch. Journ.   *The Archaeological Journal*
BABesch   *Bulletin Antieke Beschaving*
BAR   British Archaeological Reports
BBCS   *Bulletin of the Board of Celtic Studies*
BJ   *Bonner Jahrbücher*
BNJ   *British Numismatic Journal*
CSIR   *Corpus Signorum Imperii Romani*
JBAA   *Journal of the British Archaeological Association*
JHS   *Journal of Hellenic Studies*
JRA   *Journal of Roman Archaeology*
JRS   *Journal of Roman Studies*
OJA   *Oxford Journal of Archaeology*
PBSR   Papers of the British School at Rome
PPS   *Proceedings of the Prehistoric Society*
PSAS   *Proceedings of the Society of Antiquaries of Scotland*
RIB   R.G. Collingwood and R.P. Wright, *The Roman Inscriptions of Britain*
SAC   *Sussex Archaeological Collections*
TBGAS   *Transactions of the Bristol and Gloucestershire Archaeological Society*

Notes and References

Chapter 1   The Art of the Celts (pp.13–23)

Megaw and Megaw 1986 and especially idem 1989 provide a more detailed approach to Celtic Art than is attempted in this chapter. Fox 1958 is still useful.

1   For Greek acanthus see Andronicos 1984, figs 135, 136 (gold larnyx) and 156, 157 (textile); Wandsworth shield see Brailsford 1975, 14–18, 20; Stead 1985, 41 pl.xv. Celtic coins are studied by Allen 1988. Cf. pl.13 no.163 (Philip stater), copies *passim*, for instance pl.31, nos 459–63 for coins of Coritani and Dobunni.
2   On Celtic art in Ireland in the pre-Christian period see Raftery 1984.
3   Thomas 1981 demonstrates a significant Romano-British element in the development of Christianity in the British Isles. For insular art in the Dark Ages, see Youngs 1989.
4   Collingwood and Myres 1937, 247.
5   Jacobsthal 1944.
6   Jope 1987.
7   Stead 1979; *idem* 1991a.
8   Dent 1985.
9   Stead 1967 (Welwyn); *idem* 1971; Brailsford 1975, frontispiece and 83–9 (Aylesford Bucket); Birchall 1965 (Aylesford-Swarling culture).
10   Piggott 1971; Brailsford 1975, 90–7.
11   Ibid., 62–8; Lowery, Savage and Wilkins 1975; Farley 1983.
12   For the Bartlow Barrows see Gage 1834, 1837, 1842.
13   Brailsford 1975, 44–53 (Ipswich); 54–61; Stead 1991b (Snettisham).
14   Fox 1946.
15   Bradley 1990, especially chapter 4.
16   Spratling in Wainwright 1979, 125–49.
17   Henig 1972, 212, pl.xi, c.
18   See n.11.
19   Megaw and Megaw 1989, figs 329, 360; Stead 1991a, frontispiece and see pp.64–70.
20   Megaw and Megaw 1989, figs 321, 322, 359.
21   Ibid., fig.332.
22   Stead 1985.
23   Richter 1971, no.16[bis].
24   Atkinson and Piggott 1955.
25   I am grateful to Julian Munby for demonstrating to me, as long ago as 1972, that the cap and horns probably did function together. See now Henig 1974b, Megaw 1983, Jope 1983.
26   Brailsford 1975, 32–9; Megaw and Megaw 1989, fig.364.
27   See n.1.
28   Simon Palmer, 'The White Horse Project', *Oxford Archaeological Unit Annual Report 1990–91*, 14 for an interim statement.
29   Pollitt 1986, 86, ills.85 and 87c.
30   Raftery 1984, 175–8, pls 59, 60; Megaw and Megaw 1989, figs 205, 361, 362, col. pls xii–xiv. See n.13 above.
31   Compare n.11 with Gehrig 1980 and Johns 1986.
32   Lloyd-Morgan in Gregory 1991, 132 suggests links with northern and central Italy.
33   Lloyd-Morgan 1980.
34   Boon and Savory 1975.
35   Boon 1982.
36   Megaw 1970.
37   Henig and Wood 1990 and references cited; see Megaw 1970, no.280 and references for wooden figures; Deyts 1983 for the wooden sculptures from the Seine.
38   Henig 1972.

Chapter 2   Art in the Era of the Conquest (pp.24–41)

1   A large bibliography on the monument includes Toynbee 1953 and Zanker 1988.
2   Schmidt 1965, pl.63.
3   Zanker 1988, especially chapters 5 and 7.
4   Stead 1967.
5   Kennett 1976.
6   Foster 1986.
7   Cunliffe 1988, 150–3.
8   See Chapter 1; for a prototype of the helmets see, for example, Haynes 1985, 298 no.145 (a late fifth-century BC figurine from central Etruria).
9   Henig 1972; Henig and Nash 1982, 243–4.
10   Toynbee 1964a, 25–38.
11   Henig 1988b (sleeping hound). Bone and Burnett 1986, no.11 (a minim showing a boar's head) likewise seems gem based.
12   Toynbee 1964, 299–300, pl.lxixb; Hull 1958, pl.i A and B; RIB 200 and 201, pl.v; Phillips 1975 (Facilis); Mattern 1989, 770–1 nos 70 and 71.
13   Ireland 1983. See Keppie 1991 for an excellent introduction to epigraphy.

14 Richborough: D.E. Strong in Cunliffe 1968, 40–73; Colchester: *Britannia* xi, 1980, 403 no.1; Drury 1984, 37–9, fig.14 suggesting placement on the screen marking out the *temenos*.

15 RIB 12.

16 Frere 1983, 8–9, 69–72.

17 Temple: RIB 91, and see Bogaers 1979 for revised reading. Monument: RIB 89, and see Cunliffe and Fulford 1982, 29 no.107 though the second-century dating suggested by them on the basis of the nymphs' coiffure lacks foundation. For the *Pilier des Nautes*: Caillet 1985; exhibition catalogue, *Lutèce, Paris de César à Clovis*, Musée Carnavalet 1984–5, 299–314. See Henig and Nash 1982 for the early Romanization of Chichester.

18 Cunliffe 1971.

19 Collingwood and Myres 1937, 250.

20 Anganuzzi and Mariani 1987, figs 5, 6 (col.), 22 and 23 (Breno); for other parallels see Cunliffe 1971, vol.1, 146–50, for the new Fishbourne pavement see *Britannia* XII, 1981, 364–5, fig.17 and D.J. Rudkin in the 1983 revision of B. Cunliffe's site guide, 36–7. Lavagne 1979, 68–73 no.58, pls xx, xxi, xxii, 5 (Orange).

21 London: see Marsden 1975, 57, 67, 99; D. Smith in Perring and Roskams 1991, 88–94; Exeter: see D.J. Smith in Bidwell 1979, 132–4.

22 Down and Henig 1988.

23 Henig 1970.

24 *Idem* 1991a; Henig, Webster and Wilkins 1987.

25 Henig 1972, 215–6, pl.xii a and b.

26 Chichester gem, Henig 1974a, no.654; the Verulamium eagle and galley ibid. no.533; the Colchester Mars, Henig 1982 and *idem* 1990b, 155, fig.11.4.

27 *Idem* in Cunliffe 1971, vol.2, 83–8 and 1974a no.53.

28 Henig 1984b; also Murdoch 1991, 81 nos 57, 58 and 176 no.499, pl.14.

29 Henig 1988a; *idem* 1992.

30 E.g. Colchester: Marshall 1907 no.453; Henig 1990b, 155, fig.11.4; London: Chapman 1974, 274–5 no.2. For comparanda from Pompeii see Stefanelli 1992, 136 and 240–1 nos 73–82, figs 121–6 (Casa del Menandro).

31 Marsden 1975, 100–2, pl.7.

32 Inv. 464.982.

33 Brandon: *Britannia* xi, 1980, 376 (cache cited); Santon: Smith 1909.

34 Kennett 1976; Megaw and Megaw 1989, 220.

35 Exhibition catalogue, *Römer in Rumänien*, Cologne 1969, cat. nos A99, A100.

36 Johns and Potter 1983, 84–5 no.7.

37 Toynbee 1964a, 23.

38 Boon 1974, 134, fig.19, 2; Megaw and Megaw 1989, 228, ills 387 (brooch), 385 (Dowgate plaque).

39 Ibid., 236–7, ill.406.

40 Evans 1896, 186–7.

41 Charlesworth 1973, 226–8.

42 Boon and Savory 1975.

43 Cool 1986, fig.3. See also Pfeiler 1970, 51 taf.10 and Stefanelli 1992, 154 and 245, no.109, fig.157.

44 Elmswell: Toynbee 1962, 176 no.123, pl.142; Megaw and Megaw 1989, 230, ill.390; Macgregor 1976, no.336. Fulham sword: Toynbee 1964a, 299–300, pl.lxixb.

45 BM Guide Ant. RB, 1958, 56 no.3, pl.21, see Toynbee 1964a, 331.

46 Stag: Christie's *sale catalogue* 16 July 1985, 12–13, lot 38 and *Review of the National Art-Collections Fund*, 1987, 145–6. The animal eating a man: Henig 1984a, 65 ill.22. Boar: Henig and Keen 1984, fig.12, pl.11. Human figures: Ellis 1900 (not Iberian as stated) and *Britannia* i, 1970, 296 and pl.xxxvd.

47 Foster 1977.

48 Ibid., 17–19, 31 and pl.vii (Muntham Court boar), compare pl.viii (Capel St Mary lion); Toynbee 1964a, 122 and 126, pl.xxxiii.

49 *Norfolk Archaeology* xli, pt.ii, 1991, 232 (Holme Hale); Henig 1984a, 138 and 249, n.33 (Chalton); Henig and Leahy 1986 (Kirmington); for Brough see Corder and Richmond 1938.

50 Megaw and Megaw 1989, 241, ill.412 (Cadbury); Toynbee 1962, 146 no.43, pl.47 (Felmingham Hall); *eadem* 1964a, 57 pl.viiib and Denford 1992, 37, 39 and 40, fig.9 (Silkstead); Toynbee 1964a, 110, pl.xxviiib ('Copenhagen'); the Icklingham find has not yet been properly published, but was reported (with photos) in *The Independent*, 28 Sept. 1989.

51 See Henig 1984a, 65–6 ill.23.

52 *Idem* 1991b.

53 Green and Henig 1988.

54 Cunliffe and Davenport 1985, 115–6, pls xxxv–xxxix.

55 Towcester: Toynbee 1962, 148–9 no.48, pl.52; Uley: Henig 1984a, 58, ill.18; *idem* 1993b, no.62.

56 *Idem*, 1984a chapter 3.

Chapter 3 Art and the Roman Army (pp.42–57)

1 Zienkiewicz 1986, vol.ii (Caerleon); Ward-Perkins and Claridge 1976 (Pompeii).

2 Charlesworth 1969.

3 Bowman and Thomas 1983 and especially idem 1987, 130–2 (Virgil exercise) and 137–40 (Claudia Severa's letter).

4 Birley 1977, *passim*.

5 Birley 1978.

6 Ling 1991a, 10–11.

7 Lepper and Frere 1988 (Trajan's Column); Keppie and Arnold 1984, no.68 (Bridgeness slab).

8 Brewer 1986, no.31 (RIB 330).

9 RIB 665 (York; magnesian limestone); Zienkiewicz 1986, vol.ii, 22–3 (Caerleon; micaceous sandstone); RIB 463 (Chester; Purbeck marble); RIB 464 and *Britannia* ii, 1971, 290–1 no.7 and pl.xxxviiia (Chester; slate).

10 RIB 288.

11 Brewer 1986, nos 44–7 (Caerleon), 48 (Caernarfon); Tufi 1983, no.38 (Constantine at York).

12 Mattern 1989 provides an excellent survey.

13 Wright and Richmond 1955, 4–9 especially p.7.

14 For Facilis see Chapter 2; the London *beneficiarius consularis* is discussed by Bishop 1983. See Mattern 1989, 783 no.98.

15 Wright and Richmond 1955, nos 38 and 90.

16 Tufi 1983, nos 44, 57 and 55.

17 Brewer 1986, no.19; Mattern 1989, no.9.

18 Wright and Richmond 1955, no.37 for the tombstone of Nepos. For the series of draped women see for example nos 117–22 and Mattern 1989, 728–31; Tufi 1983, no.39 for the York tombstone of Flavia Augustina.

19 Tufi 1983, no.42, also nos 40 and 43; Wright and Richmond 1955, no.108 and nos 111–16 (for female banquet stele) and nos 65 and 66 for soldiers as banqueters. See also Mattern 1989, 722–5; Brewer 1986, no.18 (Caerleon funerary *mensa*).

20 Bidwell 1979, 136 and Brewer 1986, no.4 for *labra* from Exeter and Caerleon.

21 Tufi 1983, nos 10, 11, 22 and 26.

22 Wright and Richmond 1955, nos 138–40 and 163.

23 Baucchenss 1978 (from Bonn and region; mainly first century but note fine Antonine banquet scene, no.38); for the Danube region see Mócsy 1974, 130.

24 Wright and Richmond 1955, nos Ex 1 and 5; also no.163; Brewer 1986, no.6; Tufi 1983 no.21.

25 For official sculpture see Keppie and Arnold 1984, xvii–xviii and see nos 149 (Hutcheson Hill), 156 (Old Kilpatrick); 68 (Bridgeness); 150 (Braidfield); Phillips 1977a, nos 84 and 85 (Corbridge); Keppie and Arnold 1984, no.114 (Shirva); Brewer 1986, no.36 (Castell Collen).

26 Mackintosh 1986; Mattern 1989, 711–4.

27 Housesteads: Coulston and Phillips 1988, nos 202, 203 (tombstones), 349 (Ceres and Persephone), 166–9 (mother goddesses), 126 (Mithras Saecularis), 87, 88 (Neptune reliefs). Also no.94 (Chesters river-god); no.15 (Birdoswald Fortuna); nos 492–8, and see Phillips 1976a (Carlisle school).

28 Coulston and Phillips 1988, nos 70 and 72 (poor quality renditions of Mars from Housesteads); 227 (Castlesteads tombstone), 211 and 256 (Vindolanda reliefs).

29 Phillips 1977a no.215 (Risingham); Coulston and Phillips 1988, nos 99 and 100 (Housesteads victories); 272 (Stanwix victory); Keppie and Arnold 1984, no.2, also nos 7 and 9 (Birrens).

30 Toynbee 1986 (London); Tufi 1983, nos 22 and 23 (York); Coulston and Phillips 1988, no.122 (Carrawburgh altar); nos 125–7 (Housesteads).

31 Mosaics from Exeter D.J. Smith in Bidwell 1979, 132–4; Caerleon, see Rainey 1973, 31–2; Chester, see Rainey 1973, 41–2; paintings from the Fortress Baths, Caerleon, Zienkiewicz 1986, vol.i, 281–302; York principia, Davey and Ling 1982, 201–8. The Echzell paintings are discussed by Baatz 1968. See Davey and Ling 1982, 45 for fragments of wall-painting from forts.

32 Jenkins 1985.

33 Grew and Griffiths 1991.

34 For the Fulham scabbard see Toynbee 1964a, 299–300, pl.lxixb.

35 Grew and Griffiths 1991, fig.5 no.A.1. (belt plate). Toynbee 1964a, 49 and pl.v and Henig 1984a, 74–5, ill.26 (Nero).

36 Curle 1911, 168. On helmets in general see Toynbee 1964a, 290–8.

37 *Eadem* 1962, 167 no.101, pl.108.

38 Russell Robinson and Toynbee 1975; Clay 1984; Toynbee 1964a, 297, pl.lxvib.

39 Zienkiewicz in Evans 1991, 130–2, fig.8 and pl.xii.

40 Niblett 1985, fig.66, no.61 and pl.14 and see G. Webster in ibid., p.114.

41 Toynbee 1962, 168–9 no.104, pl.110; eadem 1964a, 293–4, pls lxvii and lxviii.

42 For military enamels see for example Curle 1911, 329–33 pl.lxxxix (Newstead); Pitts and St Joseph 1985, 286–8 (horse harness attachment from Inchtuthil); Birley 1977, 77 and col.pl.vii (Vindolanda); J. Webster in Evans and Metcalf 1992, 123 (Caerleon). For the Rudge Cup cf. RIB vol.ii, fasc.2, 2415.53, and the Amiens Patera, Heurgon 1951. On openwork see Webster in Evans and Metcalf 1992, 123–5; inscribed baldric and belt fittings in RIB vol.ii, fasc.3 nos 2429.1–2429.17. On the changing appearance of Roman military equipment see now Bishop and Coulston 1993.

Chapter 4   The Uses of Art in Roman Britain
(pp.58–78)

1 Haverfield 1915, 55–6.

2 Note three examples of Form 29 from Fishbourne, Cunliffe 1971, ii, fig.126 nos 1–3 exemplifying the quality of early southern Gaulish samian; for the Southwark vase see Merrifield 1969, 164, fig.46.

3 Toynbee 1964a, 408–15, see pl.xciii; Merrifield 1969, 164–6, fig.47.

4 Blair and Ramsay 1991.

5 Merrifield 1983, 75 and 77.

6 Turcan 1982 for the Lyon altar and Hull 1958, 175–7 for its equivalent at Colchester.

7 D.E. Strong in Cunliffe 1968, 40–73.

8 Erim 1982.

9 Keppie and Arnold 1984, 25–58, *passim*.

10 For Imperial sculpture see Tufi 1983, no.38 (Constantine, York); bronze fragments are recorded in Brewer 1986, nos 44–7 (Caerleon), no.48 (Caernarfon); Keppie and Arnold 1984, no.45 (Milsington); a silver arm from Tunshill is discussed by Potter and Johns 1986 and see *eisdem* 1992, 124 and 125, ills 43 and 44 (reconstruction).

11 Frere 1983, 69–72 and pl.ix (Verulamium); one of the large bronze clamps in the form of thumb has recently been discovered in the reserves of Verulamium Museum and is now displayed with the inscription; RIB 288 (Wroxeter Forum Inscription).

12 Bronze Imperial heads of Claudius and Hadrian, Toynbee 1964a, 46–8 and 50–1, pls iv and vi; for the Billingford fragments see *Britannia* xvi, 1985, 293–4, pl.xxivb; Ashill hock see Lawson 1986; for the equestrian statue from Gloucester, see Henig 1993b, no.177; for the Lincoln leg, Wacher 1974, pl.22; the cuirassed statue from Cirencester is published in Henig 1993b, no.178; see RIB 289 for the Wroxeter inscription.

13 RIB 707.

14 RIB 141 (Bath, guild); *Britannia* viii, 1977, 430–1 no.18 (York, L. Viducius Placidus); *JRS* lii, 1962, 192 no.8 (Nettleham, Q. Neratius Proxsimus) ibid. no.7 (Ancaster, Trenico). For the Arch of Dativius Victor see Esperandieu vii, 5726; for the London Arch and Screen see Blagg in Hill, Millett and Blagg 1980, 125–93; the relief of Mercury from the Cirencester gate, Henig, 1993b, no.69. For St Cuthbert's fountain at Carlisle see Bede, *Vita Sancti Cuthberti*, 27. The Cirencester altar: Henig 1984a, 82–3, ill.30; idem, 1993b, no.32 and RIB 102.

15 The Caerwent statue base, RIB 311 and Blagg 1990, 19 (following E. Frézouls).

16 Verulamium: Davey and Ling 1982, 169–91; J. Liversidge in Frere 1984, 114–40, pls vi–xxii, xxv–xxvi. For earlier Italian comparanda see Ling 1991, 31–100; his colour plates iv–viii, xivc suggest the effect of such walls.

17 Brewer 1986, no.18.

18 Toynbee 1964a, 59–63, pls x and xi (Lullingstone); Henig 1993b, no.10 (Woodchester); idem, part ii, no.1 and R. Ling in Holbrook and Bidwell 1991, 230–1, figs 97 and 98, no.1 (Exeter).

19 Monumental tombs in Belgica, see Wightman 1970, 244–6, pls 11, 14–20; myths depicted in funerary sculpture from the European provinces are discussed by Toynbee 1977; the Stanwick sculpture will be fully published by Dr T.F.C. Blagg and the present author; for the Bartlow Barrows see Gage 1834, 1836, 1842, also *VCH Essex* III, 1963, 39–43, frontispiece (enamelled bowl), pls vi–viii (other bronzes); for the bust from Walcot, Bath see Cunliffe and Fulford 1982, no.1.

20 Classicianus, RIB 12; Titus Flaminius, RIB 292 and Mattern 1989, 792 no.124.

21 M. Favonius Facilis, RIB 200, Toynbee 1964a, 185 and pl.xlvia, Phillips 1975 and Mattern 1989, 770 no.70; L. Valerius Aurelius ibid., 774 no.79 and Henig 1993b, no.142; Philus, RIB 110, Mattern 1989, 768 no.66 and Henig 1993b no.141.

22 Murrell Hill: Coulston and Phillips 1988, no.497 and Mattern 1989, 743 no.10, see Phillips 1976a, 101–8 for the Carlisle school; Chester: Wright and Richmond 1955, 49–50 no.120, pl.xxxi and

Mattern 1989, 752 no.31 (woman with mirror) and Wright and Richmond, 44 no.108, pl.xxviii, Mattern, 758 no.45 (Curatia Dinysia) and see Mattern 1989, 722–6 and 728–31 for discussion of workshop groups; South Shields: Phillips 1977a, no.247 and Mattern 1989, 790–1 no.117 (Regina); York: Tufi 1983, no.42 and Mattern 1989, 799 no.137 (Julia Velva).

23 For the Cirencester cupid see Toynbee 1962, 130–1, no.13, pl.32; Henig 1993b no.180 and references cited.

24 Pevsner 1956; Henig 1985.

25 See Ling in no.16 above. For the decor of Verulamium buildings XXVIII, 3, room 9 see Frere 1983, 237–8 and pls xxxvi and xxxviii and of building XXI, 2, room 4 (with the lion mosaic) idem, 163, pl.xviii. For mosaics in general see Rainey 1973; Neal 1981; Johnson 1982.

26 Leicester: house in insula xvi see Davey and Ling 1981, 123–31; Dover (Painted House): Philp 1989, esp. p.281; Southwark (Winchester Palace): Mackenna and Ling 1991 and Hassall and Tomlin, *Britannia* xvi, 1985, 317–22 no.1 for third-century monumental inscription from the same building. Decorative stone inlay at Fishbourne: Cunliffe 1971, *passim* especially ii, 16–35; Angmering: Scott 1938, 15–17; Buriton: Des Brisay 1992, 97–8, fig.5, p and q; Bignor: Lysons 1817, pl.xxxi, figs 3, 4, 6, 8.

27 Colchester wall-painting: Ling in Crummy 1984, 147–53, figs 141 and 142 (gladiator); gem showing Cupid with herm: Henig 1974a and 1978, no.112. Verulamium Neptune mosaic: Toynbee 1962, 196–7 no.178, pl.207; Verulamium Sea-shell: ibid. 196 no.177, pl.206. Cirencester, Dyer Street Seasons mosaic: ibid., 197 no.181, pls 210–12; Dyer Street marine scene: ibid., 197 no.182, pl.213; Fishbourne: Cunliffe 1971, 163–4, pls xlvii–l; Dorchester Neptune mosaic: Smith 1977, 122–3 no.55, pl.6. xiib. Otford villa Vergilian painting. Davey and Ling 1982, 146–8; Lullingstone nymphs: Meates 1987, 10–11, col.pls iv–vi.

28 Furniture in Britain: Liversidge 1955; see pls 44–54, 57–8 and 61 for jet, and see R. Goodburn and F. Grew in Frere 1984, 78 and pl.vd for example from Verulamium. The marble leg from Colchester is published by Walker and Matthews 1986. For the pipe-clay diners see Toynbee 1964a, 419 and pl.xcvi.

29 Side tables, Cunliffe and Fulford 1982, nos 159–89.

30 Tripods: see Thompson 1971, 101–2, pl.xxv (Lincoln), Henig 1976 (London), Bartlett 1985 (Old Harlow). For the fine Littlecote appliqués see Walters and Henig 1988. For Romano-British versions of such attachments see Toynbee 1964a, 103–4, pl.xxvi (Cirencester); Dix 1985 (near Fotheringhay, Northamptonshire). Report on the Tarrant Hinton mask by M. Henig, forthcoming in excavation report by A.G. Giles.

31 For Pliny as a moral writer see Isager 1991. For the

32 Fishbourne *askos*: Down and Henig 1988; Bartlow Barrow: Gage 1836, 303 no.ii, pls xxxiii, xxxiv Winchester grave: Biddle 1967. Note the Bacchic imagery in the Verulamium fresco with its vigorous scroll, Frere 1983, 165 and pl.xxi.

33 Dress: Wild 1985.

34 Enamelling: Bateson 1981; a good selection is shown by Allason-Jones and Miket 1984, nos 3.10 and 3.11 (belt plates), 3.128–134, 141, 142, 152, 153 (brooches), 3.374–3.387 (seal-boxes). For the Rudge Cup see RIB ii fasc.2, 2415.53 (also 2415.54 from Beadlam, Yorkshire with a legend reading 'Good Luck!') and the Amiens *Patera*, Heurgon 1951.

35 London ring: Henig 1984e; openwork rings as gifts: Johns 1981b (citing other examples), see Stefanelli 1992, 211 and 268, no.231, fig.265 for a good colour picture of one of the Corbridge rings. For the Stonham Aspal ring see Mawer 1989. A brooch set with gems is mentioned in the Marble of Thorigny. CIL XIII 3162 (Charlesworth 1973, 229–30, pl.xxviii has a gem on the loop, or is one to think of a jewel such as Stefanelli 1992, 156, fig.162 from South Russia, imitated in gilt-bronze disc-brooches, Charlesworth 1961, 36 nos 7–11, see pl.viii, 7–9); for the tetrarchic-period inscribed, openwork brooch from Erickstanebrae, Dumfriesshire see RIB ii, fasc. 3,2421.43.

36 Henig 1974a and 1978.

37 Guiraud 1988 (Gaul); Middleton 1991 (Dalmatia); Pannuti 1983 (Pompeii); Sena Chiesa 1966 (Aquileia); Henig and Whiting 1987 (Gadara); Hamburger 1968 (Caesarea).

38 Henig 1974a, *passim*. The gems illustrated are nos 12, 112, 292 and in the revised 1978 edition, App.220. No.12 is shown in *Lexicon Iconographicum Mythologiae Classicae* 582–4 (Henig, 'Amaltheia', no.10). For military preferences see Zienkiewicz 1986, ii, 117–41 and pls v–xvii (Caerleon), and Henig 1970 for the veneration of heroes.

39 Potter 1986 (interim on the Snettisham jeweller's hoard).

40 Henig 1974a and 1978, no.App.36.

41 Ibid. no.742–6, App.30 and see RIB ii fasc.3, nos 2423.10, 2423. 11, 2423. 19 with Greek inscriptions; 2423.4, 2423.18. See Henig 1993a, 27–30.

42 Ibid., 31, fig.2.4.

43 For portraits on jet pendants from Britain see Henig 1974a, nos 757–60.

44 Medusa heads: onyx cameos, Henig 1974a and 1978 nos 725–31; jet 750–5, App.53; Murdoch 1991, 31, fig.4.6 nos 1 and 500, the former = Potter and Johns 1992, 148 ill.58. For the example from Rome see Fremersdorf 1975, no.1150.

45 Henig 1984a.

46 Perring 1989; see Davey and Ling 1981, 136–8 no.26 (Lullingstone water-nymphs). For the

Stonesfield and Cirencester sculptures see Henig 1993b, nos 42 and 24.

47 Ibid. nos 180 (Cupid), 2 (Cupid and Psyche), 1 (Bacchus). See Philp 1989 for the Bacchic frescoes in the Painted House, Dover.

48 See Henig, 1974a, passim; *JRS* lii, 1962, 192 no.8 (Nettleham); *RIB* i, 309 (Caerwent); Toynbee 1978 for votive leaves.

49 Henig 1974a, 50, ill. 11 and 124, ill.51 (plate); on sceptres see ibid., 138 and Henig and Leahy 1984 and 1986. The Aldworth sceptre was brought to my attention by Paul Cannon of Newbury Museum, where the object now is.

Chapter 5 Natives and Strangers in Roman Britain
(pp.79–105)

1 Toynbee 1964a, 5–9.

2 Trow 1990.

3 Henig 1972.

4 Henig 1984b. Compare intaglio no.1 with Henig and Whiting 1987, no.161. See also Murdoch 1991, 81 nos 57, 58 and 176 no.499, pl.14.

5 Henig 1988a, no.3 (Minerva) citing Wroxeter analogue; no.13 (Methe), noting very similar intaglios from Sea Mills and Caerwent; nos 24 and 25 (horses) can be compared with a stone from Tiverton, Henig in Maxfield 1991, 77–8 no.2 and Henig 1992.

6 Marsden 1975, 100–101, pl.7.

7 Toynbee 1964a, 49 and pl.v; also Henig 1984a, 74–5 (Nero); ibid. 118, pl.xxxb (Hercules); Henig and Wilkins 1982 (Vulcan); Pitts 1979, 49 no.3, pl.v (Jupiter); Toynbee 1962, 130–1 no.13, pl.32 (Cupid); Moore, Plouviez and West 1988, back cover (leopard).

8 Frere 1970 (Gestingthorpe mould). Toynbee 1964a, 68 and *BM Guide* 1958, 54, no.17, pl.17 (London Bridge Apollo).

9 RIB 213.

10 See Chapter 4, note 12.

11 Marble sarcophagus, Rook, Walker and Denston 1984, 149–60, for the Chilgrove sculpture see Toynbee in Down 1979, 181–3, pl.11.

12 Facilis, see Toynbee 1962, 157 no.81, pl.93 and Phillips 1975; the London *beneficiarius*, Bishop 1983; Longinus, Toynbee 1962, 158 no.83, pl.92; Genialis, *idem* 1964a, 191, pl.xlvii a and Webster in Henig, 1993b no.137; also Mattern 1989, nos 70, 98 and 69.

13 Toynbee 1964a, 112–3, pl.xxixa; compare Calza and Nash 1959, 12, fig.8 and Meiggs 1973, 66–7.

14 Exeter eagle, Toynbee in Bidwell 1979, 130–2, fig.44 and pl.xx and Henig, 1993b (part 2), no.3; Wroxeter Venus/water-nymph, *Britannia* xv, 1984, 291 and 293, fig.12.

15 Beeson 1986; see Haskell and Penny 1981, 161–3, no.13 for type.

16 Walcot head, Toynbee 1964a, 58 and pl.ix.

17 Boon 1973; *idem* 1974, 116–19 and 166–7, pls 10 and 18.

18 Minerva from Sibson: Hartshorne 1847 and Toynbee 1962, 136 no.27, pl.26; for this as well as the Harlow head see Huskinson 1994, nos 10 and 11.

19 Hartshorne 1847 and Huskinson 1994, no. 35.

20 Davey and Ling 1982, 30; Ling 1991a, 168–97.

21 Colchester gladiator. Ling in Crummy 1984, 147–53; Leicester. Davey and Ling 1982, 123–31; Otford: ibid. 146–8; Dover, Philp 1989, 166–179, 219–20; Kingscote: Ling 1985, 42–4, appears to favour this rather than Achilles among the daughters of King Lycomedes, his earlier hypothesis (Davey and Ling, 119–23); Tarrant Hinton: Davey and Ling, 165–8; Ling 1985, 42; Lullingstone, see Liversidge and Weatherhead in Meates 1987, 11–40.

22 Smith 1975.

23 Johnson 1984.

24 For the second-century gold-jewellery workshop see Cool 1986, colour illustrations of two bracelets from Rhayader, Stefanelli 1992, 154 and 245, nos 109, 110, figs 157 and 158. The gold serpent-ring from Backworth is published by Charlesworth 1961, 10 and 25 no.10. Also note examples from London, Murdoch 1991, 80–1 no.53 and from house xx at Caerwent (Newport Museum) which are of silver as are those from Snettisham; for the Backworth chains and comparanda see Charlesworth, 20–21, 34–5 nos 1–3 and pl.vii and those fom Dolaucothi, Potter and Johns 1992, 167, ill.70; Stefanelli 1992, 108–10 and 234–5 nos 34 and 37, figs 72–5 for chains with wheel pendants from Pompeii. See Potter 1986 and Potter and Johns 1992, 146–7 for interim statements on the Snettisham Treasure of which a full account, edited by Catherine Johns, is in preparation; Cool 1979 for the Castlethorpe bracelets.

25 For the Bignor brooch see Grew in Frere 1982, 177–9, pl.xiiia.

26 The gems from the cache are ascribed to three hands by Marianne Maaskant-Kleibrink (1992).

27 Jet in Britain: see Toynbee 1964a, 363–8, Murdoch 1991, 31, fig.4.6, 70 no.1 and 176 no.500, M. Henig and N.P. Wickenden in Drury 1988, 107–10; in the Rhineland, Hagen 1937; from Italy (Vatican collection), Fremersdorf 1975, 124–5, nos 1140–52 especially no.1150 for the amulet.

28 See Boon and Savory 1975 for early knowledge of mercury gilding of silver. The mould from Newington-next-Hythe, Kent, is published by Jackson 1989. For the Backworth silver: Walters 1921, 46–8 no.183; Capheaton 48–51 nos 188–94; Wroxeter mirror: Toynbee 1964a, 334–5, pl.lxxviii and see Lloyd-Morgan 1981, 146–51. Gaulish comparanda for items of plate can be found in Baratte and Painter 1989 *passim*. See Esmonde Cleary 1989, 99 for the wealth of Late Roman Britain. Water Newton: Painter 1977a; Mileham:

Walters 1921, 23 no.87, pl.14 compare pewter. Potter and Johns 1992, 136, ill.51 (Icklingham, Suffolk) and Ashmolean Museum 1979.83 (University Farm, Wytham, Oxfordshire); Risley Park: Johns and Painter 1991 and see Johns 1981a and Toynbee and Painter 1986, 41–2 and pl.xxc, no.50 for background; Traprain Law: Curle 1923, for the square dishes, 59–61 nos 86 and 87, figs 38, 39 and pl.xxxviii (note also 27–8 no.8, fig.9 for the Ulysses flagon cited as Mediterranean). Ballinrees (Coleraine): Kent and Painter 1977, 125–7 esp. p.127 no.230 = Hawkes 1972, 157, fig.3, 4; Balline (Co. Limerick): Ó Riordáin 1947, 43–53 esp. 49 and pl.I.4 for fragment of square dish; Thetford: Johns and Potter 1983, 34–48, 106–31.

29 For the Foss Dyke Mars see Toynbee 1962, 131 no.16, pl.19 and Henig 1984a, 54, ill.15; the Cirencester appliqué is published by Barber, Walker, Paddock and Henig 1992. Lindgren 1980, gives an appraisal of Roman-British art, most notably bronzes and demonstrates how many works reflect its synthetic nature.

30 Hull 1958, 264, pl.xl and Toynbee 1962, 133–4, no.21, pl.33.

31 Mercury (Zenodorus type), Boucher 1976, 106–7; Manea Fen, Pitts 1979, 58 no.42, pl.10; Great Walsingham, *Britannia* xix, 1988, 456, pl.xxvi, no.3 (note also nos 1 and 2).

32 Toynbee 1964a, 83–4 pl.xviii c and d.

33 For the Amersham heads, see Henig in Farley, Henig and Taylor 1988, 364–6; one is shown (as a sceptre-head) in Henig 1984a, 139, ill.60. They are paralleled in a silver bust from the Little St Bernard pass, Baratte and Painter 1989, 230–1 no.188; for the Silchester musician see Toynbee 1962, 149 no.152, pl.55 and now A. Beeson 'The Tibia Player of Calleva Atrebatum. A New Interpretation', *Roman Research News*, no.7, Autumn 1993, p.3; for the Earith figure, Green and Henig 1988; the Catterick Vulcan, Henig and Wilson 1982.

34 Hounds: Toynbee 1964a, 126–7, pl.xxxiv, b and c; compare Zadoks-Josephus Jitta, Peters and van Es 1969, 166–7, no.72; stag: *JRS* lix, 1969, 223, pl.xiv, 6 and 7 and see Hicks 1978, 381 – see fig.272c for the Brampton head; boars: Foster 1977 and Jackson 1990, 26, frontispiece and pl.1; lions: Ferris 1988–9; Henig 1984d (key-handle); and see Henig and Munby 1973 (monster); eagles: ibid., also Kirk 1949, 31 and pl.5. and Henig and Chambers 1984; cockerel: see Rook and Henig 1981.

35 Toynbee 1964a, 50–1, pl.vi (Hadrian, London); *eadem* 1962, 135–6 no.25, pl.20 (Minerva, Bath); compare with 134–5 no.24, pl.28 (Minerva, London Mithraeum); 150 no. 60, pl.61, *eadem* 1964a, 129 and pl.xxxvb and Boon 1974, 119–20, pl.34c also *Annual Report of National Art-Collections Fund*, 1980, 98 no.2881 (Eagle, Silchester); Boon 1974, 119, pl.34g and Cunliffe and Fulford 1982,

no.153 for the lappet; Toynbee 1962, 147 no.44, pl.46, *eadem* 1964a, 146 no.43, pl.47 and Henig 1984a, 143, ill.64 (Jupiter, Felmingham Hall). The Icklingham treasure awaits scholarly study and publication, but see *The Independent*, 28 September 1989. One of the heads is bearded and somewhat reminiscent of the Felmingham Hall Jupiter.

36 Toynbee 1962, 148–9 no.48, pl.52 (Towcester mask); Henig 1984a, 58 ill.18; *idem* 1993b no.62 (Uley).

37 Ibid., nos 69 and 78 (Mercury from Cirencester and Gloucester); Merrifield 1986 (hunter god) and Toynbee 1986, no.11 (Mithras). Compare the sculptural ornament of the Bath temple (Cunliffe and Davenport 1985, 114–17, pls xxxv–xlvii) with sculpture from Avenches (Verzàr 1977, 36–44), Nyon (Espérandieu xiv, 1955, no.8499 and other sculpture in site museum); Arles (Verzàr, pl.24), and also Narbonne (Espérandieu i, 1907, nos 693, 738, 743). For other schools in Britain, see for example Huskinson 1994 (Lincoln); Tufi 1983 (York) and Phillips 1976 (Carlisle). Also note a local tradition at Chester (see Mattern 1989, 728–31 and Henig in *Transactions of the British Archaeological Association, Chester meeting 1992*, forthcoming). Phillips 1977b is an excellent resumé of the British sculptor's approach to Classical art.

38 Candelabra, see Davey and Ling 1982, 48 and 188–90 (Verulamium) and compare Ling 1991, 172 fig.186 for a much more elaborate example from Cologne. Davey and Ling 1982, 171 no.41 for the Verulamium scroll.

39 Toynbee 1962, 196–7 nos 178 and 179, pls 207 and 208.

40 Smith 1987, 9–13, also the Aquatic mosaic, 14–16 and for suggestion of a (late) third-century date, 26 and 28; *idem* 1981 for third-century mosaics in Britain, p.163 and pl.10. iii for Bignor.

41 Webster 1989 and 1991b.

42 Symonds 1992, 32–8.

43 Phillips 1977a, nos 247 and 248 (South Shields); Coulston and Phillips 1988, no.117 (Chesters); Phillips 1977a, nos 52–56 (Corbridge Dolichenum), 49 (Hercules of Tyre), compare with no.54.

44 Bulmer 1938; Feachem 1951; for convenient illustrations see also Toynbee 1962, 179 no.131, pl.155 and Potter and Johns 1992, 150, ill.60.

45 Bateson 1981; Hattatt 1989, 116–27.

46 RIB 2415.53 and 2415.54, Heurgon 1951 and D. Brown in Cunliffe 1988, 14–16 no.23.

47 Henig in Cunliffe 1988, 23 and pl.xvii, no.48 and see Graham-Campbell 1991a, 228; Youngs 1989, 23 no.1 and see nos 2–6, 7a, 8a.

48 Raftery 1984, 268–75 (Petrie crown and Cork horns); 276–82 (Monasterevin disc); Macgregor 1976, no.210 (Stichill collar), nos 231–50 (massive armlets of Pitkelloney type; Youngs 1989, nos 8b, c; Graham-Campbell 1991b, 253–6 and *idem* 1993 (plaques from Norrie's Law).

49 For the Water Newton bowl, Painter 1977a, 11–12 no.4; for hanging bowls see Youngs 1989, 47–52 nos 31–8 (no.37 for a double pelta escutcheon); Bruce-Mitford 1983, 202–315 (Sutton Hoo); Longley 1975, for a suggestion of Roman origins.

Chapter 6 Artists and their Patrons (pp.106–137)

1 Burford 1972 for a general work on the subject.

2 Fishwick 1972.

3 Blagg 1990.

4 For the Cirencester tombstones see RIB 108 and 109 and Mattern 1989, nos 67 and 69 (also 68 for a fragment); Webster in Henig 1993b, nos 137–9; Gloucester RIB 121, Rhodes 1964, no.1 and Mattern 1989, no.80; Webster in Henig 1993b, no.140.

5 RIB 110, Rhodes 1964, no.2 and Mattern 1989, no.66; Henig 1993b, no.141.

6 RIB 159, Cunliffe and Fulford 1982, no.44 and Mattern 1989, no.3 (Tancinus); also Cunliffe and Fulford no.45 and Mattern no.4 (another cavalry tombstone from Bath); RIB 149 for Priscus.

7 RIB 151 (Bath) and 105 (Cirencester); see Haverfield 1917–18, 180–5; Henig 1993b, no.116, also 117 and 120 (Matres) and 23 (Diana).

8 Bath: for Cogidubnus as a possible patron of the temple see Henig 1989, 221 and 223; the inscription on the Façade of the Four Seasons, RIB 141. Gloucester antefix: Toynbee 1962, 165 no.96 pl.103; Rhodes 1964, no.6 and Henig 1993b, no.173.

9 Cirencester: *Britannia* vi, 1975, pp.272–3 n.162, pl.xxi b and Henig 1993b, no.69 (Bath Gate relief); Phillips 1976 b and Henig 1993b, no.18 (Figured capital).

10 For the cult image at Uley: Ellison and Henig 1981; Potter and Johns 1992, 172–3, ill.74; Henig 1993b no.62; see in general Woodward and Leach 1993.

11 Clifford 1938; Henig, 1993b nos 48–60; see RIB 132 and Rhodes 1964, no.12 for inscribed Bisley relief.

12 Rhodes 1964, no.13 iii and vi; Henig 1993b, *passim* (among the celtic deities).

13 Frere 1963 (Keisby); *idem* 1961 (Wilsford and Ancaster); Ambrose and Henig 1980 (Stragglethorpe).

14 Whitwell 1970, 125 pl.viia.

15 Frere 1961, 231.

16 *Lincs Architectural and Archaeological Society* x, pt.ii, 1964, 5–8, pls 2, 3; see Whitwell 1970, 126.

17 Blagg and Henig 1986.

18 RIB 250.

19 Toynbee 1964a, 201, pl.xlviii; *eadem* 1962, 159–60 no.86, pl.88. Compare Wightman 1970, pls 14–20 for funerary sculpture in the Trier region.

20 Whitwell 1970, 42 and pl.ivb.

21 *Idem* 124–5.

22 *Idem* 124, pl. ii b; Blagg 1982.

23 Merrifield 1986 (hunter gods); *Britannia* xix, 1988, 463, pl.xxvib (Mercury); Blagg in Hill, Millett and Blagg 1980, 169–71.

24 Merrifield 1986 and see Henig 1993b, nos 110–14.

25 Toynbee 1986, nos 11–13.

26 Rhodes 1964, nos 4 and 8 and Henig 1993b, nos 91, 92.

27 Phillips 1976a; also see Coulston and Phillips 1988, nos 492–8 and Mattern 1989, nos 10–14 (Carlisle tombstones). Coulston and Phillips no.481 (Mercury on tombstone) no.482 (Mercury on altar) *Britannia* xxi, 1990, 322 fig.11 and pl.xxviiib for the Minerva relief.

28 Coulston and Phillips, no.15 (Fortuna from Birdoswald); see p.xviii for Housesteads workshop. Phillips 1977b on Romano-British sculpture in general, though he rather loses sight of the fact there was very bad work alongside many examples of inventive regional style.

29 Toynbee 1962, 159 no.85, pl.89; 160, no.87, pl.85 also Phillips 1977a, nos 247 and 248 and Mattern 1989, nos 117 and 116 (South Shields); Toynbee 140, no.35, pl.41 and Coulston and Phillips 1988, no.117 (Chesters).

30 Toynbee 1962, 135–6 no.25, pl.20 (Minerva); *eadem* 1964a, 50–1, pl.vi (Hadrian).

31 Ibid. 46–8, pl.iv; see Lawson 1986 for the Ashill hock; Toynbee 1964a, 129, and pl.xxxvb (Silchester eagle).

32 Cunliffe and Fulford 1982, 42 no.153 (Silchester lappet); Henig 1993b, nos 178, 179 (Cirencester). For the statue-bases see Chapter 4.

33 Frere 1983, 69–72, pl.ix (Verulamium); RIB 288 (Wroxeter).

34 Ireland 1983, 220–33. See Keppie 1991 for a longer introduction to the subject.

35 Ling 1985, 5–6.

36 Cunliffe 1971, vol.i, 142–5 and vol.ii, 16–33 (Fishbourne marbles); Davey and Ling 1982, 183–6 nos 43 and 44 (Verulamium wall-paintings).

37 MacKenna and Ling 1991 (Southwark), rightly draw attention to late Hadrianic and early Antonine parallels in Britain; Philp 1989 (Dover).

38 Davey and Ling 1982, 123–31 no.22 (Leicester).

39 Ling 1991a, 175–8.

40 Ling in Crummy 1984, 146–53.

41 Davey and Ling 1982, 116 no.17 see pl.cxiii (Fishbourne – fish rather than shrimp); 162–3 no.37(c) (Sparsholt); J. Liversidge in Meates 1987, 1, 9–10 and col.pl.1 (Lullingstone); Davey and Ling 1982, 196–9 no.49 (Winterton); 155–8 no.34 (Southwell).

42 Ibid. 146–8 no.30; RIB 2447.9.

43 Philp 1989, 139.

44 Davey and Ling 1982. 165–8 no.38.

45 Swain and Ling 1981, but see also Ling 1985, 44.

46 Lullingstone nymphs see Meates 1987, 6–11; see Wedlake 1982, 63–4 and 104–5 for the painting in the octagonal temple at Nettleton; for the

47 Christian paintings at Lullingstone, Liversidge and Weatherhead in Meates, 11–41.

47 Smith 1965, 1969, 1975, 1977 and 1984 are the most important; also Neal 1981 surveying and illustrating, with his own detailed paintings, a large number of mosaics.

48 RIB ii, fasc.4, 2448.11, see Johnson 1984, 409.

49 Darmon 1976, especially p.8.

50 For Thruxton see Henig and Soffe 1993 and RIB ii, fasc.4, 2448.9; for Lydney see Henig 1984a, 135–6 and RIB ii, fasc.4, 2448.3.

51 Lullingstone, RIB i, fasc.4, 2448.6 (elegiac couplet); Frampton 2448.8 (originally eight lines, metre described by Tomlin as catalectic anapaestic dimeters).

52 RIB ii, fasc.4, 2448.5.

53 Toynbee 1962, 203–5 no.200, pl.235.

54 Henig 1986; *contra*, specifically with regard to Brading, Ling 1991b, especially 148–53, but see also p.156 dismissing a cult aspect at Littlecote.

55 See Toynbee 1964a; Eriksen 1980; Black 1986, 147–50.

56 Gladiators: Neal 1981, 76 no.43 (Eccles); 92–3 no.66 and Smith 1987, 9–13 and p.28 (Rudston Venus mosaic); Toynbee 1962, 200 no.191, pls.225, 226 (Bignor cupids as gladiators); Henig 1986, 167, fig.1 (Brading gladiators). Circus racing see Humphrey 1986, 431–7 and specifically on mosaics, Smith 1987, 37(Horkstow); ibid., 20–25 (Rudston). For North African mosaics see Dunbabin 1978.

57 Cunliffe 1971, vol.i, 145–50 (Fishbourne palace); Marsden 1975, 57 and 99, fig.44 and pl.iv (London palace); D.J. Smith in Perring, Roskams and Allen 1991, 88–94 (Watling Court, London); D.J. Smith in Bidwell 1979, 132–4 (Exeter bath-house); Zienkiewicz 1986, 165–8 and G.C. Boon in ibid., 273–6 (Caerleon); Thompson 1965, 40 and 44 with frontispiece (Chester).

58 Cookson 1984 first suggested the possible complications, albeit in a somewhat convoluted manner.

59 D.J. Smith in Crummy 1984, 168–74 (Middleborough pavement); Toynbee 1962, 197 no.179, pl.208 and Neal 1981, 102–3 no.75 (Lion mosaic). See Smith 1984, 363–4 and tav.1 (Eastern tradition).

60 Smith 1984, 362–3 and tav.1 (Western tradition).

61 Merrifield 1965, pls 63–9 (London mosaics); Neal 1981, 37–8 nos 1 and 2 (Aldborough).

62 Ibid., 54–5 no.20 (Chichester, below south choir aisle of cathedral); Cunliffe 1971, vol.1, 163–4, pls xlvii–liii (Fishbourne dolphin mosaic).

63 See Smith 1984, 363–4; Neal and Walker 1988.

64 Neal 1981, 20–35.

65 Smith 1977, 107 no.3, pl.6.xiia.

66 *Idem* 1981, quoted on p.163; *idem* 1987, 28 (third-century dating of Rudston Venus); for the wolf and twins see Toynbee 1962, 198 no.184, pl.220.

67 Smith, see n.47 above is the main source; see

Johnston 1977 (Central Southern); Millett 1990, 176 for Leicester; Johnson 1982, 45–9 for the *Lindinis officina*; Cosh 1989 for the Corinian Saltire branch.

68 For Withington see Smith 1969, 112–13 and 116.

69 Johnston 1977.

70 Smith 1984, pls 2–9 illustrates the work of the Corinian Saltire School. Neal 1981, 60–1 no.25c. The hare mosaic from Beeches Road Cirencester) has not been attributed to any school by either Smith or Neal, but the design is sufficiently close to the Gloucester (Bell Lane) pavement with central figure of Bacchus (Smith 1984, 362, pl.4) to assign it to the Saltire School. The *emblema* of the London (Broad Street) mosaic (364, pl.6) looks more like a reclining Bacchus on a feline than Europa as proposed by Smith 1977, 114 no.26.

71 For this late tradition see Smith 1984, 370–2. I attribute Lullingstone to it in Henig 1985, 18. The Bellerophon scene on the new Croughton mosaic, of which I have only seen a snapshot, looks more like that at Lullingstone than those of Hinton St Mary or Frampton and consequently it may be assigned to this secondary phase.

72 For the Orpheus pavements see Smith 1983; for their style, Henig 1985, 15–16, pl.iv.

73 Rosenthal 1972; see Henig 1979, 22–3, pl.ii. and now Dark 1994, 184–91

74 Barrett 1978.

75 Henig 1984c.

76 Alcock 1989; RIB 274.

77 Glaucus: RIB 213; Cintusmus: RIB 194. For metalworking at the temple site at Woodeaton, Oxfordshire, see Kirk 1949, 28–30, sprue, fig.7 no.7 and ingots, fig.8, nos 10, 11. For images of Vulcan representing smiths see Henig and Wilson 1982; Henig 1991 (figurines); Johns 1991, 61–2 no.18 (ring); Walters 1921, nos 235, 236 and Potter and Johns 1992, 176 ill.77 (votive plaques); Tufi 1983, no.56 (sculpture from York).

78 Toynbee 1964a, 320 and pl.lxxvb; RIB ii, fasc.2, 2415.11; Potter and Johns 1992, 133–4 ill.49.

79 RIB ii, fasc.2, 2415.53 (Rudge Cup); Heurgon 1951 (Amiens *patera*); Painter 1977a nos 8 and 9 (Water Newton).

80 Risley Park *lanx* see Johns 1981a, Toynbee and Painter 1986, 41–2 and pl.xxc, no.50, Johns and Painter 1991, also Potter and Johns 1992, 210–11, ill.87. Pewter industry: Brown 1973, see also Wedlake 1982, 67–74 for moulds and other debris from Nettleton, mentioning moulds from Camerton and Lansdown; moulds have also been found near the source of the tin, for example at Leswyn St Just, Cornwall (Ashmolean Museum 1836, 147–8); the Bath ingots, one of lead and the other of pewter are published by Henig in Cunliffe 1988b, 22–4, fig.12 nos 55 and 56; for inscriptions scratched on pewter see RIB ii, fasc.2, 2417.5–8 (dedications to Sulis Minerva, Bath) and 2417.1 (dedication to Mars from Bosence, Cornwall);

2417.28 and 34 (personal gifts from Appleford and North Oxfordshire). There are a number of names of owners, e.g. 2417.23 and 24 (Martinus, from Southwark) 31 (Venusta, Silchester); 2417.32 for the Welney dish which actually reads 'VERE FELEI'.

81 RIB 712 and see Ogden 1982, 177 and 181 ill.11:8.

82 Maaskant-Kleibrink 1992 for the Snettisham gems. The mould from Alchester, Ashmolean Museum inv.1929.747, is unpublished.

83 Potter 1986 (Snettisham); Cool 1979 (Castlethorpe); *eadem* 1986 (Rhayader, Southfleet etc.).

84 Johns and Potter 1983.

85 Brooches: enamels, see Chapter 5, notes 44 and 45; distinctive brooches in the Aesica hoard, Charlesworth 1973, 225–30; the giant silver trumpet brooch once contained a gem in its head loop. See CIL XIII 3162 for the Marble of Thorigny; Hattatt 1989, 181 fig 84 no.1648 for the Abbots Ann Brooch.

86 For the jet and shale industries: Lawson 1976, especially pp. 242–3; RCHM *Eburacum Roman York*, 1962, 141–4, pls 68–70 (jet); Sunter 1987, 30–35; P. Cox in Woodward 1987a, 106–10; P. Cox and P. Woodward in Woodward 1987b, 165–72 (shale).

87 The well-known reference to the silversmiths' guild at Ephesus is in Acts 19. Several *collegia* in Britain are recorded: RIB 91 (Chichester) mentions a guild of *fabri* while 69–71 (Silchester) were set up by the guild of *peregrini*. Neither is specifically a guild of artists. Other guilds attested appear to be religious, under the patronage of deities, e.g. 141 (Bath); 247; 270; 271 (Lincoln); RIB ii, fasc.3, 2422.52 (Wendens Ambo), though this in no way rules out the possibility that they were craft associations.

88 Painter 1977a; Johns and Potter 1983; Johns and Painter 1991.

89 For furniture in general see Liversidge 1955; for shale see n.86 above; shale trenchers, Biddle 1967, 233–4 and 248–50 and a jewellery casket in Johns and Potter 1983, 33 and 131 no.83. Stone sideboards, Cunliffe and Fulford 1982, nos 159–89 and T.F.C. Blagg in Henig 1993b, nos 240–51.

90 For Central Gaulish samian see Stanfield and Simpson 1990; colour-coated wares in Gaul see especially Symonds 1990, 32–8. For the British vessels with scenes in relief rendered in barbotine see Toynbee 1964a, 408–15, pls xciii and xciva; their fascinating iconography is discussed by Webster 1989 and 1991b; also see Darling 1989, raising problems of patronage on pp.31 and 32. For face flagons made in the Oxfordshire kilns see Munby 1975 and the Horspath mould, Hassall 1952–3. Toynbee 1964a, 406, pl.xcii, b and c for masks from East Anglia. Face and head pots, see Braithwaite 1984.

91 Terracotta *antefixa*, see Toynbee 1964a, 428–31, pls xcviii–xcix; Carrawburgh incense burners, see RIB ii, fasc.4, 2457.2 and 2457.3.

Chapter 7 Art in Late Roman Britain (pp.138–173)

1 Brown 1971.
2 Esmonde Cleary 1989; Dark 1994.
3 Bloch 1963.
4 Onians 1980.
5 Brown 1971, 74.
6 Volbach 1961, 335–6, pls 122–7.
7 Foster 1991.
8 Ariadne lanx: Weitzmann 1979, 147–8 no.126; Cahn and Kaufmann-Heinimann 1984, pls 103–61 no.61; Toynbee and Painter 1986, 33 and pl.xiva, no.26; Rubens Vase: ibid., 333–4 no.313; Dietreta: Harden and Toynbee 1959 and Whitehouse 1992, especially p.115.
9 Constantine: Volbach 1961, 315–16, pls 16, 17; Christ (Catacomb of Commodilla): Dorigo 1971, pl.178; the Piazza Armerina *Dominus*: ibid., pl.101, see Wilson 1983, 85, ill.54; Dominus Iulius: Dorigo 1971, pl.146 and Weitzmann 1979, 270–1.
10 Painter 1990, 5–6. The subject of gift-exchange in Late Antiquity is currently being researched by Ida Johansen.
11 See for example Weitzmann 1979, 67–9 no.58; 107–8 no.99.
12 For Carausius and Allectus see Casey 1994. There is, of course, the fascinating possibility of Romano-British craftsment (jewellers and gem-cutters) – as well as Gauls – being employed by the British mints during this unusual decade. Certainly the style of the coins is far from Metropolitan. The subject demands detailed investigation. For the Arras Medallion see also Merrifield 1965, pl.13.
13 Lullingstone Orantes: J. Liversidge and F. Weatherhead in Meates 1987, 14–17, 33–5, pls 1–3, col.pl.xii; Walesby font: Thomas 1981, 221–5, pl.6.
14 For deities see Smith 1977, pl.6. iii and xxiiia (Venus); Henig and Soffe 1993 (Bacchus); Ling 1991b, pl.xxi (Tyche or Muse). Hinton St Mary: Toynbee 1964b, Thomas 1981, 105–6, 182 and pl.5, and see Painter 1976 for the conception of Hinton St Mary as a vault design: also Smith 1987, 38–9 for Horkstow; Orpheus mosaics: Smith 1983 and Scott 1991.
15 See n.13 with the chi-rhos, 12–14, 36–7, col.pls xi and xiii; for the dress of the figures see J.P. Wild in Meates 1987, 40–1.
16 Smith 1983, 320–1. The presence of water-nymphs in the outer spandrels and possibly of 'fish and a star about the center' suggests a fountain or at least basins of water in the room. Also see Lysons III 1817, pl.v for a well-preserved fountain in the piscina of room 7 at Bignor, surrounded by a mosaic *schema* (see also Frere 1982, plan fig.3 and 142–3 for water-supply).
17 Painter 1977b (Mildenhall); Haverfield 1914 and Toynbee 1962, 172 no.108; Toynbee and Painter 1986, 32 and pl.xic, no.23 (Corbridge).
18 Ibid., 185–6 no.142, pl.161 (Wint Hill); *Dietreta:*

Harden and Toynbee 1959, 207 no.13 (Silchester; probably figured) and 212 (Great Staughton, Huntingdonshire).
19 Johns and Potter 1983; for information on the Hoxne Treasure I am most grateful to Catherine Johns who will publish a full study. See C. Johns and R. Bland, 'The great Hoxne treasure: a preliminary report,' *JRA* 6, 1993, pp.493–6; R. Bland and C. Johns, *The Hoxne Treasure. An Illustrated Introduction* (London, 1993) and C. Johns *Jewellery of Roman Britain* (forthcoming).
20 Thomas 1981; also Watts 1991.
21 Henig 1993b, no.2; Calza and Nash 1959, pl.44.
22 *RIB* ii, 4, 2448.3 (Lydney) and 2448.9 (Thruxton), on which see further Henig and Soffe 1993; Webster 1983a, but see Goodburn 1972 for the conventional view of the site (Chedworth).
23 *RIB* i, 103; see P. Brown 1980, 19.
24 Tufi 1983, 23 no.38; Thomas 1981, pl.2 (Constantine), Henig 1978 (?Fausta). Johns and Bland 1993.
25 See Gazda 1981 on late Roman marble statuettes as objects of pagan devotion; for statuettes in Britain see Henig 1983b, Toynbee 1986 and Henig 1993b, nos 1–4, 7, 8, 14, 15.
26 Kendrick 1938, 34–6 and 98–100; see Reece 1977, 407.
27 Walters 1984, 435; for the appropriate text see Henig 1984a, 200.
28 For a sceptical approach see Ling 1991b, 147–53.
29 Henig 1986, 164–5 and 167; also Black 1986, 150–1; Henig 1984c; Beeson 1990. For the 'holy man' see Fowden 1982.
30 Henig 1985, 15–16, pl.iv; Scott 1991.
31 Henig, 'Syncretism in Roman Britain: the huntsman with the phrygian cap', *Rencontres Scientifiques de Luxembourg* 4, ed. C.M. Ternes and P.F. Burke (Luxembourg 1994), 78–92.
32 Smith 1983.
33 Walters 1984; on Julian see Athanassiadi 1992, 151–2.
34 Webster 1983b.
35 Henig 1984c.
36 For Bacchus in Roman Britain see Hutchinson 1986a and 1986b; also Henig and Soffe 1991 (Thruxton); see Toynbee 1986, 23–5 nos 6 and 7, 39–42 no.15 (marbles from site of Walbrook Mithraeum), 42–52 no.16 (silver casket and infusor).
37 For Hinton St Mary see n.14 above. Watts 1991, 179–214 deals with syncretism between paganism and Christianity but interprets the Bellerophon theme as straightforward Christian allegory (p.208). However, see Huskinson 1974, who does not accept that this was regularly the case. Hanfmann 1980, 85–7 restates the problems.
38 For Pelagius see Thomas 1981, 53–60 and Esmonde Cleary 1989, 121, 128 and 162. Both are sceptical about his effect on the British church, but

Pelagianism was clearly a problem in fifth-century Britain (AD 429), and it seems reasonable to ask whether his natal environment had affected Pelagius' own attitude to the problems of Grace and Free Will; that background was one in which robust Paganism could not be avoided, see Henig 1984a, 217–24; *idem* 1986, 163–4.

39 Bloch 1963, especially 208–16 for literary *subscriptiones* to editions of the classics.

40 For the Keynsham villa see Russell 1985. On the subjects of the *triclinium* mosaics see Stupperich 1980, 293–6; for illustrations see Toynbee 1964a, pl.lvii. Minerva and the *tibia* is found in Ovid, *Fasti* vi, 699–702; Europa in *Fasti* v, 603–20 and *Metamorphoses* ii, 832ff. The third scene is less certain and if Achilles discovered amongst the daughters of Lycomedes (Stupperich, *op. cit.*, also Ling 1981), it reduces the likelihood of an Ovidian source for the other two scenes.

41 Toynbee 1962, 203–5 no.200, pl.235; Barrett 1978, 308–9; *RIB* ii, 2448. 6, pl.vi.

42 Rosenthal 1972 for the illustrations; Henig 1979, 21–4 and now, Dark 1994, 184–91.

43 Barrett 1978, 309–13.

44 *RIB* ii, 2448.5.

45 Huntsmen: Toynbee 1964a, 239–40 and see *VCH* Somerset I (1906), fig.87 (East Coker); Toynbee 1962, 199 no.187, pl.216 (Chedworth). Hounds: Toynbee 1964b; Smith 1969, pl.3.29; Neal 1981, 87–9 no.61 (Hinton St Mary); Smith 1969, pl.3.27 (Frampton); Johnson 1985 (Cherhill). Hare: Neal 1981, 60–1 no.25c. Bacchus mosaics: Smith 1977, 108–10, nos 5–11. For the Grateley fan, see Rainey 1973, 85 and pl.Ib.

46 Hercules: Smith 1977, 144 no.129, but the third figure is certainly Minerva. I am grateful to Pat Witts and Grahame Soffe for information on Lickman's fine coloured engravings at Stourhead. Medusa: Smith 1977, 118–19 nos 39–42. Cult rooms: see Henig and Soffe 1993 (Thruxton); Walters 1984 (Littlecote); Henig 1984c and 1986, 162–4; Black 1986, 149–50 (Frampton); Henig 1986, 164–5; Black 1986, 150–1 (Brading). Ling 1991b, 148–53 makes some instructive iconographical observations about Brading but does not lead me to doubt my previous position; also see Schefold 1972 and Brilliant 1984 for discussions of mythological scenes as pendants with relation to earlier Italian fresco, but almost certainly relevant to fourth-century images. Webster 1983a for Chedworth; Hanfmann 1980, 89–90 and fig.26 gives a convincing explanation of the Trier mosaic. For the Cyprus mosaics see Daszewski 1985.

47 For earlier mosaics see Chapter 4, n.27. See Neal 1981, 90 no.63b (Kingscote); 94 no.67 and Smith 1987, 14–16 (Rudston); *idem* 1977, 122 no.53, pl.6.xa (Cirencester, Neptune); ibid., 123 no.59, pl.6.xviia (Hemsworth Neptune) and ibid., 134–5 no.104 (Hemsworth Venus) which is illustrated in Johnson (1982, 45 pl.34 Smith 1977, 135, pl.6.xxiiia (Low Ham Venus).

48 Gladiators: Toynbee 1962, 200 no.191, pls 225, 226 (Bignor); Henig 1984a, 221 ill.106 and Ling 1991, 152 and pl.xivb (Brading). Ling describes the scene but misses the point that the function here is very different from the Nennig floor, see Dorigo 1971, pl.40, Beast Fights: Smith 1987, 9–13 (Rudston); Putnam and Rainey 1972, 84 fig.8 (Dewlish); Neal 1981, 103–4 no.76 (Verulamium). The Circus: Smith 1987, 37 (Horkstow); ibid., 21–5 and Ling 1983, 18–19, pl.1 (Rudston); Humphrey 1986, 431–7 assembles the slender evidence for circus-racing in Britain.

49 Bignor: Johnson 1984, 406, pl.3. The long hair makes the identification as Venus certain. Brantingham: see Liversidge, Smith and Stead 1973, 92–9 (mosaic) and 99, 102–3 (paintings); Henig in *Lexicon Iconographicum Mythologiae Classicae* iii, 156 sees the central figure as the Tyche of Eboracum, plausibly equated with Brigantia; Ling 1991b, 154–6 sees her as a muse (?Terpsichore).

50 Davey and Ling 1981, 119–23 and Ling 1985, 42–4 (Kingscote); Davey and Ling 1981, 165–8 (Tarrant Hinton).

51 See n.49 for Brantingham; for the Trier paintings see Ling 1991a, 195–6 pl.xvib.

52 Lullingstone: J. Liversidge in Meates 1987, 11–40; J.P. Wild in ibid., 40–1. Poundbury: Davey and Ling 1981, 106–11; Sparey Green 1993, esp. p.139.

53 Painter 1977b, 26 nos 1–3, pls 1–8; Toynbee and Painter 1986, 22–4 and pl.vii, no.1; 29 and pl.xb and c, nos 18 and 19.

54 Ibid., 27–8 nos 7 and 8, pls 20–2 (Alexander and Olympias); 31–2 nos 29–31, pl.36 (spoons with chi-rhos).

55 Haverfield 1914; see Toynbee and Painter 1986, 32 and pl.xic no.23.

56 Traprain Law: Curle 1923, 13–19, no.1, pl.v (Christian flagon); 27–8, no.8. pl.xii (recognition of Ulysses); 54 no.65 (crowning of Dionysus [Bacchus]); 41–3, no.36, pl.xxi (head of Hercules); 36–9, no.30, pl.xvii (nereid on sea-panther). Balline: Ó Ríordáin 1947, 50–5, pl.iii and Toynbee 1964a, 315 and pl.lxxiiia.

57 Johns and Potter 1983, 107–8 no.50 and 119–20 no.66, col.pl.2, also 119–21 no.67; and see in general pp.34–45 (Thetford); Johns and Potter 1985; 318–19 no.7 (Canterbury); Hawkes 1972, 157 and fig.3, 4 (Ballinrees/Coleraine).

58 Johns and Potter 1991.

59 Pewter, see Chapter 6, n.80; also Isle of Ely bowl: Toynbee 1962, 176 no.121, pls 137, 138; Appleford: Brown 1973, see 193 no.24 and *RIB* ii, 2417.28 for the inscription and Brown, 193–4, fig.4 no.21; Appleshaw: Read 1898, 10 no.9 is the same as the Appleford design; 9 nos 2 and 4, figs 1 and 2 are more complicated. Comparanda in silver:

Painter 1977b, 27 no.4, pls 11–14 (Mildenhall) and Cahn and Kaufmann-Heinimann 1984, pls 79–81, no.55 (Kaiseraugst). Note also the fish-dish with central fish design on it, Read, 12 no.32, fig.9; Cahn and Kaufmann-Heinimann 1984, pl.77, 2 and see ibid., pl.78, 2 and Baratte and Painter 1989, 272–4 no.237 for the pewter fish dish from Alise-Ste-Reine. Silver comparanda: Cahn and Kaufmann-Heinimann 1984, pls 70–74, nos 53 and 54; Toynbee and Painter 1986, 43 and pl.xxiiia, no.54 (Kaiseraugst) and bronze, Cahn and Kaufmann-Heinimann, pl.76 and 77, 1 (from Cologne, Rhonetal and Morrens-Le Buy), also a heart-shaped vessel with a fish from Traprain, Curle 1923, 72–3 no.108, pl.xxvii and Cahn and Kaufmann-Heinimann, pl.78, 1. For the Bath pewter see N. Sunter and P. Brown in Cunliffe 1988b, 9–21 especially 11 no.14 (with coin of Constantine), comparing it with the 'Munich Treasure' bowls, Kent and Painter 1977, 20–1 nos 1–3 and Toynbee and Painter 1986, 24–5 and pls viib and c, and viiia, nos 2–4 (with images of Licinius); also ibid., 25 and pl.viiic (similar from Červenbreg, Bulgaria).

60 Volbach 1961, 322 no.53 and Toynbee and Painter 1986, 27–8 and pl.xa, no.16 (Missorium of Theodosius) and 324 no.63 (Stilicho diptych). Erickstanebrae brooch: *RIB* ii, 2421.43; Moray Firth brooch: Kent and Painter 1977, 28 no.21; Odiham: ibid., no.20, see *Guide to the Antiquities of Roman Britain* (British Museum 1951), 21 fig.10 no.28. Other examples of bronze nos 29 and 30; see Potter and Johns 1992, 215 no.90 for brooch of silver with niello.

61 Thetford: Johns and Potter 1983, 20–9, 78–105. Multi-gem rings nos 5 and 8; rings using filigree wires, nos 10–15, 17 – compare Kent and Painter 1977, 128–9 nos 231, 232 from New Grange and Fulford, Burnett, Henig and Johns 1989, nos 3 and 5 from Silchester; figured rings nos 23 (Faunus), 7 (woodpeckers), 5 and 6 (dolphins) – bronze ring from Canterbury shown to me by Pan Garrard of the Canterbury Archaeological Trust; for the Sussex brooch see Toynbee 1964a, 344 and pl.lxxixc and Kent and Painter 1977, 28 no.23; dolphin buckles (types IA and IIA), see Hawkes and Dunning 1961, 41–5 and 50–7, figs 13, 17, 18. For the Thetford buckle, Johns and Potter 1983, 78–9, 81 and col.pl.1.

62 For silver belts and buckles from Traprain Law see Curle 1923, 86–9 nos 146–9 and pls xxxii and xxxiii; on Late Roman belts from Britain see in general Hawkes and Dunning 1961; 62 and pl.iib for the Snodland buckle and compare portraits with those on a silver vessel from Traprain Law – Curle 1923, 53 no.63; 62 and pl.iii for a buckle in Liverpool. Note Hawkes 1972 for the splendid example of a type IB buckle from Caves Inn, with two peacocks on the plate. On belts as badge of

status see Esmonde Cleary 1989, 34, 54–6 and note Dorigo 1971, 226, iii.183 for servant holding a belt from a tomb at Silistra, Bulgaria.

63 Hawkes 1961 for quoit brooches, especially 30–1, pl.xiv for the Sarre brooch, also figured in Kent and Painter 1977, 137–8 no.293; Evison 1968 for buckles in that style, note especially pl.liii for the Mucking mounts. The relevant rings are *Proc. Soc. Antiq. London* 2nd ser. iv(i), 38–9 (Wantage); Henig 1978, nos 801–3, pl.lix and Kent and Painter, 62 nos 141–3 (Amesbury); *idem* 1985, 19; Henig and Ogden 1988, 315–17 and 326, n.59 (Richborough). A gold bracelet in the Hoxne treasure also depicts animals in the 'quoit-brooch style', see Bland and Johns 1993, 20 (illustration, bottom row).

64 For the Bath brooch and the Oldcroft pin see Chapter 5, n.47. For hanging-bowl escutcheons in 'antique revival style' see Youngs 1989, 51 no.36. On Sutton Hoo see Bruce-Mitford 1983 (silver on pp.1–191).

Chapter 8 Attitudes to Art in Roman Britain
(pp.174–189)

1 Bruce-Mitford 1978, 311–77; Hicks 1978; *eadem* 1993.

2 Webster and Backhouse 1991, 17–19 no.1 (Gospels of St Augustine); ibid., 123–4, 126, also Bruce-Mitford 1969 (Codex Amiatinus). See Wilson 1984, 49; Bruce-Mitford 1983 and Kent and Painter 1977, 130–5, nos 236–48 for the silver.

3 Cunliffe 1983.

4 Kitzinger 1993, esp. 8–13; Henderson 1993.

5 Wilson 1984, 79 pl.82 (Otley); 108 pl.132 (Whitchurch), cf. Phillips and Coulston 1988, no.209, Mattern 1989, 784–5 no.102. Note Lang 1993.

6 Biddle and Kjølbye-Biddle 1985, esp. pp.254–73. For Roman parallels cf. *Britannia* ii, 1971, 238, pl.xxxiii and Henig 1984a, 53, ill.13.

7 Hayward Gallery exhibition catalogue, *English Romanesque Art* (1984), nos 99–101; cf.Tufi 1983, no.128 (capitals); Higgitt 1973, 13–14, pls i.5 and i.4 (fonts).

8 For *spolia* in the Middle Ages see Greenhalgh 1989. For late sixteenth-century antiquarianism, see Munby 1977, 416, 418–19, fig.10.la and see Phillips 1977, no.215 and Henig 1984a, 70, ill.24; Howarth 1992.

9 Horsley 1733, 327.

10 Henig 1993b, no.180 for full references.

11 Johns 1981. See Munby 1977, 423 on Stukeley.

12 Toynbee 1962, 197–8 no.183, pl.219.

13 Taylor 1941; Levine 1978.

14 Colour illustration on back cover of Littlecote guide-book by P.A. Spreadbury, 1979. The mosaic is discussed by Colt Hoare 1822, who gives details of the discovery almost a century before on pp.118–20.

15 Lysons 1797.

16 *Idem* 1813 (*Reliquiae* i, part 3) = 'Figures of mosaic pavements discovered near Frampton in Dorsetshire' (1808), 2 and 5.

17 Ibid., 1; Henig 1984c.

18 Lysons 1817 (*Reliquiae* iii) = 'Remains of a Roman villa discovered at Bignor in Sussex' (1815).

19 *Idem* 1813 (*Reliquiae* i), Introduction iii–iv.

20 Ibid. (*Reliquiae* i, part 2) = 'Remains of two temples and other Roman antiquities discovered at Bath' (1802).

21 Fowler 1804; Artis 1828.

22 Colt Hoare 1821.

23 Ibid., 124 footnote (on Lysons) in section *De Musivis*.

24 Ecroyd Smith 1852; see Henig and Soffe 1993 on the work of John Lickman at Thruxton.

25 Ribchester helmet: Townley 1799 = *Vetusta Monumenta* iv (1815), 1–12, pls i–iii. See also Toynbee 1962, 167 no.101, pl.108. For the Barking Hall statuette, *Vet. Mon.* iv, pls xi–xv; see also Toynbee 1964a, 49 and pl.v; Henig 1984a, 75, ill.26.

26 Gage 1836, 310–11.

27 Newton 1846, 477.

28 Hartshorne 1847, 3.

29 Buckman and Newmarch 1850, 19–21 (capital) 25–47 (mosaics), also 48–69 (sections on materials and techniques employed in making mosaics).

30 Roach-Smith 1846, 287. The contents of the early issues of *JBAA* are noteworthy, for example Wright 1863 is the first attempt at examining the glyptic material from a single site. On Mayer see White 1988.

31 Roach Smith 1859, 6.

32 Ibid., 33–45 (Matres); 65–7 (Hadrian).

33 Ibid., 69–70.

34 Ibid., 49–59. Pat Witts points out to me that the animal seems to be spotted, and if so the subject has to be Bacchus on his leopard.

35 Ibid., 60–4.

36 Price 1870; see Merrifield 1965, 4–5, pls 63, 65.

37 Jenkyns 1991, 312–17 for Scottish nineteenth-century neo-classicism.

38 Kendrick 1938, ch.2 (pp.17–46).

39 Ibid., 21.

40 Ibid., 23.

41 Ibid., 40–1.

42 Ibid., esp. pp.32 and 36.

43 Ibid., 39.

44 Frere 1967, 315–22. Blagg 1989, for convenient account of recent developments. Reece's paper, announced in *Aufstieg und Niedergang der Römischen Welt* 11.12.3 (1985) will eventually appear in volume 11.12.4.

Bibliography

Alcock, J.P. 1989, 'A note on the Foss Dyke bronze figurine of Mars Gradivus', *Lincs. Hist. and Arch.* xxiv, 59–60

Allason-Jones, L. and Miket, R. 1984, *The catalogue of small finds from South Shields Roman fort*, Newcastle upon Tyne

Allen, D.F. 1988, *The coins of the ancient Celts*, Edinburgh

Ambrose, T. and Henig, M. 1980, 'A new Roman rider-relief from Stragglethorpe, Lincolnshire', *Britannia* xi, 135–8

Andronicos, M. 1984, *Vergina. The royal tombs and the ancient city*, Athens

Anganuzzi, A. and Mariani, E. 1987, 'Il mosaico di Breno' pp.52–60 in F. Rossi *et al.*, *La Valcamonica Romana ricerche e 'studi'*, Brescia

Artis, E.T. 1828, *The Durobrivae of Antoninus identified and illustrated in a series of plates exhibiting the excavated remains of that Roman station in the vicinity of Castor, Northamptonshire*, London

Atkinson, R.J.C. and Piggott, S. 1955, 'The Torrs Chamfrein', *Archaeologia* xcvi, 197–235.

Athanassiadi, P. 1992, *Julian. An intellectual biography*, second ed., London

Baatz, D. 1968, 'Romische Wandmalereien aus dem Limeskastell Echzell, Kr. Büdingen (Hessen)', *Germania* xlvi, 40–52

Baratte, F. and Painter, K. 1989, *Tresors d'orfevrerie Gallo-Romains*, ex. cat., Paris

Barber, A.J., Walker, G.T., Paddock, J. and Henig, M. 1992, 'A bust of Mars or a hero from Cirencester', *Britannia* xxiii, 217–18

Barrett, A.A. 1978, 'Knowledge of the literary classics in Roman Britain', *Britannia* ix, 307–13

Bartlett, R. 1985, 'A Roman tripod mount from Old Harlow, Essex', *Essex Journal* xx, 55–6

Bateson, J.D. 1981, *Enamel working in Iron Age, Roman and sub-Roman Britain*, BAR Brit.ser.93, Oxford

Baucchenss, G. 1978, *Corpus Signorum Imperii Romani. Deutschland. iii, 1 Germania Inferior. Bonn und Umgebung. Militärische Grabdenkmäler*, Bonn

Beeson, A.J. 1986, 'The boar of Aquae Sulis', *Popular Archaeology* vii no.5, 29–32

Beeson, A.J. 1990, 'Perseus and Andromeda as lovers. A mosaic panel from Brading and its origins', *Mosaic* 17, 13–19

Biddle, M. 1967, 'Two Flavian burials from Grange Road, Winchester', *Ant.J.* xlvii, 224–50

Biddle, M. and Kjølbye-Biddle, B. 1985, 'The Repton Stone', *Anglo-Saxon England*, xiv, 233–92

Bidwell, P.T. 1979, *The legionary bath-house and basilica and forum at Exeter*, Exeter

Birchall, A. 1965, 'The Aylesford-Swarling Culture: The problem of the Belgae reconsidered', *PPS* xxxi, 241–67

Bird, J., Chapman, H. and Clark, J. 1978 (eds), *Collectanea Londiniensia. Studies in London archaeology and history presented to Ralph Merrifield*, London and Middlesex Archaeological Society special paper no.2

Birley, E. 1978, 'The religion of the Roman army. 1895–1977', *ANRW* II, 16.2, 1506–41.

Birley, R. 1977, *Vindolanda. A Roman frontier post on Hadrian's Wall*, London

Bishop, M.C. 1983, 'The Camomile Street Soldier reconsidered', *Trans. London and Middlesex Arch.Soc.* xxxiv, 31–48

Bishop, M.C. and Coulston, J.C.N. 1993, *Roman Military Equipment from the Punic Wars to the fall of Rome*, London

Black, E.W. 1986, 'Christian and Pagan hopes of salvation in Romano-British mosaics', pp.147–58 in Henig and King, 1986

Blagg, T.F.C. 1982, 'A Roman relief carving of three female figures found at Lincoln', *Ant.J.* lxii, 125–6

Blagg, T.F.C. 1989, 'Art and architecture', pp.203–17 in M. Todd, *Research on Roman Britain 1960–89*, Britannia Monograph series no.11, London

Blagg, T.F.C. 1990, 'Architectural munificence in Britain: the evidence of inscriptions', *Britannia* xxi, 13–31

Blagg, T. and Henig, M. 1986, 'Cupid or Adonis? A new Roman relief carving from Lincoln', *Ant.J.* lxvi, 360–3

Blagg, T. and Millett, M. 1990 (eds), *The early Roman Empire in the West*, Oxford

Blair, J. and Ramsay, N. 1991, *English medieval industries*, London and Rio Grande

Bloch, H. 1963, 'The pagan revival in the West at the end of the fourth century', pp.193–218 in A. Momigliano, *The conflict between Paganism and Christianity in the fourth century*, Oxford

Boardman, J.B., Brown, M.A. and Powell, T.G.E. 1971, *The European Community in later prehistory. Studies in honour of C.F.C. Hawkes*, London

Bogaers, J.E. 1979, 'King Cogidubnus in Chichester: another reading of RIB 91', *Britannia* x, 243–54

Bone, A. and Burnett, A. 1986, 'The 1986 Selsey Treasure Trove', *BNJ* lvi, 178–80

Boon, G.C. 1973, 'Sarapis and Tutela: a Silchester coincidence', *Britannia* iv, 107–14

Boon, G.C. 1974, *Silchester. The Roman town of Calleva*, Newton Abbot

Boon, G.C. 1982, 'A coin with the head of the Cernunnos', *Seaby Coin and Medal Bulletin* no.769 (Sept. 1982), 276–82.

Boon, G.C. and Savory, H.N. 1975, 'A silver trumpet-brooch with relief decoration from Carmarthen', *Ant.J.* lv, 41–61

Boucher, S. 1976, *Recherches sur les bronzes figurés de Gaule pré-Romaine et Romaine*, École Française, Rome

Bowman, A.K. and Thomas, J.D. 1983, *Vindolanda: the Latin writing-tablets*, Britannia monograph no. 4

Bradley, R. 1990, *The Passage of Arms. An archaeological analysis of prehistoric hoards and votive deposits*, Cambridge

Brailsford, J. 1975, *Early Celtic masterpieces from Britain in the British Museum*, London

Braithwaite, G. 1984, 'Romano-British face pots and head pots', *Britannia* xv, 99–131

Brewer, R.J. 1986, *Corpus Signorum Imperii Romani Great Britain* i. 5 Wales, British Academy

Brilliant, R. 1984, 'Pendants and the mind's eye', pp. 53–89 of *Visual Narratives: Storytelling in Etruscan and Roman art*, Ithaca and London

Brown, D. 1973, 'A Roman pewter hoard from Appleford, Berks', *Oxoniensia* xxxviii, 184–206

Brown, P. 1971, *The world of Late Antiquity from Marcus Aurelius to Muhammad*, London

Brown, P. 1980, 'Art and society in Late Antiquity', pp.17–27 in Weitzmann (ed.) 1980

Bruce-Mitford, R. 1969, 'The art of the Codex Amiatinus', *JBAA* third ser. xxxii, 1–25

Bruce-Mitford, R. 1978, *The Sutton Hoo ship-burial vol.2. Arms, armour and regalia*, London

Bruce-Mitford, R. 1983, *The Sutton Hoo ship-burial vol.3. Late Roman and Byzantine silver, hanging bowls etc.*, London

Buckman, J. and Newmarch, C.H. 1850, *Illustrations of the remains of Roman Art in Cirencester, the site of ancient Corinium*, London

Burford, A. 1972, *Craftsmen in Greek and Roman society*, London

Caillet, J.-P. 1985, 'Pilier des nautes' pp.24–39 of catalogue *L'antiquité classique, le haut moyen âge et Byzance au musée de Cluny*, Paris

Calza, R. and Nash, E. 1959, *Ostia*, Florence

Casey, J. 1994, *The British Usurpers: Carausius and Allectus*, London

Charlesworth, D. 1961, 'Roman jewellery in Northumberland and Durham', *Arch.Ael.* fourth ser. xxxix, 1–36

Charlesworth, D. 1969, 'A gold signet ring from Housesteads', *Arch. Ael.* fourth ser. xlvii, 39–42

Charlesworth, D. 1973, 'The Aesica hoard', *Arch.Ael.* fifth ser.i, 225–34

Clay, P. 1984, 'A cheek-piece from a cavalry helmet found in Leicester', *Britannia* xv, 235–8

Clifford, E.M. 1938, 'Roman Altars in Gloucestershire', *TBGAS* lx, 297–307

Collingwood, R.G. and Myres, J.N.L. 1937, *Roman Britain and the English Settlements* second edition, Oxford

Colt Hoare, R. 1821, *Roman Aera* appended to vol.2 of *Auncient Wiltescire* published in 1819

Cookson, N.A. 1984, *Romano-British mosaics. A reassessment and critique of some notable stylistic affinities*, BAR Brit.ser.135, Oxford

Cool, H.E.M. 1979, 'A newly found inscription on a pair of silver bracelets from Castlethorpe, Buckinghamshire', *Britannia* x, 165–8

Cool, H.E.M. 1986, 'A Romano-British gold workshop of the second century', *Britannia* xvii, 231–7

Corder, P. and Richmond, I.A. 1938, 'A Romano-British interment, with bucket and sceptres, from Brough, East Yorkshire', *Ant.J.* xviii, 68–74

Cosh, S.R. 1989, 'The Lindinis branch of the Corinian Saltire officina', *Mosaic* 16, 14–19

Crummy, P. 1984, *Excavations at Lion Walk, Balkerne Lane, and Middleborough, Colchester, Essex* Colchester Archaeological Report 3

Coulston, J.C. and Phillips, E.J. 1988, *Corpus Signorum Imperii Romani Great Britain* i. 6. Hadrian's Wall west of the North Tyne and Carlisle, British Academy

Cunliffe, B. 1968, *Fifth report on the excavations of the Roman fort at Richborough, Kent*, Society of Antiquaries of London research report no.xxiii

Cunliffe, B. 1971, *Excavations at Fishbourne*, 2 vols. Society of Antiquaries of London research report no.xxvi

Cunliffe, B. 1983, 'Earth's Grip holds Them', pp.67–83 in Hartley and Wacher 1983

Cunliffe, B. 1988a, *Greeks, Romans and Barbarians. Spheres of interaction* (London 1988) 150–3

Cunliffe, B. 1988b, *The Temple of Sulis Minerva at Bath. vol.2. The finds from the sacred spring*, Oxford University Committee for Archaeology monograph no.16

Cunliffe, B. and Davenport, P. 1985, *The Temple of Sulis Minerva at Bath. vol.1. The site*, Oxford University Committee for Archaeology monograph no.7

Cunliffe, B.W. and Fulford, M.G. 1982, *Corpus Signorum Imperii Romani, Great Britain* i. 2 Bath and the rest of Wessex, British Academy

Curle, A.O. 1923, *The Treasure of Traprain. A Scottish hoard of Roman silver plate*, Glasgow

Curle, J. 1911, *A Roman frontier post and its people. The fort of Newstead in the Parish of Melrose*, Glasgow

Dark, K.R. 1994, *Civitas to Kingdom. British political continuity 300–800*, Leicester

Darling, M.J. 1989, 'A figured colour-coated beaker from excavations of the East gate at Lincoln', *Journal of Roman Pottery Studies* ii, 29–32

Darmon, J.P. 1976, *La mosaïque de Lillebonne*, Musée des Antiquités, Rouen

Daszewski, W.A. 1985, *Dionysos der Erlöser. Griechische Mythen im spätantiken Cypern*, Mainz

Davey, N. and Ling, R. 1981, *Wall-painting in Roman Britain*, Britannia Monograph no.3

Denford, G.T. 1992, 'Some exotic discoveries at Silkstead sandpit, Otterbourne, and the possible site of an ancient temple', *Proc.Hants.Field Club Arch.Soc.* xlviii, 27–54

Dent, J. 1985, 'Three cart burials from Wetwang, Yorkshire', *Antiquity* lix, 85–92

Des Brisay, E. 1992, 'Fieldwork at Lawn Field, Buriton, Hampshire', *Proc.Hants. Field Club Arch.Soc.* xlviii, 95–105

Deyts, S. 1983, *Les bois sculptés des Sources de la Seine*, xlii supp. à *Gallia*, Paris

Dix, B. 1985, 'A Roman figured bronze from between Fotheringhay and Nassington, Northants', *Northamptonshire Archaeology* xx, 139

Dorigo, W. 1971, *Late Roman painting. A study of pictorial records 30BC–AD 500*, English edition, London

Down, A. 1979, *Chichester Excavations 4. The Roman villas at Chilgrove and Upmarden*, Chichester

Down, A. and Henig, M. 1988, 'A Roman *askos* handle from Fishbourne', *Ant.J.* lxviii, 308–10

Drury, P.J. 1984, 'The Temple of Claudius at Colchester reconsidered', *Britannia* xv, 7–50

Drury, P.J. 1988, *The mansio and other sites in the south-eastern sector of Caesaromagus*, CBA Research Report 66, London

Dunbabin, K.M.D. 1978, *The mosaics of Roman North Africa. Studies in iconography and patronage*, Oxford

Ecroyd Smith, H. 1852, *Reliquiae Isurianae: the remains of the Roman Isurium (now Aldborough)*, London

Ellis, F. 1900, 'An ancient bronze figure from Aust Cliff, Gloucestershire', *TBGAS* xxiii, 323–5

Ellison, A. and Henig, M. 1981, 'Head of Mercury from Uley, Gloucestershire', *Antiquity* lv, 43–4

Eriksen, R.T. 1980, 'Syncretic symbolism and the Christian Roman mosaic at Hinton St Mary: a closer reading', *Proc. Dorset.Nat.Hist. Archaeol.Soc.* cii, 43–8

Erim, K.T. 1982, 'A new relief showing Claudius and Britannia from Aphrodisias', *Britannia* xiii, 277–81

Esmonde Cleary, A.S. 1989, *The ending of Roman Britain*, London

Evans, D.R. and Metcalf, V.M. 1992, *Roman Gates, Caerleon*, Oxbow Books, Oxford and Glamorgan-Gwent Archaeological Trust, Swansea

Evans, E. 1991, 'Excavations at "Sandygate", Gold Bath Road, Caerleon, Gwent', *Britannia* xxii, 103–36.

Evans, J.A. 1896, 'On two fibulae of Celtic fabric from Aesica', *Archaeologia* lv, 179–98

Farley, M. 1983, 'A mirror burial at Dorton, Buckinghamshire', *PPS* n.s. xxxi, 241–67

Farley, M., Henig, M. and Taylor, J.W. 1988, 'A hoard of late Roman bronze bowls and mounts from the Misbourne valley, near Mersham, Bucks', *Britannia* xix, 357–66

Ferris, I.M. 1988–9, 'The lion motif in Romano-British art', *Trans.South Staffs Arch. and Hist.Soc* xxx, 1–17

Fishwick, D. 1972, 'Templum Divo Claudio Constitutum', *Britannia* iii, 164–81

Foster, J. 1977, *Bronze boar figurines in Iron Age and Roman Britain*, BAR Brit.ser.39, Oxford

Foster, J. 1986, *The Lexden Tumulus. A re-appraisal of an Iron Age burial from Colchester, Essex*, BAR Brit.ser.156, Oxford

Foster, R. 1991, *Patterns of thought. The hidden meaning of the Great Pavement of Westminster Abbey*, London

Fowden, G. 1982, 'The pagan holy man in late antique society', *JHS* cii, 33–59

Fowler, W. 1804, *Engravings of the principal mosaic pavements which have been discovered during the course of the last century in various parts of Great Britain*, Winterton

Fox, C.F. 1946, *A Find of the Early Iron Age from Llyn Cerrig Bach, Anglesey*, National Museum of Wales, Cardiff

Fox, C.F. 1958, *Pattern and Purpose. A survey of Early Celtic art in Britain*, National Museum of Wales, Cardiff

Fremersdorf, F. 1975, *Catalogo del Museo Sacro V. Antikes. Islamisches und Mittelalterliches Glas etc.*, Vatican City

Frere, S.S. 1961, 'Some Romano-British sculptures from Ancaster and Wilsford, Lincolnshire', *Ant.J.* xli, 229–31

Frere, S.S. 1963, 'A Romano-British relief from Keisby, Lincs', *Ant.J.* xliii, 292

Frere, S.S. 1967, *Britannia. A history of Roman Britain*, London

Frere, S.S. 1970, 'Mould for bronze statuette from Gestingthorpe, Essex', *Britannia* i, 266–7

Frere, S.S. 1982, 'The Bignor Villa', *Britannia* xiii, 135–95

Frere, S.S. 1983, *Verulamium Excavations* vol.ii, Society of Antiquaries of London research report no.xli

Frere, S.S. 1984, *Verulamium Excavations* vol.iii, Oxford University Committee for Archaeology monograph no.1

Fulford, M.G., Burnett, A., Henig, M. and Johns, C. 1989, 'A hoard of late Roman rings and silver coins from Silchester, Hampshire', *Britannia* xx, 219–28

Gage, J. 1834, 'The Bartlow Hills in the parish of Ashdon in Essex', *Archaeologia* xxv, 1–23

Gage, J. 1836, 'The recent discovery of Roman sepulchral relics in one of the greater barrows at Bartlow', *Archaeologia* xxvi, 300–17

Gage, J. 1842, 'An account of the final excavation made at the Bartlow Hills', *Archaeologia* xxix, 1–4

Gazda, E.K. 1981, 'A marble group of Ganymede and the eagle from the age of Augustine' in J.H. Humphrey (ed.), *Excavations at Carthage* vi, 125–78

Gehrig, U. 1980, *Hildesheimer Silberschatz*, Berlin

Graham-Campbell, J. 1991a, 'Dinas Powys metalwork and the dating of enamelled zoomorphic Pennanular brooches', *BBCS* xxxviii, 220–32

Graham-Campbell, J. 1991b, 'Norrie's Law, Fife: on the nature and dating of the silver hoard', *PSAS* cxxi, 241–60

Graham-Campbell, J. 1993, 'The Norrie's Law Hoard and the dating of Pictish silver', pp.115–17 in Spearman and Higgitt 1993

Green, H.J.M. and Henig, M. 1988, 'A Roman bronze figurine from Earith, Cambridgeshire', *JBAA* cxli, 159–61

Greenhalgh, M. 1989, *The survival of Roman antiquities in the Middle Ages*, London

Gregory, T. 1991, *Excavations in Thetford, 1980–1982, Fison Way* (East Anglian Archaeology 53)

Grew, F. and Griffiths, N. 1991, 'The pre-Flavian military belt: the evidence from Britain', *Archaeologia* cix, 47–84

Guiraud, H. 1988, *Intailles et camées de l'époque romaine en Gaule* 48ᵉ supp. à Gallia

Hagen, W. 1937, 'Kaiserzeitliche Gagatarbeiten aus dem rheinischen Germanien', *Bonner Jahrbücher* cxlii, 77–144

Hamburger, A. 1968, *Gems from Caesarea Maritima*, Jerusalem

Hanfmann, G.M.A. 1980, 'The continuity of classical art: culture, myth and faith', pp.75–99 in Weitzmann (ed.), 1980

Hanson, W.F. and Keppie, L.J.F. 1980, *Roman Frontier Studies 1979*, BAR Int.ser.71, Oxford

Harden, D.B. and Toynbee, J.M.C. 1959, 'The Rothschild Lycurgus cup', *Archaeologia* xcvii, 179–212

Hartley, B. and Wacher, J. 1983, *Rome and the Northern Provinces. Papers presented to Sheppard Frere*, Trowbridge

Hartshorne, C.H. 1847, 'A statue of Minerva Custos and other Roman antiquities recently discovered . . . at Sibson and Bedford Purlieus in the county of Northampton', *Archaeologia* xxxii, 1–15

Haskell, F. and Penny, N. 1981, *Taste and the Antique. The lure of Classical sculpture 1500–1900*, New Haven and London

Hassall, M. 1952–3, 'A pottery mould from Horsepath', *Oxoniensia* xvii/xviii, 231–4

Hassall, M.W.C. and Ireland, R.I. 1979, *De Rebus Bellicis*, BAR Int.ser.63, Oxford

Hattatt, R. 1989, *Ancient brooches and other artefacts*, Oxford

Haverfield, F. 1914, 'Roman silver in Northumberland', *JRS* iv, 1–12

Haverfield, F. 1915, *The Romanization of Roman Britain*, third ed., Oxford

Haverfield, F. 1917–18, 'Roman Cirencester', *Archaeologia* lxix, 161–209

Hawkes, S.C. 1961, 'The Jutish Style. A study of Germanic animal art in southern England in the fifth century AD', *Archaeologia* xcviii, 29–74

Hawkes, S.C. 1972, 'A late Roman buckle from Tripontium', *Trans.Birmingham and Warwickshire Arch.Soc.*, 145–59

Hawkes, S.C. and Dunning, G.C. 1961, 'Soldiers and settlers in Britain, fourth to fifth century', *Med.Arch.* v, 1–70

Haynes, S. 1985, *Etruscan bronzes*, London

Henderson, G. 1993, 'Cassiodorus and Eadfrith once again', pp.82–91 in Spearman and Higgitt 1993

Henig, M. 1970, 'The veneration of heroes in the Roman Army', *Britannia* i, 249–65

Henig, M. 1972, 'The origin of some Ancient British coin types', *Britannia* iii, 209–23

Henig, M. 1974a, *A Corpus of Roman Engraved Gemstones from British Sites*, BAR Brit.ser.8, Oxford. Second ed. 1978

Henig, M. 1974b, 'A coin of Tasciovanus', *Britannia* v, 374–5

Henig, M. 1976, 'A Roman tripod-mount from the G.P.O. site, London', *Ant.J.*, lvi, 248–9

Henig, M. 1978, 'Bronze steelyard weight from Roman villa, Kingscote, Gloucestershire', *Ant.J.* lviii, 370–1

Henig, M. 1979, 'Late Antique book illustration and the Gallic prefecture', pp.17–37 in Hassall and Ireland 1979

Henig, M. 1982, 'Two gold rings from Colchester', *Trans. Essex Arch.Soc.*, xiv, third series, 153–5

Henig, M. 1983a (ed.), *A handbook of Roman Art*, Oxford

Henig, M. 1983b, 'The Maiden Castle "Diana": a case of mistaken identity?', *Proc.Dorset Nat.Hist. and Arch.Soc.* cv, 160–2

Henig, M. 1984a, *Religion in Roman Britain*, London

Henig, M. 1984b, 'A cache of Roman intaglios from Eastcheap, City of London', *Trans. London and Middlesex Arch.Soc.* xxxv, 11–15

Henig, M. 1984c, 'James Engleheart's drawing of a mosaic at Frampton', *Proc.Dorset Nat.Hist. and Arch.Soc.* cvi, 143–6

Henig, M. 1984d, 'A Roman key handle from Brampton, Norfolk', *Ant.J.* lxiv, 407–8

Henig, M. 1984e, 'Two inscribed finger rings from the City of London', *Trans. London and Middlesex Arch.Soc.* xxxv, 17–18

Henig, M. 1985, 'Graeco-Roman Art and Romano-British Imagination', *JBAA* cxxxviii, 1–22

Henig, M. 1986, 'Ita intellexit numine inductus tuo: some personal interpretations of deity in Roman religion', pp.159–69 in Henig and King 1986

Henig, M. 1988a, 'The gemstones', pp.27–33 in Cunliffe 1988b

Henig, M. 1988b, 'Verica's hound', *OJA* vii, 253–5

Henig, M. 1989, 'Religion in Roman Britain', pp.219–34 in Todd 1989

Henig, M. 1990a (ed.), *Architecture and Architectural Sculpture in the Roman Empire* Oxford University Committee for Archaeology monograph no.29

Henig, M. 1990b, 'A house for Minerva: temples, aedicula shrines and signet-rings', pp.152–62 in Henig 1990a

Henig, M. 1991a, 'Antique gems in Roman Britain', *Jewellery Studies* v, 49–54

Henig, M. 1991b, 'A bronze Vulcan from North Bradley', *Wilts Arch and Nat.Hist. Magazine* lxxxiv, 120–22

Henig, M. 1992, 'The Bath gem-workshop: further discoveries', *OJA* xi, 241–3

Henig, M. 1993a, 'Ancient Cameos in the Content Family Collection', pp.26–40 in Henig and Vickers 1993

Henig, M. 1993b, *Corpus Signorum Imperii Romani Great Britain* i.7 The Cotswold region with Devon and Cornwall, British Academy

Henig, M. and Chambers, R.A. 1984, 'Two Roman bronze birds from Oxfordshire', *Oxoniensia* xlix, 19–21

Henig, M. and Keen, L. 1984, 'Figurines from Duncliffe Hill, Motcombe, Dorset' *Proc.Dorset Nat. Hist. and Arch.Soc.* cvi, 147–8

Henig, M. and King, A. 1986 (eds), *Pagan gods and shrines of the Roman Empire*, Oxford University Committee for Archaeology monograph no.8

Henig, M. and Leahy, K.A. 1984, 'A bronze bust from Ludford Magna, Lincolnshire', *Ant.J.* lxiv, 387–9

Henig, M. and Leahy, K.A. 1986, 'A sceptre head and two votive swords from Kirmington, Lincolnshire', *Ant.J.* lxvi, 388–91

Henig, M. and Munby, J. 1973, 'Three bronze figurines', *Oxoniensia* xxxviii, 386–7

Henig, M. and Nash, D. 1982, 'Amminus and the kingdom of Verica', *OJA* i, 243–6

Henig, M. and Ogden, J. 1988, 'A late Roman gold ring and other objects from Richborough', *Ant.J.* lxviii, 315–7 and 326

Henig, M. and Soffe, G. 1993, 'The Thruxton Roman villa and its mosaic pavement', *JBAA* cxlvi, 1–28

Henig, M. and Vickers, M. 1993 (eds) *Cameos in Context. The Benjamin Zucker Lectures, 1990* (Oxford and Houlton, Maine)

Henig, M., Webster, G. and Wilkins, R. 1987, 'A bronze Dioscurus from Wroxeter and its fellow from Canterbury', *Ant.J.* lxvii, 360–2

Henig, M. and Whiting, M. 1987, *Engraved gems from Gadara in Jordan. The Sa'd collection of intaglios and cameos*, Oxford University Comittee for Archaeology monograph no.6

Henig, M. and Wilson, P.R. 1982, 'A bronze figurine from Bainesse Farm, Catterick', *Ant.J.* lxii, 370–2

Henig, M. and Wood, M. 1990, 'A cast bronze figure of Iron Age date from the Channel Island of Jersey, *OJA* ix, 237–40

Heurgon, J. 1951, 'The Amiens Patera', *JRS* xli, 22–4

Hicks, C. 1978, 'A note on the provenance of the Sutton Hoo stag', pp.378–82 in Bruce-Mitford 1978

Hicks, C. 1993, 'The Pictish Class I animals', pp. 196–202 in Spearman and Higgitt 1993

Higgitt, J.C. 1973, 'The Roman Background to Medieval England', *JBAA* 3rd.ser.xxxvi,

Hill, C., Millett, M. and Blagg, T. 1980, *The Roman riverside wall and monumental Arch in London*, London and Middlesex Archaeological Society special paper no.3

Holbrook, N. and Bidwell, P.T. 1991, *Roman finds from Exeter*, Exeter Archaeological Reports no.4

Horsley, J. 1733, *Britannia Romana or the Roman Antiquities of Britain*, London

Howarth, D. 1992, 'Sir Robert Cotton and the commemoration of famous men', *British Library Journal* xviii, 1–28

Hull, M.R. 1958, *Roman Colchester*, Society of Antiquaries of London research report no.xx

Humphrey, J.H. 1986, *Roman circuses. Arenas for chariot racing*, London

Huskinson, J. 1974, 'Some pagan mythological figures and their significance in early Christian art', *Papers of the British School at Rome* xlii, 68–97

Huskinson, J. 1994, *Corpus Signorum Imperii Romani Great Britain* i. 8 Eastern England, British Academy

Hutchinson, V.J. 1986a, *Bacchus in Roman Britain: the evidence for his cult*, BAR Brit.ser.151, Oxford

Hutchinson, V.J. 1986b, 'The cult of Bacchus in Roman Britain', pp.135–45 in Henig and King 1986

Ireland, R. 1983, 'Epigraphy', pp.220–33 in Henig 1983a

Isager, J. 1991, *Pliny on art and society*, London and New York

Jackson, R. 1989, 'A bronze mould from Dolland's Moor, Newington-next-Hythe, Kent', *Ant.J.* lxix, 327–9

Jackson, R. 1990, *Camerton. The late Iron Age and early Roman metalwork*, British Museum, London

Jacobsthal, P. 1944, *Early Celtic art*, Oxford

Jenkins, I. 1985, 'A group of silvered horse-trappings from Xanten (*Castra Vetera*)', *Britannia* xvi, 141–64

Jenkyns, R. 1991, *Dignity and decadence*, London

Johns, C. 1981a, 'The Risley Park silver lanx: A lost antiquity from Roman Britain, *Ant.J.* lxi, 53–72

Johns, C. 1981b, 'A Roman gold ring from Bedford', *Ant.J.* lxi, 343–5

Johns, C. 1986, 'The Roman silver cups from Hockwold, Norfolk', *Archaeologia* cviii, 1–13

Johns, C. 1991, 'Some unpublished jewellery from Roman Britain', *Jewellery Studies* v, 55–64

Johns, C. and Painter, K. 1991, 'The "rediscovery" of the Risley Park Roman lanx', *Minerva* ii, no.6, 6–13

Johns, C. and Potter, T. 1983, *The Thetford Treasure. Roman jewellery and silver*, London

Johnson, P. 1982, *Romano-British Mosaics*, Princes Risborough

Johnson, P. 1984, 'The mosaics of Bignor villa, England: a Gallo-Roman connection', pp.405–10 in R. Farioli Campanati, *III colloquio internazionale sul mosaico antico*, Ravenna

Johnson, P. 1985, 'The hunting dog mosaic of Cherhill, Wiltshire', *Mosaic* 12, 14–5, pl.2

Johnston, D.E. 1977, 'The Central Southern group of Romano-British mosaics', pp.195–215 in Munby and Henig 1977

Jope, E.M. 1983, 'Torrs, Aylesford and the Padstow Hobby Horse', pp.149–59 in O'Connor and Clarke 1983

Jope, E.M. 1987, 'Celtic Art: Expressiveness and Communication through 2500 years', *Proc.Brit.Acad.* lxxiii, 97–123

Kendrick, T.D. 1938, *Anglo-Saxon art to* AD *900*, London

Kennett, D.H. 1976, 'Felmersham and Ostia: a metal-work comparison', *Beds Arch Journ.* xi, 19–22

Kent, J.P.C. and Painter, K.S. 1977, *Wealth of the Roman World.* AD *300–700*, London

Keppie, L. 1991, *Understanding Roman inscriptions*, London

Keppie, L.J.F. and Arnold, B.J. 1984, *Corpus Signorum Imperii Romani Great Britain* i. 4. Scotland, British Academy

King, A. and Henig, M. 1981 (eds), *The Roman West in the third century. Contributions from archaeology and history*, BAR. Int.ser.109, Oxford

Kirk, J.R. 1949, 'Bronzes from Woodeaton, Oxon', *Oxoniensia* xiv, 1–45

Kitzinger, E. 1993, 'Interlace and icons: form and function in early Insular art', pp.3–15 in Spearman and Higgitt 1993

Lang, J. 1993, 'Survival and revival in Insular art: Northumbrian sculpture of the 8th to 10th centuries', pp.261–7 in Spearman and Higgitt 1993

Lavagne, H. 1979, *Recueil Général des Mosaïques de la Gaule* x supp à *Gallia* III. *Narbonnaise I Partie Centrale*; Paris

Lawson, A.J. 1976, 'Shale and jet objects from Silchester', *Archaeologia* cv, 241–75

Lawson, A.K. 1986, 'A fragment of life-size bronze equine statuary from Ashill, Norfolk', *Britannia* xvii, 333–9

Lepper, F. and Frere, S. 1988, *Trajan's Column. A new edition of the Cichorius plates*, Gloucester

Levine, J.M. 1978, 'The Stonesfield Pavement: Archaeology in Augustan England', *Eighteenth-Century Studies* xi, no.3, 340–61

Lindgren, C. 1980, *Classical art forms and Celtic mutations. Figural art in Roman Britain*, Park Ridge, New Jersey

Ling, R. 1983, 'The Seasons in Romano-British mosaic pavements', *Britannia* xiv, 13–22

Ling, R. 1985, *Romano-British Wall Painting*, Princes Risborough

Ling, R. 1991a, *Roman Painting*, Cambridge

Ling, R. 1991b, 'Brading, Brantingham and York. A new look at some fourth-century mosaics', *Britannia* xxii, 147–57

Liversidge, J. 1955, *Furniture in Roman Britain*, London

Lloyd-Morgan, G. 1980, 'Roman Mirrors and Pictish Symbol', pp.96–100 in Hanson and Keppie

Lloyd-Morgan, G. 1981, 'Roman mirrors and the third century', pp.145–57 in King and Henig 1981

Longley, D. 1975, *Hanging-bowls, pennanular brooches and the Anglo-Saxon connexion*, BAR Brit.ser.22, Oxford

Lowery, P.R., Savage, R.D.A. and Wilkins, R.L. 1975, 'A technical study of the designs on the British Mirror Series', *Archaeologia* cv, 99–126

Lysons, S. 1797, *An Account of Roman Antiquities discovered at Woodchester in the County of Gloucester*, London

Lysons, S. 1813–17, *Reliquiae Britannico Romanae* i–iii, London

Maaskant-Kleibrink, M. 1992, 'Three gem engravers at work in a jeweller's workshop in Norfolk. The evidence of roman engraved gems in the jeweller's hoard found at Snettisham', *BABesch* lxvii, 151–67

Macgregor, M. 1976, *Early Celtic art in north Britain. A study of decorative metalwork from the third century* BC *to the third century* AD, Leicester

MacKenna, S.A. and Ling, R.J. 1991, 'Wall paintings from the Winchester Palace site, Southwark', *Britannia* xxii, 159–71

Mackintosh, M. 1986, 'The sources of the Horseman and Fallen Enemy motif on the tombstones of the Western Roman Empire', *JBAA* cxxxix, 1–21

Marsden, P. 1975, 'The excavation of a Roman palace site in London, 1961–1972' *Trans. London and Middlesex Arch.Soc.* xxvi, 1–102

Marshall, F.H. 1907, *Catalogue of the Finger Rings, Greek, Etruscan and Roman in the Departments of Antiquities, British Museum*, London

Mattern, M. 1989, 'Die reliefverzierten römischen Grabstelen der Provinz Britannia. Themen und Typen', *Kölner Jahrbuch* xxii, 707–801

Mawer, C.F. 1989, 'A lost Roman ring from Suffolk', *Britannia* xx, 237–41

Maxfield, V.A. 1991, 'Tiverton Roman Fort (Bolham): Excavations 1981–1986', *Proc.Devon Arch.Soc.* xlix, 25–98

Meates, G.W. 1987, *The Roman villa at Lullingstone, Kent* ii. *The wall paintings and finds*, Maidstone

Megaw, J.V.S. 1970, *Art of the European Iron Age. A study of the elusive image*, Bath

Megaw, J.V.S. 1983, 'From Transdanubia to Torrs', pp.127–48 in O'Connor and Clarke 1983

Megaw, R. and Megaw, J.V.S. 1986, *Early Celtic Art in Britain and Ireland*, Princes Risborough

Megaw, R. and Megaw, J.V.S. 1989, *Celtic Art from its beginnings to the Book of Kells*, London

Meiggs, R. 1973, *Roman Ostia*, second ed., Oxford

Merrifield, R. 1965, *The Roman city of London*, London

Merrifield, R. 1969, *Roman London*, London

Merrifield, R. 1983, *London. City of the Romans*, London

Merrifield, R. 1986, 'The London hunter-god', pp.85–92 in Henig and King 1986

Middleton, S.H. 1991, *Engraved gems from Dalmatia*, Oxford University Committee for Archaeology monograph no.31

Millett, M. 1990, *The Romanisation of Britain*, Cambridge

Mócsy, A. 1974, *Pannonia and Upper Moesia: a history of the middle Danube provinces of the Roman Empire*, London

Moore, I.E., Plouviez, J. and West, S. 1988, *The archaeology of Roman Suffolk*, Bury St Edmunds

Morgan, T. 1886, *Romano-British mosaic pavements. A history of their discovery and a record and interpretation of their design*, London

Munby, J. 1975, 'Some moulded-face flagons from the Oxford kilns', *Britannia* vi, 182–8

Munby, J. 1977, 'Art, archeology and antiquaries', pp.415–36 in Munby and Henig 1977

Munby, J. and Henig, M. 1977 (eds), *Roman life and art in Britain*, BAR Brit.ser.8 Oxford

Murdoch, T. (ed.) 1991, *Treasures and trinkets. Jewellery in London from pre-Roman times to the 1930s*, Museum of London

Neal, D.S. 1981, *Roman mosaics in Britain*, Britannia monograph no.1

Neal, D.S. and Walker, B. 1988, 'A mosaic from Boughspring Roman villa, Tidenham, Gloucestershire', *Britannia* xix, 191–7

Newton, C. 1846, 'A description of four bronzes found in Colchester from the collection of Henry Vint Esq.', *Archaeologia* xxxi, 443–7

Niblett, R. 1985, *Sheepen: an early Roman industrial site at Camulodunum*, CBA Research report 57, London

O'Connor, A. and Clarke, D.V. 1983 (eds), *From the Stone Age to the 'Forty-Five*, Edinburgh

Ó Riordáin, S.P. 1947, 'Roman material in Ireland', *Proc.Royal Irish Academy*, li, c. no.3, 35–82

Ogden, J. 1982, *Jewellery of the Ancient World*, London

Onians, J. 1980, 'Abstraction and imagination in Late Antiquity', *Art History* iii, 1–24

Painter, K.S. 1976, 'The design of the Roman mosaic at Hinton St Mary', *Ant.J.* lvi, 49–54

Painter, K.S. 1977a, *The Water Newton Early Christian silver*, London

Painter, K.S. 1977b, *The Mildenhall Treasure. Roman silver from East Anglia*, London

Painter, K.S. 1990, 'The Seuso Treasure. A spectacular hoard of Roman silver', *Minerva* i no.4, 4–11

Pannuti, U. 1983, *Museo Archeologico Nazionale di Napoli. Catalogo della Collezione Glittica* I, Rome

Perring, D. 1989, 'Cellars and cults in Roman Britain', *Arch.J.* cxlvi, 279–301

Perring, D., Roskams, S. and Allen, P. 1991, *The archaeology of Roman London 2. Early development of Roman London west of the Walbrook*, CBA research report 70, London

Pevsner, N. 1956, *The Englishness of English Art*, London

Pfeiler, B. 1970, *Römischer Goldschmuck des ersten und zweiten Jahrhunderts n. Chr. nach datierten Funden*, Mainz

Phillips, E.J. 1975, 'The Gravestone of M. Favonius Facilis at Colchester', *Britannia* vi, 102–5

Phillips, E.J. 1976a, 'A workshop of Roman sculptors at Carlisle', *Britannia* vii, 101–8

Phillips, E.J. 1976b, 'A Roman figured capital in Cirencester', *JBAA* cxxix, 35–41

Phillips, E.J. 1977a, *Corpus Signorum Imperii Romani Great Britain* i. 1. Corbridge. Hadrian's Wall east of the North Tyne, British Academy

Phillips, E.J. 1977b, 'The Classical tradition in the popular sculpture of Roman Britain', pp.35–49 in Munby and Henig 1977

Philp, B. 1989, *The Roman House with Bacchic Murals at Dover*, Dover

Piggott, S. 1971, 'Firedogs in Iron Age Britain and beyond', pp.245–70 in Boardman et al

Pitts, L.F. 1979, *Roman bronze figurines from the civitates of the Catuvellauni and Trinovantes*, BAR Brit.ser.60, Oxford

Pitts, L.F. and St Joseph, J.K. 1985, *Inchtuthil. The Roman legionary fortress*, Britannia monograph series no.6, London

Pollitt, J.J. 1986, *Art in the Hellenistic Age*, Cambridge

Potter, T. 1986, 'A Roman jeweller's hoard from Snettisham, Norfolk', *Antiquity* lx, 137–9

Potter, T.W. and Johns, C.M. 1986, 'The Tunshill Victory', *Ant.J.* lxvi, 390–2

Price, J.E. 1870, *A description of the Roman tessellated pavement found in Bucklersbury with observations on analogous discoveries*, Westminster

Putnam, W.G. and Rainey, A. 1972, 'Fourth interim report on excavations at Dewlish Roman villa, 1972', *Proc.Dorset Nat.Hist and Arch.Soc.* xciv, 81–6

Raftery, B. 1984, *La Tène in Ireland. Problems of origin and chronology*, Marburg

Rainey, A. 1973, *Mosaics in Roman Britain. A gazetteer*, Newton Abbot

Read, C.H. 1898, 'List of pewter dishes and vessels found at Appleshaw and now in the British Museum', *Archaeologia* lvi, 7–12

Reece, R. 1977, 'Mosaics and carpets', pp.407–13 in Munby and Henig 1977

Rhodes, J.F. 1964, *Catalogue of the Romano-British sculptures in the Gloucester City Museum*, Gloucester

Richter, G.M.A. 1971, *Engraved gems of the Romans*, London

Rivet, A.L.F. 1969, *The Roman villa in Britain*, London

Roach Smith, C. 1846, 'Notes on a bronze head of Hadrian', *JBAA* i, 286–91

Roach Smith, C. 1859, *Illustrations of Roman London*, London

Rook, T. and Henig, M. 1981, 'A bronze cockerel from a late Romano-British context at Aston, Hertfordshire', *Ant.J.* lxi, 1981, 356–9

Rook, T., Walker, S. and Denston, C.B. 1984, 'A Roman mausoleum and associated marble sarcophagus and burials from Welwyn, Hertfordshire', *Britannia* xv, 143–62

Rosenthal, E. 1972, *The illuminations of the Vergilius Romanus*, Zurich

Russell, J. 1985, 'The Keynsham Roman villa and its hexagonal *triclinia*', *Bristol and Avon Archaeology* 4, 6–12

Russell Robinson, H. and Toynbee, J.M.C. 1976, 'The Kingsholm Cheekpiece', *Arch. J.* lv, 287–90

Schefold, K. 1972, *La peinture pompéienne. Essai sur l'évolution de sa signification*, Coll. Latomus 108, Brussels

Schmidt, E. 1965, *The Great Altar of Pergamum*, London

Scott, L. 1938, 'The Roman villa at Angmering', SAC lxxix, 3–44

Scott, S. 1991, 'An outline of a new approach for the interpretation of Romano-British mosaics, and some comments on the possible significance of the Orpheus mosaics of fourth-century Roman Britain, *Journal of Theoretical Archaeology* 2, 29–35

Sena Chiesa, G. 1966, *Gemme del Museo Nazionale di Aquileia*, Aquileia

Sieveking, G. de G. 1971, *Prehistoric and Roman Studies*, British Museum, London

Smith, D.J. 1965, 'Three fourth-century schools of mosaic in Roman Britain', pp.95–115 in M.G. Picard and M.H. Stern, *La mosaïque Gréco-Romaine*, Paris

Smith, D.J. 1969, 'The mosaic pavements' pp.71–125 in Rivet 1969

Smith, D.J. 1975, 'Roman mosaics in Britain before the fourth century', pp.269–90 in M. le Glay and H. Stern, *La mosaïque Gréco-Romaine*, Paris

Smith, D.J. 1977, 'Mythological figures and scenes in Romano-British mosaics', pp.105–193 of Munby and Henig 1977

Smith, D.J. 1981, 'Romano-British mosaics in the third century', pp.159–65 in King and Henig 1981

Smith, D.J. 1983, 'Orpheus mosaics in Britain', pp.315–28 of *Mosaïque. Recueil d'hommages à Henri Stern*, Paris

Smith, D.J. 1984, 'Roman mosaics in Britain: a synthesis', pp.357–80 in R. Farioli Campanati, *III colloquio internazionale sul mosaico antico*, Ravenna

Smith, D.J. 1987, *Roman Mosaics at Hull*, second ed.

Smith, R.A. 1909, 'A hoard of metal found at Santon Downham, Suffolk', *Proc.Cambridge Ant.Soc.* xiii, 146–63

Sparey Green, C.J. 1993, 'The mausolea painted plaster', pp.135–40 in D.E. Farwell and T.I. Molleson, *Poundbury vol. 2. The cemeteries*, Dorset Nat.Hist. and Archeol.Soc., monograph no.11

Spearman, R.M. and Higgitt, J. 1993 (eds), *The age of migrating ideas. Early Medieval art in northern Britain and Ireland*, Edinburgh and Stroud

Stanfield, J.A. and Simpson, G. 1990, *Les potiers de la Gaule Centrale*, Revue Archéologique sites, Gonfaron (second ed. of *Central Gaulish potters*, Oxford 1958)

Stead, I.M. 1967, 'A La Tène burial at Welwyn Garden City', *Archaeologia* ci, 1–62

Stead, I.M. 1971, 'The reconstruction of Iron Age buckets from Aylesford and Baldock', pp.250–82 in Sieveking 1971

Stead, I.M. 1979, *The Arras Culture*, Yorkshire Philosophical Society, York

Stead, I.M. 1985, *The Battersea Shield*, British Museum, London

Stead, I.M. 1991a, *Iron Age cemeteries in East Yorkshire*, English Heritage Archaeological Report 22, London

Stead, I.M. 1991b, 'The Snettisham Treasure: excavations in 1990', *Antiquity* lxv, 447–64

Stefanelli, L.P.B. 1992, *L'Oro dei Romani. Gioielli di età imperiale*, Rome

Strong, D. and Brown, D. (eds) 1976, *Roman crafts*, London

Stupperich, R. 1980, 'A reconsideration of some fourth-century British mosaics', *Britannia* xi, 289–301

Sunter, N. 1987, 'Excavations at Norden' in *Romano-British Industries in Purbeck*, Dorset Nat.Hist. and Arch.Soc. monograph no.6, 5–43

Swain, E.J. and Ling, R.J. 1981, 'The Kingscote wall-paintings', *Britannia* xii, 167–75

Symonds, R.P. 1992, *Rhenish Wares. Fine dark coloured pottery from Gaul and Germany*, Oxford University Committee for Archaeology Monograph no.23

Taylor, M.V. 1941, 'The Roman tessellated pavement at Stonesfield, Oxon.', *Oxoniensia* vi, 1–8

Thomas, C. 1981, *Christianity in Britain to AD 500*, London

Thompson, F.H. 1965, *Roman Cheshire*, Chester

Thompson, F.H. 1971, 'Some lost Roman bronzes from Lincoln', *Ant.J.* li, 100–3

Todd, M. (ed.) 1989, *Research on Roman Britain, 1960–89*, Britannia monograph series no.11

Townley, C. 1799, 'Account of Antiquities discovered at Ribchester', *Vetusta Monumenta* iv, 1–12

Toynbee, J.M.C. 1953, 'The Ara Pacis reconsidered', *Proc. British Academy* xxxix, 67–95

Toynbee, J.M.C. 1962, *Art in Roman Britain*, London

Toynbee, J.M.C. 1964a, *Art in Britain under the Romans*, Oxford

Toynbee, J.M.C. 1964b, 'A new Roman mosaic pavement found in Dorset', *JRS* liv, 7–14

Toynbee, J.M.C. 1976, 'Roman Sculpture in Gloucestershire', pp.62–100 in P. McGrath and J. Cannon, *Essays in Bristol and Gloucestershire History*

Toynbee, J.M.C. 1977, 'Greek myth in Roman stone', *Latomus* xxxvi, 343–412

Toynbee, J.M.C. 1978, 'A Londinium votive leaf or feather and its fellows', pp.128–47 in Bird, Chapman and Clark 1978

Toynbee, J.M.C. 1986, *The Roman art treasures from the Temple of Mithras* London and Middlesex Archaeological Society special paper no.7

Toynbee, J.M.C. and Painter, K.S. 1986, 'Silver picture plates of Late Antiquity', *Archaeologia* cviii, 15–65

Trow, S.D. 1990, 'By the northern shores of Ocean: Some observations on acculturation process at the edge of the Roman world', pp.103–18 of Blagg and Millett 1990

Tufi, S.R. 1983, *Corpus Signorum Imperii Romani Great Britain i. 3. Yorkshire*, British Academy

Turcan, R. 1982, 'L'Autel de Rome et d'Auguste "Ad Confluentem" ', *ANRW* II. 1, 607–44

Verzàr, M. 1977, *Aventicum II. Un temple du culte impérial*, Avenches

Volbach, W.F. 1961, *Early Christian art*, London

Wacher, J. 1974, *The Towns of Roman Britain*, London

Wainwright, G.J. 1979, *Gussage All Saints: an Iron Age settlement in Dorset*, London

Walker, S. and Matthews, K. 1986, 'A fragmentary marble table-leg from Colchester', *Ant.J.* lxvi, 369–71

Walters, B. 1984, 'The "Orpheus" mosaic in Littlecote Park, England', pp.433–42 in R. Farioli Campanati, *III colloquio internazionale sul mosaico antico*, Ravenna

Walters, B. and Henig, M. 1988, 'Two busts from Littlecote', *Britannia* xix, 407–10

Walters, H.B. 1921, *Catalogue of the silver plate, Greek, Etruscan and Roman in the British Museum*, London

Ward-Perkins, J. and Claridge, A. 1976, *Pompeii, A.D. 79*, Royal Academy of Arts, London. Exhibition catalogue

Watts, D. 1991, *Christians and pagans in Roman Britain*, London and New York

Webster, G. 1983a, 'The Function of Chedworth Roman "villa"', *TBGAS* ci, 5–20, reprinted in Webster 1991a, 95–111

Webster, G. 1983b, 'The possible effects on Britain of the fall of Magnentius', pp.240–54 in Hartley and Wacher 1983, reprinted in Webster 1991a, 81–94

Webster, G. 1989, 'Deities and religious scenes on Romano-British pottery', *Journal of Roman Pottery Studies* ii, 1–28

Webster, G. 1991a, *Archaeologist at large*, London

Webster, G. 1991b, 'Romano-British scenes and figures on pottery', pp.129–62 of Webster 1991a

Webster, L. and Backhouse, J. 1991, *The making of England. Anglo-Saxon art and culture. AD 600–900*, British Museum, London

Wedlake, W.J. 1982, *The excavation of the shrine of Apollo at Nettleton, Wiltshire, 1956–1971*, Society of Antiquaries of London research report no.xl,

Weitzmann, K. 1979, *Age of Spirituality. Late Antique and Early Christian art, third to seventh century*, Metropolitan Museum, New York

Weitzmann, K. 1980, *Age of Spirituality. A symposium*, Metropolitan Museum, New York

Whitehouse, D. 1992, 'Luxury glass in Late Antiquity',

pp.103–16 in G. Sena Chiesa and E.A. Arslan (eds), *Felix Temporis Reparatio*, Milan

Wightman, E.M. 1970, *Roman Trier and the Treveri*, London

White, R.H. 1988, 'Mayer and British Archaeology', pp.118–36 in M. Gibson and S.M. Wright, *Joseph Mayer of Liverpool, 1803–1886*, Society of Antiquaries occasional paper (n.s.) no.xi, London

Whitwell, J.B. 1970, *History of Lincolnshire. II. Roman Lincolnshire*, Lincoln

Wild, J.P. 1985, 'The clothing of Britannia, Gallia belgica and Germania inferior', *ANRW* 12. ii, 362–422

Wilson, D.M. 1984, *Anglo-Saxon art*, London

Woodward, A. and Leach, P. 1993, *The Uley Shrines: excavation of a ritual complex on West Hill Uley, Gloucestershire, 1977–9*, London

Woodward, P.J. 1987a, 'The excavation of a late Iron-Age trading settlement and Romano-British BB1 pottery production site at Ower, Dorset' in *Romano-British Industries in Purbeck*, Dorset Nat.Hist. and Arch.Soc. monograph no.6, 44–124

Woodward, P.J. 1987b, 'The excavation of an Iron Age and Romano-British settlement at Rope Lake Hole, Corfe Castle, Dorset', in *Romano-British Industries in Purbeck*, Dorset Nat.Hist. and Arch.Soc. monograph no.6, 125–80

Wright, R.P. and Richmond, I.A. 1955, *The Roman inscribed and sculptured stones in the Grosvenor Museum, Chester*, Chester

Wright, T. 1863, 'On Roman engraved stones found at Uriconium', *JBAA* xix, 106–11

Youngs, S. 1989, *'The Work of Angels'. Masterpieces of Celtic metalwork 6th–9th centuries AD*, British Museum, London

Zadoks-Josephus Jitta, A.N., Peters, W.J.T. and van Es, W.A. 1969, *Roman bronze statuettes from the Netherlands II south of the Limes*, Groningen

Zanker, P. 1988, *The power of images in the age of Augustus*, Ann Arbor

Zienkiewicz, J.D. 1986, *The Legionary Fortress Baths at Caerleon*, 2 vols Cardiff

Glossary

aedicula(*e*)   a small niche, generally containing the image of a deity either free-standing or in relief and serving as a shrine.

aerarius   a bronzesmith.

antefix   a vertical ornament on the edge of a roof or apex of the gable.

apodyterium   the undressing-room of a bath-house.

aquila   an eagle. The term is generally used of the legionary Eagle (standard).

askos (*askoi*)   lit. 'a wine-skin'; a container in the form of a wine-skin though the Roman custom was for a pair of these to be carried round at a feast containing water with which to dilute the wine.

avatar   term used of different manifestations or incarnations of a deity.

barbotine   a method of decorating pottery by trailing slip over its surface.

basilica   a hall with aisles and clerestory lighting; esp. used for the Roman town-hall.

basilica principiorum   the hall of the headquarters' building in a fort.

beneficiarius consularis   a soldier detached from routine duties to serve on the staff of a provincial governor, esp. for policing.

birrus   a hooded cape; one version the *birrus britannicus* was especially associated with the province.

breccia   a composite rock, consisting of angular fragments of stone cemented together by some matrix such as lime.

bucranium   a ox-scull, often included in decorative reliefs from temples and altars and also found in funerary contexts.

cameo   a gemstone so cut that the device is in relief.

canabae   lit. 'the booths', refering to the civil settlement outside a legionary fortress.

cantharus   a cup or vase with two vertical handles.

cella   the central chamber or sanctuary of a temple.

chamfrein   a frontlet, protecting the head of a horse.

chiton   a long garment worn by women (Greek).

chi-rho   a monogram formed of the first two letters, X and P of Christ's name in Greek (ΧΡΙΣΤΟΣ); see *labarum*.

cingulum   a belt.

civitas   lit. a community or state; in the north-western provinces it refers to a tribal territory with its capital.

clipeate   something circular or ovoid like a shield.

collegium   a society (or college), generally with religious and 'friendly' functions like a medieval guild.

colonia   a chartered town of Roman citizens, frequently first settled by legionary veterans (e.g. Colchester, Gloucester, Lincoln) but sometimes a status awarded as an honour (York).

cupellation   a refining process, whereby precious metal is extracted from lead and other base metals.

diatretum   a glass cage-cup made by undercutting the surface layer of a vessel so that it appears to be enclosed in an openwork cage.

dichroic (glass)   glass which shows two colours according to whether it is viewed by transmitted or reflected light.

domus   a house; the term is employed in connection with fairly grand town residences, much as the way in which 'town house' was used in the eighteenth/nineteenth centuries.

emblema(*ta*)   the device(s) in the centre of a mosaic floor or an item of silver plate.

forum   the central market-square of a town, with the *basilica* (q.v.) on one side.

frigidarium   the cold-room of a bath-house.

hacksilber   a German term for the broken pieces of silver-plate found in the bullion hoards of Late Antiquity.

honestiores   the term used for the upper orders of Late Roman society in contradistinction to the inferior *humiliores*.

imaginifer   in the army, the bearer of the standard with the emperor's image.

imbricated   resembling overlapping roof-tiles (from *imbrex* a tile).

insula   lit. 'an island', used of a city block.

intaglio   a gemstone with the device cut in negative image into the stone, enabling it to be used as a seal or signet.

labarum   the chi-rho standard used by Constantine after the Battle of the Milvian Bridge, and by his successors. It seems to be derived from the *vexillum laureum*, the standard wreathed to indicate victory.

labrum   a wash-basin.

lanx   a large plate or dish, sometimes rectangular (Corbridge, Risley Park) though great circular plates such as that from Mildenhall may have been called *lanxes*.

lapidarius   a sculptor or carver of monumental inscriptions.

lappet   A flap like those on the sides of some hats and boots or the *pteryges* (q.v.) worn by soldiers.

lararium   the domestic shrine, housing images of the household gods (*lares*) and other deities.

lunette   a moon-shaped ornament.

Mater (Matres)   a mother-goddess, in Britain and the north-western provinces, generally venerated as a triad of Matres.

ministerium   a service of silver plate.

mithraeum   the temple of the god Mithras in the form of a cave, though in Britain all examples are small basilica-like structures.

mundus muliebris   lit. 'the woman's world'; the sphere in Roman daily life and society belonging to the female sphere of interest, such as toilet, jewellery, dress.

municipium   a free chartered town with citizen rights (e.g. Verulamium), not a *colonia* (q.v.).

nebris   the animal-skin worn as a garment by a satyr.

negotiatores   merchants.

nimbed   a figure with a nimbus (a halo).

officina(e)   a workshop or studio.

optio   an officer in a century within a legion, second to the centurion.

opus interrasile   openwork; especially used of jewellery.

opus sectile   shaped slabs of marble and other coloured stones fitted together to form decorative floor- or wall-veneers.

opus signinum   lime mortar with aggregate of crushed brick used as floor covering.

orans (orantes)   Christian figures with arms raised in prayer, as in paintings from Lullingstone, Kent.

parure   a set of jewellery, intended to be worn together.

patera   an offering-dish either with or without a handle.

paenula   a travelling-cloak.

pelta(e)   a moon-shaped ornament, derived from a type of light shield, frequently employed as a decorative device in art.

petasos   a traveller's brimmed hat, used notably of the winged hat worn by the god Mercury.

pileus   the skull-cap worn by artisans, in art especially by Vulcan and Ulysses.

podium   the high platform, carrying a Roman temple.

proscaenium   the stage of a theatre.

pteryx (pteryges)   lappet (q.v.) hanging from the armoured skirt worn by a Roman soldier below his cuirass.

protome   the forepart of an animal.

putti (It.) infants, winged or unwinged, used decoratively in art = cupids.

quadrifons   a four-way arch.

repoussé   metal which has been hammered into relief from the reverse side.

rosalia (or rosaria)   a festival held in Rome and throughout the Empire, at different times from May to July when roses were in flower. Graves were decorated with the flowers and in the army the standards were hung with rose-garlands on the *rosaliae signorum*.

sacellum   the shrine at the back of the civil basilica or the *basilica principiorum* (where it was also known as the *aedes*).

sagum   the military cloak.

sarcophagus   a coffin, generally carved out of marble and embellished with sculpture.

schola   the cult-room where a *collegium* (q.v.) met.

sevir (seviri augustales)   the priesthoods of the Imperial Cult found throughout the Empire and reserved for freedmen.

signifer   the standard-bearer in the Roman army.

spolia   classical antiquities such as sculpture or gems re-used or re-set in the Middle Ages.

stemma   the pedigree (line of descent) of a manuscript.

stele   a standing slab, generally a gravestone.

tessera(e)   the small stone cubes of which a mosaic pavement was constructed.

thiasos   the company of followeres of the god Bacchus; the marine thiasos is used of the rout of sea-creatures, tritons etc. accompanying Neptune.

thyrsus   a staff tied with ribbons and tipped with a pine-cone, carried by Bacchus or a member of his *thiasos* (q.v.).

togatus   a male figure wearing the formal Roman garment, the toga.

topos   a standard theme or topic used in a rhetorical discourse.

triclinium   the dining-room in a Roman house.

torus (moulding)   a rounded convex moulding, often double (double-torus).

trabeated (building)   a buiding constructed with beams as lintels and entablatures, as opposed to an arched construction.

triconch   a room of trefoil or three-lobed plan.

triskele   a figure consisting of three legs radiating from a common centre.

Tyche/Tychai   (Greek) Fortuna; especially employed for city or territorial goddesses (tychai).

trulla(e)   a saucepan-like vessel employed in the service of food, deeper in shap but not always distinguishable from the *patera* (q.v.) in function as such vessels were also used in religious rites such as pouring libations.

vas diatreton (vasa diatreta)   see *diatreton*.

venatio (venationes)   the hunting of wild beasts, either in the countryside or in the arena; a popular subject in art.

vesica   a pointed oval shape, the sides of which are properly parts of two equal circles, passing through each other at their centres.

vicennalia   the twenty-year anniversary of a imperial accession (also *decennalia*, the ten-year anniversary).

vicus (vici)   a civilian settlement, often outside a fort, but the term was also used for unchartered communities elsewhere, even for Brough-on-Humber where the *vicus* had local officers, such as the aedile who presented a *proscaenium* (q.v.).

volute   a spiral scroll in sculpture.

Index

———

(Figures in **bold** refer to plate numbers)